10.⁰⁰

Brennan Mitchell

D0138419

The Theory of Knowledge

Classical and Contemporary Readings

The Theory of Knowledge

Classical and Contemporary Readings

LOUIS P. POJMAN

University of Mississippi

Wadsworth Publishing Company
Belmont, California
A Division of Wadsworth, Inc.

Philosophy Editor: Kenneth King
Editorial Assistant: Gay Meixel
Production Editor: Carol Dondrea, Bookman
   Productions
Print Buyer: Diana Spence
Permissions Editor: Robert Kauser
Designer: Cynthia Bassett and Judith Levinson
Copy Editor: Linda Purrington
Cover: Albert Burkhardt
Compositor: TCSystems
Printer: R.R. Donnelley and Sons Company

 This book is printed on acid-free paper that
meets Environmental Protection Agency
standards for recycled paper.

© 1993 by Wadsworth, Inc. All rights reserved. No
part of this book may be reproduced, stored in a
retrieval system, or transcribed, in any form or by
any means, without the prior written permission of
the publisher, Wadsworth Publishing Company,
Belmont, California 94002.

   3 4 5 6 7 8 9 10—97 96 95

Library of Congress Cataloging-in-Publication Data

The Theory of knowledge : classical and contemporary readings / Louis
   P. Pojman.
        p.   cm.
   Includes bibliographical references.
   ISBN 0-534-17826-X
   1. Knowledge, Theory of.   I. Pojman. Louis P.
BD143. T48   1993   92-12263
121—dc20   CIP

To
Robert Audi
and
Jim Landesman,
Two Men Worthy of the Name *Philosopher*
Whom I Am Privileged to Have as Friends,
This Book Is Dedicated

Contents

Preface

An updated anthology in epistemology is urgently needed. Although the subject is at the heart of contemporary analytic philosophy and a great deal of work has been done in it during the past two decades, no comprehensive anthology exists. The last full treatment was Ernest Nagel and Richard Brandt's *Meaning and Knowledge: Systematic Readings in Epistemology* (New York: Harcourt, Brace & World, 1965), and it provides a model for this book. I treat five of its nine major parts and add four new ones.

Many of us are convinced that epistemology is the central subject in philosophy. Understanding the concept of knowledge and the meaning of justification and all that goes under those rubrics (broadly speaking, containing the issues covered in this book) is basic to virtually everything else in philosophy. Lamentably, few philosophy departments offer courses in epistemology on a regular basis. There are many reasons for this omission, including the difficult nature of the subject matter. Another reason is that there exists no comprehensive and accessible text on the subject. I hope this volume will meet this need by collecting the best works under the main categories of the subject so that both we who are already teaching the subject on a regular basis and those who might be prompted to do so will have an adequate book available.

This text consists of ten parts and contains 55 classical and contemporary readings. Each part contains an introduction that outlines the problems dealt with in the readings. I have set forth opposing positions on virtually every issue and have chosen the readings on the basis of general importance, accessibility, and cogency of argument. Each reading is preceded by a brief synopsis. Except in unusual cases, I have not analyzed the argument in the essays—that is for the student to do. But I *have* tried to identify the aims and peculiar features of the essays, to spare the student needless agony. A selected bibliography follows each part of the book.

This work is aimed at upper-level undergraduates and graduate students. The readings have been chosen both for their overall importance (historical or contemporary) and for their accessibility. I have also chosen representatives of diverse perspectives.

Outline of the Book

I have included in this book the nine subjects I consider central to contemporary epistemology. Wherever possible I have introduced the part with a classic reading, usually from antiquity or the modern period, but in a few cases have used a reading from recent history (for example, Edmund Gettier's "Is Justified True Belief Knowledge?" is as close to a contemporary classic as there is). I have begun the anthology with two readings from Plato: the section on the ascent to knowledge from the *Republic* and the section on innate ideas from the *Meno*. So much of epistemology was discussed by Plato that one cannot appreciate the subject without having a basic acquaintance with Plato's thought. The first three of Descartes's *Meditations* are included, as are central selections from Locke, Berkeley, Hume, and Kant. There are three selections from Bertrand Russell, my favorite twentieth-century philosopher. And five essays were commissioned.

The nine topics treated are skepticism; perception; the analysis of knowledge; theories of justification: foundationalism and coherentism (and contextualism); the internalist and externalist debate; *a priori* knowledge; induction; other minds; and the ethics of belief.

Several people gave me considerable help in assembling this work. Keith DeRose, Bill Lawhead, and Michael Levin read through several parts and gave me good advice. Kent Baldner, Western Michigan Unversity; Robert Causey, University of Texas at Austin; Michael R. DePaul, University of Notre Dame; John L. King, University of North Carolina at Greensboro; George Pappas, Ohio State University; and Elizabeth Preston, University of Georgia, offered valuable critical and constructive comments on various stages of this project. Students in my epistemology class provided a good testing ground for most of the essays in this book (as well as for some that didn't make it—if they didn't find an essay helpful, I generally rejected it). Eric Durlacher, Dan Kirk, and Susan Vincent deserve special mention. The production editor, Carol Dondrea, and the copyeditor, Linda Purrington, did an excellent job improving this book in its final phases. I want to thank Ken King for encouraging me to do this book and for giving his friendship and splendid support. Trudy, my wife, supported me at every step of the way.

Over the years two philosophers have greatly influenced my epistemic views. Robert Audi and Jim Landesman have taught me more than I can say. Both of these men helped me throughout this project. I am rich in having them as friends. To them this book is dedicated.

Louis P. Pojman
Philosophy Department
University of Mississippi
December 19, 1991

The Theory of Knowledge

Classical and Contemporary Readings

Part I

The Theory of Knowledge

What can we really know? How can we be certain that we have the truth? How can we be certain that we know anything at all? What is knowledge, and how is it different from belief? If we know something, must we know that we know it?

The theory of knowledge—or *epistemology* (from the Greek, "the science of knowing")—inquires into the nature of knowledge and justification of belief. Many philosophers believe it is the central area of philosophy, for if philosophy is the quest for truth and wisdom, then we need to know how we are to obtain the truth and justify our beliefs. We need to know how to distinguish the true from the false and justified beliefs from unwarranted beliefs.

If we consult the Oxford English Dictionary, we find the following definition of the verb *to know*: "to recognize, to identify, to distinguish, to be acquainted with, to apprehend or comprehend as a fact or truth." This sort of definition gives us a ballpark understanding of the term, but it is still too broad for philosophical purposes. So let us note some typical uses of the verb *to know*:

1. "I know my friend John very well."
2. "I know how to speak English."
3. "I know that Washington, DC, is the capital of the United States."

The three sentences illustrate three different

types of knowledge: knowledge by acquaintance, competence knowledge, and descriptive or propositional knowledge. We may characterize each of them this way:

1. *Knowledge by acquaintance*: A person S knows something or someone X (where X is the direct object of the verb). We are familiar in this way with the objects in the world and with our thoughts and sensations. We have acquaintance knowledge of our pains, our beliefs, our friends, the town in which we grew up, and so forth.

2. *Competence knowledge (sometimes called skill knowledge)*. Person S knows how to D (where D stands for a verb infinitive). This is *knowhow*. You know how to speak English and get around campus (or at least your room, when it isn't too cluttered). You may know how to ride a bicycle or play the piano or swim.

3. *Propositional knowledge (or descriptive knowledge)*. Person S knows that *p* (where *p* is some statement or proposition). Propositions have truth value; that is, they are true or false. They are the objects of propositional knowledge. When we claim to know that *p* is the case, we are claiming that *p* is true. Here are three examples of propositional knowledge: "I know that the sun will rise tomorrow," "I know that I have a mind," and "I know that Columbus discovered America in 1492."

Epistemology is primarily interested in this third kind of knowledge, propositional knowledge, and it is the kind of knowledge we shall be examining in this work. But this statement of purpose only scratches the surface of what we are concerned with in the theory of knowledge.

The field of epistemology seeks to throw light on the following kinds of questions:

1. What is knowledge? That is, what are the essential characteristics of this concept?

2. Can we know anything at all? Or are we doomed to ignorance about the most important subjects in life?

3. How do we obtain knowledge? Through the use of our senses, or our intellect, or both? Let us examine each of these questions.

What is knowledge? As mentioned, propositional knowledge is knowledge of true propositions. To claim to know something is to claim to possess a truth. If you claim to know that "$10 \times 10 = 100$," you implicitly claim that the statement "$10 \times 10 = 100$" is true. It would be a misuse of language to make a statement such as "I know that $10 \times 10 = 13$, but it is false," for knowledge claims are claims about grasping the truth. Of course, we may be wrong about our knowledge claims. The drunk claims to know that there are pink elephants in the room, the child claims to know that Santa Claus exists, and two witnesses may make contradictory knowledge claims in reporting an accident. We often believe falsely that we know. Sometimes the evidence on which our knowledge claim is based is inadequate or misleading, or we misremember or misperceive. Sometimes our knowledge claims are contradicted by those of others, as when two people of different religious faiths each claims that his or hers is the only true religion or when one person claims with certainty that abortion is morally wrong and the other person claims with equal certainty that it is morally permissible.

Knowledge involves possessing the truth but includes more than having a true belief. Imagine that I am holding up four cards so that I can see their faces but you can only see their backs. I ask you to guess what types of cards I am holding. You feel a hunch (have a weak belief) that I am holding up four aces and correctly announce, "You are holding four aces in your hands." Although we both possess the truth, I have something you don't—an adequate justification for my belief that there are four aces in my hand. So knowledge differs from mere true belief in that the knower has an adequate justification for claiming truth.

Now the question shifts to the nature of

justification. What exactly does it mean to be justified in believing some proposition? Are we justified when the evidence is undeniable, such as when we believe that "2 + 2 = 4" or when we feel pain and cannot help believing that we are in pain? Can we have sufficient evidence to justify belief in physical objects? our belief in other minds? beliefs about metaphysical propositions such as the existence of God or freedom of the will? How much evidence must one have before one can claim to know a belief is true? Questions of justification will occupy us in most of this work, especially Parts V, VI, VIII, IX, and X.

Let us turn to the second question: Can we know anything at all? Or are we doomed to ignorance about the most important subjects in life? What do we really know? Could it be that we really know nothing at all? *Skepticism* is the theory that we do not have any knowledge. We cannot be completely certain that any of our beliefs are true. Radical skepticism goes even further and claims that *we cannot even be certain of the belief that we cannot be completely certain that any of our beliefs are true*. We cannot even know that we cannot have knowledge. Skepticism can also differ with regard to the skeptical thesis; for example, some skeptics claim that we cannot have empirical knowledge but allow mathematical knowledge.

Skepticism does not deny that we should not act from the best evidence available, but it insists that we can never be sure that we are correct in our truth claims. For all we know, that universe and everything in it could have been created ten minutes ago, and all our apparent memories created with it. Or the universe and everything in it may have doubled in size last night while we were sleeping. How could we check on this? It wouldn't help to use a ruler to measure our height to see if we doubled in size, would it?

Can you defeat the skeptic? Arguments for and against skepticism are examined in Part II.

Let's turn to the third question: How do we obtain knowledge? through our senses, or our intellect, or both? There are two classic theories on the acquisition of knowledge. They are called *rationalism* and *empiricism*. "Rationalism" may be a misleading name for the first theory, because both theories use reason in acquiring knowledge. It is simply that rationalists believe that reason is sufficient to discover truth, whereas empiricists hold that all knowledge originates through sense perception (through seeing, hearing, touching, tasting, and smelling).

In the first reading, Plato's "Ascent to Knowledge," we encounter a classic expression of rationalism and idealism (or "Idea-ism"). Plato distinguishes two approaches to knowledge: sense perception and reason. Sense perception cannot be adequate for possessing the truth because its objects are subject to change and decay. All one gets in this way of apprehending things is beliefs about particular objects. Knowledge, however, goes beyond the particular and grasps universal *Ideas* or *Forms*. Plato argues that all knowing is the knowing of objects, so that these Ideas must exist in the *really* real world, the world of being. The philosopher is a person who works his or her way through the world of becoming, the empirical world, to this higher reality. Plato uses the allegory of the cave to illustrate his doctrine.

The bridge between the world of being and the world of becoming is *innate ideas*. In the second selection from Plato (the *Meno*), Socrates claims to demonstrate, by teaching an uneducated slave geometry, that all learning comes about through recollection of innate ideas. The slave learns to double the size of a square simply by being prodded to consult his own native understanding. Plato believed in reincarnation, that in a previous existence we saw all essential truths but have lost awareness of them through birth. Education should be a stimulation of the soul so that a person recalls what he or she really possesses but has forgotten.

Plato thought that all knowledge was *a priori* knowledge, knowledge one has independently of sense experience—as opposed to "empirical knowledge," which comes to us from experience through the five senses. Empirical beliefs, according to Plato, are not knowledge, but simply unstable appearance. An example of *a priori* knowledge is the following mathematical equation: "5 + 7 = 12." You don't have to appeal to experience in order to see that this equation is true. The mind alone can discover its truth. René Descartes (1596–1650) in Reading II.1 and Immanuel Kant (1724–1804) in Reading VIII.1 argue for the reality of *a priori* knowledge. The whole of Part VIII considers that issue.

Empiricism is the doctrine that all knowledge originates in the senses. In Part III, we examine two classical empiricist philosophers, John Locke and Bishop George Berkeley. John Locke (1632–1704) systematically attacked the notions of innate ideas and *a priori* knowledge, arguing that if our claims to knowledge are to make sense they must be derived from the world of sense experience:

> Let us then suppose the mind to be, as we say, white paper, void of all characters, without any ideas; how comes it by that vast store, which the busy and boundless fancy of man has painted on it with an almost endless variety? Whence has it all the materials of reason and knowledge? To this I answer, in one word, from experience: in that all our knowledge is founded.

Locke goes on to set forth a representational theory of knowledge, which claims that the core of what we know is caused by the world itself, although some qualities are the products of the way our perceptual mechanisms are affected by the world. The former qualities—called *primary qualities,* such as motion, size, shape, and number—are the true building blocks of knowledge, because these qualities are accurate representatives of the objective features of the world. The *secondary qualities* are modes of appre-

hending the primary qualities; examples are taste, color, odor, and sound. Because the color or taste of the same object can appear differently to different people or to the same person at different times, secondary qualities are subjective, even though they are caused by the objective primary qualities.

The difference between rationalism and empiricism may be illustrated by the following schema with regard to two important questions:

Question 1. How do we acquire ideas?

Answer A. Rationalism: Some *nonanalytic propositions** are innate or known *a priori* (independent of experience).

Answer B. Empiricism: All propositions are acquired from experience. No nonanalytic propositions are known *a priori.*

Question 2. How is knowledge organized in the mind?

Answer A. Rationalism: The mind brings to experience principles of order from the mind's own nature.

Answer B. Empiricism: The mind arranges and stores materials that are given in experience.

The two selections of Plato in this part, as well as the two selections of Descartes's writings (II.1 and V.1), illustrate rationalism. Selections from the work of Locke (III.1), Berkeley (III.2), and Hume (II.1) illustrate classical empiricism.

---

* An *analytic* proposition is one in which the predicate term is contained in the subject—for example, "All mothers are women"—whereas a *nonanalytic* or *synthetic* proposition is one where the predicate adds something to the subject— for example, "Mary Smith has just become a mother." The nonanalytic propositions referred to by the rationalists typically are metaphysical propositions such as "God exists," "I have a free will," and "All things have sufficient reasons to explain them." See Part VII for more on this subject.

The rest of this book considers nine perennial epistemological topics:

Part II, "Skepticism": Can we have any knowledge at all?

Part III, "Perception": Can we have knowledge of the external world?

Part IV, "The Analysis of Knowledge": Is knowledge true justified belief?

Part V, "Theories of Justification (I)": Is the structure of justification foundational or coherentist or neither?

Part VI, "Theories of Justification (II)": Is the correct account of the justification process one of externalism or of internalism?

Part VII, "*A Priori* Knowledge": Is there synthetic *a priori* truth? Is the analytic–synthetic distinction itself valid?

Part VIII, "Induction": Which is the correct solution to the problem of inductive knowledge?

Part IX, "Other Minds": How do we justify our beliefs that others experience mental events, have beliefs and feelings?

Part X, "The Ethics of Belief": Are there epistemic obligations? Are there moral obligations to seek the truth or to have the best set of justified beliefs?

These topics and the questions that surround them form the heart of the philosophical enterprise. Nearly everything in philosophy refers back to them. Although, first of all, they are purely theoretical, an understanding of their significance promises to make one a more enlightened human being, more aware of the structures of the cognitive dimension of existence.

I.1 *The Ascent to Knowledge (from the Republic)*

PLATO

Plato (427–347 B.C.) is one of the greatest philosophers who ever lived and may be called the father of epistemology. The British philosopher and mathematician Alfred North Whitehead called the whole history of Western philosophy "a series of footnotes to Plato." Although this is hyperbole, Plato does raise and systematically discusses such central questions of epistemology as "What is knowledge?" "Why is knowledge superior to belief?" and "How is knowledge possible?" He is the first to discuss the problem of skepticism and set forth an idealist theory of knowledge. He provides the classic discussion of innate ideas.

In our first reading from the *Republic,* Plato distinguishes two approaches to knowledge: sense perception and reason. Sense perception has as its object the fleeting world of particular objects, which appear differently at different times. Hence it is an unstable relationship, yielding only fallible opinion or belief, but not knowledge, the ultimate truth. Reason, however, grasps that which is absolute, unchanging, and universal, the *Ideas* (or *Forms,* as they are sometimes called). Sense perception causes us to see horses, chairs, and people, but reason gives us understanding of the universal horse, chair, and person.

Sense perception may be the starting point for knowledge but it can never itself bring us to the realm of reality, the world of being. By itself it leaves us in the realm of appearances, in the world of becoming. "And the man who believes in beautiful things, but does not believe in absolute beauty, nor is able to follow if one lead him to an understanding of it—do you think that his life is real or a dream? Is it not a dream? For whether a man be asleep or awake is it not dream-like to mistake the image for the real thing?" The role of the philosopher is to use the world of sense perception to lead the soul out of the dreamlike state of becoming and into the real world of being.

In this selection Plato describes a dialogue between his teacher, Socrates, and his brother, Glaucon, in which Socrates describes the nature of the Ideas and the four levels of cognition, which each person must ascend if he or she is to attain knowledge and the liberation of the soul.

Knowledge *Versus* Opinion

[Socrates has been arguing that unless philosophers become rulers or rulers become philosophers there will never be a truly good State. Glaucon now asks

Plato, *The Republic,* trans. Benjamin Jowett, Books V, VI, and VII (Oxford: Oxford University Press, 1896). Dialogue has been edited to add speakers' names before lines spoken and to delete redundant matter accordingly.

who the true philosophers are. Socrates, to whom the "I" refers, gives his answer in terms of possession of knowledge as opposed to mere opinion.]

GL.: Who then are the true philosophers?

SOC.: Those who are lovers of the vision of truth.

GL.: That is also good; but I should like to know what you mean?

SOC.: To another I might have a difficulty in explaining; but I am sure that you will admit a proposition which I am about to make.

GL.: What is the proposition?

SOC.: That since beauty is the opposite of ugliness, they are two?

GL.: Certainly.

SOC.: And inasmuch as they are two, each of them is one?

GL.: True again.

SOC.: And of just and unjust, good and evil, and of every other class, the same remark holds; taken singly, each of them is one; but from the various combinations of them with actions and things and with one another, they are seen in all sorts of lights and appear many?

GL.: Very true.

SOC.: And this is the distinction which I draw between the sight-loving, art-loving, practical class and those of whom I am speaking, and who are alone worthy of the name of philosophers.

GL.: How do you distinguish them?

SOC.: The lovers of sounds and sights are, as I conceive, fond of tones and colors and forms and all the artificial products that are made out of them, but their mind is incapable of seeing or loving absolute beauty.

GL.: True.

SOC.: Few are they who are able to attain to the sight of this. And the man who believes in beautiful things but does not believe in absolute beauty, nor is able to follow if one lead him to an understanding of it—do you think that his life is real or a dream? Is it not a dream? For whether a man be asleep or awake is it not dream-like to mistake the image for the real thing?

GL.: I should certainly say that such an one was dreaming.

SOC.: But take the case of the other, who recognizes the existence of absolute beauty and is able to distinguish the idea from the objects which participate in the idea, neither putting the objects in the place of the idea nor the idea in the place of the objects—is he a dreamer, or is he awake?

GL.: He is wide awake.

SOC.: And may we not say that the mind of the one who knows has knowledge and that the mind of the other, who opines only, has opinion?

GL.: Certainly.

SOC.: But suppose that the latter should quarrel with us and dispute our statement, can we administer any soothing cordial or advice to him, without revealing to him that there is sad disorder in his wit?

GL.: We must certainly offer him some good advice.

SOC.: Come, then, and let us think of something to say to him. Shall we begin by assuring him that he is welcome to any knowledge which he may have, and that we rejoice at his having it? But we should like to ask him a question: Does he who has knowledge know something or nothing?

GL.: I answer that he knows something.

SOC.: Something that is or is not?*

GL.: Something that is; for how can that which is not ever be known?

SOC.: And are we assured, after looking at the matter from many points of view, that absolute being is or may be absolutely known, but that the utterly non-existent is utterly unknown?

GL.: Nothing can be more certain.

SOC.: Good. But if there be anything which is of such a nature as to be and not to be, that will have a place intermediate between pure being and the absolute negation of being?

GL.: Yes, between them.

SOC.: And, as knowledge corresponds to being and ignorance of necessity to not-being, we must find something intermediate between ignorance and knowledge for that which lies between them, if there is such a thing.

GL.: Yes.

[* Note that Plato is referring to the Ideas, which have a true existence, as opposed to the objects of sense perception, which have only appearance and dwell in the zone of becoming, between being and nothingness.—Ed.]

soc.: Would you admit the existence of opinion?

GL.: No question.

soc.: Is opinion the same faculty as knowledge or is it a different faculty?

GL.: A different faculty.

soc.: Then opinion and knowledge have to do with different kinds of matter corresponding to this difference of faculties?

GL.: Yes.

soc.: And knowledge is relative to being and knows being. But before I proceed further I will make a division. I will begin by placing faculties in a class by themselves: they are powers in us, and in all other things, by which we do as we do. Sight and hearing, for example, I should call faculties. Have I clearly explained the class which I mean?

GL.: Yes, I quite understand.

soc.: Then let me tell you my view about them. I do not see the faculties, and therefore the distinctions of shape, color, and the like, which enable me to discern the differences of some things, do not apply to them. In speaking of a faculty I think only of its sphere and its result; and that which has the same sphere and the same result I call the same faculty, but that which has another sphere and another result I call different. Would that be your way of speaking?

GL.: Yes.

soc.: Would you say that knowledge is a faculty, or in what class would you place it?

GL.: Certainly knowledge is a faculty, and the mightiest of all faculties.

soc.: And is opinion also a faculty?

GL.: Certainly; for opinion is that with which we are able to form an opinion.

soc.: And yet you were acknowledging a little while ago that knowledge is not the same as opinion?

GL.: Why, yes; how can any reasonable being ever identify that which is infallible with that which errs?

soc.: An excellent answer, proving that we are quite conscious of a distinction between them.

GL.: Yes.

soc.: Then knowledge and opinion having distinct powers have also distinct spheres or subject-matters?

GL.: That is certain.

soc.: Being is the sphere or subject-matter of knowledge, and knowledge is to know the nature of being?

GL.: Yes.

soc.: And opinion is to have an opinion?

GL.: Yes.

soc.: And do we know what we opine? or is the subject-matter of opinion the same as the subject-matter of knowledge?

GL.: Nay, that has been already disproven; if difference in faculty implies difference in the sphere or subject-matter, and if, as we were saying, opinion and knowledge are distinct faculties, then the sphere of knowledge and of opinion can not be the same.

soc.: Then if being is the subject-matter of knowledge, something else must be the subject-matter of opinion?

GL.: Yes, something else.

soc.: Well then, is not-being the subject-matter of opinion? or, rather, how can there be an opinion at all about not-being? Reflect: when a man has an opinion, has he not an opinion about something? Can he have an opinion which is an opinion about nothing?

GL.: Impossible.

soc.: He who has an opinion has an opinion about some one thing?

GL.: Yes.

soc.: And not-being is not one thing but, properly speaking, nothing?

GL.: True.

soc.: Of not-being, ignorance was assumed to be the necessary correlative; of being, knowledge?

GL.: True.

SOC.: Then opinion is not concerned either with being or with not-being?

GL.: Not with either.

SOC.: And can therefore neither be ignorance nor knowledge?

GL.: That seems to be true.

SOC.: But is opinion to be sought without and beyond either of them, in a greater clearness than knowledge, or in a greater darkness than ignorance?

GL.: In neither.

SOC.: Then I suppose that opinion appears to you to be darker than knowledge, but lighter than ignorance?

GL.: Both; and in no small degree.

SOC.: And also to be within and between them?

GL.: Yes.

SOC.: Then you would infer that opinion is intermediate?

GL.: No question.

SOC.: But were we not saying before, that if anything appeared to be a sort which is and is not at the same time, that sort of thing would appear also to lie in the interval between pure being and absolute not-being; and that the corresponding faculty is neither knowledge nor ignorance, but will be found in the interval between them?

GL.: True.

SOC.: And in that interval there has now been discovered something which we call opinion?

GL.: There has.

SOC.: Then what remains to be discovered is the object which partakes equally of the nature of being and not-being, and can not rightly be termed either, pure and simple; this unknown term, when discovered, we may truly call the subject of opinion, and assign each to their proper faculty,—the extremes to the faculties of the extremes and the mean to the faculty of the mean.

GL.: True.

SOC.: This being premised, I would ask the gentleman who is of opinion that there is no absolute or unchangeable idea of beauty—in whose opinion the beautiful is the manifold—he, I say, your lover of beautiful sights, who can not bear to be told that the beautiful is one, and the just is one, or that anything is one—to him I would appeal, saying, Will you be so very kind, sir, as to tell us whether, of all these beautiful things, there is one which will not be found ugly; or of the just, which will not be found unjust; or of the holy, which will not also be unholy?

GL.: No; the beautiful will in some point of view be found ugly; and the same is true of the rest.

SOC.: And may not the many which are doubles be also halves?—doubles, that is, of one thing, and halves of another?

GL.: Quite true.

SOC.: And things great and small, heavy and light, as they are termed, will not be denoted by these any more than by the opposite names?

GL.: True; both these and the opposite names will always attach to all of them.

SOC.: And can any one of those many things which are called by particular names be said to be this rather than not to be this?

GL.: They are like the punning riddles which are asked at feasts or the children's puzzle about the eunuch aiming at the bat, with what he hit him, as they say in the puzzle, and upon what the bat was sitting. The individual objects of which I am speaking are also a riddle, and have a double sense: nor can you fix them in your mind, either as being or not-being, or both, or neither.

SOC.: Then what will you do with them? Can they have a better place than between being and not-being? For they are clearly not in greater darkness or negation than not-being, or more full of light and existence than being.

GL.: That is quite true.

SOC.: Thus then we seem to have discovered that the many ideas which the multitude entertain about the beautiful and about all other things are tossing about in some region which is half-way between pure being and pure not-being?

GL.: We have.

SOC.: Yes; and we had before agreed that anything of this kind which we might find was to be described as matter of opinion, and not as matter of knowledge; being the intermediate flux which is caught and detained by the intermediate faculty.

GL.: Quite true.

SOC.: Then those who see the many beautiful, and who yet neither see absolute beauty, nor can follow any guide who points the way thither; who see the many just, and not absolute justice, and the like,—such persons may be said to have opinion but not knowledge?

GL.: That is certain.

SOC.: But those who see the absolute and eternal and immutable may be said to know, and not to have opinion only?

GL.: Neither can that be denied.

SOC.: The one love and embrace the subjects of knowledge, the other those of opinion? The latter are the same, as I dare say you will remember, who listened to sweet sounds and gazed upon fair colors, but would not tolerate the existence of absolute beauty.

GL.: Yes, I remember.

SOC.: Shall we then be guilty of any impropriety in calling them lovers of opinion rather than lovers of wisdom, and will they be very angry with us for thus describing them?

GL.: I shall tell them not to be angry; no man should be angry at what is true.

SOC.: But those who love the truth in each thing are to be called lovers of wisdom and not lovers of opinion.

GL.: Assuredly.

. . .

The Objects of Knowledge

SOC.: . . . I must first come to an understanding with you, and remind you of what I have mentioned in the course of this discussion, and at many other times.

GL.: What?

SOC.: The old story, that there is a many beautiful and a many good, and so of other things which we describe and define; to all of them the term "many" is applied.

GL.: True.

SOC.: And there is an absolute beauty and an absolute good, and of other things to which the term "many" is applied there is an absolute; for they may be brought under a single idea, which is called the essence of each.

GL.: Very true.

SOC.: The many, as we say, are seen but not known, and the ideas are known but not seen.

GL.: Exactly.

SOC.: And what is the organ with which we see the visible things?

GL.: The sight.

SOC.: And with the hearing, we hear, and with the other senses perceive the other objects of sense?

GL.: True.

SOC.: But have you remarked that sight is by far the most costly and complex piece of workmanship which the artificer of the senses ever contrived?

GL.: No, I never have.

SOC.: Then reflect: has the ear or voice need of any third or additional nature in order that the one may be able to hear and the other to be heard?

GL.: Nothing of the sort.

SOC.: No, indeed, and the same is true of most, if not all, the other senses—you would not say that any of them rquires such an addition?

GL.: Certainly not.

SOC.: But you see that without the addition of some other nature there is no seeing or being seen?

GL.: How do you mean?

SOC.: Sight being, as I conceive, in the eyes, and he who has eyes wanting to see; color being also present in them, still unless there be a third nature specially adapted to the purpose, the owner of the eyes will see nothing and the colors will be invisible.

GL.: Of what nature are you speaking?

SOC.: Of that which you term light.

GL.: True.

SOC.: Noble, then, is the bond which links together sight and visibility, and great beyond other bonds by no small difference of nature; for light is their bond, and light is no ignoble thing?

GL.: Nay, the reverse of ignoble.

SOC.: And which of the gods in heaven would you say was the lord of this element? Whose is that light which makes the eye to see perfectly and the visible to appear?

GL.: You mean the sun, as you and all mankind say.

SOC.: May not the relation of sight to this deity be described as follows?

GL.: How?

SOC.: Neither sight nor the eye in which sight resides is the sun?

GL.: No.

SOC.: Yet of all the organs of sense the eye is the most like the sun?

GL.: By far the most like.

SOC.: And the power which the eye possesses is a sort of effluence which is dispensed from the sun?

GL.: Exactly.

SOC.: Then the sun is not sight, but the author of sight who is recognized by sight?

GL.: True.

SOC.: And this is he whom I call the child of the good, whom the good begat in his own likeness, to be in the visible world, in relation to sight and the things of sight, what the good is in the intellectual world in relation to mind and the things of mind.

GL.: Will you be a little more explicit?

SOC.: Why, you know, that the eyes, when a person directs them towards objects on which the light of day is no longer shining, but the moon and stars only, see dimly, and are nearly blind; they seem to have no clearness of vision in them?

GL.: Very true.

SOC.: But when they are directed towards objects on which the sun shines, they see clearly and there is sight in them?

GL.: Certainly.

SOC.: And the soul is like the eye: when resting upon that on which truth and being shine, the soul perceives and understands, and is radiant with intelligence; but when turned towards the twilight of becoming and perishing, then she has opinion only, and goes blinking about, and is first of one opinion and then of another, and seems to have no intelligence?

GL.: Just so.

SOC.: Now, that which imparts truth to the known and the power of knowing to the knower is what I would have you term the idea of good, and this you will deem to be the cause of science, and of truth in so far as the latter becomes the subject of knowledge; beautiful too, as are both truth and knowledge, you will be right in esteeming this other nature as more beautiful than either; and, as in the previous instance, light and sight may be truly said to be like the sun, and yet not to be the sun, so in this other sphere, science and truth may be deemed to be like the good, but not the good; the good has a place of honor yet higher.

GL.: What a wonder of beauty that must be, which is the author of science and truth, and yet surpasses them in beauty; for you surely can not mean to say that pleasure is the good?

SOC.: God forbid; but may I ask you to consider the image in another point of view?

GL.: In what point of view?

SOC.: You would say, would you not, that the sun is not only the author of visibility in all visible things, but of generation and nourishment and growth, though he himself is not generation?

GL.: Certainly.

SOC.: In like manner the good may be said to be not only the author of knowledge to all things known, but of their being and essence, and yet the good is not essence, but far exceeds essence in dignity and power.

GL.: (With a ludicrous earnestness) By the light of heaven, how amazing!

The Four Levels of Knowledge: The Line

SOC.: You have to imagine that there are two ruling powers, and that one of them, the good, is set over the intellectual world, the other, the Sun, over the visible world. May I suppose that you have this distinction of the visible and the intelligible fixed in your mind?

The Line

D

Ideas: *Reason*

C

Mathematics:
Intelligence

B

Physical
Phenomena:
Belief

A

Images:
Imagination

GL.: I have.

SOC.: Now take a line which has been cut into two unequal parts, and divide each of them again in the same proportion, and suppose the two main divisions to answer, one to the visible and the other to the intelligible, and then compare the subdivisions in respect to their clearness and want of clearness, and you will find that the first section (A) in the sphere of the visible consists of images. And by images I mean, in the first place, shadows, and in the second place, reflections in water and in solid, smooth and polished bodies and the like. Do you understand?

GL.: Yes, I understand.

SOC.: Imagine now, the other section (B), of which this is only the resemblance, to include the animals which we see, and everything that grows or is made. Would you not admit that both the sections of this division have different degrees of truth, and that the copy is to the original as the sphere of opinion is to the sphere of knowledge?

GL.: Most undoubtedly.

SOC.: Next we proceed to consider the manner in which the sphere of the intellectual is to be divided. There are two subdivisions, in the lower (C) of which the soul uses the figures given by the former division as images; the inquiry can only be hypothetical, and instead of going upwards to a principle descends to the other end; in the higher of the two (D), the soul passes out of hypotheses, and goes up to a principle which is above hypotheses, making no use of images as in the former case, but proceeding only in and through the ideas themselves.

GL.: I do not quite understand your meaning.

SOC.: Then I will try again; you will understand me better when I have made some preliminary remarks. [Regarding C], you are aware that students of geometry, arithmetic, and the kindred sciences assume the odd and the even and the figures and three kinds of angles and the like in their several branches of science; these are their hypotheses, which they and everybody are supposed to know, and therefore they do not deign to give any account of them either to themselves or others; but they begin with them, and go on until they arrive at last, and in a consistent manner, at their conclusion.

GL.: Yes, I know.

SOC.: And do you not know also that although they make use of the visible forms and reason about them, they are thinking not of these, but of the ideals which they resemble; not of the figures which they draw, but of the absolute square and the absolute diameter, and so on. The forms which they draw or make are actual things, which have shadows and reflections in water of their own, but now they serve in turn as images, but the soul is really seeking to behold the things themselves, which can only be seen with the eye of the mind.

GL.: That is true.

SOC.: And of this I spoke as the intelligible (C), although in the search after it the soul is compelled to use hypotheses; not ascending to a first principle, because she is unable to rise above the region of hypothesis, but employing the objects of which the shadows below are resemblances in their turn as images, they having in relation to the shadows and reflections of them a greater distinctness, and therefore a higher value.

GL.: I understand, that you are speaking of the province of geometry and the sister arts.

SOC.: When I speak of the other division of the intelligible (D), you will understand me to speak of that other sort of knowledge which reason herself attains by the power of dialectic, using the hypotheses not as first principles, but only as hypotheses—that is to say, as steps and points of departure into a world which is above hypotheses, in order that she may soar beyond them to the first principle of the whole; and clinging to this and then to that which depends on this, by successive steps she descends again without the aid of any sensible object, from ideas, through ideas, and in ideas she ends.

GL.: I understand you. Not perfectly, for you seem to me to be describing a task which is really tremendous; but at any rate, I understand you to say that knowledge and being, which the science of dialectic contemplates, are clearer than the notions of the arts, as they are termed, which proceed from hypotheses only. These are also contemplated by the understanding, and not by the senses: yet, because they start from hypotheses and do not ascend to a principle, those who contemplate them appear to you not to exercise the higher reason upon them, although when a first principle is added to them they are cognizable by the higher reason. And the habit which is concerned with geometry and the cognate sciences I suppose that you would term understanding and not reason, as being intermediate between opinion and reason.

SOC.: You have quite conceived my meaning; and now, corresponding to these four divisions, let there be four faculties in the soul—Reason answering to the highest (D), Understanding to the second (C), Belief (or conviction) to the third (B), and Imaging (or perception of shadows) to the last (A). And let us suppose that the several faculties have clearness in the same degree that their objects have truth.

GL.: I understand and give my assent, and accept this arrangement of the matter.

The Allegory of the Cave

SOC.: And now, let me show in a figure how far our nature is enlightened or unenlightened:—Behold! human beings living in an underground den, which has a mouth open towards the light and reaching all along the den; here they have been from their childhood, and have their legs and necks chained so that they can not move, and can only see before them, being prevented by the chains from turning round their heads. Above and behind them a fire is blazing at a distance, and between the fire and the prisoners there is a raised way; and you will see, if you look, a low wall built along the way, like the screen which marionette players have in front of them, over which they show the puppets.

GL.: I see.

SOC.: And do you see men passing along the wall carrying all sorts of vessels, and statues and figures of animals made of wood and stone and various materials, which appear over the wall? Some of them are talking, others silent.

GL.: You have shown me a strange image, and they are strange prisoners.

SOC.: Like ourselves; and they see only their own

shadows, or the shadows of one another, which the fire throws on the opposite wall of the cave?

GL.: True; how could they see anything but the shadows if they were never allowed to move their heads?

SOC.: And of the objects which are being carried in like manner they would only see the shadows?

GL.: Yes.

SOC.: And if they were able to converse with one another, would they not suppose that they were naming what was actually before them?

GL.: Very true.

SOC.: And suppose further that the prison had an echo which came from the other side, would they not be sure to fancy when one of the passers-by spoke that the voice which they heard came from the passing shadow?

GL.: No question.

SOC.: To them, the truth would be literally nothing but the shadows of the images.

GL.: That is certain.

SOC.: And now look again, and see what will naturally follow if the prisoners are released and disabused of their error. At first, when any of them is liberated and compelled suddenly to stand up and turn his neck round and walk and look towards the light, he will suffer sharp pains; the glare will distress him, and he will be unable to see the realities of which in his former state he had seen the shadows; and then conceive some one saying to him, that what he saw before was an illusion, but that now, when he is approaching nearer to being and his eye is turned towards more real existence, he has a clearer vision—what will be his reply? And you may further imagine that his instructor is pointing to the objects as they pass and requiring him to name them,—will he not be perplexed? Will he not fancy that the shadows which he formerly saw are truer than the objects which are now shown to him?

GL.: Far truer.

SOC.: And if he is compelled to look straight at the light, will he not have a pain in his eyes which will make him turn away to take refuge in the objects of vision which he can see, and which he will conceive to be in reality clearer than the things which are now being shown to him?

GL.: True.

SOC.: And suppose once more, that he is reluctantly dragged up a steep and rugged ascent, and held fast until he is forced into the presence of the sun himself, is he not likely to be pained and irritated? When he approaches the light his eyes will be dazzled, and he will not be able to see anything at all of what are now called realities.

GL.: Not all in a moment.

SOC.: He will require to grow accustomed to the sight of the upper world. And first he will see the shadows best, next the reflections of men and other objects in the water, and then the objects themselves; then he will gaze upon the light of the moon and the stars and the spangled heaven; and he will see the sky and the stars by night better than the sun or the light of the sun by day?

GL.: Certainly.

SOC.: Last of all he will be able to see the sun, and not mere reflections of him in the water, but he will see him in his own proper place, and not in another; and he will contemplate him as he is.

GL.: Certainly.

SOC.: He will then proceed to argue that this is he who gives the season and the years, and is the guardian of all that is in the visible world, and in a certain way the cause of all things which he and his fellows have been accustomed to behold?

GL.: Clearly, he would first see the sun and then reason about him.

SOC.: And when he remembered his old habitation, and the wisdom of the den and his fellow-prisoners, do you not suppose that he would felicitate himself on the change, and pity them?

GL.: Certainly, he would.

SOC.: And if they were in the habit of conferring honors among themselves on those who were quickest to observe the passing shadows and to remark which of them went before, and which followed after, and which were together; and who were therefore best able to draw conclusions as to the future, do you think that he would care for such honors and glories, or envy the possessors of them? Would he not say with Homer,

Better to be the poor servant of a poor master,

and to endure anything, rather than think as they do and live after their manner?

GL.: Yes, I think that he would rather suffer anything than entertain these false notions and live in this miserable manner.

SOC.: Imagine once more, such an one coming suddenly out of the sun to be replaced in his old situation; would he not be certain to have his eyes full of darkness?

GL.: To be sure.

SOC.: And if there were a contest, and he had to compete in measuring the shadows with the prisoners who had never moved out of the den, while his sight was still weak, and before his eyes had become steady (and the time which would be needed to acquire this new habit of sight might be very considerable), would he not be ridiculous? Men would say of him that up he went and down he came without his eyes; and that it was better not even to think of ascending; and if any one tried to loose another and lead him up to the light, let them only catch the offender, and they would put him to death.

GL.: No question.

SOC.: This entire allegory you may now append, dear Glaucon, to the previous argument; the prison-house is the world of sight, the light of the fire is the sun, and you will not misapprehend me if you interpret the journey upwards to be the ascent of the soul into the intellectual world according to my poor belief, which, at your desire, I have expressed—whether rightly or wrongly God knows. But, whether true or false, my opinion is that in the world of knowledge the idea of good appears last of all, and is seen only with an effort; and, when seen, is also inferred to be the universal author of all things beautiful and right, parent of light and of the lord of light in this visible world, and the immediate source of reason and truth in the intellectual; and that this is the power upon which he who would act

rationally either in public or private life must have his eye fixed.

GL.: I agree, as far as I am able to understand you.

SOC.: Moreover, you must not wonder that those who attain to this beatific vision are unwilling to descend to human affairs; for their souls are ever hastening into the upper world where they desire to dwell; which desire of theirs is very natural, if our allegory may be trusted.

GL.: Yes, very natural.

SOC.: And is there anything surprising in one who passes from divine contemplations to the evil state of man, misbehaving himself in a ridiculous manner; if, while his eyes are blinking and before he has become accustomed to the surrounding darkness, he is compelled to fight in courts of law, or in other places, about the images or the shadows of images of justice, and is endeavoring to meet the conceptions of those who have never yet seen absolute justice?

GL.: Anything but surprising.

SOC.: Any one who has common sense will remember that the bewilderments of the eyes are of two kinds, and arise from the two causes, either from coming out of the light or from going into the light, which is true of the mind's eye, quite as much as of the bodily eye; and he who remembers this when he sees any one whose vision is perplexed and weak, will not be too ready to laugh; he will first ask whether that soul of man has come out of the brighter life, and is unable to see because unaccustomed to the dark, or having turned from darkness to the day is dazzled by excess of light. And he will count the one happy in his condition and state of being, and he will pity the other; or, if he have a mind to laugh at the soul which comes from below into the light, there will be more reason in this than in the laugh which greets him who returns from above out of the light into the den.

GL.: That is a very just distinction.

SOC.: But then, if I am right, certain professors of education must be wrong when they say that they can put a knowledge into the soul which was not there before, like sight into blind eyes.

GL.: They undoubtedly say this.

SOC.: Whereas, our argument shows that the power and capacity of learning exists in the soul already; and that just as the eye was unable to turn from darkness to light without the whole body, so too the instrument of knowledge can only by the movement of the whole soul be turned from the world of becoming into that of being, and learn by degrees to endure the sight of being, and of the brightest and best of being, or in other words, of the good.

GL.: Very true.

SOC.: And must there not be some art which will effect conversion in the easiest and quickest manner; not implanting the faculty of sight, for that exists already, but has been turned in the wrong direction, and is looking away from the truth?

GL.: Yes, such an art may be presumed.

SOC.: And whereas the other so-called virtues of the soul seem to be akin to bodily qualities, for even when they are not originally innate they can be implanted later by habit and exercise, the virtue of wisdom more than anything else contains a divine element which always remains, and by this conversion is rendered useful and profitable; or, on the other hand, hurtful and useless. Did you never observe the narrow intelligence flashing from the keen eye of a clever rogue—how eager he is, how clearly his paltry soul sees the way to his end; he is the reverse of blind, but his keen eye-sight is forced into the service of evil, and he is mischievous in proportion to his cleverness?
. . .

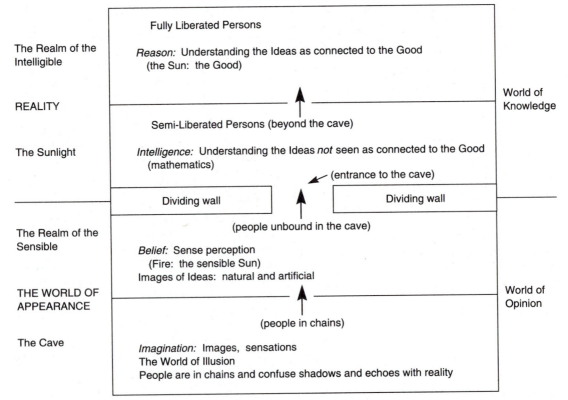

FOUR LEVELS OF KNOWLEDGE

The Realm of the Intelligible	**Fully Liberated Persons** *Reason:* Understanding the Ideas as connected to the Good (the Sun: the Good)
REALITY	World of Knowledge
The Sunlight	**Semi-Liberated Persons (beyond the cave)** *Intelligence:* Understanding the Ideas *not* seen as connected to the Good (mathematics)

(entrance to the cave)

| Dividing wall | Dividing wall |

(people unbound in the cave)

| The Realm of the Sensible | **Belief:** Sense perception
(Fire: the sensible Sun)
Images of Ideas: natural and artificial |
| THE WORLD OF APPEARANCE | World of Opinion |

(people in chains)

| The Cave | *Imagination:* Images, sensations
The World of Illusion
People are in chains and confuse shadows and echoes with reality |

I.2 Innate Ideas (from the Meno)

PLATO

This selection from Plato's dialogue *Meno* is the classic expression of the doctrine that we are born with innate ideas or *a priori* knowledge (knowledge prior to experience). Meno raises a puzzle about learning: how do you know when you have found the answer to your question? Either (1) you don't know the answer and so won't know when you've found it, or (2) you already know the answer, in which case why make the inquiry in the first place? Socrates sets about to solve this riddle about the possibility of new knowledge by showing how Meno's slave may come to be aware of what he already knows.

The dialogue begins with Meno describing Socrates' renowned ability to expose pretensions and reveal just how ignorant we all are.

MEN.: O Socrates, I used to be told, before I knew you, that you were always doubting yourself and making others doubt; and now you are casting your spells over me, and I am simply getting bewitched and enchanted, and am at my wits' end. And if I may venture to make a jest upon you, you seem to me both in your appearance and in your power over others to be very like the flat torpedo fish, who torpifies those who come near him and touch him, as you have now torpified me, I think. For my soul and my tongue are really torpid, and I do not know how to answer you; and though I have been delivered of an infinite variety of speeches about virtue before now, and to many persons—and very good ones they were, as I thought—at this moment I cannot even say what virtue is. And I think that you are very wise in not voyaging and going away from home, for if you did in other places as you do in Athens, you would be cast into prison as a magician.

SOC.: You are a rogue, Meno, and had all but caught me. . . . As to my being a torpedo, if the torpedo is torpid as well as the cause of torpidity in others, then indeed I am a torpedo, but not otherwise; for I perplex others, not because I am clear, but because I am utterly perplexed myself. And now I know not what virtue is, and you seem to be in the same case, although you did once perhaps know before you touched me. However, I have no objection to join with you in the enquiry.

MEN.: And how will you enquire, Socrates, into that which you do not know? What will you put forth as the subject of enquiry? And if you find what you want, how will you ever know that this is the thing which you did not know?

SOC.: I know, Meno, what you mean; but just see what a tiresome dispute you are introducing. You argue that a man cannot enquire either about that which he knows, or about that which he does not know; for if he knows, he has no need to enquire; and if not, he cannot; for he does not know the very subject about which he is to enquire.

MEN.: Well, Socrates, and is not the argument sound?

SOC.: I think not.

MEN.: Why not?

SOC.: I will tell you why: I have heard from certain

Plato, *Meno*, trans. Benjamin Jowett (Oxford: Oxford University Press, 1896).

wise men and women who spoke of things divine that—

MEN.: What did they say?

SOC.: They spoke of a glorious truth, as I conceive.

MEN.: What was it? and who were they?

SOC.: Some of them were priests and priestesses, who had studied how they might be able to give a reason of their profession: there have been poets also, who spoke of these things by inspiration, like Pindar, and many others who were inspired. And they say—mark, now, and see whether their words are true—they say that the soul of man is immortal, and at one time has an end, which is termed dying, and at another time is born again, but is never destroyed. And the moral is, that a man ought to live always in perfect holiness. *'For in the ninth year Persephone sends the souls of those from whom she has received the penalty of ancient crime back again from beneath into the light of the sun above, and these are they who become noble kings and mighty men and great in wisdom and are called saintly heroes in after ages.'* The soul, then, as being immortal, and having been born again many times, and having seen all things that exist, whether in this world or in the world below, has knowledge of them all; and it is no wonder that she should be able to call to remembrance all that she ever knew about virtue, and about everything; for as all nature is akin, and the soul has learned all things, there is no difficulty in her eliciting or as men say learning, out of a single recollection all the rest, if a man is strenuous and does not faint; for all enquiry and all learning is but recollection. And therefore we ought not to listen to this sophistical argument about the impossibility of enquiry: for it will make us idle, and is sweet only to the sluggard; but the other saying will make us active and inquisitive. In that confiding, I will gladly enquire with you into the nature of virtue.

MEN.: Yes, Socrates; but what do you mean by saying that we do not learn, and that what we call learning is only a process of recollection? Can you teach me how this is?

SOC.: I told you, Meno, just now that you were a rogue, and now you ask whether I can teach you, when I am saying that there is no teaching, but only recollection; and thus you imagine that you will involve me in a contradiction.

MEN.: Indeed, Socrates, I protest that I had no such intention. I only asked the question from habit; but if you can prove to me that what you say is true, I wish that you would.

SOC.: It will be no easy matter, but I will try to please you to the utmost of my power. Suppose that you call one of your numerous attendants, that I may demonstrate on him.

MEN.: Certainly. Come hither, boy.

SOC.: He is Greek, and speaks Greek, does he not?

MEN.: Yes, indeed; he was born in the house.

SOC.: Attend now to the questions which I ask him, and observe whether he learns of me or only remembers.

MEN.: I will.

SOC.: Tell me, boy, do you know that a figure like this is a square?

BOY: I do.

SOC.: And you know that a square figure has these four lines equal?

BOY: Certainly.

SOC.: And these lines which I have drawn through the middle of the square are also equal?

BOY: Yes.

SOC.: A square may be of any size?

BOY: Certainly.

SOC.: And if one side of the figure be of two feet, and the other side be of two feet, how much will the whole be? Let me explain: if in one direction the space was of two feet, and in the other direction of one foot, the whole would be of two feet taken once?

BOY: Yes.

SOC.: But since this side is also of two feet, there are twice two feet?

BOY: There are.

SOC.: Then the square is of twice two feet?

BOY: Yes.

SOC.: And how many are twice two feet? count and tell me.

BOY: Four, Socrates.

SOC.: And might there not be another square twice as large as this, and having like this the lines equal?

BOY: Yes.

SOC.: And of how many feet will that be?

BOY: Of eight feet.

SOC.: And now try and tell me the length of the line which forms the side of that double square: this is two feet—what will that be?

BOY: Clearly, Socrates, it will be double.

SOC.: Do you observe, Meno, that I am not teaching the boy anything, but only asking him questions; and now he fancies that he knows how long a line is necessary in order to produce a figure of eight square feet; does he not?

MEN.: Yes.

SOC.: And does he really know?

MEN.: Certainly not.

SOC.: He only guesses that because the square is double, the line is double.

MEN.: True.

SOC.: Observe him while he recalls the steps in regular order. (*To the Boy.*) Tell me, boy, do you assert that a double space comes from a double line? Remember that I am not speaking of an oblong, but of a figure equal every way, and twice the size of this—that is to say of eight feet; and I want to know whether you still say that a double square comes from a double line?

BOY: Yes.

SOC.: But does not this line become doubled if we add another such line here?

BOY: Certainly.

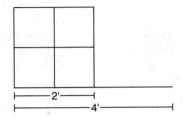

SOC.: And four such lines will make a space containing eight feet?

BOY: Yes.

SOC.: Let us describe such a figure: Would you not say that this is the figure of eight feet?

BOY: Yes.

SOC.: And are there not these four divisions in the figure, each of which is equal to the figure of four feet?

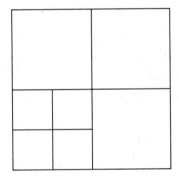

BOY: True.

SOC.: And is not that four times four?

BOY: Certainly.

SOC.: And four times is not double?

BOY: No, indeed.

SOC.: But how much?

BOY: Four times as much.

SOC.: Therefore the double line, boy, has given a space, not twice, but four times as much.

BOY: True.

SOC.: Four times four are sixteen—are they not?

BOY: Yes.

SOC.: What line would give you a space of eight feet, as this gives one of sixteen feet—do you see?

BOY: Yes.

SOC.: And the space of four feet is made from this half line?

BOY: Yes.

SOC.: Good; and is not a space of eight feet twice the size of this, and half the size of the other?

BOY: Certainly.

SOC.: Such a space, then, will be made out of a line greater than this one, and less than that one?

BOY: Yes; I think so.

SOC.: Very good; I like to hear you say what you think. And now tell me, is not this a line of two feet and that of four?

BOY: Yes.

SOC.: Then the line which forms the side of eight feet ought to be more than this line of two feet, and less than the other of four feet?

BOY: It ought.

SOC.: Try and see if you can tell me how much it will be.

BOY: Three feet.

SOC.: Then if we add a half to this line of two, that will be the line of three. Here are two and there is one; and on the other side, here are two also and there is one: and that makes the figure of which you speak?

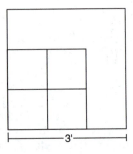

BOY: Yes.

SOC.: But if there are three feet this way and three feet that way, the whole space will be three times three feet?

BOY: That is evident.

SOC.: And how much are three times three feet?

BOY: Nine.

SOC.: And how much is the double of four?

BOY: Eight.

SOC.: Then the figure of eight is not made out of a line of three?

BOY: No.

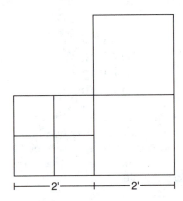

SOC.: But from what line?—tell me exactly; and if you would rather not reckon, try and show me the line.

BOY: Indeed, Socrates, I do not know.

SOC.: Do you see, Meno, what advances he has made in his power of recollection? He did not know at first, and he does not know now, what is the side of a figure of eight feet: but then he thought that he knew, and answered confidently as if he knew, and had no difficulty; now he has a difficulty, and neither knows nor fancies that he knows.

MEN.: True.

SOC.: Is he not better off in knowing his ignorance?

MEN.: I think that he is.

SOC.: If we have made him doubt, and given him the 'torpedo's shock,' have we done him any harm?

MEN.: I think not.

SOC.: We have certainly, as would seem, assisted him in some degree to the discovery of the truth; and now he will wish to remedy his ignorance, but then he would have been ready to tell all the world again and again that the double space should have a double side.

MEN.: True.

SOC.: But do you suppose that he would ever have enquired into or learned what he fancied that he knew, though he was really ignorant of it, until he had fallen into perplexity under the idea that he did not know, and had desired to know?

MEN.: I think not, Socrates.

SOC.: Then he was the better for the torpedo's touch?

MEN.: I think so.

[Although the slave boy has never been educated, he possesses innate knowledge of geometry. Socrates claims that all he is doing is helping the slave bring to consciousness that which he already knows. That is, education is recollection of innate ideas.—Ed.]

SOC.: Mark now the farther development. I shall only ask him, and not teach him, and he shall share the enquiry with me: and do you watch and see if you find me telling or explaining anything to him, instead of eliciting his opinion. Tell me, boy, is not this a square of four feet which I have drawn?

BOY: Yes.

SOC.: And now I add another square equal to the former one?

BOY: Yes.

SOC.: And a third, which is equal to either of them?

BOY: Yes.

SOC.: Suppose that we fill up the vacant corner?

BOY: Very good.

SOC.: Here, then, there are four equal spaces?

BOY: Yes.

SOC.: And how many times larger is this space than this other?

BOY: Four times.

SOC.: But it ought to have been twice only, as you will remember.

BOY: True.

SOC.: And does not this line, reaching from corner to corner, bisect each of these spaces? [BDEF]

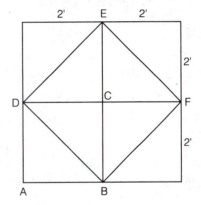

BOY: Yes.

SOC.: And are there not here four equal lines which contain this space? [BD, DE, EF, and FB]

BOY: There are.

SOC.: Look and see how much this space is.

BOY: I do not understand.

SOC.: Has not each interior line cut off half of the four spaces? [BD, DE, EF, and FB]

BOY: Yes.

SOC.: And how many spaces are there in this section? [BDEF]

BOY: Four.

SOC.: And how many in this? [ABCD]

BOY: Two.

SOC.: And four is how many times two?

BOY: Twice.

SOC.: And this space is of how many feet? [BDEF]

BOY: Of eight feet.

SOC.: And from what line do you get this figure?

BOY: From this. [BDEF]

SOC.: That is, from the line which extends from corner to corner of the figure of four feet?

BOY: Yes.

SOC.: And that is the line which the learned call the diagonal. And if this is the proper name, then you, Meno's slave, are prepared to affirm that the double space is the square of the diagonal?

BOY: Certainly, Socrates.

SOC.: What do you say of him, Meno? Were not all these answers given out of his own head?

MEN.: Yes, they were all his own.

SOC.: And yet, as we were just now saying, he did not know?

MEN.: True.

SOC.: But still he had in him those notions of his—had he not?

MEN.: Yes.

SOC.: Then he who does not know may still have true notions of that which he does not know?

MEN.: He has.

SOC.: And at present these notions have just been stirred up in him, as in a dream; but if he were frequently asked the same questions, in different forms, he would know as well as any one at last?

MEN.: I dare say.

SOC.: Without any one teaching him he will recover his knowledge for himself, if he is only asked questions?

MEN.: Yes.

SOC.: And this spontaneous recovery of knowledge in him is recollection?

MEN.: True.

SOC.: And this knowledge which he now has must he not either have acquired or always possessed?

MEN.: Yes.

SOC.: But if he always possessed this knowledge he would always have known; or if he has acquired the knowledge he could not have acquired it in this life, unless he has been taught geometry; for he may be made to do the same with all geometry and every other branch of knowledge. Now, has any one ever taught him all this? You must know about him, if, as you say, he was born and bred in your house.

MEN.: And I am certain that no one ever did teach him.

SOC.: And yet he has the knowledge?

MEN.: The fact, Socrates, is undeniable.

SOC.: But if he did not acquire the knowledge in this life, then he must have had and learned it at some other time?

MEN.: Clearly he must.

SOC.: Which must have been the time when he was not a man?

MEN.: Yes.

SOC.: And if there have been always true thoughts in him, both at the time when he was and was not a man, which only need to be awakened into knowledge by putting questions to him, his soul must have always possessed this knowledge, for he always either was or was not a man?

MEN.: Obviously.

SOC.: And if the truth of all things always existed in the soul, then the soul is immortal. Wherefore be of good cheer, and try to recollect what you do not know, or rather what you do not remember.

MEN.: I feel, somehow, that I like what you are saying.

SOC.: And I, Meno, like what I am saying. Some things I have said of which I am not altogether confident. But that we shall be better and braver and less helpless if we think that we ought to enquire, than we should have been if we indulged in the idle fancy that there was no knowing and no use in seeking to know what we do not know;—that is a theme upon which I am ready to fight, in word and deed, to the utmost of my power.

Bibliography

Audi, Robert. *Belief, Justification and Knowledge.* Belmont, CA: Wadsworth, 1988.

Ayer, A. J. *The Problem of Knowledge.* London: Penguin, 1956.

Capaldi, Nicholas. *Human Knowledge.* New York: Pegasus, 1969.

Chisholm, Roderick M. *Theory of Knowledge.* 3d ed. Englewood Cliffs, NJ: Prentice-Hall, 1988.

Dancy, John. *Introduction to Contemporary Epistemology.* London: Blackwell, 1985.

French, Peter, Theodore E. Vehling, Jr., and Howard Wettstein, eds. *Midwest Studies in Philosophy.* Vol. 5: *Studies in Epistemology.* Minneapolis: University of Minnesota Press, 1980.

Lehrer, Keith. *Theory of Knowledge.* Boulder, CO: Westview, 1990.

Locke, John. *An Essay Concerning Human Understanding.* Oxford, England: Oxford University Press, 1975.

Harman, Gilbert. *Thought.* Princeton, NJ: Princeton University Press, 1975.

Landesman, Charles, ed. *The Foundations of Knowledge.* Englewood Cliffs, NJ: Prentice-Hall, 1970.

Malcolm, Norman. *Knowledge and Certainty.* Ithaca, NY: Cornell University Press, 1963.

Moser, Paul, and Arnold Vander Nat, eds. *Human Knowledge.* Oxford, England: Oxford University Press, 1987.

Nagel, Ernest, and Richard Brandt, eds. *Meaning and Knowledge.* New York: Harcourt, Brace, & World, 1965.

O'Connor, D. J., and Brian Carr. *Introduction to the Theory of Knowledge.* Minneapolis: University of Minnesota Press, 1982.

Plato. *Phaedo, Meno, Theaetetus,* and the *Republic.*

Pollock, John L. *Contemporary Theories of Knowledge.* Totawa, NJ: Rowman & Littlefield, 1986.

Popkin, Richard. *A History of Skepticism from Erasmus to Spinoza.* Berkeley: University of California Press, 1979.

Russell, Bertrand. *Human Knowledge: Its Scope and Limits.* New York: Simon & Schuster, 1948.

Russell, Bertrand. *The Problems of Philosophy.* Oxford, England: Oxford University Press, 1912.

Part II

Skepticism

What can we really know? How can we be certain that we have the truth?
How can we be certain that we know anything at all? If we know something,
must we know that we know it? Is the skeptic right in claiming that we
know almost nothing at all?

Can we know anything at all? Or are we doomed to ignorance about the most important subjects in life? What do we really know? Could it be that we really know nothing at all? Could it be that either none of our beliefs are completely true or that none of our true beliefs are sufficiently justified to constitute knowledge? How can we show that we really do know anything at all?

Skepticism is the theory that we do not have any knowledge. We cannot be completely certain that any of our beliefs are true. There are two classic types of skepticism, both originat-ing in ancient Greek philosophy: Academic skepticism and Pyrrhonian skepticism. Academic skepticism was first formulated by Arcesilaus (about 315 to about 240 B.C.), a philosopher in Plato's Academy, and builds on Socrates' confes-sion in the *Apology,* "All that I know is that I know nothing." It argues that the only thing we can know is that we know nothing. The Academ-ics argued that there is no criterion by which we can distinguish veridical perceptions from illusions and that at best we have only probable true belief.

Pyrrhonian skepticism, named after Pyrrho

of Elis (about 360 to 270 B.C.), flourished in Alexandria in the first century B.C. The Pyrrhonians rejected Academic skepticism and dogmatism, the view that we could have knowledge, and set forth "tropes," skeptical arguments leading to *equipollence,* the balancing of reasons on both sides of an issue that led to *epoche,* the suspension of judgment. Whereas the Academics claimed to know one thing (that they didn't have any other knowledge), the Pyrrhonians denied that we could know even that. The Greek Pyrrhonist, Sextus Empiricus (second century A.D.), said that Pyrrhonism was like a purge that eliminates everything, including itself.

One other distinction regarding skepticism needs to be made: that between global and local skepticism. Global skeptics maintain universal doubt. They deny that we know that there is an external world, that there are other minds, that we can have knowledge of metaphysical truths, such as whether we have free will, whether God exists, whether we have souls, and so forth. Some superglobal skeptics even deny that we can know simple mathematical truths or that the laws of logic are valid (an evil genius could be deceiving us). In the following readings, René Descartes (1596–1650) and Keith Lehrer both represent global skepticism. The other type of skepticism is local skepticism, which admits that we can have mathematical and empirical knowledge but denies that we can have metaphysical knowledge (God's existence, the nature of matter, whether all events have antecedent causes, whether there are other minds, and so forth). David Hume (1711–1776) entertains the possibility of both forms of skepticism. As Richard Popkin accurately puts it,

> Hume sometimes held a most extreme skeptical position . . . questioning even the knowledge claims of science, mathematics, and logical reasoning, and sometimes held a limited mitigated skepticism allowing for probabilistic standards for evaluating beliefs about

what is beyond immediate experience. When Hume examined the general nature of all beliefs, he tended toward complete skepticism. When he examined metaphysics and theology, in contrast with science, he tended toward a positivistic, limited skepticism. And when he developed his own views about human nature and conduct, his doubts tended to recede and his positive views became more pronounced.[1]

Skepticism does not deny that we should act from the best evidence available, but its insists that we can never be sure that we are correct in our truth claims. For all we know, the universe and everything in it could have been created ten minutes ago, and all our apparent memories created with it. Or the universe and everything in it may have doubled in size last night while we were sleeping. How could we check on this? It wouldn't help to use a ruler to measure our height to see if we have doubled in size, would it?

How do you know that you are not the only person who exists and that everyone else is a robot who is programed to speak and smile and write exams? Can you prove that other people have consciousness? Have you ever felt their consciousness, their pain, or their sense of the color green? In fact, come to think of it, how do you know that you are not just dreaming right now? All you are experiencing is part of a dream. Soon you will awake and be surprised to discover that what you thought were dreams were really minidreams within your maxidream. How can you prove that you are not dreaming? Or perhaps you are simply a brain suspended in a tub full of a chemical solution in a scientist's laboratory and wired to a computer that is causing you to have the simulated experiences of what you now seem to be experiencing? If you are under the control of an ingenious scientist, you would never discover it, for he has arranged that you will only be able to compare your beliefs to experiences that he simulates. Your tub is your destiny!

In the first reading, from the *Meditations,* Descartes begins by rejecting all sensory perception, arguing that the senses are not reliable witnesses because they sometimes deceive. Essentially, we do not have a criterion by which to distinguish illusory experience from veridical perception. His argument may be formulated thus:

1. In order to have knowledge, we need to be able to tell the difference between a hallucination (deception) and a perception. (Where there is no relevant difference, no epistemological distinction can be made.)

2. It is impossible to distinguish between an hallucination (or deception) and a normal perception.

3. Therefore, we do not know whether any of our perceptual beliefs are true.

But Descartes goes on to doubt even our mathematical judgments. He imagines that an ingenious demon is deceiving him about everything, even about the most secure mathematical sums, so that it is possible that he is mistaken about adding 2 plus 3.

In the second selection, David Hume admits that we can know mathematical truths but claims that we cannot have empirical knowledge. He supposes that all our beliefs (or ideas) are caused by impressions (both internal and external, the passions and the perceptions). But we cannot get behind the impressions to check whether the world is really like what we are experiencing, so we can never know to what extent our impressions and ideas resemble the world. Hume goes on to argue that since all our beliefs are founded on these insecure impressions, we can have no metaphysical knowledge. We cannot even trace our belief in cause and effect, the self, the existence of God, or free will to impressions; hence they are entirely without justification. In the fourth reading, Keith Lehrer argues that knowledge entails complete justification of belief, but that if it is possible that the skeptical hypothesis is true, no one is completely justified in any belief. Hence, no one knows anything at all.

Can you defeat the skeptic? Two attempts are offered in this part of the book. In the third reading, G. E. Moore claims we *can* know there is an external world, for we can know we have bodies. There are many empirical beliefs that we can be absolutely certain of, so that skepticism may justly be refuted. In the fifth reading, Norman Malcolm distinguishes two types of knowledge, weak and strong. When I use the weak sense of knowledge, I am prepared to let an investigation determine whether my knowledge claim is true or false, whereas when I use the strong sense I will not concede that anything whatsoever could prove me mistaken.

Note

[1] Richard Popkin, "Skepticism," *Encyclopedia of Philosophy,* Vol. 7 (New York: Macmillan, 1967), p. 455.

II.1 *Global Skepticism*

RENÉ DESCARTES

René Descartes (1596–1650) was born in France and educated by the Jesuits at the College of La Fleche. In this classic work, *Meditations on First Philosophy* (1641), Descartes declares that because his education and experience in general have resulted in a shaky house of knowledge, he must use the method of universal doubt to raze the entire edifice, foundations and all, and erect new and solid foundations on which to build a permanent dwelling, an indestructible system of knowledge. This selection contains the first of six meditations on the subject of knowledge. In Reading V.1 we consider the second and third meditations.

Meditation I

Of the Things Which May Be Brought Within the Sphere of the Doubtful

It is now some years since I detected how many were the false beliefs that I had from my earliest youth admitted as true, and how doubtful was everything I had since constructed on this basis; and from that time I was convinced that I must once for all seriously undertake to rid myself of all the opinions which I had formerly accepted, and commence to build anew from the foundation, if I wanted to establish any firm and permanent structure in the sciences. But as this enterprise appeared to be a very great one, I waited until I had attained an age so mature that I could not hope that at any later date I should be better fitted to execute my design. This reason caused me to delay so long that I should feel that I was doing wrong were I to occupy in deliberation the time that yet remains to me for action. Today, then, since very opportunely for the plan I have in view I have delivered my mind from every care [and am happily agitated by no passions] and

Reprinted from the *Philosophical Works of Descartes,* trans. Elizabeth Haldane and G. Ross, vol. I, pp. 144–199 (Cambridge University Press, 1931) by permission of the publisher.

since I have procured for myself an assured leisure in a peaceable retirement, I shall at last seriously and freely address myself to the general upheaval of all my former opinions.

Now for this object it is not necessary that I should show that all of these are false—I shall perhaps never arrive at this end. But inasmuch as reason already persuades me that I ought no less carefully to withhold my assent from matters which are not entirely certain and indubitable than from those which appear to me manifestly to be false, if I am able to find in each one some reason to doubt, this will suffice to justify my rejecting the whole. And for that end it will not be requisite that I should examine each in particular, which would be an endless undertaking; for owing to the fact that the destruction of the foundations of necessity brings with it the downfall of the rest of the edifice, I shall only in the first place attack those principles upon which all my former opinions rested.

All that up to the present time I have accepted as most true and certain I have learned either from the senses or through the senses; but it is sometimes proved to me that these senses are deceptive, and it is wiser not to trust entirely to any thing by which we have once been deceived.

But it may be that although the senses sometimes deceive us concerning things which are hardly perceptible, or very far away, there are yet many others to be met with as to which we cannot reasonably have any doubt, although we recognise them by their means. For example, there is the fact that I am here, seated by the fire, attired in a dressing gown, having this paper in my hands and other similar matters. And how could I deny that these hands and this body are mine, were it not perhaps that I compare myself to certain persons, devoid of sense, whose cerebella are so troubled and clouded by the violent vapours of black bile, that they constantly assure us that they think they are kings when they are really quite poor, or that they are clothed in purple when they are really without covering, or who imagine that they have an earthenware head or are nothing but pumpkins or are made of glass. But they are mad, and I should not be any the less insane were I to follow examples so extravagant.

At the same time I must remember that I am a man, and that consequently I am in the habit of sleeping, and in my dreams representing to myself the same things or sometimes even less probable things, than do those who are insane in their waking moments. How often has it happened to me that in the night I dreamt that I found myself in this particular place, that I was dressed and seated near the fire, whilst in reality I was lying undressed in bed! At this moment it does indeed seem to me that it is with eyes awake that I am looking at this paper; that this head which I move is not asleep, that it is deliberately and of set purpose that I extend my hand and perceive it; what happens in sleep does not appear so clear nor so distinct as does all this. But in thinking over this I remind myself that on many occasions I have in sleep been deceived by similar illusions, and in dwelling carefully on this reflection I see so manifestly that there are no certain indications by which we may clearly distinguish wakefulness from sleep that I am lost in astonishment. And my astonishment is such that it is almost capable of persuading me that I now dream.

Now let us assume that we are asleep and that all these particulars, e.g. that we open our eyes, shake our head, extend our hands, and so on, are but false delusions; and let us reflect that possibly neither our hands nor our whole body are such as they appear to us to be. At the same time we must at least confess that the things which are represented to us in sleep are like painted representations which can only have been formed as the counterparts of something real and true, and that in this way those general things at least, i.e. eyes, a head, hands, and a

whole body, are not imaginary things, but things really existent. For, as a matter of fact, painters, even when they study with the greatest skill to represent sirens and satyrs by forms the most strange and extraordinary, cannot give them natures which are entirely new, but merely make a certain medley of the members of different animals; or if their imagination is extravagant enough to invent something so novel that nothing similar has ever before been seen, and that then their work represents a thing purely fictitious and absolutely false, it is certain all the same that the colours of which this is composed are necessarily real. And for the same reason, although these general things, to wit, [a body], eyes, a head, hands, and such like, may be imaginary, we are bound at the same time to confess that there are at least some other objects yet more simple and more universal, which are real and true; and of these just in the same way as with certain real colours, all these images of things which dwell in our thoughts, whether true and real or false and fantastic, are formed.

To such a class of things pertains corporeal nature in general, and its extension, the figure of extended things, their quantity or magnitude and number, as also the place in which they are, the time which measures their duration, and so on.

That is possibly why our reasoning is not unjust when we conclude from this that Physics, Astronomy, Medicine and all other sciences which have as their end the consideration of composite things, are very dubious and uncertain; but that Arithmetic, Geometry and other sciences of that kind which only treat of things that are very simple and very general, without taking great trouble to ascertain whether they are actually existent or not, contain some measure of certainty and an element of the indubitable. For whether I am awake or asleep, two and three together always form five, and the square can never have more than four sides, and it does not seem possible that truths so clear and apparent can be suspected of any falsity [or uncertainty].

Nevertheless I have long had fixed in my mind the belief that an all-powerful God existed by whom I have been created such as I am. But how do I know that He has not brought it to pass that there is no earth, no heaven, no extended body, no magnitude, no place, and that nevertheless [I possess the perceptions of all these things and that] they seem to me to exist just exactly as I now see them? And, besides, as I sometimes imagine that others deceive themselves in the things which they think they know best, how do I know that I am not deceived every time that I add two and three, or count the sides of a square, or judge of things yet simpler, if anything simpler can be imagined? But possibly God has not desired that I should be thus deceived, for He is said to be supremely good. If, however, it is contrary to His goodness to have made me such that I constantly deceive myself, it would also appear to be contrary to His goodness to permit me to be sometimes deceived, and nevertheless I cannot doubt that He does permit this.

There may indeed be those who would prefer to deny the existence of a God so powerful, rather than believe that all other things are uncertain. But let us not oppose them for the present, and grant that all that is here said of a God is a fable; nevertheless in whatever way they suppose that I have arrived at the state of being that I have reached—whether they attribute it to fate or to accident, or make out that it is by a continual succession of antecedents, or by some other method—since to err and deceive oneself is a defect, it is clear that the greater will be the probability of my being so imperfect as to deceive myself ever, as is the Author to whom they assign my origin the less powerful. To these reasons I have certainly nothing to reply, but at the end I feel constrained to confess that there is nothing in all that I formerly believed to be true, of which I cannot in some measure doubt, and that not merely through want of thought or through levity, but for reasons which are very powerful and maturely considered; so that henceforth I ought not the less carefully to refrain from giving credence to these opinions than to that which is manifestly false, if I desire to arrive at any certainty [in the sciences].

But it is not sufficient to have made these remarks, we must also be careful to keep them in mind. For these ancient and commonly held opinions still revert frequently to my mind, long and familiar custom having given them the right to occupy my mind against my inclination and rendered them almost masters of my belief; nor will I ever lose the habit of deferring to them or of placing my confidence in them, so long as I consider them as they really are, i.e. opinions in some measure doubtful, as I have just shown, and at the same time

highly probable, so that there is much more reason to believe in than to deny them. That is why I consider that I shall not be acting amiss, if, taking of set purpose a contrary belief, I allow myself to be deceived, and for a certain time pretend that all these opinions are entirely false and imaginary, until at last, having thus balanced my former prejudices with my latter [so that they cannot divert my opinions more to one side than to the other], my judgment will no longer be dominated by bad usage or turned away from the right knowledge of the truth. For I am assured that there can be neither peril nor error in this course, and that I cannot at present yield too much to distrust, since I am not considering the question of action, but only of knowledge.

I shall then suppose, not that God who is supremely good and the fountain of truth, but some evil genius not less powerful than deceitful, has employed his whole energies in deceiving me; I shall consider that the heavens, the earth, colours, figures, sound, and all other external things are nought but the illusions and dreams of which this genius has availed himself in order to lay traps for my credulity; I shall consider myself as having no hands, no eyes, no flesh, no blood, nor any senses, yet falsely believing myself to possess all these things; I shall remain obstinately attached to this idea, and if by this means it is not in my power to arrive at the knowledge of any truth, I may at least do what is in my power [i.e. suspend my judgment], and with firm purpose avoid giving credence to any false thing, or being imposed upon by this arch deceiver, however powerful and deceptive he may be. But this task is a laborious one, and insensibly a certain lassitude leads me into the course of my ordinary life. And just as a captive who in sleep enjoys an imaginary liberty, when he begins to suspect that his liberty is but a dream, fears to awaken, and conspires with these agreeable illusions that the deception may be prolonged, so insensibly of my own accord I fall back into my former opinions, and I dread awakening from this slumber, lest the laborious wakefulness which would follow the tranquility of this repose should have to be spent not in daylight, but in the excessive darkness of the difficulties which have just been discussed.

II.2 *Skepticism Regarding the Senses*

DAVID HUME

The Scottish empiricist David Hume (1711–1776) accepts that there are truths of reason, mathematical, and logical truths, but doubts whether we can have empirical and metaphysical knowledge. According to Hume, all learning is based on sensory impressions, and our ideas are mere representations of these impressions. We use these ideas to construct complex ideas, but we have no way of knowing whether the complex ideas represent reality. An example of such a complex idea is the notion of God, the thought of which is a composite made up of our ideas of power, knowledge, and goodness, each of which are joined to the notion of unlimited quantity, to make up the notions of all-powerful, all-knowing, and moral perfection. But there is no way of proving that these ideas are exemplified in reality.

In the present selection from Hume's youthful *Treatise of Human Nature* (1739), Hume asks why we believe in the individual and continued existence of physical objects ("the existence of body"). He admits that we cannot help believing in an external world, but he wants to know whether we are justified in so believing. He offers three hypotheses to answer this question. Our knowledge of the external world is based either (1) on our senses, (2) on our reason, or (3) on our imagination. He rejects the first hypothesis, because our perceptions change when there is no reason to believe that the external object changes. The senses do not preserve the continued existence of objects, yet we cannot help believing that objects do continue to exist even when we do not perceive them. He rejects the second hypothesis (that reason is the cause of our belief) because reason lacks sufficient premises to establish the existence of physical objects but rather, in order to think about the external world, takes their continued and distinct existence for granted. That leaves the third hypothesis, imagination, as the only plausible cause of our belief in the external world. Constancy and coherence of impressions are the forces that lead us to posit such a belief. But this is no proof of an external world, let alone of the veridicality of our perceptions.

We may well ask, *What causes induce us to believe in the existence of body* [external objects—Ed.]? but 'tis in vain to ask, *Whether there be body or not?* That is a point, which we must take for granted in all our reasonings.

The subject, then, of our present enquiry is concerning the *causes* which induce us to believe in the existence of body; And my reasonings on this shall begin with a distinction, which at first sight may seem superfluous, but which will contribute very much to the perfect understanding of what follows. We ought to examine apart those two questions, which are commonly confounded together, *viz.* Why we attribute a CONTINUED existence to objects, even when they are not present to the senses; and why we suppose them to have an existence DISTINCT from the mind and perception. Under this last head I comprehend their situation as well as relations, their *external* position as well as the *independence* of their existence and operation. These two questions concerning the continu'd and

Reprinted from *Treatise of Human Nature* (1739).

distinct existence of body are intimately connected together. For if the objects of our senses continue to exist, even when they are not perceiv'd, their existence is of course independent of and distinct from the perception; and *vice versa,* if their existence be independent of the perception and distinct from it, they must continue to exist, even tho' they be not perceiv'd. But tho' the decision of the one question decides the other; yet that we may the more easily discover the principles of human nature, from whence the decision arises, we shall carry along with us this distinction, and shall consider, whether it be the *senses, reason,* or the *imagination,* that produces the opinion of a *continu'd* or of a *distinct* existence. These are the only questions, that are intelligible on the present subject. For as to the notion of external existence, when taken for something specifically different from our perceptions, we have already shewn its absurdity.

To begin with the SENSES, 'tis evident these faculties are incapable of giving rise to the notion of the *continu'd* existence of their objects, after they no longer appear to the senses. For that is a contradiction in terms, and supposes that the senses continue to operate, even after they have ceas'd all manner of operation. These faculties, therefore, if they have any influence in the present case, must produce the opinion of a distinct, not of a continu'd existence; and in order to that, must present their impressions either as images and representations, or as these very distinct and external existences.

That our senses offer not their impressions as the images of something *distinct,* or *independent,* and *external,* is evident; because they convey to us nothing but a single perception, and never give us the least intimation of any thing beyond. A single perception can never produce the idea of a double existence, but by some inference either of the reason or imagination. When the mind looks farther than what immediately appears to it, its conclusions can never be put to the account of the senses; and it certainly looks farther, when from a single perception it infers a double existence, and supposes the relations of resemblance and causation betwixt them.

If our senses, therefore, suggest any idea of distinct existences, they must convey the impressions as those very existences, by a kind of fallacy and illusion. Upon this head we may observe, that all sensations are felt by the mind, such as they really are, and that when we doubt, whether they present themselves as distinct objects, or as mere impressions, the difficulty is not concerning their nature, but concerning their relations and situation. Now if the senses presented our impressions as external to, and independent of ourselves, both the objects and ourselves must be obvious to our senses, otherwise cou'd not be compar'd by these faculties. The difficulty, then, is how far we are *ourselves* the objects of our senses.

'Tis certain there is no question in philosophy more abstruse than that concerning identity, and the nature of the uniting principle, which constitutes a person. So far from being able by our senses merely to determine this question, we must have recourse to the most profound metaphysics to give a satisfactory answer to it; and in common life 'tis evident these ideas of self and person are never very fix'd nor determinate. 'Tis absurd, therefore, to imagine the senses can ever distinguish betwixt ourselves and external objects.

Add to this, that every impression, external and internal, passions, affections, sensations, pains and pleasures, are originally on the same footing; and that whatever other differences we may observe among them, they appear all of them, in their true colours, as impressions or perceptions. And indeed, if we consider the matter aright, 'tis scarce possible it shou'd be otherwise, nor is it conceivable that our senses shou'd be more capable of deceiving us in the situation and relations, than in the nature of our impressions. For since all actions and sensations of the mind are known to use by consciousness, they must necessarily appear in every particular what they are, and be what they appear. Every thing that enters the mind, being in *reality* as the perception, 'tis impossible any thing shou'd to *feeling* appear different. This were to suppose, that even where we are most intimately conscious, we might be mistaken.

But not to lose time in examining, whether 'tis possible for our senses to deceive us, and represent our perceptions as distinct from ourselves, that is as *external* to and *independent* of us; let us consider whether they really do so, and whether this error proceeds from an immediate sensation, or from some other causes.

To begin with the question concerning *external* existence, it may perhaps be said, that setting aside the metaphysical question of the identity of a thinking substance, our own body evidently belongs to us; and as several impressions appear exterior to the body, we suppose them also exterior to ourselves. The paper, on which I write at present, is beyond my hand. The table is beyond the paper. The walls of the chamber beyond the table. And in casting my eye towards the window, I perceive a great extent of fields and buildings beyond my chamber. From all this it may be infer'd, that no other faculty is requir'd, beside the senses, to convince us of the external existence of body. But to prevent this inference, we need only weigh the three following considerations. *First,* That, properly speaking, 'tis not our body we perceive, when we regard our limbs and members, but certain impressions, which enter by the senses; so that the ascribing a real and corporeal existence to these impressions, or to their objects, is an act of the mind as difficult to explain, as that which we examine at present. *Secondly,* Sounds, and tastes, and smells, tho' commonly regarded by the mind as continu'd independent qualities, appear not to have any existence in extension, and consequently cannot appear to the senses as situated externally to the body. The reason, why we ascribe a place to them, shall be consider'd afterwards. *Thirdly,* Even our sight informs us not of distance or outness (so to speak) immediately and without a certain reasoning and experience, as is acknowledg'd by the most rational philosophers.

As to the *independency* of our perceptions on ourselves, this can never be an object of the senses; but any opinion we form concerning it, must be deriv'd from experience and observation: And we shall see afterwards, that our conclusions from experience are far from being favourable to the doctrine of the independency of our perceptions. Meanwhile we may observe that when we talk of real distinct existences, we have commonly more in our eye their independency than external situation in place, and think an object has a sufficient reality, when its Being is uninterrupted, and independent of the incessant revolutions, which we are conscious of in ourselves.

Thus to resume what I have said concerning the senses; they give us no notion of continu'd existence, because they cannot operate beyond the extent, in which they really operate. They as little produce the opinion of a distinct existence, because they neither can offer it to the mind as represented, nor as original. To offer it as represented, they must present both an object and an image. To make it appear as original, they must convey a falshood; and this falshood must lie in the relations and situation: In order to which they must be able to compare the object with ourselves; and even in that case they do not, nor is it possible they shou'd, deceive us. We may, therefore, conclude with certainty, that the opinion of a continu'd and of a distinct existence never arises from the senses.

To confirm this we may observe, that there are three different kinds of impressions convey'd by the senses. The first are those of the figure, bulk, motion and solidity of bodies. The second those of colours, tastes, smells, sounds, heat and cold. The third are the pains and pleasures, that arise from the application of objects to our bodies, as by the cutting of our flesh with steel, and such like. Both philosophers and the vulgar suppose the first of these to have a distinct continu'd existence. The vulgar only regard the second as on the same footing. Both philosophers and the vulgar, again, esteem the third to be merely perceptions; and consequently interrupted and dependent beings.

Now 'tis evident, that, whatever may be our philosophical opinion, colours, sounds, heat and cold, as far as appears to the senses, exist after the same manner with motion and solidity, and that the difference we make betwixt them in this respect, arises not from the mere perception. So strong is the prejudice for the distinct continu'd existence of the former qualities, that when the contrary opinion is advanc'd by modern philosophers, people imagine they can almost refute it from their feeling and experience, and that their very senses contradict this philosophy. 'Tis also evident, that colours, sounds, &c. are originally on the same footing with the pain that arises from steel, and pleasure that proceeds from a fire; and that the difference betwixt them is founded neither on perception nor reason, but on the imagination. For as they are confest to be, both of them, nothing but perceptions arising from the particular configurations and motions of the parts of body, wherein possibly can their difference consist? Upon the whole, then, we may conclude, that as far as the senses are judges, all perceptions are the same in the manner of their existence.

We may also observe in this instance of sounds and colours, that we can attribute a distinct continu'd existence to objects without ever consulting REASON, or weighing our opinions by any philosophical principles. And indeed, whatever convincing arguments philosophers may fancy they can produce to establish the belief of objects independent of the mind, 'tis obvious these arguments are known but to very few, and that 'tis not by them, that children, peasants, and the greatest part of mankind are induc'd to attribute objects to some impressions, and deny them to others. Accordingly we find, that all the conclusions, which the vulgar form on this head, are directly contrary to those, which are confirm'd by philosophy. For philosophy informs us, that every thing, which appears to the mind, is nothing but a perception, and is interrupted, and dependent on the mind; whereas the vulgar confound perceptions and objects, and attribute a distinct continu'd existence to the very things they feel or see. This sentiment, then, as it is entirely unreasonable, must proceed from some other faculty than the understanding. To which we may add, that as long as we take our perceptions and objects to be the same, we can never infer the existence of the one from that of the other, nor form any argument from the relation of cause and effect; which is the only one that can assure us of matter of fact. Even after we distinguish our perceptions from our objects, 'twill appear presently, that we are still incapable of reasoning from the existence of one to that of the other: So that upon the whole our reason neither does, nor is it possible it ever shou'd, upon any supposition, give us an assurance of the continu'd and distinct existence of body. That opinion must be entirely owing to the IMAGINATION: which must now be the subject of our enquiry.

Since all impressions are internal and perishing existences, and appear as such, the notion of their distinct and continu'd existence must arise from a concurrence of some of their qualities with the qualities of the imagination; and since this notion does not extend to all of them, it must arise from certain qualities peculiar to some impressions. 'Twill therefore be easy for us to discover these qualities by a comparison of the impressions, to which we attribute a distinct and continu'd existence, with those, which we regard as internal and perishing.

We may observe, then, that 'tis neither upon account of the involuntariness of certain impressions, as is commonly suppos'd, nor of their superior force and violence, that we attribute to them a reality, and continu'd existence, which we refuse to others, that are voluntary or feeble. For 'tis evident our pains and pleasures, our passions and affections, which we never suppose to have any existence beyond our perception, operate with greater violence, and are equally involuntary, as the impressions of figure and extension, colour and sound, which we suppose to be permanent beings. The heat of a fire, when moderate, is suppos'd to exist in the fire; but the pain, which it causes upon a near approach, is not taken to have any being except in the perception.

These vulgar opinions, then, being rejected, we must search for some other hypothesis, by which we may discover those peculiar qualities in our impressions, which makes us attribute to them a distinct and continu'd existence.

After a little examination, we shall find, that all those objects, to which we attribute a continu'd existence, have a peculiar *constancy,* which distinguishes them from the impressions, whose existence depends upon our perception. Those mountains, and houses, and trees, which lie at present under my eye, have always appear'd to me in the same order; and when I lose sight of them by shutting my eyes or turning my head, I soon after find them return upon me without the least alteration. My bed and table, my books and papers, present themselves in the same uniform manner, and change not upon account of any interruption in my seeing or perceiving them. This is the case with all the impressions, whose objects are suppos'd to have an external existence; and is the case with no other impressions, whether gentle or violent, voluntary or involuntary.

This constancy, however, is not so perfect as not to admit of very considerable exceptions. Bodies often change their position and qualities, and after a little absence or interruption may become hardly knowable. But here 'tis observable, that even in these changes they preserve a *coherence,* and have a regular dependence on each other; which is the foundation of a kind of reasoning from causation, and produces the opinion of their continu'd existence. When I return to my chamber after an hour's absence, I find not my fire in the same situation, in which I left it: But then I am accustom'd in other instances to see a like alteration produc'd in a like time, whether I am present or absent, near or remote. This coherence, therefore, in their changes is one of the characteristics of external objects, as well as their constancy.

Having found that the opinion of the continu'd existence of body depends on the COHERENCE and CONSTANCY of certain impressions, I now proceed to examine after what manner these qualities give rise to so extraordinary an opinion. To begin with the coherence; we may observe, that tho' those internal impressions, which we regard as fleeting and perishing, have also a certain coherence or regularity in their appearances, yet 'tis of somewhat a different nature, from that which we discover in bodies. Our passions are found by experience to have a mutual connexion with and dependence on each other; but on no occasion is it necessary to suppose, that they have existed and operated, when they were not perceiv'd, in order to preserve the same dependence and connexion, of which we have had experience. The case is not the same with relation to external objects. Those require a continu'd existence, or otherwise lose, in a great measure, the regularity of their operation. I am here seated in my chamber with my face to the fire; and all the objects, that strike my senses, are contain'd in a few yards around me. My memory, indeed, informs me of the existence of many objects; but then this information extends not beyond their past existence, nor do either my senses or memory give any testimony to the continuance of their being. When therefore I am thus seated, and revolve over these thoughts, I hear on a sudden a noise as of a door turning upon its hinges; and a little after see a porter, who advances towards me. This gives occasion to many new reflexions and reasonings. First, I never have observ'd, that this noise cou'd proceed from anything but the motion of a door; and therefore conclude, that the present phaenomenon is a contradiction to all past experience, unless the door, which I remember on t'other side the chamber, be still in being. Again, I have always found, that a human body was possest of a quality, which I call gravity, and which hinders it from mounting in the air, as this porter must have done to arrive at my chamber, unless the stairs I remember be not annihilated by my absence. But this is not all. I receive a letter, which upon opening it I perceive by the hand-writing and subscription to have come from a friend, who says he is two hundred leagues distant. 'Tis evident I can never account for this phaenomenon, conformable to my experience in other instances, without spreading out in my mind the whole sea and continent between us, and supposing the effects and continu'd existence of posts and ferries, according to my memory and observation. To consider these phaenomena of the porter and letter in a certain light, they are contradictions to common experience, and may be regarded as objections to those maxims, which we form concerning the connexions of causes and effects. I am accustom'd to hear such a sound, and see such an object in motion at the same time. I have not receiv'd in this particular instance both these perceptions. These observations are contrary, unless I suppose that the door still remains, and that it was open'd without my perceiving it: And this supposition, which was at first entirely arbitrary and hypothetical, acquires a force and evidence by its being the only one, upon which I can reconcile these contradictions. There is scarce a moment of my life, wherein there is not a similar instance presented to me, and I have not occasion to suppose the continu'd existence of objects, in order to connect their past and present appearances, and give them such an union with each other, as I have found by experience to be suitable to their particular natures and circumstances. Here then I am naturally led to regard the world, as something real and durable, and as preserving its existence, even when it is no longer present to my perception.

But tho' this conclusion from the coherence of appearances may seem to be of the same nature with our reasonings concerning causes and effects; as being deriv'd from custom, and regulated by past experience; we shall find upon examination, that they are at the bottom considerably different from each other, and that this inference arises from the understanding, and from custom in an indirect and oblique manner. For 'twill readily be allow'd, that since nothing is ever really present to the mind, besides its own perceptions, 'tis not only impossible, that any habit shou'd ever be acquir'd otherwise than by the regular succession of these perceptions, but also that any habit shou'd ever exceed that degree of regularity. Any degree, therefore, of regularity in our perceptions, can never be a foundation for us to infer a greater degree of regularity in some objects, which are not perceiv'd; since this supposes a contradiction, *viz.* a habit acquir'd by what was never present to the mind. But 'tis evident, that whenever we infer the continu'd existence of the objects of sense from their coherence, and the frequency of their unions, 'tis in order to bestow on the objects a greater regularity than what is observ'd in our mere perceptions. We remark a connexion betwixt two kinds of objects in their past appearance to the senses, but are not able to observe this connexion to be perfectly constant, since the turning about of our head, or the shutting of our eyes is able to break it. What then do we suppose in this case, but that these objects still continue their usual connexion, notwithstanding their apparent interruption, and that the irregular appearances are join'd by something, of which we are insensible? But as all reasoning concerning matters of fact arises only from custom, and custom can only be the effect of repeated perceptions, the extending of custom and reasoning beyond the perceptions can never be the direct and natural effect of the constant repetition and connexion, but must arise from the cooperation of some other principles.

I have already observ'd, in examining the foundation of mathematics, that the imagination, when set into any train of thinking, is apt to continue, even when its object fails it, and like a galley put in motion by the oars, carries on its course without any new impulse. This I have assign'd for the reason, why, after considering several loose standards of equality, and correcting them by each other, we proceed to imagine so correct and exact a standard of that relation, as is not liable to the least error or variation. The same principle makes us easily entertain this opinion of the continu'd existence of body. Objects have a certain coherence even as they appear to our senses; but this coherence is much greater and more uniform, if we suppose the objects to have a continu'd existence; and as the mind is once in the train of observing a uniformity among objects, it naturally continues, till it renders the uniformity as compleat as possible. The simple supposition of their continu'd existence suffices for this purpose, and gives us a notion of a much greater regularity among objects, than what they have when we look no farther than our senses.

But whatever force we may ascribe to this principle, I am afraid 'tis too weak to support alone so vast an edifice, as is that of the continu'd existence of all external bodies; and that we must join the *constancy* of their appearance to the *coherence,* in order to give a satisfactory account of that opinion. As the explication of this will lead me into a considerable compass of very profound reasoning; I think it proper, in order to avoid confusion, to give a short sketch or abridgment of my system, and afterwards draw out all its parts in their full compass. This inference from the constancy of our perceptions, like the precedent from their coherence, gives rise to the opinion of the *continu'd* existence of body, which is prior to that of its *distinct* existence, and produces that latter principle.

When we have been accustom'd to observe a constancy in certain impressions, and have found, that the perception of the sun or ocean, for instance, returns upon us after an absence or annihilation with like parts and in a like order, as at its first appearance, we are not apt to regard these interrupted perceptions as different, (which they really are) but on the contrary consider them as individually the same, upon account of their resemblance. But as this interruption of their existence is contrary to their perfect identity, and makes us regard the first impression as annihilated, and the second as newly created, we find ourselves somewhat at a loss, and are involv'd in a kind of contradiction. In order to free ourselves from this difficulty, we disguise, as much as possible, the interruption, or rather remove it entirely, by supposing that these interrupted perceptions are connected by a real existence, of which we are insensible. This supposition, or idea of continu'd existence, acquires a force and vivacity from the memory of these broken impressions, and from that propensity, which they give us, to suppose them the same; and according to the precedent reasoning, the very essence of belief consists in the force and vivacity of the conception. . . .

But tho' we are led after this manner, by the natural propensity of the imagination, to ascribe a continu'd existence to those sensible objects or perceptions, which we find to resemble each other in their interrupted appearance; yet a very little reflection and philosophy is sufficient to make us perceive the fallacy of that opinion. I have already observ'd, that there is an intimate connexion betwixt those two principles, of a *continu'd* and of a *distinct* or *independent* existence, and that we no sooner establish the one than the other follows, as a necessary consequence. 'Tis the opinion of a continu'd existence, which first takes place, and without much study or reflection draws the other along with it, wherever the mind follows its first and most natural tendency. But when we compare experiments, and reason a little upon them, we quickly perceive, that the doctrine of the independent existence of our sensible perceptions is contrary to the plainest experience. This leads us backward upon our footsteps to perceive our error in attributing a continu'd existence to our perceptions, and is the origin of many very curious opinions, which we shall here endeavour to account for.

'Twill first be proper to observe a few of those experiments, which convince us, that our perceptions are not possest of any independent existence. When we press one eye with a finger, we immediately perceive all the objects to become double, and one half of them to be remov'd from their common and natural position. But as we do not attribute a continu'd existence to both these perceptions, and as they are both of the same nature, we clearly perceive, that all our perceptions are dependent on our organs, and the disposition of our nerves and animal spirits. This opinion is confirm'd by the seeming encrease and diminution of objects, according to their distance; by the apparent alterations in their figure; by the changes in their colour and other qualities from our sickness and distempers; and by an infinite number of other experiments of the same kind; from all which we learn, that our sensible perceptions are not possest of any distinct or independent existence.

The natural consequence of this reasoning shou'd be, that our perceptions have no more a continu'd than an independent existence; and indeed philosophers have so far run into this opinion, that they change their system, and distinguish, (as we shall do for the future) betwixt perceptions and objects, of which the former are suppos'd to be interrupted, and perishing, and different at every different return; the latter to be uninterrupted, and to preserve a continu'd existence and identity. But however philosophical this new system may be esteem'd, I assert that 'tis only a palliative remedy, and that it contains all the difficulties of the vulgar system, with some others, that are peculiar to itself. There are no principles either of the understanding or fancy, which lead us directly to embrace this opinion of the double existence of perceptions and objects, nor can we arrive at it but by passing thro'

the common hypothesis of the identity and continuance of our interrupted perceptions. Were we not first persuaded, that our perceptions are our only objects, and continue to exist even when they no longer make their appearance to the senses, we shou'd never be led to think, that our perceptions and objects are different, and that our objects alone preserve a continu'd existence. 'The latter hypothesis has no primary recommendation either to reason or the imagination, but acquires all its influence on the imagination from the former.' This proposition contains two parts, which we shall endeavour to prove as distinctly and clearly, as such abstruse subjects will permit.

As to the first part of the proposition, *that this philosophical hypothesis has no primary recommendation, either to reason or the imagination,* we may soon satisfy ourselves with regard to *reason* by the following reflections. The only existences, of which we are certain, are perceptions, which being immediately present to us by consciousness, command our strongest assent, and are the first foundation of all our conclusions. The only conclusion we can draw from the existence of one thing to that of another, is by means of the relation of cause and effect, which shews, that there is a connexion betwixt them, and that the existence of one is dependent on that of the other. The idea of this relation is deriv'd from past experience, by which we find, that two beings are constantly conjoin'd together, and are always present at once to the mind. But as no beings are ever present to the mind but perceptions; it follows that we may observe a conjunction or a relation of cause and effect between different perceptions, but can never observe it between perceptions and objects. 'Tis impossible, therefore, that from the existence or any of the qualities of the former, we can ever form any conclusion concerning the existence of the latter, or ever satisfy our reason in this particular.

'Tis no less certain, that this philosophical system has no primary recommendation to the *imagination,* and that that faculty wou'd never, of itself, and by its original tendency, have fallen upon such a principle. I confess it will be somewhat difficult to prove this to the full satisfaction of the reader; because it implies a negative, which in many cases will not admit of any positive proof. If any one wou'd take the pains to examine this question, and wou'd invent a system, to account for the direct origin of this opinion from the imagination, we shou'd be able, by the examination of that system, to pronounce a certain judgment in the present subject. Let it be taken for granted, that our perceptions are broken, and interrupted, and however like, are still different from each other; and let any one upon this supposition shew why the fancy, directly and immediately, proceeds to the belief of another existence, resembling these perceptions in their nature, but yet continu'd, and uninterrupted, and identical; and after he has done this to my satisfaction, I promise to renounce my present opinion. Mean while I cannot forbear concluding, from the very abstractedness and difficulty of the first supposition, that 'tis an improper subject for the fancy to work upon. Whoever wou'd explain the origin of the *common* opinion concerning the continu'd and distinct existence of body, must take the mind in its *common* situation, and must proceed upon the supposition, that our perceptions are our only objects, and continue to exist even when they are not perceiv'd. Tho' this opinion be false, 'tis the most natural of any, and has alone any primary recommendation to the fancy.

As to the second part of the proposition, *that the philosophical system acquires all its influence on the imagination from the vulgar one;* we may observe, that this is a natural and unavoidable consequence of the foregoing conclusion, *that it has no primary recommendation to reason or the imagination.* For as the philosophical system is found by experience to take hold of many minds, and in particular of all those, who reflect ever so little on this subject, it must derive all its authority from the vulgar system; since it has no original authority of its own. The manner, in which these two systems, tho' directly contrary, are connected together, may be explain'd, as follows.

The imagination naturally runs on in this train of thinking. Our perceptions are our only objects: Resembling perceptions are the same, however broken or uninterrupted in their appearance: This appearing interruption is contrary to the identity: The interruption consequently extends not beyond the appearance, and the perception or object really continues to exist, even when absent from us: Our sensible perceptions have, therefore, a continu'd and uninterrupted existence. But as a little reflection destroys this conclusion, that our perceptions have a continu'd existence, by shewing that they

have a dependent one, 'twou'd naturally be expected, that we must altogether reject the opinion, that there is such a thing in nature as a continu'd existence, which is preserv'd even when it no longer appears to the senses. The case, however, is otherwise. Philosophers are so far from rejecting the opinion of a continu'd existence upon rejecting that of the independence and continuance of our sensible perceptions, that tho' all sects agree in the latter sentiment, the former, which is, in a manner, its necessary consequence, has been peculiar to a few extravagant sceptics; who after all maintain'd that opinion in words only, and were never able to bring themselves sincerely to believe it.

There is a great difference betwixt such opinions as we form after a calm and profound reflection, and such as we embrace by a kind of instinct or natural impulse, on account of their suitableness and conformity to the mind. If these opinions become contrary, 'tis not difficult to foresee which of them will have the advantage. As long as our attention is bent upon the subject, the philosophical and study'd principle may prevail; but the moment we relax our thoughts, nature will display herself, and draw us back to our former opinion. Nay she has sometimes such an influence, that she can stop our progress, even in the midst of our most profound reflections, and keep us from running on with all the consequences of any philosophical opinion. Thus tho' we clearly perceive the dependence and interruption of our perceptions, we stop short in our career, and never upon that account reject the notion of an independent and continu'd existence. That opinion has taken such deep root in the imagination, that 'tis impossible ever to eradicate it, nor will any strain'd metaphysical conviction of the dependence of our perceptions be sufficient for that purpose.

But tho' our natural and obvious principles here prevail above our study'd reflections, 'tis certain there must be some struggle and opposition in the case; at least so long as these reflections retain any force or vivacity. In order to set ourselves at ease in this particular, we contrive a new hypothesis, which seems to comprehend both these principles of reason and imagination. This hypothesis is the philosophical one of the double existence of perceptions and objects; which pleases our reason, in allowing, that our dependent perceptions are interrupted and different; and at the same time is agreeable to the imagination, in attributing a continu'd existence to something else, which we call *objects*. This philosophical system, therefore, is the monstrous offspring of two principles, which are contrary to each other, which are both at once embrac'd by the mind, and which are unable mutually to destroy each other. The imagination tells us, that our resembling perceptions have a continu'd and uninterrupted existence, and are not annihilated by their absence. Reflection tells us, that even our resembling perceptions are interrupted in their existence, and different from each other. The contradiction betwixt these opinions we elude by a new fiction, which is conformable to the hypotheses both of reflection and fancy, by ascribing these contrary qualities to different existences; the *interruption* to perceptions, and the *continuance* to objects. Nature is obstinate, and will not quit the field, however strongly attack'd by reason; and at the same time reason is so clear in the point, that there is no possibility of disguising her. Not being able to reconcile these two enemies, we endeavour to set ourselves at ease as much as possible, by successively granting to each whatever it demands, and by feigning a double existence, where each may find something, that has all the conditions it desires. Were we fully convinc'd, that our resembling perceptions are continu'd, and identical, and independent, we shou'd never run into this opinion of a double existence; since we shou'd find satisfaction in our first supposition, and wou'd not look beyond. Again, were we fully convinc'd, that our perceptions are dependent, and interrupted, and different, we shou'd be as little inclin'd to embrace the opinion of a double existence; since in that case we shou'd clearly perceive the error of our first supposition of a continu'd existence, and wou'd never regard it any farther. 'Tis therefore from the intermediate situation of the mind, that this opinion arises, and from such an adherence to these two contrary principles, as makes us seek some pretext to justify our receiving both; which happily at last is found in the system of a double existence.

Another advantage of this philosophical system is its similarity to the vulgar one; by which means we can humour our reason for a moment, when it becomes troublesome and solicitous; and yet upon its least negligence or inattention, can easily return to our vulgar and natural notions. Accordingly we find, that philosophers neglect not this advantage; but immediately upon leaving their closets, mingle with the rest of mankind in those exploded opinions, that our perceptions are our only objects, and continue identically and uninterruptedly the same in all their interrupted appearances.

There are other particulars of this system, wherein we may remark its dependence on the fancy, in a very conspicuous manner. Of these, I shall observe the two following. *First,* We suppose external objects to resemble internal perceptions. I have already shewn, that the relation of cause and effect can never afford us any just conclusion from the existence or qualities of our perceptions to the existence of external continu'd objects: And I shall farther add, that even tho' they cou'd afford such a conclusion, we shou'd never have any reason to infer, that our objects resemble our perceptions. That opinion, therefore, is deriv'd from nothing but the quality of the fancy above-explain'd, *that it borrows all its ideas from some precedent perception.* We never can conceive any thing but perceptions, and therefore must make every thing resemble them.

Secondly, As we suppose our objects in general to resemble our perceptions, so we take it for granted, that every particular object resembles that perception, which it causes. The relation of cause and effect determines us to join the other of resemblance; and the ideas of these existences being already united together in the fancy by the former relation, we naturally add the latter to compleat the union. We have a strong propensity to compleat every union by joining new relations to those which we have before observ'd betwixt any ideas, as we shall have occasion to observe presently.

Having thus given an account of all the systems both popular and philosophical, with regard to external existences, I cannot forbear giving vent to a certain sentiment, which arises upon reviewing those systems. I begun this subject with premising, that we ought to have an implicit faith in our senses, and that this wou'd be the conclusion, I shou'd draw from the whole of my reasoning. But to be ingenuous, I feel myself *at present* of a quite contrary sentiment, and am more inclin'd to repose no faith at all in my senses, or rather imagination, than to place in it such an implicit confidence. I cannot conceive how such trivial qualities of the fancy, conducted by such false suppositions, can ever lead to any solid and rational system. They are the coher-

ence and constancy of our perceptions, which produce the opinion of their continu'd existence; tho'
these qualities of perceptions have no perceivable
connexion with such an existence. The constancy of
our perceptions has the most considerable effect,
and yet is attended with the greatest difficulties. 'Tis
a gross illusion to suppose, that our resembling
perceptions are numerically the same; and 'tis this
illusion, which leads us into the opinion, that these
perceptions are uninterrupted, and are still existent,
even when they are not present to the senses. This is
the case with our popular system. And as to our
philosophical one, 'tis liable to the same difficulties;
and is over-and-above loaded with this absurdity,
that it at once denies and establishes the vulgar
supposition. Philosophers deny our resembling
perceptions to be identically the same, and uninterrupted; and yet have so great a propensity to believe
them such, that they arbitrarily invent a new set of
perceptions, to which they attribute these qualities.
I say, a new set of perceptions: For we may well
suppose in general, but 'tis impossible for us distinctly to conceive, objects to be in their nature any
thing but exactly the same with perceptions. What
then can we look for from this confusion of groundless and extraordinary opinions but error and

falsehood? And how can we justify to ourselves any
belief we repose in them?

This sceptical doubt, both with respect to reason and the senses, is a malady, which can never be
radically cur'd, but must return upon us every moment, however we may chace it away, and sometimes may seem entirely free from it. 'Tis impossible
upon any system to defend either our understanding or senses; and we but expose them farther when
we endeavour to justify them in that manner. As the
sceptical doubt arises naturally from a profound and
intense reflection on those subjects, it always en-
creases, the farther we carry our reflections, whether
in opposition or conformity to it. *Carelessness and
in-attention alone can afford us any remedy.* For this
reason I rely entirely upon them; and take it for
granted, whatever may be the reader's opinion at
this present moment, that an hour hence he will be
persuaded there is both an external and internal
world; and going upon that supposition, I intend to
examine some general systems both ancient and
modern, which have been propos'd of both, before
I proceed to a more particular enquiry concerning
our impressions. This will not, perhaps, in the end
be found foreign to our present purpose.

II.3 A *Defense of Common Sense*

G. E. MOORE

G. E. Moore (1873–1958) was Professor of Philosophy at Cambridge University and one of the leading philosophers of the first half of the twentieth century. In this essay—which is a combination of two of his articles, "A Defence of Common Sense" and "Proof of the External World"—Moore argues that skepticism is decisively refuted by common sense. The essence of the argument is as follows:

1. If skepticism is true, we do not have knowledge of the external world.
2. But we do have knowledge of the external world (Moore gives many examples).

Therefore

3. Skepticism is false.

In what follows I have merely tried to state, one by one, some of the most important points in which my philosophical position differs from positions which have been taken up by *some* other philosophers. It may be that the points which I have had room to mention are not really the most important, and possibly some of them may be points as to which no philosopher has ever really differed from me. But, to the best of my belief, each is a point as to which many have really differed; although (in most cases, at all events) each is also a point as to which many have agreed with me.

I

The first point is a point which embraces a great many other points. And it is one which I cannot state as clearly as I wish to state it, except at some length. The method I am going to use for stating it is this. I am going to begin by enunciating, under the heading (1), a whole long list of propositions, which may seem, at first sight, such obvious truisms as not to be worth stating: they are, in fact, a set of

propositions, every one of which (in my own opinion) I *know,* with certainty, to be true. I shall, next, under the heading (2), state a single proposition which makes an assertion about a whole set of *classes* of propositions—each class being defined, as the class consisting of all propositions which resemble *one* of the propositions in (1) in a certain respect. (2), therefore, is a proposition which could not be stated, until the list of propositions in (1), or some similar list, had already been given. (2) is itself a proposition which may seem such an obvious truism as not to be worth stating: and it is also a proposition which (in my own opinion) I know, with certainty, to be true. But, nevertheless, it is, to the best of my belief, a proposition with regard to which many philosophers have, for different reasons, differed from me; even if they have not directly denied (2) itself, they have held views incompatible with it. My first point, then, may be said to be that (2), together with all its implications, some of which I shall expressly mention, is true.

(1) I begin, then, with my list of truisms, every one of which (in my own opinion) I *know,* with certainty, to be true. The propositions to be included in this list are the following:

There exists at present a living human body, which is *my* body. This body was born at a certain time in the past, and has existed continuously ever since, though not without undergoing changes; it was, for instance, much smaller when it was born,

Reprinted from G. E. Moore, *Philosophical Papers* (London: George Allen & Unwin, 1959) by permission of Timothy Moore.

and for some time afterwards, than it is now. Ever since it was born, it has been either in contact with or not far from the surface of the earth; and, at every moment since it was born, there have also existed many other things, having shape and size in three dimensions (in the same familiar sense in which it has), from which it has been *at various distances* (in the familiar sense in which it is now at a distance both from that mantelpiece and from that bookcase, and at a greater distance from the bookcase than it is from the mantelpiece); also there have (very often, at all events) existed some other things of this kind with which it was *in contact* (in the familiar sense in which it is now in contact with the pen I am holding in my right hand and with some of the clothes I am wearing). Among the things which have, in this sense, formed part of its environment (i.e. have been either in contact with it, or at *some* distance from it, however *great*) there have, at every moment since its birth, been large numbers of other living human bodies, each of which has, like it, (*a*) at some time been born, (*b*) continued to exist from some time after birth, (*c*) been, at every moment of its life after birth, either in contact with or not far from the surface of the earth; and many of these bodies have already died and ceased to exist. But the earth had existed also for many years before my body was born; and for many of these years, also, large numbers of human bodies had, at every moment, been alive upon it; and many of these bodies had died and ceased to exist before it was born. Finally (to come to a different class of propositions), I am a human being, and I have, at different times since my body was born, had many different experiences, of each of many different kinds: e.g. I have often perceived both my own body and other things which formed part of its environment, including other human bodies; I have not only perceived things of this kind, but have also observed facts about them, such as, for instance, the fact which I am now observing, that that mantel-piece is at present nearer to my body than that bookcase; I have been aware of other facts, which I was not at the time observing, such as, for instance, the fact, of which I am now aware, that my body existed yesterday and was then also for some time nearer to that mantelpiece than to that bookcase; I have had expectations with regard to the future, and many beliefs of other kinds, both true and false; I have thought of imaginary things and persons and incidents, in the reality of which I did not believe; I have had dreams; and I have had feelings of many different kinds. And, just as my body has been the body of a human being, namely myself, who has, during his lifetime, had many experiences of each of these (and other) different kinds; so, in the case of very many of the other human bodies which have lived upon the earth, each has been the body of a different human being, who has, during the lifetime of that body, had many different experiences of each of these (and other) different kinds.

(2) I now come to the single truism which, as will be seen, could not be stated except by reference to the whole list of truisms, just given in (1). This truism also (in my own opinion) I *know,* with certainty, to be true; and it is as follows:

In the case of *very many* (I do not say *all*) of the human beings belonging to the class (which includes myself) defined in the following way, i.e. as human beings who have had human bodies, that were born and lived for some time upon the earth, and who have, during the lifetime of those bodies, had many different experiences of each of the kinds mentioned in (1), it is true that each has frequently, during the life of his body, known, with regard to *him*self or *his* body, and with regard to some time earlier than any of the times at which I wrote down the propositions in (1), a proposition *corresponding* to each of the propositions in (1), in the sense that it asserts with regard to *him*self or *his* body and the earlier time in question (namely, in each case, the time at which he knew it), just what the corresponding proposition in (1) asserts with regard to *me* or *my* body and the time at which I wrote that proposition down.

In other words what (2) asserts is only (what seems an obvious enough truism) that each of *us* (meaning by 'us', very many human beings of the class defined) has frequently *known,* with regard to *him*self or *his* body and the time at which he knew it, everything which, in writing down my list of propositions in (1), I was claiming to know about *my*self or *my* body and the time at which I wrote that proposition down, i.e. just as *I* knew (when I wrote it down) 'There exists at present a living human body which is my body', so each of us has frequently known with regard to himself and some other time the different but corresponding proposition, which *he* could *then* have properly expressed by, 'There exists *at present* a human body which is *my* body'; just as *I* know 'Many human bodies other than mine have before now lived on the earth', so each of us has frequently known the different but corresponding proposition 'Many human bodies other than *mine* have before *now* lived on the earth'; just as *I* know 'Many human beings other than myself have before now perceived, and dreamed, and felt', so each of *us* has frequently known the different but corresponding proposition 'Many human beings other than *myself* have before *now* perceived, and dreamed, and felt'; and so on, in the case of *each* of the propositions enumerated in (1). . . .

Proof of an External World

In the preface to the second edition of Kant's *Critique of Pure Reason* some words occur, which, in Professor Kemp Smith's translation, are rendered as follows:

> It still remains a scandal to philosophy . . . that the existence of things outside of us . . . must be accepted merely on *faith,* and that, if anyone thinks good to doubt their existence, we are unable to counter his doubts by any satisfactory proof.[1]

It seems clear from these words that Kant thought it a matter of some importance to give a proof of 'the existence of things outside of us' or perhaps rather (for it seems to me possible that the force of the German words is better rendered in this way) of 'the existence of *the* things outside of us'; for had he not thought it important that a proof should be given, he would scarcely have called it a 'scandal' that no proof had been given. And it seems clear also that he thought that the giving of such a proof was a task which fell properly within the province of philosophy; for, it if did not, the fact that no proof had been given could not possibly be a scandal to *philosophy.*

Now, even if Kant was mistaken in both of these two opinions, there seems to me to be no doubt whatever that it is a matter of some importance and also a matter which falls properly within the province of philosophy, to discuss the question what sort of proof, if any, can be given of 'the existence of things outside of us'. And to discuss

this question was my object when I began to write the present lecture. But I may say at once that, as you will find, I have only, at most, succeeded in saying a very small part of what ought to be said about it.

The words 'it . . . remains a scandal to philosophy . . . that we are unable . . .' would, taken strictly, imply that, at the moment at which he wrote them, Kant himself was unable to produce a satisfactory proof of the point in question. But I think it is unquestionable that Kant himself did not think that he personally was at the time unable to produce such a proof. On the contrary, in the immediately preceding sentence, he has declared that he has, in the second edition of his *Critique,* to which he is now writing the Preface, given a 'rigorous proof' of this very thing; and has added that he believes this proof of his to be 'the only possible proof'. It is true that in this preceding sentence he does not describe the proof which he has given as a proof of 'the existence of things outside of us' or of 'the existence of the things outside of us', but describes it instead as a proof of 'the objective reality of outer intuition'. But the context leaves no doubt that he is using these two phrases, 'the objective reality of outer intuition' and 'the existence of things (*or* 'the things') outside of us', in such a way that whatever is a proof of the first is also necessarily a proof of the second. We must, therefore, suppose that when he speaks as if *we* are unable to give a satisfactory proof, he does not mean to say that he himself, as well as others, is *at the moment* unable; but rather that, until he discovered the proof which he has given, both he himself and everybody else *were* unable. Of course, if he is right in thinking that he has given a satisfactory proof, the state of things which he describes came to an end as soon as his proof was published. As soon as that happened, anyone who read it was able to give a satisfactory proof by simply repeating that which Kant had given, and the 'scandal' to philosophy had been removed once for all.

If, therefore, it were certain that the proof of the point in question given by Kant in the second edition is a satisfactory proof, it would be certain that at least one satisfactory proof can be given; and all that would remain of the question which I said I proposed to discuss would be, firstly, the question as to what *sort* of a proof this of Kant's is, and secondly the question whether (contrary to Kant's own opinion) there may not perhaps be other proofs, of the same or of a different sort, which are also satisfactory. But I think it is by no means certain that Kant's proof is satisfactory. I think it is by no means certain that he did succeed in removing once for all the state of affairs which he considered to be a scandal to philosophy. And I think, therefore, that the question whether it is possible to give *any* satisfactory proof of the point in question still deserves discussion.

But what is the point in question? I think it must be owned that the expression 'things outside of us' is rather an odd expression, and an expression the meaning of which is certainly not perfectly clear. It would have sounded less odd if, instead of 'things outside of us' I had said 'external things', and perhaps also the meaning of this expression would have seemed to be clearer; and I think we make the meaning of 'external things' clearer still if we explain that this phrase has been regularly used by philosophers as short for 'things external to *our minds*'. The fact is that there has been a long philosophical tradition, in accordance with which the three expressions 'external things', 'things external to *us*', and 'things external to *our minds*' have been used as equivalent to one another, and have, each of them, been used as if they needed no explanation. The origin of this usage I do not know. It occurs already in Descartes; and since he uses the expressions as if they needed no explanation, they had presumably been used with the same meaning before. Of the three, it seems to me that the expression 'external to *our minds*' is the clearest, since it at least makes clear that what is meant is not 'external to *our bodies*'; whereas both the other expressions might be taken to mean this: and indeed there has been a good deal of confusion, even among philosophers, as to the relation of the two conceptions 'external things' and 'things external to *our bodies*'. But even the expression 'things external to our minds' seems to me to be far from perfectly clear; and if I am to make really clear what I mean by 'proof of the existence of things outside of us', I cannot do it by merely saying that by 'outside of us' I mean 'external to our minds'.

. . .

But now, if to say of anything, e.g. my body, that it is external to *my* mind, means merely that from a proposition to the effect that it existed at a specified time, there in no case follows the further

proposition that *I* was having an experience at the time in question, then to say of anything that it is external to *our* minds, will mean similarly that from a proposition to the effect that it existed at a specified time, it in no case follows that any of *us* were having experiences at the time in question. And if by *our* minds be meant, as is, I think, usually meant, the minds of human beings living on the earth, then it will follow that any pains which animals may feel, any after-images they may see, any experiences they may have, though not external to *their* minds, yet are external to *ours*. And this at once makes plain how different is the conception 'external to our minds' from the conception 'to be met with in space'; for, of course, pains which animals feel or after-images which they see are no more to be met with in space than are pains which *we* feel or after-images which *we* see. From the proposition that there are external objects—objects that are not in any of *our* minds, it does *not* follow that there are things to be met with in space; and hence 'external to our minds' is not a mere synonym for 'to be met with in space': that is to say, 'external to our minds' and 'to be met with in space' are two different conceptions. And the true relation between these conceptions seems to me to be this. We have already seen that there are ever so many kinds of 'things', such that, in the case of each of these kinds, from the proposition that there is at least one thing of that kind there *follows* the proposition that there is at least one thing to be met with in space: e.g. this follows from 'There is at least one star', from 'There is at least one human body', from 'There is at least one shadow', etc. And I think we can say that of every kind of thing of which this is true, it is also true that from the proposition that there is at least one 'thing' of that kind there *follows* the proposition that there is at least one thing external to our minds: e.g. from 'There is at least one star' there follows not only 'There is at least one thing to be met with in space' but also 'There is at least one external thing', and similarly in all other cases. My reason for saying this is as follows. Consider any kind of thing, such that anything of that kind, if there is anything of it, must be 'to be met with in space': e.g. consider the kind 'soap-bubble'. If I say of anything which I am perceiving, 'That is a soap-bubble', I am, it seems to me, certainly implying that there would be no contradiction in asserting that it existed before I perceived it and that it will continue to exist, even if I cease to perceive it. This seems to me to be part of what is meant by saying that it is a real soap-bubble, as distinguished, for instance, from an hallucination of a soap-bubble. Of course, it by no means follows, that if it really is a soap-bubble, it did in fact exist before I perceived it or will continue to exist after I cease to perceive it: soap-bubbles are an example of a kind of 'physical object' and 'thing to be met with in space', in the case of which it is notorious that particular specimens of the kind often do exist only so long as they are perceived by a particular person. But a thing which I perceive would not be a soap-bubble unless its existence at any given time were *logically independent* of my perception of it at that time; unless that is to say, from the proposition, with regard to a particular time, that it existed at that time, it *never* follows that I perceived it at that time. But, if it is true that it would not be a soap-bubble, unless it *could* have existed at any given time without being perceived by me at that time, it is certainly also true that it would not be a soap-bubble, unless it *could* have existed at any given time, without its being true that I was having any experience of any kind at the time in question: it would not be a soap-bubble, unless, whatever time you take, from the proposition that it existed at that time it does *not* follow that I was having any experience at that time. That is to say, from the proposition with regard to anything which I am perceiving that it is a soap-bubble, there *follows* the proposition that it is external to *my* mind. But if, when I say that anything which I perceive is a soap-bubble, I am implying that it is external to *my* mind, I am, I think, certainly also implying that it is also external to all other minds: I am implying that it is not a thing of a sort such that things of that sort *can* only exist at a time when somebody is having an experience. I think, therefore, that from any proposition of the form 'There's a soap-bubble!' there does really *follow* the proposition 'There's an external object!' 'There's an object external to *all* our minds!' And, if this is true of the kind 'soap-bubble', it is certainly also true of any other kind (including the kind 'unicorn') which is such that, if there are any things of that kind, it follows that there are *some* things to be met with in space.

I think, therefore, that in the case of all kinds of 'things', which are such that if there is a pair of things, both of which are of one of these kinds, or a pair of things one of which is of one of them and one of them of another, then it will follow at once that there are some things to be met with in space, it is true also that if I can prove that there are a pair of things, one of which is of one of these kinds and another of another, or a pair both of which are of one of them, then I shall have proved *ipso facto* that there are at least two 'things outside of us'. That is to say, if I can prove that there exist now both a sheet of paper and a human hand, I shall have proved that there are now 'things outside of us'; if I can prove that there exist now both a shoe and sock, I shall have proved that there are now 'things outside of us'; etc.; and similarly I shall have proved it, if I can prove that there exist now two sheets of paper, or two human hands, or two shoes, or two socks, etc. Obviously, then, there are thousands of different things such that, if, at any time, I can prove any one of them, I shall have proved the existence of things outside of us. Cannot I prove any of these things?

It seems to me that, so far from its being true, as Kant declares to be his opinion, that there is only one possible proof of the existence of things outside of us, namely the one which he has given, I can now give a large number of different proofs, each of which is a perfectly rigorous proof; and that at many other times I have been in a position to give many others. I can prove now, for instance, that two human hands exist. How? By holding up my two hands, and saying, as I make a certain gesture with the right hand, 'Here is one hand', and adding, as I make a certain gesture with the left, 'and here is another'. And if, by doing this, I have proved *ipso facto* the existence of external things, you will all see that I can also do it now in numbers of other ways: there is no need to multiply examples.

But did I prove just now that two human hands were then in existence? I do want to insist that I did; that the proof which I gave was a perfectly rigorous one; and that it is perhaps impossible to give a better or more rigorous proof of anything whatever. Of course, it would not have been a proof unless three conditions were satisfied; namely (1) unless the premiss which I adduced as proof of the conclusion was different from the conclusion I adduced it to prove; (2) unless the premiss which I adduced was something which I *knew* to be the case, and not merely something which I believed but which was by no means certain, or something which, though in fact true, I did not know to be so;

and (3) unless the conclusion did really follow from the premiss. But all these three conditions were in fact satisfied by my proof. (1) The premiss which I adduced in proof was quite certainly different from the conclusion, for the conclusion was merely 'Two human hands exist at this moment'; but the premiss was something far more specific than this—something which I expressed by showing you my hands, making certain gestures, and saying the words 'Here is one hand, and here is another'. It is quite obvious that the two were different, because it is quite obvious that the conclusion might have been true, even if the premiss had been false. In asserting the premiss I was asserting much more than I was asserting in asserting the conclusion. (2) I certainly did at the moment *know* that which I expressed by the combination of certain gestures with saying the words 'There is one hand and here is another'. I *knew* that there was one hand in the place indicated by combining a certain gesture with my first utterance of 'here' and that there was another in the different place indicated by combining a certain gesture with my second utterance of 'here'. How absurd it would be to suggest that I did not know it, but only believed it, and that perhaps it was not the case! You might as well suggest that I do not know that I am now standing up and talking—that perhaps after all I'm not, and that it's not quite certain that I am! And finally (3) it is quite certain that the conclusion did follow from the premiss. This is as certain as it is that if there is one hand here and another here *now*, then it follows that there are two hands in existence *now*.

My proof, then, of the existence of things outside of us did satisfy three of the conditions necessary for a rigorous proof. Are there any other conditions necessary for a rigorous proof, such that perhaps it did not satisfy one of them? Perhaps there may be; I do not know; but I do want to emphasize that, so far as I can see, we all of us do constantly take proofs of this sort as absolutely conclusive proofs of certain conclusions—as finally settling certain questions, as to which we were previously in doubt. Suppose, for instance, it were a question whether there were as many as three misprints on a certain page in a certain book. A says there are, B is inclined to doubt it. How could A prove that he is right? Surely he *could* prove it by taking the book, turning to the page, and pointing

to three separate places on it, saying 'There's one misprint here, another here, and another here': surely that is a method by which it *might* be proved! Of course, A would not have proved, by doing this, that there were at least three misprints on the page in question, unless it was certain that there was a misprint in each of the places to which he pointed. But to say that he *might* prove it in this way, is to say that it *might* be certain that there was. And if such a thing as that could ever be certain, then assuredly it was certain just now that there was one hand in one of the two places I indicated and another in the other.

I did, then, just now, give a proof that there were *then* external objects; and obviously, if I did, I could *then* have given many other proofs of the same sort that there were external objects *then*, and could now give many proofs of the same sort that there are external objects *now*.

But, if what I am asked to do is to prove that external objects have existed *in the past*, then I can give many different proofs of this also, but proofs which are in important respects of a different *sort* from those just given. And I want to emphasize that, when Kant says it is a scandal not to be able to give a proof of the existence of external objects, a proof of their existence in the past would certainly *help* to remove the scandal of which he is speaking. He says that, if it occurs to anyone to question their existence, we ought to be able to confront him with a satisfactory proof. But by a person who questions their existence, he certainly means not merely a person who questions whether any exist at the moment of speaking, but a person who questions whether any have *ever* existed; and a proof that some have existed in the past would certainly therefore be relevant to *part* of what such a person is questioning. How then can I prove that there have been external objects in the past? Here is one proof. I can say: 'I held up two hands above this desk not very long ago; therefore two hands existed not very long ago; therefore at least two external objects have existed at some time in the past, Q.E.D.' This is a perfectly good proof, provided I *know* what is asserted in the premiss. But I *do* know that I held up two hands above this desk not very long ago. As a matter of fact, in this case you all know it too. There's no doubt whatever that I did. Therefore I have given a perfectly conclusive proof that external objects have existed in the past; and you will all see at once that, if this is a conclusive proof, I could have given many others of the same sort, and could now give many others. But it is also quite obvious that this sort of proof differs in important respects from the sort of proof I gave just now that there were two hands existing *then*.

I have, then, given two conclusive proofs of the existence of external objects. The first was a proof that two human hands existed at the time when I gave the proof; the second was a proof that two human hands had existed at a time previous to that at which I gave the proof. These proofs were of a different sort in important respects. And I pointed out that I could have given, then, many other conclusive proofs of both sorts. It is also obvious that I could give many others of both sorts now. So that, if these are the sort of proof that is wanted, nothing is easier than to prove the existence of external objects.

But now I am perfectly well aware that, in spite of all that I have said, many philosophers will still feel that I have not given any satisfactory proof of the point in question. And I want briefly, in conclusion, to say something as to why this dissatisfaction with my proofs should be felt.

One reason why, is, I think, this. Some people understand 'proof of an external world' as including a proof of things which I haven't attempted to prove and haven't proved. It is not quite easy to say *what* it is that they want proved—*what* it is that is such that unless they got a proof of it, they would not say that they had a proof of the existence of external things; but I can make an approach to explaining what they want by saying that if I had proved the propositions which I used as *premisses* in my two proofs, then they would perhaps admit that I had proved the existence of external things, but, in the absence of such a proof (which, of course, I have neither given nor attempted to give), they will say that I have not given what they mean by a proof of the existence of external things. In other words, they want a proof of what I assert *now* when I hold up my hands and say 'Here's one hand and here's another'; and, in the other case, they want a proof of what I assert *now* when I say 'I did hold up two hands above this desk just now'. Of course, what they really want is not merely a proof of these two propositions, but something like a general

statement as to how *any* propositions of this sort may be proved. This, of course, I haven't given; and I do not believe it can be given: if this is what is meant by proof of the existence of external things, I do not believe that any proof of the existence of external things is possible. Of course, in some cases what might be called a proof of propositions which seem like these can be got. If one of you suspected that one of my hands was artificial he might be said to get a proof of my proposition 'Here's one hand, and here's another', by coming up and examining the suspected hand close up, perhaps touching and pressing it, and so establishing that it really was a human hand. But I do not believe that any proof is possible in nearly all cases. How am I to prove now that 'Here's one hand, and here's another'? I do not believe I can do it. In order to do it, I should need to prove for one thing, as Descartes pointed out, that I am not now dreaming. But how can I prove that I am not? I have, no doubt, conclusive reasons for asserting that I am not now dreaming; I have conclusive evidence that I am awake: but that is a very different thing from being able to prove it. I could not tell you what all my evidence is; and I should require to do this at least, in order to give you a proof.

But another reason why some people would feel dissatisfied with my proofs is, I think, not merely that they want a proof of something which I haven't proved, but that they think that, if I cannot give such extra proofs, then the proofs that I have given are not conclusive proofs at all. And this, I think, is a definite mistake. They would say: 'If you cannot prove your premiss that here is one hand and here is another, then you do not know it. But you yourself have admitted that, if you did not know it, then your proof was not conclusive. Therefore your proof was not, as you say it was, a conclusive proof.' This view that, if I cannot prove such things as these, I do not know them, is, I think, the view that Kant was expressing in the sentence which I quoted at the beginning of this lecture, when he implies that so long as we have no proof of the existence of external things, their existence must be accepted merely on *faith*. He means to say, I think, that if I cannot prove that there is a hand here, I must accept it merely as a matter of faith—I cannot know it. Such a view, though it has been very common among philosophers, can, I think, be shown to be wrong—though shown only by the use of premisses which are not known to be true, unless we do know of the existence of external things. I can know things, which I cannot prove; and among things which I certainly did know, even if (as I think) I could not prove them, were the premisses of my two proofs. I should say, therefore, that those, if any, who are dissatisfied with these proofs merely on the ground that I did not know their premisses, have no good reason for their dissatisfaction.

Note

[1] B xxxix, note: Kemp Smith, p. 34. The German words are 'so bleibt es immer ein Skandal der Philosophie . . . , das Dasein der Dinge ausser uns . . . bloss auf *Glauben* annehmen zu müssen, und wenn es jemand einfällt es zu bezweifeln, ihm keinin genugtuenden Beweis entgegenstellen zu können'.

II.4 *Why Not Skepticism?*

KEITH LEHRER

Keith Lehrer is Professor of Philosophy at the University of Arizona. In this essay, Lehrer contends that refutations such as Moore's fail to answer the fundamental problem with knowledge claims, namely, that they need to show that they satisfy the justification requirement. To know that *p*, one must be completely justified in believing that *p*. Lehrer argues that we are never completely justified in our beliefs. So we do not have knowledge.

The sceptic has been mistreated. Sophisticated epistemologies have been developed in defense of dogmatic knowledge claims. Recently, theories of ignorance have been so rare that the name for such theories, *agnoiology,* sounds like the antique it is. Actually, James F. Ferrier[1] introduced both the terms *epistemology* and *agnoiology* into the philosophical lexicon, but the latter has fallen into disuse through lack of denotation. Scepticism suffers from many defects, or so say the dogmatists. Some have contended that scepticism is contradictory, others that it is meaningless, and still others that it amounts to nothing more than an ingenious

restatement of what we already believe. One problem with refutations of scepticism is that they are overly plentiful and mutually inconsistent. This should create some suspicion in the minds of the philosophically wary that some theory of ignorance, an agnoiology, might sustain the contentions of scepticism. I shall develop an agnoiology for the defense of scepticism against dogmatic knowledge claims. By so doing I hope to convince you of the tenability and importance of theories of rational belief and action based on probability without knowledge.

The form of scepticism I wish to avow is more radical than traditional sceptics have been wont to defend. Some philosophers have maintained that we do not know about anything beyond some necessary truths and some truths about our own subjective states. But they have not denied that we do

Reprinted from *The Philosophical Forum,* 2.3 (1971), 283–298, by kind permission of the author and aditor. [Footnotes have been edited—Ed.]

know about those matters. I wish to seriously consider a stronger form of scepticism, to wit, that we do not know anything.

I

Some qualification is necessary to avoid misunderstanding and to escape the burden of replying to overeasy refutations. The form of scepticism that concerns me does not embody the thesis that we know that we do not know anything. That thesis is obviously self-refuting. Rather, the contention is that no one knows anything, not even that no one knows anything. You might feel a surge of confidence in the face of such contention simply because the sceptic has admitted that he does not know that he is correct, and hence, that he does not know that you are incorrect when you affirm that you do know something. But this confidence is misplaced because scepticism entails that, just as the sceptic does not know that we do not know anything, so we do not know that we do know anything, and, moreover, that we do not know anything.

In setting out to develop an agnoiology, the sceptic looks as though he must inevitably fall into embarrassment. For, in saying why he says what he does, must he not fall back on the claim that he knows various things to be true which support his conclusion? Again the answer is negative. The sceptic is not prevented by his agnoiology from believing most of the same things that we believe; indeed, all his position debars him from is believing in such things as would entail that we have knowledge. About devils, dust, and delight, he may believe what he wishes. He may even consider some beliefs to be more prudent than others or more useful, and he surely may distinguish between what is true and what is false.

He affirms that we know nothing, but he believes most of what most men believe. He affirms much else besides, only here he must be careful not to mislead with his sceptical speech. For often when a man speaks we take him to be claiming to know, though he does not say he knows. Indeed, it is perhaps more common than not to attach such implications to the acts of speech we confront.

However, there is nothing inevitable or irreversible in this practice. When a man wishes to tell us what he thinks has transpired but does not wish to be understood as making any pretense to knowledge in the matter whereof he speaks, we may understand him without any confusion or perplexity. The agnoiologist who is about to defend scepticism must be understood as speaking in a similar manner. The premisses of his agnoiology must not be understood as claims to knowledge but only formulations of what he believes and hopes we shall concede. Not even the claim that conclusion follows from premiss would be taken as a claim to knowledge. His words are addressed to us in the full conviction that they are the truth but without any pretense to knowledge.

II

Before attempting to offer any argument for so general a thesis as one affirming universal ignorance, it is essential to include in our agnoiology an account of what knowledge entails. And here we immediately confront the problem that whatever one philosopher has said knowledge is another philosopher has rejected. Hence it is impossible to avoid controversy. Having written elsewhere on this subject, I shall have to rely on those results. I shall consequently assume that if a man knows *that p*, then it is true *that p*. It has seemed evident to most epistemologists that no one can know anything to be true which is not true. Second, I shall assume that if a man knows *that p,* then he believes *that p*. This has been controverted, but I shall not undertake any defense of the assumption here. Next, I shall assume that if a man knows *that p*, then he is completely justified in believing *that p*. A word of explanation. As I am using the locution, "completely justified," it is logically possible that a man should be completely justified in believing something even though he has no justificatory argument to support his belief. However, as an agnoiologist I shall deny the existence of such beliefs. Though completely justified true belief is a necessary condition of knowledge, it is not sufficient for reasons that might further aid the cause of scepticism.

III

We may best serve the purposes of scepticism by developing our agnoiology in an area where the dogmatist considers himself to be the most invulnerable, namely with respect to those claims to knowledge that he considers to be most certain and beyond doubt. Two classes of such claims are those concerning some logical and mathematical truths as well as those concerning some of our present conscious states. Let us consider necessary truths.

One argument against the sceptic in these matters is that such beliefs are ones where all possibility of error is excluded by logical necessity. This argument is worth a moment of consideration, because by so doing the first agnoiological strong-hold of scepticism may be secured. It is logically impossible to be mistaken in believing any necessary truth. If I believe that the axiom of choice is independent of the continuum hypothesis, and if it is a necessary truth that the axiom of choice is independent of the continuum hypothesis, then it is impossible that I should believe that the axiom of choice is independent of the continuum hypothesis and also be in error. Of course, this is also true of more mundane beliefs like my belief that there is a natural number greater than two and less than five which is prime.

However, the above-mentioned fact, if it constituted any defense of dogmatism, would constitute equally good grounds for the wildest forms of speculation concerning the necessary and the impossible. For, it is logically impossible to be mistaken when one believes any statement which is a necessary truth no matter how speculative or groundless such a belief may be. If it is necessarily true *that p*, then the statement that I am mistaken in believing *that p* would be equivalent to the conjunctive statement that I believe *that p* and it is false *that p*. If it is necessarily true *that p*, then the statement that it is false *that p* cannot possibly be true. Moreover, no conjunctive statement entailing that it is false *that p* could possibly be true either. Therefore, if it is necessarily true *that p*, then it cannot possibly be true that I am mistaken in believing *that p*. No one can possibly be mistaken in believing any necessary truth.

What the preceding proves is that if the dogmatist argues that a person knows that a statement is true whenever it is logically impossible for him to

be mistaken in believing it, then he will be committed to the implausible conclusion that a person knows a mathematical statement to be true whenever he correctly believes it to be so no matter how foolish or groundless his belief. However, this violates our assumption that a belief must be completely justified as well as true or else we lack knowledge. Before any proof was forthcoming, someone might have believed that the axiom of choice was independent of the continuum hypothesis, but he did not know it. There is a distinction of justification between being right in mathematics and knowing that one is right. Of course, our agnoiology does not imply that anyone ever does know anything but it does imply that *if* anyone knows anything, then that person must not only have true belief, but complete justification as well.

Thus the preceding argument shows that we cannot assume a man knows whereof he believes simply because it is logically impossible that he should be mistaken in what he believes. For, he may have no proof or justification for believing what he does. Indeed, we might wish to say of the man that he could have been mistaken even though it was logically impossible that he should have been mistaken. What is the force of the *could* which defies logical possibility? In what sense could he have been mistaken? The answer is—he could have been mistaken in the sense that, for all he knows, what he believes is false. This, in turn, means that what he knows does not establish that what he believes is true. And, so, if he knows nothing, then he could have been mistaken even though it is logically impossible that he should be mistaken.

The logical impossibility of error in beliefs concerning the impossible and necessary, that is, statements which if true are necessary and if false are impossible, is no bulwark against scepticism. The logical impossibility of error in such matters is perfectly consistent with complete ignorance. Thus our agnoiology shows that there is no refutation of scepticism to be built on such logical impossibility of false belief.

IV

Let us, however, leave the realm of the necessary and the impossible for that of the contingent. Suppose a man believes some contingent statement to be true, a statement which is neither logically necessary nor logically impossible. What if, in such a case, it is logically impossible for the man to believe falsely? Must not we concede that the man knows?

Before answering this question let us note how few beliefs have the character in question. Some philosophers have thought that beliefs about one's current psychological states were ones that excluded the logical possibility of error. But this is, I am convinced, mostly mistaken. Let me explain why.

First, there are almost no beliefs about one's own present states of consciousness that it is logically inconsistent to suppose should be false. The best candidates for such incorrigible beliefs are ones concerning one's present sensations or thoughts. But it is logically possible for such beliefs to be mistaken. Consider sensations first. Suppose it is affirmed that if a person believes that he is having sensation S, a pain for example, then it is logically impossible that such a belief should be mistaken. This is not so. One might believe one is having a sensation S, a pain for example, because one is having a different sensation, S*, an itch for example, and one has mistaken S* for S, that is, one has mistaken an itch for a pain. How could this happen? It might happen either because of some general belief, to wit, that itches are pains, which one has been led to believe by some authority, or one may simply be misled on this occasion because one has been told by some authority that one will experience a pain. In short, one might have some false belief which together with the sensation of an itch produces the belief that one is in pain. Beliefs about sensations can be inferential, and one can infer that one is in a conscious state that one is not in by inferring from some false belief that this is so. One might believe that sensation S* is S, just as with respect to thoughts, one might believe that some thought T* is T, and thus arrive at the mistaken conclusion that one is in state S or state T because one is in state S* or T*.

The preceding argument might be bolstered by examples to please the fancy, but the argument is so simple as to render them superfluous. For all that I have assumed is that it is logically possible for a person, under the influence of authority, to mistake one conscious state for another and thus to believe that he is in a conscious state when in fact he is not in that state. The argument applies to almost all conscious states with a notable exception. If I be-

lieve that I believe something, then the first belief does seem to be one such that it is logically impossible that I should be mistaken. For, it is logically inconsistent to suppose both that I believe that I believe something and that I do not believe anything. It would be tempting to rid oneself of such troublesome cases by saying that it does not make sense to speak of believing that one believes, but I do not believe that such a contention is correct. So, I concede that the set of incorrigible beliefs about one's own conscious states is not null.

V

The preceding argument shows how little contingent knowledge we would need to concede to the dogmatist even if we conceded that we know those beliefs to be true which are such as to exclude the logical possibility of error. But the sceptic need not concede that we know even that. It is not the logical impossibility of error that could yield knowledge but rather our *knowledge* of the logical impossibility of error. Consider the mathematical case again. If I know that something is logically impossible, for example, if I know that it is contradictory to suppose that the axiom of choice and the continuum hypothesis are not independent, then I know that the axiom of choice is independent of the continuum hypothesis. It is not the logical impossibility of error by itself that guarantees knowledge but only *knowledge* of the logical impossibility. *If* we know that it is logically impossible that certain of our beliefs are mistaken, then, no doubt, we know that those beliefs are true. But this *if* is the noose that strangles dogmatism. For, even if we agree it is logically impossible for certain contingent beliefs to be mistaken, still it does not follow that we *know* that it is logically impossible for those beliefs to be mistaken, and, hence it does not follow that we know that the beliefs are true. A sceptic may contend that we do not *know* that anything is logically impossible however strongly convinced we may be. And he may conclude that we do not know that those beliefs are true even where the logical possibility of error is excluded, because we do not know that the logical possibility of error is excluded.

. . . I have argued that scepticism is logically

consistent. . . . He denies what we assert and there is nothing inconsistent or semantically unacceptable in so doing. Language allows for such radical disagreement as that between the sceptic and his detractors. It is this resource of language that provides for possibility of speculation and innovation. Thus, the question to which we must now turn is this—if the position of scepticism is neither meaningless nor contradictory, then why not scepticism?

VIII

The most common answer stems from Thomas Reid. It is based on the assumption that some beliefs are completely justified, because they are beliefs of a special kind which are justified without any supporting justificatory argument.[2] Beliefs of this kind are *basic* beliefs. Thus, if a man believes *that p,* where this is a basic belief of kind K, then he is completely justified in believing *that p* without argument unless there is some good reason for believing *p* to be false. The kind K of basic beliefs may be specified differently by philosophers of different epistemic biases, which already offers succor to the sceptic, but dogmatists have generally agreed that at least some kinds of perceptual beliefs, memory beliefs, and beliefs concerning our conscious states are among them.

Now it is not at all difficult to conceive of some hypothesis that would yield the conclusion that beliefs of the kind in question are not justified, indeed, which if true would justify us in concluding that the beliefs in question were more often false than true. The sceptical hypothesis might run as follows. There are a group of creatures in another galaxy, call them Googols, whose intellectual capacity is 10^{100} that of men, and who amuse themselves by sending out a peculiar kind of wave that affects our brain in such a way that our beliefs about the world are mostly incorrect. This form of errror infects beliefs of every kind, but most of our beliefs, though erroneous, are nevertheless very nearly correct. This allows us to survive and manipulate our environment. However, whether any belief of any man is correct or even nearly correct depends entirely on

the whimsy of some Googol rather than on the capacities and faculties of the man. If you are inclined to wonder why the Googols do not know anything, it is because there is another group of men, call them Googolplexes, whose intellectual capacity is 10^{100} that of the Googols, and who amuse themselves by sending out a peculiar wave that affects the brains of Googols in such a way that . . . I think you can see how the story goes from here. I shall refer to this hypothesis as the *sceptical hypothesis.* On such a hypothesis our beliefs about our conscious states, what we perceive by our senses, or recall from memory, are more often erroneous than correct. Such a sceptical hypothesis as this would, the sceptic argues, entail that the beliefs in question are not completely justified.

The reply of the dogmatist to such imaginings might be that we are not only justified in those basic beliefs, we are also justified in rejecting any hypothesis, such as the sceptical one, which conflicts with those beliefs. But the sceptic may surely intercede long enough to protest that he has been ruled out by fiat. The beliefs of common sense are said to be basic and thus completely justified without any justificatory arguments. But why, the sceptic may query, should the dogmatists' beliefs be considered completely justified without argument and his hypothesis be rejected without argument? Dogmatists affirm that the beliefs of common sense are innocent until proven guilty, but why, the sceptic might inquire, should his hypothesis not receive comparable treatment before the bar of evidence? Why not regard the sceptical hypothesis as innocent until proven guilty? Indeed, the sceptic might continue, why not regard all belief as innocent until proven guilty? And, he might add, where all is innocence, nothing is justified or unjustified, which is precisely the agnoiology of scepticism.

Some opponents of scepticism have been willing to concede that unless we hold some beliefs to be justified without argument, then we must surely accept the conclusion of scepticism. But, when replying to the sceptic, it will not do to say that we must regard the beliefs of common sense as justified or else we shall wind up on the road to scepticism. For that is precisely the route the sceptic would have us travel.

Let me clarify the preceding argument. In one passage, Bishop Berkeley replies to a dogmatist by appeal to the agnoiological precept that the burden of proof always lies with the affirmative. The precept could be doubted, and generally arguments about where the burden of proof lies are unproductive. It is more reasonable to suppose that such questions are best left to courts of law where they have suitable application. In philosophy a different principle of agnoiology is appropriate, to wit, that no hypothesis should be rejected as unjustified without argument against it. Consequently, if the sceptic puts forth a hypothesis inconsistent with the hypotheses of common sense, then there is not burden of proof on either side, but neither may one side to the dispute be judged unjustified in believing his hypothesis unless an argument is produced to show that this is so. If contradictory hypotheses are put forth without reason being given to show that one side is correct and the other in error, then neither party may be fairly stigmatized as unjustified. However, if a belief is completely justified, then those with which it conflicts are unjustified. Therefore, if neither of the conflicting hypotheses is shown to be unjustified, then we must refrain from concluding that belief in one of the hypotheses is completely justified.

We have here an argument that does not prejudicially presuppose that the burden of proof rests on one side or the other but instead takes an impartial view of the matter and refuses to side with either party until some argument has been given. Thomas Reid was wont to argue that the beliefs of common sense had a right of ancient possession and were justified until shown to be unjustified. But such epistemology favors the sentiments of conservative defenders of the status quo in both philosophy and politics. And the principle that, what is, is justified, is not a better principle of epistemology than of politics or morals. It should be supplanted by the agnoiological principle of impartiality. Thus, before scepticism may be rejected as unjustified, some argument must be given to show that the infamous hypotheses employed by sceptics are incorrect and the beliefs of common sense have the truth on their side. If this is not done, then the beliefs of common sense are not completely justified, because conflicting sceptical hypotheses have not been shown to be unjustified. From this premiss it follows in a single step that we do not know those beliefs to be true because they are not completely justified. And then the sceptic wins the day.

IX

The preceding agnoiological argument can be extended to defeat a whole range of alleged refutations of scepticism. For example, some philosophers have rejected scepticism on the grounds that the sceptic is denying our standards of evidence or our criteria of justification or something of the sort. Now, of course, this may be trivially true; obviously the sceptic is denying that we are completely justified in certain beliefs which we consider to be completely justified, and if that constitutes rejecting our ordinary standards or criteria of evidence, then the sceptic is indeed denying them. But that is no argument against the sceptic; it is a restatement of his position. Unless we can show that the sceptical hypothesis is false, we cannot justly conclude that it is unjustified. In that case our beliefs, which contradict the sceptical hypotheses, are not completely justified. So much the worse for our standards or criteria of evidence.

Next, there are arguments claiming that the sceptic is making proposals which undermine our conceptual framework and change the very concepts we use to formulate our beliefs. The reply is twofold. Sometimes talking about changing concepts is a disguised way of talking about changing meaning of words. I have already argued that scepticism does not have that consequence. So I discount that contention. Other than that, the change of concepts implied by scepticism seems to me, to amount to no more than a change of belief, perhaps of very fundamental beliefs. The reply to this objection is that first, the agnoiology of the sceptic allows him to embrace most of the same beliefs we do. He need not *believe* the sceptical hypothesis to argue that if the sceptical hypothesis is true, then our more familiar beliefs are more often false than true. By thus employing the hypothesis, he has placed us in a position of either showing the hypothesis to be false, or else conceding that our beliefs are not completely justified. Thus the sceptic need not advocate ceasing to believe those fundamental hypotheses which constitute the assumptions, presuppositions, or what not of our conceptual framework. He only denies that we know those beliefs to be true.

Thus appeals to ancient rights, standards of evidence, and conceptual frameworks are all equally ineffective against the basic challenge of scepticism, to wit—either show that the sceptical hypothesis is false and unjustified or concede that beliefs inconsistent with that hypothesis are not completely justified!

X

We must now turn to a rather different sort of maneuver against the sceptic. It might be conceded that we cannot show that our beliefs are true and the sceptical hypothesis false, but contended that we can show that our beliefs are completely justified, not perhaps for the purpose of arriving at the truth, but for other epistemic ends. Thus it has been proposed that we believe whatever will facilitate explanation and increase our information. If a person is seeking to have beliefs which facilitate explanation and increase information, then he is completely justified in adopting beliefs contributing to those objectives. This argument against scepticism is, I believe, the very strongest that can be offered. For, even if we can offer no argument to show that our beliefs are true and the sceptical hypothesis false, still we may be completely justified in our beliefs in terms of objectives other than truth.

Finally, the move has an intuitive appeal. For, the sceptical hypothesis according to which most of our beliefs arise because of the deception of Googols yields results that would make it difficult to explain in a satisfactory manner what we believe to be the case and, it would make it even more difficult for us to increase our information about the world. Many generalizations about the world, and theories as well, would turn out to be incorrect on that hypothesis, thus making explanation difficult and complicated. Moreover, we would, by hypothesis, have no way of telling when our beliefs give us information about the world and when we are simply being misled by the Googols. All in all the sceptical hypothesis is quite unsatisfactory from the standpoint of explaining things and increasing our information; so unsatisfactory that anyone seeking to explain as much as possible and to increase his information as much as possible would be completely justified in rejecting it.

Is there any reply to this line of argument? The sceptic might reply that he is under no obligation to accept the ends of facilitating explanation and increasing information. But this will not refute the claim that we who do accept such ends are completely justified in believing what we do for the sake of obtaining those objectives. There is a better line of reply available to the sceptic, namely, that our disregard for truth will, in the final accounting, destroy our assets. For agnoiology shows that such pragmatic justification of belief ultimately depends on the assumption that the beliefs are true. Suppose we adopt those beliefs that are most full of explanatory power and informative content, and those admirable beliefs turn out to be false. In that case, by adopting those beliefs we shall have correctly explained nothing and increased our genuine information not at all. For any belief to correctly explain or genuinely inform it must first be true. Only what correctly explains or genuinely informs can constitute knowledge. Therefore, we must be completely justified in believing what we do simply because by so doing we shall obtain true beliefs, or else our beliefs are not completely justified in the manner requisite for knowledge.

XI

The preceding line of argument leads to an inevitable conclusion. To meet the agnoiological challenge of scepticism, we must provide some argument to show that the sceptical hypothesis is false and that the beliefs of common sense are correct. And this leads to a second equally inescapable conclusion. The challenge cannot be met. Many reasons may be given for not *believing* the sceptical hypothesis. Indeed, a sceptic himself need not believe the sceptical hypothesis, and he might agree that there are practical disadvantages in believing such a hypothesis. But he might justifiably insist that we are not completely justified in concluding that the hypothesis is *false*. The hypothesis might seem silly, it might interfere with the attempt to explain things, and it might make it very difficult to arrive at any sensible set of beliefs for conducting practical affairs and scientific investigations. There are perfectly cogent practical considerations, the sceptic might concede, for not believing the hypothesis. However, agnoiology rejects the premiss contending that inconvenient hypotheses are false. To suppose that would be to trip back into the clutches of a simplistic pragmatism from which we have been rescued all too recently.

The principal argument offered to show that sceptical hypotheses are false is simply that they conflict with our dogmatic beliefs. Since it is precisely the justification of the latter that is in question, this conflict cannot be taken to adjudicate against the sceptical hypothesis. We are not completely justified in rejecting the sceptical hypothesis, and thus we are not completely justified in believing the others. We do not know that the sceptical hypothesis is false, and thus we do not know that anything else is true. That is the agnoiology that sustains scepticism.

XII

In conclusion, let me remark that we need not mourn the passing of knowledge as a great loss. The assumption of dogmatists that some beliefs are completely justified and that they are true, is not a great asset in scientific inquiry where all contentions should be subject to question and must be defended on demand. Moreover, the sceptic is not deprived of those practical beliefs necessary to carrying on the business of practical affairs. Indeed, economists and philosophers have suggested that an analysis of rational choice requires only subjective probability, which is a coherent measure of belief, and the utilities we attach to various outcomes.

It might seem that to introduce an appeal to probabilities is to concede the day to scepticism because the probabilities must be based on observational evidence and the latter must be something we know to be true. But this objection is unsound. First, as Richard Jeffrey has shown, we may employ a concept of subjective probability in which no observation statement is assigned a probability of unity.[3] Moreover, we may reassign probabilities on the basis of sense experience without assigning the probability of unity to any such statement. Finally,

even if we do assign a probability of unity to a statement, for example, to a tautology, we need not interpret this assignment as meaning that we know the statement to be true. To be sure, the statement must have a kind of subjective certainty, but this may be analyzed in terms of the betting preferences of the subject rather than as knowledge. If there is any statement of which a person feels so certain that he would prefer to bet the statement is true rather than false no matter what the odds, then the subjective probability of that statement for that man is unity. It does not follow that he knows the statement to be true.

Finally, I would contend that just as we can give an analysis of rational decision in terms of probabilities and practical values, so we can give an analysis of rational belief on the basis of probabilities and epistemic values. In the first case we maximize practical utilities and in the second case we maximize epistemic ones. Neither analysis requires the assumption that we know anything. We can instead regard practical action and scientific inquiry as aiming at the satisfaction of objectives appropriate to each sphere. We change our beliefs to better satisfy those objectives. Thus, we may, while remaining sceptics, contend that our beliefs and actions are rational even though we agree that such beliefs are not so completely justified as to constitute knowledge. As such, all beliefs, even those we consider rational, are subject to critical review. None can be exempted from evaluation on the grounds that it is known to be true without need of supporting argument. Such are the fruits of agnoiology.

Notes

[1] James F. Ferrier, *Institutes of Metaphysics* (Edinburgh and London: William Blackwood & Sons, 1854).

[2] Thomas Reid, *The Works of Thomas Reid, D.D.* (Edinburgh: Maclaugh and Steward, 1863), p. 234.

[3] Richard Jeffrey, *The Logic of Decision* (New York: McGraw-Hill, 1965).

II.5 *Two Types of Knowledge*

Norman Malcolm

Norman Malcolm (1911–1990) was for many years Professor of Philosophy at Cornell University. Malcolm begins this essay with a quotation from the British philosopher H. A. Prichard to the effect that we can discover in ourselves whether we *know* some proposition or whether we merely *believe* it. Does knowledge light up a mental state different from that lighted up by belief? Malcolm rejects this thesis on one level of discourse, but he argues that Prichard's distinction does convey insight. Some beliefs or knowledge claims seem so self-evident that we cannot conceive of anything undermining them. Malcolm distinguishes two types of knowledge: weak and strong. Regarding our weak knowledge claims, we are willing to let further investigation determine whether we really have knowledge or not, but regarding strong knowledge we feel absolute certainty, so that no evidence could count against it.

'We must recognize that when we know something we either do, or by reflecting, can know that our condition is one of knowing that thing, while when we believe something, we either do or can know that our condition is one of believing and not of knowing: so that we cannot mistake belief for knowledge or vice versa.'[1]

This remark is worthy of investigation. Can I discover *in myself* whether I know something or merely believe it?

Let us begin by studying the ordinary usage of 'know' and 'believe.' Suppose, for example, that several of us intend to go for a walk and that you propose that we walk in Cascadilla Gorge. I protest that I should like to walk beside a flowing stream and that at this season the gorge is probably dry. Consider the following cases:

(1) You say 'I believe that it won't be dry although I have no particular reason for thinking so'. If we went to the gorge and found a flowing stream we should not say that you *knew* that there would be water but that you thought so and were right.

Originally published in *Mind* 51 (1952), 178–89. Reprinted in its revised form from *Knowledge and Certainty: Essays and Lectures by Norman Malcolm* (Englewood Cliffs, N.J.: Prentice-Hall, 1963).

(2) You say 'I believe that it won't be dry because it rained only three days ago and usually water flows in the gorge for at least that long after a rain'. If we found water we should be inclined to say that you knew that there would be water. It would be quite natural for you to say 'I knew that it wouldn't be dry'; and we should tolerate your remark. This case differs from the previous one in that here you had a *reason*.

(3) You say 'I know that it won't be dry' and give the same reason as in (2). If we found water we should have very little hesitation in saying that you knew. Not only had you a reason, but you *said* 'I know' instead of 'I believe'. It may seem to us that the latter should not make a difference—but it does.

(4) You say 'I know that it won't be dry' and give a stronger reason, e.g., 'I saw a lot of water flowing in the gorge when I passed it this morning'. If we went and found water, there would be no hesitation at all in saying that you knew. If, for example, we later met someone who said 'Weren't you surprised to see water in the gorge this afternoon?' you would reply 'No, I *knew* that there would be water; I had been there earlier in the day'. We should have no objection to this statement.

(5) Everything happens as in (4), except that

upon going to the gorge we find it to be dry. We should not say that you knew, but that you *believed* that there would be water. And this is true even though you declared that you knew, and even though your evidence was the same as it was in case (4) in which you did know.

I wish to make some comments on the usage of 'know', 'knew', 'believe', and 'believed', as illustrated in the preceding cases:

(*a*) Whether we should say that you knew, depends in part on whether you had grounds for your assertion and on the strength of those grounds. There would certainly be less hesitation to say that you knew in case (4) than in case (3), and this can be due only to the difference in the strength of the grounds.

(*b*) Whether we should say that you knew, depends in part on how *confident* you were. In case (2), if you had said 'It rained only three days ago and usually water flows in the gorge for at least that long after a rain; but, of course, I don't feel absolutely sure that there will be water', then we should *not* have said that you knew that there would be water. If you lack confidence that *p* is true then others do not say that you know that *p* is true, even though *they* know that *p* is true. Being confident is a necessary condition for knowing.

(*c*) Prichard says that if we reflect we cannot mistake belief for knowledge. In case (4) you knew that there would be water, and in case (5) you merely believed it. Was there any way that you could have discovered by reflection, in case (5), that you did not know? It would have been useless to have reconsidered your grounds for saying that there would be water, because in case (4), where you *did* know, your grounds were identical. They could be at fault in (5) only if they were at fault in (4), and they were not at fault in (4). Cases (4) and (5) differ in only one respect—namely, that in one case you did subsequently find water and in the other you did not. Prichard says that we can determine by reflection whether we know something or merely believe it. But where, in these cases, is the material that reflection would strike upon? There is none.

There is only one way that Prichard could defend his position. He would have to say that in case (4) you did *not* know that there would be water. And it is obvious that he would have said this. But this is false. It is an enormously common usage of

language to say, in commenting upon just such an incident as (4), 'He knew that the gorge would be not dry because he had seen water flowing there that morning'. It is a usage that all of us are familiar with. We so employ 'know' and 'knew' every day of our lives. We do not think of our usage as being loose or incorrect—and it is not. As philosophers we may be surprised to observe that it *can* be that the knowledge that *p* is true should differ from the belief that *p* is true *only* in the respect that in one case *p* is true and in the other false. But that is the fact.

There is an argument that one is inclined to use as a proof that you did not know that there would be water. The argument is the following: It could have turned out that you found no water; if it had so turned out you would have been mistaken in saying that you would find water; therefore you could have been mistaken; but if you could have been mistaken then you did not know.

Now it certainly *could* have turned out that the gorge was quite dry when you went there, even though you saw lots of water flowing through it only a few hours before. This does not show, however, that you did not know that there would be water. What it shows is that *although you knew you could have been mistaken.*[2] This would seem to be a contradictory result; but it is not. It seems so because our minds are fixed upon another usage of 'know' and 'knew'; one in which 'It could have turned out that I was mistaken', implies 'I did not know'.

When is 'know' used in this sense? I believe that Prichard uses it in this sense when he says that when we go through the proof of the proposition that the angles of a triangle are equal to two right angles we *know* that the proposition is true (p. 89). He says that if we put to ourselves the question: Is our condition one of knowing this, or is it only one of being convinced of it? then 'We can only answer "Whatever may be our state on other occasions, here we are knowing this." And this statement is an expression of our *knowing* that we are knowing; for we do not *believe* that we are knowing this, we know that we are' (p. 89). He goes on to say that if someone were to object that we might be making a mistake 'because for all we know we can later on discover some fact which is incompatible with a triangle's having angles that are equal to two right angles, we can answer that we *know* that there can be no such fact, for in knowing that a triangle must have such angles we also know that nothing can exist which is incompatible with this fact' (p. 90).

It is easy to imagine a non-philosophical context in which it would have been natural for Prichard to have said 'I know that the angles of a triangle are equal to two right angles'. Suppose that a young man just beginning the study of geometry was in doubt as to whether that proposition is true, and had even constructed an ingenious argument that appeared to prove it false. Suppose that Prichard was unable to find any error in the argument. He might have said to the young man: 'There must be an error in it. I know that the angles of a triangle are equal to two right angles'.

When Prichard says that 'nothing can exist which is incompatible with' the truth of that proposition, is he prophesying that no one will ever have the ingenuity to construct a flawless-looking argument against it? I believe not. When Prichard says that 'we' *know* (and implies that *he* knows) that the proposition is true and *know* that nothing can exist that is incompatible with its being true, he is not making any *prediction* as to what the future will bring in the way of arguments or measurements. On the contrary, he is asserting that *nothing* that the future might bring could ever count as evidence against the proposition. He is implying that he would not *call* anything 'evidence' against it. He is using 'know' in what I shall call its 'strong' sense. 'Know' is used in this sense when a person's statement 'I know that *p* is true' implies that the person who makes the statement would look upon nothing whatever as evidence that *p* is false.

It must not be assumed that whenever 'know' is used in connexion with mathematical propositions it is used in the strong sense. A great many people have *heard* of various theorems of geometry, e.g., the Pythagorean. These theorems are a part of 'common knowledge'. If a schoolboy doing his geometry assignment felt a doubt about the Pythagorean theorem, and said to an adult 'Are you *sure* that it is true?' the latter might reply 'Yes, I know that it is'. He might make this reply even though he could not give proof of it and even though he had never gone through a proof of it. If subsequently he was presented with a 'demonstration' that the theorem is false, or if various persons reputed to have a knowledge of geometry soberly assured him that it is false, he might be filled with doubt or even be convinced that he was mistaken. When he said 'Yes,

I know that it is true', he did not pledge himself to hold to the theorem through thick and thin. He did not absolutely exclude the possibility that something could prove it to be false. I shall say that he used 'know' in the 'weak' sense.

Consider another example from mathematics of the difference between the strong and weak senses of 'know.' I have just now rapidly calculated that 92 times 16 is 1472. If I had done this in the commerce of daily life where a practical problem was at stake, and if someone had asked 'Are you sure that $92 \times 16 = 1472$?' I might have answered 'I *know* that it is; I have just now calculated it'. But also I might have answered 'I know that it is; but I will calculate it again to *make sure*'. And here my language points to a distinction. I say that I *know* that $92 \times 16 = 1472$. Yet I am willing to *confirm* it—that is, there is something that I should *call* 'making sure'; and, likewise, there is something that I should *call* 'finding out that it is false'. If I were to do this calculation again and obtain the result that $92 \times 16 = 1372$, and if I were to carefully check this latter calculation without finding any error, I should be disposed to say that I was previously mistaken when I declared that $92 \times 16 = 1472$. Thus when I say that I know that $92 \times 16 = 1472$, I allow for the possibility of a *refutation*, and so I am using 'know' in its weak sense.

Now consider propositions like $2 + 2 = 4$ and $7 + 5 = 12$. It is hard to think of circumstances in which it would be natural for me to say that I know that $2 + 2 = 4$, because no one ever questions it. Let us try to suppose, however, that someone whose intelligence I respect argues that certain developments in arithmetic have shown that $2 + 2$ does not equal 4. He writes out a proof of this in which I can find no flaw. Suppose that his demeanour showed me that he was in earnest. Suppose that several persons of normal intelligence became persuaded that his proof was correct and that $2 + 2$ does not equal 4. What would be my reaction? I should say 'I can't see what is wrong with your proof; but it *is* wrong, because I *know* that $2 + 2 = 4$'. Here I should be using 'know' in its strong sense. I should not admit that any argument or any future development in mathematics could show that it is false that $2 + 2 = 4$.

The propositions $2 + 2 = 4$ and $92 \times 16 = 1472$ do not have the same status. There *can* be a demonstration that $2 + 2 = 4$. But a demonstration would be for me (and for any average person) only a curious exercise, a sort of *game*. We have no serious interest in proving that proposition. It does not *need* a proof. It stands without one, and would not fall if a proof went against it. The case is different with the proposition that $92 \times 16 = 1472$. We take an interest in the demonstration (calculation) because that proposition *depends* upon its demonstration. A calculation may lead me to reject it as false. But $2 + 2 = 4$ does *not* depend on its demonstration. It does not depend on anything! And in the calculation that proves that $92 \times 16 = 1472$, there are steps that do not depend on any calculation (e.g., $2 \times 6 = 12$; $5 + 2 = 7$; $5 + 9 = 14$).

There is a correspondence between this dualism in the logical status of mathematical propositions and the two senses of 'know'. When I use 'know' in the weak sense I am prepared to let an investigation (demonstration, calculation) determine whether the something that I claim to know is true or false. When I use 'know' in the strong sense I am not prepared to look upon anything as an *investigation;* I do not concede that anything whatsoever could prove me mistaken; I do not regard the matter as open to any *question;* I do not admit that my proposition could turn out to be false, that any future investigation *could* refute it or cast doubt on it.

We have been considering the strong sense of 'know' in its application to mathematical propositions. Does it have application anywhere in the realm of *empirical* propositions—for example, to propositions that assert or imply that certain physical things exist? Descartes said that we have a 'moral assurance' of the truth of some of the latter propositions but that we lack a 'metaphysical certainty'. Locke said that the perception of the existence of physical things is not 'so certain as our intuitive knowledge, or the deductions of our reason' although 'it is an assurance that deserves the name of knowledge'. Some philosophers have held that when we make judgements of perception such as that there are peonies in the garden, cows in the field, or dishes in the cupboard, we are 'taking for granted' that the peonies, cows, and dishes exist, but not knowing it in the 'strict' sense. Others have held that all empirical propositions, including judgements of perception, are merely hypotheses. The thought behind this exaggerated mode of expression is that any empirical proposition whatever

could be refuted by future experience—that is, it *could* turn out to be false. Are these philosophers right?

Consider the following propositions:

(i) The sun is about ninety million miles from the earth.

(ii) There is a heart in my body.

(iii) Here is an ink-bottle.

In various circumstances I should be willing to assert of each of these propositions that I know it to be true. Yet they differ strikingly. This I see when, with each, I try to imagine the possibility that it is false.

(i) If in ordinary conversation someone said to me 'The sun is about twenty million miles from the earth, isn't it?' I should reply 'No, it is about ninety million miles from us.' If he said 'I think that you are confusing the sun with Polaris', I should reply, 'I *know* that ninety million miles is roughly the sun's distance from the earth'. I might invite him to verify the figure in an encyclopedia. A third person who overheard our conversation could quite correctly report that I knew the distance to the sun, whereas the other man did not. But this knowledge of mine is little better than hearsay. I have seen that figure mentioned in a few books. I know nothing about the observations and calculations that led astronomers to accept it. If tomorrow a group of eminent astronomers announced that a great error had been made and that the correct figure is twenty million miles, I should not insist that they were wrong. It would surprise me that such an enormous mistake could have been made. But I should no longer be willing to say that I *know* that ninety million is the correct figure. Although I should *now* claim that I know the distance to be about ninety million miles, it is easy for me to envisage the possibility that some future investigation will prove this to be false.

(ii) Suppose that after a routine medical examination the excited doctor reports to me that the X-ray photographs show that I have no heart. I should tell him to get a new machine. I should be inclined to say that the fact that I have a heart is one of the few things that I can count on as absolutely certain. I can feel it beat. I know it's there. Furthermore, how could my blood circulate if I didn't have one? Suppose that later on I suffer a chest injury and undergo a surgical operation. Afterwards the astonished surgeons solemnly declare that they searched my chest cavity and found no heart, and that they made incisions and looked about in other likely places but found it not. They are convinced that I am without a heart. They are unable to understand how circulation can occur or what accounts for the thumping in my chest. But they are in agreement and obviously sincere, and they have clear photographs of my interior spaces. What would be my attitude? Would it be to insist that they were all mistaken? I think not. I believe that I should eventually accept their testimony and the evidence of the photographs. I should consider to be false what I now regard as an absolute certainty.

(iii) Suppose that as I write this paper someone in the next room were to call out to me 'I can't find an ink-bottle; is there one in the house?' I should reply 'Here is an ink-bottle'. If he said in a doubtful tone 'Are you sure? I looked there before', I should reply 'Yes, I know there is; come and get it'.

Now could it turn out to be false that there is an ink-bottle directly in front of me on this desk? Many philosophers have thought so. They would say that many things could happen of such a nature that if they did happen it would be proved that I am deceived. I agree that many extraordinary things could happen, in the sense that there is no logical absurdity in the supposition. It could happen that when I next reach for this ink-bottle my hand should seem to pass *through* it and I should not feel the contact of any object. It could happen that in the next moment the ink-bottle will suddenly vanish from sight; or that I should find myself under a tree in the garden with no ink-bottle about; or that one or more persons should enter this room and declare with apparent sincerity that they see no ink-bottle on this desk; or that a photograph taken now of the top of the desk should clearly show all of the objects on it except the ink-bottle. Having admitted that these things *could happen,* am I compelled to admit that if they did happen then it would be proved that there is no ink-bottle here *now*? Not at all! I could say that when my hand seemed to pass through the ink-bottle I should *then* be suffering from hallucination; that if the ink-bottle suddenly vanished it would have miraculously ceased to exist; that the other persons were conspiring to drive me mad, or were themselves victims of remarkable concurrent hallucinations; that the camera possessed some strange flaw or that there was trickery in de-

veloping the negative. I admit that in the next moment I could find myself under a tree or in the bathtub. But this is not to admit that it could be revealed in the next moment that I am now dreaming. For what I admit is that I might be instantaneously transported to the garden, but not that in the next moment I might *wake up* in the garden. There is nothing that could happen to me in the next moment that I should call 'waking up'; and therefore nothing that could happen to me in the next moment would be accepted by me now as proof that I now dream.

Not only do I not *have* to admit that those extraordinary occurrences would be evidence that there is no ink-bottle here; the fact is that I *do not* admit it. There is nothing whatever that could happen in the next moment or the next year that would by me be called *evidence* that there is not an ink-bottle here now. No future experience or investigation could prove to me that I am mistaken. Therefore, if I were to say 'I know that there is an ink-bottle here', I should be using 'know' in the strong sense.

It will appear to some that I have adopted an *unreasonable* attitude towards that statement. There is, however, nothing unreasonable about it. It seems so because one thinks that the statement that here is an ink-bottle *must* have the same status as the statements that the sun is ninety million miles away and that I have a heart and that there will be water in the gorge this afternoon. But this is a *prejudice*.

In saying that I should regard nothing as evidence that there is no ink-bottle here now, I am not *predicting* what I should do if various astonishing things happened. If other members of my family entered this room and, while looking at the top of this desk, declared with apparent sincerity that they see no ink-bottle, I might fall into a swoon or become mad. I *might* even come to believe that there is not and has not been an ink-bottle here. I cannot foretell with certainty how I should react. But if it is *not* a prediction, what is the meaning of my assertion that I should regard nothing as evidence that there is no ink-bottle here?

That assertion describes my *present* attitude towards the statement that here is an ink-bottle. It does not prophesy what my attitude *would* be if various things happened. My present attitude towards that statement is radically different from my present attitude towards those other statements (e.g., that I have a heart). I do *now* admit that certain future occurrences would disprove the latter. Whereas no imaginable future occurrence would be considered by me *now* as proving that there is not an ink-bottle here.

These remarks are not meant to be autobiographical. They are meant to throw light on the common concepts of evidence, proof, and disproof. Every one of us upon innumerable occasions of daily life takes this same attitude towards various statements about physical things, e.g., that here is a torn page, that this dish is broken, that the thermometer reads 70, that no rug is on the floor. Furthermore, the concepts of proof, disproof, doubt, and conjecture *require* us to take this attitude. In order for it to be possible that any statements about physical things should *turn out to be false* it is necessary that some statements about physical things *cannot* turn out to be false.

This will be made clear if we ask ourselves the question, When do we *say* that something turned out to be false? When do we use those words? Someone asks you for a dollar. You say 'There is one in this drawer'. You open the drawer and look, but it is perfectly empty. Your statement turned out to be false. This can be said because you *discovered* an empty drawer. It could not be said if it were only probable that the drawer is empty or were still open to question. Would it make sense to say 'I had better make sure that it is empty; perhaps there is a dollar in it after all?' Sometimes; but not always. Not if the drawer lies open before your eyes. That remark is the prelude to a search. What search can there be when the emptiness of the drawer confronts you? In certain circumstances there is nothing that you would call 'making sure' that the drawer is empty; and likewise nothing that you would call 'its turning out to be false' that the drawer is empty. You *made* sure that the drawer is empty. One statement about physical things *turned out to be false* only because you *made sure* of another statement about physical things. The two concepts cannot exist apart. Therefore it is impossible that *every* statement about physical things *could* turn out to be false.

In a certain important respect some a priori statements and some empirical statements possess the same logical character. The statements that 5 × 5 = 25 and that here is an ink-bottle, both lie beyond the reach of doubt. On both, my judgement and reasoning *rests*. If you could somehow under-

mine my confidence in either, you would not teach me *caution*. You would fill my mind with chaos! I could not even make *conjectures* if you took away those fixed points of certainty; just as a man cannot *try* to climb whose body has no support. A conjecture implies an understanding of what certainty would be. If it is not a certainty that 5 × 5 = 25 and that here is an ink-bottle, then I do not understand what it is. You cannot make me doubt either of these statements or treat them as hypotheses. You cannot persuade me that future experience could refute them. With both of them it is perfectly unintelligible to me to speak of a 'possibility' that they are false. This is to say that I know both of them to be true, in the strong sense of 'know'. And I am inclined to think that the strong sense of 'know' is what various philosophers have had in mind when they have spoken of 'perfect', 'metaphysical', or 'strict certainty'.

It will be thought that I have confused a statement about my 'sensations', or my 'sense-data', or about the way something *looks* or *appears* to me, with a statement about physical things. It will be thought that the things that I have said about the statement 'Here is an ink-bottle' could be true only if that statement is interpreted to mean something like 'There appears to me to be an ink-bottle here', i.e., interpreted so as not to assert or imply that any physical thing exists. I wish to make it clear that my statement 'Here is an ink-bottle' is *not* to be interpreted in that way. It would be utterly fantastic for me in my present circumstances to say 'There appears to me to be an ink-bottle here'.

If someone were to call me on the telephone and say that he urgently needed an ink-bottle I should invite him to come here and get this one. If he said that it was extremely urgent that he should obtain one immediately and that he could not afford to waste time going to a place where there might not be one, I should tell him that it is an absolute certainty that there is one here, that nothing could be more certain, that it is something I absolutely guarantee. But if my statement 'There is an ink-bottle here' were a statement about my 'sensations' or 'sense-data', or if it meant that there *appears* to me to be an ink-bottle here or that something here *looks* to me like an ink-bottle, and if that is all that I meant by it—then I should react quite differently to his urgent request. I should say that there is probably an ink-bottle here but that I could not *guarantee* it, and that if he needs one very desperately and at once then he had better look elsewhere. In short, I wish to make it clear that my statement 'Here is an ink-bottle' is strictly about physical things and not about 'sensations', 'sense-data', or 'appearances'.

Let us go back to Prichard's remark that we can determine by reflection whether we know something or merely believe it. Prichard would think that 'knowledge in the weak sense' is mere belief and not knowledge. This is wrong. But if we let ourselves speak this way, we can then see some justification for Prichard's remark. For then he would be asserting, among other things, that we can determine by reflection whether we know something in the strong sense or in the weak sense. This is not literally true; however, there is this truth in it—that reflection can make us realize that we are *using* 'I know it' in the strong (or weak) sense in a particular case. Prichard says that reflection can show us that 'our condition is one of knowing' a certain thing, or instead that 'our condition is one of believing and not of knowing' that thing. I do not understand what could be meant here by 'our condition'. The way I should put it is that reflection on *what we should think* if certain things were to happen may make us realize that we should (or should not) call those things 'proof' or 'evidence' that what we claim to know is not so. I have tried to show that the distinction between strong and weak knowledge does not run parallel to the distinction between a priori and empirical knowledge but cuts across it, i.e., these two kinds of knowledge may be distinguished *within* a priori knowledge and *within* empirical knowledge.

Reflection can make me realize that I am using 'know' in the strong sense; but can reflection show me that I *know* something in the strong sense (or in the weak)? It is not easy to state the logical facts here. On the one hand, if I make an assertion of the form 'I know that *p*' it does not follow that *p*, whether or not I am using 'know' in the strong

sense. If I have said to someone outside my room 'Of course, I know that Freddie is in here', and I am speaking in the strong sense, it does not *follow* that Freddie is where I claim he is. This logical fact would not be altered even if I *realized* that I was using 'know' in the strong sense. My reflection on what I should say if . . . , cannot show me that I *know* something. From the fact that I should not call anything 'evidence' that Freddie is not here, it does not follow that he *is* here; therefore, it does not follow that I *know* he is here.

On the other hand, in an actual case of my using 'know' in the strong sense, I cannot envisage a possibility that what I say to be true should turn out to be not true. If I were speaking of *another person's* assertion about something, I *could* think both that he is using 'know' in the strong sense and that nonetheless what he claims he knows to be so might turn out to be not so. But *in my own case* I cannot have this conjunction of thoughts, and this is a logical and not a psychological fact. When *I* say that I know something to be so, using 'know' in the strong sense, it is unintelligible *to me* (although perhaps not to others) to suppose that anything could prove that it is not so and, therefore, that I do not know it.

Notes

[1] H. A. Prichard, *Knowledge and Perception* (Oxford: Clarendon Press, 1950), p. 88.

[2] Some readers seem to have thought that I was denying here that 'I knew that *p*' entails 'that *p*'. That was not my intention, and my words do not have that implication. If I had said *'although you knew you were mistaken'*, I should have denied the above entailment and, also, I should have misused 'knew'. The difference between the strong and weak senses of 'know' (and 'knew') is not that this entailment holds for the strong but not for the weak sense. It holds for both. If it is false that *p*, then one does not (and did not) know that *p*.

Bibliography

Johnson, Oliver. *Skepticism and Cognition*. Berkeley: University of California Press, 1978.

Klein, Peter. *Certainty: A Refutation of Scepticism*. Minneapolis: University of Minnesota Press, 1981.

Rescher, Nicholas. *Skepticism: A Critical Reappraisal*. Totowa, NJ: Rowman & Littlefield, 1980.

Stroud, Barry. *The Significance of Philosophical Skepticism*. Oxford, England: Oxford University Press, 1984.

Unger, Peter. *Ignorance: A Case for Skepticism*. Oxford, England: Clarendon Press, 1975.

Unger, Peter. "A Defense of Skepticism." *Philosophical Review 80* (1971).

Part III

Perception: Our Knowledge of the External World

In daily life, we assume as certain many things which, on a closer scrutiny, are found to be so full of apparent contradictions that only a great amount of thought enables us to know what it is that we really may believe. In the search for certainty, it is natural to begin with our present experiences, and in some sense, no doubt, knowledge is to be derived from them. But any statement as to what it is that our immediate experience makes us know is very likely to be wrong. It seems to me that I am now sitting in a chair, at a table of a certain shape, on which I see sheets of paper with writing or print. . . . I believe that, if any other normal person comes into my room, he will see the same chairs and tables and books as I see, and that the table which I see is the same as the table which I feel pressing against my arm. All this seems to be so evident as to be hardly worth stating, except in answer to a man who doubts whether I know anything. Yet all this may be reasonably doubted, and all of it requires much careful discussion before we can be sure that we have stated it in a form that is wholly true.

BERTRAND RUSSELL
Problems of Philosophy

What do we really know? Assuming that skepticism is false and that we do know something of the external world, what exactly do we know and how do we know it? Do we ever really see the book that appears in front of us, the table that it rests on, the floor on which we stand, the walls that surround us? What is the direct object of awareness when we perceive? Three answers have traditionally been given to that question: (1) direct realism (sometimes called "naive realism" or "common-sense realism"), (2) representationalism, and (3) phenomenalism. Direct realism claims that the immediate object of perception is a physical thing that exists independently of our awareness of it. Representationalism and phenomenalism answer that the immediate object of perception is a sense datum or sense impression—which cannot exist apart from our awareness of it. But representationalism and phenomenalism divide over the relationship of sense data to the physical world. For the representationalist, the physical world exists independently of and is the cause of our perceptions. Physical objects give rise to sense data that we perceive, so we only have mediate knowledge of the external world. For phenomenalism, physical objects are simply constructions of sense data. They do not exist independently of sense impressions.

Common sense tells us that we, through our five senses, sight, hearing, touch, taste, and smell, do directly perceive the real world. It tells us that the physical world exists independently of our awareness of it and that the things we perceive are pretty much the way we perceive them. They exist here and now. Common sense supports naive or direct realism.

Science casts doubt on common sense. As Bertrand Russell succinctly says, "Naive realism leads to physics, and physics, if true, shows that naive realism is false. Therefore, naive realism, if true, is false; therefore it it false."[1] Science tells us that the physical objects we perceive are not what they seem to be, nor do we ever see things in the present. Colors are not in the objects but are the way objects appear as they reflect light. Since light takes time to reach our eyes, all that we see really existed in the past. It takes 8 minutes for the light from the sun to reach us and hundreds of years for the light from distant stars to reach us, so that when we look (through the proper filtered lenses) at the sun or at distant stars we are not seeing them as they exist in the present but as they existed 8 minutes or hundreds of years ago. In fact, there is nothing we see as it presently exists but only as it existed in the past (near or far).

Likewise, science tells us that the sounds we hear, the flavors we taste, the sensations of touch, and the odors we smell are not what they seem to be. They are mediated through our ways of perceiving, so that we seldom or never experience them as they really are in themselves.

So representationalism seems to succeed in giving an explanation of perception that is more faithful to science than is direct realism. Representationalism holds that the real world causes our appearances or perceptions by representing the physical world through sense data, mental entities that are private to individual perceivers.

In the following readings, John Locke (1632–1704) sets forth the classic expression of this view. Attacking the notion that we have innate knowledge of metaphysical truths, Locke argues that all our knowledge derives ultimately from sense experience:

> Let us then suppose the mind to be, as we say, white paper, void of all characters, without any ideas; how comes it to be furnished? Whence comes it by that vast store which the busy and boundless fancy of man has painted on it with an almost endless variety? Whence has it all the materials of reason and knowledge? To this I answer, in one word, from experience; in all that our knowledge is founded, and from that it ultimately derives itself.

Locke held a causal theory of perception in which processes in the external world impinge on the perceiver's sense organs, which in turn send messages to the brain, where they are transformed into mental events. We may diagram Locke's causal theory of perception this way:

OBJECTS AND EVENTS IN THE REAL WORLD

⬇ (Energy coming to sense organs: insensible particles reflected from the object onto the sense organ or coming into contact with the sense organ)

SENSE ORGANS

⬇ (Signals to brain)

BRAIN EVENT

⬇ (Transformation from physical to mental event)

PERCEPTUAL EXPERIENCE

The mechanical input yields the nonmechanical idea in the mind. Although the process is physical and mechanistic, it yields a nonphysical result, a mental event, the perceptual experience, that subsequent philosophers describe as a *percept* or *sense datum* or *sense impression*.

Locke divides the qualities of physical objects into two basic classes: *primary qualities* and *secondary qualities*. Primary qualities are inseparable from their objects and so truly represent them. Such qualities are solidity (or bulk), extension, figure, movement (and rest), and number. These are the true building blocks of knowledge because they accurately represent features in the world. Secondary qualities are not in the things themselves but are caused by the primary qualities. These qualities include colors, sounds, smells, tastes, touch, and sensations. These secondary qualities are types of powers or potentialities or dispositions that reside in a physical object. Fire has the power to change liquids into gases, sugar is soluble in warm water, and glass is fragile. Solubility, flammability, and fragility are dispositional qualities in bodies. Dispositional qualities cause changes in the external world.

Secondary qualities are powers that produce sensations (that is, perceptions) in the perceiver. The primary qualities (motion or whatever) cause the secondary qualities that we perceive. When, under normal circumstances, we look at an object it looks a certain color—say, red. The redness we are acquainted with is not in the object itself but in the way the light reflects off the object into our eye and is communicated to our brain. Secondary qualities are the ways things have of appearing to us.

Underneath all the qualities is substance, the foundation of matter itself. Locke assumes that there must be an ultimate source of reality that underlies the ideas presented in experience. He describes it as "something I know not what."

There are problems with representationalism. If direct realism, via physics, leads to representationalism, representationalism, on philosophical reflection, seems to lead to phenomenalism.

In the second reading in this part of the book, George Berkeley (1685–1753) holds to a type of phenomenalism that has been called "immaterialism." Berkeley criticized Locke's representationalism on several counts. First, he argued that the primary–secondary qualities distinction was unsound. The primary qualities are no more "in" the objects of perception than are the secondary ones. Second, he argued that there were logical problems in the theory that our perceptions resembled physical objects ("and idea can be like nothing but an idea"). Third, he undermined the whole notion of substance that Locke needed to maintain his theory. What is the difference, Berkeley rhetorically asked, between a "something I know not what" (Locke's notion of substance) and nothing at all? Ultimately; Locke's representationalism leads back to skepticism.

Berkeley held that ideas exist in the mind alone. All perceived qualities are mental or subjective: their reality consists in being perceived ("To be is to be perceived"). There is no material world. Physical objects are simply mental events. "The table I write on, I say, exists, that is, I see and feel it; and if I were out of my study I should say it existed, meaning thereby that if I was in my study I might perceive it, or that some other spirit actually does perceive it." All physical objects are mental phenomena that would cease to exist if they were not perceived. Why do physical objects continue to exist when no one is perceiving them? Well, someone *is* always perceiving them: God's eye keeps the world from dissolving.[2]

Contemporary phenomenalism differs with Berkeley only in this last respect. It doesn't posit God as necessary to hold the physical world in existence. Instead, it views the physical world as a construct of ideas. In Mill's words, objects are "permanent possibilities of sensation," meaning that if one were to get into the appropriate condition, one would experience the sense data. In the third reading for this part, W. T. Stace argues that the realist's view of the world as containing material objects behind the perceived world is an unjustified faith. The world of scientific discourse (for example, such terms as "atoms," "gravity," and "conservation of energy") is not to be taken literally, but instrumentally, as providing useful fictions that help us to predict experiences.

The fourth reading, by C. H. Whiteley, provides a thorough critical assessment of the phenomenalist position, analyzing its strengths and weaknesses.

Two puzzles for sense data theories, whether representational or phenomenal, which Whiteley doesn't discuss, should be noted. The first is the paradox of the nontransitivity of perception. Take three pieces of red colored paper. Suppose that we cannot distinguish between Samples A and B. They seem exactly the same color. Likewise Samples B and C are indistinguishable. But say we *can* distinguish between A and C! On the sense data account, this is puzzling, since we should be able to distinguish our sense data from one another.

The second puzzle is that of indeterminateness. Suppose we see a speckled hen. How many speckles does our sense datum hold? If we say that the number is indeterminate, we seem to have a paradox between the indeterminate sense datum and the determinate objects that are supposed to be represented.

The fifth reading, by Bertrand Russell, is a defense of representational realism, developing Locke's causal theory of perception in the light of contemporary science. According to Russell, our knowledge of physical objects is inferred from percepts in our brain. One may ask why Russell does not simply accept phenomenalism, since he makes percepts primary to our knowledge. Russell concedes that phenomenalism is not impossible, but views it as implausible for reasons similar to Whiteley's.

The sixth reading contains a contemporary defense of direct realism. John Searle holds to the similarity between beliefs and perceptions. Both are intentional in structure. Perception gives us direct access to physical objects.

Searle's essay is important because it relates perception to other intentional states such as beliefs, desires, and memory. You need to decide whether Searle deals adequately with the main criticism against direct realism, the problem of illusion.

The final reading is in part a defense of representationalism by Charles Landesman, who argues that nothing in the world exemplifies color, that it is the impact of radiant energy on the nervous system that produces the appearance of color. Such illusions as color appearances have a biological function, helping us to make closer discriminations in the world, but colors are features neither of the external world nor of the mind.

Notes

[1] Bertrand Russell, *Inquiry into Meaning and Truth* (London: Allen & Unwin, 1940), p. 15.

[2] According to Berkeley, there is no sound independent of our hearing it and no reality but a mind's experiencing it. Does this mean that when we leave our rooms, they disappear? There is an old Oxford limerick on this point:

There was a young man who said, "God
Must think it exceedingly odd
If he finds that this tree
Continues to be,
When there's no one about in the quad."

Dear Sir, your astonishment's odd
I'm always about in the quad,
And that's why the tree
Continues to be,
Since observed by,

Yours faithfully,
God

III.1 A *Representational Theory of Perception*

JOHN LOCKE

The English philosopher John Locke (1632–1704) was educated at Oxford University, where he became a tutor in Greek rhetoric and philosophy. Later he was a practicing physician and assistant to the Earl of Shaftesbury. This selection is taken from Locke's *Essay Concerning Human Understanding* (1689).

Locke's work in the theory of knowledge is the first systematic assault on Cartesian rationalism, the view that reason alone guarantees knowledge. Locke argues that if our claims to knowledge make any sense, they must be derived from the world. He rejects the rationalist notion that we have *innate ideas* (actual knowledge of metaphysical truths, such as mathematical truths, universals, and the laws of nature) because (1) there is not good deductive argument establishing the existence of such entities, (2) children and idiots do not seem to possess them, and (3) an empirical way of knowing, which seems far more reasonable, has no place for such entities.

According to Locke, the mind at birth is a *tabula rasa,* a blank slate. It is like white paper, devoid of characteristics until it receives sense perceptions. All knowledge begins with sensory experience on which the powers of the mind operate, developing complex ideas, abstractions, and the like. In place of the absolute certainty that the rationalists sought to find, Locke says that apart from the knowledge of the self, most of what we know we know in degrees of certainty derived from inductive generalizations. For example, we see the sun rise every morning and infer that it is highly probable that it will rise tomorrow—but we cannot be absolutely certain.

Locke holds a representational theory of perception in which objects in the world cause our sense organs to start processes that result in perceptual experience. We are never aware of the thing in itself, the object that is perceived and that causes the idea to arise in our mind, but only of the idea or *representation* of the object. We are directly aware of the idea but inasmuch as the object is the cause of the idea, we may be said to be *indirectly* aware of the object itself.

Locke divides our ideas into two types: primary qualities and secondary qualities. Primary qualities are inseparable from their objects and thus truly represent them. Examples of primary qualities are solidity, extension, figure, movement, and number. These are the building blocks of knowledge. Secondary qualities are not in the things themselves but are caused by primary qualities. They include colors, sounds, tastes, and touch. They are powers that objects have to do certain things. Fire has the power to change liquids into gases, sugar is soluble in warm water, and glass is fragile. Solubility, flammability, and fragility are dispositional qualities in bodies, and as such cause changes in the world.

Reprinted from *An Essay Concerning Human Understanding* (1689).

Book II.

Chapter I. Of Ideas in General, and Their Original.

1. Every man being conscious to himself that he thinks, and that which his mind is applied about, whilst thinking, being the ideas that are there, it is past doubt that men have in their minds several ideas, such as are those expressed by the words, Whiteness, Hardness, Sweetness, Thinking, Motion, Man, Elephant, Army, Drunkenness, and others. It is in the first place then to be enquired, how he comes by them. I know it is a received doctrine, that men have native ideas, and original characters, stamped upon their minds, in their very first being. This opinion I have, at large, examined already; and, I suppose, what I have said, in the foregoing book, will be much more easily admitted, when I have shewn, whence the understanding may get all the ideas it has, and by what ways and degrees they may come into the mind for which I shall appeal to every one's own observation and experience.

2. Let us then suppose the mind to be, as we say, white paper, void of all characters, without any ideas; how comes it to be furnished? Whence comes it by that vast store which the busy and boundless fancy of man has painted on it with an almost endless variety? Whence has it all the materials of reason and knowledge? To this I answer, in one word, from experience; in all that our knowledge is founded, and from that it ultimately derives itself. Our observation employed either about external sensible objects, or about the internal operations of our minds, perceived and reflected on by ourselves, is that which supplies our understandings with all the materials of thinking. These two are the fountains of knowledge, from whence all the ideas we have, or can naturally have, do spring.

3. First, Our senses, conversant about particular sensible objects, do convey into the mind several distinct perceptions of things, according to those various ways wherein those objects do affect them: And thus we come by those ideas we have of Yellow, White, Heat, Cold, Soft, Hard, Bitter, Sweet, and all those which we call sensible qualities; which when I say the senses convey into the mind, I mean, they from external objects convey into the mind what produces there those perceptions. This great source of most of the ideas we have, depending wholly upon our senses, and derived by them to the understanding, I call SENSATION.

4. Secondly, The other fountain from which experience furnisheth the understanding with ideas, is the perception of the operations of our own mind within us, as it is employed about the ideas it has got; which operations, when the soul comes to reflect on and consider, do furnish the understanding with another set of ideas, which could not be had from things without. And such are Perception, Thinking, Doubting, Believing, Reasoning, Knowing, Willing, and all the different actings of our own minds; which we being conscious of and observing in ourselves, do from these receive into our understandings as distinct ideas, as we do from bodies affecting our senses. This source of ideas every man has wholly in himself; and though it be not sense, as having nothing to do with external objects, yet it is very like it, and might properly enough be called internal sense. But as I call the other sensation, so I call this REFLECTION, the ideas it affords being such only as the mind gets by reflecting on its own operations within itself. By reflection then, in the following part of this discourse, I would be understood to mean that notice which the mind takes of its own operations, and the manner of them; by reason whereof there come to be ideas of these operations in the understanding. These two, I say, viz. external material things, as the objects of sensation; and the operations of our own minds within, as the objects of reflection; are to me the only originals from whence all our ideas take their beginnings. The term operations here I use in a large sense, as comprehending not barely the actions of the mind about its ideas, but some sort of passions arising sometimes from them, such as is the satisfaction or uneasiness arising from any thought.

5. The understanding seems to me not to have the least glimmering of any ideas, which it doth not receive from one of these two. External objects furnish the mind with the ideas of sensible qualities, which are all those different perceptions they produce in us: And the mind furnishes the understanding with ideas of its own operations.

These, when we have taken a full survey of them, and their several modes, combinations, and relations, we shall find to contain all our whole stock of ideas; and that we have nothing in our minds which did not come in one of these two ways. Let any one examine his own thoughts, and thoroughly search into his understanding; and then let him tell me, whether all the original ideas he has there, are any other than of the objects of his senses, or of the operations of his mind, considered as objects of his reflection; and how great a mass of knowledge soever he imagines to be lodged there, he will, upon taking a strict view, see that he has not any idea in his mind, but what one of these two have imprinted; though perhaps, within infinite variety compounded and enlarged by the understanding, as we shall see hereafter.

6. He that attentively considers the state of a child, at his first coming into the world, will have little reason to think him stored with plenty of ideas, that are to be the matter of his future knowledge: It is by degrees he comes to be furnished with them. And though the ideas of obvious and familiar qualities imprint themselves before the memory begins to keep a register of time or order, yet it is often so late before some unusual qualities come in the way, that there are few men that cannot recollect the beginning of their acquaintance with them: And if it were worth while, no doubt a child might be so ordered as to have but a very few even of the ordinary ideas, till he were grown up to a man. But all that are born into the world being surrounded with bodies that perpetually and diversely affect them; variety of ideas, whether care be taken of it or not, are imprinted on the minds of children. Light and colours are busy at hand every-where, when the eye is but open; sounds and some tangible qualities fail not to solicit their proper senses, and force an entrance to the mind; but yet, I think, it will be granted easily, that if a child were kept in a place where he never saw any other but black and white till he were a man, he would have no more ideas of scarlet or green, than he that from his childhood never tasted an oyster, or a pineapple, has of those particular relishes.

Chapter VIII. Some Farther Considerations Concerning Our Simple Ideas.

1. Concerning the simple ideas of sensation it is to be considered that whatsoever is so constituted in nature as to be able, by affecting our senses, to cause any perception in the mind, doth thereby produce in the understanding a simple idea; which, what-

ever be the external cause of it, when it comes to be taken notice of by our discerning faculty, it is by the mind looked on and considered there to be a real positive idea in the understanding, as much as any other whatsoever; though perhaps the cause of it be but a privation of the subject.

2. Thus the ideas of heat and cold, light and darkness, white and black, motion and rest, are equally clear and positive ideas in the mind; though perhaps some of the causes which produce them are barely privations in subjects, from whence our senses derive those ideas. These the understanding, in its view of them, considers all as distinct positive ideas, without taking notice of the causes that produce them: Which is an enquiry not belonging to the idea, as it is in the understanding, but to the nature of the things existing without us. These are two very different things, and carefully to be distinguished; it being one thing to perceive and know the idea of white or black, and quite another to examine what kind of particles they must be, and how ranged in the superficies, to make any object appear white or black.

3. A painter or dyer, who never enquired into their causes, hath the ideas of white and black, and other colours, as clearly, perfectly, and distinctly in his understanding, and perhaps more distinctly, than the philosopher, who hath busied himself in considering their natures, and thinks he knows how far either of them is in its cause positive or privative; and the idea of black is no less positive in his mind, than that of white, however the cause of that colour in the external object may be only a privation.

4. If it were the design of my present undertaking to enquire into the natural causes and manner of perception, I should offer this as a reason why a privative cause might, in some cases at least, produce a positive idea, viz. that all sensation being produced in us only by different degrees and modes of motion in our animal spirits, variously agitated by external objects, the abatement of any former motion must as necessarily produce a new sensation, as the variation or increase of it; and so introduce a new idea, which depends only on a different motion of the animal spirits in that organ.

5. But whether this be so or no, I will not here determine, but appeal to every one's own experience, whether the shadow of a man, though it consists of nothing but the absence of light (and the more the absence of light is, the more discernible is

the shadow) does not, when a man looks on it, cause as clear and positive idea in his mind, as a man himself, though covered over with clear sunshine? and the picture of a shadow is a positive thing. Indeed we have negative names, which stand not directly for positive ideas, but for their absence, such as insipid, silence, nihil, &c. which words denote positive ideas, e.g. taste, sound, being, with a signification of their absence.

6. And thus one may truly be said to see darkness. For supposing a hole perfectly dark, from whence no light is reflected, it is certain one may see the figure of it, or it may be painted: Or whether the ink I write with makes any other idea, is a question. The privative causes I have here assigned of positive ideas are according to the common opinion; but in truth it will be hard to determine, whether there be really any ideas from a privative cause, till it be determined, whether rest be any more a privation than motion.

7. To discover the nature of our ideas the better, and to discourse of them intelligibly, it will be convenient to distinguish them as they are ideas or perceptions in our minds, and as they are modifications of matter in the bodies that cause such perceptions in us: That so we may not think (as perhaps usually is done) that they are exactly the images and resemblances of some thing inherent in the subject; most of those of sensation being in the mind no more the likeness of some thing existing without us, than the names that stand for them are the likeness of our ideas, which yet upon hearing they are apt to excite in us.

8. Whatsoever the mind perceives in itself, or is the immediate object of perception, thought, or understanding, that I call idea; and the power to produce any idea in our mind I call a quality of the subject wherein that power is. Thus a snow-ball having the power to produce in us the ideas of white, cold, and round, the power to produce those ideas in us, as they are in the snow-ball, I call qualities; and as they are sensations or perceptions in our understandings, I call them ideas; which ideas, if I speak of sometimes, as in the things themselves, I would be understood to mean those qualities in the objects which produce them in us.

9. Qualities thus considered in bodies are, first, such as are utterly inseparable from the body, in what state soever it be; such as in all the alterations and changes it suffers, all the force can be used upon

it, it constantly keeps; and such as sense constantly finds in every particle of matter which has bulk enough to be perceived, and the mind finds inseparable from every particle of matter, though less than to make itself singly be perceived by our senses, v.g. Take a grain of wheat, divide it into two parts, each part has still solidity, extension, figure, and mobility; divide it again, and it retains still the same qualities; and so divide it on till the parts become insensible, they must retain still each of them all those qualities. For division (which is all that a mill, or pestle, or any other body does upon another, in reducing it to insensible parts) can never take away either solidity, extension, figure, or mobility from any body, but only makes two or more distinct separate masses of matter, of that which was but one before: All which distinct masses, reckoned as so many distinct bodies, after division make a certain number. These I call original or primary qualities of body, which I think we may observe to produce simple ideas in us, viz. solidity, extension, figure, motion or rest, and number.

10. Secondly, such qualities which in truth are nothing in the objects themselves, but powers to produce various sensations in us by their primary qualities, i.e. by the bulk, figure, texture, and motion of their insensible parts, as colours, sounds, tastes, &c. these I call secondary qualities. To these might be added a third sort, which are allowed to be barely powers, though they are as much real qualities in the subject, as those which I, to comply with the common way of speaking, call qualities, but for distinction, secondary qualities. For the power in fire to produce a new colour, or consistency, in wax or clay, by its primary qualities, is as much a quality in fire, as the power it has to produce in me a new idea or sensation of warmth or burning, which I felt not before by the same primary qualities, viz. the bulk, texture, and motion of its insensible parts.

11. The next thing to be considered is, how bodies produce ideas in us; and that is manifestly by impulse, the only way which we can conceive bodies to operate in.

12. If then external objects be not united to our minds, when they produce ideas therein, and yet we perceive these original qualities in such of them as singly fall under our senses, it is evident that some motion must be thence continued by our nerves, or animal spirits, by some parts of our bodies, to the brains or the seat of sensation, there to produce on

our minds the particular ideas we have of them. And since the extension, figure, number, and motion of bodies, of an observable bigness, may be perceived at a distance by the sight, it is evident some singly imperceptible bodies must come from them to the eyes, and thereby convey to the brain some motion, which produces these ideas which we have of them in us.

13. After the same manner that the ideas of these original qualities are produced in us, we may conceive that the ideas of secondary qualities are also produced, viz. by the operation of insensible particles on our senses. For it being manifest that there are bodies and good store of bodies, each whereof are so small, that we cannot, by any of our senses, discover either their bulk, figure, or motion as is evident in the particles of the air and water, and others extremely smaller than those, perhaps as much smaller than the particles of air and water, as the particles of air and water are smaller than peas or hail-stones: Let us suppose at present, that the different motions and figures, bulk and number of such particles, affecting the several organs of our senses, produce in us those different sensations, which we have from the colours and smells of bodies; e.g. that a violet, by the impulse of such insensible particles of matter of peculiar figures and bulks, and in different degrees and modifications of their motions, causes the ideas of the blue colour and sweet scent of that flower, to be produced in our minds; it being no more impossible to conceive that God should annex such ideas to such motions, with which they have no similitude, than that he should annex the idea of pain to the motion of a piece of steel dividing our flesh, with which that idea hath no resemblance.

14. What I have said concerning colours and smells may be understood also of tastes and sounds, and other the like sensible qualities; which, whatever reality we by mistake attribute to them, are in truth nothing in the objects themselves, but powers to produce various sensations in us, and depend on those primary qualities, viz. bulk, figure, texture, and motion of parts; as I have said.

15. From whence I think it easy to draw this observation, that the ideas of primary qualities of bodies are resemblances of them, and their patterns do really exist in the bodies themselves; but the ideas, produced in us by these secondary qualities, have no resemblance of them at all. There is nothing like our ideas existing in the bodies themselves. They are in the bodies, we denominate from them, only a power to produce those sensations in us: And what is sweet, blue, or warm in idea, is but the certain bulk, figure, and motion of the insensible parts in the bodies themselves, which we call so.

16. Flame is denominated hot and light; snow, white and cold; and manna, white and sweet, from the ideas they produce in us: Which qualities are commonly thought to be the same in those bodies that those ideas are in us, the one the perfect resemblance of the other, as they are in a mirror; and it would by most men be judged very extravagant, if one should say otherwise. And yet he that will consider that the same fire, that at one distance produces in us the sensation of warmth, does at a nearer approach produce in us the far different sensation of pain, ought to bethink himself what reason he has to say, that his idea of warmth, which was produced in him by the fire, is actually in the fire; and his idea of pain, which the same fire produced in him the same way, is not in the fire. Why are whiteness and coldness in snow, and pain not, when it produces the one and the other idea in us; and can do neither, but by the bulk, figure, number, and motion of its solid parts?

17. The particular bulk, number, figure, and motion of the parts of fire or snow are really in them, whether any one's senses perceive them or no: And therefore they may be called real qualities, because they really exist in those bodies: But light, heat, whiteness or coldness, are no more really in them, than sickness or pain is in manna. Take away the sensation of them; let not the eyes see light, or colours, nor the ears hear sounds; let the palate not taste, nor the nose smell; and all colours, tastes, odours, and sounds, as they are such particular ideas, vanish and cease, and are reduced to their causes, i.e. bulk, figure, and motion of parts.

18. A piece of manna of a sensible bulk is able to produce in us the idea of a round or square figure, and, by being removed from one place to another, the idea of motion. This idea of motion represents it as it really is in the manna moving: A circle or square are the same, whether in idea or existence, in the mind, or in the manna; and this both motion and figure are really in the manna, whether we take notice of them or no: This every body is ready to agree to. Besides, manna, by the bulk, figure, texture, and motion of its parts, has a

power to produce the sensations of sickness, and sometimes of acute pains or gripings in us. That these ideas of sickness and pain are not in the manna, but effects of its operations on us, and are nowhere when we feel them not; this also every one readily agrees to. And yet men are hardly to be brought to think, that sweetness and whiteness are not really in manna; which are but the effects of the operations of manna by the motion, size, and figure of its particles on the eyes and palate; as the pain and sickness caused by manna are confessedly nothing but the effects of its operations on the stomach and guts, by the size, motion, and figure of its insensible parts (for by nothing else can a body operate, as has been proved): As if it could not operate on the eyes and palate, and thereby produce in the mind particular distinct ideas, which in itself it has not, as well as we allow it can operate on the guts and stomach, and thereby produce distinct ideas, which in itself it has not. These ideas, being all effects of the operations of manna, on several parts of our bodies, by the size, figure, number, and motion of its parts: Why those produced by the eyes and palate should rather be thought to be really in the manna, than those produced by the stomach and guts; or why the pain and sickness, ideas that are the effect of manna, should be thought to be no-where when they are not felt; and yet the sweetness and whiteness, effects of the same manna on other parts of the body, by ways equally as unknown, should be thought to exist in the manna, when they are not seen or tasted, would need some reason to explain.

19. Let us consider the red and white colours in porphyry: Hinder light from striking on it, and its colours vanish, it no longer produces any such ideas in us; upon the return of light, it produces these appearances on us again. Can any one think any real alterations are made in the porphyry, by the presence or absence of light; and that those ideas of whiteness and redness are really in porphyry in the light, when it is plain it has no colour in the dark? it has, indeed, such a configuration of particles, both night and day, as are apt, by the rays of light rebounding from some parts of that hard stone, to produce in us the idea of redness, and from others the idea of whiteness; but whiteness or redness are not in it at any time, but such a texture, that hath the power to produce such a sensation in us.

20. Pound an almond, and the clear white colour will be altered into a dirty one, and the sweet taste into an oily one. What real alteration can the beating of the pestle make in any body, but an alteration of the texture of it?

21. Ideas being thus distinguished and understood, we may be able to give an account how the same water, at the same time, may produce the idea of cold by one hand and of heat by the other; whereas it is impossible that the same water, if those ideas were really in it, should at the same time be both hot and cold: For if we imagine warmth, as it is in our hands, to be nothing but a certain sort and degree of motion in the minute particles of our nerves, or animal spirits, we may understand how it is possible that the same water may, at the same time, produce the sensations of heat in one hand, and cold in the other; which yet figure never does, that never producing the idea of a square by one hand, which has produced the idea of a globe by another. But if the sensation of heat and cold be nothing but the increase or diminution of the motion of the minute parts of our bodies, caused by the corpuscles of any other body, it is easy to be understood, that if that motion be greater in one hand than in the other; if a body be applied to the two hands, which has in its minute particles a greater motion, than in those of one of the hands, and a less than in those of the other, it will increase the motion of the one hand, and lessen it in the other, and so cause the different sensations of heat and cold that depend thereon.

22. I have in what just goes before been engaged in physical enquiries a little farther than perhaps I intended. But it being necessary to make the nature of sensation a little understood, and to make the difference between the qualities in bodies, and the ideas produced by them in the mind, to be distinctly conceived, without which it were impossible to discourse intelligibly of them; I hope I shall be pardoned this little excursion into natural philosophy, it being necessary in our present enquiry to distinguish the primary and real qualities of bodies, which are always in them (viz. solidity, extension, figure, number, and motion, or rest, and are sometimes perceived by us, viz. when the bodies they are in are big enough singly to be discerned) from those secondary and imputed qualities, which are but the powers of several combinations of those primary ones, when they operate, without being distinctly discerned; whereby we may also come to know what ideas are, and what are not, resemblances of

some thing really existing in the bodies we denominate from them.

23. The qualities then that are in bodies rightly considered, are of three sorts.

First, the bulk, figure, number, situation, and motion, or rest of their solid parts; those are in them, whether we perceive them or no; and when they are of that size, that we can discover them, we have by these an idea of the thing as it is in itself, as is plain in artificial things. These I call primary qualities.

Secondly, The power that is in any body, by reason of its insensible primary qualities, to operate after a peculiar manner on any of our senses, and thereby produce in us the different ideas of several colours, sounds, smells, tastes, &c. These are usually called sensible qualities.

Thirdly, the power that is in any body, by reason of the particular constitution of its primary qualities, to make such a change in the bulk, figure, texture, and motion of another body, as to make it operate on our senses differently from what it did before. Thus the sun has a power to make wax white, and fire to make lead fluid. These are usually called powers.

The first of these, as has been said, I think, may be properly called real, original, or primary qualities, because they are in the things themselves, whether they are perceived or no: And upon their different modifications it is, that the secondary qualities depend.

The other two are only powers to act differently upon other things, which powers result from the different modifications of those primary qualities.

24. But though the two latter sorts of qualities are powers barely, and nothing but powers, relating to several other bodies, and resulting from the different modifications of the original qualities; yet they are generally otherwise thought of. For the second sort, viz. the powers to produce several ideas in us by our senses, are looked upon as real qualities, in the things thus affecting us: But the third sort are called and esteemed barely powers, e.g. the idea of heat, or light, which we receive by our eyes or touch from the sun, are commonly thought real qualities, existing in the sun, and some thing more than mere powers in it. But when we consider the sun, in reference to wax, which it melts or blanches, we look on the whiteness and softness produced in the

wax, not as qualities in the sun, but effects produced by powers in it: Whereas, if rightly considered, these qualities of light and warmth, which are perceptions in me when I am warmed, or enlightened by the sun, are no otherwise in the sun, than the changes made in the wax, when it is blanched or melted, are in the sun. They are all of them equally powers in the sun, depending on its primary qualities; whereby it is able, in the one case, so to alter the bulk, figure, texture, or motion of some of the insensible parts of my eyes or hands, as thereby to produce in me the idea of light or heat; and in the other it is able so to alter the bulk, figure, texture, or motion of the insensible parts of the wax, as to make them fit to produce in me the distinct ideas of white and fluid.

25. The reason why the one are ordinarily taken for real qualities, and the other only for bare powers, seems to be, because the ideas we have of distinct colours, sounds, &c. containing nothing at all in them of bulk, figure, or motion, we are not apt to think them the effects of these primary qualities, which appear not, to our senses, to operate in their production; and with which they have not any apparent congruity, or conceivable connexion. Hence it is that we are so forward to imagine, that those ideas are the resemblances of some thing really existing in the objects themselves: Since sensation discovers nothing of bulk, figure, or motion of parts in their production; nor can reason shew how bodies, by their bulk, figure, and motion, should produce in the mind the ideas of blue or yellow, &c. But in the other case, in the operations of bodies changing the qualities one of another, we plainly discover, that the quality produced hath commonly no resemblance with any thing in the thing producing it; wherefore we look on it as a bare effect of power. For though receiving the idea of heat, or light, from the sun, we are apt to think it is a perception and resemblance of such a quality in the sun; yet when we see wax, or a fair face, receive change of colour from the sun, we cannot imagine that to be the reception or resemblance of any thing in the sun, because we find not those different colours in the sun itself. For our senses being able to observe a likeness or unlikeness of sensible qualities in two different external objects, we forwardly enough conclude the production of any sensible quality, in any subject to be an effect of bare power, and not the communication of any quality, which

was really in the efficient, when we find no such sensible quality in the thing that produced it. But our senses not being able to discover any unlikeness between the idea produced in us, and the quality of the object producing it; we are apt to imagine, that our ideas are resemblances of something, in the objects, and not the effects of certain powers placed in the modification of their primary qualities, with which primary qualities the ideas produced in us have no resemblance.

26. To conclude, beside those before mentioned primary qualities in bodies, viz. bulk, figure, extension, number, and motion of their solid parts; all the rest whereby we take notice of bodies, and distinguish them one from another, are nothing else but several powers in them depending on those primary qualities; whereby they are fitted, either by immediately operating on our bodies, to produce several different ideas in us; or else by operating on other bodies, so to change their primary qualities, as to render them capable of producing ideas in us, different from what before they did. The former of these, I think, may be called secondary qualities, immediately perceivable: The latter, secondary qualities, mediately perceivable.

Chapter IX. Of Perception.

1. Perception, as it is the first faculty of the mind exercised about our ideas; so it is the first and simplest idea we have from reflection, and is by some called thinking in general. Though thinking, in the propriety of the English tongue, signifies that sort of operation in the mind about its ideas, wherein the mind is active; where it, with some degree of voluntary attention, considers any thing. For in bare naked perception, the mind is, for the most part, only passive: And what it perceives, it cannot avoid perceiving.

2. What perception is, every one will know better by reflecting on what he does himself, when he sees, hears, feels, &c. or thinks, than by any discourse of mine. Whoever reflects on what passes in his own mind, cannot miss it: And if he does not reflect, all the words in the world cannot make him have any notion of it.

3. This is certain, that whatever alterations are made in the body, if they reach not the mind; whatever impressions are made on the outward parts, if

they are not taken notice of within; there is no perception. Fire may burn our bodies, with no other effect, than it does a billet, unless the motion be continued to the brain, and there the sense of heat, or idea of pain, be produced in the mind, wherein consists actual perception.

4. How often may a man observe in himself, that whilst his mind is intently employed in the contemplation of some objects, and curiously surveying some ideas that are there, it takes no notice of impressions of sounding bodies made upon the organ of hearing, with the same alteration that uses to be for the producing the idea of sound? A sufficient impulse there may be on the organ; but it not reaching the observation of the mind, there follows no perception: And though the motion that uses to produce the idea of sound be made in the ear, yet no sound is heard. Want of sensation, in this case, is not through any defect in the organ, or that the man's ears are less affected than at other times when he does hear; but that which uses to produce the idea, though conveyed in by the usual organ, not being taken notice of in the understanding, and so imprinting no idea in the mind, there follows no sensation. So that wherever there is sense, or perception, there some idea is actually produced, and present in the understanding. . . .

8. We are further to consider concerning perception, that the ideas we receive by sensation are often in grown people altered by the judgment, without our taking notice of it. When we set before our eyes a round globe, of any uniform colour, v.g. gold, alabaster, or jet; it is certain that the idea thereby imprinted in our mind, is of a flat circle variously shadowed, with several degrees of light and brightness coming to our eyes. But we having by use been accustomed to perceive what kind of appearance convex bodies are wont to make in us, what alterations are made in the reflections of light by the difference of the sensible figures of bodies; the judgment presently, by an habitual custom, alters the appearances into their causes; so that from that which is truly variety of shadow or colour, collecting the figure, it makes it pass for a mark of figure, and frames to itself the perception of a convex figure and an uniform colour; when the idea we receive from thence is only a plane variously coloured, as is evident in painting. To which purpose I shall here insert a problem of that very ingenious and studious promoter of real knowledge, the

learned and worthy Mr. Molineaux, which he was pleased to send me in a letter some months since; and it is this: Suppose a man born blind, and now adult, and taught by his touch to distinguish between a cube and a sphere of the same metal, and nighly of the same bigness, so as to tell, when he felt one and the other, which is the cube, which the sphere. Suppose then the cube and sphere placed on a table, and the blind man be made to see: Quaere, "whether by his sight, before he touched them, he could now distinguish and tell, which is the globe, which the cube?" to which the acute and judicious proposer answers: Not. For though he has obtained the experience of how a globe, how a cube affects his touch; yet he has not yet obtained the experience, that what affects his touch so or so, must affect his sight so or so: Or that a protuberant angle in the cube, that pressed his hand unequally, shall appear to his eye as it does in the cube. I agree with this thinking gentleman, whom I am proud to call my friend, in his answer to this problem; and am of opinion, that the blind man at first sight, would not be able with certainty to say which was the globe, which the cube, whilst he only saw them: Though he could unerringly name them by his touch, and certainly distinguish them by the difference of their figures felt. This I have set down, and leave with my reader, as an occasion for him to consider how much he may be beholden to experience, improvement, and acquired notions, where he thinks he had not the least use of, or help from them: And the rather, because this observing gentleman further adds, that having, upon the occasion of my book, proposed this to divers very ingenious men, he hardly ever met with one, that at first gave the answer to it which he thinks true, till by hearing his reasons they were convinced.

9. But this is not, I think, usual in any of our ideas, but those received by sight: Because sight, the most comprehensive of all our senses, conveying to our minds the ideas of light and colours, which are peculiar only to that sense; and also the far different ideas of space, figure, and motion, the several varieties whereof change the appearances of its proper object, viz. light and colours; we bring ourselves by use to judge of the one by the other. This, in many cases, by a settled habit, in things whereof we have frequent experience, is performed so constantly and so quick, that we take that for the perception of our sensation, which is an idea formed by our judgment; so that one, viz. that of sensation, serves only to excite the other, and is scarce taken notice of itself: As a man who reads or hears with attention and understanding, takes little notice of the characters, or sounds, but of the ideas that are excited in him by them.

10. Nor need we wonder that this is done with so little notice, if we consider how quick the actions of the mind are performed: For as itself is thought to take up no space, to have no extension; so its actions seem to require no time, but many of them seem to be crowded into an instant. I speak this in comparison to the actions of the body. Any one may easily observe this in his own thoughts, who will take the pains to reflect on them. How, as it were in an instant, do our minds with one glance see all the parts of a demonstration, which may very well be called a long one, if we consider the time it will require to put it into words, and step by step shew it another? Secondly, we shall not be so much surprized, that this is done in us with so little notice, if we consider how the facility which we get of doing things, by a custom of doing, makes them often pass in us without our notice. Habits, especially such as are begun very early, come at last to produce actions in us, which often escape our observation. How frequently do we, in a day, cover our eyes with our eye-lids, without perceiving that we are at all in the dark? Men that by custom have got the use of a by-word, do almost in every sentence pronounce sounds which, though taken notice of by others, they themselves neither hear nor observe. And therefore it is not so strange, that our mind should often change the idea of its sensation into that of its judgment, and make one serve only to excite the other without our taking notice of it. . . .

15. Perception then being the first step and degree towards knowledge, and the inlet of all the materials of it; the fewer senses any man, as well as any other creature, hath, and the fewer and duller the impressions are that are made by them, and the duller the faculties are that are employed about them; the more remote are they from that knowledge, which is to be found in some men. But this being in great variety of degrees (as may be perceived amongst men) cannot certainly be discovered in the several species of animals, much less in their particular individuals. It suffices me only to have remarked here, that perception is the first op-

eration of all our intellectual faculties, and the inlet of all knowledge in our minds. And I am apt too to imagine, that it is perception in the lowest degree of it, which puts the boundaries between animals and the inferior ranks of creatures. But this I mention only as my conjecture by the by; it being indifferent to the matter in hand, which way the learned shall determine of it.

Chapter XXIII. Of Our Complex Ideas of Substances.

1. The mind being, as I have declared, furnished with a great number of the simple ideas, conveyed in by the senses, as they are found in exterior things, or by reflection on its own operations, takes notice also, that a certain number of these simple ideas go constantly together; which being presumed to belong to one thing, and words being suited to common apprehensions, and made use of for quick dispatch, are called, so united in one subject, by one name: Which, by inadvertency, we are apt afterward to talk of, and consider as one simple idea, which indeed is a complication of many ideas together; because, as I have said, not imagining how these simple ideas can subsist by themselves, we accustom ourselves to suppose some substratum wherein they do subsist, and from which they do result, which therefore we call substance.

    2. So that if any one will examine himself concerning his notion of pure substance in general, he will find he has no other idea of it at all, but only a supposition of he knows not what support of such qualities, which are capable of producing simple ideas in us; which qualities are commonly called accidents. If any one should be asked, what is the subject wherein colour or weight inheres, he would have nothing to say, but the solid extended parts: And if he were demanded, what is it that solidity and extension adhere in, he would not be in a much better case than the Indian before-mentioned, who, saying that the world was supported by a great elephant, was asked what the elephant rested on; to which his answer was, a great tortoise. But being again pressed to know what gave support to the broad-backed tortoise, replied, something he knew not what. And thus here, as in all other cases where we use words without having clear and distinct ideas, we talk like children; who being questioned

what such a thing is, which they know not, readily give this satisfactory answer, that it is some thing: Which in truth signifies no more, when so used either by children or men, but that they know not what; and that the thing they pretend to know and talk of, is what they have no distinct idea of at all, and so are perfectly ignorant of it, and in the dark. The idea then we have, to which we give the general name substance, being nothing but the supposed, but unknown support of those qualities we find existing, which we imagine cannot subsist, "sine re substante," without some thing to support them, we call that support substantia; which, according to the true import of the word, is in plain English, standing under or upholding.

    3. An obscure and relative idea of substance in general being thus made we come to have the ideas of particular sorts of substances, by collecting such combinations of simple ideas, as are by experience and observation of men's senses taken notice of to exist together, and are therefore supposed to flow from the particular internal constitution, or unknown essence of that substance. Thus we come to have the ideas of a man, horse, gold, water &c. of which substances, whether any one has any other clear idea, farther than of certain simple ideas coexistent together, I appeal to every one's own experience. It is the ordinary qualities observable in iron, or a diamond, put together, that make the true complex idea of those substances, which a smith or a jeweller commonly knows better than a philosopher; who, whatever substantial forms he may talk of, has no other idea of those substances, than what is framed by a collection of those simple ideas which are to be found in them; only we must take notice, that our complex ideas of substances, besides all those simple ideas they are made up of, have always the confused idea of some thing to which they belong, and in which they subsist. And therefore, when we speak of any sort of substance, we say it is a thing having such or such qualities: A body is a thing that is extended, figured, and capable of motion; spirit, a thing capable of thinking; and so hardness, friability, and power to draw iron, we say, are qualities to be found in a loadstone. These, and the like fashions of speaking, intimate, that the substance is supposed always some thing besides the extension, figure, solidity, motion, thinking, or other observable ideas, though we know not what it is. . . .

15. Besides the complex ideas we have of material sensible substances, of which I have last spoken, by the simple ideas we have taken from those operations of our own minds, which we experiment daily in ourselves, as thinking, understanding, willing, knowing, and power of beginning motion, &c. co-existing in some substance: We are able to frame the complex idea of an immaterial spirit. And thus by putting together the ideas of thinking, perceiving, liberty, and power of moving themselves, and other things, we have as clear a perception and notion of immaterial substances, as we have of material. For putting together the ideas of thinking and willing, or the power of moving or quieting corporeal motion, joined to substance of which we have no distinct idea, we have the idea of an immaterial spirit; and by putting together the ideas of coherent solid parts, and a power of being moved, joined with substance, of which likewise we have no positive idea, we have the idea of matter. The one is as clear and distinct an idea as the other: The idea of thinking, and moving a body, being as clear and distinct ideas, as the ideas of extension, solidity, and being moved. For our idea of substance is equally obscure, or none at all in both: It is but a supposed I know not what, to support those ideas we call accidents. It is for want of reflection that we are apt to think, that our senses shew us nothing but material things. Every act of sensation, when duly considered, gives us an equal view of both parts of nature, the corporeal and spiritual. For whilst I know, by seeing or hearing, &c. that there is some corporeal being without me, the object of that sensation; I do more certainly know, that there is some spiritual being within me, that sees and hears. This, I must be convinced, cannot be the action of bare insensible matter; nor ever could be, without an immaterial thinking being.

Book IV

Chapter I. Of Knowledge in General.

1. Since the mind, in all its thoughts and reasonings, hath no other immediate object but its own ideas, which it alone does or can contemplate; it is evident, that our knowledge is only conversant about them.

2. Knowledge then seems to me to be nothing but the perception of the connexion and agreement, or disagreement and repugnancy, of any of our ideas. In this alone it consists. Where this perception is, there is knowledge; and where it is not, there, though we may fancy, guess, or believe, yet we always come short of knowledge. For when we know that white is not black, what do we else but perceive that these two ideas do not agree? When we possess ourselves with the utmost security of the demonstration, that the three angles of a triangle are equal to two right ones, what do we more but perceive, that equality to two right ones does necessarily agree to, and is inseparable from the three angles of a triangle?

Chapter XI. Of Our Knowledge of the Existence of Other Things.

1. The knowledge of our own being we have by intuition. The existence of a God reason clearly makes known to us, as has been shown.

The knowledge of the existence of any other thing, we can have only by sensation: For there being no necessary connexion of real existence with any idea a man hath in his memory, nor of any other existence but that of God, with the existence of any particular man; no particular man can know the existence of any other being, but only when by actual operating upon him, it makes itself perceived by him. For the having the idea of any thing in our mind, no more proves the existence of that thing, than the picture of a man evidences his being in the world, or the visions of a dream make thereby a true history.

2. It is therefore the actual receiving of ideas from without, that gives us notice of the existence of other things, and makes us know that something doth exist at that time without us, which causes that idea in us, though perhaps we neither know nor consider how it does it: For it takes not from the certainty of our senses, and the ideas we receive by them, that we know not the manner wherein they are produced: V.g. whilst I write this, I have, by the paper affecting my eyes, that idea produced in my mind, which whatever object causes, I call white; by which I know that that quality or accident (i.e.

whose appearance before my eyes always causes that idea) doth really exist, and hath a being without me. And of this, the greatest assurance I can possibly have, and to which my faculties can attain, is the testimony of my eyes, which are the proper and sole judges of this thing, whose testimony I have reason to rely on as so certain, that I can no more doubt, whilst I write this, that I see white and black, and that something really exists, that causes that sensation in me, than that I write or move my hand; which is a certainty as great as human nature is capable of, concerning the existence of any thing, but a man's self alone, and of God.

3. The notice we have by our senses, of the existing of things without us, though it be not altogether so certain as our intuitive knowledge, or the deductions of our reason employed about the clear abstract ideas of our own minds; yet it is an assurance that deserves the name of knowledge. If we persuade ouselves, that our faculties act and inform us right, concerning the existence of those objects that affect them, it cannot pass for an ill-grounded confidence: For I think nobody can, in earnest, be so sceptical, as to be uncertain of the existence of those things which he sees and feels. At least, he that can doubt so far (whatever he may have with his own thoughts) will never have any controversy with me; since he can never be sure I say any thing contrary to his own opinion. As to myself, I think God has given me assurance enough of the existence of things without me; since by their different application I can produce in myself both pleasure and pain, which is one great concernment of my present state. This is certain; the confidence that our faculties do not herein deceive us is the greatest assurance we are capable of, concerning the existence of material beings. For we cannot act any thing but by our faculties; nor talk of knowledge itself, but by the help of those faculties, which are fitted to apprehend even what knowledge is. But besides the assurance we have from our senses themselves, that they do not err in the information they give us, of the existence of things without us, when they are affected by them, we are farther confirmed in this assurance by other concurrent reasons.

4. First, it is plain those perceptions are produced in us by exterior causes affecting our senses; because those that want the organs of any sense, never can have the ideas belonging to that sense produced in their minds. This is too evident to be doubted: And therefore we cannot but be assured, that they come in by the organs of that sense, and no other way. The organs themselves, it is plain, do not produce them, for then the eyes of a man in the dark would produce colours, and his nose smell roses in the winter: But we see nobody gets the relish of a pineapple, till he goes to the Indies, where it is, and tastes it.

5. Secondly, because sometimes I find, that I cannot avoid the having those ideas produced in my mind. For though when my eyes are shut, or windows fast, I can at pleasure recall to my mind the ideas of light, or the sun, which former sensations had lodged in my memory; so I can at pleasure lay by that idea, and take into my view that of the smell of a rose, or taste of sugar. But, if I turn my eyes at noon towards the sun, I cannot avoid the ideas, which the light, or sun, then produces in me. So that there is a manifest difference between the ideas laid up in my memory, (over which, if they were there only, I should have constantly the same power to dispose of them, and lay them by at pleasure) and those which force themselves upon me, and I cannot avoid having. And therefore it must needs be some exterior cause, and the brisk acting of some objects without me, whose efficacy I cannot resist, that produces those ideas in my mind, whether I will or no. Besides, there is nobody who doth not perceive the difference in himself between contemplating the sun, as he hath the idea of it in his memory, and actually looking upon it: Of which two, his perception is so distinct, that few of his ideas are more distinguishable one from another. And therefore he hath certain knowledge that they are not both memory, or the actions of his mind, and fancies only within him; but that actual seeing hath a cause without.

6. Thirdly, add to this, that many of those ideas are produced in us with pain, which afterwards we remember without the least offence. Thus the pain of heat or cold, when the idea of it is revived in our minds, gives us no disturbance; which, when felt, was very troublesome, and is again, when actually repeated; which is occasioned by the disorder the external object causes in our bodies when applied to it. And we remember the pains of hunger, thirst, or the head-ache, without

any pain at all; which would either never disturb us, or else constantly do it, as often as we thought of it, were there nothing more but ideas floating in our minds, and appearances entertaining our fancies, without the real existence of things affecting us from abroad. The same may be said of pleasure, accompanying several actual sensations: And though mathematical demonstration depends not upon sense, yet the examining them by diagrams gives great credit to the evidence of our sight, and seems to give it a certainty approaching to that of demonstration itself. For it would be very strange, that a man should allow it for an undeniable truth, that two angles of a figure, which he measures by lines and angles of a diagram, should be bigger one than the other; and yet doubt of the existence of those lines and angles, which by looking on he makes use of to measure that by.

7. Fourthly, our senses in many cases bear witness to the truth of each other's report, concerning the existence of sensible things without us. He that sees a fire, may, if he doubt whether it be any thing more than a bare fancy, feel it too; and be convinced by putting his hand in it. Which certainly could never be put into such exquisite pain, by a bare idea or phantom, unless that the pain be a fancy too: Which yet he cannot, when the burn is well, by raising the idea of it, bring upon himself again.

Thus I see, whilst I write this, I can change the appearance of the paper: And by designing the letters tell beforehand what new idea it shall exhibit the very next moment, by barely drawing my pen over it: Which will neither appear (let me fancy as much as I will) if my hands stand still; or though I move my pen, if my eyes be shut: Nor when those characters are once made on the paper, can I choose afterwards but see them as they are; that is, have the ideas of such letters as I have made. Whence it is manifest, that they are not barely the sport and play of my own imagination, when I find that the characters, that were made at the pleasure of my own thoughts, do not obey them; nor yet cease to be, whenever I shall fancy it; but continue to affect my senses constantly and regularly, according to the figures I made them. To which if we will add, that the sight of those shall, from another man, draw such sounds, as I beforehand design they shall stand for; there will be little reason left to doubt, that those words I write do really exist without me,

when they cause a long series of regular sounds to affect my ears, which could not be the effect of my imagination, nor could my memory retain them in that order.

8. But yet, if after all this any one will be so sceptical, as to distrust his senses, and to affirm that all we see and hear, feel and taste, think and do, during our whole being, is but the series and deluding appearances of a long dream, whereof there is no reality; and therefore will question the existence of all things, or our knowledge of any thing; I must desire him to consider, that if all be a dream, then he doth but dream, that he makes the question; and so it is not much matter, that a waking man should answer him. But yet, if he pleases, he may dream that I make him this answer, that the certainty of things existing in rerum natura, when we have the tesimony of our senses for it, is not only as great as our frame can attain to, but as our condition needs. For our faculties being suited not to the full extent of being, nor to a perfect, clear, comprehensive knowledge of things free from all doubt and scruple; but to the preservation of us, in whom they are; and accommodated to the use of life; they serve to our purpose well enough, if they will but give us certain notice of those things, which are convenient or inconvenient to us. For he that sees a candle burning, and hath experimented the force of its flame, by putting his finger in it, will little doubt that this is something existing without him, which does him harm, and puts him to great pain: Which is assurance enough, when no man requires greater certainty to govern his actions by, than what is as certain as his actions themselves. And if our dreamer pleases to try, whether the glowing heat of a glass furnace be barely a wandering imagination in a drowsy man's fancy; by putting his hand into it, he may perhaps be wakened into a certainty greater than he could wish, that it is something more than bare imagination. So that this evidence is as great as we can desire, being as certain to us as our pleasure or pain, i.e. happiness or misery; beyond which we have no concernment, either of knowing or being. Such an assurance of the existence of things without us is sufficient to direct us in the attaining the good, and avoiding the evil, which is caused by them; which is the important concernment we have of being made acquainted with them.

9. In fine then, when our senses do actually

convey into our understandings any idea, we cannot but be satisfied that there doth something at that time really exist without us, which doth affect our senses, and by them give notice of itself to our apprehensive faculties, and actually produce that idea which we then perceive: And we cannot so far distrust their testimony, as to doubt, that such collections of simple ideas, as we have observed by our senses to be united together, do really exist together. But this knowledge extends as far as the present testimony of our senses, employed about particular objects that do then affect them, and no farther. For if I saw such a collection of simple ideas, as is wont to be called man, existing together one minute since, and am now alone, I cannot be certain that the same man exists now, since there is no necessary connexion of his existence a minute since, with his existence now: By a thousand ways he may cease to be, since I had the testimony of my senses for his existence. And if I cannot be certain, that the man I saw last to-day is now in being, I can less be certain that he is so, who hath been longer removed from my senses, and I have not seen since yesterday, or since the last year; and much less can I be certain of the existence of men that I never saw. And therefore though it be highly probable, that millions of men do now exist, yet, whilst I am alone writing this, I have not that certainty of it which we strictly call knowledge; though the great likelihood of it puts me past doubt, and it be reasonable for me to do several things upon the confidence that there are men (and men also of my acquaintance, with whom I have to do) now in the world: But this is but probability, not knowledge.

10. Whereby yet we may observe, how foolish and vain a thing it is, for a man of a narrow knowledge, who having reason given him to judge of the different evidence and probability of things, and to be swayed accordingly; how vain, I say, it is to expect demonstration and certainty in things not capable of it; and refuse assent to very rational propositions, and act contrary to very plain and clear truths, because they cannot be made out so evident, as to surmount every the least (I will not say reason, but) pretence of doubting. He that in the ordinary affairs of life would admit of nothing but direct plain demonstration, would be sure of nothing in this world, but of perishing quickly. The wholesomeness of his meat or drink would not give him reason to venture on it: And I would fain know, what it is he could do upon such grounds, as are capable of no doubt, no objection.

III.2 An *Idealist Theory of Knowledge*

GEORGE BERKELEY

George Berkeley (1685–1753), an Irish philosopher and Anglican bishop, was educated at Trinity College, Dublin, where he subsequently taught. A deeply committed Christian, he sought to reconcile science with his faith, proving that although matter does not exist, the laws of physics, being God's laws, govern a universe made up of ideas. Only two types of things exist: minds and ideas. To exist is to be perceived (*"Esse est percipi"*), and God is that being who, perceiving all things, causes them to exist as ideas in his mind. This position is called philosophical idealism, though "idea-ism" would be a more accurate title.

Note that Berkeley's idealism differs from traditional idealism (such as Plato's) in that it is not rationalistic. It does not adhere to independently existing ideas, but rather it assumes an empirical foundation. It agrees with Locke that all ideas originate in sense experience, and proceeds to show that all we ever experience are ideas, our sensations, or sense perceptions. The only reality there is to be known is perceivers and perceptions.

Of The Principles of Human Knowledge.

Part I.

I. It is evident to any one who takes a survey of the objects of human knowledge, that they are either ideas actually imprinted on the senses, or else such as are perceived by attending to the passions and operations of the mind, or lastly, ideas formed by help of memory and imagination, either compounding, dividing, or barely representing those originally perceived in the aforesaid ways. By sight I have the ideas of light and colours with their several degrees and variations. By touch I perceive, for example, hard and soft, heat and cold, motion and resistance, and of all these more and less either as to quantity or degree. Smelling furnishes me with odours; the palate with tastes; and hearing conveys sounds to the mind in all their variety of tone and composition. And as several of these are observed to accompany each other, they come to be marked by one name, and so to be reputed as one thing. Thus, for example, a certain colour, taste, smell, figure, and consistence having been observed to go together, are accounted one distinct thing, signified by the name apple. Other collections of ideas constitute a stone, a tree, a book, and the like sensible things; which, as they are pleasing or disagreeable, excite the passions of love, hatred, joy, grief, and so forth.

II. But besides all that endless variety of ideas or objects of knowledge, there is likewise something which knows or perceives them, and exercises divers operations, as willing, imagining, remembering about them. This perceiving, active being is what I call mind, spirit, soul, or myself. By which words I do not denote any one of my ideas, but a thing entirely distinct from them, wherein they exist, or, which is the same thing, whereby they are perceived; for the existence of an idea consists in being perceived.

III. That neither our thoughts, nor passions,

Reprinted from *A Treatise Concerning the Principles of Human Knowledge* (1710).

nor ideas formed by the imagination, exist without the mind, is what every body will allow. And (to me) it seems no less evident that the various sensations or ideas imprinted on the sense, however blended or combined together (that is, whatever objects they compose), cannot exist otherwise than in a mind perceiving them. I think an intuitive knowledge may be obtained of this, by any one that shall attend to what is meant by the term exist, when applied to sensible things. The table I write on, I say, exists, that is, I see and feel it; and if I were out of my study I should say it existed, meaning thereby that if I was in my study I might perceive it, or that some other spirit actually does perceive it. There was an odour, that is, it was smelled; there was a sound, that is to say, it was heard; a colour or figure, and it was perceived by sight or touch. This is all that I can understand by these and the like expressions. For as to what is said of the absolute existence of unthinking things without any relation to their being perceived, that seems perfectly unintelligible. Their esse is percipi, nor is it possible they should have any existence, out of the minds or thinking things which perceive them.

IV. It is indeed an opinion strangely prevailing amongst men, that houses, mountains, rivers, and in a word sensible objects have an existence natural or real, distinct from their being perceived by the understanding. But with how great an assurance and acquiescence soever this principle may be entertained in the world; yet whoever shall find in his heart to call it in question, may, if I mistake not, perceive it to involve a manifest contradiction. For what are the forementioned objects but the things we perceive by sense, and what do we perceive besides our own ideas or sensations; and is it not plainly repugnant that any one of these or any combination of them should exist unperceived?

V. If we thoroughly examine this tenet, it will, perhaps, be found at bottom to depend on the doctrine of abstract ideas. For can there be a nicer strain of abstraction than to distinguish the existence of sensible objects from their being perceived, so as to conceive them existing unperceived? Light and colours, heat and cold, extension and figures, in a word the things we see and feel, what are they but so many sensations, notions, ideas, or impressions on the sense; and is it possible to separate, even in thought, any of these from perception? For my part I might as easily divide a thing from itself. I may

indeed divide in my thoughts or conceive apart from each other those things which, perhaps, I never perceived by sense so divided. Thus I imagine the trunk of a human body without the limbs, or conceive the smell of a rose without thinking on the rose itself. So far I will not deny I can abstract, if that may properly be called abstraction, which extends only to the conceiving separately such objects as it is possible may really exist or be actually perceived asunder. But my conceiving or imagining power does not extend beyond the possibility of real existence or perception. Hence as it is impossible for me to see or feel any thing without an actual sensation of that thing, so is it impossible for me to conceive in my thoughts any sensible thing or object distinct from the sensation or perception of it.

VI. Some truths there are so near and obvious to the mind, that a man need only open his eyes to see them. Such I take this important one to be, to wit, that all the choir of heaven and furniture of the earth, in a word all those bodies which compose the mighty frame of the world, have not any subsistence without a mind, that their being (esse) is to be perceived or known; that consequently so long as they are not actually perceived by me, or do not exist in my mind or that of any other created spirit, they must either have no existence at all, or else subsist in the mind of some eternal spirit: it being perfectly unintelligible and involving all the absurdity of abstraction, to attribute to any single part of them an existence independent of a spirit. To be convinced of which, the reader need only reflect and try to separate in his own thoughts the being of a sensible thing from its being perceived.

VII. From what has been said, it follows, there is not any other substance than spirit, or that which perceives. But for the fuller proof of this point, let it be considered, the sensible qualities are colour, figure, motion, smell, taste, and such like, that is, the ideas perceived by sense. Now for an idea to exist in an unperceiving thing, is a manifest contradiction; for to have an idea is all one as to perceive: that therefore wherein colour, figure, and the like qualities exist, must perceive them; hence it is clear there can be no unthinking substance or substratum of those ideas.

VIII. But say you, though the ideas themselves do not exist without the mind, yet there may be things like them whereof they are copies or resemblances, which things exist without the mind, in an unthinking substance. I answer, an idea can be like nothing but an idea; a colour or figure can be like nothing but another colour or figure. If we look but ever so little into our thoughts, we shall find it impossible for us to conceive a likeness except only between our ideas. Again, I ask whether those supposed originals or external things, of which our ideas are the pictures or representations, be themselves perceivable or no? if they are, then they are ideas, and we have gained our point; but if you say they are not, I appeal to any one whether it be sense, to assert a colour is like something which is invisible; hard or soft, like something which is intangible; and so of the rest.

IX. Some there are who make a distinction betwixt primary and secondary qualities: by the former, they mean extension, figure, motion, rest, solidity or impenetrability, and number: by the latter they denote all other sensible qualities, as colours, sounds, tastes, and so forth. The ideas we have of these they acknowledge not to be the resemblances of any thing existing without the mind or unperceived; but they will have our ideas of the primary qualities to be patterns or images of things which exist without the mind, in an unthinking substance which they call matter. By matter therefore we are to understand an inert, senseless substance, in which extension, figure and motion, do actually subsist. But it is evident from what we have already shown, that extension, figure, and motion, are only ideas existing in the mind, and that an idea can be like nothing but another idea, and that consequently neither they nor their archetypes can exist in an unperceiving substance. Hence it is plain, that the very notion of what is called matter, or corporeal substance, involves a contradiction in it.

X. They who assert that figure, motion, and the rest of the primary or original qualities, do exist without the mind, in unthinking substances, do at the same time acknowledge that colours, sounds, heat, cold, and such like secondary qualities, do not, which they tell us are sensations existing in the mind alone, that depend on and are occasioned by the different size, texture, and motion of the minute particles of matter. This they take for an undoubted truth, which they can demonstrate beyond all exception. Now if it be certain, that those original qualities are inseparably united with the other sensible qualities, and not, even in thought, capable of being abstracted from them, it plainly follows that

they exist only in the mind. But I desire any one to reflect and try, whether he can, by any abstraction of thought, conceive the extension and motion of a body, without all other sensible qualities. For my own part, I see evidently that it is not in my power to frame an idea of a body extended and moved, but I must withal give it some colour or other sensible quality which is acknowledged to exist only in the mind. In short, extension, figure, and motion, abstracted from all other qualities, are inconceivable. Where therefore the other sensible qualities are, there must these be also, to wit, in the mind and nowhere else.

XI. Again, great and small, swift and slow, are allowed to exist no where without the mind, being entirely relative, and changing as the frame or position of the organs of sense varies. The extension therefore which exists without the mind, is neither great nor small, the motion neither swift nor slow, that is, they are nothing at all. But, say you, they are extension in general, and motion in general: thus we see how much the tenet of extended, moveable substances existing without the mind, depends on that strange doctrine of abstract ideas. And here I cannot but remark, how nearly the vague and indeterminate description of matter or corporeal substance, which the modern philosophers are run into by their own principles, resembles that antiquated and so much ridiculed notion of materia prima, to be met with in Aristotle and his followers. Without extension solidity cannot be conceived; since therefore it has been shown that extension exists not in an unthinking substance, the same must also be true of solidity.

XII. That number is entirely the creature of the mind, even though the other qualities be allowed to exist without, will be evident to whoever considers, that the same thing bears a different denomination of number, as the mind views it with different respects. Thus, the same extension is one, or three, or thirty-six, according as the mind considers it with reference to a yard, a foot, or an inch. Number is so visibly relative, and dependent on men's understanding, that it is strange to think how any one should give it an absolute existence without the mind. We say, one book, one page, one line; all these are equally units, though some contain several of the others. And in each instance it is plain, the unit relates to some particular combination of ideas arbitrarily put together by the mind.

XIII. Unity, I know, some will have to be a simple or uncompounded idea, accompanying all other ideas into the mind. That I have any such idea, answering the word unity, I do not find; and if I had, methinks I could not miss finding it; on the contrary, it should be the most familiar to my understanding, since it is said to accompany all other ideas, and to be perceived by all the ways of sensation and reflection. To say no more, it is an abstract idea.

XIV. I shall further add, that after the same manner as modern philosophers prove certain sensible qualities to have no existence in matter, or without the mind, the same thing may be likewise proved of all other sensible qualities whatsoever. Thus, for instance, it is said that heat and cold are affections only of the mind, and not at all patterns of real beings, existing in the corporeal substances which excite them, for that the same body which appears cold to one hand, seems warm to another. Now why may we not as well argue that figure and extension are not patterns or resemblances of qualities existing in matter, because to the same eye at different stations, or eyes of a different texture at the same station, they appear various, and cannot therefore be the images of any thing settled and determinate without the mind? Again, it is proved that sweetness is not really in the said thing, because, the thing remaining unaltered, the sweetness is changed into bitter, as in case of a fever or otherwise vitiated palate. Is it not as reasonable to say, that motion is not without the mind, since if the succession of ideas in the mind become swifter, the motion, it is acknowledged, shall appear slower without any alteration in any external object.

XV. In short, let any one consider those arguments which are thought manifestly to prove that colours and tastes exist only in the mind, and he shall find they may with equal force be brought to prove the same thing of extension, figure, and motion. Though it must be confessed, this method of arguing doth not so much prove that there is no extension or colour in an outward object, as that we do not know by sense which is the true extension or colour of the object. But the arguments foregoing plainly show it to be impossible that any colour or extension at all, or other sensible quality whatsoever, should exist in an unthinking subject without the mind, or in truth, that there should be any such thing as an outward object.

XVI. But let us examine a little the received opinion. It is said extension is a mode or accident of matter, and that matter is the substratum that supports it. Now I desire that you would explain what is meant by matter's supporting extension: say you, I have no idea of matter, and therefore cannot explain it. I answer, though you have no positive, yet if you have any meaning at all, you must at least have a relative idea of matter; though you know not what it is, yet you must be supposed to know what relation it bears to accidents, and what is meant by its supporting them. It is evident support cannot here be taken in its usual or literal sense, as when we say that pillars support a building: in what sense therefore must it be taken?

XVII. If we inquire into what the most accurate philosophers declare themselves to mean by material substance, we shall find them acknowledge, they have no other meaning annexed to those sounds, but the idea of being in general, together with the relative notion of its supporting accidents. The general idea of being appeareth to me the most abstract and incomprehensible of all other; and as for its supporting accidents, this, as we have just now observed, cannot be understood in the common sense of those words; it must therefore be taken in some other sense, but what that is they do not explain. So that when I consider the two parts or branches which make the signification of the words material substance, I am convinced there is no distinct meaning annexed to them. But why should we trouble ourselves any further, in discussing this material substratum or support of figure and motion, and other sensible qualities? does it not suppose they have an existence without the mind? and is not this a direct repugnancy, and altogether inconceivable?

XVIII. But though it were possible that solid, figured, moveable substances may exist without the mind, corresponding to the ideas we have of bodies, yet how is it possible for us to know this? either we must know it by sense, or by reason. As for our senses, by them we have the knowledge only of our sensations, ideas, or those things that are immediately perceived by sense, call them what you will: but they do not inform us that things exist without the mind, or unperceived, like to those which are perceived. This the materialists themselves acknowledge. It remains therefore that if we have any knowledge at all of external things, it must be by reason, inferring their existence from what is immediately perceived by sense. But (I do not see) what reason can induce us to believe the existence of bodies without the mind, from what we perceive, since the very patrons of matter themselves do not pretend, there is any necessary connexion betwixt them and our ideas. I say, it is granted on all hands (and what happens in dreams, frenzies, and the like, puts it beyond dispute) that it is possible we might be affected with all the ideas we have now, though no bodies existed without, resembling them. Hence it is evident the supposition of external bodies is not necessary for the producing our ideas: since it is granted they are produced sometimes, and might possibly be produced always, in the same order we see them in at present, without their concurrence.

XIX. But though we might possibly have all our sensations without them, yet perhaps it may be thought easier to conceive and explain the manner of their production, by supposing external bodies in their likeness rather than otherwise; and so it might be at least probable there are such things as bodies that excite their ideas in our minds. But neither can this be said; for though we give the materialists their external bodies, they, by their own confession, are never the nearer knowing how our ideas are produced: since they own themselves unable to comprehend in what manner body can act upon spirit, or how it is possible it should imprint any idea in the mind. Hence it is evident, the production of ideas or sensations in our minds, can be no reason why we should suppose matter or corporeal substances, since that is acknowledged to remain equally inexplicable with or without this supposition. If therefore it were possible for bodies to exist without the mind, yet to hold they do so must needs be a very precarious opinion; since it is to suppose, without any reason at all, that God has created innumerable beings that are entirely useless, and serve to no manner of purpose.

XX. In short, if there were external bodies, it is impossible we should ever come to know it; and if there were not, we might have the very same reasons to think there were that we have now. Suppose, what no one can deny possible, an intelligence, without the help of external bodies, to be affected with the same train of sensations or ideas that you are, imprinted in the same order and with like vividness in his mind. I ask, whether that intelligence hath not all the reason to believe the existence

of corporeal substances, represented by his ideas, and exciting them in his mind, that you can possibly have for believing the same thing? Of this there can be no question; which one consideration is enough to make any reasonable person suspect the strength of whatever arguments he may think himself to have for the existence of bodies without the mind.

XXI. Were it necessary to add any further proof against the existence of matter, after what has been said, I could instance several of those errors and difficulties (not to mention impieties) which have sprung from that tenet. It has occasioned numberless controversies and disputes in philosophy, and not a few of greater moment in religion. But I shall not enter into the detail of them in this place, as well because I think arguments a posteriori are unnecessary for confirming what has been, if I mistake not, sufficiently demonstrated a priori, as because I shall hereafter find occasion to say somewhat of them.

XXII. I am afraid I have given cause to think me needlessly prolix in handling this subject. For to what purpose is it to dilate on that which may be demonstrated with the utmost evidence in a line or two, to any one that is capable of the least reflection? it is but looking into your own thoughts, and so trying whether you can conceive it possible for a sound, or figure, or motion, or colour, to exist without the mind, or unperceived. This easy trial may make you see, that what you contend for is a downright contradiction. Insomuch that I am content to put the whole upon this issue; if you can but conceive it possible for one extended moveable substance, or in general, for any one idea, or any thing like an idea, to exist otherwise than in a mind perceiving it, I shall readily give up the cause: and as for all that compacts of external bodies which you contend for, I shall grant you its existence, though you cannot either give me any reason why you believe it exists, or assign any use to it when it is supposed to exist. I say, the bare possibility of your opinion's being true, shall pass for an argument that it is so.

XXIII. But say you, surely there is nothing easier than to imagine trees, for instance, in a park, or books existing in a closet, and nobody by to perceive them. I answer, you may so, there is no difficulty in it: but what is all this, I beseech you, more than framing in your mind certain ideas which you call books and trees, and at the same time omitting to frame the idea of any one that may perceive them? but do not you yourself perceive or think of them all the while? this therefore is nothing to the purpose; it only shows you have the power of imagining or forming ideas in your mind; but it doth not show that you can conceive it possible the objects of your thought may exist without the mind: to make out this, it is necessary that you conceive them existing unconceived or unthought-of, which is a manifest repugnancy. When we do our utmost to conceive the existence of external bodies, we are all the while only contemplating our own ideas. But the mind, taking no notice of itself, is deluded to think it can and doth conceive bodies existing unthought-of or without the mind; though at the same time they are apprehended by or exist in itself. A little attention will discover to any one the truth and evidence of what is here said, and make it unnecessary to insist on any other proofs against the existence of material substance.

XXIV. It is very obvious, upon the least inquiry into our own thoughts, to know whether it be possible for us to understand what is meant by the absolute existence of sensible objects in themselves or without the mind. To me it is evident those words mark out either a direct contradiction, or else nothing at all. And to convince others of this, I know no readier or fairer way, than to entreat they would calmly attend to their own thoughts: and if by this attention the emptiness or repugnancy of those expressions does appear, surely nothing more is requisite for their conviction. It is on this therefore that I insist, to wit, that the absolute existence of unthinking things are words without a meaning, or which include a contradiction. This is what I repeat and inculcate, and earnestly recommend to the attentive thoughts of the reader.

XXV. All our ideas, sensations, or the things which we perceive, by whatsoever names they may be distinguished, are visibly inactive; there is nothing of power or agency included in them. So that one idea or object of thought cannot produce, or make any alteration in another. To be satisfied of the truth of this, there is nothing else requisite but a bare observation of our ideas. For since they and every part of them exist only in the mind, it follows that there is nothing in them but what is perceived. But whoever shall attend to his ideas, whether of sense or reflection, will not perceive in them any power or activity; there is therefore no such thing contained in them. A little attention will discover to us that the very being of an idea implies passiveness and inertness in it, insomuch that it is impossible for an idea to do any thing, or, strictly speaking, to be the cause of any thing: neither can it be the resemblance or pattern of any active being, as is evident from Sect. viii. Whence it plainly follows that extension, figure, and motion, cannot be the cause of our sensations. To say, therefore, that these are the effects of powers resulting from the configuration, number, motion, and size of corpuscles, must certainly be false.

XXVI. We perceive a continual succession of ideas, some are anew excited, others are changed or totally disappear. There is therefore some cause of these ideas whereon they depend, and which produces and changes them. That this cause cannot be any quality or idea or combination of ideas, is clear from the preceding section. It must therefore be a substance; but it has been shown that there is no corporeal or material substance: it remains therefore that the cause of ideas is an incorporeal active substance or spirit.

XXVII. A spirit is one simple, undivided, active being: as it perceives ideas, it is called the understanding, and as it produces or otherwise operates about them, it is called the will. Hence there can be no idea formed of a soul or spirit: for all ideas whatever, being passive and inert (vide Sect. xxv.), they cannot represent unto us, by way of image or likeness, that which acts. A little attention will make it plain to any one, that to have an idea which shall be like that active principle of motion and change of ideas, is absolutely impossible. Such is the nature of spirit, or that which acts, that it cannot be of itself perceived but only by the effects which it produceth. If any man shall doubt of the truth of what is here delivered, let him but reflect and try if he can frame the idea of any power or active being; and whether he hath ideas of two principal powers, marked by the names will and understanding, distinct from each other as well as from a third idea of substance or being in general, with a relative notion of its supporting or being the subject of the aforesaid powers, which is signified by the name soul or spirit. This is what some hold; but so far as I can see, the words will, soul, spirit, do not stand for different ideas, or in truth, for any idea at all, but for something which is very different from ideas, and which being an agent cannot be like unto, or represented by, any idea whatsoever. Though it must be owned at the same time, that we have some notion of soul, spirit, and the operations of the mind, such as willing, loving, hating, inasmuch as we know or understand the meaning of those words.

XXVIII. I find I can excite ideas in my mind at pleasure, and vary and shift the scene as oft as I think fit. It is no more than willing, and straightway this or that idea arises in my fancy: and by the same power it is obliterated, and makes way for another. This making and unmaking of ideas doth very properly denominate the mind active. Thus much is certain, and grounded on experience: but when we talk of unthinking agents, or of exciting ideas exclusive of volition, we only amuse ourselves with words.

XXIX. But whatever power I may have over my own thoughts, I find the ideas actually perceived by sense have not a like dependence on my will. When in broad day-light I open my eyes, it is not in my power to choose whether I shall see or no, or to determine what particular objects shall present themselves to my view; and so likewise as to the hearing and other senses, the ideas imprinted on them are not creatures of my will. There is therefore some other will or spirit that produces them.

XXX. The ideas of sense are more strong, lively, and distinct than those of the imagination; they have likewise a steadiness, order, and coherence, and are not excited at random, as those which are the effects of human wills often are, but in a regular train or series, the admirable connexion whereof sufficiently testifies the wisdom and benevolence of its author. Now the set rules or established methods, wherein the mind we depend on excites in us the ideas of sense, are called the laws of nature: and these we learn by experience, which teaches us that such and such ideas are attended with such and such other ideas, in the ordinary course of things.

XXXI. This gives us a sort of foresight, which enables us to regulate our actions for the benefit of life. And without this we should be eternally at a loss: we could not know how to act any thing that might procure us the least pleasure, or remove the least pain of sense. That food nourishes, sleep refreshes, and fire warms us; that to sow in the seed-time is the way to reap in the harvest, and, in general, that to obtain such or such ends, such or such means are conducive, all this we know, not by discovering any necessary connexion between our

ideas, but only by the observation of the settled laws of nature, without which we should be all in uncertainty and confusion, and a grown man no more know how to manage himself in the affairs of life than an infant just born.

XXXII. And yet this consistent, uniform working, which so evidently displays the goodness and wisdom of that governing Spirit whose will constitutes the laws of nature, is so far from leading our thoughts to him, that it rather sends them a wandering after second causes. For when we perceive certain ideas of sense constantly followed by other ideas, and we know this is not of our own doing, we forthwith attribute power and agency to the ideas themselves, and make one the cause of another, than which nothing can be more absurd and unintelligible. Thus, for example, having observed that when we perceive by sight a certain round luminous figure, we at the same time perceive by touch the idea or sensation called heat, we do from thence conclude the sun to be the cause of heat. And in like manner perceiving the motion and collision of bodies to be attended with sound, we are inclined to think the latter an effect of the former.

XXXIII. The ideas imprinted on the senses by the author of nature are called real things: and those excited in the imagination, being less regular, vivid, and constant, are more properly termed ideas, or images of things, which they copy and represent. But then our sensations, be they never so vivid and distinct, are nevertheless ideas, that is, they exist in the mind, or are perceived by it, as truly as the ideas of its own framing. The ideas of sense are allowed to have more reality in them, that is, to be more strong, orderly, and coherent than the creatures of the mind: but this is no argument that they exist without the mind. They are also less dependent on the spirit, or thinking substance which perceives them, in that they are excited by the will of another and more powerful spirit: yet still they are ideas, and certainly no idea, whether faint or strong, can exist otherwise than in a mind perceiving it.

XXXIV. Before we proceed any further, it is necessary to spend some time in answering objections which may probably be made against the principles hitherto laid down. In doing of which, if I seem too prolix to those of quick apprehensions, I hope it may be pardoned, since all men do not equally apprehend things of this nature; and I am willing to be understood by every one. First then it will be objected that by the foregoing principles, all that is real and substantial in nature is banished out of the world: and instead thereof a chimerical scheme of ideas takes place. All things that exist, exist only in the mind, that is, they are purely notional. What therefore becomes of the sun, moon, and stars? What must we think of houses, rivers, mountains, trees, stones; nay, even of our own bodies? Are all these but so many chimeras and illusions on the fancy? To all which, and whatever else of the same sort may be objected, I answer, that by the principles premised, we are not deprived of any one thing in nature. Whatever we see, feel, hear, or any wise conceive or understand, remains as secure as ever, and is as real as ever. There is a rerum natura, and the distinction between realities and chimeras retains its full force. This is evident from Sect. xxix., xxx., and xxxiii., where we have shown what is meant by real things in opposition to chimeras, or ideas of our own framing; but then they both equally exist in the mind, and in that sense are like ideas.

XXXV. I do not argue against the existence of any one thing that we can apprehend, either by sense or reflection. That the things I see with mine eyes and touch with my hands do exist, really exist, I make not the least question. The only thing whose existence we deny, is that which philosophers call matter or corporeal substance. And in doing of this, there is no damage done to the rest of mankind, who, I dare say, will never miss it. The atheist indeed will want the colour of an empty name to support his impiety; and the philosophers may possibly find, they have lost a great handle for trifling and disputation.

. . .

CXLV. From what hath been said, it is plain that we cannot know the existence of other spirits otherwise than by their operations, or the ideas of them excited in us. I perceive several motions, changes, and combinations of ideas, that inform me there are certain particular agents like myself, which accompany them, and concur in their production. Hence the knowledge I have of other spirits is not immediate, as is the knowledge of my ideas; but depending on the intervention of ideas, by me referred to agents or spirits distinct from myself, as effects or concomitant signs.

CXLVI. But though there be some things which convince us human agents are concerned in producing them; yet it is evident to every one, that those things which are called the works of nature, that is, the far greater part of the ideas or sensations perceived by us, are not produced by, or dependent on, the wills of men. There is therefore some other spirit that causes them, since it is repugnant that they should subsist by themselves. See Sect. xxix. But if we attentively consider the constant regularity, order, and concatenation of natural things, the surprising magnificence, beauty, and perfection of the larger, and the exquisite contrivance of the smaller parts of the creation, together with the exact harmony and correspondence of the whole, but, above all, the never enough admired laws of pain and pleasure, and the instincts or natural inclinations, appetites, and passions of animals; I say if we consider all these things, and at the same time attend to the meaning and import of the attributes, one, eternal, infinitely wise, good, and perfect, we shall clearly perceive that they belong to the aforesaid spirit, who works all in all, and by whom all things consist.

CXLVII. Hence it is evident, that God is known as certainly and immediately as any other mind or spirit whatsoever, distinct from ourselves. We may even assert, that the existence of God is far more evidently perceived than the existence of men; because the effects of nature are infinitely more numerous and considerable than those ascribed to human agents. There is not any one mark that denotes a man, or effect produced by him, which doth not more strongly evince the being of that Spirit who is the Author of nature. For it is evident that in affecting other persons, the will of man hath no other object than barely the motion of the limbs of his body; but that such a motion should be attended by, or excite any idea in the mind of another, depends wholly on the will of the Creator. He alone it is who, "upholding all things by the word of his power," maintains that intercourse between spirits, whereby they are able to perceive the existence of each other. And yet this pure and clear light, which enlightens every one, is itself invisible.

III.3 *Science and the Physical World:* A Defense of Phenomenalism

W. T. STACE

W. T. Stace (1886–1967) was born in Britain and served in the British Civil Service in Ceylon. In 1932 he came to the United States to teach philosophy at Princeton University. In this essay Stace defends a phenomenalist view of perception. Drawing on Hume's remarks on causality (see Reading VIII.1), Stace argues that the realist, one who believes in a separate material world apart from sensations, has no good arguments for his or her position. All that the principle of causality tells us is that there are regularities of experiences in the world. Modern science goes beyond its proper domain when it hypostatizes functional concepts such as "atoms," "gravity," "forces," and "the conservation of energy," and treats them as though they were things. For a phenomenalist like Stace, only sensations and the minds that perceive them exist. The rest is mental construction, useful fiction, which help us to organize our experience and predict sensations.

Stars, Atoms and Sensations

So far as I know scientists still talk about electrons, protons, neutrons, and so on. We never directly perceive these, hence if we ask how we know of their existence the only possible answer seems to be that they are an inference from what we do directly perceive. What sort of an inference? Apparently a causal inference. The atomic entities in some way impinge upon the sense of the animal organism and cause that organism to perceive the familiar world of tables, chairs, and the rest.

But is it not clear that such a concept of causation, however interpreted, is invalid? The only reason we have for believing in the law of causation is that we *observe* certain regularities or sequences. We observe that, in certain conditions, *A* is always followed by *B*. We call *A* the cause, *B* the effect. And the sequence *A–B* becomes a causal law. It follows

that all *observed* causal sequences are between sensed objects in the familiar world of perception, and that all known causal laws apply solely to the world of sense and not to anything beyond or behind it. And this in turn means that we have not got, and never could have, one jot of evidence for believing that the law of causation can be applied *outside* the realm of perception, or that that realm can have any causes (such as the supposed physical objects) which are not themselves perceived.

Put the same thing in another way. Suppose there is an observed sequence *A–B–C*, represented by the vertical lines in the diagram below.

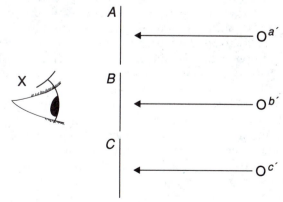

This selection is a slight abbreviation of Stace's article "Science and the Physical World" which was published in 1967 in his *Man Against Darkness and Other Essays*. It is reprinted with the permission of the University of Pittsburgh Press. © 1967 University of Pittsburgh Press.

The observer X sees, and can see, nothing except things in the familiar world of perception. What *right* has he, and what *reason* has he, to assert cause of *A*, *B*, and *C*, such as *a'*, *b'*, *c'*, which he can never observe, behind the perceived world? He has no *right*, because the law of causation on which he is relying has never been observed to operate outside the series of perceptions, and he can have, therefore, no evidence that it does so. And he has no *reason* because the phenomenon *C* is *sufficiently* accounted for by the cause *B*, *B* by *A*, and so on. It is unnecessary and superfluous to introduce a *second* cause *b'*, for *B*, *c'* for *C*, and so forth. To give two causes for each phenomenon, one in one world and one in another, is unnecessary, and perhaps even self-contradictory.

Is it denied, then, it will be asked, that the star causes light waves, that the waves cause retinal changes, that these cause changes in the optic nerve, which in turn causes movements in the brain cells, and so on? No, it is not denied. But the observed causes and effects are all in the world of perception. And no sequences of sense-data can possibly justify going outside that world. If you admit that we never observe anything except sensed objects and their relations, regularities, and sequences, then it is obvious that we are completely shut in by our sensations and can never get outside them. Not only causal relations, but all other observed relations, upon which *any* kind of inferences might be founded, will lead only to further sensible objects and their relations. No inference, therefore, can pass from what is sensible to what is not sensible.

The fact is that atoms are *not* inferences from sensations. No one denies, of course, that a vast amount of perfectly valid inferential reasoning takes place in the physical theory of the atom. But it will not be found to be in any strict logical sense inference *from sense-data to atoms*. An *hypothesis* is set up, and the inferential processes are concerned with the application of the hypothesis, that is, with the prediction by its aid of further possible sensations and with its own internal consistency.

That atoms are not inferences from sensations means, of course, that from the existence of sensations we cannot validly infer the existence of atoms. And this means that we cannot have any reason at all to believe that they exist. And that is why I propose to argue that they do not exist—or at any rate that no one could know it if they did, and that we have absolutely no evidence of their existence.

What status have they, then? Is it meant that they are false and worthless, merely untrue? Certainly not. No one supposes that the entries in the Nautical Almanac "exist" anywhere except on the pages of that book and in the brains of its compilers and readers. Yet they are "true," inasmuch as they enable us to predict certain sensations, namely, the positions and times of certain perceived objects which we call the stars. And so the formulae of the atomic theory are true in the same sense, and perform a similar function.

I suggest that they are nothing but shorthand formulae, ingeniously worked out by the human mind, to enable it to predict its experience, i.e. to predict what sensations will be given to it. By "predict" here I do not mean to refer solely to the future. To calculate that there was an eclipse of the sun visible in Asia Minor in the year 585 B.C. is, in the sense in which I am using the term, to predict.

In order to see more clearly what is meant, let us apply the same idea to another case, that of gravitation. Newton formulated a law of gravitation in terms of "forces." It was supposed that this law—which was nothing but a mathematical formula—governed the operation of these existent forces. Nowadays it is no longer believed that these forces exist at all. And yet the law can be applied just as well without them to the prediction of astronomical phenomena. It is a matter of no importance to the scientific man whether the forces exist or not. That may be said to be a purely philosophical question. And I think the philosopher should pronounce them fictions. But that would not make the law useless or untrue. If it could still be used to predict phenomena, it would be just as true as it was.

It is true that fault is now found with Newton's law, and that another law, that of Einstein, has been substituted for it. And it is sometimes supposed that the reason for this is that forces are no longer believed in. But this is not the case. Whether forces exist or not simply does not matter. What matters is the discovery that Newton's law does *not* enable us accurately to predict certain astronomical facts such as the exact position of the planet Mercury. Therefore another formula, that of Einstein, has been substituted for it which permits correct predictions. This new law, as it happens, is a formula in terms of geometry. It is pure mathematics and nothing else. It does not contain anything about forces. In its pure form it does not even contain, so I am informed, anything about "humps and hills in space-time." And it does not matter whether any such humps and hills exist. It is truer than Newton's law, not because it substitutes humps and hills for forces, but solely because it is a more accurate formula of prediction.

Not only may it be said that forces do not exist. It may with equal truth be said that "gravitation" does not exist. Gravitation is not a "thing," but a mathematical formula, which exists only in the heads of mathematicians. And as a mathematical formula cannot cause a body to fall, so gravitation cannot cause a body to fall. Ordinary language misleads us here. We speak of the law "of" gravitation, and suppose that this law "applies to" the heavenly bodies. We are thereby misled into supposing that there are *two* things, namely, the gravitation and the heavenly bodies, and that one of these things, the gravitation, causes changes in the other. In reality nothing exists except the moving bodies. And neither Newton's law nor Einstein's law is, strictly speaking, a law of gravitation. They are both laws of moving bodies, that is to say, formulae which tell us how these bodies will move.

Now, just as in the past "forces" were foisted into Newton's law (by himself, be it said), so now certain popularizers of relativity foisted "humps and hills in space-time" into Einstein's law. We hear that the reason why the planets move in curved courses is that they cannot go through these humps and hills, but have to go round them! The planets just get "shoved about," not by forces, but by the humps and hills! But these humps and hills are pure metaphors. And anyone who takes them for "existences" gets asked awkward questions as to what "curved space" is curved "in."

It is not irrelevant to our topic to consider *why* human beings invent these metaphysical monsters of forces and bumps in space-time. The reason is that they have never emancipated themselves from the absurd idea that science "explains" things. They were not content to have laws which merely told them *that* the planets will, as a matter of fact, move in such and such ways. They wanted to know "why" the planets move in those ways. So Newton replied, "Forces." "Oh," said humanity, "that explains it. We understand forces. We feel them every time someone pushes or pulls us." Thus the movements were supposed to be "explained" by entities familiar

because analogous to the muscular sensations which human beings feel. The humps and hills were introduced for exactly the same reason. They seem so familiar. If there is a bump in the billiard table, the rolling billiard ball is diverted from a straight to a curved course. Just the same with the planets. "Oh, I see!" says humanity, "that's quite simple. That *explains* everything."

But scientific laws, properly formulated, never "explain" anything. They simply state, in an abbreviated and generalized form, *what happens*. No scientist, and in my opinion no philosopher, knows *why* anything happens, or can "explain" anything. Scientific laws do nothing except state the brute fact that "when *A* happens, *B* always happens too." And laws of this kind obviously enable us to predict. If certain scientists substituted humps and hills for forces, then they have just substituted one superstition for another. For my part I do not believe that *science* has done this, though some *scientists* may have. For scientists, after all, are human beings with the same craving for "explanations" as other people.

I think that atoms are in exactly the same position as forces and the bumps and hills of space-time. In reality the mathematical formulae which are the scientific ways of stating the atomic theory are simply formulae for calculating what sensations will appear in given conditions. But just as the weakness of the human mind demanded that there should correspond to the formula of gravitation a real "thing" which could be called "gravitation itself" or "force," so the same weakness demands that there should be a real thing corresponding to the atomic formulae, and this real thing is called the atom. In reality the atoms no more cause sensations than gravitation causes apples to fall. The only causes of sensations are other sensations. And the relation of atoms to sensations to be felt is not the relation of cause to effect, but the relation of a mathematical formula to the facts and happenings which it enables the mathematician to calculate. . . .

It will not be out of place to give one more example to show how common fictitious existences are in science, and how little it matters whether they really exist or not. This example has no strange and annoying talk of "bent spaces" about it. One of the foundations of physics is, or used to be, the law of the conservation of energy. I do not know how far, if at all, this has been affected by the theory that matter sometimes turns into energy. But that does not affect the lesson it has for us. The law states, or used to state, that the amount of energy in the universe is always constant, that energy is never either created or destroyed. This was highly convenient, but it seemed to have obvious exceptions. If you throw a stone up into the air, you are told that it exerts in its fall the same amount of energy which it took to throw it up. But suppose it does not fall. Suppose it lodges on the roof of your house and stays there. What has happened to the energy which you can nowhere perceive as being exerted? It seems to have disappeared out of the universe. No, says the scientist, it still exists as *potential* energy. Now what does this blessed word "potential"—which is thus brought in to save the situation—mean as applied to energy? It means, of course, that the energy does not exist in any of its regular "forms," heat, light, electricity, etc. But this is merely negative. What positive meaning has the term? Strictly speaking, none whatever. Either the energy exists or it does not exist. There is no realm of the "potential" half-way between existence and non-existence. And this existence of energy can only consist in its being exerted. If the energy is not being exerted, then it is not energy and does not exist. Energy can no more exist without energizing than heat can exist without being hot. The "potential" existence of the energy is, then, a fiction. The actual empirically verifiable facts are that if a certain quantity of energy *e* exists in the universe and then disappears out of the universe (as happens when the stone lodges on the roof), the same amount of energy *e* will always reappear, begin to exist again, in certain known conditions. That is the fact which the law of the conservation of energy actually expresses. And the fiction of potential energy is introduced simply because it is convenient and makes the equations easier to work. They could be worked quite well without it, but would be slightly more complicated. In either case the function of the law is the same. Its object is to apprise us that if in certain conditions we have certain perceptions (throwing up the stone), then in certain other conditions we shall get certain other perceptions (heat, light, stone hitting skull, or other such). But there will always be a temptation to hypostatize the potential energy as an "existence," and to believe that it is a "cause" which "explains" the phenomena.

If the views which I have been expressing are followed out, they will lead to the conclusion that, strictly speaking, *nothing exists except sensations* (and the minds which perceive them). The rest is mental construction or fiction. But this does not mean that the conception of a star or the conception of an electron are worthless or untrue. Their truth and value consist in their capacity for helping us to organize our experience and predict our sensations.

III.4 *Phenomenalism: Its Grounds and Difficulties*

C. H. WHITELEY

C. H. Whiteley (b. 1911) was until his retirement Professor of Philosophy at the University of Birmingham in England. In this essay, Whitely analyzes Berkeley's successor, contemporary phenomenalism, identifying its strengths and weaknesses. Its strengths are that it is simpler than its competitors, it lends itself readily to verification, and it refutes skepticism. Its weaknesses are that it tends to blur the distinction between "appearance" and "reality," it cannot account for the seeming permanence of things, it has problems accounting for causation, and it leads to solipsism, the view that "the only experience in the world is my experience, and the only person existing in the universe is myself."

48. *The Non-Existence of Matter*

From such arguments as these, Berkeley draws the conclusion that Matter does not exist, or at least there is no good reason for believing that it does. This seems a most alarming conclusion. But he assures us that there is no cause for alarm, if we are careful to understand exactly what he is saying. He is denying that there is any such thing as material substance as the materialist philosophers define it; that is, a substance apart from and independent of all awareness, permanent, public, the cause of our sensations, having shape, size, position, motion. He is not denying that there are such things as tables and chairs and clouds and apples and cats, or that we know quite a lot about them and often make true statements concerning them. It is true that there is a table in this room, that it is 3 feet long, etc. It is true that grass is green and snow is white. It is true that water is a compound of oxygen and hydrogen, and malaria is caused by the bite of a mosquito. These statements are false if they are interpreted as referring to some unobservable "material" thing which is outside all experience. But there is another way of interpreting them in which they may well be true. That is to take them as descriptions, not of a mysterious unexperienceable Matter, but of sense-experiences which people have or might have.

49. *The Meaning of Words*

And this seems a reasonable way of interpreting our statements when we consider how it is that we come to understand and make use of language. When I am teaching a child the meaning of the word "table," I point to the table, so that he sees it; I put his hand to it, so that he feels it; that is, I cause him to sense certain sense-data. Surely it is with these sense-data that he thereupon associates the sound "table"; when he sees and feels similar sense-data, he repeats "table." It is by the differences in what they look like and feel like that he distinguishes tables from chairs and apples and half-crowns. It is natural to conclude that when he uses the word "table" or "apple," he is using it to describe what he sees, feels, tastes, etc., rather than to propound some theory about an invisible and intangible material substance.

The word "table" *means* a certain visible

From C. H. Whiteley, *An Introduction to Metaphysics*, Methuen & Co. Ltd., London, 1950. Reprinted by permission.

squareness and brownness, a certain tangible hardness; i.e., it means a certain type of sense-experience. When I say "There is a table in this room" I am describing the sense-data which I am now sensing, and if I do not sense such sense-data, then, being a truthful person, I do not say that there is a table in the room. If someone else says that there is, I test his statement by looking and feeling, i.e., by finding out whether the appropriate sense-data are available; if they are not, I dismiss his statement as false. If I say "Socrates drank his companions under the table," I am not describing any sense-experiences which I have now, but I am describing sense-experiences which I suppose Socrates and his companions to have had at another time and place.

We cannot, of course, identify "the table" with any one single sense-datum; an experience which was entirely unique and did not recur would not be worth naming. The function of words is not to name everything we see or hear, but to pick out the recurrent patterns in our experience. They identify our present sense-data as being of the same group or type as others which we have sensed before. A word, then, describes, not a single experience, but a group or type of experiences; the word "table" describes all the various sense-data which we normally refer to as appearances or sensations "of" the table. So a material thing is not indeed identical with any sense-datum; but neither is it something different in kind from sense-data. It is a group, or class, or system of sense-data; and nothing but sense-data goes to constitute it. So this doctrine may be expressed by saying that every statement we make about a material thing is equivalent to another statement about sense-data.

50. *Phenomenalism*

This analysis of the notion of a material thing is called Phenomenalism, since it makes of a material thing a group of phenomena, appearances, instead of a transcendent reality distinct from appearances. It is a widespread view, and has been accepted by many philosophers who do not call themselves Idealists and are far from accepting Berkeley's view that the fundamental reality is Mind. The term "idealism" itself, however, though it has shifted in mean-

ing since, does properly denote just this part of Berkeley's theory, that the material world—"the whole choir of heaven and furniture of the earth" says Berkeley—consists of what he calls "ideas" and I have been calling "sense-data." The word in this sense has nothing to do with ideals, and the theory would have been called "ideaism" but for considerations of pronunciation.

Phenomenalism, then, is the doctrine that all statements about material objects can be completely analysed into statements about sense-data. The analysis of any such statement must be very complex; and the value of the "material-object language" is that it enables us to refer in one word, such as "table," to a vast number of sense-data differing very much among themselves. The group of sense-data constituting the table includes all the different views I can obtain at different distances, from different angles, in different lights, no two of them exactly alike, but all of them variations on one central pattern; it includes sense-data of touch, and those of sound (though these last seem somewhat more loosely connected with the main visuo-tactual group); and with other kinds of material things, such as apples, sense-data of taste and smell form important constituents of the thing.

51. *Its Advantages*

This type of theory has certain clear advantages. On the representative theory, the very existence of a material world or of any given material object must always be in principle doubtful. I am directly aware of my sense-data, and so can be certain of their existence and character: but "material objects" are quite different—their existence and character can be known only by an inference, which cannot give the complete certainty which comes from observation. Descartes, for example, accepts this consequence of the theory, and will not allow himself to believe that there is a material world at all, until he has convinced himself that there exists an omnipotent and benevolent God who would never have led him to believe in the material world if it had not been real. But if Descartes really succeeded in keeping up this attitude of doubt for more than a moment, few men have been able to imitate him. We *cannot* believe that the existence of the table is in any way subject to doubt.

The phenomenalist theory, by making the existence of the table *the same thing* as the occurrence of certain sense-data, removes that doubt; for the system of sense-data constituting the table has beyond doubt come under my observation.

The theory not only removes the doubt, but makes it clear why we cannot seriously entertain it. The Plain Man was right after all: material things are seen and touched, are objects of direct awareness, and it is by seeing and touching that we know that they exist, though no material thing is straightforwardly identical with what I am seeing and touching *at this particular moment*.

So, by accepting the phenomenalist analysis, we escape being involved in any reference to an unobservable Matter. We can preserve our empiricism inviolate, and talk about the things we see and hear and smell and touch, and not about other hypothetical things beyond the reach of our observation. Science, the knowledge of nature, on this view becomes the recording, ordering and forecasting of human experiences. Therein lies its interest for us. If the physical world lay outside our experience, why should we be concerned with it?

---

52. *Criticisms of Phenomenalism*

But these advantages of phenomenalism are purchased at a cost. Along several different lines the phenomenalist interpretation of our statements about material things seem to conflict with our usual beliefs, and produces paradoxes not very easy to accept.

"Appearance and Reality"

(1) In ordinary speech we are accustomed to draw a distinction between "appearance" and "reality," and to allow that a thing may appear to be what it is not, as Descartes' stick half under water may appear bent although it is really straight. Hence we reckon some of our perceptions as "real" or "true" or "genuine," and others as "illusions." The representative theory of perception is in accordance with this way of

thinking; for on that theory our sense-data are in some respects copies of material things; some are accurate copies, and so are genuine and true, others are inaccurate copies, and so false and illusory. The representative theory differs from common sense mainly in holding that the discrepancies between the sense-datum and the material object which it represents are greater than we realise.

But what is the phenomenalist to make of this distinction? He can admit no essential difference between appearance and reality; for on his view the appearances *are* the reality. Material things consist of appearances—sense-data—and of nothing else. And these sense-data all actually occur and so are equally real. Moreover, they are what they appear to be; their reality consists in appearing, and the suggestion that they might "really" have qualities which they do not appear to have is without meaning. Thus the phenomenalist has no justification for classifying them into "real" and "unreal," or "genuine" and "counterfeit." The various sense-data which go to constitute a material object, such as my table, are of many different shapes and colours. All of them are equally real, and none of them can be *the* "real shape" or "real colour" of the table. Evidently tables are more versatile objects than we thought, and may have as many different shapes and colours as there are occasions of observing them. Why then should we come by the idea that there is only one "real shape," and the rest are mere appearances?

The phenomenalist solution of this difficulty is to allow that in a strict philosophical sense of the word "real," the distinction between reality and appearance cannot be drawn. But the purpose of the common-sense distinction between appearance and reality is not to pry into the ultimacies of metaphysics, but to enable us to deal with the experiences we encounter. What causes us to condemn an experience as an "illusion" is that it leads us astray. A mirage is an illusion because it causes us to make a mistake. But what kind of mistake? Surely, not the mistake of thinking that we now see trees and water, but the mistake of expecting that we shall soon be able to have a drink and sit in the shade. The mistake consists in the false expectation of certain other sense-data. Thus the illusoriness is not in the sense-datum itself, but in the expectation which we form when we sense it.

Error of this sort is possible because sense-data are not chaotic, but in the main are arranged in orderly series. Normally, when the visual sense-data belonging to water are obtainable, so are the gustatory sense-data of drinking water and relieving one's thirst. The mirage deceives us because, abnormally, we get the visual sense-data without the gustatory ones. Mirror-images may deceive us because the things seen in a mirror cannot be observed from the back and cannot be touched. Thus a "real" table consists of a complete set of sense-data of different senses related to one another in certain systematic ways (e.g., visual sense-data become continuously smaller and auditory ones continuously fainter as we move away from a certain region of space). When, as in the case of a table seen in a mirror, you have some members of the set but not others, you say that what is seen in the mirror is not a "real" table, or is not "really" there.

Again, the stick in water may lead us into error because sticks that "look bent" usually "feel bent" as well; and so we are surprised to find that it "feels straight," and say that though it "looks bent" it is not "really bent."

The precise interpretation of the word "real" is different in different contexts. But in general, say phenomenalists, it will be found that what we call the "real world" is not a world different from that of appearances; it is a selection from the world of appearances, a collection of appearances which are normal, systematic, and so reliable. The "unreal" consists of eccentric appearances which in one way or another fail to fit in with the normal type of sets of sense-data, and therefore causes us to form false expectations.

53. The Permanence of Material Things

(2) Sensations come and go. Few of them last for very long, and none of them lasts for ever. If we add up all the occasions in my life on which I have been looking at this table, we get a very short period indeed. And, like the rest of my species, I frequently go to sleep, and cease to perceive any material object whatsoever. That is to say, if a material thing consists of sense-data, its existence must be intermittent. Sense-data belonging to the thing exist only now and again, and most of the time they do

not exist at all. But material objects such as tables are normally supposed to be permanent things, which endure uninterruptedly for very long periods. How can a permanent object be made out of momentary sense-data?

If I am alone in the room and close my eyes, there are then no sense-data belonging to the table; are we to suppose that I can annihilate so substantial a material object simply by shutting my eyes? It seems as though the phenomenalist must deny that any such statement as "There is a table in the room" can be true unless there is someone there seeing or touching it; and he must also deny that any such statement as "The table has been here for twenty years" can be true, unless (what seems most improbable) gangs of watchers have been observing it in relays for the whole of that time.

54. Phenomenalist Analysis of Permanence

The phenomenalist answer to these difficulties involves a radical reinterpretation of the whole notion of a permanent material thing. That the existence of the table should be permanent in the way in which my waking experience is uninterrupted, that the table should last for twenty years in the way that my hearing a performance of a symphony can last for three-quarters of an hour, is of course impossible on a phenomenalist view. Whatever kind of permanence is attributed to the table must be understood in another sense.

Clearly, when I say that there is a table in the now uninhabited attic, I am not describing the sense-data of anyone. But, though the statement cannot be a description of *actual* sense-data, it can be a description of *possible* sense-data; and this is what it is according to phenomenalists. To say that there is a table there now is to say that *if* there were anyone in the room he *would be* having the kind of experience which we call seeing a table. "There is a table" means "Go and look and you will see a table." And to say that it has been there twenty years means that if at any time during those years anyone had been in the room, he could have seen or touched a table.

So we must modify our original account of the

nature of a material thing. It consists not merely of actual sense-data, but also of possible sense-data; or more precisely, of the fact that under certain conditions sense-data are obtainable. What is permanent is then not any sense-datum or group of sense-data, but the possibility of obtaining sense-data of a certain kind. Hence J. S. Mill defined matter as "the permanent possibility of sensation."

I think this much at least must be admitted: if it is true that there is a table in the attic, it is also true that if anyone with the use of normal eyes in a good light were to be in the attic now, he would have the experience of seeing the table; if it is true that the table has been there for twenty years, it is also true that if anyone has been there under those conditions at any time during those twenty years, he would have had the experience of seeing the table. That is to say, the statement about sense-data is involved in or implied by the statement about the table. According to the phenomenalist, such statements about possible sense-data constitute the whole of what the statement about the table means. All statements about material objects are equivalent to statements about what people have experienced, or would have experienced if circumstances had been different.

He points out that if we try to imagine the presence of the table in the attic, what we do is to imagine what it would look like and feel like. If we want to test the statement that it is there, we go and look. Statements which are not, in the final analysis, about actual or possible experiences, cannot be tested at all, and are therefore without meaning for us.

55. *Berkeley's Account of Permanence*

Berkeley himself gives another explanation of the permanence of material things. According to his theory, God is eternally perceiving everything, and therefore, at times when neither I nor any other human being or animal is perceiving the table, God is still perceiving it. But whether or not this is really the case, it is obviously not a correct interpretation of what we mean when we attribute continuous existence in time to the table. For if it were, we should not believe in permanent material things at

all unless we believed, not only in God, but in an omnisentient God such as Berkeley believed in.

56. *Causal Activity*

(3) According to our ordinary notions of them, material objects are causally active: they do things. The table supports the tablecloth, the fire warms the room. Material objects exercise force, have influences on one another and incidentally on ourselves, causing, among other things, our sensations of them. This continually active causal interplay makes up the system of nature, which it is the business of science to study and reduce to laws. Does not science explain what happens by referring events to their causes, which in the material realm at least are material things, exercising physical force? Surely, the room cannot be warmed by my visual sense-datum of a fire! Still less can it be warmed by the possibility of a visual sense-datum of a fire during my absence, when I am not looking at the fire but the room gets warmed all the same. When we all sit round the table and sense sense-data very similar in shape, size and colour, what is the explanation of this fact, if not that there is an independent table which is the common cause of all our similar sense-data? Berkeley himself admits, or rather insists, that an "idea" is "inert," and can *do* nothing.

57. *Phenomenalist Analysis of Causation*

To deal with this problem, we need a fresh analysis and re-interpretation of the notion of cause, parallel to the phenomenalist re-interpretation of the notion of "substance" or "thing." Such an analysis was given in David Hume's *Treatise of Human Nature* (1739), and modern phenomenalists in the main follow his line of thought. Hume's aim is to interpret statements about cause and effect in such a way that the relation between a cause and its effect shall be an observable fact, and shall contain nothing mysterious or occult. For unless the words "cause and effect" described something we could observe, they would not, according to Hume, be intelligible to us.

What, then, do I observe in cases in which I should naturally use causal language? I am watching a game of billiards. I observe the event which I might naturally describe by saying that one ball A moved across the table and made or caused another ball B to roll into a pocket. What do I actually *see:* I see a certain sequence of events: first the movement of A, then the touching of A and B, then the movement of B. This temporal sequence of movements, the one which I call the effect following on the one I call the cause, seems to be all the visible relation there is between them.

But obviously, mere temporal sequence is not the same thing as causation; *post hoc* is not the same as *propter hoc;* plenty of other things preceded the movement of my billiard ball in time which were not causes of it. Yet nothing seems to be observable but temporal sequence—first one event, then the other. Whence do I get this notion of the ball being made or caused or forced to move?

If I were pushing the ball myself, I should be aware of myself making a certain muscular effort, *trying* to make it move; and, when I observe the collision of the two balls and the ensuing movement of B, I may perhaps have a vague image of a similar kind of pushing going on between the balls. But if I do, it is clear that this feeling of muscular effort is not observed in the situation presented to my senses, but is a "projection" of my own past feelings in similar situations. For billiard balls do not have muscles, or make efforts, and even if they did, I could not observe what efforts they were making, I could only observe their movements.

Certainly when I see the collision, I expect that the second ball will move—there is a "felt tendency of the mind" to pass from the "cause" to the "effect"; but this is a psychological fact about me, not a physical fact about the balls. There seems nothing in the observed situation corresponding to the words "cause," "power," "force," which I am inclined to apply to it; only the observed sequence of one event on the other. But how, then, do I distinguish between those temporal antecedents of an event which are its causes, and those which are not? How do I establish the difference between *post hoc* and *propter hoc?*

The answer is plain enough; I repeat the experiment, and if the same sequence of events recurs, I conclude that it was a causal and not an accidental sequence. The reason I believe that the movement of the ball was caused by the impact of the other ball, and not by somebody lighting a cigarette at the same time, is that I know by long experience that balls always move when they are struck by other balls moving fairly quickly, whereas they do not usually move when men light cigarettes in their neighbourhood. When medical men inquire into the cause of cancer, what they are looking for is something which always happens to a man before he becomes ill with cancer, just as, when they say that malaria is caused by the bite of a mosquito, they mean that a man has always been bitten by a mosquito before developing malaria. The observable fact which leads us to say that C is the cause of E is the fact that events of the kind C are followed by events of the kind E, not once or sometimes, but whenever they occur.

Causality, as a fact about the world, is then, according to Hume, a relation of invariable sequence. What is required to convert *post hoc* into *propter hoc* is regular repetition. To say that every event has a cause is to say that for any event E there is another event (or complex of "conditions") C such that whenever an event of the kind C occurs, an event of the kind E follows. It is to say that the sequence of phenomena is patterned, systematic; that there are in nature discoverable regularities.

But these regularities are discoverable among the observed phenomena themselves, and not between phenomena and something transcending phenomena. Causation, thus interpreted, is a relation between sense-data. The causes, that is to say, the invariable antecedents, of sense-experience, are other sense-experiences.

Of course, not all causes are actually observed phenomena. In the analysis of cause, as in the analysis of substance, we must sometimes refer to possible sense-data which are not actual. But to say, for example, that a burst pipe was caused by the formation of a lump of ice which I have not seen, is not to desert the realm of sense-data; it is only to refer to sense-data which were not actually observed, but which might, in principle, have been observed; if I had been in a position to look at the interior of the pipe, I should have seen a lump of ice there.

Thus Hume and his followers do not deny that the relation of cause and effect is a real feature of the world; but they interpret it as a relation between sense-data, actual or possible. So the principle of causality does not carry us beyond the sphere of the observed and the observable, or compel us to admit the existence of "material substance" over and above systems of sense-data.

Thus, on this theory, the material world consists of sets of sense-experiences, together with the fact that an indefinitely large number of other similar sense-experiences might be had under certain specified conditions. Its "substances" are orderly groups of sense-data; and its causal relations are relations of regular sequence between sense-data of specified kinds. The main business of science is to discover causal laws, i.e., to reveal the patterns in that complex of experiences we call Nature. Science tells us what experiences to expect as the sequel to the experiences we are now having, and so renders our knowledge of the world systematic.

Phenomenalism Examined

We thus have, arising out of this discussion, two questions to answer. (1) Is phenomenalism true, that is, can we take the series of sense-data as complete in itself and self-explanatory, or must we postulate some other kind of reality to be its source? (2) Is idealism true, that is, if we assume some other kind of reality to exist, ought we to assume that it is mental?

61. The Relation between Sense-Data and Material Things

As to the first question, there is one point on which the argument seems to me quite conclusive. Our sense-data are not identical with physical objects, whether these are defined as the plain man, or as the physicist, or even as the phenomenalist define them. They are not identical with the physical objects of the plain man or of the physicist, for both these persons require a physical object to remain unchanged in circumstances in which the sense-data certainly change. Both hold that the table does not change its shape when I change the position from

which I look at it, whereas the sense-datum *is* changed. Unless these comparatively stable physical objects are assumed, the scientific explanation of sensation itself falls to pieces. As for the phenomenalist, even on his view no sense-datum is identical with a physical object, for the physical object is a system of possibilities, only a few of which can ever be actualised in any one experience. "This is a table" is never a mere record of what I am now observing, but involves the assertion that I and other people will be able to make further observations of a specific kind; and this possibility of further observations, which is part of what I mean when I say "This is a table," is not a matter of direct observation. So in any case our acquaintance with physical objects is not direct but mediate (to call it "inferential" would suggest a much more deliberate, self-consciously logical process than usually takes place). The properties of the sense-datum are not those of the material thing.

Yet—here is a paradox to be resolved—if I set out to describe a material thing, it seems that I invariably find myself describing sense-data. The table is square, brown, hard . . . all these, and all the other things I can say about the table, are expressed in terms of what is observed through the senses. Three alternatives are open to use here. (*a*) We can say that there is after all a real table which has some of the properties of our sense-data, though not all of them (Locke's theory). (*b*) We can say that the table consists of a set of actual and possible sense-data, which between them possess the properties which we commonly assign to "the table" (phenomenalism). (*c*) We can say that a statement like "The table is brown" is more complex than it looks. It must be understood to mean, not that anything in the world is both a table (a material object) and brown, but that there is some material object in existence such that, when it comes into a certain causal relation with a normal percipient under certain conditions, there will be a brown sense-datum in that percipient's experience.

Now for alternative (*a*) I cannot see any good reason. Once it is granted that we do not know the properties of the table directly, I cannot see any convincing reason for holding that it has any of the properties of the sense-datum. It cannot have them all; any arguments which can be brought against its having one of them are equally valid against the others; and we cannot produce any evidence of its having any of them except the observation of the sense-data themselves. We cannot, then, permit ourselves to assign to the material object any property of a sense-datum just because it belongs to that sense-datum. We are not entitled, from the square look of the sense-datum of the table, to infer that the material object is square. We are left with the other two alternatives.

62. The Paradoxes of Phenomenalism

If we take the phenomenalist alternative, let us not do so without being clearly and fully aware of what it involves. (1) It involves the denial that physical objects are permanent, or exist unperceived. It must be granted to the phenomenalists that when I say "There is a table upstairs," I am at least implying that if you were to go upstairs and look (given normal eyesight, normal lighting, etc.) you would have certain visual sense-data. But it seems quite clear to me that this is not the whole nor the essential part of what I am asserting. For when I say that the table is there, I am stating something about what exists or happens *in fact, now;* my statement is about the actual present, and not, as the phenomenalists make it, about the possible future. And if the phenomenalist account is to be accepted, we must say that this statement is a mistake. There is nothing at all in the attic now; there is no attic now at all; for there is nobody perceiving it.

(2) We must very seriously revise our opinions about the nature of causality. As a rule, we are in the habit of believing that a cause is something which actually exists or occurs, and that something which does not actually exist or occur can have no effects. This opinion must be given up if we accept the phenomenalist view. For on that view, to say that the bursting of pipes is caused by the formation of ice in them is to say that whenever one observes or could observe sense-data of the set constituting a burst pipe, one either has or could have previously observed sense-data of the set constituting a lump of ice inside that pipe. But quite clearly, in practically every instance of this rule, nobody does actually observe the ice; the sense-data of the ice are possible, not actual. That is to say, causality in such

a case is a relation between something and nothing, between an actually observed burst, and a hypothetical proposition to the effect that if something had happened which did not happen and in practice could not have happened, then something else would have happened which also did not happen. This interpretation flouts our usual assumption that what might have happened but did not happen can have no effects. The actual material agents of physics and common sense must be replaced by a set of hypothetical facts relating to unfulfilled conditions. If this is so, it is difficult to see why we should suppose that these hypothetical propositions are true. If I leave a fire in my room, I expect it to be warm on my return; but is this not because I believe that the fire is still now burning, a real present fire exercising an influence on a real present atmosphere? I cannot see what reason can be given for expecting the room to be warmed, independently of my reasons for supposing that the fire *is* burning *now* (and not that, *if* I went and looked, I should see flame). I can see reason for believing in regularities in nature holding between one event and another; but no reason at all for believing in regularities holding between one event which happened and another which might have happened but did not.

(3) A similar paradox arises with regard to other persons. According to the phenomenalist theory, all the statements I make about the consciousness of other people must be interpreted in terms of actual or possible observations of my own. A statement like "Jones is bored but he is not giving any sign of it" is a contradiction in terms, for on this theory the boredom *is* the sign. The only experiences I can intelligibly talk about or think about are my own, and whatever is not expressible in terms of actual or possible observations of mine is not intelligible to me. That is, there is no good argument for phenomenalism which is not an equally good argument for solipsism—the doctrine that the only experience in the world is my experience, and the only person existing in the universe is myself.

These paradoxical conclusions have been accepted by able philosophers, and one cannot therefore say that they are beyond belief. But they are markedly at variance with the ordinary assumptions, not only of common sense, but also of scientific investigation (for, whatever some scientists may manage to persuade themselves, they are not concerned only with the cataloguing and ordering of phenomena, but believe themselves to be dealing with permanent and independent objects). Hence we must demand very strong reasons indeed for accepting them.

III.5 A Defense of Representationalism

BERTRAND RUSSELL

Bertrand Russell (1872–1970) was a British philosopher and mathematician who taught at Cambridge University. Russell defends representational realism as the theory that is adequate to the three central factors of the perceptual process: physics, physiology, and psychology or privileged access. He elaborates on all three factors in the perceptual process, setting forth a causal theory of perception in which mental events are caused by processes in the outside world impinging on the perceiver's body and starting a chain reaction, ending with the percept in the brain. Percepts are the most indubitable things in the world, and from them we infer the reality of the external world.

When we consider perception—visual or auditory—of an external event, there are three different matters to be examined. There is first the process in the outside world, from the event to the percipient's body; there is next the process in his body, in so far as this can be known by an outside observer; lastly, there is the question, which must be faced sooner or later, whether the percipient can perceive something of the process in his body which no other observer could perceive. We will take these points in order.

If it is to be possible to "perceive" an event not in the percipient's body, there must be a physical process in the outer world such that, when a certain event occurs, it produces a stimulus of a certain kind at the surface of the percipient's body. Suppose, for example, that pictures of different animals are exhibited on a magic lantern to a class of children, and all the children are asked to say the name of each animal in turn. We may assume that the children are sufficiently familiar with animals to say "cat," "dog," "giraffe," "hippopotamus," etc., at the right moments. We must then suppose—taking the physical world for granted—that some process travels from each picture to the eyes of the various children, retaining throughout these journeys such peculiarities that, when the process reaches their eyes, it can in one case stimulate the word "cat" and in another the word "dog." All this the physical theory of light provides for. But there is one interesting point about language that should be noticed in this connection. If the usual physical theory of light is correct, the various children will receive stimuli which differ greatly according to their distance and direction from the picture, and according to the way the light falls. There are also differences in their reactions, for, though they all utter the

This selection consists of parts of Chapters XII and XIII of *The Outline of Philosophy* published by George Allen & Unwin in 1927.

word "cat," some say it loud, others soft, some in a soprano voice, some in a contralto. But the differences in their reactions are much less than the differences in the stimuli. . . .

The fact that it is possible for a number of people to perceive the same noise or the same colored pattern obviously depends upon the fact that a physical process can travel outward from a center and retain certain of its characteristics unchanged, or very little changed. The most notable of such characteristics is frequency in a wave-motion. That, no doubt, affords a biological reason for the fact that our most delicate senses, sight and hearing, are sensitive to frequencies, which determine color in what we see and pitch in what we hear. If there were not, in the physical world, processes spreading out from centers and retaining certain characters practically unchanged, it would be impossible for different percipients to perceive the same object from different points of view, and we should not have been able to discover that we all live in a common world.

We come now to the process in the percipient's body, in so far as this can be perceived by an outside observer. This raises no new philosophical problems, because we are still concerned, as before, with the perception of events outside the observer's body. The observer, now, is supposed to be a physiologist, observing, say, what goes on in the eye when light falls upon it. His means of knowing are, in principle, exactly the same as in the observation of dead matter. An event in an eye upon which light is falling causes light-waves to travel in a certain manner until they reach the eye of the physiologist. They there cause a process in the physiologist's eye and optic nerve and brain, which ends in what he calls "seeing what happens in the eye he is observing." But this event, which happens in the physiologist, is not what happened in the eye he was observing; it is only connected with this by a complicated causal chain. Thus our knowledge of physiology is no more direct or intimate than our knowledge of processes in dead matter; we do not know any more about our eyes than about the trees and fields and clouds that we see by means of them. The event which happens when a physiologist observes an eye is an event in him, not on the eye that he is observing.

. . . It may be said that we do not in fact proceed to *infer* the physical world from our perceptions, but that we begin at once with a rough-and-ready knowledge of the physical world, and only at a late stage of sophistication compel ourselves to regard our knowledge of the physical world as an inference. What is valid in this statement is the fact that our knowledge of the physical world is not at first inferential, but that is only because we take our percepts to *be* the physical world. Sophistication and philosophy come in at the stage at which we realize that the physical world cannot be identified with our percepts. When my boy was three years old, I showed him Jupiter, and told him that Jupiter was larger than earth. He insisted that I must be speaking of some other Jupiter, because, as he patiently explained, the one he was seeing was obviously quite small. After some efforts, I had to give it up and leave him unconvinced. In the case of the heavenly bodies, adults have got used to the idea that what is really there can only be *inferred* from what they see; but where rats in mazes are concerned, they still tend to think that they are seeing what is happening in the physical world. The difference, however, is only one of degree, and naive realism is as untenable in the one case as in the other. There are differences in the perceptions of two persons observing the same process; there are sometimes no discoverable differences between two perceptions of the same persons observing different processes, e.g., pure water and water full of bacilli. The subjectivity of our perceptions is thus of practical as well as theoretical importance.

. . . A lamp at the top of a tall building might produce the same visual stimulus as Jupiter, or at any rate one practically indistinguishable from that produced by Jupiter. A blow on the nose might make us "see stars." Theoretically, it should be possible to apply a stimulus direct to the optic nerve, which should give us a visual sensation. Thus when we think we see Jupiter, we may be mistaken. We are less likely to be mistaken if we say that the surface of the eye is being stimulated in a certain way, and still less likely to be mistaken if we say that the optic nerve is being stimulated in a certain way. We do not eliminate the risk of error completely unless we confine ourselves to saying that an event of a certain sort is happening in the brain; this statement may still be true if we see Jupiter in a dream.

But, I shall be asked, what do you know about

what is happening in the brain? Surely nothing. Not so, I reply. I know what is happening in the brain exactly what naive realism thinks it knows about what is happening in the outside world. But this needs explaining, and there are other matters that must be explained first.

When the light from a fixed star reaches me, I see the star if it is night and I am looking in the right direction. The light started years ago, probably many years ago, but my reaction is primarily something that is happening *now*. When my eyes are open, I see the star; when they are shut, I do not. Children discover at a fairly early age that they see nothing when their eyes are shut. They are aware of the difference between seeing and not seeing, and also of the difference between eyes open and eyes shut; gradually they discover that these two differences are correlated—I mean that they have expectations of which this is the intellectualist transcription. Again, children learn to name the colors, and to state correctly whether a thing is blue or red or yellow or whatnot. They ought not to be sure that light of the appropriate wave-length started from the object. The sun looks red in a London fog, grass looks blue through blue spectacles, everything looks yellow to a person suffering from jaundice. But suppose you ask: What color are you seeing? The person who answers, in these cases, red for the sun, blue for the grass, and yellow for the sickroom of the jaundiced patient, is answering quite truly. And in each of these cases he is stating something that he *knows*. What he knows in such cases is what I call a "percept." I shall contend later that, from the standpoint of physics, a percept is in the brain; for the present, I am only concerned to say that a percept is what is most indubitable in our knowledge of the world.

I do not in fact entertain any doubts that physics is true in its main lines. The interpretation of physical formulae is a matter as to which a considerable degree of uncertainty is possible; but we cannot well doubt that there is an interpretation which is true roughly and in the main. I shall come to the question of interpretation later; for the present, I shall assume that we may accept physics in its broad outlines, without troubling to consider how it is to be interpreted. On this basis, the above remarks on perception seem undeniable. We are often misled as to what is happening, either by peculiarities of the medium between the object and our bodies, or by

unusual states of our bodies, or by a temporary or permanent abnormality in the brain. But in all these cases *something* is really happening, as to which, if we turn our attention to it, we can obtain knowledge that is not misleading. At one time when, owing to illness, I had been taking a great deal of quinine, I became hypersensitive to noise, so that when the nurse rustled the newspaper I thought she was spilling a scuttle of coals on the floor. The interpretation was mistaken, but it was quite true that I heard a loud noise. It is commonplace that a man whose leg has been amputated can still feel pains in it; here again, he does really feel the pains, and is only mistaken in his belief that they come from his leg. A percept is an observable event, but its interpretation as knowledge of this or that event in the physical world is liable to be mistaken, for reasons which physics and physiology can make fairly clear.

Perhaps there is nothing so difficult for the imagination as to teach it to feel about space as modern science compels us to think. This is the task which must now be attempted. . . . The gist of the matter is that percepts . . . are in our heads; that percepts are what we can know with most certainty; and that percepts contain what naive realism thinks it knows about the world.

But when I say that my percepts are in my head, I am saying something which is ambiguous until the different kinds of space have been explained, for the statement is only true in connection with *physical* space. There is also a space in our percepts, and of this space the statement would not be true. When I say that there is space in our percepts, I mean nothing at all difficult to understand. I mean—to take the sense of sight, which is the most important in this connection—that in what we see at one time there is up and down, right and left, inside and outside. If we see, say, a circle on a blackboard, all these relations exist within what we see. The circle has a top half and a bottom half, a right-hand half and a left-hand half, an inside and an outside. Those relations alone are enough to make up a space of sorts. But the space of every-day life is filled out with what we derive from touch and movement—how a thing feels when we touch it, and what movements are necessary in order to grasp it. Other elements also come into the genesis of the space in which everybody believes who has not been troubled by philosophy; but it is unnecessary for our purposes to go into this question any more deeply. The point that concerns us is that a man's percepts are private to himself: what I see, no one else sees; what I hear, no one else hears; what I touch, no one else touches; and so on. True, others hear and see something very like what I hear and see, if they are suitably placed; but there are always differences. Sounds are less loud at a distance; objects change their visual appearance according to the laws of perspective. Therefore it is impossible for two persons at the same time to have exactly identical percepts. It follows that the space of percepts, like the percepts, must be private; there are as many perceptual spaces as there are percipients. My percept of a table is outside my percept of my head, in my perceptual space; but it does not follow that it is outside my head as a physical object in physical space. Physical space is neutral and public: in this space, all my percepts are in my head, even the most distant star *as I see it*. Physical and perceptual space have relations, but they are not identical, and failure to grasp the difference between them is a potent source of confusion.

To say that you see a star when you see the light that has come from it is no more correct than to say that you see New Zealand when you see a New Zealander in London. Your perception when (as we say) you see a star is causally connected, in the first instance, with what happens in the brain, the optic nerve, and the eye, then with a light-wave which, according to physics, can be traced back to the star as its source. Your sensations will be closely similar if the light comes from a lamp at the top of a mast. The physical space in which you believe the "real" star to be is an elaborate inference; what is given is the private space in which the speck of light you see is situated. It is still an open question whether the space of sight has depth, or is merely a surface, as Berkeley contended. This does not matter for our purposes. Even if we admit that sight alone shows a difference between an object a few inches from the eyes and an object several feet distant, yet you certainly cannot, by sight alone, see that a cloud is less distant than a fixed star, though you may *infer* that it is, because it can hide the star. The world of astronomy, from the point of view of sight, is a surface. If you were put in a dark room with little holes cut in the ceiling in the pattern of the stars letting light come through, there would be nothing in your immediate visual data to show that

you were not "seeing the stars." This illustrates what I mean by saying that what you see is *not* "out there" in the sense of physics.

We learn in infancy that we can sometimes touch objects we see, and sometimes not. When we cannot touch them at once, we can sometimes do so by walking to them. That is to say, we learn to correlate sensations of sight with sensations of touch, and sometimes with sensations of movement followed by sensations of touch. In this way we locate our sensations in a three-dimensional world. Those which involve sight alone we think of as "external," but there is no justification for this view. What you see when you see a star is just as internal as what you feel when you feel a headache. That is to say, it is internal from the standpoint of *physical* space. It is distant in your private space, because it is not associated with sensations of touch, and cannot be associated with them by means of any journey you can perform.

To make the matter definite, let us suppose that a physiologist is observing a living brain—no longer an impossible supposition, as it would have been formerly. It is natural to suppose that what the physiologist sees is in the brain he is observing. But if we are speaking of physical space, what the physiologist sees is in his own brain. It is in no sense in the brain that he is observing, though it is in the percept of that brain, which occupies part of the physiologist's perceptual space. Causal continuity makes the matter perfectly evident: light-waves travel from the brain that is being observed to the eye of the physiologist, at which they only arrive after an interval of time, which is finite though short. The physiologist sees what he is observing only after the light-waves have reached his eye; therefore the event which constitutes his seeing comes at the end of a series of events which travel from the observed brain into the brain of the physiologist. We cannot, without a preposterous kind of discontinuity, suppose that the physiologist's percept, which comes at the end of this series, is anywhere else but in the physiologist's head.

It is extraordinarily difficult to divest ourselves of the belief that the physical world is the world we perceive by sight and touch; even if, in our philosophic moments, we are aware that this is an error, we nevertheless fall into it again as soon as we are off our guard. The notion that what we see is "out there" in physical space is one which cannot survive while we are grasping the difference between what physics supposes to be really happening, and what our senses show us as happening; but it is sure to return and plague us when we begin to forget the argument. Only long reflection can make a radically new point of view familiar and easy.

Our illustrations hitherto have been taken from the sense of sight; let us now take one from the sense of touch. Suppose that, with your eyes shut, you let your finger-tip press against a hard table. What is really happening? The physicist says that your finger-tip and the table consist, roughly speaking, of vast numbers of electrons and protons; more correctly, each electron and proton is to be thought of as a collection of processes of radiation, but we can ignore this for our present purposes. Although you think you are touching the table, no electron or proton in your finger ever really touches an electron or proton in the table, because this would develop an infinite force. When you press, repulsions are set up between parts of your finger and parts of the table. If you try to press upon a liquid or a gas, there is room in it for the parts that are repelled to get away. But if you press a hard solid, the electrons and protons that try to get away, because electrical forces from your finger repel them, are unable to do so, because they are crowded close to others which elbow them back to more or less their original po-

sition, like people in a dense crowd. Therefore the more you press the more they repel your finger. The repulsion consists of electrical forces, which set up in the nerves a current whose nature is not very definitely known. This current runs into the brain, and there has effects which, so far as the physiologist is concerned, are almost wholly conjectural. But there is one effect which is not conjectural, and that is the sensation of touch. This effect, owing to physiological inference or perhaps to a reflex, is associated by us with the finger-tip. But the sensation is the same if, by artificial means, the parts of the nerve nearer the brain are suitably stimulated—e.g., if your hand has been amputated and the right nerves are skilfully manipulated. Thus our confidence that touch affords evidence of the existence of bodies at the place which we think is being touched is quite misplaced. As a rule we are right, but we can be wrong; there is nothing of the nature of an infallible revelation about the matter. And even in the most favorable case, the perception of touch is something very different from the mad dance of electrons and protons trying to jazz out of each other's way, which is what physics maintains is really taking place at your finger-tip.

III.6 *The Intentionality of Perception*

JOHN R. SEARLE

John R. Searle is Professor of Philosophy at the University of California at Berkeley. In this selection from his book *Intentionality,* Searle defends direct ("naive") realism. What standard forms of direct realism lacked, according to Searle, was a notion of intentionality that links the mind directly to the perceived object. Taking visual experience as the paradigm case, Searle argues that all visual experiences have intentionality in which the mind directs itself to the world, just as it does in believing. Visual experience gives us direct access to states of affairs that are perceived. From this point of view, all seing is *seeing that;* that is, is propositional (as we might say, "Seeing is believing").

Searle uses one technical phrase, "direction of fit," that needs explaining. This phrase has to do with where the responsibility lies in mind-to-world relationships. In believing, the direction of fit is from mind-to-world, since if the belief turns out to be false it is not the world's fault but our faulty judgment. In desiring, the direction of fit is just the reverse, from world-to-mind, for if the desire cannot realize itself in action, that is because of the way the world is, not the mind. Perception is like belief, the direction of fit being mind-to-world, in that the mind goes out to the world endeavoring to gain a true presentation of its object.

I

Traditionally the "problem of perception" has been the problem of how our internal perceptual experiences are related to the external world. I believe we ought to be very suspicious of this way of formulating the problem, since the spatial metaphor for internal and external, or inner and outer, resists any clear interpretation. If my body including all of its internal parts is part of the external world, as it surely is, then where is the internal world supposed to be? In what space is it internal relative to the external world? In what sense exactly are my perceptual experiences 'in here' and the world 'out there'? Nonetheless these metaphors are persistent and perhaps even inevitable, and for that reason

they reveal certain underlying assumptions we will need to explore.

My aim in this chapter is not, except incidentally, to discuss the traditional problem of perception, but rather to place an account of perceptual experiences within the context of the theory of Intentionality that was outlined in the last chapter. Like most philosophers who talk about perception, I will give examples mostly concerning vision, though the account, if correct, should be general in its application.

When I stand and look at a car, let us say a yellow station wagon, in broad daylight, at point blank range, with no visual impediments, I see the car. How does the seeing work? Well, there is a long story about how it works in physical optics and in neurophysiology, but that is not what I mean. I mean how does it work conceptually; what are the elements that go to make up the truth conditions of sentences of the form "x sees y" where x is a perceiver, human or animal, and y is, for example, a

Reprinted from *Intentionality* (Oxford, England: Oxford University Press, 1983) by permission.

material object? When I see a car, or anything else for that matter, I have a certain sort of visual experience. In the visual perception of the car I don't *see* the visual experience, I see the car; but in seeing the car I *have* a visual experience, and the visual experience is an experience *of* the car, in a sense of "of" we will need to explain. It is important to emphasize that though the visual perception always has as a component a visual experience, it is not the visual experience that is seen, in any literal sense of "see", for if I close my eyes the visual experience ceases, but the car, the thing I see, does not cease. Furthermore, in general it makes no sense to ascribe to the visual experience the properties of the thing that the visual experience is of, the thing that I see. For example, if the car is yellow and has a certain shape characteristic of a station wagon, then though my visual experience is of a yellow object in the shape of a station wagon it makes no sense to say my visual experience itself is yellow or that it is in the shape of a station wagon. Color and shape are properties accessible to vision, but though my visual experience is a component of any visual perception, the visual experience is not itself a visual object, it is not itself seen. If we try to deny this point we are placed in the absurd situation of identifying two yellow station wagon shaped things in the perceptual situation, the yellow station wagon and the visual experience.

In introducing the notion of a visual experience I am distinguishing between experience and perception in ways that will become clearer in the subsequent discussion. The notion of perception involves the notion of succeeding in a way that the notion of experience does not. Experience has to determine what counts as succeeding, but one can have an experience without succeeding, i.e., without perceiving.

But at this point the classical epistemologist will surely want to object as follows: Suppose there is no car there; suppose the whole thing is a hallucination; what do you see then? And the answer is that if there is no car there, then in the car line of business I see nothing. It may seem to me exactly as if I were seeing a car, but if there is no car I don't see anything. I may see background foliage or a garage or a street, but if I am having a hallucination of a car then I don't see a car or a visual experience or a sense datum or an impression or anything else, though I do indeed *have* the visual experience and the visual

experience may be indistinguishable from the visual experience I would have had if I had actually seen a car.

Several philosophers have denied the existence of visual experiences. I think these denials are based on a misunderstanding of the issues involved, and I will discuss this question later. But at this stage, taking for granted that there are visual experiences, I want to argue for a point that has often been ignored in discussions of the philosophy of perception, namely that visual (and other sorts of perceptual) experiences have Intentionality. The visual experience is as much *directed at* or *of* objects and states of affairs in the world as any of the paradigm Intentional states that we discussed in the last chapter, such as belief, fear, or desire. And the argument for this conclusion is simply that the visual experience has conditions of satisfaction in exactly the same sense that beliefs and desires have conditions of satisfaction. I can no more separate this visual experience from the fact that it is an experience *of* a yellow station wagon than I can separate this belief from the fact that it is a belief that it is raining; the "of" of "experience of" is in short the "of" of Intentionality.[1] In both the cases of belief and visual experience I might be wrong about what states of affairs actually exist in the world. Perhaps I am having a hallucination and perhaps it isn't actually raining. But notice that in each case what counts as a mistake, whether a hallucination or a false belief, is already determined by the Intentional state or event in question. In the case of the belief, even if I am in fact mistaken, I know what must be the case in order that I not be mistaken, and to say that is simply to say that the Intentional content of the belief determines its conditions of satisfaction; it determines under what conditions the belief is true or false. Now exactly analogously I want to say that in the case of the visual experience, even if I am having a hallucination, I know what must be the case in order that the experience not be a hallucination, and to say that is simply to say that the Intentional content of the visual experience determines its conditions of satisfaction; it determines what must be the case in order that the experience not be a hallucination in exactly the same sense that the content of the belief determines its conditions of satisfaction. Suppose we ask ourselves, "What makes the presence or absence of rain even relevant to my belief that it is raining, since after all, the belief is just a mental state?" Now, analogously, we can ask, "What makes the presence or absence of a yellow station wagon even relevant to my visual experience, since, after all, the visual experience is just a mental event?" And the answer in both cases is that the two forms of mental phenomena, belief and visual experience, are intrinsically Intentional. Internal to each phenomenon is an Intentional content that determines its conditions of satisfaction. The argument that visual experiences are intrinsically Intentional, in sum, is that they have conditions of satisfaction which are determined by the content of the experience in exactly the same sense that other Intentional states have conditions of satisfaction which are determined by the content of the states. Now by drawing an analogy between visual experience and belief I do not wish to suggest that they are alike in all respects. Later on I will mention several crucial differences.

If we apply the conceptual apparatus developed in the last chapter we can state several important similarities between the Intentionality of visual perception and, for example, belief.

1. The content of the visual experience, like the content of the belief, is always equivalent to a whole proposition. Visual experience is never simply *of* an object but rather it must always be *that* such and such is the case. Whenever, for example, my visual experience is of a station wagon it must also be an experience, part of whose content is, for example, that there is a station wagon in front of me. When I say that the content of the visual experience is equivalent to a whole proposition I do not mean that it is linguistic but rather that the content requires the existence of a whole state of affairs if it is to be satisfied. It does not just make reference to an object. The linguistic correlate of this fact is that the verbal specification of the conditions of satisfaction of the visual experience takes the form of the verbal expression of a whole proposition and not just a noun phrase, but this does not imply that the visual experience is itself verbal. From the point of view of Intentionality, all seeing is seeing *that:* whenever it is true to say that *x* sees *y* it must be true that *x* sees that such and such is the case. Thus, in our earlier example, the content of the visual perception is not made explicit in the form

I have a visual experience of (a yellow station wagon.)[2]

but a first step in making the content explicit would be, for example,

I have a visual experience (that there is a yellow station wagon there).

The fact that visual experiences have propositional Intentional contents is an immediate (and trivial) consequence of the fact that they have conditions of satisfaction, for conditions of satisfaction are always that such and such is the case.

There is an additional syntactical argument for the same conclusion. Just as verbs of desire take temporal modifiers that require us to postulate an entire proposition as the content of the desire, so the verb "see" takes spatial modifiers that under natural interpretations require us to postulate an entire proposition as the content of the visual experience. When I say, for example, "I see a station wagon *in front of me*", I don't normally just mean that I see a station wagon which *also happens to be* in front of me but rather *I see that* there is a station wagon in front of me. An additional clue that the "see that" form expresses the Intentional content of the visual experience is that this form is intensional-with-an-s with respect to the possibility of substitution whereas third person statements of the form "*x* sees *y*" are (in general) extensional. When in third-person reports of seeings we use the "sees that" form we are committed to reporting the content of the perception, how it seemed to the perceiver, in a way that we are not so committed by the use of a simple noun phrase as direct object of "see". Thus, for example,

Jones saw that the bank president was standing in front of the bank.

together with the identity statements

The bank president is the tallest man in town.

and

The bank is the lowest building in town.

do not entail

Jones saw that the tallest man in town was standing in front of the lowest building in town.

But

Jones saw the bank president.

together with the identity statement does entail

Jones saw the tallest man in town.

The most obvious explanation of this distinction is that the "see that" form reports the Intentional content of the perception. When in third-person reports we say that an agent saw that *p* we are committed to reporting the Intentional content of the visual perception, but the "see *x*" form reports only the Intentional object and does not commit the reporter to the content, to the aspect under which the Intentional object was perceived.

Exactly the same point—the fact that a whole propositional content is the Intentional content of visual perception—is also illustrated by the following distinction:

Jones saw a yellow station wagon, but did not know it was a yellow station wagon.

is perfectly consistent; but

Jones saw that there was a yellow station wagon in front of him but did not know that there was a yellow station wagon in front of him.

is odd and perhaps even self-contradictory. The "see *x*" form does not commit the reporter to reporting how it seemed to the agent, but the "see that" form does, and a report of how it seemed to the agent is, in general, a specification of the Intentional content.

2. Visual perception, like belief, and unlike desire and intention, always has the mine-to-world direction of fit. If the conditions of satisfaction are not in fact fulfilled, as in the case of hallucination, delusion, illusion, etc., it is the visual experience and not the world which is at fault. In such cases we say that "our senses deceive us" and though we do not describe our visual experiences as true or false (because these words are more appropriate when applied to certain sorts of representations, and visual experiences are more than just representations—a point I will come to in a minute) we do feel inclined to describe failure to achieve fit in terms such as "deceive", "mislead", "distort", "illusion", and "delusion"; and various philosophers have introduced the word "veridical" to describe success in achieving fit.

3. Visual experiences, like beliefs and desires, are characteristically identified and described in terms of their Intentional content. There is no way

to give a complete description of my belief without saying what it is a belief *that* and similarly there is no way to describe my visual experience without saying what it is an experience *of.* The characteristic philosophical mistake in the case of visual experience has been to suppose that the predicates which specify the conditions of satisfaction of the visual experience are literally true of the experience itself. But, to repeat a point mentioned earlier, it is a category mistake to suppose that when I see a yellow station wagon the visual experience itself is also yellow and in the shape of a station wagon. Just as when I believe that it is raining I do not literally have a wet belief, so when I see something yellow I do not literally have a yellow visual experience. One might as well say that my visual experience is six cylindered or that it gets twenty-two miles to the gallon as say that it is yellow or in the shape of a station wagon. One is tempted to the mistake of ascribing the latter (rather than the former) predicates to the visual experience, because the Intentional content specified by "yellow" and "in the shape of a station wagon" have greater immediacy to visual experiences than do the other predicates for reasons we will mention in the next section.

There are many things one can say about Intentional states and events which are not specifications of their Intentional contents and where the predicates are literally true of the states and events. One can say of a visual experience that it has a certain temporal duration or that it is pleasant or unpleasant, but these properties of the experience are not to be confused with its Intentional content, even though on occasion these same expressions might specify features of its Intentional content as well.

It is a bit difficult to know how one would argue for the existence of perceptual experiences to someone who denied their existence. It would be a bit like arguing for the existence of pains: if their existence is not obvious already, no philosophical argument could convince one. But I think by way of indirect argument one could show that the reasons philosophers have given for denying the existence of visual experiences can be answered. The first source of reluctance to speak of perceptual experiences is the fear that in recognizing such entities we are admitting sense data or some such, that is, we are admitting entities that somehow get between us and the real world. I have tried to show that a correct description of the Intentionality of visual experience does not have these consequences. The visual experience is not the object of visual perception, and the features which specify the Intentional content are not in general literally features of the experience. A second source of reluctance to concede that there are visual experiences (in, e.g., Merleau-Ponty[3]) is the fact that any attempt to focus our attention on the experience inevitably alters its character. As one proceeds through the active affairs of life one seldom concentrates one's attention on the flow of one's visual experiences, but rather on the things they are experiences of. This tempts us to think that, when we do focus our attention on the experience, we are bringing something into existence which was not there before, that visual experiences only exist as a result of adopting the 'analytic attitude' as when one does philosophy, neurophysiology, or impressionist painting. But this seems to me to misdescribe the situation. One does indeed alter the character (though not, in general, the content) of a visual experience by focussing one's attention on it, but it does not follow from this fact that the visual experience was not there all along. The fact that one shifts one's attention from the conditions of satisfaction of the visual experience to the experience itself does not show that the experience did not really exist prior to the shift in one's attention.

So far in this chapter I have argued for the following main 3 theses. There are perceptual experiences; they have Intentionality; their Intentional content is propositional in form; they have mind-to-world direction of fit, and the properties which are specified by their Intentional content are not in general literally properties of the perceptual experiences.

II

Having so far emphasized the analogies between visual experiences and other forms of Intentionality such as belief, I want in this section to point out several disanalogies. First of all, I said in Chapter I that we could justifiably call such Intentional states as beliefs and desires "representations" provided that we recognize that there is no special ontology carried by the notion of representation and that it is just a shorthand for a constellation of independently motivated notions such as conditions of satisfaction, Intentional content, direction of fit, etc. But when we come to visual and other sorts of perceptual experiences we need to say a great deal more in order to characterize their Intentionality. They do indeed have all of the features in terms of which we defined representations, but they have other intrinsic features as well which might make this term misleading. States such as beliefs and desires need not be conscious states. A person can have a belief or desire even when he is not thinking about it and he can be truly said to have such states even when asleep. But visual and other sorts of perceptual experiences are *conscious* mental *events*. The Intentionality of a representation is independent of whether it is realized in consciousness or not, but in general the Intentionality of a perceptual experience is realized in quite specific phenomenal properties of conscious mental events. For this reason the claim that there are visual experiences goes beyond the claim that the perception has Intentionality, since it is an ontological claim about how the Intentionality is realized; it is, in general, realized in conscious mental events.

Not only is the visual experience a conscious mental event but it is related to its conditions of satisfaction in ways which are quite different from beliefs and desires. If, for example, I see a yellow station wagon in front of me, the experience I have is directly of the object. It doesn't just "represent" the object, it provides direct access to it. The experience has a kind of directness, immediacy and involuntariness which is not shared by a belief I might have about the object in its absence. It seems therefore unnatural to describe visual experiences as representations, indeed if we talk that way it is almost bound to lead to the representative theory of perception. Rather, because of the special features of perceptual experiences I propose to call them "presentations". The visual experience I will say does not just represent the state of affairs perceived; rather, when satisfied, it gives us direct access to it, and in that sense it is a presentation of that state of affairs. Strictly speaking, since our account of representations was ontologically neutral, and since presentations have all the defining conditions we laid down for representations (they have Intentional content, conditions of satisfaction, direction of fit, Intentional objects, etc.), presentations are a special subclass of representations. However, as they are a special subclass, involving conscious mental events, I will sometimes oppose "presentation" to "representation" without thereby denying that presentations are representations, as one might oppose "human" to "animal" without thereby denying that humans are animals. Furthermore, when the context warrants it, I will use "Intentional state" broadly to cover both states and events.

The claim that the Intentionality of vision is characteristically realized in visual experiences which are conscious mental events is a genuine empirical ontological claim, and in that respect it contrasts with the claim that beliefs and desires contain propositions as Intentional contents. The claim that there are propositions in the sense previously explained is not an ontological empirical claim, though it is often mistakenly supposed to be so both by its defenders and by its attackers. That is, the claim that there are propositions or other representative contents adds nothing to the claim that there are certain common features of beliefs, hopes, fears, desires, questions, assertions, commands, promises, etc. But the claim that there are visual experiences really adds something to the claim that there are visual perceptions, since it tells us how the content of those perceptions is realized in our conscious life. Someone who claimed that there was a class of beings capable of perceiving optically, that is, beings capable of visual perception but who did not have visual experiences, would be making a genuine empirical claim. But if someone claimed that there was a class of beings who literally had hopes, fears, and beliefs, and who made statements, assertions, and commands, all with their various logical features, but who did not have propositional contents, they such a person doesn't know what he's talking about or else is simply refusing to adopt a notation, for the claim that there are propositional contents isn't in any way an additional empirical claim. It is rather the adoption of a certain notational device for representing common logical features of hopes, fears, beliefs, statements, etc.

Some recent empirical work bears out this crucial distinction between the ontological status of the visual experience as a conscious mental event and that of the propositional content. Weiskrantz, Warrington and their colleagues[4] have studied how certain sorts of brain lesions produce what they call "blind sight". The patient can give correct answers to questions about visual events and objects that he is presented with, but he claims to have no visual awareness of these objects and events. Now, from our point of view the interest of such cases derives from the fact that the optical stimuli the patient is subjected to apparently produce a form of Intentionality. Otherwise, the patient would not be able to report the visual events in question. But the Intentional content produced by their optical stimulation is not realized in the way that our presentational contents are realized. For us to see an object, we have to have visual experiences of a certain sort. But, assuming Weiskrantz's account is correct, the patient can in some sense "see" an object even though he does not have the relevant visual experiences. He simply reports a "feeling" that something is there, or makes a "guess" that it is there. Those who doubt the existence of visual experiences, by the way, might want to ask themselves what it is that we have that such patients seem to lack.

Another distinction between the Intentionality of perception and the Intentionality of belief is that it is part of the conditions of satisfaction (in the sense of requirement) of the visual experience that the visual experience must itself be caused by the rest of the conditions of satisfaction (in the sense of things required) of that visual experience. Thus, for example, if I see the yellow station wagon, I have a certain visual experience. But the Intentional content of the visual experience, which requires that there be a yellow station wagon in front of me in order that it be satisfied, also requires that the fact that there is a yellow station wagon in front of me must be the cause of that very visual experience. Thus, the Intentional content of the visual experience requires as part of the conditions of satisfaction that the visual experience be caused by the rest of its conditions of satisfaction, that is, by the state of affairs perceived. The content of the visual experience is therefore self-referential in a sense that I hope to be able to make fairly precise. The Intentional content of the visual experience is entirely specified by stating the conditions of satisfaction of the visual experience, but that statement makes essential reference to the visual experience itself in the conditions of satisfaction. For what the Intentional content requires is not simply that there be a state of affairs in the world, but rather that the state of affairs in the world must cause the very visual experience which is the embodiment or realization of the Intentional content. And the argument for this goes beyond the familiar proof of the "causal theory of perception";[5] the usual argument is that unless the presence and features of the object cause the agent's experience, he does not see the object. But it is essential to my account to show how these facts enter into the Intentional content. The Intentional content of the visual experience therefore has to be made explicit in the following form:

> I have a visual experience (that there is a yellow station wagon there and that there is a yellow station wagon there is causing this visual experience).

This looks puzzling, but I think it is on the right track. The Intentional content of the visual experience determines under what conditions it is satisfied or not satisfied, what must be the case in order that it be, as they say, "veridical". Well, what must be the case in the station wagon scene in order that the experience be a veridical one? At least this much: the world must be as it visually seems to me that it is, and furthermore its being that way must be what causes me to have the visual experience which constitutes its seeming to be that way. And it is this combination that I am trying to capture in the representation of the Intentional content.

The verbal representation that I have just given of the visual Intentional content is not in any sense a *translation*. It is rather a verbal specification of what the Intentional content requires if it is to be satisfied. The sense then in which the visual Intentional content is self-referential is not that it contains a verbal or other representation of itself: it certainly performs no speech act of reference to itself! Rather, the sense in which the visual experience is self-referential is simply that it figures in its own conditions of satisfaction. The visual experience itself does not *say* this but *shows* it; in my verbal representation of the Intentional content of the visual experience I have said it. Furthermore, when I say that the visual experience is causally self-referential I do not mean that the causal relation is seen, much less that the visual experience is seen. Rather, what is seen are objects and states of affairs, and part of the conditions of satisfaction of the visual experience of seeing them is that the experience itself must be caused by what is seen.

On this account perception is an Intentional and causal transaction between mind and the world. The direction of fit is mind-to-world, the direction

of causation is world-to-mind; and they are not independent, for fit is achieved only if the fit is caused by the other term of the relation of fitting, namely the state of affairs perceived. We can say either that it is part of the content of the visual experience that if it is to be satisfied it must be caused by its Intentional object; or, more cumbersomely but more accurately, it is part of the content of the visual experience, that if it is to be satisfied it must be caused by the state of affairs that its Intentional object exists and has those features that are presented in the visual experience. And it is in this sense that the Intentional content of the perceptual experience is causally self-referential.

The introduction of the notion of causal self-referentiality of certain sorts of Intentionality—a self-referentiality which is shown but not said—is a crucial addition to the conceptual apparatus of this book. The simple, and I think obvious, observation that perceptual experiences are causally self-referential is the first step in a series of arguments that we will use in attacking several vexing philosophical problems—about the nature of human action, the explanation of behavior, the nature of causation, and the analysis of indexical expressions, to mention just a few. One immediate consequence can be mentioned now: it is quite easy to see how type-identical visual experiences can have different conditions of satisfaction and therefore different Intentional contents. Two 'phenomenologically' identical experiences can have different contents because each experience is self-referential. Thus, for example, suppose two identical twins have type-identical visual experiences while looking at two different but type-identical station wagons at the same time in type-identical lighting conditions and surrounding contexts. Still, the conditions of satisfaction can be different. Twin number one requires a station wagon causing his visual experience and twin number two requires a station wagon causing his numerically different visual experience. Same phenomenology; different contents and therefore different conditions of satisfaction.

Though I think the characterization of causal self-referentiality is correct it does leave us with some difficult questions we are not yet in a position to answer. What is the sense of "cause" in the above formulations, and doesn't this account have the skeptical consequence that we can never be sure our visual experiences are satisfied since there is no neutral position from which we can observe the causal relation to see that the experience really is satisfied? All we can ever have is more of the same sorts of experiences. I will discuss both of these questions later. . . .

Yet another distinction between the form of Intentionality exemplified by visual perception and other forms of Intentionality such as beliefs and desires has to do with the character of the aspect or the point of view under which an object is seen or otherwise perceived. When I have a representation of an Intentional object in a belief or desire it will always be represented under some aspect or other, but in belief and desire aspect is not constrained in the way that the aspect of visual perception is fixed by the sheer physical features of the situation. For example, I can represent a certain famous planet under its "Morning Star" aspects, or its "Evening Star" aspects. But because the Intentionality of visual perception is realized in a quite specific way the aspect under which we perceive the objects of our perceptions plays a different sort of role than it does in other Intentional states. In visual perception the aspect under which an object is perceived is fixed by the point of view, and the other physical features of the perceptual situation, in which the object is perceived. For example, given a certain position, I can't help but see the left side of the station wagon. To see the car under some other aspect I would have to alter the physical features of the perceptual situation by, for example, walking around the car or moving it.

Furthermore, in the non-perceptual cases, though the Intentional object is always represented by way of some aspect or other, it is nonetheless the object itself that is represented and not just an aspect. That, incidentally, is why there is nothing ontologically fishy about Intentional objects on my account. The aspect under which an object is represented is not something that gets between us and the object. But in at least some cases of visual perception the situation does not seem to be quite so simple. Consider, for example, Wittgenstein's familiar duck/rabbit example.[6]

In this case we are inclined to say that in one sense the Intentional object is the same both in our perception of the duck and in our perception of the rabbit. That is, though we have two visual experiences with two different presentational contents, there is only one picture on the page before us. But in another sense we want to say that the Intentional object of the visual experience is different in the two cases. What is seen is in one case a picture duck and in the other case a picture rabbit. Now Wittgenstein copes, or rather fails to cope, with this difficulty simply by saying that these are different uses of the verb "see". But that doesn't seem to be very much help in clarifying the relation of aspects to Intentional objects. I think the solution to our puzzle is to point out that just as we can literally see objects, even though whenever we see an object we always see it under an aspect, so we can literally see aspects of objects. I literally see the duck aspect and I literally see the rabbit aspect of the drawing before me. Now on my account that will commit us to the view that we see those aspects under aspects. But why should that bother us? Actually, if we are willing to accept this view, then the parallel with other Intentional states is preserved. As we have already seen when John loves Sally or believes something about Bill, it is always under some aspect that John loves Sally and under some aspect that he believes something about Bill, even though what John's love is directed at or what his belief is about is not an aspect. But furthermore there is nothing to prevent him loving an aspect of Sally or believing something about an aspect of Bill. That is, there is nothing to prevent an aspect from being an Intentional object of a belief or other psychological attitude such as love. And similarly there is nothing to prevent an aspect from being the Intentional object of visual perceptions. As soon as we recognize that an aspect can be an Intentional object even though all Intentionality including the Intentionality of perception is under an aspect, we can see how the aspect is essential to the Intentional phenomena and yet is not itself the Intentional object.

One way to summarize the foregoing account of the Intentionality of perception is to present a table comparing the formal features of the various kinds of Intentionality discussed. To belief, desire, and visual perception I will add memory of events in one's past, since it shares some features with visual perception (like seeing, it is causally self-referential) and some with belief (like belief, it is a representation rather than a presentation). The verbs "see" and "remember", unlike the verbs "desire" and "believe", imply not only the presence of an Intentional content but also that the content is satisfied. If I really see some state of affairs then there must be more than my visual experience; the state of affairs which is the condition of satisfaction of the visual experience must exist and must cause the visual experience. And if I really remember some event then the event must have occurred and its occurrence must cause my memory of it.

A comparison of some of the formal features of the Intentionality of seeing, believing, desiring, and remembering

	Seeing	Believing	Desiring	Remembering
Nature of the Intentional component	Visual experience	Belief	Desire	Memory
Presentation or representation	Presentation	Representation	Representation	Representation
Causally self-referential	Yes	No	No	Yes
Direction of fit	Mind-to-world	Mind-to-world	World-to-mind	Mind-to-world
Direction of causation as determined by Intentional content	World-to-mind	None	None	World-to-mind

III

In my effort to give an account of the Intentionality of visual perception I am anxious not to make it look much simpler than it really is. In this section I want to call attention to some of the complexities, though the cases I mention here are only a few among many puzzles in the philosophy of perception.

We are tempted to think, *á la* Hume, that perceptions come to us pure and unsullied by language, and that we then attach labels by way of ostensive definitions to the results of our perceptual encounters. But that picture is false in a number of ways. First, there is the familiar point that perception is a function of expectation, and the expectations of human beings at least are normally realized linguistically. So language itself affects the perceptual encounter. Over a quarter of a century ago Postman and Bruner[7] did some experiments which showed that the recognition threshold for features varied greatly depending on whether or not the particular feature was expected in that situation. If the subject expects that the next color he is going to see is red, he will recognize it much more quickly than if he has no such expectation.

But secondly and more importantly from our point of view, many of our visual experiences aren't even possible without the mastery of certain Background skills and prominent among them are linguistic skills. Consider the following figure:

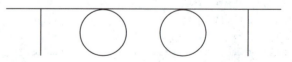

This can be seen as the word "TOOT", as a table with two large balloons underneath, as the numberal I00I with a line over the top, as a bridge with two pipelines crossing underneath, as the eyes of a man wearing a hat with a string hanging down each side, and so on. In each case, we have a different experience even though the purely physical visual stimuli, the lines on the paper in front of us and the light reflected from them, are constant. But these experiences and the differences between them are dependent on our having mastered a series of linguistically impregnated cultural skills. It is not the failure, for example, of my dog's optical apparatus that prevents him from seeing this figure as the word "TOOT". In such a case one wants to say that a certain conceptual mastery is a precondition of having visual experience; and such cases suggest that the Intentionality of visual perception is tied up in all sorts of complicated ways with other forms of Intentionality such as belief and expectation, and also with our systems of representation, most notably language. Both the Network of Intentional states and the Background of non-representational mental capacities affect perception.

But if the Network and the Background affect perception, how can the conditions of satisfaction be determined by the visual experience? There are at least three sorts of cases we will need to discuss. First, there are cases where the Network of beliefs and the Background actually affect the content of the visual experience. Consider, for example, the difference between looking at the front of a house where one takes it to be the front of a whole house and looking at the front of a house where one takes it to be a mere façade, e.g., as part of a movie set. If one believes one is seeing a whole house, the front of the house actually looks different from the way it looks if one believes one is seeing a false façade of a house, even though the optical stimuli may be identical in the two cases. And this difference in the actual character of the visual experiences is reflected in the differences between the two sets of conditions of satisfaction. It is part of the content of my visual experience when I look at a whole house that I *expect* the rest of the house to be there if, for example, I enter the house or go around to the back. In these sorts of cases the character of the visual experience and its conditions of satisfaction will be affected by the content of the beliefs that one has about the perceptual situation. I am not going beyond the content of my visual experience when I say, "I see a house" instead of "I see the façade of a house", for, though the optical stimuli may be the same, the conditions of satisfaction in the former case are that there should be a whole house there. I do not *infer* from the façade of the house to the presence of the house; I simply see a house.

A second sort of case arises where the content of the beliefs is actually inconsistent with the content of the visual experience. A good example is the appearance of the moon on the horizon. When one sees the moon on the horizon it looks a great deal bigger than it does when it is directly overhead. Yet though the visual experiences are different in the two cases there is no change in the content of one's beliefs. I do not believe the moon has grown on the horizon or shrunk overhead. Now in our first sort of example we saw there was no way we could carve off the content of the visual experience from the beliefs one has about it. The house actually looks different depending on what sort of beliefs we have about it. But in the second sort of case we want to say that the visual experience of the moon's size definitely changes with the moon's position and yet our beliefs remain constant. And what shall we say about the conditions of satisfaction of the visual experiences? Because of the holistic character of the Network of our Intentional states, we are inclined to say that the conditions of satisfaction of the visual experiences remain the same. Since we are not really at all inclined to believe that the moon has changed in size, we suppose that the two visual experiences have the same conditions of satisfaction. But I think in fact that is not the right way to describe the situation. Rather, it seems to me that where the Intentional content of our visual experience is in conflict with our beliefs, and where the beliefs override the visual experience, we nonetheless have the original Intentional content of the visual experience. The visual experiences do indeed have as part of their respective Intentional contents that the moon is smaller overhead than it is on the horizon, and the argument for this is that if we imagine that the visual experiences remained as they are now, but that the beliefs were absent, that we simply had no relevant beliefs, then we really would be inclined to believe that the moon had changed in size. It is only because we believe independently that the moon remains constant in size that we allow the Intentionality of belief to override the Intentionality of our visual experience. In these cases we believe that our eyes deceive us. A similar example is the Müller-Lyer lines:

where the Intentional content of the visual experience is in conflict with and is overridden by the Intentional content of our beliefs. These cases are in sharp contrast to the phenomenon of perceived color constancy under different lighting conditions. In the color constancy case the color looks the same in both light and shadow, even though the light reflected is quite different; and thus the content of the belief and the content of the perceptual experience are consistent, unlike the previous cases.

A third sort of case is where the visual experiences differ but the conditions of satisfaction are the same. Our "TOOT" example is of this type. Another example of this would be seeing a triangle first with one point as apex and then with another point as apex. In these last two examples we are not in the least inclined to think that anything is different in the real world corresponding to the differences in the experiences.

We have then a variety of ways in which the Network and Background of Intentionality are related to the character of the visual experience, and the character of the visual experience is related to its conditions of satisfaction.

1. The house example: Different beliefs cause different visual experiences with different conditions of satisfaction, even given the same optical stimuli.

2. The moon example: The same beliefs coexist with different visual experiences with different conditions of satisfaction even though the content of the experiences is inconsistent with the content of the beliefs and is overridden by the beliefs.

3. The triangle and "TOOT" examples: The same beliefs plus different visual experiences yield the same conditions of satisfaction of the visual experiences.

One feels there ought to be a systematic theoretical account of the relations between these various parameters, but I do not know what it is.

IV

The account of visual perception that I have been arguing for so far is, I guess, a version of 'naive' (direct, common sense) realism and it can be represented diagrammatically as shown in Figure 1. This visual perception involves at least three elements: the perceiver, the visual experience, and the object (more strictly: the state of affairs) perceived. The fact that an arrow represents the visual perception is meant to indicate that the visual experience has Intentional content, it is directed at the Intentional object, whose existence is part of its conditions of satisfaction (it is not of course meant to suggest that the visual experience exists in the physical space between the perceiver and the object).

In the case of visual hallucination the perceiver has the same visual experience but no Intentional object is present. This case can be represented diagrammatically as in Figure 2.

It is not my aim in this chapter to enter into the traditional disputes concerning the philosophy of perception; however, the thesis I am arguing for concerning the Intentionality of visual experience will perhaps be clearer if we digress a moment to contrast this naive realist view with its great historical rivals, the representative theory and phenomenalism. Both of these theories differ from naive realism in that they both treat the visual experience as itself the object of visual perception and thus they strip it of its Intentionality. According to them what is seen is always, strictly speaking, a visual experience (in various terminologies the visual experience has been called a "sensum" or a "sense datum", or an "impression"). They are thus confronted with a question that does not arise for the naive realist: What is the relationship between the sense data which we do see and the material object which apparently we do not see? This question does not arise for the naive realist because on his account

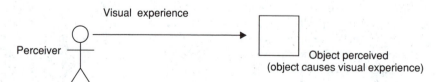

Visual experience

Perceiver

Object perceived
(object causes visual experience)

Figure 1

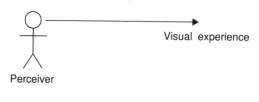

Figure 2

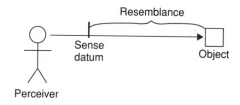

Figure 3 The representative theory

we do not see sense data at all. We see material objects and other objects and states of affairs in the world, at least much of the time; and in the hallucination cases we don't see anything, though we do indeed *have* visual experiences in both cases. Both the phenomenalists and the representative theorists try to drive the line that represents the visual experience in Figure 1 out of the horizontal axis and into the vertical so that the vehicle of the Intentional *content* of our visual perception, the visual experience, becomes itself the *object* of visual perception. The numerous arguments that have been presented for this move, notably the arguments from illusion and the argument from science, have been in my view effectively refuted by other philosophers,[8] and I will not rehearse the arguments here. The point for the purposes of the present argument is simply that once one has driven the visual experience line out of the horizontal axis and into the vertical axis in such a way that the visual experience becomes the object of perception one is then confronted with a choice as to how one is to describe the relationship between the sense datum that, according to this theory, one does perceive and the material object that one apparently does not perceive. The two favorite solutions to the problem are that the visual experience or sense datum is in some sense a copy or representation of the material object (this is the representative theory) or that the object somehow just is a collection of sense data (and this, in its various versions, is phenomenalism), each of these theories can be represented diagrammatically as in figures 3 and 4.

Even if we ignore the various objections that have been made to the view that all one ever perceives are sense data, it still seems to me that there are other decisive objections against each of these theories. The main difficulty with a representative theory of perception is that the notion of resem-

blance between the things we perceive, the sense data, and the thing that the sense data represent, the material object, must be unintelligible since the object term is by definition inaccessible to the senses. It is absolutely invisible and otherwise imperceptible. As Berkeley pointed out, it makes no sense to say that the shape and color we see resemble the shape and color of an object which is absolutely invisible or otherwise inaccessible to any of our senses. Furthermore, on this account no literal sense can even be attached to the claim that objects have such sensible qualities as shape, size, color, weight, or the other sensorily accessible qualities, whether 'primary' or 'secondary'. In short, the representative theory is unable to make sense of the notion of resemblance, and therefore it cannot make any sense of the notion of representation, since the form of representation in question requires resemblance.

The decisive objection to the phenomenalist view is simply that it reduces to solipsism. The publicly accessible material objects on the phenomenalist view become sense data, but sense data are always private. Thus, the objects I see are in an important sense my objects since they reduce to sense data and the only sense data to which I have access are my sense data. The world that I perceive is not accessible to anyone else since it consists entirely in my private sense data, and indeed the hypothesis that other people might see the same ob-

Figure 4 Phenomenalism

jects that I see becomes unintelligible, since all I see are my sense data and all they could see would be their sense data. But furthermore the hypothesis that other people even exist and perceive sense data in the sense in which I exist and perceive sense data becomes at best unknowable and at worst unintelligible since my perceptions of other people are always my perceptions of my sense data, that is my perceptions of features of myself.

Once one treats the content of perception as the object of perception, something like the above theories seems inevitable. And indeed the mistake of the sense data theorists seems to me analogous to the mistake of treating the propositional content of the belief as the object of the belief. The belief is no more about or directed at its propositional content than the visual perception is about or directed at its experiential component. However, in rejecting the sense datum hypothesis, it seems to me many 'naive realists' have failed to recognize the role of experiences and the Intentionality of experiences in the perceptual situation. In rejecting the idea that what we see are visual experiences in favor of the idea that what we see are characteristically, for example, material objects in our vicinity, many philosophers, e.g., Austin,[9] have rejected the idea that we have visual experiences at all. I want to argue that the traditional sense data theorists were correct in recognizing that we have experiences, visual and otherwise, but they mislocated the Intentionality of perception in supposing that experiences were the objects of perception, and the naive realists were correct in recognizing that material objects and events are characteristically the objects of perception, but many of them failed to realize that the material object can only be the object of visual perception because the perception has an Intentional content, and the vehicle of the Intentional content is a visual experience.

V

We are now in a poistion to return to our original question: what are the truth conditions of a sentence of the form

X sees a yellow station wagon.

But from the point of view of a theory of Intentionality this question is ill-formed because the Intentional content of vision is propositional: the correct form is, for example,

> X sees that there is a yellow station wagon in front of X.

The truth conditions are:

1. X has visual experience which has
   a. certain conditions of satisfaction
   b. certain phenomenal properties.

2. The conditions of satisfaction are: that there is a yellow station wagon in front of X and the fact that there is a yellow station wagon in front of X is causing the visual experience.

3. The phenomenal properties are such as to determine that the conditions of satisfaction are as described in 2. That is, those conditions of satisfaction are determined by the experience.

4. The form of the causal relation in the conditions of satisfaction is continuous and regular Intentional causation. (This condition is required to block certain sorts of counterexamples involving "deviant causal chains", where the conditions of satisfaction do cause the visual experience but all the same the experience is not satisfied. We will examine these cases and explore the nature of Intentional causation [later.])

5. The conditions of satisfaction are in fact satisfied. That is, there actually is a station wagon causing (in the manner described in 4) the visual experience (described in 3) which has the Intentional content (described in 2).

On this account there are, besides the perceiver, two components to visual perception, the visual experience and the scene perceived, and the relation between them is Intentional and causal.

Notes

[1] As we noted in Chapter 1 ordinary language is misleading in this regard, for we speak of an experience of pain and an experience of redness, but in the former case the experience just is the pain and the "of" is not the "of" of Intentionality, and in the latter case the experience is not itself red, and the "of" is Intentional.

[2] Notice once again that when we are just specifying the Intentional content we cannot use expresions like "see" or "perceive" since they imply success, they imply that the conditions of satisfaction are in fact satisfied. To say I have a visual experience that there is a yellow station wagon there is just to specify the Intentional content. To say I see or perceive that there is a yellow station wagon there implies that the content is satisfied.

[3] M. Merleau-Ponty, *The Phenomenology of Perception* (London: Routledge & Kegan Paul), 1962.

[4] L. Weiskrantz et al., 'Visual capacity in the hemianopic field following a restricted occipital ablation', *Brain,* vol. 97 (1974), pp. 709–28.

[5] See H. P. Grice, 'The causal theory of perception',

Proceedings of the Aristotelian Society, suppl. vol. 35 (1961), pp. 121–52.

[6] L. Wittgenstein, *Philosophical Investigations* (Oxford: Basil Blackwell, 1953), Part II, section 10.

[7] L. Postman, J. Bruner, and R. Walk, 'The perception of error', *British Journal of Psychology,* vol. 42 (1951), pp. 1–10.

[8] See, e.g., J. L. Austin, *Sense and Sensibilia* (Oxford: Oxford University Press, 1962), for a discussion of the argument from illusion.

[9] *Op. cit.*

III.7 *Why Nothing Has Color: Color Skepticism*

CHARLES LANDESMAN

Charles Landesman is Professor at Hunter College and the City University of New York Graduate Center. In this essay Landesman argues, from the perspective of representationalism, that the commonsense view that we see colors is false. Appearances to the contrary, nothing has color. "Roses are not really red; lemons not really yellow; the sky is not really blue." Landesman offers two related arguments to support his position: (1) the argument from biological purpose and (2) the argument from color science. Landesman goes on to criticize Locke's dispositional account of colors and meet objections to his position.

I

One of the great topics in the history of Western philosophy has been the distinction between appearance and reality. There is both a metaphysical and an epistemological question here. The metaphysical question is "How different is the world as it is in itself from the world as it appears to our senses and as we represent it in thought?" The epis-

temological question is "Can we gain knowledge of the world as it is in itself on the basis of the way it appears to our senses?" The two questions are linked because the greater the metaphysical difference between appearance and reality, the less reliable are the appearances in providing access to reality.

Some philosophers have accepted the commonsense view that with just a few exceptions the world as it appears faithfully reflects the world as it really is and that our senses are reliable guides to reality. They are not perfect guides; we all admit that our senses can sometimes deceive us. Remem-

This essay was commissioned for this book and appears here for the first time.

ber, Macbeth thought he saw a bloody dagger that wasn't there. But the common sense of the matter is that illusions and hallucinations occur infrequently and that in the normal case our senses provide us with a direct and accurate account of the physical world.

However, major traditions within Western philosophy reject the epistemological optimism of common sense. According to the Platonic tradition, the senses give us only a pale imitation of a reality that is grasped most directly through reason. According to the monistic systems of Parmenides and Spinoza, our commonsense view that the world consists of a plurality of things or substances is an illusion. Skeptics of many varieties claim we cannot obtain knowledge of the world as it is in itself. And scientific realism says that the physical sciences are the only reliable guides to the nature of the material world and that theories of these sciences imply that the information provided by our senses is frequently misleading.

One basic idea in our commonsense view of the world is that, as our sense of sight reveals, the material things we can perceive are colored. Roses are red, lemons are yellow, the sky is blue. Colors are as much a part of reality as are the objects that exemplify them. This idea I label *color realism*. On the contrary, *color skepticism* says that despite appearances, nothing has any color. Roses are not really red, lemons are not really yellow, the sky is not really blue. Color skepticism does not, of course, deny that things *appear* to have color. But the color skeptic asserts that colors belong to the appearances only and that no thing or substance or event or region of space actually exemplifies color. For the color skeptic, every statement we make that this or that thing has color is, literally, false. The color skeptic is not a radical skeptic who claims that nothing is as it appears to be. Rather, color skepticism is a more modest sort of departure from common sense and says merely that appearance deviates from reality with respect to color and that the appearances are misleading with respect to color.

Two arguments have convinced me to accept color skepticism. The first starts out from the fact that the senses of the various species of animals are biological systems that function to enable the animals that possess them to do what is necessary to ensure their survival and well-being. The biological purpose of a sensory system is not to attain the absolute truth about reality but to provide useful indicators to an organism to enable it to find food and to avoid enemies and other perils. It is thus very likely that different species of animals perceive the world quite differently, these differences being determined by the different indicators that are useful to them in their particular habitats. We see the world in color and in a particular array of colors. Other species may see quite different colors or may perceive the world in just black, white, and gray.

Consider an animal species whose members see things in shades of black, white, and gray. Are their visual systems more reliable with respect to the true colors of objects than ours? Are ours more reliable than theirs? From a biological point of view, these questions seem pointless. There is no question here of who is right or wrong. Their visual system supplies indicators useful to them; ours supplies indicators useful to us. The differences in color perception are due to the different ways that visual systems respond to the light that falls on them. The systems of some species may be more or less sensitive to different ranges of radiant energy, and they may respond in different ways to the same energy. From a biological point of view, colors are different "subjective" responses to the ambient light. Instead of speaking of the colors of objects, we should speak rather of the color sensations produced by the impact of light energy on the visual system. It so happens that the nervous systems of animals capable of color sight tend to "project" the color sensations onto the objects that cause them, so that these animals are made to experience the illusion that colors are objective features of physical things. But we should not take that illusion for reality; we should use our knowledge of the biological functions of the senses to correct the error induced by projection.

The second argument that I find convincing is an extension of the biological viewpoint of the first argument. Consider the sequence of events S that precede and make possible your seeing a colored object. Suppose you are looking at a tomato in a lit room. We are told by the physicist that, as a result of its atomic and molecular microstructure, the tomato absorbs some of the light that falls on it and reflects light of other wavelengths. Some of the reflected light enters the eye and causes changes in the retina, which then sends neural signals through the optic nerve to the brain, as a result of which you see the tomato and its bright red color. From the seventeenth century to the present day, scientists have been attempting to unravel the details of the process whose outline I have just given. The interdisciplinary science that attempts to understand color in all its aspects—physical, biological, and psychological—is called *color science*.

If we consider this process S by means of which we are able to see colored objects, we shall find something rather surprising. Color itself plays no role in causing us to see color. What is there about the tomato that enables us to see its red color? According to color science, it is the tomato's capacity to absorb light of certain wavelengths and reflect light of other wavelengths. What happens in the eye? A pattern of light falls on the retina and causes a complex set of chemical changes in the back of the eye. What happens in the nervous system? Various neural signals travel from the eye to certain parts of the brain. What happens then? The tomato appears to us via the sensation of red caused by the brain events. At no stage of this process does the fact that the tomato is *red* enter into the causal chain. The color drops out of the picture.

What shall we make of this? In the first place, your seeing the red tomato just consists of your being caused to have a complex of sensations by the impact of the reflected light on your visual system. In the second place, since color plays no role whatsoever in the causation of that event that consists of your seeing the tomato, there is no reason whatsoever to suppose that the tomato is red. The sensation of red that is the result of this process does all the work that common sense thinks color does. The tomato appears red; that is the subjective side of the process. On the objective side, we have the tomato with its atomic microstates, the light it reflects, and the changes in the visual system and nervous system produced by the light. We can provide a complete explanation of visual perception without supposing that colors inhere in objects or, for that matter, in anything. We are thus led to the same conclusion as that of the first argument: the reality of color consists of the impact of radiant energy on our nervous systems that produces via projection the appearances of color in objects. As far as colors in objects are concerned, the proper thing to say is "I have no need of that hypothesis."

Note that these arguments for color skepticism are based on premises drawn from the sciences.

They depend on the assumption of scientific realism that says that there is an external world and that science is the way to determine its true nature. So color skepticism as here developed cannot consistently be used in behalf of that more radical skepticism that doubts the existence of the external world or says that the external world is not knowable. Rather, color skepticism assumes that we have scientific knowledge of the external world and that we can use that knowledge as a basis for doubting that anything has color.

II

I will now consider several responses that the color realist might make to these arguments. Some color realists advocate a type of approach that identifies colors with some item in the process S. Things really do have colors, they say. Even if the whole story about color is given by the theory that describes the details of S, nevertheless colors are reducible to some phase of S.

The most famous version of this identification approach is given by Locke's theory of primary and secondary qualities. The primary qualities of objects, such as shape, size, mass, and motion, are their real qualities. The secondary qualities such as color, sound, temperature, taste, and odor are merely powers or dispositions to cause certain sensations in the minds of those who perceive them. These powers are explained in terms of the primary qualities. Thus the fact that the tomato is red is to be explained by reference to its atomic microstructure, by virtue of which it reflects certain light waves. But its being red just consists in its power of producing, as a result of this microstructure, the sensations that normal observers receive when they look at it under the appropriate illumination.

There are three major difficulties with Locke's theory. In the first place, if we reflect on our concept of color, we will recognize that it is not a concept of a mere disposition. A disposition such as the solubility of a lump of sugar or the fragility of a piece of glass is a feature that is actualized under appropriate conditions as when the sugar is placed in water or the glass is dropped on a hard surface. But colors are not like that at all. They are relatively enduring nondispositional or occurrent qualities to which the notion of actualization does not apply. Colors are spread over the surfaces of objects; they fill regions of space; they permeate objects through and through; they are intimately connected to the shapes and sizes of objects. They do not behave at all as dispositions are supposed to behave. The concept of color is no more the concept of a power than is the concept of shape.

Second, there is a hidden circularity in the dispositional theory. Which sensation, we may ask, is the redness of the tomato supposed to cause? Why, the sensation or appearance of red, of course. So in the attempt to explain what red is with respect to the tomato, Locke's view makes use of the concept of red in describing the sensation it causes. So it looks as if we have made no progress in understanding red. We have just shifted the problem from the tomato to the sensation.

Finally, if colors are causal powers, then in order for us to acquire knowledge of the colors of objects, we would have to know about some of the events that the objects are capable of causing. Yet in order for me to know that the tomato is red, all I need to know is what red colors look like; with this in hand, all I need to do is look at the tomato and classify the color it presents. I do not have to know anything about the causal powers latent in the tomato.

In another version of the identification approach, colors are reduced to the microstates that absorb and reflect light and that explain why objects seem to be of one color rather than another. Colors are nothing more than the atomic structures of objects that account for their interactions with light waves. The main problem with this microstate identification is that colors are things that we can see simply and directly. The microstates, however, are theoretical entities postulated for explanatory purposes and are not visible. This difficulty applies as well to any version of the identification approach that reduces colors to an imperceptible phase of S. Our concept of color is a concept of a quality that is directly visible. If our only access to something is via theoretical inference, it cannot plausibly be identified with color.

The final version of the identification approach that I shall mention is suggested by the biological argument for color skepticism that I gave earlier. That argument might be formulated in this way:

Colors are the ways that certain animals react to impinging radiant energy because of their possessing a nervous system that enables them to see objects; colors belong to those phases of S that are within the organism rather than to the phases that are external to the organism, as the earlier versions of the identification approach claimed. So colors do inhere in something: they inhere in organic events. So color skepticism that denies they inhere in anything must be mistaken.

The error at the basis of this argument lies in the formulation that colors are the ways in which animals react to light. Animals do react in certain ways to light, but none of these ways literally exemplify color. Consider the effect of the light on your retina when you see the tomato. That pattern of chemical changes is a phase of the process S that enables you to see the tomato, but there is no reason at all to suppose that it is actually red as you think the tomato is red. Or consider the brain events that are the effects of the activity in the retina. None of these are literally red even if they carry the message that the tomato is red. Or consider the sensation of red that is the final phase of S. Although it is true that the sensation is *of red,* it isn't true that the sensation *is red.* Somthing can present or represent a quality without actually exemplifying the quality indicated. The word *red,* for example, represents the color red even when written in black ink. A sensation of red no more needs to *be* red than a sensation of a triangle needs to *be* triangular. The ways that animals react to light are given by the intraorganic phases of S, including the sensations of color; but in none of these phases does color literally inhere.

III

Instead of adopting a version of the identification approach, a color realist may argue that colors are *emergent* features of bodies. He or she may agree that colors cannot be identified with any of the phases of S. Colors are not reducible to dispositions, to microstates, to brain events, to sensations, and so forth. However, when a material object comes to exemplify certain complex physical states, that object is *in addition* caused to possess color. Although it is wrong to say that colors are nothing but microstates, nevertheless it is right to say that they are novel qualities that come to inhere in bodies whose physical organization includes the microstates that enable them to interact with light. The microstates explain why bodies possess the colors we see in them; but the colors themselves are items that exist over and above the underlying structures that explain them.

According to this emergence theory of color, colors come to inhere in bodies that possess a certain level of complexity. An individual atom does not exemplify color, nor do two or three atoms placed side by side. But when you have enough atoms, suddenly color emerges. Suppose you have a heap of *n* atoms that lack color either individually or as a group. You add one or a few more atoms and suddenly the heap acquires a color—it is, say, a red tomato. But this sudden emergence of color seems utterly mysterious. What difference can a few atoms make that is sufficient to produce an utterly novel quality? Of course, the addition of atoms to the heap will sooner or later make a difference; as the heap increases in size, it will come to reflect enough light to become visible to those in its vicinity; the increase in size will allow it to reflect enough light to cause our visual systems to produce sensations of color. So we do not need to introduce emergent color qualities in order to explain the difference that an increase in complexity makes.

In general, we can account for all color phenomena, such as the appearances of colors, our beliefs about colors, the causes of these appearances and beliefs, and so forth, without bringing emergent colors into the explanation. Emergent colors have no role to play in color science and serve merely to satisfy our prejudice in favor of color realism. That this prejudice is so well entrenched as to be ineliminable does not make it any less a prejudice.

IV

In the course of defending color skepticism before various audiences, I have found that the most common reaction has been one of sheer incredulity and instantaneous rejection. To the extent that this reaction can be put in the form of argument, it goes like this: "How can you possibly deny that objects have color? We *see* their colors; nothing is easier to see; nothing is better supported by our sense experience. What better evidence can you have about anything than the evidence of the senses? We have the best possible reason for thinking that the colors we see are really there. Even though your arguments for color skepticism are plausible and convincing, they are not strong enough to outweigh the evidence of the senses. Such evidence is rock bottom. Even if we can't answer your arguments or diagnose their fallacies, we are assured that they are indeed fallacious and that you are trying to make the worse argument appear to be the better. In addition, you agree with everyone else that material objects have size and shape; you are not a size skeptic or a shape skeptic. So you too rely on the evidence of the senses. But your use of this evidence is unjustifiably selective. If you judge that the tomato is round on the basis of what you see, you ought also to affirm that it is red on the basis of what you see. As a matter of fact, because you have the best possible reason for thinking that is is red, you *know* that it is red. Thus in affirming color skepticism, you are contradicting things you know to be true. You are defending an indefensible position, because we are rightly convinced that even before you begin your defense, color skepticism is a lost cause."

To assess the cogency of this response, let us reflect on the following example. There are people who see spots before their eyes because certain impurities in the gel inside their eyeballs cast shadows on their retinas. Imagine a group of such individuals gathered together in the office of an ophthalmologist waiting to be examined. In speaking to one another, they discover that they agree that the world is spotty. Not one of them disagrees; they see the spots, and they think that they have the best possible reason for believing that the world is spotty.

We know they are mistaken; the world is not spotty. So they do not have the best possible reason for thinking that it is. Thus the evidence of the senses, even if supported by the agreement of others, is not, *ipso facto,* the best possible reason for believing anything. It is *one* reason, no doubt. It is a reason that can be strengthened to some extent by intersubjective agreement. But no amount of intersubjective agreement ever makes it the best possible reason because one cannot exclude *a priori* the possibility of there being evidence that, in any particular case, outweighs evidence provided by the senses.

A reason that we have for thinking that people who believe that the world is spotty are mistaken is that the world does not appear spotty to us. But why is our agreement to be trusted and theirs not? Perhaps the fact that they agree on the evidence of their senses is just as good a reason for them as our agreement is for us. Thus, we must go beyond the mere fact of agreement to bring in additional factors.

The relevant factor in this case is that there is something wrong with their eyes. That's why their agreement is not convincing. The world appears spotty to them not because it is spotty but because of the shadows cast by the impurities in the gel inside their eyeballs. To us, the world appears free of spots because it is free of spots; there is nothing the matter with our eyes that would make actual spots invisible to us. Their agreement is not based on sensory appearances whose occurrence depends on the facts that appear; there are no such facts; their experiences are not under the control of a spotty world; that is why they are not veridical. In general, when our experience is veridical and the world appears as it really is, then our experience is under the control of or depends on the facts that appear. In certain cases, we are in a position to establish or to explain failures of veridicality by identifying the causes of the experiences and finding out that these causes have nothing to do with the states of affairs that are thought to appear. Thus, the ophthalmologist is in a position to explain to his or her patients why their agreement counts for naught as evidence about the way the world is.

We are now in a position to understand why the argument against color skepticism fails, based on the evidence of the senses. We have no reason to suppose, on the basis of the scientific story about perception, that our color sensations are under the control of or are dependent on colored objects. Our visual apparatus would cause us to have the same color sensations we now have, caused in the way they are usually caused even if there were no colored objects. If we follow out the chain of causation, we do not come on colored objects. In that respect, we have no more reason for supposing that the appearances of color to us are any more likely to be veridical than are the appearances of the spots to the patients. But this way of looking at the matter also shows why the arguments for color skepticism fail to lead to shape skepticism. Normally the shapes that objects actually have play a role in the causation of the shapes they appear to have. If we follow the chain of causation, we come on shaped objects.

We have an inborn tendency to trust the evidence of the senses. If we were to try to justify this trust, we would discover that it depends on a presumption that our experiences are mostly veridical. Through experiencing failures of veridicality, we modify the tendency somewhat so that we learn to trust our senses more in some circumstances than in others. Our inborn trust is shaped and modified and qualified by the experience of error and the failures of our expectations and intentions when errors occur. We also acquire the ability to explain the sources of error, and in many such cases the explanation reaches beyond the resources of common sense and falls within the purview of science. Here is where ophthalmologists become useful. Color skepticism is an outcome of our applying our understanding of the nature of perception to the assessment both of the degree to which our experiences are veridical and of the reliability of the evidence of the senses. Thus, we have the ability to use our senses in combination with our rational faculties to develop theories that can then be applied to determine with greater exactness the actual informational content of our sense experience. Our experiences are our reactions to impinging energies, and there is no alternative but to call on scientific theory to assess what our experiences are capable of telling us about the world that causes them.

Bibliography

Armstrong, D. M. *Perception and the Physical World*. London: Routledge & Kegan Paul, 1961.

Austin, J. L. *Sense and Sensibilia*. Oxford, England: Clarendon Press, 1962.

Chisholm, Roderick. *Perceiving*. Ithaca NY: Cornell University Press, 1957.

Clay, Marjorie, and Keith Lehrer, eds. *Knowledge and Skepticism*. Boulder, CO: Westview, 1989.

Cornman, James. *Perception, Common Sense, and Science*. New Haven, CT: Yale University Press, 1975.

Dancy, John, ed. *Perception*. Oxford, England: Oxford University Press, 1987.

Dretske, Fred. *Seeing and Knowing*. London: Routledge & Kegan Paul, 1969.

Fumerton, Richard. *Metaphysical and Epistemological Problems of Perception*. Lincoln: University of Nebraska, 1985.

Gibson, James J. *Perception of the Visual World*. New York: 1950.

Ginet, Carl. *Knowledge, Perception and Memory*. Dordrecht, Netherlands: Reidel, 1975.

Hardin, C. L. *Color for Philosophers: Unweaving the Rainbow*. Indianapolis: Hackett, 1988.

Heil, John. *Perception and Cognition*. Berkeley: University of California Press, 1983.

Kelley, David. *The Evidence of the Senses*. Baton Rouge: Louisiana State University Press, 1986.

Landesman, Charles. *Color and Consciousness*. Philadelphia: Temple University Press, 1989.

MacLachlan, D. L. C. *Philosophy of Perception*. Englewood Cliffs, NJ: Prentice-Hall, 1989.

Price, H. H. *Perception*. London: Methuen, 1932.

Sellars, W. F. *Science, Perception and Reality*. London: Routledge & Kegan Paul, 1963.

Part IV

The Analysis of Knowledge

What are the criteria of knowledge? Can we give an adequate definition of *knowledge*? That is, can we state exactly what the necessary and sufficient conditions of knowledge are? Does knowing entail absolute certainty? In order to know, must we be aware of the evidence on which our knowledge is based?

Jack sees Jill get on Flight 101 for Miami and believes correctly that Jill is now in Miami, but unknown to Jack Flight 101 has been hijacked and diverted to Havana. However, Jill has fortunately taken a boat back to Miami and, two days after her original flight, has just arrived in Miami. Under these circumstances, does Jack *know* that Jill is in Miami? Many would argue that he merely has a true justified belief of this fact. His belief that Jill is in Miami is justified because normally a flight bound to Miami will land in Miami. However, while Jack's belief that Jill is in Miami is true and justified, the reason on which his belief is based is false.

Jane truly believes that the United States dropped an atomic bomb on Hiroshima in August 1945. However, she received this information from her brother John who guessed it on a multiple-choice test and, without believing one way or another, told Jane what his answer was. Jane—falsely believing that John knows what he is talking about (John is usually a reliable witness about such matters)—truly believes John's testimony, but does she *know* that the United States dropped a bomb on Hiroshima in 1945?

Joe has read in two separate newspapers that the Boston Celtics beat the Los Angeles Lakers last night by a score of 100 to 99, so Joe believes that the Celtics won the game last night. The Celtics did win the game last night, only they beat the Detroit Pistons, not the Lakers. A drunken sports reporter made a mistake and wrote down the losing team as the Lakers rather than the Pistons and the score was 109 to 90. A second newspaper simply copied his official report. Does Joe *know* that the Celtics won last night?

On the basis of these reports, Joe also believes that the Lakers didn't win last night. He is right about that, for the Lakers were idle, but does Joe *know* that the Lakers didn't win last night, or does he merely have a justified true belief?

When I was about nine or ten, a day or two before Christmas I told my brother Vincent that I had snuck into my father's workroom (something forbidden), and had discovered his Christmas present, a railroad and train set. I actually had not gone into my father's room but had made up the story to mislead my brother. But I had guessed correctly, for Vincent was indeed to be given a train set that Christmas. Vincent told my father that he knew what he was getting for Christmas, and my father, who regarded knowledge of Christmas presents as tantamount to knowledge uttered by the Oracle of Delphi and his workroom as Delphi itself, angrily spanked me for my sacrilege. While I was being spanked, I pleaded that I had not gone into my father's room and had not seen the Christmas presents. "How did you know Vincent was getting a train

set?" he asked. "I didn't know it," I responded; "I just made up the story." The question is, did Vincent, on believing my lie two days before Christmas, *know* he was going to get a train set?

Before 1963, the concept of knowledge was either left unanalyzed or defined more or less as true justified belief. I said in the introduction to Part I that Plato offered a tripartite analysis of knowledge, defining it as true belief with a rational explanation or justification (Greek *logos*). Passages asserting the tripartite analysis can be found in C. I. Lewis, Roderick Chisholm, and A. J. Ayer with similar definitions. Roughly, Person S knows that *p* if and only if

a. S believes that *p*.
b. Belief *p* is true.
c. S's belief that *p* is justified.

These three conditions constitute the necessary and sufficient conditions of knowledge. If one of them was missing, S did not know that *p*. If all of them were present, S could not fail to know that *p*. Let us call this the "tripartite analysis" of knowledge.

Alvin Plantinga reports the following anecdote. In 1962 he was drinking a cup of coffee in the cafeteria of Wayne State University with his colleague Edmund Gettier, when Gettier mentioned that he was concerned that he would be coming up for tenure next year without a lot of publications. He did have an idea of setting forth a few minor counterexamples to the traditional definition of knowledge, but he considered that a minor matter. The next year Gettier's two-and-a-half-page article on the definition of knowledge was published in *Analysis*, and epistemology has never been the same.

Gettier's analysis was based on two counterexamples to the tripartite analysis. The first is as follows. Smith and Jones have applied for a certain job, and Smith has strong evidence for conjunctive proposition (d), "Jones is the man who will get the job, and Jones has ten coins in his pocket."

Proposition (d) entails (e), "The man who will get the job has ten coins in his pocket." We may suppose that Smith sees the entailment and believes (e).

But unknown to Smith, he himself will get the job and happens to have ten coins in his pocket. So, while (d) is false, (e) is true and Smith truly and justifiably believes (e), but we would not say that Smith *knows* that the man who will get the job has ten coins in his pocket.

So the tripartite analysis fails, for he knows neither that he will get the job nor that he has ten coins in his pocket.

Keith Lehrer offers the following variation of Gettier's second counterexample.

A pupil in S's office, Mr. Nogot, has given S evidence *e* that justifies S in believing "Mr. Nogot, who is in the office, owns a Ford," from which S deduces *p*: "Someone in the office owns a Ford." But unsuspected by S, Mr. Nogot has been shamming and *p* is only true because another person in the office, Mr. Havit, owns a Ford.[1] Again the tripartite analysis seems to fail, since the true, justified belief is based on a false proposition.

Gettier's counterexamples have the following form:

1. S believes that *p*.

2. Belief *p* is true.

3. S's belief that *p* is justified.

4. Belief *p* is based on or entailed by some proposition *q*.

5. S is justified in believing *q*.

6. Belief *q* is false.

Therefore

7. S doesn't know that *p*.

Several proposals have been offered to meet the Gettier-type counterexamples. Four prominent attempts are included in this part of this book. A fifth radical reaction, represented by William Rozeboom's "Why I Know So Much More Than You Do" (Reading IV.6) rejects the traditional concept of knowledge as hopelessly confused or made up of several more adequate notions. You may finally choose that alternative, but before you do, you should consider the other four strategies, which consist in supplementing the tripartite analysis with a fourth condition. The four strategies are (1) The "no false belief" condition, (2) the conclusive reasons analysis, (3) the causal condition, and (4) the defeasibility condition.

1. *The "No False Belief" Condition*

Early on it was thought that the Gettier counterexamples could be defeated by simply stipulating that the belief that *p* must not be caused or based on a false belief. In the preceding examples, the belief that *p* is based on a false belief *q*. However, this attempt at a solution was soon found to be both too weak and too strong. It was too strong because we can think of instances of knowing where a false belief is present. For example, I believe that Joan will be elected president of the student body because I justifiably believe (1) all the fraternity members, constituting 30 percent of the student body, are committed to Joan; and (2) all the sorority members, constituting 30 percent of the student body, are committed to Joan; and (3) all the on-campus independents, constituting 30 percent of the student body, are committed to Joan. Only the off-campus independent students, constituting only 10 percent of the student body, are against Joan. But I may be wrong about Item 3. A last-minute change causes the independents to switch their vote. Nevertheless, I may still know Joan will win the election based on my justified true belief. If my belief in *h* is based on evidence *a*, *b*, *c*, and *d*, where my combination of two will justify *h*, I may hold two false beliefs and still be said to know that *h*.

The "no false belief" condition was also shown to be too weak, and examples were soon forthcoming in which no false belief was present. One of the most famous was set forth by Carl Ginet (and appears in Goldman's essay in this section, Reading IV.5). Henry is driving in the country and correctly identifies a red barn in the distance. Unknown to Henry, someone has set forth a series of red barn façades in this vicinity, so that Henry could not distinguish the real barn from the façades. Hence, Henry cannot be said to know that he is seeing a red barn even though he has a justified true belief. But Henry's failure to know is not attributed to any false proposition on which his belief is based. So the "no false belief" condition does not succeed in saving the tripartite analysis.

2. *The Conclusive Reasons Condition*

Fred Dretske set forth an ingenious solution to the Gettier puzzle in offering an account that basically argued that S knows that *p* if S has a reason (R) for *p*, such that if *p* were not the case S would not have R.[2] Smith's believing that the man who will get the job has ten coins in his pocket is not based on a conclusive reason, for the man who gets the job would get it even if he were not known to have ten coins in his pocket.

But there are problems with the conclusive reasons condition. George Pappas and Marshall Swain argue that it is too strong. Suppose S were looking at a table on which there was a cup.[3] S truly and justifiably believes that a cup is before him on the table, but unknown to him he is seeing not the cup itself but a hologram caused by rays given off by the cup. So the conclusive reasons account fails, for S would not have the reason he does for believing *p* if *p* were not the case, but we would not want to say that S *knows* that a cup is on the table.

3. *The Causal Condition*

Alvin Goldman in "A Causal Theory of Knowing" (Reading IV.2) set forth a causal theory that based justification on the way it was caused. If S knows that *p*, then S's belief that *p* must be caused by the state of affairs corresponding to *p*. Returning to the Gettier example, Smith does not know that the person who will get the job has ten coins in his pocket because that belief is not caused in the right way. In knowledge, there must be proper causal connections between the evidence and the belief. This seems promising, and perhaps it can ultimately be refined to do the work Goldman intended, but others quickly pointed out that the notion of causality is very vague here and that explaining via causality is an explanation *obscurum per obscurum* (explaining the obscure by the obscure), for it is not clear how the numbers 2 and 3 cause us to believe that they make 5 or how the future fact that I will die causes me to know this fact or that the universal proposition that all humans are mortal causes me to know the truth.

In Reading IV.4, Harman critically discusses problems connected with the causal theory of knowing. He seeks to replace it with a near relative, inference to the best explanation. We do not need to be able to reconstruct the causal chain that led to Event X in order to know X. Consider, says Harman, the case of the mad fiend. Omar suffers a fatal heart attack in the street. An hour later a mad fiend comes down the street and sees Omar lying in the gutter. He cuts off Omar's head. You walk down the street an hour later, see Omar lying there with his head detached, and immediately infer from that state of affairs that Omar is dead. Harman points out that there is no causal connection between Omar's being dead and his head being cut off. Having his head cut off did not cause Omar's death, the heart attack did. You know that Omar is dead not because of any causal relation between his death and your belief, but because of a correct explanatory inference: "Normally, if someone's head is cut off, that person is dead. This generalization accounts for the fact that Omar's head is cut off is being correlated here with Omar's being dead." Incidentally, this also serves as a counterexample to the "no false belief" condition, for you may believe that Omar is dead because someone cut off Omar's head, whereas in fact his head was cut off because he was dead. Even though you are mistaken about the cause of Omar's death, you still know that he is dead.

Harman sees his explanatory account of knowledge as an enlargement of Goldman's causal account. Inference to the best explanation is the general theory of knowledge within which the causal account functions as a special case.

In Reading IV.5, "Discrimination and Perceptual Knowledge," Goldman sets forth a descendent of his causal theory, which seeks to meet some of the criticisms of his main theory. In Goldman's revised theory, knowledge consists in the ability to discriminate between relevant alternatives. For example, in the case of Henry picking out a red barn in an area where there are barn façades, Henry, on Goldman's account, fails to know that he sees a barn, since he could not distinguish it from the façades.

4. The Defeasibility Condition

The defeasibility requirement, set forth in our readings by Lehrer and Paxson in Reading IV.3 and Harman in Reading IV.4, states that if there is no other truth (q) such that S's believing it would have destroyed his justification for believing that p, then this condition, along with the tripartite conditions, entails that S knows that p. Lehrer and Paxson set forth the following illustration of defeasibility. S sees a man named Tom

Grabit steal a book. However, unknown to S, Tom's deranged mothers lies and testifies that Tom is a thousand miles away, so it must have been his twin brother Buck who stole the book. If S had known that Mrs. Grabit had testified the way she did, he would not have been justified in believing that Tom stole the book. The statement "Mrs. Grabit testified that Tom was a thousand miles away at the time in question" would have defeated knowledge. However, one can imagine a defeater to the defeater here. If S knew that Mrs. Grabit was a deranged liar, he would have warrant to dismiss her testimony and continue to hold to his original belief about Tom.

As you may suspect, the defeasibility criterion seems vague and open-ended. Harman argues that for any inductive belief there will always be some true proposition such that if the person knew of it, his or her justification would be defeated. For a large number of knowledge claims, we can imagine some true proposition that, if we believed it, would defeat our claim to knowledge, but then we can think of some further true belief that would defeat the defeater, and some other true belief that would defeat the antidefeater, and so on. One may suspect that this condition is really appealing to omniscience. Nonetheless, many epistemologists, like Lehrer and Paxson, believe we can distinguish between defeating and nondefeating conditions. Others, like Harman, hold that the best we can do is set forth as a requirement that if a person is justified in inferring that there is no defeating counterevidence to a true, justified belief, then that person *knows* the proposition in question.

In our final reading, William Rozeboom argues that the attempts to add a supplementary account of knowledge to meet the Gettier counterexamples are misguided. We can define knowledge in terms of absolute certainty and so save the traditional analysis, but, unfortunately, the result will be to show that our concept of knowledge is inadequate for most of our epistemic purposes.

These essays represent the tip of the iceberg with regard to the literature generated by Gettier's three-page article. All the positions described have received important criticisms that you may want to look into. A bibliography, including these critical essays, appears at the end of this part of the book. Parts V and VI also contain discussion of some of the ideas discussed in this section.

Let us turn to our readings.

Notes

[1] Keith Lehrer, "Knowledge, Truth and Evidence," *Analysis* 25.5 (1965), 169.

[2] Fred Dretske, "Conclusive Reasons," *Australasian Journal of Philosophy 49* (1971), reprinted in George Pappas and Marshall Swain, eds., *Essays on Knowledge and Justification* (Ithaca, NY: Cornell University Press, 1978).

[3] George Pappas and Marshall Swain, "Some Conclusive Reasons Against 'Conclusive Reasons,'" in Pappas and Swain, 1978.

IV.1 Is *Justified True Belief* Knowledge?

EDMUND L. GETTIER

Edmund L. Gettier (b. 1927) is Professor of Philosophy at the University of Massachusetts at Amherst.

In this celebrated short essay, Gettier identifies the third condition in Plato and other accounts of knowledge as *justification* and then shows by clear counterexamples that this tripartite analysis of knowledge as true, justified belief is insufficient for knowledge. Something more than mere justification is required before a true belief can qualify as knowledge.

Various attempts have been made in recent years to state necessary and sufficient conditions for someone's knowing a given proposition. The attempts have often been such that they can be stated in a form similar to the following:[1]

(a) S knows that P   *IFF*
    (i) P is true,
    (ii) S believes that P, and
    (iii) S is justified in believing that P.

From *Analysis*, Vol. 23 (Blackwell, 1963), pp. 121–3.
Reprinted by permission of the author.

For example, Chisholm has held that the following gives the necessary and sufficient conditions for knowledge:[2]

(b) S knows that P   *IFF*
    (i) S accepts P,
    (ii) S has adequate evidence for P, and
    (iii) P is true.

Ayer has stated the necessary and sufficient conditions for knowledge as follows:[3]

(c) S knows that P   *IFF*
    (i) P is true,
    (ii) S is sure that P is true, and

(iii) S has the right to be sure that P is true.

I shall argue that (a) is false in that the conditions stated therein do not constitute a *sufficient* condition for the truth of the proposition that S knows that P. The same argument will show that (b) and (c) fail if 'has adequate evidence for' or 'has the right to be sure that' is substituted for 'is justified in believing that' throughout.

I shall begin by noting two points. First, in that sense of 'justified' in which S's being justified in believing P is a necessary condition of S's knowing that P, it is possible for a person to be justified in believing a proposition that is in fact false. Secondly, for any proposition P, if S is justified in believing P, and P entails Q, and S deduces Q from P and accepts Q as a result of this deduction, then S is justified in believing Q. Keeping these two points in mind, I shall now present two cases in which the conditions stated in (a) are true for some proposition, though it is at the same time false that the person in question knows that proposition.

Case I:

Suppose that Smith and Jones have applied for a certain job. And suppose that Smith has strong evidence for the following conjunctive proposition:

(d) Jones is the man who will get the job, and Jones has ten coins in his pocket.

Smith's evidence for (d) might be that the president of the company assured him that Jones would in the end be selected, and that he, Smith, had counted the coins in Jones's pocket ten minutes ago. Proposition (d) entails:

(e) The man who will get the job has ten coins in his pocket.

Let us suppose that Smith sees the entailment from (d) to (e), and accepts (e) on the grounds of (d), for which he has strong evidence. In this case, Smith is clearly justified in believing that (e) is true.

But imagine, further, that unknown to Smith, he himself, not Jones, will get the job. And, also, unknown to Smith, he himself has ten coins in his pocket. Proposition (e) is then true, though proposition (d), from which Smith inferred (e), is false. In our example, then, all of the following are true: (*i*) (e) is true, (*ii*) Smith believes that (e) is true, and (*iii*) Smith is justified in believing that (e) is true. But it is equally clear that Smith does not *know* that (e) is true; for (e) is true in virtue of the number of coins in Smith's pocket, while Smith does not know how many coins are in Smith's pocket, and bases his belief in (e) on a count of the coins in Jones's pocket, whom he falsely believes to be the man who will get the job.

Case II:

Let us suppose that Smith has strong evidence for the following proposition:

(f) Jones owns a Ford.

Smith's evidence might be that Jones has at all times in the past within Smith's memory owned a car, and always a Ford, and that Jones has just offered Smith a ride while driving a Ford. Let us imagine, now, that Smith has another friend, Brown, of whose whereabouts he is totally ignorant. Smith selects three place-names quite at random, and constructs the following three propositions:

(g) Either Jones owns a Ford, or Brown is in Boston;
(h) Either Jones owns a Ford, or Brown is in Barcelona;
(i) Either Jones owns a Ford, or Brown is in Brest-Litovsk.

Each of these propositions is entailed by (f). Imagine that Smith realizes the entailment of each of these propositions he has constructed by (f), and proceeds to accept (g), (h), and (i) on the basis of (f). Smith has correctly inferred (g), (h), and (i) from a proposition for which he has strong evidence. Smith is therefore completely justified in believing each of these three propositions. Smith, of course, has no idea where Brown is.

But imagine now that two further conditions hold. First, Jones does *not* own a Ford, but is at present driving a rented car. And secondly, by the sheerest coincidence, and entirely unknown to Smith, the place mentioned in proposition (h) happens really to be the place where Brown is. If these two conditions hold then Smith does *not* know that (h) is true, even though (*i*) (h) *is* true, (*ii*) Smith does believe that (h) is true, and (*iii*) Smith is justified in believing that (h) is true.

These two examples show that definition (a) does not state a *sufficient* condition for someone's knowing a given proposition. The same cases, with appropriate changes, will suffice to show that neither definition (b) nor definition (c) do so either.

Notes

[1] Plato seems to be considering some such definition at *Theatetus* 201, and perhaps accepting one at *Meno* 98.

[2] Roderick M. Chisholm, *Perceiving: a Philosophical Study,* Cornell University Press (Ithaca, New York, 1957), p. 16.

[3] A. J. Ayer, *The Problem of Knowledge,* Macmillan (London, 1956), p. 34.

IV.2 A *Causal Theory of Knowing*

ALVIN I. GOLDMAN

Alvin I Goldman is Professor of Philosophy at the University of Arizona. Goldman accepts Gettier's contention that the traditional account of empirical knowledge is deficient and seeks to repair the weakness with a causal account of knowledge. Examining Gettier's second counterexample, which involves proposition *p*, either Jones owns a Ford or Brown is in Barcelona, Goldman argues that *p* fails to qualify as knowledge, not because it is based on a false proposition but because there is no *causal* connection between the facts that Brown is in Barcelona and that Smith believes *p*. Goldman shows how perceptual and memory knowledge are such in virtue of the proper causal chains: Pattern 1 and Pattern 2 chains. In Pattern 1 chains, the state of affairs *p* is involved in the chain that causes a Person S's true belief *p*. In Pattern 2 chains, a common source causes both state of affairs *p* and S's belief that *p*. Goldman's analysis represents a radical departure from traditional epistemology, which views epistemological matters as questions of logic or justification, for rather than focusing on the reasons one has for one's belief, he views knowledge as primarily a causal issue. We will see how Goldman's views further develop in Readings IV.5 and VI.1.

Since Edmund L. Gettier reminded us recently of a certain important inadequacy of the traditional analysis of "S knows that *p*," several attempts have been made to correct that anlaysis.[1] In this paper I shall offer still another analysis (or a sketch of an analysis) of "S knows that *p*," one which will avert Gettier's problem. My concern will be with knowledge of empirical propositions only, since I think that the traditional analysis is adequate for knowledge of nonempirical truths.

Consider an abbreviated version of Gettier's second counterexample to the traditional analysis. Smith believes

(*q*) Jones owns a Ford

and has very strong evidence for it. Smith's evidence might be that Jones has owned a Ford for many

years and that Jones has just offered Smith a ride while driving a Ford. Smith has another friend, Brown, of whose whereabouts he is totally ignorant. Choosing a town quite at random, however, Smith constructs the proposition

(*p*) Either Jones owns a Ford or Brown is in Barcelona.

Seeing that *q* entails *p*, Smith infers that *p* is true. Since he has adequate evidence for *q*, he also has adequate evidence for *p*. But now suppose that Jones does *not* own a Ford (he was driving a rented car when he offered Smith a ride), but, quite by coincidence, Brown happens to be in Barcelona. This means that *p* is true, that Smith believes *p*, and that Smith has adequate evidence for *p*. But Smith does not know *p*.

A variety of hypotheses might be made to account for Smith's not knowing *p*. Michael Clark, for example, points to the fact that *q* is false, and suggests this as the reason why Smith cannot be said to know *p*. Generalizing from this case, Clark argues that, for *S* to know a proposition, each of *S*'s

Reprinted from *The Journal of Philosophy,* 64, 12 (1967), 355–372, by kind permission of the author and editor.

I wish to thank members of the University of Michigan Philosophy Department, several of whom made helpful comments on earlier versions of this paper.

grounds for it must be *true,* as well as his grounds for his grounds, etc.[2] I shall make another hypothesis to account for the fact that Smith cannot be said to know *p,* and I shall generalize this into a new analysis of *"S* knows that *p."*

Notice that what *makes p* true is the fact that Brown is in Barcelona, but that this fact has nothing to do with Smith's believing *p.* That is, there is no *causal* connection between the fact that Brown is in Barcelona and Smith's believing *p.* If Smith had come to believe *p* by reading a letter from Brown postmarked in Barcelona, then we might say that Smith knew *p.* Alternatively, if Jones did own a Ford, and his owning the Ford was manifested by his offer of a ride to Smith, and this in turn resulted in Smith's believing *p,* then we would say that Smith knew *p.* Thus, one thing that seems to be missing in this example is a causal connection between the fact that makes *p* true [or simply: the fact that *p*] and Smith's belief of *p.* The requirement of such a *causal connection* is what I wish to add to the traditional analysis.

To see that this requirement is satisfied in all cases of (empirical) knowledge, we must examine a variety of such causal connections. Clearly, only a sketch of the important kinds of cases is possible here.

Perhaps the simplest case of a causal chain connecting some fact *p* with someone's belief of *p* is that of *perception.* I wish to espouse a version of the causal theory of perception, in essence that defended by H. P. Grice.[3] Suppose that *S* sees that there is a vase in front of him. How is this to be analyzed? I shall not attempt a complete analysis of this, but a necessary condition of *S's* seeing that there is a vase in front of him is that there be a certain kind of causal connection between the presence of the vase and *S's* believing that a vase is present. I shall not attempt to describe this causal process in detail. Indeed, to a large extent, a description of this process must be regarded as a problem for the special sciences, not for philosophy. But a certain causal process—viz. that which standardly takes place when we say that so-and-so *sees* such-and-such—must occur. That our ordinary concept of sight (i.e., knowledge acquired by sight) includes a causal requirement is shown by the fact that if the relevant causal process is absent we would withhold the assertion that so-and-so *saw* such-and-such. Suppose that, although a vase is directly in front of

S, a laser photograph[4] is interposed between it and *S,* thereby blocking it from *S's* view. The photograph, however, is one of a vase (a different vase), and when it is illuminated by light waves from a laser, it looks to *S* exactly like a real vase. When the photograph is illuminated, *S* forms the belief that there is a vase in front of him. Here we would deny that *S sees* that there is a vase in front of him, for his view of the real vase is completely blocked, so that it has no causal role in the formation of his belief. Of course, *S* might *know* that there was a vase in front of him even if the photograph is blocking his view. Someone else, in a position to see the vase, might tell *S* that there is a vase in front of him. Here the presence of the vase might be a causal ancestor of *S's* belief, but the causal process would not be a (purely) *perceptual* one. *S could not be said to see* that there is a vase in front of him. For this to be true, there must be a causal process, but one of a very special sort, connecting the presence of the vase with *S's* belief.

I shall here assume that perceptual knowledge of facts is noninferential. This is merely a simplifying procedure, and not essential to my account. Certainly a percipient does not *infer* facts about physical objects from the state of his brain or from the stimulation of his sense organs. He need not know about these goings-on at all. But some epistemologists maintain that we directly perceive only sense data and that we infer physical-object facts from them. This view could be accommodated within my analysis. I could say that physical-object facts cause sense data, that people directly perceive sense data, and that they infer the physical object facts from the sense data. This kind of process would be fully accredited by my analysis, which will allow for knowledge based on inference. But for purposes of exposition it will be convenient to regard perceptual knowledge of external facts as independent of any inference.

Here the question arises about the *scope* of perceptual knowledge. By perception I can know noninferentially that there is a vase in front of me. But can I know noninferentially that the painting I am viewing is a Picasso? It is unnecessary to settle such issues here. Whether the knowledge of such facts is to be classed as inferential or noninferential, my analysis can account for it. So the scope of noninferential knowledge may be left indeterminate.

I turn next to memory, i.e., knowledge that is

based, in part, on memory. Remembering, like perceiving, must be regarded as a causal process. S remembers p at time t only if S's believing p at an earlier time is a cause of his believing p at t. Of course, not every causal connection between an earlier belief and a later one is a case of remembering. As in the case of perception, however, I shall not try to describe this process in detail. This is a job mainly for the scientist. Instead, the kind of causal process in question is to be identified simply by example, by "pointing" to paradigm cases of remembering. Whenever causal processes are of that kind—whatever that kind is, precisely—they are cases of remembering.[5]

A causal connection between earlier belief (or knowledge) of p and later belief (knowledge) of p is certainly a necessary ingredient in memory.[6] To remember a fact is not simply to believe it at t_0 and also to believe it at t_1. Nor does someone's knowing a fact at t_0 and his knowing it at t_1 entail that he remembers it at t_1. He may have perceived the fact at t_0, forgotten it, and then relearned it at t_1 by someone's telling it to him. Nor does the inclusion of a memory "impression"—a feeling of remembering—ensure that one really remembers. Suppose S perceives p at t_0, but forgets it at t_1. At t_2 he begins to believe p again because someone tells him p, but at t_2 he has no memory impression of p. At t_3 we artificially stimulate in S a memory impression of p. It does not follow that S remembers p at t_3. The description of the case suggests that his believing p at t_0 has no causal effect whatever on his believing p at t_3; and if we accepted this fact, we would deny that he remembers p at t_3.

Knowledge can be acquired by a combination of perception and memory. At t_0, the fact p causes S to believe p, by perception. S's believing p at t_0 results, via memory, in S's believing p at t_1. Thus, the fact p is a cause of S's believing p at t_1, and S can be said to know p at t_1. But not all knowledge results from perception and memory alone. In particular, much knowledge is based on *inference*.

As I shall use the term 'inference', to say that S knows p by "inference" does not entail that S went through an explicit, conscious process of reasoning. It is not necessary that he have "talked to himself," saying something like "Since such-and-such is true, p must also be true." My belief that there is a fire in the neighborhood is based on, or inferred from, my belief that I hear a fire engine. But I have not gone through a process of explicit reasoning, saying "There's a fire engine; therefore there must be a fire." Perhaps the word 'inference' is ordinarily used only where explicit reasoning occurs; if so, my use of the term will be somewhat broader than its ordinary use.

Suppose S perceives that there is solidified lava in various parts of the countryside. On the basis of this belief, plus various "background" beliefs about the production of lava, S concludes that a nearby mountain erupted many centuries ago. Let us assume that this is a highly warranted inductive inference, one which gives S adequate evidence for believing that the mountain did erupt many centuries ago. Assuming this proposition is true, does S know it? This depends on the nature of the causal process that induced his belief. If there is a continuous causal chain of the sort he envisages connecting the fact that the mountain erupted with his belief of this fact, then S knows it. If there is no such causal chain, however, S does not know that proposition.

Suppose that the mountain erupts, leaving lava around the countryside. The lava remains there until S perceives it and infers that the mountain erupted. Then S does know that the mountain erupted. But now suppose that, after the mountain has erupted, a man somehow removes all the lava. A century later, a different man (not knowing of the real volcano) decides to make it look as if there had been a volcano, and therefore puts lava in appropriate places. Still later, S comes across this lava and concludes that the mountain erupted centuries ago. In this case, S cannot be said to know the proposition. This is because the fact that the mountain did erupt is not a cause of S's believing that it erupted. A necessary condition of S's knowing p is that his believing p be connected with p by a causal chain.

In the first case, where S knows p, the causal connection may be diagrammed as in Figure 1. (p) is the fact that the mountain erupted at such-and-such a time. (q) is the fact that lava is (now) present around the countryside. 'B' stands for a belief, the expression in parentheses indicating the proposition believed, and the subscript designating the believer. (r) is a "background" proposition, describing the ways in which lava is produced and how it solidifies. Solid arrows in the diagram represent causal connections; dotted arrows represent inferences. Notice that, in Figure 1, there is not only an

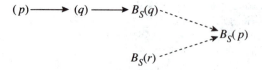

Figure 1

arrow connecting (q) with S's belief of (q), but also an arrow connecting (p) with (q). In the suggested variant of the lava case, the latter arrow would be missing, showing that there is no continuous causal chain connecting (p) with S's belief of (p). Therefore, in that variant case, S could not be said to know (p).

I have said that p is causally connected to S's belief of p, in the case diagrammed in Figure 1. This raises the question, however, of whether the inferential part of the chain is itself a causal chain. In other words, is S's belief of q a cause of his believing p? This is a question to which I shall not try to give a definitive answer here. I am inclined to say that inference *is* a causal process, that is, that when someone *bases* his belief of one proposition on his belief of a set of other propositions, then his belief of the latter propositions can be considered a cause of his belief of the former proposition. But I do not wish to rest my thesis on this claim. All I do claim is that, if a chain of inferences is "added" to a causal chain, then the entire chain is causal. In terms of our diagram, a chain consisting of solid arrows plus dotted arrows is to be considered a causal chain, though I shall not take a position on the question of whether the dotted arrows represent causal connections. Thus, in Figure 1, p is a cause of S's belief of p, whether or not we regard S's belief of q a cause of his belief of p.[7]

Consider next a case of knowledge based on "testimony." This too can be analyzed causally. p causes a person T to believe p, by perception. T's belief of p gives rise to (causes) his asserting p. T's asserting p causes S, by auditory perception, to believe that T is asserting p. S infers that T believes p, and from this, in turn, he infers that p is a fact. There is a continuous causal chain from p to S's believing p, and thus, assuming that each of S's inferences is warranted, S can be said to know p.

This causal chain is represented in Figure 2. 'A' refers to an act of asserting a proposition, the expression in parentheses indicating the proposition

asserted and the subscript designating the agent. (q), (r), (u), and (v) are background propositions. (q) and (r), for example, pertain to T's sincerity; they help S conclude, from the fact that T asserted p, that T really believes p.

In this case, as in the lava case, S knows p because he has correctly reconstructed the causal chain leading from p to the evidence for p that S perceives, in this case, T's asserting (p). This correct reconstruction is shown in the diagram by S's inference "mirroring" the rest of the causal chain. Such a correct reconstruction is a necessary condition of knowledge based on inference. To see this, consider the following example. A newspaper reporter observes p and reports it to his newspaper. When printed, however, the story contains a typographical error so that it asserts not-p. When reading the paper, however, S fails to see the word 'not', and takes the paper to have asserted p. Trusting the newspaper, he infers that p is true. Here we have a continuous causal chain leading from p to S's believing p; yet S does not know p. S thinks that p resulted in a report to the newspaper about p and that this report resulted in its printing the statement p. Thus, his reconstruction of the causal chain is mistaken. But, if he is to know p, his reconstruction must contain no mistakes. Though he need not reconstruct *every* detail of the causal chain, he must reconstruct all the important links.[8] An additional requirement for knowledge based on inference is that the knower's inferences be warranted. That is, the propositions on which he bases his belief of p must genuinely confirm p very highly, whether deductively or inductively. Reconstructing a causal chain merely by lucky guesses does not yield knowledge.

With the help of our diagrams, we can contrast the traditional analysis of knowing with Clark's analysis (*op. cit.*) and contrast each of these with my own analysis. The traditional analysis makes reference to just three features of the diagrams. First, it requires that p be true; i.e., that (p) appear in the diagram. Secondly, it requires that S believe p; i.e.,

$$(p) \rightarrow B_T(p) \rightarrow A_T(p) \rightarrow B_S(A_T(p)) \rightarrow B_S(B_T(p)) \rightarrow B_S(p)$$

Figure 2

that S's belief of p appear in the diagram. Thirdly, it requires that S's inferences, if any, be warranted; i.e., that the sets of beliefs that are at the tail of a dotted arrow must jointly highly confirm the belief at the head of these arrows. Clark proposes a further requirement for knowledge. He requires that *each* of the beliefs in S's chain of inference be *true*. In other words, whereas the traditional analysis requires a fact to correspond to S's belief of p, Clark requires that a fact correspond to *each* of S's beliefs on which he based his belief of p. Thus, corresponding to each belief on the right side of the diagram there must be a fact on the left side. (My diagrams omit facts corresponding to the "background" beliefs.)

As Clark's analysis stands, it seems to omit an element of the diagrams that my analysis requires, viz., the arrows indicating causal connections. Now Clark might reformulate his analysis so as to make implicit reference to these causal connections. If he required that the knower's beliefs include *causal beliefs* (of the relevant sort), then his requirement that these beliefs be true would amount to the requirement that there *be* causal chains of the sort I require. This interpretation of Clark's analysis would make it almost equivalent to mine, and would enable him to avoid some objections that have been raised against him. But he has not explicitly formulated his analysis that way, and it therefore remains deficient in this respect.

Before turning to the problems facing Clark's analysis, more must be said about my own analysis. So far, my examples may have suggested that, if S knows p, the fact that p is a cause of his belief of p. This would clearly be wrong, however. Let us grant that I can know facts about the future. Then, if we required that the known fact cause the knower's belief, we would have to countenance "backward" causation. My analysis, however, does not face this dilemma. The analysis requires that there be a causal *connection* between p and S's belief, not necessarily that p be a *cause* of S's belief. p and S's belief of p can also be causally connected in a way that yields knowledge if both p and S's belief of p have a common cause. This can be illustrated as follows.

T intends to go downtown on Monday. On Sunday, T tells S of his intention. Hearing T say he will go downtown, S infers that T really does intend to go downtown. And from this S concludes that T *will* go downtown on Monday. Now suppose that

T fulfills his intention by going downtown on Monday. Can S be said to know that he would go downtown? If we ever can be said to have knowledge of the future, this is a reasonable candidate for it. So let us say S did know that proposition. How can my analysis account for S's knowledge? T's going downtown on Monday clearly cannot be a cause of S's believing, on Sunday, that he would go downtown. But there is a fact that is the *common* cause of T's going downtown and of S's belief that he would go downtown, viz., T's intending (on Sunday) to go downtown. This intention resulted in his going downtown and also resulted in S's believing that he would go downtown. This causal connection between S's belief and the fact believed allows us to say that S *knew* that T would go downtown.

The example is diagrammed in Figure 3. (p) = T's going downtown on Monday. (q) = T's intending (on Sunday) to go downtown on Monday. (r) = T's telling S (on Sunday) that he will go downtown on Monday. (u) and (v) are relevant background propositions pertaining to T's honesty, resoluteness, etc. The diagram reveals that q is a cause both of p and of S's belief of p. Cases of this kind I shall call *Pattern 2* cases of knowledge. Figures 1 and 2 exemplify *Pattern 1* cases of knowledge.

Notice that the causal connection between q and p is an essential part of S's knowing p. Suppose, for example, that T's intending (on Sunday) to go downtown does not result in, or cause, T's going downtown on Monday. Suppose that T, after telling S that he would go downtown, changes his mind. Nevertheless, on Monday he is kidnapped and forced, at the point of a gun, to go downtown. Here both q and p actually occur, but they are not causally related. The diagram in Figure 3 would

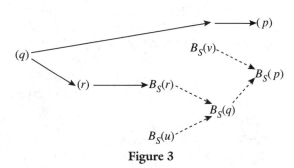

Figure 3

have to be amended by deleting the arrow connecting (q) with (p). But if the rest of the facts of the original case remain the same, S could not be said to know p. It would be false to say that S knew, on Sunday, that T would go downtown on Monday.

Pattern 2 cases of knowledge are not restricted to knowledge of the future. I know that smoke was coming out of my chimney last night. I know this because I remember perceiving a fire in my fireplace last night, and I infer that the fire caused smoke to rise out of the chimney. This case exemplifies Pattern 2. The smoke's rising out of the chimney is not a causal factor of my belief. But the fact that there was a fire in the fireplace was a cause both of my belief that smoke was coming out of the chimney and of the fact that smoke was coming out of the chimney. If we supplement this case slightly, we can make my knowledge exemplify *both* Pattern 1 and Pattern 2. Suppose that a friend tells me today that he perceived smoke coming out of my chimney last night and I base my continued belief of this fact on his testimony. Then the fact was a cause of my current belief of it, as well as an *effect* of another fact that caused my belief. In general, numerous and diverse kinds of causal connections can obtain between a given fact and a given person's belief of that fact.

Let us now examine some objections to Clark's analysis and see how the analysis presented here fares against them. John Turk Saunders and Narayan Champawat have raised the following counterexample to Clark's analysis:[9]

> Suppose that Smith believes
>   (p) Jones owns a Ford
> because his friend Brown whom he knows to be generally reliable and honest yesterday told Smith that Jones had always owned a Ford. Brown's information was correct, but today Jones sells his Ford and replaces it with a Volkswagen. An hour later Jones is pleased to find that he is the proud owner of two cars: he has been lucky enough to win a Ford in a raffle. Smith's belief in p is not only justified and true, but is fully grounded, e.g., we suppose that each link in the . . . chain of Smith's grounds is true (8).

Clearly Smith does not know p; yet he seems to satisfy Clark's analysis of knowing.

Smith's lack of knowledge can be accounted for in terms of my analysis. Smith does not know p because his believing p is not causally related to p, Jones's owning a Ford *now*. This can be seen by examining Figure 4. In the diagram, (p) = Jones's owning a Ford now; (q) = Jones's having owned a Ford (until yesterday); (r) = Jones's winning a Ford in a raffle today. (t), (u), and (v) are background propositions. (v), for example, deals with the likelihood of someone's continuing to own the same car today that he owned yesterday. The subscript 'B' designates Brown, and the subscript 'S' designates Smith. Notice the absence of an arrow connecting (p) with (q). The absence of this arrow represents the absence of a casual relation between (q) and (p). Jones's owning a Ford in the past (until yesterday) is not a cause of his owning one now. Had he continued owning the same Ford today that he owned yesterday, there would be a casual connection between q and p and, therefore, a casual connection between p and Smith's believing p. This casual connection would exemplify Pattern 2. But, as it happened, it is purely a coincidence that Jones owns a Ford today as well as yesterday. Thus, Smith's belief of p is not connected with p by Pattern 2, nor is there any Pattern 1 connection between them. Hence, Smith does not know p.

If we supplement Clark's analysis as suggested above, it can be saved from this counterexample. Though Saunders and Champawat fail to mention this explicitly, presumably it is one of Smith's beliefs that Jones's owning a Ford yesterday would *result* in Jones's owning a Ford now. This was undoubtedly one of his grounds for believing that Jones owns a Ford now. (A complete diagram of S's beliefs relevant to p would include this belief.) Since this belief is false, however, Clark's analysis would yield the correct consequence that Smith does not know p. Unfortunately, Clark himself seems not to have noticed this point, since Saunders and Champawat's putative counterexample has been allowed to stand.

Another sort of counterexample to Clark's analysis has been given by Saunders and Cham-

$$(r) \longrightarrow (p)$$
$$B_S(t) \text{ ----- } B_S(u) \text{ .. } B_S(v) \text{ --------}$$
$$(q) \rightarrow B_B(q) \rightarrow A_B(q) \rightarrow B_S(A_B(q)) \rightarrow B_S(B_B(q)) \rightarrow B_S(q) \rightarrow B_S(p)$$

Figure 4

pawat and also by Keith Lehrer. This is a counterexample from which his analysis cannot escape. I shall give Lehrer's example (*op. cit.*) of this sort of difficulty. Suppose Smith bases his belief of

(*p*) Someone in his office owns a Ford

on his belief of four propositions

(*q*) Jones owns a Ford
(*r*) Jones works in his office
(*s*) Brown owns a Ford
(*t*) Brown works in his office

In fact, Smith knows *q, r,* and *t,* but he does not know *s* because *s* is false. Since *s* is false, not *all* of Smith's grounds for *p* are true, and, therefore, on Clark's analysis, Smith does not know *p.* Yet clearly Smith does know *p.* Thus, Clark's analysis is *too strong.*

Having seen the importance of a causal chain for knowing, it is fairly obvious how to amend Clark's requirements without making them too weak. We need not require, as Clark does, that *all* of *S*'s grounds be true. What is required is that enough of them be true to ensure the existence of at least *one* causal connection between *p* and *S*'s belief of *p.* In Lehrer's example, Smith thinks that there are two ways in which he knows *p:* via his knowledge of the conjunction of *q* and *r,* and via his knowledge of the conjunction of *s* and *t.* He does not know *p* via the conjunction of *s* and *t,* since *s* is false. But there is a causal connection via *q* and *r,* between *p* and Smith's belief of *p.* And this connection is enough.

Another sort of case in which one of *S*'s grounds for *p* may be false without preventing him from knowing *p* is where the false proposition is a dispensable background assumption. Suppose *S* bases his belief of *p* on 17 background assumptions, but only 16 of these are true. If these 16 are strong enough to confirm *p,* then the 17th is dispensable. *S* can be said to know *p* though one of his grounds is false.

Our discussion of Lehrer's example calls attention to the necessity of a further clarification of the notion of a "causal chain." I said earlier that causal chains with admixtures of inferences are causal chains. Now I wish to add that causal chains with admixtures of logical connections are causal chains. Unless we allow this interpretation, it is hard to see how facts like "Someone in the office owns a Ford"

or "All men are mortal" could be *causally* connected with beliefs thereof.

The following principle will be useful: *If x is logically related to y and if y is a cause of z, then x is a cause of z.* Thus, suppose that *q* causes *S*'s belief of *q* and that *r* causes *S*'s belief of *r.* Next suppose that *S* infers *q & r from his belief of q* and of *r.* Then the facts *q* and *r* are causes of *S*'s believing *q & r.* But the fact *q & r* is logically related to the fact *q* and to the fact *r.* Therefore, using the principle enunciated above, the fact *q & r* is a cause of *S*'s believing *q & r.*

In Lehrer's case another logical connection is involved: a connection between an existential fact and an instance thereof. Lehrer's case is diagrammed in Figure 5. In addition to the usual conventions, logical relationships are represented by double solid lines. As the diagram shows, the fact *p*—someone in Smith's office owning a Ford—is logically related to the fact *q & r*—Jones's owning a Ford and Jones's working in Smith's office. The fact *q & r* is, in turn, logically related to the fact *q* and to the fact *r.* *q* causes *S*'s belief of *q* and, by inference, his belief of *q & r* and of *p.* Similarly, *r* is a cause of *S*'s belief of *p.* Since Smith's inferences are warranted, even setting aside his belief of *s & t,* he knows *p.*

In a similar way, universal facts may be causes of beliefs thereof. The fact that all men are mortal is logically related to its instances: John's being mortal, George's being mortal, Oscar's being mortal, etc. Now suppose that *S* perceives George, John, Oscar, etc. to be mortal (by seeing them die). He infers from these facts that all men are mortal, an inference which, I assume, is warranted. Since each of the facts, John is mortal, George is mortal, Oscar is mortal, etc., is a cause of *S*'s believing that fact, each is also a cause of *S*'s believing that all men are

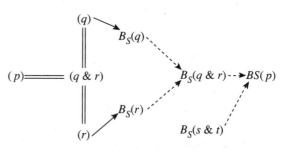

Figure 5

mortal. Moreoever, since the universal fact that all men are mortal is logically related to each of these particular facts, this universal fact is a cause of *S*'s belief of it. Hence, *S* can be said to know that all men are mortal. In analogous fashions, *S* can know various other logically compound propositions.

We can now formulate the analysis of knowing as follows:

> *S knows that p* if and only if
> *the fact p is causally connected in an*
> *"appropriate" way with S's believing p.*

"Appropriate," knowledge-producing causal processes include the following:

(1) perception

(2) memory

(3) a causal chain, exemplifying either Pattern 1 or 2, which is correctly reconstructed by inferences, each of which is warranted (background propositions help warrant an inference only if they are true)[10]

(4) combinations of (1), (2), and (3)

We have seen that this analysis is *stronger* than the traditional analysis in certain respects: the causal requirement and the correct-reconstruction requirement are absent from the older analysis. These additional requirements enable my analysis to circumvent Gettier's counterexamples to the traditional one. Buy my analysis is *weaker* than the traditional analysis in another respect. In at least one popular interpretation of the traditional analysis, a knower must be able to justify or give evidence for any proposition he knows. For *S* to know *p* at *t*, *S* must be able, at *t*, to *state* his justification for believing *p*, or his grounds for *p*. My analysis makes no such requirement, and the absence of this requirement enables me to account for cases of knowledge that would wrongly be excluded by the traditional analysis.

I know now, for example, that Abraham Lincoln was born in 1809.[11] I originally came to know this fact, let us suppose, by reading an encyclopedia article. I believed that this encyclopedia was trustworthy and that its saying Lincoln was born in 1809 must have resulted from the fact that Lincoln was indeed born in 1809. Thus, my original knowledge of this fact was founded on a warranted inference. But now I no longer remember this inference.

I remember that Lincoln was born in 1809, but not that this is stated in a certain encyclopedia. I no longer have any pertinent beliefs that highly confirm the proposition that Lincoln was born in 1809. Nevertheless, I know this proposition now. My original knowledge of it was preserved until now by the causal process of memory.

Defenders of the traditional analysis would doubtlessly deny that I really do know Lincoln's birth year. This denial, however, stems from a desire to protect their analysis. It seems clear that many things we know were originally learned in a way that we no longer remember. The range of our knowledge would be drastically reduced if these items were denied the status of knowledge.

Other species of knowledge without explicit evidence could also be admitted by my analysis. Notice that I have not closed the list of "appropriate" causal processes. Leaving the list open is desirable, because there may be some presently controversial causal processes that we may later deem "appropriate" and, therefore, knowledge-producing. Many people now doubt the legitimacy of claims to extrasensory perception. But if conclusive evidence were to establish the existence of causal processes connecting physical facts with certain persons' beliefs without the help of standard perceptual processes, we might decide to call such beliefs items of knowledge. This would be another species of knowledge in which the knower might be unable to justify or defend his belief. My analysis allows for the possibility of such knowledge, though it doesn't commit one to it.

Special comments are in order about knowledge of our own mental states. This is a very difficult and controversial topic, so I hesitate to discuss it, but something must be said about it. Probably there are some mental states that are clearly distinct from the subject's belief that he is in such a state. If so, then there is presumably a casual process connecting the existence of such states with the subject's belief thereof. We may add this kind of process to the list of "appropriate" causal processes. The more difficult cases are those in which the state is hardly distinguishable from the subject's believing that he is in that state. My being in pain and my believing that I am in pain are hardly distinct states of affairs. If there is no distinction here between the believing and the believed, how can there be a causal connection between them? For the purposes of the present analysis, we may regard identity as a "limiting" or "degenerate" case of a causal connection, just as zero may be regarded as a "limiting" or "degenerate" case of a number. It is not surprising that knowledge of one's own mental state should turn out to be a limiting or degenerate case of knowledge. Philosophers have long recognized its peculiar status. While some philosophers have regarded it as a paradigm case of knowledge, others have claimed that we have no "knowledge" of our mental states at all. A theory of knowledge that makes knowledge of one's own mental states rather different from garden-variety species of knowledge is, in so far forth, acceptable and even welcome.

In conclusion, let me answer some possible objections to my analysis. It might be doubted whether a causal analysis adequately provides the meaning of the word 'knows' or of the sentence (-schema) "*S* knows *p*." But I am not interested in giving the *meaning* of "*S* knows *p*"; only its *truth conditions*. I claim to have given one correct set of truth conditions for "*S* knows *p*." Truth conditions of a sentence do not always provide its meaning. Consider, for example, the following truth-conditions statement: "The sentence 'Team *T* wins the baseball game' is true if and only if team *T* has more runs at the end of the game than the opposing team." This statement fails to provide the meaning of the sentence 'Team *T* wins the baseball game'; for it fails to indicate an essential part of the meaning of that sentence, viz., that to win a game is to achieve the presumed goal of playing it. Someone might fully understand the truth conditions given above and yet fail to understand the meaning of the sentence because he has no understanding of the notion of "winning" in general.

Truth conditions should not be confused with verification conditions. My analysis of "*S* knows *p*" does not purport to give procedures for *finding out* whether a person (including oneself) knows a given proposition. No doubt, we sometimes do know that people know certain propositions, for we sometimes know that their beliefs are causally connected (in appropriate ways) with the facts believed. On the other hand, it may often be difficult or even impossible to find out whether this condition holds for a given proposition and a given person. For example, it may be difficult for me to find out whether I really do remember a certain fact that I seem to remember. The difficulties that exist for

finding out whether someone knows a given proposition do not constitute difficulties for my analysis, however.

In the same vein it should be noted that I have made no attempt to answer skeptical problems. My analysis gives no answer to the skeptic who asks that I start from the content of my own experience and then prove that I know there is a material world, a past, etc. I do not take this to be one of the jobs of giving truth conditions for "*S* knows that *p*."

The analysis presented here flies in the face of a well-established tradition in epistemology, the view that epistemological questions are questions of logic or justification, not causal or genetic questions. This traditional view, however, must not go unquestioned. Indeed, I think my analysis shows that the question of whether someone knows a certain proposition is, in part, a causal question, although, of course, the question of what the correct analysis is of "*S* knows that *p*" is not a causal question.

Notes

[1] "Is Justified True Belief Knowledge?" *Analysis,* 23.6 (1963), 121–123. I say "reminded" because essentially the same point was made by Russell in 1912. Cf. *The Problems of Philosophy* (Oxford, 1912), ch. 13, pp. 132 ff. New analyses have been proposed by Michael Clark, "Knowledge and Grounds: A Comment on Mr. Gettier's Paper," *Analysis* 24.2 (1963), 46–48; Ernest Sosa, "The Analysis of 'Knowledge that P,'" *ibid.,* 25.1 (1964): 1–8; and Keith Lehrer, "Knowledge, Truth and Evidence," *ibid.,* 25.5 (1965), 168–175.

[2] *Op. cit.* Criticisms of Clark's analysis will be discussed below.

[3] "The Causal Theory of Perception," *Proceedings of the Aristotelian Society,* supp. vol. 35 (1961).

[4] If a laser photograph (hologram) is illuminated by light waves, especially waves from a laser, the effect of the hologram on the viewer is exactly as if the object were being seen. It preserves three-dimensionality completely, and even gives appropriate parallax effects as the viewer moves relative to it. Cf. E. N. Leith and J. Upatnieks, "Photography by Laser," *Scientific American* (June 1965), p. 24.

[5] For further defense of this kind of procedure, with attention to perception, cf. Grice, *op. cit.*

[6] Causal connections can hold between states of affairs, such as believings, as well as between events. If a given event or state, in conjunction with other events or states, "leads to" or "results in" another event or state (or the same state obtaining at a later time), it will be called a

"cause" of the latter. I shall also speak of "facts" being causes.

[7] A fact can be a cause of a belief even if it does not *initiate* the belief. Suppose I believe that there is a lake in a certain locale, this belief having started in a manner quite unconnected with the existence of the lake. Continuing to have the belief, I go to the locale and perceive the lake. At this juncture, the existence of the lake becomes a cause of my believing that there is a lake there. This is analogous to a table top that is supported by four legs. When a fifth leg is inserted flush beneath the table top, it too becomes a cause of the table top's not falling. It has a causal role in the support of the table top even though, before it was inserted, the table top was adequately supported.

[8] Clearly we cannot require someone to reconstruct every detail, since this would involve knowledge of minute physical phenomena, for example, of which ordinary people are unaware. On the other hand, it is difficult to give criteria to identify which details, in general, are "important." This will vary substantially from case to case.

[9] "Mr. Clark's Definition of 'Knowledge'," *Analysis*, 25.1 (1964), 8–9.

[10] Perhaps background propositions that help warrant S's inference must be *known* by S, as well as true. This requirement could be added without making our analysis of "S knows that p" circular. For these propositions would not include p. In other words, the analysis of knowledge could be regarded as recursive.

[11] This kind of case is drawn from an unpublished manuscript of Gilbert Harman.

IV.3 *Knowledge: Undefeated Justified True Belief*

Keith Lehrer and Thomas D. Paxson, Jr.

Keith Lehrer is Professor of Philosophy at the University of Arizona, and Thomas Paxson is Professor of Philosophy at Southern Illinois University, Edwardsville. Confining themselves to nonbasic beliefs—those statements that are based on other statements—Lehrer and Paxson characterize nonbasic knowledge as undefeated justified true belief. That is, "Person S has nonbasic knowledge that *h* if and only if (i) *h* is true; (ii) S believes that *h*, and (iii) there is some statement *p* that completely justified S in believing that *h* and no other statement defeats this justification." This third condition is further explicated and qualified.

If a man knows that a statement is true even though there is no other statement that justifies his belief, then his knowledge is basic. Basic knowledge is completely justified true belief. On the other hand, if a man knows that a statement is true because there is some other statement that justifies his belief, then his knowledge is nonbasic. Nonbasic knowledge requires something in addition to completely justified true belief; for, though a statement completely justifies a man in his belief, there may be some true statement that *defeats* his justification. So, we must add the condition that his justification is not defeated. Nonbasic knowledge is undefeated justified true belief. These analyses will be elaborated below and subsequently defended against various alternative analyses.[1]

Reprinted from *The Journal of Philosophy*, 66.8 (1969), 225–237, by kind permission of the authors and editor.

I

We propose the following analysis of basic knowledge: S has basic knowledge that h if and only if (i) h is true, (ii) S believes that h, (iii) S is completely justified in believing that h, and (iv) the satisfaction of condition (iii) does not depend on any evidence p justifying S in believing that h. The third condition is used in such a way that it entails neither the second condition nor the first. A person can be completely justified in believing that h, even though, irrationally, he does not; and a person can be completely justified in believing that h, even though, unfortunately, he is mistaken.[2] Furthermore, the third condition does not entail that there is any statement or belief that justifies S in believing that h. The analysis, then, is in keeping with the characterization of basic knowledge given above. In basic knowledge, S is completely justified in believing that h even if it is not the case that there is any statement or belief that justifies his believing that h.

There are cases in which a person has some, perhaps mysterious, way of being right about matters of a certain sort with such consistency that philosophers and others have said that the person knows whereof he speaks. Consider, for example, the crystal-ball-gazing gypsy who is almost always right in his predictions of specific events. Peter Unger suggests a special case of this.[3] His gypsy is always right, but has no evidence to this effect and, in fact, believes that he is usually wrong. With respect to each specific prediction, however, the gypsy impulsively believes it to be true (as indeed it is). Whether or not the predictive beliefs of the ordinary gypsy and Unger's gypsy are cases of knowledge depends, we contend, on whether they are cases of basic knowledge. This in turn depends on whether the gypsies are completely justified in their beliefs. It is plausible to suggest that these are cases of knowledge, but this is only because it is also plausible to think that the gypsies in question have some way of being right that completely justifies their prognostications. We neither affirm nor deny that these are cases of knowledge, but maintain that, if they are cases of knowledge, then they are cases of *basic* knowledge.

It is consistent with our analysis of knowledge to admit that a man knows something even though no statement constitutes evidence that completely justifies his believing it. Philosophers have suggested that certain memory and perceptual beliefs are completely justified in the absence of such evidential statements. We choose to remain agnostic with respect to any claim of this sort, but such proposals are not excluded by our analysis.

II

Not all knowledge that p is basic knowledge that p, because sometimes justifying evidence is essential. Consider the following analysis of nonbasic knowledge: (i) h is true, (ii) S believes that h, and (iii*) p completely justifies S in believing that h. In this analysis, p is that (statement) which makes S completely justified in believing that h. Note that (iii*), like (iii), does not entail (ii) or (i).

This analysis of nonbasic knowledge is, of course, defective. As Edmund Gettier has shown, there are examples in which some false statement p entails and hence completely justifies S in believing that h, and such that, though S correctly believes that h, his being correct is mostly a matter of luck.[4] Consequently, S lacks knowledge, contrary to the above analysis. Other examples illustrate that the false statement which creates the difficulty need not *entail* h. Consider, for example, the case of the pyromaniac described by Skyrms.[5] The pyromaniac has found that Sure-Fire matches have always ignited when struck. On the basis of this evidence, the pyromaniac is completely justified in believing that the match he now holds will ignite upon his striking it. However, unbeknownst to the pyromaniac, this match happens to contain impurities that raise its combustion temperature above that which can be produced by the friction. Imagine that a burst of Q-radiation ignites the match just as he strikes it. His belief that the match will ignite upon his striking it is true and completely justified by the evidence. But this is not a case of knowledge, because it is not the striking that will cause the match to ignite.

Roderick Chisholm has pointed out that justifications are defeasible.[6] In the examples referred to above, there is some true statement that would defeat any justification of S for believing that h. In the case of the pyromaniac, his justification is defeated by the true statement that striking the match will not cause it to ignite. This defeats his justification for believing that the match will ignite upon his striking it.

Thus we propose the following analysis of nonbasic knowledge: S has nonbasic knowledge that h if and only if (i) h is true. (ii) S believes that h, and (iii) there is some statement p that completely justifies S in believing that h and no other statement defeats this justification. The question we must now answer is—what does it mean to say that a statement defeats a justification? Adopting a suggestion of Chisholm's, we might try the following: when p completely justifies S in believing that h, this justification is defeated by q if and only if (i) q is true, and (ii) the conjunction of p and q does not completely justify S in believing that h.[7] This definition is strong enough to rule out the example of the pyromaniac as a case of knowledge. The statement that the striking of a match will *not* cause it to ignite, which is true, is such that when it is conjoined to any statement that completely justifies the pyromaniac in believing that the match will ignite, the resultant conjunction will fail to so justify him in that belief. Given this definition of defeasibility, the analysis of nonbasic knowledge would require that a man who has nonbasic knowledge that h must have some justification for his belief that is not defeated by any true statement.

However, this requirement is somewhat unrealistic. To see that the definition of defeasibility under consideration makes the analysis of nonbasic knowledge excessively restrictive, we need only notice that there can be true statements that are misleading. Suppose I see a man walk into the library and remove a book from the library by concealing it beneath his coat. Since I am sure the man is Tom Grabit, whom I have often seen before when he attended my classes, I report that I know that Tom Grabit has removed the book. However, suppose further that Mrs. Grabit, the mother of Tom, has averred that on the day in question Tom was not in the library, indeed, was thousands of miles away, and that Tom's identical twin brother, John Grabit, was in the library. Imagine, moreover, that I am entirely ignorant of the fact that Mrs. Grabit has said these things. The statement that she has said these things would defeat any justification I have for believing that Tom Grabit removed the book, according to our present definition of defeasibility.

Thus, I could not be said to have nonbasic knowledge that Tom Grabit removed the book.

The preceding might seem acceptable until we finish the story by adding that Mrs. Grabit is a compulsive and pathological liar, that John Grabit is a fiction of her demented mind, and that Tom Grabit took the book as I believed. Once this is added, it should be apparent that I did know that Tom Grabit removed the book, and, since the knowledge must be nonbasic, I must have nonbasic knowledge of that fact. Consequently, the definition of defeasibility must be amended. The fact that Mrs. Grabit said what she did should not be allowed to defeat any justification I have for believing that Tom Grabit removed the book, because I neither entertained any beliefs concerning Mrs. Grabit nor would I have been justified in doing so. More specifically, my justification does not depend on my being completely justified in believing that Mrs. Grabit did *not* say the things in question.

To understand how the definition of defeasibility must be amended to deal with the preceding example, let us consider an example from the literature in which a justification deserves to be defeated. Suppose that I have excellent evidence that completely justifies my believing that a student in my class, Mr. Nogot, owns a Ford, the evidence consisting in my having seen him driving it, hearing him say he owns it, and so forth. Since Mr. Nogot is a student in my class who owns a Ford, someone in my class owns a Ford, and, consequently, I am completely justified in believing that someone in my class owns a Ford. Imagine that, contrary to the evidence, Mr. Nogot does not own a Ford, that I have been deceived, but that unknown to me Mr. Havit, who is also in my class, does own a Ford. Though I have a completely justified true belief, I do not know that someone in my class owns a Ford. The reason is that my sole justification for believing that someone in my class does own a Ford is and should be defeated by the true statement that Mr. Nogot does not own a Ford.

In the case of Tom Grabit, the true statement that Mrs. Grabit said Tom was not in the library and so forth, should not be allowed to defeat my justification for believing that Tom removed the book, whereas in the case of Mr. Nogot, the true statement that Mr. Nogot does not own a Ford, should defeat my justification for believing that someone in my class owns a Ford. Why should one true statement but not the other be allowed to defeat my justification? The answer is that in one case my justification depends on my being completely justified in believing the true statement to be false while in the other it does not. My justification for believing that Tom removed the book does not depend on my being completely justified in believing it to be false that Mrs. Grabit said Tom was not in the library and so forth. But my justification for believing that someone in my class owns a Ford does depend on my being completely justified in believing it to be false that Mr. Nogot does not own a Ford. Thus, a defeating statement must be one which, though true, is such that the subject is completely justified in believing it to be false.[8]

The following definition of defeasibility incorporates this proposal: when p completely justifies S in believing that h, this justification is defeated by q if and only if (i) q is true, (ii) S is completely justified in believing q to be false, and (iii) the conjunction of p and q does not completely justify S in believing that h.

This definition of defeasibility, though basically correct, requires one last modification to meet a technical problem. Suppose that there is some statement h of which S has nonbasic knowledge. Let us again consider the example in which I know that Tom Grabit removed the book. Now imagine that there is some true statement which is completely irrelevant to this knowledge and which I happen to be completely justified in believing to be false, for example, the statement that I was born in St. Paul. Since I am completely justified in believing it to be false that I was born in St. Paul, I am also completely justified in believing to be false the conjunctive statement that I was born in St. Paul and that q, whatever q is, because I am completely justified in believing any conjunction to be false if I am completely justified in believing a conjunct of it to be false. Therefore, I am completely justified in believing to be false the conjunctive statement that I was born in St. Paul and Mrs. Grabit said that Tom Grabit was not in the library and so forth. Moreover, this conjunctive statement is true, and is such that, when it is conjoined in turn to any evidential statement that justifies me in believing that Tom Grabit removed the book, the resultant extended conjunction will not completely justify me in believing that Tom Grabit removed the book. Hence, any such justification will be defeated.[9] Once again, it

turns out that I do not have nonbasic knowledge of the fact that Tom is the culprit.

In a logical nut, the problem is that the current definition of defeasibility reduces to the preceding one. Suppose there is a true statement q such that, for any p that completely justifies S in believing h, the conjunction of p and q does not completely justify me in believing that h. Moreover, suppose that I am not completely justified in believing q to be false, so that, given our current definition of defeasibility, q does not count as defeating. Nevertheless, if there is any true statement r, irrelevant to both p and q, which I am completely justified in believing to be false, then we can indirectly use q to defeat my justification for believing h. For I shall be completely justified in believing the conjunction of r and q to be false, though in fact it is true, because I am completely justified in believing r to be false. If the conjunction of q and p does not completely justify me in believing that h, then, given the irrelevance of r, neither would the conjunction of r, q and p justify me in believing that h. Hence, my justifications for believing h would be defeated by the conjunction r and q on the current definition of defeasibility as surely as they were by q alone on the preceding definition.

The defect is not difficult to repair. Though S is completely justified in believing the conjunction of r and q to be false, one consequence of the conjunction, q, undermines my justification but is not something I am completely justified in believing to be false, while another consequence, r, is one that I am completely justified in believing to be false but is irrelevant to my justification. To return to our example, I am completely justified in believing to be false the conjunctive statement that I was born in St. Paul and that Mrs. Grabit said that Tom was not in the library and so forth. One consequence of this conjunction, that Mrs. Grabit said that Tom was not in the library and so forth, undermines my justification but is not something I am completely justified in believing to be false, while the other consequence, that I was born in St. Paul, is something I am completely justified in believing to be false but is irrelevant to my justification. The needed restriction is that those consequences of a defeating statement which undermine a justification must themselves be statements that the subject is completely justified in believing to be false.

We propose the following definition of defeasibility: if *p* completely justifies *S* in believing that *h*, then this justification is defeated by *q* if and only if (i) *q* is true, (ii) the conjunction of *p* and *q* does not completely justify *S* in believing that *h*, (iii) *S* is completely justified in believing *q* to be false, and (iv) if *c* is a logical consequence of *q* such that the conjunction of *c* and *p* does not completely justify *S* in believing that *h*, then *S* is completely justified in believing *c* to be false.

With this definition of defeasibility, we complete our analysis of nonbasic knowledge. We have defined nonbasic knowledge as true belief for which some statement provides a complete and undefeated justification. We previously defined basic knowledge as true belief for which there was complete justification that did not depend on any justifying statement. We define as knowledge anything that is either basic or nonbasic knowledge. Thus, *S* knows that *h* if and only if *S* has either basic or nonbasic knowledge that *h*.

Notes

[1] This analysis of knowledge is a modification of an earlier analysis proposed by Keith Lehrer, "Knowledge, Truth and Evidence," *Analysis,* 25.5 (1965), 168–175. It is intended to cope with objections to that article raised by Gilbert H. Harman in "Lehrer on Knowledge," *Journal of Philosophy,* 63.9 (1966), 241–247, and Alvin Goldman, Brian Skyrms, and others. Criticisms of various alternative analyses of knowledge are given in Lehrer's earlier article, and the reader is referred to that article; such discussion will not be repeated here. The distinction between basic and nonbasic knowledge that is elaborated here was suggested by Arthur Danto in "Freedom and Forebearance," in *Freedom and Determinism* (New York: Random House, 1965), pp. 45–63.

[2] Harman's criticism of Lehrer's earlier article rested on his interpreting Lehrer as saying that a person can be completely justified in believing something only if he does believe it. This interpretation leads to problems and is repudiated here.

[3] "Experience and Factual Knowledge," *Journal of Philosophy,* 64.5 (1967), 152–173, esp. pp. 165–167; see also his "An Analysis of Factual Knowledge," ibid., 65.6 (1968), 157–170, esp. pp. 163–164.

[4] "Is Justified True Belief Knowledge?" *Analysis,* 23.6 (1963), 121–123.

[5] "The Explication of 'X knows that *p*'," *Journal of Philosophy,* 64.12 (1967), 373–389.

[6] *Theory of Knowledge* (Englewood Cliffs, N.J.: Prentice-Hall, 1966), p. 48.

[7] Chisholm, "The Ethics of Requirement," *American Philosophical Quarterly,* 1.2 (1964), 147–153. This definition of defeasibility would make our analysis of nonbasic knowledge very similar to one Harman derives from Lehrer's analysis and also one proposed by Marshall Swain in "The Analysis of Non-Basic Knowledge" (unpublished).

[8] In Skyrms' example of the pyromaniac cited earlier, the defeating statement is not one which the pyromaniac need believe; Skyrms suggests that the pyromaniac neither believes nor disbelieves that striking the match will cause it to ignite. Nevertheless, the pyromaniac would be completely justified in believing that striking the Sure-Fire match will cause it to ignite. Hence the statement that striking the match will *not* cause it to light is defeating.

[9] A similar objection to Lehrer's earlier analysis is raised by Harman, p. 243.

IV.4 *Inference to the Best Explanation*

GILBERT HARMAN

Gilbert Harman is Professor of Philosophy at Princeton University and is the author of *Thought* (1973), from which this selection is taken. Harman seeks to correct Goldman's causal account of empirical knowledge by replacing "cause" with "because" and by viewing the causal account as a special case of an explanatory account of knowledge. Inductive knowledge is inference to the best explanation. In the second part of his essay, Harman goes on to discuss undermining evidence to knowledge claims, modifying his formula for inferential conclusions to read "Y because X and there is no undermining evidence to this whole conclusion."

Gettier Examples and Probabilistic Rules of Acceptance

In any Gettier example we are presented with similar cases in which someone infers h from things he knows, h is true, and he is equally justified in making the inference in either case. In the one case he comes to know that h and in the other case he does not. I have observed that a natural explanation of many Gettier examples is that the relevant inference involves not only the final conclusion h but also at least one intermediate conclusion true in the one case but not in the other. And I have suggested that any account of inductive inference should show why such intermediate conclusions are essentially involved in the relevant inferences. Gettier cases are thus to be explained by appeal to the principle

P   Reasoning that essentially involves false conclusions, intermediate or final, cannot give one knowledge.

It is easy to see that purely probabilistic rules of acceptance do not permit an explanation of Gettier

examples by means of principle P. Reasoning in accordance with a purely probabilistic rule involves essentially only its final conclusion. Since that conclusion is highly probable, it can be inferred without reference to any other conclusions; in particular, there will be no intermediate conclusion essential to the inference that is true in one case and false in the other. . . .

The trouble is that purely probabilistic rules are incompatible with the natural account of Gettier examples by means of principle P. The solution is not to attempt to modify P but rather to modify our account of inference.

1. *Knowledge and Explanation: A Causal Theory*

Goldman suggests that we know only if there is the proper sort of causal connection between our belief and what we know. For example, we perceive that there has been an automobile accident only if the accident is relevantly causally responsible, by way of our sense organs, for our belief that there has been an accident. Similarly, we remember doing something only if having done it is relevantly causally responsible for our current memory of having done it. Although in some cases the fact that we know

From Gilbert Harman, *Thought* (copyright © 1973 by Princeton University Press), pp. 120–172, some selections in paraphrased and expanded form. Reprinted by kind permission of the author and Princeton University Press.

thus simply begins a causal chain that leads to our belief, in other cases the causal connection is more complicated. If Mary learns that Mr. Havit owns a Ford, Havit's past ownership is causally responsible for the evidence she has and also responsible (at least in part) for Havit's present ownership. Here the relevant causal connection consists in there being a common cause of the belief and of the state of affairs believed in.

Mary fails to know in the original Nogot-Havit case[1] because the causal connection is lacking. Nogot's past ownership is responsible for her evidence but is not responsible for the fact that one of her friends owns a Ford. Havit's past ownership at least partly accounts for why one of her friends now owns a Ford, but it is not responsible for her evidence. Similarly, the man who is told something true by a speaker who does not believe what he says fails to know because the truth of what is said is not causally responsible for the fact that it is said.

General knowledge does not fit into this simple framework. That all emeralds are green neither causes nor is caused by the existence of the particular green emeralds examined when we come to know that all emeralds are green. Goldman handles such examples by counting logical connections among the causal connections. The belief that all emeralds are green is, in an extended sense, relevantly causally connected to the fact that all emeralds are green, since the evidence causes the belief and is logically entailed by what is believed.

It is obvious that not every causal connection, especially in this extended sense, is relevant to knowledge. Any two states of affairs are logically connected simply because both are entailed by their conjunction. If every such connection were relevant, the analysis Goldman suggests would have us identify knowledge with true belief, since there would always be a relevant "causal connection" between any state of true belief and the state of affairs believed in. Goldman avoids this reduction of his analysis to justified true belief by saying that when knowledge is based on inference relevant causal connections must be "reconstructed" in the inference. Mary knows that one of her friends owns a Ford only if her inference reconstructs the relevant causal connection between evidence and conclusion.

But what does it mean to say that her inference must "reconstruct" the relevant causal connection? Presumably it means that she must infer or be able to infer something about the causal connection between her conclusion and the evidence for it. And this suggests that Mary must make at least two inferences. First she must infer her original conclusion and second she must infer something about the causal connection between the conclusion and her evidence. Her second conclusion is her "reconstruction" of the causal connection. But how detailed must her reconstruction be? If she must reconstruct every detail of the causal connection between evidence and conclusion, she will never gain knowledge by way of inference. If she need only reconstruct some "causal connection," she will always know, since she will always be able to infer that evidence and conclusion are both entailed by their conjunction.

I suggest that it is a mistake to approach the problem as a problem about what else Mary needs to infer before she has knowledge of her original conclusion. Goldman's remark about reconstructing the causal connection makes more sense as a remark about the kind of inference Mary needs to reach her original conclusion in the first place. It has something to do with principle P and the natural account of the Gettier examples.

Nogot presents Mary with evidence that he owns a Ford. She infers that one of her friends owns a Ford. She is justified in reaching that conclusion and it is true. However, since it is true, not because Nogot owns a Ford, but because Havit does, Mary fails to come to know that one of her friends owns a Ford. The natural explanation is that she must infer that Nogot owns a Ford and does not know her final conclusion unless her intermediate conclusion is true. According to this natural explanation, Mary's inference essentially involves the conclusion that Nogot owns a Ford. According to Goldman, her inference essentially involves a conclusion concerning a causal connection. In order to put these ideas together, we must turn Goldman's theory of knowledge into a theory of inference.

As a first approximation, let us take his remarks about causal connections literally, forgetting for the moment that they include logical connections. Then let us transmute his causal theory of knowing into the theory that inductive conclusions always take the form X *causes* Y, where further conclusions are reached by additional steps of inductive or deductive reasoning. In particular, we may deduce either X or Y from X *causes* Y.

This causal theory of inferring provides the following account of why knowledge requires that we be right about an appropriate causal connection. A person knows by inference only if all conclusions essential to that inference are true. That is, his inference must satisfy principle P. Since he can legitimately infer his conclusion only if he can first infer certain causal statements, he can know only if he is right about the causal connection expressed by those statements. First, Mary infers that her evidence is a causal result of Nogot's past ownership of the Ford. From that she deduces that Nogot has owned a Ford. Then she infers that his past ownership has been causally responsible for present ownership; and she deduces that Nogot owns a Ford. Finally, she deduces that one of her friends owns a Ford. She fails to know because she is wrong when she infers that Nogot's past ownership is responsible for Nogot's present ownership.

2. Inference to the Best Explanatory Statement

A better account of inference emerges if we replace "cause" with "because." On the revised account, we infer not just statements of the form X *causes* Y but, more generally, statements of the form Y *because* X or X *explains* Y. Inductive inference is conceived as inference to the best of competing explanatory statements. Inference to a causal explanation is a special case.

The revised account squares better with ordinary usage. Nogot's past ownership helps to explain Mary's evidence, but it would sound odd to say that it caused that evidence. Similarly, the detective infers that activities of the butler explain these footprints; does he infer that those activities caused the footprints? A scientist explains the properties of water by means of a hypothesis about unobservable particles that make up the water, but it does not seem right to say that facts about those particles cause the properties of water. An observer infers that certain mental states best explain someone's behavior; but such explanation by reasons might not be causal explanation.

Furthermore, the switch from "cause" to "because" avoids Goldman's *ad hoc* treatment of knowledge of generalizations. Although there is no causal relation between a generalization and those observed instances which provide us with evidence for the generalization, there is an obvious explanatory relationship. That all emeralds are green does not cause a particular emerald to be green; but it can explain why that emerald is green. And, other things being equal, we can infer a generalization only if it provides the most plausible way to explain our evidence.

We often infer generalizations that explain but do not logically entail their instances, since they are of the form, *In circumstances C, X's tend to be Y's.* Such generalizations may be inferred if they provide a sufficiently plausible account of observed instances all things considered. For example, from the fact that doctors have generally been right in the past when they have said that someone is going to get measles, I infer that doctors can normally tell from certain symptoms that someone is going to get measles. More precisely, I infer that doctors have generally been right in the past because they can normally tell from certain symptoms that someone is going to get measles. This is a very weak explanation, but it is a genuine one. Compare it with the pseudo-explanation, "Doctors are generally right when they say someone has measles because they can normally tell from certain symptoms that someone is going to get measles."

Similarly, I infer that a substance is soluble in water from the fact that it dissolved when I stirred it into some water. That is a real explanation, to be distinguished from the pseudo-explanation, "That substance dissolves in water because it is soluble in water." Here too a generalization explains an instance without entailing that instance, since water-soluble substances do not always dissolve in water.

Although we cannot simply deduce instances from this sort of generalization, we can often infer that the generalization will explain some new instance. The inference is warranted if the explanatory claim *that X's tend to be Y's will explain why the next X will be Y* is sufficiently more plausible than competitors such as *interfering factor Q will prevent the next X from being a Y.* For example, the doctor says that you will get measles. Because doctors are normally right about that sort of thing, I infer that you will. More precisely, I infer that doctors' normally being able to tell when someone will get measles will explain the doctor's being right in this case. The competing explanatory statements here are not other explanations of the doctor's being right but rather explanations of his being wrong—e.g., because he has misperceived the symptoms, or because you have faked the symptoms of measles, or because these symptoms are the result of some other disease, etc. Similarly, I infer that this sugar will dissolve in my tea. That is, I infer that the solubility of sugar in tea will explain this sugar's dissolving in the present case. Competing explanations would explain the sugar's not dissolving—e.g., because there is already a saturated sugar solution there, because the tea is ice-cold, etc. . . .

Another example is the mad-fiend case. Omar falls down drunk in the street. An hour later he suffers a fatal heart attack not connected with his recent drinking. After another hour a mad fiend comes down the street, spies Omar lying in the gutter, cuts off his head, and runs away. Some time later still, you walk down the street, see Omar lying there, and observe that his head has been cut off. You infer that Omar is dead; and in this way you come to know that he is dead. Now there is no causal connection between Omar's being dead and his head's having been cut off. The fact that Omar is dead is not causally responsible for his head's having been cut off, since if he had not suffered that fatal heart attack he still would have been lying there drunk when the mad fiend came along. And having his head cut off did not cause Omar's death, since he was already dead. Nor is there a straightforward logical connection between Omar's being dead and his having his head cut off. (Given the right sorts of tubes, one might survive decapitation.) So it is doubtful that Goldman's causal theory of knowing can account for your knowledge that Omar is dead.

If inductive inference is inference to the best explanatory statement, your inference might be parsed as follows: "Normally, if someone's head is cut off, that person is dead. This generalization accounts for the fact that Omar's having his head cut off is correlated here with Omar's being dead." Relevant competing explanatory statements in this case would not be competing explanations of Omar's being dead. Instead they would seek to explain Omar's not being dead despite his head's having been cut off. One possibility would be that doctors have carefully connected head and body with special tubes so that blood and air get from body to head and back again. You rule out that hypothesis on grounds of explanatory complications: too many questions left unanswered (why can't you see the tubes? why wasn't it done in the hospital? etc.). If you cannot rule such possibilities out, then you cannot come to know that Omar is dead. And if you do rule them out but they turn out to be true, again you do not come to know. For example, if it is all an elaborate psychological philosophical experiment, which however fails, then you do not come to know that Omar is dead even though he is dead.

4. *Statistical Inference*

Statistical inference, and knowledge obtained from it, is also better explicated by way of the notion of statistical explanation than by way of the notion of cause or logical entailment. . . .

Evidence One Does Not Possess: Three Examples

Example (1).

While I am watching him, Tom takes a library book from the shelf and conceals it beneath his coat. Since I am the library detective, I follow him as he walks brazenly past the guard at the front door. Outside I see him take out the book and smile. As I approach he notices me and suddenly runs away. But I am sure that it was Tom, for I know him well. I saw Tom steal a book from the library and that is the testimony I give before the University Judicial Council. After testifying, I leave the hearing room and return to my post in the library. Later that day, Tom's mother testifies that Tom has an identical twin, Buck. Tom, she says, was thousands of miles away at the time of the theft. She hopes that Buck did not do it; but she admits that he has a bad character.

Do I know that Tom stole the book? Let us suppose that I am right. It was Tom that took the book. His mother was lying when she said that

Tom was thousands of miles away. I do not know that she was lying, of course, since I do not know anything about her, even that she exists. Nor does anyone at the hearing know that she is lying, although some may suspect that she is. In these circumstances I do not know that Tom stole the book. My knowledge is undermined by evidence I do not possess.

Example (2).

Donald has gone off to Italy. He told you ahead of time that he was going; and you saw him off at the airport. He said he was to stay for the entire summer. That was in June. It is now July. Then you might know that he is in Italy. It is the sort of thing one often claims to know. However, for reasons of his own Donald wants you to believe that he is not in Italy but in California. He writes several letters saying that he has gone to San Francisco and has decided to stay there for the summer. He wants you to think that these letters were written by him in San Francisco, so he sends them to someone he knows there and has that person mail them to you with a San Francisco postmark, one at a time. You have been out of town for a couple of days and have not read any of the letters. You are now standing before the pile of mail that arrived while you were away. Two of the phony letters are in the pile. You are about to open your mail. I ask you, "Do you know where Donald is?" "Yes," you reply, "I know that he is in Italy." You are right about where Donald is and it would seem that your justification for believing that Donald is in Italy makes no reference to letters from San Francisco. But you do not know that Donald is in Italy. Your knowledge is undermined by evidence you do not as yet possess.

Example (3).

A political leader is assassinated. His associates, fearing a coup, decide to pretend that the bullet hit someone else. On nationwide television they announce that an assassination attempt has failed to kill the leader but has killed a secret service man by mistake. However, before the announcement is made, an enterprising reporter on the scene telephones the real story to his newspaper, which has included the story in its final edition. Jill buys a copy of that paper and reads the story of the assassination. What she reads is true and so are her assumptions about how the story came to be in the paper. The reporter, whose by-line appears, saw the assassination and dictated his report, which is now printed just as he dictated it. Jill has justified true belief and, it would seem, all her intermediate conclusions are true. But she does not know that the political leader has been assassinated. For everyone else has heard about the televised announcement. They may also have seen the story in the paper and, perhaps, do not know what to believe; and it is highly implausible that Jill should know simply because she lacks evidence everyone else has. Jill does not know. Her knowledge is undermined by evidence she does not possess.

These examples pose a problem for my strategy. They are Gettier examples and my strategy is to make assumptions about inference that will account for Gettier examples by means of principle *P*. But these particular examples appear to bring in considerations that have nothing to do with conclusions essential to the inference on which belief is based.

Some readers may have trouble evaluating these examples. Like other Gettier examples, these require attention to subtle facts about ordinary usage; it is easy to miss subtle differences if, as in the present instance, it is very difficult to formulate a theory that would account for these differences. We must compare what it would be natural to say about these cases if there were no additional evidence one does not possess (no testimony from Tom's mother, no letters from San Francisco, and no televised announcement) with what it would be natural to say about the cases in which there is the additional evidence one does not possess. We must take care not to adopt a very skeptical attitude nor become too lenient about what is to count as knowledge. If we become skeptically inclined, we will deny there is knowledge in either case. If we become too lenient, we will allow that there is knowledge in both cases. It is tempting to go in one or the other of these directions, toward skepticism or leniency, because it proves so difficult to see what general principles are involved that would mark the difference. But at least some difference between the cases is revealed by the fact that we are *more inclined* to say that there is knowledge in the examples where there is no undermining evidence a person does not possess than in the examples where there is such evidence. The problem, then, is to account for this difference in our inclination to ascribe knowledge to someone.

Evidence Against What One Knows

If I had known about Tom's mother's testimony, I would not have been justified in thinking that it was Tom I saw steal the book. Once you read the letters from Donald in which he says he is in San Francisco, you are no longer justified in thinking that he is in Italy. If Jill knew about the television announcement, she would not be justified in believing that the political leader has been assassinated. This suggests that we can account for the preceding examples by means of the following principle.

> One knows only if there is no evidence such that if one knew about the evidence one would not be justified in believing one's conclusion.

However, by modifying the three examples it can be shown that this principle is too strong.

Suppose that Tom's mother was known to the Judicial Council as a pathological liar. Everyone at the hearing realizes that Buck, Tom's supposed twin, is a figment of her imagination. When she testifies no one believes her. Back at my post in the library, I still know nothing of Tom's mother or her testimony. In such a case, my knowledge would not be undermined by her testimony; but if I were told only that she had just testified that Tom has a twin brother and was himself thousands of miles away from the scene of the crime at the time the book was stolen, I would no longer be justified in believing as I now do that Tom stole the book. Here I know even though there is evidence which, if I knew about it, would cause me not to be justified in believing my conclusion.

Suppose that Donald had changed his mind and never mailed the letters to San Francisco. Then those letters no longer undermine your knowledge. But it is very difficult to see what principle accounts for this fact. How can letters in the pile on the table in front of you undermine your knowledge while the same letters in a pile in front of Donald do not? If you knew that Donald had written letters to you saying that he was in San Francisco, you would not be justified in believing that he was still in Italy. But that fact by itself does not undermine your present knowledge that he is in Italy.

Suppose that as the political leader's associates are about to make their announcement, a saboteur cuts the wire leading to the television transmitter. The announcement is therefore heard only by those in the studio, all of whom are parties to the deception. Jill reads the real story in the newspaper as before. Now, she does come to know that the political leader has been assassinated. But if she had known that it had been announced that he was not assassinated, she would not have been justified in believing that he has, simply on the basis of the newspaper story. Here, a cut wire makes the difference between evidence that undermines knowledge and evidence that does not undermine knowledge.

We can know that h even though there is evidence e that we do not know about such that, if we did know about e, we would not be justified in believing h. If we know that h, it does not follow that we know that there is not any evidence like e. This can seem paradoxical, for it can seem obvious that, if we know that h, we know that any evidence against h can only be misleading. So, later if we get that evidence we ought to be able to know enough to disregard it.

A more explicit version of this interesting paradox goes like this.[2] "If I know that h is true, I know that any evidence against h is evidence against something that is true; so I know that such evidence is misleading. But I should disregard evidence that I know is misleading. So, once I know that h is true, I am in a position to disregard any future evidence that seems to tell against h." This is paradoxical, because I am never in a position simply to disregard any future evidence even though I do know a great many different things.

A skeptic might appeal to this paradox in order to argue that, since we are never in a position to disregard any further evidence, we never know anything. Some philosophers would turn the argument around to say that, since we often know things, we are often in a position to disregard further evidence. But both of these responses go wrong in accepting the paradoxical argument in the first place.

I can know that Tom stole a book from the

library without being able automatically to disregard evidence to the contrary. You can know that Donald is in Italy without having the right to ignore whatever further evidence may turn up. Jill may know that the political leader has been assassinated even though she would cease to know this if told that there was an announcement that only a secret service agent had been shot.

The argument for paradox overlooks the way actually having evidence can make a difference. Since I now know that Tom stole the book, I now know that any evidence that appears to indicate something else is misleading. That does not warrant me in simply disregarding any further evidence, since getting that further evidence can change what I know. In particular, after I get such further evidence I may no longer know that it is misleading. For having the new evidence can make it true that I no longer know that Tom stole the book; if I no longer know that, I no longer know that the new evidence is misleading.

Therefore, we cannot account for the problems posed by evidence one does not possess by appeal to the principle, which I now repeat:

> One knows only if there is no evidence such that if one knew about the evidence one would not be justified in believing one's conclusion.

For one can know even though such evidence exists.

A *Result Concerning Inference*

When does evidence one does not possess keep one from having knowledge? I have described three cases, each in two versions, in which there is misleading evidence one does not possess. In the first version of each case the misleading evidence undermines someone's knowledge. In the second version it does not. What makes the difference?

My strategy is to account for Gettier examples by means of principle *P*. This strategy has led us to conceive of induction as inference to the best explanation. But that conception of inference does not by itself seem able to explain these examples. So I want to use the examples in order to learn something more about inference, in particular about

what other conclusions are essential to the inference that Tom stole the book, that Donald is in Italy, or that the political leader has been assassinated.

It is not plausible that the relevant inferences should contain essential intermediate conclusions that refer explicitly to Tom's mother, to letters from San Francisco, or to special television programs. For it is very likely that there is an infinite number of ways a particular inference might be undermined by misleading evidence one does not possess. If there must be a separate essential conclusion ruling out each of these ways, inferences would have to be infinitely inclusive—and that is implausible.

Therefore it would seem that the relevant inferences must rule out undermining evidence one does not possess by means of a single conclusion, essential to the inference, that characterizes all such evidence. But how might this be done? It is not at all clear what distinguishes evidence that undermines knowledge from evidence that does not. How is my inference to involve an essential conclusion that rules out Tom's mother's testifying a certain way before a believing audience but does not rule out (simply) her testifying in that way? Or that rules out the existence of letters of a particular sort in the mail on your table but not simply the existence of those letters? Or that rules out a widely heard announcement of a certain sort without simply ruling out the announcement?

Since I am unable to formulate criteria that would distinguish among these cases, I will simply *label* cases of the first kind "undermining evidence one does not possess." Then we can say this: one knows only if there is no undermining evidence one does not possess. If there is such evidence, one does not know. However, these remarks are completely trivial.

It is somewhat less trivial to use the same label to formulate a principle concerned with inference.

> Q One may infer a conclusion only if one also infers that there is no undermining evidence one does not possess.

There is of course an obscurity in principle *Q;* but the principle is not as trivial as the remarks of the last paragraph, since the label "undermining evidence one does not possess" has been explained in terms of knowledge, whereas this is a principle concerning inference.

If we can explain "undermining" without appeal to knowledge, given Q, we can use principle P to account for the differences between the two versions of each of the three examples described above. In each case an inference involves essentially the claim that there is no undermining evidence one does not possess. Since this claim is false in the first version of each case and true in the second, principle P implies that there can be knowledge only in the second version of each case.

So there is, according to my strategy, some reason to think that there is a principle concerning inference like principle Q. That raises the question of whether there is any independent reason to accept such a principle; and reflection on good scientific practice suggests a positive answer. It is a commonplace that a scientist should base his conclusions on all the evidence. Furthermore, he should not rest content with the evidence he happens to have but should try to make sure he is not overlooking any relevant evidence. A good scientist will not accept a conclusion unless he has some reason to think that there is no as yet undiscovered evidence which would undermine his conclusion. Otherwise he would not be warranted in making his inference. So good scientific practice reflects the acceptance of something like principle Q, which is the independent confirmation we wanted for the existence of this principle.

Notice that the scientist must accept something like principle Q, with its reference to "undermining evidence one does not possess." For example, he cannot accept the following principle,

> One may infer a conclusion only if one also infers that there is no evidence at all such that if he knew that evidence he could not accept his conclusion.

There will always be a true proposition such that if he learned that the proposition was true (and learned nothing else) he would not be warranted in accepting his conclusion. If h is his conclusion, and if k is a true proposition saying what ticket will win the grand prize in the next New Jersey State lottery, then *either k or not h* is such a proposition. If he were to learn that it is true that *either k or not h* (and learned nothing else), *not h* would become probable since (given what he knows) k is antecedently very improbable. So he could no longer reasonably infer that h is true.

There must be a certain kind of evidence such

that the scientist infers there is no as yet undiscovered evidence of that kind against h. Principle Q says that the relevant kind is what I have been labelling "undermining evidence one does not possess." Principle Q is confirmed by the fact that good scientific practice involves some such principle and by the fact that principle Q together with principle P accounts for the three Gettier examples I have been discussing.

If this account in terms of principles P and Q is accepted, inductive conclusions must involve some self-reference. Otherwise there would be a regress. Before we could infer that h, we would have to infer that there is no undermining evidence to h. That prior inference could not be deductive, so it would have to be inference to the best explanatory statement. For example, we might infer that the fact that there is no sign of undermining evidence we do not possess is explained by there not being any such evidence. But, then, before we could accept that conclusion we would first have to infer that there is no undermining evidence to *it* which one does not possess. And, since that inference would have to be inference to the best explanation, it would require a previous inference that there is no undermining evidence for its conclusion; and so on *ad infinitum*.

Clearly, we do not *first* have to infer that there is no undermining evidence to h and only then infer h. For that would automatically yield the regress. Instead, we must at the same time infer both h and that there is no undermining evidence. Furthermore, we infer that there is not only no undermining evidence to h but also no undermining evidence to the whole conclusion. In other words, all legitimate inductive conclusions take the form of a self-referential conjunction whose first conjunct is h and whose second conjunct (usually left implicit) is the claim that there is no undermining evidence to the whole conjunction.

Conclusions as Total Views: Problems

[We have seen] that we could use principle P to account for many Gettier examples if we were willing to suppose that induction always has an explanatory statement as its conclusion. On that supposition reasoning would have to take the form of a series of inductive and deductive steps to appropriate intermediate conclusions that therefore become essential to our inference. However, certain difficulties indicate that this conception of inference is seriously oversimplified and that our account of Gettier examples must be modified.

[I have] already mentioned a minor complication. There is a self-referential aspect to inductive conclusions. Instead of saying that such conclusions are of the form *Y because X* we must say that they are of the form *Y because X and there is no undermining evidence to this whole conclusion.*

Another difficulty, . . . the "lottery paradox," poses a more serious problem. . . . This paradox arises given a purely probabilistic rule of acceptance, since such a rule would have us infer concerning any ticket in the next New Jersey lottery that the ticket will not win the grand prize. We might suggest that the paradox cannot arise if induction is inference to the best explanatory statement, since the hypothesis that a particular ticket fails to win the grand prize in the next New Jersey lottery does nothing to explain anything about our current evidence. However, there are two things wrong with such a suggestion. First, the paradox will arise in any situation in which, for some large number N, there are N different explanations of different aspects of the evidence, each inferable when considered apart from the other explanations, if we also know that only N − 1 of these explanations are correct. So, the paradox can arise even when we attempt to infer explanations of various aspects of one's evidence.

Furthermore, inference to the best explanatory statement need not infer explanations of the evidence. It can infer that something we already accept will explain something else. That is how I am able to infer that the sugar will dissolve when stirred into my tea or that a friend who intends to meet me on a corner in an hour will in fact be there. Moreover, we can sometimes infer explanatory statements involving statistical explanations; and, if a particular ticket does fail to win the grand prize, we can explain its not winning by describing this as a highly probable outcome in the given chance set-up. So, if induction is inference to the best explanatory statement, we should be able to infer of any ticket in a fair lottery that the conditions of the lottery will explain that ticket's failing to win the grand prize; the lottery paradox therefore arises in its original form. But

before attempting to modify the present conception of inference in order to escape the lottery paradox, let us consider a different sort of problem involving that conception.

Our present conception of reasoning takes it to consist in a series of inductive and deductive steps. We have therefore supposed that there are (at least) two kinds of inference, inductive inference and deductive inference; and we have also supposed that reasoning typically combines inferences of both sorts. But there is something fishy about this. Deduction does not seem to be a kind of inference in the same sense in which induction is. Induction is a matter of inductive acceptance. On our current conception of inference, we may infer or accept an explanatory statement if it is sufficiently more plausible than competing statements, given our antecedent beliefs. On the other hand, deduction does not seem in the same way to be a matter of "deductive acceptance." So called deductive rules of inference are not plausibly construed as rules of deductive acceptance that tell us what conclusions we may accept, given that we already have certain antecedent beliefs. For example, although the deductive rule of *modus ponens* is sometimes stated like this, "From *P* and *If P, then Q,* infer *Q*," there is no plausible rule of acceptance saying that if we believe both *P* and *If P, then Q,* we may always infer or accept *Q*. Perhaps we should stop believing *P* or *If P, then Q* rather than believe *Q*.

A contradiction logically implies everything; anything follows (deductively) from a set of logically inconsistent beliefs. Although this point is sometimes expressed by saying that from a contradiction we may deductively infer anything, that is a particular use of "infer." Logic does not tell us that if we discover that our beliefs are inconsistent we may go on to infer or accept anything and everything we happen to think of. Given the discovery of such inconsistency in our antecedent beliefs, inference should lead not to the acceptance of something more but to the rejection of something previously accepted.

This indicates that something is wrong in a very basic way with our current conception of inference. We have been supposing that inference is simply a way to acquire new beliefs on the basis of our old beliefs. What is needed is a modification of that conception to allow for the fact that inference can lead as easily to rejection of old beliefs as to the acceptance of new beliefs. Furthermore, we want to avoid the supposition that deduction is a kind of inference in the same sense in which induction is inference, and we want to avoid the lottery paradox.

Inference to the Best Total Explanatory Account

Influenced by a misleading conception of deductive inference, we have implicitly supposed that inductive inference is a matter of going from a few premises we already accept to a conclusion one comes to accept, of the form *X because Y (and there is no undermining evidence to this conclusion)*. But this conception of premises and conclusion in inductive inference is mistaken. The conception of the conclusion of induction is wrong since such inference can lead not only to the acceptance of new beliefs but also the rejection of old beliefs. Furthermore, the suggestion that only a few premises are relevant is wrong, since inductive inference must be assessed with respect to everything one believes.

A more accurate conception of inductive inference takes it to be a way of modifying what we believe by addition and subtraction of beliefs. Our "premises" are all our antecedent beliefs; our "conclusion" is our total resulting view. Our conclusion is not a simple explanatory statement but a more or less complete explanatory account. Induction is an attempt to increase the explanatory coherence of our view, making it more complete, less ad hoc, more plausible. At the same time we are conservative. We seek to minimize change. We attempt to make the least change in our antecedent view that will maximize explanatory coherence.

The conception of induction as inference to the best total explanatory account retains those aspects of our previous conception that permitted an account of Gettier examples, although that account must be modified to some extent. On the other hand, the new conception does not suppose that there is deductive inference in anything like the sense in which there is inductive inference, since deductive inference is not a process of changing beliefs. Furthermore, the new conception accounts for the fact that inference can lead us to reject something previously accepted, since such rejection can

be part of the least change that maximizes coherence.

Finally, the new conception avoids the lottery paradox. Inference is no longer conceived of as a series of steps which together might add up to something implausible as a whole. Instead, inference is taken to be a single step to one total conclusion. If there can be only one conclusion, there is no way to build up a lottery paradox.

Consider the case in which there are N explanations of various aspects of the evidence, each very plausible considered by itself, where however it is known that only $N - 1$ are correct. Competing possible conclusions must specify for each explanation whether or not that explanation is accepted. A particular explanation will be accepted not simply because of its plausibility when considered by itself but only if it is included in an inferable total explanatory account. We will not be able to infer that all N explanations are correct since, I am assuming, that would greatly decrease coherence.

Similarly, we will be able to infer that a particular ticket will fail to win the grand prize in the next New Jersey lottery only if there is a total resulting view containing this result that is to be preferred to alternative total views on grounds of maximizing coherence and minimizing change. The claim that a particular ticket fails to win will be part of an inferable total view only if that claim adds sufficiently more coherence than do claims that other tickets fail to win. Otherwise that total view will not be any better than a different total view that does not contain the claim that the first ticket fails to win.

This is a rather complicated matter and depends not only on the probabilities involved but also on how we conceive the situation and, in particular, on what claims we are interested in.[3] We can see this by considering the conditions under which we can make inferences that give us knowledge. For example, if we are simply interested in the question of whether a particular ticket will win or fail to win, we cannot include in our total view the conclusion that the ticket will fail to win, since it would not be correct to say that in such a case we know the ticket will lose. On the other hand, if we are primarily interested in a quite different question whose answer depends in part on an answer to the question of whether this ticket fails to win, we may be able to include the conclusion that it does fail in our total view, since we can often come to have relevant knowledge in such cases. Thus, we might infer and come to know that the butler is the murderer because that hypothesis is part of the most plausible total account, even though the account includes the claim that the butler did not win the lottery (for if he had won he would have lacked a motive). Or we might infer and come to know that we will be seeing Jones for lunch tomorrow even though our total view includes the claim that Jones does not win the lottery (e.g., because if he won he would have to be in Trenton tomorrow to receive his prize and would not be able to meet us for lunch).

However I am unable to be very precise about how our interests and conception of the situation affect coherence or indeed about any of the factors that are relevant to coherence.

Inference and Knowledge

Having seen that induction is inference to the best total explanatory account, we must now modify our account of knowledge and of the Gettier examples.

One problem is that we want to be able to ascribe several inferences to a person at a particular time so as to be able to say that one of the inferences yields knowledge even though another does not. Suppose that Mary has evidence both that her friend Mr. Nogot owns a Ford and that her friend Mr. Havit owns a Ford. She concludes that both own Fords and therefore that at least one of her friends owns a Ford. Nogot does not own a Ford; but Havit does. We want to be able to say that Mary can know in this case that at least one of her friends owns a Ford, because one inference on which her belief is based satisfies principle P even if another inference she makes does not. But, if inference is a matter of modifying one's total view, how can we ascribe more than a single inference to Mary?[4]

Principle P seems to be in trouble in any event. It tells us that one gets knowledge from an inference only if all conclusions essential to that inference are true. Since one's conclusion is one's total resulting view, principle P would seem to imply that one gains no knowledge from inference unless the whole of one's resulting view is true. But that is absurd. A person comes to know things through inference even though some of what he believes is false.

A similar point holds of premises. It is plausible to suppose that one comes to know by inference only if one already knows one's premises to be true. However, one's total view is relevant to inference even though it always contains things one does not know to be true.

The key to the solution of these problems is to take an inference to be a change that can be described simply by mentioning what beliefs are given up and what new beliefs are added (in addition to the belief that there is no undermining evidence to the conclusion). Mary might be described as making all the following inferences. (1) She rejects her belief that no friend of hers owns a Ford. (2) In addition she comes to believe that one of her friends owns a Ford and accepts a story about Nogot. (3) As in (2), except that she accepts a story about Havit rather than one about Nogot. (4) She does all the preceding things. All the inferences (1)–(4) might be ascribed to Mary by an appropriate reasoning instantiator F.[5] Mary knows because inference (3) adds nothing false to her view.

Given Mary's antecedent beliefs, there is a single maximal inference she makes, (4), which is the union of all the inferences she makes. An inference is warranted only if it is included in the maximal warranted inference. That is why the lottery paradox does not arise even though we allow for the possibility that Mary makes more than one inference.

In order to handle the problem about premises we must require, not that the actual premises of the inference (everything Mary believes ahead of time) be known to be true but only that the inference remain warranted when the set of antecedent beliefs is limited to those Mary antecedently knows to be true and continues to know after the inference. More precisely, let (A, B) be an inference that rejects the beliefs in the set A and adds as new beliefs those in the set B; let $B \cup C$ be the union of the sets B and C, containing anything that belongs either to B or to C or to both; and let Φ be the empty set that contains nothing. Then principle P is to be replaced by the following principle P^*, which gives necessary and sufficient conditions of inferential knowledge.

P^* S comes to know that h by inference (A, B) if and only if (i) the appropriate reasoning instantiator F ascribes (A, B) to S, (ii) S is warranted in making the inference (A, B) given his antecedent beliefs, (*iii*) there is a possibly empty set C of unrejected antecedent beliefs not antecedently known by S to be true such that the inference $(\Phi, B{\cup}C)$ is warranted when antecedent beliefs are taken to be the set of things S knows (and continues to know after the inference (A, B) is made), (iv) $B{\cup}C$ contains the belief that h, (v) $B{\cup}C$ contains only true beliefs.[6]

Reference to the set C is necessary to cover cases in which S comes to know something he already believes. Part (v) of P^* captures what was intended by our original principle P.

. . .

Summary

Our previous conception of induction as inference to the best explanatory statement fell short in three ways. It failed to account for the rejection of previously held beliefs, it failed to avoid the lottery paradox, and it treated deduction as a form of inference. The last of these is especially serious since it can lead to misguided theories in response to a form of skepticism it encourages; and it can also suggest the construction of inductive or practical logics, having to do with inductive or practical reasoning. These defects are avoided if induction is taken to be inference to the best total explanatory account. We can reject beliefs because the account we come to accept may not contain beliefs we previously accepted. Any inference we are warranted in making is included in the maximal inference we are warranted in making, so the lottery paradox cannot arise. Deductive arguments are not inferences but are explanatory conclusions that can increase the coherence of one's view.

Finally, all this means that principle P must give way to principle P^*, which says that we know

by inference only if one of our inferences remains warranted and leads to the acceptance only of truths when restricted in premises to the set of things we know ahead of time to be true.

Notes

[1] "Mary's friend Mr. Nogot convinces her that he has a Ford. He tells her that he owns a Ford, he shows her his ownership certificate, and he reminds her that she saw him drive up in a Ford. On the basis of this and similar evidence, Mary concludes that Mr. Nogot owns a Ford. From that she infers that one of her friends owns a Ford. . . . However, as it turns out in this case, Mary is wrong about Nogot. His car has just been repossessed and towed away. . . . On the other hand, Mary's friend Mr. Havit does own a Ford, so she is right in thinking that one of her friends owns a Ford . . . but she does not know that one of her friends owns a Ford" (*Thought*, p. 121).

[2] Here and in what follows I am indebted to Saul Kripke, who is, however, not responsible for any faults in my presentation.

[3] Levi.

[4] Lehrer.

[5] "Words like 'reasoning,' 'argument,' and 'inference' are ambiguous. They may refer to a process of reasoning, argument, or inference, or they may refer to an abstract structure consisting of certain propositions as premises, others as conclusions, perhaps others as intermediate steps. A functional account of reasoning says how a mental or neurophysiological process can *be* a process of reasoning by virtue of the way it functions. That is, a functional account says how the functioning of such a process allows it to be correlated with the reasoning, taken to be an abstract inference, which the process instantiates.

To be more precise, the relevant correlation is a mapping F from mental or neurophysiological processes to abstract structures of inference. If x is a process in the domain of F, then $F(x)$ is the (abstract) reasoning that x instantiates. Such a mapping F is a *reasoning instantiator*. . . . To ascribe reasoning r to someone is to presuppose the existence of a reasoning instantiator F and to claim that his belief resulted from a process x such that $F(x) = r$" (*Thought*, pp. 48–49).

[6] I have made substantive changes in the discussion of principle Q and in the statement of P^* in response to comments by Ernest Sosa.

IV.5 *Discrimination and Perceptual Knowledge*

ALVIN I. GOLDMAN

In this essay Goldman modifies his earlier causal account of knowledge, dropping the idea that the knower's belief that *p* must be connected with the fact that *p*. Instead knowledge is defined as beliefs formed by reliable mechanisms, specifically the ability to distinguish the truth of *p* from relevant alternatives. In sections II and III, Goldman works out the details of his discrimination view of perceptual knowledge, and in section IV he shows the significance of his reliabilist theory over against the "Cartesian" justificationist model of perceptual knowledge.

This paper presents a partial analysis of perceptual knowledge, an analysis that will, I hope, lay a foundation for a general theory of knowing. Like an earlier theory I proposed,[1] the envisaged theory would seek to explicate the concept of knowledge by reference to the causal processes that produce (or sustain) belief. Unlike the earlier theory, however, it would abandon the requirement that a knower's belief that *p* be causally connected with the fact, or state of affairs, that *p*.

What kinds of causal processes or mechanisms must be responsible for a belief if that belief is to count as knowledge? They must be mechanisms that are, in an appropriate sense, "reliable." Roughly, a cognitive mechanism or process is reliable if it not only produces true beliefs in actual situations, but would produce true beliefs, or at least inhibit false beliefs, in relevant counterfactual situations. The theory of knowledge I envisage, then, would contain an important counterfactual component.

To be reliable, a cognitive mechanism must enable a person to *discriminate* or *differentiate* between incompatible states of affairs. It must operate in such a way that incompatible states of the world would generate different cognitive responses. Perceptual mechanisms illustrate this clearly. A perceptual mechanism is reliable to the extent that con-

trary features of the environment (e.g., an object's being red, versus its being yellow) would produce contrary perceptual states of the organism, which would, in turn, produce suitably different beliefs about the environment. Another belief-governing mechanism is a reasoning mechanism, which, given a set of antecedent beliefs, generates or inhibits various new beliefs. A reasoning mechanism is reliable to the extent that its functional procedures would generate new true beliefs from antecedent true beliefs.

My emphasis on discrimination accords with a sense of the verb 'know' that has been neglected by philosophers. The O.E.D. lists one (early) sense of 'know' as "*to distinguish* (one thing) *from* (another)," as in "I know a hawk from a handsaw" (*Hamlet*) and "We'll teach him to know Turtles from Jayes" (*Merry Wives of Windsor*). Although it no longer has great currency, this sense still survives in such expressions as "I don't know him from Adam," "He doesn't know right from left," and other phrases that readily come to mind. I suspect that this construction is historically important and can be used to shed light on constructions in which 'know' takes propositional objects. I suggest that a person is said to know that *p* just in case he *distinguishes* or *discriminates* the truth of *p* from relevant alternatives.

A knowledge attribution imputes to someone the discrimination of a given state of affairs from possible alternatives, but not necessarily all logically possible alternatives. In forming beliefs about the

Reprinted from *The Journal of Philosophy*, 73.20 (1976), 771–791, by kind permission of the author and publisher.

world, we do not normally consider all logical possibilities. And in deciding whether someone knows that *p* (its truth being assumed), we do not ordinarily require him to discriminate *p* from all logically possible alternatives. Which alternatives are, or ought to be considered, is a question I shall not fully resolve in this paper, but some new perspectives will be examined. I take up this topic in section I.

I

Consider the following example. Henry is driving in the countryside with his son. For the boy's edification Henry identifies various objects on the landscape as they come into view. "That's a cow," says Henry, "That's a tractor," "That's a silo," "That's a barn," etc. Henry has no doubt about the identity of these objects; in particular, he has no doubt that the last-mentioned object is a barn, which indeed it is. Each of the identified objects has features characteristic of its type. Moreover, each object is fully in view, Henry has excellent eyesight, and he has enough time to look at them reasonably carefully, since there is little traffic to distract him.

Given this information, would we say that Henry *knows* that the object is a barn? Most of us would have little hesitation in saying this, so long as we were not in a certain philosophical frame of mind. Contrast our inclination here with the inclination we would have if we were given some additional information. Suppose we are told that, unknown to Henry, the district he has just entered is full of papier-mâché facsimiles of barns. These facsimiles look from the road exactly like barns, but are really just façades, without back walls or interiors, quite incapable of being used as barns. They are so cleverly constructed that travelers invariably mistake them for barns. Having just entered the district, Henry has not encountered any facsimiles; the object he sees is a genuine barn. But if the object on that site were a facsimile, Henry would mistake it for a barn. Given this new information, we would be strongly inclined to withdraw the claim that Henry *knows* the object is a barn. How is this change in our assessment to be explained?[1a]

Note first that the traditional justified-true-belief account of knowledge is of no help in explaining this change. In both cases Henry truly believes (indeed, is certain) that the object is a barn. Moreover, Henry's "justification" or "evidence" for the proposition that the object is a barn is the same in both cases. Thus, Henry should either know in both cases or not know in both cases. The presence of facsimiles in the district should make no difference to whether or not he knows.

My old causal analysis cannot handle the problem either. Henry's belief that the object is a barn is caused by the presence of the barn; indeed, the causal process is a perceptual one. Nonetheless, we are not prepared to say, in the second version, that Henry knows.

One analysis of propositional knowledge that might handle the problem is Peter Unger's non-accidentality analysis.[2] According to this theory, *S* knows that *p* if and only if it is not at all accidental that *S* is right about its being the case that *p*. In the initial description of the example, this requirement appears to be satisfied; so we say that Henry knows. When informed about the facsimiles, however, we see that it is accidental that Henry is right about its being a barn. So we withdraw our knowledge attribution. The "non-accidentality" analysis is not very satisfying, however, for the notion of "non-accidentality" itself needs explication. Pending explication, it isn't clear whether it correctly handles all cases.

Another approach to knowledge that might handle our problem is the "indefeasibility" approach.[3] On this view, *S* knows that *p* only if *S*'s true belief is justified *and* this justification is not defeated. In an unrestricted form, an indefeasibility theory would say that *S*'s justification *j* for believing that *p* is defeated if and only if there is some true proposition *q* such that the conjunction of *q* and *j* does not justify *S* in believing that *p*. In slightly different terms, *S*'s justification *j* is defeated just in case *p* would no longer be evident for *S* if *q* were evident for *S*. This would handle the barn example, presumably, because the true proposition that there are barn facsimiles in the district is such that, if it were evident for Henry, then it would no longer be evident for him that the object he sees is a barn.

The trouble with the indefeasibility approach is that it is too strong, at least in its unrestricted form. On the foregoing account of "defeat," as Gilbert Harman shows,[4] it will (almost) always be possible to find a true proposition that defeats *S*'s justification. Hence, *S* will never (or seldom) know. What is needed is an appropriate restriction on the notion of "defeat," but I am not aware of an appropriate restriction that has been formulated thus far.

The approach to the problem I shall recommend is slightly different. Admittedly, this approach will raise problems analogous to those of the indefeasibility theory, problems which will not be fully resolved here. Nevertheless, I believe this approach is fundamentally on the right track.

What, then, is my proposed treatment of the barn example? A person knows that *p,* I suggest, only if the actual state of affairs in which *p* is true is *distinguishable* or *discriminable* by him from a relevant possible state of affairs in which *p* is false. If there is a relevant possible state of affairs in which *p* is false and which is indistinguishable by him from the actual state of affairs, then he fails to know that *p*. In the original description of the barn case there is no hint of any relevant possible state of affairs in which the object in question is not a barn but is indistinguishable (by Henry) from the actual state of affairs. Hence, we are initially inclined to say that Henry knows. The information about the facsimiles, however, introduces such a relevant state of affairs. Given that the district Henry has entered is full of barn facsimiles, there is a relevant alternative hypothesis about the object, viz., that it is a facsimile. Since, by assumption, a state of affairs in which such a hypothesis holds is indistinguishable by Henry from the actual state of affairs (from his vantage point on the road), this hypothesis is not "ruled out" or "precluded" by the factors that prompt Henry's belief. So, once apprised of the facsimiles in the district, we are inclined to deny that Henry knows.

Let us be clear about the bearing of the facsimiles on the case. The presence of the facsimiles does not "create" the possibility that the object Henry sees is a facsimile. Even if there were no facsimiles in the district, it would be possible that the object on that site is a facsimile. What the presence of the facsimiles does is make this possibility *relevant;* or it makes us *consider* it relevant.

The qualifier 'relevant' plays an important role in my view. If knowledge required the elimination of all logically possible alternatives, there would be no knowledge (at least of contingent truths). If only *relevant* alternatives need to be precluded, however, the scope of knowledge could be substantial. This depends, of course, on which alternatives are relevant.

The issue at hand is directly pertinent to the dispute—at least one dispute—between skeptics and their opponents. In challenging a claim to knowledge (or certainty), a typical move of the skeptic is to adduce an unusual alternative hypothesis that the putative knower is unable to preclude: an alternative compatible with his "data." In the skeptical stage of his argument, Descartes says that he is unable to preclude the hypothesis that, instead of being seated by the fire, he is asleep in his bed and dreaming, or the hypothesis that an evil and powerful demon is making it appear to him as if he is seated by the fire. Similarly, Bertrand Russell points out that, given any claim about the past, we can adduce the "skeptical hypothesis" that the world sprang into being five minutes ago, exactly as it then was, with a population that "remembered" a wholly unreal past.[5]

One reply open to the skeptic's opponent is that these skeptical hypotheses are just "idle" hypotheses, and that a person can know a proposition even if there are "idle" alternatives he cannot preclude. The problem, of course, is to specify when an alternative is "idle" and when it is "serious" ("relevant"). Consider Henry once again. Should we say that the possibility of a facsimile before him is a serious or relevant possibility if there are no facsimiles in Henry's district, but only in Sweden? Or if a single such facsimile once existed in Sweden, but none exist now?

There are two views one might take on this general problem. The first view is that there is a "correct" answer, in any given situation, as to which alternatives are relevant. Given a complete specification of Henry's situation, a unique set of relevant alternatives is determined: either a set to which the facsimile alternative belongs or one to which it doesn't belong. According to this view, the semantic content of 'know' contains (implicit) rules that map any putative knower's circumstances into a set of relevant alternatives. An analysis of 'know' is incomplete unless it specifies these rules. The correct specification will favor either the skeptic or the skeptic's opponent.

The second view denies that a putative knower's circumstances uniquely determine a set of relevant alternatives. At any rate, it denies that the semantic content of 'know' contains rules that map a set of circumstances into a single set of relevant alternatives. According to this second view, the verb 'know' is simply not so semantically determinate.

The second view need not deny that there are *regularities* governing the alternative hypotheses a speaker (i.e., an attributer or denier of knowledge) thinks of, and deems relevant. But these regularities are not part of the semantic content of 'know'. The putative knower's circumstances do not *mandate* a unique selection of alternatives; but psychological regularities govern which set of alternatives are in fact selected. In terms of these regularities (together with the semantic content of 'know'), we can explain the observed use of the term.

It is clear that some of these regularities pertain to the (description of the) putative knower's circumstances. One regularity might be that the more *likely* it is, given the circumstances, that a particular alternative would obtain (rather than the actual state of affairs), the more probable it is that a speaker will regard this alternative as relevant. Or, the more *similar* the situation in which the alternative obtains to the actual situation, the more probable it is that a speaker will regard this alternative as relevant. It is not only the circumstances of the putative knower's situation, however, that influence the choice of alternatives. The speaker's own linguistic and psychological context are also important. If the speaker is in a class where Descartes's evil demon has just been discussed, or Russell's five-minute-old-world hypothesis, he may think of alternatives he would not otherwise think of and will perhaps treat them seriously. This sort of regularity is entirely ignored by the first view.

What I am calling the "second" view might have two variants. The first variant can be imbedded in Robert Stalnaker's framework for pragmatics.[6] In this framework, a proposition is a function from possible words into truth values; the determinants of a proposition are a sentence and a (linguistic) context. An important contextual element is what the utterer of a sentence presupposes, or takes for granted. According to the first variant of the second view, a sentence of the form '*S* knows that *p*' does not determine a unique proposition. Rather, a proposition is determined by such a sentence together with the speaker's presuppositions concerning the relevant alternatives.[7] Skeptics and non-skeptics might make different presuppositions

(both presuppositions being "legitimate"), and, if so, they are simply asserting or denying different propositions.

One trouble with this variant is its apparent implication that, if a speaker utters a knowledge sentence without presupposing a fully determinate set of alternatives, he does not assert or deny any proposition. That seems too strong. A second variant of the second view, then, is that sentences of the form '*S* knows that *p*' express vague or indeterminate propositions (if they express "propositions" at all), which can, but need not, be made more determinate by full specification of the alternatives. A person who *assents* to a knowledge sentence says that *S* discriminates the truth of *p* from relevant alternatives; but he may not have a distinct set of alternatives in mind. (Similarly, according to Paul Ziff, a person who says something is "good" says that it answers to *certain* interests;[8] but he may not have a distinct set of interests in mind.) Someone who *denies* a knowledge sentence more commonly has one or more alternatives in mind as relevant, because his denial may stem from a particular alternative *S* cannot rule out. But even the denier of a knowledge sentence need not have a full set of relevant alternatives in mind.

I am attracted by the second view under discussion, especially its second variant. In the remainder of the paper, however, I shall be officially neutral. In other words, I shall not try to settle the question of whether the semantic content of 'know' contains rules that map the putative knower's situation into a unique set of relevant alternatives. I leave open the question of whether there is a "correct" set of relevant alternatives, and if so, what it is. To this extent, I also leave open the question of whether skeptics or their opponents are "right." In defending my analysis of 'perceptually knows', however, I shall have to discuss particular examples. In treating these examples I shall assume some (psychological) regularities concerning the selection of alternatives. Among these regularities is the fact that speakers do not *ordinarily* think of "radical" alternatives, but are caused to think of such alternatives, and take them seriously, if the putative knower's circumstances call attention to them. Since I assume that radical or unusual alternatives are not *ordinarily* entertained or taken seriously, I may appear to side with the opponents of skepticism. My official analysis, however, is neutral on the issue of skepticism.

II

I turn now to the analysis of 'perceptually knows'. Suppose that Sam spots Judy on the street and correctly identifies her as Judy, i.e., believes she is Judy. Suppose further that Judy has an identical twin, Trudy, and the possibility of the person's being Trudy (rather than Judy) is a relevant alternative. Under what circumstances would we say that Sam *knows* it is Judy?

If Sam regularly identifies Judy as Judy and Trudy as Trudy, he apparently has some (visual) way of discriminating between them (though he may not know how he does it, i.e., what cues he uses). If he does have a way of discriminating between them, which he uses on the occasion in question, we would say that he *knows* it is Judy. But if Sam frequently mistakes Judy for Trudy, and Trudy for Judy, he presumably does not have a way of discriminating between them. For example, he may not have sufficiently distinct (visual) memory "schemata" of Judy and Trudy. So that, on a particular occasion, sensory stimulation from either Judy *or* Trudy would elicit a Judy-identification from him. If he happens to be right that it is Judy, this is just accidental. He doesn't *know* it is Judy.

The crucial question in assessing a knowledge attribution, then, appears to be the truth value of a counterfactual (or set of counterfactuals). Where Sam correctly identifies Judy as Judy, the crucial counterfactual is: "If the person before Sam were Trudy (rather than Judy), Sam would believe her to be Judy." If this counterfactual is true, Sam doesn't know it is Judy. If this counterfactual is false (and all other counterfactuals involving relevant alternatives are also false), then Sam may know it is Judy.

This suggests the following analysis of (noninferential) perceptual knowledge.

> S (noninferentially) *perceptually knows that p* if and only if
> (1) S (noninferentially) perceptually believes that p,
> (2) p is true, and
> (3) there is no relevant contrary q of p such that, if q were true (rather than p), then S would (still) believe that p.

Restricting attention to relevant possibilities, these conditions assert in effect that the only situation in which S would believe that p is a situation in which p is true. In other words, S's believing that p is sufficient for the truth of p. This is essentially the analysis of noninferential knowledge proposed by D. M. Armstrong in *A Materialist Theory of the Mind* (though without any restriction to "relevant" alternatives), and refined and expanded in *Belief, Truth, and Knowledge*.[9]

This analysis is too restrictive. Suppose Oscar is standing in an open field containing Dack the dachshund. Oscar sees Dack and (noninferentially) forms a belief in (P):

(P) The object over there is a dog.

Now suppose that (Q):

(Q) The object over there is a wolf.

is a relevant alternative to (P) (because wolves are frequenters of this field). Further suppose that Oscar has a tendency to mistake wolves for dogs (he confuses them with malamutes, or German shepherds). Then if the object Oscar saw were Wiley the wolf, rather than Dack the dachshund, Oscar would (still) believe (P). This means that Oscar fails to satisfy the proposed analysis with respect to (P), since (3) is violated. But surely it is wrong to deny—for the indicated reasons—that Oscar *knows* (P) to be true. The mere fact that he would erroneously take a wolf to be a dog hardly shows that he doesn't know a *dachshund* to be a dog! Similarly, if someone looks at a huge redwood and correctly believes it to be a tree, he is not disqualified from knowing it to be a tree merely because there is a very small plant he would wrongly believe to be a tree, i.e., a bonsai tree.

The moral can be formulated as follows. If Oscar believes that a dog is present because of a certain way he is "appeared to," then this true belief fails to be knowledge if there is an alternative situation in which a non-dog produces the same belief by means of the same, or a very similar, appearance. But the wolf situation is not such an alternative: although it would produce in him the same belief, it would not be by means of the same (or a similar) appearance. An alternative that disqualifies a true belief from being perceptual knowledge must be a "perceptual equivalent" of the actual state of affairs.[10] A *perceptual equivalent* of an actual state of affairs is a possible state of affairs that would produce the same, or a sufficiently similar, perceptual experience.

The relation of perceptual equivalence must obviously be relativized to *persons* (or organisms). The presence of Judy and the presence of Trudy might be perceptual equivalents for Sam, but not for the twins' own mother (to whom the twins look quite different). Similarly, perceptual equivalence must be relativized to *times,* since perceptual discriminative capacities can be refined or enhanced with training or experience, and can deteriorate with age or disease.

How shall we specify alternative states of affairs that are candidates for being perceptual equivalents? First, we should specify the *object* involved. (I assume for simplicity that only one object is in question.) As the Judy-Trudy case shows, the object in the alternative state of affairs need not be identical with the actual object. Sometimes, indeed, we may wish to allow non-actual possible objects. Otherwise our framework will be unable in principle to accommodate some of the skeptic's favorite alternatives, e.g., those involving demons. If the reader's ontological sensibility is offended by talk of possible objects, I invite him to replace such talk with any preferred substitute.

Some alternative states of affairs involve the same object but different properties. Where the actual state of affairs involves a certain ball painted blue, an alternative might be chosen involving the same ball painted green. Thus, specification of an alternative requires not only an object, but properties of the object (at the time in question). These should include not only the property in the belief under scrutiny, or one of its contraries, but other properties as well, since the property in the belief (or one of its contraries) might not be sufficiently determinate to indicate what the resultant percept would be like. For full generality, let us choose a *maximal set of* (nonrelational) *properties.* This is a set that would exhaustively characterize an object (at a single time) in some possible world.[11]

An object plus a maximal set of (nonrelational) properties still does not fully specify a perceptual alternative. Also needed are relations between the object and the perceiver, plus conditions of the environment. One relation that can affect the resultant percept is *distance.* Another relational factor is *relative orientation,* both of object vis-à-vis perceiver and perceiver vis-à-vis object. The nature of the percept depends, for example, on which side of the object faces the perceiver, and on how the perceiver's bodily organs are oriented, or situated, vis-à-vis the object. Thirdly, the percept is affected by the current state of the *environment,* e.g., the illumination, the presence or absence of intervening objects, and the direction and velocity of the wind.

To cover all such elements, I introduce the notion of a *distance-orientation-environment* relation, for short, a *DOE relation.* Each such relation is a conjunction of relations or properties concerning distance, orientation, and environmental conditions. One DOE relation is expressed by the predicate 'x is 20 feet from y, the front side of y is facing x, the eyes of x are open and focused in y's direction, no opaque object is interposed between x and y, and y is in moonlight.'

Since the health of sensory organs can affect percepts, it might be argued that this should be included in these relations, thereby opening the condition of these organs to counterfactualization. For simplicity I neglect this complication. This does not mean that I don't regard the condition of sensory organs as open to counterfactualization. I merely omit explicit incorporation of this factor into our exposition.

We can now give more precision to our treatment of perceptual equivalents. Perceptual states of affairs will be specified by ordered triples, each consisting of (1) an object, (2) a maximal set of nonrelational properties, and (3) a DOE relation. If S perceives object b at t and if b has all the properties in a maximal set J and bears DOE relation R to S at t, then the actual state of affairs pertaining to this perceptual episode is represented by the ordered triple $<b,J,R>$. An alternative state of affairs is represented by an ordered triple $<c,K,R^*>$, which may (but need not) differ from $<b,J,R>$ with respect to one or more of its elements.

Under what conditions is an alternative $<c,K,R^*>$ a perceptual equivalent of $<b,J,R>$ for person S at time t? I said that a perceptual equivalent is a state of affairs that would produce "the same, or a very similar" perceptual experience. That is not very committal. Must a perceptual equivalent produce exactly the same percept? Given our intended use of perceptual equivalence in the analysis of perceptual knowledge, the answer is clearly No. Suppose that a Trudy-produced percept would be qualitatively distinct from Sam's Judy-produced percept, but similar enough for Sam to mistake

Trudy for Judy. This is sufficient grounds for saying that Sam fails to have knowledge. Qualitative identity of percepts, then, is too strong a requirement for perceptual equivalence.

How should the requirement be weakened? We must not weaken it too much, for the wolf alternative might then be a perceptual equivalent of the dachshund state of affairs. This would have the unwanted consequence that Oscar doesn't know Dack to be a dog.

The solution I propose is this. If the percept produced by the alternative state of affairs would not differ from the actual percept in any respect that is causally relevant to S's belief, this alternative situation is a perceptual equivalent for S of the actual situation. Suppose that a Trudy-produced percept would differ from Sam's Judy-produced percept to the extent of having a different eyebrow configuration. (A difference in shape between Judy's and Trudy's eyebrows does not ensure that Sam's percepts would "register" this difference. I assume, however, that the eyebrow difference would be registered in Sam's percepts.) But suppose that Sam's visual "concept" of Judy does not include a feature that reflects this contrast. His Judy-concept includes an "eyebrow feature" only in the sense that the absence of eyebrows would inhibit a Judy-classification. It does not include a more determinate eyebrow feature, though: Sam hasn't learned to associate Judy with distinctively shaped eyebrows. Hence, the distinctive "eyebrow shape" of his actual (Judy-produced) percept is not one of the percept-features that is causally responsible for his believing Judy to be present. Assuming that a Trudy-produced percept would not differ from his actual percept in any *other* causally relevant way, the hypothetical Trudy-situation is a perceptual equivalent of the actual Judy-situation.

Consider now the dachshund-wolf case. The hypothetical percept produced by a wolf would differ from Oscar's actual percept of the dachshund in respects that *are* causally relevant to Oscar's judgment that a dog is present. Let me elaborate. There are various kinds of objects, rather different in shape, size, color, and texture, that would be classified by Oscar as a dog. He has a number of visual "schemata," we might say, each with a distinctive set of features, such that any percept that "matches" or "fits" one of these schemata would elicit a "dog" classification. (I think of a schema not as a "template," but as a set of more-or-less abstract—

though iconic—features.[12]) Now, although a dachshund and a wolf would each produce a dog-belief in Oscar, the percepts produced by these respective stimuli would differ in respects that are causally relevant to Oscar's forming a dog-belief. Since Oscar's dachshund-schema includes such features as having an elongated, sausagelike shape, a smallish size, and droopy ears, these features of the percept are all causally relevant, when a dachshund is present, to Oscar's believing that a dog is present. Since a hypothetical wolf-produced percept would differ in these respects from Oscar's dachshund-produced percept, the hypothetical wolf state of affairs is not a perceptual equivalent of the dachshund state of affairs for Oscar.

The foregoing approach requires us to relativize perceptual equivalence once again, this time to the belief in question, or the property believed to be exemplified. The Trudy-situation is a perceptual equivalent for Sam of the Judy-situation *relative to the property of being* (identical with) *Judy*. The wolf-situation is not a perceptual equivalent for Oscar of the dachshund-situation *relative to the property of being a dog*.

I now propose the following definition of perceptual equivalence:

If object b has the maximal set of properties J and is in DOE relation R to S at t, if S has some percept P at t that is perceptually caused by b's having J and being in R to S at t, and if P noninferentially causes S to believe (or sustains S in believing) of object b that it has property F, then $<c,K,R*>$ is a perceptual equivalent of $<b,J,R>$ *for S at t relative to property* F if and only if

(1) if at t object c had K and were in $R*$ to S, then this would perceptually cause S to have some percept $P*$ at t,

(2) $P*$ would cause S noninferentially to believe (or sustain S in believing) of object c that it has F, and

(3) $P*$ would not differ from P in any respect that is causally relevant to S's F-belief.

Since I shall analyze the *de re, relational*, or *transparent* sense of 'perceptually knows', I shall want to employ, in my analysis, the *de re* sense of 'believe'. This is why such phrases as 'believe . . . of object b' occur in the definition of perceptual equivalence. For present purposes, I take for granted the notion of (perceptual) *de re* belief. I assume, however, that the object *of which* a person perceptually believes a property to hold is the object he perceives, i.e., the object that "perceptually causes" the percept that elicits the belief. The notion of *perceptual causation* is another notion I take for granted. A person's percept is obviously caused by many objects (or events), not all of which the person is said to perceive. One problem for the theory of perception is to explicate the notion of perceptual causation, that is, to explain which of the causes of a percept a person is said to perceive. I set this problem aside here.[13] A third notion I take for granted is the notion of a (noninferential) *perceptual belief,* or perceptual "taking." Not all beliefs that are noninferentially caused by a percept can be considered perceptual "takings"; "indirectly" caused beliefs would not be so considered. But I make no attempt to delineate the requisite causal relation.

Several other comments on the definition of perceptual equivalence are in order. Notice that the definition is silent on whether J or K contains property F, i.e., whether F is exemplified either the actual or the alternative states of affairs. The relativization to F (in the definiendum) implies that an *F-belief* is produced in both situations, not that F is exemplified (in either or both situations). In applying the definition to cases of putative knowledge, we shall focus on cases where F belongs to J (so S's belief is true in the actual situation) but does not belong to K (so S's belief is false in the counterfactual situation). But the definition of perceptual equivalence is silent on these matters.

Though the definition does not say so, I assume it is possible for object c to have all properties in K, and possible for c to be in R^* and S while having all properties in K. I do not want condition 1 to be vacuously true, simply by having an impossible antecedent.

It might seem as if the antecedent of (1) should include a further conjunct, expressing the supposition that object b is absent. This might seem necessary to handle cases in which, if c were in R^* to S, but b remained in its actual relation R to S, then b would "block" S's access to c. (For example, b might be an orange balloon floating over the horizon, and c might be the moon.) This can be handled by the definition as it stands, by construing R^*, where necessary, as including the absence of object b from the perceptual scene. (One cannot *in general* hypothesize that b is absent, for we want to allow object c to be identical with b.)

The definition implies that there is no temporal gap between each object's having its indicated properties and DOE relation and the occurrence of the corresponding percept. This simplification is introduced because no general requirement can be laid down about how long it takes for the stimulus energy to reach the perceiver. The intervals in the actual and alternative states may differ because the stimuli might be at different distances from the perceiver.

III

It is time to turn to the analysis of perceptual knowledge, for which the definition of perceptual equivalence paves the way. I restrict my attention to perceptual knowledge of the possession, by physical objects, of nonrelational properties. I also restrict the analysis to *noninferential* perceptual knowledge. This frees me from the complex issues introduced by inference, which require separate treatment.

It may be contended that all perceptual judgment is based on inference and, hence, that the proposed restriction reduces the scope of the analysis to nil. Two replies are in order. First, although cognitive psychology establishes that percepts are affected by cognitive factors, such as "expectancies," it is by no means evident that these causal processes should be construed as inferences. Second, even if we were to grant that there is in fact no noninferential perceptual belief, it would still be of epistemological importance to determine whether noninferential perceptual knowledge of the physical world is conceptually possible. This could be explored by considering merely possible cases of noninferential perceptual belief, and seeing whether, under suitable conditions, such belief would count as knowledge.

With these points in mind, we may propose the following (tentative) analysis:

At t S noninferentially perceptually knows of object b that it has property F if and only if
(1) for some maximal set of nonrelational properties *J* and some DOE relation

R, object b has (all the members of) J
at t and is in R to S at t,

(2) F belongs to J,

(3) (A) b's having J and being in R to S at
        t perceptually causes S at t to have
        some percept P,[14]

    (B) P noninferentially causes S and T
        to believe (or sustains S in
        believing) of object b that it has
        property F, and

    (C) there is no alternative state of
        affairs $<c,K,R^*>$ such that

        (i) $<c,K,R^*>$ is a relevant
            perceptual equivalent of
            $<b,J,R>$ for S at t relative to
            property F, and

        (ii) F does not belong to K.

Conditions 1 and 2 jointly entail the truth condition for knowledge: S knows b to have F (at t) only if b does have F (at t). Condition 3B contains the belief condition for knowledge, restricted, of course, to (noninferential) perceptual belief. The main work of the conditions is done by 3C. It requires that there be no relevant alternative that is (i) a perceptual equivalent to the actual state of affairs relative to property F, and (ii) a state of affairs in which the appropriate object lacks F (and hence S's F-belief is false).

How does this analysis relate to my theme of a "reliable discriminative mechanism"? A perceptual cognizer may be thought of as a two-part mechanism. The first part constructs percepts (a special class of internal states) from receptor stimulation. The second part operates on percepts to produce beliefs. Now, in order for the conditions of the analysans to be satisfied, each part of the mechanism must be sufficiently discriminating, or "finely tuned." If the first part is not sufficiently discriminating, patterns of receptor stimulation from quite different sources would result in the same (or very similar) percepts, percepts that would generate the same beliefs. If the second part is not sufficiently discriminating, then even if different percepts are constructed by the first part, the same beliefs will be generated by the second part. To be sure, even an undiscriminating bipartite mechanism may produce a belief that, luckily, is true; but there will be other, counterfactual, situations in which such a belief would be false. In this sense, such a mechanism is unreliable. What our analysis says is that S has perceptual knowledge if and only if not only does his perceptual mechanism produce true belief, but there are no relevant counterfactual situations in which the same belief would be produced via an equivalent percept and in which the belief would be false.

Let me now illustrate how the analysis is to be applied to the barn example, where there are facsimiles in Henry's district. Let S = Henry, b = the barn Henry actually sees, and F = the property of being a barn. Conditions 1 through 3B are met by letting J take as its value the set of all nonrelational properties actually possessed by the barn at t, R take as its value the actual DOE relation the barn bears to Henry at t, and P take as its value the actual (visual) percept caused by the barn. Condition 3C is violated, however. There *is* a relevant triple that meets subclauses (i) and (ii), i.e., the triple where c = a suitable barn facsimile, K = a suitable set of properties (excluding, of course, the property of being a barn), and R^* = approximately the same DOE relation as the actual one. Thus, Henry does not (noninferentially) perceptually *know* of the barn that it has the property of being a barn.

In the dachshund-wolf case, S = Oscar, b = Dack the dachshund, and F = being a dog. The first several conditions are again met. Is 3C met as well? There is a relevant alternative state of affairs in which Wiley the wolf is believed by Oscar to be a dog, but lacks that property. This state of affairs doesn't violate 3C, however, since it isn't a *perceptual equivalent* of the actual situation relative to being a dog. So this alternative doesn't disqualify Oscar from knowing Dack to be a dog.

Is there another alternative that *is* a perceptual equivalent of the actual situation (relative to being a dog)? We can imagine a DOE relation in which fancy devices between Wiley and Oscar distort the light coming from Wiley and produce in Oscar a Dack-like visual percept. The question here, however, is whether this perceptual equivalent is *relevant*. Relevance is determined not only by the hypothetical object and its properties, but also by the DOE relation. Since the indicated DOE relation is highly unusual, this will count (at least for a nonskeptic) against the alternative's being relevant and against its disqualifying Oscar from knowing.[15]

The following "Gettierized" example, suggested by Marshall Swain, might appear to present difficulties. In a dark room there is a candle several yards ahead of S which S sees and believes to be ahead of him. But he sees the candle only indirectly, via a system of mirrors (of which he is unaware) that make it appear as if he were seeing it directly.[16] We would surely deny that S knows the candle to be ahead of him. (This case does not really fit our intended analysandum, since the believed property F is relational. This detail can be ignored, however.) Why? If we say, with Harman, that all perceptual belief is based on inference, we can maintain that S infers that the candle is ahead of him from the premise that he sees whatever he sees *directly*. This premise being false, S's knowing is disqualified on familiar grounds.

My theory suggests another explanation, which makes no unnecessary appeal to inference. We deny that S knows, I suggest, because the system of mirrors draws our attention to a perceptual equivalent in which the candle is *not* ahead of S, i.e., a state of affairs where the candle is behind S but reflected in a system of mirrors so that it appears to be ahead of him. Since the actual state of affairs involves a system of reflecting mirrors, we are impelled to count this alternative as relevant, and hence to deny that S knows.

Even in ordinary cases, of course, where S sees a candle directly, the possibility of reflecting mirrors constitutes a perceptual equivalent. In the ordinary case, however, we would not count this as relevant; we would not regard it as a "serious" possibility. The Gettierized case impels us to take it seriously because there the actual state of affairs involves a devious system of reflecting mirrors. So we have an explanation of why people are credited with knowing in ordinary perceptual cases but not in the Gettierized case.

The following is a more serious difficulty for our analysis. S truly believes something to be a tree, but there is a relevant alternative in which an electrode stimulating S's optic nerve would produce an equivalent percept, which would elicit the same belief. Since this is assumed to be a relevant alternative, it ought to disqualify S from knowing. But it doesn't satisfy our definition of a perceptual equivalent, first because the electrode would not be a perceptual cause of the percept (we would not say that S *perceives* the electrode), and second because S would not believe *of the electrode* (nor *of* anything else) that it is a tree. A similar problem arises where

the alternative state of affairs would involve S's having a hallucination.

To deal with these cases, we could revise our analysis of perceptual knowledge as follows. (A similar revision in the definition of perceptual equivalence would do the job equally well.) We could reformulate 3C to say that there must neither be a relevant perceptual equivalent of the indicated sort (using our present definition of perceptual equivalence) *nor* a relevant alternative situation in which an equivalent percept occurs and prompts a *de dicto* belief that something has F, but where there is nothing that *perceptually* causes this percept and nothing *of which* F is believed to hold. In other words, knowledge can be disqualified by relevant alternative situations where S doesn't perceive anything and doesn't have any *de re* (F) belief at all. I am inclined to adopt this solution, but will not actually make this addition to the analysis.

Another difficulty for the analysis is this. Suppose Sam's "schemata" of Judy and Trudy have hitherto been indistinct, so Judy-caused percepts sometimes elicit Judy-beliefs and sometimes Trudy-beliefs, and similarly for Trudy-caused percepts. Today Sam falls down and hits his head. As a consequence a new feature is "added" to his Judy-schema, a mole-associated feature. From now on he will believe someone to be Judy only if he has the sort of percept that would be caused by a Judy-like person with a mole over the left eye. Sam is unaware that this change has taken place and will remain unaware of it, since he isn't conscious of the cues he uses. Until today, neither Judy nor Trudy has had a left-eyebrow mole; but today Judy happens to develop such a mole. Thus, from now on Sam can discriminate Judy from Trudy. Does this mean that he will *know* Judy to be Judy when he correctly identifies her? I am doubtful.

A possible explanation of Sam's not knowing (on future occasions) is that Trudy-with-a-mole is a relevant perceptual equivalent of Judy. This is not Trudy's actual condition, of course, but it might be deemed a relevant possibility. I believe, however, that the mole case calls for a further restriction, one concerning the *genesis* of a person's propensity to form a certain belief as a result of a certain percept. A merely fortuitous or accidental genesis is not enough to support knowledge. I do not know exactly what requirement to impose on the genesis of such a propensity. The mole case intimates that the genesis should involve certain "experience" with objects, but this may be too narrow. I content myself with a very vague addition to our previous conditions, which completes the analysis:

(4) *S*'s propensity to form an *F*-belief as a result of percept *P* has an appropriate genesis.

Of course this leaves the problem unresolved. But the best I can do here is identify the problem.

IV

A few words are in order about the intended significance of my analysis. One of its purposes is to provide an alternative to the traditional "Cartesian" perspective in epistemology. The Cartesian view combines a theory of knowledge with a theory of justification. Its theory of knowledge asserts that *S* knows that *p* at *t* only if *S* is (fully, adequately, etc.) justified at *t* in believing that *p*. Its theory of justification says that *S* is justified at *t* in believing that *p* only if either (A) *p* is self-warranting for *S* at *t*, or (B) *p* is (strongly, adequately, etc.) supported or confirmed by propositions each of which is self-warranting for *S* at *t*. Now propositions about the state of the external world at *t* are not self-warranting. Hence, if *S* knows any such proposition *p* at *t*, there must be some other propositions which strongly support *p* and which are self-warranting for *S* at *t*. These must be propositions about *S*'s mental state at *t* and perhaps some obvious necessary truths. A major task of Cartesian epistemology is to show that there is some such set of self-warranting propositions, propositions that support external-world propositions with sufficient strength.

It is impossible to canvass all attempts to fulfill this project; but none have succeeded, and I do not think that any will. One can conclude either that we have no knowledge of the external world or that Cartesian requirements are too demanding. I presuppose the latter conclusion in offering my theory of perceptual knowledge. My theory requires no justification for external-world propositions that derive entirely from self-warranting propositions. It

requires only, in effect, that beliefs in the external world be suitably caused, where "suitably" comprehends a process or mechanism that not only produces true belief in the actual situation, but would not produce false belief in relevant counterfactual situations. If one wishes, one can so employ the term 'justification' that belief causation of *this* kind counts as justification. In this sense, of course, my theory does require justification. But this is entirely different from the sort of justification demanded by Cartesianism.

My theory protects the possibility of knowledge by making Cartesian-style justification unnecessary. But it leaves a door open to skepticism by its stance on relevant alternatives. This is not a failure of the theory, in my opinion. An adequate account of the term 'know' should make the temptations of skepticism comprehensible, which my theory does. But it should also put skepticism in a proper perspective, which Cartesianism fails to do.

In any event, I put forward my account of perceptual knowledge not primarily as an antidote to skepticism, but as a more accurate rendering of what the term 'know' actually means. In this respect it is instructive to test my theory and its rivals against certain metaphorical or analogical uses of 'know.' A correct definition should be able to explain extended and figurative uses as well as literal uses, for it should explain how speakers arrive at the extended uses from the central ones. With this in mind, consider how tempting it is to say of an electric-eye door that it "knows" you are coming (at least that *something* is coming), or "sees" you coming. The attractiveness of the metaphor is easily explained on my theory: the door has a reliable mechanism for discriminating between something being before it and nothing being there. It has a "way of telling" whether or not something is there: this "way of telling" consists in a mechanism by which objects in certain DOE relations to it have differential effects on its internal state. By contrast, note how artificial it would be to apply more traditional analyses of 'know' to the electric-eye door, or to other mechanical detecting devices. How odd it would be to say that the door has "good reasons," "adequate evidence," or "complete justification" for thinking something is there; or that it has "the right to be sure" something is there. The oddity of these locutions indicates how far from the mark are the analyses of 'know' from which they derive.

The trouble with many philosophical treatments of knowledge is that they are inspired by Cartesian-like conceptions of justification or vindication. There is a consequent tendency to overintellectualize or overrationalize the notion of knowledge. In the spirit of naturalistic epistemology,[17] I am trying to fashion an account of knowing that focuses on more primitive and pervasive aspects of cognitive life, in connection with which, I believe, the term 'know' gets its application. A fundamental facet of animate life, both human and infra-human, is telling things apart, distinguishing predator from prey, for example, or a protective habitat from a threatening one. The concept of knowledge has its roots in this kind of cognitive activity.

Notes

[1] "A Causal Theory of Knowing" [Reading IV.2 in this volume].

[1a] The barn facsimile example was originally suggested to me as a puzzle by Carl Ginet.

[2] "An Analysis of Factual Knowledge," *Journal of Philosophy,* 65.6 (1968), 157–170. Reprinted in M. Roth and L. Galis, eds., *Knowing* (New York: Random House, 1970), 113–130.

[3] See, for example, Keith Lehrer and Thomas Paxson, Jr., "Knowledge: Undefeated Justified True Belief" and Peter D. Klein, "A Proposed Definition of Propositional Knowledge," *Journal of Philosophy,* 68.16 (1971), 471–482.

[4] *Thought* (Princeton: Princeton University Press, 1973), p. 152.

[5] *The Analysis of Mind* (London: George Allen and Unwin, 1921), pp. 159–160.

[6] "Pragmatics," in D. Davidson and G. Harman, eds., *Semantics of Natural Language* (Dordrecht: Reidel, 1972).

[7] Something like this is suggested by Fred Dretske, in "Epistemic Operators," *Journal of Philosophy,* 67.24 (1970), 1022. I should emphasize that Dretske himself uses the phrase "relevant alternative," probably its first occurrence.

[8] That 'good' means *answers to certain interests* is claimed by Ziff in *Semantic Analysis* (Ithaca, N.Y.: Cornell University Press, 1960), chap. 6.

[9] *A Materialist Theory of the Mind* (New York: Humanities Press, 1968), pp. 189 ff., and *Belief, Truth and Knowledge* (Cambridge: Cambridge University Press, 1973), chaps. 12 and 13.

[10] My notion of a perceptual equivalent corresponds to Hintikka's notion of a "perceptual alternative." See "On the Logic of Perception," in N. S. Care and R. H. Grimm, eds., *Perception and Personal Identity* (Cleveland: The Press of Case Western Reserve University, 1969).

[11] I have in mind here purely qualitative properties. Properties like *being identical with Judy* would be given by the selected object. If the set of qualitative properties (at a given time) implied which object it is that has these properties, then specification of the object would be redundant, and we could represent states of affairs by ordered pairs of maximal sets of (qualitative) properties and DOE relations. Since this is problematic, however, I include specification of the object as well as the set of (qualitative) properties.

[12] For a discussion of iconic schemata, see Michael I. Posner, *Cognition: An Introduction* (Glenview, Ill.: Scott, Foresman, 1974), chap. 3.

[13] I take this problem up in "Perceptual Objects," forthcoming in *Synthese.*

[14] Should (3A) be construed as implying that *every* property in *J* is a (perceptual) cause of *P*? No. Many of *b*'s properties are exemplified in its interior, or at its backside. These are not causally relevant, at least in visual perception. (3A) must therefore be construed as saying that *P* is (perceptually) caused by *b*'s having (jointly) *all* the members of *J*, and leaving open which, among these members, are individually causally relevant. It follows, however, that (3A) does not require that *b*'s-having-*F*, in particular, is a (perceptual) cause of *P*, and this omission might be regarded as objectionable. "Surely," it will be argued, "*S* perceptually knows *b* to have *F* only if *b*'s-having-*F* (perceptually) causes the percept." The reason I omit this requirement is the following. Suppose *F* is the property of being a dog. Can we say that *b*'s-being-a-dog is a cause of certain light waves' being reflected? This is very dubious. It is the molecular properties of the surface of the animal that are causally responsible for this transmission of light, and hence for the percept.

One might say that even if the percept needn't be (perceptually) caused by *b*'s-having-*F*, it must at least be caused by micro-structural properties of *b* that *ensure* *b*'s-having-*F*. As the dog example again illustrates, however, this is too strong. The surface properties of the dog that reflect the light waves do not *ensure* that the object is a dog, either logically or nomologically. Something could have that surface (on one side) and still have a non-dog interior and backside. The problem should be solved, I think, by reliance on whether there are relevant perceptual equivalents. If there are no relevant perceptual equivalents in which *K* excludes being a dog, then the properties of the actual object that are causally responsible for the percept suffice to yield knowledge. We need not require either that the percept be (perceptually) caused by *b*'s-having-*F*, nor by any subset of *J* that "ensures" *b*'s having-*F*.

[15] It is the "unusualness" of the DOE relation that inclines us not to count the alternative as relevant; it is not the mere fact that the DOE relation differs from the actual one. In general, our analysis allows knowledge to be defeated or disqualified by alternative situations in which the DOE relation differs from the DOE relation in the actual state of affairs. Our analysis differs in this respect from Fred Dretske's analysis in "Conclusive Reasons." Dretske's analysis, which ours resembles on a number of points, considers only those counterfactual situations in which everything that is "logically and causally

independent of the state of affairs expressed by *P*" (p. 50) is the same as in the actual situation. (*P* is the content of *S*'s belief.) This implies that the actual DOE relation cannot be counterfactualized, but must be held fixed. (It may also imply—depending on what *P* is—that one cannot counterfactualize the perceived object nor the full set of properties *J*.) This unduly narrows the class of admissible alternatives. Many *relevant* alternatives, that do disqualify knowledge, involve DOE relations that differ from the actual DOE relation.

[16] Harman has a similar case, in *Thought*, pp. 22–23. In that case, however, *S* does not see the candle; it is not a cause of his percept. Given our causal requirement for perceptual knowledge, that case is easily handled.

[17] Cf. W. O. Quine, "Epistemology Naturalized," in *Ontological Relativity and Other Essays* (New York: Columbia University Press, 1969).

An early version of this paper was read at the 1972 Chapel Hill Colloquium. Later versions were read at the 1973 University of Cincinnati Colloquium, and at a number of other philosophy departments. For comments and criticism, I am especially indebted to Holly Goldman, Bruce Aune, Jaegwon Kim, Louis Loeb, and Kendall Walton.

IV.6 *Why I Know So Much More Than You Do*

William W. Rozeboom

Rozeboom argues that the attempts to dismiss the tripartite analysis of knowledge are misguided. It is not that our ideal of knowledge is inadequate, but that it only touches an extreme epistemic relationship, that of absolute justification. First Rozeboom shows that there is a conceptual vagueness in our use of the term *knowledge*. Then he seeks to rectify this by restricting knowledge to cases of absolute certainty. He shows that this solves the Gettier problem, but it has the result of making "knowledge" an ideal that is never instantiated. Rozeboom's conclusion is that the subject of "knowledge" is too primitive for the needs of technical epistemology and that we must work out more fine-grained concepts.

What does it mean to say that person *X* "knows" that *p*? With a unanimity remarkable for philosophers, it is generally agreed that for this to be true, it must obtain that

    (a) *p* is the case,
    (b) *X* believes that *p,* and
    (c) *X* is justified in believing *p*.

Whether conditions (*a*)–(*c*) jointly suffice for *X* to know that *p,* however, has recently been disputed by several writers.[1] I shall attempt to show

that these doubts are unfounded, and that the *justified true belief* analysis of knowledge (hereafter referred to as the "JTB thesis") is indeed adequate. But I shall then proceed to agitate related perplexities about the concept of "knowledge" and conclude with a possible heretical suggestion about its continued usefulness for technical epistemology.

—

I

Estranged from his wife and beset by financial troubles, John Duosmith has become conspicuously despondent. Today, a man's body is found in

William W. Rozeboom, "Why I Know So Much More Than You Do," *American Philosophical Quarterly*, 4 (1967), 281–90. Reprinted by permission.

Duosmith's hotel room with Duosmith's revolver in its hand, a bullet therefrom in its head, and a suicide note signed by Duosmith on the table. Mrs. Duosmith identifies the body as that of her husband, pointing out his characteristic birthmark, the private details of their recent quarrel cited in the note, and so on for many other items which make it overwhelmingly evident to Mrs. Duosmith that the corpse of John Duosmith lies before her, and hence that her husband is dead

And John Durosmith is indeed dead. But what has happened is this: Last night, Duosmith received a secret visit from his indentical twin brother Jim, a petty criminal whose existence John had concealed from his wife and who now begged John to hide him from certain colleagues seeking retribution for something Jim had done. Seeing a chance to make a new life for himself, John shot his brother and arranged the scene to appear as though he, John, had killed himself. But as John left the hotel, he was spotted by Jim's pursuers who, mistaking him for his twin, promptly executed their plans for Jim's demise. So John Duosmith is dead while his wife, for the best of reasons, also believes this to be so.

But does Mrs. Duosmith *know* that her husband is dead? Mr. Gettier and others[2] say "No," and my own linguistic intuition agrees with this judgment. The force of this and similar examples cited by Gettier *et seq.* is drawn from the principle that true beliefs grounded upon false premisses do not count as knowledge, no matter how reasonable those premisses may themselves be under the circumstances. That is,

(A) If person X believes *p*—justifiably—only because he believes *q*, while he justifiably believes *q* on the basis of evidence *e*, then *q* as well as *p* must be the case if X's belief in *p* is to qualify as "knowledge."

Consequently, if *p* is true while *q* is false in such a case, as apparently illustrated by the Duosmith episode and Gettier's examples, it follows that a person may justifiably believe true proposition *p* and still not *know* that *p*. Now in fact, these examples do *not* show this, nor can the JTB thesis ever be threatened by principle (A). But before I point out why this is so, it is best to undermine confidence that linguistic intuition can be trusted to provide as sound interpretation of cases like these.

II

It is Sunday afternoon, and Mrs. Jones is on her way to borrow an egg from her neighbor, Mrs. Togethersmith. She fears that she may be too late, however, for she is aware that every Sunday afternoon for the past several years, the Togethersmith family—Mr. and Mrs. Togethersmith and their two children—has gone for a drive in the country. As she steps outside, Mrs. Jones sees the Togethersmith car departing with Mr. Togethersmith at the wheel, and thinks to herself, "Pity, there she goes." Mrs. Jones believes that Mrs. Togethersmith is driving away because, for excellent reasons, she believes that the entire Togethersmith family is in the departing car. But in fact, while Mrs. Togethersmith, her husband, and one of their children are indeed in the departing car, the other Togethersmith child is on this one occasion attending a friend's birthday party. Insomuch as it is not true that the entire Togethersmith family is driving away, is Mrs. Jones's justified true belief, that Mrs. Togethersmith is driving away, *knowledge*? Principle (A) appears to deny this, since Mrs. Jones arrived at her true belief about Mrs. Togethersmith by means of a justified but false belief about the whereabouts of the entire Togethersmith family. But the falsehood here seems so *irrelevant*. For "The entire Togethersmith family is driving away" is equivalent to the conjunction "Mrs. Togethersmith is driving away, Mr. Togethersmith is driving away, and all the Togethersmith children are driving away," the components of which are supported by Mrs. Jones's evidence just as well separately as conjoined—in fact, it is difficult to say whether Mrs. Jones's belief about Mrs. Togethersmith derives from her belief about the Togethersmith family as a whole, or is a part-cause of it. In any event, linguistic intuition is disposed to deny that the absence of one Togethersmith child from the departing family car disqualifies Mrs. Jones's justified true belief about Mrs. Togethersmith's departure as an instance of knowledge.

But if so, what about Mr. Jones, who, wanting a 12-inch board, measures one with his new tape rule, obtains a 10-inch reading, and concludes "That's too small," when the tape rule is defective and this board is really 11 inches? (We assume that Jones has had much past experience with tape rules, all of which amply warrants his trust in the present reading.) Mr. Jones's justified belief, that this board is under 12 inches, is true even though it is derived from his false justified belief that this board is 10 inches. Since intuitively this case is no different in kind from Mrs. Duosmith's belief about her dead husband, we shoud deny that Jones *knows* this board is less than 12 inches. Yet "This board is 10 inches" is equivalent to the conjunction "This board is under 12 inches, this board is at least 10 inches, and this board is not between 10 and 12 inches," only the last component of which is false while its first component requires for its justification only a proper part of the evidence which supports Jones's belief in the whole conjunction. So by formal parallel, it might also seem that Mr. Jones's conclusion that the board in undersize should not be epistemically inferior to Mrs. Jones's belief in Mrs. Togethersmith's departure.

More intensive analysis of these two cases would show not so much that one or both violate principle (*A*) as that when a person's justified true belief *p* is accompanied by a justified false belief *q* it may well prove troublesome to decide whether or not his belief in *p* is related to his belief in *q* in such fashion that the falsity of the latter should disqualify the former as knowledge. That this is in general a failure of conception, not just an insufficiency of data concerning the believer's detailed reasoning, is shown by the following more sophisticated example.

Dr. Pillsmith, a competent practitioner of medicine, is well aware that

(1) Among persons who have not been vaccinated against Hypofluvia, 999,999 out of a million who show symptoms *S* are afflicted with this disease,

(2) Among vaccinated persons showing symptoms *S*, only one in ten is afflicted with Hypofluvia,

(3) Only one person in a million showing symptoms *S* has been vaccinated against Hypofluvia,

and that consequently,[3]

(4) More than 999,998 persons in a million who show symptoms *S* are afflicted with Hypofluvia.

Attempting to diagnose the condition of his latest patient, Dr. Pillsmith observes that

(5) Philip Blotely shows symptoms *S*,

and, lacking further information about Blotely's medical history, infers unhesitatingly from (1)–(5) both that

(6) Philip Blotely has not been vaccinated against Hypofluvia.

and that

(7) Philip Blotely has Hypofluvia.

Now it so happens that Blotely was, in fact, vaccinated against Hypofluvia, but has contracted it just the same. So Pillsmith's diagnosis (7) is both justified and true—but is it knowledge? At first it might seem that the falsity of (6) thwarts this, for were Pillsmith to surmise the truth of Blotely's vaccination, his knowledge of (2) and (5) would prevent him from justifiedly accepting (7). Yet (6) is at the same time irrelevant to the diagnosis in that Pillsmith can get to (7) from (5) and (1)–(3) by way of (4) without ever considering whether or not Blotely has been vaccinated. And if Pillsmith does make his diagnosis in this way, must (6) still be true if Pillsmith's justified belief, that Blotely has Hypofluvia, is to count as knowledge? Surely not, since falsehood (6) takes no part in the inference. Yet we can also argue that justification of (7) by (5) and (1)–(3) via (4) implicitly presupposes the truth of (6), for derivation of (4) from (1)–(3) argues in effect: Given any person with symptoms *S*, either he has or has not been vaccinated against Hypofluvia. If he hasn't, it is virtually certain that he has Hypofluvia; otherwise, Hypofluvia is counterindicated, but this is too unlikely a possibility to be considered seriously.

It seems to me that the intuition which was so sure in Sect. I that Mrs. Duosmith doesn't really know her husband is dead is quite at a loss to say whether or not Dr. Pillsmith knows that Blotely has Hypofluvia. There is quicksand underfoot here, and we must not too hastily presume that Duosmith-type examples, which apparently refute the JTB analysis of knowledge by way of principle (*A*), are all that they seem to be.

III

It is now time to make explicit an important technical detail which is usually slighted in philosophical discussions of knowledge. This is that the judgmental attitudes in which a proposition can be held are not just belief and disbelief, or belief, disbelief, and uncertainty, but a whole spectrum of credibilities spanning many shades of uncertain belief and doubt. Consequently, assertion that knowing presupposes believing is specious unless it is made clear just how strong a belief is so required. Once this question of degree is raised, however, we can easily see from the absurdity of "He knows that p but isn't entirely sure of it,"[4] or "I know that p but have some doubts about whether it is really so," that only maximal belief is acceptable for knowledge. Hence condition (b) of the JTB thesis must be explicated as "X feels completely sure of p" or "X believes p absolutely," while similarly, (c) must be read as "X is justified in believing p absolutely," "X has a right to have not the slightest doubt about p," or the like. (Also, since it may be argued that if X is justified in believing p in degree d then X is also justified to almost the same extent in believing p to a degree which is almost d, "X is justified in believing p absolutely" should be further explicated as "X has more justification for believing p absolutely than for feeling any doubt about p.")

When is absolute belief justified? While a convincing general answer is not easy to come by (see Sect. IV), a necessary condition for evidential justification is surely the following:

> (B) If person X feels completely sure of p on the basis of evidence e, then X's belief in p is justified only if e necessitates p.

That is, X is not justified in feeling certain of p in virtue of his awareness of e unless p is certain, given e. This is entirely compatible with admitting that X may be justified in feeling *almost* certain of p on grounds e if p is extremely likely, given e. It only denies that it is rational for X to close his mind completely to the possibility of not-p even though e, so long as this possibility does in fact exist. Moreover, while (B) does not specify what sense of necessity—logical, causal, or whatever—is required, it is in any case analytically true that

> (C) If e while not q, then it is not the case that e necessitates q.

Finally, I think it will be agreed that in general,

> (D) If person X feels completely sure of p only because he feels completely sure of q, but his belief in q is not justified, then neither is his belief in p justified.

(I would hold that (D) is always the case, but there is room for argument on this point when q is "basic" for X—see Sect. IV—and it is not essential here that (D) be completely universal.)

Let us now reconsider principle (A), which envisions a person's believing p on the basis of his belief q, and q on the basis of evidence e. For this to pose any threat to the JTB analysis of knowledge, the degree of belief at issue must be *absolute* belief. But it follows from (B) and (C) that X can justifiedly believe q—absolutely—on the basis of evidence e only if q is the case; so stipulation of q's truth in the final clause of (A) is in this case otiose. That is, if X feels completely sure of p only because he is convinced of q, and the latter only because he is aware of e, then to hypothesize that q is false is also, by (B) and (C), to presuppose that X's absolute belief in q is unjustified, and hence by (D) that neither is he justified in feeling completely sure of p. Thus in our Duosmith example (and similarly for Gettier's cases), while Mrs. Duosmith had excellent reason to feel *virtually* certain that her husband was dead, the bare fact that overwhelming evidence to the contrary notwithstanding, the body before her was not that of her husband shows that this evidence did not warrant her having no doubt whatsoever that her husband was dead. Likewise, for our more problematic examples in Sect. II, we can say without hesitation that Mrs. Jones, Mr. Jones, and Dr. Pillsmith did not *know* that Mrs. Togethersmith was departing, that this board was less than 12 inches, and that Blotely had Hypofluvia, respectively, because while the evidential bases for these conclusions made them extremely likely, a vestige of uncertainty still remained. In short, if the "belief" cited in principle (A) is allowed to include degrees of belief weaker than complete conviction, the truth of (A) resides in that the falsity of q is symptomatic that the degree of p-belief justified by e is less than absolute.

IV

But while the argument from principle (A) thus fails to impeach the JTB thesis, the claim that justification is always prerequisite to knowledge is far from unproblematic. Most conspicuously troublesome is that if X's knowing p requires there to exist evidence e such that X's belief in p is justified by X's awareness (i.e., knowledge) of e, then X's belief in e also requires such justification and we are off on a regress. In particular, the justification requirement might seem to exclude the possibility of perceptual knowledge and self-awareness where X's belief in p is not inferred from other beliefs but is aroused directly by sensory stimulation or given introspectively. Moreover, as will be seen, the demand for justification undergoes a remarkable transformation when we turn from other-person to first-person knowledge, while the conditions of justification even for the inferred beliefs of others are not so straightforward as they might at first appear.

Actually, no puzzle of "justification" can even discredit the JTB thesis, for the simple reason that whatever is needed for X to know that p, if X does know p then he is certainly justified in believing p. (Witness, e.g., the absurdity of "X knows that p, but he has no right to believe it so strongly.") So we can maintain that X knows that p iff p is a justified true belief of X's without concern for how murky the concept of justification may itself be. I submit, therefore, that the greatest philosophic challenge which issues from the JTB position is not to settle whether this view is entirely correct (though the import of my argument in Sect. III is that we have no good reason to doubt this), but to determine what it is about X's knowing p that accredits X's p-belief as "justified." The intent of this section is to rough out a tentative solution to this problem, which is more untidily complex than heretofore recognized, in full expectation that many more exchanges will be needed to round out the present survey in convincing detail.

Let a person's belief in p be described as "basic" if he does not believe p as a result of his believing something else. (For example, when X perceives that p, his belief in p is simply for him a *given* which becomes a basis for inference but is not derived from anything else he knows.) Then X's *basic con-*

victions are beliefs of which X feels completely sure without having inferred them from evidence. Unless knowledge can be inferred from beliefs which do not themselves qualify as knowledge (a counterintuitive possibility which I shall not discuss), the regression argument shows that if X knows anything at all, he must also have basic knowledge, i.e., justified true basic convictions, and our first task in this section is to find some acceptable sense in which a basic conviction may be said to be justified. Two alternatives present themselves: either (1) basic convictions are self-justifying, or (2) some basic convictions have nonevidential justification.

In support of (1), it might be argued that the justification of X's belief in p consists in p's bearing a certain relation $\mathfrak{I}$ to some set B of X's true basic convictions. If b_i is such that each $b_i \in B$ is also related to B in manner $\mathfrak{I}$, then all basic convictions in B are also by definition justified. For example, if "X is justified in believing p" were to be analyzed as "p is logically entailed by X's true basic convictions," then X's basic convictions are justified by the reflexivity of entailment. But this approach leaves much to be desired. For one, an intuitively acceptable $\mathfrak{I}$-relation with the needed formal properties is not easy to come by. (It is simple to argue, e.g., that logical entailment does not in itself confer evidential justification.) Further, how is the set B to be circumscribed? Does veracity suffice for a basic conviction to belong to B—i.e., for it to be justified? If so, we should have to grant that a dogmatic thinker who habitually works himself into a state of absolutely closed judgment on controversial issues without considering any of the relevant evidence is justified in holding any such belief which by chance happens to be true. But if we hold that a basic conviction can be true without necessarily being justified, whatever else is needed for the latter constitutes a non-evidential source of justification and thus carries us into alternative (2).

There are many intriguing thought experiments by which our intuitions about nonevidential belief-warrants can be bared, starting with increasingly bizarre or futuristic ways (e.g., electrical stimulation of the retina) in which sensory input might elicit true perceptual beliefs; but here it will suffice to consider just one which cuts directly to the heart of the matter. Suppose that Tom Seersmith claims to be able to foretell the outcomes of horse races. Upon investigation, we learn that when Seersmith thinks about a forthcoming race, he is often overwhelmed, quite without any reason for it, with a feeling of complete certainty that a certain horse will be the winner. Before the last Kentucky Derby, Seersmith felt sure that it would be won by a horse named Fleetfoot, and as it turned out his prediction was correct. Did Seersmith *know* that Fleetfoot was going to win, and if so, in what sense was his belief justified?

Whatever the personal peculiarity which endows Seersmith with convictions about forthcoming horse races, if his prognostication record has shown only chance accuracy in the past, we would be loath to say that Seersmith either knew or was justified in believing that Fleetfoot would win the Derby even though his belief in this instance happened to be true. Even if Seersmith's previous race predictions have usually been correct, with a hit rate high enough to convince us that there is something extraordinary about this man, we would still deny that he was justified in feeling absolutely sure that Fleetfoot would win so long as his predictions are not infallible. But suppose we discover that Seersmith's horse race prognoses *are* infallible— i.e., we become convinced that whenever Seersmith feels sure that race *r* will be won by horse *h*, it is absolutely certain that *h* will win *r*. Then surely we would be forced to admit that Seersmith knew that Fleetfoot would win the Derby, even though how he knew would baffle us. (As I follow Seersmith through prediction after prediction and see that he is *never* wrong, I find myself saying, "I can't understand it, but somehow, he *knows*!") The justification—nonevidential—for Seersmith's belief is simply that since generalization

($\forall h$) ($\forall r$) (Tom Seersmith believes that horse *h* will win race *r* $\supset$ *h* wins *r*)

is a nomological principle of our world, Seersmith's basic conviction that Fleetfoot would win the Derby was true not by mere happenstance but of nomic necessity. For if Seersmith's horse race precognitions *cannot* be wrong, what better justification could there possibly be for his having them?

Now let's change the case slightly. Tom Seersmith's brother Dick also feels occasional convictions about the outcomes of forthcoming horse races, but unlike his brother, Dick's percentage of

correct anticipations is substantially less than perfect. Careful research discloses, however, that Dick's accuracy depends critically upon the horse's name. Whenever Dick feels sure that horse *h* will win race *r*, he is never mistaken so long as *h*'s name contains exactly two syllables, but when the predicted winner's name is shorter or longer than this, Dick's precognitive effectiveness is somehow impaired. Dick, too, felt sure that Fleetfoot would win the Derby—but did he *know* this? In principle, Dick's case is exactly like that of brother Tom, since by natural law his preconvictions about bisyllabically designated horse-race victors cannot err. Yet intuition is more hesitant here, for at times Dick also feels certain that *h* will win *r* when he should not, namely, when '*h*' is not bisyllabic. And if Dick is unaware that the anticipated winner's name makes a difference for the reliability of his forecast, we might question whether he is entitled to feel such perfect confidence in his precognition even when, unknown to him, it is in fact nomologically infallible. Thus it might be denied that Dick *knew* of Fleetfoot's forthcoming victory if he did not recognize that his particular belief had stronger truth-credentials than his average forecast. But this line of argument is unsound. If Dick were aware of his general precognitive fallibility, it would indeed seem reasonable for him to have inferential meta-doubts about his belief in Fleetfoot's victory—if he had, in fact, had any. But to make a person's knowing *p* contingent upon his knowing that he knows *p* would precipitate an intolerable regress, nor should a person's true belief in *p* be disqualified as knowledge merely by his having additional erroneous convictions as well. (To hold that a person can know nothing if he ever believes falsely seems extreme to the point of absurdity, though as will be seen in Sect. V it contains an important grain of truth.) If Dick's conviction that Fleetfoot would win the Derby was truly basic for him, uninfluenced by any meta-beliefs concerning his general prognostic proficiency, then it was for him no less an instance of *knowing* than it was for brother Tom, and was justified on the very same grounds, namely, that insomuch as Dick felt certain Fleetfoot would win, it *was* certain that Fleetfoot would win.

And now one more twist, Suppose that Harry is still another Seersmith whose case is like Dick's except that Harry's precognitions of form "horse *h* will win race *r*" are always (nomologically) correct when and only when *r* is run on a dry track. Insomuch as Fleetfoot won the Derby on a dry track, was Harry's conviction that Fleetfoot would win an instance of knowledge? Harry's belief, too, was infallible in that there exists a nomic principle in virtue of which, given that Harry felt sure that Fleetfoot would win and that the track was dry, it was certain that Fleetfoot would win. But Harry differs from Dick in that Dick's infallible precognitions are intrinsically identifiable as such—i.e., whether or not a forecast by Dick falls under the law which vouchsafes its accuracy is revealed by its syllabic composition—whereas the reliability of Harry's forecast cannot be determined without additional information which does not generally become available until race time. And since Harry thus cannot discriminate his infallible precognitions from those which are not (assuming that he does not also have advance knowledge of the track conditions), it might be argued that he had no right to feel so sure that Fleetfoot would win the Derby. But this doubt is only a refinement of the one we have already rejected in Dick's case. If it is not necessary for Harry to know that he knows *p*, or to know that he can trust his belief *p* absolutely, in order for him to know *p* or for his *p*-belief to be justified, then neither can we reasonably hold that his being *able* to acquire this meta-knowledge is requisite for the latter. (How could such an ability possibly be germane except by way of the knowledge which, with its help, Harry does acquire?) Consequently, so long as a person's basic believing of *p* belongs to a class whose members are nomologically infallible, its epistemological status should not depend upon whether or not this class is defined by properties inherent in the belief itself. (It is relevant to this point that knowing what *we* know about Harry, we could win a pretty penny at the races by noting Harry's prediction and waiting to see the track conditions before deciding whether to bet.)

The principle which appears to govern our Seersmith examples (though intuition speaks only with a subdued and halting voice here) is that a basic conviction counts as "knowledge," and is by the same token justified, if and only if it not merely *is* true, as could occur by chance, but is infallibly true by virtue of its being of a kind (perhaps defined in part by relational attributes) whose accuracy is guaranteed by natural law. This is at best an uneasy conclusion, however, for without further qualification it trembles on the brink of triviality: If *V* is the attribute of veridicality, then any belief of type *V*—i.e., any which happens to be true—is also infallibly true vis-á-vis type *V* and hence qualifies as knowledge unless "natural law" is defined to exclude generalizations which are logical truths. (That we would *like* to make some such exclusion is, I think, intuitively evident, but how to accomplish it effectively is another question.) Moreover, this criterion applies only to the basic convictions of other persons, for *my* beliefs, basic or otherwise, are justified by standards rather different from this.

Suppose that I set out to determine which of us, you or I, knows the more. I start by listing all propositions which you believe (or more precisely, all which I believe that you believe) and then prune this list by deleting everything on it which, in my judgment, is either false or is unwarranted for you. To display what *I* know, however (or rather, what I believe that I know), I list all the propositions believed by me—*and stop*. For while I am perfectly willing to admit that there are facts of which I have no knowledge, I do not believe, nor can I bring myself to believe, any specific proposition of form "*p*, but I don't know that *p*." This is closely related to the oddity of "*p*, but I don't believe it," but has a significance the latter does not. I reject "*p*, but I don't believe it" because my believing this would entail my believing *p* and hence falsify the conjunction as a whole—i.e., it is impossible for me to believe a true proposition of this form. I could, however, truly believe "*p*, but I don't know it" were *p* to be the case while I believed but did not know what *p*.[5] Hence my refusal to admit, when I am convinced of *p*, that I may not know that *p*, has the force of maintaining that in *my* case, believing truly suffices for knowing. (And yet, when I reflect upon why I don't consider all *your* true beliefs to be knowledge, I am also willing to admit in general terms that some of mine may not be knowledge, either. This is an apparent inconsistency which will be resolved in Sect. V.)

This first-person/other-person difference in knowledge criteria is present even when, from your vantage point, my true belief is amply justified. Suppose that I believe mathematical theorem *T* because I have just discovered a convincing proof of it, and when I inform you that I know *T*, you ask me what grounds I have for thinking that I know this. The only reply which seems relevant is for me to recapitulate the steps by which I deduced T—except that when I do this, you quite properly point out that what I have given you is grounds for believing T whereas what you asked for is grounds for believing that I know T. My supplying of proof for T *demonstrates* to you that my belief in T is justified, but *asserts* nothing which implies this. On the other hand, if I try to give you an account of how it is that I know T, it will go something like: "Well, I know that L_1 and L_2 are logically true, so when I see that T is an immediate consequence of L_1 and L_2, this makes me aware that T is also the case." What I am telling you is that my awareness of certain facts, namely, that L_1 and L_2 are logically true and jointly entail T, is a *cause* of my knowing T. But from your perspective, my awareness of this evidence *provides* (noncausally, by fulfilling an existence requirement) the justification which is an analytic component of my knowing T. That is, in more general terms, when I have come to know p by a valid line of reasoning from unimpeachable premisses, the inferential procedure which to you is a *condition* on my knowing p is to me only the *occasion* for this. What justifies *my believing p* is simply p's being the case; for once I have convinced myself that p, I require nothing else to consider it right that I feel sure of—what more could possibly be relevant? In fact, it is nomically impossible for me to accept "p, but I have no right to believe it so absolutely," for my believing the second component of this suffices to create some doubt in me about p. (This is why I am unable—nomically, not logically—to believe "p, but I don't know it.") So I reason about p not to transmute my base belief in p into golden knowledge, but to decide whether p is the case; whereupon, having convinced myself that it is, I rebuff all challenges to my conviction's epistemic credentials by the argument "p; therefore it is reasonable for me to believe that p."

What are my criteria for the justification of *your* beliefs? We have already explored the evaluation of your basic convictions, but it remains to see what is needed for your inferred beliefs to be reasonable. Ordinarily, the degree of p-belief which I consider evidence e to warrant in you is simply the confidence in p which I sense is aroused in me by conviction that e. However, closer analysis shows this not to be definitive. Let p and q be two propositions such that q logically entails p. If, somehow, I know that you know q, what will persuade me that you have evidential justification for believing p? For my-

self, merely being cognizant of q does not in itself convince me of p (I am, after all, often unsure of consequences of my beliefs when I have not discerned that they are such consequences), so for your q-awareness to warrant your p-belief, I would normally require you to know not only that q, but that q entails p as well. But is q & $(q \vdash p)$, then *sufficient* evidence to justify your belief in p? If, either thoughtlessly or with good reason, I presume that our minds work alike, I will agree that it is; for belief in the former would cause me to believe the latter as well. But suppose I have learned that you just don't seem to grasp the significance of logical relationships: specifically, that you often accept propositions of form "α, and α entails β" while simultaneously doubting or even disbelieving β. Then I would no longer consider your belief in q & $(q \vdash p)$ to be evidential justification for your believing p, for I could not regard the former as the *source* of the latter, nor would I have reason to regard your p-belief as knowledge insomuch as your veridicality in this instance may simply be the chance success of irrational thought. Conversely suppose I discover instead that your thinking is superrational in that for any two propositions α and β such that α entails β, and you believe α, your mere thinking of β when you believe α suffices for you to be convinced of β as well—i.e., you believe all logical consequences of your beliefs, so long as they come to mind at all, whether or not you are also aware of the entailment relations among these propositions. In this case, I must concede that your knowledge of q is fully adequate in itself to justify, and hence to dignify as knowledge, your belief in p. For if you accept all logical consequences of your convictions, rather than just a proper subclass of these constrained by your logistical perceptiveness, on what grounds can I hold your belief processes to be epistemically defective?

The preceding arguments show, first impressions to the contrary notwithstanding, that my other-person epistemology has exactly the same justificational standards for inferred beliefs as it does for basic ones. In both cases, the critical determinant is not whether the belief in question is "reasonable" in accord with some impersonal normative ideal, but whether it has arisen in circumstances which guarantee its accuracy. (This applies also to beliefs with derivational status intermediate between basic and inferred, thus bypassing the problems these would generate were the criteria of justification qualitatively different for the two extremes. For example, suppose that for a certain pair of attributes P and Q, whenever you perceive that $P(a)$ for an object a you find yourself also convinced that $Q(a)$. If I know that in our world P nomically implies Q, I must count your belief in $Q(a)$ as knowledge, justified by your awareness of $P(a)$, even if you are not consciously aware that $(\forall x([P(x)\supset Q(x)].^6)$ Harmony between first-person and other-person justification, however, is more elusive. At one level, these show a common pattern: Whenever I consider my/your conviction in p to be justified, I presume there to exist an argument of form "S; hence my/ your belief in p is necessarily correct," where S is some state of reality.[7] But when it is my belief which is at issue, S is p itself; whereas I want the S which warrants your p-belief to do so nomically rather than logically. That I should adopt so flagrant an epistemological double standard is not a conclusion which I find esthetically pleasing, but if there is a deeper unity here I have yet to find it.

V

However lacking in clarity (and perhaps consistency) the epistemic concept of "justification" may be, it nonetheless appears that knowing p analytically requires not only that the knower feel completely certain of p, but also that there be some sense in which, considering the circumstances, it *is* completely certain that p. But since I reject the argument "p; therefore you are justified in feeling sure of p," and also doubt that our *de facto* world contains any nomic regularities perfect enough to vouchsafe any belief beyond all possibility of error, I do not think that you strictly know anything at all. Whereas in my own case, I have too much faith in my own fallibility to feel *absolutely* sure of anything, even if some of my perceptual beliefs fall short of this only negligibly. My admission (with high but not complete conviction) that probably not all of my beliefs are entirely correct, plus inability to meta-distinguish those which are true from those which are not, causally prevents me from ever entirely achieving an absolute extremity of belief, while my professional skills as scientist and philosopher en-

able me to find genuine even if minuscule chinks of uncertainty in any proposition I examine, even those which arise perceptually or feel analytically true. So technically speaking, I know nothing either.[8]

In short, my conception of "knowledge"—and presumably yours as well—is so impossibly idealized that no real-life belief episode ever satisfies it. Whenever you or I assert, as we often do, "I am aware that . . . ," "He knows that . . . ," etc., we are uttering falsehoods which would come closer to the truth if revised as "I approximate awareness that . . . ," "He almost knows that . . . ," or the like. The paradigm-case rejoinder, that what we mean by "know" is defined by these ordinary-life, applications, no more shows that this usage is literally correct than the everyday paradigmatic ascriptions of "spherical" to roundish objects of irregular curvature demonstrates that a thing's surface does not really have to be a constant distance from its center in order for it to be literally a sphere. On matters philosophical as well as scientific, ordinary language teems with simplistic presuppositions and coarse-grained, uncritical categories which do slovenly justice to reality; and intellectual maturity—represented most illustriously by technical science but by no means restricted thereto—consists first of all in learning to relinquish these cognitive crudities for a more sophisticated grasp of complexity and precise detail. It is all very well to recognize that the conceptual fluency of idealized approximations is often more convenient for everyday affairs than is the encumbrance of needless exactitude, but it is folly to construe the success of this practical usage as a sign that what is so asserted is precisely correct, or to begrudge its abandonment when, like outgrown clothing, its inaccuracies being to chafe. In particular, there is no more reason for us to agonize philosophically over the esoterics of everyday knowledge-talk—e.g., why justified true beliefs at practical levels of assurance should sometimes be called knowledge and sometimes not—than for geometricians to puzzle over why some common-sense spheres have a larger cubed-surface-to-squared volume ratio than do others.

To conclude, then, I propose that the subject of "knowledge" is no longer of serious philosophical concern for the simple reason that this concept is far too primitive for the needs of technical epistemology. No harm will be done, I suppose, by retaining a special name for true beliefs at the theoretical limit of absolute conviction and perfect infallibility so long as we appreciate that this ideal is never instantiated, but such sentimentality must not be allowed to impede development of conceptual resources for mastering the panorama of partial certainties which are more literally relevant to the real world. So far, however, the normative theory of practical belief has scarcely advanced beyond surmise that the structure of propositional credibilities is isomorphic to the probability calculus, and has not even begun to think technically about such vital subtleties as the ramifications of uncertainty in basic beliefs, reciprocal nondemonstrative supports among partially confirmed propositions, the credibility interplay between beliefs and meta-beliefs, and the like. With problems of "How strongly should X believe p?" lying dark and unfathomed before us, we stand to profit from continued epistemological preoccupation with the nature of "knowledge" to just about the same extent as would psychology from a return to study of the "soul."

Notes

[1] See Gettier (8), Clark (7), Sosa (17), Saunders and Champawat (16), Lehrer (12), and Harman (9). The justified-true-belief view of knowledge has been well stated by Ayer (3, ch. 1), Chisholm (5, ch. 1), and Woozley (18, ch. 8, though Woozley rashly puts the justification condition as having *evidence* for what one knows), and recently defended in one respect or another by Arner (2), Saunders (15), and Harrison (10). While condition (*b*) has occasionally been disputed on the rather foolish ground that "believes" is sometimes understood to imply "does not feel sure of," the necessity of (*a*) and (*b*) for knowing that *p* is essentially noncontroversial. The status of (*c*), however, is more problematic. Armstrong (1, p. 120), Malcolm (13, p. 225ff.), and Sosa (17) contend from an overly narrow equating of "justification" with "evidence" that justification is not always requisite to knowing. In contrast, Gettier (8), Clark (7), Lehrer (12), and Harman (9) accept the necessity of (*c*) for knowing *p* but deny its sufficiency given (*a*, *b*), while Saunders and Champawat (16) question the possibility of finding *any* set of conditions which are necessary and sufficient for all instances of "knowledge."

Though not strictly addressed to the analysis of "knowing," recent discussion by Chisholm (6), Brown (4), and Saunders (14) concerning self-justifying beliefs, and Hintikka's (11) widely acclaimed exploration of the modal logic of knowledge and belief are also background context for the present work.

[2] See n.1.

[3] Since for any three attributes A, B, and C,

$$Pr(A/B) = Pr(C/B) \times Pr(A/BC) +$$
$$Pr(\overline{C}/B) \times Pr(A/\overline{B}C) \geq [1 - PR(C/B)] \times Pr(A/\overline{B}C).$$

[4] At first thought, this might seem to make sense as a variant of "He really knows that *p* but can't bring himself to admit it." But *not admitting to belief in* is not at all the same as *having some doubts about*, and "He knows that *p* but won't admit it" implies not "He is not sure of *p* and won't admit that *p*," but either "He doesn't really have any doubt about *p* but can't bring himself to say so," or "He still isn't really convinced of *p* even though he has overwhelming evidence for it."

[5] While Hintikka (11) has proposed essentially the same analysis of "*p*, but I don't believe it" as offered here, his modal system allows that a person *can* defensibly claim to believe "*p*, but I don't know it." However, Hintikka's intuitive apologia for this (11, p. 83) construes it to involve a degree of *p*-belief less than perfect conviction, and the fact that his system does not recognize the unacceptability of "I don't know that *p* even though I am absolutely sure of it" would seem to reveal a lacuna in its axioms.

[6] I say "not consciously aware" rather than simply "unaware" to suggest the glide from inference episodes of the most paradigmatically rational sort down to believings which are patterned *as though* they were accompanied by additional supportive knowledge which the believer does not, in fact, have in any conceptualized form.

[7] The scope of "necessary" here is of course $N(S \supset$ my-or-your *p*-belief is correct), not $S \supset N$ (my-or-your *p*-belief is correct).

[8] Hence the title of this paper is something of a misnomer. Although my knowledge-criteria are enormously more liberal for me than for you, their extension is in both cases the null class.

References

1. Armstrong, D. M. *Perception and the Physical World*. London, Routledge & Kegan Paul, 1961.

2. Arner, D. "On Knowing." *The Philosophical Review*, vol. 68 (1959), pp. 84–92.

3. Ayer, A. J. *The Problem of Knowledge*. London, Macmillan, 1956.

4. Brown, R. "Self-Justifying Statements." *The Journal of Philosophy*, vol. 62 (1965), pp. 145–150.

5. Chisholm, R. M. *Perceiving: A Philosophical Study*. Ithaca, Cornell University Press, 1957.

6. Chisholm, R. "Theory of Knowledge." In: *Philosophy*, R. M. Chisholm, *et al*. Englewood Cliffs, Prentice-Hall, 1964.

7. Clark, M. "Knowledge and Grounds: a Comment on Mr. Gettier's Paper." *Analysis,* vol. 24 (1963), pp. 46–48.

8. Gettier, E. L. "Is Justified True Belief Knowledge?" *Analysis,* vol. 23 (1963), pp. 121–123.

9. Harman, G. H. "Lehrer on Knowledge." *The Journal of Philosophy,* vol. 63 (1966), pp. 241–246.

10. Harrison, J. "Does Knowing Imply Believing?" *The Philosophical Quarterly,* vol. 15 (1963), pp. 322–332.

11. Hintikka, J. *Knowledge and Belief.* Ithaca, Cornell University Press, 1962.

12. Lehrer, K. "Knowledge, Truth and Evidence." *Analysis,* vol. 25 (1965), pp. 168–175.

13. Malcolm, N. *Knowledge and Certainty.* Englewood Cliffs, Prentice-Hall, 1963.

14. Saunders, J. T. "Beliefs Which Are Grounds for Themselves." *Philosophical Studies,* vol. 16 (1965), pp. 88–90.

15. ——"Does Knowledge Require Grounds?" *Philosophical Studies,* vol. 17 (1966), pp. 7–13.

16. ——and Champawat, N. "Mr. Clark's Definition of 'Knowledge'." *Analysis,* vol. 25 (1964), pp. 8–9.

17. Sosa, E. "The Analysis of 'Knowledge that p'," *Analysis,* vol. 25 (1964), pp. 1–8.

18. Woozley, A. D. *Theory of Knowledge.* London, Hutchinson, 1949.

Bibliography

Audi, Robert. *Belief, Justification and Knowledge.* Belmont, CA: Wadsworth, 1988.

Dancy, Jonathan. *An Introduction to Contemporary Epistemology.* Oxford, England: Blackwell, 1985. Chap. 2.

Fumerton, Richard. *Metaphysical and Epistemological Problems of Perception.* Lincoln: University of Nebraska, 1985.

Harman, Gilbert. *Thought.* Princeton, NJ: Princeton University Press, 1973.

Nozick, Robert. *Philosophical Explanations.* Cambridge MA: Harvard University Press, 1981.

Pappas, George, ed. *Justification and Knowledge.* Dordrecht, Netherlands: Reidel, 1979.

Pappas, George, and Marshall Swain, eds. *Essays on Knowledge and Justification.* Ithaca, NY: Cornell University Press, 1978.

Roth, Michael, and Leon Galis, eds. *Knowing: Essays in the Theory of Knowledge.* New York: Random House, 1970.

Shope, Robert. *The Analysis of Knowledge.* Princeton NJ: Princeton University Press, 1983.

Swain, Marshall. *Reasons and Knowledge.* Ithaca, NY: Cornell University Press, 1981.

Part V

Theories of Justification (I): Foundationalism and Coherentism

Now of the thinking states by which we grasp truth, some are unfailingly true; others admit of error-opinion, for example, and calculation, whereas scientific knowlege and intuition are always true; further, no other kind of thought except intuition is more accurate than scientific knowledge, whereas primary premises are more knowable than demonstrations, and all scientific knowledge is discursive. From these considerations it follows that there will be no scientific knowledge of the primary, and since, except intuition, nothing can be truer than scientific knowledge, it will be intuition that apprehends the primary premises.

ARISTOTLE
Posterior Analytics, II, 19

Until recently most epistemologists have held that there are self-evident first principles that are immediately known to the understanding and sufficient to build a complete system of knowledge. For Plato these principles were the forms the knowledge of which was latent as innate ideas within us. For Aristotle and Aquinas they were the basic truths, such as the axioms of mathematics and logic, which are grasped immediately by the understanding. Aquinas wrote,

> Now a truth can come into the mind in two ways, namely, as known in itself, and

as known through another. What is known in itself is like a principle, and is perceived immediately by the mind. And so the habit which perfects the intellect in considering such a truth is called 'understanding'; it is a firm and easy quality of mind which sees into principles. A truth, however, which is known through another is understood by the intellect, not immediately, but through an inquiry of reason of which it is the terminus. (*Summa Theologica,* Ia. Q84, a. 2)

Descartes, in the first reading in this part of the book, holds that knowledge of the existence and mental nature of the self is grasped noninferentially by the understanding. Furthermore, each person can have infallible knowledge of his or her psychological states, beliefs, and desires. For example, I can know infallibly that I am in pain, that I seem to see a tree in front of me, and that I believe that there is a tree in front of me, although I cannot know that there really is a tree in front of me. In addition, Descartes thought we had immediate knowledge of certain metaphysical truths such as that there must be as much reality in the total cause as in the effect—a proposition that enabled him to deduce the existence of a perfect divine being, who in turn guaranteed the veracity of our empirical beliefs. Self-evident truths were "clear and distinct," having a luminous aura about them that the intuition could not fail to grasp as obvious truth.

Empiricists such as Locke believed we could have knowledge of physical objects, especially the primary qualities (as we saw in Part III).

What all these philosophers have in common is the theory that we can have immediate and infallible knowledge of first principles or basic propositions, from which we can deduce further truths. The properly basic beliefs are known immediately through the *intuition* (sometimes called the "faculty of intuition"). All other knowledge is inferred deductively from these basic beliefs.

Two related notions are tied together in this notion of immediate and infallible or indubitable knowledge: self-evidence and incorrigibility. A proposition is self-evident just in the case that if one understands and considers it, one cannot help but believe and know it. It is obvious, luminous, certain. Examples of such propositions are the law of noncontradiction and basic truths of arithmetic such as $1 + 1 = 2$. A belief is incorrigible for someone S if and only if it's not possible for S to believe the proposition and the proposi-

tion be false. Examples are appearance statements such as "I seem to see a red object" and Descartes's "Cogito, ergo sum," "I think, therefore I am." Both have been considered certain, but only propositions are self-evident. Incorrigibility is primarily a property of beliefs, but these terms often overlap. There is no clear consensus on their definitions.

This traditional view, that we may have infallible noninferential knowledge on which all other knowledge is based, we call "classical foundationalism." Note the architectural metaphor "foundation." Descartes spoke of tearing down the superstructure and destroying the foundations of our epistemically unjustified house and of laying a new, infallible foundation with indubitable propositions, and thereupon erecting a solid and certain superstructure, a house of knowledge. As such, we may divide all beliefs into two kinds: basic beliefs and inferred beliefs. We may define the primary epistemic unit "*properly basic belief*" this way: "A belief that *p* is properly basic for a person S if and only if it is (1) basic (noninferential) for S and (2) properly so (justified noninferentially)." A nonbasic justified belief is one that is inferentially based on one or more properly basic beliefs.

The relationship is asymmetrical, in that the basic beliefs transfer justification and knowledge to the derived belief but not vice versa. The resulting treelike relationship is shown as follows:

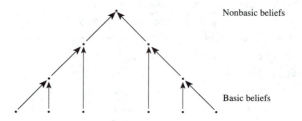

Nonbasic beliefs

Basic beliefs

From indubitable first premises, Descartes deduced the existence of God as an omnibenevolent being whose nature excluded deception. Since God implanted our perceptual mechanisms within us, it will follow that we can know we are not being deceived when we believe things about objects in the world. Normally, if I seem to see a tree, I really do see one. Only under abnormal circumstances will I be deceived about such matters. Yet, because I can be deceived, I should withhold the attribution of knowledge to such empirical judgments. Induction can never be a means of knowledge, but only of belief.

Philosophers have pointed to the problems with Descartes's (1) arguments for the existence of God, (2) notion that "there is as much reality in the total cause as in the effect," (3) notion of clear and distinct ideas, and (4) notion of infallibility or incorrigibility. It is generally conceded that Descartes fails to establish (1), (2), and (3) and that (4) is at least a dubitable notion. Whether our appearance beliefs—for example, "I am in pain" or "I seem to see a red object"—are really infallible or incorrigible is a matter of debate. It is hard to prove either way.

Most contemporary foundationalists are not of the classical variety. They tend to relativize the idea of self-evidence or proper basicality to individuals. What is self-evident to you may not be self-evident for me. You may see immediately that $13 \times 13 = 169$ or even that $69 \times 69 = 4,761$, while I may have to work these sums out from simpler self-evident truths, such as $3 \times 3 = 9$; $3 \times 10 = 30$, $10 \times 13 = 130$, and the like.

Perhaps there are some self-evident, incorrigible truths, such as simple mathematical statements and truths of logic, as well as the *cogito* ("I think, therefore I am"), but this doesn't give us enough of a foundation to build a sturdy superstructure. It doesn't even include empirical beliefs.

So the trend has been for foundationalists to take on the label "moderate" or "minimal" before "foundationalism." Such foundationalism accepts the foundational model of distinguishing basic from nonbasic beliefs but rejects the possibility of an infallible belief system and accepts fallibilism, the theory that many of our most cherished beliefs could be false.

The following are features of modest foundationalism:

1. An asymmetrical relationship exists between the foundations and the superstructure.

2. Doubts about any psychological beliefs (beliefs about our mental states, such as our desires) being indubitable or incorrigible are allowed.

3. Almost any belief can be basic for a person under certain circumstances. No particular type of content is required.

4. The foundational relationship is justification of belief rather than knowledge, although knowledge is the goal of believing.

5. Superstructure beliefs may be only inductively based on basic beliefs. That is, the transmission of justification from the basic to the nonbasic beliefs is more flexible than allowed by classical foundationalism.

6. Coherence is allowed some scope in the justification process. As an example, for Robert Audi coherence plays a negative role in foundational structures. If someone shows that our belief set is incoherent, it cannot be justified. For Audi and Alston, a justification of a belief can be "overdetermined." That is, it may be justified by appeal to properly basic beliefs, and it may also be justified by its cohering within a whole system of beliefs.

7. One must distinguish between *having* a justification for a belief and being able to *show* that one has such a justification. Moderate foundationalists argue that for the justification to obtain it is not necessary for a person to be able to show that he or she is justified.

The two selections by Robert Audi contain many of these points.

The Regress Problem

A driving force behind contemporary foundationalists is the problem of stopping the regress of inferential justification. Suppose you believe that eating vegetables will promote your health. I ask you why you believe that. You answer that your belief is based on your beliefs about nutrition. Vegetables have the kind of vitamins necessary for the proper maintenance of the human body. But suppose I ask you why you believe that vegetables contain the kind of vitamins necessary for the proper maintenance of the human body. Well, you'd either appeal to "common knowledge" or start discussing chemistry and physiology. Where would the demand for a justification stop? Does it matter?

Structurally, your Belief A that vegetables promote health is based on your Belief B that vegetables contain necessary vitamins, which in turn is based on Belief C having to do with chemistry and physiology. Or you could argue that A is based on D, inductive knowledge that vegetables generally promote physical health.

Another way of putting the matter is to say that we infer Belief A from Belief B and B from C and so on. Four kinds of such inference chains may be identified.

1. Belief A is itself inferred directly from Belief B, which is unjustified.

2. Belief A owes its justification to Belief B, which is based on Belief C and so on *ad infinitum*.

3. Belief A owes its justification to Belief B, which is based on Belief C, which is based on Belief A, doubling back in a circle.

4. Belief A owes its justification to Belief B, which is based on a foundational or noninferential belief that needs no further justification.

There are problems with each type of chain. Wittgenstein seems to have held the first option, because he remarked that "at the foundation of well-founded beliefs lies belief that is not founded." Perhaps contextualism (see the discussion later in this part introduction) fits this category, but it is hard to see, without more qualifications, how unjustified beliefs can yield a justified belief.

Regarding the infinite regress chain, it is difficult to believe that creatures like us have an infinite set of beliefs, and, even if we did, it would be impossible ever to show that such a justified belief was justified. Perhaps we have an infinite set of mathematical beliefs ("2 is greater than 1," "3 is larger than 2," and so forth), but it is doubtful whether the notion of an infinite set (or infinite sets of all our justified beliefs) has anything to commend it. No one has given a good argument for the infinite regress chain, though it hasn't been disproven, either.

The circular scheme is the model for coherentism. On the face of it, it seems to beg the question. For example, suppose you ask me why I believe in the Bible and I say, "Because it's inspired by God." Then you ask me why I believe in God, and I say, "I believe in God because the Bible says God exists." Arguing in a circle can be done by any fool and proves nothing. However, as we shall see, if the circle is big enough and the interrelations are intricate enough, many philosophers will accept something like the circular scheme. It is called coherentism.

The final pattern, which posits self-justified beliefs ("unmoved movers" to use Chisholm's phrase) at the base of every inferential chain, is the one foundationalists choose. Every justified belief either itself is a properly basic (justified) belief or ends in a chain of beliefs the last of which is self-justified. On the face of it, foundationalism seems the most satisfactory solution to the regress problem. It stops the chain of justification and does so in a way that does not beg the question.

Nonetheless, as noted in the readings, there are several problems with foundationalism. First, strong foundationalism contains too little content to sustain the edifice of knowledge; weaker foundationalism is too compromising to offer us justification. That is, classical foundationalism with its appeal to infallible knowledge doesn't seem adequate to yield much inferred knowledge or justified belief but tends toward skepticism about the external world, other minds, induction, and the like. Moderate or weak foundationalism, however, doesn't give us the strong justification, let alone knowledge, that we would like to have. In fact, as it compromises and accepts coherence constraints, it tends to become indistinguishable from moderate coherentism.

Second, the epistemic ascent argument set forth by Wilfrid Sellars and Laurence BonJour (see the third reading in this part) maintains that foundationalism cannot explain, without appealing to an unwarranted stipulation, how a justification terminates. Let A represent the property of being a properly basic belief; then for a Belief B to qualify as properly basic, the premises of the following justificatory argument must themselves be justified:

1. S's Belief B has Property A.

2. Beliefs having Property A are highly likely to be true.

3. Therefore, S's Belief B is highly likely to be true.

BonJour argues that for foundationalists to be justified in believing that B is properly basic, they must depend on this argument, so that their justification is not immediate or basic but inferential.

Foundationalists have attempted to set forth reasons why the ascent argument is not decisive against them.[1]

Coherentist Theories of Justification

There have always been coherence theories of truth, theories that claim that the truth resides in the absolute system of knowledge. Hegel, F. H. Bradley, and Brand Blanshard held the view that truth was defined not as correspondence of propositions with facts but as integrated and absolute wholes in which individual propositions received justification and relative truth credentials. Every true belief is entailed by every other proposition in the coherent system.

However, most contemporary coherentists, such as W. V. Quine, Wilfrid Sellars, Gilbert Harman, Keith Lehrer, and Laurence BonJour, reject the coherence theory of truth as an implausible metaphysical doctrine and adhere instead to a coherentist theory of justification. Individual beliefs are justified by the entire system of beliefs in which they cohere. All justification is inferential, so the notion of proper basicality is a contradiction in terms.

There are several versions of coherentism, but one important objection has been applied against all forms: the isolation objection. This objection states that the coherence of a theory is an inadequate justification of the theory, because by itself it doesn't supply the necessary criteria to distinguish it from illusory but consistent theories. Fairytales may sometimes be coherent as may dreams and hallucinations. Astrology may be as coherent as astronomy, Newtonian physics as coherent as Einsteinian physics, but surely, the objection runs, we want to connect our theories with empirical data. Consistency may, generally, be a necessary condition for justification (although see Fumerton's critique in Reading V.5), but it is not a sufficient condition for justification.

One version of coherentism that has tried to meet the isolation objection is Laurence Bon-Jour's moderate (or "impure") coherentism, which is included as the fourth reading in this part of the book. BonJour tries to show how observation beliefs get worked into a coherentist network. He appeals to a principle of introspection (that introspective beliefs of the appropriate kind are very likely to be true) and from there gets to spontaneous beliefs about the physical world. The details are worked out in your reading.

Two insightful discussions end the section on the foundationalist-coherentist debate, Ernest Sosa's "The Raft and the Pyramid," which closely analyzes the strengths and weaknesses of various forms of each of these theories; and Robert Audi's "Fallible Foundationalism and Holistic Coherentism," where Audi outlines a moderate foundationalism sympathetic to the insights of coherentism.

Contextualism

Finally, an alternative to the foundationalist-coherentist controversy has recently been set forth by several philosophers, ranging from Thomas Kuhn to Bernard Williams and David Annis. Annis, whose reading concludes this part of the book, gives the most lucid description of this theory, called "contextualism," and argues that justification is relative to social practices with differing norms. He distinguishes an "issue context" from an "objector context." The issue context of a belief is the specific concern someone raises about it, while the objector context refers to the group that raises objections to the believer about the belief in question. A belief is contextually basic for a person relative to an appropriate objector group at a specific time if that group lets the person hold the belief without supporting reasons. In different contexts, different beliefs take on proper basicality, but there is no general epistemic criterion for justifying beliefs independent of those arising from social practices and social approval.

Contextualism is still in its infancy, but has already been criticized as being unduly relativistic.

Note

[1] See Roderick Chisholm, *Theory of Knowledge*, 3d ed. (Englewood Cliffs, NJ: Prentice-Hall, 1985), and Paul Moser, *Epistemic Justification* (Dordrecht, Netherlands: Reidel, 1985), chap. 4.

V.1 *Classical Foundationalism*

RENÉ DESCARTES

A biographical sketch of Descartes (1596–1650) is included in the introduction to Reading II.1. The following reading is a continuation of the *Meditations,* which we encountered in the section on skepticism. There he uses his method of universal doubt to undermine inadequate epistemic foundations. "I realized that for once I had to raze everything in my life, down to the very bottom, so as to begin again from the first foundations, if I wanted to establish anything firm and lasting in the sciences." In the second and third meditations, which make up this reading, Descartes begins to construct the solid foundations for a firm edifice of science. Only what can withstand universal doubt, only what is indubitable will be allowed into the foundations. He suddenly comes to the realization that even if a demon is deceiving him about everything else, the demon cannot deceive him about his own existence. "We must come to the definite conclusion that this proposition: I am, I exist, is necessarily true each time that I pronounce it, or that I mentally conceive it." From here he goes on to discover that he is essentially mind and, using the mind's understanding, concludes that he can have infallible knowledge about psychological states:

Finally, I am the same who feels, that is to say, who perceives certain things, as by the organs of sense, since in truth I see light, I hear noise, I feel heat. But it will be said that these phenomena are false and that I am dreaming. Let it be so; still it is at least quite certain that it seems to me that I see light, that I hear noise and that I feel heat. That cannot be false.

Using the same method, Descartes goes on to prove the existence of God, who since he is perfectly good would not have created us in such a way as to be deceived about our normal empirical judgments.

In his *Rules for the Direction of the Mind* (1644), Descartes says that there are only two rational methods for arriving at knowledge: intuition and deduction.

By *intuition* I understand, not the fluctuating testimony of the senses, nor the misleading judgment that proceeds from the blundering constructions of imagination, but the conception which an unclouded and attentive mind gives us so readily and distinctly that we are wholly freed from doubt about that which we understand. Or, what comes to the same thing, *intuition* is the undoubting conception of an unclouded and attentive mind, and springs from the light of reason alone; it is more certain than deduction itself, in that it is simpler. . . . Thus each individual can mentally have intuition of the fact that he exists, and that he thinks; that the triangle is bounded by three lines only, the sphere by a single superficies. (*The Philosophical Works of Descartes,* Vol. 1, p. 7)

Intuition, the natural light of reason, along with deductive reasoning, is our only guarantee to erecting an absolute science comparable to Euclidian geometry. Induction is an inadequate guide to truth and must be held in suspicion. We turn to the reading.

Meditation II
Of the Nature of the Human Mind; and That It Is More Easily Known Than the Body

The Meditation of yesterday filled my mind with so many doubts that it is no longer in my power to forget them. And yet I do not see in what manner I can resolve them; and, just as if I had all of a sudden fallen into very deep water, I am so disconcerted that I can neither make certain of setting my feet on the bottom, nor can I swim and so support myself on the surface. I shall nevertheless make an effort and follow anew the same path as that on which I yesterday entered, i.e., I shall proceed by setting aside all that in which the least doubt could be supposed to exist, just as if I had discovered that it was absolutely false; and I shall ever follow in this road until I have met with something which is certain, or at least, if I can do nothing else, until I have

Reprinted from *The Philosophical Works of Descartes,* trans. Elizabeth Haldane and G. Ross, Vol. 1 (Cambridge University Press, 1931) by permission of the publisher.

learned for certain that there is nothing in the world that is certain. Archimedes, in order that he might draw the terrestrial globe out of its place, and transport it elsewhere, demanded only that one point should be fixed and immoveable; in the same way I shall have the right to conceive high hopes if I am happy enough to discover one thing only which is certain and indubitable.

I suppose, then, that all the things that I see are false; I persuade myself that nothing has ever existed of all that my fallacious memory represents to me. I consider that I possess no senses; I imagine that body, figure, extension, movement and place are but the fictions of my mind. What, then, can be esteemed as true? Perhaps nothing at all, unless that there is nothing in the world that is certain.

But how can I know there is not something different from those things that I have just considered, of which one cannot have the slightest doubt? Is there not some God, or some other being by whatever name we call it, who puts these reflections into my mind? That is not necessary, for is it not possible that I am capable of producing them myself? I myself, am I not at least something? But I have already denied that I had senses and body. Yet I hesitate, for what follows from that? Am I so dependent on body and senses that I cannot exist without these? But I was persuaded that there was nothing in all the world, that there was no heaven, no earth, that there were no minds, nor any bodies: was I not then likewise persuaded that I did not exist? Not at all; of a surety I myself did exist since I persuaded myself of something [or merely because I thought of something]. But there is some deceiver or other, very powerful and very cunning, who ever employs his ingenuity in deceiving me. Then without doubt I exist also if he deceives me, and let him deceive me as much as he will, he can never cause me to be nothing so long as I think that I am something. So that after having reflected well and carefully examined all things, we must come to the definite conclusion that this proposition: I am, I exist, is necessarily true each time that I pronounce it, or that I mentally conceive it.

But I do not yet know clearly enough what I am, I who am certain that I am; and hence I must be careful to see that I do not imprudently take some other object in place of myself, and thus that I do not go astray in respect of this knowledge that I hold to be the most certain and most evident of all that I have formerly learned. That is why I shall now consider anew what I believed myself to be before I embarked upon these last reflections; and of my former opinions I shall withdraw all that might even in a small degree be invalidated by the reasons which I have just brought forward, in order that there may be nothing at all left beyond what is absolutely certain and indubitable.

What then did I formerly believe myself to be? Undoubtedly I believed myself to be a man. But what is a man? Shall I say a reasonable animal? Certainly not; for then I should have to inquire what an animal is, and what is reasonable; and thus from a single question I should insensibly fall into an infinitude of others more difficult; and I should not wish to waste the little time and leisure remaining to me in trying to unravel subtleties like these. But I shall rather stop here to consider the thoughts which of themselves spring up in my mind, and which were not inspired by anthing beyond my own nature alone when I applied myself to the consideration of my being. In the first place, then, I considered myself as having a face, hands, arms, and all that system of members composed of bones and flesh as seen in a corpse which I designated by the name of body. In addition to this I considered that I was nourished, that I walked, that I felt, and that I thought, and I referred all these actions to the soul: but I did not stop to consider what the soul was, or if I did stop, I imagined that it was something extremely rare and subtle like a wind, a flame, or an ether, which was spread throughout my grosser parts. As to body I had no manner of doubt about its nature, but thought I had a very clear knowledge of it; and if I had desired to explain it according to the notions that I had then formed of it, I should have described it thus: By the body I understand all that which can be defined by a certain figure: something which can be confined in a certain place, and which can fill a given space in such a way that every other body will be excluded from it; which can be perceived either by touch, or by sight, or by hearing, or by taste, or by smell: which can be moved in many ways not, in truth, by itself, but by something which is foreign to it, by which it is touched [and from which it receives impressions]: for to have the power of self-movement, as also of feeling or of thinking, I did not consider to appertain to the nature of body: on the contrary, I was rather astonished to find that faculties similar to them existed in some bodies.

But what am I, now that I suppose that there is a certain genius which is extremely powerful, and, if I may say so, malicious, who employs all his powers in deceiving me? Can I affirm that I possess the least of all those things which I have just said pertain to the nature of body? I pause to consider, I revolve all these things in my mind, and I find none of which I can say that it pertains to me. It would be tedious to stop to enumerate them. Let us pass to the attributes of soul and see if there is any one which is in me? What of nutrition or walking [the first mentioned]? But if it is so that I have no body it is also true that I can neither walk or take nourishment. Another attribute is sensation. But one cannot feel without body, and besides I have thought I perceived many things during sleep that I recognised in my waking moments as not having been experienced at all. What of thinking? I find here that thought is an attribute that belongs to me: it alone cannot be separated from me. I am, I exist, that is certain. But how often? Just when I think; for it might possibly be the case if I ceased entirely to think, that I should likewise cease altogether to exist. I do not now admit anything which is not necessarily true: to speak accurately I am not more than a thing which thinks, that is to say a mind or a soul, or an understanding, or a reason, which are terms whose significance was formerly unknown to me. I am, however, a real thing and really exist: but what thing I have answered: a thing which thinks.

And what more? I shall exercise my imagination [in order to see if I am not something more]. I am not a collection of members which we call the human body: I am not a subtle air distributed through these members, I am not a wind, a fire, a vapour, a breath, nor anything at all which I can imagine or conceive; because I have assumed that all these were nothing. Without changing that supposition I find that I only leave myself certain of the fact that I am somewhat. But perhaps it is true that these same things which I supposed were nonexistent because they are unknown to me, are really not different from the self which I know. I am not sure about this, I shall not dispute about it now; I can only give judgment on things that are known to me. I know that I exist, and I inquire what I am, I whom I know to exist. But it is very certain that the knowledge of my existence taken in its precise significance does not depend on things whose existence is not yet known to me; consequently it does not depend on those which I can feign in imagination. And indeed the very term *feign* in imagination proves to me my error, for I really do this if I image myself a something, since to imagine is nothing else than to contemplate the figure or image of a corporeal thing. But I already know for certain that I am, and that it may be that all these images, and, speaking generally, all things that relate to the nature of body are nothing but dreams [and chimeras]. For this reason I see clearly that I have as little reason to say, 'I shall stimulate my imagination in order to know more distinctly what I am,' than if I were to say, 'I am now awake, and I perceive somewhat that is real and true: but because I do not yet perceive it distinctly enough, I shall go to sleep of express purpose, so that my dreams may represent the perception with greatest truth and evidence.' And, thus, I know for certain that nothing of all that I can understand by means of my imagination belongs to this knowledge which I have of myself, and that it is necessary to recall the mind from this mode of thought with the utmost diligence in order that it may be able to know its own nature with perfect distinctness.

But what then am I? A thing which thinks. What is a thing which thinks? It is a thing which doubts, understands, [conceives], affirms, denies, wills, refuses, which also imagines and feels.

Certainly it is no small matter if all these things pertain to my nature. But why should they not so pertain? Am I not that being who now doubts nearly everything, who nevertheless understands certain things, who affirms that one only is true, who denies all the others, who desires to know more, is averse from being deceived, who imagines many things, sometimes indeed despite his will, and who perceives many likewise, as by the intervention of the bodily organs? Is there nothing in all this which is as true as it is certain that I exist, even though I should always sleep and though he who has given me being employed all his ingenuity in deceiving me? Is there likewise any one of these attributes which can be distinguished from my thought, or which might be said to be separated from myself? For it is so evident of itself that it is I who doubts, who understands, and who desires, that there is no reason here to add anything to explain it. And I have certainly the power of imagining likewise; for although it may happen (as I formerly supposed) that none of the things which I imagine are true, nevertheless this power of imagining does not cease to be really in use, and it forms part of my thought. Finally, I am the same who feels, that is to say, who perceives certain things, as by the organs of sense, since in truth I see light, I hear noise, I feel heat. But it will be said that these phenomena are false and that I am dreaming. Let it be so; still it is at least quite certain that it seems to me that I see light, that I hear noise and that I feel heat. That cannot be false; properly speaking it is what is in me called feeling; and used in this precise sense that is no other thing than thinking.

From this time I begin to know what I am with a little more clearness and distinction than before; but nevertheless it still seems to me, and I cannot prevent myself from thinking, that corporeal things, whose images are framed by thought, which are tested by the senses, are much more distinctly known than that obscure part of me which does not come under the imagination. Although really it is very strange to say that I know and understand more distinctly these things whose existence seems to me dubious, which are unknown to me, and which do not belong to me, than others of the truth of which I am convinced, which are known to me and which pertain to my real nature, in a word, than myself. But I see clearly how the case stands: my mind loves to wander, and cannot yet suffer itself to be retained within the just limits of truth. Very good, let us once more give it the freest rein, so that, when afterwards we seize the proper occasion for pulling up, it may the more easily be regulated and controlled.

Let us begin by considering the commonest matters, those which we believe to be the most distinctly comprehended, to wit, the bodies which we touch and see; not indeed bodies in general, for these general ideas are usually a little more confused, but let us consider one body in particular. Let us take, for example, this piece of wax: it has been taken quite freshly from the hive, and it has not yet lost the sweetness of the honey which it contains; it still retains somewhat of the odour of the flowers from which it has been culled; its colour, its figure, its size are apparent; it is hard, cold, easily handled, and if you strike it with the finger, it will emit a sound. Finally all the things which are requisite to cause us distinctly to recognise a body, are met with in it. But notice that while I speak and approach the fire what remained of the taste is exhaled, the smell evaporates, the colour alters, the figure is destroyed, the size increases, it becomes liquid, it heats, scarcely can one handle it, and when one strikes it, no sound is emitted. Does the same wax remain after this change? We must confess that it remains; none would judge otherwise. What then did I know so distinctly in this piece of wax? It could certainly be nothing of all that the senses brought to my notice, since all these things which fall under taste, smell, sight, touch, and hearing, are found to be changed, and yet the same wax remains.

Perhaps it was what I now think, viz. that this wax was not that sweetness of honey, nor that agreeable scent of flowers, nor that particular whiteness, nor that figure, nor that sound, but simply a body which a little while before appeared to me as perceptible under these forms, and which is now perceptible under others. But what, precisely, is it that I imagine when I form such conceptions? Let us attentively consider this, and, abstracting from all that does not belong to the wax, let us see what remains. Certainly nothing remains excepting a certain extended thing which is flexible and movable. But what is the meaning of flexible and movable? Is it not that I imagine that this piece of wax being round is capable of becoming square and of passing from a square to a triangular figure? No, certainly it is not that, since I imagine it admits of an infinitude of similar changes, and I nevertheless do not know how to compass the infinitude by my imagination, and consequently this conception which I have of the wax is not brought about by the faculty of imagination. What now is this extension? Is it not also unknown? For it becomes greater when the wax is melted, greater when it is boiled, and greater still when the heat increases; and I should not conceive [clearly] according to truth what wax is, if I did not think that even this piece that we are considering is capable of receiving more variations in extension than I have ever imagined. We must then grant that I could not even understand through the imagination what this piece of wax is, and that it is my mind alone which perceives it. I say this piece of wax in particular, for as to wax in general it is yet clearer. But what is this piece of wax which cannot be understood excepting by the [understanding or] mind? It is certainly the same that I see, touch, imagine, and finally it is the same which I have always believed it to be from the beginning. But what must particularly be observed is that its perception is neither an act of vision, nor of touch, nor of imagination, and has never been such although it may have appeared formerly to be so, but only an intuition of the mind, which may be imperfect and confused as it was formerly, or clear and distinct as it is at present, according as my attention is more or less directed to the elements which are found in it, and of which it is composed.

Yet in the meantime I am greatly astonished when I consider [the great feebleness of mind] and its proneness to fall [insensibly] into error; for although without giving expression to my thoughts I consider all this in my own mind, words often impede me and I am almost deceived by the terms of ordinary language. For we say that we see the same wax, if it is present, and not that we simply judge that it is the same from its having the same colour and figure. From this I should conclude that I knew the wax by means of vision and not simply by the intuition of the mind; unless by chance I remember that, when looking from a window and saying I see men who pass in the street, I really do not see them, but infer that what I see is men, just as I say that I see wax. And yet what do I see from the window but hats and coats which may cover automatic machines? Yet I judge these to be men. And similarly solely by the faculty of judgment which rests in my mind, I comprehend that which I believed I saw with my eyes.

A man who makes it his aim to raise his knowledge above the common should be ashamed to derive the occasion for doubting from the forms of speech invented by the vulgar; I prefer to pass on and consider whether I had a more evident and perfect conception of what the wax was when I first perceived it, and when I believed I knew it by means of the external senses or at least by the common sense as it is called, that is to say by the imaginative faculty, or whether my present conception is clearer now that I have most carefully examined what it is, and in what way it can be known. It would certainly be absurd to doubt as to this. For what was there in this first perception which was distinct? What was there which might not as well have been perceived by any of the animals? But when I distinguish the wax from its external forms, and when, just as if I had taken from it its vestments, I consider it quite naked, it is certain that although some error may still be found in my judgment, I can nevertheless not perceive it thus without a human mind.

But finally what shall I say of this mind, that is, of myself, for up to this point I do not admit in myself anything but mind? What then, I who seem to perceive this piece of wax so distinctly, do I now know myself, not only with much more truth and certainty, but also with much more distinctness and clearness? For if I judge that the wax is or exists from the fact that I see it, it certainly follows much more clearly that I am or that I exist myself from the fact that I see it. For it may be that what I see is not really wax, it may also be that I do not possess eyes with which to see anything; but it cannot be that when I see, or (for I no longer take account of the distinction) when I think I see, that I myself who think am nought. So if I judge that the wax exists from the fact that I touch it, the same thing will follow, to wit, that I am; and if I judge that my imagination, or some other cause, whatever it is, persuades me that the wax exists, I shall still conclude the same. And what I have here remarked of wax may be applied to all other things which are external to me [and which are met with outside of me]. And further, if the [notion or] perception of wax has seemed to me clearer and more distinct, not only after the sight or the touch, but also after many other causes have rendered it quite manifest to me, with how much more [evidence] and distinctness must it be said that I now know myself, since all the reasons which contribute to the knowledge of wax, or any other body whatever, are yet better proofs of the nature of my mind! And there are so many other things in the mind itself which may contribute to the elucidation of its nature, that those which depend on body such as these just mentioned, hardly merit being taken into account.

But finally here I am, having insensibly reverted to the point I desired, for, since it is now manifest to me that even bodies are not properly speaking known by the senses or by the faculty of imagination, but by the understanding only, and since they are not known from the fact that they are seen or touched, but only because they are understood, I see clearly that there is nothing which is easier for me to know than my mind. But because it is difficult to rid oneself so promptly of an opinion to which one was accustomed for so long, it will be well that I should halt a little at this point, so that by the length of my meditation I may more deeply imprint on my memory this new knowledge.

Meditation III

Of God: That He Exists

I shall now close my eyes, I shall stop my ears, I shall call away all my senses, I shall efface even from my thoughts all the images of corporeal things, or at least (for that is hardly possible) I shall esteem them as vain and false; and thus holding converse only with myself and considering my own nature, I shall try little by little to reach a better knowledge of and a more familiar acquaintanceship with myself. I am a thing that thinks, that is to say, that doubts, affirms, denies, that knows a few things, that is ignorant of many [that loves, that hates], that wills, that desires, that also imagines and perceives; for as I remarked before, although the things which I perceive and imagine are perhaps nothing at all apart from me and in themselves, I am nevertheless assured that these modes of thought that I call perceptions and imaginations, inasmuch only as they are modes of thought, certainly reside [and are met with] in me.

And in the little that I have just said, I think I have summed up all that I really know, or at least all that hitherto I was aware that I knew. In order to try to extend my knowledge further, I shall now look around more carefully and see whether I cannot still discover in myself some other things which I have not hitherto perceived. I am certain that I am a thing which thinks; but do I not then likewise know what is requisite to render me certain of a truth? Certainly in this first knowledge there is nothing that assures me of its truth, excepting the clear and distinct perception of that which I state, which would not indeed suffice to assure me that what I say is true, if it could ever happen that a thing which I conceived so clearly and distinctly could be false; and accordingly it seems to me that already I can establish as a general rule that all things which I perceive very clearly and very distinctly are true.

At the same time I have before received and admitted many things to be very certain and manifest, which yet I afterwards recognised as being dubious. What then were these things? They were the earth, sky, stars and all other objects which I apprehended by means of the senses. But what did I clearly [and distinctly] perceive in them? Nothing more than that the ideas or thoughts of these things were presented to my mind. And not even now do I deny that these ideas are met with in me. But there was yet another thing which I affirmed, and which, owing to the habit which I had formed of believing it, I thought I perceived very clearly, although in truth I did not perceive it at all, to wit, that there were objects outside of me from which these ideas proceeded, and to which they were entirely similar. And it was in this that I erred, or, if perchance my judgment was correct, this was not due to any knowledge arising from my perception.

But when I took anything very simple and easy in the sphere of arithmetic or geometry into consideration, e.g., that two and three together made five, and other things of the sort, were not these present to my mind so clearly as to enable me to affirm that they were true? Certainly if I judged that since such matters could be doubted, this would not have been so for any other reason than that it came into my mind that perhaps a God might have endowed me with such a nature that I may have been deceived even concerning things which seemed to me most manifest. But every time that this preconceived opinion of the sovereign power of a God presents itself to my thought, I am constrained to confess that it is easy to Him, if He wishes it, to cause me to err, even in matters in which I believe myself to have the best evidence. And, on the other hand, always when I direct my attention to things which I believe myself to perceive very clearly, I am so persuaded of their truth that I let myself break out into words such as these: Let who will deceive me, He can never cause me to be nothing while I think that I am, or some day cause it to be true to say that I have never been, it being true now to say that I am, or that two and three make more or less than five, or any such thing in which I see a manifest contradiction. And, certainly, since I have no reason to believe that there is a God who is a deceiver, and as I have not yet satisfied myself that there is a God at all, the reason for doubt which depends on this opinion alone is very slight, and so to speak metaphysical. But in order to be able altogether to remove it, I must inquire whether there is a God as soon as the occasion presents itself; and if I find that there is a God, I must also inquire whether He may be a deceiver; for without a knowledge of these two truths I do not see that I can ever be certain of anything.

And in order that I may have an opportunity of inquiring into this in an orderly way [without interrupting the order of meditation which I have proposed to myself, and which is little by little to pass from the notions which I find first of all in my mind to those which I shall later on discover in it] it is requisite that I should here divide my thoughts into certain kinds, and that I should consider in which of these kinds there is, properly speaking, truth or error to be found. Of my thoughts some are, so to speak, images of the things, and to these alone is the title 'idea' properly applied; examples are my thought of a man or of a chimera, of heaven, of an angel, or [even] of God. But other thoughts possess other forms as well. For example in willing, fearing, approving, denying, though I always perceive something as the subject of the action of my mind, yet by this action I always add something else to the idea which I have of that thing; and of the thoughts of this kind some are called volitions or affections, and others judgments.

Now as to what concerns ideas, if we consider them only in themselves and do not relate them to anything else beyond themselves, they cannot properly speaking be false; for whether I imagine a goat or a chimera, it is not less true that I imagine the one than the other. We must not fear likewise that falsity can enter into will and into affections, for although I may desire evil things, or even things that never existed, it is not the less true that I desire them. Thus there remains no more than the judgments which we make, in which I must take the greatest care not to deceive myself. But the principal error and the commonest which we may meet with

in them, consists in my judging that the ideas which are in me are similar or comfortable to the things which are outside me; for without doubt if I considered the ideas only as certain modes of my thoughts, without trying to relate them to anything beyond, they could scarcely give me material for error.

But among these ideas, some appear to me to be innate, some adventitious, and others to be formed [or invented] by myself; for, as I have the power of understanding what is called a thing, or a truth, or a thought, it appears to me that I hold this power from no other source than my own nature. But if I now hear some sound, if I see the sun, or feel heat, I have hitherto judged that these sensations proceeded from certain things that exist outside of me; and finally it appears to me that sirens, hippogryphs, and the like, are formed out of my own mind. But again I may possibly persuade myself that all these ideas are of the nature of those which I term adventitious, or else that they are all innate, or all fictitious; for I have not yet clearly discovered their true origin.

And my principal task in this place is to consider, in respect to those ideas which appear to me to proceed from certain objects that are outside me, what are the reaons which cause me to think them similar to these objects. It seems indeed in the first place that I am taught this lesson by nature; and, secondly, I experience in myself that these ideas do not depend on my will nor therefore on myself— for they often present themselves to my mind in spite of my will. Just now, for instance, whether I will or whether I do not will, I feel heat, and thus I persuade myself that this feeling, or at least this idea of heat, is produced in me by something which is different from me, i.e., by the heat of the fire near which I sit. And nothing seems to me more obvious than to judge that this object imprints its likeness rather than anything else upon me.

Now I must discover whether these proofs are sufficiently strong and convincing. When I say that I am so instructed by nature, I merely mean a certain spontaneous inclination which impels me to believe in this connection, and not a natural light which makes me recognise that it is true. But these two things are very different; for I cannot doubt that which the natural light causes me to believe to be true, as, for example, it has shown me that I am from the fact that I doubt, or other facts of the same kind. And I possess no other faculty whereby to distinguish truth from falsehood, which can teach me that what this light shows me to be true is not really true, and no other faculty that is equally trustworthy. But as far as [apparently] natural impulses are concerned, I have frequently remarked, when I had to make active choice between virtue and vice, that they often enough led me to the part that was worse; and this is why I do not see any reason for following them in what regards truth and error.

And as to the other reason, which is that these ideas must proceed from objects outside me, since they do not depend on my will, I do not find it any the more convincing. For just as these impulses of which I have spoken are found in me, notwithstanding that they do not always concur with my will, so perhaps there is in me some faculty fitted to produce these ideas without the assistance of any external things, even though it is not yet known by me; just as, apparently, they have hitherto always been found in me during sleep without the aid of any external objects.

And finally, though they did proceed from objects different from myself, it is not a necessary consequence that they should resemble these. On the contrary, I have noticed that in many cases there was a great difference between the object and its idea. I find, for example, two completely diverse ideas of the sun in my mind; the one derives its origin from the senses, and should be placed in the category of adventitious ideas; according to this idea the sun seems to be extremely small; but the other is derived from astronomical reasonings, i.e. is elicited from certain notions that are innate in me, or else it is formed by me in some other manner; in accordance with it the sun appears to be several times greater than the earth. These two ideas cannot, indeed, both resemble the same sun, and reason makes me believe that the one which seems to have originated directly from the sun itself, is the one which is most dissimilar to it.

All this causes me to believe that until the present time it has not been by a judgment that was certain [or premeditated], but only by a sort of blind impulse that I believed that things existed outside of, and different from me, which, by the organs of my senses, or by some other method whatever it might be, conveyed these ideas or images to me [and imprinted on me their similitudes].

But there is yet another method of inquiring whether any of the objects of which I have ideas within me exist outside of me. If ideas are only taken as certain modes of thought, I recognise amongst them no difference or inequality, and all appear to proceed from me in the same manner; but when we consider them as images, one representing one thing and the other another, it is clear that they are very different one from the other. There is no doubt that those which represent to me substances are something more, and contain so to speak more objective reality within them [that is to say, by representation participate in a higher degree of being or perfection] than those that simply represent modes or accidents; and that idea again by which I understand a supreme God, eternal, infinite, [immutable], omniscient, omnipotent, and Creator of all things which are outside of Himself, has certainly more objective reality in itself than those ideas by which finite substances are represented.

Now it is manifest by the natural light that there must at least be as much reality in the efficient and total cause as in its effect. For, pray, whence can the effect derive its reality, if not from its cause? And in what way can this cause communicate this reality to it, unless it possessed it in itself? And from this it follows, not only that something cannot proceed from nothing, but likewise that what is more perfect—that is to say, which has more reality within itself—cannot proceed from the less perfect. And this is not only evidently true of those effects which possess actual or formal reality, but also of the ideas in which we consider merely what is termed objective reality. To take an example, the stone which has not yet existed not only cannot now commence to be unless it has been produced by something which possesses within itself, either formally or eminently, all that enters into the composition of the stone [i.e. it must possess the same things or other more excellent things than those which exist in the stone] and heat can only be produced in a subject in which it did not previously exist by a cause that is of an order [degree or kind] at least as perfect as heat, and so in all other cases. But further, the idea of heat, or of a stone, cannot exist in me unless it has been placed within me by some cause which possesses within it at least as much reality as that which I conceive to exist in the heat or the stone. For although this cause does not transmit anything of its actual or formal reality to my idea, we must not for that reason imagine that it is necessarily a less real cause; we must remember that [since every idea is a work of the mind] its nature is such that it demands of itself no other formal reality than that which it borrows from my thought, of which it is only a mode [i.e. a manner or way of thinking]. But in order that an idea should contain some one certain objective reality rather than another, it must without doubt derive it from some cause in which there is at least as much formal reality as this idea contains of objective reality. For if we imagine that something is found in an idea which is not found in the cause, it must then have been derived from nought; but however, imperfect may be this mode of being by which a thing is objectively [or by representation] in the understanding by its idea, we cannot certainly say that this mode of being is nothing, nor, consequently, that the idea derives its origin from nothing.

Nor must I imagine that, since the reality that I consider in these ideas is only objective, it is not essential that this reality should be formally in the causes of my ideas, but that it is sufficient that it should be found objectively. For just as this mode of objective existence pertains to ideas by their proper nature, so does the mode of formal existence pertain to the causes of those ideas (this is at least true of the first and principal) by the nature peculiar to them. And although it may be the case that one idea gives birth to another idea, that cannot continue to be so indefinitely; for in the end we must reach an idea whose cause shall be so to speak an archetype, in which the whole reality [or perfection] which is so to speak objectively [or by representation] in these ideas is contained formally [and really]. Thus the light of nature causes me to know clearly that the ideas in me are like [pictures or] images which can, in truth, easily fall short of the perfection of the objects from which they have been derived, but which can never contain anything greater or more perfect.

And the longer and the more carefully that I investigate these matters, the more clearly and distinctly do I recognise their truth. But what am I to conclude from it all in the end? It is this, that if the objective reality of any one of my ideas is of such a nature as clearly to make me recognise that it is not in me either formally or eminently, and that consequently I cannot myself be the cause of it, it follows of necessity that I am not alone in the world, but

that there is another being which exists, or which is the cause of this idea. On the other hand, had no such an idea existed in me, I should have had no sufficient argument to convince me of the existence of any being beyond myself; for I have made very careful investigation everywhere and up to the present time have been able to find no other ground.

But of my ideas, beyond that which represents me to myself, as to which there can here be no difficulty, there is another which represents a God, and there are others representing corporeal and inanimate things, others angels, others animals, and others again which represent to me men similar to myself.

As regards the ideas which represent to me other men or animals, or angels, I can however easily conceive that they might be formed by an admixture of the other ideas which I have of myself, of corporeal things, and of God, even although there were apart from me neither men nor animals, nor angels, in all the world.

And in regard to the ideas of corporeal objects, I do not recognise in them anything so great or so excellent that they might not have possibly proceeded from myself; for if I consider them more closely, and examine them individually, as I yesterday examined the idea of wax, I find that there is very little in them which I perceive clearly and distinctly. Magnitude or extension in length, breadth, or depth, I do so perceive; also figure which results from a termination of this extension, the situation which bodies of different figure preserve in relation to one another, and movement or change of situation; to which we may also add substance, duration and number. As to other things such as light, colours, sounds, scents, tastes, heat, cold and the other tactile qualities, they are thought by me with so much obscurity and confusion that I do not even know if they are true or false, i.e., whether the ideas which I form of these qualities are actually the ideas of real objects or not [or whether they only represent chimeras which cannot exist in fact]. For although I have before remarked that it is only in judgments that falsity, properly speaking, or formal falsity, can be met with, a certain material falsity may nevertheless be found in ideas, i.e. when these ideas represent what is nothing as though it were something. For example, the ideas which I have of cold and heat are so far from clear and distinct that by their means I cannot tell whether cold is merely a privation of heat, or heat a privation of cold, or whether both are real qualities, or are not such. And inasmuch as [since ideas resemble images] there cannot be any ideas which do not appear to represent some things, if it is correct to say that cold is merely a privation of heat, the idea which represents it to me as something real and positive will not be improperly termed false, and the same holds good of other similar ideas.

To these it is certainly not necessary that I should attribute any author other than myself. For if they are false, i.e. if they represent things which do not exist, the light of nature shows me that they issue from nought, that is to say, that they are only in me in so far as something is lacking to the perfection of my nature. But if they are true, nevertheless because they exhibit so little reality to me that I cannot even clearly distinguish the thing represented from non-being, I do not see any reason why they should not be produced by myself.

As to the clear and distinct idea which I have of corporeal things, some of them seem as though I might have derived them from the idea which I possess of myself, as those which I have of substance, duration, number, and such like. For [even] when I think that a stone is a substance, or at least a thing capable of existing of itself, and that I am a substance also, although I conceive that I am a thing that thinks and not one that is extended, and that the stone on the other hand is an extended thing which does not think, and that thus there is a notable difference between the two conceptions—they seem, nevertheless, to agree in this, that both represent substances. In the same way, when I perceive that I now exist and further recollect that I have in former times existed, and when I remember that I have various thoughts of which I can recognise the number, I acquire ideas of duration and number which I can afterwards transfer to any object that I please. But as to all the other qualities of which the ideas of corporeal things are composed, to wit, extension, figure, situation and motion, it is true that they are not formally in me, since I am only a thing that thinks; but because they are merely certain modes of substance [and so to speak the vestments under which corporeal substance appears to us] and because I myself am also a substance, it would seem that they might be contained in me eminently.

Hence there remains only the idea of God, concerning which we must consider whether it is something which cannot have proceeded from me myself. By the name God I understand a substance that is infinite [eternal, immutable], independent, all-knowing, all-powerful, and by which I myself and everything else, if anything else does exist, have been created. Now all these characteristics are such that the more diligently I attend to them, the less do they appear capable of proceeding from me alone; hence, from what has been already said, we must conclude that God necessarily exists.

For although the idea of substance is within me owing to the fact that I am substance, nevertheless I should not have the idea of an infinite substance—since I am finite—if it had not proceeded from some substance which was veritably infinite.

Nor should I imagine that I do not perceive the infinite by a true idea, but only by the negation of the finite, just as I perceive repose and darkness by the negation of movement and of light; for, on the contrary, I see that there is manifestly more reality in infinite substance than in finite, and therefore that in some way I have in me the notion of the infinite earlier than the finite—to wit, the notion of God before that of myself. For how would it be possible that I should know that I doubt and desire, that is to say, that something is lacking to me, and that I am not quite perfect, unless I had within me some idea of a Being more perfect than myself, in comparison with which I should recognise the deficiencies of my nature?

And we cannot say that this idea of God is perhaps materially false and that consequently I can derive it from nought [i.e. that possibly it exists in me because I am imperfect], as I have just said is the case with ideas of heat, cold and other such things; for, on the contrary, as this idea is very clear and distinct and contains within it more objective reality than any other, there can be none which is of itself more true, nor any in which there can be less suspicion of falsehood. The idea, I say, of this Being who is absolutely perfect and infinite, is entirely true; for although, perhaps, we can imagine that such a Being does not exist, we cannot nevertheless imagine that His idea represents nothing real to me, as I have said of the idea of cold. This idea is also very clear and distinct; since all that I conceive clearly and distinctly of the real and the true, and of what conveys some perfection, is in its entirety contained in this idea. And this does not cease to be true although I do not comprehend the infinite, or though in God there is an infinitude of things which I cannot comprehend, nor possibly even reach in any way by thought; for it is of the nature of the infinite that my nature, which is finite and limited, should not comprehend it; and it is sufficient that I should understand this, and that I should judge that all things which I clearly perceive and in which I know that there is some perfection, and possibly likewise an infinitude of properties of which I am ignorant, are in God formally or eminently, so that the idea which I have of Him may become the most true, most clear, and most distinct of all the ideas that are in my mind.

But possibly I am something more than I suppose myself to be, and perhaps all those perfections which I attribute to God are in some way potentially in me, although they do not yet disclose themselves, or issue in action. As a matter of fact I am already sensible that my knowledge increases [and perfects itself] little by little, and I see nothing which can prevent it from increasing more and more into infinitude; nor do I see, after it has thus been increased [or perfected], anything to prevent my being able to acquire by its means all the other perfections of the Divine nature; nor finally why the power I have of acquiring these perfections, if it really exists in me, shall not suffice to produce the ideas of them.

At the same time I recognise that this cannot be. For, in the first place, although it were true that every day my knowledge acquired new degrees of perfection, and that there were in my nature many things potentially which are not yet there actually, nevertheless these excellences do not pertain to [or make the smallest approach to] the idea which I have of God in whom there is nothing merely potential [but in whom all is present really and actually]; for it is an infallible token of imperfection in my knowledge that it increases little by little. And further, although my knowledge grows more and more, nevertheless I do not for that reason believe that it can ever be actually infinite, since it can never reach a point so high that it will be unable to attain to any greater increase. But I understand God to be actually infinite, so that He can add nothing to His supreme perfection. And finally I perceive that the objective being of an idea cannot be produced by a being that exists potentially only, which properly speaking is nothing, but only by a being which is formal or actual.

To speak the truth, I see nothing in all that I have just said which by the light of nature is not manifest to anyone who desires to think attentively on the subject; but when I slightly relax my attention, my mind, finding its vision somewhat obscured and so to speak blinded by the images of sensible objects, I do not easily recollect the reason why the idea that I possess of a being more perfect than I, must necessarily have been placed in me by a being which is really more perfect; and this is why I wish here to go on to inquire whether I, who have this idea, can exist if no such being exists.

And I ask, from whom do I then derive my existence? Perhaps from myself or from my parents, or from some other source less perfect than God; for we can imagine nothing more perfect than God, or even as perfect as He is.

But [were I independent of every other and] were I myself the author of my being, I should doubt nothing and I should desire nothing, and finally no perfection would be lacking to me; for I should have bestowed on myself every perfection of which I possessed any idea and should thus be God. And it must not be imagined that those things that are lacking to me are perhaps more difficult of attainment than those which I already possess; for, on the contrary, it is quite evident that it was a matter of much greater difficulty to bring to pass that I, that is to say, a thing or a substance that thinks, should emerge out of nothing, than it would be to attain to the knowledge of many things of which I am ignorant, and which are only the accidents of this thinking substance. But it is clear that if I had of myself possessed this greater perfection of which I have just spoken [that is to say, if I had been the author of my own existence], I should not at least have denied myself the things which are the more easy to acquire [to wit, many branches of knowledge of which my nature is destitute]; nor should I have deprived myself of any of the things contained in the idea which I form of God, because there are none of them which seem to me specially difficult to acquire: and if there were any that were more difficult to acquire, they would certainly appear to me to be such (supposing I myself were the origin

↓ *our mental capability is infinite, in that our potential for learning is infinite. Ha.*

of the other things which I possess) since I should discover in them that my powers were limited.

But though I assume that perhaps I have always existed just as I am at present, neither can I escape the force of this reasoning, and imagine that the conclusion to be drawn from this is, that I need not seek for any author of my existence. For all the course of my life may be divided into an infinite number of parts, none of which is in any way dependent on the other; and thus from the fact that I was in existence a short time ago it does not follow that I must be in existence now, unless some cause at this instant, so to speak, produces me anew, that is to say, conserves me. It is as a matter of fact perfectly clear and evident to all those who consider with attention the nature of time, that, in order to be conserved in each moment in which it endures, a substance has need of the same power and action as would be necessary to produce and create it anew, supposing it did not yet exist, so that the light of nature shows us clearly that the distinction between creation and conservation is solely a distinction of the reason.

All that I thus require here is that I should interrogate myself, if I wish to know whether I possess a power which is capable of bringing it to pass that I who now am shall still be in the future; for since I am nothing but a thinking thing, or at least since thus far it is only this portion of myself which is precisely in question at present, if such a power did reside in me, I should certainly be conscious of it. But I am conscious of nothing of the kind, and by this I know clearly that I depend on some being different from myself.

Possibly, however, this being on which I depend is not that which I call God, and I am created either by my parents or by some other cause less perfect than God. This cannot be, because, as I have just said, it is perfectly evident that there must be at least as much reality in the cause as in the effect; and thus since I am a thinking thing, and possess an idea of God within me, whatever in the end be the cause assigned to my existence, it must be allowed that it is likewise a thinking thing and that it possesses in itself the idea of all the perfections which I attribute to God. We may again inquire whether this cause derives its origin from itself or from some other thing. For if from itself, it follows by the reasons

before brought forward, that this cause must itself be God; for since it possesses the virtue of self-existence, it must also without doubt have the power of actually possessing all the perfections of which it has the idea, that is, all those which I conceive as existing in God. But if it derives its existence from some other cause than itself, we shall again ask, for the same reason, whether this second cause exists by itself or through another, until from one step to another, we finally arrive at an ultimate cause, which will be God.

And it is perfectly manifest that in this there can be no regression into infinity, since what is in question is not so much the cause which formerly created me, as that which conserves me at the present time.

Nor can we suppose that several causes may have concurred in my production, and that from one I have received the idea of one of the perfections which I attribute to God, and from another the idea of some other, so that all these perfections indeed exist somewhere in the universe, but not as complete in one unity which is God. On the contrary, the unity, the simplicity or the inseparability of all things which are in God is one of the principal perfections which I conceive to be in Him. And certainly the idea of this unity of all Divine perfections cannot have been placed in me by any cause from which I have not likewise received the ideas of all the other perfections; for this cause could not make me able to comprehend them as joined together in an inseparable unity without having at the same time caused me in some measure to know what they are [and in some way to recognise each one of them].

Finally, so far as my parents [from whom it appears I have sprung] are concerned, although all that I have ever been able to believe of them were true, that does not make it follow that it is they who conserve me, nor are they even the authors of my being in any sense, in so far as I am a thinking being; since what they did was merely to implant certain dispositions in that matter in which the self—i.e. the mind, which alone I at present identify with myself—is by me deemed to exist. And thus there can be no difficulty in their regard, but we must of necessity conclude from the fact alone that I exist, or that the idea of a Being supremely perfect—that is of God—is in me, that the proof of God's existence is grounded on the highest evidence.

It only remains to me to examine into the manner in which I have acquired this idea from God; for I have not received it through the senses, and it is never presented to me unexpectedly, as is usual with the ideas of sensible things when these things present themselves, or seem to present themselves, to the external organs of my senses; nor is it likewise a fiction of my mind, for it is not in my power to take from or to add anything to it; and consequently the only alternative is that it is innate in me, just as the idea of myself is innate in me.

And one certainly ought not to find it strange that God, in creating me, placed this idea within me to be like the mark of the workman imprinted on his work; and it is likewise not essential that the mark shall be something different from the work itself. For from the sole fact that God created me it is most probable that in some way He has placed His image and similitude upon me, and that I perceive this similitude (in which the idea of God is contained) by means of the same faculty by which I perceive myself—that is to say, when I reflect on myself I not only know that I am something [imperfect], incomplete and dependent on another, which incessantly aspires after something which is better and greater than myself, but I also know that He on whom I depend possesses in Himself all the great things towards which I aspire [and the ideas of which I find within myself], and that not indefinitely or potentially alone, but really, actually and infinitely;

and that thus He is God. And the whole strength of the argument which I have here made use of to prove the existence of God consists in this, that I recognise that it is not possible that my nature should be what it is, and indeed that I should have in myself the idea of a God, if God did not veritably exist—a God, I say, whose idea is in me, i.e. who possesses all those supreme perfections of which our mind may indeed have some idea but without understanding them all, who is liable to no errors or defect [and who has none of all those marks which denote imperfection]. From this it is manifest that He cannot be a deceiver, since the light of nature teaches us that fraud and deception necessarily proceed from some defect.

But before I examine this matter with more care, and pass on to the consideration of other truths which may be derived from it, it seems to me right to pause for a while in order to contemplate God Himself, to ponder at leisure His marvellous attributes, to consider, and admire, and adore, the beauty of this light so resplendent, at least as far as the strength of my mind, which is in some measure dazzled by the sight, will allow me to do so. For just as faith teaches us that the supreme felicity of the other life consists only in this contemplation of the Divine Majesty, so we continue to learn by experience that a similar meditation, though incomparably less perfect, causes us to enjoy the greatest satisfaction of which we are capable in this life.

V.2 *Contemporary Foundationalism*

ROBERT AUDI

Robert Audi is Professor of Philosophy at the University of Nebraska. In this essay Audi outlines the main theses of contemporary modest foundationalism, distinguishing it from classical foundationalism and arguing that it has "perhaps unexpected advantages" over other epistemic theories.

As I sit reading on a quiet summer evening, I sometimes hear a distinctive patter outside my open window. I immediately believe that it is raining. It may then occur to me that if I do not bring in the lawn chairs, the cushions will be soaked. But this I do not believe immediately, even if the thought strikes me in an instant; I believe it on the basis of my prior belief that it is raining. The first belief is perceptual, being grounded directly in what I hear. The second is inferential, being grounded not in what I perceive, but in what I believe: my belief that it is raining expresses a premise for my belief that the cushions will be soaked.

There are many beliefs of both kinds. Perception is a constant source of beliefs; and, from beliefs we have through perception, many arise inferentially. The latter, inferential beliefs, are then based on the former, perceptual beliefs. When I see a headlight beam cross my window and immediately believe, perceptually, that there is a bright light moving out there, I may, on the basis of that belief, come to believe, inferentially, that a car has turned into my driveway. From this proposition in turn I might infer that my doorbell is about to ring, and from that I might infer still further propositions. On the plausible assumption that knowledge implies belief, the same holds for knowledge: much of it is perceptually grounded, and much of it is inferential.[1] There is no definite limit on how many inferences one may draw in such a chain, and people differ in how many they tend to draw. Could it be, however, that despite the apparent obviousness of

these points, there really *is* no non-inferential knowledge or belief, even in perceptual cases? Might every belief be based on some other and no belief be simply grounded in perception? If inference can take us forward indefinitely beyond perceptual beliefs, why may it not take us backward indefinitely from them? To see how this might occur, we must consider more systematically how beliefs arise, what justifies them, and when they are sufficiently well grounded to constitute knowledge.

I. *The Sources of Belief and Knowledge*

Imagine that when the rain began I had not trusted my ears. I might then have believed only that there was a pattering sound, and only on that basis, and after considering the situation, come to believe that it was raining. We need not stop here, however. For suppose I do not trust my sense of hearing at all. I might then believe only that it *seems* to me that there is a patter, and only on that basis believe that there is such a sound. All right, you may say, but surely this cannot go much further, and in fact there is no need to go even this far. But *can* we go further? What theoretical reason is there to stop at all? It is not as if we had to articulate all our beliefs. Little of what we believe is at any one time before our minds being inwardly voiced. Indeed, perhaps we can have an infinite number of beliefs, as some think we do in the case of arithmetic: we believe, it is said, such things as that 2 is larger than 1, that 3 is larger than

---

This essay was commissioned for this anthology and appears here for the first time.

2, and so forth.[2] Another possibility is a cognitive circle: one believes p on the basis of q, q on the basis of r, and so on until one reaches some proposition, say z, which one believes on the basis of p. Debate about these matters continues on both the philosophy of mind and epistemology. In the philosophy of mind, the issue is whether a person's cognitive system can sustain an infinite set of beliefs or a circular cognitive chain; in epistemology, the main question is whether, even if it could, this would help in accounting for knowledge or justification.

The epistemological position associated with the view that even if there could be infinite or circular beliefs chains, they could not be sources of knowledge or justification, is foundationalism. Foundationalism is a long-established and leading view in epistemology; but despite the amount of attention it has received in the past fifteen to twenty years it has too rarely been carefully formulated and continues to be widely misunderstood.[3] Foundationalism is so called because it considers knowledge—and indeed justified belief, which is commonly regarded as a major part of knowledge—to be possible only through *foundational beliefs*. These beliefs are construed as non-inferential in the way perceptual beliefs are: based on experience rather than inference. The underlying idea is in part this: If knowledge or justified belief arises through inference, it requires belief of at least one premise, and that belief can produce knowledge or justified belief of a proposition inferred from the premise only if the premise belief is itself an instance of knowledge or at least justified. But if the premise belief is justified, it must be so by virtue of *something*—otherwise it would be self-justified, and hence a kind of foundational belief after all. If, however, experience cannot serve to justify it, then the belief must derive its justification from yet another set of premises, and the problem arises all over again: what justifies that set?

In the light of such points, the foundationalist concludes that if—as common sense would certainly have us suppose—some of our beliefs are justified or constitute knowledge, then some of our beliefs are justified, or constitute knowledge, simply because they arise (in a certain way) from experience. If we construe experience broadly enough to include logical reflection and rational intuition, then there appear to be at least four basic sources of

knowledge and justified belief. Perception is one experiential source; consciousness is another and grounds, for example, my knowledge that I am thinking about the structure of justification; reflection is still another and is, for instance, the basis of my justified belief that if person A is older than B and B is older than C, then A is older than C. And memory is yet another source, because I can be justified in believing that, say, I left a light on simply by virtue of the sense of recalling my doing so.[4]

Particularly in the perceptual cases, the foundationalist tends to see experience as a mirror of nature.[5] This seems to foundationalists a good metaphor because it suggests at least two important points: first, that some experiences are *produced* by external states of the world, somewhat as light produces mirror images; and second, that (normally) the experiences in some way *match* their causes; for instance in the color and shape I sense in my visual field.[6] If I want to focus on one perceptual belief at a time, I might think of a thermometer model; it suggests both the causal connections just sketched, but also, perhaps even more than the mirror metaphor, *reliable* responses to the external world.[7] From this causal responsiveness perspective, it is at best unnatural to regard perceptual beliefs as inferential: they are not formed by inference from anything else believed, but directly reflect the objects and events that cause them. To assess foundationalism, then, we must consider whether all knowledge and all justified beliefs could arise from a regress or circle, or whether some must be non-inferential and in that sense foundational, as where they originate in experience that reflects reality. Because even a finite circle can generate an infinite regress by repeated rotation around it, this is called the "epistemic regress problem." The foundationalist uses it to produce a supporting argument. That argument is my next concern.

II. *The Epistemic Regress Argument*

Let us start by formulating the regress problem more sharply and then proceed to state the regress argument which foundationalists propose as a partial solution to the problem.[8] First, suppose I have knowledge, even if only of something so simple as there being a patter outside my window. Could all my knowledge be inferential? Imagine that this is possible by virtue of an infinite epistemic regress—roughly, an infinite series of knowings, each based (inferentially) on the next. Just assume that a belief constituting inferential knowledge is based on knowledge of some other proposition, or at least on a further belief of another proposition; the further knowledge or belief might be based on knowlege of, or belief about, something still further, and so on. Call this sequence an *epistemic chain;* it is simply a chain of beliefs, with at least the first constituting knowledge, and each belief linked to the previous one by being based on it. A standard view is that there are just four kinds: an epistemic chain might be infinite or circular, hence in either case unending and in that sense regressive; third, it might terminate with a belief that is not knowledge; and fourth, it might terminate with a belief constituting direct knowledge. The epistemic regress problem is above all to assess these chains as possible sources (or at least carriers) of knowledge or justification.

The foundationalist response to the regress problem is to offer a regress argument favoring the fourth possibility as the only genuine one. The argument can be best formulated along these lines:

1. If one has any knowledge, it occurs in an epistemic chain (possibly including the special case of a single link, such as a perceptual or *a priori* belief, which constitutes knowledge by virtue of being anchored directly in experience or reason).

2. The only possible kinds of epistemic chains are the four mutually exclusive kinds just sketched.

3. Knowledge can occur only in the last kind of chain.

4. Hence, if one has any knowledge, one has some direct knowledge.[9]

Some preliminary clarification is in order before we appraise this argument. First, the conclusion, being conditional, does not presuppose that there *is* any knowledge. This preserves neutrality with respect to skepticism, as is appropriate, because the issue concerns *conceptual* requirements for the possession of knowledge. The argument would have existential import, and so would not be purely

conceptual, if it presupposed that there *is* knowledge and hence that at least one knower exists. Second, I take the first line of the argument to imply that inferential knowledge depends on at least one epistemic chain for its status *as* knowledge. I thus take the argument to imply the further conclusion that any inferential knowledge one has exhibits (inferential) *epistemic dependence* on some appropriate inferential connection, via some epistemic chain, to some non-inferential knowledge one has. Thus, the argument shows not only that if there is inferential knowledge, there *is* non-inferential knowledge; but also that if there is inferential knowledge, that very knowledge is *traceable* to some non-inferential knowledge as its foundation.

The second point suggests a third: if two epistemic chains should *intersect,* as where a belief that *p* is both foundationally grounded in experience and part of a circular chain, then if the belief is knowledge, that knowledge *occurs in* only the former chain, though the knowledge *qua belief* belongs to both chains. Knowledge, then, does not occur in a chain merely because the belief constituting it does. Fourth, the argument concerns the structure, not the content, of a body of knowledge and of its constituent epistemic chains. The argument may thus be used regardless of the purported items of knowledge to which one applies it in any particular person. It does not presuppose that, to have knowledge, there are specific things one must believe, or that a body of knowledge must have some one definite content.

A similar argument applies to justification. We simply speak of *justificatory chains* and proceed in a parallel way, substituting justification for knowledge. The conclusion would be that if there are any justified beliefs, there are some non-inferentially justified beliefs, and that if one has any inferentially justified belief, it shows (inferential) *justificatory dependence* on an epistemic chain appropriately linking it to some non-inferentially justified belief one has, that is, to a foundational belief. In discussing foundationalism, I shall often focus on justification.

Detailed assessment of the regress argument is impossible here. I shall simply comment on some important aspects of it to provide a better understanding of foundationalism and of some major objections to it.

The possibility of an infinite epistemic chain

has seldom seemed to philosophers to be likely to solve the regress problem. Let me suggest one reason to think that it is doubtful that human beings are even capable of having infinite sets of beliefs. Recall the claim that we can have an infinite set of arithmetical beliefs, say that 2 is twice 1, that 4 is twice 2, and so on. Surely for a finite mind there will be some point or other at which the relevant proposition cannot be grasped. The required formulation (or entertaining of the proposition) would, at some point on the way "toward" infinity, become too lengthy to permit understanding it. Thus, even if we could read or entertain it part by part, when we got to the end we would be unable to remember enough of the first part to grasp and thereby believe what the formulation expresses. Granted, we could believe that the *formulation* just read expresses a truth; but this is not sufficient for believing the *truth* it expresses. That truth is a specific mathematical statement; believing, of a formulation we cannot even get before our minds or remember in toto, that it expresses *some* mathematical truth is not enough for believing, or even grasping, the true statement in question. Because we cannot understand the formulation as a whole, we cannot grasp that truth, and what we cannot grasp we cannot believe. I doubt that any other lines of argument show that we can have infinite sets of beliefs; nor, if we can, is it clear how infinite epistemic chains could account for any of our knowledge. I thus propose to consider only the other kinds of chain.

The possibility of a circular epistemic chain as a basis of knowledge has been taken much more seriously. The standard objection has been that such circularity is vicious, because you would ultimately have to know something on the basis of itself—say *p* on the basis of *q, q* on the basis of *r*, and *r* on the basis of *p*. A standard reply has been that if the circle is wide enough and its content sufficiently rich and coherent, the circularity is innocuous. I bypass this difficult matter, because I believe that coherentism as most plausibly formulated does not depend on circular chains.[10]

The third alternative, namely that an epistemic chain terminates in a belief which is not knowledge, has been at best rarely affirmed; and there is little plausibility in the hypothesis that knowledge can originate through a belief of a proposition that Person S does not know. If there are exceptions,

it is where, although I do not know that *p,* I am justified, to *some* extent, in believing *p,* as in making a reasonable estimate that there are at least thirty books on a certain shelf. Here is a different case. Suppose it vaguely seems to me that I hear strains of music. If, on the basis of the resulting somewhat justified belief that there is music playing, I believe that my daughter has come home, and she has, do I know this? The answer is not clear. But that would not help anyone who claims knowledge can arise from belief which does not constitute knowledge. For it is equally unclear, and for the same sort of reason, whether my belief that there is music playing is *sufficiently* reasonable—say, in terms of how good my perceptual grounds are—to give me knowledge that music is playing. The stronger our tendency to say that I know she is home, the stronger our inclination to say that I do after all know that there are strains of music in the air. Notice something else. In the only cases where the third kind of chain seems likely to ground knowledge (or justification), there is a degree—apparently a substantial degree—of justification. If there can be an epistemic chain which ends with belief that is not knowledge only because it ends, in this way, with justification, then we are apparently in the general vicinity of knowledge. We seem to be at most a few degrees of justification away. Knowledge is not emerging from nothing, as it were (the picture originally painted by the third alternative) but from something characteristically much like it—justified true belief. There would thus be a foundation after all: not bedrock, but perhaps ground that is nonetheless firm enough to yield a foundation we can build on.

The fourth possibility is that epistemic chains that originate with knowledge end in non-inferential knowledge: knowledge not inferentially based on further knowledge (or further justified belief). That knowledge, in turn, is apparently grounded in experience, say in my auditory impression of music or my intuitive sense that if Person A is taller than B, then B is shorter than A. This non-inferential grounding of my knowledge can explain how it is (epistemically) direct: it arises non-inferentially—and so without any intermediary premise which must be known along the way—from (I shall assume) one of the four classical kinds of foundational material, namely, perception, memory, introspection, or reason.

Such direct grounding in experience (including reason) also seems to explain why a belief so grounded may be expected to be *true;* for experience seems to connect the beliefs they ground to the reality constituting their object, in such a way that what is believed about that reality tends to be the case. This, at least, seems to explain best why we have those beliefs. In any event, the ground-level knowledge could not be inferential; otherwise the chain would not end without a further link: every inference needs a premise. Let me illustrate all this. Normally when I know music is playing, that is just because I hear it; hence the chain grounding my knowledge that my daughter has come home is anchored in my auditory perception, which in turn reflects the musical reality represented by my knowledge and explains both my perception and, through that, my believing the proposition I know to be true.

The non-inferentially grounded epistemic chains in question may differ in many ways. They differ *compositionally,* in the sorts of beliefs constituting them, and *causally,* in the kind of causal relation holding between one belief and its successor. This relation, for instance, may or may not involve the predecessor belief's being necessary or sufficient for its successor: perhaps I would have believed, on grounds other than the music, my daughter was home, and perhaps not, depending on how many indications are accessible to me. Such chains also differ *structurally,* in the kind of *epistemic transmission* they show; it may be deductive, as where I infer a theorem from an axiom by rigorous rules of deductive inference, or inductive, as where I infer from a knife's good performance that other knives of that kind will also cut well; or the transmission of knowledge or justification may combine deductive and inductive elements. Epistemic chains also differ *foundationally,* in their ultimate grounds, the anchors of the chains; the grounds may, as illustrated, be perceptual or rational, and they may vary in justificational strength.

Different proponents of the fourth possibility have held various views about the character of the *foundational knowledge;* that is, the beliefs constituting the knowledge that makes up the final link and anchors the chain in experience or reason. Some,

including Descartes, have thought that the appropriate beliefs must be infallible, or at least indefeasibly justified.[11] But in fact all that the fourth possibility requires is *non-inferential knowledge,* knowledge not (inferentially) based on other knowledge (or other justified belief). Non-inferential knowledge need not be of self-evident propositions, nor constituted by indefeasibly justified belief, the kind whose justification cannot be defeated. The case of introspective beliefs, which are paradigms of those that are non-inferentially justified, supports this view, and we shall see other reasons to hold it.

III. *Fallibilist Foundationalism*

If the regress argument is as important as I think in supporting and shaping epistemological foundationalism, then we can now formulate some foundationalist theses in the light of it. Let us start with two versions of what I shall call *generic foundationalism.* The first concerns knowledge:

> I. For any person, S, and any time, *t,* the structure of S's knowledge, at *t,* is foundational, and (thus) any inferential (hence non-foundational) knowledge S has depends on non-inferential (thus in a sense foundational) knowledge of S's.

The second position, regarding justification, is the thesis that

> II. For any S and any *t,* the structure of S's body of justified beliefs is, at *t,* foundational, and therefore any inferentially (hence non-foundationally) justified beliefs S has depend on non-inferentially (thus in a sense foundationally) justified beliefs of S's.

Different foundationalist theories may diverge in the kind and degree of dependence they assert. I especially want to contrast fallibilist (moderate) and strong foundationalist theses, particularly in the case of justification.

I take *fallibilist foundationalism,* as applied to justification, to be the inductivist thesis that

> III. For any S and any *t,* (a) the structure of S's body of justified beliefs is, at *t,*

foundational in the sense indicated by thesis II; (b) the justification of S's foundational beliefs is at least typically defeasible; (c) the inferential transmission of justification need not be deductive: and (d) non-foundationally justified beliefs need not derive *all* their justification from foundational ones, but only enough so that they would remain justified if (other things remaining equal) any other justification they have (say, from coherence) were eliminated.[12]

This is fallibilistic in at least three ways: foundational beliefs may turn out to be unjustified or false or both; superstructure beliefs may be only inductively, hence fallibly, justified by foundational ones and hence can be false even when the latter are true; and the possibility of *discovering* error or lack of justification, even in foundational beliefs, is left open: they may be found to conflict either with other such beliefs or with sufficiently well-supported superstructure beliefs. Even foundationalism as applied to knowledge can be fallibilistic; for granting that false propositions cannot be known, foundationalism about knowledge does not entail that someone's *grounds* for knowledge (at any level) are indefeasible. Perceptual grounds, for example, may be overridden; and one can fail (or cease) to know a proposition not because it is (or is discovered to be) false, but because one ceases to be justified in believing it.

Fallibilistic foundationalism contrasts markedly with what we might call *Cartesian foundationalism*. There are three main elements in that view. The first is *axiomatism* about foundations, the requirement (which goes back at least to Aristotle) of indubitable or clearly self-evident propositions as objects of the foundational beliefs: if I can rationally doubt that p, my belief of it is not strong enough to be a good foundation. The second is *deductivism* about transmission, the requirement that a superstructure belief—say, that p—can be justified by a foundational belief—say, that q—only if p is validly deducible from q. It is not enough that p is inductively supported by q, with however high probability, because then p could be false even if q is true. The third is a *second-order* requirement to the effect that, for any foundational knowledge or justified belief—for example, that one hears music—one can

come to know or justifiedly believe that it *is* knowledge or justified belief; for instance, one can come to know that one does in fact know that there is music. I call this view Cartesian not because it is certain that Descartes held just this, but because something close to it is evident in his work and, almost equally important, this view has been associated with him in the literature about foundationalism. It is this third requirement that I am least confident he would hold; but in the *Meditations* there is no question that he is seeking foundations which one can *cite*, from a higher level of reflection, as certain and indubitable. For one thing, it is easier to understand the way he attempts to overcome skepticism in the way he does on the assumption that when he finds appropriate foundations, he supposes that they can be known or at least justifiedly taken to be such. Only then, he may have thought, can someone really know that the skeptic is wrong.

Fallibilist foundationalism, then, is far weaker than Cartesian foundationalism; and because the latter has been so influential in shaping philosophers' views of foundationalism in general, this point must be kept in mind in appraising the general foundationalist position. Moreover, we can construct weaker versions of foundationalism than III. For instance, one might hold only that justified foundational beliefs are necessary conditions for the existence of justified beliefs; this would allow coherence to be a necessary condition as well. One might even hold that justified foundational beliefs are not necessary but only sufficient, in which case one could have a mixed foundational theory that allows sources quite different from experience to produce justification. But I am not seeking a minimal formulation, or a mixed theory; my purpose has been only to set forth a plausible contemporary version of the theory, and, properly clarified, III. will serve well as an indication of a kind of foundationalism that can be defended against the most plausible objections coherentists and others have—especially in recent decades—brought against it. Those objections have been treated elsewhere.[13] Here I shall simply point out some of the very general considerations supporting a fallibilist foundationalism.

First, the theory provides a plausible and reasonably straightforward solution to the regress problem. It selects what seems the best option among the four, and does not interpret that option in a way that makes knowledge or justification either impossible, as the skeptic would have it, or too easy to achieve, as they would be if they required no grounds at all or only grounds obtainable without the effort of observing, thinking, or in some other way taking account of experience.

Second, in working from the experiential and rational sources fallibilist foundationalism takes as basic to justification and knowledge, it accords with reflective common sense: the sorts of beliefs it says we are non-inferentially justified in holding, or can generally take to constitute non-inferential knowledge, are pretty much those which, on reflection, we think people are justified in holding, or in supposing to be knowledge, without any more than the evidence of the senses or of intuition. We do not, for instance, normally ask people for reasons to think it is raining when they can see clearly out an unobstructed window and say that it is; and if a person should give a reason, "I see it" is usually as good as any. *Prima facie,* in accepting it we are accepting an experiential, not an inferential, ground.

Third, fallibilist foundationalism is psychologically plausible, in two major ways: the account it suggests of the experiential and inferential genesis of many of our beliefs apparently fits what is known about their origins and development; and, far from positing infinite or circular belief chains, whose psychology is at least puzzling,[14] it allows (indeed encourages) a fairly simple account of the structure of cognition. Beliefs arise both from experience and from inference; some serve to unify others, especially those based on them; and their relative strengths, their changes, and their mutual interactions are all explicable within the moderate foundationalist assumptions suggested.

Fourth, fallibilist foundationalism serves to integrate our epistemology with our psychology and even biology, particularly in the crucial case of perceptual beliefs: what causally explains why we hold them—sensory experience—is also what justifies them. From an evolutionary point of view, moreover, many of the kinds of beliefs the theory takes to be non-inferentially justified—introspective and memorial beliefs as well as perceptual ones—are plainly essential to survival. We may need a map, and not merely a mirror, of the world to navigate it; but if experience does not generally mirror reality, we are in no position to move to the abstract level on which we can draw a good map. If a mirror without a map is insufficiently discriminating, a map without a mirror is insufficiently reliable.

Fifth, contrary to what has sometimes been thought about foundationalism in general, the fallibilist version is not dogmatic;[15] on the contrary, it leads us to expect cognitive pluralism. Given that different people have different experiences, and that anyone's experiences change over time, people should be expected to differ from one another in their non-inferentially justified beliefs and, in their own case, across time; and given that logic does not dictate what is to be inferred from one's premises, people should be expected to differ considerably in their inferential beliefs as well. Logic does, to be sure, tell us what *may* be inferred, but it neither forces inferences nor, when we draw them, selects which among the permissible ones we will make. Particularly in the case of inductive inference, as where we infer a hypothesis as the best explanation of some puzzling event, our imagination comes into play; and even if we were to build from the same foundations as our neighbors, we would often produce quite different superstructures.

These points do not, of course, establish foundationalism; that is an immense task beyond any single essay. But they do bring out some perhaps unexpected advantages of a sufficiently moderate version of the theory, and I believe that, taken together with a balanced perspective on the problems besetting alternative theories—most notably coherentism—they strongly argue that a fallibilist foundationalism is a viable position to be reckoned with whatever may be someone's ultimate outlook in epistemology.

Notes

[1] That knowing a proposition implies believing it is not uncontroversial, but most epistemologists accept the implication. For defense of the implication, see e.g., Gilbert H. Harman, *Thought* (Princeton, NJ: Princeton University Press, 1973), and Robert Audi, *Belief, Justification, and Knowledge* (Belmont, CA: Wadsworth, 1988).

[2] See, e.g., Richard Foley, "Justified Inconsistent Beliefs," *American Philosophical Quarterly 16* (1979). I have criticized the infinite belief view in "Believing and Affirming," *Mind 91* (1982).

[3] For an indication of this misunderstanding see, e.g., William P. Alston, "Two Types of Foundationalism," *Journal of Philosophy 83* (1976), and my "The Architecture of Reason," *Proceedings and Addresses of the American Philosophical Association 62* (1988). This essay, like those, seeks to formulate foundationalism in a way that corresponds with plausible contemporary developments in the foundationalist tradition.

[4] Note that memory differs from the other three in this: it is apparently not a *basic* source of knowledge, as it is of justification; i.e., one cannot know something from memory unless one has *come* to know it in some other mode, e.g., through perception. This is discussed in Chapter 2 of my *Belief, Justification, and Knowledge* (Belmont, CA: Wadsworth, 1988). Cp. Carl Ginet, *Knowledge, Perception, and Memory* (Boston: Reidel, 1973) and George S. Pappas, "Suddenly He Knows," in Steven Luper-Foy, ed., *The Possibility of Knowledge: Nozick and His Critics* (Totowa, NJ: Rowman & Littlefield, 1987).

[5] The view that such experience is a mirror of nature is criticized at length by Richard Rorty in *Philosophy and the Mirror of Nature* (Princeton, NJ: Princeton University Press, 1979). He has in mind, however, a Cartesian version of foundationalism, which is not the only kind and which implies features of the "mirror" that are not entailed by the uses implied in this essay.

[6] This does not entail that there are *objects* in the visual field which have their own phenomenal colors and shapes; the point is only that there is some sense in which experiences *characterized by* color and shape (however that is to be analyzed) represent the colors and shapes apparently instantiated in the external world.

[7] This model comes from D. M. Armstrong. See especially *Belief, Truth and Knowledge* (Cambridge, England: Cambridge University Press, 1973). His theory of justification and knowledge is *reliabilist,* in taking both to be analyzable in terms of their being produced or sustained by reliable processes (such as tactile belief production), those that (normally) yield true beliefs more often than false. Foundationalism may, but need not, be reliabilist; and this essay is intended to be neutral with respect to the choice between reliabilist and internalist views. I have briefly sketched internalism in "Fallibilist Foundationalism and Holistic Coherentism" (Reading V.7 in this book) and I have assessed the controversy between the two kinds of theory in "Justification, Truth, and Reliability," *Philosophy and Phenomenological Research 49* (1988). For further discussion see Paul K. Moser, *Knowledge and Evidence* (New York: Cambridge University Press, 1989), and R.M. Chisholm, *Theory of Knowledge*, 3rd ed. (Englewood Cliffs, NJ: Prentice-Hall, 1989).

[8] This section draws on my "Foundationalism, Coherentism, and Epistemological Dogmatism," *Philosophical Perspectives 2* (1988).

[9] The locus classicus of this argument is the *Posterior Analytics,* Book II. But while Aristotle's version agrees with the one given here insofar as his main conclusion is that "not all knowledge is demonstrative," he also says, "since the regress must end in immediate truths, those truths must be indemonstrable" (72b19–24), whereas I hold that direct knowledge does *not* require indemonstrability. There might be appropriate premises; S's foundational belief is simply not based on them (I also question the validity of the inference in the second quotation, but I suspect Aristotle had independent grounds for its conclusion).

[10] In "Fallibilist Foundationalism and Holistic Coherentism" (Reading V.7), I set forth such a coherentism. As to circular versions, for some major difficulties they face see my "Psychological Foundationalism," *Monist 62* (1978).

[11] In Meditation I, e.g., Descartes says that "reason already persuades me that I ought no less carefully to withhold my assent from matters which are not entirely certain and indubitable than from those which appear to me manifestly to be false" (from the Haldane and Ross translation).

[12] Clause d needs the "other things being equal" clause because removal of justification from one source can affect justification from another even without being a basis of it; and the *level* of justification in question I take to be (as in the counterpart formulation of coherentism) approximately that appropriate to knowledge. The formulation should hold, however, for any given level.

[13] For a reply to some of them, see my "Fallibilist Foundationalism and Holistic Coherentism" (Reading V.7), and for further defense of foundationalism and a wealth of relevant references, see Chisholm (1989) and Moser (1989).

[14] In "Psychological Foundationalism," *Monist 62* (1978), I argued that circular epistemic chains are at best deeply problematic; and in "Believing and Affirming," cited in note 2, I have explained some difficulties about the view that we have infinite sets of beliefs.

[15] Keith Lehrer, e.g., has maintained that foundationalism is dogmatic, in *Knowledge* (Oxford, England: Oxford University Press, 1974). I have replied to the dogmatism charge in general in "Foundationalism, Coherentism, and Epistemological Dogmatism," cited in note 8.

V.3   A *Critique of Foundationalism*

Laurence BonJour

Laurence BonJour is Professor of Philosophy at the University of Washington. After rehearsing the regress argument and foundationalism's claim to meet its challenge, BonJour distinguishes three different versions of foundationalism: (1) strong or classical foundationalism, which holds that basic beliefs yield knowledge and are infallible; (2) modest (strong) foundationalism, which holds that basic beliefs yield knowledge but are not infallible; and (3) weak foundationalism, which holds that the basic beliefs have a relatively low degree of warrant so that they need to be augmented by inferential relationships (coherence) with other minimally warranted beliefs. Weak foundationalism is a hybrid between strong foundationalism and coherence views.

      At the core of the essay is BonJour's critique of foundationalism through what is sometimes called the argument from epistemic ascent. The argument says that regarding whatever feature we pick out as being the kind that yields proper basicality we need to ask for a justification of positing that feature, but if we do that we seem to be calling for additional justification, so that our basic beliefs aren't really foundational after all. Then BonJour takes up the two foundationalist attempts to answer this criticism: the externalist solution and the standard foundational solution: "givenness." He argues that neither is successful in meeting the problem.

The idea that empirical knowledge has, and must have, a *foundation* has been a common tenet of most major epistemologists, both past and present. There have been, as we shall see further below, many importantly different variants of this idea. But the common denominator among them, the central thesis of epistemological foundationism, as I shall understand it here, is the claim that certain empirical beliefs possess a degree of epistemic justification or warrant which does not depend, inferentially or otherwise, on the justification of other empirical beliefs, but is instead somehow immediate or intrinsic. It is these noninferentially justified beliefs, the unmoved (or self-moved) movers of the epistemic realm, as Chisholm has called them,[1] that constitute the foundation upon which the rest of empirical knowledge is alleged to rest.

      In recent years, the most familiar foundationist views have been subjected to severe and continuous attack. But this attack has rarely been aimed directly at the central foundationist thesis itself, and new versions of foundationism have been quick to emerge, often propounded by the erst-while critics themselves. Thus foundationism has become a philosophical hydra, difficult to come to grips with and seemingly impossible to kill. The purposes of this essay are, first, to distinguish and clarify the main dialectical variants of foundationism, by viewing them as responses to one fundamental problem which is both the main motivation and the primary obstacle for foundationism; and second, as a result of this discussion to offer schematic reasons for doubting whether any version of foundationism is finally acceptable.

Reprinted from the *American Philosophical Quarterly* 15 (1978): 1–13, by permission of the editor and the author. Copyright 1978, *American Philosophical Quarterly*. [Footnotes edited.—Ed.]

The main reason for the impressive durability of foundationism is not any overwhelming plausibility attaching to the main foundationist thesis in itself, but rather the existence of one apparently decisive argument which seems to rule out all non-skeptical alternatives to foundationism, thereby showing that *some* version of foundationism must be true (on the assumption that skepticism is false). In a recent statement by Quinton, this argument runs as follows:

> If any beliefs are to be justified at all, . . . there must be some terminal beliefs that do not owe their . . . credibility to others. For a belief to be justified it is not enough for it to be accepted, let alone merely entertained: there must also be good reason for accepting it. Furthermore, for an inferential belief to be justified the beliefs that support it must be justified themselves. There must, therefore, be a kind of belief that does not owe its justification to the support provided by others. Unless this were so no belief would be justified at all, for to justify any belief would require the antecedent justification of an infinite series of beliefs. The terminal . . . beliefs that are needed to bring the regress of justification to a stop need not be strictly self-evident in the sense that they somehow justify themselves. All that is required is that they should not owe their justification to any other beliefs.[2]

I shall call this argument the *epistemic regress argument,* and the problem which generates it, the *epistemic regress problem.* Since it is this argument which provides the primary rationale and argumentative support for foundationism, a careful examination of it will also constitute an exploration of the foundationist position itself. The main dialectical variants of foundationism can best be understood as differing attempts to solve the regress problem, and the most basic objection to the foundationist approach is that it is doubtful that any of these attempts can succeed. (In this essay, I shall be concerned with the epistemic regress argument and the epistemic regress problem only as they apply to empirical knowledge. It is obvious that an analogous problem arises also for *a priori* knowledge, but there it seems likely that the argument would take a different course. In particular, a foundationist approach might be inescapable in an account of *a priori* knowledge.)

I

This epistemic regress problem arises directly out of the traditional conception of knowledge as *adequately justified true belief*[3]—whether this be taken as a fully adequate definition of knowledge or, in light of the apparent counterexamples discovered by Gettier,[4] as merely a necessary but not sufficient condition. (I shall assume throughout that the elements of the traditional conception are at least necessary for knowledge.) Now the most natural way to justify a belief is by producing a justificatory argument: belief A is justified by citing some other (perhaps conjunctive) belief B, from which A is inferable in some acceptable way and which is thus offered as a reason for accepting A.[5] Call this *inferential justification*. It is clear, as Quinton points out in the passage quoted above, that for A to be genuinely justified by virtue of such a justificatory argument, B must itself be justified in some fashion; merely being inferable from an unsupported guess or hunch, e.g., would confer no genuine justification upon A.

Two further points about inferential justification, as understood here, must be briefly noted. First, the belief in question need not have been *arrived at* as the result of an inference in order to be inferentially justified. This is obvious, since a belief arrived at in some other way (e.g., as a result of wishful thinking) may later come to be maintained solely because it is now seen to be inferentially justifiable. Second, less obviously, a person for whom a belief is inferentially justified need not have explicitly rehearsed the justificatory argument in question to others or even to himself. It is enough that the inference be available to him if the belief is called into question by others or by himself (where such availability may itself be less than fully explicit) and that the availability of the inference be, in the final analysis, his reason for holding the belief. It seems clear that many beliefs which are quite sufficiently justified to satisfy the justification criterion for knowledge depend for their justification on inferences which have not been explicitly formulated and indeed which could not be explicitly formulated without considerable reflective effort (e.g., my current belief that this is the same piece of paper upon which I was typing yesterday).

Suppose then that belief *A* is (putatively) justified via inference, thus raising the question of how the justifying premise-belief *B* is justified. Here again the answer may be in inferential terms: *B* may be (putatively) justified in virtue of being inferable from some further belief *C*. But then the same question arises about the justification of *C*, and so on, threatening an infinite and apparently vicious regress of epistemic justification. Each belief is justified only if an epistemically prior belief is justified, and that epistemically prior belief is justified only if a still prior belief is justified, etc., with the apparent result that justification can never get started—and hence that there is no justification and no knowledge. The foundationist claim is that only through the adoption of some version of foundationism can this skeptical consequence be avoided.

Prima facie, there seem to be only four basic possibilities with regard to the eventual outcome of this potential regress of epistemic justification: (i) the regress might terminate with beliefs for which no justification of any kind is available, even though they were earlier offered as justifying premises; (ii) the regress might proceed infinitely backwards with ever more new premise-beliefs being introduced and then themselves requiring justification; (iii) the regress might circle back upon itself, so that at some point beliefs which appeared earlier in the sequence of justifying arguments are appealed to again as premises; (iv) the regress might terminate because beliefs are reached which are justified—unlike those in alternative (i)—but whose justification does not depend inferentially on other empirical beliefs and thus does not raise any further issue of justification with respect to such beliefs. The foundationist opts for the last alternative. His argument is that the other three lead inexorably to the skeptical result, and that the second and third have additional fatal defects as well, so that some version of the fourth, foundationist alternative must be correct (assuming that skepticism is false).

With respect to alternative (i), it seems apparent that the foundationist is correct. If this alternative were correct, empirical knowledge would rest ultimately on beliefs which were, from an epistemic standpoint at least, entirely arbitrary and hence incapable of conferring any genuine justification. What about the other two alternatives?

The argument that alternative (ii) leads to a skeptical outcome has in effect already been sketched in the original formulation of the problem. One who opted for this alternative could hope to avoid skepticism only by claiming that the regress, though infinite, is not vicious; but there seems to be no plausible way to defend such a claim. Moreover, a defense of an infinite regress view as an account of how empirical knowledge is actually justified—as opposed to how it might in principle be justified—would have to involve the seemingly dubious thesis that an ordinary knower holds a literally infinite number of distinct beliefs. Thus it is not surprising that no important philosopher, with the rather uncertain exception of Peirce, seems to have advocated such a position.

Alternative (iii), the view that justification ultimately moves in a closed curve, has been historically more prominent, albeit often only as a dialectical foil for foundationism. At first glance, this alternative might seem even less attractive than the second. Although the problem of the knower having to have an infinite number of beliefs is no longer present, the regress itself, still infinite, now seems undeniably vicious. For the justification of each of the beliefs which figure in the circle seems now to presuppose *its own* epistemically prior justification: such a belief must, paradoxically, be justified before it can be justified. Advocates of views resembling alternative (iii) have generally tended to respond to this sort of objection by adopting a holistic conception of justification in which the justification of individual beliefs is subordinated to that of the closed systems of beliefs which such a view implies; the property of such systems usually appealed to as a basis for justification is internal *coherence*. Such coherence theories attempt to evade the regress problem by abandoning the view of justification as essentially involving a linear order of dependence (though a non-linear view of justification has never been worked out in detail).[6] Moreover, such a coherence theory of empirical knowledge is subject to a number of other familiar and seemingly decisive objections. Thus alternative (iii) seems unacceptable, leaving only alternative (iv), the foundationist alternative, as apparently viable.

As thus formulated, the epistemic regress argument makes an undeniably persuasive case for foundationism. Like any argument by elimination, however, it cannot be conclusive until the surviving alternative has itself been carefully examined. The foundationist position may turn out to be subject to equally serious objections, thus forcing a reexamination of the other alternatives, a search for a further non-skeptical alternative, or conceivably the reluctant acceptance of the skeptical conclusion. In particular, it is not clear on the basis of the argument thus far whether and how foundationism can itself solve the regress problem; and thus the possibility exists that the epistemic regress argument will prove to be a two-edged sword, as lethal to the foundationist as it is to his opponents.

II

The most straightforward interpretation of alternative (iv) leads directly to a view which I will here call *strong foundationism*. According to strong foundationism, the foundational beliefs which terminate the regress of justification possess sufficient epistemic warrant, independently of any appeal to inference from (or coherence with) other empirical beliefs, to satisfy the justification condition of knowledge and qualify as acceptable justifying premises for further beliefs. Since the justification of these *basic beliefs,* as they have come to be called, is thus allegedly not dependent on that of any other empirical belief, they are uniquely able to provide secure starting-points for the justification of empirical knowledge and stopping-points for the regress of justification.

The position just outlined is in fact a fairly modest version of strong foundationism. Strong foundationists have typically made considerably stronger claims on behalf of basic beliefs. Basic beliefs have been claimed not only to have sufficient non-inferential justification to qualify as knowl-

edge, but also to be *certain, infallible, indubitable,* or *incorrigible* (terms which are usually not very carefully distinguished). And most of the major attacks on foundationism have focused on these stronger claims. Thus it is important to point out that nothing about the basic strong foundationist response to the regress problem demands that basic beliefs be more than adequately justified. There might of course be other reasons for requiring that basic beliefs have some more exalted epistemic status or for thinking that in fact they do. There might even be some sort of indirect argument to show that such a status is a consequence of the sorts of epistemic properties which are directly required to solve the regress problem. But until such an argument is given (and it is doubtful that it can be), the question of whether basic beliefs are or can be certain, infallible, etc., will remain a relatively unimportant side-issue.

Indeed, many recent foundationists have felt that even the relatively modest version of strong foundationism outlined above is still too strong. Their alternative, still within the general aegis of the foundationist position, is a view which may be called *weak foundationism*. Weak foundationism accepts the central idea of foundationism—viz. that certain empirical beliefs possess a degree of independent epistemic justification or warrant which does not derive inference or coherence relations. But the weak foundationist holds that these foundational beliefs have only a quite low degree of warrant, much lower than that attributed to them by even modest strong foundationism and insufficient by itself to satisfy the justification condition for knowledge or to qualify them as acceptable justifying premises for other beliefs. Thus this independent warrant must somehow be augmented if knowledge is to be achieved, and the usual appeal here is to coherence with other such minimally warranted beliefs. By combining such beliefs into larger and larger coherent systems, it is held, their initial, minimal degree of warrant can gradually be enhanced until knowledge is finally achieved. Thus weak foundationism, like the pure coherence theories mentioned above, abandons the linear conception of justification.[7]

Weak foundationism thus represents a kind of hybrid between strong foundationism and the coherence views discussed earlier, and it is often thought to embody the virtues of both and the vices of neither. Whether or not this is so in other respects, however, relative to the regress problem weak foundationism is finally open to the very same basic objection as strong foundationism, with essentially the same options available for meeting it. As we shall see, the key problem for any version of foundationism is whether it can itself solve the regress problem which motivates its very existence, without resorting to essentially *ad hoc* stipulation. The distinction between the two main ways of meeting this challenge both cuts across and is more basic than that between strong and weak foundationism. This being so, it will suffice to concentrate here on strong foundationism, leaving the application of the discussion to weak foundationism largely implicit.

The fundamental concept of strong foundationism is obviously the concept of a basic belief. It is by appeal to this concept that the threat of an infinite regress is to be avoided and empirical knowledge given a secure foundation. But how can there be any empirical beliefs which are thus basic? In fact, though this has not always been noticed, the very idea of an epistemically basic empirical belief is extremely paradoxical. For on what basis is such a belief to be justified, once appeal to further empirical beliefs is ruled out? Chisholm's theological analogy, cited earlier, is most appropriate: a basic belief is in effect an epistemological unmoved (or self-moved) mover. It is able to confer justification on other beliefs, but apparently has no need to have justification conferred on it. But is such a status any easier to understand in epistemology than it is in theology? How can a belief impart epistemic "motion" to other beliefs unless it is itself in "motion"? And, even more paradoxically, how can a belief epistemically "move" itself?

This intuitive difficulty with the concept of a basic empirical belief may be elaborated and clarified by reflecting a bit on the concept of epistemic justification. The idea of justification is a generic one, admitting in principle of many specific varieties. Thus the acceptance of an empirical belief might be morally justified, i.e., justified as morally obligatory by reference to moral principles and standards; or pragmatically justified, i.e., justified by reference to the desirable practical consequences which will

result from such acceptance; or religiously justified, i.e., justified by reference to specified religious texts or theological dogmas; etc. But none of these other varieties of justification can satisfy the justification condition for knowledge. Knowledge requires *epistemic* justification, and the distinguishing characteristic of this particular species of justification is, I submit, its essential or internal relationship to the cognitive goal of truth. Cognitive doings are epistemically justified, on this conception, only if and to the extent that they are aimed at this goal—which means roughly that one accepts all and only beliefs which one has good reason to think are true. To accept a belief in the absence of such a reason, however appealing or even mandatory such acceptance might be from other standpoints, is to neglect the pursuit of truth; such acceptance is, one might say, *epistemically irresponsible*. My contention is that the idea of being epistemically responsible is the core of the concept of epistemic justification.

A corollary of this conception of epistemic justification is that a satisfactory defense of a particular standard of epistemic justification must consist in showing it to be truth-conducive, i.e., in showing that accepting beliefs in accordance with its dictates is likely to lead to truth (and more likely than any proposed alternative). Without such a meta-justification, a proposed standard of epistemic justification lacks any underlying rationale. Why after all should an epistemically responsible inquirer prefer justified beliefs to unjustified ones, if not that the former are more likely to be true? To insist that a certain belief is epistemically justified, while confessing in the same breath that this fact about it provides no good reason to think that it is true, would be to render nugatory the whole concept of epistemic justification.

These general remarks about epistemic justification apply in full measure to any strong foundationist position and to its constituent account of basic beliefs. If basic beliefs are to provide a secure foundation for empirical knowledge, if inference from them is to be the sole basis for the justification of other empirical beliefs, then that feature, whatever it may be, in virtue of which a belief qualifies as basic must also constitute a good reason for thinking that the belief is true. If we let 'Φ' represent this feature, then for a belief B to qualify as basic in an acceptable foundationist account, the premises of the following justificatory argument must themselves be at least justified:

(i)   Belief B has feature Φ.
(ii) Beliefs having feature Φ are highly likely to be true.

Therefore, B is highly likely to be true.

Notice further that while either premise taken separately might turn out to be justifiable on an *a priori* basis (depending on the particular choice of Φ), it seems clear that they could not both be thus justifiable. For B is *ex hypothesi* an empirical belief, and it is hard to see how a particular empirical belief could be justified on a purely *a priori* basis. And if we now assume, reasonably enough, that for B to be justified for a particular person (at a particular time) it is necessary, not merely that a justification for B exist in the abstract, but that the person in question be in cognitive possession of that justification, we get the result that B is not basic after all since its justification depends on that of at least one other empirical belief. If this is correct, strong foundationism is untenable as a solution to the regress problem (and an analogous argument will show weak foundationism to be similarly untenable).

The foregoing argument is, no doubt, exceedingly obvious. But how is the strong foundationist to answer it? *Prima facie,* there seem to be only two general sorts of answer which are even remotely plausible, so long as the strong foundationist remains within the confines of the traditional conception of knowledge, avoids tacitly embracing skepticism, and does not attempt the heroic task of arguing that an empirical belief could be justified on a purely *a priori* basis. First, he might argue that although it is indeed necessary for a belief to be justified and *a fortiori* for it to be basic that a justifying argument of the sort schematized above be in principle available in the situation, it is *not* always necessary that the person for whom the belief is basic (or anyone else) know or even justifiably believe that it is available; instead, in the case of basic beliefs at least, it is sufficient that the premises for an argument of that general sort (or for some favored particular variety of such argument) merely be *true,* whether or not that person (or anyone else) justifiably believes that they are true. Second, he might grant that it is necessary both that such justification

exist and that the person for whom the belief is basic be in cognitive possession of it, but insist that his cognitive grasp of the premises required for that justification does not involve further empirical beliefs which would then require justification, but instead involves cognitive states of a more rudimentary sort which do not themselves require justification: *intuitions or immediate apprehensions.* I will consider each of these alternatives in turn.

III

The philosopher who has come the closest to an explicit advocacy of the view that basic beliefs may be justified even though the person for whom they are basic is not in any way in cognitive possession of the appropriate justifying argument is D. M. Armstrong. In his recent book, *Belief, Truth and Knowledge,* Armstrong presents a version of the epistemic regress problem (though one couched in terms of knowledge rather than justification) and defends what he calls an "Externalist" solution:

> According to 'Externalist' accounts of non-inferential knowledge, what makes a true non-inferential belief a case of *knowledge* is some natural relation which holds between the belief-state . . . and the situation which makes the belief true. It is a matter of a certain relation holding between the believer and the world [157].

Armstrong's own candidate for this "natural relation" is "that there must be a *law-like connection* between the state of affairs *Bap* [i.e. *a*'s believing that *p*] and the state of affairs that makes '*p*' true such that, given *Bap*, it must be the case that *p*." [166] A similar view seems to be implicit in Dretske's account of perceptual knowledge in *Seeing and Knowing,* with the variation that Dretske requires for knowledge not only that the relation in question obtain, but also that the putative knower *believe* that it obtains—though *not* that this belief be justified. In addition, it seems likely that various views of an ordinary-language stripe which appeal to facts about how language is learned either to justify basic belief or to support the claim that no justification is required would, if pushed, turn out to be positions of this general sort. Here I shall mainly confine myself to Armstrong, who is the only one of these philosophers who is explicitly concerned with the regress problem.

There is, however, some uncertainty as to how views of this sort in general and Armstrong's view in particular are properly to be interpreted. On the one hand, Armstrong might be taken as offering an account of how basic beliefs (and perhaps others as well) satisfy the adequate-justification condition for knowledge; while on the other hand, he might be taken as simply repudiating the traditional conception of knowledge and the associated concept of epistemic justification, and offering a surrogate conception in its place—one which better accords with the "naturalistic" world-view which Armstrong prefers. But it is only when understood in the former way that externalism (to adopt Armstrong's useful term) is of any immediate interest here, since it is only on that interpretation that it constitutes a version of foundationism and offers a direct response to the anti-foundationist argument set out above. Thus I shall mainly focus on this interpretation of externalism, remarking only briefly at the end of the present section on the alternative one.

Understood in this way, the externalist solution to the regress problem is quite simple: the person who has a basic belief need not be in possession of any justified reason for his belief and indeed, except in Dretske's version, need not even think that there is such a reason; the status of his belief as constituting knowledge (if true) depends solely on the external relation and not at all on his subjective view of the situation. Thus there are no further empirical beliefs in need of justification and no regress.

Now it is clear that such an externalist position succeeds in avoiding the regress problem and the anti-foundationist argument. What may well be doubted, however, is whether this avoidance deserves to be considered a *solution,* rather than an essentially *ad hoc* evasion, of the problem. Plainly the sort of "external" relation which Armstrong has in mind would, if known, provide a basis for a justifying argument along the lines sketched earlier, roughly as follows:

(i)   Belief B is an instance of kind K.
(ii) Beliefs of kind K are connected in a law-like way with the sorts of states of affairs which would make them true, and therefore are highly likely to be true.

Therefore, B is highly likely to be true.

But precisely what generates the regress problem in the first place is the requirement that for a belief B to be epistemically justified for a given person P, it is necessary, not just that there be justifiable or even true premises available in the situation which could in principle provide a basis for a justification of B, but that P himself know or at least justifiably believe some such set of premises and thus be in a position to employ the corresponding argument. The externalist position seems to amount merely to waiving this general requirement in cases where the justification takes a certain form, and the question is why this should be acceptable in these cases when it is not acceptable generally. (If it were acceptable generally, then it would seem that any true belief would be justified for any person, and the distinction between knowledge and true belief would collapse.) Such a move seems rather analogous to solving a regress of causes by simply stipulating that although most events must have a cause, events of a certain kind need not.

Whatever plausibility attaches to externalism seems to derive from the fact that if the external relation in question genuinely obtains, then P will not go wrong in accepting the belief, and it is, in a sense, not an accident that this is so. But it remains unclear how these facts are supposed to justify P's acceptance of B. It is clear, of course, that an external observer who knew both that P accepted B and that there was a law-like connection between such acceptance and the truth of B would be in a position to construct an argument to justify *his own* acceptance of B. P could thus serve as a useful epistemic instrument, a kind of cognitive thermometer, for such an external observer (and in fact the example of a thermometer is exactly the analogy which Armstrong employs to illustrate the relationship which is supposed to obtain between the person who has the belief and the external state of affairs [166ff.]). But P himself has no reason at all for thinking that *B* is likely to be true. From his perspective, it *is* an accident that the belief is true.[8] And thus his acceptance of *B* is no more rational or responsible from an epistemic standpoint than would be the acceptance of a subjectively similar belief for which the external relation in question failed to obtain.[9]

Nor does it seem to help matters to move from Armstrong's version of externalism, which requires only that the requisite relationship between the believer and the world obtain, to the superficially less radical version apparently held by Dretske, which requires that *P* also believe that the external relation obtains, but does not require that this latter belief be justified. This view may seem slightly less implausible, since it at least requires that the person have some idea, albeit unjustified, of why *B* is likely to be true. But this change is not enough to save externalism. One way to see this is to suppose that the person believes the requisite relation to obtain on some totally irrational and irrelevant basis, e.g. as a result of reading tea leaves or studying astrological charts. If *B* were an ordinary, non-basic belief, such a situation would surely preclude its being justified, and it is hard to see why the result should be any different for an allegedly basic belief.

Thus it finally seems possible to make sense of externalism only by construing the externalist as simply abandoning the traditional notion of epistemic justification and along with it anything resembling the traditional conception of knowledge. (As already remarked, this may be precisely what the proponents of externalism intend to be doing, though most of them are not very clear on this point.) Thus consider Armstrong's final summation of his conception of knowledge:

> *Knowledge of the truth of particular matters of fact* is a belief which must be true, where the 'must' is a matter of law-like necessity. Such knowledge is a reliable representation or 'mapping' of reality [220].

Nothing is said here of reasons or justification or evidence or having the right to be sure. Indeed the whole idea, central to the western epistemological tradition, of knowledge as essentially the product of reflective, critical, and rational inquiry has seemingly vanished without a trace. It is possible of course that such an altered conception of knowledge may be inescapable or even in some way desirable, but it constitutes a solution to the regress problem or any problem arising out of the traditional conception of knowledge only in the radical and relatively uninteresting sense that to reject that conception is also to reject the problems arising out of it. In this essay, I shall confine myself to less radical solutions.

IV

The externalist solution just discussed represents a very recent approach to the justification of basic beliefs. The second view to be considered is, in contrast, so venerable that it deserves to be called the standard foundationist solution to the problem in question. I refer of course to the traditional doctrine of cognitive givenness, which has played a central role in epistemological discussions at least since Descartes. In recent years, however, the concept of the given, like foundationism itself, has come under serious attack. One upshot of the resulting discussion has been a realization that there are many different notions of givenness, related to each other in complicated ways, which almost certainly do not stand or fall together. Thus it will be well to begin by formulating the precise notion of givenness which is relevant in the present context and distinguishing it from some related conceptions.

In the context of the epistemic regress problem, givenness amounts to the idea that basic beliefs are justified by reference not to further *beliefs*, but rather to states of affairs in the world which are "immediately apprehended" or "directly presented" or "intuited." This justification by reference to non-cognitive states of affairs thus allegedly avoids the need for any further justification and thereby stops the regress. In a way, the basic gambit of givenism (as I shall call positions of this sort) thus resembles that of the externalist positions considered above. In both cases the justificatory appeal to further beliefs which generates the regress problem is avoided for basic beliefs by an appeal directly to the noncognitive world; the crucial difference is that for the givenist, unlike the externalist, the justifying state of affairs in the world is allegedly apprehended *in some way* by the believer.

The givenist position to be considered here is significantly weaker than more familiar versions of the doctrine of givenness in at least two different respects. In the first place, the present version does not claim that the given (or, better, the apprehension thereof) is certain or even incorrigible. As discussed above, these stronger claims are inessential to the strong foundationist solution to the regress problem. If they have any importance at all in this context it is only because, as we shall see, they might be thought to be entailed by the only very obvious intuitive picture of how the view is supposed to work. In the second place, givenism as understood here does not involve the usual stipulation that only one's private mental and sensory states can be given. There may or may not be other reasons for thinking that this is in fact the case, but such a restriction is not part of the position itself. Thus both positions like that of C. I. Lewis, for whom the given is restricted to private states apprehended with certainty, and positions like that of Quinton, for whom ordinary physical states of affairs are given with no claim of certainty or incorrigibility being involved, will count as versions of givenism.

As already noted, the idea of givenness has been roundly criticized in recent philosophical discussion and widely dismissed as a piece of philosophical mythology. But much at least of this criticism has to do with the claim of certainty on behalf of the given or with the restriction to private, subjective states. And some of it at least has been mainly concerned with issues in the philosophy of mind which are only distantly related to our present epistemological concerns. Thus even if the objections offered are cogent against other and stronger versions of givenness, it remains unclear whether and how they apply to the more modest version at issue here. The possibility suggests itself that modest givenness may not be a myth, even if more ambitious varieties are, a result which would give the epistemological foundationist all he really needs, even though he has usually, in a spirit of philosophical greed, sought considerably more. In what follows, however, I shall sketch a line of argument which, if correct, will show that even modest givenism is an untenable position.

The argument to be developed depends on a problem within the givenist position which is surprisingly easy to overlook. I shall therefore proceed in the following way. I shall first state the problem in an initial way, then illustrate it by showing how it arises in one recent version of givenism, and finally consider whether any plausible solution is possible. (It will be useful for the purposes of this discussion to make two simplifying assumptions, without which the argument would be more complicated, but not essentially altered. First, I shall assume that the basic belief which is to be justified by reference to the given or immediately apprehended state of affairs is just the belief that this same state of affairs obtains. Second, I shall assume that the given or immediately apprehended state of affairs is not itself a belief or other cognitive state.)

Consider then an allegedly basic belief that-*p* which is supposed to be justified by reference to a given or immediately apprehended state of affairs that-*p*. Clearly what justifies the belief is not the state of affairs simpliciter, for to say that would be to return to a form of externalism. For the givenist, what justifies the belief is the *immediate apprehension* or *intuition* of the state of affairs. Thus we seem to have three items present in the situation: the belief, the state of affairs which is the object of the belief, and the intuition or immediate apprehension of that state of affairs. The problem to be raised revolves around the nature of the last of these items, the intuition or immediate apprehension (hereafter I will use mainly the former term). It *seems* to be a cognitive state, perhaps somehow of a more rudimentary sort than a belief, which involves the thesis or assertion that-*p*. Now if this is correct, it is easy enough to understand in a rough sort of way how an intuition can serve to justify a belief with this same assertive content. The problem is to understand why the intuition, involving as it does the cognitive thesis that-*p,* does not *itself* require justification. And if the answer is offered that the intuition is justified by reference to the state of affairs that-*p*, then the question will be why this would not require a second intuition or other apprehension of the state of affairs to justify the original one. For otherwise one and the same cognitive state must somehow constitute both an apprehension of the state of affairs and a justification of that very apprehension, thus pulling itself up by its own cognitive bootstraps. One is reminded here of Chisholm's claim that certain cognitive states justify themselves but that extremely paradoxical remark hardly constitutes an explanation of how this is possible.

If, on the other hand, an intuition is not a cognitive state and thus involves no cognitive grasp of the state of affairs in question, then the need for a justification for the intuition is obviated, but at the serious cost of making it difficult to see how the intuition is supposed to justify the belief. If the person in question has no cognitive grasp of that state of affairs (or of any other) by virtue of having such an intuition, then how does the intuition give him a *reason* for thinking that his belief is true or likely to be true? We seem again to be back to an externalist position, which it was the whole point of the category of intuition or givenness to avoid.

As an illustration of this problem, consider Quinton's version of givenism, as outlined in his book *The Nature of Things*. As noted above, basic beliefs may, according to Quinton, concern ordinary perceptible states of affairs and need not be certain or incorrigible. (Quinton uses the phrase "intuitive belief" as I have been using "basic belief" and calls the linguistic expression of an intuitive belief a "basic statement"; he also seems to pay very little attention to the difference between beliefs and statements, shifting freely back and forth between them, and I will generally follow him in this.) Thus "this book is red" might, in an appropriate context, be a basic statement expressing a basic or intuitive belief. But how are such basic statements (or the correlative beliefs) supposed to be justified? Here Quinton's account, beyond the insistence that they are not justified by reference to further beliefs, is seriously unclear. He says rather vaguely that the person is "aware" [129] or "directly aware" [139] of the appropriate state of affairs, or that he has "direct knowledge" [126] of it, but he gives no real account of the nature or epistemological status of this state of "direct awareness" or "direct knowledge," though it seems clear that it is supposed to be a cognitive state of some kind. (In particular, it is not clear what "direct" means, over and above "non-inferential.")

The difficulty with Quinton's account comes out most clearly in his discussion of its relation to the correspondence theory of truth:

> The theory of basic statements is closely connected with the correspondence theory of truth. In its classical form that theory holds that to each true statement, whatever its form may be, a fact of the same form corresponds. The theory of basic statements indicates the point at which correspondence is established, at which the system of beliefs makes its justifying contact with the world [139].

And further on he remarks that the truth of basic statements "is directly determined by their correspondence with fact" [143]. (It is clear that "determined" here means "epistemically determined.") Now it is a familiar but still forceful idealist objection to the correspondence theory of truth that if the theory were correct we could never know whether any of our beliefs were true, since we have no perspective outside our system of beliefs from which to see that they do or do not correspond. Quinton, however, seems to suppose rather blithely that intuition or direct awareness provides just such a perspective, from which we can in some cases apprehend both beliefs and world and judge whether or not they correspond. And he further supposes that the issue of justification somehow does not arise for apprehensions made from this perspective, though without giving any account of how or why this is so.

My suggestion here is that no such account can be given. As indicated above, the givenist is caught in a fundamental dilemma: if his intuitions or immediate apprehensions are construed as cognitive, then they will be both capable of giving justification and in need of it themselves; if they are noncognitive, then they do not need justification but are also apparently incapable of providing it. This, at bottom, is why epistemological givenness is a myth.

Once the problem is clearly realized, the only possible solution seems to be to split the difference by claiming that an intuition is a semi-cognitive or quasi-cognitive state, which resembles a belief in its capacity to confer justification, while differing from a belief in not requiring justification itself. In fact, some such conception seems to be implicit in most if not all givenist positions. But when stated thus baldly, this "solution" to the problem seems hopelessly contrived and *ad hoc*. If such a move is acceptable, one is inclined to expostulate, then once again any sort of regress could be solved in similar fashion. Simply postulate a final term in the regress which is sufficiently similar to the previous terms to satisfy, with respect to the penultimate term, the sort of need or impetus which originally generated the regress; but which is different enough from previous terms so as not itself to require satisfaction by a further term. Thus we would have semi-events, which could cause but need not be caused; semi-explanatia, which could explain but need not be explained; and semi-beliefs, which could justify but need not be justified. The point is not that such a move is always incorrect (though I suspect that it is), but simply that the nature and possibility of such a convenient regress-stopper needs at the very least to be clearly and convincingly established and explained before it can constitute a satisfactory solution to any regress problem.

The main account which has usually been offered by givenists of such semi-cognitive states is well suggested by the terms in which immediate or intuitive apprehensions are described: "immediate," "direct," "presentation," etc. The underlying idea here is that of *confrontation:* in intuition, mind or consciousness is directly confronted with its object, without the intervention of any sort of intermediary. It is in this sense that the object is *given* to the mind. The root metaphor underlying this whole picture is vision: mind or consciousness is likened to an immaterial eye, and the object of intuitive awareness is that which is directly before the mental eye and open to its gaze. If this metaphor were to be taken seriously, it would become relatively simple to explain how there can be a cognitive state which can justify but does not require justification. (If the metaphor is to be taken seriously enough to do the foundationist any real good, it becomes plausible to hold that the intuitive cognitive states which result would after all have to be infallible. For if all need for justification is to be precluded, the envisaged relation of confrontation seemingly must be conceived as too intimate to allow any possibility of error. To the extent that this is so, the various arguments which have been offered against the no-

tion of infallible cognitive states count also against this version of givenism.)

Unfortunately, however, it seems clear that the mental eye metaphor will not stand serious scrutiny. The mind, whatever else it may be, is not an eye or, so far as we know, anything like an eye. Ultimately the metaphor is just far too simple to be even minimally adequate to the complexity of mental phenomena and to the variety of conditions upon which such phenomena depend. This is not to deny that there is considerable intuitive appeal to the confrontational model, especially as applied to perceptual consciousness, but only to insist that this appeal is far too vague in its import to adequately support the very specific sorts of epistemological results which the strong foundationist needs. In particular, even if empirical knowledge at some point involves some sort of confrontation or seeming confrontation, this by itself provides no clear reason for attributing epistemic justification or reliability, let alone certainty, to the cognitive states, whatever they may be called, which result.

Moreover, quite apart from the vicissitudes of the mental eye metaphor, there are powerful independent reasons for thinking that the attempt to defend givenism by appeal to the idea of a semi-cognitive or quasi-cognitive state is fundamentally misguided. The basic idea, after all, is to distinguish two aspects of a cognitive state, its capacity to justify other states and its own need for justification, and then try to find a state which possesses only the former aspect and not the latter. But it seems clear on reflection that these two aspects cannot be separated, that it is one and the same feature of a cognitive state, viz., its assertive content, which both enables it to confer justification on other states and also requires that it be justified itself. If this is right, then it does no good to introduce semi-cognitive states in an attempt to justify basic beliefs, since to whatever extent such a state is capable of conferring justification, it will to that very same extent require justification. Thus even if such states do exist, they are of no help to the givenist in attempting to answer the objection at issue here.

Hence the givenist response to the antifoundationist argument seems to fail. There seems to be no way to explain how a basic cognitive state, whether called a belief or an intuition, can be directly justified by the world without lapsing back into externalism—and from there into skepticism. I shall conclude with three further comments aimed at warding off certain likely sorts of misunderstanding. First. It is natural in this connection to attempt to justify basic beliefs by appealing to *experience*. But there is a familiar ambiguity in the term "experience," which in fact glosses over the crucial distinction upon which the foregoing argument rests. Thus "experience" may mean either an *experiencing* (i.e., a cognitive state) or something *experienced* (i.e., an object of cognition). And once this ambiguity is resolved, the concept of experience seems to be of no particular help to the givenist. Second. I have concentrated, for the sake of simplicity, on Quinton's version of givenism in which ordinary physical states of affairs are among the things which are given. But the logic of the argument would be essentially the same if it were applied to a more traditional version like Lewis's in which it is private experiences which are given; and I cannot see that the end result would be different—though it might be harder to discern, especially in cases where the allegedly basic belief is a belief about another cognitive state. Third. Notice carefully that the problem raised here with respect to givenism is a logical problem (in a broad sense of "logical"). Thus it would be a mistake to think that it can be solved simply by indicating some sort of state which seems intuitively to have the appropriate sorts of characteristics; the problem is to understand how it is *possible* for any state to have those characteristics. (The mistake would be analogous to one occasionally made in connection with the free-will problem: the mistake of attempting to solve the logical problem of how an action can be not determined but also not merely random by indicating a subjective act of effort or similar state, which seems intuitively to satisfy such a description.)

Thus foundationism appears to be doomed by its own internal momentum. No account seems to be available of how an empirical belief can be genuinely justified in an epistemic sense, while avoiding all reference to further empirical beliefs or cognitions which themselves would require justification. How then is the epistemic regress problem to be solved? The natural direction to look for an answer is to the coherence theory of empirical knowledge

and the associated non-linear conception of justification which were briefly mentioned above. But arguments by elimination are dangerous at best: there may be further alternatives which have not yet been formulated, and the possibility still threatens that the epistemic regress problem may in the end be of aid and comfort only to the skeptic.

Notes

[1] Roderick M. Chisholm, *Theory of Knowledge*, 1st. ed., p. 30.

[2] Anthony Quinton, *The Nature of Things*, p. 119. This is an extremely venerable argument, which has played a central role in epistemological discussion at least since Aristotle's statement of it in the *Posterior Analytics*, Book I, ch. 2–3. (Some have found an anticipation of the argument in the *Theaetetus* at 209E–210B, but Plato's worry in that passage appears to be that the proposed definition of knowledge is circular, not that it leads to an infinite regress of justification.)

[3] "Adequately justified" because a belief could be justified to some degree without being sufficiently justified to qualify as knowledge (if true). But it is far from clear just how much justification is needed for adequacy. Virtually all recent epistemologists agree that certainty is not required. But the lottery paradox shows that adequacy cannot be understood merely in terms of some specified level of probability. (For a useful account of the lottery paradox, see Robert Ackermann, *Belief and Knowledge*, pp. 39–50). Armstrong, in *Belief, Truth and Knowledge*, argues that what is required is that one's reasons for the belief be "conclusive," but the precise meaning of this is less than clear. Ultimately, it may be that the concept of knowledge is simply too crude for refined epistemological discussion, so that it may be necessary to speak instead of degrees of belief and corresponding degrees of justification. I shall assume (perhaps controversially) that the proper solution to this problem will not affect the issues to be discussed here, and speak merely of the reasons or justification making the belief *highly likely* to be true, without trying to say exactly what this means.

[4] See Edmund Gettier, "Is Justified True Belief Knowledge?" [Reading IV.1—Ed.]. Also Ackermann, *Belief and Knowledge*, chap. 5, and the corresponding references.

[5] For simplicity, I will speak of inference relations as obtaining between beliefs rather than, more accurately, between the propositions which are believed. "Inference" is to be understood here in a very broad sense; any relation between two beliefs which allows one, if accepted, to serve as a good reason for accepting the other will count as inferential.

[6] The original statement of the non-linear view was by Bernard Bosanquet in *Implication and Linear Inference*

(London, 1920). For more recent discussions, see Gilbert Harman, *Thought;* and Nicholas Rescher, "Foundationalism, Coherentism, and the Idea of Cognitive Systematization."

[7] For discussions of weak foundationalism, see Bertrand Russell, *Human Knowledge,* part 2, chap. 2, and part 5, chaps. 6 and 7; Nelson Goodman, "Sense and Certainty," *Philosophical Review* 61 (1952): 160–167; Israel Scheffler, *Science and Subjectivity,* chap. 5; and Roderick Firth, "Coherence, Certainty, and Epistemic Priority."

[8] One way to put this point is to say that whether a belief is likely to be true or whether in contrast it is an accident that it is true depends significantly on how the belief is described. Thus it might be true of one and the same belief that it is "a belief connected in a law-like way with the state of affairs which it describes" and also that it is "a belief adopted on the basis of no apparent evidence"; and it might be likely to be true on the first description and unlikely to be true on the second. The claim here is that it

is the believer's own conception which should be considered in deciding whether the belief is justified. (Something analogous seems to be true in ethics: the moral worth of a person's action is correctly to be judged only in terms of that person's subjective conception of what he is doing and not in light of what happens, willy-nilly, to result from it.)

[9] Notice, however, that if beliefs standing in the proper external relation should happen to possess some subjectively distinctive feature (such as being spontaneous and highly compelling to the believer), and if the believer were to notice empirically, that beliefs having this feature were true a high proportion of the time, he would then be in a position to construct a justification for a new belief of that sort along the lines sketched at the end of section II. But of course a belief justified in that way would no longer be basic.

V.4 Holistic Coherentism

Laurence BonJour

In this essay Laurence BonJour attempts to set forth a version of coherentism that avoids the weaknesses of previous versions. Whereas these versions were *linear*—that is, the justification moves in a circle, so that the first premise ends up as the last one, the justifying premise—BonJour's version is *holistic* in that the whole systematic set of inferentially related beliefs mutually supports each individual belief. BonJour next takes us through the various steps of the argument and meets objections to his proposal. Finally, he further marks off his version by showing how it meets the isolation criticism, namely that coherentism lacks a tie-in with empirical beliefs. BonJour's version integrates an observational requirement, which meets this need but still manages to derive its authority from inferential relations with other beliefs.

In a paper written for a commemorative symposium on the philosophy of C. I. Lewis, Roderick Firth remarks that Lewis liked to confront his Harvard epistemology students with a fundamental

Reprinted from *Philosophical Studies* 30 (1976): 281–312, by permission of the publisher and the author. Copyright 1976, D. Reidel Publishing Company. [Footnotes edited. —Ed.]

choice between a foundation theory of knowledge based on "the given," like that advocated so ably in Lewis's own books, and "a coherence theory like that of Bosanquet."[1] As Firth notes, there are many different philosophical views which have been called "coherence theories," including theories of truth and of meaning; but what Lewis seems to have had primarily in mind is a coherence theory of *epistemic justification:* the view that the epistemic warrant or authority of empirical statements derives *entirely* from coherence and not at all from any sort of "foundation." Since Lewis's strong version of foundationism is by now everywhere in eclipse, it seems appropriate to examine the Bosanquetian alternative.

The purpose of this essay is to explore, and tentatively defend, a view of the Bosanquetian sort, which I shall call "the coherence theory of empirical knowledge" (hereafter CTEK). As discussed here, the CTEK is not to be identified with any specific historical view, though it has obvious affinities with some. It is intended rather as an idealized reconstruction of a relatively pure coherence theory, one which avoids all versions of foundationism.[2]

Views like the CTEK, though often employed as dialectical bogeymen, have rarely been treated as serious epistemological alternatives, since they have been thought to be subject to obvious and overwhelming objections. Thus the essential first step in a defense of such a view is to provide a sketch of its overall shape and rationale and show on this basis that these supposedly fatal objections can be answered. Such a preliminary defense of the CTEK, aimed at establishing its epistemological viability, is the goal of this essay. . . .

II

The underlying motivation for the CTEK is the conviction that all foundationist accounts of empirical knowledge are untenable. The crucial problem is much the same for both versions of foundationism: what is the source or rationale of the non-inferential epistemic warrant which allegedly attaches to a basic belief (in strong foundationism) or to an initially credible belief (in weak foundationism)? If an empirical, contingent belief *B,* one which is not knowable *a priori,* is to have such warrant for a given person, it seems that he must have some *reason* for thinking that *B* is true or likely to be true (the degree of likelihood required depending on whether *B* is held to be basic or only initially credible). And it is hard to see what such a reason could consist in other than the justified be-

liefs both (a) that *B* has some property or feature Φ, and (b) that beliefs having the property or feature Φ are likely, to the appropriate degree, to be true. Such justified beliefs would provide the basis for a justifying argument for *B,* and reliance on them would of course mean that *B* was not basic or initially credible after all. But how can a person be justified in accepting a contingent belief if he does not believe, and *a fortiori* does not know, anything about it which makes it at all likely to be true? A standard of epistemic justification which yields this result would seem clearly to have severed the vital connection between epistemic justification and truth, thus leaving itself without any ultimate rationale. It is for reasons of this sort that the CTEK holds that the justification of particular empirical beliefs is always inferential in character, and that there can in principle be no basic (or initially credible) empirical beliefs and no foundation for empirical knowledge.

This picture of the CTEK, however, though accurate as far as it goes, is seriously misleading because it neglects the systematic or holistic character of the view. The best way to see this is to return to the regress problem.

Having rejected foundationism, the CTEK must hold that the regress of justification moves in a circle (or at least a closed curve), since this is the only alternative to a genuinely infinite regress involving an infinite number of distinct beliefs. But this response to the regress problem will seem obviously inadequate to one who approaches the issue with foundationist preconceptions. For surely, it will be argued, such an appeal to circularity does not solve the regress problem. Each step in the regress is an argument whose premises must be justified *before* they can confer justification on the conclusion. To say that the regress moves in a circle is to say that at some point one (or more) of the beliefs which figured earlier as conclusions is now appealed to as a justifying premise. And this situation, far from solving the regress problem, yields the patently absurd result that the justification of such a belief (qua conclusion) depends on *its own* logically prior justification (qua premise): it cannot be justified unless it is *already* justified. And thus neither it nor anything which depends on it can be justified. Since justification is always finally circular in this way according to the CTEK, there can be on that view no genuine justification and no knowledge.

The tacit premise in this seemingly devastating line of argument is the idea that inferential justification is essentially *linear* in character, involving a linear sequence of beliefs along which warrant is transferred from the earlier beliefs in the sequence to the later beliefs via connections of inference. It is this linear conception of inferential justification that ultimately generates the regress problem. If it is accepted, the idea that justification moves in a circle will be obviously unacceptable, and only *strong* foundationism will be left as an alternative. (Even weak foundationism cannot accept a purely linear view of justification, since its initially credible beliefs are not sufficiently justified to serve as first premises for everything else.) Thus the basic response of the CTEK to the regress problem is not the appeal to circularity, which would be futile by itself, but rather the rejection of the linear conception of inferential justification.[3]

The alternative is a holistic or systematic conception of inferential justification (and hence of empirical justification in general, since all empirical justification is inferential for the CTEK): beliefs are justified by being inferentially related to other beliefs in the overall context of a coherent system. To make this view clear, it is necessary to distinguish two levels at which issues of justification can be raised. Thus the issue at hand may be merely the justification of a particular belief, or a small set of beliefs, in the context of a cognitive system whose overall justification is taken for granted; or it may be the global issue of the justification of the cognitive system itself. According to the CTEK it is the latter, global issue which is fundamental for the determination of epistemic justification. Confusion arises, however, because it is only issues of the former, more limited, sort which tend to be raised explicitly in actual cases.

At the level at which only the justification of a particular belief (or small set of such beliefs) is at issue, justification appears linear. A given justificandum belief is justified explicitly by citing other premise-beliefs from which it may be inferred. Such premise-beliefs can themselves be challenged, with justification being provided for them in the same fashion. But there is no serious danger of a regress at this level since the justification of the overall epistemic system (and thus of at least most of its component beliefs) is *ex hypothesi* not at issue. One thus quickly reaches premise-beliefs which are dialectically acceptable in that context.

If on the other hand no dialectically acceptable stopping point is reached, if the premise-beliefs which are offered by way of justification continue to be challenged, then the epistemic dialogue would, if ideally continued, eventually move in a circle, giving the appearance of a regress and in effect challenging the entire cognitive system. At this global level, however, the CTEK no longer conceives the relation between the various particular beliefs as one of linear dependence, but rather as one of mutual or reciprocal support. There is no ultimate relation of epistemic priority among the members of such a system and consequently no basis for a true regress. The component beliefs are so related that each can be justified in terms of the others; the direction in which the justifying argument actually moves depends on which belief is under scrutiny in a particular context. The apparent circle of justification is not vicious because the justification of particular beliefs depends finally not on other particular beliefs, as in the linear conception of justification, but on the overall system and its coherence.

Thus the fully explicit justification of a particular belief would involve four distinct steps of argument, as follows:

1. The inferability of that particular belief from other particular beliefs, and further inference relations among particular beliefs.

2. The coherence of the overall system of beliefs.

3. The justification of the overall system of beliefs.

4. The justification of the particular belief in question, by virtue of its membership in the system.

According to the CTEK, each of these steps depends on the ones which precede it. It is the neglecting of steps 2 and 3, the ones pertaining explicitly to the cognitive system, that is the primary source of the linear conception of justification and thus of the regress problem. This is a seductive mistake. Since the very same inferential connections between particular beliefs are involved in both step 1 and step 4, it is fatally easy to conflate these two, leaving out the two intermediary steps which involve explicit reference to the system.

Of the three transitions represented in this schematic argument, only the third, from step 3 to step 4, is reasonably unproblematic, depending as it does on the inferential relations that obtain between the justificandum belief and other beliefs of the system; in effect it is this transition that is made when an inferential justification is offered in an ordinary context. But the other two transitions are highly problematic, and the issues which they raise are crucial for understanding and assessing the CTEK.

The transition from step 1 to step 2, from the inference relations obtaining between particular beliefs to the coherence of the system as a whole, is rendered problematic by the serious vagueness and unclarity of the central conception of coherence. It is clear that coherence depends on the various sorts of inferential, evidential, and explanatory relations which exist among the members of a set of propositions, especially upon the more systematic of these. Thus various detailed investigations by philosophers and logicians of such topics as explanation, confirmation, etc., may be taken to provide some of the essential ingredients of a general account of coherence. But the main job of giving such a general account, and in particular one which will provide a basis for *comparative* assessments of coherence, has scarcely been begun. Nevertheless, while the absence of such an account represents a definite lacuna in the CTEK, it cannot provide the basis for a decisive or even a very serious objection to the theory. This is so because coherence (or something very closely resembling it) is, and seemingly must be, a basic ingredient of rival epistemological theories as well. We have already seen that weak foundationism makes an explicit appeal to coherence. And it seems that even strong foundationism must appeal to coherence if it is to make sense of knowledge of the past, theoretical knowledge, etc. In fact, all of the leading proponents of alternatives to the CTEK employ the notion of coherence (sometimes by other names)[4] in their accounts.

Thus the problem of giving an adequate account of coherence is one which may safely be neglected by the sort of preliminary defense of the CTEK which is offered here. There are, however, some essential points concerning the concept which should be noted. First, coherence is not to be equated with consistency. A coherent system must be consistent, but a consistent system need not be very coherent. Coherence has to do with systematic connections between the components of a system, not just with their failure to conflict. Second, coherence will obviously be a matter of degree. For a system of beliefs to be justified, according to the CTEK, it must not be merely coherent to some extent, but more coherent than any currently available alternative. Third, coherence is closely connected with the concept of explanation. Exactly what the connection is I shall not try to say here. But it is clear that the coherence of a system is enhanced to the extent that observed facts (in a sense to be explicated below) can be explained within it and reduced to the extent that this is not the case. Since explanation and prediction are at the very least closely allied, much the same thing can be said about prediction as well.

The problems relating to the other problematic transition in the schematic argument, that from step 2 to step 3, are more immediately serious. What is at issue here is the fundamental question of the connection between coherence and justification: why, if a body of beliefs is coherent, is it thereby epistemically justified? The force of this question is best brought out by formulating three related objections to the CTEK, centering on this point, which are usually thought to destroy all plausibility which it might otherwise have:

(I) According to the CTEK, the system of beliefs which constitutes empirical knowledge is justified *solely* by reference to coherence. But coherence will never suffice to pick out one system of beliefs, since there will always be many other alternative, incompatible systems of belief which are equally coherent and hence equally justified according to the CTEK.

(II) According to the CTEK, empirical beliefs are justified only in terms of relations to other beliefs and to the system of beliefs; at no point does any relation to the world come in. But this means that the alleged system of empirical knowledge is deprived of all *input* from the world. Surely such a self-enclosed system of beliefs cannot constitute empirical knowledge.

(III) An adequate epistemological theory must establish a connection between its account of justification and its account of *truth;* i.e., it must be shown that justification, as viewed by that theory, is *truth-conducive,* that one who seeks justified beliefs is at least likely to find true ones. But the only way in which the CTEK can do this is by adopting a coherence theory of truth and the absurd idealistic metaphysics which goes along with it.

Of these three objections, (III) is the most basic and (I) is the most familiar. It is (II), however, which must be dealt with first, since the answer to it is essential for dealing with the other two objections. Fundamentally, the point made in (II) must simply be accepted: there must be some sort of input into the cognitive system from the world. Thus the answer to (II) must consist in showing how the CTEK can allow for such input. I shall attempt to lay the groundwork for this in the next section by offering a schematic account of how the crucial concept of *observation* fits into the CTEK, following which I shall return in the final section to the objections.

▬▬

III

It may be thought that the suggestion that there is room in the CTEK for an appeal to observation involves an immediate contradiction in terms. For surely, the argument might go, it is essential to the very conception of observation that observational beliefs are *non-inferential* in character; and it is equally essential to the conception of the CTEK, as explained above, that *all* justified beliefs are *inferential.* Thus the CTEK can accord no significant epistemic role to observation (which surely constitutes an immediate *reductio ad absurdum* of the theory).

But this argument is mistaken. It rests on a confusion between two quite different ways in which a belief may be said to be inferential (or non-inferential). In the first place, there is the issue of how the belief was arrived at, of its *origin* in the thinking of the person in question: was it arrived at via an actual process of reasoning or inference from other beliefs, or in some other way? In the second place, there is the issue of how the belief is *justified*

or *warranted* (if at all): is it justified by virtue of inferential relations to other beliefs, or in some other way? Thus there are two distinct senses in which a belief may be inferential (and corresponding senses in which it may be non-inferential). And the immediate force of the above objection rests on a failure to distinguish these senses, for it is in the *first* sense (inferential or non-inferential *origin*) that an observational belief is paradigmatically non-inferential; while it is in the *second* sense (inferential or non-inferential *warrant*) that the CTEK insists that all justified belief might be arrived at in some non-inferential way (e.g., as a hunch) and only subsequently justified, via inference.

Proponents of the foundation theory will no doubt argue that this distinction at best only momentarily staves off the force of the objection, since observational beliefs are in fact non-inferential in both senses, even if somewhat more obviously so in the first sense, so that the contradiction remains. The CTEK, on the other hand, holds that observational beliefs are non-inferential in only the first sense, that their epistemic authority or warrant derives from inferential relations to other beliefs and thus ultimately from coherence, in the way outlined above. The immediate task here is to elaborate this latter view by showing in some detail how the justification of observational beliefs might be plausibly viewed as deriving from inference. In doing so I shall neglect, for the moment, the systematic dimension of coherence and concentrate more narrowly on the inferential relations which pertain immediately to observation, according to the CTEK.

It is best to begin by considering some examples before attempting a more general account. Consider, as a first example, the following simple case. As I look at my desk, I come to have the belief, among many others, that there is a red book on the desk. This belief is *cognitively spontaneous:* it is not arrived at via any sort of conscious ratiocinative process, but simply occurs to me, strikes me, in a coercive manner over which I have no control; thus it is clearly non-inferential in the first of the two senses distinguished above. Let us suppose, as would ordinarily be the case, that this belief is indeed an instance of knowledge. The question now becomes: how is it justified or warranted? The strong foundationist will claim either that the belief is itself a basic belief, or else that it is justified via inference from a further belief, presumably about my experience, which is basic. But what account can the CTEK offer as an alternative? What sort of inferential justification might be available for such a belief?

Once the question is put in this way, the main elements of the answer are, I think, readily discernible. First, the belief in question is a visual belief, i.e., it is produced by my sense of sight; and I am, or at least can be, introspectively aware of this fact. Second, the conditions of observation are of a specifiable sort: the lighting is good, my eyes are functioning normally, and there are no interfering circumstances; and again, I know or can know these facts about the conditions, via other observations and introspections. Finally, it is a true law about me (and indeed about a large class of relevantly similar observers) that my spontaneous visual beliefs in such conditions about that sort of subject matter (viz., medium-sized physical objects) are highly reliable, i.e., very likely to be true; and, once more, I know this law. Putting these elements together, I am in a position to offer the following justification for my belief:

(i) I have a spontaneous visual belief that there is a red book on the desk.

(ii) Spontaneous visual beliefs about the color and general classification of medium-sized physical objects are, in (specified) conditions, very likely to be true.

(iii) The conditions are as specified in (ii).

Therefore, my belief that there is a red book on the desk is very likely to be true.

Therefore, (probably) there is a red book on the desk.

There are two points which may be noted quickly about this justifying argument. First, all of the premises are empirical. Second, instead of assuming a listing of the conditions, I could have spoken instead in (ii) and (iii) of "standard conditions"; this would have had the effect of reducing the empirical content of (ii) and packing this content instead into (iii), but would have altered nothing of any real significance.

Consider now, more briefly, some contrasting examples. In all of the following cases I fail to have

knowledge, despite the presence of a spontaneous visual belief. According to the account offered by the CTEK, the reason that I fail to know is that in each case one of the essential premises for an analogous justifying argument is unavailable to me. (a) Far on the other side of the campus a figure is coming toward me. I spontaneously believe that it is my friend George, and in fact it is; but the belief is not knowledge, because beliefs produced under those conditions (i.e., at very great distance) are not generally reliable, i.e., not likely enough to be true. (b) Watching the traffic, I spontaneously believe that the car going by is a Lotus, and in fact it is; but the belief is not knowledge, although the conditions of observation are excellent, because I am not very familiar with cars and my perceptual beliefs about them are not very reliable. (I am apt to think that almost any fancy sports car is a Lotus.) (c) Peering into the darkness, I spontaneously believe that there is a man in the bushes, and in fact there is; but the belief is not knowledge, both because the conditions are poor and because I am a bit paranoid and quite apt to imagine people in the bushes who are not there. (d) In a fun house (a house of mirrors), I spontaneously believe that there is a little fat man directly in front of me, across the room, and in fact there is; but the belief is not knowledge, because I do not know the conditions of perception (which are in fact quite normal) and hence am unable to supply the appropriate premise.

I submit that the contrast between these latter cases where I fail to have knowledge and the former one where I do have knowledge, and between analogous cases of the same sort, provides good evidence that arguments like the one sketched above are indeed involved in the justification of observation knowledge. It is an interesting exercise to attempt to give an account of the difference between such cases in strong foundationist terms.

There is one other sort of case which needs to be discussed. Looking at my desk, I come to know that there is no blue book on it. This knowledge clearly results from observation, but the sort of account sketched above is inapplicable, since I do not have a spontaneous visual belief that there is no blue book on the desk. I do not somehow see the absence of such a book; rather I simply fail to see its presence, i.e., I fail to have a spontaneous visual belief that there *is* a blue book on the desk, and my belief that there is not is an inference from my failure to spontaneously believe that there is. What this example illustrates is that spontaneous visual beliefs are reliable in two distinct senses: not only are they (in specifiable circumstances, about specifiable subject matter) very likely to be true, but they are also very likely to be produced (in specifiable circumstances, about specifiable subject matter), if they would be true if produced. It is this second sort of reliability that allows me to reason, in the case in point:

(i) I have no spontaneous visual belief that there is a blue book on my desk.
(ii) If there were a blue book on my desk, then, in (specified) conditions, it is highly likely that such a belief would be produced.
(iii) The conditions are as specified in (ii)

Therefore, (probably) there is not a blue book on my desk.

Clearly knowledge justified in this way is closely connected with observation, whether or not it should itself be called observational. (It is also an interesting question, which I shall not pause to discuss here, whether all negative observational or observation-related knowledge must be justified in this indirect fashion.)

The crucial point, for present purposes, is that all of the premises of this justifying argument (as of the earlier one) are empirical premises, including most especially the crucial general premise (ii) in each argument. It is not an *a priori* truth, but rather an empirical discovery, that certain sorts of cognitively spontaneous beliefs are epistemically reliable and others are not; that waking visual beliefs are reliable and that visual beliefs produced in dreams, though similar in other respects, are not reliable. There are possible worlds in which the positions of these two sorts of experience are exactly reversed, in which reliable visual beliefs occur during sleep and unreliable ones while awake. (In such worlds, of course, the causal genesis of dreams, and of waking visual beliefs as well, will no doubt be different in important ways, but this difference need not be reflected in the subjective character of the beliefs or in the known conditions.) Thus the reason that visual perceptual beliefs are epistemically justified or warranted is that we have empirical background

knowledge which tells us that beliefs of that specific sort are epistemically reliable. This is the basic claim of the CTEK for *all* varieties of observation.

On the basis of these examples, I offer the following tentative sketch of a concept of observation compatible with the CTEK. According to this view, any mode of observation must involve three essential elements.

First, there must be a process of some sort which produces cognitively spontaneous beliefs about a certain range of subject matter. The process involved may be very complicated, involving such things as sense organs; the state of the mind and/or brain as a result of previous training or innate capacities; perhaps also the sorts of entities or events which philosophers have variously referred to by such terms as "immediate experience," "raw feels," and "sensa;" instruments of various kinds; perhaps even occult abilities of some sort (such as clairvoyance); etc.

Second, the beliefs thus produced must be *reliable* with respect to the subject matter in question in the two distinct ways discussed above (under specifiable conditions): on the one hand, it must be very likely that such beliefs, when produced, are true (if the requisite conditions are satisfied); and, on the other hand, if the person is in a situation in which a particular belief about that range of subject matter would be true (and if the requisite conditions are satisfied), then it must be very likely that such a belief will in fact be produced. This second sort of reliability is crucial; on it depends, in large part at least, the possibility of negative observational knowledge.

Third, and most important from the standpoint of the CTEK, the person must *know* all of these things, at least in a rough and ready way. He must be able to recognize beliefs which result from the process in question (though he need not know anything about the details of the process). He must know that such beliefs are reliable in the two senses specified. And he must know in a given case that any necessary conditions for reliability are satisfied. He will then be in a position, in a particular case, to offer the following justification for such a spontaneous belief:

(i) I have a spontaneous belief that P (about subject matter S) which is an instance of kind K.

(ii) Spontaneous beliefs about S which are instances of K are very likely to be true, if conditions C are satisfied.

(iii) Conditions C are satisfied.

Therefore, my belief that P is (probably) true.

Therefore, (probably) P.

And he will also be in a position to argue for a negative conclusion on the basis of observation, in the following way:

(i) I have no spontaneous belief that P (about subject matter S) which is an instance of kind K.

(ii) If P, then if conditions C are satisfied, it is very likely that I would have a spontaneous belief that P which was an instance of K.

(iii) Conditions C are satisfied.

Therefore, (probably) not-P.

These two schematic arguments are the basic schemata for the justification of observational knowledge, according to the CTEK.

The foregoing account of observation is obviously highly schematic and would require much more discussion to be complete. For present purposes, however, it will suffice to add five supplementary comments, by way of clarification, elaboration, and anticipation of possible objections, following which I shall return to a discussion of the main objection to the CTEK.

First, it needs to be asked what the exact status of the various inferences outlined above is supposed to be, relative to the actual cognitive state of a person who has observational knowledge. For it is only too obvious that such a person need not go explicitly through any such process of inference in order to have observational knowledge (on pain of making actual instances of observational knowledge vanishingly rare). But it is equally obvious that the inferences in question, in order to be a correct account of the observational knowledge of such a person, must be somehow relevant to his particular cognitive state and not merely an account which could be added, totally from the outside, by a philosopher. Thus the claim of the CTEK here (and indeed the analogous claim of foundation theories for the inferences which they typically postulate)

must be that such inferences are in some way tacitly or implicitly involved in the cognitive state of a person who has observational knowledge, even though he does not rehearse them explicitly and indeed might well be unable to do so even if challenged. It is not necessary that the belief actually originate via inference, however tacit or even unconscious; but it must be the case that a tacit grasp of the *availability* of the inference is the basis for the continuing acceptance of the belief and for the conviction that it is warranted. It has to be claimed, in other words, that such inferences are indeed an adequate philosophical unpacking or explication of what is really involved in the observational knowledge of an ordinary person, even though he may never be explicitly conscious of them. Such a claim on the part of the CTEK, as also on the part of foundation theories, is obviously very difficult to establish. Ultimately, it must simply be asserted that careful reflection on actual cases of observational knowledge will reveal that something like this is tacitly involved, though ultimately it may have to be conceded that any philosophically adequate account of knowledge is an idealization which is only loosely approximated by ordinary cognition. (It is worth remarking, however, that the inferential apparatus postulated by the CTEK, on the above account, is surely more common-sensical and less esoteric than is the analogous apparatus typically postulated by the foundation theories.)

Second. It is obvious that the knowledge represented by the third premises of the illustrative and schematic justifying arguments set out above, viz., the knowledge of the conditions of observation, will itself normally be largely or wholly based on observation and must be justified in the same way. This means that the element of coherence enters in immediately—with many observational beliefs, which may be from the same sense or from different senses, serving (directly or indirectly) as premises for each other's justification.

Third. As was emphasized above, the second premises of the various arguments are empirical premises. More specifically, each such premise is an empirical *law* about certain classes of beliefs. But it is obvious that such laws cannot be viewed in general as having been arrived at inductively, since no inductive argument as ordinarily construed would be possible unless one was *already* in a position to make warranted observations. Confirming evidence is available from within the coherent system for such laws, and any such law can be empirically tested within the context of the others; but the cognitive system as a whole could not have been developed piecemeal from the ground up.

Fourth. A more difficult problem is how the first premises of the various arguments are to be justified. It is obvious that such premises, for the most part at least, are to be regarded as the products of introspection, but how is introspective knowledge to be understood within the CTEK? It is tempting to treat introspection as just one more mode of observation, which would then be justified along the lines of the justification-schemata set forth above. Unfortunately, however, this will not quite do. Justifying an introspective belief along those lines would require as a first premise the claim that one had a spontaneous introspective belief of a certain sort. Thus, to return to the original example of my perceiving a red book on my desk, if premise (i) of the justifying argument for the claim is taken as the introspective belief to be justified, the first premise of the justifying argument would have to be:

(i) I have a spontaneous introspective belief that I have a spontaneous visual belief that there is a red book on the desk.

This is all right by itself. But now if justification is demanded for this premise, and one attempts to give it along similar lines, the first premise required for the new justifying argument will be:

(i) I have a spontaneous introspective belief that I have a spontaneous introspective belief that I have a spontaneous visual belief that there is a red book on the desk.

And since the challenge can be repeated again and again, we are seemingly off on a new regress, one which cannot be handled by the strategy set forth above, since the chain of arguments clearly does not move in a circle. I am not convinced that this regress is logically vicious, but it does not represent a plausible account of our actual introspective knowledge.

How then is introspective knowledge to be handled by the CTEK—that is if it is to avoid collapsing back into the foundationist view that introspective beliefs are basic? The key to the answer is that although an introspective belief *could* be justified along the lines of the earlier justification-schema, only one of the three premises of such an argument is really indispensable for the work of justification. Thus premise (iii), concerning conditions of observation, can be dispensed with because introspection, unlike other modes of observation, is almost entirely impervious to conditions. And premise (i), the premise which produced our current difficulty, can also be dispensed with. It is a fact about human perceivers that their beliefs about introspective matters are in accord with and reflect their spontaneous introspective beliefs. This is a weak and unproblematic version of privileged access, which is traceable to the fact that in introspective matters we are always in the proper position to have spontaneous beliefs; and thus, unlike the situation with other modes of observation, there is no chance for a disparity between our potential spontaneous beliefs and our other beliefs about the same introspective subject matter to develop. Consequently the reliability which attaches to spontaneous introspective beliefs also attaches to beliefs about introspective subject matter generally, whether spontaneous or not, and there is thus no need for premise (i) which stipulates that I have such a spontaneous belief.

Thus the only premise that is essential for a justification of introspective beliefs along the lines of CTEK is the one corresponding to premise (ii) of the schematic argument, with the references to conditions of observation and to cognitive spontaneity excised:

(*) Introspective beliefs (of certain sorts) are very likely to be true.

Here the phrase "introspective beliefs" is to be taken to mean simply "beliefs about introspective subject matter"; such beliefs need not be cognitively spontaneous. It is premise (*) that underlies introspective knowledge, according to the CTEK.[5]

The appeal to premise (*) may perhaps give the appearance that the CTEK is only verbally distinct from foundationalism, for it might be taken to be equivalent to treating introspective beliefs as basic or at least as initially credible. This would be a mistake. The basic difference is that premise (*), according to the CTEK, is an *empirical* premise, which must and does receive justification from within the rest of our cognitive system and which is subject to being reassessed and modified in light of that system. This fact about (*) is reflected in the parenthetical clause; all instances of introspection are not equally reliable, and the distinction among them must be made empirically. When an introspective belief is justified by appeal to premise (*), the appeal is still ultimately to coherence. Therefore, according to the CTEK, although introspective beliefs do play a unique and pivotal role in empirical knowledge, they do not constitute a foundation for that knowledge, as that notion has traditionally been understood; the basic thesis of foundationism can still be consistently rejected. (Indeed, the CTEK does *not* insist that some premise like premise (*) must be maintained by any acceptable cognitive system. It is logically conceivable that no such premise might be true, that no variety of introspection might be consistently reliable, so that *any* premise of this sort would fail to yield coherent results in the long run. This point will be considered further below, together with its bearing on the possibility of empirical knowledge.)

Fifth. It is worth noting explicitly that the conception of observation advanced here is implicitly much broader than the standard conceptions of sense-perception and introspection. On this view any process of empirical belief-production whose results are epistemically reliable counts as a mode of observation, whether or not it involves the traditional senses. Thus, for example, if there are people who have spontaneous clairvoyance or telepathic beliefs which are reliable, then for such people clairvoyance or telepathy is at least a potential mode of observation (though they must *know* that the beliefs in question are reliable if they are to have knowledge on this basis). Or, more interestingly, if (as often seems to be the case) a scientist who masters the use of an instrument such as a Geiger counter or cloud chamber develops the capacity to have reliable spontaneous beliefs about theoretical entities and processes such as radioactivity or subatomic particles, then these beliefs count as observational on the present account and can be justified directly, without reference to sense-experience, along the lines sketched above.

IV

This schematic account of the role of observation in the CTEK provides the essential ingredient for answering the three objections to that theory that were set out in Section II, above. The first two objections can be dealt with very simply and directly, while the third will require a more extended discussion and even then must be dealt with here in a less conclusive fashion.

I begin with objection (II), which alleges that a consequence of the CTEK is that empirical knowledge has no *input* from the world. In light of the discussion of observation, it should now be clear that the CTEK can allow for input into the cognitive system from the world, while insisting that this input must be understood in *causal* rather than epistemic terms. The world impinges upon the system of knowledge by causing cognitively spontaneous beliefs of various sorts, but these beliefs are epistemically justified or warranted only from within the system, along the lines set out above. And, in principle at least, any sort of causal impact of the world that is capable of producing such beliefs in a reliable way is capable of being justified as a species of observation.

Moreover, such observational beliefs need not merely augment the overall system, but may force the alteration or abandonment of parts of it—either because the observational belief is directly inconsistent with one or more other beliefs in the system or because such alteration will enhance the overall coherence of the system. (Of course the observational belief could itself be rejected for a similar reason, though if this is done very often the law which specifies the degree of reliability of that sort of observational belief will also have to be revised.) In this way, the CTEK provides an account of how a system of beliefs can be tested against the results of observation.

Thus the CTEK clearly allows for the *possibility* of input from the world into the cognitive system, a possibility which is in fact realized in our cognitive system. But does it not also admit the possibility of empirical knowledge without such input? Suppose that a cognitive system either fails to attribute reliability to any observational beliefs at all, or else fails to attribute reliability to those introspective beliefs which are needed for the reliable recognition of other reliable observational beliefs. Such a state of affairs might be built into the system from the outset, or might result gradually from repeated revision of the system if conflicts between putative observations and other component beliefs were always adjudicated by rejecting the observation. Clearly such a system would fail to have any effective input from the world. And yet on the account of the CTEK given so far, it seems that such a system (or rather the contingent part thereof) might constitute empirical knowledge if only it were sufficiently coherent. And surely this is an absurd result.

This point is essentially sound. Any adequate account of empirical knowledge must *require,* not merely allow, input from the world into the cognitive system—for without such input any agreement between the system and the world would be purely fortuitous, and thus the beliefs of the system would not be knowledge. Thus the CTEK must require that for a cognitive system to be even a candidate for the status of empirical knowledge, it must include laws attributing a high degree of reliability to a reasonable variety of kinds of cognitively spontaneous beliefs, including those kinds of introspective beliefs which are required for the recognition of other sorts of reliable cognitively spontaneous beliefs. Call this "the observational requirement." It provides the basic answer to objection (II).[6]

It is important to understand clearly the status of this requirement within the CTEK. The need for the requirement is *a priori:* it is an *a priori* truth, according to the CTEK, that a cognitive system must attribute reliability to cognitively spontaneous beliefs to the degree indicated *if* it is to contain empirical knowledge. But it is *not* an *a priori* truth that the antecedent of this conditional is satisfied and hence also not an *a priori* truth that its consequent must be satisfied. Whether any cognitively spontaneous beliefs are in fact reliable is an empirical issue to be decided within the cognitive system purely on the basis of coherence. It is logically conceivable, according to the CTEK, that no variety of cognitively spontaneous belief is sufficiently reliable and hence that any system satisfying the observation requirement would become incoherent in the long run, so that coherence could be preserved only

by denying reliability to enough cognitively spontaneous beliefs to violate the observation requirement. The observation requirement does *not* say that such a result must be incorrect, but only that if it were correct there would be no empirical knowledge.

Thus the observation requirement functions within the CTEK as a regulative meta-principle of epistemological assessment. It does not impinge directly on the operations of the coherence machinery, but rather provides a partial basis for categorizing the results of that process. This is the main difference between the CTEK and that very weak version of weak foundationism which would attribute initial credibility to all cognitively spontaneous beliefs and then require the preservation of a reasonably high proportion of them. For such a version of foundationism, it is true *prior* to the workings of coherence that cognitively spontaneous beliefs have this minimal degree of credibility—for which no empirical justification is thus ever offered. Whereas for the CTEK *all* epistemic warrant for empirical propositions is ultimately a matter of coherence.

What then is the status of those contingent and seemingly empirical beliefs which appear within a cognitive system that violates the observation requirement? I would suggest that their status is quite analogous to, if not indeed identical with, that of imaginative or fictional accounts. It is a consequence of the holism advocated by the CTEK that the distinction between the category of empirical description and these other categories is not to be drawn with respect to particular beliefs but only with regard to systems of beliefs. And the empirical thrust of a cognitive system is precisely the implicit claim that its component beliefs will agree, in general at least, with those classes of cognitively spontaneous beliefs which it holds to be reliable. Thus the observation requirement might be viewed as a weak analogue of the old positivist verifiability criterion of empirical meaningfulness, now transposed so as to apply to systems rather than to individual statements.

The answer to objection (I), the alternative coherent system objection, is already implicit in the foregoing discussion. For once it is clear that the CTEK involves the possibility that a system which is coherent at one time may be rendered incoherent by subsequent observational input, and once the requirement is accepted that any putative system of empirical knowledge must allow for this possibility, objection (I) in effect divides into two parts. Part one is the claim that *at a given moment* there may be many equally coherent empirical systems among which the CTEK provides no basis for decision. This claim is correct, but does not provide any basis for a serious objection, since the same thing will be true for any theory of knowledge imaginable. The important issue is whether these equally coherent systems will remain equally coherent and still distinct under the impact of observation in the long run. Thus the second and crucial part of objection (I) will be the claim that even in the long run, and with the continuing impact of observation, there will be multiple, equally coherent empirical systems among which it will not be possible to decide. But, once the role of observation in the CTEK is appreciated, there seems little if any reason to accept this claim. The role of observation undercuts the idea that such alternatives can be simply constructed at will: such systems might be coherent at the beginning, but there is no reason to think that they would remain so as observations accumulate. This point is obvious enough if the observational components of the different systems involve the same concepts. But even if the observational components, or even the entire systems, involve different concepts so that they are not directly commensurable, there is no reason to think that one objective world will go on providing coherent input to incompatible systems in the long run.

This brings us to objection (III), surely the most penetrating and significant of the three. Objection (III) contends that the CTEK will be unable to establish the vital connection between justification and truth, will be unable to show that its account of justification is truth-conducive, unless it also adopts the coherence theory of *truth*. It is certainly correct that a connection of this sort must be established by any adequate epistemology, even though this issue is rarely dealt with in a fully explicit fashion. Truth is after all the *raison d'être* of the cognitive enterprise. The only possible ultimate warrant for an account of epistemic justification must therefore consist in showing that accepting such an account and seeking beliefs which are in accord with it is likely to yield the truth, or at least

more likely than would be the case on any alternative account. And the objection is also right that one who adopts a coherence theory of justification is in danger of being driven dialectically to espouse the coherence theory of truth as well. For the easiest and most straightforward way to establish a connection between a coherence account of justification and truth itself is to simply identify truth with justification-in-the-long-run, i.e., with coherence-in-the-long-run. Essentially this move was made by the absolute idealists and, in a different way, by Peirce. I assume here that such a coherence theory of truth is mistaken, that truth is to be understood at least roughly along the lines of the traditional correspondence theory. But if this is right, then the only way finally to justify the CTEK and answer objection (III) is to provide an argument to show that following the epistemic standards set by the CTEK is, in the long run, *likely* at least to lead to correspondence.

I believe that it is possible to give such an argument, though I cannot undertake to provide a detailed account of it here. The main difficulty is an extrinsic one: no one has succeeded so far in giving an adequate account of the correspondence theory of truth, and such an account is an indispensable ingredient of the envisaged argument. It is possible, however, to provide a rough sketch of the way in which the argument would go, given a very rough and intuitive conception of the correspondence theory: a proposition is true if it accords with an actual situation in the world, and otherwise false. (The argument is relative to the assumption that the observation requirement can be satisfied; if there were no possibility of reliable input from the world, then no set of epistemic standards would be likely to yield the truth.)

Suppose then that we have a hypothetical cognitive system which is coherent and satisfies the observation requirement as stipulated above, but fails to accord with reality. Our task is to show that such a system is unlikely to *remain* coherent (and continue to satisfy the observation requirement) unless it is revised in the direction of greater accord with reality. The way in which such revision *might* take place is obvious enough. If the lack of accord between the system and reality involves observable matters, then if the appropriate observations are actually made, they will produce inconsistency or incoherence within the system and force its revision. If the observations themselves are not rejected by such a revision, then the effect is to bring the system more into accord with reality. And this process *might* be repeated over and over until complete accord with reality is achieved in the very long run.

This, as I say, is what *might* happen. But is it *likely* to happen? The best way to show that it is likely to happen is to consider in turn each of the various seemingly plausible ways in which it might fail to happen, despite the lack of accord between system and reality stipulated above, and show that these are *un*likely.

First. The process described above, whereby the system is revised in the direction of greater accord with the world, depends essentially on the occurrence of observational beliefs which conflict with other parts of the system and thus force the revision of the system. But any such revision involves a choice as to which of the conflicting beliefs to retain, and the system will come to accord more closely with reality only if this choice results in the retention of the observational beliefs and the exclusion of their competitors. Thus the most obvious way in which such revision in the direction of truth might fail to occur is that the choice be made consistently in favor of the non-observational beliefs in question, rejecting the observational beliefs. In the short run, it is quite likely that such a revision would produce a more justified result than would the alternate choice in favor of observation. But this could happen in the long run. For if an inquirer or community of inquirers were to follow in the long run such a policy, deliberate or not, of resolving most such decisions in favor of the antecedent system and against the observational belief, this would inevitably have the effect of undermining the law that such observations are reliable and thus eventually violating the observation requirement. Thus this first possibility may be ruled out.

Second. Another way in which the envisaged revision in favor of truth might fail to take place is that, although the situations in the world which conflicted with the system were in fact observable, it might be the case that the inquirer or inquirers in question were simply never in the proper position to make the requisite observations, and so the conflict between the system and world would never be

discovered. This possibility cannot be completely ruled out. But the longer the period of inquiry in question becomes, the more unlikely it is that this situation would continue, and this unlikelihood is increased as the supposed discrepancy between system and world is made larger.

Third. So far the assumption has been that the lack of accord between system and world involves aspects of the world which are observable. But suppose that this is not the case, that the aspects of the world in question are unobservable. There are various ways in which this might be so. First, and most basically, it might be the case that the aspects in question simply had not causal effects which were detectable by the sense organs or sensitive faculties of our community of inquirers, so that there would be no way that such inquirers could learn to observe those aspects. Second, it might be the case that, although the aspects in question did have causal impact on our inquirers, these inquirers simply had not learned to make observations of the appropriate sort. Third, it might be the case that although the aspects in question were in principle observable by our inquirers, there were barriers of some sort which prevented them from actually making the observations. Such barriers would include distance in space or time, impossibly hostile environments of various sorts, etc.

This sort of situation must be acknowledged as possible and even likely. The question is whether it could be overcome, given only the resources allowed by the CTEK, and if so, how likely it is that such an overcoming would occur. The answer to the first part of the question is that it *could* be overcome, in either of two ways. In the first place, the unobservability of the aspects of the world in question might be overcome: the barriers might be transcended, the inquirers might learn to make the requisite observations, and/or new instruments might be developed which would create an appropriate causal linkage between these aspects and the sense organs of our observers. (See the remarks about instrumental observation at the end of Section III.) All of these things could happen, but there is no way to show that they are likely to happen in general. Thus the more important way in which the situation of unobservability might be overcome is by the development of *theories* concerning the unobservable aspects of the world. It is via theory construction that we come to know about the unobservable aspects of the world.

But is there any reason to think that such theory construction is likely to take place? The only possible answer on behalf of the CTEK, as indeed on behalf of any theory of knowledge, is that if enough aspects of the world are observable and if the unobservable aspects of the world have enough causal impact on the observable ones, then a fully coherent account of the observable aspects will in the long run lead to theories about the unobservable aspects. The main consideration here is that coherence essentially involves both prediction and explanation. An account of the observable world which was unable to predict and explain the observable effects of unobservable entities and processes would be to that extent incoherent. Thus to suppose that an ideally coherent account could be given of the observable aspects without any mention of the unobservable aspects would be in effect to suppose both that the world divides into two parts with no significant causal interaction between the two, and that this division coincides with that between the observable and the unobservable. And this is surely unlikely, even if one does not bring in the fact that the observable/unobservable line is not fixed once and for all.

Fourth. There is one other apparently possible way to be considered in which there could be a lack of accord between one's cognitive system and reality without revision in the direction of truth being likely to take place. This alleged possibility is difficult to make fully clear, but it goes at least roughly as follows. Suppose that the conceptual picture which is given by the cognitive system, though failing to accord with the world, is isomorphic with it in the following way: for each kind of thing K, property of things P, etc., in the world, there is a corresponding but distinct kind of thing K^*, property of things P^*, etc., in the conceptual picture, and analogously for other kinds, properties, and whatever other categories of things are found in the world. The observational dispositions of the community of inquirers are such that they have observational beliefs about K^*s when what they are actually observing is As, etc. Under these conditions, the conceptual picture of the world would be fully coherent and would be in no danger of being rendered incoherent by observations, and

yet *ex hypothesi* it would fail to accord with the world.

Notice, however, that for this situation to occur, the laws, conceptual connections, etc., which pertain to the conceptually depicted kinds, properties, etc., must exactly mirror those which pertain to the actual kinds, properties, etc., of the world. If it is a true law in the world that instances of K_1 are always accompanied by instances of K_2, then it must be a law in the conceptual depiction that instances of K_1^* are always accompanied by instances of K_2^*, etc. For any discrepancy in such inferential patterns between the conceptual depiction and the world would be a basis for a potential conflicting observation. But despite this exact mirroring of all inferential patterns, it must still be the case that the kinds, properties, etc., of the world are not identical with those of the system. Thus one possible response by a proponent of the CTEK would be simply the denial that this sort of situation is indeed possible, on the grounds that the associated inferential patterns determine the kinds, properties, etc., completely, so that if these are the same there is no room left for a difference between the conceptually depicted world and the actual world. I think that there is merit in this claim, but a defense of it is impossible here. In any case, it will suffice for present purposes merely to make the weaker claim that this sort of situation in which the inference patterns match but the kinds, etc., are still different is very unlikely, i.e., that the fact that one set of inference patterns mirror the other is a very good reason for supposing that the kinds, etc., are identical.

The foregoing considerations are an attempt to make plausible the following conclusions: it is highly unlikely, though not impossible, that a cognitive system which failed to accord with the world and which satisfied the observation requirement would be coherent and remain coherent under the impact of new observation, unless it was gradually revised in the direction of greater accord with the world. This is so because all of the apparent ways in which such revision could fail to take place represent highly unlikely situations. This is obviously only a sketch of a line of argument which would have to be greatly elaborated in various ways to be really adequate. Here it is intended only to suggest the sort of answer which the CTEK can make to objection (III), how it can establish the truth-conduciveness of its view of justification, without resorting to the desperate expedient of the coherence theory of truth.

Thus the standard objections to views like the CTEK turn out to be in fact far less conclusive than has usually been thought, and that it is reasonable to suppose that they can be successfully answered, once the role of observation in the theory is fully understood and appreciated. This in turn suggests that views like the CTEK are potentially viable accounts of empirical knowledge, worthy of far more serious attention than they have usually been given.

Notes

[1] Roderick Firth, "Coherence, Certainty, and Epistemic Priority." Reprinted in Chisholm and Swartz, ed., *Empirical Knowledge,* p. 459.

[2] Whether or not the view presented here is an entirely *pure* coherence theory is mainly an issue of taxonomy. As will be seen, it does *not* hold that the only factor which determines the acceptability of a set of propositions as putative empirical knowledge is its internal coherence. It does claim, however, that the epistemic justification attaching to an empirical proposition always derives entirely from considerations of coherence—and thus is never immediate or intrinsic, as the foundationist claims.

[3] The original critique of the linear account of inference was by Bosanquet in *Implication and Linear Inference.* A more recent version is offered by Rescher in "Foundationalism, Coherentism, and the Idea of Cognitive Systematization." Harman's account of inference in *Thought* is in many ways a modernized version of Bosanquet.

[4] Thus Lewis calls it "congruence" and Chisholm calls it "concurrence." See Lewis, *op. cit.,* chap. 11, and Chisholm, *Theory of Knowledge,* chap 3.

[5] It might be thought that the justification of an introspective belief using premise (*) would still require the additional premise that the person indeed has the introspective belief in question—which would suffice to generate a regress. There is no doubt that the thesis that the person has the introspective belief in question figures in the justification. I would argue, however, that it does not figure as a *premise,* which would then require further justification, because the existence of that belief is *presupposed* by the very raising of the issue of justification in the first place.

[6] The observation requirement, as stated, may seem too weak. It may be thought that at least two further requirements should be added: (a) that each of the kinds of cognitively spontaneous beliefs in question result from a unique causal process; and (b) that the various causal processes in question actually produce reliable beliefs. These additional requirements are indeed part of the notion of observation as set forth above. But they need not be made a part of this requirement, because failure to satisfy them will make it extremely unlikely that a cognitive system will both remain coherent and continue to satisfy the observation requirement as stated, in the long run. (A point worth adding is that the ability to have epistemically reliable cognitively spontaneous beliefs is presumably acquired via training, linguistic or otherwise, since it presupposes the grasp of a conceptual system. Such training, however, though presumably a causally necessary condition for the satisfaction of the observation requirement, is not a part of it.)

The observation requirement should also be understood to include the requirement, common to all adequate theories of knowledge, that a user of the system must make a reasonable attempt to seek out relevant observations if his results are to be justified.

V.5 A *Critique of Coherentism*

RICHARD FUMERTON

Richard Fumerton is Professor of Philosophy at the University of Iowa. In this essay he argues that fundamental difficulties face any attempt to define justified belief in terms of coherence among beliefs. To be plausible, a coherence theory must embrace internalism, but a coherentist cannot give a reasonable account of our access to our own beliefs. Moreover, even rather strong coherence seems at once neither sufficient nor necessary for the justification of our beliefs.

One of the most prominent attempts to avoid both skepticism and a vicious regress of justification without embracing foundationalism is the coherence theory of justification. Like the foundationalist, the coherence theorist usually accepts the principle that only justified beliefs can justify other beliefs, but unlike the foundationalist, the coherence theorist wants also to assert that the only thing that can justify a belief is another set of beliefs. The crudest and most implausible version of a coherence theory simply endorses the legitimacy of circular reasoning, at least when the circles are "big" enough. I can justify my belief that *P* by appealing to *E*, justify my belief that *E* by appealing to *F*, justify my belief that *F* by appealing to *G*, and justify my belief that *G* by appealing once again to *P*. More sophisticated coherence theorists will point out that this caricature of a coherence theory overlooks its characteristic rejection of the notion of *linear* justification in favor of a holistic conception of justification. When we attempt to justify a belief by showing its coherence with other beliefs, we never appeal directly to *P* as the sole support of itself (as in the example just given). Rather, we try to justify our belief that *P* by appealing to the way in which *P* coheres with other propositions we believe, *Q*, *R*, *S*, and *T*. We justify our belief that *Q* by appealing to its coherence with *P*, *R*, *S*, and *T*; we justify our belief that *S*, by pointing out its coher-

ence with *P*, *Q*, *R*, and *T*; and so on. We try not so much to lift ourselves by our bootstraps as to give ourselves a helpful tug. There are, of course, many different versions of a coherence theory of justification. Some coherentists restrict their thesis to empirical beliefs; others allow a kind of privileged epistemic status to a subset of beliefs after which coherence is the sole source of justification. In what follows I restrict my comments to pure coherentism and argue that pure coherentism is fundamentally flawed. Pure coherentism is the view that all beliefs are to be justified by virtue of their coherence with other beliefs.

The first step in evaluating a coherence theory is to force the coherentist to make clear his criteria for coherence and his concept of truth and to explain how the two fit together. Perhaps the most natural theory of truth to go with a coherence theory of justification is a coherence theory of truth, but one cannot simply assume that the two go together in arguing against a coherence theory of justification. The two views share a number of problems, however.

The most obvious concern with a coherence theory of truth is that no concept of coherence developed so far has ruled out the possibility of two internally consistent, coherent systems of beliefs that are nevertheless incompatible. This possibility seems to force the proponent of a coherence theory of truth into either abandoning the law of noncontradiction or into relativizing the concept of truth. Because most coherentists are as fond of the law of noncontradiction as anyone else, presumably the

This essay was commissioned for this book and appears here for the first time.

most plausible alternative is to relativize truth. Strictly speaking, one should not speak of a proposition being true; one should only speak of its being true relative to a given system of beliefs where I suppose one can distinguish as many different relativized conceptions of truth as one can distinguish systems of beliefs.

This radical relativization of truth is paralleled by a radical subjectivity with respect to justification on a coherence theory of justification. It seems we can justify believing any proposition provided we "choose" the rest of our beliefs so as to avoid incoherence. The "choice" between systems of beliefs seems completely and utterly arbitrary. One philosopher's *reductio* is often another philosopher's welcome consequence of a view, and to be sure many contemporary philosophers will embrace with open arms this radical subjectivity with respect to the concept of justification. Moreover, they will rightly protest my description of the dilemma as one of an arbitrary "choice" between beliefs. Fortunately for us, they might point out, we don't so much choose beliefs as find ourselves caused to have them. So we are not faced with the insurmountable problem of having to make a nonarbitrary choice between infinitely many internally coherent systems of beliefs. Our real-life decision is that of making (usually) relatively minor adjustments within a system that already exists, the core of which doesn't change much. As to the possibility of another kind of being with a radically different system of beliefs, all of which are justified relative to one another, the coherentist will probably allow such a possibility without flinching.

There is, however, another more serious kind of problem, a regress problem, that affects both coherence theories of truth and coherence theories of justification. It has always seemed to me that a coherence theory of truth was quite literally unintelligible because of a vicious metaphysical regress. The truth of *P* must be relativized to a system of beliefs, say *P, Q, R,* and *S*. The truth of *P* relative to this system *consists* in the coherence of these beliefs. But the very statement of the theory seems to take as unproblematic the existence of beliefs. Given the theory, however, its being true that I believe *P* must itself be defined in terms of coherence, presumably coherence among beliefs in a set including the metabelief that I believe that *P*. Again, it will only be true

I have this metabelief "I believe that *P*" if meta-metabeliefs cohere in the relevant way. But how do we ever get anything that ends this regress to actually ground truth? I don't in fact have an infinite number of increasingly more complex metabeliefs (it's too difficult to keep them straight after even the first three or four levels). And even if it were possible to have an infinite number of more and more complex metabeliefs, it is not clear this would provide a satisfactory solution to the regress problem, for we will still never get a *ground* of truth until the regress ends.

If a coherence theory of truth faces a vicious ontological regress, an epistemological coherence theory (combined, say, with a correspondence theory of truth) faces a vicious epistemological regress. Almost all coherence theorists explicitly or implicitly accept a version of *internalism*. Roughly, they accept the idea that the conditions that define a belief's being justified are conditions to which the believer has, or at least could have, access. It is not enough that my beliefs actually do cohere in order for them to be justified. I must be aware of, or at least have the ability to be aware of, that coherence. Thus, for example, I may have a complex set of mathematical beliefs that do in fact cohere beautifully, but if I am completely unaware of any of the logical or probabilistic connections among these beliefs, it is surely implausible to suppose that these beliefs are justified *for me*. But how exactly does a coherence theorist understand our access to our beliefs and the coherence that holds between them? One could try to stay within the framework of a coherence theory and hold that our justification for believing that we have a certain belief is our awareness of a coherence between our metabelief that we believe *P* and other beliefs. But now we need to be aware of coherence between our meta-metabelief that we do in fact have the metabelief that *P* and other beliefs, and so on, *ad infinitum*. One of the most sophisticated defenses of a coherence theory of justification for empirical beliefs has been provided by Laurence BonJour in his book *The Structure of Empirical Knowledge*.[1] A confirmed internalist, BonJour, to his credit, is well aware of this problem and seeks to deal with it by arguing that the coherence theorist needs a *doxastic presumption*. The doxastic presumption amounts to the presumption that my beliefs about what I believe are correct, but when the smoke clears it is obvious BonJour must recognize that the belief constituting this presumption is an unjustified belief. He may protest it is in the nature of a presumption to deflect questions about justification, but one can be sure the skeptic will not be so easily deterred from asking the obviously relevant question concerning the epistemic status of my belief that I have these beliefs. And in his more candid moments, BonJour himself seems to recognize that his coherence theory combined with internalism yields comprehensive skepticism with respect to empirical belief.[2]

In short, if one is going to be a coherence theorist one had better abandon internalism. But if one abandons internalism it is not clear what motivation one has for being a coherence theorist, particularly when more straightforward versions of externalism (reliabilism, for example) avoid some of the other problems facing coherentism (sketched later).

Even if one avoids the regress problem just sketched (for example) by combining an externalist epistemology with one's coherence theory of justification, there are innumerable other technical problems with defending the view. Most of those problems involve developing a plausible conception of coherence. In *The Structure of Empirical Knowledge*, BonJour argues that the coherence theorist must stress the importance of probabilistic connections between beliefs. Mere logical coherence is too weak. One can have a logically consistent set of beliefs that have nothing to do with one another. He also goes on to suggest (p. 97) that it would be far too strong to require that each belief in a system of beliefs be deducible from the rest, presumably because he thinks it would be too difficult to satisfy such a requirement. In fact, however, it is probably too *easy* to satisfy such a requirement, at least for someone lucky enough to have the concept of material implication and disposed to make obvious inferences. Whenever I believe P and also believe Q, I will believe that P materially implies Q, and that Q materially implies P. But if this is so my belief that P will be entailed by my other beliefs (Q and Q materially implies P), my belief that Q will be entailed by my other beliefs (P and P materially implies Q), and my belief that P materially implies Q will be entailed by my other beliefs (P and Q). But it is obvious that as long as my beliefs are logically consistent and I

am a logician who understands material implication, I will undoubtedly satisfy the very requirement that BonJour thought was too difficult a requirement to satisfy because of the very strong conception of coherence it presupposed. Ironically, belief systems in which every belief is entailed by the rest are a dime a dozen. It is actually harder to come by belief systems in which there are lots of nondeductive probabilistic connections.[3]

Some coherence theorists will try to "tighten up" the relevant sort of coherence required for justification by turning to explanatory coherence as one of the most important kinds of coherence that should be exemplified by a system of beliefs. Thus, for example, a belief might be said to be justified if it fits into a set of beliefs in which each belief is explained or explains "better" than it would in some alternative system of beliefs. The interpretation of such a view rests heavily on the criteria offered for determining good explanation, criteria that in this context will exclude reference to the truth of the explanans. I might, for example, endorse Hempel's famous D–N (deductive-nomological) model as capturing the formal structure of an explanation and construe the best explanatory system of beliefs as the system in which the most is explained with the fewest D–N explanations. Another question that must be answered involves the relevant comparison class of systems of beliefs referred to. Must my beliefs fare better than all possible systems of beliefs, or merely all systems of beliefs that I have the conceptual capacity to entertain?[4]

Explanatory coherence may initially seem like a relevant criterion of justification, especially if one is inclined to think there is such a thing as reasoning to the best explanation construed as an alternative to inductive reasoning.[5] It is important to realize, however, that with an explanatory coherence theory of justification I cannot simply give myself unproblematically justified beliefs for which I can find plausible explanations. The explanandum beliefs must in turn be justified, presumably by virtue of the fact that they explain still other beliefs. But is it at all plausible to suppose that the justification for all your beliefs—your belief that you are in pain, for example—consists solely in the fact that it explains or is explained by other things you believe? How does the theory accommodate justified beliefs in analytic truths, synthetic necessary truths (if there are any), and principles of reasoning? Do such beliefs even admit of explanatory coherence? And does an explanatory theory of coherence help at all with the radical problem of subjectivity sketched earlier? Certainly if anything like a D–N model of explanation were correct, one would have no difficulty coming up with systems of beliefs that meet the formal requirements (excluding truth, of course) of adequate explanation, no matter what the content of those beliefs happened to be. If one uses criteria such as comprehensiveness and simplicity of explanations as a way of choosing between alternative explanations, you will have to deal with obvious counterintuitive consequences. If you want an example of an intuitively implausible system of beliefs with maximum explanatory power and simplicity, look at Berkeley's theory of perception. But furthermore one needs to explain how a coherence theory of justification allows one to rely on such things as simplicity as a plausible criterion of truth. If simpler theories are true more often than complex theories, it is a contingent fact, and my belief that it is so could only be justified by its coherence with other beliefs. One cannot simply presuppose the truth of this belief in defending a coherence theory of justification.

Whatever else coherence involves, virtually all proponents of both coherence theories of justification and truth have always assumed that coherence *minimally* involves logical consistency. Earlier I argued that logical coherence was too easy to come by to provide a useful criterion of justification. It may also be too *strong* a requirement for justified belief. Far from being sufficient for having a justified belief, coherence is not even necessary. In "Justified Inconsistent Beliefs," Richard Foley argues (quite correctly) by appealing to lottery-like examples that one can justifiably believe a number of propositions, P, Q, R, and S, such that the conjunction (P and Q and R and S) constitutes a contradiction.[6] If Persons A through J have an equal chance of winning a lottery, I can justifiably believe A will lose, B will lose, C will lose, . . . and J will lose, and also justifiably believe either A or B or C, . . . or J will win. The propositions believed are inconsistent but are nevertheless each justifiably believed. The argument is simple, but it strikes at the very heart of the coherentist's intuitions. As would be expected of an argument so potentially decisive,

its premises are not uncontroversial. A surprising number of philosophers think there is a lottery *paradox,* that there is something wrong with allowing that someone could be justified in believing of each participant in the lottery that he will lose *and* that one of them will win. I have never understood what the paradox is supposed to be, however. What reason is there for denying that one can have justified inconsistent beliefs regarding the outcome of the lottery?

In "A Solution to the Problem of Induction," John Pollock attempts to resolve the lottery "paradox."[7] His strategy is to grant that one has a *prima facie* reason for thinking that Person A will lose the lottery while pointing out that one has equally strong *prima facie* reasons for believing that B will lose, that C will lose, . . . and that J will lose. Furthermore, we also know that if B and C and . . . J lose, A will win. We are, then, in a position to present the following valid argument for the claim that A will win the lottery:

B will lose.

C will lose.

.

.

.

J will lose.

If B will lose, and C will lose, and . . . J will lose, then A will win.

Therefore, A will win.

The availability of this argument is supposed to balance our initial reason for thinking Person A will lose, thus leaving us with no more reason to believe A will lose than that he will win! It is hard for me to see how one could accept so paradoxical a solution to a paradox. Pollock is assuming a principle that seems problematic, to say the least. To justifiably infer the conclusion of the argument from its premises, one needs to be justified in believing the *conjunction* that B will lose, and C will lose, and . . . , J will lose. And that one can justifiably believe *each* of B through J will lose does not imply that one can justifiably believe they *all* will. More generally, it seems obviously fallacious to infer, from the fact that I justifiably believe *P* and justifiably believe *Q*, that I can justifiably believe (*P* and *Q*).

In *Knowledge*, Lehrer offers a highly sophisticated coherence theory of what he calls complete justification and discusses the lottery "paradox" within the framework of that theory.[8] His main concern is to show how his theory can accommodate the natural intuition that we cannot be completely justified in believing of any particular participant that he will lose the lottery, but in the course of making this claim he argues that an ideally rational person interested in maximizing true belief and minimizing false belief will not allow inconsistent beliefs in his system of beliefs. I suspect he would argue for this claim by observing that, if we have beliefs whose objects, in conjunction, are inconsistent, we are assured of at least one false belief, thus guaranteeing that we frustrate at least one of the ends of an ideal truth seeker. But as Lehrer himself notes, the goal of a rational person is not just to avoid falsehood. The rational person is also interested in arriving at true beliefs, and by purging ourselves of beliefs about the outcome of the lottery we guarantee that we will forgo a great number of true beliefs. If S and R have the same set of beliefs, excluding those concerning the outcome of the lottery, and S believes of each participant that he will lose while R withholds belief in these propositions, it is not hard to calculate that S is going to end up with a better "winning" percentage of true beliefs over false beliefs.

There is in fact no reason to assume we cannot have justified inconsistent beliefs, and since we can, the most minimal sort of coherence is not even a *necessary* condition for justification.

Notes

[1] Laurence BonJour, *The Structure of Empirical Knowledge* (Cambridge, MA: Harvard University Press, 1985).

[2] BonJour (1985); see particularly the last paragraph on p. 105.

[3] BonJour (1985) worries particularly about the apparent incoherence of a person's beliefs if that person's system of beliefs contains two subsets (call them *x* and *y*) which are themselves logically unrelated (p. 97). But the preceding point applies here again, of course. In addition to the beliefs that comprise *x* and the beliefs that comprise *y*, the subject can easily see that these subsets justify the beliefs that *x* materially implies *y* and that *y* materially implies *x*, and when we add these beliefs to the system we have logical entailment again.

[4] See Lehrer's discussion of this issue in *Knowledge* (Oxford, England: Clarendon Press, 1974), p. 161.

[5] A view I have challenged in "Induction and Reasoning to the Best Explanation", *Philosophy of Science 47* (1980).

[6] Richard Foley, "Justified Inconsistent Beliefs," *American Philosophical Quarterly 16* (1979), pp. 247–258.

[7] John Pollock, "A Solution to the Problem of Induction," *Nous,* 1984.

[8] Lehrer, 1974.

V.6 *The Raft and the Pyramid: Coherence versus Foundations in the Theory of Knowledge*

ERNEST SOSA

Ernest Sosa is Professor of Philosophy at Brown University. In this essay, Sosa compares the "solid security of the ancient foundationalist pyramid and the risky adventure of the new coherentist raft."

Contemporary epistemology must choose between the solid security of the ancient foundationalist pyramid and the risky adventure of the new coherentist raft. Our main objective will be to understand, as deeply as we can, the nature of the controversy and the reasons for and against each of the two options. But first of all we take note of two underlying assumptions.

1. *Two Assumptions*

(A1) Not everything believed is known, but nothing can be known without being at least believed (or accepted, presumed, taken for granted, or the like) in some broad sense. What additional requirements must a belief fill in order to be knowledge? There are surely at least the following two: (a) it must be true, and (b) it must be justified (or warranted, reasonable, correct, or the like).

(A2) Let us assume, moreover, with respect to the second condition A1(b): first, that it involves a normative or evaluative property; and, second, that the relevant sort of justification is that which pertains to knowledge: epistemic

Reprinted from *Midwest Studies in Philosophy, Vol. 5: Studies in Epistemology* (Minneapolis: University of Minnesota Press, 1980), 3–25, by permission of the author and the publisher. Copyright 1980, University of Minnesota Press.

(or theoretical) justification. Someone seriously ill may have two sorts of justification for believing he will recover: the practical justification that derives from the contribution such belief will make to his recovery and the theoretical justification provided by the lab results, the doctor's diagnosis and prognosis, and so on. Only the latter is relevant to the question whether he knows.

2. *Knowledge and Criteria*

a. There are two key questions of the theory of knowledge:

(i) What do we know?
(ii) How do we know?

The answer to the first would be a list of bits of knowledge or at least of types of knowledge: of the self, of the external world, of other minds, and so on. An answer to the second would give criteria (or canons, methods, principles, or the like) that would explain how we know whatever it is that we do know.

b. In developing a theory of knowledge, we can begin either with a(i) or with a(ii). Particularism would have us begin with an answer to a(i) and only then take up a(ii) on the basis of that answer. Quite to the contrary, methodism would reverse that order. The particularist thus tends to be antiskeptical on principle. But the methodist is as such equally receptive to skepticism and to the contrary. Hume, for example, was no less a methodist than Descartes. Each accepted, in effect, that only the obvious and what is proved deductively on its basis can possibly be known.

c. What, then, is the obvious? For Descartes it is what we know by intuition, what is clear and distinct, what is indubitable and credible with no fear of error. Thus for Descartes basic knowledge is always an infallible belief in an indubitable truth. All other knowledge must stand on that basis through deductive proof. Starting from such criteria (canons, methods, etc.), Descartes concluded that knowledge extended about as far as his contemporaries believed.[1] Starting from similar criteria, however, Hume concluded that both science and common sense made claims far beyond their rightful limits.

d. Philosophical posterity has rejected Descartes's theory for one main reason: that it admits too easily as obvious what is nothing of the sort. Descartes's reasoning is beautifully simple: God exists; no omnipotent perfectly good being would descend to deceit; but if our common sense beliefs were radically false, that would represent deceit on His part. Therefore, our common sense beliefs must be true or at least cannot be radically false. But in order to buttress this line of reasoning and fill in details, Descartes appeals to various principles that appear something less than indubitable.

e. For his part, Hume rejects all but a minuscule portion of our supposed common sense knowledge. He establishes first that there is no way to prove such supposed knowledge on the basis of what is obvious at any given moment through reason or experience. And he concludes, in keeping with this methodism, that in point of fact there really is no such knowledge.

3. *Two Metaphors: The Raft and the Pyramid*

Both metaphors concern the body or system of knowledge in a given mind. But the mind is of course a more complex marvel than is sometimes supposed. Here I do not allude to the depths plumbed by Freud, nor even to Chomsky's. Nor need we recall the labyrinths inhabited by statesmen and diplomats, nor the rich patterns of some novels or theories. We need look no further than the most common, everyday beliefs. Take, for instance, the belief that driving tonight will be dangerous. Brief reflection should reveal that any of us with that belief will join to it several other closely related beliefs on which the given belief depends for its existence or (at least) its justification. Among such beliefs we could presumably find some or all of the following: that the road will be icy or snowy; that driving on ice or snow is dangerous; that it will rain or snow tonight; that the temperature will be below freezing; appropriate beliefs about the forecast and its reliability; and so on.

How must such beliefs be interrelated in order to help justify my belief about the danger of driving tonight? Here foundationalism and coherentism disagree, each offering its own metaphor. Let us have a closer look at this dispute, starting with foundationalism.

Both Descartes and Hume attribute to human knowledge an architectonic structure. There is a nonsymmetric relation of physical support such that any two floors of a building are tied by that relation: one of the two supports (or at least helps support) the other. And there is, moreover, a part with a special status: the foundation, which is supported by none of the floors while supporting them all.

With respect to a body of knowledge K (in someone's possession), foundationalism implies that K can be divided into parts K_1, K_2, . . . such that there is some nonsymmetric relation R (analogous to the relation of physical support) which orders those parts in such a way that there is one—call it F—that bears R to every other part while none of them bears R in turn to F.

According to foundationalism, each piece of knowledge lies on a pyramid such as the following:

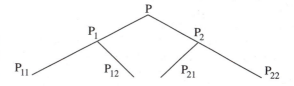

The nodes of such a pyramid (for a proposition P relative to a subject S and a time *t*) must obey the following requirements:

   a. The set of all nodes that succeed (directly) any given node must serve jointly as a base that properly supports that node (for S at *t*).

   b. Each node must be a proposition that S is justified in believing at *t*.

   c. If a node is not self-evident (for S at *t*), it must have successors (that serve jointly as a base that properly supports that node).

   d. Each branch of an epistemic pyramid must terminate.

For the foundationalist Descartes, for instance, each terminating node must be an indubitable proposition that S believes at *t* with no possibility of error. As for the nonterminal nodes, each of them represents inferential knowledge, derived by deduction from more basic beliefs.

   Such radical foundationalism suffers from a fatal weakness that is twofold: (a) there are not so many perfectly obvious truths as Descartes thought; and (b) once we restrict ourselves to what is truly obvious in any given context, very little of one's supposed common sense knowledge can be proved on that basis. If we adhere to such radical foundationalism, therefore, we are just wrong in thinking we know so much.

   Note that in citing such a "fatal weakness" of radical foundationalism, we favor particularism as against the methodism of Descartes and Hume. For we reject the methods or criteria of Descartes and Hume when we realize that they plunge us in a deep skepticism. If such criteria are incompatible with our enjoyment of the rich body of knowledge that we commonly take for granted, then as good particularists we hold on to the knowledge and reject the criteria.

   If we reject radical foundationalism, however, what are we to put in its place? Here epistemology faces a dilemma that different epistemologists resolve differently. Some reject radical foundationalism but retain some more moderate form of foundationalism in favor of a radically different coherentism. Coherentism is associated with idealism—of both the German and the British variety—and has recently acquired new vigor and interest.

   The coherentists reject the metaphor of the pyramid in favor of one that they owe to the positivist Neurath, according to whom our body of knowledge is a raft that floats free of any anchor or tie. Repairs must be made afloat, and though no part is untouchable, we must stand on some in order to replace or repair others. Not every part can go at once.

   According to the new metaphor, what justifies a belief is not that it be an infallible belief with an indubitable object, nor that it have been proved deductively on such a basis, but that it cohere with a comprehensive system of beliefs.

4. A *Coherentist Critique* of *Foundationalism*

What reasons do coherentists offer for their total rejection of foundationalism? The argument that follows below summarizes much of what is alleged against foundationalism. But first we must distinguish between subjective states that incorporate a propositional attitude and those that do not. A propositional attitude is a mental state of someone with a proposition for its object: beliefs, hopes, and fears provide examples. By way of contrast, a headache does not incorporate any such attitude. One can of course be conscious of a headache, but the headache itself does not constitute or incorporate any attitude with a proposition for its object. With this distinction in the background, here is the anti-foundationalist argument, which has two lemmas—a(iv) and b(iii)—and a principal conclusion.

   a.   (i) If a mental state incorporates a propositional attitude, then it does not give us direct contact with reality, e.g., with pure experience, unfiltered by concepts or beliefs.

         (ii) If a mental state does not give us direct

contact with reality, then it provides no guarantee against error.

(iii) If a mental state provides no guarantee against error, then it cannot serve as a foundation for knowledge.

(iv) Therefore, if a mental state incorporates a propositional attitude, then it cannot serve as a foundation for knowledge.

b. (i) If a mental state does not incorporate a propositional attitude, then it is an enigma how such a state can provide support for any hypothesis, raising its credibility selectively by contrast with its alternatives. (If the mental state has no conceptual or propositional content, then what logical relation can it possibly bear to any hypothesis? Belief in a hypothesis would be a propositional attitude with the hypothesis itself as object. How can one depend logically for such a belief on an experience with no propositional content?)

(ii) If a mental state has no propositional content and cannot provide logical support for any hypothesis, then it cannot serve as a foundation for knowledge.

(iii) Therefore, if a mental state does not incorporate a propositional attitude, then it cannot serve as a foundation for knowledge.

c. Every mental state either does or does not incorporate a propositional attitude.

d. Therefore, no mental state can serve as a foundation for knowledge. (From a(iv), b(iii), and c.)

According to the coherentist critic, foundationalism is run through by this dilemma. Let us take a closer look.[2]

In the first place, what reason is there to think, in accordance with premise b(i), that only propositional attitudes can give support to their own kind? Consider practices—e.g., broad policies or customs. Could not some person or group be justified in a practice because of its consequences: that is,

could not the consequences of a practice make it a good practice? But among the consequences of a practice may surely be found, for example, a more just distribution of goods and less suffering than there would be under its alternatives. And neither the more just distribution nor the lower degree of suffering is a propositional attitude. This provides an example in which propositional attitudes (the intentions that sustain the practice) are justified by consequences that are not propositional attitudes. That being so, is it not conceivable that the justification of belief that matters for knowledge be analogous to the objective justification by consequences that we find in ethics?

Is it not possible, for instance, that a belief that there is something red before one be justified in part because it has its origins in one's visual experience of red when one looks at an apple in daylight? If we accept such examples, they show us a source of justification that serves as such without incorporating a propositional attitude.

As for premise a(iii), it is already under suspicion from our earlier exploration of premise b(i). A mental state M can be nonpropositional and hence not a candidate for so much as truth, much less infallibility, while it serves, in spite of that, as a foundation of knowledge. Leaving that aside, let us suppose that the relevant mental state is indeed propositional. Must it then be infallible in order to serve as a foundation of justification and knowledge? That is so far from being obvious that it seems more likely false when compared with an analogue in ethics. With respect to beliefs, we may distinguish between their being true and their being justified. Analogously, with respect to actions, we may distinguish between their being optimal (best of all alternatives, all things considered) and their being (subjectively) justified. In practical deliberation on alternatives for action, is it inconceivable that the most *eligible* alternative *not* be objectively the best, all things considered? Can there not be another alternative—perhaps a most repugnant one worth little if any consideration—that in point of fact would have a much better total set of consequences and would thus be better, all things considered? Take the physician attending to Frau Hitler at the birth of little Adolf. Is it not possible that if he had acted less morally, that would have proved better in the fullness of time? And if that is so in ethics, may not its likeness hold good in epistemology? Might there not be justified (reasonable, warranted) beliefs that are not even true, much less infallible? That seems to me not just a conceivable possibility, but indeed a familiar fact of everyday life, where observational beliefs too often prove illusory but no less reasonable for being false.

If the foregoing is on the right track, then the antifoundationalist is far astray. What has led him there?

As a diagnosis of the antifoundationalist argument before us, and more particularly of its second lemma, I would suggest that it rests on an Intellectualist Model of Justification.

According to such a model, the justification of belief (and psychological states generally) is parasitical on certain logical relations among propositions. For example, my belief (i) that the streets are wet, is justified by my pair of beliefs (ii) that it is raining, and (iii) that if it is raining, the streets are wet. Thus we have a structure such as this:

B(Q) is justified by the fact that B(Q) is grounded on (B(P), B(P⊃Q)).

And according to an Intellectualist Model, this is parasitical on the fact that

P and (P⊃Q) together logically imply Q.

Concerning this attack on foundationalism I will argue (a) that it is useless to the coherentist, since if the antifoundationalist dilemma impales the foundationalist, a form of it can be turned against the coherentist to the same effect; (b) that the dilemma would be lethal not only to foundationalism and coherentism but also to the very possibility of substantive epistemology; and (c) that a form of it would have the same effect on normative ethics.

(a) According to coherentism, what justifies a belief is its membership in a coherent and comprehensive set of beliefs. But whereas being grounded on B(P) and B(P⊃Q) is a property of a belief B(Q) that yields immediately the logical implication of Q and P and (P⊃Q) as the logical source of that property's justificatory power, the property of being a member of a coherent set is not one that immediately yields any such implication.

It may be argued, nevertheless, (i) that the property of being a member of a coherent set would supervene in any actual instance on the property of being a member of a particular set *a* that is in fact coherent, and (ii) that this would enable us to preserve our Intellectualist Model, since (iii) the justification of the member belief B(Q) by its membership in *a* would then be parasitical on the logical relations among the beliefs in *a* which constitute the coherence of that set of beliefs, and (iv) the justification of B(Q) by the fact that it is part of a coherent set would then be *indirectly* parasitical on logical relations among propositions after all.

But if such an indirect form of parasitism is allowed, then the experience of pain may perhaps be said to justify belief in its existence parasitically on the fact that P logically implies P! The Intellectualist Model seems either so trivial as to be dull, or else sharp enough to cut equally against both foundationalism and coherentism.

(b) If (i) only propositional attitudes can justify such propositional attitudes as belief, and if (ii) to do so they must in turn be justified by yet other propositional attitudes, it seems clear that (iii) there is no hope of constructing a complete epistemology, one which would give us, in theory, an account of what the justification of any justified belief would supervene on. For (i) and (ii) would rule out the possibility of a finite regress of justification.

(c) If only propositional attitudes can justify propositional attitudes, and if to do so they must in turn be justified by yet other propositional attitudes, it seems clear that there is no hope of constructing a complete normative ethics, one which would give us, in theory, an account of what the justification of any possible justified action would supervene upon. For the justification of an action presumably depends on the intentions it embeds and the justification of these, and here we are already within the net of propositional attitudes from which, for the Intellectualist, there is no escape.

It seems fair to conclude that our coherentist takes his antifoundationalist zeal too far. His antifoundationalist argument helps expose some valuable insights but falls short of its malicious intent. The foundationalist emerges showing no serious damage. Indeed, he now demands equal time for a positive brief in defense of his position.

5. *The Regress Argument*

a. The regress argument in epistemology concludes that we must countenance beliefs that are justified in the absence of justification by other beliefs. But it reaches that conclusion only by rejecting the possibility in principle of an infinite regress of justification. It thus opts for foundational beliefs justified in some noninferential way by ruling out a chain or pyramid of justification that has justifiers, and justifiers of justifiers, and so on *without end*. One may well find this too short a route to foundationalism, however, and demand more compelling reasons for thus rejecting an infinite regress as vicious. We shall find indeed that it is not easy to meet this demand.

b. We have seen how even the most ordinary of everyday beliefs is the tip of an iceberg. A closer look below the surface reveals a complex structure that ramifies with no end in sight. Take again my belief that driving will be dangerous tonight, at the tip of an iceberg, (I), that looks like this:

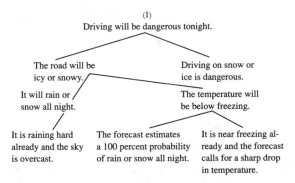

(I)
Driving will be dangerous tonight.

The road will be icy or snowy.

Driving on snow or ice is dangerous.

It will rain or snow all night.

The temperature will be below freezing.

It is raining hard already and the sky is overcast.

The forecast estimates a 100 percent probability of rain or snow all night.

It is near freezing already and the forecast calls for a sharp drop in temperature.

The immediate cause of my belief that driving will be hazardous tonight is the sound of raindrops on the windowpane. All but one or two members of the underlying iceberg are as far as they can be from my thoughts at the time. In what sense, then, do they form an iceberg whose tip breaks the calm surface of my consciousness?

Here I will assume that the members of (I) are beliefs of the subject, even if unconscious or subconscious, that causally buttress and thus justify his prediction about the driving conditions.

Can the iceberg extend without end? It may appear obvious that it cannot do so, and one may jump to the conclusion that any piece of knowledge must be ultimately founded on beliefs that are *not* (inferentially) justified or warranted by other beliefs. This is a doctrine of *epistemic foundationalism*.

Let us focus not so much on the *giving* of justification as on the *having* of it. *Can* there be a belief that is justified in part by other beliefs, some of which are in turn justified by yet other beliefs, and so on without end? Can there be endless regress of justification?

c. There are several familiar objections to such a regress:

(i) *Objection:* "It is incompatible with human limitations. No human subject could harbor the required infinity of beliefs." *Reply:* It is mere presumption to fathom with such assurance the depths of the mind, and especially its unconscious and dispositional depths. Besides, our object here is the nature of epistemic justification in itself and not only that of such justification as is accessible to humans. Our question is not whether humans could harbor an infinite iceberg of justification. Our question is rather whether *any* mind, no matter how deep, could do so. Or is it ruled out *in principle* by the very nature of justification?

(ii) *Objection:* "An infinite regress is indeed ruled out in principle, for if justification were thus infinite how could it possibly end? *Reply:* (i) If the end mentioned is *temporal,* then why must there be such an end? In the first place, the subject may be eternal. Even if he is not eternal, moreover, why must belief acquisition and justification occur seriatim? What precludes an infinite body of beliefs acquired at a single stroke? Human limitations may rule this out for humans, but we have yet to be shown that it is precluded in principle, by the very nature of justification. (ii) If the end mentioned is justificatory on the other hand, then to ask how justification could possibly end is just to beg the question.

(iii) *Objection:* "Let us make two assumptions: first, that S's belief of q justifies his belief of p only if it works together with a justified belief on his part that q provides good evidence for p; and, second, that if S is to be justified in believing p on the basis of his belief of q and is to be justified in believing q on the basis of his belief of r, then S must be justified in believing that r provides good evidence for p via q. These assumptions imply that an actual regress of justification requires belief in an infinite proposition. Since no one (or at least no human) can believe an infinite proposition, no one (no human) can be a subject of such an actual regress."[3]

Reply: Neither of the two assumptions is beyond question, but even granting them both, it may still be doubted that the conclusion follows. It is true that each finitely complex belief of form "r provides good evidence for p via $q_1 \ldots q_n$" will *omit* how some members of the full infinite regress are epistemically tied to belief of p. But that seems irrelevant given the fact that for each member r of the regress, such that r is tied epistemically to belief of p, there *is* a finite belief of the required sort ("r provides good evidence for p via $q_1 \ldots q_n$") that ties the two together. Consequently, there is no apparent reason to suppose—even granted the two assumptions— that an infinite regress will require a single belief in an infinite proposition, and not just an infinity of beliefs in increasingly complex finite propositions.

(iv) *Objection:* "But if it is allowed that justification extend infinitely, then it is too easy to justify any belief at all or too many beliefs altogether. Take, for instance, the belief that there are per-

fect numbers greater than 100. And suppose a mind powerful enough to believe every member of the following sequence:

(σ1) There is at least one perfect number > 100
There are at least two perfect numbers > 100
"   three   "

If such a believer has no other belief about perfect numbers save the belief that a perfect number is a whole number equal to the sum of its whole factors, then surely he is *not* justified in believing that there are perfect numbers greater than 100. He is quite unjustified in believing any of the members of sequence (σ1), in spite of the fact that a challenge to any can be met easily by appeal to its successor. Thus it cannot be allowed after all that justification extend infinitely, and an infinite regress is ruled out." *Reply:* We must distinguish between regresses of justification that are actual and those that are merely potential. The difference is *not* simply that an actual regress is composed of actual beliefs. For even if all members of the regress are actual beliefs, the regress may still be *merely potential* in the following sense: while it is true that *if* any member *were* justified then its predecessors *would* be, still none is in fact justified. Anyone with our series of beliefs about perfect numbers in the absence of any further relevant information on such numbers would presumably be the subject of such a merely potential justificatory regress.

(v) *Objection:* "But defenders of infinite justificatory regresses cannot distinguish thus between actual regresses and those that are merely potential. There is no real distinction to be drawn between the two. For if any regress ever justifies the belief at its head, then every regress must always do so. But obviously not every regress does so (as we have seen by examples), and hence no regress can do so."[4]

Reply: One can in fact distinguish between actual justificatory regresses and merely potential ones, and one can do so both abstractly and by examples.

What an actual regress has that a merely potential regress lacks is the property of containing only justified beliefs as members. What they both share is the property of containing no member without successors that would jointly justify it.

Recall our regress about perfect numbers greater than 100; i.e., there is at least one; there are at least two; there are at least three; and so on. Each member has a successor that would justify it, but no member is justified (in the absence of further information external to the regress). That is therefore a merely potential infinite regress. As for an actual regress, I see no compelling reason why someone (if not a human, then some more powerful mind) could not hold an infinite series of actually justified beliefs as follows:

(σ2) There is at least one even number
There are at least two even numbers
" three "

It may be that no one could be the subject of such a series of justified beliefs unless he had a proof that there is a denumerable infinity of even numbers. But even if that should be so, it would not take away the fact of the infinite regress of potential justifiers, each of which is actually justified, and hence it would not take away the fact of the actual endless regress of justification.

The objection under discussion is confused, moreover, on the nature of the issue before us. Our question is *not* whether there can be an infinite potential regress, each member of which would be justified by its successors,

such that the belief at its head is justified in virtue of its position there, at the head of such a regress. The existence and even the possibility of a single such regress with a belief at its head that was *not* justified in virtue of its position there would of course settle that question in the negative. Our question is, rather, whether there can be an actual infinite regress of justification, and the fact that a belief at the head of a potential regress might still fail to be justified despite its position does *not* settle this question. For even if there can be a merely potential regress with an unjustified belief at its head, that leaves open the possibility of an infinite regress, each member of which is justified by its immediate successors working jointly, where every member of the regress is in addition actually justified.

6. The Relation of Justification and Foundationalist Strategy

The foregoing discussion is predicated on a simple conception of justification such that a set of beliefs β conditionally justifies (*would* justify) a belief X iff, necessarily, if all members of β are justified then X is also justified (if it exists). The fact that on such a conception of justification actual endless regresses—such as (σ2)—seem quite possible blocks a straightforward regress argument in favor of foundations. For it shows that an actual infinite regress cannot be dismissed out of hand.

Perhaps the foundationalist could introduce some relation of justification—presumably more complex and yet to be explicated—with respect to which it could be argued more plausibly that an actual endless regress is out of the question.

There is, however, a more straightforward strategy open to the foundationalist. For he *need not* object to the possibility of an endless regress of justification. His essential creed is the more positive belief that every justified belief must be at the head of a terminating regress. Fortunately, to affirm the universal necessity of a terminating regress is *not* to deny the bare possibility of a nonterminating regress. For a single belief can trail at once regresses of both sorts: one terminating and one not. Thus the proof of the denumerably infinite cardinality of the set of evens may provide for a powerful enough intellect a *terminating* regress for each member of the *endless* series of justified beliefs:

(σ2) There is at least one even number
         There are at least two even numbers
         "   three   "

At the same time, it is obvious that each member of (σ2) lies at the head of an actual endless regress of justification, on the assumption that each member is conditionally justified by its successor, which is in turn actually justified.

"Thank you so much," the foundationalist may sneer, "but I really do not need that kind of help. Nor do I need to be reminded of my essential creed, which I know as well as anyone. Indeed my rejection of endless regresses of justification is only a means of supporting my view that every justified belief must rest ultimately on foundations, on a terminating regress. You reject that strategy much too casually, in my view, but I will not object here. So we put that strategy aside. And now, my helpful friend, just what do we put in its place?"

Fair enough. How then could one show the need for foundations if an endless regress is not ruled out?

---

7. Two Levels of Foundationalism

a. We need to distinguish, first, between two forms of foundationalism: one *formal,* the other *substantive.* A type of *formal foundationalism* with respect to a normative or evaluative property Φ is the view that the conditions (actual and possible) within which Φ would apply can be specified in general, perhaps recursively. *Substantive foundationalism* is only a particular way of doing so, and coherentism is another.

Simpleminded hedonism is the view that:
    (i) every instance of pleasure is good,

    (ii) everything that causes something good is itself good, and
    (iii) everything that is good is so in virtue of (i) or (ii) above.

Simpleminded hedonism is a type of formal foundationalism with respect to the good.

Classical foundationalism in epistemology is the view that:

    (i) every infallible, indubitable belief is justified.
    (ii) every belief deductively inferred from justified beliefs is itself justified, and
    (iii) every belief that is justified is so in virtue of (i) or (ii) above.

Classical foundationalism is a type of formal foundationalism with respect to epistemic justification.

Both of the foregoing theories—simpleminded hedonism in ethics, and classical foundationalism in epistemology—are of course flawed. But they both remain examples of formal foundationalist theories.

b. One way of arguing in favor of formal foundationalism in epistemology is to formulate a convincing formal foundationalist theory of justification. But classical foundationalism in epistemology no longer has for many the attraction that it had for Descartes, nor has any other form of epistemic foundationalism won general acceptance. Indeed epistemic foundationalism has been generally abandoned, and its advocates have been put on the defensive by the writings of Wittgenstein, Quine, Sellars, Rescher, Aune, Harman, Lehrer, and others. It is lamentable that in our headlong rush away from foundationalism we have lost sight of the different types of foundationalism (formal vs. substantive) and of the different grades of each type. Too many of us now see it as a blur to be decried and avoided. Thus our present attempt to bring it all into better focus.

c. If we cannot argue from a generally accepted foundationalist theory, what reason is there to accept formal foundationalism? There is no reason to think that the conditions (actual and possible) within which an object is spherical are generally specifiable in nongeometric terms. Why should we think that the conditions (actual and possible) within which a belief is epistemically justified are generally specifiable in nonepistemic terms?

So far as I can see, the main reason for accepting formal foundationalism in the absence of an actual, convincing formal foundationalist theory is the very plausible idea that epistemic justification is subject to the supervenience that characterizes normative and evaluative properties generally. Thus, if a car is a good car, then any physical replica of that car must be just as good. If it is a good car in virtue of such properties as being economical, little prone to break down, etc., then surely any exact replica would share all such properties and would thus be equally good. Similarly, if a belief is epistemically justified, it is presumably so in virtue of its character and its basis in perception, memory, or inference (if any). Thus any belief exactly like it in its character and its basis must be equally well justified. Epistemic justification is supervenient. The justification of a belief supervenes on such properties of it as its content and its basis (if any) in perception, memory, or inference. Such a doctrine of supervenience may itself be considered, with considerable justice, a grade of foundationalism. For it entails that every instance of justified belief is founded on a number of its nonepistemic properties, such as its having a certain basis in perception, memory, and inference, or the like.

But there are higher grades of foundationalism as well. There is, for instance, the doctrine that the conditions (actual and possible) within which a belief would be epistemically justified *can be specified* in general, perhaps recursively (and by reference to such notions as perception, memory, and inference).

A higher grade yet of formal foundationalism requires not only that the conditions for justified belief be specifiable, in general, but that they be specifiable by a simple, comprehensive theory.

d. Simpleminded hedonism is a formal foundationalist theory of the highest grade. If it is true, then in every possible world goodness supervenes on pleasure and causation in a way that is recursively specifiable by means of a very simple theory.

Classical foundationalism in epistemology is also a formal foundationalist theory of the highest grade. If it is true, then in every possible world epistemic justification supervenes on infallibility cum indubitability and deductive inference in a way

that is recursively specifiable by means of a very simple theory.

Surprisingly enough, coherentism may also turn out to be formal foundationalism of the highest grade, provided only that the concept of coherence is itself both simple enough and free of any normative or evaluative admixture. Given these provisos, coherentism explains how epistemic justification supervenes on the nonepistemic in a theory of remarkable simplicity: a belief is justified if it has a place within a system of beliefs that is coherent and comprehensive.

It is a goal of ethics to explain how the ethical rightness of an action supervenes on what is not ethically evaluative or normative. Similarly, it is a goal of epistemology to explain how the epistemic justification of a belief supervenes on what is not epistemically evaluative or normative. If coherentism aims at this goal, that imposes restrictions on the notion of coherence, which must now be conceived innocent of epistemically evaluative or normative admixture. Its substance must therefore consist of such concepts as explanation, probability, and logical implication—with these conceived, in turn, innocent of normative or evaluative content.

e. We have found a surprising kinship between coherentism and substantive foundationalism, both of which turn out to be varieties of a deeper foundationalism. This deeper foundationalism is applicable to any normative or evaluative property Φ, and it comes in three grades. The *first* or lowest is simply the supervenience of Φ: the idea that whenever something has Φ its having it is founded on certain others of its properties which fall into certain restricted sorts. The *second* is the explicable supervenience of Φ: the idea that there are formulable principles that explain in quite general terms the conditions (actual and possible) within which Φ applies. The *third* and highest is the easily explicable supervenience of Φ: the idea that there is a *simple* theory that explains the conditions within which Φ applies. We have found the coherentist and the substantive foundationalist sharing a primary goal: the development of a formal foundationalist theory of the highest grade. For they both want a simple theory that explains precisely how epistemic justification supervenes, in general, on the nonepistemic. This insight gives us an unusual viewpoint on some recent attacks against foundationalism. Let us now consider as an example a certain simple form of argument distilled from the recent antifoundationalist literature.[5]

8.   *Doxastic Ascent Arguments*

Several attacks on foundationalism turn on a sort of "doxastic ascent" argument that calls for closer scrutiny.[6] Here are two examples:

A. A belief B is foundationally justified for S in virtue of having property F only if S is justified in believing (1) that most at least of his beliefs with property F are true, and (2) that B has property F. But this means that belief B is not foundational after all, and indeed that the very notion of (empirical) foundational belief is incoherent.

It is sometimes held, for example, that perceptual or observational beliefs are often justified through their origin in the exercise of one or more of our five senses in standard conditions of perception. The advocate of doxastic ascent would raise a vigorous protest, however, for in his view the mere fact of such sensory prompting is impotent to justify the belief prompted. Such prompting must be coupled with the further belief that one's senses work well in the circumstances, or the like. For we are dealing here with *knowledge,* which requires not blind faith but *reasoned* trust. But now surely the further belief about the reliability of one's senses itself cannot rest on blind faith but requires its own backing of reasons, and we are off on the regress.

B. A belief B of proposition P is foundationally justified for S only if S is justified in believing that there are no factors present that would cause him to make mistakes on the matter of the proposition P. But, again, this means that belief B is not foundational after all and indeed that the notion of (empirical) foundational belief is incoherent.

From the vantage point of formal foundationalism, neither of these arguments seems persuasive. In the first place, as we have seen, what makes a belief foundational (formally) is its having a property that is nonepistemic (not evaluative in the epistemic or cognitive mode), and does not involve inference from other beliefs, but guarantees, via a necessary principle, that the belief in question is justified. A belief B is made foundational by having some such nonepistemic property that yields its justification. Take my belief that I am in pain in a context where it is caused by my being in pain. The property that my belief then has, of being a self-attribution of pain caused by one's own pain is, let us suppose, a nonepistemic property that yields the justification of any belief that has it. So my belief that I am in pain is in that context foundationally justified. Along with my belief that I am in pain, however, there come other beliefs that are equally well justified, such as my belief that I am in pain only if I am justified in believing that someone is in pain. Those who object to foundationalism as in A or B above are hence mistaken in thinking that their premises would refute foundationalism. The fact is that they would not touch it. For a belief is no less foundationally justified for having its justification yoked to that of another closely related belief.

The advocate of arguments like A and B must apparently strengthen his premises. He must apparently claim that the beliefs whose justification is entailed by the foundationally justified status of belief B must in some sense function as a *necessary source* of the justification of B. And this would of course preclude giving B foundationally justified status. For if the *being justified* of those beliefs is an *essential* part of the source of the justification of B, then it is ruled out that there be a wholly *nonepistemic* source of B's justification.

That brings us to a second point about A and B, for it should now be clear that these cannot be selectively aimed at foundationalism. In particular, they seem neither more nor less valid objections to coherentism than to foundationalism, or so I will now argue about each of them in turn.

A′. A belief X is justified for S in virtue of membership in a coherent set only if S is justified in believing (1) that most at least of his beliefs with the property of thus cohering are true, and (2) that X has that property.

Any coherentist who accepts A seems bound to accept A′. For what could he possibly appeal to as a relevant difference? But A′ is a quicksand of endless depth. (How is he justified in believing A′(1)?

Partly through justified belief that *it* coheres? And what would justify *this*? And so on . . .)

B'. A belief X is justified for S only if S is justified in believing that there are no factors present that would cause him to make mistakes on the subject matter of that belief.

Again, any coherentist who accepts B seems bound to accept B'. But this is just another road to the quicksand. (For S is justified in believing that there are no such factors only if . . . and so on.)

Why are such regresses vicious? The key is again, to my mind, the doctrine of supervenience. Such regresses are vicious because they would be logically incompatible with the supervenience of epistemic justification on such nonepistemic facts as the totality of a subject's beliefs, his cognitive and experiential history, and as many other nonepistemic facts as may seem at all relevant. The idea is that there is a set of such nonepistemic facts surrounding a justified belief such that no belief could possibly have been surrounded by those very facts without being justified. Advocates of A or B run afoul of such supervenience, since they are surely committed to the more general views derivable from either A or B by deleting 'foundationally' from its first sentence. In each case the more general view would then preclude the possibility of supervenience, since it would entail that the source of justification *always* includes an *epistemic* component.

9. Coherentism and Substantive Foundationalism

a. The notions of coherentism and substantive foundationalism remain unexplicated. We have relied so far on our intuitive grasp of them. In this section we shall consider reasons for the view that substantive foundationalism is superior to coherentism. To assess these reasons, we need some more explicit account of the difference between the two.

By coherentism we shall mean any view according to which the ultimate sources of justification for any belief lie in relations among that belief and other beliefs of the subject: explanatory relations, perhaps, or relations of probability or logic.

According to substantive foundationalism, as it is to be understood here, there are ultimate sources of justification other than relations among beliefs. Traditionally these additional sources have pertained to the special content of the belief or its special relations to the subjective experience of the believer.

b. The view that justification is a matter of relations among beliefs is open to an objection from alternative coherent systems or detachment from reality, depending on one's perspective. From the latter perspective the body of beliefs is held constant and the surrounding world is allowed to vary, whereas from the former perspective it is the surrounding world that is held constant while the body of beliefs is allowed to vary. In either case, according to the coherentist, there could be no effect on the justification for any belief.

Let us sharpen the question before us as follows. Is there reason to think that there is at least one system B', alternative to our actual system of beliefs B, such that B' contains a belief X with the following properties:

   (i) in our present nonbelief circumstances we would not be justified in having belief X even if we accepted along with that belief (as our total system of beliefs) the entire belief system B' in which it is embedded (no matter how acceptance of B' were brought about); and

   (ii) that is so despite the fact that belief X coheres within B' at least as fully as does some actual justified belief of ours within our actual belief system B (where the justification of that actual justified belief is alleged by the coherentist to derive solely from its coherence within our actual body of beliefs B).

The coherentist is vulnerable to counterexamples of this sort right at the surface of his body of beliefs, where we find beliefs with minimal coherence, whose detachment and replacement with contrary beliefs would have little effect on the coherence of the body. Thus take my belief that I have a headache when I do have a splitting headache, and let us suppose that this *does* cohere within my present body of beliefs. (Thus I have no reason to doubt my present introspective beliefs, and so on.

And if my belief does *not* cohere, so much the worse for coherentism, since my belief is surely justified.) Here then we have a perfectly justified or warranted belief. And yet such a belief may well have relevant relations of explanation, logic, or probability with at most a small set of other beliefs of mine at the time: say, that I am not free of headache, that I am in pain, that someone is in pain, and the like. If so, then an equally coherent alternative is not far to seek. Let everything remain constant, *including* the splitting headache, except for the following: replace the belief that I have a headache with the belief that I do *not* have a headache, the belief that I am in pain with the belief that I am *not* in pain, the belief that someone is in pain with the belief that someone is *not* in pain, and so on. I contend that my resulting hypothetical system of beliefs would cohere as fully as does my actual system of beliefs, and yet my hypothetical belief that I do *not* have a headache would not therefore be justified. What makes this difference concerning justification between my actual belief that I have a headache and the hypothetical belief that I am free of headache, each as coherent as the other within its own system, if not the actual splitting headache? But the headache is *not* itself a belief nor a relation among beliefs and is thus in no way constitutive of the internal coherence of my body of beliefs.

Some might be tempted to respond by alleging that one's belief about whether or not one has a headache is always *infallible*. But since we could devise similar examples for the various sensory modalities and propositional attitudes, the response given for the case of headache would have to be generalized. In effect, it would have to cover "peripheral" beliefs generally—beliefs at the periphery of one's body of beliefs, minimally coherent with the rest. These peripheral beliefs would all be said to be infallible. That is, again, a possible response, but it leads to a capitulation by the coherentist to the radical foundationalist on a crucial issue that has traditionally divided them: the infallibility of beliefs about one's own subjective states.

What is more, not all peripheral beliefs are about one's own subjective states. The direct realist is probably right that some beliefs about our surroundings are uninferred and yet justified. Consider my present belief that the table before me is oblong.

This presumably coheres with such other beliefs of mine as that the table has the same shape as the piece of paper before me, which is oblong, and a different shape than the window frame here, which is square, and so on. So far as I can see, however, there is no insurmountable obstacle to replacing that whole set of coherent beliefs with an equally coherent set as follows: that the table before me is square, that the table has the same shape as the square window frame, and a different shape than the piece of paper, which is oblong, and so on. The important points are (a) that this replacement may be made without changing the rest of one's body of beliefs or any aspect of the world beyond, including one's present visual experience of something oblong, not square, as one looks at the table before one; and (b) that it is so, in part, because of the fact (c) that the subject need not have any beliefs about his present sensory experience.

Some might be tempted to respond by alleging that one's present experience is *self-intimating,* i.e., always necessarily taken note of and reflected in one's beliefs. Thus if anyone has visual experience of something oblong, then he believes that he has such experience. But this would involve a further important concession by the coherentist to the radical foundationalist, who would have been granted two of his most cherished doctrines: the infallibility of introspective belief and the self-intimation of experience.

10. *The Foundationalist's Dilemma*

The antifoundationalist zeal of recent years has left several forms of foundationalism standing. These all share the conviction that a belief can be justified not only by its coherence within a comprehensive system but also by an appropriate combination of observational content and origin in the use of the senses in standard conditions. What follows presents a dilemma for any foundationalism based on any such idea.

a. We may surely suppose that beings with observational mechanisms radically unlike ours might also have knowledge of their environment. (That seems possible even if the radical difference in observational mechanisms precludes overlap in substantive concepts and beliefs.)

b. Let us suppose that there is such a being, for whom experience of type ϕ (of which we have no notion) has a role with respect to his beliefs of type ϕ analogous to the role that our visual experience has with respect to our visual beliefs. Thus we might have a schema such as the following:

Human	Extraterrestrial being
Visual experience	ϕ experience
Experience of something red	Experience of something F
Belief that there is something red before one	Belief that there is something F before one

c. It is often recognized that our visual experience intervenes in two ways with respect to our visual beliefs: as cause and as justification. But these are not wholly independent. Presumably, the justification of the belief that something here is red derives at least in part from the fact that it originates in a visual experience of something red that takes place in normal circumstances.

d. Analogously, the extraterrestrial belief that something here has the property of being F might be justified partly by the fact that it originates in a ϕ experience of something F that takes place in normal circumstances.

e. A simple question presents the foundationalist's dilemma: regarding the epistemic principle that underlies our justification for believing that something here is red on the basis of our visual experience of something red, is it proposed as a fundamental principle or as a derived generalization? Let us compare the famous Principle of Utility of value theory, according to which it is best for that to happen which, of all the possible alternatives in the circumstances, would bring with it into the world the greatest balance of pleasure over pain, joy over sorrow, happiness over unhappiness, content over discontent, or the like. Upon this fundamental principle one may then base various generalizations, rules of thumb, and maxims of public health,

nutrition, legislation, etiquette, hygiene, and so on. But these are all then derived generalizations which rest for their validity on the fundamental principle. Similarly, one may also ask, with respect to the generalizations advanced by our foundationalist, whether these are proposed as fundamental principles or as derived maxims or the like. This sets him face to face with a dilemma, each of whose alternatives is problematic. If his proposals are meant to have the status of secondary or derived maxims, for instance, then it would be quite unphilosophical to stop there. Let us turn, therefore, to the other alternative.

f. On reflection it seems rather unlikely that epistemic principles for the justification of observational beliefs by their origin in sensory experience could have a status more fundamental than that of derived generalizations. For by granting such principles fundamental status we would open the door to a multitude of equally basic principles with no unifying factor. There would be some for vision, some for hearing, etc., without even mentioning the corresponding extraterrestrial principles.

g. It may appear that there is after all an idea, however, that unifies our multitude of principles. For they all involve sensory experience and sensible characteristics. But what is a sensible characteristic? Aristotle's answer appeals to examples: colors, shapes, sounds, and so on. Such a notion might enable us to unify perceptual epistemic principles under some more fundamental principle such as the following.

If σ is a sensible characteristic, then the belief that there is something with σ before one is (prima facie) justified if it is based on a visual experience of something with σ in conditions that are normal with respect to σ.

h. There are at least two difficulties with such a suggestion, however, and neither one can be brushed aside easily. First, it is not clear that we can have a viable notion of sensible characteristics on the basis of examples so diverse as colors, shapes, tones, odors, and so on. Second, the authority of such a principle apparently derives from contingent circumstances concerning the reliability of beliefs prompted by sensory experiences of certain sorts. According to the foundationalist, our visual beliefs are justified by their origin in our visual experience or the like. Would such beliefs be equally well justified in a world where beliefs with such an origin were nearly always false?

   i. In addition, finally, even if we had a viable notion of such characteristics, it is not obvious that fundamental knowledge of reality would have to derive causally or otherwise from sensory experience of such characteristics. How could one impose reasonable limits on extraterrestrial mechanisms for noninferential acquisition of beliefs? Is it not possible that such mechanisms need not always function through sensory experience of any sort? Would such beings necessarily be denied any knowledge of the surroundings and indeed of any contingent spatio-temporal fact? Let us suppose them to possess a complex system of true beliefs concerning their surroundings, the structures below the surface of things, exact details of history and geography, all constituted by concepts none of which corresponds to any of our sensible characteristics. What then? Is it not possible that their basic beliefs should all concern fields of force, waves, mathematical structures, and numerical assignments to variables in several dimensions? This is no doubt an exotic notion, but even so it still seems conceivable. And if it is in fact possible, what then shall we say of the noninferential beliefs of such beings? Would we have to concede the existence of special epistemic principles that can validate their noninferential beliefs? Would it not be preferable to formulate more abstract principles that can cover both human and extraterrestrial foundations? If such more abstract principles are in fact accessible, then the less general principles that define the human foundations and those that define the extraterrestrial foundations are both derived principles whose validity depends on that of the more abstract principles. In this the human and extraterrestrial epistemic principles would resemble rules of good nutrition for an infant and an adult. The infant's rules would of course be quite unlike those valid for the adult. But both would still be based on a more fundamental principle that postulates the ends of well-being and good health. What more fundamental principles might support both human and extraterrestrial

knowledge in the way that those concerning good health and well-being support rules of nutrition for both the infant and adult?

---

11. *Reliabilism: An Ethics of Moral Virtues and an Epistemology of Intellectual Virtues*

In what sense is the doctor attending Frau Hitler justified in performing an action that brings with it far less value than one of its accessible alternatives? According to one promising idea, the key is to be found in the rules that he embodies through stable dispositions. His action is the result of certain stable virtues, and there are no equally virtuous alternative *dispositions* that, given his cognitive limitations, he might have embodied with equal or better total consequences, and that would have led him to infanticide in the circumstances. The important move for our purpose is the stratification of justification. Primary justification attaches to virtues and other dispositions, to stable dispositions to act, through their greater contribution of value when compared with alternatives. Secondary justification attaches to particular acts in virtue of their source in virtues or other such justified dispositions.

   The same strategy may also prove fruitful in epistemology. Here primary justification would apply to *intellectual* virtues, to stable dispositions for belief acquisition, through their greater contribution toward getting us to the truth. Secondary justification would then attach to particular beliefs in virtue of their source in intellectual virtues or other such justified dispositions.[7]

   That raises parallel questions for ethics and epistemology. We need to consider more carefully the concept of a virtue and the distinction between moral and intellectual virtues. In epistemology, there is reason to think that the most useful and illuminating notion of intellectual virtue will prove broader than our tradition would suggest and must give due weight not only to the subject and his intrinsic nature but also to his environment and to his epistemic community. This is a large topic, however, to which I hope some of us will turn with more space, and insight, than I can now command.[8]

Summary

1. *Two assumptions:* (A1) that for a belief to constitute knowledge it must be (a) true and (b) justified; and (A2) that the justification relevant to whether or not one knows is a sort of epistemic or theoretical justification to be distinguished from its practical counterpart.

2. *Knowledge and criteria.* Particularism is distinguished from methodism: the first gives priority to particular examples of knowledge over general methods or criteria, whereas the second reverses that order. The methodism of Descartes leads him to an elaborate dogmatism whereas that of Hume leads him to a very simple skepticism. The particularist is, of course, antiskeptical on principle.

3. *Two metaphors: the raft and the pyramid.* For the foundationalist every piece of knowledge stands at the apex of a pyramid that rests on stable and secure foundations whose stability and security do not derive from the upper stories or sections. For the coherentist a body of knowledge is a free-floating raft every plank of which helps directly or indirectly to keep all the others in place, and no plank of which would retain its status with no help from the others.

4. *A coherentist critique of foundationalism.* No mental state can provide a foundation for empirical knowledge. For if such a state is propositional, then it is fallible and hence no secure foundation. But if it is *not* propositional, then how can it possibly serve as a foundation for belief? How can one infer or justify anything on the basis of a state that, having no propositional content, must be logically dumb? An analogy with ethics suggests a reason to reject this dilemma. Other reasons are also advanced and discussed.

5. *The regress argument.* In defending his position, the foundationalist often attempts to rule out the very possibility of an infinite regress of justification (which leads him to the necessity for a foundation). Some of his arguments to that end are examined.

6. *The relation of justification and foundationalist strategy.* An alternative foundationalist strategy is exposed, one that does not require ruling out the possibility of an infinite regress of justification.

7. *Two levels of foundationalism.* Substantive foundationalism is distinguished from formal foundationalism, three grades of which are exposed: first, the supervenience of epistemic justification; second, its explicable supervenience; and, third, its supervenience explicable by means of a simple theory. There turns out to be a surprising kinship between coherentism and substantive foundationalism, both of which aim at a formal foundationalism of the highest grade, at a theory of the greatest simplicity that explains how epistemic justification supervenes on nonepistemic factors.

8. *Doxastic ascent arguments.* The distinction between formal and substantive foundationalism provides an unusual viewpoint on some recent attacks against foundationalism. We consider doxastic ascent arguments as an example.

9. *Coherentism and substantive foundationalism.* It is argued that substantive foundationalism is superior, since coherentism is unable to account adequately for the epistemic status of beliefs at the "periphery" of a body of beliefs.

10. *The foundationalist's dilemma.* All foundationalism based on sense experience is subject to a fatal dilemma.

11. *Reliabilism.* An alternative to foundationalism of sense experience is sketched.

Notes

1 But Descartes's methodism was at most partial. James Van Cleve has supplied the materials for a convincing argument that the way out of the Cartesian circle is through a particularism of basic knowledge. See James Van Cleve, "Foundationalism, Epistemic Principles, and the Cartesian Circle." But this is, of course, compatible with methodism on inferred knowledge. Whether Descartes subscribed to such methodism is hard (perhaps impossible) to determine, since in the end he makes room for all the kinds of knowledge required by particularism. But his language when he introduces the method of hyperbolic doubt, and the order in which he proceeds, suggest that he did subscribe to such methodism.

2 Cf. Laurence BonJour, "Holistic Coherentism" [Reading V.4—Ed.] and, especially, Michael Williams, *Groundless Belief;* and BonJour, "A Critique of Foundationalism" [Reading V.3—Ed.].

3 Cf. Richard Foley, "Inferential Justification and the Infinite Regress," *American Philosophical Quarterly* 15 (1978): 311–16.

4 Cf. John Post, "Infinite Regresses of Justification and of Explanation," *Philosophical Studies* 34 (1980).

5 The argument of this whole section is developed in greater detail in my paper "The Foundations of Foundationalism."

6 For some examples of the influence of doxastic ascent arguments, see Wilfrid Sellars's writing in epistemology: "Empiricism and the Philosophy of Mind," especially section VIII, and particularly p. 168. Also I. T. Oakley, "An Argument for Skepticism Concerning Justified Belief," *American Philosophical Quarterly* 13 (1976): 221–28; and BonJour, "A Critique of Foundationalism" [Reading V.3—Ed.].

7 This puts in a more traditional perspective the contemporary effort to develop a "causal theory of knowing." From our viewpoint, this effort is better understood not as an attempt to *define* propositional knowledge, but as an attempt to formulate fundamental principles of justification.

Cf. the work of D. Armstrong, *Belief, Truth, and Knowledge,* and that of F. Dretske, A. Goldman, and M. Swain, whose relevant already published work is included in *Essays on Knowledge and Justification,* ed. G. Pappas and M. Swain (Ithaca and London, 1978). But the theory is still under development by Goldman and by Swain, who have reached general conclusions about it similar to those suggested here, though not necessarily—so far as I know—for the same reasons or in the same overall context.

8 I am indebted above all to Roderick Chisholm: for his writings and for innumerable discussions. The main ideas in the present essay were first presented in a seminar of 1976–77 at the University of Texas. I am grateful to Anthony Anderson, David and Jean Blumenfeld, Laurence BonJour, and Martin Perlmutter, who made that seminar a valuable stimulus. Subsequent criticism by my colleague James Van Cleve has also been valuable and stimulating.

V.7 *Fallibilist Foundationalism and Holistic Coherentism*

ROBERT AUDI

Robert Audi is Professor of Philosophy at the University of Nebraska. Audi writes, "This essay is a study of the foundationalism–coherentism controversy with special attention to each position as a response to the epistemic regress problem. The essay distinguishes two ways of formulating that problem—dialectical and structural—and shows their importance for developing a properly qualified foundationalism. Coherentism is also clarified in the light of the regress problem. A central thrust of the essay is that a fallibilist foundationalism can both avoid many of the influential criticisms of foundationalist theories and accommodate many of the insights associated with coherentism."

Foundationalism and coherentism each contain significant epistemological truths.[1] Both positions are, moreover, intellectually influential even outside epistemology. But most philosophers defending either position have been mainly concerned to argue for their view and against the other side, which they have often interpreted through just one leading proponent. It is not surprising, then, that although the foundationalism–coherentism controversy remains a focus of epistemological attention, philosophers in each tradition often feel misunderstood by those in the other. The unclarity—and unwarranted stereotyping—about both foundationalism and coherentism go beyond what one would expect from terminological and philosophical diversity: there are genuine obscurities and misconceptions. Because both positions, and especially foundationalism, are responses to the epistemic regress problem, I begin with a brief account of that perennial conundrum.

This essay was commissioned for this anthology and appears here for the first time.

I. *Two Conceptions of the Epistemic Regress Problem*

There is wide agreement that the epistemic regress argument gives crucial support to foundationalism, and even coherentists, who reject the argument, grant that the regress problem which generates it is important in motivating their views.[2] Let us start, then, with a statement of that problem.

There are at least two major contexts—often not distinguished—in which the regress problem arises. Central to one context is pursuit of the question how we know or are justified in believing some particular thing, most typically a proposition about the external world; for example, that one saw a bear in the woods. This context is often colored by conceiving such questions as skeptical challenges. The challenges are often spearheaded by the question "How do you know?" Central to the other main context in which the regress problem arises are the questions of what *grounds* our knowledge or justification. We must consider the regress problem raised in both ways.

Suppose I am asked how I know that *p*, say that there are books in my study. The skeptic, for instance, issues the question as a challenge. I might reply by citing a ground of the belief in question, say *q:* I have a clear recollection of books in my study. The skeptic then challenges the apparent presupposition that I know the ground holds; after all, if I do have a ground, it is natural to think that I should be able (at least on reflection) not just to produce it but also to justify it: how else can I be entitled to take it as a ground? Thus, if "How do you know?" is motivated by a skeptical interest in knowledge, the question of how I know is likely to be reiterated, at least if *q* is not self-evident; for unless *q* is self-evident, and in that sense a self-certifying ground for *p*, the questioner—particularly if skeptical—will accept my citing *q* as answering, "How do you know that *p*?" only on the assumption that I *also* know that *q*. How far can this questioning go? How far should it go?

For epistemologists, the problem posed by "How do you know?" and "What justifies you?" is to answer such questions without making one or another apparently inevitable move that ultimately undermines the possibility of knowledge or justification, and hence confirms skepticism. The way the issue initially appears, we have three unpleasant options. The first is to rotate regressively in a vicious circle, say from *p* to *q* as a ground for *p*, then to *r* as a ground for *q*, and then back to *p* as a ground for *r*. The second option is to fall into a vicious regress, in the usual sense in which a regress is an infinite series: from *p* to *q* as a ground for *p*, then to *r* as a ground for *q*, then to *s* as a ground for *r*, and so on to infinity. The third option is to stop at a purported ground, say *s*, that does not constitute knowledge or even justified belief; but if one neither knows nor justifiedly believes *s*, it is at best difficult to see how citing *s* can answer the question how one knows that *p*. The fourth option is to stop with something known or justifiedly believed, say *r*, but *not* known on the basis of any further knowledge or justified belief. Here the problem as many see it is that *r*, not being believed on any further ground, is just an arbitrary way of stopping the regress and is only capriciously taken to be known or justifiedly believed. Thus, *citing r* as a final answer to the chain of queries seems dogmatic. I want to call this difficulty—how to answer, dialectically, questions about how one knows or about what justifies one—the *dialectical form of the regress problem*.[3]

Imagine, by contrast, that we consider either the entire body of a person's apparent knowledge, as Aristotle seems to have done,[4] or a representative item of apparent knowledge, say my belief that there are books in my study, and ask on what this apparent knowledge is grounded (or based) and whether, if it is grounded on some further belief, *all* our knowledge or justified belief could be so grounded. We are now asking a structural question about knowledge, not requesting a verbal response in defense of a claim to it. No dialectic need even be imagined; we are considering a person's overall knowledge, or some presumably representative item of it, and asking how that body of knowledge is structured or how that item of knowledge is grounded. Again we get a regress problem: how to specify my grounds without vicious circularity or regress or, on the other hand, stopping with a belief that does not constitute knowledge (or is not justified), or seems only capriciously regarded as knowledge. Call this search for appropriate grounds of knowledge the *structural form of the regress problem*.

To see how the two forms of the regress problem differ, think of them as arising from different ways of asking, "How do you know?" It can be asked with *skeptical force*, as a challenge to people who either claim to know something or (more commonly) presuppose that some belief they confidently hold represents knowledge. Here the question is roughly equivalent to "Show me that you know." It can also be asked with *informational force*, as where someone simply wants to know by what *route*, such as observation or testimony, someone came to know something. Here the question is roughly equivalent to "How do you know?" The skeptical form of the question does *not* presuppose that the person in question really has any knowledge, and, asked in this way, the question tends to generate the dialectical form of the regress. The informational form of the question typically *does* presuppose that the person knows the proposition in question. It is easy to assume that it does not matter in which way we formulate the problem. But it *does* matter, for at least four reasons.

Knowing Versus Showing We Know

First, the dialectical form of the regress problem invites us to think that an adequate answer to "How do you know?" *shows* that we know. This is so particularly *in* the context of a concern to reply to skepticism. For the skeptic is not interested in the information most commonly sought when people ask how someone knows, say information about the origin of the belief; for example, in firsthand observation as opposed to testimony. It is, however, far from clear that an adequate answer to the how question must be an adequate answer to the show question. If by citing the testimony of a credible witness who saw the accident I tell you how I know there were injuries, you may be satisfied; but I have not shown that I know (as I might by taking you to the scene), and the skeptic who, with the force of a challenge, asks how I know will not be satisfied. I have answered the informational form of the question, but not the skeptical form.

First-Order Versus Second-Order Knowledge

Second, when the regress problem is dialectically formulated, any full non-skeptical answer to "How do you know that *p*?" will tend to imply an epistemic ascription, say "I know that *q*." Thus, my answer is admissible only if I both have the concept of knowledge—because I would otherwise not understand what I am attributing to myself—*and* am at least dialectically warranted in asserting that I do know that *q*. If you ask, informationally, how I know there were injuries, I simply say (for instance) that I heard it from Janet, who saw them. But if you ask, skeptically, how I know it, I will realize you will not accept evidence I merely *have,* but only evidence I *know;* and I will thus tend to say something to the effect that I *know* that Janet saw the injuries. Because this in effect claims knowledge of knowledge, it succeeds only if I meet the second-order standard for having knowledge that I know. If, however, the regress problem is structurally formulated, it is then sufficient for a solution that there *be* propositions which, whether or not I believe them *prior* to being questioned, are both warranted for me (reasonable for me *to* believe) and together justify the proposition originally in question. For this to be true of me, I need only meet a first-order standard—for example, to remember the accident—and thereby be justified in believing there were injuries.

Having, Giving, and Showing a Solution

Third, and largely implicit in the first two points, the two formulations of the regress problem differ as to what must hold for there to *be,* and for S to *give,* an adequate answer to "How do you know?" or "What justifies you?" On the structural formulation, if there *are* warranted propositions of the kind just described, as where I am warranted in believing there were injuries, the problem (as applied to *p,* the proposition in question) *has* a solution; and if I *cite* them in answering "How do you know that *p*?" I *give* a solution to the problem. By contrast, when the problem is dialectically formulated, it is taken to have a solution only if there not only *are* such propositions, but I can also show by *argument* that there are; and to give a solution, I must not merely cite these propositions but also show that they are justified and that they in turn justify *p.* Thus, I cannot adequately say how I know there are books in my study by citing my recollection unless I can show by argument that it is warranted and justifies concluding that books are indeed there. In raising the structural form of the problem, it is assumed only that if I know that *p,* I have grounds of this knowledge that are expressible in propositions warranted for me; it is not assumed that I can formulate the grounds or show that they imply knowledge. The structural form thus encourages us to conceive solutions as *propositional,* in the sense that they depend on the evidential propositions warranted for me; the dialectical form encourages conceiving solutions, as *argumental,* since they depend on what *arguments* about the evidence are accessible to me. I must be able to enter the dialectic with good arguments for *p,* not simply to be warranted in believing evidence propositions that justify *p.*

The Process of Justification Versus the Property of Justification

Fourth, a dialectical formulation, at least as applied to justification—which is widely considered an element in knowledge—tends to focus our attention on the *process* of justification (i.e., of justifying a proposition), although the initial question concerns whether the relevant belief has the *property* of justification (i.e., of being justified). The skeptical forms of the questions "How you know?" and "What justifies you?" tend to start a process of argument; "Show me that you know" demands a response, and what is expected is a process of justifying the belief that *p*. The informational form of those questions tends to direct someone to cite a ground, such as clear recollection, and the knowledge or (property of) justification in question may be simply taken to be based on this ground. "By what route (or on what basis) do you know?" need not start a process (although it may). It implies that providing a good ground—one in virtue of which the belief that *p* has the property of being justified—will fully answer the question.

If I am correct in thinking that the dialectical and structural formulations of the regress problem are significantly different, which is preferable in appraising the foundationalism–coherentism controversy? One consideration is neutrality; we should try to avoid bias toward any particular epistemological theory. The dialectical formulation, however, favors coherentism, or at least non-foundationalism. Let me explain.

Foundationalists typically posit beliefs that are grounded in experience or reason and are direct in two senses. First, they are *psychologically direct:* non-inferential (in the most common sense of that term), and thus not held on the basis of (hence through) some further belief. Second, they are *epistemically direct:* they do not depend (inferentially) for their status as knowledge, or for any justification they have, on other beliefs, justification, or knowledge. The first kind of direct belief has no psychological intermediary of the relevant kind—namely, belief. The second kind has no evidential intermediary, such as knowledge of a premise for the belief in question. Roughly, epistemically direct beliefs are not inferentially *based on* other beliefs or knowledge, and this point holds whether or not there is any actual *process* of inference.[5] Now imagine that, in dealing with the dialectical form of the regress problem, say in answering the question how I know I have reading material for tonight, I cite, as an appropriate ground, my knowing there are books in my study. In choosing this an an example of knowledge, I express a belief that I do in fact know there are books in the study. But am I warranted in this *second-order* belief, as I appear to be warranted simply in believing there *are* books in the study (the

former belief is construed as a second-order belief on the assumption that knowing entails believing, and the belief that one knows is thus in some sense a belief about another belief)? Clearly it is far less plausible to claim that my second-order belief that I *know* there are books in my study is epistemically direct, than to claim this status for my *perceptual* belief that there *are* books in it; for the latter seems non-inferentially based on my seeing them, whereas the former seems inferential; for example, based on beliefs about epistemic status. Thus, foundationalists are less likely to seem able to answer the dialectical formulation of the problem, because doing that requires positing direct second-order knowledge (or at least direct, second-order justified belief). In short, the dialectical form of the problem seems to require foundationalists to posit foundations of a higher order, and a greater degree of complexity, than they are generally prepared to posit. The same point emerges if we note that "How do you know?" can be repeated, and in some fashion answered, indefinitely. Since this question (or a similar one) is central to the dialectical formulation, that formulation tends to be inimical to foundationalism, which posits at least one kind of natural place to stop the regress.

It might seem, on the other hand, that the structural formulation, which stresses our actual cognitive makeup, is inimical toward coherentism. For given our knowledge of cognitive psychology, it is difficult to see how a normal person might *have* anything approaching an infinite chain of beliefs constituting knowings; hence, an infinite chain of answers to "How do you know?" seems out of the question. But this only cuts against an infinite regress approach, not against any finitistic coherentism, which seems the only kind ever plausibly defended. Indeed, even assuming—as coherentists may grant—that much of our knowledge in fact arises, non-inferentially, from experiential states such as seeing, the structural formulation of the problem allows *both* that, as foundationalists typically claim, there is non-inferential knowledge and that, as coherentists typically claim, non-inferential beliefs are dialectically defensible indefinitely and (when true) capable of constituting knowledge only by virtue of coherence. The structural formulation may not demand that such defenses be available indefinitely; but it also does not preclude this nor even limit the mode of defense to circular reasoning.

I believe, then, that the structural formulation is not significantly biased against coherentism. Nor is it biased in favor of internalism over externalism about justification, where internalism is roughly the view that what justifies a belief, such as a visual impression, is internal in the sense that someone can become (in some way) aware of it through reflection or introspection (internal processes), and externalism denies that what justifies a belief is always accessible to S in this sense. The dialectical formulation, by contrast, tends to favor internalism, because it invites us to see the regress problem as solved in terms of what propositions warranted for someone are *also* accessible to one in answering, "How do you know that *p*?" If the structural formulation is biased, I am not aware of good reasons to think so, and I will work with it here.

II. *The Epistemic Regress Argument and Fallibilist Foundationalism*

If we formulate the regress problem structurally, then a natural way to state the famous epistemic regress argument is along the following lines. (1) If one has any knowledge, it occurs in an epistemic chain, a chain of beliefs, that *p*, that *q*, and so on, each based on the next which expresses a ground for its predecessor, as *q* might be a ground for *p* (we include the special case of a single link, such as a perceptual or *a priori* belief that *p*, which constitutes knowledge by virtue of being anchored directly in experience or reason). (2) The only possible kinds of epistemic chains are (a) circular, running from *p* to *q* to *r*, and so on until we come to one based on *p*; (b) infinitely regressive, running from *p* to *q* and so on to infinity; (c) terminal and ending in belief that is not knowledge; and (d) terminal, but ending with a belief constituting direct knowledge. (3) Knowledge can occur only in the last kind of chain. Hence, (4) if one has any knowledge, one has some direct knowledge.[6] The conclusion is of course a version of foundationalism about knowledge; and the parallel argument with justification substituted for knowledge has at least equal force in

supporting foundationalism about justification: the view that if someone has any justified beliefs, someone has some non-inferentially justified belief. Both views are, however, quite generic and leave much to be determined, such as how *well* justified foundational beliefs must be if they are to justify a superstructure belief based on them. In assessing the foundationalist–coherentist controversy, then, we need a more detailed formulation.

The most plausible kind of foundationalism will be fallibilist (moderate) in at least the following respects—and I shall concentrate on foundationalism about justification, although much that is said will also hold for foundationalism about knowledge. First, as a purely philosophical thesis about the *structure* of justification, foundationalism should be neutral with respect to skepticism and should not entail that there *are* justified beliefs. Second, if it is fallibilistic, it must allow that a justified belief, even a foundational one, is nevertheless false. To require justification of a kind that entails truth is to require that justified beliefs be infallible. Third, superstructure beliefs may be only inductively, hence fallibly, justified by foundational ones and thus can be false even when the latter are true. Just as one's warranted beliefs may be fallible, one's inferences may be, leading from truth to falsity: if the proposition is sufficiently supported by evidence one justifiedly believes, one may justifiedly hold it on the basis of that evidence, even if one could turn out to be in error. Fourth, a fallibilist foundationalism must allow for *discovering* error or lack of justification, in foundational as well as in superstructure beliefs: foundational beliefs may be discovered to conflict either with other such beliefs or with sufficiently well supported superstructure beliefs.

These four points are quite appropriate to the inspiration of the theory as expressed in the regress argument: it requires epistemic unmoved movers, but not unmovable movers. Solid ground is enough, even if bedrock is better. There are also different kinds of bedrock, and not all of them have the invulnerability apparently belonging to beliefs of luminously self-evident truths of logic. Even foundationalism as applied to knowledge can be fallibilistic; for granting that false propositions cannot be known, foundationalism about knowledge does not entail that one's *grounds* for knowledge (at any level) are indefeasible. Perceptual grounds, for example, may be overridden; and one can fail (or cease) to know a proposition not because it is (or is discovered to be) false, but because one ceases to be justified in believing it.

I take *fallibilist foundationalism,* then, as applied to justification, to be the view that for any person, S, and any time, *t,* (1) the structure of S's body of justified beliefs is, at *t,* foundational in the sense that any indirectly justified beliefs S has depend for their justification on directly (hence foundationally) justified beliefs of S's; (2) the justification of S's foundational beliefs is at least typically defeasible; (3) the inferential transmission of justification need not be deductive: and (4) non-foundationally justified beliefs need not derive *all* their justification from foundational ones, but only enough so that they would remain justified if (other things remaining equal) any other justification they have (say, from coherence) were eliminated.[7] This principle is not only fallibilistic; it also allows for coherence to play some role in justification, though a restricted one. But there remains a strong contrast between the two accounts, as we shall see when we have before us a plausible formulation of coherentism.

III. *Holistic Coherentism*

It is very difficult to explain what coherence is. It is not mere consistency, though *in*consistency is the clearest case of incoherence. Whatever coherence is, it is a cognitively *internal* relation, in the sense that it is a matter of how your beliefs (or other cognitive items) are related *to one another,* not to anything outside your system of beliefs, such as your perceptual experience. Coherence is sometimes connected with explanation; it is widely believed that propositions that stand in an explanatory relation cohere with one another and that this coherence counts toward that of a person's beliefs of the propositions in question. If the wilting of the leaves is explained by smoke from a chemical fire, then presumably the proposition expressing the first event coheres with the proposition expressing the second (even if the coherence is not obvious). Probability is also relevant: if the probability of one proposition you be-

lieve is raised by that of a second proposition you believe, this at least counts toward the coherence of the first of the beliefs with the second. The relevant notions of explanation and probability are themselves philosophically problematic, but our intuitive grasp of them can still help us understand coherence.

Because I am particularly concerned to clarify foundationalism in contrast to coherentism, I want to focus on the roles fallibilist foundationalism allows for coherence in relation to justification. Coherence may play at least the following two important roles.

The first role fallibilist foundationalism allows for coherence, or at least for incoherence, is negative: incoherence may defeat justification or knowledge, even the justification of a directly justified, hence foundational, belief (or one constituting knowledge), as where my justification for believing I am hallucinating books prevents me from knowing, or remaining justified in believing, certain propositions incoherent with it, say that the books in my study are before me. If this is not ultimately a role for coherence itself—which is the opposite and not merely the absence of incoherence—it *is* a role crucial for explaining points stressed by coherentism. Coherentists have noted, for instance, such things as the defeasibility of the justification of a memorial belief owing to its incoherence with perceptual beliefs, as where I take myself to remember an oak tree in a certain spot on my uncle's farm, yet, standing near the very spot, can find no trace of such a tree. Because fallibilist foundationalism does not require indefeasible justification on the part of the relevant memory belief, there is no anomaly in its defeat by perceptual evidence.

Second, fallibilist foundationalism can employ an *independence principle*—one of a family of principles commonly emphasized by coherentists, although foundationalists need not attribute its truth to coherence. This principle says that the larger the number of independent mutually coherent factors I believe to support the truth of a proposition, the better my justification for believing it (other things being equal). The principle can explain, for instance, why my justification for believing, from what I hear, that my daughter has come home increases as I acquire new beliefs supporting that conclusion, say a smell of grilled cheese. I now have a confirmatory belief which comes through a different sense (smell) and does not depend for its justification on my other evidence beliefs.

Similar principles consistent with foundationalism can accommodate other cases in which coherence enhances justification, say those in which a proposition's explaining, and thereby cohering with, something I justifiably believe tends to confer some justification on that proposition. Suppose I check three suitcases at the airline ticket counter. Imagine that as I await them at the baggage terminal I see two on the conveyor at a distance and, as I cannot yet see them perfectly, tentatively believe they are mine. The propositions that (1) the first is mine, (2) the second is, and (3) these two are side by side—which I am fully justified in believing, because I can clearly see how close they are to each other—would be explained by the hypothesis that my three suitcases are now coming off together; and that hypothesis, in turn, derives some justification from its explaining what I already believe. When I believe the further proposition, independent of propositions 1 to 3, that my third suitcase is coming just behind the second, the level of my justification for the hypothesis rises.

Let us now try to formulate a plausible version of coherentism as applied to justification. The central idea underlying coherentism is that a belief is justified by its coherence with other beliefs one holds. The unit of coherence may be as large as one's entire set of beliefs, although some may be more significant in producing the coherence than others, say because of differing degrees of their closeness in subject matter to the belief in question. This conception of coherentism would be accepted by a proponent of the circular view, but the thesis I want to explore differs from that view in not being *linear*: it does not take justification for believing p, or knowledge that p, to emerge from an inferential line running from premises for p to that proposition as a conclusion from them, and from other premises to the first set of premises, and so on until we return to the original proposition as a premise. On the circular view, no matter how wide the circle or how rich its constituent beliefs, there is a line from any one belief in a circular epistemic chain to any other. In practice I may never trace the entire line, as by inferring one thing I know from a second, the second from a third, and so on until I reinfer the first.

Still, in this view there is such a line for every belief constituting knowledge.

Coherentism need not, however, be linear, and I believe that the most plausible versions are instead holistic.[8] A moderate version of *holistic coherentism* might be expressed as follows: for any S and any t, if S has any justified beliefs at t, then, at t (1) they are each justified by virtue of their coherence with one or more others of S's beliefs, and (2) they would remain justified even if (other things remaining equal) any justification they derive from sources other than coherence were eliminated. The holism here is minimal, because the unit of coherence may be as small as one pair of beliefs—although it may also be as large as the entire system of beliefs (including the belief in question, because we may take "self-coherence" as a limiting case). But the formulation also applies to the more typical cases of holistic coherentism; in these cases a justified belief coheres with a substantial number of other beliefs, and some beliefs, like those expressing basic principles of our thinking, can be justified only by coherence with a large and diverse group of related beliefs.

To illustrate holistic coherentism, consider a question that evokes a justification. Ken wonders how, from my closed study, I know (or why I believe) that my daughter is home. I say that there is music playing in the house. He next wants to know how I can recognize my daughter's music from behind my closed doors. I reply that what I hear is the wrong sort of thing to come from any nearby house. He then asks how I know that it is not from a passing car. I say that the volume is too steady. He now wonders whether I can distinguish, with my door closed, my daughter's vocal music from the singing of a neighbor in her yard. I reply that I hear an accompaniment. In giving each justification, I apparently go only one step along the inferential line: initially, for instance, just to my belief that there is music playing in the house. For my belief that my daughter is home *is* based on this belief about the music. After that, I do not even mention anything that this belief, in turn, is based on; rather, I defend my beliefs as appropriate, in terms of an entire pattern of interrelated beliefs I hold. And I may appeal to many different parts of the pattern. For coherentism, then, beliefs representing knowledge do not lie at one end of a grounded chain; they fit a coherent pattern and are justified through their fitting it in an appropriate way.

Consider a variant of the case. Suppose I had seemed to hear music of neither the kind my daughter plays nor the kind the neighbors play nor the sort I expect from passing cars. The proposition that this is what I hear does not cohere well with my belief that the music is played by my daughter. Suddenly I recall that she was bringing a friend, and I remember that her friend likes such music. I might now be justified in believing my daughter is home. When I finally hear her voice, I know she is. The crucial thing here is how, initially, a kind of *incoherence* prevents justification of my belief that she is home, and how, as relevant pieces of the pattern develop, I become justified in believing, and (presumably) come to know, that she is. Arriving at a justified belief, on this view, is more like answering a question by looking up diverse information that suggests the answer than like deducing a theorem from axioms.

Such examples show how a holistic coherentism can respond to the regress argument *without* embracing the possibility of an epistemic circle (although its proponents need not reject that either). It may deny that there are only the four kinds of possible epistemic chains I have specified. There is apparently another, not generally noted: that the chain terminates with belief which is *psychologically direct* but *epistemically indirect* or, if we are talking of coherentism about justification, *justificationally indirect*. Hence, the last link is, as belief, direct, because it is non-inferential; yet, as knowledge, it is *indirect,* not in the usual sense that it is inferential, but rather in the broad sense that the belief constitutes knowledge only by virtue of receiving support from other knowledge or belief. Thus, my belief that there is music playing is psychologically direct because it is simply grounded, causally, in my hearing and is not (inferentially) based on any other belief; yet my *knowledge* that there is music is not epistemically direct. It is epistemically, but not inferentially, based on the coherence of my belief that there is music with my other beliefs, presumably including many that constitute knowledge themselves. It is thus knowledge *through,* though not by inference from, other knowledge—or at least through justified beliefs; hence it is epistemically indirect and thus non-foundational.

There is another way to see how this attack on the regress argument is constructed. The coherentist grants that the belief element *in* my knowledge is non-inferentially grounded in perception and is in that sense direct; but the claim is that the belief constitutes knowledge only by virtue of coherence with my other beliefs. The strategy, then—call it the *wedge strategy*—is to sever the connection foundationalism usually posits between the psychological and the epistemic: in the common cases, foundationalists tend to hold, the basis of one's *knowledge* that *p*, say a perceptual experience, is also the basis of one's belief that *p;* similarly, for justified belief, the basis of its justification is usually also that of the belief itself. For the coherentist using the wedge strategy, the epistemic ground of a belief need not be a psychological ground. Knowledge and justification are a matter of how well the system of beliefs hangs together, not of how well grounded they are—and they may indeed hang; one could have a body of justified beliefs, at least some of them constituting knowledge, even if *none* of them is justified by a belief or experience in which it is psychologically grounded.

In a sense, of course, coherentism does posit a *kind* of foundation for justification and knowledge: namely, coherence. But so long as coherentists deny that justification and knowledge can be *non-inferentially* grounded in experience or reason, this point alone simply shows that they take justification and knowledge to be based on something. It is still grounded in the coherence of elements which themselves admit of justification and derive their justification (or status as knowledge) from coherence with other such items rather than from grounding in elements such as sensory impressions (say of music), which, though not themselves justified or unjustified, confer justification on beliefs they ground.

Apparently, then, the circularity objection to coherentism can be met by construing the thesis holistically and countenancing psychologically direct beliefs. One could insist that if a non-inferential, thus psychologically direct, belief constitutes knowledge, it *must* be direct knowledge. But the coherentist would reply that in that case there will be two kinds of direct knowledge: the kind the foundationalist posits, which derives from grounding in a basic experiential or rational source, and the kind the coherentist posits, which derives from coherence with other beliefs and not from being based on those sources. This is surely a plausible response.

Is the holistic coherentist trying to have it both ways? Not necessarily. Holistic coherentism can grant that a variant of the regress argument holds for belief, because the only kind of belief chain that it is psychologically realistic to attribute to us is the kind terminating in direct (non-inferential) belief. But even on the assumption that knowledge is constituted by (certain kinds of) beliefs, it does not follow that direct belief which is knowledge is also direct *knowledge*. Epistemic dependence, in this view, does not imply inferential or psychological dependence; hence, a non-inferential belief can depend for its status as knowledge on other beliefs. Thus, the coherentist may grant a kind of *psychological foundationalism*, which says (in part) that if we have any beliefs at all, we have some direct (non-inferential) ones, yet deny epistemological foundationalism, which requires that there be knowledge which is epistemically (and normally also psychologically) direct, if there is any knowledge at all. Holistic coherentism may grant experience and reason the status of psychological foundations of our belief systems. But it denies that they are the basic sources of justification or knowledge.

IV. *Foundationalism, Coherentism, and Defeasibility*

Drawing on the preceding results, this section considers how fallibilist foundationalism and holistic coherentism differ and, related to that, how the controversy is sometimes obscured by failing to take account of the differences.

One kind of case seems both to favor foundationalism and to show something about justification which coherentism in any form misses. It might seem that coherence theories of justification are decisively refuted by the possibility of S's having, if just momentarily, only a single belief which is nonetheless justified, say that there is music playing. For this belief would be justified without cohering with any others one has. But could I have just a single belief? Could I, for instance, believe that

there is music playing yet not believe, say, that there are (or could be) musical instruments, melodies, and chords? It is not clear that I could; and foundationalism does not assume this possibility, although the theory may easily be wrongly criticized for implying it. Foundationalism is in fact consistent with *one* kind of coherentism—*conceptual coherentism*. This is a coherence theory of the acquisition of concepts which says that a person acquires concepts, say of musical pieces, only in relation to one another and must acquire an entire family of related concepts in order to acquire any concept.

It remains questionable, however, whether my justification for believing that there is music playing ultimately *derives* from the coherence of the belief with others; that is, whether coherence is even partly the basis of my justification in holding this belief.[9] Let us first note an important point. Suppose the belief turns out to be *in*coherent with a second, such as my belief that I am standing before the phonograph playing the music, yet see no movement of its turntable; now the belief may *cease* to be justified, because if I really hear the phonograph, I should see its turntable moving. But this shows only that the belief's justification is *defeasible*—liable to being either overridden (roughly, outweighed) or undermined—should sufficiently serious incoherence arise. It does not show that the justification derives from coherence. In this case the justification of my belief grounded in hearing may be overridden: my better-justified beliefs, including the belief that a phonograph with a motionless turntable cannot play, may make it more reasonable for me to believe that there is *not* music playing in the house.

The case raises another question regarding the possibility that coherence is the source of my justification, as opposed to providing a constraint on it. Could incoherence override the justification of my belief if I were not *independently* justified in believing that a proposition incoherent with certain other ones is, or probably is, false; for example, in believing that if I do not see the turntable moving, then I do not hear music from the phonograph? For if I lacked such independent justification, should I not suspend judgment on, or even reject, the other propositions and retain my original belief? And aren't the relevant other beliefs or propositions— those that can override or defeat my justification—

precisely the kind for which, directly or inferentially, we have some degree of justification through the experiential and rational sources, such as visual perception of a stockstill turntable?

A similar question arises regarding the crucial principles themselves: could incoherence play the defeating role it does if we did not have a kind of foundational justification for principles to the effect that certain kinds of evidences or beliefs override certain other kinds? More generally, can we *use,* or even benefit from, considerations of coherence in acquiring justification, or in correcting mistaken presuppositions of justification, if we do not bring to the various coherent or incoherent patterns, principles not derived from those very patterns? If, without such principles to serve as justified standards that guide belief formation and belief revision, we can become justified by coherence, then coherence would seem to be playing the kind of generative role that foundational sources are held to play in producing justification. One could become justified in believing *p* by virtue of coherence even if one had no justified principles by which one could, for instance, inferentially connect the justified belief that *p* with others that cohere with it.

There is a second case, in which one's justification is simply undermined: one ceases to be justified in believing the proposition in question, though one does not become justified in believing it false. Suppose I seem to see a black cat, yet there no longer appears to be one there if I move five feet to my left. This experience could justify my believing, and lead me to believe, that I might be hallucinating. This belief in turn is to a degree incoherent with, and undermines the justification of, my visual belief that the cat is there, though it does not by itself justify my believing that *no* cat is there. Again, however, I am apparently justified, independently of coherence, in believing a proposition relevant to my overall justification for an apparently foundational perceptual belief: namely, the proposition that my seeing the cat there is incoherent with my merely hallucinating it there. The same seems to hold for the proposition that my seeing the cat there coheres with my feeling fur if I extend my hand to the feline focal point of my visual field. Such considerations suggest that coherence has the role it does in justification only because *some* beliefs are justified independently of it.

Both examples illustrate an important distinction that is often missed.[10] It is between defeasibility and epistemic dependence or, alternatively, between *negative epistemic dependence* (which is a form of defeasibility) and *positive epistemic dependence* (the kind beliefs bear to the source(s) from which they *derive* any justification they have or, if they represent knowledge, their status as knowledge). The defeasibility of a belief's justification by incoherence does not imply that, as coherentists must hold, its justification positively depends on coherence. If my garden is my source of food, I (positively) depend on it. The fact that people could poison the soil does not make their non-malevolence part of my food *source,* or imply a (positive) dependence on them, such as I have on the sunshine. Moreover, it is the sunshine which (with rainfall and other conditions) explains both my having the food and the amount that I have. The non-malevolence is necessary for, but does not explain, this; it alone, under the relevant conditions of potential for growth, does not even tend to produce food.

So it is with perceptual experience as a source of justification. Foundationalists need not deny that a belief's justification negatively depends on something else, for as we have seen they need not claim that justification must be indefeasible. It may arise, unaided by coherence, from a source like perception; yet it remains defeasible from various quarters—including conflicting perceptions. Negative dependence, however, does not imply positive dependence. Justification can be defeasible by incoherence, and thus overridden or undermined should incoherence arise, without owing its existence to coherence. Fallibilist foundationalism does not, then, turn out to be a blend of coherentism, and it remains open just what positive role, if any, it must assign to coherence in explicating justification.

There is a further point which fallibilist foundationalism should stress, and in appraising the point we learn more about both coherentism and justification. If I set out to *show* that my belief is justified—as the dialectical formulation of the regress problem invites one to think stopping the regress of justification requires—I do have to cite propositions that cohere with the one to be shown to be justified for me, say that there is music in my house. In some cases, these are not even propositions I already believe. Often, in defending my original belief, I form new beliefs, such as the belief I acquire, in moving my head, that I can vividly see the changes in perspective that go with seeing a black cat. More important, these beliefs are highly appropriate to the *process of self-consciously justifying* my belief; and the result of that process is showing that the original belief is justified, together with my forming the second-order belief that the original belief is justified. Thus, coherence is important in showing that a belief is justified. In *that* sense, coherence is a pervasive element in justification: it is pervasive in the process of *justifying,* especially when that is construed as showing that I have justification.

Why, however, should the second-order beliefs appropriate to *showing* that a belief is justified be necessary for its *being* justified? They need not be. Indeed, why should my simply having a justified belief imply even that I could be justified in holding the second-order beliefs appropriate to showing it is justified? It would seem that just as a little child can be of good character even if unable to defend its character against attack, I can have a justified belief even if, in response to someone who doubts this, I could not show that I do. Supposing S has the sophistication to form a second-order belief that his belief there is a cat before him is justified, the latter belief can be justified so long as the former is *true;* and it can be *true* that S's belief about the cat is justified even if S is not justified in holding it or is unable to show it is true. Justifying a second-order belief is a sophisticated process. The process is particularly sophisticated if the second-order belief concerns a special property like the justification of the original belief. Simply being justified in a belief about, say, the sounds around me, is a much simpler matter. But confusion is easy here, particularly if the governing context is an imagined dialectic with a skeptic. Take, for instance, the question how a simple perceptual belief "is justified." The very phrase is ambiguous: the question could be "By what process, say of reasoning, has the belief been (or might it be) justified?" or, on the other hand, "In virtue of what is the belief justified?" These are very different questions. The first invites us to conceive justification as a process of which the belief is a beneficiary, the second to conceive it as a property

that a belief has, whether in virtue of its content, its genesis, or other characteristics of it. Both aspects of the notion are important, but unfortunately much of our talk about justification makes it easy to run them together. A justified belief could be one that *has* justification or one that *has been* justified; and a request for someone's justification could be a request for a list of justifying factors or for a recounting of the process by which the person justified the belief.

Once we forswear the mistakes just pointed out, what argument is left to show the (positive) dependence of perceptual justification on coherence? I doubt that any plausible one remains, though given how hard it is to discern what coherence is, we cannot be confident that no plausible argument is forthcoming. Granted, I could point to the oddity of saying such things as "I am justified in believing that there is music playing, but I cannot justify this belief." Why is this odd if not because, when I have a justified belief, I can give a justification for it by appeal to beliefs that cohere with it? But consider this. Typically, in asserting something, say that there were lawsuits arising from an accident, I imply that, in some way or other, I *can* justify what I say, especially if the belief I express is, like this one, not plausibly thought to be grounded in a basic source such as perception. In the quoted sentence, I deny that I can justify what I claim. The foundationalist must explain why that is odd, given that I can be justified in believing propositions even when I cannot show that I am (and may not even believe I am). The main point needed to explain this is that it is apparently my *asserting* that my belief is justified, rather than its being so, that gives the appearance that I must be able to give a justification of the belief. Compare "*She* is justified in believing that there is music playing, but (being an intuitive and unphilosophical kind of person) she cannot justify that proposition." This has no disturbing oddity, because the person said to have justification is not the one claiming it. Because she might be shocked to be asked to justify the proposition and might not know how to justify it, this statement might be true of her. We must not stop here, however. There are at least two further points.

First, there is quite a difference between *showing* that one is justified and simply *giving* a justification. I can give my justification for believing there is music simply by indicating that I hear it. But this does not show that I am justified, at least in the sense of "show" usual in epistemology. That task requires not just exhibiting what justifies me, but indicating conditions for being justified *and* showing that I meet them. It is one thing to cite a justifier, such as a clear perception; it is quite another to show that the justifier meets a sufficiently high standard to *be* a justifier of the belief it grounds. Certainly skeptics—and probably most coherentists as well—have in mind something more like the latter process when they ask for a justification. Similarly, where a regress of justification is, for fallibilist foundationalism, stopped by giving a (genuine) justification for the proposition in question, and the regress problem can be considered soluble because such stopping is possible, the skeptic will not countenance any stopping place, and certainly not any solution, that is not dialectically defended by argument showing that I am justified.

To be sure, it may be that at least typically when we do have a justified belief we can give a justification for it. When I justifiedly believe that there is music playing, I surely can give a justification: that I hear it. But I need not *believe* that I hear it, *before* the question of justification arises. That question leads me to focus on my circumstances, in which I first had a belief solely about the music. I also had a *disposition,* based on my auditory experience, to form the belief that *I hear* the music, and this is largely why, in the course of justifying that belief, I then *form* the further belief that I do hear it. But a disposition to believe something does not imply an actual belief of it, not even a dispositional one, as opposed to one manifesting itself in consciousness. If I am talking loudly and excitedly in a restaurant, I may be disposed to believe this—so much so that if I merely think of the proposition that I am talking loudly, I will form the belief that I am, and lower my voice. But this disposition does not imply that I *already* believe that proposition—if I did, I would not be talking loudly in the first place. In the musical case, I tend to form the belief that I hear the music if, as I hear it, the question whether I hear it arises; yet I need not have subliminally believed this already. The justification I offer, then, is not by appeal to coherence with other beliefs I already had—such as that I saw the turntable moving—but by reference to what has traditionally

been considered a basic source of both justification and knowledge: perception. It is thus precisely the kind of justification which foundationalists are likely to consider appropriate for a non-inferential belief. Indeed, one consideration favoring foundationalism about both justification and knowledge, at least as an account of our everyday epistemic practices, including much scientific practice, is that typically we cease to offer justification or to defend a knowledge claim precisely when we reach a basic source.

V. Coherence, Foundations, and Justification

There is far more to say in clarifying both foundationalism and coherentism. But if what I have said so far is correct, then we can at least understand their basic thrusts. We can also see how coherentism may respond to the regress argument—in part by distinguishing psychological from epistemic directness. And we can see how foundationalism may reply to the charge that, once made moderate enough to be plausible, it depends on coherence criteria rather than on grounding in experience and reason: the response is in part to distinguish negative from positive epistemic dependence and to argue that foundationalism does not make justification depend positively on coherence, but only, negatively, on (avoiding) incoherence.

We may still wonder, however, if fallibilist foundationalism concedes enough to coherentism. Granted that it need not restrict the role of coherence any more than is required by the regress argument, it still denies that coherence is (independently) necessary for justification. As most plausibly developed, fallibilist foundationalism also denies that coherence is a *basic* (non-derivative) source of justification—or at least that if it is, it can produce *enough* justification to render a belief unqualifiedly justified or (given truth and certain other conditions) to make it knowledge. One drop of even the purest water will not quench a thirst. The moderate holistic coherentism just formulated is parallel in this: although it may grant foundationalism its typical psychological picture of how belief systems are structured, it denies that foundational justification is (independently) necessary for justification and that it is a basic source of justification, except possibly of degrees of justification too slight for knowledge or unqualifiedly justified belief.

The issue here is the difference in the two conceptions of justification: broadly, foundationalists tend to hold that justification belongs to a belief, whether inferentially or directly, by virtue of its grounding in experience or reason; coherentists tend to hold that justification belongs to a belief by virtue of its coherence with one or more other beliefs. This is apparently a difference concerning basic sources. To be sure, my formulation may make coherentism sound foundationalistic, because justification is grounded not in an inferential relation to premises but in coherence itself, which sounds parallel to experience or reason. But note three contrasts with foundationalism: (1) the source of coherence is *cognitive,* because the coherence is an internal property of the belief system, whereas foundationalism makes no such restriction; (2) coherence is an inferential or at least epistemic generator, in the sense that it arises from such relations among beliefs, or their propositional objects, as entailment, inductive support, and explanation of one belief or proposition by another, whereas experiential and rational sources are a non-inferential generator of belief (these sources can produce and thereby explain belief, but they do not explain it in the way coherentism requires); and (3) S has *inferential access* to the coherence-making relations: S can wield them in inferentially justifying the belief that *p*, whereas foundationalism does not require such access to its basic sources. Still, I want to pursue just how deep the difference between foundationalism and coherentism is; for once foundationalism is moderately expressed and grants conceptual coherentism, and once coherentism is (plausibly) construed as consistent with psychological foundationalism, it may appear that the views differ far less than usually supposed.

It should help if we first contrast fallibilist foundationalism with *strong foundationalism* and compare their relation to coherentism. If we use Descartes's version as a model, strong foundationalism is deductivist, takes foundational beliefs as indefeasibly justified, and allows coherence at most a limited generative role. To meet these conditions,

it may reduce the basic sources of justification to reason and some form of introspection. Moreover, being committed to the indefeasibility of foundational justification, it would not grant that incoherence can defeat such justification. Strong foundationalism would also concede to coherentists, and hence to any independence principle they countenance, at most a minimal positive role, say by insisting that if a belief is supported by two or more independent cohering sources, its justification is increased at most "additively"; that is, only by combining the justification transmitted separately from each relevant basic source.

By contrast, what fallibilist foundationalism denies regarding coherence is only that it is a basic (hence sufficient) source of justification. Thus, coherence by itself does not ground justification, and hence the independence principle does not apply to sources that have *no* justification; at most, the principle allows coherence to raise the level of justification originally drawn from other sources to a level higher than it would have if those sources did not mutually cohere. Similarly, if inference is a basic source of coherence (as some coherentists seem to believe), it is not a basic source of justification. It may enhance justification, as where I strengthen my justification for believing someone's testimony by inferring the same point from someone else's. But inference *alone* does not generate justification. Suppose I believe several propositions without a shred of evidence and merely through wishful thinking; I might infer any number of others, yet even if by good luck I arrive at a highly coherent set of beliefs, I do not automatically gain justification for believing any of them. If I am floating in the middle of the ocean, strengthening my boat with added nails and planks may make it hang together more tightly and thereby make me feel secure; but if nothing indicates my location, there is no reason to expect this work to get me any closer to shore. Coherence may, to be sure, enable me to draw a beautiful map; but if there are no experiences I may rely on to connect it with reality, I may follow it forever to no avail. Even to be justified in *believing* it will correspond with reality, I must have some experiential source to work from.

A natural coherentist reply is that when we consider examples of justified belief, not only do we always find some coherence, we also apparently find enough of it to account for the justification. This reply is especially plausible if—as I suggest—coherentism as usually formulated is modified to include, in the coherence base, *dispositions to believe*. Consider my belief that music is playing. It coheres both with my beliefs about what records are in the house, what music my daughter prefers, my auditory capacities, and so on, *and* with many of my dispositions to believe, say to form the belief that no one else in the house would play that music. Because such dispositions can themselves be well grounded (say in perception) or poorly grounded (say in prejudice), they admit of justification and, when they produce beliefs, can lead to reasonable inferences. These dispositions are thus appropriate for the coherence base, and including them among generators of coherence is particularly useful in freeing coherentism from implausibly positing all the beliefs needed for the justificational capacities it tends to take to underlie justified belief. Given this broad conception of coherence, it is surely plausible to take coherence as at least necessary for justified belief. And it might be argued that its justification is based on coherence, not on grounding in experience.

Let us grant both that the case of the music does exhibit a high degree of coherence among my beliefs and dispositions to believe, and even that the coherence is necessary for the justification of my belief. It does not follow that the justification is based on the coherence. Coherence could still be at best a *consequential necessary condition* for justification, one that holds as a result of the justification itself or what that is based on, as opposed to a *constitutive necessary condition,* one that either expresses part of what it *is* for a belief to be justified or constitutes a basic ground of it. The relation of coherence to the properties producing it might be analogous to that of heat to friction: a necessary product of them, but not part of what constitutes them.

If coherence is a constitutive necessary condition for justification, there should be cases in which the experiential and rational sources are absent, yet there is sufficient coherence for justified belief. But this is precisely what we do not easily find, if we ever find it: if I discover a set of my beliefs that intuitively cohere very well yet receive no support from what I believe (or at least am disposed to believe) on the basis of experience or reason, I am not inclined

to attribute justification to any of them. To be sure, if the unit of coherence is large enough to include my actual beliefs, then because I have so many that *are* grounded in experience or reason (indeed, few that are not), I will almost certainly not in fact have any beliefs which, intuitively, seem justified yet are not coherent with some of my beliefs so grounded. This complicates assessment of the role of coherence in justification. But we can certainly imagine beings (or ourselves) artificially endowed with coherent sets of beliefs *not* grounded in experience or reason; and when we do, it appears that coherence does not automatically confer justification.

We might conclude, then, that it is more nearly true that coherence is based on justification than that the latter is based on the former. Further, the data we have so far considered can be explained on the hypothesis that both coherence among beliefs and their justification are based on the beliefs' being grounded (in an appropriate way) in the basic sources. Particularly if a coherence theory of the acquisition concepts is true, we perhaps cannot have a belief justified by a basic source without having beliefs—or at least dispositions to believe—related in an intimate (and intuitively coherence-generating) way to that belief. We certainly cannot have a justified belief unless no incoherence defeats its justification. Given these two points, it is to be expected that on a fallibilist foundationalism, justification will normally imply coherence, both in the positive sense involving mutual support and in the weak sense of the absence of potential incoherence. There is some reason to think, then, that coherence is not a basic source of justification and is at most a consequentially necessary condition for it.

There is at least one more possibility to be considered, however: that *given* justification from foundational sources, coherence can generate more justification than S would have from those sources alone. If so, we might call coherence a *conditionally basic* source, in that, where there is already some justification from other sources, it can produce new justification. This bears on interpreting the independence principle. It is widely agreed that our justification increases markedly when we take into account independent sources of evidence, as where I confirm—by going closer to enhance my auditory impression and by visually confirming that a phonograph is playing—that there is music playing. Perhaps what explains the dramatic increase in my overall justification here is not just "additivity" of foundational justification, but coherence as a further source of justification.

There is plausibility in this reasoning, but it is not cogent. For one thing, there really are no such additive quantities of justification. Perhaps we simply combine degrees of justification, so far as we can, on analogy with combinations of independent probabilities. Thus, the probability of at least one heads on two fair coin tosses is not $1/2 + 1/2$ (the two independent probabilities), which would give the event a probability of 1 and make it a certainty; the probability is $3/4$; that is, $1 - 1/4$, which is the probability of two tails. Moreover, the relevant probability rules do not seem to depend on coherence; they seem to be justifiable by *a priori* reasoning in the way beliefs grounded in reason are commonly thought to be justifiable, and they appear to be among the principles we must *presuppose* if we are to give an account of how coherence contributes to justification.

There remains a contrast between, say, having six independent credible witnesses tell me that *p* on separate occasions which I do not connect with one another, and having them do so on a single occasion when I can note the coherence of their stories. In the first case, although my isolated beliefs cohere, I have no belief that they do, nor even a sense of their collective weight. This is not, to be sure, a case of six increments of isolated foundational justification versus a case of six cohering items of evidence. Both cases exhibit coherence; but in the second there is an additional belief (or justified disposition to believe): *that* six independent witnesses agree. Foundationalists as well as coherentists can plausibly explain how this additional belief increases the justification I have in the first case. It would be premature, then, to take such cases to show that coherence is even a conditionally basic source of justification.

Conclusion

The foundationalism–coherentism controversy cannot be settled in a single essay. But we can now appreciate some often neglected dimensions of the issue. One dimension is the formulation of the regress problem itself; another is the distinction between defeasibility and epistemic dependence; still another is that between consequential and constitutive necessary conditions; and yet another is between an unqualifiedly and a conditionally basic source. Even if coherence is neither a constitutive necessary condition for justification nor even a conditionally basic source of it, there is still reason to consider it important for justification. It may even be a *mark* of justification, a common effect of the same causes as it were, or a virtue with the same foundations. Coherence is certainly significant as indicating a negative constraint on justification; for incoherence is a paradigm of what defeats justification.

I have argued for the importance of the regress problem in the controversy between foundationalism and coherentism. It matters considerably whether we conceive the problem dialectically or structurally, at least insofar as we cast foundationalism and coherentism in terms of their capacity to solve it. Indeed, while both coherentism and foundationalism can be made plausible on either conception, coherentism is perhaps best understood as a response to the problem *in* some dialectical formulation, and foundationalism is perhaps best understood as a response to it in some structural form. Taking account of both formulations of the regress problem, I have suggested plausible versions of both foundationalism and coherentism. Neither has been established, although fallibilist foundation has emerged as the more plausible of the two. In clarifying them, I have stressed a number of distinctions: between the process and the property of justification, between dispositional beliefs and dispositions to believe, between epistemically and psychologically foundational beliefs, between defeasibility and epistemic dependence, between constitutive and consequential necessary conditions for justification, and between unqualified and conditionally basic sources of it. Against this background, we can see how fallibilist foundationalism avoids some of the objections commonly thought to refute foundationalism, including its alleged failure to account for the defeasibility of most and perhaps all our justification, and for the role of coherence in justification. Indeed, fallibilist foundationalism can even account for coherence as a mark of justification; the chief tension between the two theories concerns not whether coherence is crucial for justification, but whether it is a basic source of it.

Of the problems that remain for foundationalism and coherentism, the one most readily clarified here—and particularly by the distinction between defeasibility and epistemic dependence—is the dogmatism objection, which in its most general form is the claim that if we can have knowledge or justified belief without being able to show that we do, then the way is open to claim just about anything we like, defending it by cavalierly noting that we can be justified without being able to show that we are. It turns out, however, that fallibilist foundationalism is not damaged by this objection and coherentism is not immune to it. Far from being dogmatic, fallibilist foundationalism implies that even where we have a justified belief we cannot show to be justified, we may (and at least normally can) *give* a justification for it. As to coherentism, it, too, may be a refuge for dogmatists, at least those clever enough to find a coherent pattern by which to rationalize the beliefs they dogmatically hold. More positively, a fallibilist foundationalism can account for the main connections between coherence and justification and can provide principles of justification to explain how justification that can be plausibly attributed to coherence can also be traced—by sufficiently complex and sometimes inductive paths—to basic sources in experience and reason.[11]

Notes

[1] For recent statements of foundationalism, see, for example, Chisholm (1966 and 1977) and especially his "A Version of Foundationalism" in (1982); Alston, (1976); Audi (1978); Moser (1985); and Foley (1987). For detailed statements of coherentism, see, for example, Sellars (1973), Lehrer (1974), Harman (1975), and BonJour (1985). For useful discussion of the controversy between foundationalism and coherentism, see Delaney (1976), which defends a kind of foundationalism, and Blanshard (1964), which defends his earlier views against objections by critics quoted in the same chapter.

[2] BonJour, for example, says that the regress problem is "perhaps the most crucial in the entire theory of knowledge" (1985, p. 18); and he considers it the chief motivation for foundationalism (p. 17) and regards the failure of foundationalism as "the main motivation for a coherence theory" (p. 149).

[3] Chisholm seems to raise the problem in this way when he says, "If we try Socratically to formulate our justification for any particular claim to know ("My justification for thinking that I know that *A* is the fact that *B*"), and if we are relentless in our inquiry ("and my

justification for thinking that I know that *B* is the fact that *C*"), we will arrive, sooner or later, at a kind of stopping place ("but my justification for thinking that I know that *N* is simply the fact that *N*"). An example of *N* might be the fact that I seem to remember having been here before or that something now looks blue to me" (1966, p. 2); compare his (1977), especially pp. 19–20. In these and other passages, Chisholm seems to be thinking of the regress problem dialectically and taking a foundational belief to be a second-order belief. To be sure, he is talking about justification of any "claim to know"; but this and similar locutions—such as "knowledge claim"—have often been taken to apply to expressions of first-order knowledge, as where I say that it is raining, on the basis of perceptions I would normally take to yield knowledge that it is.

[4] See *Posterior Analytics,* Book III. Having opened Book I with the statement that "All instruction given or received by way of argument proceeds from pre-existent knowledge" (71a1–2), and thereby established a concern with the structure and presuppositions of knowledge, he formulated the regress argument as a response to the question of what is required for the existence of (what he called *scientific*) knowledge (72b4–24). (The translation is by W. D. Ross.)

[5] In Audi (1986), I have developed a detailed account of what it is for one belief to be based on another in the relevant (broadly inferential) sense.

[6] This argument is a distant descendent of one given by Aristotle in the *Posterior Analytics,* Book II, and is discussed in some detail in my "Contemporary Foundationalism" (Reading V.2 in this book). For other discussions of it, see the works cited in note 1 and, on the possibility of justification by infinite regress, see Harker (1984).

[7] The "other things being equal" clause is needed to allow for loss of justification from one source somehow producing new justification from another even without being a basis of that justification. There are different *degrees* of justification on the part of beliefs, and here, as in discussing coherentism, my concern is roughly the degree appropriate for knowledge.

[8] This applies to Sellars, Lehrer, and BonJour and is evident in the works cited in note 1. Their coherentist positions are not linear. For a statement of an internal difficulty besetting linear coherentism and probably also the most plausible versions of holistic coherentism, see Audi (1982a).

[9] With this question in mind, it is interesting to read Davidson (1983). Compare Kim (1988), "What Is 'Naturalized Epistemology'?" (Reading VI.4).

[10] This distinction seems to have been often missed—for example, in Kornblith (1980)—as I have argued (especially in relation to Kornblith's paper) in Audi (1983).

[11] This essay was prepared for this book but draws substantially on my "Foundationalism, Coherentism, and Epistemological Dogmatism," *Philosophical Perspectives 2* (1988), 407–459 (edited by James E. Tomberlin). I thank Louis P. Pojman for many helpful comments on an earlier draft.

References

Alston, William P. 1976, "Two Types of Foundationalism." *Journal of Philosophy 83* (1976), 7.

Audi, Robert. 1974, "The Limits of Self-Knowledge." *Canadian Journal of Philosophy 4* (1974), 2.

Audi, Robert. "Psychological Foundationalism." *Monist 62* (1978), 4.

Audi, Robert. "Axiological Foundationalism." *Canadian Journal of Philosophy 12* (1982a), 1.

Audi, Robert. "Believing and Affirming." *Mind 91* (1982b).

Audi, Robert. "Foundationalism, Epistemic Dependence, and Defeasibility." *Synthese 55* (1983), 1.

Audi, Robert. "Belief, Reason, and Inference." *Philosophical Topics 14* (1986), 1.

Aune, Bruce. *Knowledge, Mind and Nature*. Atascadero, CA: Ridgeview, 1967.

Blanshard, Brand. "Coherence and Correspondence." In Sydney and Beatrice Rome, eds., *Philosophical Interrogations*. New York, 1964.

BonJour, Laurence. *The Structure of Empirical Knowledge*. Cambridge, MA: Harvard University Press, 1985.

Chisholm, Roderick M. *Theory of Knowledge*. Englewood Cliffs, NJ: Prentice-Hall, 1966 and 1977.

Chisholm, Roderick M. "A Version of Foundationalism." In *The Foundations of Knowing*. Minneapolis: University of Minnesota Press, 1982.

Clark, Romane. "Vicious Infinite Regress Arguments." In James Tomberlin, ed., *Philosophical Perspectives 2*. Atascadero, CA: Ridgeview, 1988.

Cornman, James, and Keith Lehrer. *Philosophical Problems and Arguments*, 2d ed. New York: Macmillan, 1974.

Davidson, Donald. "A Coherence Theory of Truth and Knowledge." In Dieter Hendrich, ed., *Kant oder Hegel*. Stuttgart, 1983.

Delaney, C. F. 1976. "Foundations of Empirical Knowledge—Again." *New Scholasticism 50* (1976), 1.

Foley, Richard. *The Theory of Epistemic Rationality*. Cambridge, MA: Harvard University Press, 1987.

Kornblith, Hilary. "Beyond Foundationalism and the Coherence Theory." *Journal of Philosophy 77* (1980).

Lehrer, Keith. *Knowledge*. Oxford, England: Oxford University Press, 1974.

Lehrer, Keith. "Metaknowledge: Undefeated Justification." *Synthese*. In press.

Moser, Paul K. *Empirical Justification*. Boston: Reidel, 1985.

Plantinga, Alvin. "Coherentism and the Evidentialist Objection to Belief in God." In Robert Audi and William Wainwright, eds., *Rationality, Religious Belief, and Moral Commitment*. Ithaca: Cornell University Press, 1986.

Quinton, Anthony. *The Nature of Things*. London: Routledge & Kegan Paul, 1973.

Sellars, Wilfrid. "Givenness and Explanatory Coherence." *Journal of Philosophy 70* (1973).

Shatz, David. "Foundationalism, Coherentism, and the Levels Gambit." *Synthese 55* (1983), 1.

Tomberlin, James E., ed. *Philosophical Perspectives*. Vol. 2: *Epistemology*. Atascadero, CA: Ridgeview, 1988.

V.8 A Contextual Theory of Epistemic Justification

David Annis

David Annis is Professor of Philosophy at Ball State University. In this essay Annis offers an alternative to the foundationalist–coherentist controversy: "contextualism." This theory rejects both the idea of intrinsically basic beliefs in the foundational sense and the thesis that coherence is sufficient for justification. He argues that justification is relative to the varying norms of social practices.

I. Foundationalism, Coherentism, and Contextualism

Foundationalism is the theory that every empirical statement which is justified ultimately must derive at least some of its justification from a special class of basic statements which have at least some degree of justification independent of the support such statements may derive from other statements. Such *minimal* foundationalism does not require certainty or incorrigibility; it does not deny the revisability of *all* statements, and it allows an important role for intrasystematic justification or coherence.[1] The main objections to foundationalism have been (a) the denial of the existence of basic statements and (b) the claim that even if such statements were not mythical, such an impoverished basis would never justify all the various statements we normally take to be justified.

Opposed to foundationalism has been the coherence theory of justification. According to coherentism a statement is justified if and only if it coheres with a certain kind of system of statements. Although there has been disagreement among coherentists in explaining what coherence is and specifying the special system of statements, the key elements in these explanations have been consistency,

connectedness, and comprehensiveness. The chief objection to the theory has been that coherence within a consistent and comprehensive set of statements is not sufficient for justification.[2] Theorists of epistemic justification have tended to stress foundationalism and coherentism and in general have overlooked or ignored a third kind of theory, namely, *contextualism*. The contextualist denies that there are basic statements in the foundationalist's sense and that coherence is sufficient for justification. According to contextualism both theories overlook contextual parameters essential to justification. In what follows I develop a version of a contextualist theory.[3]

II. The Basic Model— Meeting Objections

The basic model of justification to be developed here is that of a person's being able to meet certain objections. The objections one must meet and whether or not they are met are relative to certain goals. Since the issue is that of epistemic justification, the goals are epistemic in nature. With respect to one epistemic goal, accepting some statement may be reasonable, whereas relative to a different goal it may not be. Two of our epistemic goals are having true beliefs and avoiding having false beliefs. Other epistemic goals such as simplicity, conservation of existing beliefs, and maximization of ex-

Reprinted from the *American Philosophical Quarterly* 15 (1978): 213–19, by permission of the author and the editor. Copyright 1978, *American Philosophical Quarterly*.

planatory power will be assumed to be subsidiary to the goals of truth and the avoidance of error.[4]

Given these goals, if a person S claims that some statement h is true, we may object (A) that S is not in a position to know that h or (B) that h is false. Consider (A). Suppose we ask S how he knows that h and he responds by giving us various reasons e_1, e_2, . . ., e_n for the truth of h. We may object that one of his reasons e_1–e_n is false, e_1–e_n does not provide adequate support for h, S's specific reasoning from e_1–e_n to h is fallacious, or that there is evidence i such that the conjunction of e_1–e_n and i does not provide adequate support for h. These objections may be raised to his reasons for e_1–e_n as well as to his responses to our objections.

There are also cases where a person is not required to give reasons for his claim that h is true. If S claims to see a brown book across the room, we usually do not require reasons. But we may still object that the person is not in a position to know by arguing, for example, that the person is not reliable in such situations. So even in cases where we do not in general require reasons, objections falling into categories (A) or (B) can be raised.

But it would be too strong a condition to require a person to be able to meet all *possible* objections falling into these categories. In some distant time new evidence may be discovered as the result of advances in our scientific knowledge which would call into question the truth of some statement h. Even though we do not in fact have that evidence now, it is logically possible that we have it, so it is a possible objection to h now. If the person had to meet the objection, he would have to be in a different and better epistemic position than the one he is presently in, that is, he would have to have new evidence in order to respond to the objection. The objectors also would have to be in a better position to raise the objection. But the objections to be raised and answered should not require the participants to be in a new epistemic position. What is being asked is whether the person in his present position is justified in believing h. Thus the person only has to answer *current* objections, that is, objections based on the current evidence available.

Merely uttering a question that falls into one of our categories does not make it an objection S must answer. To demand a response the objection must be an expression of a *real* doubt. According to

Peirce, doubt is an uneasy and dissatisfied state from which we struggle to free ourselves. Such doubt is the result of "some surprising phenomenon, some experience which either disappoints an expectation, or breaks in upon some habit of expectation."[5] As Dewey puts it, it is only when "jars, hitches, breaks, blocks, . . . incidents occasioning an interruption of the smooth straight forward course of behavior" occur that doubt arises.[6] Thus for S to be held accountable for answering an objection, it must be a manifestation of a real doubt where the doubt is occasioned by a real life situation. Assuming that the subjective probabilities a person assigns reflect the person's actual epistemic attitudes and that these are the product of his confrontation with the world, the above point may be expressed as follows. S is not required to respond to an objection if *in general* it would be assigned a low probability by the people questioning S.

If an objection must be the expression of a real doubt caused by the jars of a real life situation, then such objections will be primarily *local* as opposed to *global*. Global objections call into question the totality of beliefs held at a certain time or a whole realm of beliefs, whereas local objections call into question a specific belief. This is not to say that a real situation might not occur that would prompt a global objection. If having experienced the nuclear radiation of a third world war, there were a sudden and dramatic increase in the error rate of perceptual beliefs of the visual sort, we would be more hesitant about them as a class.

It must be assumed that the objecting audience has the epistemic goals of truth and the avoidance of error. If they were not critical truth seekers, they would not raise appropriate objections. To meet an objection i, S must respond in such a way as to produce within the objecting group a general but not necessarily universal rejection of i or at least the general recognition of the diminished status of i as an objection. In the latter case S may, for example, point out that although i might be true, it only decreases the support of e_i (one of his reasons for believing h) a very small amount, and hence he is still justified in believing h. There are of course many ways in which S can handle an objection. He might indicate that it is not of the type (A) or (B) and so is not relevant. He may respond that it is just an *idle* remark not prompted by real doubt; that is, there is no reason for thinking that it is true. He may ask the objector for his reasons, and he can raise any of the objections of the type (A) or (B) in response. Again the give and take is based on real objections and responses.

III. *The Social Nature of Justification*

When asking whether S is justified in believing h, this has to be considered relative to an *issue-context*. Suppose we are interested in whether Jones, an ordinary non-medically trained person, has the general information that polio is caused by a virus. If his response to our question is that he remembers the paper reporting that Salk said it was, then this is good enough. He has performed adequately given the issue-context. But suppose the context is an examination for the M.D. degree. Here we expect a lot more. If the candidate simply said what Jones did, we would take him as being very deficient in knowledge. Thus relative to one issue-context a person may be justified in believing h but not justified relative to another context.

The issue-context is what specific issue involving h is being raised. It determines the level of understanding and knowledge that S must exhibit, and it determines an appropriate objector-group. For example in the context of the examination for the M.D. degree, the appropriate group is not the class of ordinary non-medically trained people, but qualified medical examiners.

The importance (value or utility) attached to the outcome of accepting h when it is false or rejecting h when it is true is a component of the issue-context. Suppose the issue is whether a certain drug will help cure a disease in humans without harmful effects. In such a situation we are much more demanding than if the question were whether it would help in the case of animals. In both cases the appropriate objector-group would be the same, namely, qualified researchers. But they would require quite a bit more proof in the former case. Researchers do in fact strengthen or weaken the justificatory conditions in relation to the importance of the issue. If accepting h when h is false would have critical consequences, the researcher

may increase the required significance level in testing h.

Man is a social animal, and yet when it comes to the justification of beliefs philosophers tend to ignore this fact. But this is one contextual parameter that no adequate theory of justification can overlook. According to the contextualist model of justification sketched above, when asking whether some person S is justified in believing h, we must consider this relative to some specific issue-context which determines the level of understanding and knowledge required. This in turn determines the appropriate objector-group. For S to be justified in believing h relative to the issue-context, S must be able to meet all current objections falling into (A) and (B) which express a real doubt of the qualified objector-group where the objectors are critical truth seekers. Thus social information—the beliefs, information, and theories of others—plays an important part in justification, for it in part determines what objections will be raised, how a person will respond to them, and what responses the objectors will accept.

Perhaps the most neglected component in justification theory is the *actual* social practices and norms of justification of a culture or community of people. Philosophers have looked for universal and a priori principles of justification. But consider this in the context of scientific inquiry. There certainly has been refinement in the methods and techniques of discovery and testing in science. Suppose that at a time t in accordance with the best methods then developed for discovery and testing in a scientific domain by critical truth seekers, S accepts theory T. It is absurd to say that S is not justified in accepting T since at a later time a refinement of those techniques would lead to the acceptance of a different theory. Thus relative to the standards at t, S is justified in accepting T.

The same conclusion follows if we consider a case involving two different groups existing at the same time instead of two different times as in the above example. Suppose S is an Earth physicist and accepts T on the basis of the best methods developed by Earth physicists at t. Unknown to us the more advanced physicists on Twin Earth reject T. S is still justified in accepting T.

To determine whether S is justified in believing h we must consider the actual standards of justification of the community of people to which he belongs. More specifically we determine whether *S* is justified in believing *h* by specifying an issue-context raised within a community of people *G* with certain social practices and norms of justification. This determines the level of understanding and knowledge *S* is expected to have and the standards he is to satisfy. The appropriate objector-group is a subset of *G*. To be justified in believing *h*, *S* must be able to meet their objections in a way that satisfies their practices and norms.

It follows that justification theory must be *naturalized*. In considering the justification of beliefs we cannot neglect the actual social practices and norms of justification of a group. Psychologists, sociologists, and anthropologists have started this study, but much more work is necessary.[7]

The need to naturalize justification theory has been recognized in recent philosophy of science. Positivists stressed the *logic* of science—the structure of theories, confirmation, explanation—in abstraction from science as actually carried on. But much of the main thrust of recent philosophy of science is that such an approach is inadequate. Science as *practiced* yields justified beliefs about the world. Thus the study of the actual practices, which have changed through time, cannot be neglected. The present tenor in the philosophy of science is thus toward a historical and methodological realism.[8]

From the fact that justification is relative to the social practices and norms of a group, it does not follow that they cannot be criticized nor that justification is somehow subjective. The practices and norms are epistemic and hence have as their goals truth and the avoidance of error. Insofar as they fail to achieve these goals they can be criticized. For example the Kpelle people of Africa rely more on the authority of the elders than we do. But this authority could be questioned if they found it led to too many false perceptual beliefs. An objection to a practice must of course be real; that is, the doubt must be the result of some jar or hitch in our experience of the world. Furthermore such objections will always be local as opposed to global. Some practice or norm and our experiences of the world yield the result that another practice is problematic. A real objection presupposes some other accepted practice. This however does not commit us to some

form of subjectivism. Just as there is no theory-neutral observation language in science, so there is no standard-neutral epistemic position that one can adopt. But in neither case does it follow that objectivity and rational criticism are lost.[9]

IV. *The Regress Argument*

Philosophers who have accepted foundationalism have generally offered a version of the infinite regress argument in support of it. Two key premises in the argument are the denial of a coherence theory of justification and the denial that an infinite sequence of reasons is sufficient to justify a belief. But there is another option to the conclusion of the argument besides foundationalism. A contextualist theory of the sort offered above stops the regress and yet does not require basic statements in the foundationalist's sense.

Suppose that the Joneses are looking for a red chair to replace a broken one in their house. The issue-context is thus not whether they can discern subtle shades of color. Nor is it an examination in physics where the person is expected to have detailed knowledge of the transmission of light and color perception. Furthermore nothing of great importance hinges on a correct identification. Mr. Jones, who has the necessary perceptual concepts and normal vision, points at a red chair a few feet in front of him and says "here is a red one." The appropriate objector-group consists of normal perceivers who have general knowledge about the standard conditions of perception and perceptual error. In such situations which we are all familiar with, generally, there will be no objections. His claim is accepted as justified. But imagine that someone objects that there is a red light shining on the chair so it may not be red. If Jones cannot respond to this objection when it is real, then he is not in an adequate cognitive position. But suppose he is in a position to reply that he knows about the light and the chair is still red since he saw it yesterday in normal light. Then we will accept his claim.

A belief is *contextually basic* if, given an issue-context, the appropriate objector-group does not require the person to have reasons for the belief in order to be in a position to have knowledge. If the objector-group requires reasons, then it is not basic in the context. Thus in the first situation above Jones's belief that there is a red chair here is contextually-basic, whereas it is not basic in the second situation.

Consider the case either where the objector-group does not require S to have reasons for his belief that h in order to be in a position to have knowledge and where they accept his claim, or the case where they require reasons and accept his claim. In either case there is no regress of reasons. If an appropriate objector-group, the members of which are critical truth seekers, have no real doubts in the specific issue-context, then the person's belief is justified. The belief has withstood the test of verifically motivated objectors.

V. *Objections to the Theory*

There are several objections to the contextualist theory offered, and their main thrust is that the conditions for justification imposed are too stringent. The objections are as follows. First according to the theory offered, to be justified in believing h one must be able to meet a restricted class of objections falling into categories (A) and (B). But this ignores the distinction between *being* justified and *showing* that one is justified. To be justified is just to satisfy the principles of justification. To show that one is justified is to demonstrate that one satisfies these principles, and this is much more demanding.[10] For example S might have evidence that justifies his belief that h even though he is not able to articulate the evidence. In this case S would not be able to show that he was justified.

Second, if to be justified in believing h requires that one be able to meet the objection that h is false, then the theory ignores the distinction between truth and justification. A person can be justified in believing a statement even though it is false.

Finally the theory requires S to be in a position to answer all sorts of objections from a variety of perspectives. But this again is to require too much. For example assume that two scientists in different countries unaware of each other's work perform a certain experiment. The first scientist, S_1, gets one

result and concludes that h. The second scientist, S_2, does not get the result (due to incorrect measurements). To require of S_1 that he be aware of S_2's experiment and be able to refute it is to impose an unrealistic burden on him in order for his belief to be justified. It is to build a *defeasibility* requirement into the justification condition. One approach to handling the Gettier problem has been to add the condition that in order to have knowledge, besides having justified true belief, the justification must not be defeated. Although there have been different characterizations of defeasibility, a core component or unrestricted version has been that a statement i defeats the justification evidence e provides h just in case i is true and the conjunction of i and e does not provide adequate support for h.[11] But according to the contextualist theory presented in order for S to be justified in believing h, he must be able to meet the objection that there is defeating evidence.

In reply to the first objection, the theory offered does not ignore the distinction between being justified and showing that one is justified. It is not required of S that he be able to state the standards of justification and demonstrate that he satisfies them. What is required is that he be able to meet real objections. This may *sometimes* require him to discuss standards, but not always. Furthermore the example given is not a counterexample since it is not a case of justified belief. Consider a case where relative to an issue-context we would expect S to have reasons for his belief that h. Suppose when asked how he knows or what his reasons are he is not able to say anything. We certainly would not take him as justified in his belief. We may not be able to articulate all our evidence for h, but we are required to do it for some of the evidence. It is not enough that we have evidence for h; it must be *taken* by us as evidence, and this places us "in the logical space of reasons, of justifying and being able to justify what one says."[12]

The first point in response to the next objection is that *epistemic* justification makes a claim to knowledge. To be *epistemically* justified in believing h is to be in a position to know h. Furthermore if the goals of epistemic justification are truth and the avoidance of error, then one *ought not* accept false statements. From an epistemic point of view to do so is objectionable. Hence the falsity of h at least counts against the person's being justified.

However, the contextualist account offered does not ignore the distinction between truth and justification. Meeting an objection does not entail showing the objection is false. It only requires general agreement on the response. So the objection may still be true. Thus *S* may be justified in believing *h* since he can meet the objection when *h* is in fact false. Furthermore an objection in order to require a response has to be the expression of a real doubt. Since it is possible for verifically motivated objectors not to be aware of the falsity of *h*, this objection will not be raised, so *S* may be justified in believing *h* even though it is false.

The situation is complex, however, since there are cases where the falsity of *h* implies *S* is not justified in believing *h*. Suppose that Jones is at a party and wonders whether his friend Smith is there. Nothing of great importance hinges on his presence; he simply wonders whether he is there. Perhaps he would not mind a chat with Smith. He looks about and asks a few guests. They have not seen him there. In such a situation Jones is justified in believing Smith is not there.

Imagine now that Jones is a police officer looking for Smith, a suspected assassin, at the party. Merely looking about casually and checking with a few guests is certainly not adequate. If Smith turns out to be hiding in one of the closets, we will not conclude that Jones was justified in his belief only it turned out false. He displayed gross negligence in not checking more thoroughly. There are cases where relative to an issue-context we require the person *S* to put himself in such an epistemic position that *h* will not turn out to be false. In this case the falsity of *h* is *non-excusable*. To be justified in believing *h* in non-excusable cases, *S* must be able to meet the objection that *h* is false. This is not required in excusable cases.

Assume that *h* is some very complicated scientific theory and *S* puts himself in the very best evidential position at the time. Even if the truth of *h* is very important, the falsity of *h* is excusable. The complexity of the issue and the fact that *S* put himself in the best position possible excuses *S* from the falsity of *h*, so he is still justified. But not all excusable cases involve a complex *h* nor being in the best position possible. Suppose that Smith has an identical twin brother but the only living person who knows this is the brother. Furthermore there are no

records that there was a twin brother. If Jones returns a book to Smith's house and mistakenly gives it to the brother (where the issue-context is simply whether he returned the borrowed book and nothing of great importance hinges on to whom he gave it), he is still justified in his belief that he gave it to his friend Smith. Although Jones could have put himself in a better position (by asking questions about their friendship), there was no reason for him in the context to check further. People did not generally know about the twin brother, and Smith did not notice any peculiar behavior. Given the issue-context, members of the appropriate objector-group would not *expect* Jones to check further. So he evinces no culpability when his belief turns out to be false. Excusability thus depends on the issue-context and what the appropriate objector-group, given their standards of justification and the information available, expect of *S*.

Part of assimilating our epistemic standards, as is the case with both legal and moral standards, is learning the conditions of excusability. Such conditions are highly context-dependent, and it would be extremely difficult if not impossible to formulate rules to express them. In general we learn the conditions of excusability case by case. One need only consider moral and legal negligence to realize the full complexity of excuses, an area still to be studied despite Austin's well-known plea a number of years ago.

In response to the third objection it should be noted that epistemic justification is not to be taken lightly. Accepting *h* in part determines what other things I will believe and do. Furthermore I can infect the minds of others with my falsehoods and thus affect their further beliefs and actions. So to be epistemically justified requires that our claims pass the test of criticism. This point has motivated some philosophers to build a defeasibility requirement into the conditions of justification.[13]

The contextualist theory presented above, however, does not do this. There may be a defeating statement *i*, but *S* need meet this objection only if the objector-group raises it. For them to raise it, *i* must be the expression of real doubt. But it is perfectly possible for verifically motivated people to be unaware of *i*.

Furthermore the concept of epistemic excusability applies to defeating evidence. Suppose there is defeating evidence *i*. *S* may still be justified in his belief that *h* in the issue-context, even though he is unable to meet the objection. Relative to the issue-context, the appropriate objector-group with their standards of justification and available information may not expect of *S* that he be aware of *i*. Perhaps the issue involving *h* is very complicated. Thus his failure to meet the defeating evidence is excusable.

In the experiment case we can imagine issue-contexts where we would expect the first scientist to know of the experiment of the other scientist. But not all issue-contexts demand this. Nevertheless we may still require that he be in a position to say something about the other experiment if informed about it. For example he might indicate that he knows the area well, has performed the experiment a number of times and gotten similar results, it was performed under carefully controlled conditions, so he has every reason for believing that the experiment is replicable with similar results. Thus there must be something wrong with the other experiment. Requiring the scientist to be able to respond in the *minimal* way seems not to be overly demanding.

VI. *Summary*

Contextualism is an alternative to the traditional theories of foundationalism and coherentism. It denies the existence of basic statements in the foundationalist's sense (although it allows contextually basic statements), and it denies that coherence as it traditionally has been explained is sufficient for justification. Both theories overlook contextual parameters essential to justification, such as the issue-context and thus the value of *h*, social information, and social practices and norms of justification. In particular, the social nature of justification cannot be ignored.

Notes

[1] For a discussion of minimal foundationalism see William P. Alston, "Has Foundationalism Been Refuted?"; James W. Cornman, "Foundationalism versus Nonfoundational Theories of Empirical Justification"; David B. Annis, "Epistemic Foundationalism."

[2] Recent discussions of coherentism are found in Keith Lehrer, *Knowledge,* chaps. 7–8; Nicholas Rescher, "Foundationalism, Coherentism, and the Idea of Cognitive Systematization" and his *The Coherence Theory of Truth.* Criticism of Lehrer's coherence theory is to be found in Cornman, "Foundational Versus Nonfoundational Theories of Empirical Justification," and in my review of Lehrer in *Philosophia* 6 (1976): 209–13. Criticism of Rescher's version is found in Mark Pastin's "Foundationalism Redux," unpublished, an abstract of which appears in *The Journal of Philosophy* 61 (1974): 709–10.

[3] Historically the key contextualists have been Peirce, Dewey, and Popper. But contextualist hints, suggestions, and theories are also to be found in Robert Ackermann, *Belief and Knowledge;* Bruce Aune, *Knowledge, Mind and Nature;* John Austin, *Sense and Sensibilia* (London, 1962); Isaac Levi, *Gambling with Truth* (New York, 1967); Stephen Toulmin, *The Uses of Argument* (London, 1958) and *Human Understanding* (Princeton, New Jersey, 1972); Carl Wellman, *Challenge and Response: Justification in Ethics* (Carbondale, Illinois, 1971); F. L. Will, *Induction and Justification;* Ludwig Wittgenstein, *Philosophical Investigations* (New York, 1953) and *On Certainty.*

[4] For a discussion of epistemic goals see Levi, *Gambling with Truth.*

[5] C. S. Peirce, *Collected Papers,* vol. 6, ed. Charles Hartshorne and Paul Weiss (Harvard, 1965), p. 469.

[6] John Dewey, *Knowing and the Known* (Boston, 1949), p. 315. See also Wittgenstein's *On Certainty.*

[7] See, for example, Michael Cole et al., *The Cultural Context of Learning and Thinking* (New York, 1971).

[8] For a discussion of the need to naturalize justification theory in the philosophy of science, see Frederick Suppe, "Afterword—1976" in the 2nd edition of his *The Structure of Scientific Theories* (Urbana, Illinois, 1977).

[9] See Frederick Suppe's "The Search for Philosophic Understanding of Scientific Theories" and his "Afterword–1976" in *The Structure of Scientific Theories* for a discussion of objectivity in science and the lack of a theory-neutral observation language.

[10] Alston discusses this distinction in "Has Foundationalism Been Refuted?" See also his "Two Types of Foundationalism."

[11] The best discussion of defeasibility is Marshall Swain's "Epistemic Defeasibility."

[12] Wilfrid Sellars, *Science, Perception and Reality,* p. 169.

[13] Carl Ginet, "What Must Be Added to Knowing to Obtain Knowing That One Knows?," *Synthese* 21 (1970): 163–86.

Bibliography

Alston, William. "Concepts of Epistemic Justification." *Monist 68* (1985). Reprinted in his book *Epistemic Justification: Essays in the Theory of Knowledge*. Ithaca, NY: Cornell University Press, 1990.

Alston, William. "Two Types of Foundationalism." *Journal of Philosophy 73* (1976). Also in his book *Epistemic Justification: Essays in the Theory of Knowledge*. Ithaca, NY: Cornell University Press, 1990.

Ayer, A. J. *The Foundations of Empirical Knowledge*. New York: St. Martin's Press, 1955.

Blanshard, Brand. *The Nature of Thought*. 2 vols. London: Allen & Unwin, 1940.

BonJour, Laurence. *The Structure of Empirical Knowledge*. Cambridge, MA: Harvard University Press, 1985.

Butchvarov, Panayot. *The Concept of Knowledge*. Evanston, IL: Northwestern University Press, 1970.

Chisholm, Roderick. *The Foundations of Knowing*. Minneapolis: University of Minnesota Press, 1982.

Chisholm, Roderick, and Robert Schwartz, eds. *Empirical Knowledge*. Englewood Cliffs, NJ: Prentice-Hall, 1973.

Foley, Richard. *The Theory of Epistemic Rationality*. Cambridge, MA: Harvard University Press, 1987.

Goldman, Alvin. *Epistemology and Cognition*. Cambridge, MA: Harvard University Press, 1986.

Lehrer, Keith. *Knowledge*. Oxford, England: Clarendon Press, 1974.

Lehrer, Keith. *Theory of Knowledge*. Boulder, CO: Westview, 1990.

Lewis, C. I. *An Analysis of Knowledge and Valuation*. La Salle, IL: Open Court, 1946.

Moser, Paul. *Empirical Justification*. Boston: Reidel, 1985.

Moser, Paul, ed. *Empirical Knowledge*. Totowa, NJ: Rowman & Littlefield, 1986.

Pappas, George, ed. *Justification and Knowledge*. Dordrecht, Netherlands: Reidel, 1979.

Pappas, George, and Marshall Swain, eds. *Essays on Knowledge and Justification*. Ithaca, NY: Cornell University Press, 1978.

Pollock, John. *Contemporary Theories of Knowledge*. Totowa, NJ: Rowman & Littlefield, 1986.

Rescher, Nicholas. *The Coherence Theory of Truth*. Oxford, England: Clarendon Press, 1973.

Sellars, Wilfrid. *Science, Perception and Reality*. London: Routledge & Kegan Paul, 1963.

Sosa, Ernest. "The Foundations of Foundationalism." *Nous 14* (1980).

Van Cleve, James. "Foundationalism, Epistemic Principles and the Cartesian Circle." *Philosophical Review 88* (1979).

Part VI

Justification (II): Externalism and Internalism

Bishop James Ussher (1581–1656), Primate of All Ireland, calculated the genealogies in the Bible and determined that the creation of the heavens and earth, as well as the first humans, took place in the year 4004 B.C. (October 23 at noon), about 6,000 years ago. Modern science totally rejects Ussher's theory. The fossil record, the dating of the age of rocks that posits that the earth is about 5 billion years old, the evidence from astronomy that the universe is at least 15 billion years old, our best evidence for evolutionary theory—all purport to refute Bishop Ussher's conclusions. But suppose that Ussher is right about the age of the universe and that the Genesis account of the creation is accurate, so that all our evidence for evolution and the longevity of the universe is systematically misleading. The carbon 14 test for dating organic materials does not function reliably after about 5,500 years. The fossils of dinosaurs were hidden in the earth to mislead unbelievers. Our evidence for an ancient universe is fraudulent, but is such that finite minds like ours could never comprehend the truth unaided by revelation. If we had not sinned, our noetic devices would have processed all this information reliably, but as it is, sin has corrupted our belief-forming mechanisms so that they are unreliable about such matters. Only through conversion wherein divine grace sets our mechanisms back in proper working order can we become knowledgeable of the hidden truth.

According to internalists or *justificationists,* so long as we are following the best evidence available to us, we are justified in believing the evolutionary account and the creationists are unjustified in their lucky true belief. The externalists (*reliabilists*) argue that this is not the case. So long as a reliable process caused creationists to believe the way they did, they have knowledge as well as justification.

Actually, there are two kinds of externalists: reliabilists and naturalists, the former (D. M. Armstrong, and Alvin Goldman in the first reading of this part of the book) hold that reliable processes are justifactory. Naturalists, such as W. V. Quine in the third reading, reject the notion of justification altogether. Knowledge is a matter of having beliefs caused in the proper way. The idea of justification implies normativity, but we are not responsible for our beliefs, so the idea of evaluation is misplaced.

There are several advantages of externalism. It defeats the skeptic, dissolves the problems of induction and other minds, and makes sense of perceptual knowledge.

It defeats skepticism. Since knowledge is defined as true beliefs caused in the proper manner, it doesn't matter whether the subject can give an account of his or her beliefs or is even conscious of those beliefs. In a similar vein, externalism dissolves the problem of induction and other minds, because these beliefs are seen as being caused by reliable processes (see Levin, Reading IX.4).

With regard to perception, we often cannot give an account of our beliefs. We may not even know why we hold them. Suppose you come to dinner at my home, and after dinner I take you into another room and give you a quiz. "Do you know what color the walls in the dining room were and what pictures were hanging on them?" I ask. You pause, for you don't remember even noticing the walls or the pictures, but you correctly say, "The walls were red and a couple of pictures of Oxford were on one wall and a Renoir picture was on the other." "How did you know that?" I ask. You admit that you don't know how you knew. Your perceptual mechanisms picked up the information, stored it in your mind or brain, and let you retrieve it at the appropriate moment. Were you justified in believing that the walls were red and that pictures of Oxford were on one wall? What if you thought you were only guessing? What if you didn't really believe what you said, but only said what came to your mind unbidden via the unconscious?

The externalist says you knew the color of the walls and what pictures were hanging there, just as long as a reliable mechanism caused your beliefs. The internalist has trouble with this sort of case and either says it is a borderline case of justification or is an unjustified true belief.

But there are weaknesses with externalism. First of all, exactly what is to count as a reliable belief-forming mechanism is vague. What percentage of true beliefs must the process be able to produce before it is admitted to be reliable? The major problem, however, is that it seems to dissolve the notion of normativity. Knowledge is more than simply having true beliefs or properly caused beliefs. A long tradition, going back to Plato in the *Theaetetus,* holds that knowledge requires the ability to give reasons, a justification. Appropriate causation of a belief seems necessary but not sufficient for justification, for we can imagine counterexamples where a belief that p has been properly caused, but where we would not want to say that the subject knew p. Laurence BonJour offers the following counterexample:

Samantha believes herself to have the power of clairvoyance, though she has no reason for or against this belief. One day she comes to believe, for no apparent reason, that the President is in New York City. She maintains this belief, appealing to her alleged clairvoyance power, even though she is at the same time aware of a massive amount of apparently cogent evidence, consisting of news reports, press releases, allegedly live television pictures, and so on, indicating that the President is at that time in Washington, D.C. Now the President is in fact in New York City, the evidence to the contrary being part of a massive official hoax mounted in the face of an assassination threat. Moreover, Samantha does in fact have completely reliable clairvoyant power under the conditions which were then satisfied, and her belief about the President did result from the operation of that power.[1]

In this case the reliability requirement is met, but we would hesitate to say that Samantha knows that the president is in New York or is justified in her belief.

Likewise, even if it turned out that Bishop Ussher was right in dating the creation of the heavens and the earth to the year 4004 B.C. and that present-day creationists had their correct beliefs formed in reliable ways (their belief-forming mechanisms were unconsciously tied into information patterns going back to Creation, though they didn't have good reasons to believe this), as long as they weren't able to give good reasons for their beliefs, we would deny that they were epistemically justified in their belief.

Finally, reliabilists seem to be driven to giving counterfactual accounts of knowing and so are heirs to all the problems inherent in such accounts, as well as specifying the relevant belief-forming mechanism in specific cases.

In the first reading, Alvin I. Goldman de-

velops a causal account of foundational justification called "historical reliabilism," in contrast with the traditional "current time slice" theories of justification. Current time slice or synchronic theories view the justificatory status of a belief as a function of what is true for the believer at the time of the believing. Historical reliabilism holds that the justificatory status is a function of the belief's prior history, aspecifically of whether it was produced in the right way. Goldman's theory is objectivist and externalist.

In the second reading, Keith Lehrer nicely maps out the geography of the internalist–externalist debate and argues against Goldman's account and for internalism.

In the third reading, W. V. Quine argues for a more radical version of externalism than Goldman and the reliabilists. According to Quine, normative epistemology is an outmoded enterprise that must be turned over to psychology. With the failure of Rudolf Carnap's project for constructing a foundational system of knowledge and with our understanding of the indeterminacy of translation, all hope of reviving the "old epistemology" is fruitless. What is left is a descriptive inquiry into the relationship between sensory inputs and the "torrential output," our picture of the world.

In the fourth reading, Jaegwon Kim rejects Quine's naturalism and all such endeavors to eliminate the normative element in epistemology. To give up normativity in the name of science is to give up the notion of knowledge itself, as well as the idea of rationality on which science itself depends.

The justificationist contends that epistemology naturalized is not a rival account to internalism but is a change in subject matter.

In the fifth reading, John Pollock sets forth a theory diametrically opposed to Goldman's objective externalism, one that is subjective and internalist. The justification of a belief depends solely on the internal states of the believer: states directly accessible to the mechanisms in our central nervous system that direct our reasoning.

In the final reading, Alvin Plantinga argues that the classical version of internalism, exemplified in Descartes and Locke, which links justification with duties and closely relates it to knowledge, is incoherent and suggests a replacement in terms of properly functioning belief-forming mechanisms. Regarding Ussher's estimated dating of the creation of the heavens and the earth, Plantinga would very likely say that Ussher and creationists were *warranted* and have knowledge of these propositions just in case they are true and the beliefs were formed in a suitable way, even if they cannot give reasons for these beliefs. Plantinga's critique of the notion of epistemic duties overlaps this part of the book and Part X, "The Ethics of Belief."

Let us turn to our first reading, the groundbreaking article by Alvin Goldman, "What Is Justified Belief?"

Note

[1] Laurence BonJour, *The Structure of Empirical Knowledge* (Cambridge, MA: Harvard University Press, 1985), p. 38.

VI.1   *Reliabilism: What Is Justified Belief?*

ALVIN I. GOLDMAN

Alvin I. Goldman is Professor of Philosophy at the University of Arizona. Two of his earlier essays appear in Part IV (Readings IV.2 and IV.5). This essay is a successor to these earlier causal accounts in which Goldman argues that (1) all present versions of internalism are plagued with insuperable obstacles, (2) the absence of a causal requirement is common to each of these inadequate principles, and (3) the theory that best satisfies the causal requirement is an external version of justification, namely "reliabilism," which defines the justificatory status of a belief in terms of the reliability of the process that caused it. The reliability of a process consists in its tendency to produce true beliefs rather than false ones. This is an externalist and objective theory of justification, because the agent need not have access to the causal mechanisms that produce justified beliefs.

The aim of this essay is to sketch a theory of justified belief. What I have in mind is an explanatory theory, one that explains in a general way why certain beliefs are counted as justified and others as unjustified. Unlike some traditional approaches, I do not try to prescribe standards for justification that differ from, or improve upon, our ordinary standards. I merely try to explicate the ordinary standards, which are, I believe, quite different from those of many classical, e.g., "Cartesian," accounts.

Many epistemologists have been interested in justification because of its presumed close relationship to knowledge. This relationship is intended to be preserved in the conception of justified belief presented here. In previous papers on knowledge,[1] I have denied that justification is necessary for

Reprinted from *Justification and Knowledge*, ed. G. S. Pappas (Dordrecht: D. Reidel, 1979), 1–23, by permission of the author and the publisher. Copyright 1979, D. Reidel Publishing Company.

knowing, but there I had in mind "Cartesian" accounts of justification. On the account of justified belief suggested here, it *is* necessary for knowing, and closely related to it.

The term "justified," I presume, is an evaluative term, a term of appraisal. Any correct definition or synonym of it would also feature evaluative terms. I assume that such definitions or synonyms might be given, but I am not interested in them. I want a set of *substantive* conditions that specify when a belief is justified. Compare the normal term "right." This might be defined in other ethical terms or phrases, a task appropriate to meta-ethics. The task of normative ethics, by contrast, is to state substantive conditions for the rightness of actions. Normative ethics tries to specify non-ethical conditions that determine when an action is right. A familiar example is act-utilitarianism, which says an action is right if and only if it produces, or would produce, at least as much net happiness as any alternative open to the agent. These necessary and sufficient conditions clearly involve no ethical notions. Analogously, I want a theory of justified belief to specify in non-epistemic terms when a belief is justified. This is not the only kind of theory of justifiedness one might seek, but it is one important kind of theory and the kind sought here.

In order to avoid epistemic terms in our theory, we must know which terms are epistemic. Obviously, an exhaustive list cannot be given, but here are some examples: "justified," "warranted," "has (good) grounds," "has reason (to believe)," "knows that," "sees that," "apprehends that," "is probable" (in an epistemic or inductive sense), "shows that," "establishes that," and "ascertains that." By contrast, here are some sample non-epistemic expressions: "believes that," "is true," "causes," "it is necessary that," "implies," "is deducible from," and "is probable" (either in the frequency sense or the propensity sense). In general, (purely) doxastic, metaphysical, modal, semantic, or syntactic expressions are not epistemic.

There is another constraint I wish to place on a theory of justified belief, in addition to the constraint that it be couched in non-epistemic language. Since I seek an explanatory theory, i.e., one that clarifies the underlying source of justificational status, it is not enough for a theory to state "correct" necessary and sufficient conditions. Its conditions must also be appropriately deep or revelatory. Suppose, for example, that the following sufficient condition of justified belief is offered: "If *S* senses redly at *t* and *S* believes at *t* that he is sensing redly, then *S*'s belief at *t* that he is sensing redly is justified." This is not the kind of principle I seek; for, even if it is correct, it leaves unexplained *why* a person who senses redly and believes that he does, believes this justifiably. Not every state is such that if one is in it and believes one is in it, this belief is justified. What is distinctive about the state of sensing redly, or "phenomenal" states in general? A theory of justified belief of the kind I seek must answer this question, and hence it must be couched at a suitably deep, general, or abstract level.

A few introductory words about my *explicandum* are appropriate at this juncture. It is often assumed that whenever a person has a justified belief, he knows that it is justified and knows what the justification is. It is further assumed that the person can state or explain what his justification is. On this view, a justification is an argument, defense, or set of reasons that can be given in support of a belief. Thus, one studies the nature of justified belief by considering what a person might *say* if asked to defend, or justify, his belief. I make none of these sorts of assumptions here. I leave it an open question whether, when a belief *is* justified, the believer *knows* it is justified. I also leave it an open question whether, when a belief is justified, the believer can *state* or *give* a justification for it. I do not even assume that when a belief is justified there is something "possessed" by the believer which can be called a "justification." I do assume that a justified belief gets its status of being justified from some processes or properties that make it justified. In short, there must be some justification-conferring processes or properties. But this does not imply that there must be an argument, or reason, or anything else, "possessed" at the time of belief by the believer.

I

A theory of justified belief will be a set of principles that specify truth-conditions for the schema ⌈*S*'s belief in *p* at time *t* is justified⌉, i.e., conditions for the satisfaction of this schema in all possible cases. It will be convenient to formulate candidate theories in a recursive or inductive format, which would include (A) one or more base clauses, (B) a set of recursive clauses (possibly null), and (C) a closure clause. In such a format, it is permissible for the predicate "is a justified belief" to appear in recursive clauses. But neither this predicate, nor any other epistemic predicate, may appear in (the antecedent of) any base clause.[2]

Before turning to my own theory, I want to survey some other possible approaches to justified belief. Identification of problems associated with other attempts will provide some motivation for the theory I shall offer. Obviously, I cannot examine all, or even very many, alternative attempts. But a few sample attempts will be instructive.

Let us concentrate on the attempt to formulate one or more adequate base-clause principles.[3] Here is a classical candidate:

(1) If S believes p at t, and p is indubitable for S (at t), then S's belief in p at t is justified.

To evaluate this principle, we need to know what "indubitable" means. It can be understood in at least two ways. First, "p is indubitable for S" might mean: "S has no *grounds* for doubting p." Since "ground" is an epistemic term, however, principle (1) would be inadmissible in this reading, for epistemic terms may not legitimately appear in the antecedent of a base-clause. A second interpretation would avoid this difficulty. One might interpret "p is indubitable for S" psychologically, i.e., as meaning "S is psychologically incapable of doubting p." This would make principle (1) admissible, but would it be correct? Surely not. A religious fanatic may be psychologically incapable of doubting the tenets of his faith, but that doesn't make his belief in them justified. Similarly, during the Watergate affair, someone may have been so blinded by the aura of the presidency that even after the most damaging evidence against Nixon had emerged he was still incapable of doubting Nixon's veracity. It doesn't follow that his belief in Nixon's veracity was justified.

A second candidate base-clause principle is this:

(2) If S believes p at t and p is self-evident, then S's belief in p at t is justified.

To evaluate this principle, we again need an interpretation of its crucial term, in this case "self-evident." On one standard reading, "evident" is a synonym for "justified." "*Self*-evident" would therefore mean something like "directly justified," "intuitively justified," or "non-derivatively justified." On this reading "self-evident" is an epistemic phrase, and principle (2) would be disqualified as a base-clause principle.

However, there are other possible readings of "p is self-evident" on which it isn't an epistemic phrase. One such reading is: "It is impossible to understand p without believing it."[4] According to this interpretation, trivial analytic and logical truths might turn out to be self-evident. Hence, any belief in such a truth would be a justified belief, according to (2).

What does "it is *impossible* to understand p without believing it" mean? Does it mean "*humanly* impossible"? That reading would probably make (2) an unacceptable principle. There may well be propositions which humans have an innate and irrepressible disposition to believe, e.g., "Some events have causes." But it seems unlikely that people's inability to refrain from believing such a proposition makes every belief in it justified.

Should we then understand "impossible" to mean "impossible in principle," or "logically impossible"? If that is the reading given, I suspect that (2) is a vacuous principle. I doubt that even trivial logical or analytic truths will satisfy this definition of "self-evident." Any proposition, we may assume, has two or more components that are somehow organized or juxtaposed. To understand the proposition one must "grasp" the components and their juxtaposition. Now in the case of *complex* logical truths, there are (human) psychological operations that suffice to grasp the components and their juxtaposition but do not suffice to produce a belief that the proposition is true. But can't we at least *conceive* of an analogous set of psychological operations even for simple logical truths, operations which perhaps are not in the repertoire of human cognizers but which might be in the repertoire of some conceivable beings? That is, can't we conceive of psychological operations that would suffice to grasp the components and componential-juxtaposition of these simple propositions but do not suffice to produce *belief* in the propositions? I think we can conceive of such operations. Hence, for any proposition you choose, it will be possible for it to be understood without being believed.

Finally, even if we set these two objections aside, we must note that self-evidence can at best confer justificational status on relatively few beliefs, and the only plausible group are beliefs in necessary truths. Thus, other base-clause principles will be needed to explain the justificational status of beliefs in contingent propositions.

The notion of a base-clause principle is naturally associated with the idea of "direct" justifiedness, and in the realm of contingent propositions first-person-current-mental-state propositions have often been assigned this role. In Chisholm's terminology, this conception is expressed by the notion of a "*self-presenting*" state or proposition. The sentence "I am thinking," for example, expresses a self-presenting proposition. (At least I shall *call* this sort of content a "proposition," though it only has a truth value given some assignment of a subject who utters or entertains the content and a time of entertaining.) When such a proposition is true for person S at time t, S is justified in believing it at t: in Chisholm's terminology, the proposition is "evident" for S at t. This suggests the following base-clause principle:

(3) If p is a self-presenting proposition, and p is true for S at t, and S believes p at t, then S's belief in p at t is justified.

What, exactly, does "self-presenting" mean? In the second edition of *Theory of Knowledge*, Chisholm offers this definition: "h is self-presenting for S at $t = df.$ h is true at t; and necessarily, if h is true at t, then h is evident for S at t."[5] Unfortunately, since "evident" is an epistemic term, "self-presenting" also becomes an epistemic term on this definition, thereby disqualifying (3) as a legitimate base-clause. Some other definition of self-presentingness must be offered if (3) is to be a suitable base-clause principle.

Another definition of self-presentation readily comes to mind. "Self-presentation" is an approximate synonym of "self-intimation," and a proposition may be said to be self-intimating if and only if whenever it is true of a person that person believes it. More precisely, we may give the following definition:

(SP) Proposition p is self-presenting if and only if: necessarily, for any S and any t, if p is true for S at t, then S believes p at t.

On this definition, "self-presenting" is clearly not an epistemic predicate, so (3) would be an admissible principle. Moreover, there is initial plausibility in the suggestion that it is *this* feature of first-person-current-mental-state propositions—viz., their truth guarantees their being believed—that makes beliefs in them justified.

Employing this definition of self-presentation, is principle (3) correct? This cannot be decided until we define self-presentation more precisely. Since the operator "necessarily" can be read in different ways, there are different forms of self-presentation and correspondingly different versions of principle (3). Let us focus on two of these readings: a "*nomological*" reading and a "*logical*" reading. Consider first the nomological reading. On this definition a proposition is self-presenting just in case it is nomologically necessary that if p is true for S at t, then S believes p at t.[6]

Is the nomological version of principle (3)—call it "(3_N)"—correct? Not at all. We can imagine cases in which the antecedent of (3_N) is satisfied, but we would not say that the belief is justified. Suppose, for example, that p is the proposition expressed by the sentence "I am in brain-state B," where "B" is shorthand for a certain highly specific neural state description. Further suppose it is a nomological truth that anyone in brain-state B will ipso facto *believe* he is in brain-state B. In other words, imagine that an occurrent belief with the content "I am in brain-state B" is realized whenever one is in brain-state B.[7] According to (3_N), any such belief is justified. But that is clearly false. We can readily imagine circumstances in which a person goes into brain-state B and therefore has the belief in question, though this belief is by no means justified. For example, we can imagine that a brain-surgeon operating on S artificially induced brain-state B. This results, phenomenologically, in S's suddenly believing—out of the blue—that he is in brain-state B, without any relevant antecedent beliefs. We would hardly say, in such a case, that S's belief that he is in brain-state B is justified.

Let us turn next to the logical version of (3)—call it "(3_L)"—in which a proposition is defined as self-presenting just in case it is logically necessary that if p is true for S at t, then S believes p at t. This stronger version of principle (3) might seem more promising. In fact, however, it is no more successful than (3_N). Let p be the proposition "I am awake" and assume that it is logically necessary that if this proposition is true for some person S and time t, then S believes p at t. This assumption is consistent with the further assumption that S frequently believes p when it is false, e.g., when he is dreaming. Under these circumstances, we would hardly accept the contention that S's belief in this proposition is always justified. Nor should we accept the contention that the belief is justified when it is *true*. The truth of the proposition logically guarantees that the belief is *held*, but why should it guarantee that the belief is *justified*?

The foregoing criticism suggests that we have things backwards. The idea of self-presentation is that truth guarantees belief. This fails to confer justification because it is compatible with there being belief without truth. So what seems necessary— or at least sufficient—for justification is that belief should guarantee truth. Such a notion has usually gone under the label of "*infallibility*" or "*incorrigibility*." It may be defined as follows:

> (INC) Proposition p is incorrigible if and only if: necessarily, for any S and any t, if S believes p at t, then p is true for S at t.

Using the notion of incorrigibility, we may propose principle (4).

> (4) If p is an incorrigible proposition, and S believes p at t, then S's belief in p at t is justified.

As was true of self-presentation, there are different varieties of incorrigibility, corresponding to different interpretations of "necessarily." Accordingly, we have different versions of principle (4). Once again, let us concentrate on a nomological and a logical version, (4_N) and (4_L) respectively.

We can easily construct a counterexample to (4_N) along the lines of the belief-state/brain-state counterexample that refuted (3_N). Suppose it is nomologically necessary that if anyone believes he is in brain-state B then it is true that he is in brain-state B, for the only way this belief-state is realized is through brain-state B itself. It follows that "I am in brain-state B" is a nomologically incorrigible proposition. Therefore, according to (4_N), whenever anyone believes this proposition at any time, that

belief is justified. But we may again construct a brain-surgeon example in which someone comes to have such a belief but the belief isn't justified.

Apart from this counterexample, the general point is this. Why should the fact that S's believing p guarantees the truth of p imply that S's belief is justified? The nature of the guarantee might be wholly fortuitous, as the belief-state/brain-state example is intended to illustrate. To appreciate the point, consider the following related possibility. A person's mental structure might be such that whenever he believes that p will be true (of him) a split second later, then p is true (of him) a split second later. This is because, we may suppose, his believing it brings it about. But surely we would not be compelled in such a circumstance to say that a belief of this sort is justified. So why should the fact that S's believing p guarantees the truth of p *precisely at the time of belief* imply that the belief is justified? There is no intuitive plausibility in this supposition.

The notion of *logical* incorrigibility has a more honored place in the history of conceptions of justification. But even principle (4_L), I believe, suffers from defects similar to those of (4_N). The mere fact that belief in p logically guarantees its truth does not confer justificational status on such a belief.

The first difficulty with (4_L) arises from logical or mathematical truths. Any true proposition of logic or mathematics is logically necessary. Hence, any such proposition p is logically incorrigible, since it is logically necessary that, for any S and any t, if S believes p at t then p is true (for S at t). Now assume that Nelson believes a certain very complex mathematical truth at time t. Since such a proposition is logically incorrigible, (4_L) implies that Nelson's belief in this truth at t is justified. But we may easily suppose that this belief of Nelson is not at all the result of proper mathematical reasoning, or even the result of appeal to trustworthy authority. Perhaps Nelson believes this complex truth because of utterly confused reasoning, or because of hasty and ill-founded conjecture. Then his belief is not justified, contrary to what (4_L) implies.

The case of logical or mathematical truths is admittedly peculiar, since the truth of these propositions is assured independently of any beliefs. It might seem, therefore, that we can better capture the idea of "belief logically guaranteeing truth" in cases where the propositions in question are *contingent*. With this in mind, we might restrict (4_L) to *contingent* incorrigible propositions. Even this amendment cannot save (4₍L₎), however, since there are counterexamples to it involving purely contingent propositions.

Suppose that Humperdink has been studying logic—or, rather, pseudo-logic—from Elmer Fraud, whom Humperdink has no reason to trust as a logician. Fraud has enunciated the principle that any disjunctive proposition consisting of at least 40 distinct disjuncts is very probably true. Humperdink now encounters the proposition *p*, a contingent proposition with 40 disjuncts, the 7th disjunct being "I exist." Although Humperdink grasps the proposition fully, he doesn't notice that it is entailed by "I exist." Rather, he is struck by the fact that it falls under the disjunction rule Fraud has enunciated (a rule I assume Humperdink is not *justified* in believing). Bearing this in mind, Humperdink forms a belief in *p*. Now notice that *p* is logically incorrigible. It is logically necessary that if anyone believes *p*, then *p* is true (of him at that time). This simply follows from the fact that, first, a person's believing anything entails that he exists, and second, "I exist" entails *p*. Since *p* is logically incorrigible, principle (4₍L₎) implies that Humperdink's belief in *p* is justified. But surely, given our example, that conclusion is false. Humperdink's belief in *p* is not at all justified.

One thing that goes wrong in this example is that while Humperdink's belief in *p* logically implies its truth, Humperdink doesn't *recognize* that his believing it implies its truth. This might move a theorist to revise (4₍L₎) by adding the requirement that *S* "recognize" that *p* is logically incorrigible. But this, of course, won't do. The term "recognize" is obviously an epistemic term, so the suggested revision of (4₍L₎) would result in an inadmissible base-clause.

II

Let us try to diagnose what has gone wrong with these attempts to produce an acceptable base-clause principle. Notice that each of the foregoing attempts confers the status of "justified" on a belief without restriction on *why* the belief is held, i.e., on what *causally initiates* the belief or *causally sustains* it.

The logical versions of principles (3) and (4), for example, clearly place no restriction on causes of belief. The same is true of the nomological versions of (3) and (4), since nomological requirements can be satisfied by simultaneity or cross-sectional laws, as illustrated by our brain-state/belief-state examples. I suggest that the absence of causal requirements accounts for the failure of the foregoing principles. Many of our counterexamples are ones in which the belief is caused in some strange or unacceptable way, e.g., by the accidental movement of a brain-surgeon's hand, by reliance on an illicit, pseudo-logical principle, or by the blinding aura of the presidency. In general, a strategy for defeating a noncausal principle of justifiedness is to find a case in which the principle's antecedent is satisfied but the belief is caused by some faulty belief-forming process. The faultiness of the belief-forming process will incline us, intuitively, to regard the belief as unjustified. Thus, correct principles of justified belief must be principles that make causal requirements, where "cause" is construed broadly to include sustainers as well as initiators of belief (i.e., processes that determine, or help to overdetermine, a belief's continuing to be held).[8]

The need for causal requirements is not restricted to base-clause principles. Recursive principles will also need a causal component. One might initially suppose that the following is a good recursive principle: "If *S* justifiably believes *q* at *t*, and *q* entails *p*, and *S* believes *p* at *t*, then *S*'s belief in *p* at *t* is justified." But this principle is unacceptable. *S*'s belief in *p* doesn't receive justificational status simply from the fact that *p* is entailed by *q* and *S* justifiably believes *q*. If what causes *S* to believe *p* at *t* is entirely different, *S*'s belief in *p* may well not be justified. Nor can the situation be remedied by adding to the antecedent the condition that *S* justifiably believes that *q* entails *p*. Even if he believes this, and believes *q* as well, he might not put these beliefs together. He might believe *p* as a result of some other wholly extraneous considerations. So once again, conditions that fail to require appropriate causes of a belief don't guarantee justifiedness.

Granted that principles of justified belief must make reference to causes of belief, what kinds of causes confer justifiedness? We can gain insight into this problem by reviewing some faulty processes of belief-formation, i.e., processes whose belief-outputs would be classed as unjustified. Here are some examples: confused reasoning, wishful thinking, reliance on emotional attachment, mere hunch or guesswork, and hasty generalization. What do these faulty processes have in common? They share the feature of *unreliability:* they tend to produce *error* a large proportion of the time. By contrast, which species of belief-forming (or belief-sustaining) processes are intuitively justification-conferring? They include standard perceptual processes, remembering, good reasoning, and introspection. What these processes seem to have in common is *reliability:* the beliefs they produce are generally true. My positive proposal, then, is this. The justificational status of a belief is a function of the reliability of the process or processes that cause it, where (as a first approximation) reliability consists in the tendency of a process to produce beliefs that are true rather than false.

To test this thesis further, notice that justifiedness is not a purely categorical concept, although I treat it here as categorical in the interest of simplicity. We can and do regard certain beliefs as more justified than others. Furthermore, our intuitions of comparative justifiedness go along with our beliefs about the comparative reliability of the belief-causing processes.

Consider perceptual beliefs. Suppose Jones believes he has just seen a mountain-goat. Our assessment of the belief's justifiedness is determined by whether he caught a brief glimpse of the creature at a great distance, or whether he had a good look at the thing only 30 yards away. His belief in the latter sort of case is (*ceteris paribus*) more justified than in the former sort of case. And, if his belief is true, we are more prepared to say he *knows* in the latter case than in the former. The difference between the two cases seems to be this. Visual beliefs formed from brief and hasty scanning, or where the perceptual object is a long distance off, tend to be wrong more often than visual beliefs formed from detailed and leisurely scanning, or where the object is in reasonable proximity. In short, the visual processes in the former category are less reliable than those in the latter category. A similar point holds for memory beliefs. A belief that results from a hazy and indistinct memory impression is counted as less justified than a belief that arises from a distinct memory impression, and our inclination to classify those beliefs as "*knowledge*" varies in the same way. Again,

the reason is associated with the comparative reliability of the processes. Hazy and indistinct memory impressions are generally less reliable indicators of what actually happened, so beliefs formed from such impressions are less likely to be true than beliefs formed from distinct impressions. Further, consider beliefs based on inference from observed samples. A belief about a population that is based on random sampling, or on instances that exhibit great variety, is intuitively more justified than a belief based on biased sampling, or on instances from a narrow sector of the population. Again, the degree of justifiedness seems to be a function of reliability. Inferences based on random or varied samples will tend to produce less error or inaccuracy than inferences based on non-random or non-varied samples.

Returning to a categorical concept of justifiedness, we might ask just *how* reliable a belief-forming process must be in order that its resultant beliefs be justified. A precise answer to this question should not be expected. Our conception of justification is *vague* in this respect. It does seem clear, however, that *perfect* reliability isn't required. Belief-forming processes that *sometimes* produce error still confer justification. It follows that there can be justified beliefs that are false.

I have characterized justification-conferring processes as ones that have a "tendency" to produce beliefs that are true rather than false. The term "tendency" could refer either to *actual* long-run frequency, or to a "propensity," i.e., outcomes that would occur in merely *possible* realizations of the process. Which of these is intended? Unfortunately, I think our ordinary conception of justifiedness is vague on this dimension too. For the most part, we simply assume that the "observed" frequency of truth versus error would be approximately replicated in the actual long-run, and also in relevant counterfactual situations, i.e., ones that are highly "realistic" or conform closely to the circumstances of the actual world. Since we ordinarily assume these frequencies to be roughly the same, we make no concerted effort to distinguish them. Since the purpose of my present theorizing is to capture our ordinary conception of justifiedness, and since our ordinary conception is vague on this matter, it is appropriate to leave the theory vague in the same respect.

We need to say more about the notion of a belief-forming "*process.*" Let us mean by a "process" a *functional operation* or procedure, i.e., something that generates a *mapping* from certain states— "inputs"—into other states—"outputs." The outputs in the present case are states of believing this or that proposition at a given moment. On this interpretation, a process is a *type* as opposed to a *token*. This is fully appropriate, since it is only types that have statistical properties such as producing truth 80 percent of the time; and it is precisely such statistical properties that determine the reliability of a process. Of course, we also want to speak of a process as *causing* a belief, and it looks as if types are incapable of being causes. But when we say that a belief is caused by a given process, understood as a functional procedure, we may interpret this to mean that it is caused by the particular *inputs* to the process (and by the intervening events "through which" the functional procedure carries the inputs into the output) on the occasion in question.

What are some examples of belief-forming "processes" construed as functional operations? One example is reasoning processes, where the inputs include antecedent beliefs and entertained hypotheses. Another example is functional procedures whose inputs include desires, hopes, or emotional states of various sorts (together with antecedent beliefs). A third example is a memory process, which takes as input beliefs or experiences at an earlier time and generates as output beliefs at a later time. For example, a memory process might take as input a belief *at t_1* that Lincoln was born in 1809 and generate as output a belief *at t_n* that Lincoln was born in 1809. A fourth example is perceptual processes. Here it isn't clear whether inputs should include states of the environment, such as the distance of the stimulus from the cognizer, or only events within or on the surface of the organism, e.g., receptor stimulations. I shall return to this point in a moment.

A critical problem concerning our analysis is the degree of generality of the process-types in question. Input-output relations can be specified very broadly or very narrowly, and the degree of generality will partly determine the degree of reliability. A process-type might be selected so narrowly that only one instance of it ever occurs, and

hence the type is either completely reliable or completely unreliable. (This assumes that reliability is a function of *actual* frequency only.) If such narrow process-types were selected, beliefs that are intuitively unjustified might be said to result from perfectly reliable processes, and beliefs that are intuitively justified might be said to result from perfectly unreliable processes.

It is clear that our ordinary thought about process-types slices them broadly, but I cannot at present give a precise explication of our intuitive principles. One plausible suggestion, though, is that the relevant processes are *content-neutral*. It might be argued, for example, that the process of *inferring p whenever the Pope asserts p* could pose problems for our theory. If the Pope is infallible, this process will be perfectly reliable; yet we would not regard the belief-outputs of this process as justified. The content-neutral restriction would avert this difficulty. If relevant processes are required to admit as input beliefs (or other states) with *any* content, the aforementioned process will not count, for its input beliefs have a restricted propositional content, viz., "*the Pope asserts p.*"

In addition to the problem of "generality" or "abstractness" there is the previously mentioned problem of the "*extent*" of belief-forming processes. Clearly, the causal ancestry of beliefs often includes events outside the organism. Are such events to be included among the "inputs" of belief-forming processes? Or should we restrict the extent of belief-forming processes to "*cognitive*" events, i.e., events within the organism's nervous system? I shall choose the latter course, though with some hesitation. My general grounds for this decision are roughly as follows. Justifiedness seems to be a function of how a cognizer deals with his environmental input, i.e., with the goodness or badness of the operations that register and transform the stimulation that reaches him. ("Deal with," of course, does not mean *purposeful* action, nor is it restricted to *conscious* activity). A justified belief is, roughly speaking, one that results from cognitive operations that are, generally speaking, good or successful. But "*cognitive*" operations are most plausibly construed as operations of the cognitive faculties, i.e., "information-processing" equipment *internal* to the organism.

With these points in mind, we may now advance the following base-clause principle for justified belief.

(5) If *S*'s believing *p* at *t* results from a reliable cognitive belief-forming process (or set of processes), then *S*'s belief in *p* at *t* is justified.

Since "reliable belief-forming process" has been defined in terms of such notions as belief, truth, statistical frequency, and the like, it is not an epistemic term. Hence, (5) is an admissible base-clause.

It might seem as if (5) promises to be not only a successful base clause, but the only principle needed whatever, apart from a closure clause. In other words, it might seem as if it is a necessary as well as a sufficient condition of justifiedness that a belief be produced by reliable cognitive belief-forming processes. But this is not quite correct, given our provisional definition of "reliability."

Our provisional definition implies that a reasoning process is reliable only if it generally produces beliefs that are true, and similarly, that a memory process is reliable only if it generally yields beliefs that are true. But these requirements are too strong. A reasoning procedure cannot be expected to produce true belief if it is applied to false premises. And memory cannot be expected to yield a true belief if the original belief it attempts to retain is false. What we need for reasoning and memory, then, is a notion of "*conditional reliability*." A process is conditionally reliable when a sufficient proportion of its output-beliefs are true *given that its input-beliefs are true*.

With this point in mind, let us distinguish *belief-dependent* and *belief-independent* cognitive processes. The former are processes *some* of whose inputs are belief-states.[9] The latter are processes *none* of whose inputs are belief-states. We may then replace principle (5) with the following two principles, the first a base-clause principle and the second a recursive-clause principle.

(6$_A$) If *S*'s belief in *p* at *t* results ("immediately") from a belief-independent process that is (unconditionally) reliable, then *S*'s belief in *p* at *t* is justified.
(6$_B$) If *S*'s belief in *p* at *t* results ("immediately") from a belief-dependent process that is (at least) conditionally reliable,

and if the beliefs (if any) on which this process operates in producing *S*'s belief in *p* at *t* are themselves justified, then *S*'s belief in *p* at *t* is justified.[10]

If we add to (6$_A$) and (6$_B$) the standard closure clause, we have a complete theory of justified belief. The theory says, in effect, that a belief is justified if and only if it is "*well-formed*," i.e., it has an ancestry of reliable and/or conditionally reliable cognitive operations. (Since a dated belief may be overdetermined, it may have a number of distinct ancestral trees. These need not all be full of reliable or conditionally reliable processes. But at least one ancestral tree must have reliable or conditionally reliable processes throughout.)

The theory of justified belief proposed here, then, is an *Historical* or *Genetic* theory. It contrasts with the dominant approach to justified belief, an approach that generates what we may call (borrowing a phrase from Robert Nozick) "*Current Time-Slice*" theories. A Current Time-Slice theory makes the justificational status of a belief wholly a function of what is true of the cognizer *at the time* of belief. An Historical theory makes the justificational status of a belief depend on its prior history. Since my Historical theory emphasizes the reliability of the belief-generating processes, it may be called "*Historical Reliabilism*."

The most obvious examples of Current Time-Slice theories are "Cartesian" Foundationalist theories, which trace all justificational status (at least of contingent propositions) to current mental states. The usual varieties of Coherence theories, however, are equally Current Time-Slice views, since they too make the justificational status of a belief wholly a function of *current* states of affairs. For Coherence theories, however, these current states include all other beliefs of the cognizer, which would not be considered relevant by Cartesian Foundationalism. Have there been other Historical theories of justified belief? Among contemporary writers, Quine and Popper have Historical epistemologies, though the notion of "justification" is not their avowed *explicandum*. Among historical writers, it might seem that Locke and Hume had Genetic theories of sorts. But I think that their Genetic theories were only theories of ideas, not of knowledge or justification. Plato's theory of recollection, however, is a good example of a Genetic theory of knowing.[11] And it might be argued that Hegel and Dewey had Genetic epistemologies (if Hegel can be said to have had a clear epistemology at all).

The theory articulated by (6_A) and (6_B) might be viewed as a kind of "Foundationalism" because of its recursive structure. I have no objection to this label, as long as one keeps in mind how different this "diachronic" form of Foundationalism is from Cartesian, or other "synchronic" varieties of, Foundationalism.

Current Time-Slice theories characteristically assume that the justificational status of a belief is something which the cognizer is able to know or determine at the time of belief. This is made explicit, for example, by Chisholm.[12] The Historical theory I endorse makes no such assumption. There are many facts about a cognizer to which he lacks "privileged access," and I regard the justificational status of his beliefs as one of those things. This is not to say that a cognizer is necessarily ignorant, at any given moment, of the justificational status of his current beliefs. It is only to deny that he necessarily has, or can get, knowledge or true belief about this status. Just as a person can know without knowing that he knows, so he can have justified belief without knowing that it is justified (or believing justifiably that it is justified).

A characteristic case in which a belief is justified though the cognizer doesn't know that it's justified is where the original evidence for the belief has long since been forgotten. If the original evidence was compelling, the cognizer's original belief may have been justified, and this justificational status may have been preserved through memory. But since the cognizer no longer remembers how or why he came to believe, he may not know that the belief is justified. If asked now to justify his belief, he may be at a loss. Still, the belief *is* justified, though the cognizer can't demonstrate or establish this.

The Historical theory of justified belief I advocate is connected in spirit with the causal theory of knowing I have presented elsewhere.[13] I had this in mind when I remarked near the outset of the essay that my theory of justified belief makes justifiedness come out closely related to knowledge. Justified beliefs, like pieces of knowledge, have appropriate histories; but they may fail to be knowledge either because they are false or because they founder on some other requirement for knowing of the kind discussed in the post-Gettier knowledge-trade.

There is a variant of the Historical conception of justified belief that is worth mentioning in this context. It may be introduced as follows. Suppose S has a set B of beliefs at time t_0, and some of these beliefs are *un*justified. Between t_0 and t_1 he reasons from the entire set B to the conclusion p, which he then accepts at t_1. The reasoning procedure he uses is a very sound one, i.e., one that is conditionally reliable. There is a sense or respect in which we are tempted to say that S's belief in p at t_1 is "justified." At any rate, it is tempting to say that the *person* is justified in believing p at t. Relative to his antecedent cognitive state, he did as well as could be expected: the *transition* from his cognitive state at t_0 to his cognitive state at t_1 was entirely sound. Although we may acknowledge this brand of justifiedness—it might be called "*Terminal-Phase Reliabilism*"—it is not a kind of justifiedness so closely related to knowing. For a person to know proposition p, it is not enough that the *final phase* of the process that leads to his belief in p be sound. It is also necessary that some entire history of the process be sound (i.e., reliable or conditionally reliable).

Let us return now to the Historical theory. In the next section, I shall adduce reasons for strengthening it a bit. Before looking at these reasons, however, I wish to review two quite different objections to the theory.

First, a critic might argue that *some* justified beliefs do not derive their justificational status from their causal ancestry. In particular, it might be argued that beliefs about one's current phenomenal states and intuitive beliefs about elementary logical or conceptual relationships do not derive their justificational status in this way. I am not persuaded by either of these examples. Introspection, I believe, should be regarded as a form of retrospection. Thus, a justified belief that I am "now" in pain gets its justificational status from a relevant, though brief, causal history.[14] The apprehension of logical or conceptual relationships is also a cognitive process that occupies time. The psychological process of "seeing" or "intuiting" a simple logical truth is very fast, and we cannot introspectively dissect it into constituent parts. Nonetheless, there are mental operations going on, just as there are mental operations that occur in *idiots savants*, who are unable to report the computational processes they in fact employ.

A second objection to Historical Reliabilism focuses on the reliability element rather than the causal or historical element. Since the theory is intended to cover all possible cases, it seems to imply that for any cognitive process C, if C is reliable in possible world W, then any belief in W that results from C is justified. But doesn't this permit easy counterexamples? Surely we can imagine a possible world in which wishful thinking is reliable. We can imagine a possible world where a benevolent demon so arranges things that beliefs formed by wishful thinking usually come true. This would make wishful thinking a reliable process in that possible world, but surely we don't want to regard beliefs that result from wishful thinking as justified.

There are several possible ways to respond to this case, and I am unsure which response is best, partly because my own intuitions (and those of other people I have consulted) are not entirely clear. One possibility is to say that in the possible world imagined, beliefs that result from wishful thinking *are* justified. In other words, we reject the claim that wishful thinking could never, intuitively, confer justifiedness.[15]

However, for those who feel that wishful thinking couldn't confer justifiedness even in the world imagined, there are two ways out. First, it may be suggested that the proper cirterion of justifiedness is the propensity of a process to generate beliefs that are true *in a non-manipulated environment*, i.e., an environment in which there is no purposeful arrangement of the world either to accord or conflict with the beliefs that are formed. In other words, the suitability of a belief-forming process is only a function of its success in *"natural"* situations, not situations of the sort involving benevolent or malevolent demons or any other such manipulative creatures. If we reformulate the theory to include this qualification, the counterexample in question will be averted.

Alternatively, we may reformulate our theory, or reinterpret it, as follows. Instead of construing the theory as saying that a belief in possible world W is justified if and only if it results from a cognitive process that is reliable in W, we may construe it as saying that a belief in possible world W is justified if and only if it results from a cognitive process that is reliable in *our world*. In short, our conception of justifiedness is derived as follows. We note certain cognitive processes in the actual world, and form beliefs about which of these are reliable. The ones we believe to be reliable are then regarded as justification-conferring processes. In reflecting on hypothetical beliefs, we deem them justified if and only if they result from processes already picked out as justification-conferring, or processes very similar to those. Since wishful thinking is not among these processes, a belief formed in a possible world W by wishful thinking would not be deemed justified, even if wishful thinking is reliable *in W*. I am not sure that this is a correct reconstruction of our intuitive conceptual scheme, but it would accommodate the benevolent demon case, at least if the proper thing to say in that case is that the wishful-thinking-caused beliefs are unjustified.

Even if we adopt this strategy, however, a problem still remains. Suppose that wishful thinking turns out to be reliable *in the actual world!*[16] This might be because, unbeknownst to us at present, there is a benevolent demon who, lazy until now, will shortly start aranging things so that our wishes come true. The long-run performance of wishful thinking will be very good, and hence even the new construal of the theory will imply that beliefs resulting from wishful thinking (in *our* world) are justified. Yet this surely contravenes our intuitive judgment on the matter.

Perhaps the moral of the case is that the standard format of a "conceptual analysis" has its shortcomings. Let me depart from that format and try to give a better rendering of our aim and the theory that tries to achieve that aim. What we really want is an *explanation* of why we count, or would count, certain beliefs as justified and others as unjustified. Such an explanation must refer to our *beliefs* about reliability, not to the actual *facts*. The reason we *count* beliefs as justified is that they are formed by what we *believe* to be reliable belief-forming processes. Our beliefs about which belief-forming processes are reliable may be erroneous, but that does not affect the adequacy of the explanation. Since we *believe* that wishful thinking is an unreliable belief-forming process, we regard beliefs formed by wishful thinking as unjustified. What matters, then, is what we *believe* about wishful thinking, not what is *true* (in the long run) about wishful thinking. I am not sure how to express this point in the standard format of conceptual analysis, but it identifies an important point in understanding our theory.

III

Let us return, however, to the standard format of conceptual analysis, and let us consider a new objection that will require some revisions in the theory advanced until now. According to our theory, a belief is justified in case it is caused by a process that is in fact reliable, or by one we generally believe to be reliable. But suppose that although one of *S*'s beliefs satisfies this condition, *S* has no reason to believe that it does. Worse yet, suppose *S* has reason to believe that his belief is caused by an *un*reliable process (although *in fact* its causal ancestry is fully reliable). Wouldn't we deny in such circumstances that *S*'s belief is justified? This seems to show that our analysis, as presently formulated, is mistaken.

Suppose that Jones is told on fully reliable authority that a certain class of his memory beliefs are almost all mistaken. His parents fabricate a wholly false story that Jones suffered from amnesia when he was seven but later developed *pseudo*-memories of that period. Though Jones listens to what his parents say and has excellent reason to trust them, he persists in believing the ostensible memories from his seven-year-old past. Are these memory beliefs justified? Intuitively, they are not justified. But since these beliefs result from genuine memory and original perceptions, which are adequately reliable processes, our theory says that these beliefs are justified.

Can the theory be revised to meet this difficulty? One natural suggestion is that the actual reliability of a belief's ancestry is not enough for justifiedness; in addition, the cognizer must be *justified in believing* that the ancestry of his belief is reliable. Thus one might think of replacing (6_A), for example, with (7). (For simplicity, I neglect some of the details of the earlier analysis.)

(7) If *S*'s belief in *p* at *t* is caused by a reliable cognitive process, and *S* justifiably believes at *t* that his *p*-belief is so caused, then *S*'s belief in *p* at *t* is justified.

It is evident, however, that (7) will not do as a base clause, for it contains the epistemic term "justifiably" in its antecedent.

A slightly weaker revision, without this problematic feature, might next be suggested, viz.,

(8) If *S*'s belief in *p* at *t* is caused by a reliable cognitive process, and *S* believes at *t* that his *p*-belief is so caused, then *S*'s belief in *p* at *t* is justified.

But this won't do the job. Suppose that Jones believes that his memory beliefs are reliably caused despite all the (trustworthy) contrary testimony of his parents. Principle (8) would be satisfied, yet we wouldn't say that these beliefs are justified.

Next, we might try (9), which is stronger than (8) and, unlike (7), formally admissible as a base clause.

(9) If *S*'s belief in *p* at *t* is caused by a reliable cognitive process, and *S* believes at *t* that his *p*-belief is so caused, and this meta-belief is caused by a reliable cognitive process, then *S*'s belief in *p* at *t* is justified.

A first objection to (9) is that it wrongly precludes unreflective creatures—creatures like animals or young children, who have no beliefs about the genesis of their beliefs—from having justified beliefs. If one shares my view that justified belief is, at least roughly, *well-formed* belief, surely animals and young children can have justified beliefs.

A second problem with (9) concerns its underlying rationale. Since (9) is proposed as a substitute for (6_A), it is implied that the reliability of a belief's own cognitive ancestry does not make it justified. But, the suggestion seems to be, the reliability of a *meta-belief*'s ancestry confers justifiedness on the first-order belief. Why should that be so? Perhaps one is attracted by the idea of a "trickle-down" effect: if an n + 1-level belief is justified, its justification trickles down to an n-level belief. But even if the trickle-down theory is correct, it doesn't help here. There is no assurance from the satisfaction of (9)'s antecedent that the meta-belief itself is *justified*.

To obtain a better revision of our theory, let us

re-examine the Jones case. Jones has strong evidence against certain propositions concerning his past. He doesn't *use* this evidence, but if he *were* to use it properly, he would stop believing these propositions. Now the proper use of evidence would be an instance of a (conditionally) reliable process. So what we can say about Jones is that he *fails* to use a certain (conditionally) reliable process that he could and should have used. Admittedly, had he used this process, he would have "worsened" his doxastic states: he would have replaced some true beliefs with suspension of judgment. Still, he couldn't have known this in the case in question. So he failed to do something which, epistemically, he should have done. This diagnosis suggests a fundamental change in our theory. The justificational status of a belief is not only a function of the cognitive process *actually* employed in producing it, it is also a function of processes that could and should be employed.

With these points in mind, we may tentatively propose the following revision of our theory, where we again focus on a base-clause principle but omit certain details in the interest of clarity.

(10) If S's belief in p at t results from a reliable cognitive process, and there is no reliable or conditionally reliable process available to S which, had it been used by S in addition to the process actually used, would have resulted in S's not believing p at t, then S's belief in p at t is justified.

There are several problems with this proposal. First, there is a technical problem. One cannot use an additional belief-forming (or doxastic-state-forming) process *as well as* the original process if the additional one would result in a different doxastic state. One wouldn't be using the original process at all. So we need a slightly different formulation of the relevant counterfactual. Since the basic idea is reasonably clear, however, I won't try to improve on the formulation here. A second problem concerns the notion of "*available*" belief-forming (or doxastic-state-forming) processes. What is it for a process to be "available" to a cognizer? Were scientific procedures "available" to people who lived in pre-scientific ages? Furthermore, it seems implausible to say that all "available" processes ought to be used, at least if we include such processes as gathering *new* evidence. Surely a belief can sometimes be

justified even if additional evidence-gathering would yield a different doxastic attitude. What I think we should have in mind here are such additional processes as calling previously acquired evidence to mind, assessing the implications of that evidence, etc. This is admittedly somewhat vague, but here again our ordinary notion of justifiedness is vague, so it is appropriate for our analysans to display the same sort of vagueness.

This completes the sketch of my account of justified belief. Before concluding, however, it is essential to point out that there is an important use of "justified" which is not captured by this account but can be captured by a closely related one.

There is a use of "justified" in which it is not implied or presupposed that there is a *belief* that is justified. For example, if S is trying to decide whether to believe p and asks our advice, we may tell him that he is "justified" in believing it. We do not thereby imply that he *has* a justified *belief*, since we know he is still suspending judgment. What we mean, roughly, is that he *would* or *could* be justified if he were to believe p. The justificational status we ascribe here cannot be a function of the causes of S's believing p, for there is no belief by S in p. Thus, the account of justifiedness we have given thus far cannot explicate *this* use of "justified." (It doesn't follow that this use of "justified" has no connection with causal ancestries. Its proper use may depend on the causal ancestry of the cognizer's cognitive state, though not on the causal ancestry of his believing p.)

Let us distinguish two uses of "justified": an *ex post* use and an *ex ante* use. The *ex post* use occurs when there exists a belief, and we say of *that belief* that it is (or isn't) justified. The *ex ante* use occurs when no such belief exists, or when we wish to ignore the question of whether such a belief exists. Here we say of the *person*, independent of his doxastic state vis-à-vis p, that p is (or isn't) suitable for him to believe.[17]

Since we have given an account of *ex post* justifiedness, it will suffice if we can analyze *ex ante* justifiedness in terms of it. Such an analysis, I believe, is ready at hand. S is *ex ante* justified in believing p at t just in case his total cognitive state at t is such that from that state he could come to believe p in such a way that this belief would be *ex post* justified. More precisely, he is *ex ante* justified in believing p at t just in case a reliable belief-forming operation is available to him such that the application of that operation to his total cognitive state at t would result, more or less immediately, in his believing p and this belief would be *ex post* justified. Stated formally, we have the following:

> (11) Person S is *ex ante* justified in believing p at t if and only if there is a reliable belief-forming operation available to S which is such that if S applied that operation to this total cognitive state at t, S would believe p at t-plus-delta (for a suitably small delta) and that belief would be *ex post* justified.

For the analysans of (11) to be satisfied, the total cognitive state at t must have a suitable causal ancestry. Hence, (11) is implicitly an Historical account of *ex ante* justifiedness.

As indicated, the bulk of this essay was addressed to *ex post* justifiedness. This is the appropriate analysandum if one is interested in the connection between justifiedness and knowledge, since what is crucial to whether a person *knows* a proposition is whether he has an actual *belief* in the proposition that is justified. However, since many epistemologists are interested in *ex ante* justifiedness, it is proper for a general theory of justification to try to provide an account of that concept as well. Our theory does this quite naturally, for the account of *ex ante* justifiedness falls out directly from our account of *ex post* justifiedness.[18]

Notes

[1] "A Causal Theory of Knowing"; "Innate Knowledge," in S. P. Stich, ed., *Innate Ideas* (Berkeley: University of California Press, 1975); and "Discrimination and Perceptual Knowledge."

[2] Notice that the choice of a recursive format does not prejudice the case for or against any particular theory. A recursive format is perfectly general. Specifically, an explicit set of necessary and sufficient conditions is just a special case of a recursive format, i.e., one in which there is no recursive clause.

[3] Many of the attempts I shall consider are suggested by material in William P. Alston, "Varieties of Privileged Access."

[4] Such a definition (though without the modal term) is given, for example, by W. V. Quine and J. S. Ullian in *The Web of Belief*, p. 21. Statements are said to be self-evident just in case "to understand them is to believe them."

[5] Page 22.

[6] I assume, of course, that "nomologically necessary" is *de*

re with respect to "S" and "t" in this construction. I shall not focus on problems that may arise in this regard, since my primary concerns are with different issues.

[7] This assumption violates the thesis that Davidson calls "The Anomalism of the Mental." Cf. "Mental Events" in L. Foster and J. W. Swanson, eds., *Experience and Theory* (Amherst: University of Massachusetts Press, 1970). But it is unclear that this thesis is a necessary truth. Thus, it seems fair to assume its falsity in order to produce a counterexample. The example neither entails nor precludes the mental–physical identity theory.

[8] Keith Lehrer's example of the gypsy lawyer is intended to show the inappropriateness of a causal requirement. (See *Knowledge*, pp. 124–25.) But I find this example unconvincing. To the extent that I clearly imagine that the lawyer fixes his belief solely as a result of the cards, it seems intuitively wrong to say that he *knows*—or has a *justified belief*—that his client is innocent.

[9] This definition is not exactly what we need for the purposes at hand. As Ernest Sosa points out, introspection will turn out to be a belief-dependent process, since sometimes the input into the process will be a belief (when the introspected content is a belief). Intuitively, however, introspection is not the sort of process which may be merely conditionally reliable. I do not know how to refine the definition so as to avoid this difficulty, but it is a small and isolated point.

[10] It may be objected that principles (6_A) and (6_B) are jointly open to analogues of the lottery paradox. A series of processes composed of reliable but less-than-perfectly-reliable processes may be extremely unreliable. Yet applications of (6_A) and (6_B) would confer justifiedness on a belief that is caused by such a series. In reply to this objection, we might simply indicate that the theory is intended to capture our ordinary notion of justifiedness, and this ordinary notion has been formed without recognition of this kind of problem. The theory is not wrong *as* a theory of the ordinary (naive) conception of justifiedness. On the other hand, if we want a theory to do more than capture the ordinary conception of justifiedness, it might be possible to strengthen the principles to avoid lottery-paradox analogues.

[11] I am indebted to Mark Pastin for this point.

[12] Cf. *Theory of Knowledge*, 2nd ed., pp. 17, 114–16.

[13] Cf. "A Causal Theory of Knowing." The reliability aspect of my theory also has its precursors in earlier papers of mine on knowing: "Innate Knowledge" and "Discrimination and Perceptual Knowledge."

[14] The view that introspection is retrospection was taken by Ryle, and before him (as Charles Hartshorne points out to me) by Hobbes, Whitehead, and possibly Husserl.

[15] Of course, if people in world W learn *inductively* that wishful thinking is reliable, and regularly base their beliefs on this inductive inference, it is quite unproblematic and straightforward that their beliefs are justified. The only interesting case is where their beliefs are formed *purely* by wishful thinking, without using inductive inference. The suggestion contemplated in this paragraph of the text is that, in the world imagined, even pure wishful thinking would confer justifiedness.

[16] I am indebted here to Mark Kaplan.

[17] The distinction between *ex post* and *ex ante* justifiedness is similar to Roderick Firth's distinction between *doxastic* and *propositional* warrant. See his "Are Epistemic Concepts Reducible to Ethical Concepts?" in Alvin I. Goldman and Jaegwon Kim, eds., *Values and Morals, Essays in Honor of William Frankena, Charles Stevenson, and Richard Brandt* (Dordrecht: D. Reidel, 1978).

[18] Research on this essay was begun while the author was a fellow of the John Simon Guggenheim Memorial Foundation and of the Center for Advanced Study in the Behavioral Sciences. I am grateful for their support. I have received helpful comments and criticism from Holly S. Goldman, Mark Kaplan, Fred Schmitt, Stephen P. Stich, and many others at several universities where earlier drafts of the paper were read.

VI.2 A *Critique of Externalism*

KEITH LEHRER

Keith Lehrer is Professor of Philosophy at the University of Arizona. We have already encountered his defense of skepticism (Reading II.4) and his analysis of knowledge (Reading IV.3). In this selection from his book *Theory of Knowledge*, Lehrer argues against all forms of externalism, both reliabilism, which transforms properly caused beliefs into justification (as is the case with Goldman, Reading VI.1), and the more radical naturalism that repudiates justification as necessary for knowledge (see Quine, Reading VI.3). But it is the justificatory type of externalism that Lehrer concentrates on. After identifying the strength of externalism as defeating the threat of skepticism, Lehrer sets forth two fundamental objections to externalism: (1) that possession of correct information is inadequate for knowledge and (2) that we may be justified in a belief even when it has not been caused (or sustained) by a reliable process. Note the idea of trustworthiness in Lehrer's account.

Our analysis of complete and undefeated justification in terms of coherence and truth within an acceptance system brings us into conflict with an important competing theory of knowledge called *externalism*. The fundamental doctrine of externalism is that what must be added to true belief to obtain knowledge is the appropriate connection between belief and truth. An earlier account presented by Goldman affirmed that the appropriate connection is causal. This is a very plausible sort of account of perceptual knowledge. The fact that I see something, the hand I hold before me, for example, causes me to believe that I see a hand. The fact that my seeing a hand causes me to believe I see a hand results, it is claimed, in my knowing that I see a hand. According to such an analysis, it is the history of my belief, a matter of external causation, rather than coherence with some internal system, that yields knowledge. The central tenet of externalism is that some relationship to the external world accounting for the truth of our belief suffices to convert true belief to knowledge without our having any idea of that relationship. It is not our conception of how we are related to a fact that yields knowledge but simply our being so related to it.

Reprinted from Keith Lehrer, *Theory of Knowledge,* 1990, by permission of the author and Westview Press, Boulder, Colorado. Footnotes have been deleted.

The early analysis, though providing a plausible account of perceptual knowledge, was a less plausible account of our knowledge of generalities, that men do not become pregnant, for example, or that neutrinos have a zero rest mass, or that there is no largest prime number. For here the nature of the required causal relationship between what is believed and the belief of it evades explication. That objection is, however, one of detail. Later analyses of others, and of Goldman himself, aim at preserving the thesis of externalism that some relationship of the belief to what makes it true yields knowledge, whether we have any idea of that relationship or not. Armstrong and Dretske have argued that the relationship should be construed as nomological, one resulting from some law of nature connecting the belief with what makes it true. This account is closely connected with the proposal of Nozick that belief track truth in a sense explicated, in part, by the counterfactual claim that the person would not have believed what she did if it were not for the truth of the belief. Goldman now claims that justified belief must be the result of a belief-forming process that reliably yields truth. Beliefs resulting from such a process are justified, he contends, while other externalists deny that justification is necessary for knowledge. They all agree, however, that a belief resulting from a certain kind of process or relationship connecting belief with truth can yield knowledge without the sustenance or support of any other beliefs or system of beliefs.

Naturalism

Assuming that the required relationship is something like causation, externalist theories are *naturalistic*. What is a naturalistic theory? It is one in which all the terms used in the analysis are ones that describe phenomena of nature, such as causation, for example, or that can be reduced to such terms. Hume's theory of belief was naturalistic in this sense. He restricted his account of human knowledge to relations of causation, contiguity, and resemblance. It was, however, Quine who introduced the term *epistemology naturalized* and suggested that inquiry into the nature of human knowledge be restricted to accounts of how belief arises and is altered. Other philosophers have adopted the term to refer simply to all those accounts of knowledge couched in naturalistic vocabulary or reducible to such a vocabulary. The early account of Goldman considered above according to which S knows that p if and only if S's believing that p is caused in the appropriate way by the fact that p is, in this extended sense, an example of epistemology naturalized. Other early naturalistic accounts offered by Armstrong and Dretske rested on the assumption that the conversion relation was based on nomological rather than causal relations, that is, relations articulated in laws of nature. Dretske's basic idea was that the reasons we have for believing what we do should be nomologically connected with the truth of what is believed, that is, that it should be a law of nature that a person having such reasons for believing what she does will have a true belief. Assuming a naturalistic account of having a reason which Dretske supplies, such an account is also naturalistic.

One interesting aspect of some externalistic theories which naturalize epistemology is the way in which they attempt to avoid the problems of foundationalism. According to Dretske or Nozick, for example, there is no need either to justify beliefs or posit self-justified beliefs blindly because, contrary to the traditional analysis, the justification of beliefs is not required to convert true beliefs into knowledge. Beliefs or true beliefs having the appropriate sort of naturalistic external relationships to the facts are, as a result of such relationship, converted into knowledge without being justified. It is the way true beliefs are connected to the world that makes them knowledge rather than the way in which we might attempt to justify them. Notice how plausible this seems for perceptual beliefs. It is the way my belief that I see a bird is related to the facts, for example, when my seeing a bird causes the belief that I do, which accounts for my knowing that I see a bird, rather than some justification I have for that belief. What matters for knowledge is how the belief arises, not how I might reason on behalf of it. The traditional analysis says that knowledge is true belief coupled with the right sort of justification. One sort of externalist analysis says that knowledge is true belief coupled with the right sort of naturalistic relation. It is plausible to assume that the naturalistic relationship will be one concerning how the belief arises, in short, the natural history of the belief. Looked at in this way, the justification requirement can be eliminated altogether in favor of the right sort of historical account.

The Advantages of Externalism

Before turning to details and objections, it is useful to notice the advantages of externalism. First of all, according to some externalists, the need for justification and a theory of justification is eliminated as a component of an analysis of knowledge. On such an account, it is admitted that inference may play some role in the natural history of a true belief, but it is also possible to hold that some beliefs are noninferential. They are beliefs arising from experience without the intervention of inference. This may be offered as an account of what the foundationalist was searching for, but in the wrong place. True beliefs that arise in the appropriate way from experience are knowledge because of the way they arise. There is no need to affirm that such beliefs are self-justified to maintain that they convert to knowledge. We might think of such beliefs as naturalized basic beliefs. Such basic beliefs might, of course, serve as the premises for inferring other beliefs and such inference might convert those beliefs to knowledge as well. It is the history of the belief rather than some sort of justification of the belief that converts it to knowledge.

A Reply to Skepticism

It is helpful, as well, to notice how neatly this sort of theory deals with traditional and modern forms of skepticism. The skeptic, confronted with a commonsense perceptual claim, that I see a tree, for example, has traditionally raised some skeptical doubt, the Cartesian one, for example, that we might be deceived by an evil demon who supplies us with deceptive sensations which lead us to believe we see external objects when we do not see them at all. Or consider the case of a small object, a 'braino', implanted in our brain which, when operated by a computer, provides us with sensory states which are all produced by the computer influencing the brain

rather than by the external objects we believe to exist. In neither case, affirms the skeptic, do I know I see a tree. The reply is simple. If my beliefs are, indeed, produced by the demon or by the braino, then they are false and I am ignorant. On the other hand, if the beliefs are true and produced in the appropriate way, then I do know.

To this the skeptic is wont to reply that I only know that I see a tree if I know that it is not the demon or the braino that produces my belief and, furthermore, to insist that I do not know this. Why do I not know that there is no demon or braino? I do not know so because my experience would be exactly the same if there were; that is what the demon and braino do, produce exactly the same experiences as I would have if I were to see a tree. I have no evidence whatever against these skeptical hypotheses and, therefore, the skeptic concludes, I do not know them to be false. The reply of the externalist is simple. I do not need to *know* that the skeptical hypotheses are false to know that I see a tree, though, of course, the skeptical hypotheses must *be* false. Otherwise, my belief that I see a tree will be false. All that is necessary is that my belief be true and that it arise in the appropriate way, that it have a suitable history, for knowledge to arise. If my belief is true and has arisen in the appropriate way, then I know that I see a tree, even if I do not know that the conflicting skeptical hypotheses are false. I might never have considered such skeptical machinations. Confronted with them, I might be astounded by them and find them so bizarre as not to be worthy of consideration.

The skeptic might retort that I cannot so easily escape the clutches of skepticism. For example, she might suggest that when I claim to know that I am seeing a car, a Mazda RX7, for example, I must have the information required to tell a Mazda RX7 from cars of another sort, and lacking such information, I do not know that I see a Mazda RX7. Hence, I must know that the car is not a Toyota MR2 or a Porsche 944, which bear some resemblance to a Mazda RX7. Going on, the skeptic might argue that to know that I see a Mazda RX7, I must have the information required to tell seeing a Mazda RX7 from experiences of another sort, those supplied by the demon or braino, and lacking such information, I do not know that I am seeing a Mazda RX7, or even that I am seeing a car. So, the skeptic concludes, just as I must know that the car I am seeing is not of another manufacture, so I must know that my experiences are not of skeptical manufacture. That, she insists, is precisely what I do not know. Skepticism wins.

Relevant Alternatives: A Reply to the Skeptic

The reply of the externalist is a combination of counterassertion and explanation. The counterassertion is that my true belief that I see a tree arising in the way it does is knowledge, even if I do not know that it has arisen in that way rather than in the way the skeptic suggests. If the skeptical hypothesis is true and the belief has not arisen in the way I suppose, then I lack knowledge, but if it has arisen in the way I suppose, then I have knowledge, even if I do not know competing hypotheses about the origin of the belief to be false. It does not matter whether I know that the belief originated in the appropriate manner. All that matters is that it have originated in that way. Then I know. The explanation about the Mazda, for example, is that there will be some cases, but not all, in which some information excluding other alternatives, will be necessary for knowledge. The alternative that I am seeing a Porsche 944 and not a Mazda RX7 is a relevant alternative. The alternative that I am being deceived by an evil demon or a braino is not. What is the difference? My information about what a Mazda RX7 looks like must be sufficient to enable me to distinguish it from other cars, and that information plays a role in the formation of my belief that I am seeing a Mazda RX7. In other cases, particularly those suggested by the skeptic in which there is no such distinguishing information, no such information enters into the appropriate origination of the belief. Where the distinguishing information is a necessary component in the suitable generation of the belief, the alternatives to be distinguished from the truth are relevant, but where it is not a necessary component, the alternatives are not relevant ones. To be sure, a skeptic might find the distinction between relevant and irrelevant alternatives capricious and question-begging as a counterargument. Nevertheless, the initial reply to the skeptic to the effect that true belief originating in the appropriate manner is knowledge, even if we do not know the skeptical hypotheses to be false, is a straightforward

consequence of epistemology naturalized whether or not it satisfies the demands of the skeptic.

Knowing That One Knows: Rejection of Deductive Closure

There remains, of course, the question whether I know that I know that I see a tree when I do not know that the skeptical hypotheses are false. If I know that I see a tree, then it follows that the skeptical hypotheses concerning the demon and braino are false. It follows, first of all, from the fact that if I know that I see a tree, then I do see a tree, and, therefore, my experiences are not a result of demonic bewitchment or computer wizardry. It follows, further, from my knowing that I see a tree that my belief originates in the appropriate natural way and not from the demon or braino. In short, it follows both from the fact known and from the knowing of the fact that the skeptical hypotheses are false.

Some naturalists in epistemology would deny that I know that the skeptical hypotheses are false or that I need to know this in order to know that I know that I see a tree. They do this by denying what they call a *deductive closure* condition, namely, the condition that if I know that p and that q is a logical consequence of knowing that p, then I, therefore, know that q. Thus, I might know that p, and know that q is a consequence of knowing that p, even though I do not know that q.

The denial of closure is directly relevant to replying to the skeptic. I might know that I see a tree, know that the falsity of the demon hypothesis is a consequence of my seeing a tree, even though I do not know that the demon hypothesis is false. If, however, I might know that I see a tree without knowing that the demon hypothesis is false, then might I also know that I know that I see a tree without knowing that the demon hypothesis is false? On the naturalist account, it appears that we may answer in the affirmative. If I can know something without knowing what I know to be the consequences of it, then I can know that I know something without knowing what I know to be the consequences of my knowing it.

The falsity of the demon hypothesis is something I know to be a consequence of my knowing that I see a tree, but I may, nevertheless, know that I see a tree without knowing what I know to be a consequence of my knowing it, to wit, the falsity of the demonic hypothesis. Once we deny the closure condition, we may agree with the skeptic that the falsity of the skeptical hypotheses is a necessary condition of what we know, while cheerfully admitting that we do not know that the skeptical hypotheses are false. Such are the joys of naturalism and rejection of the closure condition. Given that the appropriate origination of a true belief converts it to knowledge, it becomes obvious that the closure condition must be rejected. My true belief that I see a tree may originate in the appropriate way without a belief in the logical consequences of that true belief originating in the appropriate way. Indeed, I might fail to believe in the truth of the logical consequences. It may strike one as odd that a person should know that she sees a tree, know that the falsity of the skeptical hypothesis is a consequence, and yet fail to know the skeptical hypothesis to be false. The oddity is in the eye of the epistemologist, however, for there is no logical contradiction in this position.

The Naturalistic Relation

The advantages of naturalism are robust, but the theory must be true, not merely advantageous, to solve the problems with which we began. To ascertain whether the theory is true, we must have some account of the naturalistic relationship that is supposed to convert true belief into knowledge. Before proceeding to consideration of such accounts, however, let us consider the rejection of the justification condition. At least one defender of epistemology naturalized, Goldman in his later work, is inclined to argue that the notion of justification is a naturalistic notion. One might be a naturalist about justification and maintain that justification is reducible to some naturalistic relationship. In fact, a philosopher eager to connect the naturalistic analysis with the traditional one might argue that a person has the requisite sort of justification for knowledge if and only if true belief arises in the appropriate

naturalistic manner. This would provide us with a naturalistic reduction of justification. Thus, the externalist theory can be construed as a naturalistic account of justification or as a repudiation of a nonnaturalistic account of justification. As we shall see later, however, there are objections to externalist accounts of justification that might lead an externalist to prefer the repudiation strategy.

What exactly is the external relationship that converts true belief into knowledge? It is typical of epistemological theories to take some sort of example as a paradigm of knowledge, to fine-tool the theory to fit that sort of example and, at least at the outset, to ignore less felicitous examples whose subsequent consideration necessitates rather substantial modification of the theory. That is the history of externalism. The paradigm example is perception. In the case of perception, it is indeed very plausible to contend that what converts perceptual belief into knowledge is the way that the belief arises in perceptual experience. My belief that I see a tree is converted into knowledge by being caused by my actually seeing a tree. Another kind of example is communication. You tell me that Holly Smith is Department Head and that causes me to believe that Holly Smith is Department Head. Do I know that Holly Smith is Department Head as a result of this causation? It might be contended, and has been, that if my informant knows that what he tells me is true, then I know because he knows and his communication caused me to believe this. Of course, his knowing remains to be explicated. The assumption is that there is a causal chain beginning with the fact that Holly Smith is Department Head and ending with my believing it which accounts for my knowing it.

Thus, following Goldman's early proposal, we might consider the following as characteristic of externalistic theories which eliminate the justification condition.

(CK) S knows that p if and only if S believes that p and this belief is caused in the appropriate way by the fact that p.

This account leaves us with the need to explain the difference between being caused in an appropriate way and being caused in a way that is not appropriate. Typical cases of perception provide a model of the appropriate kind of causation.

Dretske has suggested that when x is something S perceives, then

> (DK) S knows that x is F if and only if S's belief that x is F is caused or causally sustained by the information that x is F received from the source x by S.

Dretske's analysis, though restricted to perceptual knowledge, highlights two needed qualifications recognized by other authors as well. The first is that the belief need not be caused but only causally sustained by the information that p. This is necessary because the originating causation of a belief might involve an error which is corrected by subsequent information one receives.

If I see two men in the distance, I might take the one on the left to be Buchanan and believe that I see Buchanan when, in fact, it is not Buchanan, as I note when I move closer, but Harnish instead. At the same time, I note that the other man, the one on the right, is Buchanan and that Buchanan and Harnish are dressed in such a way that each appears to be the other in preparation for Tolliver's Halloween party. My belief that I see Buchanan was caused by my seeing Harnish dressed as Buchanan, and I continue to hold that belief subsequently when I receive the further information which corrects my mistake about the man on the right but sustains my belief that I see Buchanan and, indeed, that I saw him earlier, though I did not recognize him. Moreover, on this sort of account the appropriate kind of causal relation is explicated in terms of receiving information from a source.

The foregoing analyses are, however, too restricted in scope to provide us with a general analysis of knowledge. There is more to knowledge than perceptual knowledge, and not all knowledge that p can be supposed to be caused by the fact that p. The most obvious example is general knowledge, my knowledge that all human beings die, for example. That fact includes the fact of death of as yet unborn humans which cannot now cause me to believe that all humans die or causally sustain that belief. Our knowledge that all neutrinos have zero rest mass is yet more difficult to account for on such a model, since no one has ever perceived a neutrino at rest. Assuming there to be mathematical knowledge, for example, that integers are infinite, the causal theory seems inappropriate. The integers appear to lie out-

side the temporal order and to be incapable of causing anything.

Accounts of knowledge in terms of causation or the receipt of information fail to provide an account of our knowledge of general and theoretical truths. Moreover, it is easy to see that externalism in no way requires such a restrictive conception of the external relationship. Causal or information-receiving analyses of knowledge have the virtue of explicating knowledge in a way that explains the connection between truth and belief, between reality and thought, and provides an answer to skepticism. We may, however, maintain the connection between truth and belief without committing ourselves to a restrictive causal connection. Instead, we may require that the *history* of the belief connect the belief with truth.

There are two popular accounts of how the history of a belief might connect the belief with truth. The first and perhaps best known is the later account of Goldman according to which true belief is converted to knowledge *via* justification when the belief is the result of a reliable belief-forming process. Goldman's basic idea, which he has modified and refined, is as follows:

> If S's believing that p at t results from a reliable cognitive belief-forming process (or set of processes), then S's belief in p at t is justified.

The refinements include an account of reliable rules, methods, and processes. The other account, offered by Nozick, requires that a belief must track truth in order to convert to knowledge in the sense that the person would believe that p if p were true and would not believe that p if p were not true.

The two theories share some advantages. Both retain the reply to the skeptic considered above. They both accomplish this without assuming that we have any guarantee that our beliefs are true, moreover. That my belief is the outcome of a reliable belief-forming process does not presuppose that I have any guarantee of the truth of the belief. Similarly, I might believe that something is true when I would not have believed it, had it not been true even though I have no guarantee that this is so. Thus, given either account of knowledge, the skeptic may be answered while allowing, what seems obvious, that we are fallible in the way in which we form our beliefs, even those converting to knowledge. The result is a fallibilistic epistemology without the postulation of self-justified beliefs.

Objections to Externalism: Information Without Knowledge

There is, however, a general objection to all externalist theories which is as simple to state as it is fundamental. It is that a person who has no idea that her beliefs are caused or causally sustained by a reliable belief-forming process might fail to know because of her ignorance of this. Alternatively, the person who has no idea that she would not have believed what she did had it not been true might fail to know because of her ignorance of that. Any purely externalist account faces the fundamental objection that a person totally ignorant of the external factors connecting her belief with truth, might be ignorant of the truth of her belief as a result. All externalist theories share a common defect, to wit, that they provide accounts of the possession of information rather than of the attainment of knowledge. The appeal of such theories is their naturalistic character. They assimilate knowledge to other natural causal relationships between objects. Our attainment of knowledge is just one natural relationship between facts among all the rest. It is a relationship of causality, or nomological correlation, or frequency correlation, or counterfactual dependence. But this very attractive feature of such theories is their downfall. The relationship in question may suffice for the recording of information, but if we are ignorant of the relationship, we lack knowledge. As in our refutation of foundationalism, what is missing from the accounts of externalists is the needed supplementation of background information. To convert the specified relationships into knowledge, we need the additional information of the existence of those relationships. Such additional information is, however, precisely the sort of information required for coherence and complete justification.

The general problem with externalism can be seen most graphically by considering the analogy proposed by Armstrong. He suggested that the right model of knowledge is a thermometer. The relationship between the reading on a thermometer and the temperature of the object illustrates the theories mentioned above. Suppose that the thermometer is an accurate one and that it records a temperature of 104 degrees for some oil it is used to measure. We can say, with Armstrong, that there is a nomological connection between the temperature and the thermometer reading, with Dretske that the thermometer receives the information, with Nozick that the thermometer would not record a temperature of 104 degrees if it were not true that the oil was at 104 degrees, and with Goldman that the reading is the outcome of a reliable temperature-recording process. The problem with the analogy is that the thermometer is obviously ignorant of the temperature it records. The question is—why?

One might be inclined to suggest that the thermometer is ignorant of temperature only because it lacks the capacity of thought. If, contrary to fact, the thermometer could entertain the thought that the oil is 104 degrees, would that suffice? Would the thermometer know that the temperature is 104 degrees? What are we to say of this fanciful thought experiment? One might protest, of course, that it is too farfetched to turn the philosophical lathe. The thermometer does record information accurately, however, and, given the capacity for thought, it may be said that the thermometer not only contains the information but possesses that information as well. But our thoughtful thermometer does not *know* that the temperature of the oil is 104 degrees as a result of thinking that this is so. The reason is that it might have no idea that it is an accurate temperature-recording device. If it has no idea that this is so, then, even if it thinks the temperature of the oil is 104 degrees when it records that temperature, it has no idea that the recorded temperature is correct. To obtain the benefits of these reflections, however, it is necessary to move to the human case.

Suppose a person, whom we shall name Mr. Truetemp, undergoes brain surgery by an experimental surgeon who invents a small device which is both a very accurate thermometer and a computational device capable of generating thoughts. The device, call it a tempucomp, is implanted in Truetemp's head so that the very tip of the device, no larger than the head of a pin, sits unnoticed on his scalp and acts as a sensor to transmit information about the temperature to the computational system in his brain. This device, in turn, sends a message to his brain causing him to think of the temperature recorded by the external sensor. Assume that the tempucomp is very reliable, and so his thoughts are correct temperature thoughts. All told, this is a reliable belief-forming process. Now imagine, finally, that he has no idea that the tempucomp has been inserted in his brain, is only slightly puzzled about why he thinks so obsessively about the temperature, but never checks a thermometer to determine whether these thoughts about the temperature are correct. He accepts them unreflectively, another effect of the tempucomp. Thus, he thinks and accepts that the temperature is 104 degrees. It is. Does he know that it is? Surely not. He has no idea whether he or his thoughts about the temperature are reliable. What he accepts, that the temperature is 104 degrees, is correct, but he does not know that his thought is correct. His thought that the temperature is 104 degrees is correct information, but he does not know this. Though he records the information because of the operations of the tempucomp, he is ignorant of the facts about the tempucomp and about his temperature telling reliability. Yet, the sort of causal, nomological, statistical, or counterfactual relationships required by externalism may all be present. Does he know that the temperature is 104 degrees when the thought occurs to him while strolling in Pima Canyon? He has no idea why the thought occurred to him or that such thoughts are almost always correct. He does not, consequently, know that the temperature is 104 degrees when that thought occurs to him.

The preceding example is not presented as a decisive objection against externalism and should not be taken as such. It is possible to place some constraint on relationships or processes converting belief to knowledge to exclude production by the tempucomp. The fundamental difficulty remains, however. It is that more than the possession of correct information is required for knowledge. One must have some way of knowing that the information is correct. Consider another example. Someone informs me that Professor Haller is in my office. Suppose I have no idea whether the person telling me this is trustworthy. Even if the information I receive is correct and I believe what I am told, I do not know that Haller is in my office, because I have no idea of whether the source of my information is trustworthy. The nomological, statistical, or counterfactual relationships or processes may be trustworthy, but I lack this information.

When we considered the distinction between belief and acceptance in the third chapter, we noted the argument to the effect that a person who receives the information that p and believes that p as a result may fail to know that p. The reason is that the person may not know that the information she thus receives and believes is correct information. If a person does not know that the information, that p, which she receives is correct information, then she does not know that p. All forms of externalism fail to deal with this problem adequately. To know that the information one possesses is correct, one requires background information about that information. One requires information about whether the received information is trustworthy or not, and lacking such information, one falls short of knowledge. This is a line of argumentation we have already encountered, in earlier chapters. A necessary condition of knowledge is coherence with background information, with an acceptance system, informing us of the trustworthiness of the information we possess.

Externalism and Justification

Some forms of externalism repudiate justification as a condition of knowledge, according to Nozick and Dretske, for example. Such accounts may provide an interesting account of what it is like for belief to constitute correct information or to track truth, but they provide no account of knowledge. The reason is that no one knows that what she accepts is true when it would have been just as reasonable for her to have accepted the opposite on the basis of her information. A necessary normative condition of a person knowing that p is that it be more reasonable for her to accept that p than to accept the denial of p on the basis of her information. This condition implies the need for a justification condition of the sort we have proposed.

One may, as Goldman illustrates, combine externalism with the affirmation of a justification condition, but such an account, if it takes account of background information in an acceptable manner, will introduce a coherence factor. Goldman insists, for example, that a justified belief resulting from a reliable belief-forming process must not be undermined by other evidence the subject possesses. The condition requiring that the belief not be undermined by other evidence is a kind of negative coherence condition to the effect that the belief not be incoherent with background information. Nevertheless, the source of justification on this account is the reliability of the belief-forming process, that is, the fact that the belief has the sort of history frequently producing true beliefs. As a result of providing a justification condition, a normative constraint is supplied.

The objection raised against externalism in general still applies to such a theory, however. A person totally ignorant of the reliability of the process producing his belief would not know that what he believes is true, even if he had no information that would undermine his belief. The example of Mr. Truetemp illustrates this perfectly. He has no evidence that his thoughts about the temperature are incorrect. Had he taken time to consider evidence, he would have discovered that his thoughts about the temperature are correct, but he did not consider any evidence concerning the matter, and that is why he does not know that his thoughts about the temperature are correct.

Take a more commonplace example. If I read a thermometer at the local gas station, and it says that the temperature is 104 degrees, I do not know simply from reading the thermometer that the temperature is 104 degrees. I may not have any evidence that it is untrustworthy, but the competitor to the effect that gas station thermometers are often inaccurate is not one I can beat or neutralize, at least not without inquiring about the thermometer. Whether or not the belief-forming process is reliable, which perhaps it is, I do not know whether the information about the temperature is trustworthy or not. Indeed, I may have no view on the matter. I may believe what I see out of habit, but this is not knowledge. This is a central problem for externalism, to wit, that ignorance of our reliability or of other external relationships leaves us ignorant of whether our information is trustworthy. Trust sharpens the epistemic blade.

The Invincibility Objection

There is another objection to historical reliabilism that leads to an important lesson. The objection raised by Cohen is that if we are deceived in such a way that we are invincibly ignorant of the deception, we are justified in what we believe, nonetheless. Cohen's example was the Cartesian demon who deceives us in all our perceptual beliefs. The details of the deception may vary, but let us suppose that the demon clouds our senses and supplies us with deceptive sensory data leading us to believe that we perceive the world though we actually perceive nothing at all. Since our perceptual beliefs are virtually all erroneous, the process that produces them is not reliable. Yet, Cohen suggests, we are certainly justified in our beliefs. We may have done the best we could to ensure that we were not deceived, attended to what we observe with the greatest circumspection, and noticed no error. Having done the best we could, indeed, the best anyone could do, we are certainly justified in believing what we do.

The intuition is reinforced by noting the difference between two people, one who examines his sensory data with the sort of care that would keep him virtually free from error in normal circumstances, and one who forms perceptual beliefs so casually that he would frequently err under the best of circumstances. The former puts together all his information and concludes that he is seeing the path of an alpha particle in a cloud chamber. The other believes this because some person, whom he knows to be scientifically ignorant, has told him that this is what he is seeing. We would wish to say that the former but not the latter was justified in believing that he sees the path of an alpha particle in a cloud chamber, even though both beliefs are produced by processes that are unreliable, given the interventions of the demon.

Externalism might be modified to meet the objection, and Goldman has suggested more than one way. The example shows that it is internal factors, not external ones, that make us justified and explain the difference between the circumspect and casual observers above. The sort of justification appealed to in the example is personal justification as explicated in the last chapter. The circumspect observer wins the justification round arising when the skeptic claims that casual observations are often in error by replying that his observation is circumspect and not casual. The casual observer loses that round to the skeptic.

The Absentminded Demon

There is, however, an important lesson to be learned from reliabilism. It is that the sort of justification required for knowledge is not entirely an internal matter, either. On the contrary, the needed form of justification depends on the appropriate match between what one accepts about how one is related to the world and what is actually the case. To see this, consider a minor amendment in the preceding example in which the demon, in a moment of cosmic absentmindedness, forgets for a moment to cloud our senses, with the result that we really perceive what we think we do. If this moment is one that occurs very briefly as we suddenly awake and is immediately followed by further slumber to conceal the demonic error, we might believe we perceive what, in this instance, we actually do perceive. I might perceive my hand for the first time and believe I see a hand, only to lose consciousness after this formidable event. Do I know that I see a hand in that brief moment? I believe I do, but, since such beliefs are almost all false, I am almost totally untrustworthy in such matters as is everybody else, though accepting myself to be worthy of trust.

I am as much deceived about my trustworthiness in this case as I would be when confronted with a convincing liar who tells me almost all falsehoods about some party he attended except for one fact which, in a moment of absentmindedness, he accurately conveyed, namely, that he arrived before the host. If I accept all that he tells me and also that he is a trustworthy source of information about the event, I may be personally justified in accepting all that he says, but I do not know that the one truth he has conveyed is a truth. I do not know that he arrived before the host. The reason is that my assumption that my informant is trustworthy is in error, even if he has told me the truth in this one instance, and this error is sufficient to deprive me of the sort of justification I require for knowledge.

This is the truth about justification contained in reliabilism.

Complete Justification and Reliabilism

The account that we have offered of complete justification in the last chapter is sufficient to deal with the sort of problem we have just considered. To be personally justified in accepting what another says, one must accept that the person is trustworthy, for, otherwise, the skeptic can win the justification game by claiming that informants are sometimes untrustworthy, or more directly, that the informant from whom I received the information is an untrustworthy informant. Thus, to be personally justified, I must accept that the informant is trustworthy. Since that is false, however, I will not be justified in accepting that my informant arrived before the host on the basis of my verific system, what is left of my acceptance system when all errors are deleted. I will not be verifically justified, and so I will not be completely justified either. Hence, the account offered above incorporates the reliabilist insight and explains how we fail to obtain knowledge when the source of information is unreliable.

The appeal of reliabilism and the other forms of externalism may, moreover, be easily understood in terms of the coherence theory and the account of complete justification contained therein. To oversimplify a bit, personal justification depends on our background information about the relationship of acceptance to the truth of what is accepted, about nomological or statistical correlations, about counterfactual dependence, or about reliable processes. This information is contained in my acceptance system. I know that I see my cat sitting on papers on the desk. I accept that I would not believe that I see a cat if it were not true that I see him. I accept that my believing I see a cat is correlated with my seeing a cat, though I would not put it that way. I accept that always, or almost always, I see a cat when I think I see one because my accepting that I see a cat results from a reliable process. It is my acceptance of these things that converts merely accepting that I see a cat into personal justification, into victory in the justification game. For that victory to be converted into complete justification, however, what I accept about these things must also be true. The conversion of mere acceptance into personal justification depends on my accepting the things about myself whose bare existence the externalist mistakenly assumes to be sufficient to convert true belief into knowledge. The conversion also depends, as the externalist says it does, on these things I accept about myself being true. The error of externalism is to fail to notice that the subject of knowledge must accept that the externalist conditions hold true. The insight of externalism is the claim that the conditions must, indeed, hold true.

Causation and Justification: The Basing Relation

The truth contained in reliabilism is, however, concealed by an error. What a person originally believes as a result of prejudice may later be accepted on the basis of scientific evidence. Therefore, the reliabilist must be in error when he claims that it is what originates a belief that converts it into a justified belief and knowledge. This is, in effect, to confuse the *reason* a person has for believing something with the *cause* of his believing it. The confusion is such a common one that we might name it the *causal fallacy*.

It is easy to see how the fallacy arises. When a person's justification for her belief is based on evidence, then she believes what she does *because* of the evidence. This suggests a causal account of what is involved when the justification of a belief is based on evidence. It suggests that the notion of a justification being based on evidence should be explicated in causal terms. Following this proposal, a person's justification for her belief is based on certain evidence if and only if her belief is causally related in some specified way to the evidence. How to specify the exact way in which the belief must be causally related to the evidence would remain a problem on this approach, but it would be a problem of detail rather than of principle. All such theories must be rejected, however.

Often the evidence on which a justification is based does causally explain the existence of the be-

lief, and it may even be admitted that sometimes the belief is justified because of the way in which it is causally explained by the evidence. Nevertheless, it is also possible for a justified belief to be causally independent of the evidence that justifies it. Indeed, it may well be that the evidence in no way explains why the person holds the belief, even though her justification for the belief is based on the evidence. The evidence that justifies a person's belief may be evidence she acquired because she already held the belief, rather than the other way round. This is to be expected, since it is common sense to distinguish between the reasons that justify a belief and the causes that produce it. The causes of belief are various, and, though the reasons we have for a belief sometimes cause the belief to arise, the belief may also arise from some other cause than having the reasons that justify it. Having the reasons we do may justify the belief, however, even though they have no causal influence upon the belief at all.

An example will illustrate. It is easy to imagine the case of someone who comes to believe something for the wrong reason and, consequently, cannot be said to be justified in his belief, but who, as a result of his belief, uncovers some evidence which completely justifies his belief. Suppose that a man, Mr. Raco, is racially prejudiced and, as a result, believes that the members of some race are susceptible to some disease to which members of his race are not susceptible. This belief, we may imagine, is an unshakable conviction. It is so strong a conviction that no evidence to the contrary would weaken his prejudiced conviction, and no evidence in favor would strengthen it. Now imagine that Mr. Raco becomes a doctor and begins to study the disease in question. Imagine that he reads all that is known about the disease and discovers that the evidence, which is quite conclusive, confirms his conviction. The scientific evidence shows that only members of the race in question are susceptible to the disease. We may imagine as well that Mr. Raco has become a medical expert perfectly capable of understanding the canons of scientific evidence, though, unfortunately, he becomes no less prejudiced as a result of this. Nevertheless, he understands and appreciates the evidence as well as any medical expert and, as a result, has reason for his belief that justifies it. He has discovered that his conviction is confirmed by the scientific evidence. He knows that only members of the other race are susceptible to the disease in question. Yet, the reasons that justify him in this belief do not causally explain the belief. The belief is the result of prejudice, not reason, but it is confirmed by reason which provides the justification for the belief. Prejudice gives Mr. Raco conviction, but reason gives him justification.

Harman and others, most notably Marshall Swain and Alvin Goldman, have suggested that a belief is based on evidence only if the evidence conditionally or partially explains the belief. The idea is that, even if the belief is not originated by the evidence on which it is based, it must be causally sustained by the evidence. Again, in the typical case, this will be true. Usually, the reasons a person has for a belief can be expected to have some causal influence on the belief, even if they do not originate that belief. It is, unfortunately, difficult to evaluate the claim that the reasons that justify a belief must always partially explain or causally sustain the belief because a sufficiently precise account of partial explanation and causal sustenance is lacking. There appears to be no better reason for supposing that the evidence that justifies a belief must partially explain or causally sustain the belief than for supposing that it must originate it. The explanation for this is that we may suppose that the evidence justifying Mr. Raco's beliefs does not in any way explain or causally sustain his belief. What explains and sustains his belief is his prejudice. His belief is neither strengthened nor explained by his discovering the evidence for it. His prejudice gives him the strongest level of conviction, and the evidence adds nothing to the strength of it.

One might, however, suggest that his conviction is conditionally or counterfactually explained or sustained by the evidence, nonetheless. It might be proposed that if Mr. Raco were not to believe what he does out of prejudice, he would believe it as a result of the evidence. This is again likely, but it need not be so. Imagine that Mr. Raco is so dependent on his prejudice that if he were to cease to believe what he does out of prejudice, he would become quite mad and become uninfluenced by reason. To avoid such an objection one might propose, as Swain did, that to say the belief is sustained by the evidence is only to say that if Mr. Raco were not to believe what he does out of prejudice but were to continue to believe it nonetheless, then he

would believe it as a result of the evidence. Perhaps this is to be expected, but must it be so? Again suppose that were Mr. Raco to cease to believe what he does out of prejudice, he would become quite mad and uninfluenced by reason; then were he to believe the same thing though not out of prejudice, he would believe it as a result of madness.

The point is the one with which he began. Though evidence ordinarily has some influence over belief or would have if other factors were to lose their influence, this is really incidental to justification. The analogy between justification and validity explains why. If a person validly deduces a conclusion from something he knows, this may cause him to believe the conclusion or influence his belief in the conclusion. But the validity of the inference does not depend on this causal influence. If valid deduction had no influence whatever on whether a person believed the conclusion, that would not undermine the validity of the inference. Similarly, if someone justifies some conclusion on the basis of something he knows, this may cause him to believe the conclusion or influence his belief in the conclusion. The justification of his conclusion, however, does not depend on the causal influence. Thus, a person may justify a second belief in terms of a first belief and the justification of the second belief may be based on the first without the second belief being causally influenced thereby.

The preceding discussion rests on a distinction between explaining why a person believes something, on the one hand, and explaining how he knows it, on the other. When a person knows that his belief is true, the explanation of why he believes what he does may have something to do with his having the evidence he does, but it need not. The explanation may rest on political, erotic, or other extraneous influences, but the explanation of how a person knows that his belief is true, when the justification of the belief is based on evidence, must be in terms of the evidence. It is how a person knows that is explained by evidence. Why he believes what he does may be explained by anything whatever. Therefore, a justification of a belief that is known to be true is based on certain evidence if and only if his having that evidence explains how he knows that the belief is true. The evidence explains how the person knows, moreover, if and only if the evidence justifies the person's belief. The manner in which evidence justifies a belief is explained in the account of complete justification in the last chapter. Evidence that justifies a belief consists of that part of the acceptance system of a person which yields complete justification.

The idea of evidence explaining how a person knows may be further clarified by recalling once again that our primary concern is to provide a theory to explain how people know that the information that they possess is correct. If the evidence that a person has justifies her belief that *p*, then the evidence explains how she knows that the information that *p* is correct. She knows this from the evidence. Similarly, if a person is asked how she knows that *p*, her reply will be to justify the claim that *p* in terms of her evidence. It is appeal to her evidence that shows that she knows and how she knows. Thus, a justification based on evidence explains how a person knows that *p* if that justification would be a correct answer to the question 'How do you know that *p*?'

Reliability and the Justification Game

The example of Mr. Raco, a person originally believing out of racial prejudice that the members of some race suffer a disease which members of other races do not suffer and later accepting this on the basis of scientific evidence, shows that a belief need not be produced or, as the example further indicated, even sustained by the evidence that justifies accepting it. Reliability enters into justification not by originating belief but by backing acceptance in the justification game. Consider the justification game played by the prejudiced man before obtaining the scientific information.

CLAIMANT: The members of that race suffer a disease to which members of other races are not susceptible.

SKEPTIC: You believe what you do as the result of prejudice.

CLAIMANT: It is more reasonable for me to accept that I do not believe what I do as a result of prejudice than to accept that I believe what I do as a result of prejudice. (I am quite unprejudiced concerning members of the race in question, it is just that they are inferior.)

This personal justification would fail to convert into verific and complete justification. The claimant's error concerning his prejudice would disqualify this move in the verific justification game.

After acquiring the scientific information, the claimant is in a position to neutralize the claim of the skeptic in the justification game by making the following reply to the claim of the skeptic above:

CLAIMANT: It is as reasonable for me to accept that I believe what I do out of prejudice and that the best scientific evidence shows that what I thus believe is, in fact, true than to accept merely that I believe what I do out of prejudice. (In the standard medical reference work concerning this disease, it is stated that only members of the race in question are susceptible to the disease. This has been confirmed by recent studies cited in . . .)

This move succeeds in the verific justification game. The claimant wins the round, and his move cannot be disqualified. Whatever his moral failings, as a result of obtaining scientific understanding, he is victorious in the justification game. He is, therefore, personally and verifically justified in accepting what he does.

The preceding reflections illustrate the point that the evidence which justifies a person in accepting something must explain how the person knows that *p* rather than why he believes it. The scientific evidence explains how the person knows by explaining how he is victorious in the justification game. Usually, what makes a person victorious in the justification game is closely connected to what makes him believe what he does. But the connection is not essential to justification. As a result, the reliability essential to justification is not the reliability of the process which produces or causally sustains belief. What is essential is the reliability or trustworthiness of the evidence for what we accept to guide us to acceptance of what is true rather than false. The trustworthiness of the evidence makes us trustworthy in the matter, whatever our general defects. In epistemology as in life generally, you do not have to be perfect in order to be justified.

Externalism, Foundationalism, and Coherence: An Ecumenical Reconsideration

The foregoing articulation of the coherence theory of justification suggests that there is some merit in the foundation theory and in externalism which we have preserved in our theory. It is, therefore, time to turn from criticism to ecumenicalism. The foundation theory held some introspective, perceptual, and memory beliefs to be self-justified. We argued that the justification of all such beliefs depends on background information concerning our trustworthiness in such matters. Thus, it is coherence with such information in our acceptance system that produces the justification. Nevertheless, we concede that some beliefs are justified without inference because we accept ourselves to be trustworthy in such matters, and that a principle of our trustworthiness is needed to convert mere acceptance into justified acceptance.

Moreover, though the principle of our trustworthiness must cohere with what we accept about our successes and failures in past epistemic employments, the principle of our own trustworthiness provides its own personal justification. We are, at least in part, personally justified in accepting that we are trustworthy precisely because we accept that we are. If we did not accept that we were trustworthy, there would be an unbeatable skeptical challenge to any claim we made in the justification game, to wit, that we are untrustworthy in what we accept. To beat that move, we must accept that we are trustworthy. So, there appears to be at least one thing that we accept, one important and fundamental thing, that is self-justified as the foundationalist contended, even if it is not those introspective, perceptual, and memory beliefs that he most favors. To be personally justified one must accept some principle of trustworthiness which is, in part, self-justified.

To be verifically and completely justified as well, some principle of trustworthiness we accept must be true. Otherwise, the skeptical challenge that we are not trustworthy in what we accept would not be beaten in the verific justification game. The insight of externalism is the contention that there must be some truth connection between our accepting something and the truth of what we accept. It is our acceptance of our trustworthiness and the correctness of what we thus accept that yields the truth connection.

Externalism is motivated by the doubt about whether what we accept can supply the truth connection. The reason for the doubt is the assumption that it is psychologically unrealistic to suppose that beliefs about our beliefs are necessary for knowledge. Such higher order beliefs about beliefs are not, of course, necessary for receiving and relaying information. Even a thermometer is capable of that. Such beliefs are, however, necessary for knowledge. Is it unrealistic to suppose that people believe themselves to be trustworthy? Some unrealistic theory of belief may yield that consequence, but our theory of acceptance avoids it. The mental state of acceptance is a functional state, one that plays a role in thought, inference, and action. We think, infer, and act in a way manifesting our trust in what we accept.

Thus, it is appropriate and not at all unrealistic to suppose that, in addition to the other things we accept, we accept our own trustworthiness as well. We have supplied the truth that supplies the truth connection required by the externalist in the form of a self-justified principle of our own trustworthiness. We cannot be accused of chauvinism in claiming that complete justification is the result of coherence with an acceptance system incorporating the principle. Unless we are trustworthy in what we accept, neither we nor our adversaries can be justified in what we accept and we must all concede the day to the skeptic. If we are trustworthy, as we accept ourselves to be, what we accept will cohere with our acceptance system and our verific system to yield complete justification. The attainment of knowledge, like so many other benefits in life, rests on self-trust.

VI.3 *Epistemology Naturalized*

W. V. QUINE

W. V. Quine for many years was Professor of Philosophy at Harvard University. Quine argues that epistemology centered in normative justification is dead. Because foundationalism (especially Carnap's ambitious effort) has failed as an attempt to ground our knowledge claims, we should give up traditional epistemology altogether and concentrate on empirical psychology. Whereas "old epistemology aspired to contain . . . natural science . . . epistemology in its new setting, conversely, is contained in natural science, as a chapter of psychology." The new epistemology-psychology turns into the descriptive examination of the relation "between the meager input [of sensory stimulation] and the torrential output [our three-dimensional picture of the world]." With the demise of "old epistemology" go all concerns about normativity or justification.

Quine begins his essay with an examination of the twofold goal of traditional epistemology: (1) the conceptual reduction, whereby physical terms are reduced to terms referring to phenomenal features of sensory experience; and (2) a doctrinal reduction, whereby truths about the physical world are *correctly* obtained from sensory experience. Quine argues that the twofold goal failed and that there is no "correct" or normative function left.

Epistemology is concerned with the foundations of science. Conceived thus broadly, epistemology includes the study of the foundations of mathematics as one of its departments. Specialists at the turn of the century thought that their efforts in this particular department were achieving notable success: mathematics seemed to reduce altogether to logic. In a more recent perspective this reduction is seen to be better describable as a reduction to logic and set theory. This correction is a disappointment epistemologically, since the firmness and obviousness that we associate with logic cannot be claimed for set theory. But still the success achieved in the foundations of mathematics remains exemplary by comparative standards, and we can illuminate the rest of epistemology somewhat by drawing parallels to this department.

Studies in the foundations of mathematics divide symmetrically into two sorts, conceptual and doctrinal. The conceptual studies are concerned with meaning, the doctrinal with truth. The conceptual studies are concerned with clarifying concepts by defining them, some in terms of others. The doctrinal studies are concerned with establishing laws by proving them, some on the basis of others. Ideally the more obscure concepts would be defined in terms of the clearer ones so as to maximize clarity, and the less obvious laws would be proved from the more obvious ones so as to maximize certainty. Ideally the definitions would generate all the concepts from clear and distinct ideas, and the proofs would generate all the theorems from self-evident truths.

The two ideals are linked. For, if you define all the concepts by use of some favored subset of them, you thereby show how to translate all theorems into these favored terms. The clearer these terms are, the likelier it is that the truths couched in them will be obviously true, or derivable from obvious truths. If

Reprinted from Quine, *Ontological Relativity and Other Essays* (New York: Columbia University Press, 1969), 68–90, by permission of the author and the publisher. Copyright 1969, Columbia University Press.

in particular the concepts of mathematics were all reducible to the clear terms of logic, then all the truths of mathematics would go over into truths of logic; and surely the truths of logic are all obvious or at least potentially obvious, i.e., derivable from obvious truths by individually obvious steps.

This particular outcome is in fact denied us, however, since mathematics reduces only to set theory and not to logic proper. Such reduction still enhances clarity, but only because of the interrelations that emerge and not because the end terms of the analysis are clearer than others. As for the end truths, the axioms of set theory, these have less obviousness and certainty to recommend them than do most of the mathematical theorems that we would derive from them. Moreover, we know from Gödel's work that no consistent axiom system can cover mathematics even when we renounce self-evidence. Reduction in the foundations of mathematics remains mathematically and philosophically fascinating, but it does not do what the epistemologist would like of it: it does not reveal the ground of mathematical knowledge, it does not show how mathematical certainty is possible.

Still there remains a helpful thought, regarding epistemology generally, in that duality of structure which was especially conspicuous in the foundations of mathematics. I refer to the bifurcation into a theory of concepts, or meaning, and a theory of doctrine, or truth; for this applies to the epistemology of natural knowledge no less than to the foundations of mathematics. The parallel is as follows. Just as mathematics is to be reduced to logic, or logic and set theory, so natural knowledge is to be based somehow on sense experience. This means explaining the notion of body in sensory terms; here is the conceptual side. And it means justifying our knowledge of truths of nature in sensory terms; here is the doctrinal side of the bifurcation.

Hume pondered the epistemology of natural knowledge on both sides of the bifurcation, the conceptual and the doctrinal. His handling of the conceptual side of the problem, the explanation of body in sensory terms, was bold and simple: he identified bodies outright with the sense impressions. If common sense distinguishes between the material apple and our sense impressions of it on the ground that the apple is one and enduring while the impressions are many and fleeting, then, Hume held, so much the worse for common sense;

the notion of its being the same apple on one occasion and another is a vulgar confusion.

Nearly a century after Hume's *Treatise*, the same view of bodies was espoused by the early American philosopher Alexander Bryan Johnson.[1] "The word iron names an associated sight and feel," Johnson wrote.

What then of the doctrinal side, the justification of our knowledge of truths about nature? Here, Hume despaired. By his identification of bodies with impressions he did succeed in construing some singular statements about bodies as indubitable truths, yes; as truths about impressions, directly known. But general statements, also singular statements about the future, gained no increment of certainty by being construed as about impressions.

On the doctrinal side, I do not see that we are further along today than where Hume left us. The Humean predicament is the human predicament. But on the conceptual side there has been progress. There the crucial step forward was made already before Alexander Bryan Johnson's day, although Johnson did not emulate it. It was made by Bentham in his theory of fictions. Bentham's step was the recognition of contextual definition, or what he called paraphrasis. He recognized that to explain a term we do not need to specify an object for it to refer to, nor even specify a synonymous word or phrase; we need only show, by whatever means, how to translate all the whole sentences in which the term is to be used. Hume's and Johnson's desperate measure of identifying bodies with impressions ceased to be the only conceivable way of making sense of talk of bodies, even granted that impressions were the only reality. One could undertake to explain talk of bodies in terms of talk of impressions by translating one's whole sentence about bodies into whole sentences about impressions, without equating the bodies themselves to anything at all.

This idea of contextual definition, or recognition of the sentence as the primary vehicle of meaning, was indispensable to the ensuing developments in the foundations of mathematics. It was explicit in Frege, and it attained its full flower in Russell's doctrine of singular descriptions as incomplete symbols.

Contextual definition was one of two resorts that could be expected to have a liberating effect upon the conceptual side of the epistemology of natural knowledge. The other is resort to the resources of set theory as auxiliary concepts. The epistemologist who is willing to eke out his austere ontology of sense impressions with these set-theoretic auxiliaries is suddenly rich: he has not just his impressions to play with, but sets of them, and sets of sets, and so on up. Constructions in the foundations of mathematics have shown that such set-theoretic aids are a powerful addition; after all, the entire glossary of concepts of classical mathematics is constructible from them. Thus equipped, our epistemologist may not need either to identify bodies with impressions or to settle for contextual definition; he may hope to find in some subtle construction of sets upon sets of sense impressions a category of objects enjoying just the formula properties that he wants for bodies.

The two resorts are very unequal in epistemological status. Contextual definition is unassailable. Sentences that have been given meaning as wholes are undeniably meaningful, and the use they make of their component terms is therefore meaningful, regardless of whether any translations are offered for those terms in isolation. Surely Hume and A. B. Johnson would have used contextual definition with pleasure if they had thought of it. Recourse to sets, on the other hand, is a drastic ontological move, a retreat from the austere ontology of impressions. There are philosophers who would rather settle for bodies outright than accept all these sets, which amount, after all, to the whole abstract ontology of mathematics.

This issue has not always been clear, however, owing to deceptive hints of continuity between elementary logic and set theory. This is why mathematics was once believed to reduce to logic, that is, to an innocent and unquestionable logic, and to inherit these qualities. And this is probably why Russell was content to resort to sets as well as to contextual definition when in *Our Knowledge of the External World* and elsewhere he addressed himself to the epistemology of natural knowledge, on its conceptual side.

To account for the external world as a logical construct of sense data—such, in Russell's terms, was the program. It was Carnap, in his *Der logische Aufbau der Welt* of 1928, who came nearest to executing it.

This was the conceptual side of epistemology; what of the doctrinal? There the Humean predicament remained unaltered. Carnap's constructions, if carried successfully to completion, would have enabled us to translate all sentences about the world into terms of sense data, or observation, plus logic and set theory. But the mere fact that a sentence is *couched* in terms of observation, logic, and set theory does not mean that it can be *proved* from observation sentences by logic and set theory. The most modest of generalizations about observable traits will cover more cases than its utterer can have had occasion actually to observe. The hopelessness of grounding natural science upon immediate experience in a firmly logical way was acknowledged. The Cartesian quest for certainty had been the remote motivation of epistemology, both on its conceptual and its doctrinal side; but that quest was seen as a lost cause. To endow the truths of nature with the full authority of immediate experience was as forlorn a hope as hoping to endow the truths of mathematics with the potential obviousness of elementary logic.

What then could have motivated Carnap's heroic efforts on the conceptual side of epistemology, when hope of certainty on the doctrinal side was abandoned? There were two good reasons still. One was that such constructions could be expected to elicit and clarify the sensory evidence for science, even if the inferential steps between sensory evidence and scientific doctrine must fall short of certainty. The other reason was that such constructions would deepen our understanding of our discourse about the world, even apart from questions of evidence; it would make all cognitive discourse as clear as observation terms and logic and, I must regretfully add, set theory.

It was sad for epistemologists, Hume and others, to have to acquiesce in the impossibility of strictly deriving the science of the external world from sensory evidence. Two cardinal tenets of empiricism remained unassailable, however, and so remain to this day. One is that whatever evidence there *is* for science *is* sensory evidence. The other, to which I shall return, is that all inculcation of meanings of words must rest ultimately on sensory evidence. Hence the continuing attractiveness of the idea of a *logischer Aufbau* in which the sensory content of discourse would stand forth explicitly.

If Carnap had successfully carried such a construction through, how could he have told whether it was the right one? The question would have had no point. He was seeking what he called a *rational reconstruction*. Any construction of physicalistic discourse in terms of sense experience, logic, and set theory would have been seen as satisfactory if it made the physicalistic discourse come out right. If there is one way there are many, but any would be a great achievement.

But why all this creative reconstruction, all this make-believe? The stimulation of his sensory receptors is all the evidence anybody has had to go on, ultimately, in arriving at his picture of the world. Why not just see how this construction really proceeds? Why not settle for psychology? Such a surrender of the epistemological burden to psychology is a move that was disallowed in earlier times as circular reasoning. If the epistemologist's goal is validation of the grounds of empirical science, he defeats his purpose by using psychology or other empirical science in the validation. However, such scruples against circularity have little point once we have stopped dreaming of deducing science from observations. If we are out simply to understand the link between observation and science, we are well advised to use any available information, including that provided by the very science whose link with observation we are seeking to understand.

But there remains a different reason, unconnected with fears of circularity, for still favoring creative reconstruction. We should like to be able to *translate* science into logic and observation terms and set theory. This would be a great epistemological achievement, for it would show all the rest of the concepts of science to be theoretically superfluous. It would legitimize them—to whatever degree the concepts of set theory, logic, and observation are themselves legitimate—by showing that everything done with the one apparatus could in principle be done with the other. If psychology itself could deliver a truly translational reduction of this kind, we should welcome it; but certainly it cannot, for certainly we did not grow up learning definitions of physicalistic language in terms of a prior language of set theory, logic, and observation. Here, then, would be good reason for persisting in a rational reconstruction: we want to establish the essential innocence of physical concepts, by showing them to be theoretically dispensable.

The fact is, though, that the construction which Carnap outlined in *Der logische Aufbau der Welt* does not give translational reduction either. It would not even if the outline were filled in. The crucial point comes where Carnap is explaining how to assign sense qualities to positions in physical space and time. These assignments are to be made in such a way as to fulfill, as well as possible, certain desiderata which he states, and with growth of experience the assignments are to be revised to suit. This plan, however illuminating, does not offer any key to *translating* the sentences of science into terms of observation, logic, and set theory.

We must despair of any such reduction. Carnap had despaired of it by 1936, when, in "Testability and Meaning,"[2] he introduced so-called *reduction forms* of a type weaker than definition. Definitions had shown always how to translate sentences into equivalent sentences. Contextual definition of a term showed how to translate sentences containing the term into equivalent sentences lacking the term. Reduction forms of Carnap's liberalized kind, on the other hand, do not in general give equivalences; they give implications. They explain a new term, if only partially, by specifying some sentences which are implied by sentences containing the term, and other sentences which imply sentences containing the term.

It is tempting to suppose that the countenancing of reduction forms in this liberal sense is just one further step of liberalization comparable to the earlier one, taken by Bentham, of countenancing contextual definition. The former and sterner kind of rational reconstruction might have been represented as a fictitious history in which we imagined our ancestors introducing the terms of physicalistic discourse on a phenomenalistic and set-theoretic basis by a succession of contextual definitions. The new and more liberal kind of rational reconstruction is a fictitious history in which we imagine our ancestors introducing those terms by a succession rather of reduction forms of the weaker sort.

This, however, is a wrong comparison. The fact is rather that the former and sterner kind of rational reconstruction, where definition reigned, embodied no fictitious history at all. It was nothing more nor less than a set of directions—or would have been, if successful—for accomplishing everything in terms of phenomena and set theory that we now accomplish in terms of bodies. It would have been a true reduction by translation, a legitimation by elimination. *Definire est eliminare.* Rational reconstruction by Carnap's later and looser reduction forms does none of this.

To relax the demand for definition, and settle for a kind of reduction that does not eliminate, is to renounce the last remaining advantage that we supposed rational reconstruction to have over straight psychology; namely, the advantage of translational reduction. If all we hope for is a reconstruction that links science to experience in explicit ways short of translation, then it would seem more sensible to settle for psychology. Better to discover how science is in fact developed and learned than to fabricate a fictitious structure to a similar effect.

The empiricist made one major concession when he despaired of deducing the truths of nature from sensory evidence. In despairing now even of translating those truths into terms of observation and logico-mathematical auxiliaries, he makes another major concession. For suppose we hold, with the old empiricist Peirce, that the very meaning of a statement consists in the difference its truth would make to possible experience. Might we not formulate, in a chapter-length sentence in observational language, all the difference that the truth of a given statement might make to experience, and might we not then take all this as the translation? Even if the difference that the truth of the statement would make to experience ramifies indefinitely, we might still hope to embrace it all in the logical implications of our chapter-length formulation, just as we can axiomatize an infinity of theorems. In giving up hope of such translation, then, the empiricist is conceding that the empirical meanings of typical statements about the external world are inaccessible and ineffable.

How is this inaccessibility to be explained? Simply on the ground that the experiential implications of a typical statement about bodies are too complex for finite axiomatization, however lengthy? No; I have a different explanation. It is that the typical statement about bodies has no fund of experiential implications it can call its own. A substantial mass of theory, taken together, will commonly have experiential implications; this is how we make verifiable predictions. We may not be able to explain why we arrive at theories which make successful predictions, but we do arrive at such theories.

Sometimes also an experience implied by a the-

ory fails to come off; and then, ideally, we declare the theory false. But the failure falsifies only a block of theory as a whole, a conjunction of many statements. The failure shows that one or more of those statements is false, but it does not show which. The predicted experiences, true and false, are not implied by any one of the component statements of the theory rather than another. The component statements simply do not have empirical meanings, by Peirce's standard, but a sufficiently inclusive portion of theory does. If we can aspire to a sort of *logischer Aufbau der Welt* at all, it must be to one in which the texts slated for translation into observational and logico-mathematical terms are mostly broad theories taken as wholes, rather than just terms or short sentences. The translation of a theory would be a ponderous axiomatization of all the experiential difference that the truth of the theory would make. It would be a queer translation, for it would translate the whole but none of the parts. We might better speak in such a case not of translation but simply of observational evidence for theories; and we may, following Peirce, still fairly call this the empirical meaning of the theories.

These considerations raise a philosophical question even about ordinary unphilosophical translation, such as from English into Arunta or Chinese. For, if the English sentences of a theory have their meaning only together as a body, then we can justify their translation into Arunta only together as a body. There will be no justification for pairing off the component English sentences with component Arunta sentences, except as these correlations make the translation of the theory as a whole come out right. Any translations of the English sentences into Arunta sentences will be as correct as any other, so long as the net empirical implications of the theory as a whole are preserved in translation. But it is to be expected that many different ways of translating the component sentences, essentially different individually, would deliver the same empirical implications for the theory as a whole; deviations in the translation of one component sentence could be compensated for in the translation of another component sentence. Insofar, there can be no ground for saying which of two glaringly unlike translations of individual sentences is right.[3]

For an uncritical mentalist, no such indeterminacy threatens. Every term and every sentence is a label attached to an idea, simple or complex, which is stored in the mind. When on the other hand we take a verification theory of meaning seriously, the indeterminacy would appear to be inescapable. The Vienna Circle espoused a verification theory of meaning but did not take it seriously enough. If we recognize with Peirce that the meaning of a sentence turns purely on what would count as evidence for its truth, and if we recognize with Duhem that theoretical sentences have their evidence not as single sentences but only as larger blocks of theory, then the indeterminacy of translation of theoretical sentences is the natural conclusion. And most sentences, apart from observation sentences, are theoretical. This conclusion, conversely, once it is embraced, seals the fate of any general notion of propositional meaning or, for that matter, state of affairs.

Should the unwelcomeness of the conclusion persuade us to abandon the verification theory of meaning? Certainly not. The sort of meaning that is basic to translation, and to the learning of one's own language, is necessarily empirical meaning and nothing more. A child learns his first words and sentences by hearing and using them in the presence of appropriate stimuli. These must be external stimuli, for they must act both on the child and on the speaker from whom he is learning.[4] Language is socially inculcated and controlled; the inculcation and control turn strictly on the keying of sentences to shared stimulation. Internal factors may vary *ad libitum* without prejudice to communication as long as the keying of language to external stimuli is undisturbed. Surely one has no choice but to be an empiricist so far as one's theory of linguistic meaning is concerned.

What I have said of infant learning applies equally to the linguist's learning of a new language in the field. If the linguist does not lean on related languages for which there are previously accepted translation practices, then obviously he had no data but the concomitances of native utterance and observable stimulus situation. No wonder there is indeterminacy of translation—for of course only a small fraction of our utterances report concurrent external stimulation. Granted, the linguist will end up with unequivocal translations of everything; but only by making many arbitrary choices—arbitrary

even though unconscious—along the way. Arbitrary? By this I mean that different choices could still have made everything come out right that is susceptible in principle to any kind of check.

Let me link up, in a different order, some of the points I have made. The crucial consideration behind my argument for the indeterminacy of translation was that a statement about the world does not always or usually have a separable fund of empirical consequences that it can call its own. That consideration served also to account for the impossibility of an epistemological reduction of the sort where every sentence is equated to a sentence in observational and logico-mathematical terms. And the impossibility of that sort of epistemological reduction dissipated the last advantage that rational reconstruction seemed to have over psychology.

Philosophers have rightly despaired of translating everything into observational and logico-mathematical terms. They have despaired of this even when they have not recognized, as the reason for this irreducibility, that the statements largely do not have their private bundles of empirical consequences. And some philosophers have seen in this irreducibility the bankruptcy of epistemology. Carnap and the other logical positivists of the Vienna Circle had already pressed the term "metaphysics" into pejorative use, as connoting meaninglessness; and the term "epistemology" was next. Wittgenstein and his followers, mainly at Oxford, found a residual philosophical vocation in therapy: in curing philosophers of the delusion that there were epistemological problems.

But I think that at this point it may be more useful to say rather that epistemology still goes on, though in a new setting and a clarified status. Epistemology, or something like it, simply falls into place as a chapter of psychology and hence of natural science. It studies a natural phenomenon, viz., a physical human subject. This human subject is accorded a certain experimentally controlled input— certain patterns of irradiation in assorted frequencies, for instance—and in the fullness of time the subject delivers as output a description of the three-dimensional external world and its history. The relation between the meager input and the torrential output is a relation that we are prompted to study for somewhat the same reasons that always prompted epistemology; namely, in order to see how evidence relates to theory, and in what ways one's theory of nature transcends any available evidence.

Such a study could still include, even, something like the old rational reconstruction, to whatever degree such reconstruction is practicable; for imaginative constructions can afford hints of actual psychological processes, in much the way that mechanical simulations can. But a conspicuous difference between old epistemology and the epistemological enterprise in this new psychological setting is that we can now make free use of empirical psychology.

The old epistemology aspired to contain, in a sense, natural science; it would construct it somehow from sense data. Epistemology in its new setting, conversely, is contained in natural science, as a chapter of psychology. But the old containment remains valid too, in its way. We are studying how the human subject of our study posits bodies and projects his physics from his data, and we appreciate that our position in the world is just like this. Our very epistemological enterprise, therefore, and the psychology wherein it is a component chapter, and the whole of natural science wherein psychology is a component book—all this is our own construction or projection from stimulations like those we were meting out to our epistemological subject. There is thus reciprocal containment, though containment in different senses: epistemology in natural science and natural science in epistemology.

This interplay is reminiscent again of the old threat of circularity, but it is all right now that we have stopped dreaming of deducing science from sense data. We are after an understanding of science as an institution or process in the world, and we do not intend that understanding to be any better than the science which is its object. This attitude is indeed one that Neurath was already urging in Vienna Circle days, with his parable of the mariner who has to rebuild his boat while staying afloat in it.

One effect of seeing epistemology in a psychological setting is that it resolves a stubborn old enigma of epistemological priority. Our retinas are irradiated in two dimensions, yet we see things as three-dimensional without conscious inference. Which is to count as observation—the unconscious two-dimensional rejection or the conscious three-dimensional apprehension? In the old epistemological context the conscious form had priority, for

we were out to justify our knowledge of the external world by rational reconstruction, and that demands awareness. Awareness ceased to be demanded when we gave up trying to justify our knowledge of the external world by rational reconstruction. What to count as observation now can be settled in terms of the stimulation of sensory receptors, let consciousness fall where it may.

The Gestalt psychologists' challenge to sensory atomism, which seemed so relevant to epistemology forty years ago, is likewise deactivated. Regardless of whether sensory atoms or Gestalten are what favor the forefront of our consciousness, it is simply the stimulations of our sensory receptors that are best looked upon as the input to our cognitive mechanism. Old paradoxes about unconscious data and inference, old problems about chains of inference that would have to be completed too quickly—these no longer matter.

In the old anti-psychologistic days the question of epistemological priority was moot. What is epistemologically prior to what? Are Gestalten prior to sensory atoms because they are noticed, or should we favor sensory atoms on some more subtle ground? Now that we are permitted to appeal to physical stimulation, the problem dissolves; A is epistemologically prior to B if A is causally nearer than B to the sensory receptors. Or, what is in some ways better, just talk explicitly in terms of causal proximity to sensory receptors and drop the talk of epistemological priority.

Around 1932 there was debate in the Vienna Circle over what to count as observation sentences, or *Protokollsätze*. One position was that they had the form of reports of sense impressions. Another was that they were statements of an elementary sort about the external world, e.g., "A red cube is standing on the table." Another, Neurath's, was that they had the form of reports of relations between percipients and external things: "Otto now sees a red cube on the table." The worst of it was that there seemed to be no objective way of settling the matter: no way of making real sense of the question.

Let us now try to view the matter unreservedly in the context of the external world. Vaguely speaking, what we want of observation sentences is that they be the ones in closest causal proximity to the sensory receptors. But how is such proximity to be gauged? The idea may be rephrased this way: observation sentences are sentences which, as we learn language, are most strongly conditioned to concurrent sensory stimulation rather than to stored collateral information. Thus let us imagine a sentence queried for our verdict as to whether it is true or false, queried for our assent or dissent. Then the sentence is an observation sentence if our verdict depends only on the sensory stimulation present at the time.

But a verdict cannot depend on present stimulation to the exclusion of stored information. The very fact of our having learned the language evinces much storing of information, and of information without which we should be in no position to give verdicts on sentences however observational. Evidently then we must relax our definition of observation sentence to read thus: a sentence is an observation sentence if all verdicts on it depend on present sensory stimulation and on no stored information beyond what goes into understanding the sentence.

This formulation raises another problem: how are we to distinguish between information that goes into understanding a sentence and information that goes beyond? This is the problem of distinguishing between analytic truth, which issues from the mere meanings of words, and synthetic truth, which depends on more than meanings. Now I have long maintained that this distinction is illusory. There is one step toward such a distinction, however, which does make sense: a sentence that is true by mere meanings of words should be expected, at least if it is simple, to be subscribed to by all fluent speakers in the community. Perhaps the controversial notion of analyticity can be dispensed with, in our definition of observation sentence, in favor of this straightforward attribute of community-wide acceptance.

This attribute is of course no explication of analyticity. The community would agree that there have been black dogs, yet none who talk of analyticity would call this analytic. My rejection of the analyticity notion just means drawing no line between what goes into the mere understanding of the sentences of a language and what else the community sees eye-to-eye on. I doubt that an objective distinction can be made between meaning and such collateral information as is community-wide.

Turning back then to our task of defining observation sentences, we get this: an observation sentence is one on which all speakers of the language give the same verdict when given the same concurrent stimulation. To put the point negatively, an observation sentence is one that is not sensitive to differences in past experience within the speech community.

This formulation accords perfectly with the traditional role of the observation sentence as the court of appeal of scientific theories. For by our definition the observation sentences are the sentences on which all members of the community will agree under uniform stimulation. And what is the criterion of membership in the same community? Simply, general fluency of dialogue. This criterion admits of degrees, and indeed we may usefully take the community more narrowly for some studies than for others. What count as observation sentences for a community of specialists would not always so count for a larger community.

There is generally no subjectivity in the phrasing of observation sentences, as we are now conceiving them; they will usually be about bodies. Since the distinguishing trait of an observation sentence is intersubjective agreement under agreeing stimulation, a corporeal subject matter is likelier than not.

The old tendency to associate observation sentences with a subjective sensory subject matter is rather an irony when we reflect that observation sentences are also meant to be the intersubjective tribunal of scientific hypotheses. The old tendency was due to the drive to base science on something firmer and prior in the subject's experience; but we dropped that project.

The dislodging of epistemology from its old status of first philosophy loosed a wave, we saw, of epistemological nihilism. This mood is reflected somewhat in the tendency of Polányi, Kuhn, and the late Russell Hanson to belittle the role of evidence and to accentuate cultural relativism. Hanson ventured even to discredit the idea of observation, arguing that so-called observations vary from observer to observer with the amount of knowledge that the observers bring with them. The veteran physicist looks at some apparatus and sees an x-ray tube. The neophyte, looking at the same place, observes rather "a glass and metal instrument replete with wires, reflectors, screws, lamps, and pushbuttons." One man's observation is another man's closed book or flight of fancy. The notion of observation as the impartial and objective source of evidence for science is bankrupt. Now my answer to the x-ray example was already hinted a little while back: what counts as an observation sentence varies with the width of community considered. But we can also always get an absolute standard by taking in all speakers of the language, or most. It is ironical that philosophers, finding the old epistemology untenable as a whole, should react by repudiating a part which has only now moved into clear focus.

Clarification of the notion of observation sentence is a good thing, for the notion is fundamental in two connections. These two correspond to the duality that I remarked upon early in this essay: the duality between concept and doctrine, between knowing what a sentence means and knowing whether it is true. The observation sentence is basic to both enterprises. Its relation to doctrine, to our knowledge of what is true, is very much the traditional one: observation sentences are the repository of evidence for scientific hypotheses. Its relation to meaning is fundamental too, since observation sentences are the ones we are in a position to learn to understand first, both as children and as field linguists. For observation sentences are precisely the ones that we can correlate with observable circumstances of the occasion of utterance or assent, independently of variations in the past histories of individual informants. They afford the only entry to a language.

The observation sentence is the cornerstone of semantics. For it is, as we just saw, fundamental to the learning of meaning. Also, it is where meaning is firmest. Sentences higher up in theories have no empirical consequences they can call their own; they confront the tribunal of sensory evidence only in more or less inclusive aggregates. The observation sentence, situated at the sensory periphery of the body scientific, is the minimal verifiable aggregate; it has an empirical content all its own and wears it on its sleeve.

The predicament of the indeterminacy of translation has little bearing on observation sentences. The equating of an observation sentence of our language to an observation sentence of another language is mostly a matter of empirical generalization; it is a matter of identity between the range of stimulations that would prompt assent to the one sentence and the range of stimulations that would prompt assent to the other.

It is no shock to the preconceptions of old Vienna to say that epistemology now becomes semantics. For epistemology remains centered as always on evidence, and meaning remains centered as always on verification; and evidence is verification. What is likelier to shock preconceptions is that meaning, once we get beyond observation sentences, ceases in general to have any clear applicability to single sentences; also that epistemology merges with psychology, as well as with linguistics.

This rubbing out of boundaries could contribute to progress, it seems to me, in philosophically interesting inquiries of a scientific nature. One possible area is perceptual norms. Consider, to begin with, the linguistic phenomenon of phonemes. We form the habit, in hearing the myriad variations of spoken sounds, of treating each as an approximation to one or another of a limited number of norms—around thirty altogether—constituting so to speak a spoken alphabet. All speech in our language can be treated in practice as sequences of just those thirty elements, thus rectifying small deviations. Now outside the realm of language also there is probably only a rather limited alphabet of perceptual norms altogether, toward which we tend unconsciously to rectify all perceptions. These, if experimentally identified, could be taken as epistemological building blocks, the working elements of experience. They might prove in part to be culturally variable, as phonemes are, and in part universal.

Again there is the area that the psychologist Donald T. Campbell calls evolutionary epistemology. In this area there is work by Hüseyin Yilmaz, who shows how some structural traits of color perception could have been predicted from survival value. And a more emphatically epistemological topic that evolution helps to clarify is induction, now that we are allowing epistemology the resources of natural science.

Notes

[1] A. B. Johnson, *A Treatise on Language* (New York, 1836; Berkeley, 1947).

[2] Carnap, *Philosophy of Science* 3 (1936): 419–71; 4 (1937): 1–40.

[3] See Quine, *Ontological Relativity* (New York, 1969), pp. 2ff.

[4] See ibid., p. 28.

VI.4 *What Is "Naturalized Epistemology"?*

Jaegwon Kim

Jaegwon Kim is Professor of Philosophy at Brown University. In this essay Kim defends the traditional view that epistemology is centered in the notion of justification and, as such, it is primarily normative. Attempts such as Quine's to reduce it to psychology are misguided, for if we eliminate the normative component, justification, from epistemology, we eliminate knowledge, because our concept of knowledge is inseparably tied to that of justification. At the core of Kim's critique is the argument that the notion of rationality that Quine's analysis depends on is a normative one and that we cannot help but evaluate our beliefs in relation to our notion of rationality. Finally, Kim argues that just as the notion of supervenience of value on fact helps clarify the way normativity functions in ethics, so it does in epistemology also.

1. *Epistemology As a Normative Inquiry*

Descartes' epistemological inquiry in the *Meditations* begins with this question: What propositions are worthy of belief? In the *First Meditation* Descartes canvasses beliefs of various kinds he had formerly held as true and finds himself forced to conclude that he ought to reject them, that he ought not to accept them as true. We can view Cartesian epistemology as consisting of the following two projects: to identify the criteria by which we ought to regulate acceptance and rejection of beliefs, and to determine what we may be said to know according to those criteria. Descartes' epistemological agenda has been the agenda of Western epistemology to this day. The twin problems of identifying criteria of justified belief and coming to terms with the skeptical challenge to the possibility of knowledge have defined the central tasks of theory of knowledge since Descartes. This was as true of the empiricists, of Locke and Hume and Mill, as of those who more closely followed Descartes in the rationalist path.[1]

It is no wonder then that modern epistemology has been dominated by a single concept, that of *justification,* and two fundamental questions involving it: What conditions must a belief meet if we are justified in accepting it as true? and What beliefs are we in fact justified in accepting? Note that the first question does not ask for an "analysis" or "meaning" of the term "justified belief". And it is generally assumed, even if not always explicitly stated, that not just any statement of a necessary and sufficient condition for a belief to be justified will do. The implicit requirement has been that the stated conditions must constitute "criteria" of justified belief, and for this it is necessary that the conditions be stated *without the use of epistemic terms.* Thus, formulating conditions of justified belief in such terms as "adequate evidence", "sufficient ground", "good reason", "beyond a reasonable doubt", and so on, would be merely to issue a promissory note redeemable only when these epistemic terms are themselves explained in a way that accords with the requirement.[2]

This requirement, while it points in the right direction, does not go far enough. What is crucial is this: *the criteria of justified belief must be formulated*

Reprinted from *Philosophical Perspectives: Epistemology* (Atascadero, CA: Ridgeview Publishing Company, 1988) by permission. Footnotes have been edited.

on the basis of descriptive or naturalistic terms alone, without the use of any evaluative or normative ones, whether epistemic or of another kind.[3] Thus, an analysis of justified belief that makes use of such terms as "intellectual requirement"[4] and "having a right to be sure"[5] would not satisfy this generalized condition; although such an analysis can be informative and enlightening about the inter-relationships of these normative concepts, it will not, on the present conception, count as a statement of *criteria* of justified belief, unless of course these terms are themselves provided with nonnormative criteria. What is problematic, therefore, about the use of epistemic terms in stating criteria of justified belief is not its possible circularity in the usual sense; rather it is the fact that these epistemic terms are themselves essentially normative. We shall later discuss the rationale of this strengthened requirement.

As many philosophers have observed,[6] the two questions we have set forth, one about the criteria of justified belief and the other about what we can be said to know according to those criteria, constrain each other. Although some philosophers have been willing to swallow skepticism just because what we regard as correct criteria of justified belief are seen to lead inexorably to the conclusion that none, or very few, of our beliefs are justified, the usual presumption is that our answer to the first question should leave our epistemic situation largely unchanged. That is to say, it is expected to turn out that according to the criteria of justified belief we come to accept, we know, or are justified in believing, pretty much what we reflectively think we know or are entitled to believe.

Whatever the exact history, it is evident that the concept of justification has come to take center stage in our reflections on the nature of knowledge. And apart from history, there is a simple reason for our preoccupation with justification: it is the only specifically epistemic component in the classic tripartite conception of knowledge. Neither belief nor truth is a specifically epistemic notion: belief is a psychological concept and truth a semantical-metaphysical one. These concepts may have an implicit epistemological dimension, but if they do, it is likely to be through their involvement with essentially normative epistemic notions like justification, evidence, and rationality. Moreover, justification is

what makes knowledge itself a normative concept. On surface at least, neither truth nor belief is normative or evaluative (I shall argue below, though, that belief does have an essential normative dimension). But justification manifestly is normative. If a belief is justified for us, then it is *permissible* and *reasonable,* from the epistemic point of view, for us to hold it, and it would be *epistemically irresponsible* to hold beliefs that contradict it. If we consider believing or accepting a proposition to be an "action" in an appropriate sense, belief justification would then be a special case of justification of action, which in its broadest terms is the central concern of normative ethics. Just as it is the business of normative ethics to delineate the conditions under which acts and decisions are justified from the moral point of view, so it is the business of epistemology to identify and analyze the conditions under which beliefs, and perhaps other propositional attitudes, are justified from the epistemological point of view. It probably is only an historical accident that we standardly speak of "normative ethics" but not of "normative epistemology". Epistemology is a normative discipline as much as, and in the same sense as, normative ethics.

We can summarize our discussion thus far in the following points: that justification is a central concept of our epistemological tradition, that justification, as it is understood in this tradition, is a normative concept, and in consequence that epistemology itself is a normative inquiry whose principal aim is a systematic study of the conditions of justified belief. I take it that these points are uncontroversial, although of course there could be disagreement about the details—for example, about what it means to say a concept or theory is "normative" or "evaluative".

2. *The Foundationalist Strategy*

In order to identify the target of the naturalistic critique—in particular, Quine's—it will be useful to take a brief look at the classic response to the epistemological program set forth by Descartes. Descartes' approach to the problem of justification is a familiar story, at least as the textbook tells it: it takes the form of what is now commonly called "foundationalism". The foundationalist strategy is to divide the task of explaining justification into two stages: first, to identify a set of beliefs that are "directly" justified in that they are justified without deriving their justified status from that of any other belief, and then to explain how other beliefs may be "indirectly" or "inferentially" justified by standing in an appropriate relation to those already justified. Directly justified beliefs, or "basic beliefs", are to constitute the foundation upon which the superstructure of "nonbasic" or "derived" beliefs is to rest. What beliefs then are directly justified, according to Descartes? Subtleties aside, he claimed that beliefs about our own present conscious states are among them. In what does their justification consist? What is it about these beliefs that make them directly justified? Somewhat simplistically again, Descartes' answer is that they are justified because they are *indubitable,* that the attentive and reflective mind *cannot but assent* to them. How are nonbasic beliefs justified? By "deduction"—that is, by a series of inferential steps, or "intuitions", each of which is indubitable. If, therefore, we take Cartesian indubitability as a psychological notion, Descartes' epistemological theory can be said to meet the desideratum of providing nonepistemic, naturalistic criteria of justified belief.

Descartes' foundationalist program was inherited, in its essential outlines, by the empiricists. In particular, his "mentalism", that beliefs about one's own current mental state are epistemologically basic, went essentially unchallenged by the empiricists and positivists, until this century. Epistemologists have differed from one another chiefly in regard to two questions: first, what else belonged in our corpus of basic beliefs, and second, how the derivation of the nonbasic part of our knowledge was to proceed. Even the Logical Positivists were, by and large, foundationalists, although some of them came to renounce Cartesian mentalism in favor of a "physicalist basis". In fact, the Positivists were foundationalists twice over: for them "observation", whether phenomenological or physical, served not only as the foundation of knowledge but as the foundation of all "cognitive meaning"—that is, as both an epistemological and a semantic foundation.

3. *Quine's Arguments*

It has become customary for epistemologists who profess allegiance to a "naturalistic" conception of knowledge to pay homage to Quine as the chief contemporary provenance of their inspiration—especially to his influential paper "Epistemology Naturalized". [Reading VI.3 in this book.—Ed.] Quine's principal argument in this paper against traditional epistemology is based on the claim that the Cartesian foundationalist program has failed—that the Cartesian "quest for certainty" is "a lost cause". While this claim about the hopelessness of the Cartesian "quest for certainty" is nothing new, using it to discredit the very conception of normative epistemology is new, something that any serious student of epistemology must contend with.

Quine divides the classic epistemological program into two parts: *conceptual reduction* whereby physical terms, including those of theoretical science, are reduced, via definition, to terms referring to phenomenal features of sensory experience, and *doctrinal reduction* whereby truths about the physical world are appropriately obtained from truths about sensory experience. The "appropriateness" just alluded to refers to the requirement that the favored epistemic status ("certainty" for classic epistemologists, according to Quine) of our basic beliefs be transferred, essentially undiminished, to derived beliefs, a necessary requirement if the derivational process is to yield knowledge from knowledge. What derivational methods have this property of preserving epistemic status? Perhaps there are none, given our proneness to err in framing derivations as in anything else, not to mention the possibility of lapses of attention and memory in following lengthy proofs. But logical deduction comes as close to being one as any; it can at least be relied on to transmit truth, if not epistemic status. It could perhaps be argued that no method can preserve certainty unless it preserves (or is known to preserve) truth; and if this is so, logical deduction is the only method worth considering. I do not know whether this was the attitude of most classic epistemologists; but Quine assumes that if deduction doesn't fill their bill, nothing will.

Quine sees the project of conceptual reduction as culminating in Carnap's *Der Logische Aufbau der*

Welt. As Quine sees it, Carnap "came nearest to executing" the conceptual half of the classic episte-mological project. But coming close is not good enough. Because of the holistic manner in which empirical meaning is generated by experience, no reduction of the sort Carnap and others so eagerly sought could in principle be completed. For defini-tional reduction requires point-to-point meaning relations between physical terms and phenomenal terms, something that Quine's holism tells us can-not be had. The second half of the program, doc-trinal reduction, is in no better shape; in fact, it was the one to stumble first, for, according to Quine, its impossibility was decisively demonstrated long be-fore the *Aufbau,* by Hume in his celebrated discus-sion of induction. The "Humean predicament" shows that theory cannot be logically deduced from observation; there simply is no way of deriving theory from observation that will transmit the lat-ter's epistemic status intact to the former.

I don't think anyone wants to disagree with Quine in these claims. It is not possible to "validate" science on the basis of sensory experience, if "vali-dation" means justification through logical deduc-tion. Quine of course does not deny that our theories depend on observation for evidential support; he has said that sensory evidence is the only evidence there is. To be sure, Quine's argument against the possibility of conceptual reduction has a new twist: the application of his "holism". But his conclusion is no surprise; "translational phenomenalism" has been moribund for many years. And, as Quine him-self notes, his argument against the doctrinal reduc-tion, the "quest for certainty", is only a restatement of Hume's "skeptical" conclusions concerning in-duction: induction after all is not deduction. Most of us are inclined, I think, to view the situation Quine describes with no great alarm, and I rather doubt that these conclusions of Quine's came as news to most epistemologists when "Epistemology Naturalized" was first published. We are tempted to respond: of course we can't define physical concepts in terms of sense-data; of course observation "un-derdetermines" theory. That is why observation is observation and not theory.

So it is agreed on all hands that the classical epistemological project, conceived as one of deduc-tively validating physical knowledge from indubita-ble sensory data, cannot succeed. But what is the moral of this failure? What should be its philosophi-cal lesson to us? Having noted the failure of the Cartesian program, Quine goes on.

> The stimulation of his sensory receptors is all the evidence anybody has had to go on, ultimately, in arriving at his picture of the world. Why not just see how this construction really proceeds? Why not settle for psychology? Such a surrender of the epistemological burden to psychology is a move that was disallowed in earlier times as circular reasoning. If the epistemologist's goal is validation of the grounds of empirical science, he defeats his purpose by using psychology or other empirical science in the validation. However, such scruples against circularity have little point once we have stopped dreaming of deducing science from observation. If we are out simply to understand the link between observation and science, we are well advised to use any available information, including that provided by the very science whose link with observation we are seeking to understand. [p. 75—Ed.]

And Quine has the following to say about the fail-ure of Carnap's reductive program in the *Aufbau:*

> To relax the demand for definition, and settle for a kind of reduction that does not eliminate, is to renounce the last remaining advantage that we supposed rational reconstruction to have over straight psychology; namely, the advantage of translational reduction. If all we hope for is a reconstruction that links science to experience in explicit ways short of translation, then it would seem more sensible to settle for psychology. Better to discover how science is in fact developed and learned than to fabricate a fictitious structure to a similar effect.

If a task is entirely hopeless, if we know it cannot be executed, no doubt it is rational to abandon it; we would be better off doing something else that has some hope of success. We can agree with Quine that the "validation"—that is, logical deduction—of sci-ence on the basis of observation cannot be had; so it is rational to abandon this particular epistemological program, if indeed it ever was a program that anyone seriously undertook. But Quine's recommendations go further. In particular, there are two aspects of Quine's proposals that are of special interest to us: first, he is not only advising us to quit the program of "validating science", but urging us to take up another specific project, an empirical psychological study of our cognitive processes; second, he is also claiming that this new program replaces the old, that both programs are part of something appropriately called "epistemology". Naturalized epistemology is to be a kind of epistemology after all, a "successor subject" to classical epistemology.

How should we react to Quine's urgings? What should be our response? The Cartesian project of validating science starting from the indubitable foundation of first-person psychological reports (perhaps with the help of certain indubitable first principles) is not the whole of classical epistemology—or so it would seem at first blush. In our characterization of classical epistemology, the Cartesian program was seen as one possible response to the problem of epistemic justification, the two-part project of identifying the criteria of epistemic justification and determining what beliefs are in fact justified according to those criteria. In urging "naturalized epistemology" on us, Quine is not suggesting that we give up the Cartesian foundationalist solution and explore others within the same framework—perhaps, to adopt some sort of "coherentist" strategy, or to require of our basic beliefs only some degree of "initial credibility" rather than Cartesian certainty, or to permit some sort of probabilistic derivation in addition to deductive derivation of nonbasic knowledge, or to consider the use of special rules of evidence, like Chisholm's "principles of evidence", or to give up the search for a derivational process that transmits undiminished certainty in favor of one that can transmit diminished but still useful degrees of justification. Quine's proposal is more radical than that. He is asking us to set aside the entire framework of justification-centered epistemology. That is what is new in Quine's proposals. Quine is asking us to put in its place a purely descriptive, causal-nomological science of human cognition.

How should we characterize in general terms the difference between traditional epistemological programs, such as foundationalism and coherence theory, on the one hand and Quine's program of naturalized epistemology on the other? Quine's stress is on the *factual* and *descriptive* character of his program; he says, "Why not see how [the construction of theory from observation] *actually proceeds?* Why not settle for psychology?"; again, "Better to *discover how science is in fact developed and learned than* . . ." We are given to understand that in contrast traditional epistemology is not a descriptive, factual inquiry. Rather, it is an attempt at a "validation" or "rational reconstruction" of science. Validation, according to Quine, proceeds via deduction, and rational reconstruction via definition. However, their *point* is justificatory—that is, to rationalize our sundry knowledge claims. So Quine is asking us to set aside what is "rational" in rational reconstruction.

Thus, it is normativity that Quine is asking us to repudiate. Although Quine does not explicitly characterize traditional epistemology as "normative" or "prescriptive", his meaning is unmistakable. Epistemology is to be "a chapter of psychology", a law-based predictive-explanatory theory, like any other theory within empirical science; its principal job is to see how human cognizers develop theories (their "picture of the world") from observation ("the stimulation of their sensory receptors"). Epistemology is to go out of the business of justification. We earlier characterized traditional epistemology as essentially normative; we see why Quine wants us to reject it. Quine is urging us to replace a normative theory of cognition with a descriptive science.

---

4. *Losing Knowledge from Epistemology*

If justification drops out of epistemology, knowledge itself drops out of epistemology. For our concept of knowledge is inseparably tied to that of justification. As earlier noted, knowledge itself is a normative notion. Quine's nonnormative, naturalized epistemology has no room for our concept of knowledge. It is not surprising that, in describing naturalized epistemology, Quine seldom talks about knowledge; instead, he talks about "science" and "theories" and "representations". Quine would have us investigate how sensory stimulation "leads" to "theories" and "representation" of the world. I take it that within the traditional scheme these "theories" and "representations" correspond to beliefs, or systems of beliefs; thus, what Quine would have us do is to investigate how sensory stimulation leads to the formation of beliefs about the world.

But in what sense of "lead"? I take it that Quine has in mind a causal or nomological sense. He is urging us to develop a theory, an empirical theory, that uncovers lawful regularities governing the processes through which organisms come to develop beliefs about their environment as a causal result of having their sensory receptors stimulated in certain ways. Quine says:

> [Naturalized epistemology] studies a natural phenomenon, viz., a physical human subject. This human subject is accorded experimentally controlled input—certain patterns of irradiation in assorted frequencies, for instance—and in the fullness of time the subject delivers as output a description of the three-dimensional external world and its history. *The relation between the meager input and torrential output* is a relation that we are prompted to study for somewhat the same reasons that always prompted epistemology; namely, in order to see *how evidence relates to theory,* and in what ways one's theory of nature transcends any available evidence. [p. 83–Ed.]

The relation Quine speaks of between "meager input" and "torrential output" is a causal relation; at least it is qua causal relation that the naturalized epistemologist investigates it. It is none of the naturalized epistemologist's business to assess whether, and to what degree, the input "justifies" the output, how a given irradiation of the subject's retinas makes it "reasonable" or "rational" for the subject to emit certain representational output. His interest is strictly causal and nomological: he wants us to look for patterns of lawlike dependencies characterizing the input-output relations for this particular organism and others of a like physical structure.

If this is right, it makes Quine's attempt to relate his naturalized epistemology to traditional epistemology look at best lame. For in what sense is the study of causal relationships between physical stimulation of sensory receptors and the resulting cognitive output a way of "seeing how evidence relates to theory" in an epistemologically relevant sense? The causal relation between sensory input and cognitive output is a relation between "evidence" and "theory"; however, it is not an *evidential relation*. This can be seen from the following consideration: the nomological patterns that Quine urges us to look for are certain to vary from species to species, depending on the particular way each biological (and possibly nonbiological) species processes information, but the evidential relation in its proper normative sense must abstract from such factors and concern itself only with the degree to which evidence supports hypothesis.

In any event, the concept of evidence is inseparable from that of justification. When we talk of "evidence" in an epistemological sense we are talking about justification: one thing is "evidence" for another just in case the first tends to enhance the reasonableness or justification of the second. And such evidential relations hold in part because of the "contents" of the items involved, not merely because of the causal or nomological connections between them. A strictly nonnormative concept of evidence is not our concept of evidence; it is something that we do not understand.

None of us, I think, would want to quarrel with Quine about the interest or importance of the psychological study of how our sensory input causes our epistemic output. This is only to say that the study of human (or other kinds of) cognition is of interest. That isn't our difficulty; our difficulty is whether, and in what sense, pursuing Quine's "epistemology" is a way of doing epistemology—that is, a way of studying "how evidence relates to theory". Perhaps, Quine's recommendation that we discard justification-centered epistemology is worth pondering; and his exhortation to take up the study of psychology perhaps deserves to be heeded also. What is mysterious is why this recommendation has to be coupled with the rejection of normative epistemology (if normative epistemology is not a possible inquiry, why shouldn't the would-be epistemologist turn to, say, hydrodynamics or ornithology rather than psychology?). But of course Quine is saying more; he is saying that an understandable, if misguided, motivation (that is, seeing "how evidence relates to theory") does underlie our proclivities for indulgence in normative epistemology, but that we would be better served by a scientific study of human cognition than normative epistemology.

But it is difficult to see how an "epistemology" that has been purged of normativity, one that lacks an appropriate normative concept of justification or evidence, can have anything to do with the concerns of traditional epistemology. And unless naturalized epistemology and classical epistemology share some of their central concerns, it's difficult to see how one could *replace* the other, or be a way (a better way) of doing the other. To be sure, they both investigate "how evidence relates to theory". But putting the matter this way can be misleading, and has perhaps misled Quine: the two disciplines do not investigate the same relation. As lately noted, normative epistemology is concerned with the evidential relation properly so-called—that is, the relation of justification—and Quine's naturalized epistemology is meant to study the causal-nomological relation. For epistemology to go out of the business of justification is for it to go out of business.

5. *Belief Attribution and Rationality*

Perhaps we have said enough to persuade ourselves that Quine's naturalized epistemology, while it may be a legitimate scientific inquiry, is not a kind of epistemology, and, therefore, that the question whether it is a better kind of epistemology cannot arise. In reply, however, it might be said that there was a sense in which Quine's epistemology and traditional epistemology could be viewed as sharing a common subject matter, namely this: they both concern beliefs or "representations". The only difference is that the former investigates their causal histories and connections whereas the latter is concerned with their evidential or justificatory properties and relations. This difference, if Quine is right, leads to another (so continues the reply): the former is a feasible inquiry, the latter is not.

I now want to take my argument a step further:

I shall argue that the concept of belief is itself an essentially normative one, and in consequence that if normativity is wholly excluded from naturalized epistemology it cannot even be thought of as being about beliefs. That is, if naturalized epistemology is to be a science of beliefs properly so called, it must presuppose a normative concept of belief.

Briefly, the argument is this. In order to implement Quine's program of naturalized epistemology, we shall need to identify, and individuate, the input and output of cognizers. The input, for Quine, consists of physical events ("the stimulation of sensory receptors") and the output is said to be a "theory" or "picture of the world"—that is, a set of "representations" of the cognizer's environment. Let us focus on the output. In order to study the sensory input-cognitive output relations for the given cognizer, therefore, we must find out what "representations" he has formed as a result of the particular stimulations that have been applied to his sensory transducers. Setting aside the jargon, what we need to be able to do is to attribute *beliefs,* and other contentful intentional states, to the cognizer. But belief attribution ultimately requires a "radical interpretation" of the cognizer, of his speech and intentional states; that is, we must construct an "interpretive theory" that simultaneously assigns meanings to his utterances and attributes to him beliefs and other propositional attitudes.

Even a cursory consideration indicates that such an interpretation cannot begin—we cannot get a foothold in our subject's realm of meanings and intentional states—unless we assume his total system of beliefs and other propositional attitudes to be largely and essentially rational and coherent. As Davidson has emphasized, a given belief has the content it has in part because of its location in a network of other beliefs and propositional attitudes; and what at bottom grounds this network is the evidential relation, a relation that regulates what is reasonable to believe given other beliefs one holds. That is, unless our cognizer is a "rational being", a being whose cognitive "output" is regulated and constrained by norms of rationality—typically, these norms holistically constrain his propositional attitudes in virtue of their contents—we cannot intelligibly interpret his "output" as consisting of beliefs. Conversely, if we are unable to interpret our subject's meanings and propositional attitudes in a way that satisfies a minimal standard of rationality, there is little reason to regard him as a "cognizer", a being that forms representations and constructs theories. This means that there is a sense of "rational" in which the expression "rational belief" is redundant; every belief must be rational in certain minimal ways. It is not important for the purposes of the present argument what these minimal standards of rationality are; the only point that matters is that unless the output of our cognizer is subject to evaluation in accordance with norms of rationality, that output cannot be considered as consisting of beliefs and hence cannot be the object of an epistemological inquiry, whether plain or naturalized.

We can separate the core of these considerations from controversial issues involving the so-called "principle of charity", minimal rationality, and other matters in the theory of radical interpretation. What is crucial is this: for the interpretation and attribution of beliefs to be possible, not only must we assume the overall rationality of cognizers, but also we must continually evaluate and re-evaluate the putative beliefs of a cognizer in their evidential relationship to one another and other propositional attitudes. It is not merely that belief attribution requires the umbrella assumption about the overall rationality of cognizers. Rather, the point is that *belief attribution requires belief evaluation,* in accordance with normative standards of evidence and justification. If this is correct, rationality in its broad and fundamental sense is not an optional property of beliefs, a virtue that some beliefs may enjoy and others lack; it is a precondition of the attribution and individuation of belief—that is, a property without which the concept of belief would be unintelligible and pointless.

Two objections might be raised to counter these considerations. First, one might argue that at best they show only that the normativity of belief is an epistemological assumption—that we need to assume the rationality and coherence of belief systems when we are trying to *find out* what beliefs to attribute to a cognizer. It does not follow from this epistemological point, the objection continues, that the concept of belief is itself normative. In replying to this objection, we can by-pass the entire issue of whether the rationality assumption concerns only the epistemology of belief attribution. Even if this premise (which I think is incorrect) is granted, the point has already been made. For it is an essential part of the business of naturalized epistemology, as a theory of how beliefs are formed as a result of sensory stimulation, to *find out* what particular beliefs the given cognizers have formed. But this is precisely what cannot be done, if our considerations show anything at all, unless the would-be naturalized epistemologist continually evaluates the putative beliefs of his subjects in regard to their rationality and coherence, subject to the overall constraint of the assumption that the cognizers are largely rational. The naturalized epistemologist cannot dispense with normative concepts or disengage himself from valuational activities.

Second, it might be thought that we could simply avoid these considerations stemming from belief attribution by refusing to think of cognitive output as consisting of "beliefs", namely as states having propositional contents. The "representations" Quine speaks of should be taken as appropriate neural states, and this means that all we need is to be able to discern neural states of organisms. This requires only neurophysiology and the like, not the normative theory of rational belief. My reply takes the form of a dilemma: either the "appropriate" neural states are identified by seeing how they correlate with beliefs, in which case we still need to contend with the problem of radical interpretation, or beliefs are entirely by-passed. In the latter case, belief, along with justification, drops out of Quinean epistemology, and it is unclear in what sense we are left with an inquiry that has anything to do with knowledge.

6. The "Psychologistic" Approach to Epistemology

Many philosophers now working in theory of knowledge have stressed the importance of systematic psychology to philosophical epistemology. Reasons proffered for this are various, and so are the conceptions of the proper relationship between psychology and epistemology. But they are virtually unanimous in their rejection of what they take to be the epistemological tradition of Descartes and its modern embodiments in philosophers like Russell, C. I. Lewis, Roderick Chisholm, and A. J. Ayer; and they are united in their endorsement of the naturalistic approach of Quine we have been considering. Traditional epistemology is often condemned as "aprioristic", and as having lost sight of human knowledge as a product of natural causal processes and its function in the survival of the organism and the species. Sometimes, the adherents of the traditional approach are taken to task for their implicit antiscientific bias or indifference to the new developments in psychology and related disciplines. Their own approach in contrast is hailed as "naturalistic" and "scientific", better attuned to significant advances in the relevant scientific fields such as "cognitive science" and "neuroscience", promising philosophical returns far richer than what the aprioristic method of traditional epistemology has been able to deliver. We shall here briefly consider how this new naturalism in epistemology is to be understood in relation to the classic epistemological program and Quine's naturalized epistemology.

Let us see how one articulate proponent of the new approach explains the distinctiveness of his position vis-à-vis that of the traditional epistemologists. According to Philip Kitcher, the approach he rejects is characterized by an "apsychologistic" attitude that takes the difference between knowledge and true belief—that is, justification—to consist in "ways which are independent of the causal antecedents of a subject's states". Kitcher writes.

> . . . we can present the heart of [the apsychologistic approach] by considering the way in which it would tackle the question of whether a person's true belief that *p* counts as knowledge that *p*. The idea would be to disregard the psychological life of the subject, looking just at the various propositions she believes. If *p* is 'connected in the right way' to other propositions which are believed, then we count the subject as knowing that *p*. Of course, apsychologistic epistemology will have to supply a criterion for propositions to be 'connected in the right way' . . . but proponents of this view of knowledge will emphasize that the criterion is to be given in *logical* terms. We are concerned with logical

relations among propositions, not with psychological relations among mental states.

On the other hand, the psychologistic approach considers the crucial difference between knowledge and true belief—that is, epistemic justification—to turn on "the factors which produced the belief", focusing on "processes which produce belief, processes which will always contain, at their latter end, psychological events".

It is not entirely clear from this characterization whether a psychologistic theory of justification is to be *prohibited* from making *any* reference to logical relations among belief contents (it is difficult to believe how a theory of justification respecting such a blanket prohibition could succeed); nor is it clear whether, conversely, an apsychologistic theory will be permitted to refer at all to beliefs qua psychological states, or exactly what it is for a theory to do so. But such points of detail are unimportant here; it is clear enough, for example, that Goldman's proposal to explicate justified belief as belief generated by a reliable belief-forming process nicely fits Kitcher's characterization of the psychologistic approach. This account, one form of the so-called "reliability theory" of justification, probably was what Kitcher had in mind when he was formulating his general characterization of epistemological naturalism. However, another influential form of the reliability theory does not qualify under Kitcher's characterization. This is Armstrong's proposal to explain the difference between knowledge and true belief, at least for noninferential knowledge, in terms of "a *law-like* connection between the state of affairs [of a subject's believing that *p*] and the state of affairs that makes '*p*' true such that, given the state of affairs [of the subject's believing that *p*], it must be the case that *p*." There is here no reference to the causal *antecedents* of beliefs, something that Kitcher requires of apsychologistic theories.

Perhaps, Kitcher's preliminary characterization needs to be broadened and sharpened. However, a salient characteristic of the naturalistic approach has already emerged, which we can put as follows: justification is to be characterized in terms of *causal* or *nomological* connections involving beliefs as *psychological states* or *processes,* and not in terms of the *logical* properties or relations pertaining to the *contents* of these beliefs.

If we understand current epistemological naturalism in this way, how closely is it related to Quine's conception of naturalized epistemology? The answer, I think, is obvious: not very closely at all. In fact, it seems a good deal closer to the Cartesian tradition than to Quine. For, as we saw, the difference that matters between Quine's epistemological program and the traditional program is the former's total renouncement of the latter's normativity, its rejection of epistemology as a normative inquiry. The talk of "replacing" epistemology with psychology is irrelevant and at best misleading, though it could give us a momentary relief from a sense of deprivation. When one abandons justification and other valuational concepts, one abandons the entire framework of normative epistemology. What remains is a descriptive empirical theory of human cognition which, if Quine has his way, will be entirely devoid of the notion of justification or any other evaluative concept.

As I take it, this is not what most advocates of epistemological naturalism are aiming at. By and large they are not Quinean eliminativists in regard to justification, and justification in its full-fledged normative sense continues to play a central role in their epistemological reflections. Where they differ from their nonnaturalist adversaries is the specific way in which criteria of justification are to be formulated. Naturalists and nonnaturalists ("apsychologists") can agree that these criteria must be stated in descriptive terms—that is, without the use of epistemic or any other kind of normative terms. According to Kitcher, an apsychologistic theory of justification would state them primarily in terms of *logical* properties and relations holding for propositional contents of beliefs, whereas the psychologistic approach advocates the exclusive use of *causal* properties and relations holding for beliefs as events or states. Many traditional epistemologists may prefer criteria that confer upon a cognizer a position of special privilege and responsibility with regard to the epistemic status of his beliefs, whereas most self-avowed naturalists prefer "objective" or "externalist" criteria with no such special privileges for the cognizer. But these differences are among those that arise within the familiar normative framework, and are consistent with the exclusion of normative terms in the statement of the criteria of justification.

Normative ethics can serve as a useful model here. To claim that basic ethical terms, like "good" and "right", are *definable* on the basis of descriptive or naturalistic terms is one thing; to insist that it is the business of normative ethics to provide *conditions* or *criteria* for "good" and "right" in descriptive or naturalistic terms is another. One may properly reject the former, the so-called "ethical naturalism", as many moral philosophers have done, and hold the latter; there is no obvious inconsistency here. G. E. Moore is a philosopher who did just that. As is well known, he was a powerful critic of ethical naturalism, holding that goodness is a "simple" and "nonnatural" property. At the same time, he held that a thing's being good "follows" from its possessing certain naturalistic properties. He wrote:

> I should never have thought of suggesting that goodness was 'non-natural', unless I had supposed that it was 'derivative' in the sense that, whenever a thing is good (in the sense in question) its goodness . . . 'depends on the presence of certain non-ethical characteristics' possessed by the thing in question: I have always supposed that it did so 'depend', in the sense that, if a thing is good (in my sense), then that it is so *follows* from the fact that it possesses certain natural intrinsic properties . . .

It makes sense to think of these "natural intrinsic properties" from which a thing's being good is thought to follow as constituting naturalistic criteria of goodness, or at least pointing to the existence of such criteria. One can reject ethical naturalism, the doctrine that ethical concepts are definitionally eliminable in favor of naturalistic terms, and at the same time hold that ethical properties, or the ascription of ethical terms, must be governed by naturalistic criteria. It is clear, then, that we are here using "naturalism" ambiguously in "epistemological naturalism" and "ethical naturalism". In our present usage, epistemological naturalism does not include (nor does it necessarily exclude) the claim that epistemic terms are definitionally reducible to naturalistic terms. (Quine's naturalism is eliminative, though it is not a definitional eliminativism.)

If, therefore, we locate the split between Quine and traditional epistemology at the descriptive vs. normative divide, then currently influential naturalism in epistemology is not likely to fall on Quine's side. On this descriptive vs. normative issue, one can side with Quine in one of two ways: first, one rejects, with Quine, the entire justification-based epistemological program; or second, like ethical naturalists but unlike Quine, one believes that epistemic concepts are naturalistically definable. I doubt that very many epistemological naturalists will embrace either of these alternatives.

7. *Epistemic Supervenience—Or Why Normative Epistemology Is Possible*

But why should we think that there *must be* naturalistic criteria of justified belief and other terms of epistemic appraisal? If we take the discovery and systematization of such criteria to be the central task of normative epistemology, is there any reason to think that this task can be fruitfully pursued, that normative epistemology is a possible field of inquiry? Quine's point is that it is not. We have already noted the limitation of Quine's negative arguments in "Epistemology Naturalized", but is there a positive reason for thinking that normative epistemology is a viable program? One could consider a similar question about the possibility of normative ethics.

I think there is a short and plausible initial answer, although a detailed defense of it would involve complex general issues about norms and values. The short answer is this: we believe in the supervenience of epistemic properties on naturalistic ones, and more generally, in the supervenience of all valuational and normative properties on naturalistic conditions. This comes out in various ways. We think, with R. M. Hare, that if two persons or acts coincide in all descriptive or naturalistic details, they cannot differ in respect of being good or right, or any other valuational aspects. We also think that if something is "good"—a "good car", "good drop shot", "good argument"—then that must be so "in virtue of" its being a "certain way", that is, its having certain "factual properties". Being a good car, say, cannot be a brute and ultimate fact: a car is good *because* it has a certain contextually indicated set of properties having to do with performance, reliability, comfort, styling, economy, etc. The same goes for justified belief: if a belief is justified, that must be so *because* it has certain factual, nonepistemic properties, such as perhaps that it is "indubitable", that it is seen to be entailed by another belief that is independently justified, that it is appropriately caused by perceptual experience, or whatever. That it is a justified belief cannot be a brute fundamental fact unrelated to the kind of belief it is. There must be a *reason* for it, and this reason must be grounded in the factual descriptive properties of that particular belief. Something like this, I think, is what we believe.

Two important themes underlie these convictions: first, values, though perhaps not reducible to facts, must be "consistent" with them in that objects that are indiscernible in regard to fact must be indiscernible in regard to value; second, there must be nonvaluational "reasons" or "grounds" for the attribution of values, and these "reasons" or "grounds" must be *generalizable*—that is, they are covered by *rules* or *norms*. These two ideas correspond to "weak supervenience" and "strong supervenience" that I have discussed elsewhere. Belief in the supervenience of value upon fact, arguably, is fundamental to the very concepts of value and valuation. Any valuational concept, to be significant, must be governed by a set of criteria, and these criteria must ultimately rest on factual characteristics and relationships of objects and events being evaluated. There is something deeply incoherent about the idea of an infinitely descending series of valuational concepts, each depending on the one below it as its criterion of application.

It seems to me, therefore, that epistemological supervenience is what underlies our belief in the possibility of normative epistemology, and that we do not need new inspirations from the sciences to acknowledge the existence of naturalistic criteria for epistemic and other valuational concepts. The case of normative ethics is entirely parallel: belief in the possibility of normative ethics is rooted in the belief that moral properties and relations are supervenient upon nonmoral ones. Unless we are prepared to disown normative ethics as a viable philosophical inquiry, we had better recognize normative epistemology as one, too. We should note, too, that epistemology is likely to parallel normative ethics in regard to the degree to which scientific results are relevant or useful to its development. Saying this of course leaves large room for disagreement concerning how relevant and useful, if at all, empirical psychology of human motivation and action can be to the development and confirmation of normative ethical theories. In any event, once the normativity of epistemology is clearly taken note of, it is no surprise that epistemology and normative ethics share the same metaphilosophical fate. Naturalized epistemology makes no more, and no less, sense than naturalized normative ethics.

Notes

[1] In making these remarks I am only repeating the familiar textbook history of philosophy; however, what *our* textbooks say about the history of a philosophical concept has much to do with *our* understanding of that concept.

[2] Alvin Goldman explicitly states this requirement as a desideratum of his own analysis of justified belief in "What Is Justified Belief?," in George S. Pappas (ed.), *Justification and Knowledge* (Dordrecht: Reidel, 1979), p. 1. Roderick M. Chisholm's definition of "being evident" in his *Theory of Knowledge,* 2nd ed. (Englewood Cliffs, N.J.: Prentice-Hall, 1977) does not satisfy this requirement as it rests ultimately on an unanalyzed epistemic concept of one

belief being *more reasonable than* another. What does the real "criteriological" work for Chisholm is his "principles of evidence." See especially (A) on p. 73 of *Theory of Knowledge,* which can usefully be regarded as an attempt to provide nonnormative, descriptive conditions for certain types of justified beliefs.

[3] The basic idea of this stronger requirement seems implicit in Roderick Firth's notion of "warrant-increasing property" in his "Coherence, Certainty, and Epistemic Priority," *Journal of Philosophy* 61 (1964): 545–57. It seems that William P. Alston has something similar in mind when he says, ". . . like any evaluative property, epistemic justification is a supervenient property, the application of which is based on more fundamental properties" (at this point Alston refers to Firth's paper cited above), in "Two Types of Foundationalism" (*Journal of Philosophy* 73 (1976): 165–85 (the quoted remark occurs on p. 170). Although Alston doesn't further explain what he means by "more fundamental properties," the context makes it plausible to suppose that he has in mind nonnormative, descriptive properties. See Section 7 below for further discussion.

[4] See Chisholm, ibid., p. 14. Here Chisholm refers to a "person's responsibility or duty *qua* intellectual being."

[5] This term was used by A. J. Ayer to characterize the difference between lucky guessing and knowing; see *The Problem of Knowledge* (New York & London: Penguin Books, 1956), p. 33.

[6] Notably by Chisholm in *Theory of Knowledge,* 1st ed., ch. 4.

VI.5 *Epistemic Norms*

JOHN L. POLLOCK

John L. Pollock is Professor of Philosophy at the University of Arizona. In this essay Pollock defends a subjectivist and internalist version of epistemic justification, the very opposite of Goldman's reliabilism, which, as we saw (Reading VI.1), was objectivist and externalist. A belief's justification is a function "exclusively of the internal states of the believer, . . . those states that are directly accessible to the mechanisms in our central nervous system that direct our reasoning," although we need not have conscious beliefs about them. Although one need not be able to give reasons to be justified, one must have direct, nonepistemic access to those internal states. That is, a psychological state must be present that guides our reasoning whether or not we realize it. Pollock rejects the traditional intellectualist model of justification, which says that we must be able to give our reasons for our beliefs before they are justified, and in its place he sets forth a subjective, internal model wherein the norms become internalized and unconscious, as they do in riding a bicycle.

1. *Introduction*

Historically, the main concern in epistemology has been to explain how we are justified in holding the various kinds of beliefs we have about the world. When we ask whether a belief is justified, what we want to know is whether it is all right to believe it. Justification is a matter of "epistemic permissibility". It is not a novel observation that epistemic justification is a normative notion, but by emphasizing the normative character of epistemic justification and downplaying its role in knowledge I hope to avoid some confusions that (I will argue) have plagued recent discussions of epistemic justification. I will think of epistemic justification as being concerned with questions of the form, "When is it permissible (from an epistemological point of view) to believe that *P*?" This is the concept of epistemic justification that I am concerned with exploring.

Reprinted from Synthese **71** (1987) 61–95. © 1987 by D. Reidel Publishing Company by permission. Footnote deleted.

Norms are general descriptions of the circumstances under which various kinds of normative judgments are correct. Epistemic norms are norms describing when it is epistemically permissible to hold various beliefs. A belief is justified if it is licensed by correct epistemic norms. Assuming that what justifies a belief is the reasoning underlying it ("reasoning" construed broadly), epistemic norms are the norms governing "right reasoning". Epistemologists have commonly supposed that epistemic norms are much like moral norms and that they are used in evaluating reasoning in the same way moral norms are used in evaluating actions. One of the main contentions of this paper will be that this parallel is not at all exact and that epistemologists have been misled in important ways by supposing the analogy to be better than it is. A proper understanding of epistemic norms will provide us with a radically new perspective on epistemology, and from the point of view of this perspective new light can be thrown on a number of central epistemological problems.

Perhaps the most fundamental disagreement about epistemic norms is that involved in the internalism/externalism debate. Contemporary epistemologists have divided into two camps. In the one camp we have the traditionally oriented *internalists,* according to whom the justifiedness of a belief is a function exclusively of the internal states of the believer. This means that if one is in the same internal states in two possible circumstances, then no matter how those circumstances differ with respect to things other than one's internal states, there will be no difference in what beliefs are justified under those circumstances. In the other camp we have the *externalists* who maintain that more than the internal states of the believer can be relevant to the justifiedness of his beliefs. The internalism/ externalism distinction is notoriously unclear in one respect. It is formulated in terms of an undefined notion of an internal state. It is fairly clear what kinds of states people have in mind when they talk about internalism and externalism, but it is hard to give a general characterization of these states.

The internalist tries to map out the structure of our epistemic norms entirely in terms of relations between internal states. For example, an internalist may tell us that something's looking red to me gives me a prima facie reason to think that it is red. The internalist alleges that by compiling a list of such epistemic rules he has described our epistemic norms and thus provided an adequate account of epistemic justification. Externalists typically object that such lists of rules leave the concept of justification unexplained and mysterious. The externalist insists instead that the purpose of reasoning is to achieve certain epistemic goals (most notably the acquisition of true beliefs) and hence correct epistemic norms should be those enabling us to achieve these goals. There are two ways external considerations could be brought to bear on epistemic norms, and they have not been clearly distinguished in most recent discussions of externalism. On the one hand, our epistemic norms could be *formulated in terms of* external considerations. A typical example of such a norm might be, "It is permissible to hold a belief if it is generated by a reliable belief-forming process". I will call this variety of externalism *belief externalism.* I contrast to this, *norm externalism* acknowledges that the rules comprising our epistemic norms must be internalist, but employs external considerations in the selection of the norms themselves. The distinction between belief and norm externalism is analogous to the distinc-

tion between act and rule utilitarianism. Externalism (simpliciter) is the disjunction of belief externalism and norm externalism. A number of philosophers who are usually considered externalists appear to vacillate between belief externalism and norm externalism. The difference between these two varieties of externalism will prove important.

Reliabilism is that version of belief externalism that seeks to formulate epistemic norms in terms of considerations of reliability. Reliabilism is the most common variety of belief externalism, but it is important to realize that it is not the only possible variety. Any theory proposing non-internalist norms is a version of belief externalism. Non-internalist norms need not proceed in terms of reliability. Some examples of belief externalists who are not reliabilists will be discussed in section 3.

To my mind the most telling objection to existing internalist theories is that they are simultaneously incomplete and ad hoc. They are incomplete in that they leave the concept of epistemic justification unanalyzed, and they are ad hoc in that they propose arrays of epistemic rules without giving any systematic account of why those should be the right rules. The methodology of internalism has been to describe our reasoning, rather than to justify it or explain it. These two points are connected. As long as we take the concept of epistemic justification to be primitive and unanalyzed, there is no way to *prove* that a particular epistemic rule is a correct rule. All we can do is collect rules that seem intuitively right, but we are left without any way of justifying or supporting our intuitions. Herein lies the main attraction of externalism. Externalist theories begin by proposing analyses of epistemic justification from which epistemic rules can be derived. Epistemic justification is no longer taken as primitive, and there is no longer any need to simply posit epistemic rules. Of course, the success of this approach turns upon whether externalist analyses of epistemic justification can be successful. There is a wide variety of externalist theories, and each is subject to its own difficulties. One cannot, however, do a successful job of refuting generic externalism by refuting individual externalist theories one at a time. Instead, my strategy will be to raise a general difficulty that, I believe, will demonstrate the impossibility of any externalist theory. Confronting this difficulty will ultimately enable us to understand the source of epistemic norms and the nature of epistemic justification, thus resolving what I take to be the primary and most glaring problem for internalism and leading us to a novel "naturalistic" internalism.

2. How Do *Epistemic* Norms Regulate?

In order to get a grasp on the nature of epistemic norms, let us begin by asking their purpose. It is important to distinguish between two uses of norms (epistemic or otherwise). On the one hand, there are third person uses of norms wherein we use the norms to evaluate the behavior of others. Various norms may be appropriate for third person evaluations, depending upon the purpose we have in making the evaluations. For example, we may want to determine whether a person is a good scientist because we are trying to decide whether to hire him. To be contrasted with third person uses of norms are first person uses. First person uses of norms are, roughly speaking, action-guiding. For example, I might appeal to *Fowler's Modern English Usage* to decide whether to use "that" or "which" in a sentence. Epistemological questions are inherently first person. The traditional epistemologist asks, "How is it possible for me to be justified in my beliefs about the external world, about other minds, about the past, etc.?" These are questions about what to believe. Epistemic norms are the norms in terms of which these questions are to be answered, so these norms are used in a first person reason-guiding capacity.

If reasoning is governed by epistemic norms, just how is it governed? There is a model of this regulative process that is often implicit in epistemological thinking, but when we make the model explicit it is *obviously* wrong. This model assimilates the functioning of epistemic norms to the functioning of explicitly articulated norms. For example, naval officers are supposed to "do it by the book", which means that whenever they are in doubt about what to do in a particular situation they are supposed to consult explicit regulations governing all

aspects of their behavior and act accordingly. Explicitly articulated norms are also found in driving manuals, etiquette books, etc. Without giving the matter much thought, there is a tendency to suppose that all norms work this way, and in particular to suppose that this is the way epistemic norms work. I will call this "the intellectualist model". It takes little reflection to realize that epistemic norms cannot function in accordance with the intellectualist model. If we had to make an explicit appeal to epistemic norms in order to acquire justified beliefs we would find ourselves in an infinite regress, because to apply explicitly formulated norms we must first acquire justified beliefs about how they apply to this particular case. For example, if we are to reason by making explicit appeal to a norm telling us that it is permissible to move from the belief that something looks red to us to the belief that it is red, we would first have to become justified in believing that that norm is included among our epistemic norms, and we would have to become justified in believing that we believe that the object looks red to us. In order to become justified in holding those beliefs, we would have to apply other epistemic norms, and so on ad infinitum. Thus it is clear that epistemic norms cannot guide our reasoning in this way.

If the intellectualist model is wrong, then how do epistemic norms govern reasoning? At this point we might raise the possibility that they do not. Perhaps epistemic norms are only of use in third person evaluations. But it cannot really be true that epistemic norms play *no role at all* in first person deliberations. We can certainly subject our reasoning to self-criticism. Every philosopher has detected invalid arguments in his own reasoning. This might suggest that epistemic norms are only relevant in a negative way. Our reasoning is innocent until proven guilty. We can use reasoning to criticize reasoning, and hence we can use reasoning in applying epistemic norms to other reasoning, but we cannot be required to reason about norms *before* we can do any reasoning. This would avoid the infinite regress.

But as theoretically attractive as the "innocent until proven guilty" picture might be, it cannot be right. There are a number of natural processes that lead to belief formation. Among these are such "approved" processes as vision, inductive reasoning, deductive reasoning, memory, etc., and also some "unapproved" but equally natural processes like wishful thinking. The latter is just as natural as the former. For example, a friend of mine recently drove to Albuquerque. The morning she left the weather turned unseasonably cold. As she was leaving we joked about her driving into a snow storm. As it turned out, that is exactly what happened. After she had left and I learned how bad the weather was, it occurred to me to wonder whether she had taken a coat (in fact, she had not). I found myself thinking, "Oh, she must have", and dismissing the matter from my mind. Then I realized that was just wishful thinking. I had no reason to believe she had taken a coat. The point here is that wishful thinking is a natural belief-forming process, but we do not accord it the same status as some other belief-forming processes like vision. Although we have a natural tendency to form beliefs by wishful thinking, we also seem to "naturally" know better. This is not just a matter of after-the-fact criticism. We know better than to indulge in wishful thinking at the very time we do it. It seems that *while* we are reasoning we are being guided by epistemic norms that preclude wishful thinking but permit belief formation based upon perception, induction, etc. This is of more than casual significance, because it might be impossible to rule out wishful thinking by after-the-fact reasoning. This is because the after-the-fact reasoning might include wishful thinking again, and the new wishful thinking could legitimize the earlier wishful thinking. If epistemic norms play no regulative role in our reasoning while it is going on, there is no reason to think they will be able to play a successful corrective role in after-the-fact evaluations of reasoning. In order for the corrective reasoning to be successful it must itself be normatively correct. Epistemic norms must, and apparently do, play a role in guiding our epistemic behavior at the very time it is occurring. But how can they?

Epistemic norms cannot play a merely negative, corrective, role in guiding reasoning, nor can they function in a way that requires us to make judgments before we can make judgments. What is left? I think that our perplexity reflects an inadequate understanding of the way action-guiding norms usually function. The case of making an explicit appeal to norms in order to decide what to do is the exception rather than the rule. You may make reference to a driving manual when you are first learning to drive a car, but once you learn how to drive a car you do not look things up in the manual anymore. You do not usually give any explicit thought to what to do—you just do it. This does not mean, however, that your behavior is no longer being guided by those norms you learned when you first learned to drive. Similarly, when you first learned to ride a bicycle you were told to turn the handlebars to the right when the bicycle leaned right. You learned to ride in accordance with that norm, and that norm still governs your bike riding behavior but you no longer have to think about it. The point here is that *norms can govern your behavior without your having to think about them.* The intellectualist model of the way norms guide behavior is almost always wrong. This is an obvious point, but it has been insufficiently appreciated. It is of major importance in understanding epistemic norms. Reasoning is more like riding a bicycle than being in the navy.

What makes it possible for your bike riding behavior to be governed by norms without your thinking about the norms is that you *know how* to ride a bicycle. Knowing how to ride a bicycle consists of knowing what to do under various circumstances, e.g., knowing to turn right when the bike leans right. Knowing what to do and being aware of it constitutes knowing what you *should* do. Moral philosophers have talked about different senses of "should", distinguishing particularly between moral uses of "should" and goal directed uses of "should". An example of the latter is "If you want the knife to be sharp then you should sharpen it on the whetstone". But the use of "should" in "In riding a bicycle, when the bicycle leans to the right you should turn the handlebars to the right" is of neither of these varieties. It is perhaps more like the goal directed kind of "should", but we are not saying that that is what you should do to achieve the goal of riding a bicycle. Rather, that is part of what is involved *in* riding a bicycle—that is *how* to ride a bicycle.

What we know in knowing how to ride a bicycle can be regarded as normative—we know what we should do under various circumstances. Knowing what we should do under various circumstances does not involve our being able to give a general description of what we should do under various circumstances. This is just to make the familiar observation that knowing how to ride a bicycle does not automatically enable one to write a treatise on bicycle riding. This is true for two different reasons. First, knowing how to ride a bicycle requires us to know what to do in each situation *as it arises*, but it does not require us to be able to say what we should do before the fact. Second, even when a situation has actually arisen, our knowing what to do in that situation need not be propositional knowledge. In the case of knowing that we should turn the handlebars to the right when the bicycle leans right, it is plausible to suppose that most bicycle riders do have propositional knowledge of this; but consider knowing how to hit a tennis ball with a tennis racket. I know how to do it—as the situation unfolds, at each instant I know what to do—but even at that instant I cannot give a description of what I should do. Knowing what to do is the same thing as knowing to do it, and that need not involve propositional knowledge.

We are now in a position to give a rough explanation of how action-guiding norms can govern behavior in a non-intellectualist manner. When we learn how to do something *X*, we "acquire" a plan of how to do it, and that plan becomes internalized. When we subsequently undertake to do *X*, our behavior is automatically channeled into that plan. This is just a fact of psychology. We form habits or conditioned reflexes. Norms for doing *X* constitute a description of this plan for doing *X*. The sense in which the norms guide our behavior in doing *X* is that the norms describe the way in which, once we have learned how to do *X*, our behavior is automatically channeled in undertaking to do *X*.

Now let us apply this to epistemic norms. We know how to reason. That means that under various circumstances we know what to do in reasoning. This entails that there are things we should do, and hence that there are epistemic norms that guide our reasoning. The way epistemic norms can guide our reasoning without our having to think about them is no longer mysterious. They describe an internalized pattern of behavior that we automatically follow in reasoning, in the same way we automatically follow a pattern in bicycle riding. This is what epistemic norms are. They are the internalized

norms that are used automatically when we reason. Once we realize that they are just one more manifestation of the general phenomenon of automatic behavior governed by internalized norms, epistemic norms should no longer seem puzzling. We would like to have a better understanding of the psychological process wherein behavior is generated in conformance with internalized norms, and I will say more about this below. But in the meantime, much of the mystery surrounding epistemic norms evaporates once we recognize that the governing process is a general one and its application to epistemic norms and reasoning is not much different from its application to any other kind of action-guiding norms. Of course, unlike most norms our epistemic norms may be innate, in which case there is no process of internalization that is required to make them available for use in guiding our reasoning.

I have described how our epistemic norms work. This is to describe our *actual* epistemic norms. Internalists typically assume that whatever our actual epistemic norms are, they are the correct epistemic norms. I have taken it to be part of the definition of internalism that our epistemic norms are at least not subject to criticism on externalist grounds. Of course, this is precisely where internalists disagree with norm externalists. Let us turn then to a reconsideration of externalism in the light of our new understanding of epistemic norms.

3. *The Refutation of Externalism*

3.1. *Belief Externalism*

Now that we understand how epistemic norms work in guiding our reasoning, it is easy to see that they must be internalist norms. This is because when we learn how to do something we acquire a set of norms for doing it and these norms are internalized in a way enabling our central nervous system to follow them in an automatic way without our having to think about them. This has implications for the content of our norms. For example, I have been describing one of our bike riding norms as telling us that if the bicycle leans to the right then we should turn the handlebars to the right, but that is not really what we learn when we learn to ride a bicycle. The automatic processing systems in our brain do not have access to whether the bicycle is leaning to the right. What they do have access to are things like (1) our *thinking* that the bicycle is leaning to the right, and (2) certain balance sensations emanating from our inner ear. What we learn (roughly) is to turn the handlebars to the right if we either experience those balance sensations or think on some other basis that the bicycle is leaning to the right. In general, the circumstance-types to which our norms appeal in telling us to do something in circumstances of those types must be directly accessible to our automatic processing systems. The sense in which they must be directly accessible is that our automatic processing system must be able to access them without our first having to make a *judgment* about whether we are in circumstances of that type. We must have non-epistemic access.

This general observation about action-guiding norms has immediate implications for the nature of our epistemic norms. It implies that reason-guiding epistemic norms cannot appeal to external considerations of reliability. This is because such norms could not be internalized. Like *leaning to the right,* considerations of reliability are not directly accessible to our automatic processing systems. There is in principle no way that we can learn to make inferences of various kinds only if they are *in fact* reliable. Of course, we could learn to make certain inferences only if we *think* they are reliable, but that would be an internalist norm appealing to *thoughts* about reliability rather than an externalist norm appealing to reliability itself. Similar observations apply to any externalist norms. Consequently, it is in principle impossible for us to actually employ externalist norms. I take this to be a conclusive refutation of belief externalism.

I introduced the internalism/externalism distinction by saying that internalist theories make justifiedness a function exclusively of what internal states the believer is in, where internal states are those that are "directly accessible" to the believer. The notion of direct accessibility was purposely left vague, but it can now be clarified. I propose to define internal states to be those states that are directly accessible to the mechanisms in our central nervous system that direct our reasoning. The sense in which they are *directly* accessible is that access to them does not require us to first have beliefs about them. This definition makes the internalist/

externalist distinction precise in a way that agrees at least approximately with the way it has generally been used, although it is impossible to make it agree with everything everyone has said about it because different philosophers have drawn the distinction in different ways.

I have characterized internalist theories in terms of direct accessibility, but I have not said anything in a general way about which states are directly accessible. It seems clear that directly accessible states must be in some sense "psychological", but I doubt that we can say much more than that from the comfort of our armchair. That is an empirical question to be answered by psychologists. Despite the fact that we do not have a general characterization of direct accessibility, it is perfectly clear in many specific cases that particular states to which philosophers have appealed are not directly accessible. In light of this, the preceding refutation of belief externalism can be applied to a remarkably broad spectrum of theories, and it seems to me to constitute an absolutely conclusive refutation of those theories. I have indicated how it applies to theories formulating epistemic norms in terms of reliability. It applies in the same way to a much wider class of theories that proceed generally in terms of probability. For example, a few philosophers endorse the *Simple Rule:*

A belief is justified iff what is believed is sufficiently probable.

If the simple rule is to provide us with a reason-guiding norm, then a belief's being sufficiently probable must be directly accessible. No objective probability can have that property. Thus it is impossible to use the simple rule, interpreted in terms of objective probabilities, as a reason-guiding norm. This objection could be circumvented by replacing the simple rule by its "doxastic counterpart":

A belief is justified iff the epistemic agent believes it to be highly probable.

But this rule formulates an internalist norm (albeit, an implausible one).

It might be supposed that we could breathe life back into the simple rule by interpreting it in terms of subjective probability. Here we must be careful to distinguish between subjective probability as actual degree of belief and subjective probability as rational degree of belief. Interpreted in terms of actual degrees of belief, the simple rule would amount to the claim that a belief is justified iff it is firmly held, which is an internalist norm, but a preposterous one. Interpreted in terms of rational degrees of belief it becomes an externalist norm. Rational degree of belief is the unique degree of belief one rationally ought to have in a proposition, given one's overall doxastic state. I have serious doubts about the intelligibility of this notion. Is there any reason to believe that there is a unique rational degree of belief a person ought to have in a proposition? But even if we waive this difficulty, ascertaining what this unique rational degree of belief should be is immensely difficult. The rational degree of belief one ought to have in a proposition is certainly not a directly accessible property of it, and hence this version of the simple rule also succumbs to our general objection to belief externalism.

Many other epistemological theories succumb to this objection to belief externalism. For example, Keith Lehrer's coherence theory proceeds in terms of probability and hence is akin to reliabilist theories in various ways, but it makes use of probability in a complicated way that disqualifies it from being a reliabilist theory. Leaving out a few details, Lehrer's proposal is:

> r competes with h for S iff prob(h/r) is less than prob(h) and the disjunction d which is logically equivalent to r and contains as disjuncts members m_1, m_2, and so forth of the epistemic partition of h for S in numerical order, is such that no disjunction d' of any of those members can be formed where prob(h/d') = prob(h).
>
> S is completely justified in believing h if and only if prob(h) is greater than prob$(\sim h)$ and for any r, if r competes with h for s, then prob(h) is greater than prob(r).[1]

But a proposition's being more probable than any of its competitors is most assuredly not a directly accessible property of it, and hence Lehrer's theory becomes incapable of supplying us with a reason-guiding norm.

This same kind of objection applies to a broad class of coherence theories. In Pollock (1979), I distinguished between *holistic coherence theories* and *linear coherence theories*. A linear coherence theory takes a classical view of reasons according to which

one belief is a reason for a second by virtue of some internal relation between them, and differs from a foundations theory only in the overall use it makes of reasons and reasoning. Such a theory is immune from the present objections. A holistic coherence theory, on the other hand, adopts a holistic view of reasons according to which what licenses a belief is its being suitably related to the set of *all* the beliefs one holds. Lehrer's coherence theory is of the holistic variety. A holistic coherence theory requires a relationship between a justified belief and the set of all the beliefs one holds, but that will not normally be a directly accessible property of the justified belief, and hence the norm proposed by the holistic theory will be an externalist norm. Thus it cannot be reason-guiding.

The present account of epistemic norms is efficient in dispatching a wide variety of epistemological theories, but it also has some positive consequences. I take foundationalist theories to require that all justification derives ultimately from "epistemologically basic beliefs". These are typically taken to be beliefs about how we are appeared to, what we seem to remember, and so forth. In earlier publications I have rejected foundationalist theories on the grounds that we rarely have such beliefs, and in their place I have endorsed *direct realism,* according to which justification typically derives from nondoxastic states like *being appeared to really* (without your having to believe that you are appeared to really). The need for the move from foundationalism to direct realism seems to me to be compelling, but the move itself can seem puzzling. How can it be possible for nondoxastic states to justify beliefs when we are not aware that we are in them? This really only seems puzzling because we are implicitly assuming the intellectualist model of the way epistemic norms regulate belief. Given the way epistemic norms actually operate, all that is required is that the input states be directly accessible. Belief states are directly accessible, but so are a variety of nondoxastic states like perceptual states and memory states. Thus there is no reason why epistemic norms cannot appeal to those states, and the move to direct realism ceases to be puzzling.

Is there any way to salvage belief externalism in the face of the objection that it cannot give reasonable accounts of first person reason-guiding epistemic norms? The possibility remains that belief externalism might provide norms for third person evaluations. I think it is noteworthy in this connection that externalists tend to take a third person point of view in discussing epistemology. If externalist norms played a role in third person evaluations, we would then have both externalist and internalist norms that could be applied to individual beliefs and they might conflict. What would this show? It would not show anything—they would just be different norms evaluating the same object from different points of view. I can imagine a persistent externalist insisting, "Well, if the two sets of norms conflict, which way should we reason—which set of norms should we follow?" But that question does not make any sense. Asking what we should do is asking for a normative judgment, and before we can answer the question we must inquire to what norms the "should" is appealing. To make this clearer consider an analogous case. We can evaluate beliefs from both an epistemic point of view and a prudential point of view. Suppose Helen has good reasons for believing that her father is Jack the Ripper, but suppose coming to believe that would be psychologically crushing. Then we might say that, epistemically, she should believe it, but prudentially she should not. If one then insists upon asking, "Well, should she believe it or not?", the proper response is, "In what sense of 'should', epistemic or prudential?" Similarly, if externalist and internalist norms conflict and one asks, "Which way should we reason?", the proper response is to ask to which set of forms the "should" is appealing. The point is that different norms serve different purposes, and when they conflict that does not show that there is something wrong with one of the sets of norms—it just shows that the different norms are doing different jobs. The job of internalist norms is reason-guiding, and as such they are the norms traditionally sought in epistemology. Externalist norms (if any sense can be made of them) may also have a point, but they cannot be used to solve traditional epistemological problems pertaining to epistemic justification.

3.2. Norm Externalism

Recall that there are two kinds of externalism. Belief externalism advocates the adoption of externalist norms. I regard belief externalism as having been decisively refuted by the preceding considerations.

Norm externalism, on the other hand, acknowledges that we must employ internalist norms in our reasoning, but proposes that alternative sets of internalist norms should be evaluated in terms of external considerations. For example, it may be alleged that one set of internalist norms is better than another if the first is more reliable in producing true beliefs. Both internalism and norm externalism endorse internalist norms, but they differ in that the internalist alleges that our epistemic norms are not subject to criticism on externalist grounds. It is hard to see how they could be subject to criticism on internalist grounds, so the internalist has typically assumed that our epistemic norms are immune from criticism—whatever our actual epistemic norms are, they are the correct epistemic norms. That, however, seems odd. On the surface, it seems it must be at least logically possible for two people to employ different epistemic norms. They could then hold the same belief under the same circumstances and on the basis of the same evidence and yet the first could be conforming to his norms and the second not conforming to his. If a person's epistemic norms are always beyond criticism, it would follow that the first person is justified in his beliefs and the second is not, despite the fact that their beliefs are based upon the same evidence. That would at least be peculiar. Because it seems that it must be possible for different people to employ different epistemic norms, this makes a strong *prima facie* case for norm externalism.

Action-guiding norms are not generally immune from criticism. Typically, action guiding norms tell us how to do one thing *by* doing something else. For example, knowing how to ride a bicycle consists of knowing what more basic actions to perform—leg movements, arm movements, and the like—in order to ride the bicycle. An action that is performed by doing something else is a *nonbasic* action. Norms describing how to perform nonbasic actions can be subject to external evaluation. There may be more than one way to perform the nonbasic action, and some ways may be better (more efficient, more reliable, etc.) than others. If I know how to do it in one way and you know how to do it in another way, you know how to do it better than I if the norms governing your behavior are better than the norms governing mine. For example, we may both know how to hit the target with a bow and arrow, but you may know how to do it more reliably than I. It thus becomes an empirical question whether acting in accordance with a proposed norm will constitute your doing what you want to be doing and whether another norm might not be better.

Reasoning is not, strictly speaking, an action, but it is something we do, and we do it by doing other simpler things. We reason by adopting new beliefs and rejecting old beliefs under a variety of circumstances. Our norms for reasoning tell us when it is permissible or impermissible to do this. It seems that the norms we actually employ should be subject to external criticism just like any other norms. The norm externalist proposes that we should scrutinize them and possibly replace them by other norms. Because of the direct accessibility problem, we cannot replace them by norms making an explicit appeal to reliability, but we might discover that (1) under certain circumstances inferences licensed by our natural norms are unreliable, and (2) under certain circumstances inferences not licensed by our natural norms are highly reliable. The norm externalist proposes that we should then alter our epistemic norms, adopting new internalist norms allowing us to make the inferences described under (2) and prohibiting those described under (1).

We must distinguish between two construals of the norm externalist proposal. He might be telling us that when we *discover* old reasoning patterns to be unreliable or new reasoning patterns to be reliable then we should alter our norms and our reasoning accordingly. Alternatively, he might be telling us that if old patterns simply *are* unreliable and new patterns *are* reliable, independently of our knowing or believing that they are, then we should alter our reasoning. The first construal seems like an eminently reasonable proposal, and it is one that has been made explicitly by various externalists. For example, in discussing how reliabilist considerations bear on reasoning, Goldman (1980, p. 47) writes:

At the start a creature forms beliefs from automatic, preprogrammed doxastic processes. . . . Once the creature distinguishes between more and less reliable belief-forming processes, it has taken the first step toward doxastic appraisal. . . . The creature can also begin doxastic self-criticism,

in which it proposes *regulative* principles to itself.

But this involves a fundamental misconception. Our epistemic norms are not subject to criticism in this way. Our *reasoning* is subject to such criticism, and the criticism can dictate changes in our reasoning, but this does not lead to changes in our epistemic norms. This is because, unlike other norms, our epistemic norms already accommodate criticism based on reliability. The point is twofold. First, discovering that certain kinds of inferences are unreliable under certain circumstances constitutes a defeater for those inferences and hence makes us unjustified in reasoning in that way, and this is entirely in accordance with our natural unmodified epistemic norms. For example, we discover that color vision is unreliable in dim lighting, and once we discover this we should cease to judge colors on that basis under those circumstances. But this does not require an alteration of our epistemic norms, because color vision only provides us with defeasible reasons for color judgments, and our discovery of unreliability constitutes a defeater for those reasons. This is entirely in accordance with the norms we already have. Second, discovering that some new inferences are reliable under certain circumstances provides us with justification for making those inferences under those circumstances, but this is licensed by the norms we already have. That is precisely what induction is all about. For example, I might discover that I am clairvoyant and certain kinds of "visions" provide reliable indications of what is about to happen. Once I make this discovery it becomes reasonable for me to base beliefs about the future on such visions. Again, this is entirely in accordance with the norms we already have and does not require us to alter those norms in any way. The general point is that the kinds of reliability considerations to which the norm externalist appeals can lead us to reason differently (refrain from some old inferences and adopt some new inferences), but this does not lead to any change in our epistemic norms. Epistemic norms are unique in that they involve a kind of feedback, having the result that the sort of external criticism that could lead to the modification of other action-guiding norms does not necessitate any modification of epistemic norms.

I have had several externalists respond to this

objection by protesting that they do not see the point of distinguishing between considerations of reliability leading us to alter our reasoning, and those considerations leading us to alter our norms. But if all the externalist means is that considerations of reliability can lead us to alter our reasoning, then he is not disagreeing with anyone. In particular, he is not disagreeing with paradigmatic internalists like Chisholm and me. Norm externalism becomes nothing but a pretentious statement of a platitude.

The alternative construal of norm externalism takes it to be telling us that if old patterns of reasoning are unreliable and new patterns are reliable, then regardless of whether we *know* these facts about reliability, we should not reason in accordance with the old patterns and we should reason in accordance with the new patterns. What could the point of this claim be? It cannot be taken as a recommendation about how to reason, because it is not a recommendation anyone could follow. We can only alter our reasoning in response to facts about reliability if we are appraised of those facts. However, normative judgments do not always have the force of recommendations. This is connected with the distinction that is often made in ethics between subjective and objective senses of "should". To say that a person subjectively should do X is to say, roughly, that given what he believes (perhaps falsely) to be the case he has an obligation to do X. To say that he objectively should do X is to say, roughly, that if he were appraised of all the relevant facts then he would have an obligation to do X. Judgments about what a person subjectively should do can serve as recommendations, but judgments about what a person objectively should do can only serve as external evaluations having some purpose other than guiding behavior. The subjective/objective distinction can be regarded as a distinction between evaluating the person and evaluating his act. The subjective sense of "should" has to do with moral responsibility, while the objective sense has to do with what act might best have been performed.

We can draw a similar subjective/objective distinction in epistemology. The epistemic analogue of moral responsibility is epistemic justification. A person is being "epistemically responsible" just in case his beliefs are justified. In other words, epistemic justification corresponds to *subjective* moral ob-

ligation. What determines whether a belief is justified is what else the epistemic agent *believes* about the world (and what other directly accessible states he is in)—not what is in fact true about the world. This seems to show that whatever considerations of *de facto* reliability may bear upon, it is not epistemic justification. They must instead bear upon the epistemic analogue of objective obligation. What is the analogue? There is one clear analogue: objective epistemic justification is a matter of what you should believe if you were apprised of all the relevant truths. But what you should believe if you were apprised of all the relevant truths is just *all the truths*. In other words, the epistemic analogue of objective justification is *truth*. There is nothing here to give solace to a norm externalist.

Goldman draws a somewhat different distinction between two senses of "justified" in epistemology. He distinguishes between "theoretical" evaluations of reasoning and "regulative" evaluations (the latter being reason-guiding). He suggests that the theoretical sense of justification is the sense required for knowledge and that it is to be distinguished from the reason-guiding sense. He suggests further that his Historical Reliabilism concerns the theoretical sense. The proposal is that it is knowledge that provides the point of a norm externalist's evaluation of epistemic norms in terms of considerations of reliability unknown to the epistemic agent. I do not believe that, but even if it were true it would not affect my overall point. The sense of epistemic justification with which I am concerned in this paper is the reason-guiding sense, and if it is acknowledged that norm externalism bears only upon another sense of justification then my main point has been conceded.

To summarize the discussion of externalism, one can be an externalist by being either a belief externalist or a norm externalist. These exhaust the ways in which externalist considerations might be brought to bear on our epistemic norms. The belief externalist tries to formulate epistemic norms directly in terms of externalist considerations, but it is impossible to construct reason-guiding norms in this way. The norm externalist proposes instead to recommend changes in reason-guiding norms on the basis of considerations of reliability. But this appeal to reliability is redundant because it is already incorporated in our unadulterated internalist norms. Thus, as far as I can see, externalism has nothing to contribute to the solution to traditional epistemological problems. Justified beliefs are those resulting from normatively correct reasoning. Consequently, any evaluation of the justifiedness of a belief must be reason-guiding and hence must be beyond the pale of externalism.

Note

[1] Lehrer, *Knowledge* (Oxford: Clarendon Press, 1974), p. 201.

VI.6 *Justification in the 20th Century*

ALVIN PLANTINGA

Alvin Plantinga is Professor of Philosophy at the University of Notre Dame. In this essay Plantinga examines the notion of "classical internalism," which holds (1) that justification is essentially deontological (that is, a matter of doing one's epistemic duty), (2) that justification is necessary and nearly sufficient for knowledge, and (3) that the justification of a belief involves its fitting the believer's evidence. Plantinga identifies these theses in the work of Descartes and Locke, and shows that contemporary internalism is based on their views of the matter. He argues that the concept of justification is incoherent. All three theses are plagued with difficulties. Finally, Plantinga suggests that the externalist notion of *warrant* in terms of proper functioning of one's epistemic faculties is a more promising way of characterizing the normative element that classical internalism sought to capture.

I. *The Received Tradition*

It would be colossal understatement to say that Anglo-American epistemology of this century has made much of the notion of *epistemic justification*. First, there is the widely celebrated "justified true belief" (JTB) account or analysis of knowledge, an analysis we imbibed with our mothers' milk. According to the inherited lore of the epistemological tribe, the JTB account enjoyed the status of epistemological orthodoxy until Edmund Gettier shat-

Reprinted from *Philosophy and Phenomenological Research* (1990) by permission of the author and publisher.

tered it in 1963 with his three page paper "Is Justified True Belief Knowledge?"[1] After 1963 the justified true belief account of knowledge was seen to be defective and lost its exalted status; but even those convinced by Gettier that justification (along with truth) isn't *sufficient* for knowledge still mostly think it *necessary* and *nearly* sufficient for knowledge: the basic shape or contours of the concept of knowledge is given by justified true belief, even if a quasi-technical fillip or addendum ("the fourth condition") is needed to appease Gettier.

There is an interesting historical irony here: it isn't easy to find many explicit statements of a JTB analysis of knowledge prior to Gettier; it is almost as if a distinguished critic created a tradition in the very act of destroying it.[2] Still, there are *some* fairly clear statements of a justified true belief analysis of knowledge prior to Gettier. Thus, according to C. I. Lewis, "Knowledge is belief which not only is true but also is justified in its believing attitude."[3] And A. J. Ayer speaks of knowledge as "the right to be sure"[4]; for reasons that will be clearer a bit further along, I believe this is a statement of a JTB account of knowledge.

So one element in the received epistemological tradition in the 20th century is that justification is necessary and (with truth) nearly sufficient (sufficient up to Gettier problems) for knowledge. But what exactly *is* justification? Here we are offered a wide and indeed confusing assortment of alternatives. I begin by calling to mind some contemporary examples in which this notion figures.

In the third edition of *Theory of Knowledge* (Prentice-Hall, 1989) Roderick Chisholm speaks of the question 'What is Knowledge?' and suggests that

> The traditional or classic answer—and the one proposed in Plato's dialogue, the Theaetetus—is that knowledge is *justified* true belief (p. 90). (See also the quotation from *The Foundations of Knowing* in footnote 2.)

According to Roderick Firth,

> To decide whether Watson knows that the coachman did it we must decide whether or not Watson is justified in believing that the coachman did it. Thus if Watson believes that the coachman did it, we must decide whether his conclusion is based rationally on the evidence.[5]

Lawrence BonJour[6] holds that the traditional JTB account of knowledge is "at least approximately correct"; furthermore,

> We cannot, in most cases at least, bring it about directly that our beliefs are true, but we can presumably bring it about directly (though perhaps only in the long run) that they are epistemically justified (p. 8).
>
> It follows that one's cognitive endeavors are epistemically justified only if and to the extent that they are aimed at this goal, which means very roughly that one accepts all and only those beliefs which one has good reason to think are true. To accept a belief in the

absence of such a reason . . . is to neglect the pursuit of truth; such acceptance is, one might say, *epistemically irresponsible*. My contention here is that the idea of avoiding such irresponsibility, of being epistemically responsible in one's believings, is the core of the notion of epistemic justification (p. 8).

> If a given putative knower is himself to be epistemically responsible in accepting beliefs in virtue of their meeting the standards of a given epistemological account, then it seems to follow that an appropriate metajustification for those principles must, in principle at least, be available to *him*. (p. 10).

Earl Conee and Richard Feldman claim that

> Doxastic attitude D toward proposition p is epistemically justified for S at t if and only if having D toward p fits the evidence S has at t.[7]

Conee (*Monist*, July, 1988) adds that

> A person has a justified belief only if the person has reflective access to evidence that the belief is true. . . . Such examples make it reasonable to conclude that there is epistemic justification for a belief only where the person has cognitive access to evidence that supports the truth of the belief. Justifying evidence must be internally available (p. 398).

William P. Alston considers and rejects an account of justification in terms of responsibility or duty fulfillment and proposes instead that

> S is J_{eg} ['e' for 'evaluative' and 'g' for 'grounds'] justified in believing that p iff S's believing that p, as S did, was a good thing from the epistemic point of view, in that S's belief that p was based on adequate grounds and S lacked sufficient overriding reasons to the contrary.[8]

"Adequate grounds," furthermore, "are those sufficiently indicative of the truth of p."[9] Alston also reports that he finds "widely shared and strong intuitions in favor of some kind of accessibility requirement for justification."[10] In "Justification and Truth" (*Philosophical Studies* 46 [1984] Stewart

Cohen holds that the demon hypothesis entails that "our experience is just as it would be if our cognitive processes were reliable" (281) and hence that we would be justified in believing as we do in fact, when our cognitive processes are reliable. So reliability, he argues, can't be a necessary condition of justification. He also seems to join BonJour in thinking of justification as a matter of epistemic responsibility (pp. 282, 284). And (Keith) Lehrer and Cohen (*Synthese* 55 [1983]: 192–93):

> Imagine that, unknown to us, our cognitive processes, those involved in perception, memory and inference, are rendered unreliable by the actions of a powerful demon or malevolent scientist. It would follow on reliabilist views that under such conditions the beliefs generated by those processes would not be justified. This result is unacceptable. The truth of the demon hypothesis also entails that our experiences and our reasonings are just what they would be if our cognitive processes were reliable, and therefore, that we would be just as well justified in believing what we do if the demon hypothesis were true as if it were false. Contrary to reliabilism, we aver that under the conditions of the demon hypothesis our beliefs would be justified in an epistemic sense. Justification is a normative concept. It is an evaluation of how well one has pursued one's epistemic goals. Consequently, if we have reason to believe that perception, for example, is a reliable process, then the mere fact that it turns out not to be reliable, because of some improbable contingency, does not obliterate our justification for perceptual belief. This is especially clear when we have good reason to believe that the contingency, which, in fact, makes our cognitive processes unreliable, does not obtain.

According to the early Alvin Goldman, on the other hand:

> The justificational status of a belief is a function of the reliability of the process or processes that cause it, where (as a first approximation) reliability consists in the

tendency of a process to produce beliefs that are true rather than false.[11]

And according to the later Goldman of *Epistemology and Cognition*[12]:

> (PI*) A cognizer's belief in p at time t is justified if and only if it is the final member of a finite sequence of doxastic states of the cognizer such that some (single) right J-rule system licenses the transition of each member of the sequence from some earlier state(s) (p. 83),

where

> (ARI) A J-rule system R is right if and only if R permits certain (basic) psychological processes, and the instantiation of these processes would result in a truth ration of belief that meets some specified high threshold (greater than .5) (p. 106).

Now: how shall we understand this blooming, buzzing confusion with respect to justification? There seem to be at least four central ideas in the above quotations. First, there is the pervasive connection between justification and knowledge. Second (BonJour, Cohen, the first Alstonian notion), justification is a matter of *epistemic responsibility;* a belief is justified if the person holding it isn't guilty of epistemic irresponsibility in forming and maintaining it. Third (Alston, Conee, Lehrer and Cohen, Cohen), there is the suggestion that there is an *internalist* component to justification (although Goldman seems to demur). The believer must have cognitive access to something important lurking in the neighborhood—whether or not he *is* justified, for example, or to the *grounds* of his justification, that by virtue of which he is justified (Alston), or to the connection between those grounds and the justified belief. Of course not just any old cognitive accessibility will suffice. The distance from Baghdad to Jerusalem is cognitively accessible to me (I own an atlas); but that isn't the right sort of accessibility. Instead, what is required is some kind of *special* access; perhaps S can determine by reflection alone, for example, whether he is justified (Alston, Conee, Lehrer and Cohen, BonJour). There is also a suggestion of another kind of internalism: justification depends only on states, like experience and belief, that are in a recognizable if hard to characterize sense internal to the believer. And finally, there is to be found in many of the quotations the idea that justification is a matter of *having evidence,* or at least depends upon evidence (Alston, Firth, Conee, Conee and Feldman, Chisholm).

So we have several different suggestions as to what justification is: being formed responsibly, being reliably produced, being such that the believer has adequate evidence, being formed on the basis of an internally accessible and truth conducive ground, being an evaluation of how well the believer has pursued her epistemic goals. There is also the connection with knowledge, with internalism, and with evidence. How shall we understand this welter of views as to the nature of justification? And how does it happen that justification is associated, in this way, with evidence? And what is the source of the internalist requirement and how does it fit in? And why is justification associated, in this way, with knowledge?

II. *Classical Internalism*

Here what we need is history: archeology, as Foucault says (although, *pace* Foucault, there is no reason to think we will uncover a hidden political agenda). We must go back to the fountainheads of western epistemological thought, those twin towers of Western epistemology, Descartes and Locke. For *some* topics—the nature of proper names, perhaps, or the question of serious actualism (that is, the question whether objects can have properties in possible worlds in which they do not exist) a grasp of history of the topic is not obviously essential to a grasp of the topic. Not so for epistemic justification: to understand the contemporary situation of that notion we must take a careful look at its history, in particular at some of the ideas of Descartes, and perhaps even more importantly, Locke. And here what is of first importance is to see that for Descartes and Locke the notion of *duty* or *obligation* play a central role in the whole doxastic enterprise. Firth, Chisholm and other contemporaries point out that there is a strong normative component in such basic epistemological concepts as justification and warrant; Chisholm (as we shall see) goes on to

claim that this normative component is really deontological, having to do with (moral) duties, obligations, requirements. In the contemporary context it required a real insight to see clearly the normative character of these epistemic concepts. For Descartes and Locke, however, deontological notions enter in a way that is explicit *in excelsis*.

Following Augustine (*De Libero Arbitrio*) Descartes gives his classical account of the origin of error:

> But if I abstain from giving my judgment on any thing when I do not perceive it with sufficient clearness and distinctness, it is plain that I act rightly. . . . But if I determine to deny or affirm, I no longer make use as I should of my free will, and if I affirm what is not true, it is evident that I deceive myself; even though I judge according to truth, this comes about only by chance, and I do not escape the blame of misusing my freedom; for the light of nature teaches us that the knowledge of the understanding should always precede the determination of the will. It is in the misuse of the free will that the privation which constitutes the characteristic nature of error is met with.[13]

As Descartes sees the matter, error is due to a misuse of free will, a misuse for which one is guilty and blameworthy (". . . and I do not escape the blame of misusing my freedom. . . .") There is a *duty* or *obligation* not to affirm a proposition unless we perceive it with sufficient clarity and distinctness; that there is such a duty is something we are taught by "the light of nature." According to Descartes, *being justified* is being within our rights, flouting no epistemic duties, doing no more than what is permitted. We are justified when we regulate or order our beliefs in such a way as to conform to the duty not to affirm a proposition unless we perceive it with sufficient clarity and distinctness.

Locke is if anything even more explicit about this deontological component of the epistemic:

> Faith is nothing but a firm assent of the mind: which if it be regulated, as is our duty, cannot be afforded to anything, but upon good reason; and so cannot be opposite to it. He that believes, without having any reason

for believing, may be in love with his own fancies; but neither seeks truth as he ought, nor pays the obedience due his maker, who would have him use those discerning faculties he has given him, to keep him out of mistake and error. He that does not this to the best of his power, however he sometimes lights on truth, is in the right but by chance; and I know not whether the luckiness of the accident will excuse the irregularity of his proceeding. This at least is certain, that he must be accountable for whatever mistakes he runs into: whereas he that makes use of the light and faculties God has given him, and seeks sincerely to discover truth, by those helps and abilities he has, may have this satisfaction in doing his duty as a rational creature, that though he should miss truth, he will not miss the reward of it. For he governs his assent right, and places it as he should, who in any case or matter whatsoever, believes or disbelieves, according as reason directs him. He that does otherwise, transgresses against his own light, and misuses those faculties, which were given him. . . .[14]

Here again there is the clear affirmation that we have an epistemic or doxastic duty: a duty, for example, not to afford a firm assent of the mind "to anything, but upon good reason." To act in accord with these duties or obligations is to be within one's rights; it is to do only what is permissible; it is to be subject to no blame or disapprobation; it is to have flouted no duties; it is to be deontologically approvable; it is, in a word, to be justified.

Now perhaps Descartes accepts a justified true belief account of knowledge; for he thinks that one is justified only in accepting just those propositions that are clear and distinct; and those propositions are just the ones he thinks we know. Locke, however, clearly does not; for him, knowledge and belief are two quite different states, and duty or obligation applies only to the latter. Your duty, he says, is to regulate your beliefs in such a way that you believe a proposition only if you have good reasons for it; those reasons would be propositions that are certain for you, and of which, accordingly, you have knowledge. But knowledge itself does not involve fulfillment of duty, epistemic or otherwise; indeed, here the dual concepts of obligation and permission do not really apply. Knowledge, he says, is a matter of noticing connections among ideas, and is only of what is certain. But if a proposition is certain for me, he holds, then there is no question of regulating my belief with respect to it. The reason is that I have no control with respect to such propositions, so that whether I believe is not up to me. Speaking of self-evident propositions, he says "all such affirmations, and negations, are made without any possibility of doubt, uncertainty or hesitation, and must necessarily be assented to, as soon as understood. . . ." (IV vii, 4). While Locke speaks here of just one of the several kinds of items of which we can have certainty, he clearly thinks the same thing about the others.

So Locke does not equate warrant—that quantity enough of which is sufficient, with truth, for knowledge—with epistemic justification, or, as we could call it to remind ourselves of the reference to duty and obligation, *deontological* epistemic justification. Nevertheless, deontological justification is of the very first importance for him as it is for Descartes. His central thought is that being justified in holding a belief is having fulfilled one's epistemic duties in forming or continuing to hold that belief. This thought is the *fons et origo* of the whole internalist tradition. It is this notion of deontological justification that is also the source of internalism: deontology implies internalism. But Locke is also the source (the proximate source, anyway) of the idea that justification is a matter of *evidence;* we can also understand the contemporary association of evidence with justification in terms of Locke's ideas.

I want to explain how justification requires internalism; but first we must make a detour through a steep and thorny area of ethics. Most of us will agree that a person is guilty, properly blamed, properly subject to censure and moral disapproval, if and only if she fails to do her duty (where among her duties might be that of refraining from doing something). So

(a) you are properly blamed for failing to do something **A** if and only if it is your duty to do **A** (and you fail to do it).

Of course we also think that someone who has done no more than what she nonculpably thinks duty permits or requires, is not culpable or guilty in doing what she does, even if we think that what she has done is wrong. You are the governor and it is up to you to decide whether a certain prisoner is to suffer the death penalty. You reflect as carefully and impartially as you can and make your decision; perhaps you believe that it is your duty in the circumstances not to commute the death sentence and let the law take its course. Then I will not properly hold you blameworthy or guilty for doing what you do, even if I think you made the wrong decision. You can't be faulted for doing what you think is the right thing to do—provided, of course, that you came to that judgment in a nonculpable way. (If you formed the judgment out of vengefulness, or pride, or lordly contempt for those whom you take to be your inferiors, then things are very different.) So we also have

> (b) If a person nonculpably believes that doing **A** is morally required or permitted, then she is not guilty (not to be blamed) for doing **A;** and if she nonculpably believes that refraining from doing **A** is morally required or permitted, then she is not guilty (not to be blamed) for refraining from doing **A.**

It is plausible to add, still further, that if I believe that it is my duty, all things considered, to do **A,** then I am guilty, culpable, morally blameworthy if I do not do **A.**

Sadly enough, however, these principles taken together appear to lead to trouble. For suppose I nonculpably think I am permitted to do **A.** Then by (b) I am not guilty and not to be blamed for doing **A;** but then by (a) doing **A** is not my duty. So if I nonculpably think it is not my duty to do something **A,** then it is not my duty to do **A;** and if I nonculpably think it is not my duty to refrain from doing **A,** then it is not my duty to refrain from doing it. Furthermore (given the addition to (b)), we can argue similarly that if I think it is my duty to do **A,** then I am culpable if I do not do **A,** in which case it is my duty to do **A.**

But isn't this wrong? You and I might argue at considerable and heated length about what duty requires in a given set of circumstances. Perhaps I think you ought to commute that sentence; you think the right thing to do is to let it stand. And you couldn't sensibly claim that since you do in fact

believe that is your duty, and believe that nonculpably, you automatically win the argument. It isn't given in advance that I am always right about what my duty requires, so long as I am nonculpable in holding the opinion I hold. If that were so, why should I come to you, asking for advice as to what my duty really is, in a given situation? So (a) and (b) both seem correct; taken together, however, they seem to entail a proposition that is clearly false.

Here, as Aquinas says, we must make a distinction. An attractive way out of this quandary is offered by the distinction between *objective* and *subjective* duty or rightness. You are guilty or blameworthy if you fail to do your *subjective* duty, but not necessarily guilty for failing to do your *objective* duty. Guilt, being properly blamed, being properly subject to censure, these things go with violation of subjective duty. Perhaps my objective duties are constituted by virtue of their being, of the options open to me, the ones that contribute most to the greatest good; or perhaps they are constituted by God's commands; or perhaps they are the ones that bear a certain particular relation of fittingness to the circumstances. Then a person might well not know or be able to see that a given action was the right one, the dutiful one, in the circumstances. Perhaps I suffer from a certain sort of moral blindness; I simply cannot see that I have an obligation to care for my aging parents. Then I am not blameworthy for failing to care for them, unless my moral blindness itself somehow arises from dereliction of duty. Assume, just for purposes of argument, that the ground of the obligation not to steal is the divine command "Thou shalt not steal." I could hardly be blamed for stealing if I (nonculpably) didn't know that stealing is wrong or didn't know, of a given act of stealing I am performing, that it is wrong, or didn't know, of a given act of taking something, that it is indeed an act of stealing. You are guilty, or to blame, or properly subject to censure only if, as we say, you *knowingly* flout your duty. Ignorance may be no excuse in the law; but nonculpable ignorance is an excusing condition in morality. Indeed, it is sometimes also an excusing condition in the law; according to the M'Naghten Rule you aren't legally culpable if you can't tell right from wrong.

Now how, exactly, does this help with respect to the above quandary? Well, the problem was that

(a) and (b) seemed to entail that I couldn't make a nonculpable mistake about what my duty was; but that seemed wrong, since it is perfectly sensible for you to challenge my belief as to what duty requires, even if you don't for a moment believe that I arrived at that belief culpably. And the resolution is that while I can't make a nonculpable error about my *subjective* duty, the same does not hold for my *objective* duty; but what we dispute about, when we dispute about what my duty, in a given circumstance is, is not my subjective duty but my objective duty. It is easy enough, in the right circumstances, to make a mistake about *that*.[15]

Given that no one is guilty for doing what she nonculpably believes is right, you might expect that we would ordinarily be receptive to the claim of ignorance as an excusing condition. The fact is, however, that in many circumstances we are extremely reluctant to accept such a claim. I take part in a racist lynching: you will not be impressed by my claim that, after careful reflection, I considered that the right thing to do. We are deeply suspicious of such claims. We are not ordinarily receptive to the claim, on the part of a murderer or thief, that, after due consideration, she thought the course she took most morally appropriate of those open to her. And the reason, I think, is that there are many moral views we don't think someone of sound mind could nonculpably come to accept. We think a properly functioning human being will find injustice—the sort depicted, for example, in the story the prophet Nathan told King David—despicable and odious. We think a person who engages in that sort of behavior really knows better, and has perhaps allowed himself to be temporarily blinded by greed or pride or lust. There is a link between objective and subjective duty—a link provided, we think, by our nature. Any normal adult who gives the matter a moment's thought can see that injustice of that sort is wicked and reprehensible. Indeed, we needn't limit ourselves to adults: small children often exhibit a very well developed sense of justice and fairness.

So for a large and important class of cases we think objective and subjective duty coincide, and do so because of our cognitive constitution; there is a large class of cases in which a properly functioning human being can just see (all else being equal) that a certain course of action is wrong. Now it is this same thought—the thought that in a large class of cases objective and subjective duty coincide—that underlies classical internalism. This coincidence of objective and subjective duty is the driving force behind the classical internalism of Descartes and Locke. We can see this in more detail as follows.

The First Internalist Motif

According to Locke and Descartes, epistemic justification is *deontological* justification. And here they are clearly thinking of *subjective* duty or obligation; they are thinking of guilt and innocence, blame and blamelessness. If I do not have certainty but believe anyway, says Descartes, "I do not escape the blame of misusing my freedom." Locke, clearly enough, is also thinking of subjective duty ("This at least is certain, that he must be accountable for whatever mistakes he runs into . . ."). But then the first internalist motif follows immediately:

> M1. *Epistemic justification (i.e., subjective epistemic justification, being such that I am not blameworthy) is entirely up to me and within my power.*

All that is required is that I do my subjective duty, act in such a way that I am blameless. All I have to do is my duty; and, given that ought implies can, I am guaranteed to be able to do that. So justification is entirely within my power; whether or not my beliefs are justified is up to me, within my control. My system of beliefs may be wildly skewed and laughably far from the truth; I may be a brain in a vat or a victim of a malicious Cartesian demon; but whether my beliefs have justification is still up to me.

The Second Internalist Motif

Descartes and Locke, as I say, are speaking there of subjective duty. But of course they are also speaking of *objective* duty. Locke holds that it is my duty to regulate my belief in such a way that I believe only what I have good reasons for, i.e., only what is epistemically probable with respect to my total evidence. One who does otherwise, he says, "transgresses against his own light, and misuses those faculties, which were given him." Such a person, he says, "neither seeks truth as he ought, nor pays the obedience due his maker, who would have him use those discerning faculties he has given him, to keep him out of mistake and error." To regulate my belief in this way is my *objective* duty; what makes an act of believing permissible or right is its being appropriately supported by the believer's total evidence. But Locke also holds that this is my *subjective* duty; if I do not regulate my belief in this way I am blameworthy, guilty of dereliction of epistemic duty. (Merely *trying* to regulate it thus is not sufficient; I must *succeed* in so doing if I am not to be blameworthy.) Objective and subjective duty thus coincide. Similarly for Descartes: if you give assent to what is not certain then (*ceteris paribus*) you are blameworthy, have flouted subjective duty as well as objective duty. So the second internalist motif:

> M2. *For a large, important, and basic class of objective epistemic duties, objective and subjective duty coincide; what you objectively ought to do matches that which is such that if you don't do it you are guilty and blameworthy.*

And the link is provided by our nature: in a large and important class of cases, a properly functioning human being can simply see whether a given belief is or isn't (objectively) justified for him. (Just as we think, in the more general moral case, that certain heinous acts are such that a properly functioning human being can't make a nonculpable mistake as to whether those acts are morally acceptable.)

The second internalist motif has three corollaries.

First: if it is your subjective duty to regulate your belief in this way, then you must be able to see or tell that regulating belief this way is indeed your duty. Locke and Descartes clearly hold that a dutiful, conscientious person whose cognitive faculties are functioning properly will not make a mistake as to what is the right method or practice for regulating belief. Descartes claims that it is clear to us that we must not give assent to what is uncertain: "the light of nature," he says, "teaches us that the knowledge of the understanding should always precede the determination of the will." And Locke says that the person who does not regulate his belief according to the evidence "*transgresses against his own light, and misuses those faculties, which were given him . . .*" (my emphasis). So the first corollary:

> C1. *In a large and important set of cases, a properly functioning person can simply see (can't make a nonculpable mistake about) what objective epistemic duty requires.*

To see the second corollary, we must note first that (according to both Descartes and Locke) I don't determine *directly*, so to speak, what it is that I am obliged to believe and withhold. According to Locke, I determine whether a given belief is acceptable for me or justified for me by determining something else: whether it is supported by what is certain for me—whether, that is, it is probable with respect to what I know. Similarly for Descartes: I don't *directly* determine whether a proposition is acceptable or justified for me; I do it by determining whether or not it is *clear and distinct* for me. So I have a way of determining when a belief is justified for me; to use a medieval expression, I have a *ratio cognoscendi* for whether a belief is justified for me. As we have seen, Descartes and Locke think that a well-formed human being cannot (in those basic cases) make a conscientious error as to whether a given belief is justified for her; but then, in those cases, she will also be unable to make a conscientious mistake about whether a given belief has the property by which she *determines* whether that belief is justified for her. Locke and Descartes therefore believe that a well-formed, conscientious human being will (at least in that large and important basic class of cases) be able to tell whether a given belief has the property that forms the *ratio cognoscendi* for justification. So the second corollary:

> C2. *In a large, important, and basic class of cases a properly functioning human person can simply see (can't make a nonculpable mistake about) whether a proposition has the property by means of which she tells whether a proposition is justified for her.*

As we have just seen, Locke and Descartes hold that I have a means of telling whether a given proposition is justified for me; I do it by determining whether it is supported by my total evidence (Locke) or whether it is certain for me (Descartes). But note that what *confers* justification on a belief for me, the *ground* of its justification, is, as they see it, the very same property as *that by which I determine* whether it is justified for me. According to Locke, the ratio *essendi* (to invoke the other half of that medieval contrast) of justification is the property of being supported by the believer's total evidence, while according to Descartes it is the property of being certain for the believer. But then the ground of justification (the justification-making property) is identical with the property by which we determine whether a belief has justification: *ratio cognoscendi* coincides with *ratio essendi*.* (This is not, of course, inevitable; in the case of measles, velocity, blood pressure, weight, and serum cholesterol our *ratio cognoscendi* does not coincide with the *ratio essendi*.)

If so, however, then there is another kind of error a properly functioning dutiful human being cannot make; such a person is so constructed that (in that class of basic cases) she cannot conscientiously come to believe, of the justification making property, that a given belief has it when in fact it does not. According to Locke, a properly functioning human being couldn't both be appropriately dutiful in forming his beliefs (in these cases), and also mistakenly believe, of some proposition, that it was supported by his total evidence; according to Descartes, such a person in such a case could not mistakenly come to think that a belief was certain for her when in fact it was not. We have a certain guaranteed access to the *ratio cognoscendi* of justification; but if *ratio cognoscendi* and *ratio essendi* coincide, then we also have guaranteed access to the latter. So the third corollary:

> C3. *In a large, important and basic class of epistemic cases a properly functioning human person can simply see (can't make a nonculpable mistake about) whether a proposition has the property that confers justification upon it for her.*

Now the fact of the matter seems to be, *contra* Locke, that cases in which it is obvious what my total evidence supports are, after all, relatively few and far between. It is easy enough to make a nonculpable mistake about what my total evidence supports; it is often very difficult to tell whether a belief has (what Locke sees as) the *ratio cognoscendi* of justification. Perhaps Locke sometimes saw this; significantly enough, he sometimes retreats to the weaker view that what confers justification is the belief's being such that *upon reflection I think* it is supported by my evidence. Here it seems clear that I do have the requisite special access.

The Third Internalist Motif

There is still another and somewhat less well defined internalist motif here. According to Locke and Descartes, I have a sort of guaranteed access to whether a belief is justified for me and also to what makes it justified for me: I cannot (if I suffer from no cognitive deficiency) nonculpably but mistakenly believe that a belief is justified or has the justification-making property. This is the source of another internalist motif; for it is only certain of my states and properties to which it is at all plausible to think that I have that sort of access. Clearly you don't have this sort of access to the pH level of your blood, or the size of your liver, or whether your pancreas is now functioning properly. The sorts of things about which it is plausible to hold that you can't make a mistake, will be, for example, whether you believe that Albuquerque is in New Mexico, whether you are now being appeared to redly, whether you are trying to get to Boston on time, or whether you are trying to bring it about that, for every proposition you consider, you believe it if and only if it is true. So the justification-making property will have to attach to such states as my believing thus and so, my being appeared to in such and such a fashion, my aiming at a given state of affairs, my trying to do something or other, and the like. These states are the ones such that it is plausible to hold of them that I cannot make a nonculpable mistake as to whether I exhibit them. But they are also, in some recognizable, if hard to define sense, internal to me—internal to me as a knower or a cognizing being. Thinking of justification in the deontological way characteristic of classical internalism induces *epistemic* internalism: and that in turn induces internalism of this different but related sort. It isn't easy to think of a name for internalism of this sort, but perhaps the name 'personal internalism' (calling attention to the way in which my beliefs, desires, experience and aims are crucial to me as a person) is no worse than some others.

Of course it is not *necessary* that the things to which a person has this special access are internal in

---

[* The phrase *ratio essendi* refers to what a thing is in itself, its essence; *ratio cognoscendi* refers to what we know about a thing, our understanding of it.—Ed.]

this sense; there could be a being who had guaranteed and indeed logically incorrigible access to properties that were not in this way internal to him. If the bulk of the theistic tradition is right, God is essentially omniscient: but then it is impossible (impossible in the broadly logical sense) that he err on any topic whatever, internal to him or not. Not so for us.

III. *Back to the Present*

Suppose we return to the 20th century; we are now in a better position, I think, to understand the swirling diversity that it presents with respect to justification. According to the 20th century received tradition, as we saw earlier, (1) justification is necessary and (along with truth) nearly sufficient for knowledge, (2) there is a strong connection between justification and evidence, and (3) justification involves internalism of those two kinds (epistemic and personal internalism). Further, justification itself is taken as a matter of epistemic responsibility or aptness for epistemic duty fulfillment (Firth, Lehrer, Cohen, Chisholm), as an "evaluation" of how well you have fulfilled your epistemic goals (Lehrer and Cohen), as being believed or accepted on the basis of an adequate truth conducive ground (Alston), as being produced by a reliable belief producing mechanism (Goldman), and as being supported by or fitting the evidence (Conee, Conee and Feldman, Firth, many others). The project was to try to understand this diversity, and to see what underlies (1) the close connection of justification with knowledge, (2) the internalist requirement laid upon epistemic justification, and (3) the stress upon evidence in connection with justification. I think it is now easier to see answers to these questions.

First, the basic Cartesian/Lockean idea of justification as fulfillment of epistemic duty or obligation is, of course, directly reflected in the work of those, who, like BonJour, Cohen and, preeminently, Chisholm, see justification as epistemic responsibility or aptness for epistemic duty fulfillment. (To be responsible, after all, is to live up to one's duties and obligations.) It is instructive here

to consider at a bit greater length the work of Roderick Chisholm, whose thought has quite properly dominated American epistemology for more than 30 years. Most of our contemporaries don't spend much time asking what justification *is;* they are less interested in an *analysis* of justification than in other questions, such as under what conditions a belief *has* justification. Chisholm is no exception. His principal interest, perhaps, has been in stating epistemological principles: noncontingent conditionals whose antecedents specify a nonepistemic relation between a person **S** and a proposition **A,** and whose consequents specify that **A** has a certain epistemic status for **S**—*certainty,* perhaps, or *acceptability,* or *being evident* or *being beyond reasonable doubt.* In stating these principles, of course, he is not saying what justification is, but saying instead under what nonepistemic conditions a given proposition has a given degree of it (for a given person). But he does also say what it is, and here he seems solidly in the tradition of Locke and Descartes. The classical Chisholm,[16] concurs with the fundamental deontological intuition of Classical Internalism: there are epistemic duties or obligations or requirements. We human beings are rational creatures; we are capable of grasping concepts, believing propositions, and reasoning. Rational creatures—human beings, but also angels, Alpha-Centaurians, what have you—are subject to epistemic duty or obligation; with ability comes responsibility. Justification, for a person is, in essence, being in the condition of having satisfied these duties or obligations. And a *belief* is justified for a person, in essence, when holding that belief is apt for fulfilling those epistemic duties.

What, exactly, are those epistemic duties? Chisholm states the fundamental epistemic obligation or requirement differently in different places: thus in *Foundations of Knowing,*

> Epistemic reasonability could be understood in terms of the general requirement to try to have the largest possible set of logically independent beliefs that is such that the true beliefs outnumber the false beliefs (p. 7);

but in *Theory of Knowledge* (2nd ed.),

> We may assume that every person is subject to a purely intellectual requirement: that of

trying his best to bring it about that for any proposition **p** he considers, he accepts **p** if and only if **p** is true. One might say that this is the person's responsibility or duty *qua* intellectual being. . . . One way, then, of re-expressing the locution '**p** is more reasonable than **q** for **S** at **t**' to say this: '**S** is so situated at **t** that his intellectual requirement, his responsibility as an intellectual being, is better fulfilled by **p** than by **q**' (p. 14).

Neither of these is exactly right; but for present purposes the important point is that Chisholm sees us as subject to an epistemic obligation or requirement: to try to achieve a certain condition—call it 'epistemic excellence'—which consists in a certain relation to the truth; and justification depends on conformity to that duty. Chisholm also endorses, at least by implication, the First Internalist Motif. On his view it is sufficient for my beliefs' having justification for me that I do my epistemic duty, fulfill my epistemic obligation. But then whether my beliefs have positive epistemic status for me is up to me and within my control. All I have to do is my duty, which is to try to achieve epistemic excellence; and I can certainly try (whether or not I can actually succeed). The second motif is also reflected in Chisholm's thought. If you ask him what epistemic duty requires, he will presumably reply "that you try to achieve epistemic excellence." But then he is clearly speaking of objective duty. (Otherwise the right response would be, "Do whatever you nonculpably think is right.") But he also thinks, clearly enough, that if I don't try to achieve epistemic excellence (and this duty is not overridden by others) then I will be guilty: objective and subjective duty coincide. And the third motif is also reflected in Chisholm's way of thinking. My duty is to *try* to bring it about that I am in a state of intellectual excellence; my trying to do so is something to which I have the right kind of cognitive access, and is also internal to me in the personal sense.

Of course Chisholm's view differs in crucial respects from the classical view of Descartes and Locke: for example, they limit knowledge to what is certain, but he does not. And this is an effect of an even deeper difference between Chisholm and, at any rate, Locke. For according to Chisholm justification is necessary and nearly sufficient for knowledge. Indeed, certainly, on Chisholm's view the highest degree of positive epistemic status, *just is* the highest degree of justification: a belief or proposition **A** is certain for me just if there is no other proposition such that believing it is more reasonable for me than believing **A**—that is (given his explanations of reasonability) just if there is no proposition such that I can better fulfill my epistemic duty by believing it than by believing **A**. Locke, on the other hand, doesn't think of justification as involved in that of which we are certain—self-evident beliefs, for example—and he also holds that knowledge is only of that of which we are certain.

Turn now to the second notion of the nature of justification: that it is or essentially involves having adequate evidence for the belief in question (Alston, Conee and Feldman, many others). According to the 'Evidentialism' of Conee and Feldman, you are justified in believing **B** just if you have sufficient evidence for it, or (as they put it) just if it fits your evidence. (Thus Conee: "Such examples make it reasonable to conclude that there is epistemic justification of a belief only where the person has cognitive access to evidence that supports the belief.") Indeed, this equation of being justified with having evidence is so pervasive that the justified true belief analysis of knowledge has often been put as the idea that you know if and only if your belief is true and you have adequate evidence for it. Again, this is easily understood in terms of the original constellation of ideas surrounding justification to be found in Locke and Descartes. For them deontological epistemic justification is the central notion; and the central duty here, particularly in the case of Locke, is to believe a proposition that isn't certain for you (one that isn't self-evident or incorrigible) only if you have evidence for it—evidence, as they saw it, from propositions that are certain for you.

Two further points here. (a) Conee and Feldman do not make the deontological connection: they don't say that the *ratio essendi* of justification is duty fulfillment, with the chief duty being that of believing (or, more plausibly, trying to bring it about that you believe) only that which fits your evidence. But there are plenty of contemporaries and near contemporaries who do. As we all know, W. K. Clifford (that "delicious *enfant terrible*," as

William James calls him) trumpets that "it is wrong, always, everywhere, and for anyone to believe anything upon insufficient evidence"; his is only the most strident in a vast chorus of voices insisting that the or a primary intellectual duty is that of believing only on the basis of evidence. (A few others in the choir: Sigmund Freud, Brand Blanshard, H. H. Price, Bertrand Russell, and Michael Scriven). And (b) there are two quite different possibilities for the evidentialist; she might be holding, on the one hand, that the very *nature* of justification is believing (or trying to bring it about that you believe) on the basis of evidence (that justification just *is* believing or trying to believe in that way) or she might hold, more plausibly, that the *nature* of justification is fulfillment of epistemic duty, the chief among those duties being that of believing or trying to believe only on the basis of evidence. (Since Conee and Feldman do not mention epistemic obligation, it seems likely that they are to be taken the first way.)

Lehrer and Cohen speak of epistemic justification as an evaluation of how well you have accomplished your epistemic goals. Here the idea is not that you have duties or obligations; it is rather that you have or may have epistemic goals: and you are justified to the degree that your epistemic behavior is a good way of attaining those goals. And here the word 'rationality' might be more appropriate than 'justification'. What is really at issue here is *Zweckrationalität,* means-end rationality, appropriateness of your means to your goals. This notion is similar to Richard Foley's conception of epistemic rationality, powerfully expounded in *The Theory of Epistemic Rationality*. Lehrer and Cohen's notion isn't directly connected with the classical deontological conception of justification; however it does have a sort of indirect connection. If you become doubtful that there are any specifically epistemic duties, or perhaps think there are some, but doubt that fulfilling them can play a large role in the formation and governance of belief, then this notion of means-ends rationality may seem an attractive substitute. Perhaps there is no such thing as epistemic duty; even so, however, there is such a thing as pursuing your epistemic goals well or badly.

Finally, there is the conception of justification to be found in both the old and the new Goldman. According to the old Goldman (to a first approxi-

mation), a belief is justified if and only if it is produced by a reliable belief producing process or mechanism. According to the new, a belief is justified if it is the last item in a cognitive process which is licensed by a right set of J rules; and a set of J rules is right in case it has a high truth ratio in nearby possible worlds. Here I think there is little connection with the classical notion of justification as involving fulfillment of epistemic duty. True, in the later Goldman there is the notion of a *rule,* and of a process *permitted* by a rule. But rules of this sort have nothing to do with duty or obligation; there is nothing deontological about them. Goldman's use of the term, I think, is to be understood another way: suppose you just use the term 'justification' as a *name* for what is necessary for knowledge and (together with truth) sufficient for it up to Gettier problems; and suppose you also think, with Goldman, that fulfillment of epistemic duty, no matter how fervent and conscientious, is nowhere nearly sufficient for knowledge. Then you might find yourself using the term in just the way he uses it. Here there is only a fairly distant analogical connection with the classical conception.

So much for the main contemporary conceptions of justification; they can all be understood, I think, in terms of their relation to the classical deontological conception. But the same can be said for the contemporary connection between justification and internalism. According to Conee, "Justifying evidence must be internally available"; his idea is that the evidence in question can't be evidence you could get from the encyclopedia, for example, but must rather be evidence you can come up with just by reflection. Alston, furthermore, "find[s] widely shared and strong intuitions in favor of some kind of accessibility requirement for justification." Here there seems to be a clear connection with the classical connection between deontological justification and internalism in the epistemic sense. Of course internalism in the personal sense is also widespread (and this is what we should expect, given the relation between internalism in the two senses). Thus Lehrer and Cohen argue that reliabilism must be wrong about justification: "The truth of the demon hypothesis (where my beliefs are mostly false) also entails that our experiences and our reasonings are just what they would be if our cognitive processes were reliable, and therefore, that we would be just as well justified in believing what we do if the demon hypothesis were true as if it were false" (above, p. 47). Here the idea, clearly, is that only what is internal to me as a knower in the personal sense, in the way in which my beliefs and experiences are, is relevant to justification; this may be understood, I think, as a sort of reflection of the connection between deontological justification and internalism to be found in the classical tradition. Note that an equivocation lurks here. Lehrer and Cohen think of justification a certain way (perhaps deontologically in the case of Cohen and perhaps in terms of means-ends rationality in the case of Lehrer and Cohen) and think justification so thought of is necessary for knowledge. Goldman, on the other hand, doesn't think justification thought of like *that* is necessary for knowledge; and *he* uses 'justification' more like a *name* for the property of quantity enough of which is sufficient (along with truth) for knowledge.

Now classical internalism has a certain deep integrity. The central notion is that we have epistemic duties or obligations; this induces internalism of both the epistemic and the nonepistemic sorts; and the central duty, Locke thinks, is to believe a proposition that is not certain only on the basis of evidence. Classical Chisholmian Internalism exhibits all of these features, except that according to Chisholm the central epistemic duty is to try to achieve epistemic excellence. Other contemporary accounts, however, sometimes seize on one or another of the elements of the classical package, often in such a way that the integrity of the original package is lost, or at least no longer clearly visible. Thus Conee and Feldman see justification as a matter of having adequate evidence, and hold that this evidence must be internally available to the believer; this makes sense if combined, as in Locke, with the idea that justification is fundamentally a deontological matter of duty fulfillment. They say nothing about the latter, however, which leaves the internalism unmotivated and the connection between the evidentialism and the internalism obscure.

Lehrer and Cohen speak of justification as "an evaluation of how well you have pursued your epistemic goals." The internalism they display fits at best dubiously with this conception of justification. Suppose justification is an evaluation of how well you are pursuing your epistemic goals; it is then presumably an evaluation of the appropriateness of the means you use to the goals you choose. Suppose your doxastic goal is, e.g., believing truth, or attaining salvation, or achieving fame and fortune: why would there be any necessity that you be able to tell, just by reflection, let's say, how well suited your means are for achieving those goals? And why think that only what pertains in a direct way to your experiences and beliefs is relevant to this question of how well those means fit those goals? What reason is there to think that an evaluation of how well you were pursuing your epistemic goals would have to measure something such that only your beliefs and your experiences would be relevant to it? The internalism of the classical conception lingers, but its root and foundation is no longer present.

Finally, I wish to consider William Alston's illuminating account of justification. Of all our contemporaries, Alston, I believe, is clearest and most perceptive about the nature of justification and its connection with epistemic duty and the other notions lurking in the neighborhood. Nevertheless the concept of justification that emerges from his work seems to me to be improperly unintegrated; it isn't clear to me that there is a good reason for picking out that particular notion as important for epistemology, or for our understanding of contemporary epistemology. Alston begins by asking the following question: what *is* this favorable status which, according to the central core of the idea of justification, accrues to a justified belief? Here he notes an important watershed:

As I see it, the major divide in this terrain has to do with whether believing and refraining from believing are subject to obligation, duty, and the like. If they are, we can think of the favorable evaluative status of a certain belief as consisting in the fact that in holding that belief one has fulfilled one's obligations, or refrained from violating one's obligations to achieve the fundamental aim in question [i.e., "the aim of maximizing truth and minimizing falsity in a large body of beliefs"]. If they are not so subject, the favorable status will have to be thought of in some other way.[17]

There is a hint, here, that the notion of justification as a matter of permission, of freedom from blameworthiness, of fulfillment of epistemic duty and obligation—in a word, the classical deontological notion of justification—is more natural, or at any rate more familiar than alternatives. Elsewhere he gives considerably more than a hint:

> I must confess that I do not find 'justified' an apt term for a favorable or desirable state or condition, when what makes it desirable is cut loose from considerations of obligation and blame. Nevertheless, since the term is firmly ensconced in the literature as the term to use for any concept that satisfies the four conditions [applicable to beliefs or believings, is positively evaluative and more specifically *epistemically* evaluative, and comes in degrees] set out in section II, I will stifle my linguistic scruples and employ it for a non-deontological concept.[18]

Alston's scruples seem eminently warranted; it is only by way of some sort of analogical extension that the term 'justification' could properly be used for a non-deontological notion. Exploring the family of deontological ideas of justification with care and insight, Alston pays particular and subtle attention to the ways in which doxastic phenomena can be within our voluntary control. His verdict is that none of the deontological notions will do the job: even the most promising of the bunch, he says, "does not give us what we expect of epistemic justification. The most serious defect is that it does not hook up in the right way with an adequate, truth conducive ground. I may have done what could reasonably be expected of me in the management and cultivation of my doxastic life, and still hold a belief on outrageously inadequate grounds."

So the deontological answer to the question 'what sort of evaluation is involved in justification?' can't be right. "Perhaps it was misguided all along," he says, "to think of epistemic justification as freedom from blameworthiness. Is there any alternative, given the non-negotiable point that we are looking for a concept of epistemic evaluation?" (ibid, p. 69). The answer, of course, is that there are *many* alternatives. After another careful exploration of the field, he chooses his candidate:

> S is J$_{eg}$ ['e' for 'evaluative' and 'g' for 'grounds'] justified in believing that *p* iff S's believing that *p*, as S did, was a good thing

from the epistemic point of view, in that S's belief that *p* was based on adequate grounds and S lacked sufficient overriding reasons to the contrary (ibid., p. 77).

So a justified belief is one that has adequate grounds. Alston adds that the justifying grounds in question must be accessible to the believer in question, thus honoring the classical connection between justification and internalism. In the classical case, as I have been arguing, there is a natural and inevitable connection between justification and accessibility, a connection rooted in the deontological conception of justification. Once one gives up the deontology, however, what is the reason or motivation for retaining the internalism? In support of the internalist requirement, Alston cites the fact that he finds

> widely shared and strong intuitions in favor of some kind of accessibility requirement for justification. We expect that if there is something that justifies my belief that *p*, I will be able to determine what it is. We find something incongruous, or conceptually impossible, in the notion of my being justified in believing that *p* while totally lacking any capacity to determine what is responsible for that justification.[19]

Again, this makes perfect sense if we think of justification deontologically; and the reason he finds those widespread intuitions favoring an internalist requirement, I suggest, is a testimony to the hold the classical conception has upon us; but once we give up that deontology, what is the reason for the internalism? *Is* there any longer any reason for it? Cut off the deontology, and the internalism looks like an arbitrary appendage.

Alston's conception of justification, I think, lacks the integrity of the classical conception. He clearly sees the incoherence of the 20th century received tradition, uniting as it does the notion that justification is necessary and nearly sufficient for knowledge, with the notion that justification is fundamentally a matter of doing one's epistemic duty. Looking (naturally enough) for a coherent conception, he turns to another notion. But why does he choose the one he does? Perhaps the idea is to find the (or a) closest coherent conception—that is, a conception that is coherent, and as similar to the

20th century tradition with respect to justification as any other coherent conception. Perhaps he's right; perhaps the concept he suggests is the closest coherent conception to the 20th century tradition with respect to justification: that doesn't guarantee that the conception in question helps us understand knowledge, or justification, or other important epistemological ideas.

IV. *The Incoherence of the Received Tradition*

Alston, I said, sees the incoherence of the received tradition; by way of conclusion, I shall argue briefly that the 20th century received epistemological tradition with respect to justification is indeed mistaken and incoherent. The shape of this tradition is clear: it involves first the idea that justification is necessary and nearly sufficient for knowledge; second, the idea that justification is fundamentally a matter of responsibility, of fulfillment of epistemic duty; third, the idea that justification for a belief essentially involves its fitting the believer's evidence, and fourth, the internalist connection. More than one element here is deeply questionable. For example, there is the question whether our beliefs are sufficiently within our control for deontological justification to have the right kind of bearing on belief formation and maintenance; I have little to add to Alston's discerning discussion of this question and shall therefore say nothing about it.

But second, conceding the tradition all it might like by way of control over our beliefs, it is still clear that justification is neither necessary for warrant nor anywhere nearly sufficient for it. First, it is nowhere nearly sufficient. It is not the case that justification is the fundamental component of warrant, with no more than an epicycle or quasi-technical codicil needed in order to mollify Gettier; not at all. Concede the dubious premiss that there are intellectual duties of the sort Locke and Chisholm suggest; concede the control over our beliefs that go with that idea: it is still easy to see, I think, that a person can be doing her epistemic duty to the maximum and nevertheless (by way of the depredations of a brain lesion or the machinations of a Cartesian demon or Alpha-Centaurian cognitive scientist) be such that her beliefs have little or no warrant. I have given examples to prove this point elsewhere[20]; here I shall give just one example.

Suppose our epistemic duty, as Chisholm puts it in *Foundations of Knowing,* is to "try to have the largest possible set of logically independent beliefs that is such that the true beliefs outnumber the false beliefs"—more generally, suppose our epistemic duty is to try to achieve epistemic excellence. And suppose further that I develop a rare sort of brain lesion that causes me to believe that I will be the next president of the United States. I have no evidence for that proposition, never having won or even run for public office; my only political experience was an unsuccessful bid for the vice-presidency of my sophomore class in college. Nevertheless, due to my cognitive dysfunction, the belief that I will be the next president seems to me obviously true—as obvious as the most obvious truths of elementary logic or arithmetic; it has all the phenomenological panache of *Modus Ponens* itself. Now: am I so situated that I can better fulfill my obligation to the truth by *withholding* than by accepting this proposition? Surely not. That I will be the next president seems to me to be utterly and obviously true, as obvious as $2 + 1 = 3$; and I haven't the slightest awareness that my cognitive faculties are playing me false here. So if I am trying to achieve epistemic excellence, I will put this proposition down among the ones I accept. The way for me to try to achieve epistemic excellence in these circumstances, surely, is for me to act on what I (nonculpably) believe about how best to achieve this end. But this proposition seems obviously true to me; so, naturally enough, I believe that the way to achieve epistemic excellence here is to accept it. We may add that I am exceptionally dutiful, enormously concerned with my epistemic duty; I am eager to bring it about that I am in the right relation to the truth, and am trying my level best to do so; indeed, I am fanatical on the subject and devote most of my energy to trying to achieve epistemic excellence. Then, surely, I am doing my epistemic duty in accepting the proposition in question; nevertheless that proposition has little by way of warrant or positive epistemic status for me. Even if, by some mad chance, I will in fact be the next president, I surely do not know that I will be.

So justification isn't sufficient for warrant. But

it isn't necessary either. Suppose there is the sort of epistemic duty Chisholm suggests: a duty to try to bring it about that I attain and maintain the condition of epistemic excellence; and suppose I am dutiful, but a bit confused. I come nonculpably to believe that the Alpha Centaurians thoroughly dislike the thought that I am perceiving something that is red; I also believe that they are monitoring my beliefs, and if I form the belief that I see something red, will bring it about that I have a set of beliefs most of which are absurdly false, thus depriving me of any chance for epistemic excellence. I then acquire an epistemic duty to try to withhold the beliefs I naturally form when I am appeared to redly: such beliefs as that I see a red ball, or a red fire engine, or whatever. I have the same epistemic inclinations everyone else has: when I am appeared to redly, I am powerfully inclined to believe that I see something that is red. By dint of heroic and unstinting effort, however, I am able to train myself to withhold the belief (on such occasions) that I see something red; of course it takes enormous effort and requires great willpower. On a given morning I go for a walk in London; I am appeared to redly several times (postboxes, traffic signals, redcoats practising for a re-enactment of the American revolution); each time I successfully resist the belief that I see something red, but only at the cost of prodigious effort. I become exhausted, and resentful. Finally I am appeared to redly in a particularly flagrant and insistent fashion by a large red London bus. "To hell with epistemic duty" I say, and relax blissfully into the belief that I am now perceiving something red. Then this would be a belief that was unjustified for me; in accepting it I would be going contrary to epistemic duty; yet could it not constitute knowledge?

According to the 20th century received tradition in Anglo-American epistemology—a tradition going back at least to Locke—justification is essentially deontological; it is also necessary and nearly sufficient for warrant. But this position is deeply incoherent: epistemic justification (taken in traditional deontological fashion) may be an important epistemic value or virtue, but it is neither necessary nor anywhere nearly sufficient for knowledge. Knowledge surely contains a normative element; but the normativity is not that of deontology.[21] Perhaps this incoherence in the received tradition is

the most important thing to see here: the tension between the idea that justification is a deontological matter, a matter of fulfilling duties, being permitted or within one's rights, conforming to one's intellectual obligations, on the one hand; and, on the other, the idea that justification is necessary and sufficient (perhaps with a codicil to propitiate Gettier) for warrant. To put it another way, what we need to see clearly is the vast difference between justification and warrant. The lesson to be learned is that these two are not merely uneasy bedfellows; they are worlds apart.[22]

Notes

[1] *Analysis* 23 (1963), pp. 121–23.

[2] Thus, for example, in Roderick Chisholm's *Perceiving* (1957) there is an analysis of knowledge, but one that makes no explicit reference to justification:

"S knows that h is true" means (i) S accepts h; (ii) S has adequate evidence for h and (iii) h is true (p. 16).

In the first edition of *Theory of Knowledge,* published in 1966, which was after Gettier but before it was widely recognized what Gettier had done in the JTB analysis, Chisholm again offers an analysis of knowledge, and again one in which justification plays no explicit role:

S knows at *t* that *h* is true, provided (1) S believes *h* at *t*; (2) *h* is true; and (3) *h* is evident at *t* for S.

In *The Foundations of Knowing* (1986), however, Chisholm speaks of "the traditional definition of knowledge": "Now we are in a position to define the type of justification presupposed by the traditional definition of knowledge. . . ." And after defining it he goes on to say, "And so we retain the traditional definition of knowledge:

S knows that p = Dfp; S believes that p; and S is justified in believing that p" (p. 47).

[3] *An Analysis of Knowledge and Valuation* (La Salle, Illinois: Open Court, 1946), p. 9.

[4] *The Problem of Knowledge* (London: Macmillan, 1956), p. 28.

[5] "Are Epistemic Concepts Reducible to Ethical Concepts?" in *Values and Morals,* ed. A. Goldman and J. Kim (Dordrecht: D. Reidel Publishing Co., 1978), p. 219.

[6] *The Structure of Empirical Knowledge* (Cambridge, Massachusetts: Harvard University Press, 1985).

[7] "Evidentialism," *Philosophical Studies,* 1985, p. 15.

[8] "Concepts of Epistemic Justification," *The Monist* (January, 1985), p. 71. See also the more extended quotations from Alston below, p. 67 ff.

[9] "An Externalist's Internalism," *Synthese* 74 (March, 1988), p. 269.

[10] Ibid., p. 272.

[11] "What is Justified Belief" in *Justification and Knowledge: New Studies in Epistemology,* ed. George Pappas (Dordrecht: D. Reidel, 1979), p. 10.

[12] Cambridge, Massachusetts: Harvard University Press, 1986.

[13] Meditation 4. P. 176 in Vol. I of *Philosophical Works of Descartes,* ed. Haldane and Ross (Dover, 1955 [first edition Cambridge University Press, 1911]).

[14] *An Essay Concerning Human Understanding,* Essay IV, xvii, 24.

[15] Can we explain subjective duty in terms of objective duty or *vice versa?* Or, if that is too much to hope for, can we at least state an interesting relation between the two? Perhaps: according to Alan Donagan (*The Theory of Morality,* chapter 2.3, pp. 52–57; and chapter 4, pp. 112 ff.) my subjective duty is that which it would be objectively right to blame me for not doing. In the other direction, a proposition states an objective duty for me if and only if it is true, and is such that if I knew it, then it would state a subjective duty for me.

[16] Roughly, the Chisholm from *Perceiving* (Ithaca, New York: Cornell University Press, 1957) to *The Foundations of Knowing* (Minneapolis: University of Minnesota Press, 1982). Some of Chisholm's more recent work appears to take a different (and Brentanoesque) direction; his most recent work (the third edition of *Theory of Knowledge* [New York: Prentice-Hall, 1989], for example, and his so far unpublished "Firth and the Ethics of Belief"), on the other hand, seems once more to fit with Classical Chisholmian Internalism.

[17] "Concepts of Epistemic Justification," p. 59.

[18] Ibid., p. 86 (footnote 21).

[19] "An Externalist's Internalism," *Synthese* 74 (March, 1988), p. 272.

[20] "Chisholm Internalism," in *Philosophical Analysis: a Defense by Example,* ed. David Austin (Dordrecht: D. Reidel, 1987); "Justification and Theism," *Faith and Philosophy,* October, 1987; "Positive Epistemic Status and Proper Function" in *Philosophical Perspectives,* 2; *Epistemology,* 1988, ed. James Tomberlin (Atascadero, California: Ridgeview Publishing Co., 1988); and *Warrant* (not committed for publication).

[21] In *Warrant* (forthcoming, I hope) I argue that the sort of normativity involved is that connected with the notion of proper function. Thus, for example, your heart ought to pump at between 50 and 75 strokes per minute at rest; and you ought to be able to see that if all men are mortal and Socrates is a man, then he is mortal.

[22] I don't mean to suggest, of course, that no one else has seen this point. On the contrary; it has been seen clearly by, for example, William Alston, Fred Dretske, Alvin Goldman, Ernest Sosa, and others.

Bibliography

Armstrong, David M. *Belief, Truth and Knowledge.* Cambridge, England: Cambridge University Press, 1973.

Chisholm, Roderick. *Theory of Knowledge,* 3d ed. Englewood Cliffs, NJ: Prentice-Hall, 1989.

Chisholm, Roderick. *The Foundations of Knowing.* Minneapolis: University of Minnesota Press, 1957.

Cohen, Stewart. "Justification and Truth." *Philosophical Studies 46* (1984).

Dretske, Fred. *Knowledge and the Flow of Information.* Cambridge, MA: MIT Press, 1981.

Feldman, Richard. "Reliabilism and Justification." *Monist 68* (1985).

Feldman, Richard, and Earl Conee. "Evidentialism." *Philosophical Studies 48* (1985).

Goldman, Alvin I. *Epistemology and Cognition,* Chap. 5. Cambridge, MA: Harvard University Press, 1985.

Kornblith, Hilary, ed. *Naturalized Epistemology.* Cambridge, MA: MIT Press, 1985.

Moser, Paul. *Epistemic Justification,* Chap. 4. Dordrecht, Netherlands: Reidel, 1985.

Pappas, George, ed. *Justification and Knowledge.* Dordrecht, Netherlands: Reidel, 1979.

Pollock, John L. *Contemporary Theories of Knowledge.* Totowa, NJ: Rowman & Littlefield, 1986.

Stroud, Barry. *The Significance of Skepticism,* Chap. 6. Oxford, England: Clarendon Press, 1984.

Swain, Marshall. *Reasons and Knowledge*. Ithaca, NY: Cornell University Press, 1981.

Tomberlin, James, ed. *Philosophical Perspectives*. Vol. 2: *Epistemology*. Atascadero, CA: Ridgeview, 1988. This volume contains several essays relevant to this part of this book.

Part VII
A Priori *Knowledge*

I. *Classifications and Definitions*

The problem of synthetic *a priori* knowledge involves epistemological, metaphysical, and semantic considerations. The terms *a priori* and *a posteriori* are Latin expressions developed by scholastic philosophers in the Middle Ages. *A priori* literally means "from what is prior," and *a posteriori* means "from what is posterior." Leibniz (1646–1716) used *a posteriori* to signify contingent truths of fact, truths about what is discover-

able by experience, and used *a priori* to signify truths of reason, truths that depend on the principle of identity (A = A), which the mind could discover without the aid of the senses. Immanuel Kant (1724–1804) further refined these notions to refer to judgments depending on empirical experience and judgments that do not, respectively. He further combined *a priori* knowledge with synthetic propositions giving rise to the present problem: is there synthetic *a priori* knowledge? For Kant, synthetic *a priori* knowledge is knowledge that is not derived from particular sensations but is presupposed in all our experience. It is logically necessary (that is, it could not be otherwise; it is true in all possible worlds), whereas synthetic *a posteriori* knowledge is contingent (that is, it could have been otherwise and is not true in all possible worlds).

A classification of the relevant concepts is as follows:

A. Epistemological categories
   1. *A priori* knowledge does not depend on evidence from sense experience (Plato's innate ideas and Leibniz's "Truths of Reason"); for example, mathematics and logic.
   2. *A posteriori* knowledge depends on evidence from sense experience (Plato's appearance and Leibniz's "truths of fact")—empirical knowledge.

B. Metaphysical categories
   1. *Necessary truths*—true in all possible worlds (for example, the statement that "God exists" according to the ontological argument)

   2. *Contingent truths*—true in the actual world but not in all possible worlds (for example, the fact that you exist and were born after January 1, 1800)

C. Semantical categories
   1. *Analytic*—predicate is *contained* in the subject, explicative, not ampliative (for example, "All mothers are women").
   2. *Synthetic*—predicate is not contained in the subject but adds something to the subject, ampliative, not explicative (for example, "Mary is a mother").

II. *Combinations*

If we combine these categories, using the epistemological and the semantic as the dominant ones (and subordinating the metaphysical categories), we arrive at the following chart:

	Analytic	**Synthetic**
A Priori	Entailments Identity Statements Tautologies Definitions *Examples* "All bachelors are unmarried." "All bodies are extended."	**Mathematics** "5 + 7 = 12" **Exclusionary** "Nothing red is green." **Presuppositions of Experience** Space, Time, and Causality **Moral Judgments** The Categorical Imperative "It's always wrong to torture for the fun of it." **The Laws of Logic** The Principle of Noncontradiction **Metaphysical** God's existence Freedom of the Will

A Posteriori	[NONE]	*Examples*
		
		All empirical statements:
		  "All bodies are heavy."
		  "All copper conducts electricity."
		  "John is a bachelor."

Kant rejected the idea of analytic *a posteriori* knowledge because the very idea of an analytic judgment depends solely on the relations of the concepts involved and is discoverable by determining whether its denial entails a contradiction. That is, the analytic makes no reference to experience, whereas the *a posteriori* depends on experience.

Generally rationalists assert, while empiricists deny, the existence of synthetic *a priori* knowledge. That is, while empiricists believe experience is the basis of all our knowledge, except analytic truths, the rationalist holds that reason can discover truths that are neither empirical nor analytic. For a radical rationalist such as Kant, all knowledge is grounded in self-evident, *a priori* nonempirical knowledge.

The essential claim of those who hold to synthetic *a priori* knowledge is that *the mind is able to grasp connections between ideas (concepts) that are not strictly analytically related.*

III. *The Kantian Theory About Synthetic* A Priori *Knowledge*

The primary question of Kant's *Critique of Pure Reason* is "How are synthetic *a priori* judgments possible?" Ewing has shown that Kant makes four claims about synthetic *a priori* judgments:

1. They are logically necessary—wholes that determine their own parts.

2. They are not derivable from particular sensations (although empirical experience is the trigger to cause them to arise).

3. They are presupposed in all of our experience.

4. They are contributed by our minds.

Our synthetic *a priori* "knowledge" is merely of the presuppositions or conditions of experience, and, as such, only of the *appearance* of the world to us, constructed as we are. We can have no *a priori* knowledge of the reality (the *Ding an Sich*). As red-tinted glasses cause us to see the world in shades of red, so the constraints of synthetic *a priori* categories cause us to experience the world causally, temporally, and spatially.

As mentioned earlier, all *a priori* knowledge is necessary and has universal application. It is true in all possible worlds, whereas statements known *a posteriori* are contingent. They could have turned out to be false rather than true.

In the second reading in this part of the book, A. J. Ayer gives a conventionalist critique of the notion of the synthetic *a priori*. He argues that all the supposed *a priori* knowledge can be reduced to analytic truths.

Nevertheless, there is reason to hold to the idea of synthetic *a priori* knowledge. A. C. Ewing sets forth some considerations in its favor in the third reading. Knowledge of mathematical, logical, and other statements can best be construed as *a priori*. Furthermore, there is a transcendental argument in its favor: Ayers's very statement that "there can be no synthetic *a priori* truths" is itself a synthetic *a priori* statement, so that if it's true, it's false. Even if all other cases are doubtful, the laws of logic seem to function as synthetic *a priori* truths. The principle of noncontradiction is necessary for the very possibility of thought, including the thought of the principle itself. Its denial is self-refuting, because to deny the principle depends on the very principle it is denying: If the principle of noncontradiction is not true, then the denial of its denial is just as valid as the denial itself.

A key to the distinction between analytic and synthetic *a priori* judgments is found in the notion of *containment*. When I say all bachelors are unmarried, we understand that the idea of "unmarried" is already present or contained in the notion of "bachelor," so I have not added anything to the concept of "bachelor." But when I say that if something is red it is not green, the notion of "not being green" does not seem to be contained in the concept "red," yet I do not need to look and see that the proposition is true. I can understand it immediately, using reason alone. The proposition "If something is red, it is not green" is not an analytic proposition but neither is it an empirical proposition. It is a necessary truth, known *a priori*. It is a *synthetic a priori* judgment.

But some philosophers doubt that the notion of *containment* is sturdy enough to bear the weight of the analytic–synthetic distinction. W. V. Quine in his classic essay "Two Dogmas of Empiricism" (Reading VII.4) argues that *containment* is a vague metaphor, and that its vagueness spreads over the entire analytic–synthetic distinction. The separating line between the ana-lytic and the *a priori* is so unclear that we might well throw out the analytic–synthetic distinction itself.

H. P. Grice and P. F. Strawson take issue with Quine's rejection of the analytic–synthetic distinction, arguing that there is a presumption in its favor. They argue both that the rejection of the distinction leads to absurd consequences and that we don't need a formal definition of synonymy for it to make sense.

In the final reading, Roderick Chisholm surveys and defends the traditional theses about synthetic *a priori* and analytic knowledge.

VII.1 A Priori *Knowledge*

IMMANUEL KANT

Immanuel Kant (1724–1804), who was born in a deeply pietistic Lutheran family in Königsberg, Germany, lived in that town his entire life, and taught at the University of Königsberg. He lived a duty-bound, methodical life, so regular that citizens were said to have set their clocks by his walks. Kant is one of the premier philosophers in the Western tradition. In his monumental work *The Critique of Pure Reason* (1781), he inaugurated a revolution in the theory of knowledge.

Kant began as a rationalist but on reading Hume was struck with the cogency of his argument. Hume "woke me from my dogmatic slumbers," Kant wrote, and henceforth accepted the idea that all our knowledge begins with experience. But Kant thought that Hume had made an invalid inference in concluding that all our knowledge arises from experience. Kant sought to demonstrate that the rationalists had an invaluable insight, which had been lost in their flamboyant speculation, that something determinate in the mind causes us to know what we know.

Kant argued that the mind is so structured and empowered that it imposes interpretive categories on our experience, so we do not simply experience the world, as the empiricists alleged, but interpret it through the constitutive mechanisms of the mind. This is sometimes called Kant's Copernican revolution.

In this selection, Kant makes his famous distinction between *a priori* and *a posteriori* knowledge. *A priori* knowledge is what we know *prior* to experience. It is opposed to *a posteriori* knowledge, which is based *on* experience. For Hume, all knowledge of matters of fact is *a posteriori* and only analytic statements (such as mathematical truths or statements such as 'All mothers are women') are known *a priori*. Kant rejects this formula. For him it is possible to have *a priori* knowledge of matters of fact. "But though all our knowledge begins with experience, it does not follow that it all arises out of experience." Indeed, he thinks that mathematical truth is not analytic but synthetic (the predicate adds something to the subject) and that there is other synthetic *a priori* knowledge, such as our knowledge of time, space, causality, and the moral law. The schema looks like this:

	A Priori	A Posteriori
Analytic	Tautologies and entailments ("All bachelors are unmarried.")	None
Synthetic	Causality, space, and time (5 + 7 = 12, the moral law)	Empirical judgments ("There are people in this room.")

Translated by Paul Carus, *Kant's Prolegomena* (Chicago 1902). Some notes omitted.

After a brief selection from the preface of the *Critique of Pure Reason* (1781), we turn to the preamble of Kant's *Prolegomena to Any Future Metaphysic* (1783).

Until now we have assumed that all our knowledge must conform to objects. But every attempt to extend our knowledge of objects by establishing something in regard to them *a priori,* by means of concepts, has, on this assumption, ended in failure. Therefore, we must see whether we may have better success in our metaphysical task if we begin with the assumption that objects must conform to our knowledge. In this way we would have knowledge of objects *a priori.* We should then be proceeding in the same way as Copernicus in his revolutionary hypothesis. After he failed to make progress in explaining the movements of the heavenly bodies on the supposition that they all revolved around the observer, he decided to reverse the relationship and made the observer revolve around the heavenly body, the sun, which was at rest. A similar experiment can be done in metaphysics with regard to the intuition of objects. If our intuition must conform to the constitution of the object, I do not see how we could know anything of the object *a priori,* but if the object of sense must conform to the constitution of our faculty of intuition, then *a priori* knowledge is possible. (From the Preface of *Critique of Pure Reason* (1781), my translation).

Prolegomena: Preamble on the Peculiarities of All Metaphysical Knowledge

§ 1. *Of the Sources of Metaphysics*

If it becomes desirable to organize any knowledge as science, it will be necessary first to determine accurately those peculiar features which no other science has in common with it, constituting its peculiarity; otherwise the boundaries of all sciences become confused, and none of them can be treated thoroughly according to its nature.

The peculiar characteristic of a science may consist of a simple difference of object, or of the sources of knowledge, or of the kind of knowledge, or perhaps of all three conjointly. On these, therefore, depends the idea of a possible science and its territory.

First, as concerns the sources of metaphysical knowledge, its very concept implies that they cannot be empirical. Its principles (including not only its maxims but its basic notions) must never be derived from experience. It must not be physical but metaphysical knowledge, namely, knowledge lying beyond experience. It can therefore have for its basis neither external experience, which is the source of physics proper, nor internal, which is the basis of empirical psychology. It is therefore *a priori* knowledge, coming from pure understanding and pure reason.

But so far metaphysics would not be distinguishable from pure mathematics; it must therefore be called *pure philosophical* knowledge; and for the meaning of this term I refer to the *Critique of the Pure Reason,*[1] where the distinction between these two employments of reason is sufficiently explained. So far concerning the sources of metaphysical knowledge.

§ 2. *Concerning the Kind of Knowledge Which Can Alone Be Called Metaphysical*

a. On the Distinction between Analytical and Synthetical Judgments in General.—The peculiarity of its sources demands that metaphysical knowledge must consist of nothing but *a priori* judgments. But whatever be their origin or their logical form, there is a distinction in judgments, as to their content, according to which they are either merely *explicative,* adding nothing to the content of knowledge, or *expansive,* increasing the given knowledge. The former may be called *analytical,* the latter *synthetical,* judgments.

Analytical judgments express nothing in the predicate but what has been already actually thought in the concept of the subject, though not so distinctly or with the same (full) consciousness.

When I say: "All bodies are extended," I have not amplified in the least my concept of body, but have only analyzed it, as extension was really thought to belong to that concept before the judgment was made, though it was not expressed. This judgment is therefore analytical. On the contrary, this judgment, "All bodies have weight," contains in its predicate something not actually thought in the universal concept of body; it amplifies my knowledge by adding something to my concept, and must therefore be called synthetical.

b. The Common Principle of All Analytical Judgments Is the Law of Contradiction.—All analytical judgments depend wholly on the law of contradiction, and are in their nature *a priori* cognitions, whether the concepts that supply them with matter be empirical or not. For the predicate of an affirmative analytical judgment is already contained in the concept of the subject, of which it cannot be denied without contradiction. In the same way its opposite is necessarily denied of the subject in an analytical, but negative, judgment, by the same law of contradiction. Such is the nature of the judgments: "All bodies are extended," and "No bodies are unextended (that is, simple)."

For this very reason all analytical judgments are *a priori* even when the concepts are empirical, as, for example, "Gold is a yellow metal"; for to know this I require no experience beyond my concept of gold as a yellow metal. It is, in fact, the very concept, and I need only analyze it without looking beyond it.

c. Synthetical Judgments Require a Different Principle from the Law of Contradiction.—There are synthetical *a posteriori* judgments of empirical origin; but there are also others which are certain *a priori,* and which spring from pure understanding and reason. Yet they both agree in this, that they cannot possibly spring from the principle of analysis, namely, the law of contradiction, alone. They require a quite different principle from which they may be deduced, subject, of course, always to the law of contradiction, which must never be violated, even though everything cannot be deduced from it. I shall first classify synthetical judgments.

1. *Judgments of Experience* are always synthetical. For it would be absurd to base an analytical judgment on experience, as our concept suffices for the purpose without requiring any testimony from experience. That body is extended is a judgment established *a priori,* and not an empirical judgment.

For before appealing to experience, we already have all the conditions of the judgment in the concept, from which we have but to elicit the predicate according to the law of contradiction, and thereby to become conscious of the necessity of the judgment, which experience could not in the least teach us.

2. *Mathematical Judgments* are all synthetical. This fact seems hitherto to have altogether escaped the observation of those who have analyzed human reason; it even seems directly opposed to all their conjectures, though it is incontestably certain and most important in its consequences. For as it was found that the conclusions of mathematicians all proceed according to the law of contradiction (as is demanded by all apodictic certainty), men persuaded themselves that the fundamental principles were known from the same law. This was a great mistake, for a synthetical proposition can indeed be established by the law of contradiction, but only by presupposing another synthetical proposition from which it follows, but never by that law alone.

First of all, we must observe that all strictly mathematical judgments are *a priori,* and not empirical, because they carry with them necessity, which cannot be obtained from experience. But if this be not conceded to me, very good; I shall confine my assertion to *pure mathematics,* the very notion of which implies that it contains pure *a priori* and not empirical knowledge.

It must at first be thought that the proposition $7 + 5 = 12$ is a mere analytical judgment, following from the concept of the sum of seven and five, according to the law of contradiction. But on closer examination it appears that the concept of the sum of $7 + 5$ contains merely their union in a single number, without its being at all thought what the particular number is that unites them. The concept of twelve is by no means thought by merely thinking of the combination of seven and five; and, analyze this possible sum as we may, we shall not discover twelve in the concept. We must go beyond these concepts, by calling to our aid some intuition which corresponds to one of the concepts—that is, either our five fingers or five points (as Segner has it in his *Arithmetic*)—and we must add successively the units of the five given in the intuition to the concept of seven. Hence our concept is really amplified by the proposition $7 + 5 = 12$, and we add to the first concept a second concept not thought in it. Arithmetical judgments are therefore synthetical, and the more plainly according as we take larger numbers; for in such cases it is clear that, however closely we analyze our concepts without calling intuition to our aid, we can never find the sum by such mere dissection.

Just as little is any principle of geometry analytical. That a straight line is the shortest path between two points is a synthetical proposition. For my concept of straight contains nothing of quantity, but only a quality. The concept "shortest" is therefore altogether additional and cannot be obtained by any analysis of the concept "straight line." Here, too, intuition must come to aid us. It alone makes the synthesis possible. What usually makes us believe that the predicate of such apodictic judgments is already contained in our concept, and that the judgment is therefore analytical, is the duplicity of the expression. We must think a certain predicate as attached to a given concept, and necessity indeed belongs to the concepts. But the question is not what we must join in thought *to* the given concept, but what we actually think together with and in it, though obscurely; and so it appears that the predicate belongs to this concept necessarily indeed, yet not directly but indirectly by means of an intuition which must be present.

Some other principles, assumed by geometers, are indeed actually analytical, and depend on the law of contradiction; but they only serve, as identical propositions, as a method of concatenation, and not as principles—for example $a = a$, the whole is equal to itself, or $a + b > a$, the whole is greater than its part. And yet even these, though they are recognized as valid from mere concepts, are admitted in mathematics only because they can be represented in some intuition.

The essential and distinguishing feature of pure mathematical knowledge among all other *a priori* knowledge is that it cannot at all proceed from concepts, but only by means of the construction of concepts.[2] As therefore in its propositions it must proceed beyond the concept to that which its corresponding intuition contains, these propositions neither can, nor ought to, arise analytically, by dissection of the concept, but are all synthetical.

I cannot refrain from pointing out the disadvantage resulting to philosophy from the neglect of this easy and apparently insignificant observation. Hume being prompted to cast his eye over the whole field of *a priori* cognitions in which human

understanding claims such mighty possessions (a calling he felt worthy of a philosopher) heedlessly severed from it a whole, and indeed its most valuable, province, namely, pure mathematics; for he imagined its nature or, so to speak, the state constitution of this empire depended on totally different principles, namely, on the law of contradiction alone; and although he did not divide judgments in this manner formally and universally as I have done here, what he said was equivalent to this: that mathematics contains only analytical, but metaphysics synthetical, *a priori* propositions. In this, however, he was greatly mistaken, and the mistake had a decidedly injurious effect upon his whole conception. But for this, he would have extended his question concerning the origin of our synthetical judgments far beyond the metaphysical concept of causality and included in it the possibility of mathematics *a priori* also, for this latter he must have assumed to be equally synthetical. And then he could not have based his metaphysical propositions on mere experience without subjecting the axioms of mathematics equally to experience, a thing which he was far too acute to do. The good company into which metaphysics would thus have been brought would have saved it from the danger of a contemptuous ill-treatment, for the thrust intended for it must have reached mathematics, which was not and could not have been Hume's intention. Thus that acute man would have been led into considerations which must needs be similar to those that now occupy us, but which would have gained inestimably by his inimitably elegant style.

3. *Metaphysical Judgments,* properly so called, are all synthetical. We must distinguish judgments pertaining to metaphysics from metaphysical judgments properly so called. Many of the former are analytical, but they only afford the means for metaphysical judgments, which are the whole end of the science and which are always synthetical. For if there be concepts pertaining to metaphysics (as, for example, that of substance), the judgments springing from simple analysis of them also pertain to metaphysics, as, for example, substance is that which only exists as subject, etc.; and by means of several such analytical judgments we seek to approach the definition of the concepts. But as the analysis of a pure concept of the understanding (the kind of concept pertaining to metaphysics) does not proceed in any different manner from the dissection

of any other, even empirical, concepts, not belonging to metaphysics (such as, air is an elastic fluid, the elasticity of which is not destroyed by any known degree of cold), it follows that the concept indeed, but not the analytical judgment, is properly metaphysical. This science has something peculiar in the production of its *a priori* cognitions, which must therefore be distinguished from the features it has in common with other rational knowledge. Thus the judgment that all the substance in things is permanent is a synthetical and properly metaphysical judgment.

If the *a priori* concepts which constitute the materials and tools of metaphysics have first been collected according to fixed principles, then their analysis will be of great value; it might be taught as a particular part (as a *philosophia definitiva*), containing nothing but analytical judgments pertaining to metaphysics, and could be treated separately from the synthetical which constitute metaphysics proper. For indeed these analyses are not of much value except in metaphysics, that is, as regards the synthetical judgments which are to be generated by these previously analyzed concepts.

The conclusion drawn in this section then is that metaphysics is properly concerned with synthetical propositions *a priori,* and these alone constitute its end, for which it indeed requires various dissections of its concepts, namely, analytical judgments, but wherein the procedure is not different from that in every other kind of knowledge, in which we merely seek to render our concepts distinct by analysis. But the generation of *a priori* knowledge by intuition as well as by concepts, in fine, of synthetical propositions *a priori,* especially in philosophical knowledge, constitutes the essential subject of metaphysics.

§ 3. *A Remark on the General Division of Judgment into Analytical and Synthetical*

This division is indispensable, as concerns the critique of human understanding, and therefore deserves to be called classical in such critical investigation, though otherwise it is of little use. But this is the reason why dogmatic philosophers, who always seek the sources of metaphysical judgments in metaphysics itself, and not apart from it in the pure laws of reason generally, altogether neglected this appar-

ently obvious distinction. Thus the celebrated Wolff and his acute follower Baumgarten came to seek the proof of the principle of sufficient reason, which is clearly synthetical, in the principle of contradiction. In Locke's *Essay,* however, I find an indication of my division. For in the fourth book (Chapter III, § 9, seq.), having discussed the various connections of representations in judgments, and their sources, one of which he makes "identity or contradiction" (analytical judgments) and another the coexistence of ideas in a subject (synthetical judgments), he confesses (§ 10) that our (*a priori*) knowledge of the latter is very narrow and almost nothing. But in his remarks on this species of knowledge, there is so little of what is definite and reduced to rules that we cannot wonder if no one, not even Hume, was led to make investigations concerning this sort of proposition. For such general and yet definite principles are not easily learned from other men, who have had them only obscurely in their minds. One must hit on them first by one's own reflection; then one finds them elsewhere, where one could not possibly have found them at first because the authors themselves did not know that such an idea lay at the basis of their observations. Men who never think independently have nevertheless the acuteness to discover everything, after it has been once shown them, in what was said long since, though no one was ever able to see it there before.

§ 4. *The General Question of the Prolegomena: Is Metaphysics at All Possible?*

Were a metaphysics which could maintain its place as a science really in existence, could we say: "Here is metaphysics; learn it and it will convince you irresistibly and irrevocably of its truth"? This question would then be useless, and there would only remain that other question (which would rather be a test of our acuteness than a proof of the existence of the thing itself): "How is the science possible, and how does reason come to attain it?" But human reason has not been so fortunate in this case. There is no single book to which you can point as you do to Euclid, and say: "This is metaphysics; here you may find the noblest objects of this science, the knowledge of a highest being and of a future existence, proved from principles of pure reason." We can be shown indeed many propositions, demonstrably certain and never questioned; but these are all analytical, and rather concern the materials and the scaffolding for metaphysics than the extension of knowledge, which is our proper object in studying it (§ 2). Even supposing you produce synthetical judgments (such as the law of sufficient reason, which you have never proved, as you ought to, from pure reason *a priori*, though we gladly concede its truth), you lapse, when you try to employ them for your principal purpose, into such doubtful assertions that in all ages one metaphysics has contradicted another, either in its assertions or their proofs, and thus has itself destroyed its own claim to lasting assent. Nay, the very attempts to set up such a science are the main cause of the early appearance of skepticism, a mental attitude in which reason treats itself with such violence that it could never have arisen save from complete despair of ever satisfying its most important aspirations. For long before men began to inquire into nature methodically, they consulted abstract reason, which had to some extent been exercised by means of ordinary experience; for reason is ever present, while laws of nature must usually be discovered with labor. So metaphysics floated to the surface, like foam, which dissolved the moment it was scooped off. But immediately there appeared a new supply on the surface, to be ever eagerly gathered up by some; while others, instead of seeking in the depths the cause of the phenomenon, thought they showed their wisdom by ridiculing the idle labor of their neighbors.

Weary therefore of dogmatism, which teaches us nothing, and of skepticism, which does not even promise us anything—even the quiet state of a contented ignorance—disquieted by the importance of knowledge so much needed, and rendered suspicious by long experience of all knowledge which we believe we possess or which offers itself in the name of pure reason, there remains but one critical question on the answer to which our future procedure depends, namely, "Is metaphysics at all possible?" But this question must be answered, not by sceptical objections to the asseverations of some actual system of metaphysics (for we do not as yet admit such a thing to exist), but from the conception, as yet only problematical, of a science of this sort.

In the *Critique of Pure Reason* I have treated this question synthetically, by making inquiries into pure reason itself and endeavoring in this source to determine the elements as well as the laws of its pure use according to principles. The task is difficult and requires a resolute reader to penetrate by degrees into a system based on no data except reason itself, and which therefore seeks, without resting upon any fact, to unfold knowledge from its original germs. The *Prolegomena*, however, are designed for preparatory exercises; they are intended to point out what we have to do in order to make a science actual if it is possible, rather than to propound it. The *Prolegomena* must therefore rest upon something already known as trustworthy, from which we can set out with confidence and ascend to sources as yet unknown, the discovery of which will not only explain to us what we knew but exhibit a sphere of many cognitions which all spring from the same sources. The method of prolegomena, especially of those designed as a preparation for future metaphysics, is consequently analytical.

But it happens, fortunately, that though we cannot assume metaphysics to be an actual science, we can say with confidence that there is actually given certain pure *a priori* synthetical cognitions, pure mathematics and pure physics; for both contain propositions which are unanimously recognized, partly apodictically certain by mere reason, partly by general consent arising from experience and yet as independent of experience. We have therefore at least some uncontested synthetical knowledge *a priori* and need not ask *whether* it be possible, for it is actual, but *how* it is possible, in order that we may deduce from the principle which makes the given knowledge possible the possibility of all the rest.

§ 5. *The General Problem: How Is Knowledge from Pure Reason Possible?*

We have already learned the significant distinction between analytical and synthetical judgments. The possibility of analytical propositions was easily comprehended, being entirely founded on the law of contradiction. The possibility of synthetical *a posteriori* judgments, of those which are gathered from experience, also requires no particular explanations, for experience is nothing but a continued synthesis of perceptions. There remain therefore only synthetical propositions *a priori,* of which the possibility must be sought or investigated, because they must depend upon other principles than the law of contradiction.

But here we need not first establish the possibility of such propositions so as to ask whether they are possible. For there are enough of them which indeed are of undoubted certainty; and, as our present method is analytical, we shall start from the fact that such synthetical but purely rational knowledge actually exists; but we must now inquire into the ground of this possibility and ask *how* such knowledge is possible, in order that we may, from the principles of its possibility, be enabled to determine the conditions of its use, its sphere and its limits. The real problem upon which all depends, when expressed with scholastic precision, is therefore: "How are synthetic propositions *a priori* possible?"

For the sake of popular understanding I have above expressed this problem somewhat differently, as an inquiry into purely rational knowledge, which I could do for once without detriment to the desired insight, because, as we have only to do here with metaphysics and its sources, the reader will, I hope, after the foregoing reminders, keep in mind that when we speak of knowing by pure reason we do not mean analytical but synthetical knowledge.[3]

Metaphysics stands or falls with the solution of this problem; its very existence depends upon it. Let anyone make metaphysical assertions with ever so much plausibility, let him overwhelm us with conclusions; but if he has not previously proved able to answer this question satisfactorily, I have a right to say: This is all vain, baseless philosophy and false wisdom. You speak through pure reason and claim, as it were, to create cognitions *a priori* not only by dissecting given concepts, but also by asserting connections which do not rest upon the law of contradiction, and which you claim to conceive quite independently of all experience; how do you arrive at this, and how will you justify such pretensions? An appeal to the consent of the common sense of mankind cannot be allowed, for that is a witness whose authority depends merely upon rumor. Says Horace:

"Quodcunque ostendis mihi sic, incredulus odi."[4]

The answer to this question is as indispensable as it is difficult; and although the principal reason that it was not sought long ago is that the possibility of the question never occurred to anybody, there is yet another reason, namely, that a satisfactory answer to this one question requires a much more persistent, profound, and painstaking reflection than the most diffuse work on metaphysics, which on its first appearance promised immortal fame to its author. And every intelligent reader, when he carefully reflects what this problem requires, must at first be struck with its difficulty, and would regard it as insoluble and even impossible did there not actually exist pure synthetical cognitions *a priori*. This actually happened to David Hume, though he did not conceive the question in its entire universality as is done here and as must be done if the answer is to be decisive for all metaphysics. For how is it possible, says that acute man, that when a concept is given me I can go beyond it and connect with it another which is not contained in it, in such a manner as if the latter *necessarily* belonged to the former? Nothing but experience can furnish us with such connections (thus he concluded from the difficulty which he took to be impossibility), and all that vaunted necessity or, what is the same thing, knowledge assumed to be *a priori* is nothing but a long habit of accepting something as true, and hence of mistaking subjective necessity for objective.

Should my reader complain of the difficulty and the trouble which I shall occasion him in the solution of this problem, he is at liberty to solve it himself in an easier way. Perhaps he will then feel under obligation to the person who has undertaken for him a labor of so profound research and will rather feel some surprise at the facility with which, considering the nature of the subject, the solution has been attained. Yet it has cost years of work to solve the problem in its whole universality (using the term in the mathematical sense, namely, for that which is sufficient for all cases), and finally to exhibit it in the analytical form, as the reader will find it here.

All metaphysicians are therefore solemnly and legally suspended from their occupations till they shall have adequately answered the question, "How are synthetic cognitions *a priori* possible?" For the answer contains the only credentials which they must show when they have anything to offer us in the name of pure reason. But if they do not possess these credentials, they can expect nothing else of reasonable people, who have been deceived so often, than to be dismissed without further inquiry.

If they, on the other hand, desire to carry on their business, not as a science, but as an art of wholesome persuasion suitable to the common sense of man, this calling cannot in justice be denied them. They will then speak the modest language of a rational belief; they will grant that they are not allowed even to conjecture, far less to know, anything which lies beyond the bounds of all possible experience, but only to assume (not for speculative use, which they must abandon, but for practical use only) the existence of something possible and even indispensable for the guidance of the understanding and of the will in life. In this manner alone can they be called useful and wise men, and the more so as they renounce the title of metaphysicians. For the latter profess to be speculative philosophers; and since, when judgments *a priori* are under discussion, poor probabilities cannot be admitted (for what is declared to be known *a priori* is thereby announced as necessary), such men cannot be permitted to play with conjectures, but their assertion must be either science or nothing at all.

It may be said that the entire transcendental philosophy, which necessarily precedes all metaphysics, is nothing but the complete solution of the problem here propounded, in systematic order and completeness, and hence we have hitherto never had any transcendental philosophy. For what goes by its name is properly a part of metaphysics, whereas the former science is intended only to constitute the possibility of the latter and must therefore precede all metaphysics. And it is not surprising that when a whole science, deprived of all help from other sciences and consequently in itself quite new, is required to answer a single question satisfactorily, we should find the answer troublesome and difficult, nay, even shrouded in obscurity.

As we now proceed to this solution according to the analytical method, in which we assume that such cognitions from pure reason actually exist, we can only appeal to two sciences of theoretical knowledge (which alone is under consideration here), namely, pure mathematics and pure natural science. For these alone can exhibit to us objects in intuition, and consequently (if there should occur in them a cognition *a priori*) can show the truth or conformity of the cognition to the object *in concreto*, that is, its actuality, from which we could proceed

to the ground of its possibility by the analytical method. This facilitates our work greatly for here universal considerations are not only applied to facts, but even start from them, while in a synthetic procedure they must strictly be derived *in abstracto* from concepts.

But in order to rise from these actual and, at the same time, well-grounded pure cognitions *a priori* to a possible knowledge of the kind as we are seeking, namely, to metaphysics as a science, we must comprehend that which occasions it—I mean the mere natural, though in spite of its truth still suspect, cognition *a priori* which lies at the basis of that science, the elaboration of which without any critical investigation of its possibility is commonly called metaphysics. In a word, we must comprehend the natural conditions of such a science as a part of our inquiry, and thus the transcendental problem will be gradually answered by a division into four questions:

1. How is pure mathematics possible?

2. How is pure natural science possible?

3. How is metaphysics in general possible?

4. How is metaphysics as a science possible?

It may be seen that the solution of these problems, though chiefly designed to exhibit the essential matter of the *Critique,* has yet something peculiar, which for itself alone deserves attention. This is the search for the sources of given sciences in reason itself, so that its faculty of knowing something *a priori* may by its own deeds be investigated and measured. By this procedure these sciences gain, if not with regard to their contents, yet as to their proper use; and while they throw light on the higher question concerning their common origin, they give, at the same time, an occasion better to explain their own nature.

Notes

[1] *Critique of Pure Reason,* "Methodology," Ch. I, Sec. 2.

[2] *Critique of Pure Reason,* "Methodology," Ch. I, Sec. 1.

[3] It is unavoidable that, as knowledge advances, certain expressions which have become classical after having been used since the infancy of science will be found inadequate and unsuitable, and a newer and more appropriate

application of the terms will give rise to confusion. [This is the case with the term "analytical."] The analytical method, so far as it is opposed to the synthetical, is very different from one that consists of analytical propositions; it signifies only that we start from what is sought, as if it were given, and ascend to the only conditions under which it is possible. In this method we often use nothing but synthetical propositions, as in mathematical analysis, and it were better to term it the *regressive* method, in

contradistinction to the *synthetic* or *progressive*. A principal part of logic too is distinguished by the name of analytic, which here signifies the logic of truth in contrast to dialectic, without considering whether the cognitions belonging to it are analytical or synthetical.

4 ["To all that which thou provest me thus, I refuse to give credence, and hate"—*Epistle* II, 3, 188.]

VII.2 *An Empiricist Critique of* A Priori *Knowledge*

A. J. AYER

A. J. Ayer (1910–1989) was for many years Professor of Philosophy at Oxford University. In this essay from his early work, *Language, Truth, and Logic,* Ayer argues that we have no reason to believe in synthetic *a priori* truth. All the candidates for such knowledge can be explained either as tautologies or as analytic truth.

. . . Having admitted that we are empiricists, we must now deal with the objection that is commonly brought against all forms of empiricism; the objection, namely, that it is impossible on empiricist principles to account for our knowledge of necessary truths. For, as Hume conclusively showed, no general proposition whose validity is subject to the test of actual experience can ever be logically certain. No matter how often it is verified in practice, there still remains the possibility that it will be confuted on some future occasion. The fact that a law has been substantiated in $n - 1$ cases affords no logical guarantee that it will be substantiated in the nth case also, no matter how large we take n to be. And this means that no general proposition refer-

ring to a matter of fact can ever be shown to be necessarily and universally true. It can at best be a probable hypothesis. And this, we shall find, applies not only to general propositions, but to all propositions which have a factual content. They can none of them ever become logically certain. This conclusion, which we shall elaborate later on, is one which must be accepted by every consistent empiricist. It is often thought to involve him in complete scepticism; but this is not the case. For the fact that the validity of a proposition cannot be logically guaranteed in no way entails that it is irrational for us to believe it. On the contrary, what is irrational is to look for a guarantee where none can be forthcoming; to demand certainty where probability is all that is obtainable. We have already remarked upon this, in referring to the work of Hume. And we shall make the point clearer when we come to treat of probability, in explaining the use which we make of empirical propositions. We shall discover that there is nothing perverse or paradoxical about the view that all the "truths" of science and common sense are hypotheses; and consequently that the fact that

This selection is Chapter IV, except for small omissions, of Ayer's *Language, Truth and Logic,* published in Great Britain by Victor Gollancz, Ltd., in 1936, and in the United States by Dover Publications, Inc. It is here reprinted with the kind permission of the publishers. Footnotes omitted.

it involves this view constitutes no objection to the empiricist thesis.

Where the empiricist does encounter difficulty is in connection with the truths of formal logic and mathematics. For whereas a scientific generalization is readily admitted to be fallible, the truths of mathematics and logic appear to everyone to be necessary and certain. But if empiricism is correct no proposition which has a factual content can be necessary or certain. Accordingly the empiricist must deal with the truths of logic and mathematics in one of the two following ways: he must say either that they are not necessary truths, in which case he must account for the universal conviction that they are; or he must say that they have no factual content, and then he must explain how a proposition which is empty of all factual content can be true and useful and surprising.

If neither of these courses proves satisfactory, we shall be obliged to give way to rationalism. We shall be obliged to admit that there are some truths about the world which we can know independently of experience; that there are some properties which we can ascribe to all objects, even though we cannot conceivably observe that all objects have them. And we shall have to accept it as a mysterious inexplicable fact that our thought has this power to reveal to us authoritatively the nature of objects which we have never observed. Or else we must accept the Kantian explanation which, apart from the epistemological difficulties which we have already touched on, only pushes the mystery a stage further back.

It is clear that any such concession to rationalism would upset the main argument of this book. For the admission that there were some facts about the world which could be known independently of experience would be incompatible with our fundamental contention that a sentence says nothing unless it is empirically verifiable. And thus the whole force of our attack on metaphysics would be destroyed. It is vital, therefore, for us to be able to show that one or other of the empiricist accounts of the propositions of logic and mathematics is correct. If we are successful in this, we shall have destroyed the foundations of rationalism. For the fundamental tenet of rationalism is that thought is an independent source of knowledge, and is moreover a more trustworthy source of knowledge than expe-

rience; indeed some rationalists have gone so far as to say that thought is the only source of knowledge. And the ground for this view is simply that the only necessary truths about the world which are known to us are known through thought and not through experience. So that if we can show either that the truths in question are not necessary or that they are not "truths about the world," we shall be taking away the support on which rationalism rests. We shall be making good the empiricist contention that there are no "truths of reason" which refer to matters of fact.

The course of maintaining that the truths of logic and mathematics are not necessary or certain was adopted by Mill. He maintained that these propositions were inductive generalizations based on an extremely large number of instances. The fact that the number of supporting instances was so very large accounted, in his view, for our believing these generalizations to be necessarily and universally true. The evidence in their favor was so strong that it seemed incredible to us that a contrary instance should ever arise. Nevertheless it was in principle possible for such generalizations to be confuted. They were highly probable, but, being inductive generalizations, they were not certain. The difference between them and the hypotheses of natural science was a difference in degree and not in kind. Experience gave us very good reason to suppose that a "truth" of mathematics or logic was true universally; but we were not possessed of a guarantee. For these "truths" were only empirical hypotheses which had worked particularly well in the past; and, like all empirical hypotheses, they were theoretically fallible.

I do not think that this solution of the empiricist's difficulty with regard to the propositions of logic and mathematics is acceptable. In discussing it, it is necessary to make a distinction which is perhaps already enshrined in Kant's famous dictum that, although there can be no doubt that all our knowledge begins with experience, it does not follow that it all arises out of experience. When we say that the truths of logic are known independently of experience, we are not of course saying that they are innate, in the sense that we are born knowing them. It is obvious that mathematics and logic have to be learned in the same way as chemistry and history have to be learned. Nor are we denying that the first person to discover a given logical or mathematical truth was led to it by an inductive procedure. It is very probable, for example, that the principle of the syllogism was formulated not before but after the validity of syllogistic reasoning had been observed in a number of particular cases. What we are discussing, however, when we say that the logical and mathematical truths are known independently of experience, is not a historical question concerning the way in which these truths were originally discovered, nor a psychological question concerning the way in which each of us comes to learn them, but an epistemological question. The contention of Mill's which we reject is that the propositions of logic and mathematics have the same status as empirical hypotheses; that their validity is determined in the same way. We maintain that they are independent of experience in the sense that they do not owe their validity to empirical verification. We may come to discover them through an inductive process; but once we have apprehended them we see that they are necessarily true, that they hold good for every conceivable instance. And this serves to distinguish them from empirical generalizations. For we know that a proposition whose validity depends upon experience cannot be seen to be necessarily and universally true.

In rejecting Mill's theory, we are obliged to be somewhat dogmatic. We can do no more than state the issue clearly and then trust that his contention will be seen to be discrepant with the relevant logical facts. The following considerations may serve to show that of the two ways of dealing with logic and mathematics which are open to the empiricist, the one which Mill adopted is not the one which is correct.

The Irrefutability of the Propositions of Mathematics and Logic

The best way to substantiate our assertion that the truths of formal logic and pure mathematics are necessarily true is to examine cases in which they might seem to be confuted. It might easily happen, for example, that when I came to count what I had taken to be five pairs of objects, I found that they amounted only to nine. And if I wished to mislead people I might say that on this occasion twice five was not ten. But in that case I should not be using the complex sign "$2 \times 5 = 10$" in the way in which it is ordinarily used. I should be taking it not as the expression of a purely mathematical proposition, but as the expression of an empirical generalization, to the effect that whenever I counted what appeared to me to be five pairs of objects I discovered that they were ten in number. This generalization may very well be false. But if it proved false in a given case, one would not say that the mathematical proposition "$2 \times 5 = 10$" had been confuted. One would say that I was wrong in supposing that there were five pairs of objects to start with, or that one of the objects had been taken away while I was counting, or that two of them had coalesced, or that I had counted wrongly. One would adopt as an explanation whatever empirical hypothesis fitted in best with the accredited facts. The one explanation which would in no circumstances be adopted is that ten is not always the product of two and five.

To take another example: if what appears to be a Euclidean triangle is found by measurement not to have angles totalling 180 degrees, we do not say that we have met with an instance which invalidates the mathematical proposition that the sum of the three angles of a Euclidean triangle is 180 degrees. We say that we have measured wrongly, or, more probably, that the triangle we have been measuring is not Euclidean. And this is our procedure in every case in which a mathematical truth might appear to be confuted. We always preserve its validity by adopting some other explanation of the occurrence.

The same thing applies to the principles of formal logic. We may take an example relating to the so-called law of excluded middle, which states that a proposition must be either true or false, or, in other words, that it is impossible that a proposition and its contradictory should neither of them be true. One might suppose that a proposition of the form "*x* has stopped doing *y*" would in certain cases constitute an exception to this law. For instance, if my friend has never yet written to me, it seems fair to say that it is neither true nor false that he has stopped writing to me. But in fact one would refuse to accept such an instance as an invalidation of the law of excluded middle. One would point out that the proposition "My friend has stopped writing to me" is not a simple proposition, but the conjunction of the two propositions "My friend wrote to me in the past" and "My friend does not write to me now": and, furthermore, that the proposition "My friend has not stopped writing to me" is not, as it appears to be, contradictory to "My friend has stopped writing to me," but only contrary to it. For it means "My friend wrote to me in the past, and he still writes to me." When, therefore, we say that such a proposition as "My friend has stopped writing to me" is sometimes neither true nor false, we are speaking inaccurately. For we seem to be saying that neither it nor its contradictory is true. Whereas what we mean, or anyhow should mean, is that neither it nor its apparent contradictory is true. And its apparent contradictory is really only its contrary. Thus we preserve the law of excluded middle by showing that the negating of a sentence does not always yield the contradictory of the proposition originally expressed.

There is no need to give further examples. Whatever instance we care to take, we shall always find that the situations in which a logical or mathematical principle might appear to be confuted are accounted for in such a way as to leave the principle unassailed. And this indicates that Mill was wrong in supposing that a situation could arise which would overthrow a mathematical truth. The principles of logic and mathematics are true universally simply because we never allow them to be anything else. And the reason for this is that we cannot abandon them without contradicting ourselves, without sinning against the rules which govern the use of language, and so making our utterances self-stultifying. In other words, the truths of logic and mathematics are analytic propositions or tautologies. In saying this we are making what will be held to be an extremely controversial statement, and we must now proceed to make its implications clear.

The Nature of Analytic Propositions

The most familiar definition of an analytic proposition, or judgment, as he called it, is that given by Kant. He said that an analytic judgment was one in which the predicate B belonged to the subject A as something which was covertly contained in the concept of A. He contrasted analytic with synthetic judgments, in which the predicate B lay outside the subject A, although it did stand in connection with it. Analytic judgments, he explains, "add nothing through the predicate to the concept of the subject, but merely break it up into those constituent concepts that have all along been thought in it, although confusedly." Synthetic judgments, on the other hand, "add to the concept of the subject a predicate which has not been in any wise thought in it, and which no analysis could possibly extract from it." Kant gives "all bodies are extended" as an example of an analytic judgment, on the ground that the required predicate can be extracted from the concept of "body," "in accordance with the principle of contradiction"; as an example of a synthetic judgment, he gives "all bodies are heavy." He refers also to "7 + 5 = 12" as a synthetic judgment, on the ground that the concept of twelve is by no means already thought in merely thinking the union of seven and five. And he appears to regard this as tantamount to saying that the judgment does not rest on the principle of contradiction alone. He holds, also, that through analytic judgments our knowledge is not extended as it is through synthetic judgments. For in analytic judgments "the concept which I already have is merely set forth and made intelligible to me."

I think that this is a fair summary of Kant's account of the distinction between analytic and synthetic propositions, but I do not think that it succeeds in making the distinction clear. For even if we pass over the difficulties which arise out of the use of the vague term "concept," and the unwarranted assumption that every judgment, as well as every German or English sentence, can be said to have a subject and a predicate, there remains still this crucial defect. Kant does not give one straightforward criterion for distinguishing between analytic and synthetic propositions; he gives two distinct criteria, which are by no means equivalent. Thus his ground for holding that the proposition "7 + 5 = 12" is synthetic is, as we have seen, that the subjective intension of "7 + 5" does not comprise the subjective intension of "12"; whereas his ground for holding that "all bodies are extended" is an analytic proposition is that it rests on the principle of contradiction alone. That is, he employs a psychological criterion in the first of these examples, and a logical criterion in the second, and takes their equivalence for granted. But, in fact, a proposition which is synthetic according to the former criterion may very well be analytic according to the latter. For, as we have already pointed out, it is possible for symbols to be synonymous without having the same intensional meaning for anyone: and accordingly from the fact that one can think of the sum of seven and five without necessarily thinking of twelve, it by no means follows that the proposition "7 + 5 = 12" can be denied without self-contradiction. From the rest of his argument, it is clear that it is this logical proposition, and not any psychological proposition, that Kant is really anxious to establish. His use of the psychological criterion leads him to think that he has established it, when he has not.

I think that we can preserve the logical import of Kant's distinction between analytic and synthetic propositions, while avoiding the confusions which mar his actual account of it, if we say that a proposition is analytic when its validity depends solely on the definitions of the symbols it contains, and synthetic when its validity is determined by the facts of experience. Thus, the proposition "There are ants which have established a system of slavery" is a synthetic proposition. For we cannot tell whether it is true or false merely by considering the definitions of the symbols which constitute it. We have to resort to actual observation of the behavior of ants. On the other hand, the proposition "Either some ants are parasitic or none are" is an analytic proposition. For one need not resort to observation to discover that there either are or are not ants which are parasitic. If one knows what is the function of the words "either," "or," and "not," then one can see that any proposition of the form "Either *p* is true or *p* is not true" is valid, independently of experience. Accordingly, all such propositions are analytic.

It is to be noticed that the proposition "Either some ants are parasitic or none are" provides no information whatsoever about the behavior of ants, or, indeed, about any matter of fact. And this applies to all analytic propositions. They none of them provide any information about any matter of fact. In other words, they are entirely devoid of factual content. And it is for this reason that no experience can confute them.

When we say that analytic propositions are devoid of factual content, and consequently that they say nothing, we are not suggesting that they are senseless in the way that metaphysical utterances are senseless. For, although they give us no information about any empirical situation, they do enlighten us by illustrating the way in which we use certain symbols. Thus if I say, "Nothing can be colored in different ways at the same time with respect to the same part of itself," I am not saying anything about the properties of any actual thing; but I am not talking nonsense. I am expressing an analytic proposition, which records our determination to call a color expanse which differs in quality from a neighboring color expanse a different part of a given thing. In other words, I am simply calling attention to the implications of a certain linguistic usage. Similarly, in saying that if all Bretons are Frenchmen, and all Frenchmen Europeans, then all Bretons are Europeans, I am not describing any matter of fact. But I am showing that in the statement that all Bretons are Frenchmen, and all Frenchmen Europeans, the further statement that all Bretons are Europeans is implicitly contained. And I am thereby indicating the convention which governs our usage of the words "if" and "all."

We see, then, that there is a sense in which analytic propositions do give us new knowledge. They call attention to linguistic usages, of which we might otherwise not be conscious, and they reveal unsuspected implications in our assertions and beliefs. But we can see also that there is a sense in which they may be said to add nothing to our knowledge. For they tell us only what we may be said to know already. Thus, if I know that the existence of May Queens is a relic of tree-worship, and I discover that May Queens still exist in England, I can employ the tautology "If *p* implies *q*, and *p* is true, *q* is true" to show that there still exists a relic of tree-worship in England. But in saying that there are still May Queens in England, and that the existence of May Queens is a relic of tree-worship, I have already asserted the existence in England of a relic of tree-worship. The use of the tautology does, indeed, enable me to make this concealed assertion explicit. But it does not provide me with any new knowledge, in the sense in which empirical evidence that the election of May Queens had been forbidden by law would provide me with new knowledge. If one had to set forth all the information one possessed, with regard to matters of fact, one would not write down any analytic propositions. But one would make use of analytic propositions in compiling one's encyclopedia, and would thus come to include propositions which one would otherwise have overlooked. And, besides enabling one to make one's list of information complete, the formulation of analytic propositions would enable one to make sure that the synthetic propositions of which the list was composed formed a self-consistent system. By showing which ways of combining propositions resulted in contradictions, they would prevent one from including incompatible propositions and so making the list self-stultifying. But in so far as we had actually used such words as "all" and "or" and "not" without falling into self-contradiction, we might be said already to know what was revealed in the formulation of analytic propositions illustrating the rules which govern our usage of these logical particles. So that here again we are justified in saying that analytic propositions do not increase our knowledge. . . .

The Propositions of Geometry

The mathematical propositions which one might most pardonably suppose to be synthetic are the propositions of geometry. For it is natural for us to think, as Kant thought, that geometry is the study of the properties of physical space, and consequently that its propositions have factual content. And if we believe this, and also recognize that the truths of geometry are necessary and certain, then we may be inclined to accept Kant's hypothesis that space is the form of intuition of our outer sense, a form imposed by us on the matter of sensation, as the only possible explanation of our *a priori* knowledge of these synthetic propositions. But while the view that pure geometry is concerned with physical space was plausible enough in Kant's day, when the geometry of Euclid was the only geometry known, the subsequent invention of non-Euclidean geometries has shown it to be mistaken. We see now that the axioms of a geometry are simply definitions, and that the theorems of a geometry are simply the logical consequences of these definitions. A geometry is not in itself about physical space; in itself it cannot be said to be "about" anything. But we can use a geometry to reason about physical space. That

is to say, once we have given the axioms a physical interpretation, we can proceed to apply the theorems to the objects which satisfy the axioms. Whether a geometry can be applied to the actual physical world or not, is an empirical question which falls outside the scope of the geometry itself. There is no sense, therefore, in asking which of the various geometries known to us are false and which are true. In so far as they are all free from contradiction, they are all true. What one can ask is which of them is the most useful on any given occasion, which of them can be applied most easily and most fruitfully to an actual empirical situation. But the proposition which states that a certain application of a geometry is possible is not itself a proposition of that geometry. All that the geometry itself tells us is that if anything can be brought under the definitions, it will also satisfy the theorems. It is therefore a purely logical system, and its propositions are purely analytic propositions.

It might be objected that the use made of diagrams in geometrical treatises shows that geometrical reasoning is not purely abstract and logical, but depends on our intuition of the properties of figures. In fact, however, the use of diagrams is not essential to completely rigorous geometry. The diagrams are introduced as an aid to our reason. They provide us with a particular application of the geometry, and so assist us to perceive the more general truth that the axioms of the geometry involve certain consequences. But the fact that most of us need the help of an example to make us aware of those consequences does not show that the relation between them and the axioms is not a purely logical relation. It shows merely that our intellects are unequal to the task of carrying out very abstract processes of reasoning without the assistance of intuition. In other words, it has no bearing on the nature of geometrical propositions, but is simply an empirical fact about ourselves. Moreover, the appeal to intuition, though generally of psychological value, is also a source of danger to the geometer. He is tempted to make assumptions which are accidentally true of the particular figure he is taking as an illustration, but do not follow from his axioms. It has, indeed, been shown that Euclid himself was guilty of this, and consequently that the presence of the figure is essential to some of his proofs. This shows that his system is not, as he presents it, completely rigorous, although of course it can be made so. It does not show that the presence of the figure is essential to a truly rigorous geometrical proof. To suppose that it did would be to take as a necessary feature of all geometries what is really only an incidental defect in one particular geometrical system.

We conclude, then, that the propositions of pure geometry are analytic. And this leads us to reject Kant's hypothesis that geometry deals with the form of intuition of our outer sense. For the ground for this hypothesis was that it alone explained how the propositions of geometry could be both true *a priori* and synthetic: and we have seen that they are not synthetic. Similarly our view that the propositions of arithmetic are not synthetic but analytic leads us to reject the Kantian hypothesis that arithmetic is concerned with our pure intuition of time, the form of our inner sense. And thus we are able to dismiss Kant's transcendental aesthetic without having to bring forward the epistemological difficulties which it is commonly said to involve. For the only argument which can be brought in favor of Kant's theory is that it alone explains certain "facts." And now we have found that the "facts" which it purports to explain are not facts at all. For while it is true that we have *a priori* knowledge of necessary propositions, it is not true, as Kant supposed, that any of these necessary propositions are synthetic. They are without exception analytic propositions, or, in other words, tautologies.

We have already explained how it is that these analytic propositions are necessary and certain. We saw that the reason why they cannot be confuted in experience is that they do not make any assertion about the empirical world. They simply record our determination to use words in a certain fashion. We cannot deny them without infringing the conventions which are presupposed by our very denial, and so falling into self-contradiction. And this is the sole ground of their necessity. As Wittgenstein puts it, our justification for holding that the world could not conceivably disobey the laws of logic is simply that we could not say of an unlogical world how it would look. And just as the validity of an analytic proposition is independent of the nature of the external world, so is it independent of the nature of our minds. It is perfectly conceivable that we should have employed different linguistic conventions from those which we actually do employ. But whatever these conventions might be, the tautologies in which we recorded them would always be neces-

sary. For any denial of them would be self-stultifying.

We see, then, that there is nothing mysterious about the apodictic certainty of logic and mathematics. Our knowledge that no observation can ever confute the proposition "7 + 5 = 12" depends simply on the fact that the symbolic expression "7 + 5" is synonymous with "12," just as our knowledge that every oculist is an eye-doctor depends on the fact that the symbol "eye-doctor" is synonymous with "oculist." And the same explanation holds good for every other *a priori* truth.

How Can Tautologies Be Surprising?

What is mysterious at first sight is that these tautologies should on occasion be so surprising, that there should be in mathematics and logic the possibility of invention and discovery. As Poincaré says: "If all the assertions which mathematics puts forward can be derived from one another by formal logic, mathematics cannot amount to anything more than an immense tautology. Logical inference can teach us nothing essentially new, and if everything is to proceed from the principle of identity, everything must be reducible to it. But can we really allow that these theorems which fill so many books serve no other purpose than to say in a round-about fashion 'A = A'?" Poincaré finds this incredible. His own theory is that the sense of invention and discovery in mathematics belongs to it in virtue of mathematical induction, the principle that what is true for the number 1, and true for $n + 1$ when it is true for n, is true for all numbers. And he claims that this is a synthetic *a priori* principle. It is, in fact, *a priori,* but it is not synthetic. It is a defining principle of the natural numbers, serving to distinguish them from such numbers as the infinite cardinal numbers, to which it cannot be applied. Moreover, we must remember that discoveries can be made, not only in arithmetic, but also in geometry and formal logic, where no use is made of mathematical induction. So that even if Poincaré were right about mathematical induction, he would not have provided a satisfactory explanation of the paradox that a mere body of tautologies can be so interesting and so surprising.

The true explanation is very simple. The power of logic and mathematics to surprise us depends, like their usefulness, on the limitations of our reason. A being whose intellect was infinitely powerful would take no interest in logic and mathematics. For he would be able to see at a glance everything that his definitions implied, and, accordingly, could never learn anything from logical inference which he was not fully conscious of already. But our intellects are not of this order. It is only a minute proportion of the consequences of our definitions that we are able to detect at a glance. Even so simple a tautology as "91 × 79 = 7189" is beyond the scope of our immediate apprehension. To assure ourselves that "7189" is synonymous with "91 × 79" we have to resort to calculation, which is simply a process of tautological transformation— that is, a process by which we change the form of expressions without altering their significance. The multiplication tables are rules for carrying out this process in arithmetic, just as the laws of logic are rules for the tautological transformation of sentences expressed in logical symbolism or in ordinary language. As the process of calculation is carried out more or less mechanically, it is easy for us to make a slip and so unwittingly contradict ourselves. And this accounts for the existence of logical and mathematical "falsehoods," which otherwise might appear paradoxical. Clearly the risk of error in logical reasoning is proportionate to the length and the complexity of the process of calculation. And in the same way, the more complex an analytic proposition is, the more chance it has of interesting and surprising us.

It is easy to see that the danger of error in logical reasoning can be minimized by the introduction of symbolic devices, which enable us to express highly complex tautologies in a conveniently simple form. And this gives us an opportunity for the exercise of invention in the pursuit of logical enquiries. For a well-chosen definition will call our attention to analytic truths, which would otherwise have escaped us. And the framing of definitions which are useful and fruitful may well be regarded as a creative act.

Having thus shown that there is no inexplicable paradox involved in the view that the truths of logic and mathematics are all of them analytic, we may safely adopt it as the only satisfactory explanation of their *a priori* necessity. And in adopting it we vindicate the empiricist claim that there can be no *a priori* knowledge of reality. For we show that the truths of pure reason, the propositions which we know to be valid independently of all experience, are so only in virtue of their lack of factual content. To say that a proposition is true *a priori* is to say that it is a tautology. And tautologies, though they may serve to guide us in our empirical search for knowledge, do not in themselves contain any information about any matter of fact.

VII.3 *In Defense of* A Priori *Knowledge*

A. C. EWING

A. C. Ewing (born 1899) was for many years Lecturer in Moral Science at Cambridge University. In this selection from his book *The Fundamental Questions of Philosophy,* Ewing tries to meet Ayer's objections (Reading VII.2) and argues for the existence of synthetic *a priori* knowledge. He argues that deductive inferences as well as mathematical truths are synthetic *a priori* truths and that the statement that there is no synthetic *a priori* knowledge is itself a synthetic *a priori* judgment.

Meaning of the Distinction; "A Priori" *Character of Mathematics*

In the theory of knowledge, the first point that confronts us is the sharp distinction between two kinds of knowledge which have been called respectively *a priori* and empirical. Most of our knowledge we obtain by observation of the external world (sense-perception) and of ourselves (introspection). This is called empirical knowledge. But some knowledge we can obtain by simply thinking. That kind of knowledge is called *a priori*. Its chief exemplifications are to be found in logic and mathematics. In order to see that $5 + 7 = 12$ we do not need to take five things and seven things, put them together, and then count the total number. We can know what the total number will be simply by thinking.

Another important difference between *a priori* and empirical knowledge is that in the case of the former we do not see merely that something, S, is in fact P, but that it must be P and why it is P. I can discover that a flower is yellow (or at least produces sensations of yellow) by looking at it, but I cannot thereby see why it is yellow or that it must be

yellow. For anything I can tell it might equally well have been a red flower. But with a truth such as that $5 + 7 = 12$ I do not see merely that it is a fact but that it must be a fact. It would be quite absurd to suppose that $5 + 7$ might have been equal to 11 and just happened to be equal to 12, and I can see that the nature of 5 and 7 constitutes a fully adequate and intelligible reason why their sum should be 12 and not some other number. It is indeed conceivable that some of the things which make the two groups of 5 and 7 might, when they were put together, fuse like drops of water, or even vanish, so that there were no longer 12 things; but what is inconceivable is that there could *at the same time* be $5 + 7$ things of a certain kind at once in a certain place and yet less than 12 things of that kind in that place. Before some of the things fused or vanished they would be $5 + 7$ in number and also 12 in number, and after the fusion or disappearance they would be neither $5 + 7$ nor 12. When I say in this connection that something is inconceivable, I do not mean merely or primarily that we cannot conceive it—this is not a case of a mere psychological inability like the inability to understand higher mathematics. It is a positive insight: we definitely see it to be impossible that certain things could happen. This we do not see in the case of empirical propositions which are false: they are not true but might for anything we know have been true. It is even conceivable, so far as we can see, that the fundamental laws of motion might have been quite different from what they are, but we can see that

This selection is part of Chapter II of *The Fundamental Problems of Philosophy* (1951). It is reprinted here with the permission of Routledge and Kegan Paul, London.

there could not have been a world which contradicted the laws of arithmetic. This is expressed by saying that empirical propositions are *contingent,* but true *a priori* propositions *necessary.* What we see to be necessary is not indeed that arithmetic should apply to the universe. It is conceivable that the universe might have been constituted entirely of a homogeneous fluid, and then, since there would have been no distinction between different things, it is difficult to see how arithmetic could have applied to it. What we do see is that arithmetic must be true of whatever can be numbered at all.

We must not be misled here by the fact that in order to come to understand arithmetic we originally required examples. Once we have learned the beginnings of arithmetic in the kindergarten with the help of examples, we do not need examples any more to grasp it, and we can see the truth of many arithmetic propositions, e.g., that $3112 + 2467 = 5579$, of which we have never had examples. We have probably never taken 3112 things and 2467 things, put them together and counted the resulting set, but we still know that this is what the result of the counting would be. If it were empirical knowledge, we could not know it without counting. The examples are needed, not to prove anything, but only in order to enable us to come to understand in the first instance what is meant by number.

In geometry we indeed stand more in need of examples than in arithmetic, though I think this is only a psychological matter. In arithmetic we only need examples at the most elementary stage, but in geometry most people need a drawn figure, or at least an image of one in their minds, to see the validity of most proofs. But we must distinguish between an illustration and the basis of a proof. If the particular figure were not merely an illustration but the basis of the theorem, the latter would have to be proved by measuring it, but a measurement with a ruler or protractor never figures in Euclid's proofs. That the proof is not really based on the figure drawn is shown by the fact that we can still follow a proof concerning the properties of right-angled triangles even if the figure used to illustrate it is so badly drawn that it is obviously not a right-angled triangle at all. Again, if geometry were empirical, it would be a very hazardous speculation from the single example before us on the black-board to conclude that all triangles had a property. It might be an individual idiosyncrasy of some triangles and not others. These considerations should be conclusive of themselves, but we might add that recent developments in geometry have had the effect of much loosening the connection between geometrical proofs and the empirical figure. It is possible to work out non-Euclidean geometries where we cannot depend on figures.

The "A Priori" *in Logic*

Another important field for *a priori* knowledge is logic. The laws of logic must be known *a priori* or not at all. They certainly are not a matter for empirical observation, and the function of logical argument is just to give us conclusions which we have not discovered by observation. The argument would be superfluous if we had observed them already. We are able to make inferences because there is sometimes a logical connection between one or more propositions (the premise or premises) and another proposition, the conclusion, such that the latter must be true if the former is. Then, if we know the former, we can assert the latter on the strength of it, thus anticipating any experience. To take an example, there is a story that Mr. X., a man of high reputation and great social standing, had been asked to preside at a big social function. He was late in coming, and so a Roman Catholic priest was asked to make a speech to pass the time till his arrival. The priest told various anecdotes, including one which recorded his embarrassment when as confessor he had to deal with his first penitent and the latter confessed to a particularly atrocious murder. Shortly afterwards Mr. X. arrived, and in his own speech he said: "I see Father ——— is here. Now, though he may not recognize me, he is an old friend of mine, in fact I was his first penitent." It is plain that such an episode would enable one to infer that Mr. X. had committed a murder without having observed the crime. The form of inference involved: The first penitent was a murderer, Mr. X. was the first penitent, therefore Mr. X. was a murderer—is of the famous kind to which logicians have given the name of *syllogism.* The importance of syllogisms has often been exaggerated, but they are as important as any kind of inference, and we cannot deny that in many cases a syllogism has given people information of which they were not in any ordinary sense aware before they used the syllogism and which they did not acquire by observation. Inference is only possible because there are special connections between the propositions involved such that one necessarily follows from others. It is a chief function of logic to study these connections, of which that expressed in the syllogism is by no means the only one.

(A *syllogism* consists of three propositions, two forming the *premises* and the other the *conclusion*. Each proposition can be expressed by a subject and predicate connected by the verb to be, the *copula*, and if we call everything which stands as either subject or predicate a *term*, there must be three and only three terms in the syllogism. The one common to the two premises is called the *middle term*, and it is on this common element that the inference depends. The other two, having been connected by means of it, occur without it in the conclusion. Thus in the usual example of the syllogism—All men are mortal, Socrates is a man, ∴ Socrates is mortal—man is the middle term connecting Socrates with mortality so that we could, even if he had not already died, know that he was mortal.)

Other Cases of the "A Priori"

A priori knowledge, while most prominent in mathematics and logic, is not limited to these subjects. For instance, we can see *a priori* that the same surface cannot have two different colors all over at the same time, or that a thought cannot have a shape. Philosophers have been divided into *rationalists* and *empiricists* according to whether they stressed the *a priori* or the empirical element more. The possibility of metaphysics depends on *a priori* knowledge, for our experience is quite inadequate to enable us to make on merely empirical grounds any sweeping generalizations of the kind the metaphysician desires. The term *a priori* covers both self-evident propositions, i.e. those which are seen to be true in their own right, and those which are derived

by inference from propositions themselves self-evident.

The Linguistic Theory of the "A Priori" and the Denial That "A Priori" Propositions or Inferences Can Give New Knowledge

At the present time even empiricist philosophers recognize the impossibility of explaining away *a priori* propositions as merely empirical generalizations, but they are inclined to the view that *a priori* propositions and *a priori* reasoning are merely concerned with language, and so cannot tell us anything new about the real world. Thus it is said that, when we make an inference, the conclusion is just part of the premises expressed in different language.[1] If so, inference would be of use merely for clarifying our language and would involve no real advance in knowledge. Some inferences are of this type, e.g. A is a father, therefore A is male. But are they all? That would be hard indeed to square with the *prima facie* novelty of many conclusions. Take, for instance, the proposition that the square on the hypotenuse of a right-angled triangle is equal to the sum of the squares on the other two sides. Such a proposition can be inferred from the axioms and postulates of Euclid, but it certainly does not seem to be included in their meaning. Otherwise we should know it as soon as we understood the axioms and postulates. The example I gave of the murder discovered by a logical argument seems to be another case of a fact not known at all beforehand by the reasoner which is discovered by his reasoning. Extreme empiricist philosophers contend that this appearance of novelty is really illusory, and that in some sense we knew the conclusion all along; but they have never succeeded in making clear in what sense we did so. It is not enough to say that the conclusion is implicit in the premises. "Implicit" means "implied by," and of course a conclusion is implied by its premises, if the inference is correct at all. But this admission leaves quite open the question whether or not a proposition can follow from a different one which does not contain it as part of itself; and since we obviously can by deductive inference come to know things which we did not know before in any ordinary sense of "know," we must treat the empiricist's claim as unjustified till he has produced a clearly defined sense of "implicit in" or "contained in" which leaves room for that novelty in inference which we all cannot help really admitting. In any ordinary sense of "know" the conclusion is not in the cases I have mentioned known prior to the inference, and since the premises are and indeed must be known before we know the conclusion, it is therefore in no ordinary sense of "part" part of the premises.

It is indeed sometimes said that the premises include the conclusion in a confused form, but it is obvious that the beginner in geometry cannot be said to be aware of Pythagoras's theorem even in a confused form though he may know all the premises from which it can be deduced. Nor does awareness of the propositions that A was B's first penitent and that B's first penitent was a murderer include even confusedly the awareness that A was a murderer as long as the premises are not combined. When they are combined therefore something new appears that was not present to consciousness before in any way; there is a new discovery. We can also show by definite logical argument that the interpretation we are discussing does not enable one to avoid the admission of novelty in inference. For, what is it to know something in a confused form? It is surely to know some general attributes present in a whole but not others. To be aware of p even confusedly must involve discriminating some general attributes in p, and those are given in the premises, which are admittedly understood in some degree. If we do not discriminate any attributes, the confusion is too great for argument to be possible at all. Now it is admitted that, when we reach the conclusion, we do discriminate attributes which we did not discriminate before, even if they are alleged to have been contained in the confused whole which was present to our minds before we started inferring. It is further admitted that the conclusion follows necessarily from the premises. Therefore the general attributes which we discriminated at the time when we knew only the premises and not the conclusion must be linked with the attributes we discriminate afterwards in such a way that the latter follow necessarily from the former. So we still have

to admit that sheer *a priori* inference can enable us to discover new attributes. In some cases it may take a good while to draw the inference, in other cases it may be practically instantaneous as soon as the premises are known and combined, but whether it takes a long or a short time to draw the inference cannot be relevant to the principle.

Nevertheless, the view that inference cannot yield new conclusions dies hard, and so it will not be superfluous to bring further arguments. (1) "This has shape" admittedly follows logically from "this has size" and vice versa. If the view I am criticizing were true, "this has size" would, therefore, have to include in its meaning "this has shape," and "this has shape" would also have to include in its meaning "this has size." But this would only be possible if the two sentences meant exactly the same thing, which they obviously do not. (2) Take an argument such as—Montreal is to the north of New York, New York is to the north of Washington, therefore Montreal is to the north of Washington. If the view I am discussing is true, the conclusion is part of the premises. But it is not part of either premise by itself, otherwise both premises would not be needed. So the only way in which it could be part of both together would be if it were divisible into two propositions one of which was part of the first and the other part of the second. I defy anybody to divide it in this way. (3) The proposition "Socrates was a philosopher" certainly entails the proposition "if Socrates had measles some philosophers have had measles," but it cannot be that the second proposition is included in the first. For the first proposition certainly does not include the notion of measles.

What is really the same view is often expressed by saying that all *a priori* propositions are "analytic." A distinction has commonly been drawn between *analytic* propositions, in which the predicate is in the notion of the subject already formed before the proposition is asserted, so that the proposition gives no new information, and *synthetic* propositions in which the predicate is not so contained and which are thus capable of giving new information.[2] Analytic propositions are essentially verbal, being all true by definition, e.g. all fathers are male. As an example of a synthetic proposition we could take any proposition established by experience such as "I am cold" or "It is snowing," but empiricists often

assert that there are no synthetic *a priori* propositions. That this view cannot be justified may be
shown at once. The proposition that there are no
synthetic *a priori* propositions, since it cannot be
established by empirical observations, would be, if
justified, itself a synthetic *a priori* proposition, and
we cannot affirm it as a synthetic *a priori* proposition that there are no synthetic *a priori* propositions.
We may therefore dismiss off-hand any arguments
for the theory. Such arguments, whatever they
were, would have to involve synthetic *a priori* propositions. Further, the view must be false if it is ever
true that the conclusion of an inference is not part of
its premises. For, if the proposition—S is Q—ever
follows validly from—S is P, the proposition—all
that is SP is SQ, must be true *a priori*. But, unless
the concept Q is part of the concept SP, the proposition—all that is SP is SQ—cannot be analytic.
Therefore our arguments against the view that in all
valid inferences the conclusion is part of the premises expressed in different language are also arguments against the view that all *a priori* propositions
are analytic.

The analytic view seems plausible when we are
concerned with the simplest propositions of logic
and arithmetic, but we must not assume that a
proposition is analytic because it is obvious.
Though it may be very difficult to determine precisely where analytic propositions end and synthetic
propositions begin, we cannot use this as a ground
for denying the latter. It is very difficult to say
precisely where blue ends and green begins, since
the different shades run into each other impercepti-
bly, but we cannot therefore argue that all blue is
really green. Taking arithmetic, even if there is a
good deal of plausibility in saying that $2 + 2$ is
included in the meaning of "4," there is none in
saying $95 - 91$ or $(216/2) - [(287 + 25)/3]$ are
so included. Yet, if the analytic view were true, all
the infinite numerical combinations which could be
seen *a priori* to be equal to 4 would have to be
included in the meaning of "4."

Some empiricists, without committing themselves to the view that all *a priori* propositions are
analytic, still say these are a matter of arbitrary
choice or verbal convention. They are influenced
here by a modern development in the view of geometry. It used to be held that the axioms of Euclid
expressed a direct insight into the nature of physical

space, but this is denied by modern scientists, and
the view is taken that they are arbitrary postulates
which geometricians make because they are interested in what would follow *if* they were true.
Whether they are true or not is then a matter of
empirical fact to be decided by science. But, even if
this suggests that the premises of our *a priori* arguments may be arbitrary postulates, this does not
make the subsequent steps arbitrary. From the postulates of Euclid it follows that the three angles of a
triangle are equal to two right angles. If the original
postulates are arbitrary, it is not certain that the
conclusion is true of the real world; but it is still not
an arbitrary matter that it follows from the postulates. The postulates may well be false, but there
can be no doubt that *if* they were true the conclusions must be so, and it is in this hypothetical working out of the consequences of postulates which
may not be true that pure geometry consists. The *a
priori* necessity of pure geometry is not therefore in
the least invalidated by modern developments.
What is *a priori* is that the conclusions follow from
the axioms and postulates, and this is not at all
affected by the (empirical) discovery that not all the
axioms and postulates exactly apply to the physical
world. (Applied Euclidean geometry is possible in
practice because it is an empirical fact that they
approximately apply. The divergencies only show
themselves when we consider unusually great veloc-
ities or distances.)

If not only the postulates but the successive
stages in the inference were themselves arbitrary,
we might just as well infer from the same premises
that the angles of a triangle were equal to a million
right angles or to none at all. All point in inference
would be lost. Dictators may do a great deal, but
they cannot alter the laws of logic and mathematics;
these laws would not change even if by a system of
intensive totalitarian education every human being
were persuaded to fall in with a world dictator's
whim in the matter and believe they were different
from what they are. Nor can they change with alterations in language, though they may be expressed
differently. That the truth of *a priori* propositions
does not just depend on the nature of language can
be easily seen when we consider that, even if we do
not know any Fijian or Hottentot, we can know
that also in these languages and not only in the
languages we know the proposition $5 + 7 = 12$

must be true. It is of course true that by altering the meaning of the words we could make the proposition we expressed by "5 + 7 = 12" false, e.g. if I used "12" in a new sense to mean what other people mean by "11," but then it would be a different proposition. I could play the same trick with empirical propositions and say truly, e.g., that "fire does not burn" or "there is an elephant in this room" if I used "burn" to mean "drown" or "elephant" to mean "table." This does not in the least impair the obviousness of the contrary propositions established by experience. Finally, as we argued above that the proposition that there can be no synthetic *a priori* propositions would itself, if justified, have to be a synthetic *a priori* proposition, so we may argue that the proposition that all *a priori* propositions are a matter of arbitrary linguistic convention would, if true, have to be itself a matter of arbitrary linguistic convention. It therefore could not be vindicated by any argument and would be merely a matter of a new usage of words arbitrarily established by the persons who assert it, since it certainly does not express the usual meaning of "*a priori* propositions." So we must reject any attempt to explain away the *a priori* as a genuine source of new knowledge. If the attempt had succeeded, we should have had to admit that philosophy in anything like its old sense was impossible, for philosophy clearly cannot be based merely on observation.

The views we have been criticizing contain the following elements of truth. (1) *A priori* propositions can be seen to be true and the conclusions of an inference seen to follow from their premises without any further observation, provided we understand the meaning of the words used. But to say that q follows from p once we understand the meaning of the words is not to say that q is part of the meaning of the words used to express p. "Follow from" and "be part of" are not synonyms. (2) If

q follows from p you cannot assert p and deny q without contradicting yourself, but this is only to say that in that case the denial of q implies the denial of p. It is not to say that q is part of what you assert when you assert p, unless we already assume that what is implied is always part of what implies it, i.e. beg the question at issue. (3) An *a priori* proposition cannot be fully understood without being seen to be true. It may be impossible to understand something fully without understanding something else not included in it at all, so it may still be synthetic.

People have been inclined to deny synthetic *a priori* propositions because they could not see how one characteristic could necessarily involve another, but that this could not happen would be itself a synthetic *a priori* metaphysical proposition. People have also thought that it was necessary to give some sort of explanation of *a priori* knowledge, and could not see how this could be done except in terms of language. To this I should reply that there is no reason to suppose that *a priori* knowledge requires some special explanation any more than does our ability to attain knowledge empirically by observation. Why not take it as an ultimate fact? Human beings certainly cannot explain everything, whether there is ultimately an explanation for it or not.

Notes

[1] This theory is not applied to *inductive* inference.

[2] This definition would have to be amended slightly to suit modern logicians who (I think, rightly) deny that all propositions are of the subject-predicate form, but this would not alter the principle though importing a complication of detail with which we need not deal here.

VII.4 *Two Dogmas of Empiricism*

W. V. Quine

W. V. Quine (born 1908) argues against two fundamental theses of empiricism: the analytic–synthetic distinction and the belief that individual observation statements are the fundamental unit of meaning. In the first part of this essay, he seeks to undermine the distinction between analytic and synthetic statements that underlies both the Kantian project and contemporary empiricism. One version of the argument appeals to the notion of *containment:* the predicate term is contained in the subject. Quine contends that the notion of *containment* is a vague metaphor and that its vagueness spreads over the entire analytic–synthetic distinction. Furthermore, the concept of analyticity rests on the concept of synonymy, on having the same meaning. That is, if it is analytic that "A bachelor is an unmarried male" this is because the terms "bachelor" and "unmarried male" are already synonymous. But, Quine argues, to say that these terms are synonymous is to presuppose that they are analytic. Hence the argument is circular.

In the second part of this essay, Quine attacks the notion of radical reductionism, which is tied to the verification theory of meaning and assumes that individual observation statements are the basic unit of meaning. Quine rejects this atomistic view, holding instead a "pragmatic coherentism." That is, all our beliefs form a holistic web, so that individual statements are never confirmed or falsified in isolation but only with reference to the holistic web. The most successful system of beliefs is that of science because it allows us to make correct predictions. This workability of our belief system is the pragmatic aspect of epistemology.

Modern empiricism has been conditioned in large part by two dogmas. One is a belief in some fundamental cleavage between truths which are *analytic,* or grounded in meanings independently of matters of fact, and truths which are *synthetic,* or grounded in fact. The other dogma is *reductionism:* the belief that each meaningful statement is equivalent to some logical construct upon terms which refer to immediate experience. Both dogmas, I shall argue, are ill-founded. One effect of abandoning them is, as we shall see, a blurring of the supposed boundary between speculative metaphysics and natural science. Another effect is a shift toward pragmatism.

1. *Background for Analyticity*

Kant's cleavage between analytic and synthetic truths was foreshadowed in Hume's distinction between relations of ideas and matters of fact, and in Leibniz's distinction between truths of reason and truths of fact. Leibniz spoke of truths of reason as true in all possible worlds. Picturesqueness aside, this is to say that the truths of reason are those which could not possibly be false. In the same vein

W. V. Quine, 'Two Dogmas of Empiricism', reprinted by permission of the publishers from *A Logical Point of View,* 2nd. Edition, Rev., by W. V. Quine, Cambridge, Massachusetts: Harvard University Press, © 1953, 1961, 1980 by the President and Fellows of Harvard College; © 1981 by W. V. Quine. Notes have been deleted.

we hear analytic statements defined as statements whose denials are self-contradictory. But this definition has small explanatory value; for the notion of self-contradictoriness, in the quite broad sense needed for this definition of analyticity, stands in exactly the same need of clarification as does the notion of analyticity itself. The two notions are the two sides of a single dubious coin.

Kant conceived of an analytic statement as one that attributes to its subject no more than is already conceptually contained in the subject. This formulation has two shortcomings: it limits itself to statements of subject-predicate form, and it appeals to a notion of containment which is left at a metaphorical level. But Kant's intent, evident more from the use he makes of the notion of analyticity than from his definition of it, can be restated thus: a statement is analytic when it is true by virtue of meanings and independently of fact. Pursuing this line, let us examine the concept of *meaning* which is presupposed.

Meaning, let us remember, is not to be identified with naming. Frege's example of 'Evening Star' and 'Morning Star', and Russell's of 'Scott' and 'the author of *Waverley*', illustrate that terms can name the same thing but differ in meaning. The distinction between meaning and naming is no less important at the level of abstract terms. The terms '9' and 'the number of the planets' name one and the same abstract entity but presumably must be regarded as unlike in meaning; for astronomical observation was needed, and not mere reflection on meanings, to determine the sameness of the entity in question.

The above examples consist of singular terms, concrete and abstract. With general terms, or predicates, the situation is somewhat different but parallel. Whereas a singular term purports to name an entity, abstract or concrete, a general term does not; but a general term is *true* of an entity, or of each of many, or of none. The class of all entities of which a general term is true is called the *extension* of the term. Now paralleling the contrast between the meaning of a singular term and the entity named, we must distinguish equally between the meaning of a general term and its extension. The general terms 'creature with a heart' and 'creature with kidneys', for example, are perhaps alike in extension but unlike in meaning.

Confusion of meaning with extension, in the case of general terms, is less common than confusion of meaning with naming in the case of singular terms. It is indeed a commonplace in philosophy to oppose intension (or meaning) to extension, or, in a variant vocabulary, connotation to denotation.

The Aristotelian notion of essence was the forerunner, no doubt, of the modern notion of intension or meaning. For Aristotle it was essential in men to be rational, accidental to be two-legged. But there is an important difference between this attitude and the doctrine of meaning. From the latter point of view it may indeed be conceded (if only for the sake of argument) that rationality is involved in the meaning of the word 'man' while two-leggedness is not; but two-leggedness may at the same time be viewed as involved in the meaning of 'biped' while rationality is not. Thus from the point of view of the doctrine of meaning it makes no sense to say of the actual individual, who is at once a man and a biped, that his rationality is essential and his two-leggedness accidental or vice versa. Things had essences, for Aristotle, but only linguistic forms have meanings. Meaning is what essence becomes when it is divorced from the object of reference and wedded to the word.

For the theory of meaning a conspicuous question is the nature of its objects: what sort of things are meanings? A felt need for meant entities may derive from an earlier failure to appreciate that meaning and reference are distinct. Once the theory of meaning is sharply separated from the theory of reference, it is a short step to recognizing as the primary business of the theory of meaning simply the synonymy of linguistic forms and the analyticity of statements; meanings themselves, as obscure intermediary entities, may well be abandoned.

The problem of analyticity then confronts us anew. Statements which are analytic by general philosophical acclaim are not, indeed, far to seek. They fall into two classes. Those of the first class, which may be called *logically true,* are typified by:

(1) No unmarried man is married.

The relevant feature of this example is that it not merely is true as it stands, but remains true under any and all reinterpretations of 'man' and 'married'. If we suppose a prior inventory of *logical* particles, comprising 'no', 'un-', 'not', 'if', 'then', 'and', etc., then in general a logical truth is a statement which is true and remains true under all reinterpretations of its components other than the logical particles.

But there is also a second class of analytic statements, typified by:

(2) No bachelor is married.

The characteristic of such a statement is that it can be turned into a logical truth by putting synonyms for synonyms; thus (2) can be turned into (1) by putting 'unmarried man' for its synonym 'bachelor'. We still lack a proper characterization of this second class of analytic statements, and therewith of analyticity generally, inasmuch as we have had in the above description to lean on a notion of 'synonymy' which is no less in need of clarification than analyticity itself.

Our problem, however, is analyticity; and here the major difficulty lies not in the first class of analytic statements, the logical truths, but rather in the second class, which depends on the notion of synonymy.

2. Definition

There are those who find it soothing to say that the analytic statements of the second class reduce to those of the first class, the logical truths, by *definition;* 'bachelor', for example, is *defined* as 'unmarried man'. But how do we find that 'bachelor' is defined as 'unmarried man'? Who defined it thus, and when? Are we to appeal to the nearest dictionary, and accept the lexicographer's formulation as law? Clearly this would be to put the cart before the horse. The lexicographer is an empirical scientist, whose business is the recording of antecedent facts; and if he glosses 'bachelor' as 'unmarried man' it is because of his belief that there is a relation of synonymy between those forms, implicit in general or preferred usage prior to his own work. The notion of synonymy presupposed here has still to be clarified, presumably in terms relating to linguistic behaviour. Certainly the 'definition' which is the lexicographer's report of an observed synonymy cannot be taken as the ground of the synonymy.

Definition is not, indeed, an activity exclusively of philologists. Philosophers and scientists frequently have occasion to 'define' a recondite term by paraphrasing it into terms of a more familiar vocabulary. But ordinarily such a definition, like the philologist's, is pure lexicography affirming a relation of synonymy antecedent to the exposition in hand.

Just what it means to affirm synonymy, just what the interconnections may be which are necessary and sufficient in order that two linguistic forms be properly describable as synonymous, is far from clear; but, whatever these interconnections may be, ordinarily they are grounded in usage. Definitions reporting selected instances of synonymy come then as reports upon usage.

There is also, however, a variant type of definitional activity which does not limit itself to the reporting of pre-existing synonymies. I have in mind what Carnap calls *explication*—an activity to which philosophers are given, and scientists also in their more philosophical moments. In explication the purpose is not merely to paraphrase the definiendum into an outright synonym, but actually to improve upon the definiendum by refining or supplementing its meaning. But even explication, though not merely reporting a pre-existing synonymy between definiendum and definiens, does rest, nevertheless, on *other* pre-existing synonymies. The matter may be viewed as follows. Any word worth explicating has some contexts which, as wholes, are clear and precise enough to be useful; and the purpose of explication is to preserve the usage of these favoured contexts while sharpening the usage of other contexts. In order that a given definition be suitable for purposes of explication, therefore, what is required is not that the definiendum in its antecedent usage be synonymous with the definiens, but just that each of these favoured contexts of the definiendum, taken as a whole in its antecedent usage, be synonymous with the corresponding context of the definiens.

Two alternative definientia may be equally appropriate for the purposes of a given task of explication and yet not be synonymous with each other; for they may serve interchangeably within the favoured contexts but diverge elsewhere. By cleaving to one of these definientia rather than the other, a definition of explicative kind generates, by fiat, a relation of synonymy between definiendum and definiens which did not hold before. But such a definition still owes its explicative function, as seen, to pre-existing synonymies.

There does, however, remain still an extreme sort of definition which does not hark back to prior synonymies at all: namely, the explicitly conventional introduction of novel notations for purposes of sheer abbreviation. Here the definiendum becomes synonymous with the definiens simply because it has been created expressly for the purpose of being synonymous with the definiens. Here we have a really transparent case of synonymy created by definition; would that all species of synonymy were as intelligible. For the rest, definition rests on synonymy rather than explaining it.

The word 'definition' has come to have a dangerously reassuring sound, owing no doubt to its frequent occurrence in logical and mathematical writings. We shall do well to digress now into a brief appraisal of the role of definition in formal work.

In logical and mathematical systems either of two mutually antagonistic types of economy may be striven for, and each has its peculiar practical utility. On the one hand, we may seek economy of practical expression—ease and brevity in the statement of multifarious relations. This sort of economy calls usually for distinctive concise notations for a wealth of concepts. Second, however, and oppositely, we may seek economy in grammar and vocabulary; we may try to find a minimum of basic concepts such that, once a distinctive notation has been appropriated to each of them, it becomes possible to express any desired further concept by mere combination and iteration of our basic notations. This second sort of economy is impractical in one way, since a poverty in basic idioms tends to a necessary lengthening of discourse. But it is practical in another way: it greatly simplifies theoretical discourse *about* the language, through minimizing the terms and the forms of construction wherein the language consists.

Both sorts of economy, though prima facie incompatible, are valuable in their separate ways. The custom has consequently arisen of combining both sorts of economy by forging in effect two languages, the one a part of the other. The inclusive language, though redundant in grammar and vocabulary, is economical in message lengths, while the part, called primitive notation, is economical in grammar and vocabulary. Whole and part are correlated by rules of translation whereby each idiom not in primitive notation is equated to some complex built up of primitive notation. These rules of translation are the so-called *definitions* which appear in formalized systems. They are best viewed not as adjuncts to one language but as correlations between two languages, the one a part of the other.

But these correlations are not arbitrary. They are supposed to show how the primitive notations can accomplish all purposes, save brevity and convenience, of the redundant language. Hence the definiendum and its definiens may be expected, in each case, to be related in one or another of the three ways lately noted. The definiens may be a faithful paraphrase of the definiendum into the narrower notion, preserving a direct synonymy as of antecedent usage; or the definiens may, in the spirit of explication, improve upon the antecedent usage of the definiendum; or finally, the definiendum may be a newly created notation, newly endowed with meaning here and now.

In formal and informal work alike, thus, we find that definition—except in the extreme case of the explicitly conventional introduction of new notations—hinges on prior relations of synonymy. Recognizing then that the notion of definition does not hold the key to synonymy and analyticity, let us look further into synonymy and say no more of definition.

3. *Interchangeability*

A natural suggestion, deserving close examination, is that the synonymy of two linguistic forms consists simply in their interchangeability in all contexts without change of truth value—interchangeability, in Leibniz's phrase, *salva veritate*. Note that synonyms so conceived need not even be free from vagueness, as long as the vaguenesses match.

But it is not quite true that the synonyms 'bachelor' and 'unmarried man' are everywhere interchangeable *salva veritate*. Truths which become false under substitution of 'unmarried man' for 'bachelor' are easily constructed with the help of 'bachelor of arts' or 'bachelor's buttons'; also with the help of quotation, thus:

'Bachelor' has less than ten letters.

Such counter-instances can, however, perhaps be set aside by treating the phrases 'bachelor of arts' and 'bachelor's buttons' and the quotation " 'bachelor' " each as a single indivisible word and then stipulating that the interchangeability *salva veritate* which is to be the touchstone of synonymy is not supposed to apply to fragmentary occurrences inside of a word. This account of synonymy supposing it acceptable on other counts, has indeed the drawback of appealing to a prior conception of 'word' which can be counted on to present difficulties of formulation in its turn. Nevertheless, some progress might be claimed in having reduced the problem of synonymy to a problem of wordhood. Let us pursue this line a bit, taking 'word' for granted.

The question remains whether interchangeability *salva veritate* (apart from occurrences within words) is a strong enough condition for synonymy, or whether, on the contrary, some heteronymous expressions might be thus interchangeable. Now let us be clear that we are not concerned here with synonymy in the sense of complete identity in psychological associations or poetic quality; indeed no two expressions are synonymous in such a sense. We are concerned only with what may be called *cognitive* synonymy. Just what this is cannot be said without successfully finishing the present study; but we know something about it from the need which arose for it in connection with analyticity in §1. The sort of synonymy needed there was merely such that any analytic statement could be turned into a logical truth by putting synonyms for synonyms. Turning the tables and assuming analyticity, indeed, we could explain cognitive synonymy of terms as follows (keeping to the familiar example): to say that 'bachelor' and 'unmarried man' are cognitively synonymous is to say no more nor less than that the statement:

(3) All and only bachelors are unmarried men is analytic.

What we need is an account of cognitive synonymy not presupposing analyticity—if we are to explain analyticity conversely with help of cognitive synonymy as undertaken in §1. And indeed such an independent account of cognitive synonymy is at present up for consideration, namely, interchangeability *salva veritate* everywhere except within words. The question before us, to resume the thread at last, is whether such interchangeability is a sufficient condition for cognitive synonymy. We can quickly assure ourselves that it is, by examples of the following sort. The statement:

(4) Necessarily all and only bachelors are bachelors

is evidently true, even supposing 'necessarily' so narrowly construed as to be truly applicable only to analytic statements. Then, if 'bachelor' and 'unmarried man' are interchangeable *salva veritate*, the result:

(5) Necessarily all and only bachelors are unmarried men

of putting 'unmarried man' for an occurrence of 'bachelor' in (4) must, like (4), be true. But to say that (5) is true is to say that (3) is analytic, and hence that 'bachelor' and 'unmarried man' are cognitively synonymous.

Let us see what there is about the above argument that gives it its air of hocus-pocus. The condition of interchangeability *salva veritate* varies in its force with variations in the richness of the language at hand. The above argument supposes we are working with a language rich enough to contain the adverb 'necessarily', this adverb being so construed as to yield truth when and only when applied to an analytic statement. But can we condone a language which contains such an adverb? Does the adverb really make sense? To suppose that it does is to suppose that we have already made satisfactory sense of 'analytic'. Then what are we so hard at work on right now?

Our argument is not flatly circular, but something like it. It has the form, figuratively speaking, of a closed curve in space.

Interchangeability *salva veritate* is meaningless until relativized to a language whose extent is specified in relevant respects. Suppose now we consider a language containing just the following materials. There is an indefinitely large stock of one-place predicates (for example, 'F' where 'Fx' means that x is a man) and many-place predicates (for example,

'G' where 'Gxy' means that x loves y), mostly having to do with extra-logical subject-matter. The rest of the language is logical. The atomic sentences consist each of a predicate followed by one or more variables 'x', 'y', etc.; and the complex sentences are built up of the atomic ones by truth functions ('not', 'and', 'or', etc.) and quantification. In effect such a language enjoys the benefits also of descriptions and indeed singular terms generally, these being contextually definable in known ways. Even abstract singular terms naming classes, classes of classes, etc., are contextually definable in case the assumed stock of predicates includes the two-place predicate of class membership. Such a language can be adequate to classical mathematics and indeed to scientific discourse generally, except in so far as the latter involves debatable devices such as contrary-to-fact conditionals or modal adverbs like 'necessarily'. Now a language of this type is extensional, in this sense: any two predicates which agree extensionally (that is, are true of the same objects) are interchangeable *salva veritate*.

In an extensional language, therefore, interchangeability *salva veritate* is no assurance of cognitive synonymy of the desired type. That 'bachelor' and 'unmarried man' are interchangeable *salva veritate* in an extensional language assures us of no more than that (3) is true. There is no assurance here that the extensional agreement of 'bachelor' and 'unmarried man' rests on meaning rather than merely on accidental matters of fact, as does the extensional agreement of 'creature with a heart' and 'creature with kidneys'.

For most purposes extensional agreement is the nearest approximation to synonymy we need care about. But the fact remains that extensional agreement falls far short of cognitive synonymy of the type required for explaining analyticity in the manner of §1. The type of cognitive synonymy required there is such as to equate the synonymy of 'bachelor' and 'unmarried man' with the analyticity of (3), not merely with the truth of (3).

So we must recognize that interchangeability *salva veritate,* if construed in relation to an extensional language, is not a sufficient condition of cognitive synonymy in the sense needed for deriving analyticity in the manner of §1. If a language contains an intensional adverb 'necessarily' in the sense lately noted, or other particles to the same effect, then interchangeability *salva veritate* in such a language does afford a sufficient condition of cognitive synonymy; but such a language is intelligible only in so far as the notion of analyticity is already understood in advance.

The effort to explain cognitive synonymy first, for the sake of deriving analyticity from it afterward as in §1, is perhaps the wrong approach. Instead we might try explaining analyticity somehow without appeal to cognitive synonymy. Afterward we could doubtless derive cognitive synonymy from analyticity satisfactorily enough if desired. We have seen that cognitive synonymy of 'bachelor' and 'unmarried man' can be explained as analyticity of (3). The same explanation works for any pair of one-place predicates, of course, and it can be extended in obvious fashion to many-place predicates. Other syntactical categories can also be accommodated in fairly parallel fashion. Singular terms may be said to be cognitively synonymous when the statement of identity formed by putting '=' between them is analytic. Statements may be said simply to be cognitively synonymous when their biconditional (the result of joining them by 'if and only if') is analytic. If we care to lump all categories into a single formulation, at the expense of assuming again the notion of 'word' which we appealed to early in this section, we can describe any two linguistic forms as cognitively synonymous when the two forms are interchangeable (apart from occurrences within 'words') *salva* (no longer *veritate* but) *analyticitate*. Certain technical questions arise, indeed, over cases of ambiguity or homonymy; let us not pause for them, however, for we are already digressing. Let us rather turn our backs on the problem of synonymy and address ourselves anew to that of analyticity.

4. *Semantical Rules*

Analyticity at first seemed most naturally definable by appeal to a realm of meanings. On refinement, the appeal to meanings gave way to an appeal to synonymy or definition. But definition turned out to be a will-o'-the-wisp, and synonymy turned out to be best understood only by dint of a prior appeal to analyticity itself. So we are back at the problem of analyticity.

I do not know whether the statement 'Everything green is extended' is analytic. Now does my indecision over this example really betray an incomplete understanding, an incomplete grasp of the 'meanings', of 'green' and 'extended'? I think not. The trouble is not with 'green' or 'extended', but with 'analytic'.

It is often hinted that the difficulty in separating analytic statements from synthetic ones in ordinary language is due to the vagueness of ordinary language and that the distinction is clear when we have a precise artificial language with explicit 'semantical rules'. This, however, as I shall now attempt to show, is a confusion.

The notion of analyticity about which we are worrying is a purported relation between statements and languages: a statement S is said to be *analytic* for a language L, and the problem is to make sense of this relation generally, that is, for variable 'S' and 'L'. The gravity of this problem is not perceptibly less for artificial languages than for natural ones. The problem of making sense of the idiom 'S is analytic for L', with variable 'S' and 'L', retains its stubbornness even if we limit the range of the variable 'L' to artificial languages. Let me now try to make this point evident.

For artificial languages and semantical rules we look naturally to the writings of Carnap. His semantical rules take various forms, and to make my point I shall have to distinguish certain of the forms. Let us suppose, to begin with, an artificial language L_0 whose semantical rules have the form explicitly of a specification, by recursion or otherwise, of all the analytic statements of L_0. The rules tell us that such and such statements, and only those, are the analytic statements of L_0. Now here the difficulty is simply that the rules contain the word 'analytic', which we do not understand! We understand what expressions the rules attribute analyticity to, but we do not understand what the rules attribute to those expressions. In short, before we can understand a rule which begins 'A statement S is analytic for language L_0 if and only if . . .,' we must understand the general relative term 'analytic for'; we must understand 'S is analytic for L' where 'S' and 'L' are variables.

Alternatively we may, indeed, view the so-called rule as a conventional definition of a new simple symbol 'analytic-for-L_0', which might better be written untendentiously as 'K' so as not to seem to throw light on the interesting word 'analytic'. Obviously any number of classes K, M, N, etc. of statements of L_0 can be specified for various purposes or for no purpose; what does it mean to say that K, as against M, N, etc., is the class of the 'analytic' statements of L_0?

By saying what statements are analytic for L_0 we explain 'analytic-for-L_0' but not 'analytic', not 'analytic for'. We do not begin to explain the idiom 'S is analytic for L' with variable 'S' and 'L' even if we are content to limit the range of 'L' to the realm of artificial languages.

Actually we do know enough about the intended significance of 'analytic' to know that analytic statements are supposed to be true. Let us then turn to a second form of semantical rule, which says not that such and such statements are analytic but simply that such and such statements are included among the truths. Such a rule is not subject to the criticism of containing the un-understood word 'analytic'; and we may grant for the sake of argument that there is no difficulty over the broader term 'true'. A semantical rule of this second type, a rule of truth, is not supposed to specify all the truths of the language; it merely stipulates, recursively or otherwise, a certain multitude of statements which, along with others unspecified, are to count as true. Such a rule may be conceded to be quite clear. Derivatively, afterward, analyticity can be demarcated thus: a statement is analytic if it is (not merely true but) true according to the semantical rule.

Still there is really no progress. Instead of appealing to an unexplained word 'analytic', we are now appealing to an unexplained phrase 'semantical rule'. Not every true statement which says that the statements of some class are true can count as a semantical rule—otherwise *all* truths would be 'analytic' in the sense of being true according to semantical rules. Semantical rules are distinguishable, apparently, only by the fact of appearing on a page under the heading 'Semantical Rules'; and this heading is itself then meaningless.

We can say indeed that a statement is *analytic-for-L_0* if and only if it is true according to such and such specifically appended 'semantical rules', but then we find ourselves back at essentially the same case which was originally discussed: 'S is analytic-for-L_0 if and only if . . . .' Once we seek to explain

'*S* is analytic for *L*' generally for variable '*L*' (even allowing limitation of '*L*' to artificial languages), the explanation 'true according to the semantical rules of *L*' is unavailing; for the relative term 'semantical rule of' is as much in need of clarification, at least, as 'analytic for'.

It may be instructive to compare the notion of semantical rule with that of postulate. Relative to a given set of postulates, it is easy to say what a postulate is: it is a member of the set. Relative to a given set of semantical rules, it is equally easy to say what a semantical rule is. But given simply a notation, mathematical or otherwise, and indeed as thoroughly understood a notation as you please in point of the translations or truth conditions of its statements, who can say which of its true statements rank as postulates? Obviously the question is meaningless—as meaningless as asking which points in Ohio are starting-points. Any finite (or effectively specifiable infinite) selection of statements (preferably true ones, perhaps) is as much *a* set of postulates as any other. The word 'postulate' is significant only relative to an act of enquiry; we apply the word to a set of statements just in so far as we happen, for the year or the moment, to be thinking of those statements in relation to the statements which can be reached from them by some set of transformations to which we have seen fit to direct our attention. Now the notion of semantical rule is as sensible and meaningful as that of postulate, if conceived in a similarly relative spirit—relative, this time, to one or another particular enterprise of schooling unconversant persons in sufficient conditions for truth of statements of some natural or artificial language *L*. But from this point of view no one signalization of a subclass of the truths of *L* is intrinsically more a semantical rule than another; and, if 'analytic' means 'true by semantical rules', no one truth of *L* is analytic to the exclusion of another.

It might conceivably be protested that an artificial language *L* (unlike a natural one) is a language in the ordinary sense *plus* a set of explicit semantical rules—the whole constituting, let us say, an ordered pair; and that the semantical rules of *L* then are specifiable simply as the second component of the pair *L*. But, by the same token and more simply, we might construe an artificial language *L* outright as an ordered pair whose second component is the class of its analytic statements; and then the analytic statements of *L* become specifiable simply as the statements in the second component of *L*. Or better still, we might just stop tugging at our bootstraps altogether.

Not all the explanations of analyticity known to Carnap and his readers have been covered explicitly in the above considerations, but the extension to other forms is not hard to see. Just one additional factor should be mentioned which sometimes enters: sometimes the semantical rules are in effect rules of translation into ordinary language, in which case the analytic statements of the artificial language are in effect recognized as such from the analyticity of their specified translations in ordinary language. Here certainly there can be no thought of an illumination of the problem of analyticity from the side of the artificial language.

From the point of view of the problem of analyticity the notion of an artificial language with semantical rules is a *feu follet par excellence*. Semantical rules determining the analytic statements of an artificial language are of interest only in so far as we already understand the notion of analyticity; they are of no help in gaining this understanding.

Appeal to hypothetical languages of an artificially simple kind could conceivably be useful in clarifying analyticity, if the mental or behavioural or cultural factors relevant to analyticity—whatever they may be—were somehow sketched into the simplified model. But a model which takes analyticity merely as an irreducible character is unlikely to throw light on the problem of explicating analyticity.

It is obvious that truth in general depends on both language and extra-linguistic fact. The statement 'Brutus killed Caesar' would be false if the world had been different in certain ways, but it would also be false if the word 'killed' happened rather to have the sense of 'begat'. Thus one is tempted to suppose in general that the truth of a statement is somehow analysable into a linguistic component and a factual component. Given this supposition, it next seems reasonable that in some statements the factual component should be null; and these are the analytic statements. But, for all its a priori reasonableness, a boundary between analytic and synthetic statements simply has not been drawn. That there is such a distinction to be drawn at all is an unempirical dogma of empiricists, a metaphysical article of faith.

5. The Verification Theory and Reductionism

In the course of these sombre reflections we have taken a dim view first of the notion of meaning, then of the notion of cognitive synonymy, and finally of the notion of analyticity. But what, it may be asked, of the verification theory of meaning? This phrase has established itself so firmly as a catchword of empiricism that we should be very unscientific indeed not to look beneath it for a possible key to the problem of meaning and the associated problems.

The verification theory of meaning, which has been conspicuous in the literature from Peirce onward, is that the meaning of a statement is the method of empirically confirming or infirming it. An analytic statement is that limiting case which is confirmed no matter what.

As urged in §1, we can as well pass over the question of meanings as entities and move straight to sameness of meaning, or synonymy. Then what the verification theory says is that statements are synonymous if and only if they are alike in point of method of empirical confirmation or infirmation.

This is an account of cognitive synonymy not of linguistic forms generally, but of statements. However, from the concept of synonymy of statements we could derive the concept of synonymy for other linguistic forms, by considerations somewhat similar to those at the end of §3. Assuming the notion of 'word', indeed, we could explain any two forms as synonymous when the putting of the one form for an occurrence of the other in any statement (apart from occurrences within 'words') yields a synonymous statement. Finally, given the concept of synonymy thus for linguistic forms generally, we could define analyticity in terms of synonymy and logical truth as in §1. For that matter, we could define analyticity more simply in terms of just synonymy of statements together

with logical truth; it is not necessary to appeal to synonymy of linguistic forms other than statements. For a statement may be described as analytic simply when it is synonymous with a logically true statement.

So, if the verification theory can be accepted as an adequate account of statement synonymy, the notion of analyticity is saved after all. However, let us reflect. Statement synonymy is said to be likeness of method of empirical confirmation or infirmation. Just what are these methods which are to be compared for likeness? What, in other words, is the nature of the relation between a statement and the experiences which contribute to or detract from its confirmation?

The most naive view of the relation is that it is one of direct report. This is *radical reductionism.* Every meaningful statement is held to be translatable into a statement (true or false) about immediate experience. Radical reductionism, in one form or another, well antedates the verification theory of meaning explicitly so called. Thus Locke and Hume held that every idea must either originate directly in sense experience or else be compounded of ideas thus originating; and taking a hint from Tooke we might rephrase this doctrine in semantical jargon by saying that a term, to be significant at all, must be either a name of a sense datum or a compound of such names or an abbreviation of such a compound. So stated, the doctrine remains ambiguous as between sense data as sensory events and sense data as sensory qualities; and it remains vague as to the admissible ways of compounding. Moreover, the doctrine is unnecessarily and intolerably restrictive in the term-by-term critique which it imposes. More reasonably, and without yet exceeding the limits of what I have called radical reductionism, we may take full statements as our significant units— thus demanding that our statements as wholes be translatable into sense-datum language, but not that they be translatable term by term.

This emendation would unquestionably have been welcome to Locke and Hume and Tooke, but historically it had to await an important reorientation in semantics—the reorientation whereby the primary vehicle of meaning came to be seen no longer in the term but in the statement. This reorientation, explicit in Frege ((1), §60), underlies

Russell's concept of incomplete symbols defined in use; also it is implicit in the verification theory of meaning, since the objects of verification are statements.

Radical reductionism, conceived now with statements as units, set itself the task of specifying a sense-datum language and showing how to translate the rest of significant discourse, statement by statement, into it. Carnap embarked on this project in the *Aufbau*.

The language which Carnap adopted as his starting-point was not a sense-datum language in the narrowest conceivable sense, for it included also the notations of logic, up through higher set theory. In effect, it included the whole language of pure mathematics. The ontology implicit in it (that is, the range of values of its variables) embraced not only sensory events but classes, classes of classes, and so on. Empiricists there are who would boggle at such prodigality. Carnap's starting-point is very parsimonious, however, in its extra-logical or sensory part. In a series of constructions in which he exploits the resources of modern logic with much ingenuity, Carnap succeeds in defining a wide array of important additional sensory concepts which, but for his constructions, one would not have dreamed were definable on so slender a basis. He was the first empiricist who, not content with asserting the reducibility of science to terms of immediate experience, took serious steps toward carrying out the reduction.

If Carnap's starting-point is satisfactory, still his constructions were, as he himself stressed, only a fragment of the full programme. The construction of even the simplest statements about the physical world was left in a sketchy state. Carnap's suggestions on this subject were, despite their sketchiness, very suggestive. He explained spatio-temporal point-instants as quadruples of real numbers and envisaged assignment of sense qualities to point-instants according to certain canons. Roughly summarized, the plan was that qualities should be assigned to point-instants in such a way as to achieve the laziest world compatible with our experience. The principle of least action was to be our guide in constructing a world from experience.

Carnap did not seem to recognize, however, that his treatment of physical objects fell short of reduction not merely through sketchiness, but in principle. Statements of the form 'Quality q is at point-instant $x;y;z;t$' were, according to his canons, to be apportioned truth values in such a way as to maximize and minimize certain overall features, and with growth of experience the truth values were to be progressively revised in the same spirit. I think this is a good schematization (deliberately oversimplified, to be sure) of what science really does; but it provides no indication, not even the sketchiest, of how a statement of the form 'Quality q is at $x;y;z;t$' could ever be translated into Carnap's initial language of sense data and logic. The connective 'is at' remains an added undefined connective; the canons counsel us in its use but not in its elimination.

Carnap seems to have appreciated this point afterward; for in his later writings he abandoned all notion of the translatability of statements about the physical world into statements about immediate experience. Reductionism in its radical form has long since ceased to figure in Carnap's philosophy.

But the dogma of reductionism has, in a subtler and more tenuous form, continued to influence the thought of empiricists. The notion lingers that to each statement, or each synthetic statement, there is associated a unique range of possible sensory events such that the occurrence of any of them would add to the likelihood of truth of the statement, and that there is associated also another unique range of possible sensory events whose occurrence would detract from that likelihood. This notion is of course implicit in the verification theory of meaning.

The dogma of reductionism survives in the supposition that each statement, taken in isolation from its fellows, can admit of confirmation or infirmation at all. My counter-suggestion, issuing essentially from Carnap's doctrine of the physical world in the *Aufbau*, is that our statements about the external world face the tribunal of sense experience not individually but only as a corporate body.

The dogma of reductionism, even in its attenuated form, is intimately connected with the other dogma—that there is a cleavage between the analytic and the synthetic. We have found ourselves led, indeed, from the latter problem to the former through the verification theory of meaning. More directly, the one dogma clearly supports the other in this way: as long as it is taken to be significant in general to speak of the confirmation and infirmation of a statement, it seems significant to speak also of a limiting kind of statement which is vacuously confirmed, *ipso facto,* come what may; and such a statement is analytic.

The two dogmas are, indeed, at root identical. We lately reflected that in general the truth of statements does obviously depend both upon language and upon extra-linguistic fact; and we noted that this obvious circumstance carries in its train, not logically but all too naturally, a feeling that the truth of a statement is somehow analysable into a linguistic component and a factual component. The factual component must, if we are empiricists, boil down to a range of confirmatory experiences. In the extreme case where the linguistic component is all that matters, a true statement is analytic. But I hope we are now impressed with how stubbornly the distinction between analytic and synthetic has resisted any straightforward drawing. I am impressed also, apart from prefabricated examples of black and white balls in an urn, with how baffling the problem has always been of arriving at any explicit theory of the empirical confirmation of a synthetic statement. My present suggestion is that it is nonsense, and the root of much nonsense, to speak of a linguistic component and a factual component in the truth of any individual statement. Taken collectively, science has its double dependence upon language and experience; but this duality is not significantly traceable into the statements of science taken one by one.

The idea of defining a symbol in use was, as remarked, an advance over the impossible term-by-term empiricism of Locke and Hume. The statement, rather than the term, came with Frege to be recognized as the unit accountable to an empiricist critique. But what I am now urging is that even in taking the statement as unit we have drawn our grid too finely. The unit of empirical significance is the whole of science.

6. *Empiricism Without the Dogmas*

The totality of our so-called knowledge or beliefs, from the most casual matters of geography and history to the profoundest laws of atomic physics or even of pure mathematics and logic, is a man-made fabric which impinges on experience only along the edges. Or, to change the figure, total science is like a field of force whose boundary conditions are experience. A conflict with experience at the periphery occasions readjustments in the interior of the field. Truth values have to be redistributed over some of our statements. Re-evaluation of some statements entails re-evaluation of others, because of their logical interconnections—the logical laws being in turn simply certain further statements of the system, certain further elements of the field. Having re-evaluated one statement we must re-evaluate some others, which may be statements logically connected with the first or may be the statements of logical connections themselves. But the total field is so underdetermined by its boundary conditions, experience, that there is much latitude of choice as to what statements to re-evaluate in the light of any single contrary experience. No particular experiences are linked with any particular statements in the interior of the field, except indirectly through considerations of equilibrium affecting the field as a whole.

If this view is right, it is misleading to speak of the empirical content of an individual statement—especially if it is a statement at all remote from the experiential periphery of the field. Furthermore, it becomes folly to seek a boundary between synthetic statements, which hold contingently on experience, and analytic statements, which hold come what may. Any statement can be held true come what may, if we make drastic enough adjustments elsewhere in the system. Even a statement very close to the periphery can be held true in the face of recalcitrant experience by pleading hallucination or by amending certain statements of the kind called logical laws. Conversely, by the same token, no statement is immune to revision. Revision even of the logical law of the excluded middle has been proposed as a means of simplifying quantum mechanics; and what difference is there in principle between such a shift and the shift whereby Kepler superseded Ptolemy, or Einstein Newton, or Darwin Aristotle?

For vividness I have been speaking in terms of varying distances from a sensory periphery. Let me try now to clarify this notion without metaphor. Certain statements, though *about* physical objects and not sense experience, seem peculiarly germane to sense experience—and in a selective way: some statements to some experiences, others to others. Such statements, especially germane to particular experiences, I picture as near the periphery. But in this relation of 'germaneness' I envisage nothing more than a loose association reflecting the relative likelihood, in practice, of our choosing one statement rather than another for revision in the event of recalcitrant experience. For example, we can imagine recalcitrant experiences to which we would surely be inclined to accommodate our system by re-evaluating just the statement that there are brick houses on Elm Street, together with related statements on the same topic. We can imagine other recalcitrant experiences to which we would be inclined to accommodate our system by re-evaluating just the statement that there are no centaurs, along with kindred statements. A recalcitrant experience can, I have urged, be accommodated by any of various alternative re-evaluations in various alternative quarters of the total system; but, in the cases which we are now imagining, our natural tendency to disturb the total system as little as possible would lead us to focus our revisions upon these specific statements concerning brick houses or centaurs. These statements are felt, therefore, to have a sharper empirical reference than highly theoretical statements of physics or logic or ontology. The latter statements may be thought of as relatively centrally located within the total network, meaning merely that little preferential connection with any particular sense data obtrudes itself.

As an empiricist I continue to think of the conceptual scheme of science as a tool, ultimately, for predicting future experience in the light of past experience. Physical objects are conceptually imported into the situation as convenient intermediaries—not by definition in terms of experience, but simply as irreducible posits comparable, epistemologically, to the gods of Homer. For my part I do, *qua* lay physicist, believe in physical objects and not in Homer's gods; and I consider it a scientific error to believe otherwise. But in point of epistemological footing the physical objects and the gods differ only in degree and not in kind. Both sorts of entities enter our conception only as cultural posits. The myth of physical objects is epistemologically superior to most in that it has proved more effica-

cious than other myths as a device for working a manageable structure into the flux of experience.

Positing does not stop with macroscopic physical objects. Objects at the atomic level are posited to make the laws of macroscopic objects, and ultimately the laws of experience, simpler and more manageable; and we need not expect or demand full definition of atomic and subatomic entities in terms of macroscopic ones, any more than definition of macroscopic things in terms of sense data. Science is a continuation of common sense, and it continues the common-sense expedient of swelling ontology to simplify theory.

Physical objects, small and large, are not the only posits. Forces are another example; and indeed we are told nowadays that the boundary between energy and matter is obsolete. Moreover, the abstract entities which are the substance of mathematics—ultimately classes and classes of classes and so on up—are another posit in the same spirit. Epistemologically these are myths on the same footing with physical objects and gods, neither better nor worse except for differences in the degree to which they expedite our dealings with sense experiences.

The overall algebra of rational and irrational numbers is underdetermined by the algebra of rational numbers, but is smoother and more convenient; and it includes the algebra of rational numbers as a jagged or gerrymandered part. Total science, mathematical and natural and human, is similarly but more extremely underdetermined by experience. The edge of the system must be kept squared with experience; the rest, with all its elaborate myths or fictions, has as its objective the simplicity of laws.

Ontological questions, under this view, are on a par with questions of natural science. Consider the question whether to countenance classes as entities. This, as I have argued elsewhere, is the question whether to quantify with respect to variables which take classes as values. Now Carnap (6) has maintained that this is a question not of matters of fact but of choosing a convenient language form, a convenient conceptual scheme or framework for science. With this I agree, but only on the proviso that the same be conceded regarding scientific hypotheses generally. Carnap ((6), p. 32 n) has recognized that he is able to preserve a double standard for ontological questions and scientific hypotheses only by assuming an absolute distinction between the analytic and the synthetic; and I need not say again that this is a distinction which I reject.

The issue over there being classes seems more a question of convenient conceptual scheme; the issue over there being centaurs, or brick houses on Elm Street, seems more a question of fact. But I have been urging that this difference is only one of degree, and that it turns upon our vaguely pragmatic inclination to adjust one strand of the fabric of science rather than another in accommodating some particular recalcitrant experience. Conservatism figures in such choices, and so does the quest for simplicity.

Carnap, Lewis, and others take a pragmatic stand on the question of choosing between language forms, scientific frameworks; but their pragmatism leaves off at the imagined boundary between the analytic and the synthetic. In repudiating such a boundary I espouse a more thorough pragmatism. Each man is given a scientific heritage plus a continuing barrage of sensory stimulation; and the considerations which guide him in warping his scientific heritage to fit his continuing sensory promptings are, where rational, pragmatic.

Bibliographical References

Carnap, Rudolf (1), *Der logische Aufbau der Welt* (Berlin, 1928).

——— (2), *The Logical Syntax of Language* (New York: Harcourt Brace, and London: Kegan Paul, 1937). Translation, with extensions, of *Logische Syntax der Sprache* (Vienna: Springer, 1934).

——— (3), *Meaning and Necessity* (Chicago: University of Chicago Press, 1947).

——— (4), *Logical Foundations of Probability* (Chicago: University of Chicago Press, 1950).

——— (5), 'Testability and Meaning', *Philosophy of Science*, 3 (1936), 419–71; 4 (1937), 1–40 (reprinted, New Haven: Graduate Philosophy Club, Yale University, 1950).

——— (6), 'Empiricism, Semantics, and Ontology', *Revue internationale de philosophie*, 4 (1950), 20–40. Reprinted in Linsky.

Duhem, Pierre, *La Théorie physique: son objet et sa structure* (Paris, 1906).

Frege, Gottlob (1), *Foundations of Arithmetic* (New York: Philosophical Library, 1950).

VII.5 In Defense of a Dogma

H. P. Grice and Peter F. Strawson

Until their recent retirements, H. P. Grice was a Fellow at St. John's College, Oxford University, and Peter F. Strawson was a Professor of Philosophy at Oxford University. In this essay, Grice and Strawson seek to rebut Quine's contention that the analytic synthetic distinction is invalid (see Reading VII.4). They argue against Quine that if the idea of synonymy is meaningless, then so is the idea of having meaning at all. Grice and Strawson argue that Quine has failed to make his case that the notion of analyticity is obscure.

In his article "Two Dogmas of Empiricism," Professor Quine advances a number of criticisms of the supposed distinction between analytic and synthetic statements, and of other associated notions. It is, he says, a distinction which he rejects. We wish to show that his criticisms of the distinction do not justify his rejection of it. . . .

Is there . . . a presumption in favor of the distinction's existence? Prima facie, it must be admitted that there is. An appeal to philosophical tradition is perhaps unimpressive and is certainly unnecessary. But it is worth pointing out that Quine's objection is not simply to the words "analytic" and "synthetic," but to a distinction which they are supposed to express, and which at different times philosophers have supposed themselves to be expressing by means of such pairs of words or phrases as "necessary" and "contingent," "a priori" and "empirical," "truth of reason" and "truth of fact"; so Quine is certainly at odds with a philosophical tradition which is long and not wholly disreputable. But there is no need to appeal only to tradition; for there is also present practice. We can appeal, that is, to the fact that those who use the terms "analytic" and "synthetic" do to a very considerable extent agree in the applications they make of them. They apply the term "analytic" to more or

less the same cases, withhold it from more or less the same cases, and hesitate over more or less the same cases. This agreement extends not only to cases which they have been *taught* so to characterize, but to new cases. In short, "analytic" and "synthetic" have a more or less established philosophical *use;* and this seems to suggest that it is absurd, even senseless, to say that there is no such distinction. For, in general, if a pair of contrasting expressions are habitually and generally used in application to the same cases, *where these cases do not form a closed list,* this is a sufficient condition for saying that there are *kinds* of cases to which the expressions apply; and nothing more is needed for them to mark a distinction.

In view of the possibility of this kind of argument, one may begin to doubt whether Quine really holds the extreme thesis which his words encourage one to attribute to him. It is for this reason that we made the attribution tentative. For on at least one natural interpretation of this extreme thesis, when we say of something true that it is analytic and of another true thing that it is synthetic, it simply never is the case that we thereby mark a distinction between them. And this view seems terribly difficult to reconcile with the fact of an established philosophical usage (i.e., of general agreement in application in an open class). For this reason, Quine's thesis might be better represented not as the thesis that there is *no difference at all* marked by the use of these expressions, but as the thesis that the nature

From *The Philosophical Review* 65 (1965). Notes have been deleted.

of, and reasons for, the difference or differences are totally misunderstood by those who use the expressions, that the stories they tell themselves *about* the difference are full of illusion.

We think Quine might be prepared to accept this amendment. If so, it could, in the following way, be made the basis of something like an answer to the argument which prompted it. Philosophers are notoriously subject to illusion, and to mistaken theories. Suppose there were a particular mistaken theory about language or knowledge, such that, seen in the light of this theory, some statements (or propositions or sentences) appeared to have a characteristic which no statements really have, or even, perhaps, which it does not make sense to suppose that any statement has, and which no one who was not consciously or subconsciously influenced by this theory would ascribe to any statement. And suppose that there were other statements which, seen in this light, did not appear to have this characteristic, and others again which presented an uncertain appearance. Then philosophers who were under the influence of this theory would tend to mark the supposed presence or absence of this characteristic by a pair of contrasting expressions, say "analytic" and "synthetic." Now in these circumstances it still could not be said that there was no distinction at all being marked by the use of these expressions, for there would be at least the distinction we have just described (the distinction, namely, between those statements which appeared to have and those which appeared to lack a certain characteristic), and there might well be other assignable differences too, which would account for the difference in appearance; but it certainly could be said that *the* difference these philosophers supposed themselves to be marking by the use of the expressions simply did not exist, and perhaps also (supposing the characteristic in question to be one which it was absurd to ascribe to any statement) that these expressions, as so used, were senseless or without meaning. We should only have to suppose that such a mistaken theory was very plausible and attractive, in order to reconcile the fact of an established philosophical usage for a pair of contrasting terms with the claim that *the* distinction which the terms purported to mark did not exist at all, though not with the claim that there simply did not exist a difference of any kind between the classes of statements so characterized. We think that the former claim would probably be sufficient for Quine's purposes. But to establish such a claim on the sort of grounds we have indicated evidently requires a great deal more argument than is involved in showing that certain explanations of a term do not measure up to certain requirements of adequacy in philosophical clarification—and not only more argument, but argument of a very different kind. For it would surely be too harsh to maintain that the *general* presumption is that philosophical distinctions embody the kind of illusion we have described. On the whole, it seems that philosophers are prone to make too few distinctions rather than too many. It is their assimilations, rather than their distinctions, which tend to be spurious.

So far we have argued as if the prior presumption in favor of the existence of the distinction which Quine questions rested solely on the fact of an agreed *philosophical* usage for the terms "analytic" and "synthetic." A presumption with only this basis could no doubt be countered by a strategy such as we have just outlined. But, in fact, if we are to accept Quine's account of the matter, the presumption in question is not only so based. For among the notions which belong to the analyticity-group is one which Quine calls "cognitive synonymy," and in terms of which he allows that the notion of analyticity could at any rate be formally explained. Unfortunately, he adds, the notion of cognitive synonymy is just as unclarified as that of analyticity. To say that two expressions x and y are cognitively synonymous seems to correspond, at any rate roughly, to what we should ordinarily express by saying that x and y have the same meaning or that x means the same as y. If Quine is to be consistent in his adherence to the extreme thesis, then it appears that he must maintain not only that the distinction we suppose ourselves to be marking by the use of the terms "analytic" and "synthetic" does not exist, but also that the distinction we suppose ourselves to be marking by the use of the expressions "means the same as," "does not mean the same as" does not exist either. At least, he must maintain this insofar as the notion of *meaning the same as*, in its application to predicate-expressions, is supposed to differ from and go beyond the notion of *being true of just the same objects as*. (This latter notion—which we might call that of "coextensionality"—he is prepared to allow to be intelligible, though, as he rightly says, it is not sufficient for the explanation of analyticity.) Now since he cannot claim this time that the pair of expressions in question (viz., "means the same," "does not mean the same") is the special property of philosophers, the strategy outlined above of countering the presumption in favor of their marking a genuine distinction is not available here (or is at least enormously less plausible). Yet the denial that the distinction (taken as different from the distinction between the coextensional and the non-coextensional) really exists, is extremely paradoxical. It involves saying, for example, that anyone who seriously remarks that "bachelor" means the same as "unmarried man" but that "creature with kidneys" does not mean the same as "creature with a heart"—supposing the last two expressions to be coextensional—*either* is not in fact drawing attention to any distinction at all between the relations between the members of each pair of expressions *or* is making a philosophical mistake about the nature of the distinction between them. In either case, what he says, taken as he intends it to be taken, is senseless or absurd. More generally, it involves saying that it is always senseless or absurd to make a statement of the form "Predicates *x* and *y* in fact apply to the same objects, but do not have the same meaning." But the paradox is more violent than this. For we frequently talk of the presence or absence of relations of synonymy between kinds of expressions—e.g., conjunctions, particles of many kinds, whole sentences—where there does not appear to be any obvious substitute for the ordinary notion of synonymy, in the way in which coextensionality is said to be a substitute for synonymy of predicates. Is all such talk meaningless? Is all talk of correct or incorrect *translation* of sentences of one language into sentences of another meaningless? It is hard to believe that it is. But if we do successfully make the effort to believe it, we have still harder renunciations before us. If talk of sentence-synonymy is meaningless, then it seems that talk of sentences having a meaning at all must be meaningless too. For if it made sense to talk of a sentence having a meaning, or meaning something, then presumably it would make sense to ask "What does it mean?" And if it made sense to ask "What does it mean?" of a sentence, then sentence-synonymy could be roughly defined as follows: Two sentences are synonymous if and only if any true answer to the question "What does it mean?" asked of one of them, is a true answer to the same question, asked of the other. We do not, of course, claim any clarifying power for this definition. We want only to point out that if we are to give up the notion of sentence-synonymy as senseless, we must give up the notion of sentence-significance (of a sentence having meaning) as senseless too. But then perhaps we might as well give up the notion of sense. . . .

We have argued so far that there is a strong presumption in favor of the existence of the distinction, or distinctions, which Quine challenges—a presumption resting both on philosophical and on ordinary usage—and that this presumption is not in the least shaken by the fact, if it is a fact, that the distinctions in question have not been, in some sense, adequately clarified. It is perhaps time to look at what Quine's notion of adequate clarification is.

The main theme of his article can be roughly summarized as follows. There is a certain circle or family of expressions, of which "analytic" is one, such that if any one member of the circle could be taken to be satisfactorily understood or explained, then other members of the circle could be verbally, and hence satisfactorily, explained in terms of it. Other members of the family are: "self-contradictory" (in a broad sense), "necessary," "synonymous," "semantical rule," and perhaps (but again in a broad sense) "definition." The list could be added to. Unfortunately each member of the family is in as great need of explanation as any other. We give some sample quotations: "The notion of self-contradictoriness (in the required broad sense of inconsistency) stands in exactly the same need of clarification as does the notion of analyticity itself." Again, Quine speaks of "a notion of synonymy which is in no less need of clarification than analyticity itself." Again, of the adverb "necessarily," as a candidate for use in the explanation of synonymy, he says, "Does the adverb *really make sense?* To suppose that it does is to suppose that we have already *made satisfactory sense* of 'analytic.'" To make "satisfactory sense" of one of these expressions would seem to involve two things. (1) It would seem to involve providing an explanation which does not incorporate any expression belonging to the family-circle. (2) It would seem that the explanation provided must be of the same general character as those rejected explanations which do incorporate members of the family-circle (i.e., it must specify some feature common and peculiar to all cases to which, for example, the word "analytic" is to be applied; it must have the same general form as an explanation beginning, "a statement is analytic if and only if . . ."). It is true that Quine does not explicitly state the second requirement; but since he does not even consider the question whether any other kind of explanation would be relevant, it seems reasonable to attribute it to him. If we take these two conditions together, and generalize the result, it would seem that Quine requires of a satisfactory explanation of an expression that it should take the form of a pretty strict definition but should not make use of any member of a group of interdefinable terms to which the expression belongs. We may well begin to feel that a satisfactory explanation is hard to come by. The other element in Quine's position is one we have already commented on in general, before enquiring what (according to him) is to count as a satisfactory explanation. It is the step from "We have not made satisfactory sense (provided a satisfactory explanation) of *x*" to "*x* does not make sense."

It would seem fairly clearly unreasonable to insist *in general* that the availability of a satisfactory explanation in the sense sketched above is a necessary condition of an expression's making sense. It is perhaps dubious whether *any* such explanations can *ever* be given. (The hope that they can be is, or was, the hope of reductive analysis in general.) Even if such explanations can be given in some cases, it would be pretty generally agreed that there [are] other cases in which they cannot. One might think, for example, of the group of expressions which includes "morally wrong," "blameworthy," "breach of moral rules," etc.; or of the group which includes the propositional connectives and the words "true" and "false," "statement," "fact," "denial," "assertion." Few people would want to say that the expressions belonging to either of these groups were senseless on the ground that they have not been formally defined (or even on the ground that it was impossible formally to define them) except in terms of members of the same group. It might, however, be said that while the unavailability of a satisfactory explanation in the special sense described was not a

generally sufficient reason for declaring that a given expression was senseless, it was a sufficient reason in the case of the expressions of the analyticity group. But anyone who said this would have to advance a reason for discriminating in this way against the expressions of this group. The only plausible reason for being harder on these expressions than on others is a refinement on a consideration which we have already had before us. It starts from the point that "analytic" and "synthetic" themselves are technical philosophical expressions. To the rejoinder that other expressions of the family concerned, such as "means the same as" or "is inconsistent with," or "self-contradictory," are not at all technical expressions, but are common property, the reply would doubtless be that, to qualify for inclusion in the family circle, these expressions have to be used in specially adjusted and precise senses (or pseudo-senses) which they do not ordinarily possess. It is the fact, then, that all the terms belonging to the circle are *either* technical terms *or* ordinary terms used in specially adjusted senses, that might be held to justify us in being particularly suspicious of the claims of members of the circle to have any sense at all, and hence to justify us in requiring them to pass a test for significance which would admittedly be too stringent if generally applied. This point has some force, though we doubt if the special adjustments spoken of are in every case as considerable as it suggests. (This seems particularly doubtful in the case of the word "inconsistent"—a perfectly good member of the non-technician's meta-logical vocabulary). But though the point has some force, it does not have whatever force would be required to justify us in insisting that the expressions concerned should pass exactly that test for significance which is in question. The fact, if it is a fact, that the expressions cannot be explained in precisely the way which Quine seems to require, does not mean that they cannot be explained at all. There is no need to try to pass them off as expressing innate ideas. They can be and are explained, though in other and less formal ways than that which Quine considers. (And the fact that they are so explained fits with the facts, first, that there is a generally agreed philosophical use for them, and second, that this use is technical or specially adjusted.) To illustrate the point briefly for one member of the analyticity family. Let us suppose we are trying to explain to someone the notion of *logical impossibility* (a member of the family which Quine presumably regards as no clearer than any of the others) and we decide to do it by bringing out the contrast between logical and natural (or causal) impossibility. We might take as our examples the logical impossibility of a child of three's being an adult, and the natural impossibility of a child of three's understanding Russell's Theory of Types. We might instruct our pupil to imagine two conversations one of which begins by someone (X) making the claim:

> (1) "My neighbor's three-year-old child understands Russell's Theory of Types,"

and the other of which begins by someone (Y) making the claim:

> (1′) "My neighbor's three-year-old child is an adult."

It would not be inappropriate to reply to X, taking the remark as a hyperbole:

> (2) "You mean the child is a particularly bright lad."

If X were to say:

> (3) "No, I mean what I say—he really does understand it,"

one might be inclined to reply:

> (4) "I don't believe you—the thing's impossible."

But if the child were then produced, and did (as one knows he would not) expound the theory correctly, answer questions on it, criticize it, and so on, one would in the end be forced to acknowledge that the claim was literally true and that the child was a prodigy. Now consider one's reaction to Y's claim. To begin with, it might be somewhat similar to the previous case. One might say:

> (2′) "You mean he's uncommonly sensible or very advanced for his age."

If Y replies:

> (3′) "No, I mean what I say,"

we might reply:

> (4′) "Perhaps you mean that he won't grow

any more, or that he's a sort of freak, that he's already fully developed."

Y replies:

> (5′) "No, he's not a freak, he's just an adult."

At this stage—or possibly if we are patient, a little later—we shall be inclined to say that we just don't understand what Y is saying, and to suspect that he just does not know the meaning of some of the words he is using. For unless he is prepared to admit that he is using words in a figurative or unusual sense, we shall say, not that we don't believe him, but that his words have *no* sense. And whatever kind of creature is ultimately produced for our inspection, it will not lead us to say what Y said was literally true, but at most to say that we now see what he meant. As a summary of the difference between the two imaginary conversations, we might say that in both cases we would tend to begin by supposing that the other speaker was using words in a figurative or unusual or restricted way; but in the face of his repeated claim to be speaking literally, it would be appropriate in the first case to say that we did not believe him and in the second case to say that we did not understand him. If, like Pascal, we thought it prudent to prepare against very long chances, we should in the first case know what to prepare for; in the second, we should have no idea.

We give this as an example of just one type of informal explanation which we might have recourse to in the case of one notion of the analyticity group. (We do not wish to suggest it is the only type.) Further examples, with different though connected types of treatment, might be necessary to teach our pupil the use of the notion of logical impossibility in its application to more complicated cases—if indeed he did not pick it up from the one case. Now of course this type of explanation does not yield a formal statement of necessary and sufficient conditions for the application of the notion concerned. So it does not fulfill one of the conditions which Quine seems to require of a satisfactory explanation. On the other hand, it does appear to fulfill the other. It breaks out of the family circle. The distinction in which we ultimately come to rest is that between not believing something and not understanding something; or between incredulity yielding to conviction, and incomprehension yielding to comprehension. It would be rash to maintain that *this* distinction does not need clarification; but it would be absurd to maintain that it does not exist. In the face of the availability of this informal type of explanation for the notions of the analyticity group, the fact that they have not received another type of explanation (which it is dubious whether *any* expressions *ever* receive) seems a wholly inadequate ground for the conclusion that the notions are pseudo-notions, that the expressions which purport to express them have no sense. To say this is not to deny that it would be philosophically desirable, and a proper object of philosophical endeavor, to find a more illuminating general characterization of the notions of this group than any that has been so far given. But the question of how, if at all, this can be done is quite irrelevant to the question of whether or not the expressions which belong to the circle have an intelligible use and mark genuine distinctions.

So far we have tried to show that sections 1 to 4 of Quine's article—the burden of which is that the notions of the analyticity group have not been satisfactorily explained—do not establish the extreme thesis for which he appears to be arguing. . . .

There are two further points worth making which arise out of the first two sections.

(1) One concerns what Quine says about *definition* and *synonymy*. He remarks that definition does not, as some have supposed, "hold the key to synonymy and analyticity," since "definition—except in the extreme case of the explicitly conventional introduction of new notations—hinges on prior relations of synonymy." But now consider what he says of these extreme cases. He says: "Here the definiendum becomes synonymous with the definiens simply because it has been expressly created for the purpose of being synonymous with the definiens. Here we have a really transparent case of synonymy created by definition; would that all species of synonymy were as intelligible." Now if we are to take these words of Quine seriously, then his position *as a whole* is incoherent. It is like the position of a man to whom we are trying to explain, say, the idea of one thing fitting into another thing, or two things fitting together, and who says: "I can

understand what it means to say that one thing fits into another, or that two things fit together, in the case where one was specially made to fit the other; but I cannot understand what it means to say this in any other case." Perhaps we should not take Quine's words here too seriously. But if not, then we have the right to ask him exactly what state of affairs he thinks *is* brought about by explicit definition, what relation between expressions *is* established by this procedure, and why he thinks it unintelligible to suggest that the same (or a closely analogous) state of affairs, or relation, should exist in the absence of this procedure. For our part, we should be inclined to take Quine's words (or some of them) seriously, and reverse his conclusions; and maintain that the notion of synonymy by explicit convention would be unintelligible if the notion of synonymy by usage were not presupposed. There cannot be law where there is no custom, or rules where there are not practices (though perhaps we can understand better what a practice is by looking at a rule).

(2) The second point arises out of a paragraph . . . of Quine's [article]. We quote:

> I do not know whether the statement "Everything green is extended" is analytic. Now does my indecision over this example really betray an incomplete understanding, an incomplete grasp, of the "meanings" of "green" and "extended"? I think not. The trouble is not with "green" or "extended," but with "analytic."

If, as Quine says, the trouble is with "analytic," then the trouble should doubtless disappear when "analytic" is removed. So let us remove it, and replace it with a word which Quine himself has contrasted favorably with "analytic" in respect of perspicuity—the word "true." Does the indecision at once disappear? We think not. The indecision over "analytic" (and equally, in this case, the indecision over "true") arises, of course, from a further indecision: viz., that which we feel when confronted with such questions as "Should we count a *point* of green light as *extended* or not?" As is frequent enough in such cases, the hesitation arises from the fact that the boundaries of application of words are not determined by usage in all possible directions. But the example Quine has chosen is particularly unfortunate for his thesis, in that it is only too evident that our hesitations are not *here* attributable to obscurities in "analytic." It would be possible to choose other examples in which we should hesitate between "analytic" and "synthetic" and have few qualms about "true." But no more in these cases than in the sample case does the hesitation necessarily imply any obscurity in the notion of analyticity; since the hesitation would be sufficiently accounted for by the same or a similar kind of indeterminacy in the relations between the words occurring within the statement about which the question, whether it is analytic or synthetic, is raised.

VII.6 *Truths of Reason*

Roderick Chisholm

Roderick Chisholm was until his recent retirement Professor of Philosophy at Brown University and is considered by many to be the elder statesman of U.S. epistemology. In this selection, Chisholm explicates the meaning of *a priori* propositions (once we understand the proposition, we see that it is true), and defends the analytic–synthetic distinction, and the notion of synthetic *a priori* knowledge.

> There are also two kinds of truths: those of reasoning and those of fact. The truths of reasoning are necessary, and their opposite is impossible. Those of fact, however, are contingent, and their opposite is possible. When a truth is necessary, we can find the reason by analysis, resolving the truth into simpler ideas and simpler truths until we reach those that are primary.
>
> Leibniz, *Monadology* 33

A *Traditional Metaphysical View*

Reason, according to one traditional view, functions as a source of knowledge. This view, when it is clearly articulated, may be seen to involve a number of metaphysical presuppositions and it is, therefore, unacceptable to many contemporary philosophers. But the alternatives to this view, once *they* are clearly articulated, may be seen to be at least problematic and to imply an extreme form of skepticism.

According to this traditional view, there are certain *truths of reason* and some of these truths of reason can be known *a priori*. These truths pertain to certain abstract or eternal objects—things such as properties, numbers, and propositions or states of affairs, things that would exist even if there weren't any contingent things such as persons and physical objects. To present the traditional view, we will first illustrate such truths and then we will try to explain what is meant by saying that we know some of these truths *a priori*.

Some of the truths of reason concern what we

Reprinted from *Theory of Knowledge* (Englewood Cliffs, NJ: Prentice-Hall, 1977) by permission. Notes have been edited.

might call relations of "inclusion" and "exclusion" that obtain among various properties. The relation of *inclusion* among properties is illustrated by these facts: The property of being square includes that of being rectangular, and that of being red includes that of being colored. The relation of *exclusion* is exemplified by these facts: The property of being square excludes that of being circular, and that of being red excludes that of being blue. To say that one property excludes another, therefore, is to say more than that the one fails to include the other. Being red fails to include being heavy, but it does not exclude being heavy; if it excluded being heavy, as it excludes being blue, then nothing could be both red and heavy.[1]

Other examples of such inclusion and exclusion are these: Being both red and square includes being red and excludes being circular; being both red and warm-if-red includes being warm; being both non-warm and warm-if-red excludes being red.

These relations are all such that they hold *necessarily*. And they would hold, therefore, even if there weren't any contingent things.

One can formulate more general truths about the relations of inclusion and exclusion. For example, every property F and every property G is such that F's excluding G includes G's excluding F; F's excluding G includes F's including not-G; F excludes non-F, and includes F-or-G. And such truths as these are necessary.

States of affairs or propositions are analogous to properties. Like properties, they are related by inclusion and exclusion; for example, "some men being Greeks" includes, and is included by, "some Greeks being men," and excludes "no Greeks being men." States of affairs, like properties, may be compound; for example, "some men being Greek and Plato being Roman"; "Socrates being wise or Xantippe being wise." The conjunctive state of affairs, "Socrates being a man and all men being mortal," includes "Socrates being mortal" and excludes "no men being mortal." Such truths about states of affairs are examples of truths of logic. And such truths, according to the traditional doctrine, are all necessary. They would hold even if there had been no Socrates or Greeks or men.

Other truths of reason are those of mathematics; for example, the truths expressed by "2 and 3 are 5" and "7 and 5 are 12."

Not All Knowledge of Necessity Is A Posteriori

When it is said that these truths of reason are known (or are capable of being known) "*a priori*," what is meant may be suggested by contrasting them with what is known "*a posteriori*." A single example may suggest what is intended when it is said that these truths may be known without being known *a posteriori*.

Corresponding to "Being red excludes being blue," which is a truth about properties, the following general statement is a truth about individual things: "Necessarily, every individual thing, past, present, or future, is such that if it is red then it is not blue." If the latter truth were known *a posteriori*, then it would be justified by some induction or inductions; our evidence presumably would consist in the fact that a great variety of red things and a great variety of nonblue things have been observed in the past, and that up to now, no red things have been blue. We might thus inductively confirm "Every individual thing, past, present, or future, is such that if it is red then it is not blue." Reflecting upon this conclusion, we may then go on to make still another step. We will proceed to the further conclusion, "Being red excludes being blue," and then deduce, "Necessarily, every individual thing, past, present, or future, is such that if it is red then it is not blue."

Thus, there might be said to be three steps involved in an inductive justification of "Necessarily, being red excludes being blue": (1) the accumulation of instances—"This red thing is not blue," "That blue thing is not red," and so on—along with the summary statement, "No red thing observed up to now has been blue"; (2) the inductive inference from these data to "Every individual thing, past, present, and future, is such that if it is red then it is not blue"; (3) the step from this inductive conclusion to "Being red excludes being blue," or "Necessarily, every individual thing, past, present, or future, is such that if it is red then it is not blue."

Why *not* say that such "truths of reason" are thus known *a posteriori*?

For one thing, some of these truths pertain to properties that have never been exemplified. If we take "square," "rectangular," and "circular" in the precise way in which these words are usually interpreted in geometry, we must say that nothing is square, rectangular, or circular; things in nature, as Plato said, "fall short" of having such properties. Hence, to justify "Necessarily, being square includes being rectangular and excludes being circular," we cannot even take the first of the three steps illustrated above; there being no squares, we cannot collect instances of squares that are rectangles and squares that are not circles.

For another thing, application of induction would seem to presuppose a knowledge of the "truths of reason." In setting out to confirm an inductive hypothesis, we must be able to recognize what its consequences would be. Ordinarily, to recognize these we must apply deduction; we take the hypothesis along with other things that we know and we see what is then implied. All of this, it would seem, involves apprehension of truths of reason—such truths as may be suggested by "For all states of affairs, *p* and *q,* the conjunctive state of affairs, composed of *p* and of either not-*p* or *q,* includes *q,*" and "All *A*'s being *B* excludes some *A*'s not being *B*." Hence, even if we are able to justify some of the "truths of reason" by inductive procedures, any such justification will presuppose others, and we will be left with some "truths of reason" which we have not justified by means of induction.

And finally, the last of the three steps described above—the step from the inductive generalization "Every individual thing, past, present, and future, is such that if it is red then it is not blue" to "Being red excludes being blue," or "Necessarily, every individual thing, past, present, and future, is such that if it is red then it is not blue"—remains obscure.

How do we reach this final step? What justifies us in saying that *necessarily,* every individual thing, past, present, and future, is such that if it is red then it is not blue? The English philosopher, William Whewell, wrote that the mere accumulation of instances cannot afford the slightest ground for the necessity of a generalization upon those instances. "Experience," he said, "can observe and record what has happened; but she cannot find, in any case, or in any accumulation of cases, any reason for what *must* happen. She may see objects side by side, but she cannot see a reason why they must ever be side by side. She finds certain events to occur in succession; but the succession supplies, in its occur-

rence, no reasons for its recurrence; she contemplates external objects; but she cannot detect any internal bond, which indissolubly connects the future with the past, the possible with the real. To learn a proposition by experience, and to see it to be necessarily true, are two altogether different processes of thought. . . . If anyone does not clearly comprehend this distinction of necessary and contingent truths, he will not be able to go along with us in our researches into the foundations of human knowledge; nor indeed, to pursue with success any speculation on the subject."[2]

Intuitive Induction

Plato suggested that in order to acquire a knowledge of necessity, we should turn away from "the twilight of becoming and perishing" and contemplate the world of "the absolute and eternal and immutable."[3] According to Aristotle, however, and to subsequent philosophers in the tradition with which we are here concerned, one way of obtaining the requisite intuition is to consider the particular things of this world.

As a result of perceiving a particular blue thing, or a number of particular blue things, we may come to know what it is for a thing to be blue, and thus, we may be said to know what the property of being blue is. And as a result of perceiving a particular red thing, or a number of particular red things, we may come to know what it is for a thing to be red, and thus, to know what the property of being red is. Then, having this knowledge of what it is to be red and of what it is to be blue, we are able to see that being red excludes being blue, and that this is necessarily so.

Thus, Aristotle tells us that as a result of perceiving Callias and a number of other particular men, we come to see what it is for a thing to have the property of being human. And then, by considering the property of being human, we come to see that being human includes being animal, and that this is necessarily so.[4]

Looking to these examples, we may distinguish four stages:

1. There is the perception of the individual

things—in the one case, the perception of the particular red things and blue things, and in the other, the perception of Callias and the other particular men.

2. There is a process of abstraction—we come to see what it is for a thing to be red and for a thing to be blue, and we come to see what it is for a thing to be a man.

3. There is the intuitive apprehension of certain relations holding between properties—in the one case, apprehension of the fact that being red excludes being blue, and in the other, apprehension of the fact that being rational and animal includes being animal.

4. Once we have acquired this intuitive knowledge, then, *ipso facto,* we also know the truth of reason expressed by "Necessarily, everything is such that if it is red then it is not blue" and "Necessarily, everything is such that if it is human then it is animal."

Aristotle called this process "induction." But since it differs in essential respects from what subsequently came to be known as "induction," some other term, say, "intuitive induction," may be less misleading.

If we have performed an "intuitive induction" in the manner described, then we may say that by contemplating the relation between properties we are able to know that being red excludes being blue and thus to know that *necessarily,* everything is such that if it is red then it is not blue. And we can say, therefore, that the universal generalization, as well as the proposition about properties, is known *a priori.* The order of justification thus differs from that of the enumerative induction considered earlier, where one attempts to justify the statement about properties by reference to a generalization about particular things.

There is a superficial resemblance between "intuitive induction" and "induction by simple enumeration," since in each case, we start with particular instances and then proceed beyond them. Thus, when we make an induction by enumeration, we may proceed from "This *A* is *B*," "That *A* is *B*," and so on, to "In all probability, all *A*'s are *B*'s," or to "In all probability, the next *A* is *B*." But in an induction by enumeration, the function of the particular instances is to *justify* the conclusion. If we find subsequently that our perceptions of the particular instances were unveridical, say, that the things we took to be *A*'s were not *A*'s at all, then the inductive argument would lose whatever force it may have had. In an "intuitive induction," however, the particular perceptions are only incidental to the conclusion. This may be seen in the following way.

Let us suppose that the knowledge expressed by the two sentences "Necessarily, being red excludes being blue" and "Necessarily, being human includes being animal" is arrived at by intuitive induction; and let us suppose further that in each case, the process began with the perception of certain particular things. Neither conclusion depends for its *justification* upon the particular perceptions which led to the knowledge concerned. As Duns Scotus put it, the perception of the particular things is only the "occasion" of acquiring the knowledge. If we happen to find our perception was unveridical, this finding will have no bearing upon the result. "If the senses from which these terms were received were all false, or what is more deceptive, if some were false and others true, I still maintain that the intellect would not be deceived about such principles. . . ."[5] If what we take to be Callias is not a man at all, but only a clever imitation of a man, then, if the imitation is clever enough, our deceptive experience will still be an occasion for contemplating the property of being human—the property of being both rational and animal—and thus, for coming to know that being human includes being animal.

Leibniz thus observes: ". . . if I should discover any demonstrative truth, mathematical or other, while dreaming (as might in fact be), it would be just as certain as if I had been awake. This shows us how intelligible truth is independent of the truth of the existence outside of us of sensible and material things."[6]

It may be, indeed, that to perform an intuitive induction—i.e., to "abstract" a certain property, contemplate it, and then see what it includes and excludes—we need only to *think* of some individual thing as having that property. By thinking about a blue thing and a red thing, for example, we may come to see that being blue excludes being red. Thus, Ernst Mach spoke of "experiments in the imagination."[7] And E. Husserl, whose language may have been needlessly Platonic, said, "The Eidos, the *pure essence,* can be exemplified intuitively in the data of experience, data of perception, memory, and so forth, but just as readily *also in the mere data of fancy*. . . ."[8]

According to this traditional account, then, once we have acquired some concepts (once we know, with respect to certain attributes, just *what* it is for something to have those attributes), we will also be in a position to know just *what* it is for a proposition or state of affairs to be necessary—to be necessarily such that it is true or necessarily such that it obtains. Then, by contemplating or reflecting upon certain propositions or states of affairs, we will be able to see that *they* are necessary.

This kind of knowledge has traditionally been called *a priori*.

Axioms

Speaking very roughly, we might say that one mark of an *a priori* proposition is this: once you understand it, you see that it is true. We might call this the traditional conception of the *a priori*. Thus Leibniz remarks: "You will find in a hundred places that the Scholastics have said that these propositions are evident, *ex terminis,* as soon as the terms are understood. . . ."[9]

If we say an *a priori* proposition is one such that "once you understand it then you see that it is true," we must take the term "understand" in a somewhat rigid sense. You couldn't be said to "understand" a proposition, in the sense intended, unless you can grasp *what* it is for that proposition to be true. The properties or attributes that the proposition implies—those that would be instantiated if the proposition were true—must be properties or attributes that you can grasp in the sense that we have tried to explicate. To "understand" a proposition, in the sense intended, then, it is not enough merely to be able to say what *sentence* in your language happens to express that proposition. The proposition must be one that you have contemplated and reflected upon.

One cannot *accept* a proposition, in the sense in which we have been using the word "accept," unless one also *understands* that proposition. We might say, therefore, that an *a priori* proposition is one

such that, if you accept it, then it becomes certain for you. (For if you accept it, then you understand it, and as soon as you understand it, it becomes certain for you.) This account of the *a priori,* however, would be somewhat broad. We know some *a priori* propositions on the basis of others and these propositions are not themselves such that, once they are understood, then they are certain.

But let us begin by trying to characterize more precisely those *a priori* propositions which are not known on the basis of any *other* propositions.

Leibniz said that these propositions are the "first lights." He wrote: "The immediate apperception of our existence and of our thoughts furnishes us with the first truths *a posteriori,* or of fact, i.e., the *first experiences,* as the identical propositions contain the first truths *a priori,* or of reason, i.e., the *first lights.* Both are incapable of proof, and may be called *immediate*. . . ."

The traditional term for those *a priori* propositions which are "incapable of proof" is *axiom*. Thus Frege wrote: "Since the time of antiquity an axiom has been taken to be a thought whose truth is known without being susceptible to demonstration by a logical chain of reasoning."[10] In *one* sense, of course, every true proposition *h* is capable of proof, for there will always be other true propositions from which we can derive *h* by means of some principle of logic. What did Leibniz and Frege mean, then, when they said that an axiom is "incapable of proof"?

The answer is suggested by Aristotle. An axiom, or "basic truth," he said, is a proposition "which has no other proposition prior to it"; there is no proposition which is "better known" than it is. We could say that if one proposition is "better known" than another, then accepting the one proposition is more reasonable than accepting the other. Hence, if an axiomatic proposition is one such that no other proposition is better known than it is, then it is one that is certain. (It will be recalled that we characterized *certainty* in Chapter 1. We there said that a proposition *h* is *certain* for a person *S*, provided that *h* is evident for *S* and provided that there is no other proposition *i* which is such that it is *more* reasonable for *S* to accept *i* than it is for him to accept *h*.) Hence Aristotle said that an axiom is a "primary premise." Its ground does not lie in the fact that it is seen to follow from *other* propositions.

Therefore we cannot prove such a proposition by making use of any premises that are "better known" than it is. (By "a proof," then, Aristotle, Leibniz, and Frege meant more than "a valid derivation from premises that are true.")

Let us now try to say what it is for a proposition or state of affairs to be an *axiom*:

D3.1 *h* is an *axiom* = Df *h* is necessarily such that (i) it is true and (ii) for every *S*, if *S* accepts *h*, then *h* is certain for *S*.

The following propositions among countless others may be said to be axioms in our present sense of the term:

If some men are Greeks, then some Greeks are men.
If Jones is ill and Smith is away, then Jones is ill.
The sum of 5 and 3 is 8.
The product of 4 and 2 is 8.

For most of us, i.e., for those of us who really *do* consider them, they may be said to be *axiomatic* in the following sense.

D3.2 *h* is *axiomatic* for *S* = Df (i) *h* is an axiom and (ii) *S* accepts *h*.

We may assume that any conjunction of axioms is itself an axiom. But it does not follow from this assumption that any conjunction of propositions which are axiomatic for a subject *S* is itself axiomatic for *S*. If two propositions are axiomatic for *S* and if *S* does not accept their conjunction, then the conjunction is not axiomatic for *S*. (Failure to accept their conjunction need not be a sign that *S* is unreasonable. It may be a sign merely that the conjunction is too complex an object for *S* to grasp.)

We have suggested that our knowledge of what is axiomatic is a subspecies of our *a priori* knowledge, that is to say, some of the things we know *a priori* are *not* axiomatic in the present sense. They are *a priori* but they are not what Aristotle called "primary premises."

What would be an example of a proposition that is *a priori* for *S* but not axiomatic for *S*? Consider the last two axioms on our list above; i.e.,

The sum of 5 and 3 is 8.
The product of 4 and 2 is 8.

Let us suppose that their conjunction is also an axiom and that *S* accepts this conjunction; therefore the conjunction is axiomatic for *S*. Let us suppose further that the following proposition is axiomatic for *S*:

If the sum of 5 and 3 is 8 and the product of 4 and 2 is 8, then the sum of 5 and 3 is the product of 4 and 2.

We will say that, if, in such a case, *S* accepts the proposition

The sum of 5 and 3 is the product of 4 and 2

then that proposition is *a priori* for *S*. Yet the proposition may not be one which is such that it is certain for anyone who accepts it. It may be that one can consider *that* proposition without thereby seeing that it is true.

There are various ways in which we might now attempt to characterize this broader concept of the *a priori*. Thus we might say: "You know a proposition *a priori* provided you accept it and it is implied by propositions that are axiomatic for you." But this would imply that *any* necessary proposition that you happen to accept is one that you know *a priori* to be true. (Any necessary proposition *h* is implied by any axiomatic proposition *e*. Indeed any necessary proposition *h* is implied by *any* proposition *e*—whether or not *e* is axiomatic and whether or not *e* is true or false. For if *h* is necessary, then, it is necessarily true that, for any proposition *e*, either *e* is false or *h* is true. And to say "*e* implies *h*" is to say it is necessarily true that either *e* is false or *h* is true.) *Some* of the necessary propositions that we accept may *not* be propositions that we know *a priori*. They may be such that, if we know them, we know them *a posteriori*—on the basis of authority. Or they may be such that we cannot be said to know them at all.

To capture the broader concept of the *a priori*, we might say that a proposition is known *a priori* provided it is axiomatic that the proposition follows from something that is axiomatic. But let us say, more carefully:

D3.3 *h* is known *a priori* by *S* = Df There is an *e* such that (i) *e* is axiomatic for *S*, (ii) the proposition, *e* implies *h*, is axiomatic for *S*, and (iii) *S* accepts *h*.

We may add that a person knows a proposition *a posteriori* if he knows the proposition but doesn't know it *a priori*. . . .

A Priori *and* A Posteriori

Kant had said, . . . that "necessity is a mark of the *a priori*." We may accept Kant's dictum, if we take it to mean that what is known *a priori* is necessary.

But is it possible to know a necessary proposition to be true and not to know this *a priori*? In other words, can we know some necessary propositions *a posteriori*?

A possible example of a proposition that is known *a posteriori* and is yet necessary might be a logical theorem which one accepts on the ground that reputable logicians assert it to be true. Whether there are in fact any such propositions depends upon two things, each of them somewhat problematic.

The first is that such a proposition cannot be said to be *known* to be true unless such testimonial evidence is sufficient for knowledge. And this is a question we cannot discuss in the present book.

The second is that such a proposition cannot be said to be known to be true unless it is one that the man *accepts*. But when a man, as we say, accepts a theorem on the basis of authority and not on the basis of demonstration, is it the theorem *itself* that he accepts or is it what Brentano calls a "surrogate" for the theorem? If a man reads a logical text, finds there a formula which expresses a certain logical principle, and then, knowing that the author is reputable, concludes that the formula is true, it may well be that the man does *not* accept the logical principle. What he accepts is, rather, the contingent proposition to the effect that a certain formula in a book expresses a logical principle that is true.

But if we waive these difficulties, then perhaps we may say that there is an analytic *a posteriori*—or at least that some of the logical truths that we know are such that we know them only *a posteriori*.

But even if some of the things we know *a posteriori* are logically true, there is at least this additional epistemic relation holding between the necessary and the *a priori*:

If a man knows—or someone once knew—*a posteriori* that a certain necessary proposition is true, then *someone* knows *a priori* that some necessary proposition is true. If the first man bases his knowledge on the testimony of authority, and if this authority in turn bases his knowledge upon the testimony of some other authority, then sooner or later there will be an "ultimate authority" who knows some proposition *a priori*.

Skepticism with Respect *to the* A Priori

Let us now consider a skeptical objection to what we have been saying.

"You have said what it is for a proposition to be axiomatic for a person and you have given examples of propositions which, you say, are axiomatic for you and presumably for others. But how do you know that those propositions are axiomatic? How do you know that they satisfy the terms of your definitions?

"If you really do know that they are axiomatic, then you must have some *general principle* by means of which you can apply your definitions. There must be something about your experience that guarantees these propositions for you and you must *know* that it guarantees them. But what could the principle be?

"The most you can say, surely, is that such propositions just *seem* to be true, or that when you reflect on them you find you cannot doubt them and that you cannot help but accept them. But, as the history of science makes clear, such facts as these provide no guarantee that the propositions in question are true. Notoriously, there have been ever so many false propositions which reasonable people have found they couldn't doubt. And some of these may well have been taken as axiomatic. Consider the logical paradoxes, for example. People found they couldn't help but believe certain propositions, and as a result they became entangled in contradictions."

The objection may be summarized as follows:

1. You cannot know that a given proposition is axiomatic for you unless the proposition is one such that, when you contemplate it, you have a kind of experience—say, a strong feeling of conviction—that provides you with a guarantee that the proposition is true. But

2. there is no experience which will provide such a guarantee. Therefore

3. you cannot really know, with respect to any proposition that it is one that is axiomatic.

Is this a valid argument? The conclusion certainly follows from the premises. And, knowing the history of human error, we can hardly question the second of the two premises. But what of the first premise? If we cannot find any reason to accept the first premise, then we do not need to accept the conclusion. How, then, would the skeptic defend his first premise?

There is a certain more general principle to which the skeptic might appeal in the attempt to defend the first premise. I will call this principle the *generalizability thesis* and formulate it as follows. "You cannot *know* that any given proposition p is true unless you also know two other things. The first of these things will be a certain more *general* proposition q; q will not imply p but it will specify the conditions under which propositions of a certain type are true. And the second thing will be a proposition r, which enables you to *apply* this general proposition to p. In other words, r will be a proposition to the effect that the first proposition p satisfies the conditions specified in the second proposition q."

But if the generalizability thesis is true, no one knows anything. Consider the application of the thesis to a single proposition p. According to the thesis, if we know p, then we know two further propositions—a general proposition q and a proposition r that applies q to p. Applying the generalizability thesis to each of the two propositions, q and r, we obtain four more propositions; applying it to each of them, we obtain eight more propositions; . . . and so on *ad indefinitum*. The generalizability thesis implies, therefore, that we cannot know any proposition to be true unless we know all the members of such an infinite hierarchy of propositions. And therefore it implies that we cannot know any proposition to be true.

The skeptic may reply: "But in *objecting* to my general principle, you are presupposing that we *do*

know something. And this begs the question." The proper rejoinder is: "But in *affirming* your general principle, you are presupposing that we *don't* know anything. And *that* begs the question."

The general reply to a skepticism that addresses itself to an entire area of knowledge can only be this: we do have the knowledge in question, and therefore, any philosophical theory implying that we do not is false. This way of looking at the matter may seem especially plausible in the present instance. It is tempting to say of skepticism, with respect to the truths of reason, what Leonard Nelson said of skepticism, with respect to the truths of mathematics. The advocate of such a skepticism, Nelson said, has invited us to "sacrifice the clearest and most lucid knowledge that we possess—indeed, the *only* knowledge that is clear and lucid *per se*. I prefer to strike the opposite course. If a philosophy, no matter how attractive or plausible or ingenious it may be, brings me into conflict with mathematics, I conclude that not mathematics but my philosophy is on the wrong track."[11] There is certainly no *better* ground for skepticism with respect to our knowledge of the truths of reason than there is for skepticism with respect to our knowledge of physical things.

And so what of the skeptic's question, "How do you know that the proposition that 2 and 4 are 6 is one that is axiomatic?" Let us recall what we said in connection with his earlier question about self-presenting states. The question was: "How do you know that seeming to have a headache is a self-presenting state?" In dealing with that question, we avoided falling into the skeptic's trap. We said that the only possible answer to such a question is that we *do* know that seeming to have a headache is self-presenting state. We should follow a similar course in the present case.

"Linguisticism"

It has been suggested that the sentences giving rise to the problem of the synthetic *a priori* are really "postulates about the meanings of words" and, therefore, that they do not express what is synthetic *a priori*. But if the suggestion is intended literally, then it would seem to betray the confusion between use and mention that we encountered earlier. A *postulate* about the meaning of the word "red," for example, or a sentence expressing such a postulate, would presumably mention the word "red." It might read, "The word 'red' may be taken to refer to a certain color," or perhaps, "Let the word 'red' be taken to refer to a certain color." But, "Everything that is red is colored," although it uses the words "red" and "colored," does not mention them at all. It is not the case, therefore, that, "Red is a color," refers only to words and the ways in which they are used.

A popular conception of the truths of reason is the view according to which they are essentially "linguistic." Many have said, for example, that the sentences formulating the truths of logic are "true in virtue of the rules of language" and, hence, that they are "true in virtue of the way in which we use words."[12] What could this possibly mean?

The two English *sentences,* "Being round excludes being square," and, "Being rational and animal includes being animal," plausibly could be said to "owe their truth," in part, to the way in which we use words. If we used "being square" to refer to the property of being heavy and not to that of being square, then the first sentence (provided the other words in it had their present use) would be false instead of true. And if we used the word "and" to express the relation of disjunction instead of conjunction, then the second sentence (again, provided that the other words in it had their present use) would also be false instead of true. But as W. V. Quine has reminded us, "even so factual a sentence as 'Brutus killed Caesar' owes its truth not only to the killing but equally to our using the component words as we do."[13] Had "killed," for example, been given the use that "was survived by" happens to have, then, other things being the same, "Brutus killed Caesar" would be false instead of true.

It might be suggested, therefore, that the truths of logic and other truths of reason stand in this peculiar relationship to language: they are true "*solely* in virtue of the rules of our language" or "*solely* in virtue of the ways in which we use words." But if we take the phrase "solely in virtue of" in the way in which it would naturally be taken, then the suggestion is obviously false.

To say of a sentence that it is true *solely* in virtue of the ways in which we use words or that it is true *solely* in virtue of the rules of our language, would be to say that the only condition that needs to obtain in order for the sentence to be true is that we use words in certain ways or that there be certain rules pertaining to the way in which words are to be used. But let us consider what conditions must obtain if the English sentence, "Being round excludes being square," is to be true. One such condition is indicated by the following sentence which we may call "T":

The English sentence, "Being square excludes being round," is true, if and only if, being square excludes being round.

Clearly, the final part of T, the part following the second "if," formulates a necessary condition for the truth of the English sentence, "Being round excludes being square," but it refers to a relationship among properties and not to rules of language or ways in which we use words. Hence we cannot say that the *only* conditions that need to obtain in order for, "Being round excludes being square," to be true is that we use words in certain ways or that there be certain rules pertaining to the ways in which words are to be used; and therefore, the sentence cannot be said to be true solely in virtue of the ways in which we use words.

There would seem to be no clear sense, therefore, in which the *a priori* truths of reason can be said to be primarily "linguistic."

Analyzing the Predicate out of the Subject

The terms "analytic" and "synthetic" were introduced by Kant in order to contrast two types of categorical judgment. It will not be inaccurate to interpret "judgment," in Kant's sense, to mean the same as what we mean by "proposition." The terms "analytic" and "synthetic" are used in much of contemporary philosophy to refer instead to the types of *sentence* that express the types of judgment to which Kant referred. And perhaps Kant's view is best expressed by reference to sentences: an analytic *judgment* or *proposition* is one that is expressible in a certain type of *sentence*. But what type of sentence?

An analytic judgment, according to Kant, is a judgment in which "the predicate adds nothing to the concept of the subject." If I judge that all squares are rectangles, then, in Kant's terminology, the concept of the subject of my judgment is the property of being square, and the concept of the predicate is the property of being rectangular. Kant uses the term "analytic," since, he says, the concept of the predicate helps to "break up the concept of the subject into those constituent concepts that have all along been thought in it." Since being square is the conjunctive property of being equilateral and rectangular, the predicate of the judgment expressed by "All squares are rectangular" may be said to "analyze out" what is contained in the subject. An analytic judgment, then, may be expressed in the form of an explicit redundancy: e.g., "Everything is such that if it is both equilateral and rectangular then it is rectangular." To deny such an explicit redundancy would be to affirm a *contradictio in adjecto,* for it would be to judge that there are things which both have and do not have a certain property—in the present instance, that there is something that both is and is not rectangular. Hence, Kant said that "the common principle of all analytic judgments is the law of contradiction."[14]

What might it mean to say, with respect to a sentence of the form "Everything that is an *S* is a *P*" that the predicate-term can be analyzed out of the subject-term?

One thing that might be meant is this: that what the sentence expresses can *also* be expressed in a sentence in which the predicate-term is the same as the subject term. Thus the predicate of "Everything that is a man is a rational animal" could be said to be analyzed out of the subject, since what the sentence expresses can also be expressed by saying "Everything that is a rational animal is a rational animal." But not all of the traditional examples of propositions that are analytic may be expressed in sentences wherein the subject term and the predicate-term are the same.

Consider the sentence:

1. All squares are rectangles.

What this sentence expresses may also be put as:

2. Everything that is an equilateral thing and a rectangle is a rectangle.

Sentence (2) provides us with a paradigm case of a sentence in which the predicate-term ("a rectangle") may be said to be analyzed out of the subject-term ("an equilateral thing and a rectangle").

We may note that, in sentence (2), the predicate-term is *also* part of the subject-term. Shall we say, then, that the predicate of a sentence is *analyzed out* of the subject if the predicate is the same as the subject or if the subject is a conjunction of two terms one of which is the predicate? This definition would be somewhat broad, for it would require us to say that in the following sentence the predicate is analyzed out of the subject:

3. Everything that is a square and a rectangle is a rectangle.

But (3) does not exhibit the type of analysis that is to be found in (2). Thus in (3) the subject-term ("a square and a rectangle") is redundant (given "a square" in the subject we don't *need* to add "a rectangle"), but in (2) the subject-term ("an equilateral thing and a rectangle") is not redundant.

We could say, somewhat more exactly, that a predicate-term is *analyzed out* of a subject-term provided the subject-term is such that either it is itself the predicate-term or it is a conjunction of independent terms one of which is the predicate-term. But what is it for two terms to be "independent"?

We may say, of certain pairs of terms in a given language, that one of the terms *logically implies* the other in that language. Thus in English "square" logically implies "rectangle," and "red thing" logically implies "colored thing." These terms may be said to be such that in English they are *true of,* or *apply to,* certain things. And the English language is necessarily such that "rectangle" applies to everything that "square" applies to, and it is also necessarily such that "colored thing" applies to everything that "red" applies to. To say, then, "*T logically implies R* in language *L*" is to say this: *L* is necessarily such that *R* applies in *L* to all those things to which *T* applies in *L*.

Now we may say what it is for two terms to be

independent—what it is for two terms to be logically independent of each other in a given language.

Two terms are *logically independent* of each other in a given language provided only that the terms and their negations are such that no one of them logically implies the other in that language. Thus "red thing" and "square" are logically independent in English, for the four terms, "red thing," "square," "nonred thing," and "nonsquare" are such that no one of them implies the other in English.

We can now say, somewhat more exactly, what it is for the predicate-term *P*, of a sentence in a given language *L*, to be *analyzed out* of the subject-term *S*. First of all, the sentence will be an "All *S* is *P*" sentence; that is to say, the sentence will be necessarily such that it is true in *L*, if and only if, for every *x*, if *S* applies to *x* in *L*, then *P* applies to *x* in *L*. And second, either the subject-term *S* is itself the same as *P* or it is a conjunction of logically independent terms one of which is *P*.

Finally, we may define the Kantian sense of "analytic proposition" as follows: A proposition is analytic provided only it may be expressed in a sentence in which the predicate-term is analyzed out of the subject-term.

To see how the definitions may be applied, consider the following sentences, each of which may be said to express an analytic proposition, in the traditional sense of the term "analytic":

All fathers are parents.
No bachelors are married.
All dogs are dogs or cats.

What these three sentences express in English may also be put as follows:

Everything that is a male and a parent is a parent.
Everything that is a male human and a thing that is unmarried is a thing that is ummarried.
Everything that is (i) a dog or a cat and (ii) a dog or a noncat is a dog or a cat.

The last three sentences are sentences in which the predicate is analyzed out of the subject. And therefore the propositions expressed by the first sentences are all analytic.

The Synthetic A Priori

Kant raised the question: Is there a synthetic *a priori*? Are there synthetic propositions that we know *a priori* to be true?

If we construe "analytic proposition" in the way in which we have tried to spell out (by reference to the predicate of a sentence being "analyzed out of" the subject), and if, as many philosophers do, we take "synthetic proposition" to mean the same as "proposition which is not analytic," then Kant's question may not be particularly interesting. For, it would seem, there are many propositions which we know *a priori* and which are not analytic, in this restricted sense of the term "analytic." Among them are such propositions as:

If there are more than 7 dogs, then there are more than 5 dogs.
If there are either dogs or cows but no cows, then there are dogs.
If all men are mortal and Socrates is a man, then Socrates is mortal.

But when philosophers ask whether there are synthetic propositions that we know *a priori* to be true, they are not usually thinking of such propositions as these. They are thinking rather of propositions which can be expressed naturally in English in the form "All *S* are *P*." Given what we have said about the nature of analytic propositions, we may put the question, "Is there a synthetic *a priori*?" somewhat more exactly as follows:

Are there any propositions which are such that: (i) they are known by us *a priori*; (ii) they can be expressed in English in the form "Everything which is *S* is *P*"; and yet (iii) they are *not* such that in English their predicate-terms can be analyzed out of their subject-terms?

Let us consider, then, certain possible examples of "the synthetic *a priori*," so conceived.

1. One important candidate for the synthetic *a priori* is the knowledge that might be expressed by saying either "Being square includes being a shape" or "Necessarily, everything that is square is a thing that has a shape." The sentence "Everything that is square is a thing that has a shape" recalls our paradigmatic "Everything that is square is a rectangle." In the case of the latter sentence, we were able to

"analyze the predicate out of the subject": We replaced the subject-term "square" with a conjunctive term, "equilateral thing and a rectangle," and were thus able to express our proposition in the form:

Everything that is an *S* and a *P* is a *P*

where the terms replacing "*S*" and "*P*" are such that neither is implied by the other or by the negation of the other. But can we do this with "Everything that is square has a shape"?

The problem is to fill in the blank in the following sentence:

Everything that is a ——— and a thing that has a shape is a thing that has a shape

in the appropriate way. This means we should find a term such that: (i) the resulting sentence will express what is expressed by "Everything that is square has a shape"; (ii) the term will neither imply nor be implied by "thing that has a shape"; and (iii) the negation of our term will neither imply nor be implied by "thing that has a shape." With what term, then, can we fill the blank?

We might try "either a square or a thing that does not have a shape," thus obtaining "Everything that is (i) either a square or a thing that does not have a shape and (ii) a thing that has a shape is a thing that has a shape." But the sentence thus obtained is not one in which the predicate is analyzed out of the subject. The two terms making up the subject, namely (i) "either a square or a thing that does not have a shape" and (ii) "a thing that has a shape," are such that, in our language, any negation of the second logically implies the first (i.e., "not such as to be a thing that has a shape" logically implies "either a square or a thing that does not have a shape"). We do not have a sentence, therefore, in which the predicate can be said to be analyzed out of the subject; for the two terms making up the subject are not logically independent in our language.

What if we fill in the blank by "square," thus obtaining "Everything that is a square and a thing that has a shape is a thing that has a shape"? This will not help us, for the two terms making up the subject—"square" and "a thing that has a shape"—are such that, in our language, the first logically implies the second; hence they are not logically

independent of each other; and therefore the sentence is not one in which the predicate is analyzed out of the subject. And if we drop the second term from the subject, as we can without any loss, we will be back where we started.

And so we have not found a way of showing that "Everything that is square has a shape" is analytic. But the sentence expresses what we know *a priori* to be true. And therefore, it would seem, there is at last some presumption in favor of the proposition that there is a synthetic *a priori*.

There are indefinitely many other propositions presenting essentially the same difficulties as "Everything that is square has a shape." Examples are: "Everything red is colored"; "Everyone who hears something in C-sharp minor hears a sound." The sentences express what is known *a priori,* but no one has been able to show that they are analytic.

It has been suggested that the sentences giving rise to the problem of the synthetic *a priori* are really "postulates about the meanings of words," and therefore, that they do not express what is synthetic *a priori.* But if the suggestion is intended literally, then it would seem to betray the confusion between use and mention that we encountered earlier. A postulate about the meaning of the word "red," for example, or a sentence expressing such a postulate, would presumably mention the word "red." It might read, "The word 'red' may be taken to refer to a certain color," or perhaps, "Let the word 'red' be taken to refer to a certain color." But "Everything that is red is colored," although it uses the words "red" and "colored," doesn't mention them at all. Thus, there would seem to be no clear sense in which it could be said really to be a "meaning postulate" or to refer in any way to words and how they are used.

2. What Leibniz called the "disparates" furnish us with a second candidate for the synthetic *a priori.* These are closely related to the type of sentence just considered, but involve problems that are essentially different. An example of a sentence concerned with disparates would be our earlier "Being red excludes being blue" or (alternatively put) "Nothing that is red is blue." Philosophers have devoted considerable ingenuity to trying to show that "Nothing that is red is blue" can be expressed as a sentence that is analytic, but so far as I have been able to determine, all of these attempts have been

unsuccessful. Again, it is recommended that the reader try to re-express "Nothing that is red is blue" in such a way that the predicate may be "analyzed out" of the subject in the sense we have described above.

3. It has also been held, not without plausibility, that certain ethical sentences express what is synthetic *a priori*. Thus, Leibniz, writing on what he called the "supersensible element" in knowledge, said: ". . . but to return to *necessary truths,* it is generally true that we know them only by this natural light, and not at all by the experience of the senses. For the senses can very well make known, in some sort, what is, but they cannot make known what *ought to be* or what could not be otherwise." Or consider the sentence, "All pleasures, as such, are intrinsically good, or good in themselves, whenever and wherever they may occur." If this sentence expresses something that is known to be true, then what it expresses must be synthetic *a priori*. To avoid this conclusion, some philosophers deny that sentences about what is intrinsically good, or good in itself, *can* be known to be true.

given terms, if the one applies to something in that language then the other also applies to that thing in that language.[15]

But these three propositions, even if they are true, are not sufficient to yield the conclusion (4) that the distinction between the analytic and the synthetic is untenable. If we attempt to formulate the additional premise that would be needed to make the argument valid, we will see that it must involve a philosophical generalization—a generalization concerning what conditions must obtain if the distinction between the analytic and the synthetic is to be tenable. And how would the generalization be defended? This question should be considered in the light of what we have said about skepticism and the problem of the criterion. Of the philosophical generalizations that would make the above argument valid, none of them, so far as I know, has ever been defended. It is not accurate, therefore, to say that the distinction between the analytic and the synthetic has been *shown* to be untenable.

An Untenable Dualism?

But many philosophers now believe that the distinction between the analytic and the synthetic has been shown to be untenable; we should consider what reasons there might be for such a belief. Ordinarily, it is defended by reference to the following facts. (1) In drawing a distinction between analytic and synthetic sentences, one must speak of *necessity,* as we have done, or employ concepts, e.g., that of *synonymy,* that can be explicated only by reference to necessity. Thus we have spoken of a language being *necessarily* such that, if a given term applies to a thing in that language, then a certain other term also applies to that thing in that language. (2) There is no reliable way of telling, merely by observing a man's behavior, whether the language he then happens to be using is one which is *necessarily* such that if a given term applies to something in that language then a certain other term applies to that thing in that language. And (3) it is not possible, by reference merely to linguistic behavior, to say what it is for a language to be *necessarily* such that, for two

Notes

[1] "Being red excludes being blue" should not be taken to rule out the possibility of a thing being red in one part and blue in another; it tells us only that being red in one part at one time excludes being blue in exactly that same part at exactly that same time. The point might be put even more exactly by saying that it is necessarily true that anything that is red has a part that is not blue.

[2] William Whewell, *Philosophy of the Inductive Sciences Founded upon Their History, I* (London: J. W. Parker & Son, 1840), pp. 59–61.

[3] *Republic,* 479, 508.

[4] *Posterior Analytics,* 100a–100b.

[5] *Philosophical Writings,* ed. and trans. Alan Wolter (New York: Thomas Nelson & Sons, 1962), p. 109 (the Nelson philosophical texts); cf. p. 103.

[6] *The Philosophical Works of Leibniz,* ed. G. M. Duncan (New Haven: The Tuttle, Morehouse & Taylor Co., 1908), p. 161.

[7] *Erkenntnis und Irrtum* (Leipzig: Felix Meiner, 1905), pp. 180ff.

[8] E. Husserl, *Ideas: General Introduction to Phenomenology* (New York: The Macmillan Company, 1931), p. 57.

[9] G. W. Leibniz, *New Essays Concerning Human Understanding,* Book IV, Chapter 7 (Open Court edition), p. 462. Compare Alice Ambrose and Morris Lazerowitz, *Fundamentals of Symbolic Logic* (New York: Holt, Rinehart

and Winston, Inc., 1962): "A proposition is said to be true *a priori* if its truth can be ascertained by examination of the proposition alone or if it is deducible from propositions whose truth is so ascertained, and by examination of nothing else. . . . Understanding the words used in expressing these propositions is sufficient for determining that they are true." P. 17.

[10] Gottlob Frege, *Kleine Schriften* (Hildesheim: Georg Olms Verlagsbuchhandlung, 1967), p. 262.

[11] Leonard Nelson, *Socratic Method and Critical Philosophy* (New Haven: Yale University Press, 1949), p. 184.

[12] See Anthony Quinton, "The *A Priori* and the Analytic," in Robert Sleigh, ed., *Necessary Truth* (Englewood Cliffs, NJ: Prentice-Hall, Inc., 1972), pp. 89–109.

[13] W. V. Quine, "Carnap and Logical Truth," *The Philosophy of Rudolf Carnap*, P. A. Schilpp, ed., (La Salle, IL: Open Court Publishing Co., 1963), p. 386.

[14] *Prolegomena to Any Future Metaphysics,* sec. 2.

[15] Cf. W. V. Quine, "Two Dogmas of Empiricism," in *From a Logical Point of View,* esp. pp. 20–37, and Morton White, "The Analytic and the Synthetic: An Untenable Dualism," in *Semantics and the Philosophy of Language,* ed. Leonard Linsky, (Urbana: University of Illinois Press, 1952), pp. 272–286.

Bibliography

Harris, J. F., and R. H. Severens, eds. *Analyticity: Selected Readings*. Chicago: Quadrangle Books, 1970.

Kitcher, Philip. "A Priori Knowledge." *Philosophical Review 76* (1980).

Kripke, Saul. *Naming and Necessity*. Cambridge, MA: Harvard University Press, 1980.

Moser, Paul K., ed. *A Priori Knowledge*. Oxford, England: Oxford University Press, 1987.

Pap, Arthur. *The A Priori in Physical Theory*. New York: King's Crown Press, 1946.

Plantinga, Alvin. *The Nature of Necessity*. Oxford, England: Clarendon Press, 1974.

Sleigh, R. C., ed. *Necessary Truths*. Englewood Cliffs, NJ: Prentice-Hall, 1972.

Part VIII

The Justification of Induction

From a single experience, we sometimes make an inductive leap to the many; from *some* experiences of a certain kind, we often make a leap to judgments about *all* experiences of that kind. A child puts a hand on a red-hot stove and pulls away in pain and thereby learns never to put a hand on such a stove again. Another child forgets to look to the left when crossing a street and barely misses getting run down by a speeding vehicle, thereby learning never to cross the street without looking in both directions first. People who get food poisoning from eating a certain kind of mushroom learn never to eat that variety again. From the fact that some people have died, we infer that all people eventually die. From experiencing vegetables nourishing and cigarettes causing cancer, we generalize that vegetables always nourish and cigarettes always tend to cause cancer. From limited past experience, we generalize that water always boils at sea level at 100 degrees centigrade, that the sun continues to rise, that the laws of motion and gravity always function.

From limited experiences, we generalize

about future experiences. The food we eat, the friends we keep, the chairs we unthinkingly trust to support us, the way we walk, the buildings and trees we steer clear of, the clothes we wear, the sentences we speak, the cars we drive and the ways we drive them, the rules we obey, and the laws of nature we rely on all bear testimony to our faith in the principle of induction with its probability functions. Probability, said Locke, is the guide to life. We cannot, experience tells us, live without it. Our existence as well as science itself is based on the principle of induction that tells us to reason from past frequencies to future likelihoods, from the limited known of the past and present to the unknown of the past, present, and future.

But though inductive probability is psychologically inescapable, we have trouble providing a rational justification for it. What argument is there for our belief that the laws of motion and the law of gravity will continue to exist next year or the year after? Why don't the laws of nature die or grow old and fragile like people or the laws of society? How do we know that the sun will rise tomorrow or the week after? or that vegetables will continue to nourish us and cigarettes continue to cause cancer, rather than just the reverse? Why do we assume that the future will be like the past and present?

It was David Hume (1711–1776) who first raised the problem of *induction,* although he never used that term. Hume pointed out that the contrary of every matter of fact is always logically possible, because, unlike the truths of reason (logic and mathematics), it is never contradictory to deny a matter of fact. It is not logically necessary that the earth is now rotating or revolving around the sun, nor that it will do so tomorrow. These are mere contingent truths. "That the sun will not rise tomorrow is no less intelligible a proposition, and implies no more a contradiction than the affirmation that it will rise." And if the sun's not rising is possible, what reason do we have for thinking it won't actually happen?

What is our justification for our belief regarding matters of fact? Hume asks. He replies that we justify that belief by our belief in causal laws and relationships. We believe that a causal order rooted in nature's laws operates to produce all that is. But what is the foundation of all our reasoning concerning cause and effect? "Experience," Hume replies. All our experience corroborates such relations. But, Hume relentlessly continues, "what is the foundation of all conclusions from experience?" His reply: "In reality, all arguments from experience are founded on the similarity which we discover among natural objects, and by which we are induced to expect effects similar to those which we have found to follow from such objects." Only a fool or a lunatic would pretend to dispute this faith in causality based on experience.

But experience "only shows us a number of uniform effects, resulting from certain objects and teaches us that those particular objects, at that particular time, were endowed with such powers and forces, when a new object, endowed with similar sensible qualities, is produced, we expect similar powers and forces, and look for a like effect. From a body of like color and consistence with bread we expect like nourishment and support. But this surely is a step or progress of the mind, which wants to be explained."

Reasoning from the proposition "I have always found so and so to happen in the past" to the proposition "So and so will continue to happen in the future" is a great leap that stands in need of justification.

We must admit, contends Hume, "that the inference is not intuitive; neither is it demonstrative. Of what nature is it then? To say it is experiential is begging the question. For all inferences from experience suppose, as their foundation, that the future will resemble the past. . . . It is impossible, therefore, that any argument from experience can prove this resemblance of the past to the future; since all these arguments are founded on the supposition of that resemblance."

Why may not the future turn out to be quite different from the past? "What logic, what processes of argument secure you against this supposition?"

Hume shows that our belief that the future would be like the past was based on our belief in the uniformity of nature, which in turn was based on our past experience, which is an inadequate premise for arguing for the future. The argument "The uniformity of nature has been reliable in the past so it will likely be reliable in the future" is not a sound deductive argument, because the conclusion contains more information than the premises. Inductive generalizations are, in the words of C. E. Peirce, "ampliative"—adding more data than the premises contain.

Hume's point is that we cannot justify the principle of induction via either a deductive or an inductive argument. Here is what he has in mind. Suppose we attempt to justify the principle of induction by means of a deductive argument. What premises should we use? Well, whatever they are, they must be known to be true. But because we do not know the future, the premises must be confined to the present and past. And because a valid deductive argument may not include in the conclusion any claims or information not already implicit in the premises, this argument can only include statements about the past and the present, not the future. But it is just the future that we are concerned with, so deductive arguments all fail to justify the principle of induction.

Suppose we try to justify the principle of induction by means of an inductive argument. We argue that the principle of induction has had a high probability of success until now, so we may conclude that it probably will continue to have a high probability of success in the future. But, the skeptic asks, what justifies us making the leap from the past to the future? A belief in the uniformity of nature? But, he (or she) continues, how do we know that the uniformity of nature will function in the future? Because it always has

in the past, we respond. But now we are going around in circles, for we are appealing to the very principle that we would establish through induction—the principle of induction—and thus are begging the question.

Therefore neither a deductive nor an inductive argument establishes the principle of induction.

Since Hume's time there have been many attempts to justify induction. The general consensus says Hume is correct that no deductive argument can establish the truth of induction. But three other types of argumentation *have* enjoyed popularity: sophisticated *inductivism, pragmatic* arguments, and the *dissolution* argument. Each is represented in the readings in this part of the book. In "Will the Future Be Like the Past?" F. L. Will uses the metaphor of a contained expanse that successfully moves on to new territory to argue that there is something correct about using higher-order inductivism to establish lower-order induction. Hans Reichenbach in "The Pragmatic Justification of Induction" argues that the principle of induction is the only game in town. If this principle doesn't bring successful predictions, nothing will. In "Dissolving the Problem of Induction," Peter F. Strawson argues that it is a mistake to try to justify what is presupposed by the idea of justification itself.

In the final reading, Nelson Goodman goes one up on Hume. Instead of solving Hume's riddle, he sets forth a new riddle of induction, that of distinguishing between proper and improper projectable properties; that is, properties we are warranted in projecting into the future. To illustrate his problem, Goodman asks us to imagine a new color word *grue,* which is defined in terms of our old color words *green* and *blue.* An object is grue if and only if it is green at some time t before the year 2000 or blue at some time t during or after the year 2000.

All the emeralds we have so far observed have been observed before 2000, and so are grue. So, using the principle that the future will be like the past, we conclude that the emeralds we see after 2000 will be grue. But a grue emerald after 2000 is, by definition, blue. So the greenness of emeralds so far inductively supports the non-greenness of emeralds in the future, but that is a paradox.

We might protest that the grue and the green emerald seem exactly the same and that we see no reason whatsoever for imagining the property grue. But, avers Goodman, the point is that this intuitive judgment needs to be justified in terms of distinguishing between legitimate projectable regularities and illegitimate ones. Inductive logic itself doesn't do that for us. What does? Goodman's challenge is for new rules by which to sort out what is justifiably projectable and what is not.

VIII.1 *The Problem of Induction*

DAVID HUME

The Scottish philosopher David Hume (1711–1776) pointed out the problem of justifying our belief in induction in *An Enquiry Concerning Human Understanding* (1748) from which this selection is taken. Within the context of a discussion of causality, Hume argues that there is no way of proving or establishing as probable that the future will resemble the past. You cannot use a deductive argument, for a sound deductive argument disallows claims in the conclusion that are not found in the premises and the premises only contain information about the past and present, not the future. You cannot establish the principle of the induction by appealing to inductive experience, for that is assuming exactly the point in question: the validity of induction. Hume admits that we all take the principle of induction for granted and use it successfully every day, but philosophical curiosity prompts him to wonder at the difficulty of justifying the principle.

Sceptical Doubts Concerning the Operations of the Understanding

Part I

All the objects of human reason or enquiry may naturally be divided into two kinds, to wit, *Relations of Ideas*, and *Matters of Fact*. Of the first kind are the

Reprinted from *An Enquiry Concerning Human Understanding* (1748).

sciences of Geometry, Algebra, and Arithmetic; and in short, every affirmation which is either intuitively or demonstratively certain. *That the square of the hypotenuse is equal to the squares of the two sides,* is a proposition which expresses a relation between these figures. *That three times five is equal to the half of thirty,* expresses a relation between these numbers. Propositions of this kind are discoverable by the mere operation of thought, without dependence on what is anywhere existent in the universe. Though there never were a circle or triangle in nature, the truths demonstrated by Euclid would for ever retain their certainty and evidence.

Matters of fact, which are the second objects of human reason, are not ascertained in the same manner; nor is our evidence of their truth, however great, of a like nature with the foregoing. The contrary of every matter of fact is still possible; because it can never imply a contradiction, and is conceived by the mind with the same facility and distinctness, as if ever so comfortable to reality. *That the sun will not rise tomorrow* is no less intelligible a proposition, and implies no more contradiction than the affirmation, *that it will rise*. We should in vain, therefore, attempt to demonstrate its falsehood. Were it demonstratively false, it would imply a contradiction, and could never be distinctly conceived by the mind.

It may, therefore, be a subject worthy of curiosity, to enquire what is the nature of that evidence which assures us of any real existence and matter of fact, beyond the present testimony of our senses, or the records of our memory. This part of philosophy, it is observable, has been little cultivated, either by the ancients or moderns; and therefore our doubts and errors, in the prosecution of so important an enquiry, may be the more excusable; while we march through such difficult paths without any guide or direction. They may even prove useful, by exciting curiosity, and destroying that implicit faith and security, which is the bane of all reasoning and free enquiry. The discovery of defects in the common philosophy, if any such there be, will not, I presume, be a discouragement, but rather an incitement, as is usual, to attempt something more full and satisfactory than has yet been proposed to the public.

All reasonings concerning matter of fact seem to be founded on the relation of *Cause and Effect*. By means of that relation alone we can go beyond the evidence of our memory and senses. If you were to ask a man, why he believes any matter of fact, which is absent; for instance, that his friend is in the country, or in France; he would give you a reason; and this reason would be some other fact; as a letter received from him, or the knowledge of his former resolutions and promises. A man finding a watch or any other machine in a desert island, would conclude that there had once been men in that island. All our reasonings concerning fact are of the same nature. And here it is constantly supposed that there is a connection between the present fact and that which is inferred from it. Were there nothing to bind them together, the inference would be entirely precarious. The hearing of an articulate voice and rational discourse in the dark assures us of the presence of some person: Why? because these are the effects of the human make and fabric, and closely connected with it. If we anatomize all the other reasonings of this nature, we shall find that they are founded on the relation of cause and effect, and that this relation is either near or remote, direct or collateral. Heat and light are collateral effects of fire, and the one effect may justly be inferred from the other.

If we would satisfy ourselves, therefore, concerning the nature of that evidence, which assures us of matters of fact, we must enquire how we arrive at the knowledge of cause and effect. . . .

This proposition, *that causes and effects are discoverable, not by reason but by experience,* will readily be admitted with regards to such objects, as we remember to have once been altogether unknown to us; since we must be conscious of the utter inability, which we then lay under, of foretelling what would arise from them. Present two smooth pieces of marble to a man who has no tincture of natural philosophy; he will never discover that they will adhere together in such a manner as to require great force to separate them in a direct line, while they make so small a resistance to a lateral pressure. Such events, as bear little analogy to the common course of nature, are also readily confessed to be known only by experience; nor does any man imagine that the explosion of gunpowder, or the attraction of a loadstone, could ever be discovered by arguments *a priori*. In like manner, when an effect is supposed to depend upon an intricate machinery or secret structure of parts, we make no difficulty in attributing all our knowledge of it to experience. Who will assert that he can give the ultimate reason, why milk or bread is proper nourishment for a man, not for a lion or a tiger?

But the same truth may not appear, at first sight, to have the same evidence with regard to events, which have become familiar to us from our first appearance in the world, which bear a close analogy to the whole course of nature, and which are supposed to depend on the simple qualities of objects, without any secret structure of parts. We are apt to imagine that we could discover these effects by the mere operation of our reason, without experience. We fancy, that were we brought on a sudden into this world, we could at first have inferred that one Billiard-ball would communicate motion to another upon impulse; and that we needed not to have waited for the event, in order to pronounce with certainty concerning it. Such is the influence of custom, that, where it is strongest, it not only covers our natural ignorance, but even conceals itself, and seems not to take place, merely because it is found in the highest degree.

But to convince us that all the laws of nature, and all the operations of bodies without exception, are known only by experience, the following reflections may, perhaps, suffice. Were any object presented to us, and were we required to pronounce concerning the effect, which will result from it, without consulting past observation; after what manner, I beseech you, must the mind proceed in this operation? It must invent or imagine some event, which it ascribes to the object as its effect; and it is plain that this invention must be entirely arbitrary. The mind can never possibly find the effect in the supposed cause, by the most accurate scrutiny and examination. For the effect is totally different from the cause, and consequently can never be discovered in it. Motion in the second Billiard-ball is a quite distinct event from motion in the first; nor is there anything in the one to suggest the smallest hint of the other. A stone or piece of metal raised into the air, and left without any support, immediately falls: but to consider the matter *a priori,* is there anything we discover in this situation which can beget the idea of a downward, rather than an upward, or any other motion, in the stone or metal?

And as the first imagination or invention of a particular effect, in all natural operations, is arbitrary, where we consult not experience; so must we also esteem the supposed tie or connection between the cause and effect, which binds them together, and renders it impossible that any other effect could result from the operation of that cause. When I see, for instance, a Billiard-ball moving in a straight line towards another; even suppose motion in the second ball should by accident be suggested to me, as the result of their contact or impulse; may I not conceive, that a hundred different events might as well follow from that cause? May not both these balls remain at absolute rest? May not the first ball return in a straight line, or leap off from the second in any line or direction? All these suppositions are consistent and conceivable. Why then should we give the preference to one, which is no more consistent or conceivable than the rest? All our reasonings *a priori* will never be able to show us any foundation for this preference.

In a word, then, every effect is a distinct event from its cause. It could not, therefore, be discovered in the cause, and the first invention or conception of it, *a priori,* must be entirely arbitrary. And even after it is suggested, the conjunction of it with the cause must appear equally arbitrary; since there are always many other effects, which, to reason, must seem fully as consistent and natural. In vain, therefore, should we pretend to determine any single event, or infer any cause of effect, without the assistance of observation and experience. . . .

Part II

But we have not yet attained any tolerable satisfaction with regard to the question first proposed. Each solution still gives rise to a new question as difficult as the foregoing, and leads us on to farther enquiries. When it is asked, *What is the nature of all our reasonings concerning matter of fact?* the proper answer seems to be, that they are founded on the relation of cause and effect. When again it is asked, *What is the foundation of all our reasonings and conclusions concerning that relation?* it may be replied in one word, Experience. But if we still carry on our sifting humor, and ask, *What is the foundation of all conclusions from experience?* this implies a new question, which may be of more difficult solution and explication. Philosophers, that give themselves airs of superior wisdom and sufficiency, have a hard task when they encounter persons of inquisitive dispositions, who push them from every corner to which they retreat, and who are sure at last to bring them to some dangerous dilemma. The best expedient to prevent this confusion, is to be modest in our pretensions; and even to discover the difficulty ourselves before it is objected to us. By this means, we may make a kind of merit of our very ignorance.

I shall content myself, in this section, with an easy task, and shall pretend only to give a negative answer to the question here proposed. I say then, that, even after we have experience of the operations of cause and effect, our conclusions from that experience are *not* founded on reasoning, or any process of the understanding. This answer we must endeavor both to explain and to defend. . . .

In reality, all arguments from experience are founded on the similarity which we discover among natural objects, and by which we are induced to expect effects similar to those which we have found to follow from such objects. And though none but a fool or madman will ever pretend to dispute the authority of experience, or to reject that great guide of human life, it may surely be allowed a philosopher to have so much curiosity at least as to examine the principle of human nature, which gives this mighty authority to experience, and makes us draw advantage from that similarity which nature has placed among different objects. From causes which appear *similar* we expect similar effects. This is the sum of all our experimental conclusions. Now it seems evident that, if this conclusion were formed by reason, it would be as perfect at first, and upon one instance, as after ever so long a course of experience. But the case is far otherwise. Nothing so like as eggs; yet no one, on account of this appearing similarity, expects the same taste and relish in all of them. It is only after a long course of uniform experiments in any kind, that we attain a firm reliance and security with regard to a particular event. Now where is that process of reasoning which, from one instance, draws a conclusion, so different from that which it infers from a hundred instances that are nowise different from that single one? This question I propose as much for the sake of information, as with an intention of raising difficulties. I cannot find, I cannot imagine any such reasoning. But I keep my mind still open to instruction, if any one will vouchsafe to bestow it on me.

Should it be said that, from a number of uniform experiments, we *infer* a connection between the sensible qualities and the secret powers; this, I must confess, seems the same difficulty, couched in different terms. The question still recurs, on what process of argument this inference is founded? Where is the medium, the interposing ideas, which join propositions so very wide of each other? It is confessed that the color, consistence, and other sensible qualities of bread appear not, of themselves, to have any connection with the secret powers of nourishment and support. For otherwise we could infer these secret powers from the first appearance of these sensible qualities, without the aid of experience; contrary to the sentiment of all philosophers,

and contrary to plain matter of fact. Here, then, is our natural state of ignorance with regard to the powers and influence of all objects. How is this remedied by experience? It only shows us a number of uniform effects, resulting from certain objects, and teaches us that those particular objects, at that particular time, were endowed with such powers and forces. When a new object, endowed with similar sensible qualities, is produced, we expect similar powers and forces, and look for a like effect. From a body of like color and consistence with bread we expect like nourishment and support. But this surely is a step or progress of the mind, which wants to be explained. When a man says, *I have found, in all past instances, such sensible qualities conjoined with such secret powers:* And when he says, *Similar sensible qualities will always be conjoined with similar secret powers,* he is not guilty of a tautology, nor are these propositions in any respect the same. You say that the one proposition is an inference from the other. But you must confess that the inference is not intuitive; neither is it demonstrative: Of what nature is it, then? To say it is experimental, is begging the question. For all inferences from experience suppose, as their foundation, that the future will resemble the past, and that similar powers will be conjoined with similar sensible qualities. If there be any suspicion that the course of nature may change, and that the past may be no rule for the future, all experience becomes useless, and can give rise to no inference or conclusion. It is impossible, therefore, that any arguments from experience can prove this resemblance of the past to the future; since all these arguments are founded on the supposition of that resemblance. Let the course of things be allowed hitherto ever so regular; that alone, without some new argument or inference, proves not that, for the future, it will continue so. In vain do you pretend to have learned the nature of bodies from your past experience. Their secret nature, and consequently all their effects and influence, may change, without any change in their sensible qualities. This happens sometimes, and with regard to some objects: Why may it [not] happen always, and with regard to all objects? What logic, what process of argument secures you against this supposition? My practice, you say, refutes my doubts. But you mistake the purport of my question. As an agent, I am quite satisfied in the point; but as a philosopher, who has some share of curiosity, I will not say scepticism, I want to learn the foundation of this inference. No reading, no enquiry has yet been able to remove my difficulty, or give me satisfaction in a matter of such importance. Can I do better than propose the difficulty to the public, even though, perhaps, I have small hopes of obtaining a solution? We shall, at least, by this means, be sensible of our ignorance, if we do not augment our knowledge.

I must confess that a man is guilty of unpardonable arrogance who concludes, because an argument has escaped his own investigation, that therefore it does not really exist. I must also confess that, though all the learned, for several ages, should have employed themselves in fruitless search upon any subject, it may still, perhaps, be rash to conclude positively that the subject must, therefore, pass all human comprehension. Even though we examine all the sources of our knowledge, and conclude them unfit for such a subject, there may still remain a suspicion, that the enumeration is not complete, or the examination not accurate. But with regard to the present subject, there are some considerations which seem to remove all this accusation of arrogance or suspicion of mistake.

It is certain that the most ignorant and stupid peasants—nay infants, nay even brute beasts—improve by experience, and learn the qualities of natural objects, by observing the effects which result from them. When a child has felt the sensation of pain from touching the flame of a candle, he will be careful not to put his hand near any candle; but will expect a similar effect from a cause which is similar in its sensible qualities and appearance. If you assert, therefore, that the understanding of the child is led into this conclusion by any process of argument or ratiocination, I may justly require you to produce that argument; nor have you any pretense to refuse so equitable a demand. You cannot say that the argument is abstruse, and may possibly escape your enquiry; since you confess that it is obvious to the capacity of a mere infant. If you hesitate, therefore, a moment, or if, after reflection, you produce any intricate or profound argument, you, in a manner, give up the question, and confess that it is not reasoning which engages us to suppose the past resembling the future, and to expect similar effects from causes which are, to appearance, similar. This is the proposition which I intended to enforce in the present section. If I be right, I pretend not to have made any mighty discovery.

And if I be wrong, I must acknowledge myself to be indeed a very backward scholar; since I cannot now discover an argument which, it seems, was perfectly familiar to me long before I was out of my cradle.

Sceptical Solution of These Doubts
Part I

. . . Nature will always maintain her rights, and prevail in the end over any abstract reasoning whatsoever. Though we should conclude, for instance, as in the foregoing section, that, in all reasonings from experience, there is a step taken by the mind which is not supported by any argument or process of the understanding; there is no danger that these reasonings, on which almost all knowledge depends, will ever be affected by such a discovery. If the mind be not engaged by argument to make this step, it must be induced by some other principle of equal weight and authority; and that principle will preserve its influence as long as human nature remains the same. What that principle is may well be worth the pains of enquiry.

Suppose a person, though endowed with the strongest faculties of reason and reflection, to be brought on a sudden into this world; he would, indeed, immediately observe a continual succession of objects, and one event following another, but he would not be able to discover anything farther. He would not, at first, by any reasoning, be able to reach the idea of cause and effect; since the particular powers, by which all natural operations are performed, never appear to the senses; nor is it reasonable to conclude, merely because one event, in one instance, precedes another, that therefore the one is the cause, the other the effect. Their conjunction may be arbitrary and casual. There may be no reason to infer the existence of one from the appearance of the other. And in a word, such a person, without more experience, could never employ his conjecture or reasoning concerning any matter of fact, or be assured of anything beyond what was immediately present to his memory and senses.

Suppose, again, that he has acquired more experience, and has lived so long in the world as to have observed familiar objects or events to be constantly conjoined together; what is the consequence of this experience? He immediately infers the existence of one object from the appearance of the other. Yet he has not, by all his experience, acquired any idea or knowledge of the secret power by which the one object produces the other; nor is it, by any process of reasoning, he is engaged to draw this inference. But still he finds himself determined to draw it: And though he should be convinced that his understanding has no part in the operation, he would nevertheless continue in the same course of thinking. There is some other principle which determines him to form such a conclusion.

This principle is Custom or Habit. For wherever the repetition of any particular act or operation produces a propensity to renew the same act or operation, without being impelled by any reasoning or process of the understanding, we always say, that this propensity is the effect of *Custom*. By employing that word, we pretend not to have given the ultimate reason of such a propensity. We only point out a principle of human nature, which is universally acknowledged, and which is well known by its effects. Perhaps we can push our enquiries no farther, or pretend to give the cause of this cause; but must rest contented with it as the ultimate principle, which we can assign, of all our conclusions from experience. It is sufficient satisfaction, that we can go so far, without repining at the narrowness of our faculties because they will carry us no farther. And it is certain we here advance a very intelligible proposition at least, if not a true one, when we assert that, after the constant conjunction of two objects—heat and flame, for instance, weight and solidity—we are determined by custom alone to expect the one from the appearance of the other. This hypothesis seems even the only one which explains the difficulty, why we draw, from a thousand instances, an inference which we are not able to draw from one instance, that is, in no respect, different from them. Reason is incapable of any such variation. The conclusions which it draws from considering one circle are the same which it would form upon surveying all the circles in the universe. But no man, having seen only one body move after being impelled by another, could infer that every other body will move after a like impulse. All inferences from experience, therefore, are effects of custom, not of reasoning.

Custom, then, is the great guide of human life. It is that principle alone which renders our experience useful to us, and makes us expect, for the future, a similar train of events with those which have appeared in the past. Without the influence of custom, we should be entirely ignorant of every matter of fact beyond what is immediately present to the memory and senses. We should never know how to adjust means to ends, or to employ our natural powers in the production of any effect. There would be an end at once of all action, as well as of the chief part of speculation.

But here it may be proper to remark, that though our conclusions from experience carry us beyond our memory and senses, and assure us of matters of fact which happened in the most distant places and most remote ages, yet some fact must always be present to the senses or memory, from which we may first proceed in drawing these conclusions. A man, who should find in a desert country the remains of pompous buildings, would conclude that the country had, in ancient times, been cultivated by civilized inhabitants, but did nothing of this nature occur to him, he could never form such an inference. We learn the events of former ages from history; but then we must peruse the volumes in which this instruction is contained, and thence carry up our inferences from one testimony to another, till we arrive at the eyewitnesses and spectators of these distant events. In a word, if we proceed not upon some fact, present to the memory or senses, our reasonings would be merely hypothetical; and however the particular links might be connected with each other, the whole chain of inferences would have nothing to support it, nor could we ever, by its means, arrive at the knowledge of any real existence. If I ask why you believe any particular matter of fact, which you relate, you must tell me some reason; and this reason will be some other fact, connected, with it. But as you cannot proceed after this manner, *in infinitum,* you must at last terminate in some fact, which is present to your memory or senses; or must allow that your belief is entirely without foundation.

What, then, is the conclusion of the whole matter? A simple one; though, it must be confessed, pretty remote from the common theories of philosophy. All belief of matter of fact or real existence is derived merely from some object, present to the memory or senses, and a customary conjunction between that and some other object. Or in other words; having found in many instances, that any two kinds of objects—flame and heat, snow and cold—have always been conjoined together, if flame or snow be presented anew to the senses, the mind is carried by custom to expect heat or cold, and to *believe* that such a quality does exist, and will discover itself upon a nearer approach. This belief is the necessary result of placing the mind in such circumstances. It is an operation of the soul, when we are so situated, as unavoidable as to feel the passion of love, when we receive benefits; or hatred, when we meet with injuries. All these operations are a species of natural instincts, which no reasoning or process of the thought and understanding is able either to produce or to prevent.

VIII.2 *On Induction*

Bertrand Russell

Bertrand Russell (1872–1970), one of the greatest philosophers in the twentieth century, in his pithy *Problems of Philosophy* (1912) offers the clearest elaboration of Hume's problem that we can have no knowledge of the future. At best, arguments supporting the principle of induction give us justification for past futures but not future futures. He points out that fundamental laws of science are in question in Hume's challenge and that the principle is as unproved as it is undeniable.

In almost all our previous discussions we have been concerned in the attempt to get clear as to our data in the way of knowledge of existence. What things are there in the universe whose existence is known to us owing to our being acquainted with them? So far, our answer has been that we are acquainted with our sense-data, and, probably, with ourselves. These we know to exist. And past sense-data which are remembered are known to have existed in the past. This knowledge supplies our data.

But if we are to be able to draw inferences from these data—if we are to know of the existence of matter, of other people, of the past before our individual memory begins, or of the future, we must know general principles of some kind by means of which such inferences can be drawn. It must be known to us that the existence of some one sort of thing, A, is a sign of the existence of some other sort of thing, B, either at the same time as A or at some earlier or later time, as, for example, thunder is a sign of the earlier existence of lightning. If this were not known to us, we could never extend our knowledge beyond the sphere of our private experience; and this sphere, as we have seen, is exceedingly limited. The question we have now to consider is whether such an extension is possible, and if so, how it is effected.

Let us take as an illustration a matter about which none of us, in fact, feel the slightest doubt. We are all convinced that the sun will rise tomorrow. Why? Is this belief a mere blind outcome of past experience, or can it be justified as a reasonable belief? It is not easy to find a test by which to judge whether a belief of this kind is reasonable or not, but we can at least ascertain what sort of general beliefs would suffice, if true, to justify the judgement that the sun will rise to-morrow, and the

Reprinted from *The Problems of Philosophy* (Oxford, England: Oxford University Press, 1912) by permission of the publisher.

many other similar judgements upon which our actions are based.

It is obvious that if we are asked why we believe that the sun will rise to-morrow, we shall naturally answer, "Because it always has risen every day." We have a firm belief that it will rise in the future, because it has risen in the past. If we are challenged as to why we believe that it will continue to rise as heretofore, we may appeal to the laws of motion: the earth, we shall say, is a freely rotating body, and such bodies do not cease to rotate unless something interferes from outside, and there is nothing outside to interfere with the earth between now and to-morrow. Of course it might be doubted whether we are quite certain that there is nothing outside to interfere, but this is not the interesting doubt. The interesting doubt is as to whether the laws of motion will remain in operation until to-morrow. If this doubt is raised, we find ourselves in the same position as when the doubt about the sunrise was first raised.

The *only* reason for believing that the laws of motion will remain in operation is that they have operated hitherto, so far as our knowledge of the past enables us to judge. It is true that we have a greater body of evidence from the past in favour of the laws of motion than we have in favour of the sunrise, because the sunrise is merely a particular case of fulfilment of the laws of motion, and there are countless other particular cases. But the real question is: Do *any* number of cases of a law being fulfilled in the past afford evidence that it will be fulfilled in the future? If not, it becomes plain that we have no ground whatever for expecting the sun to rise to-morrow, or for expecting the bread we shall eat at our next meal not to poison us, or for any of the other scarcely conscious expectations that control our daily lives. It is to be observed that all such expectations are only *probable*; thus we have not to seek for a proof that they *must* be fulfilled, but only for some reason in favour of the view that they are *likely* to be fulfilled.

Now in dealing with this question we must, to begin with, make an important distinction, without which we should soon become involved in hopeless confusions. Experience has shown us that, hitherto, the frequent repetition of some uniform succession or coexistence has been a *cause* of our expecting the same succession or coexistence on the next occa-sion. Food that has a certain appearance generally has a certain taste, and it is a severe shock to our expectations when the familiar appearance is found to be associated with an unusual taste. Things which we see become associated, by habit, with certain tactile sensations which we expect if we touch them; one of the horrors of a ghost (in many ghost-stories) is that it fails to give us any sensations of touch. Uneducated people who go abroad for the first time are so surprised as to be incredulous when they find their native language not under-stood.

And this kind of association is not confined to men; in animals also it is very strong. A horse which has been often driven along a certain road resists the attempt to drive him in a different direction. Do-mestic animals expect food when they see the per-son who usually feeds them. We know that all these rather crude expectations of uniformity are liable to be misleading. The man who has fed the chicken every day throughout its life at last wrings its neck instead, showing that more refined views as to the uniformity of nature would have been useful to the chicken.

But in spite of the misleadingness of such ex-pectations, they nevertheless exist. The mere fact that something has happened a certain number of times causes animals and men to expect that it will happen again. Thus our instincts certainly cause us to believe that the sun will rise tomorrow, but we may be in no better a position than the chicken which unexpectedly has its neck wrung. We have therefore to distinguish the fact that past uniformi-ties *cause* expectations as to the future, from the question whether there is any reasonable ground for giving weight to such expectations after the question of their validity had been raised.

The problem we have to discuss is whether there is any reason for believing in what is called "the uniformity of nature." The belief in the uniformity of nature is the belief that everything that has happened or will happen is an instance of some general law to which there are *no* exceptions. The crude expectations which we have been considering are all subject to exceptions, and therefore liable to disappoint those who entertain them. But science habitually assumes, at least as a working hypothesis, that general rules which have exceptions can be replaced by general rules which have no exceptions.

"Unsupported bodies in air fall" is a general rule to which balloons and aeroplanes are exceptions. But the laws of motion and the law of gravitation, which account for the fact that most bodies fall, also account for the fact that balloons and aeroplanes can rise; thus the laws of motion and the law of gravitation are not subject to these exceptions.

The belief that the sun will rise to-morrow might be falsified if the earth came suddenly into contact with a large body which destroyed its rotation; but the laws of motion and the law of gravitation would not be infringed by such an event. The business of science is to find uniformities, such as the laws of motion and the law of gravitation, to which, so far as our experience extends, there are no exceptions. In this search science has been remarkably successful, and it may be conceded that such uniformities have held hitherto. This brings us back to the question: Have we any reason, assuming that they have always held in the past, to suppose that they will hold in the future?

It has been argued that we have reason to know that the future will resemble the past, because what was the future has constantly become the past, and has always been found to resemble the past, so that we really have experience of the future, namely of times which were formerly future, which we may call past futures. But such an argument really begs the very question at issue. We have experience of past futures, but not of future futures, and the question is: Will future futures resemble past futures? This question is not to be answered by an argument which starts from past futures alone. We have therefore still to seek for some principle which shall enable us to know that the future will follow the same laws as the past.

The reference to the future in this question is not essential. The same question arises when we apply the laws that work in our experience to past things of which we have no experience—as, for example, in geology, or in theories as to the origin of the Solar System. The question we really have to ask is: "When two things have been found to be often associated, and no instance is known of the one occurring without the other, does the occurrence of one of the two, in a fresh instance, give any good ground for expecting the other?" On our answer to this question must depend the validity of the whole of our expectations as to the future, the whole of the results obtained by induction, and in fact practically all the beliefs upon which our daily life is based.

It must be conceded, to begin with, that the fact that two things have been found often together and never apart does not, by itself, suffice to *prove* demonstratively that they will be found together in the next case we examine. The most we can hope is that the oftener things are found together, the more probable it becomes that they will be found together another time, and that, if they have been found together often enough, the probability will amount *almost* to certainty. It can never quite reach certainty, because we know that in spite of frequent repetitions there sometimes is a failure at the last, as in the case of the chicken whose neck is wrung. Thus probability is all we ought to seek.

It might be urged, as against the view we are advocating, that we know all natural phenomena to be subject to the reign of law, and that sometimes, on the basis of observation, we can see that only one law can possibly fit the facts of the case. Now to this view there are two answers. The first is that, even if *some* law which has no exceptions applies to our case, we can never, in practice, be sure that we have discovered that law and not one to which there are exceptions. The second is that the reign of law would seem to be itself only probable, and that our belief that it will hold in the future, or in unexamined cases in the past, is itself based upon the very principle we are examining.

The principle we are examining may be called the *principle of induction,* and its two parts may be stated as follows:

(*a*) When a thing of a certain sort A has been found to be associated with a thing of a certain other sort B, and has never been found dissociated from a thing of the sort B, the greater the number of cases in which A and B have been associated, the greater is the probability that they will be associated in a fresh case in which one of them is known to be present;

(*b*) Under the same circumstances, a sufficient number of cases of association will make the probability of a fresh association nearly a certainty, and will make it approach certainty without limit.

As just stated, the principle applies only to the verification of our expectation in a single fresh instance. But we want also to know that there is a probability in favour of the general law that things of the sort A are *always* associated with things of the sort B, provided a sufficient number of cases of association are known, and no cases of failure of association are known. The probability of the general law is obviously less than the probability of the particular case, since if the general law is true, the particular case must also be true, whereas the particular case may be true without the general law being true. Nevertheless the probability of the general law is increased by repetitions, just as the probability of the particular case is. We may therefore repeat the two parts of our principle as regards the general law, thus:

(*a*) The greater the number of cases in which a thing of the sort A has been found associated with a thing of the sort B, the more probable it is (if no cases of failure of association are known) that A is always associated with B;

(*b*) Under the same circumstances, a sufficient number of cases of the association of A with B will make it nearly certain that A is always associated with B, and will make this general law approach certainty without limit.

It should be noted that probability is always relative to certain data. In our case, the data are merely the known cases of coexistence of A and B. There may be other data, which *might* be taken into account, which would gravely alter the probability. For example, a man who had seen a great many white swans might argue, by our principle, that on the data it was *probable* that all swans were white, and this might be a perfectly sound argument. The argument is not disproved by the fact that some swans are black, because a thing may very well happen in spite of the fact that some data render it improbable. In the case of the swans, a man might know that color is a very variable characteristic in many species of animals, and that, therefore, an induction as to color is peculiarly liable to error. But this knowledge would be a fresh datum, by no means proving that the probability relatively to our previous data had been wrongly estimated. The fact, therefore, that things often fail to fulfil our expectations is no evidence that our expectations will not *probably* be fulfilled in a given case or a given class of cases. Thus our inductive principle is at any rate not capable of being *disproved* by an appeal to experience.

The inductive principle, however, is equally incapable of being *proved* by an appeal to experience. Experience might conceivably confirm the inductive principle as regards the cases that have been already examined; but as regards unexamined cases, it is the inductive principle alone that can justify any inference from what has been examined to what has not been examined. All arguments which, on the basis of experience, argue as to the future or the unexperienced parts of the past or present, assume the inductive principle; hence we can never use experience to prove the inductive principle without begging the question. Thus we must either accept the inductive principle on the ground of its intrinsic evidence, or forego all justification of our expectations about the future. If the principle is unsound, we have no reason to expect the sun to rise tomorrow, to expect bread to be more nourishing than a stone, or to expect that if we throw ourselves off the roof we shall fall. When we see what looks like our best friend approaching us, we shall have no reason to suppose that his body is not inhabited by the mind of our worst enemy or of some total stranger. All our conduct is based upon associations which have worked in the past, and which we therefore regard as likely to work in the future; and this likelihood is dependent for its validity upon the inductive principle.

The general principles of science, such as the belief in the reign of law, and the belief that every event must have a cause, are as completely dependent upon the inductive principle as are the beliefs of daily life. All such general principles are believed because mankind have found innumerable instances of their truth and no instances of their falsehood. But this affords no evidence for their truth in the future, unless the inductive principle is assumed.

Thus all knowledge which, on the basis of experience tells us something about what is not experienced, is based upon a belief which experience can neither confirm nor confute, yet which, at least in its more concrete applications, appears to be as firmly rooted in us as many of the facts of experience. The existence and justification of such beliefs—for the inductive principle, as we shall see, is not the only example—raises some of the most difficult and most debated problems of philosophy.

VIII.3 *Will the Future Be Like the Past?*

F. L. WILL

F. L. Will was for many years Professor of Philosophy at the University of Illinois. After a brief exposition of Hume's argument that we cannot establish conclusions about the future with certainty and after a description of Maynard Keynes's attempt to justify induction, Will argues that we can have knowledge "about nature's behavior and how the future will resemble the past." Will asks us to imagine our world as an enclosure beyond which no one can go or make observations. Outside the enclosure is the land of the future. The Humean skeptic is like the person in a static enclosure, but the correct analogy is that of an ever-expanding enclosure with a constantly receding border so that as our predictions of the future are realized, we obtain knowledge of nature's laws and the future. Because the new territory brought into the enclosure constantly conforms to induction, we have that reason to trust induction.

Hume's Scepticism

The standard argument for complete inductive scepticism, for the belief that inductive procedures have no rational and no empirical justification whatever, is the one stated in a small variety of ways in the writings of Hume. If one consults these writings in search of an answer to the question of inductive validity one finds the same clear answer argued first in technical detail in the *Treatise*, secondly compressed into a few non-technical paragraphs in the *Abstract of a Treatise of Human Nature*, and thirdly, presented again in a non-technical but somewhat fuller version in a chapter in the *Enquiry Concerning Human Understanding*. There is no basis whatever for any conclusion concerning future matters, according to this argument; there is no way whatever in which such conclusions can be established to be certainly true or even probable. For in the first place no such conclusion can be demonstrated by reasoning alone, since they are all conclu-

sions about matters of fact, and since it is the case that the denial of any assertion of a matter of fact is not self-contradictory. But if one gives up the rationalistic aspiration to demonstrate propositions about matters of fact or existence *a priori,* and turns instead to experience, this road, though apparently more promising at first, likewise ends by leading one exactly nowhere. Clearly no statement about future matters of fact can be established by observation. Future things cannot be observed. Any event or state of affairs which can be observed is by definition not in the future. The only recourse which remains therefore is the inductive procedure of employing present or past observations and inferring therefrom the nature of the future. But this procedure to which we are all forced, or rather, to which we all should be forced, if we did not, in company with the animals, use it naturally from birth, is in the light of close analysis completely indefensible. For such reasoning assumes, and is quite invalid without the assumption, that the future will be like the past.

> . . . all inferences from experience suppose, as their foundation, that the future will resemble the past, and that similar powers will be conjoined with similar sensible

Reprinted from *Mind* (Oxford, England: Oxford University Press, 1947) by permission. Notes omitted.

qualities. If there be any suspicion that the course of nature may change, and that the past may be no rule for the future, all experience becomes useless, and can give rise to no inference or conclusion. (*Enquiry*, Section IV.)

Will the future "resemble the past"? Or be "conformable to the past"? These are the ways in which in the *Enquiry* Hume expresses the question concerning the uniformity of nature, restricting to its reference toward the future the question which already had been asked in broader terms in the *Treatise*. There, without the temporal restriction, it is argued that the principle of inductive conclusions, the principle upon which reason would proceed if reason determined us in these matters, is *"that instances, of which we have had no experience, must resemble those, of which we have had experience, and that the course of nature continues always uniformly the same."* (Bk. I, Pt. III, Sect. VI.)

However the principle is stated, the argument about it remains the same. It is indispensable, if inductive conclusions are to be justified; but just as it is absolutely indispensable, so, and this is the measure of our logical misfortune, it cannot be established as certain or as probable in any way. It cannot be established by any demonstrative argument. For it is clearly an assertion of a matter of fact, and therefore the kind of assertion whose denial is non-contradictory and conceivable.

That there are no demonstrative arguments in the case seems evident; since it implies no contradiction that the course of nature may change, and that an object, seemingly like those which we have experienced, may be attended with different or contrary effects. May I not clearly and distinctly conceive that a body, falling from the clouds, and which, in all other respects, resembles snow, has yet the taste of salt or the feeling of fire? Is there any more intelligible proposition than to affirm, that all the trees will flourish in December and January, and decay in May and June? Now whatever is intelligible, and can be distinctly conceived, implies no contradiction and can never be proved false by any demonstrative argument or abstract

reasoning *a priori*. (*Enquiry*, Sect. IV. Cf. *Treatise, loc. cit.*)

Any further doubts about the doubtfulness of this principle which is the main-spring of inductive inference are quickly disposed of. No one who understands the principle with its reference to unobserved instances will suggest that it can be simply observed to be true. It is still true that one cannot observe the future, or the unobserved generally. And, finally, no one who has a sound logical conscience and appreciates the indispensability of the principle to induction generally will tolerate the suggestion that the principle may be established by inductions from experience. Such a process would be circular.

> It is impossible, therefore, that any arguments from experience can prove this resemblance of the past to the future; since all these arguments are founded on the supposition of that resemblance.

And again:

> . . . all our experimental conclusions proceed upon the supposition that the future will be conformable to the past. To endeavour, therefore, the proof of this last supposition by probable arguments, or arguments regarding existence, must be evidently going in a circle, and taking that for granted, which is the very point in question. (*Enquiry*, Sect. IV.)

On this point the *Treatise* (*loc. cit.*) and the *Abstract* speak with one voice. One final quotation from the latter may serve to summarise the conclusion.

> 'Tis evident that *Adam* with all his science, would never have been able to *demonstrate*, that the course of nature must continue uniformly the same, and that the future must be conformable to the past. What is possible can never be demonstrated to be false; and 'tis possible the course of nature may change, since we can conceive such a change. Nay, I will go farther, and assert, that he could not so much as prove by any *probable* arguments, that the future must be conformable to the past. All probable arguments are built on the

supposition, that there is this conformity betwixt the future and the past, and therefore can never prove it. This conformity is a *matter of fact,* and if it must be proved, will admit of no proof but from experience. But our experience in the past can be a proof of nothing for the future, but upon a supposition, that there is a resemblance betwixt them. This therefore is a point, which can admit of no proof at all, and which we take for granted without any proof. (*Abstract,* 1938 ed., p. 15.)

Is *Inductive Reasoning Really Circular?*

. . . It would be more promising in respect to logical neatness and precision for one to consider the alleged circularity of all inductive procedure, which is the central point of the above argument, while using as test case some specific scientific law or principle rather than some affirmation as vague and imprecise as that the future will resemble the past. But, for the purpose of analysing the sceptic's views and meeting the arguments by which these views have been defended, such a procedure would have this deficiency, that no matter what specific scientific generalisation were chosen, one reply which would be sure to be made would consist of an appeal beyond this generalisation to some general beliefs about uniformity, some general Principle of Uniformity which, it would be urged, is assumed somehow in the inductive establishment of this and other scientific generalisations. Since the sceptical argument has been presented in terms of general Principles of Uniformity, and it is in these terms that it is alleged to demonstrate the logical circularity of all inductive reasoning, it seems worth while to attempt to deal with this argument, if one can, in the same terms—in terms of some alleged Principle of Uniformity for which it has been claimed in recent philosophy that it does serve as a wide and basic inductive assumption.

In his *Treatise on Probability,* J. M. Keynes attempts to formulate a set of principles which, if assumed to be true of a given area of subject-matter, would justify, in accordance with the principles of probability, the employment of inductive methods in that area. One of the principles which he discusses, the simplest and at the same time the one for which it seems, at first view, most plausible to contend that it may serve as a broad inductive assumption, is the one to which he gave the name of the "Principle of the Uniformity of Nature." This Principle affirms that nature is uniform in a specific way; and that is in respect to position in space and time. "It involves," writes Keynes, "the assertion of a generalised judgment of irrelevance, namely, of the irrelevance of mere position in time and space to generalisations which have no reference to particular positions in time and space." (P. 226. *Cf.* also pp. 255–256, 263, 276.) It is this principle, he argues, which

. . . supplies the answer, if it is correct, to the criticism that the instances, on which generalisations are based, are all alike in being past, and that any generalisation, which is applicable to the future, must be based, for this reason, upon imperfect analogy. We judge directly that the resemblance between instances, which consists in their being past, is in itself irrelevant, and does not supply a valid ground for impugning a generalisation. (p. 256)

It is, however, difficult to interpret this so-called Principle in such a way that it makes a statement which is both definite and is not at the same time refuted in some areas of experience. Keynes observes that what this Principle affirms is "that the same total cause always produces the same effect" (p. 248), and this is so; but the difficulty here is that of giving a definite meaning to the important adjective "same" as it applies to causes and effects. Unless there is a specifiable meaning applicable to causes in all fields, the formula "same cause—same effect" is not a univocal principle affirming the presence of a specific kind of uniformity in every area of natural phenomena. Yet, when one sets out to specify just what kind of sameness is meant when this formula is employed, one discovers that there is a great variety of interpretations of this word in different fields of inquiry, and that what determines whether a given set of circumstances is regarded as the same cause, for example, varies from field to field, depending upon the nature of the subject-matter as that is revealed in the various generalisations which are regarded as established for that subject-matter. These generalisations exhibit among themselves great differences in scope and precision, as well as in the degree of confidence with which they are accepted. They include, for example, the generalisations about the coherence and constancy of properties which are involved in our belief in and distinctions among various kinds of material objects. And they include the more precise generalisations, frequently expressed in the form of mathematical equations, which would normally be referred to as "scientific laws," as well as broader generalisations formulated in various accepted Principles and Theories. When this is understood, when one sees that in the employment of the Principle of Uniformity what determines the kind of sameness to which the Principle affirms that differences in mere position in space and time are irrelevant is the specific generalisations, the laws, principles, and so on, which have been established in that field, one is in a better position to understand this so-called Principle and its alleged employment as a general inductive assumption. In any given field the Principle of Uniformity states that mere differences in space and time are irrelevant in just this sense, that there are certain generalisations, true of this field, which describe the conditions under which certain objects exist and events occur, and in which differences in mere position in space and time make little or no detectable difference. That this is so, accordingly, is not an inductive assumption in that field in the sense that it is specified and made before all inductive inquiry in the field. It is an inductive assumption in the more usual sense that conclusions of previous experience and inquiries are available for employment in any field as bases for further investigation in that field.

The primary purpose here is not to elucidate and specify the variations of meaning which such a Principle or formula must undergo if it is to be understood as applying to the great variety of fields in which inductive inquiry is carried on, to the great variety in the kinds of uniformity which the generalisations in these fields describe. The primary purpose is to inquire whether the sceptics are right in insisting that it is impossible to provide a genuine evidence for beliefs about uniformity or whether, on the contrary, it is possible to furnish empirical evidence for these beliefs which, in its employment, does not involve circular reasoning. It is granted that what the Principle of Uniformity affirms in any field, if "Principle" it may be called, is that there is uniformity in that field in this sense and no other; that there are certain specific generalisations which apply to that field and in which mere differences of position in time and space are regarded as irrelevant. In the light of this interpretation of uniformity the question briefly is, how can such a broad affirmation be confirmed or verified by induction without circularity?

For purposes of simplicity, in order to secure the clearest statement of the argument in the fewest words, it will be useful in what follows to abbreviate the statement of this Principle of Uniformity and also to consider it only in reference to time. If it can be shown that what the Principle affirms concerning the irrelevance of time in specific generalisations can be confirmed inductively, it can also be shown in exactly the same way that it is possible to confirm the Principle in its spatial reference also. So abbreviated and restricted, the Principle asserts that, in the specific way just defined, differences in time make no difference. Can this interpretation of the assertion that the future will resemble the past be confirmed? What, if any, is the evidence for it?

It follows directly from the interpretation which has just been given of this principle what the evidence for it must be. If the Principle affirms no more for any given area of fact than the validity in that area of certain generalisations which are uniform with respect to space and time, then the evidence for the Principle must be whatever evidence there is for these particular generalisations. This includes all the observations in the past and present which confirm the presence in that area of the uniformities of which these general statements speak. Belief in the uniformity in a given area is not something which is specifiable apart from the laws, principles, and other generalisations regarded as established in that area, but is itself belief in just the kind of uniformities which these generalisations describe and define. If it is correct, then, to say of any generalisation, *e.g.* of any scientific law, that it is confirmed or verified by empirical evidence, is it not correct to say that, to that extent, there is evidence for belief in the uniformity of nature?

Past and Future

The sceptic's answer to this question repeats that final rejoinder of Hume. Granted that there is empirical evidence which has been used to establish various scientific laws, all that it is evidence for, he insists, is the assertion that *in the past* these laws were true, that in the past differences in time have made no difference. This evidence is absolutely worthless for inferences which speak about the future unless it is possible to assume that the future will be like the past. But stop! That is part of what one is trying to show, that is, that mere differences in temporal position, whether past or future, make no difference in these laws of nature. That the future will be like the past means, among other things, that in the future these laws will hold, that in this specific respect differences in time will make no difference. This cannot be inductively confirmed, the sceptic is saying, because any inductive argument for it assumes it and is therefore, as evidence, completely valueless.

One major source of the plausibility of the sceptic's reasoning lies in the analogies which knowing the future easily suggests and in terms of which one is apt to think and be misled. Is this not, one may ask, like any case of sampling? And must one not take care, when reasoning inductively from samples, that one's samples are fair? If a scientist reasons concerning the behaviour of oxygen, nitrogen, or hydrogen on Mars, if such elements there be on Mars, on the basis of the known behaviour of these elements on the earth, he is assuming that in some respects the samples of the elements on the other planet are like those we have here. Similarly in reasoning about the future behaviour of these elements on the basis of present and past behaviour one must assume that future samples of these elements will be like present and past ones. Now if it is the case that past samples may be regarded as evidence about future ones only upon such an assumption, then no examination of past samples, however extensive, can be regarded as yielding evidence for the assumption itself. Any reasoning which did attempt to employ such samples as evidence for the assumption would be forced to use the assumption as a principle in the reasoning and would therefore beg the whole question at issue.

A physical representation of the kind of analogy presented here might be as follows: Suppose that there was somewhere in the world an enclosure beyond which it was impossible for anyone ever to go or to make any observations. Nothing could be seen, heard, or in any other way perceived beyond the border. The territory beyond the enclosure, forever barred from human perception, is the land of Future. The territory within the enclosure is the land of Present and Past, but since it is overwhelmingly the latter, it all goes under the name of Past. Now suppose that someone within the enclosure is interested in some proposition about the way things behave beyond the enclosure, say, a simple and homely proposition about chickens, to the effect that beyond the enclosure roosters fight more than hens. And he wonders what evidence, if any, there is for this proposition. Of course he cannot observe this to be true. He must base it upon his observation in the land of Past; and if he does base it upon the observed fact that roosters in the land of Past fight more than hens, he must assume that in this respect chickens beyond the enclosure behave like chickens within it, so that, knowing that in the latter area roosters are the more pugnacious, he may employ this knowledge as evidence that things are this way also in the former area. This is an assumption which no empirical evidence, confined as it must be to evidence in Past, can be employed to support. Any attempt to support it with such evidence must itself assume that in respect to the phenomena involved differences between Past and Future are negligible; and since that is exactly what the reasoning is attempting to establish, the process is patently circular.

This is the kind of metaphor which makes friends, and influences people, in this case, to draw the wrong conclusions. There are several faults in the analogy. The chief one is that, as represented, the border between Past and Future is stationary, while in the temporal situation it is not. To duplicate the temporal situation in this respect the analogy should represent the border as constantly moving, revealing as it does constantly, in territory which has hitherto been Future, hens and roosters similar as regards difference in disposition to those already observed in Past. The matter of evidence for the proposition about hens and roosters is then also different. If this proposition is in a position analogous to the beliefs about uniformity which are represented in modern scientific laws, the situation is something like this. Previously inhabitants in Past had drawn more sweeping conclusions concerning the difference between the disposition to fight of male and female chickens. They have discovered recently that in respect to young chicks and pullets this generalisation did not hold. They have therefore revised the proposition to exclude all the known negative instances and speak only and more surely of the behaviour of hens and roosters, meaning by these latter terms just fully grown and developed female and male chickens.

So far as there is any record, chickens in Past have verified this rule; so far as there is any record, every chicken revealed by the ever-receding border has likewise verified it; so far as there is any record there has not been one negative instance. Is it not the case that the inhabitants of Past do have evidence for the proposition that all chickens obey this rule, those already in Past, which they call "Past-chickens," and those also which are not yet in Past but which will be subsequently revealed by the moving border, and which they call not unnaturally "Future-chickens"? They have a vast number of positive instances of the rule, and no negative instances, except those in respect to which the rule has already been revised. In view of the present evidence that in all cases, year after year and century after century, the progressively revealed chickens have verified and do verify this rule, must one not conclude that the inhabitants of past do have evidence for this proposition, and that anyone is wrong who says that they have actually no evidence one way or other?

The sceptic, however, is still prepared to argue his case, and his argument, in terms of the present analogy, has a now familiar ring. That the inhabitants of Past have no evidence whatsoever about the behaviour of Future-chickens, he will insist; and as grounds he will point out that although the border does progressively recede and reveal chickens like those previously observed in Past, these are really not Future-chickens. By the very fact that they have been revealed they are no longer Future-chickens, but are now Past-chickens. Observation of them is not observation of Future-chickens, and any attempt to reason from such observation to conclusions about Future-chickens must therefore assume that Future-chickens are like Past-chickens. For the inhabitants of Past, in these efforts to know the land

beyond the border, this is both an inescapable and unknowable presumption.

What should one say of an argument of this kind? Only through some logical slip, one feels strongly, would it be possible to arrive at such a conclusion. One would have thought that the receding border was a matter upon which the inhabitants of Past may legitimately congratulate themselves in the light of their interest in learning what Future-chickens, when they become Past, are going to be like. If the border had not yet begun to recede they would indeed be in an unfortunate position for securing such knowledge. But happily this is not the case. The border is constantly receding. And granting that it will constantly recede, revealing always more of the land of Future, and even granting also that this means that there is an inexhaustible area to be revealed, the inhabitants of Past are in the fortunate position that with the progressive recession they may learn more and more about chickens, Past and Future. They may derive hypotheses from their experience of what has already been revealed and proceed further to test these by the progressive revelations of Future, in the light of which they may be confirmed, refuted, or revised. The sceptic's argument amounts to the assertion that all this apparent good fortune is really illusory and that the sorry Pastians are actually in no better position with respect to knowing about Future-chickens and Future-things generally than they would be if the border never moved at all. For the movement of the border does not reveal Future-chickens, since Future is by definition the land beyond the border. No matter how much or how little is revealed, by the very fact that it is revealed and on this side of the border it is not Future but Past, and therefore, since the land of Future always is beyond observation, no empirical method can produce any evidence that what is in that land is in any way similar to what is not. That this rendering of the sceptic's position, though in the language of the above metaphor, is undistorted and fair may be seen by consulting the words of an illustrious modern sceptic and follower of Hume, Bertrand Russell. In his chapter, "On Induction," in *The Problems of Philosophy*, Russell expressed the matter in this fashion:

> It has been argued that we have reason to know that the future will resemble the past, because what was the future has constantly

become the past, and has always been found to resemble the past, so that we really have experience of the future, namely of times which were formerly future, which we may call past futures. But such an argument really begs the very question at issue. We have experience of past futures, but not of future futures, and the question is: Will future futures resemble past futures? This question is not to be answered by an argument which starts from past futures alone. We have therefore still to seek for some principle which shall enable us to know that the future will follow the same laws as the past.

This is the central difficulty urged by Hume, Russell, and others in arguing that there can never be any empirical evidence that the future will be like the past. Empirically, in Russell's language, it is possible to have evidence only that this has been true of past and possibly present futures, not that it will be true of future futures. It is the situation in the land of Past all over again. There are generalisations which are constantly being confirmed by experience. But every time a confirming instance occurs it is nullified as evidence by the argument that it is not really a confirming instance at all. For by the fact that it has occurred it is an instance of a past future, and therefore it tells nothing whatever about future futures. In treating of the land of Past it was suggested that there is involved in arguing in this manner a logical slip or error. It remains to investigate how this is the case.

Suppose that in 1936, to take but a short span of time, a man says that in the above-defined sense the future will be like the past. In 1936, if he could somehow have shown that 1937 would be like 1936, this would have been evidence for his statement, as even a sceptic would admit. But in 1937, when he does establish that 1937 is like 1936, it has somehow ceased to be evidence. So long as he did not have it, it was evidence; as soon as he gets it it ceases to be. The constant neutralisation of the evidence which is effected in this argument is effected by the same kind of verbal trick which children play upon one another in fun. Child A asks child B what he is going to do to-morrow. B replies that he is going to play ball, go swimming, or what not. Thereupon A says, "You can't do that."

B: Why not?

A: Because to-morrow never comes. When to-morrow comes it won't be to-morrow; it will be to-day. You can never play to-morrow; you can only play to-day.

Again, if a prophet announces that next year will bring a utopia, and if each succeeding year, when the predicted utopia does not come, he defends himself by pointing out that he said "next year" and that obviously this is not next year, no reasonable person would pay much attention to him. Such a person would realise, on a moment's reflection, that the prophet is being deceptive with the word "next." In 1936 "next year" means "1937"; in 1937 it means "1938." Since every year "next year" means a different year, a year yet to come, what the prophet says can never be verified or disproved. If in 1936 he meant by this phrase 1937, as he sensibly should, then this statement can be verified or refuted in 1937. But if, when 1937 comes, he insists that he did not mean 1937, but "next year," and if in 1938 he again insists that he did not mean that year, and so on, then what he seems to be meaning by "next year" is the $n + 1$th year where n is the ever-progressing number of the present year. No one should alter his present activities or his plans for the future on the basis of such a prediction, for, of course, it really is not a prediction. While in the form of a statement about the future it does not say anything about the future, anything which could possibly be true or false in the infinity of time, if infinity it is, which yet remains to transpire. For what the prophet is saying is that utopia will come next year, and by his own interpretation of the words "next year" he is affirming that next year will never come. In other words, at the time which never comes, and hence when nothing occurs, a utopia will occur. This is not even sensible speech; it is a contradiction.

In a similar though less simple way those who employ the sceptical argument about uniformity to show that there is no evidence whatever for any statement about the future are being themselves deceived and are deceiving others by their use of expressions like "next," "future," "future future," and "past future." The man who said in 1936 that the future would be like the past, that mere differences in temporal position make no difference in the behaviour of nature which is described in scientific laws, meant, as he sensibly should, that this was true of the years 1937, 1938, and so on. He said something of the form "all A's are B's" and it has been possible since 1936 to examine the A's of 1937 to 1946 and to see whether what he said is confirmed or disproved by the available evidence. If, however, now that it is 1946, and all this evidence is in, he should remark that since it is 1946 the years 1937–46 are no longer future and therefore have ceased to be evidence for the proposition, then he is guilty of using, or rather abusing the word "future" in the way in which the prophet in the previous example was abusing the word "next." For the only basis for his contention that the observed A's are not confirming evidence, or what is that same thing, that they are confirming instances only if one assumes quite circularly that the future is like the past,

is in his illusive use of the word "future." Time does pass, and, because it does, the present is a constantly changing one; and the point of reference for the use of words like "future" and "past" is accordingly different. The correct conclusion to be drawn from the fact that time passes is that the future is constantly being revealed and that, in consequence, we have had and shall have the opportunity to learn more and more accurately what the laws of nature's behaviour are and how therefore the future will be like the past. But this sceptical man has his eyes fixed in fatal fascination upon the movement of time, the constantly changing present. And seeing that, as the present changes, what was once future is not now future, but present, and will shortly be past, he is led to draw the conclusion that after all, for any present whatever, the future is forever hidden behind a veil.

VIII.4 *The Pragmatic Justification of Induction*

Hans Reichenbach

Hans Reichenbach (1891–1953) was born in Germany, taught at the University of Berlin, and was Professor of Philosophy at the University of California, Los Angeles, from 1938 until his death.

    Reichenbach agrees with Hume that neither a deductive nor an inductive demonstration for inductive inference is possible. Nevertheless, we have good practical reasons for trusting induction. Our situation is like that of a cancer patient who will die unless he undergoes an operation. The operation may not succeed, but it's his only hope for continued life. Likewise, the principle of induction is our only hope for guidance in life and in science. Living by inductive principles is our best bet, for if there are laws of nature and we follow them, we will be able to predict and, to a degree, control the future. If there are no such laws, it doesn't matter what we do, for nature will prove to be lawless and chaotic.

The nontautological character of induction has been known a long time; Bacon had already emphasized that it is just this character to which the importance of induction is due. If inductive inference can teach us something new, in opposition to deductive inference, this is because it is not a tautology. This useful quality has, however, become the center of the epistemological difficulties of induction. It was David Hume who first attacked the principle from this side; he pointed out that the apparent constraint of the inductive inference, although submitted to by everybody, could not be justified. We believe in induction; we even cannot get rid of the belief when we know the impossibility of a logical demonstration of the validity of inductive inference; but as logicians we must admit that this belief is a deception—such is the result of Hume's criticism. We may summarize his objections in two statements:

    1. We have no logical demonstration for the validity of inductive inference.

Reprinted from *Experience and Prediction* (University of Chicago Press, 1938) by permission of the University of Chicago Press.

    2. There is no demonstration a posteriori for the inductive inference; any such demonstration would presuppose the very principle which it is to demonstrate.

    These two pillars of Hume's criticism of the principle of induction have stood unshaken for two centuries, and I think they will stand as long as there is a scientific philosophy. . . .

    Inductive inference cannot be dispensed with because we need it for the purpose of action. To deem the inductive assumption unworthy of the assent of a philosopher, to keep a distinguished reserve, and to meet with a condescending smile the attempts of other people to bridge the gap between experience and prediction is cheap self-deceit; at the very moment when the apostles of such a higher philosophy leave the field of theoretical discussion and pass to the simplest actions of daily life, they follow the inductive principle as surely as does every earth-bound mind. In any action there are various means to the realization of our aim; we have to make a choice, and we decide in accordance with the inductive principle. Although there is no means which will produce with certainty the desired effect, we do not leave the choice to chance but prefer the means indicated by the principle of induction. If we sit at the wheel of a car and want to turn the car to the right, why do we turn the wheel to the right? There is no certainty that the car will follow the wheel; there are indeed cars which do not always so behave. Such cases are fortunately exceptions. But if we should not regard the inductive prescription and consider the effect of a turn of the wheel as entirely unknown to us, we might turn it to the left as well. I do not say this to suggest such an attempt; the effects of skeptical philosophy applied in motor traffic would be rather unpleasant. But I should say a philosopher who is to put aside his principles any time he steers a motor-car is a bad philosopher.

It is no justification of inductive belief to show that it is a habit. It is a habit; but the question is whether it is a good habit, where "good" is to mean "useful for the purpose of actions directed to future events." If a person tells me that Socrates is a man, and that all men are mortal, I have the habit of believing that Socrates is mortal. I know, however, that this is a good habit. If anyone had the habit of believing in such a case that Socrates is not mortal, we could demonstrate to him that this was a bad habit. The analogous question must be raised for inductive inference. If we should not be able to demonstrate that it is a good habit, we should either cease using it or admit frankly that our philosophy is a failure.

Science proceeds by induction and not by tautological transformations of reports. [Francis] Bacon is right about Aristotle; but the *novum organon* [i.e., induction as opposed to deduction] needs a justification as good as that of the *organon*. Hume's criticism was the heaviest blow against empiricism; if we do not want to dupe our consciousness of this by means of the narcotic drug of aprioristic rationalism, or the soporific of skepticism, we must find a defense for the inductive inference which holds as well as does the formalistic justification of deductive logic.

§39. The Justification of the Principle of Induction

We shall now begin to give the justification of induction which Hume thought impossible. In the pursuit of this inquiry, let us ask first what has been proved, strictly, by Hume's objections.

Hume started with the assumption that a justification of inductive inference is only given if we can show that inductive inference must lead to success. In other words, Hume believed that any justified application of the inductive inference presupposes a demonstration that the conclusion is true. It is this assumption on which Hume's criticism is based. His two objections directly concern only the question of the truth of the conclusion; they prove that the truth of the conclusion cannot be demonstrated. The two objections, therefore, are valid only in so far as the Humean assumption is valid. It is this question to which we must turn: Is it necessary, for the justification of inductive inference, to show that its conclusion is true?

A rather simple analysis shows us that this assumption does not hold. Of course, if we were able to prove the truth of the conclusion, inductive inference would be justified; but the converse does not hold: a justification of the inductive inference does not imply a proof of the truth of the conclusion. The proof of the truth of the conclusion is only a sufficient condition for the justification of induction, not a necessary condition.

The inductive inference is a procedure which is to furnish us the best assumption concerning the future. If we do not know the truth about the future, there may be nonetheless a best assumption about it, i.e., a best assumption relative to what we know. We must ask whether such a characterization may be given for the principle of induction. If this turns out to be possible, the principle of induction will be justified.

An example will show the logical structure of our reasoning. A man may be suffering from a grave disease; the physician tells us: "I do not know whether an operation will save the man, but if there *is* any remedy, it is an operation." In such a case, the operation would be justified. Of course, it would be better to know that the operation will save the man; but, if we do not know this, the knowledge formulated in the statement of the physician is a sufficient justification. If we cannot realize the sufficient conditions of success, we shall at least realize the necessary conditions. If we were able to show that the inductive inference is a necessary condition of success, it would be justified; such a proof would satisfy any demands which may be raised about the justification of induction.

Now obviously there is a great difference between our example and induction. The reasoning of the physician presupposes inductions; his knowledge about an operation as the only possible means of saving a life is based on inductive generalizations, just as are all other statements of empirical character. But we wanted only to illustrate the logical structure of our reasoning. If we want to regard such a reasoning as a justification of the principle of induction, the character of induction as a necessary condition of success must be demonstrated in a way which does not presuppose induction. Such a proof, however, can be given.

If we want to construct this proof, we must begin with a determination of the aim of induction. It is usually said that we perform inductions with the aim of foreseeing the future. This determination is vague; let us replace it by a formulation more precise in character:

> *The aim of induction is to find series of events whose frequency of occurrence converges toward a limit.*

We choose this formulation because we found that we need probabilities and that a probability is to be defined as the limit of a frequency; thus our determination of the aim of induction is given in such a way that it enables us to apply probability methods. If we compare this determination of the aim of induction with determinations usually given, it turns out to be not a confinement to a narrow aim but an expansion. What we usually call "foreseeing the future" is included in our formulation as a special case; the case of knowing with certainty for every event A the event B following it would correspond in our formulation to a case where the limit of the frequency is of the numerical value 1. Hume thought of this case only. Thus our inquiry differs from that of Hume in so far as it conceives the aim of induction in a generalized form. But we do not omit any possible applications if we determine the principle of induction as the means of obtaining the limit of a frequency. If we have limits of frequency, we have all we want, including the case considered by Hume; we have then the laws of nature in their most general form, including both statistical and so-called causal laws—the latter being nothing but a special case of statistical laws, corresponding to the numerical value 1 of the limit of the frequency. We are entitled, therefore, to consider the determi-

nation of the limit of a frequency as the aim of the inductive inference.

Now it is obvious that we have no guaranty that this aim is at all attainable. The world may be so disorderly that it is impossible for us to construct series with a limit. Let us introduce the term "predictable" for a world which is sufficiently ordered to enable us to construct series with a limit. We must admit, then, that we do not know whether the world is predictable. . . .

These considerations lead, however, to a more precise formulation of the logical structure of the inductive inference. We must say that, if there is any method which leads to the limit of the frequency, the inductive principle will do the same; if there is a limit of the frequency, the inductive principle is a sufficient condition to find it. If we omit now the premise that there is a limit of the frequency, we cannot say that the inductive principle is the necessary condition of finding it because there are other methods using a correction c_n. There is a set of equivalent conditions such that the choice of one of the members of the set is necessary if we want to find the limit; and, if there is a limit, each of the members of the set is an appropriate method for finding it. We may say, therefore, that the *applicability* of the inductive principle is a necessary condition of the existence of a limit of the frequency.

The decision in favor of the inductive principle among the members of the set of equivalent means may be substantiated by pointing out its quality of embodying the smallest risk; after all, this decision is not of a great relevance, as all these methods must lead to the same value of the limit if they are sufficiently continued. It must not be forgotten, however, that the method of clairvoyance is not, without further ado, a number of the set because we do not know whether the correction c_n occurring here is submitted to the condition of convergence to zero. This must be proved first, and it can only be proved by using the inductive principle, viz., a method known to be a member of the set: this is why clairvoyance, in spite of all occult pretensions, is to be submitted to the control of scientific methods, i.e., by the principle of induction.

It is in the analysis expounded that we see the solution of Hume's problem. Hume demanded too much when he wanted for a justification of the inductive inference a proof that its conclusion is true. What his objections demonstrate is only that such a proof cannot be given. We do not perform, however, an inductive inference with the pretension of obtaining a true statement. What we obtain is a wager; and it is the best wager we can lay because it corresponds to a procedure the applicability of which is the necessary condition of the possibility of predictions. To fulfill the conditions sufficient for the attainment of true predictions does not lie in our power; let us be glad that we are able to fulfil at least the conditions necessary for the realization of this intrinsic aim of science. . . .

. . . With this result the application of the system of scientific inductions finds a justification similar to, and even better than, that of the single induction: *the system of scientific inductions is the best posit we know concerning the future.*

We found that the posits of the highest level are always blind posits; thus the system of knowledge, as a whole, is a blind posit. Posits of the lower levels have appraised weights; but their serviceableness depends on the unknown weights of the posits of higher levels. The uncertainty of knowledge as a whole therefore penetrates to the simplest posits we can make—those concerning the events of daily life. Such a result seems unavoidable for any theory of prediction. We have no certainty as to foreseeing the future. We do not know whether the predictions of complicated theories, such as the quantum theory or the theory of albumen molecules, will turn out to be true; we do not even know whether the simplest posits concerning our immediate future will be confirmed, whether they concern the sun's rising or the persistence of the conditions of our personal environment. There is no principle of philosophy to warrant the reliability of such predictions; that is our answer to all attempts made within the history of philosophy to procure for us such certainty, from Plato, through all varieties of theology, to Descartes and Kant. In spite of that, we do not renounce prediction; the arguments of skeptics like Hume cannot shake our resolution: at least to *try* predictions. We know with certainty that among all procedures for foreseeing the future, known to us as involving success if success is possible, the procedure of concatenated inductions is the best. We try it as our best posit in order to have our chance—if we do not succeed, well, then our trial was in vain.

Is this to say that we are to renounce any belief in success? There is such a belief; everyone has it when he makes inductions; does our solution of the inductive problem oblige us to dissuade him from this firm belief?

This is not a philosophical but a social question. As philosophers we know that such a belief is not justifiable; as sociologists we may be glad that there is such a belief. Not everyone is likely to act according to a principle if he does not believe in success; thus belief may guide him when the postulates of logic turn out to be too weak to direct him.

Yet our admission of this belief is not the attitude of the skeptic who, not knowing a solution of his own, permits everyone to believe what he wants. We may admit the belief because we know that it will determine the same actions that logical analysis would determine. Though we cannot justify the belief, we can justify the logical structure of the inference to which it fortunately corresponds as far as the practical results are concerned. This happy coincidence is certainly to be explained by Darwin's idea of selection; those animals were to survive whose habits of belief corresponded to the most useful instrument for foreseeing the future. There is no reason to dissuade anybody from doing with belief something which he ought to do in the same way if he had no belief.

This remark does not merely apply to the belief in induction as such. There are other kinds of belief which have crystallized round the methods of expanding knowledge. Men of scientific research are not always of so clear an insight into philosophical problems as logical analysis would require: they have filled up the world of research work with mystic concepts; they talk of "instinctive presentiments," of "natural hypotheses," and one of the best among them told me once that he found his great theories because he was convinced of the harmony of nature. If we were to analyze the discoveries of these men, we would find that their way of proceeding corresponds in a surprisingly high degree to the rules of the principle of induction, applied however to a domain of facts where average minds did not see their traces. In such cases, inductive operations are imbedded within a belief which as to its intension differs from the inductive principle, although its function within the system of operations of knowledge amounts to the same. The mysticism of scientific discovery is nothing but a superstructure of images and wishes; the supporting structure below is determined by the inductive principle.

I do not say this with the intention to discredit the belief—to pull the superstructure down. On the contrary, it seems to be a psychological law that discoveries need a kind of mythology; just as the inductive inference may lead us in certain cases to the preference of methods different from it, it may lead us also to the psychological law that sometimes those men will be best in making inductions who believe they possess other guides. The philosopher should not be astonished at this.

This does not mean that I should advise him to share any of these kinds of belief. It is the philosopher's aim to know what he does; to understand thought operations and not merely to apply them instinctively, automatically. He wants to look through the superstructure and to discover the supporting structure. Belief in induction, belief in a uniformity of the world, belief in a mystic harmony between nature and reason—they belong, all of them, to the superstructure; the solid foundation below is the system of inductive operations. The difficulty of a logical justification of these operations misled philosophers to seek a justification of the superstructure, to attempt an ontological justification of inductive belief by looking for necessary qualities of the world which would insure the success of inductive inferences. All such attempts will fail—because we shall never be able to give a cogent proof of any material presumption concerning nature. The way toward an understanding of the step from experience to prediction lies in the logical sphere; to find it we have to free ourselves from one deep-rooted prejudice: from the presupposition that the system of knowledge is to be a system of true propositions. If we cross out this assumption within the theory of knowledge, the difficulties dissolve, and with them dissolves the mystical mist lying above the research methods of science. We shall then interpret knowledge as a system of posits, or wagers; with this the question of justification assumes as its form the question whether scientific knowledge is our best wager. Logical analysis shows that this demonstration can be given, that the inductive procedure of science is distinguished from other methods of prediction as leading to the most favorable posits. Thus we wager on the predictions of science and wager on the predictions of practical wisdom: we wager on the sun's rising tomorrow, we wager that food will nourish us tomorrow, we wager that our feet will carry us tomorrow. Our stake is not low; all our personal existence, our life itself, is at stake. To confess ignorance in the face of the future is the tragic duty of all scientific philosophy; but, if we are excluded from knowing true predictions, we shall be glad that at least we know the road toward our best wagers.

VIII.5 *Dissolving the Problem of Induction*

PETER F. STRAWSON

Peter F. Strawson until his recent retirement was Professor of Philosophy at Oxford University. Ludwig Wittgenstein, who influenced Strawson's thought, wrote that his aim in philosophy was "to show the fly the way out of the fly-bottle . . . aiming at *complete* clarity, [which] means that philosophical problems should *completely* disappear" (*Philosophical Investigations,* sections 309, 133). Strawson applies this therapeutic model of philosophy to the problem and argues that just as the questions of whether deductive arguments in general are valid or the law is legal, show that the questioner fails to understand the concepts in question, the question whether induction is justified shows that the questioner does not understand what induction is all about. Induction is precisely our standard of empirical rationality. "Every successful method or recipe for finding out about the unobserved must be one which has inductive support; for to say that a recipe is successful is to say that it has been repeatedly applied with success."

What reason have we to place reliance on inductive procedures? Why should we suppose that the accumulation of instances of *A*s which are *B*s, however various the conditions in which they are observed, gives any good reason for expecting the next *A* we encounter to be a *B*? It is our habit to form expectations in this way; but can the habit be rationally justified? When this doubt has entered our minds it may be difficult to free ourselves from it. For the doubt has its source in a confusion; and some attempts to resolve the doubt preserve the confusion; and other attempts to show that the doubt is senseless seem altogether too facile. The root-confusion is easily described; but simply to describe it seems an inadequate remedy against it. So the doubt must be examined again and again, in the light of different attempts to remove it.

If someone asked what grounds there were for supposing that deductive reasoning was valid, we might answer that there were in fact no grounds for supposing that deductive reasoning was always valid; sometimes people made valid inferences, and sometimes they were guilty of logical fallacies. If he said that we had misunderstood his question, and that what he wanted to know was what grounds there were for regarding deduction *in general* as a valid method of argument, we should have to answer that his question was without sense, for to say that an argument, or a form or method of argument, was valid or invalid would *imply* that it was deductive; the concepts of validity and invalidity had application only to individual deductive arguments or forms of deductive argument. Similarly, if a man asked what grounds there were for thinking it reasonable to hold beliefs arrived at inductively, one might at first answer that there were good and bad inductive arguments, that sometimes it was reasonable to hold a belief arrived at inductively and sometimes it was not. If he, too, said that his question had been misunderstood, that he wanted to know whether induction in general was a reasonable method of inference, then we might well think his question senseless in the same way as the question whether deduction is in general valid; for to call a particular belief reasonable or unreasonable is to apply inductive standards, just as to call a particular argument valid or invalid is to apply deductive standards. The parallel is not wholly convincing; for

Reprinted from *Introduction to Logical Theory* (New York: John Wiley & Sons, 1952) by permission of the publisher.

words like 'reasonable' and 'rational' have not so precise and technical a sense as the word 'valid'. Yet it is sufficiently powerful to make us wonder how the second question could be raised at all, to wonder why, in contrast with the corresponding question about deduction, it should have seemed to constitute a genuine problem.

Suppose that a man is brought up to regard formal logic as the study of the science and art of reasoning. He observes that all inductive processes are, by deductive standards, invalid; the premises never entail the conclusions. Now inductive processes are notoriously important in the formation of beliefs and expectations about everything which lies beyond the observation of available witnesses. But an *invalid* argument is an *unsound* argument; an *unsound* argument is one in which *no good reason* is produced for accepting the conclusion. So if inductive processes are invalid, if all the arguments we should produce, if challenged, in support of our beliefs about what lies beyond the observation of available witnesses are unsound, then we have no good reason for any of these beliefs. This conclusion is repugnant. So there arises the demand for a justification, not of this or that particular belief which goes beyond what is entailed by our evidence, but a justification of induction in general. And when the demand arises in this way it is, in effect, the demand that induction shall be shown to be really a kind of deduction; for nothing less will satisfy the doubter when this is the route to his doubts.

Tracing this, the most common route to the general doubt about the reasonableness of induction, shows how the doubt seems to escape the absurdity of a demand that induction in general shall be justified by inductive standards. The demand is that induction should be shown to be a rational process; and this turns out to be the demand that one kind of reasoning should be shown to be another and different kind. Put thus crudely, the demand seems to escape one absurdity only to fall into another. Of course, inductive arguments are not deductively valid; if they were, they would be deductive arguments. Inductive reasoning must be assessed, for soundness, by inductive standards. Nevertheless, fantastic as the wish for induction to be deduction may seem, it is only in terms of it that we can understand some of the attempts that have been made to justify induction.

VIII

The first kind of attempt I shall consider might be called the search for the supreme premise of inductions. In its primitive form it is quite a crude attempt; and I shall make it cruder by caricature. We have already seen that for a particular inductive step, such as 'The kettle has been on the fire for ten minutes, so it will be boiling by now,' we can substitute a deductive argument by introducing a generalization (e.g., 'A kettle always boils within ten minutes of being put on the fire') as an additional premise. This manoeuvre shifted the emphasis of the problem of inductive support on to the question of how we established such generalizations as these, which rested on grounds by which they were not entailed. But suppose the manoeuvre could be repeated. Suppose we could find one supremely general proposition, which taken in conjunction with the evidence for any accepted generalization of science or daily life (or at least of science) would entail that generalization. Then, so long as the status of the supreme generalization could be satisfactorily explained, we could regard all sound inductions to unqualified general conclusions as, at bottom, valid deductions. The justification would be found, for at least these cases. The most obvious difficulty in this suggestion is that of formulating the supreme general proposition in such a way that it shall be precise enough to yield the desired entailments, and yet not obviously false or arbitrary. Consider, for example, the formula: 'For all f, g, wherever n cases of $f. g$, and no cases of $f. \sim g$, are observed, then all cases of f are cases of g.' To turn it into a sentence, we have only to replace 'n' by some number. But what number? If we take the value of 'n' to be 1 or 20 or 500, the resulting statement is obviously false. Moreover, the choice of any number would seem quite arbitrary; there is no privileged number of favourable instances which we take as decisive in establishing a generalization. If, on the other hand, we phrase the proposition vaguely enough to escape these objections—if, for example, we phrase it as 'Nature is uniform'—then it becomes too vague to provide the desired entailments. It should be noticed that the impossibility of framing a general proposition of the kind required is really a special case of the impossibility of framing precise rules for the assessment of evidence. If we could frame a rule which would tell us precisely when we had *conclusive* evidence for a generalization, then it would yield just the proposition required as the supreme premise.

Even if these difficulties could be met, the question of the status of the supreme premise would remain. How, if a non-necessary proposition, could it be established? The appeal to experience, to inductive support, is clearly barred on pain of circularity. If, on the other hand, it were a necessary truth and possessed, in conjunction with the evidence for a generalization, the required logical power to entail the generalization (e.g., if the latter were the conclusion of a hypothetical syllogism, of which the hypothetical premise was the necessary truth in question), then the evidence would entail the generalization independently, and the problem would not arise: a conclusion unbearably paradoxical. In practice, the extreme vagueness with which candidates for the role of supreme premise are expressed prevents their acquiring such logical power, and at the same time renders it very difficult to classify them as analytic or synthetic: under pressure they may tend to tautology; and, when the pressure is removed, assume an expansively synthetic air.

In theories of the kind which I have here caricatured the ideal of deduction is not usually so blatantly manifest as I have made it. One finds the 'Law of the Uniformity of Nature' presented less as the suppressed premise of crypto-deductive inferences than as, say, the 'presupposition of the validity of inductive reasoning'.

. . .

══

X

Let us turn from attempts to justify induction to attempts to show that the demand for a justification is mistaken. We have seen already that what lies behind such a demand is often the absurd wish that induction should be shown to be some kind of deduction—and this wish is clearly traceable in the two attempts at justification which we have examined. What other sense could we give to the demand? Sometimes it is expressed in the form of a request for proof that induction is a *reasonable* or *rational* procedure, that we have *good grounds* for placing reliance upon it. Consider the uses of the phrases 'good grounds', 'justification', 'reasonable', &c. Often we say such things as 'He has *every justification* for believing that *p*'; 'I have *very good reasons* for believing it'; 'There are *good grounds* for the view that *q*'; 'There is *good evidence* that *r*'. We often talk, in such ways as these, of justification, good grounds or reasons or evidence for certain beliefs. Suppose such a belief were one expressible in the form 'Every case of *f* is a case of *g*'. And suppose someone were asked what he meant by saying that he had good grounds or reasons for holding it. I think it would be felt to be a satisfactory answer if he replied: 'Well, in all my wide and varied experience I've come across innumerable cases of *f* and never a case of *f* which wasn't a case of *g*.' In saying this, he is clearly claiming to have *inductive* support, *inductive* evidence, of a certain kind, for his belief; and he is also giving a perfectly proper answer to the question, what he meant by saying that he had ample justification, good grounds, good reasons for his belief. It is an analytic proposition that it is reasonable to have a degree of belief in a statement which is proportional to the strength of the evidence in its favour; and it is an analytic proposition, though not a proposition of mathematics, that, other things being equal, the evidence for a generalization is strong in proportion as the number of favourable instances, and the variety of circumstances in which they have been found, is great. So to ask whether it is reasonable to place reliance on inductive procedures is like asking whether it is reasonable to proportion the degree of one's convictions to the strength of the evidence. Doing this is what 'being reasonable' *means* in such a context.

As for the other form in which the doubt may be expressed, viz., 'Is induction a justified, or justifiable, procedure?', it emerges in a still less favourable light. No sense has been given to it, though it is easy to see why it seems to have a sense. For it is generally proper to inquire of *a particular belief*, whether its adoption is justified; and, in asking this, we are asking whether there is good, bad, or any, evidence for it. In applying or withholding the epithets 'justified', 'well founded', &c., in the case of specific beliefs, we are appealing to, and applying, inductive standards. But to what standards are we appealing when we ask whether the application of inductive standards is justified or well grounded? If we cannot answer, then no sense has been given to the question. Compare it with the question: Is the law legal? It makes perfectly good sense to inquire of a particular action, of an administrative regulation, or even, in the case of some states, of a particular enactment of the legislature, whether or not it is legal. The question is answered by an appeal to a legal system, by the application of a set of legal (or constitutional) rules or standards. But it makes no sense to inquire in general whether the law of the land, the legal system as a whole, is or is not legal. For to what legal standards are we appealing?

The only way in which a sense might be given to the question, whether induction is in general a justified or justifiable procedure, is a trivial one which we have already noticed. We might interpret it to mean 'Are all conclusions, arrived at inductively, justified?', i.e., 'Do people always have adequate evidence for the conclusions they draw?' The answer to this question is easy, but uninteresting: it is that sometimes people have adequate evidence, and sometimes they do not.

XI

It seems, however, that this way of showing the request for a general justification of induction to be absurd is sometimes insufficient to allay the worry that produces it. And to point out that 'forming rational opinions about the unobserved on the evidence available' and 'assessing the evidence by inductive standards' are phrases which describe the same thing, is more apt to produce irritation than relief. The point is felt to be 'merely a verbal' one; and though the point of this protest is itself hard to see, it is clear that something more is required. So the question must be pursued further. First, I want to point out that there is something a little odd about talking of 'the inductive method', or even 'the inductive policy', as if it were just one possible method among others of arguing from the observed to the unobserved, from the available evidence to the facts in question. If one asked a meteorologist what method or methods he used to forecast the weather, one would be surprised if he answered: 'Oh, just the inductive method.' If one asked a doctor by what means he diagnosed a certain disease, the answer 'By induction' would be felt as an impa-

tient evasion, a joke, or a rebuke. The answer one hopes for is an account of the tests made, the signs taken account of, the rules and recipes and general laws applied. When such a specific method of prediction or diagnosis is in question, one can ask whether the method is justified in practice; and here again one is asking whether its employment is inductively justified, whether it commonly gives correct results. This question would normally seem an admissible one. One might be tempted to conclude that, while there are many different specific methods of prediction, diagnosis, &c., appropriate to different subjects of inquiry, all such methods could properly be called 'inductive' in the sense that their employment rested on inductive support; and that, hence, the phrase 'non-inductive method of finding out about what lies deductively beyond the evidence' was a description without meaning, a phrase to which no sense had been given; so that there could be no question of justifying our selection of one method, called 'the inductive,' of doing this.

However, someone might object: 'Surely it is possible, though it might be foolish, to use methods utterly different from accredited scientific ones. Suppose a man, whenever he wanted to form an opinion about what lay beyond his observation or the observation of available witnesses, simply shut his eyes, asked himself the appropriate question, and accepted the first answer that came into his head. Wouldn't this be a non-inductive method? Well, let us suppose this. The man is asked: 'Do you usually get the right answer by your method?' He might answer: 'You've mentioned one of its drawbacks; I never do get the right answer; but it's an extremely easy method.' One might then be inclined to think that it was not a method of finding things out at all. But suppose he answered: Yes, it's usually (always) the right answer. Then we might be willing to call it a method of finding out, though a strange one. But, then, by the very fact of its success, it would be an inductively supported method. For each application of the method would be an application of the general rule, 'The first answer that comes into my head is generally (always) the right one'; and for the truth of this generalization there would be the inductive evidence of a long run of favourable instances with no unfavourable ones (if it were 'always'), or of a sustained high proportion of successes to trials (if it were 'generally').

So every successful method or recipe for finding out about the unobserved must be one which has inductive support; for to say that a recipe is successful is to say that it has been repeatedly applied with success; and repeated successful application of a recipe constitutes just what we mean by inductive evidence in its favour. Pointing out this fact must not be confused with saying that 'the inductive method' is justified by its success, justified because it works. This is a mistake, and an important one. I am not seeking to 'justify the inductive method', for no meaning has been given to this phrase. *A fortiori*, I am not saying that induction is justified by its success in finding out about the unobserved. I am saying, rather, that any successful method of finding out about the unobserved is necessarily justified by induction. This is an analytic proposition. The phrase 'successful method of finding things out which has no inductive support' is self-contradictory. Having, or acquiring, inductive support is a necessary condition of the success of a method.

Why point this out at all? First, it may have a certain therapeutic force, a power to reassure. Second, it may counteract the tendency to think of 'the inductive method' as something on a par with specific methods of diagnosis or prediction and therefore, like them, standing in need of (inductive) justification.

VIII.6 *The New Riddle of Induction*

NELSON GOODMAN

Nelson Goodman until his retirement was Professor of Philosophy at Harvard University. In this selection, taken from his book *Fact, Fiction and Forecast*, Goodman argues that beside Hume's puzzle over induction, there is a second problem: what are the rules for deciding which properties are projectable into the future? Why does seeing another black raven confirm our hypothesis that all ravens are black or that the next raven we see will be black but the seeing of three bachelors in a room not count as evidence that tomorrow we will see three bachelors in this room? Inventing a new color term *grue*, made up from our color terms *green* and *blue*, Goodman illustrates the problem of projectability.

Confirmation of a hypothesis by an instance depends rather heavily upon features of the hypothesis other than its syntactical form. That a given piece of copper conducts electricity increases the credibility of statements asserting that other pieces of copper conduct electricity, and thus confirms the hypothesis that all copper conducts electricity. But the fact that a given man now in this room is a third son does not increase the credibility of statements asserting that other men now in this room are third sons, and so does not confirm the hypothesis that all men now in this room are third sons. Yet in both cases our hypothesis is a generalization of the

Reprinted from *Fact, Fiction and Forecast* (Cambridge, MA: Harvard University Press, 1984) by permission. Notes have been edited.

evidence statement. The difference is that in the former case the hypothesis is a *lawlike* statement; while in the latter case, the hypothesis is a merely contingent or accidental generality. Only a statement that is *lawlike*—regardless of its truth or falsity or its scientific importance—is capable of receiving confirmation from an instance of it; accidental statements are not. Plainly, then, we must look for a way of distinguishing lawlike from accidental statements.

So long as what seems to be needed is merely a way of excluding a few odd and unwanted cases that are inadvertently admitted by our definition of confirmation, the problem may not seem very hard or very pressing. We fully expect that minor defects will be found in our definition and that the necessary refinements will have to be worked out patiently one after another. But some further examples will show that our present difficulty is of a much graver kind.

Suppose that all emeralds examined before a certain time t are green.[1] At time t, then, our observations support the hypothesis that all emeralds are green; and this is in accord with our definition of confirmation. Our evidence statements assert that emerald a is green, that emerald b is green, and so on; and each confirms the general hypothesis that all emeralds are green. So far, so good.

Now let me introduce another predicate less familiar than "green". It is the predicate "grue" and it applies to all things examined before t just in case they are green but to other things just in case they are blue. Then at time t we have, for each evidence statement asserting that a given emerald is green, a parallel evidence statement asserting that that emerald is grue. And the statements that emerald a is grue, that emerald b is grue, and so on, will each confirm the general hypothesis that all emeralds are grue. Thus according to our definition, the prediction that all emeralds subsequently examined will be green and the prediction that all will be grue are alike confirmed by evidence statements describing the same observations. But if an emerald subsequently examined is grue, it is blue and hence not green. Thus although we are well aware which of the two incompatible predictions is genuinely confirmed, they are equally well confirmed according to our present definition. Moreover, it is clear that if we simply choose an appropriate predicate, then on

the basis of these same observations we shall have equal confirmation, by our definition, for any prediction whatever about other emeralds—or indeed about anything else.[2] As in our earlier example, only the predictions subsumed under lawlike hypotheses are genuinely confirmed; but we have no criterion as yet for determining lawlikeness. And now we see that without some such criterion, our definition not merely includes a few unwanted cases, but is so completely ineffectual that it virtually excludes nothing. We are left once again with the intolerable result that anything confirms anything. This difficulty cannot be set aside as an annoying detail to be taken care of in due course. It has to be met before our definition will work at all.

Nevertheless, the difficulty is often slighted because on the surface there seem to be easy ways of dealing with it. Sometimes, for example, the problem is thought to be much like the paradox of the ravens. We are here again, it is pointed out, making tacit and illegitimate use of information outside the stated evidence: the information, for example, that different samples of one material are usually alike in conductivity, and the information that different men in a lecture audience are usually not alike in the number of their older brothers. But while it is true that such information is being smuggled in, this does not by itself settle the matter as it settles the matter of the ravens. There the point was that when the smuggled information is forthrightly declared, its effect upon the confirmation of the hypothesis in question is immediately and properly registered by the definition we are using. On the other hand, if to our initial evidence we add statements concerning the conductivity of pieces of other materials or concerning the number of older brothers of members of other lecture audiences, this will not in the least affect the confirmation, according to our definition, of the hypothesis concerning copper or of that concerning other lecture audiences. Since our definition is insensitive to the bearing upon hypotheses of evidence so related to them, even when the evidence is fully declared, the difficulty about accidental hypotheses cannot be explained away on the ground that such evidence is being surreptitiously taken into account.

A more promising suggestion is to explain the matter in terms of the effect of this other evidence not directly upon the hypothesis in question but *in*directly through other hypotheses that *are* confirmed, according to our definition, by such evidence. Our information about other materials does by our definition confirm such hypotheses as that all pieces of iron conduct electricity, that no pieces of rubber do, and so on; and these hypotheses, the explanation runs, impart to the hypothesis that all pieces of copper conduct electricity (and also to the hypothesis that none do) the character of lawlikeness—that is, amenability to confirmation by direct positive instances when found. On the other hand, our information about other lecture audiences *dis*confirms many hypotheses to the effect that all the men in one audience are third sons, or that none are; and this strips any character of lawlikeness from the hypothesis that all (or the hypothesis that none) of the men in *this* audience are third sons. But clearly if this course is to be followed, the circumstances under which hypotheses are thus related to one another will have to be precisely articulated.

The problem, then, is to define the relevant ways in which such hypotheses must be alike. Evidence for the hypothesis that all iron conducts electricity enhances the lawlikeness of the hypothesis that all zirconium conducts electricity, but does not similarly affect the hypothesis that all the objects on my desk conduct electricity. Wherein lies the difference? The first two hypotheses fall under the broader hypothesis—call it "*H*"—that every class of things of the same material is uniform in conductivity; the first and third fall only under some such hypothesis as—call it "*K*"—that every class of things that are either all of the same material or all on a desk is uniform in conductivity. Clearly the important difference here is that evidence for a statement affirming that one of the classes covered by *H* has the property in question increases the credibility of any statement affirming that another such class has this property; while nothing of the sort holds true with respect to *K*. But this is only to say that *H* is lawlike and *K* is not. We are faced anew with the very problem we are trying to solve: the problem of distinguishing between lawlike and accidental hypotheses.

The most popular way of attacking the problem takes its cue from the fact that accidental hypotheses seem typically to involve some spatial or temporal restriction, or reference to some particular individual. They seem to concern the people in some particular room, or the objects on some particular person's desk; while lawlike hypotheses characteristically concern all ravens or all pieces of copper whatsoever. Complete generality is thus very often supposed to be a sufficient condition of lawlikeness; but to define this complete generality is by no means easy. Merely to require that the hypothesis contain no term naming, describing, or indicating a particular thing or location will obviously not be enough. The troublesome hypothesis that all emeralds are grue contains no such term; and where such a term does occur, as in hypotheses about men in *this room,* it can be suppressed in favor of some predicate (short or long, new or old) that contains no such term but applies only to exactly the same things. One might think, then, of excluding not only hypotheses that actually contain terms for specific individuals but also all hypotheses that are equivalent to others that do contain such terms. But, as we have just seen, to exclude only hypotheses of which *all* equivalents contain such terms is to exclude nothing. On the other hand, to exclude all hypotheses that have *some* equivalent containing such a term is to exclude everything; for even the hypothesis

All grass is green

has as an equivalent

All grass in London or elsewhere is green.

The next step, therefore, has been to consider ruling out predicates of certain kinds. A syntactically universal hypothesis is lawlike, the proposal runs, if its predicates are 'purely qualitative' or 'non-positional'.[3] This will obviously accomplish nothing if a purely qualitative predicate is then conceived either as one that is equivalent to some expression free of terms for specific individuals, or as one that is equivalent to no expression that contains such a term; for this only raises again the difficulties just pointed out. The claim appears to be rather that at least in the case of a simple enough predicate we can readily determine by direct inspection of its meaning whether or not it is purely qualitative. But even aside from obscurities in the notion of 'the meaning' of a predicate, this claim seems to me wrong. I simply do not know how to tell whether a predicate is qualitative or positional, except perhaps by completely begging the question at issue and asking whether the predicate is 'well-behaved'—that is, whether simple syntactically universal hypotheses applying it are lawlike.

This statement will not go unprotested. "Consider", it will be argued, "the predicates 'blue' and 'green' and the predicate 'grue' introduced earlier, and also the predicate 'bleen' that applies to emeralds examined before time t just in case they are blue and to other emeralds just in case they are green. Surely it is clear", the argument runs, "that the first two are purely qualitative and the second two are not; for the meaning of each of the latter two plainly involves reference to a specific temporal position." To this I reply that indeed I do recognize the first two as well-behaved predicates admissible in lawlike hypotheses, and the second two as ill-behaved predicates. But the argument that the former but not the latter are purely qualitative seems to me quite unsound. True enough, if we start with "blue" and "green", then "grue" and "bleen" will be explained in terms of "blue" and "green" and a temporal term. But equally truly, if we start with "grue" and "bleen," then "blue" and "green" will be explained in terms of "grue" and "bleen" and a temporal term; "green", for example, applies to emeralds examined before time t just in case they are grue, and to other emeralds just in case they are bleen. Thus qualitativeness is an entirely relative matter and does not by itself establish any dichotomy of predicates. This relativity seems to be completely overlooked by those who contend that the qualitative character of a predicate is a criterion for its good behavior.

Of course, one may ask why we need worry about such unfamiliar predicates as "grue" or about accidental hypotheses in general, since we are unlikely to use them in making predictions. If our definition works for such hypotheses as are normally employed, isn't that all we need? In a sense, yes; but only in the sense that we need no definition, no theory of induction, and no philosophy of knowledge at all. We get along well enough without them in daily life and in scientific research. But if we seek a theory at all, we cannot excuse gross anomalies resulting from a proposed theory by pleading that we can avoid them in practice. The odd cases we have been considering are clinically pure cases that, though seldom encountered in practice, nevertheless display to best advantage the symptoms of a widespread and destructive malady.

We have so far neither any answer nor any promising clue to an answer to the question what distinguishes lawlike or confirmable hypotheses from accidental or non-confirmable ones; and what may at first have seemed a minor technical difficulty has taken on the stature of a major obstacle to the development of a satisfactory theory of confirmation. It is this problem that I call the new riddle of induction.

Notes

[1] Although the example used is different, the argument to follow is substantially the same as that set forth in my note 'A Query on Confirmation' [*Journal of Philosophy*, XLIII (1946), 383–385.]

[2] For instance, we shall have equal confirmation, by our present definition, for the prediction that roses subsequently examined will be blue. Let "emerose" apply just to emeralds examined before time t, and to roses examined later. Then all emeroses so far examined are grue, and this confirms the hypothesis that all emeroses are grue and hence the prediction that roses subsequently examined will be blue. The problem raised by such antecedents has been little noticed, but is no easier to meet than that raised by similarly perverse consequents.

[3] Carnap took this course in his paper 'On the Application of Inductive Logic', *Philosophy and Phenomenological Research*, vol. 8 (1947), pp. 133–47, which is in part a reply to my 'A Query on Confirmation'. The discussion was continued in my note 'On Infirmities of Confirmation Theory', *Philosophy and Phenomenological Research*, vol. 8 (1947), pp. 149–51; and in Carnap's 'Reply to Nelson Goodman', same journal, same volume, pp. 461–2.

Bibliography

Goodman, Nelson. *Fact, Fiction and Forecast.* Cambridge, MA: Harvard University Press, 1955.

Jeffrey, Richard. *The Logic of Decision.* 2d ed. Chicago: University of Chicago Press, 1983.

Kyburg, Henry E., Jr. *Probability and the Logic of Rational Belief.* Middletown, CT: Wesleyan University Press, 1961.

Mill, John Stuart. *System of Logic.* 10th ed. London: Longman's Green and Co., 1879.

Reichenbach, Hans. *Experience and Prediction.* Chicago: University of Chicago Press, 1938.

Skyrms, Brian. *Choice and Chance.* Belmont, CA: Wadsworth, 1986.

Stove, D. C. *Probability and Hume's Inductive Scepticism.* Oxford, England: Clarendon Press, 1973.

Strawson, P. F. *Introduction to Logical Theory.* New York: Wiley, 1952.

Swinburne, Richard, ed. *The Justification of Induction.* Oxford, England: Oxford University Press, 1974.

Will, Frederick. *Induction and Justification.* Ithaca, NY: Cornell University Press, 1973.

Part IX

Other Minds

By what evidence do I know, or by what considerations am I led to believe, that there exist other sentient creatures; that the walking and speaking figures which I see and hear, have sensations and thoughts, or in other words, possess Minds?

JOHN STUART MILL[1]
An Examination of Sir William Hamilton's Philosophy

We are certain that other people have conscious states of mind and feelings like ourselves. Most of us are also certain that animals, such as dogs, cats, chimpanzees, apes, and gorillas, have feelings. We normally take these things for granted. But can we justify our certainty about conscious states and feelings in others?

The traditional view is that a form of the argument from analogy can be used to justify our belief in other minds. The classic expression of this view is Mill's brief discussion in *An Examination of Sir William Hamilton's Philosophy*

(1865): "I conclude it from certain things, which my experience of my own states of feeling proves to me to be marks of it." These marks or evidences are of two sorts: antecedent and subsequent bodily states. The antecedent states are necessary for the feelings, and the subsequent states are effects of feelings.

> I conclude that other human beings have feelings like me, because, first, they have bodies like me, which I know, in my own case, to be the antecedent condition of feelings; and because, secondly, they

exhibit the acts, and other outward signs, which in my own case I know by experience to be caused by feelings. I am conscious in myself of a series of facts connected by an uniform sequence, of which the beginning is modification of my body, the middle is feelings, the end is outward demeanor. In the case of other human beings I have the evidence of my senses for the first and last links of the series, but not for the intermediate link. I find, however, that the sequence between the first and last is as regular and constant in those other cases as it is in mine. In my own case I know that the first link produces the last through the intermediate link, and could not produce it without. Experience, therefore, obliges me to conclude that there must be an intermediate link; which must either be the same in others as in myself, or a different one: I must either believe them to be alive, or to be automatons: and by believing them to be alive, that is, by supposing the link to be of the same nature as in the case of which I have experience, and which is in all other respects similar, I bring other human beings, as phenomena, under the same generalizations which I know by experience to be the true theory of my own existence.[2]

The argument may be stated as follows: There are three causal states in myself: (1) the initial modification in my body (as when I step on a nail); (2) my feeling (the pain) caused by stepping on a nail, and (3) my subsequent bodily change (a scream, the contorted facial expression, the sudden lifting of my foot). When other people step on nails, I behold the first and third conditions but not the second. I see the same kind of physical states I experience in myself, but I do not experience the other person's feelings. But I can infer that the other person has feelings from the fact that he (or she) behaves the same

way I behave in similar circumstances. Although I cannot prove the other being has feelings, this argument from analogy allows me to conclude it is probable that he (or she) has feelings.

There are problems with the argument from analogy, some of which are discussed in the readings in this part of the book. One problem is that it is impossible to check up on the correctness of the conclusion that the other body is experiencing feelings like my own. I can introspect into my own mind to see whether I am angry or fearful, but I can't "extrospect" into my neighbor's mind to see whether he or she is angry or fearful. Another problem is that the argument from analogy only gives us probability, yet we feel certain other people have minds. Proponents of the traditional view have responses to these objections, some of which you will discover in the readings.

However, the main one is that the argument from analogy seems to be a generalization from only one particular. Normally inductive reasoning goes from many particular instances to an inductive generalization, but the argument from analogy regarding other minds proceeds from only one instance, my own, to a generalization about all other living animals and human beings. This generalization seems unwarranted, as though a primitive being who had only seen one tree, an apple tree, generalized that all trees are probably apple trees.

An opposite strategy, the behaviorist argument, is to discount consciousness altogether and to concentrate on an organism's behavior. If a human or a dog engages in behavior similar to mine when stepping on a nail, I infer that it is in pain. The problem of other minds is thus solved by reducing mental states to physical states.

But the behaviorist argument has serious problems, among them being the fact that we can feign behavior. I may be in pain and *not* show it, as when I have a headache, or I may pretend to be in pain to get sympathy from the school nurse as I ask for permission to leave school early. I may smile when I am sad, and good actors can cry when they have nothing in the world about which to be sad. So behavior is neither a necessary nor a sufficient condition for mental states.

Furthermore, the statement "He has a pain" may seem to be about pain behavior when said by someone else about me, but the statement "I have a pain" when said by me is not about behavior but about a feeling. Yet the first statement refers to what I am avowing when I say, "I have a pain." Hence the apparent behavioral statement "He has a pain" in fact refers to a feeling, not merely behavior. Note that "He does not have a pain," when said by someone else of me, contradicts "I have a pain" when said by me. First-person avowals such as "I have a pain" are self-evidently primary here, so behaviorism is to be rejected. However, it may be, as modified behaviorists such as Wittgenstein and Malcolm argue, that behavioral criteria are necessary requirements for our attributions of psychological phenomena. In Wittgenstein's words, "An 'inner process' stands in need of outward criteria."

In the first reading in this part of the book, Bertrand Russell defends a version of the traditional argument from analogy.

H. H. Price sets forth a sophisticated version of the analogical argument, based not on bodily states but on *language understanding*. It is by being able to verify meaningful utterances that I infer that others have minds like my own. If, while lost on a mountain, I hear a voice saying there is a sheep path behind the rock on my right, I will infer that there is another mind in the vicinity. I would do so even if the voice were coming from a tree or a gorse bush (a spiny yellow-flowered shrub, called Scotch broom in the United States).

In the third reading, Norman Malcolm criticizes both the analogical argument and Price's language understanding argument, the latter of which is detached from the requisite criteria. Under no circumstances would we believe that just because meaningful utterances came from trees or gorse bushes these objects had minds. Malcolm rejects a pure behaviorist theory, but contends that behavioral criteria are central to our belief in other minds, that we learn about pain by noticing others crying, grimacing, limping, or holding their legs. These features continue to be natural expressions of such behavior, so that it would not make sense to suppose a tree or gorse bush could have pain.

In the final reading, Michael Levin examines the problem of other minds from a reliabilist perspective, explaining how the belief has come about and why it is an intractable problem. We believe in other minds because evolution has selected this survival-oriented feature in us. A full explication of other minds eludes us because the nature of consciousness eludes us.

Note

[1] John Stuart Mill, *An Examination of Sir William Hamilton's Philosophy* (London: Longmans, 1889), pp. 243–244.
[2] Ibid.

IX.1 *The Analogy Argument for Other Minds*

BERTRAND RUSSELL

Bertrand Russell (1872–1970) notes that our belief in other minds requires a postulate that is not required for our belief in physics, "since physics can be content with knowledge of structure." He argues for a version of the analogical argument that is broadly inductive.

The postulates hitherto considered have been such as are required for knowledge of the physical world. Broadly speaking, they have led us to admit a certain degree of knowledge as to the space-time structure of the physical world, while leaving us completely agnostic as regards its qualitative character. But where other human beings are concerned, we feel that we know more than this; we are convinced that other people have thoughts and feelings that are qualitatively fairly similar to our own. We are not content to think that we know only the space-time structure of our friends' minds, or their capacity for initiating causal chains that end in sensations of our own. A philosopher might pretend to think that he knew only this, but let him get cross with his wife and you will see that he does not regard her as a mere spatio-temporal edifice of which he knows the logical properties but not a glimmer of the intrinsic character. We are therefore justified in inferring that his skepticism is professional rather than sincere.

The problem with which we are concerned is the following. We observe in ourselves such occurrences as remembering, reasoning, feeling pleasure, and feeling pain. We think that sticks and stones do not have these experiences, but that other people do. Most of us have no doubt that the higher animals feel pleasure and pain, though I was once assured by a fisherman that "Fish have no sense nor feeling." I failed to find out how he had acquired this knowledge. Most people would disagree with him, but would be doubtful about oysters and starfish. However this may be, common sense admits an increasing doubtfulness as we descend in the animal kingdom, but as regards human beings it admits no doubt.

It is clear that belief in the minds of others requires some postulate that is not required in physics, since physics can be content with a knowledge of structure. My present purpose is to suggest what this further postulate may be.

It is clear that we must appeal to something that may be vaguely called "analogy." The behavior of other people is in many ways analogous to our own, and we suppose that it must have analogous causes. What people say is what we should say if we had certain thoughts, and so we infer that they probably have these thoughts. They give us information which we can sometimes subsequently verify. They behave in ways in which we behave when we are pleased (or displeased) in circumstances in which we should be pleased (or displeased). We may talk over with a friend some incident which we have both experienced, and find that his reminiscences dovetail with our own; this is particularly convincing when he remembers something that we have forgotten but that he recalls to our thoughts. Or again: you set your boy a problem in arithmetic, and with luck he gets the right answer; this persuades you that he is capable of arithmetical reasoning. There are, in short, very many ways in which my responses to stimuli differ from those of "dead" matter, and in all these ways other people resemble

From Bertrand Russell, *Human Knowledge: Its Scope and Limits,* Part VI, Chap. 8. Copyright, 1948, by Bertrand Russell. Reprinted by permission of Simon and Schuster, Inc.

me. As it is clear to me that the causal laws governing my behavior have to do with "thoughts," it is natural to infer that the same is true of the analogous behavior of my friends.

The inference with which we are at present concerned is not merely that which takes us beyond solipsism, by maintaining that sensations have causes about which *something* can be known. This kind of inference, which suffices for physics, has already been considered. We are concerned now with a much more specific kind of inference, the kind that is involved in our knowledge of the thoughts and feelings of others—assuming that we have such knowledge. It is of course obvious that such knowledge is more or less doubtful. There is not only the general argument that we may be dreaming; there is also the possibility of ingenious automata. There are calculating machines that do sums much better than our schoolboy sons; there are gramophone records that remember impeccably what So-and-so said on such-and-such an occasion; there are people in the cinema who, though copies of real people, are not themselves alive. There is no theoretical limit to what ingenuity could achieve in the way of producing the illusion of life where in fact life is absent.

But, you will say, in all such cases it was the thoughts of human beings that produced the ingenious mechanism. Yes, but how do you know this? And how do you know that the gramophone does *not* "think"?

There is, in the first place, a difference in the causal laws of observable behavior. If I say to a student, "Write me a paper on Descartes' reasons for believing in the existence of matter," I shall, if he is industrious, cause a certain response. A gramophone record might be so constructed as to respond to this stimulus, perhaps better than the student, but if so it would be incapable of telling me anything about any other philosopher, even if I threatened to refuse to give it a degree. One of the most notable peculiarities of human behavior is change of response to a given stimulus. An ingenious person could construct an automaton which would always laugh at his jokes, however often it heard them; but a human being, after laughing a few times, will yawn, and end by saying, "How I laughed the first time I heard that joke."

But the differences in observable behavior between living and dead matter do not suffice to prove that there are "thoughts" connected with living bodies other than my own. It is probably possible theoretically to account for the behavior of living bodies by purely physical causal laws, and it is probably impossible to refute materialism by external observation alone. If we are to believe that there are thoughts and feelings other than our own, that must be in virtue of some inference in which our own thoughts and feelings are relevant, and such an inference must go beyond what is needed in physics.

I am, of course, not discussing the history of how we come to believe in other minds. We find ourselves believing in them when we first begin to reflect; the thought that Mother may be angry or pleased is one which arises in early infancy. What I am discussing is the possibility of a postulate which shall establish a rational connection between this belief and data, e.g., between the belief "Mother is angry" and the hearing of a loud voice.

The abstract schema seems to be as follows. We know, from observation of ourselves, a causal law of the form "A causes B," where A is a "thought" and B a physical occurrence. We sometimes observe a B when we cannot observe any A; we then infer an unobserved A. For example: I know that when I say, "I'm thirsty," I say so, usually, because I am thirsty, and therefore, when I hear the sentence "I'm thirsty" at a time when I am not thirsty, I assume that someone else is thirsty. I assume this the more readily if I see before me a hot, drooping body which goes on to say, "I have walked twenty desert miles in this heat with never a drop to drink." It is evident that my confidence in the "inference" is increased by increased complexity in the datum and also by increased certainty of the causal law derived from subjective observation, provided the causal law is such as to account for the complexities of the datum.

It is clear that in so far as plurality of causes is to be suspected, the kind of inference we have been considering is not valid. We are supposed to know "A causes B," and also to know that B has occurred; if this is to justify us in inferring A, we must know that *only* A causes B. Or, if we are content to infer that A is probable, it will suffice if we can know that in most cases it is A that causes B. If you hear thunder without having seen lightning, you confidently infer that there was lightning, because you are convinced that the sort of noise you heard is seldom caused by anything except lightning. As this example shows, our principle is not only employed to establish the existence of other minds but is habitually assumed, though in a less concrete form, in physics. I say "a less concrete form" because unseen lightning is only abstractly similar to seen lightning, whereas we suppose the similarity of other minds to our own to be by no means purely abstract.

Complexity in the observed behavior of another person, when this can all be accounted for by a simple cause such as thirst, increases the probability of the inference by diminishing the probability of some other cause. I think that in ideally favorable circumstances the argument would be formally as follows:

From subjective observation I know that A, which is a thought or feeling, causes B, which is a bodily act, e.g., a statement. I know also that, whenever B is an act of my own body, A is its cause. I now observe an act of the kind B in a body not my own, and I am having no thought or feeling of the kind A. But I still believe, on the basis of self-observation, that only A can cause B; I therefore infer that there was an A which caused B, though it

was not an A that I could observe. On this ground I infer that other people's bodies are associated with minds, which resemble mine in proportion as their bodily behavior resembles my own.

In practice, the exactness and certainty of the above statement must be softened. We cannot be sure that, in our subjective experience, A is the only cause of B. And even if A is the only cause of B in our experience, how can we know that this holds outside our experience? It is not necessary that we should know this with any certainty; it is enough if it is highly probable. It is the assumption of probability in such cases that is our postulate. The postulate may therefore be stated as follows:

If, whenever we can observe whether A and B are present or absent, we find that every case of B has an A as a causal antecedent, then it is probable that most B's have A's as causal antecedents, even in cases where observation does not enable us to know whether A is present or not.

This postulate, if accepted, justifies the inference to other minds, as well as many other inferences that are made unreflectingly by common sense.

IX.2 *The Argument from Language Understanding*

H. H. PRICE

H. H. Price (1899–1984) first rejects the traditional form of the analogical argument as well as an argument from intuition for the existence of other minds and then sets forth his own sophisticated version of the analogical argument based on information theory or "understanding of language." Our evidence for the existence of other minds comes from communication situations in which other bodies make utterances that show purposive behavior and convey information that can be verified.

Price's version of the analogical argument is stated thus: "Situations a and b resemble each other in respect of a characteristic C_1; situation a also has the characteristic C_2; therefore situation b probably has the characteristic C_2 likewise. The noises I am now aware of closely resemble certain ones which I have been aware of before . . . , and the resemblance covers both their qualities and their manner of combination." I need not see the bodies that utter information, nor must they be bodies like my own. A tree or bush that spoke would satisfy our conditions for the attribution of psychological states. Finally, Price applies his analysis to the question of how we learn that other minds experience emotions and volitions.

I

In ordinary life everyone assumes that he has a great deal of knowledge about other minds or persons. This assumption has naturally aroused the curiosity of philosophers; though perhaps they have not been as curious about it as they ought to have been, for they have devoted many volumes to our consciousness of the material world, but very few to our consciousness of one another. It was thought at one time that each of us derives his knowledge of other minds from the observation of other human organisms. I observe (it was said) that there are a number of bodies which resemble my own fairly closely in their shape, size, and manner of movement; I conclude by analogy that each of these bodies is animated by a mind more or less like myself. It was admitted that this argument was not demonstrative. At the best it would only provide evidence for the existence of other minds, not proof; and one's alleged knowledge of other minds would only be, at the most, well-grounded opinion. It was further admitted, by some philosophers, that our belief in the existence of other minds was probably not *reached* by an argument of this sort, indeed was not reached by an argument at all, but was an uncritical and unquestioning taking-for-granted, a mere piece of primitive credulity; but, it was claimed, the belief can only be justified by an argument of this sort.

This theory, which may be called the Analogical Theory, has come in for a good deal of criticism, and has now been generally abandoned. Perhaps it has sometimes been abandoned for the wrong reasons; for some of its critics (not all) seem to have overlooked the distinction between the genesis of a belief and its justification. However this may be, I shall not discuss the theory any further at present. My aim in this paper is to consider certain other theories which have been or might be suggested in

From H. H. Price, "Our Evidence for the Existence of Other Minds," *Philosophy*, Vol. 13 (1938). Reprinted by permission.

its place, and to develop one of them at some length.

With the abandonment of the Analogical Theory a very different view, which I shall call the Intuitive Theory, came into favour. It was maintained that each of us has a direct and intuitive apprehension of other minds, just as he has of his own, or at least that he intuitively apprehends some other minds on some occasions, for instance in a conversation or a quarrel. It was said that there is social consciousness as well as self-consciousness, a direct awareness of the "thou" as well as a direct awareness of the "me." I wish to emphasize that this consciousness was held to be a form of knowing, not merely belief (however well-grounded), still less taking for granted. And I think it would have been said to be knowing by acquaintance—extrospective acquaintance as we might call it—though doubtless this acquaintance would make possible a certain amount of "knowledge about," just as when I am acquainted with a noise I may know about the noise that it is shrill or louder than some previous noise.

This view might be worked out in several different ways. Do I have extrospective acquaintance with foreign selves, or only with foreign psychical events, from which foreign selves can somehow be inferred? Or would it be said that foreign selves, and my own self too, are only logical constructions out of extrospectible or introspectible data? Again, is my extrospective acquaintance confined to human minds, or does it extend to sub-human and super-human ones, if such there be? It is certain that some who held this kind of theory thought that it did extend to super-human minds at any rate; for they thought that religious experience, or at any rate one of the types of experience covered by that label, was an extrospective acquaintance with the Divine Mind. And I suppose that some might claim an extrospective acquaintance with what we may call ex-human minds, minds which once animated human bodies, but now animate them no longer (and perhaps with ex-animal minds, if there are any?).

We should also have to ask just what the special circumstances are which make this extrospective acquaintance possible. For clearly it does not occur in all circumstances. Otherwise we should never be deceived by waxworks; we could tell at a glance whether the man we see lying by the roadside is unconscious, or dead, or only shamming; and we should know at once whether the words we hear are uttered by a gramophone or by an animate and conscious human organism.

I do not propose to pursue these questions any further. I only mention them to suggest that the theory requires a more detailed and thorough working out than it has yet received. But perhaps it is well to add that it derives no support whatever from the phenomena of telepathy. No doubt there is strong empirical evidence for the occurrence of telepathy. But the telepathic relation appears to be causal, not cognitive; it is more like infection than like knowledge. An event E_1 in mind No. 1 causes an event E_2 in mind No. 2, without any discoverable physical intermediary. It may be that E_2 resembles E_1 fairly closely. For instance, E_1 might be the seeing of a certain scene accompanied by a feeling of horror, and E_2 might be the imaging of a visual image closely resembling that scene, accompanied by a similar feeling of horror. But E_2 is not a *knowing* of E_1; just as, when you have scarlet fever and I catch it from you, my fever is not a knowing of yours. . . .

II

The suggestion I wish to examine is that one's evidence for the existence of other minds is derived primarily from the understanding of language. I shall use the word "language" in a wide sense, to include not only speech and writing, but also signals such as waving a red flag, and gestures such as beckoning and pointing. One might say, the suggestion is that one's evidence for the existence of other minds comes from *communication*-situations. But this would be question-begging. For communication is by definition a relation between two or more minds. Thus if I have reason to believe that a communication is occurring, I must already have reason to believe that a mind other than my own exists. However, it would be true, according to the theory which I am about to consider, that the study of communication is of fundamental importance. For according to it one's most important evidence for the existence of another mind is always also evidence for the occurrence of communication between that mind and oneself. Even so, the word "communication" has to be taken in a wide sense, as the word "language" has to be. Utterances which I am not intended to hear, and writings or signals which I am not intended to see, will have to be counted as communications, provided I do in fact observe and understand them. In other words, we shall have to allow that there is such a thing as involuntary communication.

Let us consider some instances. Suppose I hear a foreign body[1] utter the noises "Look! there is the bus." I understand these noises. That is to say, they have for me a *symbolic* character, and on hearing them I find myself entertaining a certain proposition, or if you like entertaining a certain thought. (It does not matter how they came to have this symbolic character for me. The point is that they do have it now, however they got it.) As yet I only *entertain* what they symbolize, with perhaps some slight inclination towards belief; for as yet I have no decisive ground for either belief or disbelief. However, I now proceed to look round; and sure enough there is the bus, which I had not seen before, and perhaps was not expecting yet. This simple occurrence, of hearing an utterance, understanding it and then verifying it for oneself, provides some evidence that the foreign body which uttered the noises is animated by a mind like one's own. And at the same time it provides evidence that the mind in question is or recently has been in a determinate state. Either it has been itself observing the bus, or it has been observing some other physical object or event from which the advent of the bus could be inferred.

Now suppose that I frequently have experiences of this sort in connection with this particular foreign body. Suppose I am often in its neighbourhood, and it repeatedly produces utterances which I can understand, and which I then proceed to verify for myself. And suppose that this happens in many different kinds of situations. I think that my evidence for believing that this body is animated by a mind like my own would then become very strong. It is true that it will never amount to demonstration. But in the sphere of matters of fact it is a mistake to expect demonstration. We may expect it in the spheres of Pure Mathematics and Formal Logic, but not elsewhere. So much at least we may learn from Hume. If I have no direct extrospective acquaintance with other minds, the most that can be demanded is adequate *evidence* for their existence. If anyone demands *proof* of it his demand is nonsensical, at least if the word "proof" is used in the strict sense which it bears in Pure Mathematics. It is not that the demand unfortunately cannot be fulfilled, owing to the limitations of human knowledge. It is that it cannot really be made at all. The words which purport to formulate it do not really formulate anything.

To return to our argument: the evidence will be strongest where the utterance I hear gives me new information; that is to say, where it symbolizes something which I do *not* already believe, but which I subsequently manage to verify for myself. For if I did already believe it at the time of hearing, I cannot exclude the possibility that it was my own believing which caused the foreign body to utter it. And this might happen even if my own believing were, as we say, "unconscious"; as when I have been believing for many hours that to-day is Saturday, though until this moment I have not thought about the matter. I know by experience that my believings can cause my own body to utter symbolic noises; and for all I can tell they may sometimes cause a foreign body to do the same. Indeed, there is some empirical evidence is favour of this suggestion. The utterances of an entranced medium at a spiritualistic séance do sometimes seem to be caused by the unspoken beliefs of the sitters. That one mind—my own—can animate two or more bodies at the same time is therefore not an absurd hypothesis, but only a queer one. It cannot be ruled out of court *a priori*, but must be refuted by specific empirical evidence.

It might, however, be suggested that we are demanding too much when we require that the foreign utterance should convey new information. Would it not be sufficient if the information, though not new, was, so to speak, *intrusive*—if it broke in upon my train of thought, and had no link, either logical or associative, with what I was thinking a moment before? Thus, suppose that while I am engaged in a mathematical calculation I suddenly hear a foreign body say "to-day is Saturday." I did in a sense believe this already. I have received no new information. Still, the utterance has no logical relevance to the propositions which were occupying my mind, and there was nothing in them to suggest it by association. Would not the hearing of this utterance provide me with evidence for the existence of another mind? I admit that it would, but I think the evidence would be weak. For I know by experience that my powers of concentration are exceedingly limited. Sentences proceeding from my own unconscious sometimes break in upon my train of thought in just this intrusive way. It is true that they usually present themselves to my mind in the form of verbal images. But occasionally they are actually uttered in audible whispers, and sometimes they are uttered aloud. How can I tell that these same unconscious processes in myself may not sometimes cause a foreign body to utter such intrusive noises? Their intrusive character is no bar to their unconscious origin. What we require is that they should symbolize something which I did not believe beforehand at all, even unconsciously. It is still better if they symbolize something which I *could* not have believed beforehand because I was not in a position to make the relevant perceptual observations. For instance, I hear a foreign body say "there is a black cloud on the horizon" at a time when my back is turned to the window, and then I turn round and see the cloud for myself. Or I am walking in pitch darkness in a strange house, and hear someone say "there are three steps in front of you," which I had no means of guessing beforehand; and I then verify the proposition for myself by falling down the steps.

III

It follows from what has been said that if there were a foreign body which never uttered anything but platitudes, I should be very doubtful whether it was independently animated, no matter how closely it resembled my own. In the instance given ("to-day is Saturday," when I already believe that to-day *is* Saturday) the platitude was a *singular* platitude, stating a particular matter of fact. But there are also *general* platitudes. Among these some are empirical, such as "there is always a sky above us," "all cats have whiskers"; while others are *a priori*, such as "2 + 2 = 4," or "it is either raining or not raining," and are true at all times and in all possible worlds. If

there was a body which uttered only singular platitudes, I should be inclined to conclude (as we have said) that it was not independently animated; I should suspect that its noises were caused by my own believings, conscious and unconscious. If it uttered nothing but general platitudes, I might doubt whether it was animated at all. I should be inclined to think that it was a mere mechanism, a sort of talking penny-in-the-slot machine, especially if its repertoire of platitudes was limited; though it might occur to me to wonder whether any intelligent being had constructed it.

So far, then, it appears that if the noises uttered by a foreign body (or its visible gesticulations) are to provide adequately strong evidence for the existence of another mind, they must give me information. They must symbolize something which I did not know or believe beforehand, and which I then proceed to verify for myself. If these conditions are fulfilled, I have evidence of the occurrence of a foreign act of perceiving—an act of perceiving which did not form part of my own mental history. But it is not really necessary that the information conveyed should be a singular proposition, restricted to one single perceptible situation. It might be general, as if I hear a foreign body say "some cats have no tails," or "all gold dissolves in *aqua regia*." Neither of these is restricted to one single perceptible object or situation. Still, they are both empirical, and there is a sense in which even the second can be empirically verified, or at any rate confirmed, by suitable observations and experiments. Clearly such utterances as these do give me evidence for the existence of another mind; but not in the way that the previous utterances did, such as "there is the bus," or "there is a black cloud on the horizon now." They do not show that a specific perceptual act falling outside my own mental history is now occurring, or has just occurred. In one way they show something less—merely that some perceivings of cats or of gold have occurred at some time or other. But in another way they show something more: namely, that a foreign act of *thinking* is occurring or has recently occurred, directed upon the *universals* "cat," "tail," "gold," and "aqua regia." (Or if it be objected that even perceiving involves some thinking, directed upon universals in abstraction from their instances.) . . .

IV

In the situations hitherto mentioned the noises which I hear and understand are uttered by a foreign organism which I observe. And the foreign organism is more or less similar to my own. But of course I need not actually observe it. It suffices if I hear an intelligible and informative utterance proceeding from a megaphone or a telephone, from the next room or from behind my back. It may, however, be thought that such a foreign organism must be in principle observable if I am to have evidence of the existence of another mind, and further that it must be more or less similar to my own organism. But I believe that both of these opinions are mistaken, as I shall now try to show by examples.

There is a passage in the Old Testament which reads, "Thou shalt hear a voice behind thee saying, 'This is the way, walk ye in it.'" Now suppose that something like this did actually occur. For instance, I am lost on a mountain-top, and I hear a voice saying that on the other side of such-and-such a rock there is a sheep-track which leads down the mountain. After the best search that I can make, I can find no organism from which the voice could have proceeded. However, I go to the rock in question, and I do find a sheep-track which leads me down safely into the valley. Is it not clear that I should then have good evidence of the existence of another mind? The fact that so far as I can discover there was no organism, human or other, from which the voice proceeded makes no difference, provided I hear the noises, understand them, and verify the information which they convey. Now suppose I go up the mountain many times, and each time I hear an intelligible set of noises, conveying information which is new to me and subsequently verified; but I never find an organism from which they could have proceeded, search as I may. I should then have reason for concluding that the place was "haunted" by an unembodied mind. Such things do not happen, no doubt. But still there is no contradiction whatever in supposing them. The point is that if they did happen they would provide perfectly good evidence for the existence of another mind. And this is sufficient to show that the presence of an observable organism is not essential;

a fortiori, the presence of an observable organism more or less resembling my own is not essential. . . .

It appears then that I could conceivably get strong evidence of the existence of another mind even if there was no observable organism with which such a mind could be connected. This incidentally is a new and fatal argument against the old Analogical Theory which was referred to at the beginning of this paper. For that theory maintained that one's evidence of the existence of other minds could *only* come from observing foreign bodies which resemble one's own. It is also clear that even when I do observe a foreign body producing the relevant utterances, that body need not be in the least like my own. There is no logical absurdity in the hypothesis of a rational parrot or a rational caterpillar. And if there was such a creature, I could have as good evidence of its rationality as I have in the case of my human neighbours; better evidence indeed than I can have in the case of a human idiot. There is no *a priori* reason why even vegetable organisms should not give evidence of being animated by rational minds, though as it happens they never do. If the rustlings of the leaves of an oak formed intelligible words conveying new information to me, and if gorse-bushes made intelligible gestures, I should have evidence that the oak or the gorse-bush was animated by an intelligence like my own. . . .

V

I have now tried to show by a number of examples that it is the perceiving and understanding of noises and other symbols which gives one evidence for the existence of other minds. I think it is clear that the situations I have described do provide evidence for this conclusion. But exactly *how* they do so is not yet clear. Before we discuss this question, however, there are three preliminary points to be made.

First, it is necessary to insist that there is nothing recondite about this evidence for the existence of other minds. It is not the sort of evidence which only philosophers or scientists or other experts can discover. Perhaps I have spoken as if it were suddenly presented to the notice of an intelligent and reflective adult, who has reached years of discretion without ever finding any good reasons for believing in the existence of another mind, and now finds some for the first time. But of course this is not really the position. The evidence I have spoken of is available to anyone, however youthful and inexperienced, as soon as he has learned the use of language. All that is required is that he should be able to receive information by means of words or other symbols, and that he should be able to distinguish between observing something and being told about it. (Perhaps he is not *self*-conscious until he is able to draw this distinction. If so, we may agree with those who say that consciousness of self and consciousness of others come into being simultaneously, though not with their further contention that consciousness of others is a form of acquaintance or intuitive knowledge.) Thus by the time that he has reached years of discretion evidence of the sort described is exceedingly familiar to him, little though he may have reflected upon it.

The second point is more serious. It may be objected that one cannot learn to understand language unless one *already* believes (or knows?) that the noises one hears are produced by a mind other than oneself. For if not, how would it ever occur to one that those queer noises which one hears are symbols at all? Must one not assume from the start that these noises are *intended* to stand for something? Then, but not otherwise, one can proceed to discover what in particular they stand for.

To this I reply, at first it does not occur to one that the noises *are* symbols. One has to discover this for oneself. And one discovers it by learning to *use* them as symbols in one's own thinking. One begins by merely noticing a correlation between a certain type of object and a certain type of noise, as one might notice a correlation between any other two types of entities which are frequently combined, say, thunder and lightning. The correlation is at first far from complete, for one sometimes observes the object without hearing the noise. But gradually one comes to imitate the noise for oneself. And thus the correlation becomes more nearly complete; if no foreign body says "cat" when I see a cat, I shall say "cat" myself. Thus a strong association is set up in my mind between that type of noise and that type of object. The next step after this is certainly a mysterious one, the more so as it is perhaps not literally a "next" step, but merely the continuation and com-

pletion of something which has been going on from the start. But the mystery has nothing to do with awareness of other people's intentions. It has to do with what used to be called the abstraction of universals from particulars. We must suppose that all conscious beings have the power of recognizing that two or more particulars are similar to each other. No consciousness devoid of this power would be of the faintest use to its possessor; so it must be assumed that the lower animals, if they are conscious at all, can recognize at least some similarities, namely, those which are important for their biological welfare. But only some conscious beings can single out within the similar particulars that common factor in respect of which they are similar, and can conceive of it in abstraction; that is, at times when they are not actually perceiving or remembering any particular of the sort in question. This conceiving of universals in the absence of their instances is what we commonly call thinking. And it is for this that symbols are required; conversely, noises and the like only become symbols in so far as they are used as means to such conceiving. For example, I have seen many cats, and for some time I have found that the noise "cat" occurs when I see one (whether it is uttered by a foreign body or by myself, or by both). I must now attend to the common feature of all these objects, and learn to associate the noise with that. Then, when I hear the noise in future, whether uttered by myself or not, it will bring that common feature—that universal—before my mind, even if no cat is actually being perceived by me. When this happens, and not till then, the noise "cat" has become a symbol for me. The process is very puzzling, and I do not profess to have given anything like an adequate account of it. But whatever difficulties there may be about it, it does not seem to presuppose at any stage that one has a prior knowledge of other minds, or even a prior belief in their existence. . . .

VI

We may now return to the main argument. We have described a number of situations in which the perceiving and understanding of symbols gives one evidence of the existence of another mind. But how exactly do they provide evidence for this conclusion? Let us confine ourselves for simplicity to the cases in which the evidence comes from the hearing of sounds. Two conditions, we have seen, must be fulfilled. The first, and most important, is that they must have a symbolic character. And they must be symbolic *for me*. It is obvious that the characteristic of being symbolic is a relational character. An entity S is only a symbol in so far as it stands for some object—whatever the right analysis of "standing for" may be. It is no less obvious, though sometimes forgotten, that the relation is not a simple two-term relation. It involves at least three terms: the entity S, the object O, and in addition a mind or minds. S symbolizes O *to someone*. The relation is more like "to the right of" than it is like "larger than." A is to the right of B from somewhere, from a certain limited set of places. From other places it is not to the right of B, but to the left of it, or in front of it or behind it.

But if the hearing or seeing of S, or its presentation to me in the form of an image, is to provide me with evidence of the existence of another mind, it is not sufficient that S should symbolize some object to someone. It must symbolize some object *to me*. I myself must understand it. Otherwise all I know about it is that it is a noise or black mark having such-and-such sensible qualities. It is true that if I heard sounds uttered in the Arabic language, which I do not understand, I could reasonably conclude to the existence of another mind. But only by analogy. The sounds have some similarity to others which *are* symbolic to me; I therefore assume that they, too, might come to be symbolic to me if I took the trouble.

Secondly, it is essential, I think, that the sounds should symbolize to me something *true or false*. They must propound *propositions* to me. It is not, however, necessary that they should have the grammatical form of a statement. A single word may propound a proposition. Thus the word "snake" may be equivalent to "there is a snake in the immediate neighbourhood." Again, the phrase "the bus" may be equivalent to "the bus is now approaching." Must the proposition propounded be such that I can *test* it, whether in fact I do test it or not? It must certainly be such that I know what the world would be like if it were true. Otherwise I have not understood the symbols: for me they are not symbols at

all. But it is not necessary that I should be able to discover by direct observation that the world is in fact like that, or is not. Otherwise I could not understand statements about the remote past, whereas actually I can understand them perfectly well.

The third condition is the one which we have already emphasized. The noises must not only be symbolic to me; they must give me information. The proposition which they propound must be new to me. That is, it must be new to me as a whole, though of course its constituents and their mode of combination must be familiar to me; otherwise I do not understand the utterance. If it is not new (i.e. new as a whole) the noises do still give evidence of the occurrence of a mental act other than the present act which understands them, and even of a mental act which is in a sense "foreign." But as we have seen, it might conceivably be an unconscious mental act of my own. And this greatly diminishes the evidential value of the utterance.

Now suppose these conditions are fulfilled. I hear noises which are symbolic to me; they propound to me something true or false; and what they propound is new to me. For instance, I hear the noises "here is a black cat" at a time when I do not myself see the cat and was not expecting it to appear. How exactly does this situation provide me with evidence of the existence of another mind? (It is well to insist once again that evidence, not proof, is all that can be demanded.)

It might be said: I have direct access to a number of cognitive acts by my own introspection. I find that these acts are usually accompanied by noises, audible or imaged. Moreover, I find by introspection that an act directed upon one sort of object, e.g. a cat, is usually accompanied by one sort of noise; and that an act directed upon another sort of object, e.g. blackness, is usually accompanied by another sort of noise. Thus there is a correspondence between the noises and the acts. Differences in the noises are accompanied by differences in the "direction" of the acts. When the object of the act is complex, I usually find a corresponding complexity in the noise. If n_1 usually accompanies an act directed upon O_1 and n_2 usually accompanies an act directed upon O_2, then I find that the complex noise $n_1 n_2$ is usually accompanied by an act directed upon the complex object $O_1 O_2$. And the structure of the complex noise (the way the constituent noises are arranged) varies with the structure of the object-complex upon which the accompanying act is directed. In this way, it may be said, I know from introspection that, when the noise-complex "here is a black cat" occurs, it is usually accompanied by a specific sort of cognitive act, namely, by the seeing and recognizing of a black cat. But this time it cannot have been a cognitive act of my own, for *I* was not seeing any black cat at the time when the noise-complex occurred. It must therefore have been a foreign cognitive act, an act extraneous to myself, and therefore presumably forming part of the history of some *other* mind.

However, such an account of the matter is not altogether satisfactory. The relation between the noises and the mental acts is really much more intimate than this. It is not a mere accompanying. If it were, the noises would not be functioning as *symbols*. When I am thinking I am always aware of symbols of some sort or another. But they do not just occur along with the thinking. The occurrence of them, whether in a sensible or an imaged form, is an integral part of the thinking itself. One might even define thinking as awareness by means of symbols. Perhaps, indeed, I can *perceive* without symbols. But in fact symbols usually are present to my mind in perceiving as well. And if they are present, again they do not merely accompany the perceiving. They enable me to analyse what I perceive, to recognize and classify the various factors in it, so that the perceiving turns into what philosophers call perceptual judgment, a piece of intelligent or thoughtful perceiving.

Thus the argument should be restated as follows: I know from introspection that noises of this sort frequently function as *instruments to* a certain sort of mental act (not merely accompany it). Therefore they are probably functioning as instruments to an act of that sort in the present case. But in the present case the act is not mine.

But there is still a further amendment to be made. There is a sense in which the noises *are* functioning as symbolic instruments to a mental act of my own. For after all, I do understand them. It is true that I am not seeing the black cat. But I do entertain the thought that a black cat is in the neighbourhood. And I think this *by means of* the noises that I hear. But if the noises are in any case functioning as instruments to a mental act of my own, what

need have I to suppose that there is also some other mental act—some foreign one—to which they are instrumental?

To clear up this point, we must distinguish two different ways in which symbols can be instrumental to cognitive acts. We must distinguish *spontaneous* thinking from *imposed* thinking. In the present case, my entertaining of the thought that there is a black cat in the room is *imposed* by the noises which I hear. What causes me to use these noises as symbols is the noises themselves, or rather my hearing of them. When I hear them, they arouse certain cognitive dispositions in me (dispositions arising from my learning of English, which are there whether I like it or not); and the result is that I am forced to use them for the entertaining of a certain determinate thought, one which but for them I should not on this occasion have entertained.

But how did these noises happen to present themselves to me? I did not originate them, either consciously, or—so far as I can discover—unconsciously either. And how did they happen to be arranged in just that way? They are so arranged that they make up a whole which is for me a single complex symbol, symbolizing something true or false about the world. That is how they manage to impose an act of thought upon me, which many of the noises I hear do not, striking and complicated though they be. How did this remarkable combination of events come about? How is it that each of the noises was for me a symbol, and how is it, moreover, that they were so combined as to make a single complex symbol, symbolizing something true or false? Well, I know from my own experience how it might have happened, because I know what happens in *spontaneous* thinking. In the spontaneous acts of thinking which introspection reveals to me, noises often function as symbolic instruments. And when they do, they are not usually found in isolation. They are ordered into complexes, each of which is symbolic as a whole and signifies something true or false. It would not be correct to say that I find two acts occurring at once: on the one hand, an act of spontaneous thinking, on the other an act of spontaneously producing symbols and ordering them into a symbol-complex which is true or false as a whole. What happens is that the producing of the significant symbol-complex occurs *in the process of performing* the spontaneous act of thinking. Sometimes this spontaneous act of thinking is concerned with something which I am perceiving. It is then a so-called perceptual judgment.

Thus I can now guess how the noises which I hear have come about, and how they have come to be such and so arranged that I am made to use them as instruments for an act of imposed thinking. For I know by introspection that just such noises, and just such an arrangement of them, are often produced in the course of acts of spontaneous thinking. This makes it likely that here, too, they were produced in the course of an act of spontaneous thinking. But in this case no spontaneous thinking of that particular sort was occurring in myself. Therefore in this case the spontaneous act of thinking must have been a *foreign* act, occurring in some other mind. If the noises are "here is a black cat," the act was probably a perceptual judgment, occasioned by the perceiving of a black cat. But if on investigating the matter for myself I find no black cat, the evidence for a foreign act of thinking still stands. (As we pointed out earlier, false information is just as evidential as true.) Only I shall then have to conclude that this act of thinking was not a perceptual judgment after all, but a piece of fiction-making or story-telling.

In this instance the noise-complex was already familiar to me as a whole. I have often seen black cats and said to myself "here is a black cat." But this is not always so. When I hear a complex noise and find myself using it as an instrument for an act of imposed thinking, it frequently happens that the complex as a whole is one which I am not familiar with. Thus the noise-complex, "the steward of Common-Room keeps a tame mongoose," may be one which I have never myself made use of in an act of spontaneous thinking.

Still, if I hear it, it will impose an act of thinking on me; not less so if I am sure that what I am being made to think of is false. And it will accordingly provide me with evidence of a foreign act of spontaneous thinking. This is because I often have used the *constituents* of the noise-complex in the course of my own spontaneous thinkings, for instance the noises "mongoose" and "steward" and "Common-Room." Moreover, although this actual combination of noises is new to me, the *manner* of combina-

tion, the structure which the noise-complex has, is perfectly familiar. I have often used it myself in the course of my spontaneous thinkings. Thus the noise-complex as a whole functions as a symbol for me, and imposes an act of thinking on me, even though I have never made use of it in any of my own spontaneous thinkings.

VII

We must now raise certain general questions about this argument for the existence of other minds. Though very different in detail from the one used by the old Analogical Theory, it is clearly an argument from analogy. The form of the argument is: situations a and b resemble each other in respect of a characteristic C_1; situation a also has the characteristic C_2; therefore situation b probably has the characteristic C_2 likewise. The noises I am now aware of closely resemble certain ones which I have been aware of before (in technical phraseology, they are *tokens* of the same *type*), and the resemblance covers both their qualities and their manner of combination. Those which I was aware of before functioned as symbols in acts of spontaneous thinking. Therefore these present ones probably resemble them in that respect too; they too probably function as instruments to an act of spontaneous thinking, which in this case is not my own.

But the argument is not only analogical. The hypothesis which it seeks to establish may also be considered in another way. It provides a simple *explanation* of an otherwise mysterious set of occurrences. It explains the curious fact that certain noises not originated by me nevertheless have for me a symbolic character, and moreover are combined in complexes which are symbolic for me as wholes (i.e. propound propositions). Many varieties of sounds occur in the world, and of these only a relatively small proportion are symbolic for me. Those which are symbolic for me can occur in a variety of combinations, and the number of mathematically possible combinations of them is very large; of these combinations only a small proportion "make sense," that is, result in noise-complexes which are symbolic for me *as wholes*. But if there is another mind which uses the same symbols as I do and combines them according to the same principles, and if this mind has produced these noises in the course of an act of spontaneous thinking: then I can account for the occurrence of these noises, and for the fact that they are combined in one of these mathematically-improbable combinations. When I say that these facts are "explained" or "accounted for" by our hypothesis, I mean that if the hypothesis is true these facts are instances of a rule which is already known to hold good in a large number of instances. The rule is, that symbolically-functioning noises combined in symbolically-functioning combinations are produced in the course of acts of spontaneous thinking; and the instances in which it is already known to hold good have been presented to me by introspection.

It may be objected by some that the hypothesis is worthless because it is *unverifiable*. Accordingly it may be said that it has no explanatory power at all, nor can any argument (analogical or other) do anything to increase its probability. For being unverifiable, it is nonsensical; that is, the words which purport to formulate it do not really formulate anything which could conceivably be true or even false.

Now it is true that the hypothesis of the existence of other minds is "unverifiable" in a very narrow sense of that word, namely, if verifying a proposition entails observing some event or situation which makes it true. I cannot *observe* another mind or its acts—unless extrospective acquaintance is possible, which there is no reason to believe it is. But the hypothesis is a perfectly conceivable one, in the sense that I know very well what the world would have to be like if the hypothesis were true— what sorts of entities there must be in it, and what sort of events must occur in them. I know from introspection what acts of thinking and perceiving are, and I know what it is for such acts to be combined into the unity of a single mind (however difficult it may be to give a satisfactory philosophical *theory* of such unity). Moreover, the hypothesis *is* verifiable in what is called the "weak" sense. I know what it would be like to find evidence to support it, because I have in fact found a great deal of evidence which does support it; and this evidence can be increased without assignable limit. It seems to me to be a mistake to demand that all the different types of hypothesis should be verifiable in the

same manner. What is to be demanded is, first, that the hypothesis should be conceivable (otherwise certainly it is nonsense); and secondly that it should be verifiable or refutable in its own appropriate manner, in accordance with the methods suitable to that particular sort of subject-matter.

However, it is instructive to ask what one would be left with if one refused to entertain the hypothesis of the existence of other minds on the ground of its unverifiability. It would still remain the case that one thinks by means of symbols. Further, the distinction between spontaneous and imposed thinking would still hold good. Nor could one possibly deny that in imposed thinking one acquires information which one did not possess before. It is a rock-bottom fact, and one must accept it whatever philosophy one holds, that the thinking imposed by heard or seen symbols enlarges one's consciousness of the world far beyond the narrow limits to which one's own perception and one's own spontaneous thinking would confine it.[2] An extreme empiricist must accept this fact like anyone else. But the purity of his principles prevents him from attempting any explanation of it, since they force him to conclude that the hypothesis of other minds is nonsensical. So he must just be content to accept the fact itself. Or perhaps he may say: what I *mean* by asserting that there are other minds is simply this fact, that my own consciousness of the world is constantly being enlarged by the hearing of noises and the seeing of marks which are symbolic to me, and by the consequent acts of imposed thinking which go on in me; so that "you" is just a label for certain pieces of information which I get in this fashion, and "Jones" is a label for certain other pieces of information, and so on. In that case he, too, can admit that there are other minds. Indeed, he can say it is a certainty that there are, and not merely (as we have suggested) a hypothesis for which there is strong evidence. But obviously he is giving a very strange sense to the phrase "other minds," a sense utterly different from the one which he gives to the phrase "my own mind."

If I am right, there is no need to go to such lengths. One has evidence of the existence of other minds in the ordinary literal sense of the word "mind," the sense in which one applies the word to oneself. Nevertheless, the argument I have offered does have its sceptical side. Any mind whose existence is to be established by it must be subject to certain restrictive conditions, which follow from the nature of the argument itself. In the first place, it must use symbols which I can understand; and I shall only be able to do this if I am able to use them myself. It is true that I may be able to guess that certain noises or marks are symbolic even if I cannot myself understand them. But this, as we have seen, is because they have a fairly close resemblance to other noises or marks which I do understand. If I never understood *any* of the noises or marks which I hear or see, I should have no evidence for the existence of other minds. (Strictly speaking we ought to add "tactual data" as well. They, too, may be symbols for the person who feels them, as the case of Helen Keller shows.)

There is a second restriction of great importance: any mind whose existence is to be established by such an argument must be aware of the same world as I am aware of. It must be such that the world which I am aware of is *public* to me and to it, *common* to both of us. This restriction really follows from the first. Unless the foreign symbols refer to objects which I too am aware of they will not be for me symbols at all. These public entities need not be sense-data. Sense-data might still be private, as many philosophers hold. It might even be, as some hold, that the sense-datum analysis of perception is mistaken from beginning to end, and that sensing is not a cognitive process at all, but is merely the being in a certain state ("seeing bluely," or the like). But still, if I am to have evidence of your existence, there must be publicity *somewhere*. Somehow or other we must both have access to one and the same world; if not by sensing, then by some other form of consciousness which sensing makes possible. Suppose this was not so. Suppose that there is another mind which is not aware of the same world which I am aware of, and suppose that it somehow produces noises which I hear or marks which I see. When it makes these noises, obviously I shall not have the faintest idea what it is talking about. How can I, since *ex hypothesi* the noises do not refer to any objects which I am aware of? But this is equivalent to saying that I have no reason whatever for

thinking that it is *talking* at all. And so I shall have no reason whatever for believing that it exists, or even for suspecting that it does. The noises which I hear, even though in fact they state the profoundest truths, will be for me mere noises, like the soughing of the wind or the roaring of waves.

It appears, then, that any evidence which I can have of the existence of another mind must also be evidence that the other mind is aware of the same world as I am aware of myself. Philosophers have sometimes suggested that each mind perhaps lives in a private world of its own. Probably no one believes this. But some people have been worried by the suggestion. They have suspected that though incredible it could not be rationally refuted, and have had recourse to mysterious acts of faith to get them out of their difficulty. But the difficulty does not exist, for this speculation of philosophers is nothing but a baseless fancy. The theory is such that there could not conceivably be any evidence in favour of it. Any relevant evidence one can get is bound from the nature of the case to tell against it. Any evidence that I can get of your existence is bound also to be evidence that you do not *live* in a private world, but in the public world which is common to all intelligences, or all those which can have any good reason to believe in one another's existence.

Notes

[1] I use a phrase "a foreign body" to mean "a body other than my own." As we shall see, it need not be a *human* body.

[2] Here we may note that even the most rigorous course of Cartesian doubt requires the use of symbols. One cannot doubt without symbols to bring before one's mind the proposition which is to be doubted. And philosophical doubt, which is concerned with complicated and highly abstract matters, is scarcely conceivable without the use of *verbal* symbols. We may conjecture that Descartes himself conducted his doubt in French, with some admixture of Latin.

IX.3 *The Behavioral Criterion and the Problem of Other Minds*

NORMAN MALCOLM

Norman Malcolm (1911–1990) argues that all versions of the argument from analogy are unsound because they lack a criterion for determining whether another "walking and speaking figure" has thoughts or feelings. Examining versions of this argument by Mill, Stuart Hampshire, and H. H. Price, Malcolm draws attention to the need for a behavioral criterion for our attributions of psychological phenomena. While rejecting crude behaviorism that reduces psychological attributions to behavioral states, Malcolm argues for the necessity of behavioral criteria to our understanding of other minds. His unstated motto is that of his teacher, Ludwig Wittgenstein: "An 'inner process' stands in need of outward criteria." The very way in which a child learns a language informs us that facial expression and bodily movement are tied in with our understanding of psychological states. Furthermore, first-person psychological avowals such as "I'm in pain" are themselves primitive, natural behavioral expressions of pain.

I

I believe that the argument from analogy for the existence of other minds still enjoys more credit than it deserves, and my first aim will be to show that it leads nowhere. J. S. Mill is one of many who have accepted the argument and I take his statement of it as representative. He puts to himself the question, "By what evidence do I know, or by what considerations am I led to believe, that there exist other sentient creatures; that the walking and speaking figures which I see and hear, have sensations and thoughts, or in other words, possess Minds?" His answer is the following:

> I conclude that other human beings have feelings like me, because, first, they have bodies like me, which I know, in my own case, to be the antecedent condition of feelings; and because, secondly, they exhibit the acts, and other outward signs, which in my own case I know by experience to be caused by feelings. I am conscious in myself of a series of facts connected by an uniform sequence, of which the beginning is modifications of my body, the middle is feelings, the end is outward demeanor. In the case of other human beings I have the evidence of my senses for the first and last links of the series, but not for the intermediate link. I find, however, that the sequence between the first and last is as regular and constant in those other cases as it is in mine. In my own case I know that the first link produces the last through the intermediate link, and could not produce it without. Experience, therefore, obliges me to conclude that there must be an intermediate link; which must either be the same in others as in myself, or a different one: I must either believe them to be alive, or to be automatons: and by believing them to be alive, that is, by supposing the link to be of the same nature as in the case of which I

From Norman Malcolm, *Knowledge and Certainty*. This selection was first published as "Knowledge of Other Minds," *The Journal of Philosophy,* Vol. 56 (1959).

have experience, and which is in all other respects similar, I bring other human beings, as phenomena, under the same generalizations which I know by experience to be the true theory of my own existence.[1]

I shall pass by the possible objection that this would be very *weak* inductive reasoning, based as it is on the observation of a single instance. More interesting is the following point: suppose this reasoning could yield a conclusion of the sort "It is probable that that human figure (pointing at some person other than oneself) has thoughts and feelings." Then there is a question as to whether this conclusion can *mean* anything to the philosopher who draws it, because there is a question as to whether the sentence "That human figure has thoughts and feelings" can mean anything to him. Why should this be a question? Because the assumption from which Mill starts is that he has *no criterion* for determining whether another "walking and speaking figure" does or does not have thoughts and feelings. If he had a criterion he could apply it, establishing with certainty that this or that human figure does or does not have feelings (for the only plausible criterion would lie in behavior and circumstances that are open to view), and there would be no call to resort to tenuous analogical reasoning that yields at best a probability. If Mill has no criterion for the existence of feelings other than his own then in that sense he does not understand the sentence "That human figure has feelings" and therefore does not understand the sentence "It is *probable* that that human figure has feelings."

There is a familiar inclination to make the following reply: "Although I have no criterion of verification still I *understand,* for example, the sentence 'He has a pain.' For I understand the meaning of 'I have a pain,' and 'He has a pain' means that he has the *same* thing I have when I have a pain." But this is a fruitless maneuver. If I do not know how to establish that someone has a pain then I do not know how to establish that he has the *same* as I have when I have a pain.[2] You cannot improve my understanding of "He has a pain" by this recourse to the notion of "the same," unless you give me a criterion for saying that someone *has* the same as I have. If you can do this you will have no use for the argument from analogy: and if you cannot then you do not

understand the supposed conclusion of that argument. A philosopher who purports to rely on the analogical argument cannot, I think, escape this dilemma.

There have been various attempts to repair the argument from analogy. Mr. Stuart Hampshire has argued[3] that its validity as a method of inference can be established in the following way: others sometimes infer that I am feeling giddy from my behavior. Now I have direct, noninferential knowledge, says Hampshire, of my own feelings. So I can check inferences made about me against the facts, checking thereby the accuracy of the "methods" of inference.

> All that is required for testing the validity of any method of factual inference is that each one of us should sometimes be in a position to confront the conclusions of the doubtful method of inference with what is known by him to be true independently of the method of inference in question. Each one of us is certainly in this position in respect of our common methods of inference about the feelings of persons other than ourselves, in virtue of the fact that each one of us is constantly able to compare the results of this type of inference with what he knows to be true directly and non-inferentially; each one of us is in the position to make this testing comparison, whenever he is the designated subject of a statement about feelings and sensations. I, Hampshire, know by what sort of signs I may be misled in inferring Jones' and Smith's feelings, because I have implicitly noticed (though probably not formulated) where Jones, Smith and others generally go wrong in inferring my feelings [pp. 4–5].

Presumably I can also note when the inferences of others about my feelings do not go wrong. Having ascertained the reliability of some inference-procedures I can use them myself, in a guarded way, to draw conclusions about the feelings of others, with a modest but justified confidence in the truth of those conclusions.

My first comment is that Hampshire has apparently forgotten the purpose of the argument from analogy, which is to provide some probability that "the walking and speaking figures which I see and hear, have sensations and thoughts" (Mill). For the reasoning that he describes involves the assumption that other human figures *do* have thoughts and sensations: for they are assumed to *make inferences* about me from *observations* of my behavior. But the philosophical problem of the existence of other minds *is* the problem of whether human figures other than oneself do, among other things, make observations, inferences, and assertions. Hampshire's supposed defense of the argument from analogy is an *ignoratio elenchi*.

If we struck from the reasoning described by Hampshire all assumption of thoughts and sensations in others we should be left with something roughly like this: "When my behavior is such-and-such there come from nearby human figures the sounds 'He feels giddy.' And generally I do feel giddy at the time. Therefore when another human figure exhibits the same behavior and I say 'He feels giddy,' it is probable that he does feel giddy." But the reference here to the sentence-like sounds coming from other human bodies is irrelevant, since I must not assume that those sounds express inferences. Thus the reasoning becomes simply the classical argument from analogy: "When my behavior is such-and-such I feel giddy; so probably when another human figure behaves the same way he feels the same way." This argument, again, is caught in the dilemma about the criterion of the *same*.

The version of analogical reasoning offered by Professor H. H. Price[4] is more interesting. He suggests that "one's evidence for the existence of other minds is derived primarily from the understanding of language" (p. 429). His idea is that if another body gives forth noises one understands, like "There's the bus," and if these noises give one new information, this "provides some evidence that the foreign body which uttered the noises is animated by a mind like one's own. . . . Suppose I am often in its neighborhood, and it repeatedly produces utterances which I can understand, and which I then proceed to verify for myself. And suppose that this happens in many different kinds of situation. I think that my evidence for believing that this body is animated by a mind like my own would then become very strong" (p. 430). The body from which these informative sounds proceed need not

be a human body. "If the rustling of the leaves of an oak formed intelligible words conveying new information to me, and if gorse bushes made intelligible gestures, I should have evidence that the oak or the gorse bush was animated by an intelligence like my own" (p. 436). Even if the intelligible and informative sounds did not proceed from a body they would provide evidence for the existence of a (disembodied) mind (p. 435).

Although differing sharply from the classical analogical argument, the reasoning presented by Price is still analogical in form: I know by introspection that when certain combinations of sounds come from me they are "symbols in acts of spontaneous thinking"; therefore similar combinations of sounds, not produced by me, "probably function as instruments to an act of spontaneous thinking, which in this case is not my own" (p. 446). Price says that the reasoning also provides an *explanation* of the otherwise mysterious occurrence of sounds which I understand but did not produce. He anticipates the objection that the hypothesis is nonsensical because unverifiable. "The hypothesis is a perfectly conceivable one," he says, "in the sense that I know very well what the world would have to be like if the hypothesis were true—what sorts of entities there must be in it, and what sorts of events must occur in them. I know from introspection what acts of thinking and perceiving are, and I know what it is for such acts to be combined into the unity of a single mind . . ." (pp. 446–47).

I wish to argue against Price that no amount of intelligible sounds coming from an oak tree or a kitchen table could create any probability that it has sensations and thoughts. The question to be asked is: What would show that a tree or table *understands* the sounds that come from it? We can imagine that useful warnings, true descriptions and predictions, even "replies" to questions, should emanate from a tree, so that it came to be of enormous value to its owner. How should we establish that it understood those sentences? Should we "question" it? Suppose that the tree "said" that there was a vixen in the neighborhood, and we "asked" it "What is a vixen?" and it "replied," "A vixen is a female fox." It might go on to do as well for "female" and "fox." This performance might incline us to say that the tree understood the words, in contrast to the possible case in which it answered "I don't know" or did not answer at all. But would it show that the tree understood the words in the same sense that a person could understand them? With a person such a performance would create a presumption that he could make correct *applications* of the word in question: but not so with a tree. To see this point think of the normal teaching of words (e.g., "spoon," "dog," "red") to a child and how one decides whether he understands them. At a primitive stage of teaching one does not require or expect definitions, but rather that the child should *pick out* reds from blues, dogs from cats, spoons from forks. This involves his looking, pointing, reaching for and going to the right things and not the wrong ones. That a child says "red" when a red thing and "blue" when a blue thing is put before him, is indicative of a mastery of those words *only* in conjunction with the other activities of looking, pointing, trying to get, fetching and carrying. Try to suppose that he says the right words but looks at and reaches for the wrong things. Should we be tempted to say that he has mastered the use of those words? No, indeed. The disparity between words and behavior would make us say that he does not understand the words. In the case of a tree there could be no disparity between its words and its "behavior" because it is logically incapable of behavior of the relevant kind.

Since it has nothing like the human face and body it makes no sense to say of a tree, or an electronic computer, that it is looking or pointing at or fetching something. (Of course one can always *invent* a sense for these expressions.) Therefore it would make no sense to say that it did or did not understand the above words. Trees and computers cannot either pass or fail the tests that a child is put through. They cannot even take them. That an object was a source of intelligible sounds or other signs (no matter how sequential) would not be enough by itself to establish that it had thoughts or sensations. How informative sentences and valuable predictions could emanate from a gorse bush might be a grave scientific problem, but the explanation could never be that the gorse bush has a mind. Better no explanation than nonsense!

It might be thought that the above difficulty holds only for words whose meaning has a "perceptual content" and that if we imagined, for example,

that our gorse bush produced nothing but pure mathematical propositions we should be justified in attributing thought to it, although not sensation. But suppose there was a remarkable "calculating boy" who could give right answers to arithmetical problems but could not apply numerals to reality in empirical propositions, i.e., he could not *count* any objects. I believe that everyone would be reluctant to say that he *understood* the mathematical signs and truths that he produced. If he could count in the normal way there would not be this reluctance. And "counting in the normal way" involves looking, pointing, reaching, fetching, and so on. That is, it requires the human face and body, and human behavior—or something similar. Things which do not have the human form, or anything like it, not merely do not but *cannot* satisfy the criteria for thinking. I am trying to bring out part of what Wittgenstein meant when he said, "We only say of a human being and what is like one that it thinks" (*Investigations,* §360), and "The human body is the best picture of the human soul" (*ibid.,* p. 178).

I have not yet gone into the most fundamental error of the argument from analogy. It is present whether the argument is the classical one (the analogy between my body and other bodies) or Price's version (the analogy between my language and the noises and signs produced by other things). It is the mistaken assumption that *one learns from one's own case* what thinking, feeling, sensation are. Price gives expression to this assumption when he says: "I know from introspection what acts of thinking and perceiving are . . ." (*op. cit.,* p. 447). It is the most natural assumption for a philosopher to make and indeed seems at first to be the only possibility. Yet Wittgenstein has made us see that it leads first to solipsism and then to nonsense. I shall try to state as briefly as possible how it produces those results.

A philosopher who believes that one must learn what thinking, fear, or pain is "from one's own case," does not believe that the thing to be observed is one's behavior, but rather something "inward." He considers behavior to be related to the inward states and occurrences merely as an accompaniment or possibly an effect. He cannot regard behavior as a *criterion* of psychological phenomena: for if he did he would have no use for the analogical argument (as was said before) and also the priority given to "one's own case" would be pointless. He believes that he notes something in himself that he calls "thinking" or "fear" or "pain," and then he tries to infer the presence of the *same* in others. He should then deal with the question of what his criterion of the *same* in others is. This he cannot do because it is of the essence of his viewpoint to reject circumstances and behavior as a criterion of mental phenomena in others. And what else could serve as a criterion? He ought, therefore, to draw the conclusion that the notion of thinking, fear, or pain in others is in an important sense meaningless. He has no idea of what would count for or against it.[5] "That there should be thinking or pain other than my own is unintelligible," he ought to hold. This would be a rigorous solipsism, and a correct outcome of the assumption that one can know only from one's own case what the mental phenomena are. An equivalent way of putting it would be: "When I say 'I am in pain,' by 'pain' I mean a certain inward state. When I say '*He* is in pain,' by 'pain' I mean *behavior*. I cannot attribute pain to others *in the same sense* that I attribute it to myself."

Some philosophers before Wittgenstein may have seen the solipsistic result of starting from "one's own case." But I believe he is the first to have shown how that starting point destroys itself. This may be presented as follows: one supposes that one inwardly picks out something as thinking or pain and thereafter identifies it whenever it presents itself in the soul. But the question to be pressed is, Does one make *correct* identifications? The proponent of these "private" identifications has nothing to say here. He feels sure that he identifies correctly the occurrences in his soul; but feeling sure is no guarantee of being right. Indeed he has no idea of what being *right* could mean. He does not know how to distinguish between actually making correct identifications and being under the impression that he does. (See *Investigations*, §§258–59.) Suppose that he identified the emotion of anxiety as the sensation of pain? Neither he nor anyone else could know about this "mistake." Perhaps he makes a mistake *every* time! Perhaps all of us do! We ought to see now that we are talking nonsense. We do not know what a *mistake* would be. We have no standard, no examples, no customary practice, with which to

compare our inner recognitions. The inward identification cannot hit the bull's-eye, or miss it either, because there is no bull's-eye. When we see that the ideas of correct and incorrect have no application to the supposed inner identification, the latter notion loses its appearance of sense. Its collapse brings down both solipsism and the argument from analogy.

II

This destruction of the argument from analogy also destroys the *problem* for which it was supposed to provide a solution. A philosopher feels himself in a difficulty about other minds because he assumes that first of all he is acquainted with mental phenomena "from his own case." What troubles him is how to make the transition from his own case to the case of others. When his thinking is freed of the illusion of the priority of his own case, then he is able to look at the familiar facts and to acknowledge that the circumstances, behavior, and utterances of others actually are his *criteria* (not merely his evidence) for the existence of their mental states. Previously this had seemed impossible.

But now he is in danger of flying to the opposite extreme of behaviorism, which errs by believing that through observation of one's own circumstances, behavior, and utterances one can find out that one is thinking or angry. The philosophy of "from one's own case" and behaviorism, though in a sense opposites, make the common assumption that the first-person, present-tense psychological statements are verified by self-observation. According to the "one's own case" philosophy the self-observation cannot be checked by others; according to behaviorism the self-observation would be by means of outward criteria that are available to all. The first position becomes unintelligible; the second is false for at least many kinds of psychological statements. We are forced to conclude that the first-person psychological statements are not (or hardly ever) verified by self-observation. It follows that they have no verification at all; for if they had a verification it would have to be by self-observation.

But if sentences like "My head aches" or "I wonder where she is" do not express observations then what do they do? What is the relation between my declaration that my head aches and the fact that my head aches, if the former is not the report of an observation? The perplexity about the existence of *other* minds has, as the result of criticism, turned into a perplexity about the meaning of one's own psychological sentences about oneself. At our starting point it was the sentence "*His* head aches" that posed a problem; but now it is the sentence "*My* head aches" that puzzles us.

One way in which this problem can be put is by the question, "How does *one know when to say* the words 'My head aches'?" The inclination to ask this question can be made acute by imagining a fantastic but not impossible case of a person who has survived to adult years without ever experiencing pain. He is given various sorts of injections to correct this condition, and on receiving one of these one day, he jumps and exclaims, "Now I feel pain!" One wants to ask, "How did he *recognize* the new sensation as a pain?"

Let us note that if the man gives an answer (*e.g.,* "I knew it must be pain because of the way I jumped") then he proves by that very fact that he has not mastered the correct use of the words "I feel pain." They cannot be used to state a *conclusion.* In telling us *how* he did it he will convict himself of a misuse. Therefore the question "How did he recognize his sensation?" requests the impossible. The inclination to ask it is evidence of our inability to grasp the fact that the use of this psychological sentence has nothing to do with recognizing or identifying or observing a state of oneself.

The fact that this imagined case produces an especially strong temptation to ask the "How?" question shows that we have the idea that it must be more difficult to give the right name of one's sensation *the first time*. The implication would be that it is not so difficult *after* the first time. Why should this be? Are we thinking that then the man would have a paradigm of pain with which he could compare his sensations and so be in a position to know right off whether a certain sensation was or was not a pain? But the paradigm would be either something "outer" (behavior) or something "inner" (perhaps a memory impression of the sensation). If the former

then he is misusing the first-person sentence. If the latter then the question of whether he compared *correctly* the present sensation with the inner paradigm of pain would be without sense. Thus the idea that the use of the first-person sentences can be governed by paradigms must be abandoned. It is another form of our insistent misconception of the first-person sentence as resting somehow on the identification of a psychological state.

These absurdities prove that we must conceive of the first-person psychological sentences in some entirely different light. Wittgenstein presents us with the suggestion that the first-person sentences are to be thought of as similar to the natural nonverbal, behavioral expressions of psychological states. "My leg hurts," for example, is to be assimilated to crying, limping, holding one's leg. This is a bewildering comparison and one's first thought is that two sorts of things could not be more unlike. By saying the sentence one can make a *statement;* it has a *contradictory;* it is *true* or *false;* in saying it one *lies* or *tells the truth;* and so on. None of these things, exactly, can be said of crying, limping, holding one's leg. So how can there be any resemblance? But Wittgenstein knew this when he deliberately likened such a sentence to "the primitive, the natural, expressions" of pain, and said that it is "new pain-behavior" (*ibid.,* §244). This analogy has at least two important merits: first, it breaks the hold on us of the question "How does one *know when to say* 'My leg hurts'?" for in the light of the analogy this will be as nonsensical as the question "How does one know when to cry, limp, or hold one's leg?"; second, it explains how the utterance of a first-person psychological sentence by another person can have *importance* for us, although not as an identification—for in the light of the analogy it will have the same importance as the natural behavior which serves as our preverbal criterion of the psychological states of others.

Notes

[1] J. S. Mill, *An Examination of Sir William Hamilton's Philosophy,* 6th ed. (London: Longmans, 1889), pp. 243–44.

[2] "It is no explanation to say: the supposition that he has a pain is simply the supposition that he has the same as I. For *that* part of the grammar is quite clear to me: that is, that one will say that the stove has the same experience as I, *if* one says: it is in pain and I am in pain" (Ludwig Wittgenstein, *Philosophical Investigations* [New York: Macmillan Company, 1953], §350).

[3] "The Analogy of Feeling," *Mind,* LXI (1952), 1–12.

[4] "Our Evidence for the Existence of Other Minds," *Philosophy,* XIII (1938), 425–56.

[5] One reason why philosophers have not commonly drawn this conclusion may be, as Wittgenstein acutely suggests, that they assume that they have "an infallible paradigm of identity in the identity of a thing with itself" (*Investigations,* §215).

IX.4 *Why We Believe in Other Minds*

Michael Levin

Michael Levin is Professor of Philosophy at the City College of New York and the City University of New York Graduate Center. In this reading, Levin appeals to an evolutionary and reliabilist view of knowledge to explain what causes us to believe in other minds. However, Levin does not think the epistemological question (What are our reasons for believing in other minds?) will be solved until we solve the metaphysical question "What *makes* an event a mental event?" Only when we accept an identity theory between mental states and physical states will we have a solution to the problem of other minds.

I. *The Problem*

One does not hear very much about the problem of other minds these days. It is not that the problem has been solved, but, I think, that its intractability has sapped its interest. It is time for a new approach, one not beholden to the traditional analogical argument or neo-traditional criteriological arguments. That is what I undertake here.

Let me prepare the way for my positive thesis by explaining why all traditional thinking that sets the problem as one of justified inference from the first-person case (i.e., all traditional thinking) must fail. The problem of other minds is normally posed

Reprinted from *Philosophy and Phenomenological Research,* Vol. XLIV, No. 3, March 1984 by permission.

this way: on what basis do *I infer* that various organisms I observe are conscious, and is this inference *justified*? Each stressed word contains a hefty assumption which usually goes unchallenged and indeed unnoticed. First is the assumption that each individual, as a sort of information-processing atom, goes from non-belief to belief about the existence of other consciousnesses. Second is the assumption that the process by which this transition is effected is inference. Now, these two assumptions can both be true even if the inference involved is faulty; in that case nobody would *know* of other minds, even though there would now be some understanding of the process which creates *belief* in other minds. However, since such a process that culminated in unwarranted belief would be vain and unlikely—we all suppose pre-theoretically that we *know* there are other minds—philosophers write as if our retention of the belief depends on the soundness of the inference. In all this, the purely causal question, "By what process—reasonable or not—do we come to believe in other minds?", is ignored.

All three assumptions are wrong, but it is easiest to create a presumption against them corporately by concentrating on the second one. It is rather unlikely that anyone *infers* the existence of other minds for the simple reason that creatures incapable of inference, at least of complicated inference, believe in them or hold beliefs that entail the existence of other minds. Mr. Lion surely believes that Mrs. Lion is amenable to mating, a belief triggered when Mrs. Lion nips him. When my wife scolds him, my 16-month-old believes that his mommy is angry, to the full extent to which he believes anything. Yet lions and babies are incapable of inference, certainly of sophisticated inference. Even if we attribute unconscious inferential aptitudes to them, they do not seem to have the data requisite for an inference to someone else's amorousness or anger. Any advocate of any inferential theory must thus make one of three unattractive moves. He must say that babies and animals really *do not* believe in other minds, or that these beliefs are unjustified and must be replaced by justified beliefs (in the human case) as the baby reaches maturity, or that the inferential powers of lesser creatures are so powerful that they exceed that required according to some psychologists for the perception of depth and texture. Each alternative, I think, is less plausible than the simple assumption that lesser creatures know about other minds just as we do.

Since, then, there are ostensibly non-inferential beliefs about other minds indistinguishable from the heteropsychological beliefs of mature humans, the latter beliefs probably do not involve inference either. And if they do not involve inference, the question of whether the inference is sound lapses.

Let me ground these reflections by mentioning some post-Wittgensteinian efforts to speak to, if not solve, the other-minds problem. Alvin Plantinga argues[1] that belief in other minds is exactly as good as belief in God; every feature of the analogical argument—which he takes to be the best available—is matched by a feature of the argument from design. Doubts about the latter require doubts about the former. Without discussing

whether Plantinga has made his *tu quoque* convincingly, I would point out an important asymmetry Plantinga ignores. We all do believe in other minds, so much so that an adequacy condition on any theory of belief in other minds is that it leads to the conclusion that we know that there are other minds. A theory which represents inference to other minds as too tenuous to be warranted is thereby an inadequate theory. However, no such constraint exists for belief in God. There are too many sincere atheists for God's existence to be considered a pre-theoretical desideratum. Consequently, I take the upshot of Plantinga's argument to be, if it is correct, that there is more to belief in other minds than Plantinga's parallel exhibits. That one constraint on any theory of inferential belief in other minds is that the inference must succeed suggests that inference is not the source of the conviction.

Take, again, Dennett's recent work on consciousness and his hints about its connection to other minds.[2] Dennett takes a conscious being to be simply a functionally related group of intentional subsystems, i.e., to be a conscious being is to be describable by an appropriate sort of design diagram. In particular, what a conscious being is conscious of is largely what enters (what serves as) the "buffer memory" in the flow-chart. Dennett recognizes that whether something is conscious must be distinguished from whether an instantiation of an appropriate flow-chart would *seem* conscious, and he rightly points out that we could go wrong—if, e.g., the real-time operation of the instantiation were relatively slow. But what is most striking about Dennett's theory is that, combined with the inferential theory, it implies that nobody believes in other minds. For surely nobody says to himself: On the basis of what I see of my wife's behavior it will be predictively useful to posit a buffer memory, a speech center, and so on; therefore I will adopt a highly refined form of the "intentional stance" toward her. The point is not that Dennett's theory of consciousness is wrong, but that my belief in my wife's consciousness did not come about through inference that (what Dennett describes as) consciousness holds in my wife's case.

Even what I have called "traditional" approaches may be fruitfully classified by their failure to deal with this problem. As C. D. Broad noted, the basis for any heteropsychological inference has to be "the perception of a foreign body of a certain kind, which moves, alters its expression, makes noises, and so on, in certain characteristic ways."[3] This leaves the inferential approach with just two paths.

(1) The existence of other minds is not entailed by this data.

Two problems of increasing difficulty then arise:

(a) How could such an inference ever be justified?

and

(b) Given the first-person origin of the inference, how could the inferrer even find the conclusion well-formed?

Since, barring telepathy, the inferrer is restricted to data about his own consciousness, must he not identify pain with what *he* experiences under suitable conditions? If so, he could never even form a belief in other minds.

(2) Belief in other minds is entailed by the physicalistic data.

This leads either to behaviorism (about others) or to more refined theories, which, while not identifying mental states with behavioral dispositions, detect various conceptually necessary connections between mind and behavior.

Both approaches have well-known and fatal flaws. If (1) correctly described how we thought, we would never arrive at and perhaps not even formulate belief in other minds. (2) may describe a possible and permissible inference, but it hardly captures what anyone believes. When I see you writhing after banging your thumb with a hammer, I believe this behavior is contingently connected with pain, something in you that is just like what happens to me when I bang my thumb. (1) and (2), in different ways, fail to justify *our* belief in other minds.

Let me end this section by mentioning the view that the mental states of others are *theoretical entities,* and that belief in other minds is just one more inference from data (your behavior) to an explanatory theory (you are in such-and-such a constellation of mental states). This view is said by its advocates to be an improvement on the weak analogical

and behavioristic criteriological theories, since the soundness of the inference it proposes is to be gauged by the usual canons of theory evaluation, thus demonstrating that there is no *special* other-minds problem. Surely, however, this gambit is at bottom *just* the analogical argument. After all, what happens is that I know from my own case that the typical cause and effect of a given external event is a constellation of psychological states, or "belief-desire profile." When I see you behave similarly, I suppose ("posit") a similar belief-desire profile in you. As Sussman remarks, "Surely, dubbing mental events 'theoretical entities' does not mark progress" (op. cit., p. 284).

II. A *Hypothesis*

My alternative is a Darwinian story. Darwin himself wrote with great penetration about the expression of emotion in animals and men; it is regretable only that he did not connect it with classical epistemology. Here is the story:

An adult human's belief in other minds is the result of natural selection. Creatures who can detect the thoughts and feelings of human and non-human fellow creatures have an evolutionary advantage over those who cannot, because they can better predict what their fellow creatures are going to do. This is how, and why, belief in other minds got selected in. The same advantage would accrue to pre-human creatures, so this hypothesis predicts that pre-human creatures have heteropsychological beliefs implanted by natural selection. This coheres well with the fact, previously stressed, that dogs and other animals *seem* to hold beliefs about the attitudes of other creatures toward them. It predicts as well, although not so clearly, that we will find evidence of such beliefs in human infants who are not old enough to perform inferences.

More specifically, I suggest that what natural selection has implanted is a tendency to form certain anticipations and undergo certain feelings when presented with certain characteristic facial expressions and bodily carriages. I *infer* nothing when I see you writhe; by so far ill-understood neural mechanisms your writhing *causes* me to think you are in pain. Moreover, *I* infer nothing. The mechanisms themselves have been selected in because they helped my ancestors. My genes prewired these responses into my nervous system, so they are not my doing. Whether my belief is *knowledge* becomes a nearly uninteresting question, for the *warrant* for my heteropsychological beliefs is independent of my beliefs themselves and my continuing to hold them. I have not adopted such beliefs because I saw their epistemic merit, nor does continuing to hold them depend on my continuing to find meritorious the inference on which they are based. There is no inference. Whether to call my beliefs "knowledge" is a matter for spectators of my responses to decide.

There is an obvious Humean twist to this hypothesis. Our belief in other minds is founded not on reason but instinct, today's surrogate for Hume's "human nature." The advance over Hume is two-fold: we now know in impressive detail how and why such instincts get built in, and I will argue below that the Darwinian picture gives us good reasoning for supposing that other minds *do* exist and even that, inference or not, we *know* it.

III. *Evidence*

The evidence for this hypothesis is simple and strong, some of it already alluded to. From as early as three weeks, human infants react to faces. A human infant will smile if presented with even a highly schematic picture of a smiling face. As they mature, infants' reactions increase in complexity and *clearly* indicate that their laughing and cooing is not reflexive, but the expression of inner states of enjoyment. Children see such pictures as pictures of a happy person. Children too little to control their own bodies or even to have a clear sense that they are separate entities will cringe and cry at raised voices. Since they could not have *found out* that yelling means anger, they did not.

Infants thus display obviously inherited—because ubiquitous and early—reactions which are prototypical of responses to the inner states of others. The signs of happiness make children happy, and the signs of anger frighten them. It is well worth noting that these observations are quite incompatible with Goodman's widely discussed theory of art, at least to the extent that that theory has empirical import. Goodman holds that all representation is conventional, that nothing "in itself" looks like anything, and he denies that anything can be recognized as a picture of anything else without training in some tradition of representation. But children do recognize even simple and abstract face-pictures as pictures *of faces;* they react to such pictures just as they react to human faces. The evidence is overwhelming that they do this without training. (The point needs no argument for anyone who has had children.) Many philosophers and social scientists have made much of a Papuan's purported inability to recognize a black-and-white 3-in. by 5-in. snapshot of his chief taken from 50 feet away, of his need to learn to see it as a chief-picture. In reality, all such findings exhibit are the *limits* of our innate recognition capacities. When the same Papuan was, in Hume's phrase, "still in his cradle," he would have gooed at a full-face sketch of his chief.[4]

Animals, who can "sense" love or fear, supply similar evidence. They certainly seem able to tell when members of their own and related species mean them well or ill. Such detection certainly seems to be the having of full-blooded beliefs. After all, being afraid of a snarl is *believing* that the snarl means harm.

A quite different kind of evidence for my hypothesis is its consilience with evolutionary theory. It is just what we should expect if structures and behaviors are selected for their tendency to confer fitness. It is useful to know about the minds of others because what is on someone's mind is a good guide to what he will do, in particular if he will attack you. Any caveman ancestor unable to tell by looking if a visitor to his cave is spoiling for a fight is more likely than a more discriminating competitor to get into fights he would rather avoid. He will consequently be less fit than such a competitor—that is, less likely to have children who themselves will have children. Similarly, those able to read positive emotions with great difficulty at best (by induction from his own case) will waste much time approaching females whose disinterest would be evident to more discriminating competitors. Such obtuse strains are likely to have been selected out, if they ever existed.[5]

It might seem that evolution could have saved trouble by making its creatures practical behaviorists, by programming them, that is, to go from "scowling face" to "fight coming up" without a mentalistic detour. However, apart from the fact that evolution only rarely selects in belief in error (the continued existence of material objects?), the wide range of behaviors and their narrow dependence on context evidently made it impossible for evolution to select in behavioristically accurate and simultaneously useful beliefs. There is no saying what a man *with a scowl* will do. Will he shout? Pick up a club? Pick up a gun? Initiate a class-action lawsuit? Evolution cannot select in any direct beliefs about what behavior scowls portend. Reliable conditionals like "If a man who has just been bitten by your dog marches toward you, he will probably threaten to sue" are too special to get selected in. What nature wants is one easy-to-select belief that will do the predictive job of this multiplicity of purely behavioral conditionals. The belief for the job is obviously that someone with a scowl is angry. What the old analogical theory can teach us is *how* that one belief can do this job. Since one is aware of one's *own* behavioral tendencies when one is in various internal-states-plus-context, and one can easily imagine oneself in situations one is actually not in, nature seems to have implanted a tendency in us to believe that others are in states you recognize from your own case, and a tendency to project the behavioral tendencies one can detect in oneself on to others. And since there are true generalizations connecting inner states with behavior, our tendency to project leads *reliably* to expectations about what others would do. That is why it got selected in. When I see a scowler with a knife, I spontaneously imagine *myself* scowling with a knife, imagine what I would feel (thus in effect imagining what he feels), what I would *do* if I felt that way, and thence expect the scowler to act that way. Now I am prepared.

Note that evolution thus indirectly reduces a problem of theory construction ("How could the hypothesis that there are other minds ever occur to anyone?") to the problem of concept-formation ("How can anyone understand the idea of a mental state not his own?"). I argue below that this solves what is chiefly puzzling about the other minds conundrum.

IV. *Difficulties*

1. On my theory, what evolution selects in from a phenomenological point of view are mainly patterns of response and affect. Are such patterns genuine beliefs?

The answer is a "yes" qualified by a few general words about the nature of belief. Contemporary thinking on the subject seems to divide into two schools. *Literalists* take beliefs or believing to be isolable items in thought with a distinct propositional content. Such items might be sentences, vivid sentences, sentences accompanied by Frege's assent operator, or vivid images. *Ascriptionalists,* by contrast, can find no such thing as "believing *p*" as the literalist understands it. For them, all that two *p*-believers may have in common is *p*-believing; it is we outside observers who ascribe *p*-belief and other intentional states to creatures we observe. The ascription is predictively fruitful, but it is more akin to an editorial than a news item. (See Dennett, op. cit., xvii and chap. I; this theme runs through all of Quine's writing on intentional idioms.)

Ascriptionalism offers the insight that, often enough, what we call *p*-believing does amount to no more than acting like someone who believes *p*. We can organize Jones' behavior conceptually by attributing to him the belief that there is a mailbox on the corner, because he puts a letter he wants to mail into a box on the corner. Phenomenologically, there may be nothing more running through Jones' mind than "Ah, here's the box," which is followed by insertion of the letter. Obviously, if we buy ascriptionalism, we will agree that the editorial judgment we impose on Jones' reactions to Smith—"Jones believes Smith is angry"—exhausts what can be said about Jones' doxastic state.

Ascriptionalism is not so much troubled by circularity as by the fact that as-if talk of belief, and of anything else, makes sense only if there are corresponding literal descriptions. To say that Jones acts like a *p*-believer is to say that he acts like someone who *really* believes *p*. And how will we understand that unless we have in mind something about really believing *p*? In the end ascriptionalism hands everything over to literalism. But we do not need such indirect considerations—there obviously are central cases of belief which feature either inner sentences or nonsentential contents used just the way language-users use sentences. Thus, many child psychologists hold that a baby who believes that a ball he has been shown still exists behind the sofa is using a vivid mental image of the ball as a surrogate for the ball itself.

What I would emphasize in all this is the degree to which, my animadversions notwithstanding, the ascriptionalist is right, especially as concerns ascription of belief in the psychological states of others. Even though some people literally have the sentence "There are other minds" go through their head in assertoric mode—I'm thinking chiefly of philosophers persuaded by some or other standard argument—belief in other minds is typically a matter of so acting and feeling that an outsider will find it advantageous to think of the subject as if he literally had heteropsychological sentences running through his mind. This is the germ of truth in Wittgenstein's gnomic suggestion in the *Investigations* that we do not *believe* that another person has a mind; we "treat him as a soul." (Unfortunately, Wittgenstein overstates his case, and uncharacteristically *contrasts* belief with other attitudinal states.) Even if all evolution implants are patterns of response to characteristic facial expressions and bodily stances, that amounts to the implantation of belief in other minds. Being frightened of a face is to believe it portends ill. As an unlearned response to Mrs. Lion's posture, Mr. Lion acts as if he thought Mrs. Lion is amenable to mating. If this does not warrant saying that Mr. Lion believes that Mrs. Lion is amenable to mating, we have no warrant for saying that Jones believes there is a mailbox on the corner.

2. But what of those cases in which belief in other minds is literally maintained? How has nature selected that in?

Two distinct but not always distinguished problems have dogged thinking about other minds. One is: starting from an autopsychological perspective, what could ever prompt me to believe that another creature has psychological states (that are not mine)? The other is: starting from an autopsychological perspective, how could I ever form the idea of a psychological state that is not mine? The second problem is clearly easier than, because pre-

supposed by, the first. To form the other-minds hypothesis, I must already somehow have contrived the other-minds idea. Now my overall hypothesis suggests that, once the second problem has been solved, there may not be anything like the first one: I may be so constructed that as soon as I form the other-minds idea, I am inclined by nature to believe in its veridicality. On the evolutionary theory, the second problem is the *only* one.

The standard difficulty about the second idea is a supposed logical link between my concept of "pain" and my concept of "my pain." Because I cannot experience the pain of another and must learn "pain" from my own case, it is natural to suppose that what "pain" means to me is "what *I* have when my skin is damaged." If this is so, evolution can do nothing to overcome my solipsism. If a form of words like "someone else's pain" is meaningless, neither nature nor anything else can implant the corresponding idea in us, because there is no such idea. Fortunately, recent work in the theory of reference supplies the leverage with which to pry the concept of a psychological state off the concept of *my* psychological state (and without appeal to the obscure no-ownership theory), even though I must learn these concepts from my own case. It had been thought until recently that the descriptions by which people, in particular children, learn the word "pain" amount to an analytic definition of "pain." Were this so, pain would necessarily be what happens when I bang my finger, and "someone else's pain" would make no sense. It seems preferable, however, to construe these topic-neutral descriptions as contingent reference-fixers for "pain," which tie "pain" to that inner state which is, contingently, caused by the events the topic-neutral descriptions describe. It is thus no part of the meaning of "pain" in my idiolect that pains are something *I* undergo. In particular, the idea that someone else is in pain is the idea of something going on like what goes on when I smash my finger, except that it is not happening to me. I can make this split because the link between pain and contusion for me was always contingent. When I see someone else smash his finger, I can make perfect sense of something going on in him like what goes on in me when I smash my finger.

Before pressing on, I should mention the resistence of philosophers to this use of similarity. They argue that unless I can say what the similarity consists in, I have merely disguised the problem and not really explained how one can conceive the pain of another. This is a mistake. Geach and other writers would have a point if "pain" in my idiolect did make some essential reference to myself, for then "what is similar to my pain but not mine" would presumably be contradictory. The reason "It is 5 o'clock on the Sun" cannot be explained as "It is the same time as it is when it is 5 o'clock on the Earth, only on the Sun" is that clock-timings carry essential reference to the Earth. It is 5 o'clock at some point on the Earth when the Sun is in a certain position in the sky above that point. Obviously, since the Sun cannot be above itself in the sky, clock-timing cannot coherently be extended to the sun. However, since on the reference-fixing view of the connection between "pain" and my adventures there is no analytic connection between "pain" and "me," there is nothing any more problematic in "what is similar to my pain" than there is in "what is similar to my face" or "what is similar to a blue object." Imagine, then, that I have a general sense of similarity and a spontaneous tendency, when I see a man bang his finger, to form the idea of something going on in him which is like what goes on in me when I bang my finger. Now in imagining this I am *not* imagining that *I* am in his position, nor am I imagining what it would be like for *me* to be him. If I were imagining these things, it would still be my own state I was thinking of, and the problem of concept-formation would be unsolved. Rather, what I spontaneously imagine is *what it is like to be him*. In imagining the experience I of course call upon my own past sufferings, but only in the way I call upon my own past sightings of trees when I imagine what a tree no one is looking at looks like. In the latter case, even though I am necessarily calling upon my experience of what trees seen by me look like, I can clearly succeed in visualizing the unseen tree. Similarly, I can use my own pains to imagine what it must be like to be someone who just banged his thumb.

I earlier skated over the problem of how we know which behaviors mental states cause. Giving some account of this is important for my project, because I argued that the foregoing tendency to project heteropsychological ideas got selected in

because of its predictive utility. Again, the story is part reason, part instinct. I know what various mental events are likely to cause from my own case in two different ways. I know by ordinary induction what sophisticated mental states are likely to cause me to do. I have discovered that I write better if faced with space limitations. On the other hand, I believe non-inferentially that fear will make me tremble because I *feel* a tendency to tremble when I am afraid. The feeling of course is not logically infallible, and it should perhaps not even be called a "feeling" since it has predictive content, but that is how one feels impelled to describe it. Now, these feelings are usually accurate for the simple reason that the struggle for survival would have bred out strains that tended to make spontaneous misreadings of what their felt impulses portended. As a product of this selection, then, my hunches about where my mental states are likely to take me tend to be correct, and, because correct, useful.

The rest of the story now falls into place. Since in point of fact the same feelings tend to lead to the same behaviors in everybody, my tendency to

(a) read my impulses to behave off my mental states

and

(b) spontaneously use my own mental states to imagine what it is like to be someone else when presented with the right perceptual cues

enhances my predictive control of the world and hence my fitness. I suggest that this is how literal beliefs about other minds have gotten selected in.

3. On my account, does anyone *know* there are other minds?

It is tempting to say that the present account bars any warrant for belief in other minds, for it represents the belief as not based on reason, and, evidently, only beliefs based on reason (or on observation) can have warrant. In particular, it is usually supposed that a belief is warranted if the reasons the believer has for holding it actually justify it. Since if I am right I have *no* reasons for believing in other minds, my belief cannot be warranted. This is of course the other side of the Humean coin—the more prominent side being that my belief will not change even if I am forced to admit that I have no reason for belief in other minds.

All this moves much too quickly. We could be warranted in believing in other minds, and hence know there are other minds, even if our belief is not the result of reasoning. Fall in with me in embracing the causal theory of knowledge, in the simple form which takes knowledge to be belief caused by a reliable process. One reliable process is observation, another is sound reasoning. A third is the generate-and-eliminate process of evolution, where what is generated (and, if unsuccessful, eliminated) are beliefs. Nature implants various beliefs in its creatures. Creatures laden with some beliefs die, creatures laden with others prosper. Since life itself hinges on the accuracy of these beliefs, the beliefs that survive the evolutionary screening are almost certain to be *true*. A strain will die unless its innate beliefs about what is edible are true. Thus, evolution's generate-and-eliminate strategy is a reliable belief-producing mechanism. It is not infallible, but neither is perception. Consequently, the beliefs it selects are knowledge. If there are other minds (and there probably are, since nature selected in the belief that there are and nature does not lie), we *know* there are.

But what about warrant (or whatever else *YOU* suppose necessary for knowledge)? The word "warrant" and its cognates tend to be used with troublesome ambiguity. The trouble is that it encourages epistemologists to conflate knowing with knowing that one knows, and hence failure to know that one knows with failure to know. The ambiguity is this. Sometimes a person's belief is said to be warranted if it has been produced in the right way, without it being required that he *know* that it was produced in the right way; that is, without it being required that he know it was warranted. The bombardier was entitled to believe he was over the target even though he did not know how the bombsight was constructed. On the other hand, "warrant" is sometimes used in such a way that a belief is said to be warranted only if the believer knows what his warrant is and knows that it is a warrant. The detective knows who the criminal was on the basis of the footprint only if he knows *why* footprints evidence the passage of a foot. Now if, like me, you embrace the causal theory of knowledge, you will naturally be drawn to the first sense

of "warrant" as the one to be used in epistemic adjudication. You will say that a belief is warranted if *there is* a warrant for it for the person in question, whether he realizes it or not.

This decision is consilient with the causal theory because the causal theory puts no premium at all on having arrived at beliefs via reasoning, and hence on knowing what reasoning is good reasoning. On this decision plus the causal theory, true beliefs implanted by evolution are warranted; what we usually do not know is that they are warranted. Thus, even given a more traditional "warrant" or "reasoning" definition of "knowledge," everybody knows there are other minds. What few know is that they know there are other minds. Indeed, this approach promises a wholesale reconciliation of causal and justificationist theories. Causal theorists write as if they have supplanted justificationists: it does not matter what my reasons are, so long as my belief is caused in the right way. Justificationists have, at least implicitly, championed a non-causal criterion for knowledge: what matters is that my premises bear the right logical relation to my conclusions. If, however, *A* may be justified in believing *p* even if *A* does not realize it—and in particular *A* is justified in believing *p* if *A*'s *p*-belief is caused by a reliable process—a belief which is knowledge by causalist lights is also knowledge by justificationist lights.

4. But *are* there other minds? Does not appeal to the evolutionary selection of true beliefs in this context beg the chief question?

There are several ways of answering this point. The Quinean would begin by pointing out that we must believe our pre-theoretical picture of the world when asking the causal question, "Where does our belief in other minds come from?" This pre-theoretical stance includes belief in other minds, and since there is no transcendental perspective from which to judge the entire body of our current beliefs, there is no point in questioning our commitment to other minds. For us, "true" is coextensive with what our best current theory of the world asserts.

I think this sort of "no *pou stō*" globalism is better than such potted versions of it as the foregoing would suggest. However, I will not try to cloak myself in Quine's mantle. Instead, I would offer the following considerations. Everyone believes in other minds. That is the datum from which the evolutionary picture starts. (So the evolutionary picture *already* entails a plurality of minds, but I won't press that.) The best explanation for this datum, the evolutionary hypothesis I have sketched, attributes minds to others at a number of points. Ergo, we have as good reason as we need to believe that there really are the other minds our instincts force us to believe in anyway. The attribution of minds to others comes out in many places, particularly the explanation of the success of our spontaneous attribution of minds to others. The explanation for this success is simply that the attribution is correct.

It might seem, on closer inspection, that the evolutionary story really presumes, not the existence of other minds, but the existence of other beings who act the way we, on the basis of our natural assumption that they have minds, expect them to act. As long as there were some pre-established harmony between the behavior of a population of zombies and my expectations about them based on an erroneous belief that they were not zombies, my belief would get selected in. Thus, it might seem, the selection of creatures who impute minds to others can be explained either by an imputation of minds to others, or by the hypothesis that whatever mind-believers there were surrounded by mindless creatures who act like minded ones.

I am drawn to this criticism because, if sound, it would exonerate me from the charge of question begging. It would show that my evolutionary hypothesis can be stated without creating a world of sentient beings. However, I do not think the alternative explanation it holds out is a real one. It is unlikely that you have been shaped by evolution to believe in other minds because the world is and has been full of creatures who merely act as if they had minds. This is so simply because there was not any such thing as "behaving as if one had a mind," on this hypothesis, until you came along. We would have to believe that, miraculously, evolution foresaw that *you* would have a mind, and shaped creatures that behaved like you were going to behave, so that when you came along your projection of your own tendencies onto others would, miraculously, always lead to correct predictions. I agree that this is possible, but if we take evolution as a typical process in the natural world, it is very unlikely.

One can if one wants always stipulate away the possibility of knowing that there are other minds. Even if mental states are brain states, I can observe your neurons all I please and never be sure you are sentient. (This, as I argue in the next section, shows that you can never be sure that mental states are physical.) Telepathy itself can be made not to count, since even if I can read your mind—even if by an act of will I can make the world and my stream of consciousness appear to me as it appears to you— what I am having are *my* visual and introspective experiences, or *my* experience of your experience, which we have all learned to admit may not be accurate renderings of the experience numerically yours. If one wants to, one can make a necessary condition for knowing you have a mind not merely believing you have a mind, nor imagining what it is to be you by a process which is usually trustworthy, but *being you*. Why do that? Why make the stakes impossibly high?

V. *Why the Problem of Other Minds Refuses to Be Solved*

The epistemological problem of other minds is so hard to solve because it is very closely tied to a metaphysical question. The tie is not obvious, the metaphysical question is easily transformed into a cluster of pseudoquestions, and the result is sheer confusion.

The metaphysical question is: what *makes* an event a mental event? If an identity theorist says that brain event type or token B is mental event M, it is very natural to ask: what does B have that B'—the secretion of stomach acid, say—does not have. Why is B a *mental* event, and B' not? Once asked, no answer will be found adequate. If the materialist says "B is an event involving the right kind of hardware," the original impulse will manifest itself again in the question, "What's so special about that hardware?" If we say that B is a conscious event because B plays a certain functional role, it is still tempting to ask why *such* events are mental events, why *such* a role confers consciousness on an event. The impulse will not be allayed even by the assumption that one or another of these identifications is correct *de facto*. I feel the impulse in myself, and I daresay anyone who has thought about the mind-body problem feels it.

Before pursuing this question its own right, let us see how it makes epistemological trouble. It seems clear to me that anyone who grants that x is y, but also wants to know what makes x y, is really supposing that there is *something more* to being y than being x, some little extra ingredient or feature that x has to have to be y, or that x has and *so* is y. After all, no one asks what makes H_2O water, or why George Washington is the first American President. If you *really* think x is y, and not merely assent to the formula, you will think that the y-making ingredient is just *being x*, and you will not ask what makes x be y. Thus, in particular, anyone who verbally agrees that B is M, but cannot quell the puzzle about what makes B M, really does not believe that B is M—he believes instead that being $B + b$ is what being M is. Imagine someone with this muddled and inconsistent conviction about the identity of M and B being convinced that B or a B-like event is going on in another human organism O. He would continue to find it possible to doubt that O is in M because what he would not see is the extra ingredient b that he *really* wants to see if he is to admit he has witnessed M. This confusion gets expressed as the question, "How do I know that when O undergoes B it is the same for him as it is for me?" Now someone who really believes that being M is even contingently being B will not ask this; but up to the present time human beings who think about mental phenomena—even materialists who would never dream of toying with epiphenomenalism—do feel the urge to ask just this. That is why observing B objectively will never calm solipsistic worries.

The only way to dynamite the logjam is to address the underlying question. What does someone mean who asks why one thing is another, when he knows *that* the one is the other? The *most* one can mean by asking why H_2O, rather than CO_2, is water is a request to be shown that in fact all the properties of water are properties of clusters of H_2O molecules, and to be shown that all the behavior of water can be explained on the assumption that it is "just" H_2O. (Since H_2O *is* water, it makes no sense to take the question on its face value—namely, what *makes* H_2O water? For something to be responsible for H_2O's being water means that H_2O would not be water were it not for that other factor, which is at odds with the patent fact that

where H_2O is, there is water.) In short, "what makes x y?" is really a way of expressing scepticism about the proffered identity of x and y. So, in particular, philosophers will only become *convinced* of other minds in their philosophic vocation when they are shown that all the characteristics of mental states are characteristics of physical states (or some appropriate kind of state).

Notes

[1] *God and Other Minds* (Ithaca: Cornell University Press, 1967).

[2] *Brainstorms* (Cambridge: MIT Press, 1978), especially pp. 172–73.

[3] *Mind and Its Place in Nature* (Boston: Routledge and Kegan Paul, 1925), 318. Broad actually calls this "a necessary part" of the basis, chiefly because of his phenomenalism. Broad is aware that nobody comes to believe in other minds by inference from this basis, and he takes quite seriously the idea of instinctive beliefs cued by these "characteristic expressions." However, he does not develop this point along Darwinian lines, as I do below, and he embraces the assumption that if belief in other minds is to be justified, there must *be* a sound argument from the basis to the indicated conclusion, even if no one uses it. I reject this in IV below.

[4] In 1979 the American Museum of Natural History mounted an exhibit entitled *Ice Age Art: Man's Earliest Masterpieces,* which contained paintings, shallow relief and sculpture done over 35,000 years ago. It is impossible to view these items or the exhibit catalogue without remarking on their "fidelity" and naturalistic "realism," even though their creators plainly did not share with us any tradition of training or representational convention. I take it as *obvious* that there is something non-conventional and innate about how humans represent the world. Anyone who finds this anthropological material compatible with Goodman's theory must be so defining "intrinsic" as to *make* "intrinsic representationality" impossible.

[5] There is controversy over whether evolution selects for fitness in organisms or in genes, where "gene" is understood to denote the shortest stretch of a chromosome capable of self-reproduction. After all, a gene's best evolutionary strategy is to instruct its host organism to sacrifice itself whenever so doing can save a bunch of its host's siblings, and hence a bunch of partial copies of itself. This ill-named "selfish gene theory" does make it clear that what favors survival may not favor the survival of organisms. However, under most circumstances what helps me reproduce is precisely what helps my genes reproduce, so it does no harm in the present context to adopt the popular picture of more and less fit *organisms* in competition.

Bibliography

Ayer, A. J. *The Problem of Knowledge*. Middlesex, England: Penguin, 1956. Chap. 5.

Broad, C. D. *Mind and Its Place in Nature*. Totowa, NJ: Littlefield, 1960.

Mill, John Stuart. *An Examination of Sir William Hamilton's Philosophy,* 6th ed. New York: Longmans, Green, 1889.

Plantinga, Alvin. *God and Other Minds*. Ithaca, NY: Cornell University Press, 1967.

Russell, Bertrand. *Human Knowledge: Its Scope and Limits*. New York: Simon & Schuster, 1948.

Strawson, P. F. *Individuals*. London: Methuen, 1959.

Whiteley, C. A. "Behaviorism." *Mind 70* (1961).

Part X

The Ethics of Belief

Our passional nature not only lawfully may, but must, decide an option between propositions, whenever it is a genuine option that cannot by its nature be decided on intellectual grounds; for to say under such circumstances, "Do not decide, but leave the question open," is itself a passional decision,—just like deciding yes or no,—and is attended with the same risk of losing truth.

WILLIAM JAMES
The Will to Believe

It is wrong always, everywhere, and for anyone, to believe anything upon insufficient evidence.

W. K. CLIFFORD
"The Ethics of Belief," *Lectures and Essays*

Do we have a moral duty to believe propositions to the degree that the evidence supports them? What sorts of duties are there in relation to believing? To have a duty to do something implies we *can* do it—but is believing within our power? Or is it forced on us? More generally, what is the relationship between the will and belief? Can we obtain beliefs directly on willing to have them? Can we only obtain beliefs indirectly via the will: willing a belief and then actively participating in a process that will be likely to bring about that belief?

The readings in this part of the book deal with the various sorts of duties we may be said to have regarding belief acquisition. Three types of duties are found in the literature. First of all, there are *epistemic* duties, duties to believe according to the evidence or duties to inculcate the sort of belief-forming mechanisms that will ensure justified beliefs. This is echoed in Locke's dictum that "the one unerring mark by which a man may know whether he is a lover of truth for truth's sake is the not entertaining any proposition with greater assurance than the proofs it is built upon will warrant."

Secondly, there is the view that holds that we

have *moral* duties to believe according to the available evidence. There is something morally wrong about violating an epistemic duty to believe according to the evidence. This view is put forward by Clifford in the first reading: "It is wrong always, everywhere, and for anyone, to believe anything upon insufficient evidence."

Finally, there are *pragmatic* or *prudential* duties, duties to believe propositions insofar as they lead to the best outcomes. Hume, Mill, James, and H. H. Price hold this view. Price sets forth the thesis this way:

> Even if it were in our power to be wholly rational all of the time, it still would not follow that there is anything morally blameworthy about assenting unreasonably (against the evidence or without regard to the evidence) or that we ought to be chastised for doing so. There is nothing wicked about such assents. It is however true, and important, that unreasonable assent is contrary to our *long term interest*. It is to our long term interest to believe true propositions rather than false ones. And if we assent reasonably (i.e. in accordance with the evidence), it is likely that in the long run the propositions we believe will be more often true than false (*Belief*, p. 238).

The only "ought" regarding belief acquisition is a prudential one. A person is free to seek whatever goals he or she desires: happiness, salvation, convenience, esthetic pleasure, and so forth. It is simply in one's long-term interest generally to seek to have true beliefs.

The question whether we *ought* to believe propositions for such and such reasons raises the prior question of whether we *can* believe propositions simply by willing to do so. The doctrine that we can obtain beliefs directly on willing to believe them is called "volitionalism" or "voluntarism." I generally use the former term. In the readings, Clifford, James, and Meiland all accept volitionalism, whereas Feldman and I doubt it. But even if we reject volitionalism, this does not entail a rejection of the view that we have epistemic duties or moral duties with regard to doxastic states, for we may be able to influence or obtain beliefs *indirectly* via certain processes, such as auto-suggestion, hypnotism, focusing on aspects of evidence, developing better belief-forming mechanisms, and the like.

In the first reading, "The Ethics of Belief," the British philosopher W. K. Clifford (1845–1879) assembles reason's roadblock to pragmatic justifications for acquiring beliefs not fully supported by the evidence. Clifford argues that there is an ethics to believing that makes all believing without sufficient evidence immoral. Pragmatic justifications are not justifications at all but counterfeits of genuine justifications, which must always be based on evidence.

Clifford illustrates his thesis with the example of a shipowner who sends an emigrant ship to sea. He knows that the ship is old and not well built, but he fails to have the ship inspected. Dismissing from his mind all doubts and suspicions of the unseaworthiness of the vessel, he trusts in Providence to care for it. In this way, the shipowner acquires a sincere and comfortable conviction of its safety. After the ship sinks, killing all the passengers, he collects his insurance money without a trace of guilt.

Clifford comments that although the shipowner sincerely believed that all was well with the ship, his sincerity in no way exculpates him because "he had no right to believe on such evidence as was before him." We have an obligation to get ourselves in a position where we will only believe propositions on sufficient evidence. Furthermore, it is not a valid objection to say that what the shipowner had an obligation to do was *act* in a certain way (inspect the ship), not *believe* in a certain way. Although he *does* have an obligation to inspect the ship, the objection overlooks the function of believing as action guiding. "No man holding a strong belief on one side of a question, or even wishing to hold a belief on one side, can investigate it with such fairness and completeness as if he were really in doubt and unbiassed; so that the existence of a belief not founded on fair inquiry unfits a man for the performance of this necessary duty." The general conclusion is that it is always wrong for anyone to believe anything on insufficient evidence.

The classic response to Clifford's ethics of belief is William James's "The Will to Believe" (1896), the second reading in this part of the book. James argues that life would be greatly impoverished if we confined our beliefs to such a Scrooge-like epistemology as Clifford proposes. In everyday life, where the evidence for important propositions is often unclear, we must live by faith or cease to act at all. Although we may not make leaps of faith just anywhere, sometimes practical considerations force us to make a decision regarding propositions that do not have their truth value written on their faces.

In "The Sentiment of Rationality" (1879), James defines 'faith' as "a belief in something concerning which doubt is still theoretically possible; and as the test of belief is willingness to act, one may say that faith is the readiness to act in a cause the prosperous issue of which is not certified to us in advance." In "The Will to Believe," he speaks of "belief" as a live, momentous hypothesis, on which we cannot avoid a decision, for not to choose is, in effect, to choose against the hypothesis. There is a good illustration of this notion of faith in "The Sentiment of Rationality." A mountain climber in the Alps finds himself in a position from which he can only escape by means of an enormous leap. If he tries to calculate the evidence, only believing on sufficient evidence, he will be paralyzed by emotions of fear and mistrust, and hence be lost. Without evidence of being able to perform this feat successfully, the climber would be better off getting

himself to believe that he can and will make the leap. "In this case . . . the part of wisdom clearly is to believe what one desires; for the belief is one of the indispensable preliminary conditions of the realization of its object. *There are then cases where faith creates its own verification.*"

James claims that religion may be just such a genuine option for many people, and where it is, the individual has the right to believe the better story rather than the worse. To do so, one must will to believe what the evidence alone is inadequate to support.

In the third reading, "What Ought We to Believe? Jack Meiland argues that pragmatic reasons may override epistemic reasons in belief formation, so that it is sometimes permissible and even our moral duty to believe against the evidence. Loyalty to a friend or fear of disastrous psychological consequences may be sufficient reasons for rejecting the available evidence in forming beliefs.

In the fourth reading, I first argue against volitionalism on two grounds: it is psychologically aberrant and conceptually incoherent, so that our ability to obtain beliefs directly on willing to have them is, at best, a rare phenomenon. Secondly, in opposition to Meiland, I argue that we do have moral duties to believe according to the best evidence in the sense that we can indirectly get ourselves in the position where the best justified belief is likely to obtain.

In the final reading, "Epistemic Obligations," Richard Feldman distinguishes epistemic obligations from prudential and moral obligations, arguing that while the latter do depend on voluntary control, the former do not. They are more like institutional obligations (legal and financial). Feldman next discusses the difference between epistemic goals and epistemic obligations. He sets forth a version of evidentialism, according to which we have epistemic duties to believe in accordance with our evidence.

X.1 *The Ethics of Belief*

W. K. CLIFFORD

In this essay, the British philosopher W. K. Clifford (1845–1879) sets forth a classic version of evidentialism, arguing that there is an ethics to believing that makes all believing without sufficient evidence immoral. Pragmatic justifications are not justifications at all but counterfeits of genuine justifications, which must always be based on evidence. It is never morally permissible to violate our epistemic duties. Clifford opens his essay with the illustration of a shipowner who violates his epistemic duty and thus causes a disaster.

A shipowner was about to send to sea an emigrant ship. He knew that she was old, and not over-well built at the first; that she had seen many seas and climes, and often had needed repairs. Doubts had been suggested to him that possibly she was not seaworthy. These doubts preyed upon his mind and made him unhappy; he thought that perhaps he ought to have her thoroughly overhauled and refitted, even though this should put him to great expense. Before the ship sailed, however, he succeeded in overcoming these melancholy reflections. He said to himself that she had gone safely through so many voyages and weathered so many storms that it was idle to suppose she would not come safely home from this trip also. He would put his trust in Providence, which could hardly fail to protect all these unhappy families that were leaving their fatherland to seek for better times elsewhere. He would dismiss from his mind all ungenerous suspicions about the honesty of builders and contractors. In such ways he acquired a sincere and comfortable conviction that his vessel was thoroughly safe and seaworthy; he watched her departure with a light heart, and benevolent wishes for the success of the exiles in their strange new home that was to be; and he got his insurance money when she went down in midocean and told no tales.

What shall we say of him? Surely this, that he

was verily guilty of the death of those men. It is admitted that he did sincerely believe in the soundness of his ship; but the sincerity of his conviction can in no wise help him, because *he had no right to believe on such evidence as was before him*. He had acquired his belief not by honestly earning it in patient investigation, but by stifling his doubts. And although in the end he may have felt so sure about it that he could not think otherwise, yet inasmuch as he had knowingly and willingly worked himself into that frame of mind, he must be held responsible for it.

Let us alter the case a little, and suppose that the ship was not unsound after all; that she made her voyage safely, and many others after it. Will that diminish the guilt of her owner? Not one jot. When an action is once done, it is right or wrong forever; no accidental failure of its good or evil fruits can possibly alter that. The man would not have been innocent, he would only have been not found out. The question of right or wrong has to do with the origin of his belief, not the matter of it; not what it was, but how he got it; not whether it turned out to be true or false, but whether he had a right to believe on such evidence as was before him.

There was once an island in which some of the inhabitants professed a religion teaching neither the doctrine of original sin nor that of eternal punishment. A suspicion got abroad that the professors of this religion had made use of unfair means to get their doctrines taught to children. They were ac-

Reprinted from W. K. Clifford's *Lectures and Essays,* 1879.

cused of wresting the laws of their country in such a way as to remove children from the care of their natural and legal guardians; and even of stealing them away and keeping them concealed from their friends and relations. A certain number of men formed themselves into a society for the purpose of agitating the public about this matter. They published grave accusations against individual citizens of the highest position and character, and did all in their power to injure those citizens in the exercise of their professions. So great was the noise they made, that a Commission was appointed to investigate the facts; but after the Commission had carefully inquired into all the evidence that could be got, it appeared that the accused were innocent. Not only had they been accused on insufficient evidence, but the evidence of their innocence was such as the agitators might easily have obtained, if they had attempted a fair inquiry. After these disclosures the inhabitants of that country looked upon the members of the agitating society, not only as persons whose judgment was to be distrusted, but also as no longer to be counted honorable men. For although they had sincerely and conscientiously believed in the charges they had made, *yet they had no right to believe on such evidence as was before them*. Their sincere convictions, instead of being honestly earned by patient inquiring, were stolen by listening to the voice of prejudice and passion.

Let us vary this case also, and suppose, other things remaining as before, that a still more accurate investigation proved the accused to have been really guilty. Would this make any difference in the guilt of the accusers? Clearly not; the question is not whether their belief was true or false, but whether they entertained it on wrong grounds. They would no doubt say, "Now you see that we were right after all; next time perhaps you will believe us." And they might be believed, but they would not thereby become honorable men. They would not be innocent, they would only be not found out. Every one of them, if he chose to examine himself *in foro conscientiae,* would know that he had acquired and nourished a belief, when he had no right to believe on such evidence as was before him; and therein he would know that he had done a wrong thing.

It may be said, however, that in both of these supposed cases it is not the belief which is judged to be wrong, but the action following upon it. The shipowner might say, "I am perfectly certain that my ship is sound, but still I feel it my duty to have her examined, before trusting the lives of so many people to her." And it might be said to the agitator, "However convinced you were of the justice of your cause and the truth of your convictions, you ought not to have made a public attack upon any man's character until you had examined the evidence on both sides with the utmost patience and care."

In the first place, let us admit that, so far as it goes, this view of the case is right and necessary; right, because even when a man's belief is so fixed that he cannot think otherwise, he still has a choice in regard to the action suggested by it, and so cannot escape the duty of investigating on the ground of the strength of his convictions; and necessary, because those who are not yet capable of controlling their feelings and thoughts must have a plain rule dealing with overt acts.

But this being premised as necessary, it becomes clear that it is not sufficient, and that our previous judgment is required to supplement it. For it is not possible so to sever the belief from the action it suggests as to condemn the one without condemning the other. No man holding a strong belief on one side of a question, or even wishing to hold a belief on one side, can investigate it with such fairness and completeness as if he were really in doubt and unbiassed; so that the existence of a belief not founded on fair inquiry unfits a man for the performance of this necessary duty.

Nor is that truly a belief at all which has not some influence upon the actions of him who holds it. He who truly believes that which prompts him to an action has looked upon the action to lust after it, he has committed it already in his heart. If a belief is not realized immediately in open deeds, it is stored up for the guidance of the future. It goes to make a part of that aggregate of beliefs which is the link between sensation and action at every moment of all our lives, and which is so organized and compacted together that no part of it can be isolated from the rest, but every new addition modifies the structure of the whole. No real belief, however trifling and fragmentary it may seem, is ever truly insignificant; it prepares us to receive more of its like, confirms those which resembled it before, and weakens others; and so gradually it lays a stealthy train in our inmost thoughts, which may some day explode into overt action, and leave its stamp upon our character forever.

And no one man's belief is in any case a private matter which concerns himself alone. Our lives are guided by that general conception of the course of things which has been created by society for social purposes. Our words, our phrases, our forms and processes and modes of thought, are common property, fashioned and perfected from age to age; an heirloom which every succeeding generation inherits as a precious deposit and a sacred trust to be handed on to the next one, not unchanged but enlarged and purified, with some clear marks of its proper handiwork. Into this, for good or ill, is woven every belief of every man who has speech of his fellows. An awful privilege, and an awful responsibility, that we should help to create the world in which posterity will live.

In the two supposed cases which have been considered, it has been judged wrong to believe on insufficient evidence, or to nourish belief by suppressing doubts and avoiding investigation. The reason of this judgment is not far to seek: it is that in both these cases the belief held by one man was of great importance to other men. But for as much as no belief held by one man, however seemingly trivial the belief, and however obscure the believer, is ever actually insignificant or without its effect on the fate of mankind, we have no choice but to extend our judgment to all cases of belief whatever. Belief, that sacred faculty which prompts the decisions of our will, and knits into harmonious working all the compacted energies of our being, is ours not for ourselves, but for humanity. It is rightly used on truths which have been established by long experience and waiting toil, and which have stood in the fierce light of free and fearless questioning. Then it helps to bind men together, and to strengthen and direct their common action. It is desecrated when given to unproved and unquestioned statements, for the solace and private pleasure of the believer; to add a tinsel splendor to the plain straight road of our life and display a bright mirage beyond it; or even to drown the common sorrows of our kind by a self-deception which allows them not only to cast down, but also to degrade us. Whoso would deserve well of his fellows in this matter will guard the purity of his belief with a very fanaticism of jealous care, lest at any time it should rest on an unworthy object, and catch a stain which can never be wiped away.

It is not only the leader of men, statesman, philosopher, or poet, that owes this bounden duty to mankind. Every rustic who delivers in the village alehouse his slow, infrequent sentences, may help to kill or keep alive the fatal superstitions which clog his race. Every hard-worked wife of an artisan may transmit to her children beliefs which shall knit society together, or rend it in pieces. No simplicity of mind, no obscurity of station, can escape the universal duty of questioning all that we believe.

It is true that this duty is a hard one, and the doubt which comes out of it is often a very bitter thing. It leaves us bare and powerless where we thought that we were safe and strong. To know all about anything is to know how to deal with it under all circumstances. We feel much happier and more secure when we think we know precisely what to do, no matter what happens, than when we have lost our way and do not know where to turn. And if we have supposed ourselves to know all about anything, and to be capable of doing what is fit in regard to it, we naturally do not like to find that we are really ignorant and powerless, that we have to begin again at the beginning, and try to learn what the thing is and how it is to be dealt with—if indeed anything can be learned about it. It is the sense of power attached to a sense of knowledge that makes men desirous of believing, and afraid of doubting.

This sense of power is the highest and best of pleasures when the belief on which it is founded is a true belief, and has been fairly earned by investigation. For then we may justly feel that it is common property, and holds good for others as well as for ourselves. Then we may be glad, not that *I* have learned secrets by which I am safer and stronger, but that *we men* have got mastery over more of the world; and we shall be strong, not for ourselves, but in the name of Man and in his strength. But if the belief has been accepted on insufficient evidence, the pleasure is a stolen one. Not only does it deceive ourselves by giving us a sense of power which we do not really possess, but it is sinful, because it is stolen in defiance of our duty to mankind. That duty is to guard ourselves from such beliefs as from a pestilence, which may shortly master our own body and then spread to the rest of the town. What would be thought of one who, for the sake of a sweet fruit, should deliberately run the risk of bringing a plague upon his family and his neighbors?

And, as in other such cases, it is not the risk only which has to be considered; for a bad action is always bad at the time when it is done, no matter what happens afterwards. Every time we let ourselves believe for unworthy reasons, we weaken our powers of self-control, of doubting, of judicially and fairly weighing evidence. We all suffer severely enough from the maintenance and support of false beliefs and the fatally wrong actions which they lead to, and the evil born when one such belief is entertained is great and wide. But a greater and wider evil arises when the credulous character is maintained and supported, when a habit of believing for unworthy reasons is fostered and made permanent. If I steal money from any person, there may be no harm done by the mere transfer of possession; he may not feel the loss, or it may prevent him from using the money badly. But I cannot help doing this great wrong towards Man, that I make myself dishonest. What hurts society is not that it should lose its property, but that it should become a den of thieves; for then it must cease to be society. This is why we ought not to do evil that good may come; for at any rate this great evil has come, that we have done evil and are made wicked thereby. In like manner, if I let myself believe anything on insufficient evidence, there may be no great harm done by the mere belief; it may be true after all, or I may never have occasion to exhibit it in outward acts. But I cannot help doing this great wrong toward Man, that I make myself credulous. The danger to society is not merely that it should believe wrong things, though that is great enough; but that it should become credulous, and lose the habit of testing things and inquiring into them; for then it must sink back into savagery.

The harm which is done by credulity in a man is not confined to the fostering of a credulous character in others, and consequent support of false beliefs. Habitual want of care about what I believe leads to habitual want of care in others about the truth of what is told to me. Men speak the truth to one another when each reveres the truth in his own mind and in the other's mind; but how shall my friend revere the truth in my mind when I myself am careless about it, when I believe things because I want to believe them, and because they are comforting and pleasant? Will he not learn to cry, "Peace," to me, when there is no peace? By such a course I shall surround myself with a thick atmosphere of falsehood and fraud, and in that I must live. It may matter little to me, in my cloud-castle of sweet illusions and darling lies; but it matters much to Man that I have made my neighbors ready to deceive. The credulous man is father to the liar and the cheat; he lives in the bosom of this his family, and it is no marvel if he should become even as they are. So closely are our duties knit together, that whoso shall keep the whole law, and yet offend in one point, he is guilty of all.

To sum up: it is wrong always, everywhere, and for anyone, to believe anything upon insufficient evidence.

If a man, holding a belief which he was taught in childhood or persuaded of afterwards, keeps down and pushes away any doubts which arise about it in his mind, purposely avoids the reading of books and the company of men that call in question or discuss it, and regards as impious those questions which cannot easily be asked without disturbing it—the life of that man is one long sin against mankind.

X.2 *The Will to Believe*

William James

William James (1842–1910), a U.S. philosopher and psychologist, was born in New York City and educated at Harvard. He was the brother of Henry James, the novelist. William James struggled through much of his life with ill health. He was assailed by doubts over freedom of the will and the existence of God, and he developed the philosophy of pragmatism in part as a response to these difficulties. His principal works are *The Principles of Psychology* (1890), *The Varieties of Religious Experience* (1902), and *The Will to Believe* (1897), from which this selection is taken.

This essay has been regarded as the classic response to Clifford's ethics of belief (see the previous reading). James argues that life would be greatly impoverished if we confined our beliefs to such a Scrooge-like epistemology as Clifford proposes. In everyday life, where the evidence for important propositions is often unclear, we must live by faith or cease to act at all. Although we may not make leaps of faith just anywhere, sometimes practical considerations force us to make a decision regarding propositions that do not have their truth value written on their faces. 'Belief' is defined as a live, momentous optional hypothesis, on which we cannot avoid a decision, for not to choose is, in effect, to choose against the hypothesis. James claims that religion may be such an optional hypothesis for many people, and where it is, the individual has the right to believe the better story rather than the worse. To do so, he or she must will to believe what the evidence alone is inadequate to support.

I

Let us give the name of hypothesis to anything that may be proposed to our belief; and just as the electricians speak of live and dead wires, let us speak of any hypothesis as either *live* or dead. A live hypothesis is one which appeals as a real possibility to him to whom it is proposed. If I ask you to believe in the Mahdi, the notion makes no electric connection with your nature—it refuses to scintillate with any credibility at all. As an hypothesis it is completely

Reprinted from William James, *The Will to Believe* (New York: Longmans, Green & Co., 1897).

dead. To an Arab, however (even if he be not one of the Mahdi's followers), the hypothesis is among the mind's possibilities: It is alive. This shows that deadness and liveness in an hypothesis are not intrinsic properties, but relations to the individual thinker. They are measured by his willingness to act. The maximum of liveness in an hypothesis means willingness to act irrevocably. Practically, that means belief; but there is some believing tendency wherever there is willingness to act at all.

Next, let us call the decision between two hypotheses an *option*. Options may be of several kinds. They may be first, *living* or *dead*; secondly, *forced* or *avoidable*; thirdly, *momentous* or *trivial*; and for our purposes we may call an option a *genuine* option when it is of a forced, living, and momentous kind.

1. A living option is one in which both hypotheses are live ones. If I say to you: "Be a theosophist or be a Mohammedan," it is probably a dead option, because for you neither hypothesis is likely to be alive. But if I say: "Be an agnostic or be a Christian," it is otherwise: trained as you are, each hypothesis makes some appeal, however small, to your belief.

2. Next, if I say to you: "Choose between going out with your umbrella or without it," I do not offer you a genuine option, for it is not forced. You can easily avoid it by not going out at all. Similarly, if I say, "Either love me or hate me," "Either call my theory true or call it false," your option is avoidable. You may remain indifferent to me, neither loving nor hating, and you may decline to offer any judgment as to my theory. But if I say, "Either accept this truth or go without it," I put on you a forced option, for there is no standing place outside of the alternative. Every dilemma based on a complete logical disjunction, with no possibility of not choosing, is an option of this forced kind.

3. Finally, if I were Dr. Nansen and proposed to you to join my North Pole expedition, your option would be momentous; for this would probably be your singular opportunity, and your choice now would either exclude you from the North Pole sort of immortality altogether or put at least the chance of it into your hands. He who refuses to embrace a unique opportunity loses the prize as surely as if he tried and failed. *Per contra*, the option is trivial when the opportunity is not unique, when the stake is insignificant, or when the decision is reversible if it later prove unwise. Such trivial options abound in the scientific life. A chemist finds an hypothesis live enough to spend a year in its verification: he believes in it to that extent. But if his experiments prove inconclusive either way, he is quit for his loss of time, no vital harm being done.

It will facilitate our discussion if we keep all these distinctions well in mind.

II

The next matter to consider is the actual psychology of human opinion. When we look at certain facts, it seems as if our passional and volitional nature lay at the root of all our convictions. When we look at others, it seems as if they could do nothing when the intellect had once said its say. Let us take the latter facts up first.

Does it not seem preposterous on the very face of it to talk of our opinions being modifiable at will? Can our will either help or hinder our intellect in its perceptions of truth? Can we, by just willing it, believe that Abraham Lincoln's existence is a myth, and that the portraits of him in *McClure's Magazine* are all of some one else? Can we, by any effort of our will, or by any strength of wish that it were true, believe ourselves well and about when we are roaring with rheumatism in bed, or feel certain that the sum of the two one-dollar bills in our pocket must be a hundred dollars? We can say any of these things, but we are absolutely impotent to believe them; and of just such things is the whole fabric of the truths that we do believe in made up—matters of fact, immediate or remote, as Hume said, and relations between ideas, which are either there or not there for us if we see them so, and which if not there cannot be put there by any action of our own.

In Pascal's *Thoughts* there is a celebrated passage known in literature as Pascal's wager. In it he tries to force us into Christianity by reasoning as if our concern with truth resembled our concern with the stakes in a game of chance. Translated freely his words are these: You must either believe or not believe that God is—which will you do? Your human reason cannot say. A game is going on between you and the nature of things which at the day of judgment will bring out either heads or tails. Weigh what your gains and your losses would be if you should stake all you have on heads, or God's existence: if you win in such case, you gain eternal beatitude; if you lose, you lose nothing at all. If there were an infinity of chances, and only one for God in this wager, still you ought to stake your all on God; for though you surely risk a finite loss by this procedure, any finite loss is reasonable, even a certain one is reasonable, if there is but the possibility of infinite gain. Go, then, and take holy water, and have masses said; belief will come and stupefy your scruples. . . . Why should you not? At bottom, what have you to lose?

You probably feel that when religious faith expresses itself thus, in the language of the gaming-table, it is put to its last trumps. Surely Pascal's own personal belief in masses and holy water had far other springs; and this celebrated page of his is but an argument for others, a last desperate snatch at a weapon against the hardness of the unbelieving heart. We feel that a faith in masses and holy water adopted wilfully after such a mechanical calculation would lack the inner soul of faith's reality; and if we were ourselves in the place of the Deity, we should probably take particular pleasure in cutting off believers of this pattern from their infinite reward. It is evident that unless there be some preexisting tendency to believe in masses and holy water, the option offered to the will by Pascal is not a living option. Certainly no Turk ever took to masses and holy water on its account; and even to us Protestants these means of salvation seem such foregone impossibilities that Pascal's logic, invoked for them specifically, leaves us unmoved. As well might the Mahdi write to us, saying, "I am the Expected One whom God has created in his effulgence. You shall be infinitely happy if you confess me; otherwise you shall be cut off from the light of the sun. Weigh, then, your infinite gain if I am genuine against your finite sacrifice if I am not!" His logic would be that of Pascal; but he would vainly use it on us, for the hypothesis he offers us is dead. No tendency to act on it exists in us to any degree.

The talk of believing by our volition seems, then, from one point of view, simply silly. From another point of view it is worse than silly, it is vile. When one turns to the magnificent edifice of the physical sciences, and sees how it was reared; what thousands of disinterested moral lives of men lie buried in its mere foundations; what patience and postponement, what choking down of preference, what submission to the icy laws of outer fact are wrought into its very stones and mortar; how absolutely impersonal it stands in its vast augustness— then how besotted and contemptible seems every little sentimentalist who comes blowing his voluntary smoke-wreaths, and pretending to decide things from out of his private dream! Can we wonder if those bred in the rugged and manly school of science should feel like spewing such subjectivism out of their mouths? The whole system of loyalties which grow up in the schools of science go dead against its toleration; so that it is only natural that those who have caught the scientific fever should pass over to the opposite extreme, and write sometimes as if the incorruptibly truthful intellect ought positively to prefer bitterness and unacceptableness to the heart in its cup.

> It fortifies my soul to know
> That though I perish, Truth is so

sings Clough, while Huxley exclaims: "My only consolation lies in the reflection that, however bad our posterity may become, so far as they hold by the plain rule of not pretending to believe what they have no reason to believe, because it may be to their advantage so to pretend [the word 'pretend' is surely here redundant], they will not have reached the lowest depth of immorality." And that delicious *enfant terrible* Clifford writes: "Belief is desecrated when given to unproved and unquestioned statements for the solace and private pleasure of the believer. . . . Whoso would deserve well of his fellows in this matter will guard the purity of his belief with a very fanaticism of jealous care, lest at any time it should rest on an unworthy object, and catch a stain which can never be wiped away. . . . If [a] belief has been accepted on insufficient evidence [even though the belief be true, as Clifford on the same page explains] the pleasure is a stolen one. . . . It is sinful because it is stolen in defiance of our duty to mankind. That duty is to guard ourselves from such beliefs as from a pestilence which may shortly master our own body and then spread to the rest of the town. . . . It is wrong always, everywhere, and for every one, to believe anything upon insufficient evidence."

III

All this strikes one as healthy, even when expressed, as by Clifford, with somewhat too much of robustious pathos in the voice. Free will and simple wishing do seem, in the matter of our credences, to be only fifth wheels to the coach. Yet if any one should thereupon assume that intellectual insight is what remains after wish and will and sentimental preference have taken wing, or that pure reason is what then settles our opinions, he would fly quite as directly in the teeth of facts.

It is only our already dead hypotheses that our willing nature is unable to bring to life again. But what has made them dead for us is for the most part a previous action of our willing nature of an antagonistic kind. When I say "willing nature," I do not mean only such deliberate volitions as may have set up habits of belief that we cannot now escape from—I mean all such factors of belief as fear and hope, prejudice and passion, imitation and partisanship, the circumpressure of our caste and set. As a matter of fact, we find ourselves believing, we hardly know how or why. Mr. Balfour gives the name of "authority" to all those influences, born of the intellectual climate, that make hypotheses possible or impossible for us, alive or dead. Here in this room, we all of us believe in molecules and the conservation of energy, in democracy and necessary progress, in Protestant Christianity and the duty of fighting for "the doctrine of the immortal Monroe," all for no reasons worthy of the name. We see into these matters with no more inner clearness, and probably with much less, than any disbeliever in them might possess. His unconventionality would probably have some grounds to show for its conclusions; but for us, not insight, but the *prestige* of the opinions, is what makes the spark shoot from them and light up our sleeping magazines of faith. Our reason is quite satisfied, in nine hundred and ninety-nine cases out of every thousand of us, if it can find a few arguments that will do to recite in case our credulity is criticized by some one else. Our faith is faith in some one else's faith, and in the greatest matters this is the most the case. . . .

Evidently, then our non-intellectual nature does influence our convictions. There are passional tendencies and volitions which run before and others which come after belief, and it is only the latter that are too late for the fair; and they are not too late when the previous passional work has been already in their own direction. Pascal's argument, instead of being powerless, then seems a regular clincher, and is the last stroke needed to make our faith in masses and holy water complete. The state of things is evidently far from simple; and pure insight and

logic, whatever they might do ideally, are not the only things that really do produce our creeds.

IV

Our next duty, having recognized this mixedup state of affairs, is to ask whether it be simply reprehensible and pathological, or whether, on the contrary, we must treat it as a normal element in making up our minds. The thesis I defend is, briefly stated, this: *Our passional nature not only lawfully may, but must, decide an option between propositions, whenever it is a genuine option that cannot by its nature be decided on intellectual grounds; for to say, under such circumstances, "Do not decide, but leave the question open," is itself a passional decision—just like deciding yes or no—and is attended with the same risk of losing the truth.* . . .

VII

One more point, small but important, and our preliminaries are done. There are two ways of looking at our duty in the matter of opinion—ways entirely different, and yet ways about whose difference the theory of knowledge seems hitherto to have shown very little concern. *We must know the truth;* and *we must avoid error*—these are our first and great commandments as would-be knowers; but they are not two ways of stating an identical commandment, they are two separable laws. Although it may indeed happen that when we believe the truth A, we escape as an incidental consequence from believing the falsehood B, it hardly ever happens that by merely disbelieving B we necessarily believe A. We may in escaping B fall into believing other falsehoods, C or D, just as bad as B; or we may escape B by not believing anything at all, not even A.

Believe truth! Shun error!—these, we see, are two materially different laws; and by choosing between them we may end by coloring differently our whole intellectual life. We may regard the chase for truth as paramount, and the avoidance of error as secondary; or we may, on the other hand, treat the avoidance of error as more imperative, and let truth take its chance. Clifford, in the instructive passage which I have quoted, exhorts us to the latter course. Believe nothing, he tells us, keep you mind in suspense forever, rather than by closing it on insufficient evidence incur the awful risk of believing lies. You, on the other hand, may think that the risk of being in error is a very small matter when compared with the blessings of real knowledge, and be ready to be duped many times in your investigation rather than postpone indefinitely the chance of guessing true. I myself find it impossible to go with Clifford. We must remember that these feelings of our duty about either truth or error are in any case only expressions of our passional life. Biologically considered, our minds are as ready to grind out falsehood as veracity, and he who says, "Better go without belief forever than believe a lie!" merely shows his own preponderant private horror of becoming a dupe. He may be critical of many of his desires and fears, but this fear he slavishly obeys. He cannot imagine any one questioning its binding force. For my own part, I have also a horror of being duped; but I can believe that worse things than being duped may happen to a man in this world: so Clifford's exhortation has to my ears a thoroughly fantastic sound. It is like a general informing his soldiers that it is better to keep out of battle forever than to risk a single wound. Not so are victories either over enemies or over nature gained. Our errors are surely not such awfully solemn things. In a world where we are so certain to incur them in spite of all our caution, a certain lightness of heart seems healthier than this excessive nervousness on their behalf. At any rate, it seems the fittest thing for the empiricist philosopher.

VIII

And now, after all this introduction, let us go straight at our question. I have said, and now repeat it, that not only as a matter of fact do we find our passional nature influencing us in our opinions, but that there are some options between opinions in which this influence must be regarded both as an inevitable and as a lawful determinant of our choice.

I fear here that some of you my hearers will begin to scent danger, and lend an inhospitable ear. Two first steps of passion you have indeed had to admit as necessary—we must think so as to avoid dupery, and we must think so as to gain truth; but the surest path to those ideal consummations, you will probably consider, is from now onwards to take no further passional step.

Well, of course, I agree as far as the facts will allow. Wherever the option between losing truth and gaining it is not momentous, we can throw the chance of *gaining truth* away, and at any rate save ourselves from any chance of *believing falsehood*, by not making up our minds at all till objective evidence has come. In scientific questions, this is almost always the case; and even in human affairs in general, the need of acting is seldom so urgent that a false belief to act on is better than no belief at all. Law courts, indeed, have to decide on the best evidence attainable for the moment, because a judge's duty is to make law as well as to ascertain it, and (as a learned judge once said to me) few cases are worth spending much time over: the great thing is to have them decided on *any* acceptable principle, and got out of the way. But in our dealings with objective nature we obviously are recorders, not makers, of the truth; and decisions for the mere sake of deciding promptly and getting on to the next business would be wholly out of place. Throughout the breadth of physical nature facts are what they are quite independently of us, and seldom is there any such hurry about them that the risks of being duped by believing a premature theory need be faced. The questions here are always trivial options, the hypotheses are hardly living (at any rate not living for us spectators), the choice between believing truth or falsehood is seldom forced. The attitude of sceptical balance is therefore the absolutely wise one if we would escape mistakes. What difference, indeed, does it make to most of us whether we have or have not a theory of the Röntgen rays, whether we believe or not in mind-stuff, or have a conviction about the causality of conscious states? It makes no difference. Such options are not forced on us. On every account it is better not to make them, but still keep weighing reasons *pro et contra* with an indifferent hand.

I speak, of course, here of the purely judging mind. For purposes of discovery such indifference is to be less highly recommended, and science would be far less advanced than she is if the passionate desires of individuals to get their own faiths confirmed had been kept out of the game. See for example the sagacity which Spencer and Weismann now display. On the other hand, if you want an absolute duffer in an investigation, you must, after all, take the man who has no interest whatever in its results: he is the warranted incapable, the positive fool. The most useful investigator, because the most sensitive observer, is always he whose eager interest in one side of the question is balanced by an equally keen nervousness lest he become deceived. Science has organized this nervousness into a regular *technique,* her so-called method of verification; and she has fallen so deeply in love with the method that one may even say she has ceased to care for truth by itself at all. It is only truth as technically verified that interests her. The truth of truths might come in merely affirmative form, and she would decline to touch it. Such truth as that, she might repeat with Clifford, would be stolen in defiance of her duty to mankind. Human passions, however, are stronger than technical rules. "*Le coeur a ses raisons,*" as Pascal says, "*que la raison ne connait pas*", and however indifferent to all but the bare rules of the game the umpire, the abstract intellect, may be, the concrete players who furnish him the materials to judge of are usually, each one of them, in love with some pet "live hypothesis" of his own. Let us agree, however, that wherever there is no forced option, the dispassionately judicial intellect with no pet hypothesis, saving us, as it does, from dupery at any rate, ought to be our ideal.

The question next arises: Are there not somewhere forced options in our speculative questions, and can we (as men who may be interested at least as much in positively gaining truth as in merely escaping dupery) always wait with impunity till the coercive evidence shall have arrived? It seems *a priori* improbable that the truth should be so nicely adjusted to our needs and powers as that. In the great boarding-house of nature, the cakes and the butter and the syrup seldom come out so even and leave the plates so clean. Indeed, we should view them with scientific suspicion if they did.

IX

Moral questions immediately present themselves as questions whose solution cannot wait for sensible proof. A moral question is a question not of what sensibly exists, but of what is good, or would be good if it did exist. Science can tell us what exists; but to compare the *worths,* both of what exists and of what does not exist, we must consult not science, but what Pascal calls our heart. . . .

Turn now from these wide questions of good to a certain class of questions of fact, questions concerning personal relations, states of mind between one man and another. *Do you like me or not?*— for example. Whether you do or not depends, in countless instances, on whether I meet you halfway, am willing to assume that you must like me, and show you trust and expectation. The previous faith on my part in your liking's existence is in such cases what makes your liking come. But if I stand aloof, and refuse to budge an inch until I have objective evidence, until you shall have done something apt, as the absolutists say, *ad extorquendum assensum meum,* ten to one your liking never comes. How many women's hearts are vanquished by the mere sanguine insistence of some man that they *must* love him! He will not consent to the hypothesis that they cannot. The desire for a certain kind of truth here brings about that special truth's existence; and so it is in innumerable cases of other sorts. . . . *And where faith in a fact can help create the fact,* that would be an insane logic which should say that faith running ahead of scientific evidence is the "lowest kind of immorality" into which a thinking being can fall. Yet such is the logic by which our scientific absolutists pretend to regulate our lives!

X

In truths dependent on our personal action, then, faith based on desire is certainly a lawful and possibly an indispensable thing.

But now, it will be said, these are all childish human cases, and have nothing to do with great cosmical matters, like the question of religious faith. Let us then pass on to that. Religions differ so much in their accidents that in discussing the religious question we must make it very generic and broad. What then do we now mean by the religious hypothesis? Science says things are; morality says some things are better than other things; and religion says essentially two things.

First, she says that the best things are the more eternal things, the overlapping things, the things in the universe that throw the last stone, so to speak, and say the final word. "Perfection is eternal"—this phrase of Charles Secrétan seems a good way of putting this first affirmation of religion, an affirmation which obviously cannot yet be verified scientifically at all.

The second affirmation of religion is that we are better off even now if we believe her first affirmation to be true.

Now, let us consider what the logical elements of this situation are *in case the religious hypothesis in both its branches be really true.* (Of course, we must admit that possibility at the outset. If we are to discuss the question at all, it must involve a living option. If for any of you religion be a hypothesis that cannot, by any living possibility, be true, then you need go no farther. I speak to the "saving remnant" alone.) So proceeding, we see, first, that religion offers itself as a *momentous* option. We are supposed to gain, even now, by our belief, and to lose by our non-belief, a certain vital good. Secondly, religion is a *forced* option, so far as that good goes. We cannot escape the issue by remaining sceptical and waiting for more light, because, although we do avoid error in that way *if religion be untrue,* we lose the good, *if it be true,* just as certainly as if we positively chose to disbelieve. It is as if a man should hesitate indefinitely to ask a certain woman to marry him because he was not perfectly sure that she would prove an angel after he brought her home. Would he not cut himself off from that particular angel-possibility as decisively as if he went and married some one else? Scepticism, then, is not avoidance of option; it is option of a certain particular kind of risk. *Better risk loss of truth than chance of error*—that is your faith-vetoer's exact position. He is actively playing his stake as much as the believer is; he is backing the field against the reli-

gious hypothesis, just as the believer is backing the religious hypothesis against the field. To preach scepticism to us as a duty until "sufficient evidence" for religion be found, is tantamount therefore to telling us, when in presence of the religious hypothesis, that to yield to our fear of its being error is wiser and better than to yield to our hope that it may be true. It is not intellect against all passions, then; it is only intellect with one passion laying down its law. And by what, forsooth, is the supreme wisdom of this passion warranted? Dupery for dupery, what proof is there that dupery through hope is so much worse than dupery through fear? I, for one, can see no proof; and I simply refuse obedience to the scientist's command to imitate his kind of option, in a case where my own stake is important enough to give me the right to choose my own form of risk. If religion be true and the evidence for it be still insufficient, I do not wish, by putting your extinguisher upon my nature (which feels to me as if it had after all some business in this matter), to forfeit my sole chance in life of getting upon the winning side—that chance depending, of course, on my willingness to run the risk of acting as if my passional need of taking the world religiously might be prophetic and right.

All this is on the supposition that it really may be prophetic and right, and that, even to us who are discussing the matter, religion is a live hypothesis which may be true. Now, to most of us religion comes in a still further way that makes a veto on our active faith even more illogical. The more perfect and more eternal aspect of the universe is represented in our religions as having personal form. The universe is no longer a mere *It* to us, but a *Thou,* if we are religious; and any relation that may be possible from person to person might be possible here. For instance, although in one sense we are passive portions of the universe, in another we show a curious autonomy, as if we were small active centers on our own account. We feel, too, as if the appeal of religion to us were made to our own active good-will, as if evidence might be forever withheld from us unless we met the hypothesis halfway to take a trivial illustration: just as a man who in a company of gentlemen made no advances, asked a warrant for every concession, and believed no one's word without proof, would cut himself off by such churlishness from all the social rewards that a more trusting spirit would earn—so here, one who should shut himself up in snarling logicality and try to make the gods extort his recognition willy-nilly, or not get it at all, might cut himself off forever from his only opportunity of making the gods' acquaintance. This feeling, forced on us we know not whence that by obstinately believing that there are gods (although not to do so would be so easy both for our logic and our life) we are doing the universe the deepest service we can, seems part of the living essence of the religious hypothesis. If the hypothesis *were* true in all its parts, including this one, then pure intellectualism, with its veto on our making willing advances, would be an absurdity; and some participation of our sympathetic nature would be logically required. I therefore, for one, cannot see my way to accepting the agnostic rules for truth-seeking, or wilfully agree to keep my willing nature out of the game. I cannot do so for this plain reason, that *a rule of thinking which would absolutely prevent me from acknowledging certain kinds of truth if those kinds of truth were really there, would be an irrational rule.* That for me is the long and short of the formal logic of the situation, no matter what the kinds of truth might materially be.

I confess I do not see how this logic can be escaped. But sad experience makes me fear that some of you may still shrink from radically saying with me *in abstracto,* that we have the right to believe at our own risk any hypothesis that is live enough to tempt our will. I suspect, however, that if this is so, it is because you have go away from the abstract logical point of view altogether, and are thinking (perhaps without realizing it) of some particular religious hypothesis which for you is dead. The freedom to "believe what we will" you apply to the case of some patent superstition; and the faith you think of is the faith defined by the schoolboy when he said, "Faith is when you believe something that you know ain't true." I can only repeat that this is misapprehension. *In concreto,* the freedom to believe can only cover living options which the intellect of the individual cannot by itself resolve; and living options never seem absurdities to him who has them to consider. When I look at the religious question as it really puts itself to concrete men, and when I think of all the possibilities which both

practically and theoretically it involves, then this command that we shall put a stopper on our heart, instincts, and courage, and *wait*—acting of course meanwhile more or less as if religion were not true—till doomsday, or till such time as our intellect and senses working together may have raked in evidence enough—this command, I say, seems to me the queerest idol ever manufactured in the philosophic cave. Were we scholastic absolutists, there might be more excuse. If we had an infallible intellect with its objective certitudes, we might feel ourselves disloyal to such a perfect organ of knowledge in not trusting to it exclusively, in not waiting for its releasing word. But if we are empiricists, if we believe that no bell in us tolls to let us know for certain when truth is in our grasp, then it seems a piece of idle fantasticality to preach so solemnly our duty of waiting for the bell. Indeed we *may* wait if we will—I hope you do not think that I am denying that—but if we do so, we do so at our peril as much as if we believed. In either case we *act,* taking our life in our hands. No one of us ought to issue vetoes to the other, nor should we bandy words of abuse. We ought, on the contrary, delicately and profoundly to respect one another's mental freedom: then only shall we bring about the intellectual republic; then only shall we have that spirit of inner tolerance without which all our outer tolerance is soulless, and which is empiricism's glory; then only shall we live and let live, in speculative as well as in practical things.

I began by a reference to Fitz-James Stephen; let me end by a quotation from him. "What do you think of yourself? What do you think of the world? . . . These are questions with which all must deal as it seems good to them. They are riddles of the Sphinx, and in some way or other we must deal with them. . . . In all important transactions of life we have to take a leap in the dark. . . . If we decide to leave the riddles unanswered, that is a choice; if we waver in our answer, that, too, is a choice: but whatever choice we make, we make it at our peril. If a man chooses to turn his back altogether on God and the future, no one can prevent him; no one can show beyond reasonable doubt that he is mistaken. If a man thinks otherwise and acts as he thinks, I do not see that any one can prove that he is mistaken. Each must act as he thinks best;

and if he is wrong, so much the worse for him. We stand on a mountain pass in the midst of whirling snow and blinding mist, through which we get glimpses now and then of paths which may be deceptive. If we stand still we shall be frozen to death. If we take the wrong road we shall be dashed to pieces. We do not certainly know whether there is any right one. What must we do? 'Be strong and of a good courage.' Act for the best, hope for the best, and take what comes.

. . . If death ends all, we cannot meet death better."

X.3 *What Ought We to Believe?*

JACK MEILAND

Jack Meiland is Professor of Philosophy at the University of Michigan. In this selection he argues that we have no special duties to believe according to the evidence, but that every epistemic state must be judged from the perspective of our moral duties. The only ethics of belief are ethical concerns *per se*. In every prospective belief acquisition, we need to ask not what the evidence demands, but what our moral commitments demand.

Lady Britomart: Barbara, I positively forbid you to listen to your father's abominable wickedness. And you, Adolphus, ought to know better than to go about saying that wrong things are true. What does it matter whether they are true if they are wrong?
Undershaft: What does it matter whether they are wrong if they are true?

—GEORGE BERNARD SHAW
Major Barbara, Act III

One of the cornerstones of modern Western thought is the doctrine that belief ought to be based solely on sufficient evidence. John Passmore puts it in this way:

> Modern philosophy was founded on the doctrine, uncompromisingly formulated by Descartes, that to think philosophically is to accept as true only that which recommends itself to Reason. To be unphilosophical, in contrast, is to be seduced by the enticements of Will, which beckons men beyond the boundaries laid down by Reason into the wilderness of error. In England, Locke had acclimatized this Cartesian ideal. There is 'one unerring mark,' he wrote, 'by which a man may know whether he is a lover of truth for truth's sake:' namely '*the not entertaining any proposition with greater assurance than the proofs it is built upon will warrant.*'

Reprinted from "What Ought We to Believe? or the Ethics of Belief Revisited," *American Philosophical Quarterly,* vol. 17, 1980 by permission.

Nineteenth-century agnosticism reaffirmed this Lockean dictum, with a striking degree of moral fervor. The *locus classicus* is a passage in W. K. Clifford's 'The Ethics of Belief:' 'It is wrong everywhere and for anyone, to believe anything upon insufficient evidence.'[1]

Of course, this doctrine has a more ancient pedigree than Passmore indicates. One way of interpreting Plato's Socrates yields this same ideal about belief:

> Socrates astonished, fascinated and exasperated his fellow Athenians. He seems to have been, as nearly as possible, the completely rational man. What is reasonable to believe is what the evidence warrants; what is reasonable to do is what is conducive to the highest good. How could this be otherwise? Furthermore, how could you not believe and act according to the dictates of reason; are you not, after all, a rational being?[2]

The doctrine expressed in these passages is a normative doctrine. It tell us what is reasonable or rational, and it urges us to do the reasonable or rational thing as it is here described. We may put this doctrine in the following way: belief in a factual issue may legitimately be based only (solely and wholly) on considerations of evidential fact. Let us call this doctrine "evidentialism."[3] Expressed in normative principles, this doctrine is: (i) one ought not to believe on insufficient evidence; (ii) one ought to believe whatever is backed by sufficient evidence. I want to examine this normative doctrine about belief.

I

Suppose that Jones and Smith have been business partners and exceptionally close friends for more than thirty-five years. One day Jones discovers a discrepancy in the business's accounts. Upon investigation he comes into the possession of evidence which is sufficient (in anyone's eyes) to justify the belief that Smith has been secretly syphoning off money from the business. Now Jones is in the fol-

lowing predicament. He is, and knows that he is, the type of person who is unable to conceal his feelings and beliefs from others. He thus knows that if he decides that Smith has indeed been stealing money from the firm, it will definitely affect his behavior toward Smith. Even if Jones tries to conceal his belief, he knows that he will inevitably act in a remote, cold, censorious and captious manner toward Smith and that eventually both the friendship and the business partnership will break up. Jones decides that this price is too high and therefore decides not to believe that Smith stole money from the firm. In fact, he goes farther: he decides that Smith did not steal money from the firm.

I take this to be a clear violation of the normative principle that one should believe whatever is backed by sufficient evidence (where it is, of course, understood that this principle assumes that the person has this evidence and is aware of the relation between this evidence and the proposition in question). Other realistic examples of this sort are not hard to find. Take the classical case in which a wife finds a blonde hair on her husband's coat, a handkerchief with lipstick on it in his pocket, a scrap of paper with a phone number scrawled on it, and so on until everyone would agree that the evidence is sufficient that the husband has been seeing another woman. However, the wife believes that their marriage is basically sound and can weather this storm. Like Jones, she knows that she cannot conceal her suspicions and hence decides to believe that her husband is not being unfaithful to her. And let us further suppose that in these two examples, things turn out as hoped. The money stops disappearing, and Jones and Smith remain fast friends and partners for many years thereafter. The husband eventually stops seeing the other woman, becomes more attentive to his wife, and the marriage continues stronger than ever for many years. In these circumstances, it does *not* seem to me right to say that Jones and the wife should have believed Smith and the husband to be guilty just because there was sufficient evidence to justify these beliefs. And even if the partnership and the marriage did not last, I think that Jones and the wife were *not* wrong (as W. K. Clifford puts it) to hold beliefs (that Smith and the husband were innocent) on the basis of insufficient evidence. Moreover, these beliefs do not seem to me to be unreasonable or irrational in the least. If things do turn out as Jones and the wife hope, then some very precious things—a strong friendship, a good marriage—will have been preserved by their having certain beliefs even though the evidence is insufficient.

Thus, the doctrine of evidentialism—that belief should be determined solely by factual evidence—seems to me in general to be unacceptable.

One objection that is likely to arise is this. "Jones and the wife did not have to believe that Smith and the husband were innocent in order to achieve the results they desired. Instead, Jones and the wife could have believed them to be guilty, or at least suspected them of guilt, and yet ignored these beliefs or suspicions. This would preserve the evidentialist principle about belief and at the same time secure the desirable results." This objection simply ignores an important feature of the case, namely that Jones and the wife just are not people who can ignore these things. We all know people who are unable to dissemble about matters close to their hearts. So I do not take these examples to be at all unrealistic, and this objection can be safely dismissed.

Two more interesting objections are these. First, it may be claimed that Jones and the wife are engaging in "rationalization," and that rationalizing is a very bad practice. Hence, we should not consider them to have done the right thing in adopting these beliefs. However, I do not think that they are engaging in this practice, at least if we understand rationalization to be the practice of holding certain beliefs because they are expedient by allowing the person to mask his or her true motivations from him or herself. In these examples, Jones and the wife are very clear about their motivations: they are adopting certain beliefs in order to save their friendship or marriage. Second, it might be objected that Jones and the wife are engaging in self-deception. They are deceiving themselves about the true nature of Smith's behavior or the husband's behavior by deliberately adopting these beliefs. I think that this charge lacks force too, for the reasons just given. They know that the evidence is sufficient for the belief that Smith and the husband are guilty and they are not hiding this fact from themselves. But suppose that we accept, for the sake of argument, that they are deceiving themselves about this matter. I believe that this only shifts the question—

from whether it is wrong to believe on the basis of insufficient evidence to the question of whether self-deception is always wrong.

II

Another, quite different, sort of objection runs as follows: "Your position treats believing as though it were some kind of voluntary action, as though one could decide to believe *p* or not to believe *p*. But in fact, believing is not voluntary. One either does believe *p* or does not believe *p* depending on whether the facts or information at one's disposal coerce one into believing. Since believing is not a voluntary matter, we cannot decide whether or not to believe *p*." I think that this is an important objection because it does bring out that feature of my position, namely that I take belief to be, in some cases at least, a voluntary matter. But one thing to notice initially is that my position shares this feature with the evidentialist position as exemplified by Passmore's quotation from Clifford. When Clifford says that it is wrong to believe on the basis of insufficient evidence, I take him to be making a moral judgment. (Passmore also takes Clifford in this way—hence Passmore's talk about "moral fervor.") If we accept that "ought" implies "can," then Clifford has no business telling us that we ought to believe only on the basis of sufficient evidence unless he too thinks that belief is in these cases a voluntary matter. Hence the above objection is an objection to both the evidentialist position and my own position. Evidentialists should take note of this.

In order to deal with this objection, we must distinguish various situations in which belief occurs. The kind of situation with which we are principally concerned is that in which the evidence is sufficient. I take "sufficient" here to mean that the evidence justifies the belief. If the wife believed that her husband is deceiving her solely on the basis of a handerkerchief with lipstick on it, we would say that her belief is not justified. There are many other reasonable explanations of why he has a handkerchief with lipstick on it in his pocket, and thus the evidence is not sufficient to justify her belief. This belief is not a reasonable one if this is the only evidence for it. On the other hand, if the wife discovers her husband in the arms of another woman, we would probably say that the evidence is more than sufficient. We would say that the evidence is incontrovertible or conclusive. Here the belief is not only justified but almost forced upon the wife. Now, in this discussion I am considering only cases which lie between these two extremes—that is, situations in which the belief is reasonable or justified on the evidence but in which one is not forced to have that belief by the "evidence."

Given these distinctions, we can see that the objector is telling us this: every situation in which the evidence is sufficient is a situation in which belief is forced upon the person. The objector is denying that there is a middle ground between unreasonable (unjustified) belief on the one hand and forced belief on the other hand. I believe that the objector is wrong. Consider this case: a jury, having heard the evidence, convicts a person of a crime; the defendant's attorney, however, remains dubious of the verdict and, after several years of further investigation, turns up conclusive evidence of his client's innocence; nevertheless, at the time of the trial, everyone (including the defense attorney) who had followed the trial closely believed the jury's verdict to be fair and eminently justified. Now, my point here is *not* that a belief can be justified (be supported by sufficient evidence) and yet turn out to be false. Instead, my point is that a person (in this example, the defense attorney) can be in possession of evidence which everyone (including himself) agrees is sufficient to justify a certain belief (that his client is guilty), that this person can be fully aware of how the evidence is related to that belief (thus ruling out cases in which the person is unaware that the evidence justifies the belief), and yet not have that belief or indeed have the contradictory belief. The defense attorney agrees that the evidence is sufficient and that the trial was perfectly fair, and yet he continues to believe that his client is innocent. Sufficient evidence does not result in some logical or psychological necessity which forces the belief in question upon the person. If the evidence is conclusive and the person realizes this, then perhaps that person must hold that belief. But this is not so if the evidence is less than conclusive, for example sufficient.

III

The problem with which I am dealing in this paper is a problem about facts and values. But it is not the much-discussed problem of whether solely factual statements can justify value statements. Instead, it is the problem of whether value considerations can justify, or help to justify, beliefs about purely factual matters. This question about facts, values, and the justification of belief is just as important as the problem of justifying value statements. As Passmore has pointed out, the view that beliefs about factual matters should be based solely on factual material is a cornerstone of modern rationality. I have tried to show that this modern presupposition is mistaken. Indeed, since I believe that Jones and the wife are being eminently rational in believing "against" the evidence, I think that this modern presupposition is itself irrational.

Why is this modern presupposition (which I have called "evidentialism") about the connection between evidence and belief so wide-spread and pervasive? Some important reasons are not hard to discover.

Probably the most important reason is this. Many people probably feel that if any other factor (than factual evidence) were allowed to be influential in determining belief, belief could become an intensely subjective matter, and people would be out of touch with the real world. People would live in fantasy worlds with very undesirable results. Mere survival would become precarious; and, more generally, people would not be able to achieve the results that they desire. If there is a sabertoothed tiger outside one's cave, and if one does not believe that the tiger is there, one is very likely to be eaten up. This yields a clear application of the principle of the survival of the fittest, with the fittest in this case being those who believe that which is supported by evidence (for example, the low growling noise outside the cave, the previous signs of a tiger in the neighborhood, and so on). Thus, the modern presupposition that we are examining has this strong practical basis.

But if we support this modern presupposition by giving it a practical basis, this has a very important implication, namely that this presupposition is therefore open to a critique based also on "practical" reasons. In particular, we could base such a critique on value considerations which also fall into the realm of the practical, and there would be no possibility that such a critique would be irrelevant. I have tried to suggest the outlines of such a critique in this paper.

This general point about the kinds of considerations which are relevant in evaluating this modern presupposition is put forward with admirable clarity and force by Ralph Barton Perry:

> This being the case, belief becomes a question of conduct. Shall I or shall I not induce in others or in myself beliefs which do not have full evidential warrant? . . . It is clear that over and above the theoretical justification of belief there is here implied a *practical maxim* to the effect that I *ought to promote only beliefs that are theoretically justified,* that is, beliefs that are formally correct and empirically verified. . . . It is extremely difficult to persuade the scientist, trained as he is to accept the compulsions of mathematics and experimentation, to see that the *right* of these compulsions to exclusive control over belief is not itself to be established by such compulsions. . . . It is clear, then, that the inculcation of belief by the employment of its non-evidential causes, on the one hand, and the scrupulous restriction of belief within the limits of evidential proof, on the other, are practical alternatives.[4]

IV

Someone might want to object to what I have said by arguing that in my description of my two cases, I have overlooked some other beliefs which Jones and the wife have and which do obey the principle that one ought to believe whatever has sufficient evidence. For example, one might say of the wife that she believes that if she believes that her husband has not been unfaithful to her, then she will be happier and her marriage might be saved. Now, this belief is one about which it is plausible to say that she has sufficient evidence for it. She need only consult her own feelings and certain general principles (almost truisms) about the behavior of errant husbands. And this is the belief on which she is acting. So she is still acting in an eminently rational way while nevertheless following the principle of sufficient evidence as the sole warrant of belief.

Let us call this more complex belief "B_1." That is, B_1 is the belief that if she believes that her husband has not been unfaithful to her, then she will be happier and her marriage might be saved. Notice that B_1 itself mentions another belief which we will call B_2, namely the belief that her husband has not been unfaithful to her. Let us admit, for the sake of argument, that the wife has sufficient evidence for B_1 and, moreover, believes B_1 on the basis of that evidence. However, it is clear that the wife will actually gain the desirable results of happiness and a rescued marriage only if she does believe B_2—that her husband has not been unfaithful to her—as well. B_1 alone is not sufficient to bring about these desirable results. Consequently, whatever other beliefs she may have on the basis of sufficient evidence, she ought to believe that her husband has not been unfaithful to her—and *that* belief still does not have the backing of sufficient evidence. Thus, it is still the case that her most reasonable or rational course of action in this case is to hold a belief "against" the evidence.

V

Our topic in this paper may appropriately be called "the Ethics of Belief." But there are at least two different projects that can appropriately bear this title. In this and the following sections, I want to specify my project more exactly by differentiating it from another project which has received some attention in the past and then to explain my position by contrasting it with another position in this same area.

One project in the area of the Ethics of Belief is that of *defining* epistemic terms—terms such as "believe," "know," "evident" and so on—by using value, ethical, or "practical" concepts. Thus, A. J.

Ayer has attempted to define "knows" in terms of "has a right to be sure." And Roderick Chisholm has attempted to define "evident" in terms of the notion of obligation.[5]

Another, and quite different, project in this area is an inquiry into the question of whether we have rights or obligations to believe certain propositions where these rights or obligations are determined by value, ethical, or "practical" factors. I am engaged here only in this second type of project. If epistemic terms are definable by the use of value or "practical" concepts, perhaps it would follow that we have rights or duties to believe or to refrain from believing. If so, then these two types of projects would not be logically independent of one another. However, my claim is that however these epistemic terms are to be defined, what we are justified in believing, what it is reasonable to believe, depends at least partly on value and "practical" factors. Thus, I am not concerned with defining epistemic terms but only with the factors that determine these rights and duties. I believe that carrying out this second type of project does not logically imply any position concerning the definition of epistemic terms.[6]

===

VI

In order to see more perspicuously exactly what position I wish to defend and how I defend it, I will first fill in more completely the evidentialist position as it is held or would be agreed to by a great many philosophers, scientists, and other intellectuals today. The evidentialist position maintains that there exists what we might call "purely evidential warrant." That is, evidentialism maintains that a person can be justified or not justified in believing *p* simply on the basis of the evidence alone. In an excellent article on C. I. Lewis' ethics of belief, Chisholm formulates the following "practical syllogism:"

> Anyone having just the evidence in question is warranted in accepting the conclusion.
> I am in the position of having just that evidence.
> Therefore I am justified in accepting the conclusion.[7]

This syllogism illustrates evidentialism very well. Evidentialism agrees that a person can have a right (or even an obligation) to believe *p*, but this right (or obligation) is said to arise solely from the relation between the evidence and the conclusion. There will, of course, be differences among the holders of evidentialism as to the amount and kind of evidence needed and about just what the evidence does or does not justify. For example, one evidentialist might say that one has a right to believe *p* only if the evidence is sufficient, while another evidentialist might say that one has a right to believe *p* just as long as he does not have sufficient evidence for not-*p*. But evidentialists are firmly united in believing that there is an objective justificatory relation between evidence and conclusion which by itself warrants belief and which is the same for everyone (see the major premise of Chisholm's "practical syllogism" quoted above) regardless of any "personal" or "subjective" factors pertaining to the believer.

Evidentialists are united in another doctrine too. They hold that it is not correct to call the act of believing *p* "right" or "wrong" because of the content of the belief. Suppose that there is a belief which many people find distasteful, disgusting, or even vile—for example, the Nazi belief that some people are racially inferior to others. Many evidentialists would criticize people who hold this belief for holding it—saying that it is wrong of these people to believe this—but they would make this criticism solely on the grounds that there is insufficient evidence for this belief. When they say that it is wrong to hold this belief, this can be a moral evaluation. That is, they can be saying that it is morally wrong to hold this Nazi belief. But such evaluation is always based on the relation between evidence and conclusion, not on the content of the belief itself. To put this in another way, evidentialists would maintain that it is morally wrong to hold this Nazi belief but only (for example) on the grounds that it is morally wrong to hold *any* belief for which there is insufficient evidence.

Evidentialism also includes another very important doctrine. Suppose that a person holds this Nazi belief and puts it into practice by, for example, agitating for the deportation of certain racial groups. Evidentialism would allow a person to condemn this action morally, but it would not allow a person to condemn the belief because it led to this agitation. Evidentialism holds that there is a chasm between belief and action such that moral condemnation of the action which stems from that belief does not reach across this chasm and apply to the holding of the belief too. This chasm is founded on the idea that the only factor relevant to the holding of factual beliefs is evidence. It is also founded on the idea that facts have no moral or value character in themselves, and that consequently the holding of factual beliefs should have no such moral character (except in so far as it may be a moral matter to believe on the basis of evidence).

My cases of Jones and Smith, and the husband and wife, are designed specifically to show that this chasm does not exist. The specific feature which I have expressly built into these cases is that Jones and the wife are people whose beliefs automatically or involuntarily influence their actions. They are people who, as we say, cannot in the long run hide their feelings, attitudes, and beliefs. There are such people. But I do not want my case to rest on the existence of a few such people. I think that we are all people like this with respect to some beliefs and some attitudes. Few of us are consummate dissemblers. Many things are not that important to us, and about these things we can hide our true feelings and perhaps fool all of the people all of the time. But I think that for each of us there are some things which we probably cannot hide in the long run. What this shows is that there are cases of a not uncommon sort in which the alleged gap between belief and action simply does not exist. These are cases which the evidentialist position simply cannot handle correctly. The evidentialist position hold that one is morally responsible for actions but not for beliefs (except possibly on a purely epistemic basis). But our cases are cases in which having a certain belief is tantamount to behaving in certain ways. Moreover, if I am right, adopting those beliefs is a voluntary matter.[8] Consequently, moral responsibility and moral predication in general should cross the alleged chasm between behavior and belief. By this I mean that if that behavior is behavior which one ought to prevent oneself from engaging in, and if one can (as I claim) prevent this behavior by adopting a certain belief, then one ought to adopt that belief, apart from the epistemic warrant or lack thereof for that belief. Here I am not concerned

about what kind of "ought" this is (nor am I concerned as to whether it represents obligation). It may be a moral "ought"; it may be prudential; it may be of some other kind. I believe that the argument holds for all of the various kinds of "oughts."

Because evidentialism cannot handle cases like these correctly, I believe that we need a new theory about what we ought to believe.

VII

Another way of seeing the inadequacy of evidentialism is as follows. Evidentialism rests squarely on the notion of "purely evidential warrant." It holds that if there are some types of things which ought or ought not to be believed, this should be determined solely by the state of the evidence. (Consider again Chisholm's major premise: "Anyone having just the evidence in question is warranted in accepting the conclusion.") This seems clearly wrong to me. It seems to me that the justification of belief must depend, at least in part, on the believer's situation. To see this, let's go back to our husband and wife case and add a private detective hired by the wife to investigate her husband's activities. It is easy to imagine a situation in which the detective succeeds in gathering evidence on the basis of which we would say that it is reasonable for him to believe that the husband is seeing another woman. But the very same evidence may not justify the wife in believing this. Because of the relationship between husband and wife in this case, the wife should not lightly or too quickly believe that about her husband. And this is not—or not only—because if she did believe it, she would then act in certain ways. It is not only a matter of not acting hastily; she should also not believe hastily either. Her situation in life requires that she be very careful about this—more careful than, say, her neighbors or her husband's employer or even the private detective. That she and her husband have had a good marriage, full of mutual trust and confidence for fifteen years, requires that any belief on her part that her husband is seeing another woman be based on very, very substantial evidence. Evidentialists will reply that they agree with this and that in fact evidentialism gains support by being able to account for what I have just said. The evidentialist account would be as follows: through living with her husband for fifteen years, the wife has accumulated much evidence that he is not the type of man who would betray his wife with another woman; this is why the wife should not lightly decide that he is unfaithful; but this is sheerly a matter of the weight of evidence on both sides, as evidentialism requires. This account, while formally satisfactory from the evidentialist point of view, strikes me as lacking a proper appreciation of the human reality of this situation. I believe that she has a duty to her husband, arising from their commitment to one another over a long period, to require a stronger basis for belief in his treachery than does, say, the private detective. We might even say "she owes him that." It is not a matter of her having much evidence to the contrary. Instead, it is a matter of obligation toward someone to whom she has been very close.

VIII

At this point, someone might say that my position is ambiguous as between the following two alternatives:

(I) The (weaker) thesis that extra-factual considerations can sometimes be allowed to count as legitimately influencing or determining belief.

(II) The (stronger) thesis that extra-factual considerations should always count (to some extent) in the holding of beliefs.

I think that my position does seem ambiguous as between these because neither of these alternatives exactly captures my position. On the one hand, I want to hold that there can be cases in which what a person should believe is determined solely by the state of the factual evidence. On the other hand, I want to hold that in *all* cases, extra-factual considerations are relevant.

To see what I mean here, suppose that we add another person to our case of the husband and wife. This person has no special relationship to either the husband or the wife and (let us try to imagine) is investigating the question of the husband's infidel-

ity from a totally detached, disinterested point of view. (Perhaps this is just one of a number of cases of suspected infidelity which this person is investigating as part of a research project in social psychology.) In such a case, it seems that this investigator's belief about the supposed infidelity should be determined solely by the factual evidence.

I would agree with this. But I think that in order to judge that this is so, one must find out that this investigator has no special relationship to these people and in general that his situation does not require that he take extra-factual considerations into account. Perhaps we can put this by saying that one role which extra-factual matters should have in the determination of belief is that extra-factual matters should decide whether the person's belief is to be determined solely by factual evidence. Thus, I agree with the weaker thesis (I) that extra-factual considerations should sometimes legitimately influence belief, with its implication that in other cases only the factual evidence should determine belief. Our instance of the detached investigator is one of the latter cases. But I also agree with the stronger thesis (II) that extra-factual considerations should always count (to some extent) in the holding of beliefs, since I believe that extra-factual considerations must always be consulted in order to decide what factors should determine a person's beliefs in a given case.

In saying that there are cases in which a person's beliefs should be determined solely by factual evidence, I may seem to be conceding to the evidentialist everything he wants. For in such cases at least, I seem to be allowing the existence of a purely evidential warranting relation. This question will be taken up further in the next section. But here I think we can see immediately that my position has not merged with that of the evidentialist. Consider again Chisholm's syllogism, and in particular its major premise: "*Anyone* having just the evidence in question is warranted in accepting the conclusion." This is unacceptable to me. The wife and the investigator may have exactly the same factual evidence, and yet one may be thereby warranted in accepting that the husband has been unfaithful while the other is not so warranted.

It is *no* part of my purpose to claim that the state of the evidence never has any bearing on whether a given belief is justified. In that sense, I agree that there is such a thing as purely evidential warrant (where this means only that the evidence has a bearing on whether the belief is justified). What I deny is that evidence by itself can justify belief without consideration of and control by value and situational factors. Even when we are dealing with the case of the detached investigator, we can know that this is such a case, a case in which evidence should determine belief, only by considering value and situational factors. Thus, value and situational factor control the bearing of the evidence in *all* cases. Some cases will be such that the decision will be to allow the evidence to determine belief. And this might give rise to the *mistaken* doctrine that *every* case is a case of this sort. That is, it might give rise to the mistaken doctrine that there is such a thing as purely evidential warrant in the sense in which the evidence is supposed to justify belief apart from any other factor. This is mistaken because simply in order to identify those cases in which evidence should be allowed to determine belief, we must employ value and situational factors.

But, it may be objected, this position ignores certain obvious data which demonstrate a direct, basic, and underivative relationship between evidence and proposition regardless of value and situational factors. Suppose, the objector might continue, that a blonde hair is found on the husband's coat and that this is the total evidence available. The objector would say that it would be unreasonable for anyone, regardless of values or situation, to believe that the husband was seeing another woman. Thus, he would conclude, there is a basic and independent relationship between evidence and proposition which determines the reasonableness, or at least the unreasonableness, of belief. I think that this objection is mistaken, however, because even here one may imagine a situation in which the person should believe that the husband is seeing another woman—a situation in which the stakes are extremely high and the time available very short so that the person ought to go on what evidence he has available, however slim that evidence. Here again, the case is controlled by value and situational factors.

Finally, it must be pointed out that I am urging that extra-factual considerations impinge on the holding of beliefs in *two* different, though related,

ways. First, extra-factual considerations (such as the wife's relationship to her husband, as contrasted with the investigator's lack of relationship to either of them) determine which factors should influence belief. For example, they determine whether a given case is one in which belief should be determined solely by factual evidence. Now, let us suppose that we have a case in which it is decided that belief should *not* be controlled solely by factual evidence. What other factors, then, should influence belief? Here is the second way in which extra-factual considerations should bear on belief: They should influence the selection of a particular belief from the alternative beliefs available. So we may put the matter in this way: extra-factual considerations should be consulted in every case to see which factor should determine belief; and in some of these cases extra-factual considerations will themselves be among the factors that should influence belief. In the case of the wife, her relationship of fifteen years standing to her husband shows that evidence alone (unless it is conclusive) should not determine belief; and her desire to continue the marriage turns out to be one of the factors that should influence what she does believe. In the case of the detached investigator, the lack of special situational factors shows that his belief should be determined by evidence alone.

IX

But more still needs to be said about the role, if any, of the idea of purely evidential warrant in the position I am defending here. Does this position allow a role for this idea? It may seem to some readers that in the previous section I was explicitly denying any role to this notion while nevertheless secretly allowing it a place. Let's begin our discussion of this matter with the following objection: "You seem to deny that there is such a thing as purely evidential warrant, a relation between evidence and conclusion which exists independently of extra-factual considerations, since you claim that extra-factual considerations are relevant in every case. Yet, on the other hand, you do allow that we may, in many or all cases, describe exactly what evidence a person has for a given proposition. Surely, then, talk of purely evidential warrant can find a home here. For on the basis of such a description of the evidence, we can go on to talk about how much support this person has for a belief that this proposition is true. This evidence provides support for that belief. And that is all that one means when talking about 'purely evidential warrant.'"

This objection is important and must be taken seriously because it will help us to clarify the issues here. What I have said so far in this paper may seem ambiguous as between the following two possibilities: (1) I could be denying that there is such a thing as purely evidential warrant; or (2) I could be saying that there is such a thing as purely evidential warrant but that it never determines by itself what we ought to believe.

I believe that the problem here arises from a fundamental ambiguity in the notion of "purely evidential warrant" itself. This notion is a compound notion, and we must separate its parts in order to understand what is going on here. These parts are as follows: (1) the evidential component; (2) the warranting component. When E is evidence for C, E stands in a certain relationship to C. Philosophers will differ over the correct analysis of this evidential relationship. For example, Carnap believed that the notion of evidence was captured by his concept of "degree of confirmation" and thus that the evidential relationship is a logical relationship between two statements or propositions. In any case, if we accept the broad distinction between fact and value now employed in so many areas of philosophy, I think that it is clear that the evidential relation is a factual relation between propositions. (I am, of course, using "factual" in a way in which logical relations between propositions are "factual" relations. In other contexts, it would be important to contrast "logical" and "factual.") But the warranting relation is not a factual relation, in this sense of the term "factual." When we talk about one or more propositions as warranting belief in another propositon, we are talking about the reasonableness, the rationality, or the "oughtness" of believing that latter proposition on the basis of the former propositions. Warranting will be different things on different occasions. On one occasion, one proposition may warrant belief in another in the sense of making it reasonable or justified for a person to believe the latter. On another occasion, we

may feel that one proposition warrants belief in another proposition in the sense that the person *ought* to believe the latter on the basis of the former. But whatever warranting is on a given occasion, it always falls on the "value" side of the fact-value dichotomy. It has to do with "reasonableness," "justification," and "oughtness."

The important consequence of this is that if one accepts some fairly strong form of the fact-value dichotomy, then it follows that the existence of an evidential relation between two propositions does not imply anything *by itself* about the way in which the first proposition does or does not warrant belief in the second proposition. In order to move from the existence of an evidential relation to the existence of a warranting relation, we require some "bridging" principles, some principles which license this move. Now, my position is that these "bridge" principles are practical principles, in a broad sense of the term "practical." They are principles which mention or have some other connection with values and ends.

We began this section by noting that what I have said in this paper may seem ambiguous as between two possibilities: (1) denying that there is such a thing as "purely evidential warrant"; (2) admitting that there is such a thing but denying that it ever determines by itself what we ought to believe. Now this ambiguity can be cleared up. I do agree, with the evidentialists, that there often is a relation between two propositions which we may call the *evidential* relation and which exists independently of value and situational factors. But it does not follow from this that belief in the proposition for which there is evidence (even sufficient evidence) is thereby *warranted*. This does not follow unless we adopt some "practical" bridging principle which allows this to follow. So while there is a "purely *evidential* relation"—a relation between propositions which is "purified" of dependence on values and ends—there is no "purely evidential *warranting* relation." For the warranting relation will depend on a practical bridge principle and thus not be independent of values and ends. Warranting has and must have a practical basis.

But even if we were to agree on this point, there still is the question of what bridge principles to adopt. Several possibilities suggest themselves immediately:

P$_1$: If S has sufficient evidence for C, then S ought (absolutely) to believe C.

P$_2$: If S has sufficient evidence for C, then S ought (prima-facie) to believe C.

Earlier in this paper, I have tried to show that P$_1$ is not an acceptable principle. This is what my cases of Jones and the wife are principally intended to show. These cases do *not* show that P$_2$ is unacceptable. P$_2$ is a plausible principle and one which many people will be inclined to adopt. Nevertheless—and here my earlier point arises again—P$_2$ (or whatever bridge principle we do adopt) needs to be justified by a practical argument.

Now, let us suppose that we do justify P$_2$ by a practical argument and that we accept P$_2$ on this basis. This means that even sufficient evidence provides only a prima facie reason for believing C. What, then, could "outweigh" sufficient evidence in a particular case such that one on balance ought not to believe C? My answer is that extra-factual considerations can bring about this result. The cases of Jones and the wife again show this, too. Thus, we can see that the practical bears on the question "What ought we to believe?" at several crucial points. First, the practical bears on the justification of bridge principles which determine in general the relation between evidence and belief—that is, which determine in general how evidence is to be weighed in deciding what to believe. Second, since P$_1$ is not a satisfactory principle, practical factors will also be involved in decisions about particular beliefs in particular cases. Here, the potential believer's values, ends, and situation will have a definite bearing on whether he or she ought to adopt a particular belief.[9]

Notes

[1] John Passmore, *A Hundred Years of Philosophy* (Harmondsworth, 1968), p. 95.

[2] Dorothy Walsh, *Literature and Knowledge* (Middletown, Conn., 1969), p. 21.

[3] I owe the term "evidentialism" to Nicholas Rescher.

[4] Ralph Barton Perry, "The Right to Believe," in *In the Spirit of William James* (Bloomington, Ind., 1958), pp. 178 and 181. Incidentally, it should be apparent that my position in this paper is very different from that of William James in his essay "The Will to Believe." James would

appear to allow factors other than factual evidence to determine belief only when the evidence is not sufficient, whereas I am arguing here that extra-factual considerations should sometimes do so even when there is sufficient evidence to justify belief on one side or the other. There are other very large differences as well between our positions.

[5] A. J. Ayer, *The Problem of Knowledge* (London, 1954), pp. 31–35; Roderick Chisholm, "Evidence as Justification," *The Journal of Philosophy,* vol. 58 (1961), pp. 739–748. These attempts have been criticised by Herbert Heidelberger, "On Defining Epistemic Expressions," *The Journal of Philosophy,* vol. 60 (1963), pp. 344–348.

[6] In his book *Perceiving: A Philosophical Study* (Ithaca, 1957, p. 15) Chisholm attempts to define various epistemic notions in terms of the idea of something's being "worthy of one's belief." Roderick Firth criticises this attempt, in part by showing that it leads to the result that a certain view is ruled out *a priori* by Chisholm's definitions:

> This objection to Chisholm's definitions becomes even more telling when we ask, in the case of "tender" and "courageous," whether the fact that S has adequate evidence for h is the *only* acceptable ground for holding that S ought to believe h, and whether, consequently, there is even a material equivalence between the definiendum and the proposed definiens. There are many people who would answer these questions in the negative and maintain that a proposition h is sometimes more worthy of our belief than non-h even though we lack adequate evidence for h and actually have adequate evidence for non-h. Perhaps the most noteworthy of such people are those who believe that certain kinds of *faith* are morally good, or at least justified, even when there is a preponderance of contrary evidence. Theological writings provide the most notable illustrations of such an "ethics of belief," but a corresponding position may be taken with respect to faith in human beings. Some people would hold, for example, that there are situations in which a husband ought to believe that his wife is virtuous even in the face of adequate evidence to the contrary. These would be cases, to use an alternative idiom, in which a certain proposition h (viz., that his wife is virtuous) is judged to be more worthy of the husband's belief than non-h, even though it would be reasonable, considering only the evidence, for the husband to believe non-h. There is no need, for present purposes, to discuss the merits or defects of this ethical position; it is sufficient to observe that Chisholm's definitions have the undesirable effect of ruling it out *a priori*. It is surely an *open question* (logically) whether this ethical position is valid; and to close the question by definition is to make the mistake which Moore called "the naturalistic fallacy." ("Chisholm and the Ethics of Belief," *The Philosophical Review,* vol. 68 (1959), pp. 496–497.)

Now, this brief description of the husband and wife case is all that Firth says about it. He does not fill in any of the details of the case because his purpose is only to show that this kind of view should not be ruled out *a priori*. He is not trying to make this kind of case a plausible one, nor is he trying to make any positive point about what we ought to believe or have a right to believe.

My description of the husband and wife case is detailed and concrete because I want to make a positive point about the ethics of belief. I want to defend and make plausible the position which Firth only claims should not be ruled out *a priori*. The crucial feature that I have included in my description of these cases is that Jones and the wife are unable to conceal their strong beliefs, so that for them having a belief of this sort leads inevitably to their behaving in certain ways. This is discussed in greater detail a bit later in this paper.

[7] Roderick Chisholm, "Lewis' Ethics of Belief," in Paul Schilpp (ed.), *The Philosophy of C. I. Lewis* (LaSalle, 1968), p. 226.

[8] In addition to the arguments for voluntarism about beliefs given earlier in this paper, see the splendid arguments for voluntarism given by Roderick Chisholm in "Lewis' Ethics of Belief," *op. cit.,* pp. 223–227. A different view is taken by Bernard Williams in "Deciding to Believe," in Howard Kiefer and Milton Munitz (eds.), *Language, Belief, and Metaphysics* (Albany, 1970), p. 106.

[9] I am indebted to a number of people for their comments on earlier versions of this paper, principally John G. Bennett, Richard Burke, Gary Gutting, John Kekes, Richard Henson, Mark Pastin, Nicholas Rescher, and Richard A. Watson.

X.4 *Believing, Willing, and the Ethics of Belief*

Louis P. Pojman

In this essay I try to do three things. First, in the introduction I give an overview of various relations between acts of the will and belief-acquisitions. In Part I, I argue against the thesis that we can obtain beliefs directly on willing to have them. There is something both psychologically aberrant and conceptually incoherent about obtaining and sustaining beliefs through acts of will. In Part II, I argue that while we can obtain beliefs indirectly via the will, there is a *prima facie* duty not to do so. I argue that Meiland's thesis to the contrary is incorrect. I use the term *volit* to mean the act of obtaining a belief directly on willing to have it.

Introduction: Varieties of Volitionalism

It is a widely held view that we can obtain beliefs and withhold beliefs directly on performing an act of the will. This thesis is sometimes identified with

the view that believing is a basic act, an act that is under our direct control. Descartes holds a *global* version of this thesis: the will is limitless in relation to belief acquisition and we must be directly responsible for our beliefs, especially our false beliefs, for otherwise we could draw the blasphemous conclusion that God is responsible for them.[1] Kierkegaard at times seems to hold this thesis. Sometimes a less global or *local* version of this doctrine is held, asserting that only some beliefs are under our direct control—those beliefs that are not irresistible or forced on us. Aquinas, Locke, Newman, James, Pieper, Chisholm, and Meiland are representatives of this position, holding that we

This is a revised version of "Believing and Willing" (*Canadian Journal of Philosophy, 15,* no. 1, 1985) and chapters XIII and XIV of *Religious Belief and the Will* (London: Routledge & Kegan Paul, 1986).

may *volit* (obtain a belief directly on willing it) just in case the evidence is not sufficient or irresistible in forming a belief.[2] I call the thesis that some or all of our beliefs are basic acts of will "direct volitionalism." I contrast this view with the thesis that some beliefs arise indirectly from basic acts, acts of will, and intentions—a thesis I call "indirect volitionalism."

I want to make another distinction at the outset regarding the relation of believing to willing in belief acquisition: the distinction between *describing* volitional acts and *prescribing* them. I call those types of volitionalism *descriptive* that merely describe the process of coming to believe through *voliting* (obtaining a belief directly on willing to have it). I call those types of volitionalism *prescriptive* that include a normative element. Direct prescriptive volitionalism states that it is permissible or obligatory to acquire certain beliefs directly by willing to have them. Indirect prescriptive volitionalism states that it is permissible or obligatory to take the necessary steps to acquire beliefs based on nonepistemic considerations. A schematic representation of the various theses I have in mind looks like this:

acquisition. In Part I, I first set forth the criteria a fully successful volitional belief acquisition would need to meet and show why we should be skeptical about whether any instances obtain, and then offer two arguments against direct descriptive volitionalism: the phenomenological argument, which proceeds on the basis of an introspective account of the nature of belief acquisition, and the "logic of belief" argument, which shows a conceptual connection between believing and nonvolitional states. In Part II, I turn to indirect prescriptive volitionalism and the ethics of belief and argue that we have a duty not to get ourselves to believe against the evidence.

I

What role does the will play in forming a belief? Is belief formation in some sense within our direct control? Or does the judgment come naturally as a spontaneous response to the total evidence (includ-

	Direct	Indirect
Descriptive	1. One can acquire beliefs directly simply by willing to believe certain propositions.	2. One can acquire beliefs indirectly by willing to believe propositions and then taking the necessary steps to bring it about that one believes the propositions.
Prescriptive	3. One can acquire beliefs directly by willing to believe propositions, and one is justified in so doing.	4. One can acquire beliefs indirectly by willing to believe propositions as described in thesis 2, and one is justified in purposefully bringing it about that one acquires beliefs in this way.

This schema is not meant to be an exhaustive set of relations between believing and willing, but to capture the central theses regarding that relationship in the history of philosophy.

Direct volitionalism has to do with the nature of believing and the type of control that we have over our belief states; prescriptive volitionalism has to do with the ethics of belief, with our duties in regard to the acquisition and sustainment of beliefs. In what follows I discuss these two types of volitionalism both in their direct and indirect forms, contrasting them with the standard mode of belief

ing background information and assumptions)? If receiving evidence in entertaining propositions is like placing weights on balanced scales, can the will influence the outcome? In the standard model of belief acquisition, the judgment is not a separate act but simply the result of the weighing process. It is as though the weighing process exhibited the state of evidence, and then the mind simply registered the state of the scales. In the volitional model, the judgment is a special action over and above the weighing process. It is as though the mind recognized the state of the scales but were allowed to choose whether to accept that state or to influence it by putting a mental finger on one side or the other, depending on desire. The nonvolitionalist need not deny that desire unconsciously influences our belief acquisitions, but does resist the notion that beliefs can be formed by conscious acts of will. And the volitionalist need not maintain that such volits can occur any time one wants them to. There may be times when it is impossible to move the weights through any effort of the will. Here the analogy with freedom of the will is apposite. Just as the metaphysical libertarian need not claim that every act is within our control, but only some significant acts; likewise, the doxastic libertarian need not claim that every belief is within our control, but only some significant beliefs. It is sometimes possible to place the mental finger on the doxastic scales and influence the formation of a judgment or belief.

In what follows I seek to show that problems affect the volitional notion of belief formation. Although it is not possible to prove that no one *ever* volits or that it is impossible to do so (as Bernard Williams mistakenly claims), I offer two arguments to undermine the thesis that we acquire beliefs by consciously willing to have them. I also indicate the legitimate role the will does play in belief acquisition. My first argument is called "the phenomenological argument against direct descriptive volitionalism." It involves an introspective analysis of the phenomena of belief acquisition, showing that there is something psychologically aberrant about the notion of voliting. The second argument, the 'logic of belief' argument against direct descriptive volitionalism, demonstrates a conceptual connection between belief and truth, that there is something incoherent about holding that a particular belief is held decisively on the basis of wanting to have that belief.

The Phenomenological Argument Against Direct Descriptive Volitionalism

First of all we must understand what is involved in direct volitionalism (in this section "volitionalism" stands for "direct descriptive volitionalism" unless otherwise stated). The following features seem necessary and jointly sufficient conditions for a minimally interesting thesis of volitionalism:

1. *The acquisition is a basic act.* That is, some of our beliefs are obtained by acts of will directly on being willed. Believing itself need not be an action—it may be dispositional. The volitionalist need not assert that *all* belief acquisitions occur via the fiat of the will, only that *some* of them do.

2. *The acquisition must be done in full consciousness of what one is doing.* The paradigm cases of acts of will are those in which the agent deliberates over two courses of action and decides on one of them. However, acts of will may take place with greater or lesser awareness. Here our notion of will is ambiguous between two meanings: "desiring" and "deciding." Sometimes by "act of will" we mean simply a desire that manifests itself in action, such as my being hungry and finding myself going to the refrigerator or tired and finding myself heading for bed. We are not always aware of our desires or intentions. There is difference between this type of willing and the sort where we are fully aware of a decision to perform an act. If we obtain beliefs via the will in the weaker sense of desiring of which we are only dimly aware, how can we ever be sure that it was really an act of will that caused the belief directly rather than the will simply being an accompaniment of the belief? That is, there is a difference between willing to believe and believing willingly. The latter case is not an instance of acquiring a belief by fiat of the will, only the former is. To make his or her case, the volitionalist must assert that the acts of will that produce beliefs are decisions of which we are fully aware.

3. *The belief must be acquired independently of evidential considerations.* That is, the evidence is not decisive in forming the belief. Perhaps the belief may be influenced by evidence (testimony, memory, inductive experience, and the like), so that the leap of faith cannot occur just any time over any proposition, but only over propositions that have some evidence in their favor but are still inadequately supported by that evidence. They have an initial subjective probability of, or just under, 0.5. According to Descartes, we ought to withhold belief in such situations where the evidence is exactly equal, whereas with Kierkegaard religious and existential considerations may justify leaps of believing even when the evidence is weighted against the proposition in question. William James prescribes such leaps only when the option was forced, living,

and momentous. It may not be possible to volit in the way Kierkegaard prescribes without a miracle of grace, as he suggests, but the volitionalist would have to assert that volitional belief goes beyond all evidence at one's disposal and hence the believer must acquire the belief through an act of choice that goes beyond evidential considerations. Recurring to our earlier metaphor of the weights, it is possible to place our volitional finger on the mental scales of evidence assessment, tipping them one way or the other.

In sum, then, a volit is an act of will whereby I acquire a belief directly on willing to have the belief, and it is an act made in full consciousness and independently of evidential considerations. The act of acquiring a belief may itself not be a belief but a way of moving from mere entertainment of a proposition to its acceptance.

There is much to be said in favor of volitionalism. It seems to extend the scope of human freedom to an important domain, and it seems to fit our experience of believing where we are conscious of having made a choice. The teacher who sees that the evidence against a pupil's honesty is great and yet decides to trust him, believing that somehow he is innocent in spite of the evidence, and the theist who believes in God in spite of insufficient evidence, both seem to be everyday examples confirming our inclination toward a volitional account of belief formation. We suspect, at times, that many of our beliefs, while not formed through *fully* conscious volits, have been formed through *half-aware* desires, for on introspection we note that past beliefs have been acquired in ways that could not have taken the evidence seriously into consideration. Volitionalism seems a good explanatory theory to account for a great deal of our cognitive experience.

Nonetheless, certain considerations may make us question whether on reflection volitionalism is the correct account of our situation. I argue that it is not the natural way in which we acquire beliefs, and that while it may not be logically impossible that some people volit, it seems psychologically odd and even conceptually incoherent. In this section I shall look at the psychology of belief acquisition and in the next the logic of that experience. I turn then to the phenomenological argument against volitionalism, which schematically goes something like this:

1. Phenomenologically speaking, acquiring a belief is a happening in which the world forces itself on a subject.

2. A happening in which the world forces itself upon a subject is not a thing the subject does (is not a basic act) or chooses.

3. Therefore, phenomenologically speaking, acquiring a belief is not something a subject does or chooses.

This describes the standard mode of belief acquisition and, it will be urged, is the way all beliefs occur. The first premise appeals to our introspective data and assumes that acquiring a belief has a spontaneous, unbidden, involuntary, or forced aspect attached to it. The second premise merely points out the active–passive distinction—that there is a difference between doing something and having something happen to oneself. Hence, the conclusion states that as a happening believing is not something one does or chooses. The phenomenological argument asks us to look within ourselves to see if acquiring a belief is not different from entertaining a proposition, the latter of which can be done at will. The first premise is based on the view that beliefs are psychological states about states of affairs. They are, to use Cambridge University philosopher Frank Ramsey's metaphor, mappings in the mind by which we steer our lives. As such the states of affairs that beliefs represent exist independently of the mind; they exist independently of whether we want them to exist. Insofar as beliefs presume to represent the way the world is, and hence serve as effective guides to action, the will seems superfluous. Believing seems more like seeing than looking, falling than jumping, catching a cold than catching a ball, getting drunk than taking a drink, blushing than smiling, getting a headache than giving one to someone else. Indeed, this involuntary, passive aspect seems true on introspection of most propositional attitudes: anger, envy, fearing, suspecting, doubting, though not necessarily of imagining or entertaining a proposition, where an active element may often be present.

The heart of the argument is in the first premise, and that premise can only be established by considering a number of different types of belief acquisition to see if they all exhibit this passive or nonvolitional feature: having the world force itself on one. Although such an investigation might never end, I can, at least, consider typical cases of belief formation of various types. Let me begin with perceptual beliefs. If I am in a normal physiological condition and open my eyes, I cannot help but see certain things; for example, this piece of white paper in front of me. It seems intuitively obvious that I don't have to choose, before I believe I see it, to have a belief that I see this piece of white paper. Here "seeing is believing." This is not to deny a certain active element in perception. I can explore my environment, focus in on certain features, turn from others. I can direct my perceptual mechanism, but once I do this the perceptions I obtain come of themselves whether or not I will to have them. I may even have an aversion to white paper and not want to have such a perception. Likewise, if I am in a normal physiological state and someone nearby turns on loud music, I hear it. I cannot help believing that I hear it. Belief is forced on me.

Consider, next, memorial beliefs. The typical instances of believing what I seem to remember require no special choosings. I may choose to search my memory for the name of my friend's wife, but what I finally come up with, what I seem to remember, comes of itself, has its own weight attached to it. I do not *choose* to believe my memory report that my friend's wife's name is Pam. Normally, I *cannot help* believing it. There may be times when we only faintly recollect, but the fact that we only weakly believe our memory reports does not imply a volitional element in the belief formation. Although there are times (especially when considering events in the distant past or in childhood) when we are not sure whether what we seem to remember actually occurred, even here it seems that it is typically the evidence of the memory that impresses us sufficiently to tip the scales of judgment one way or the other.

This analysis can be extended to abstract and logical beliefs. Very few volitionalists affirm that we choose to believe that the law of noncontradiction has universal application or that "2 + 2 = 4." These sorts of beliefs seem almost undeniably nonvolitional, and some volitionalists would even withhold the designation "belief" from them, classifying them as cases of knowledge *simpliciter*. In any case,

all agree that in these cases if one understands what is being asserted, one is compelled to believe (or know) these propositions. They are paradigms of doxastic happenings that force themselves on us regardless of whether we will to believe them.

A similar process is at work regarding theoretical beliefs, including scientific, religious, ideological, political, and moral beliefs. Given a whole network of background beliefs, some views or theories are simply going to win out in our noetic structure over others. We sometimes find ourselves forced to accept theories that conflict with and even overthrow our favorite explanations. Accepting a theory as the best explanation, or as probably true, doesn't entail that we must act on it. We may believe an explanation to be true but find it so unedifying or personally revulsive that we are at a loss for what action to take. Such might be the case when a libertarian finds herself forced by argument to accept the doctrine of determinism or when a person loses his religious faith. After *"perestroika"* and the recent anticommunist revolution in the Soviet Union, I saw two bright Russian law students weeping. When asked why they were weeping, one student said, "We were taught that communism was the truth which would win out over capitalism. We've been proved wrong, and we don't know what to do." When doxastic revolutions break out, chaos results, and we suddenly find ourselves without relied-on anchors to stabilize us or maps to guide us.

We can also accept a theory as the best explanation among a set of weak hypotheses without believing it. There is an attitude of accepting a proposition, acting on it as an experimental hypothesis, without assenting to its truth. A behavioral analysis would conflate such acceptance with belief, but there is no reason to accept behaviorism. Sometimes we accept a theory little by little as evidence from various parts of it makes sense to us. At other times, it is as though we suddenly saw the world differently—what was once a cosmic duck is now seen as a cosmic rabbit. The term "seeing" is appropriate, because even as we do not choose what we see when we look at an object (although we can focus on part of it, neglect another part, and so forth), so we do not choose to believe a theory and thereby come to believe it. Rather, we cannot do otherwise in these cases. Nothing I have said, of course, is meant to deny that the will plays an indirect role in acquiring such beliefs.

Finally, and most importantly, there is the matter of testimony beliefs that arise on the basis of reports of others. This is the kind of belief emphasized by Pieper and Meiland. Certainly, this seems a more complex type of believing than perceptions or memory beliefs. Often we read reports in newspapers or hear rumors or predictions and hesitate before siding one way or the other. Sometimes the news seems shocking or threatening to our whole noetic structure. Here one may have the phenomenal feel, at first glance, that a decision is being made by the agent. For example, I hear a report that someone I know well and esteem highly has cheated his company of $50,000. The evidence seems the sort I normally credit as reliable, but I somehow resist accepting it. Have I willed to withhold belief or disbelief? I don't think so. Although I am stunned by the evidence, I have a great deal of background evidence, which I cannot immediately express in detail but which I have within my noetic structure, subconsciously, but which plays a role in putting the fresh data into a larger perspective.

Perhaps I find myself believing willingly that, in spite of the evidence, my friend is innocent. Does this "believing willingly" against the evidence constitute an act of will? I don't think so. Here the reader will recall the distinction between (1) willing to believe and thereby believing and (2) believing willingly, where one feels drawn toward a belief state and willingly goes along with it. One can identify with and feel good about what one comes to believe, but in neither case is the will directly causative. In addition, there is the experience of viewing the objective evidence as roughly counterbalanced, but where one feels inclined one way or the other. Here something like our intuitions or unconscious processes play a decisive role in belief formation, but these are not things we have direct control over. Within our noetic structure are dispositional beliefs and dispositions to believe that influence belief formation. There is no need to appeal to acts of will to explain instances of anomalous belief acquisition.

Normally, however, I find myself immediately and automatically assenting to testimony. If I am lost in a new neighborhood and looking for a supermarket, I may ask someone for directions. Under favorable circumstances, I will believe what she tells me because I have learned through experience that normally people will give reliable directions if they can. Even if I have to deliberate about the testimony, wondering whether the witness is credible, I don't come to a conclusion on the basis of willing to believe one way or the other but because the complex factors in the situation incline me one way or the other. One of these factors may be my wants and wishes that influence my focus; but once the belief comes, it comes as produced by the evidence and not by the choice.

It may be that given enough time and resources we can come to believe almost anything indirectly by willing the appropriate means and acting on them. For example, we believe that the world is spherical and not flat, and no amount of effort seems sufficient to overturn this belief; but perhaps if we had good prudential reasons to do so (for example, if someone offered us a million dollars if we could get ourselves to believe that the world was flat), we might go to a hypnotist, take drugs, or use elaborate autosuggestion until we actually acquired the belief.

Perhaps the volitionalist will respond that there is really little difference between a case of autosuggestion and a case of voliting. Consider the following cases, which progressively tend toward a state of successful autosuggestive belief acquisition:

1. It might be virtually impossible for anyone to use autosuggestion to come to believe that one does not exist.

2. It may take several days for the average person to get him- or herself to believe through autosuggestion that the earth is flat.

3. It may take several hours to get oneself to believe that one's spouse is faithful where there is good evidence to the contrary.

4. It may only take several minutes for a garden-variety racist to get into a state of believing that people of another race are full human beings.

5. It may take some people only a few seconds to acquire the belief that the tossed coin will come up heads.

6. With practice, some people could get themselves, in an imperceptively short amount of time, to acquire the belief that the tossed coin will come up heads.

7. Some masters at autosuggestion may be able to acquire beliefs about tossed coins without any time intervening between the volition and the belief formation.

Perhaps it is strange, stupid, or even perversely immoral to engage in such autosuggestive belief acquisition, but Cases 2 and 5 seem psychologically possible (leave aside for the moment the likely damage to our belief-forming mechanisms and our noetic structure as a whole). It is conceivable that 6 and 7 obtain. In throwing dice, one sometimes has the feeling that the lucky (unlucky) number will turn up in a way that resembles this sort of phenomenon. Perhaps there are some people who can believe some propositions at will the way people can blush, wiggle their ears, and sneeze as basic acts. If 7 is psychologically possible, then the first premise and the conclusion of the phenomenological argument must be altered to take account of these anomalies, so that the revised argument would read as follows:

1. Acquiring a belief is *typically* a happening in which the world forces itself upon a subject.

2. And happenings in which the world forces itself on a subject are not things the subject does or chooses.

3. Therefore, acquiring a belief is not *typically* something a subject does or chooses.

However, while we can never entirely rule out such behavior, it seems dubious whether we actually do perform such acts. It is hard to know whether such a case would be a case of imagining a state of affairs or believing a proposition, for the distinction is blurred at this point. At some point, to imagine that p becomes a belief that p. For most of us, most of the time, however, such belief acquisitions are not possible. Consider the proposition "This coin will land heads." Do you have any sense of yes-ness or no-ness, assent or dissent, regarding it? Or suppose that the local torturer holds out his two fists and says to you, "If you choose the fist with the penny in it, you will receive $100,000, but if you pick the empty fist, you will be tortured for the next week. The only stipulation on your choosing

the correct fist is that when you choose it, you must not only point to it but *believe* that the coin is in that hand and not in the other (a lie detector will monitor your reaction)." I take it that most of us would be in for some hard times.

The last illustration nicely brings out the difference between acting and believing. It is relatively easy to *do* crazy things if there are practical grounds for them. We can easily act when the evidence is equally balanced (for example, call heads while the coin is in the air), but believing is typically more passive in nature, not a doing, but a guide to doing. The phenomenological argument shows that volitionalism is abnormal and bizarre, but it does not rule out the possibility of acquiring beliefs by voliting.

Another possible use of the will regarding belief acquisition needs to be addressed: the veto phenomenon. Some philosophers (Locke and Holyer) hold that the will can act as a veto on belief inclinations, halting would-be beliefs in the process of formation. This is a negative type of volition, for it does not claim that we can actually attain beliefs by the fiat of the will, only that we can prevent some from getting hold of us by putting up a doxastic roadblock just in the nick of time. What seems to occur is this:

1. S entertains proposition p (this is sometimes under our direct control).

2. S is inclined to believe that p or S suspects that p (this is not normally under our control).

3. The veto phenomenon occurs by raising doubts, suspending judgment, or "tabling" the proposition under focus.

4. S looks at further evidence or looks at the old evidence in a fresh light and forms a judgment. (Although the "looking" is under our direct control, the "seeing" or judgment is not.)

Is the veto event under our direct control, or is it caused by a counterclaim, a sense that there is counterevidence, or a sense that there is something wrong with our first inclination? For example, I am interviewing Candidate A for a vacant position in our department and have a strong inclination to believe her to be the right person for the job, but I suddenly remember that we still have two candidates to interview and realize that my inclination to believe that "A is *the* best candidate for the job" is founded on insufficient evidence. I must modify the proposition to state that she is a good candidate. Here it seems that another belief (that there are other good candidates still to be interviewed) comes into play and forces the other belief aside. No act of will is present to my consciousness. But even if I do feel a will to believe or withhold judgment in these sorts of cases, it doesn't follow that the will causes the belief. It may well be an accompaniment. Nevertheless, there are other types of vetoing where I may clearly prevent a belief from forming on the basis of the evidence. Consider the situation where John tells Joan that her father has embezzled some money from his company, and before he is finished presenting the evidence Joan stops him, crying, "Stop it, please, I can't bear to hear any more!" It seems plausible to suppose that something analogous to her stopping John from providing the incriminating evidence that would cause a belief to form, may also occur within us when we begin to consider evidence for a position we deplore. We may inwardly turn away from the evidence, focus on something else, and so fail to form a belief in the matter. This seems a case of self-deception, but in any case, the veto power seems to be sometimes under our direct control. Nevertheless, it does not show that we actually can acquire beliefs by voliting, but shows only that the will has a negative role to play in preventing beliefs from fixing themselves in us.

Cartesia

Although our analysis hasn't ruled out the possibility of voliting, it does support the claim that there is something peculiar about the phenomenon. If voliters exist, they are like people who can wiggle their ears, blush, vomit, or regulate their heartbeats at will. But unlike these volitional phenomena, believing at will seems to involve a conceptual confusion. Typically, I take it, believing is representational in nature, purporting to mirror our world and our relations with the world, so that every instance of volitional–nonrepresentational believing deviates

from that relationship in a fundamental way. To see this better, imagine a society, Cartesia, whose members all volit. They attain beliefs as we engage in coughing, both voluntarily and involuntarily. Regarding every proposition, voliting will be a serious consideration. When a member of Cartesia hears that her spouse has been unfaithful, she must ask herself, not simply what the evidence is for this charge but whether she has an obligation to believe that her spouse is faithful in spite of sufficient evidence. Such people have no difficulty in making Kierkegaardian leaps of faith against sufficient evidence, let alone where the evidence is counterbalanced. For example, when they throw coins up into the air, they form convictions about the way the coins will land. No doubt they will have a strong normative component regarding voliting in order to regulate the activity. There will have to be elaborate classification systems covering obligatory volits, permissible volits, little white volits, immoral volits, and illegal volits punishable by the state.

Such a society is hard to imagine, but in it there would have to be a distinction between voliting-type beliefs and nonvoliting-type beliefs. The latter alone would be treated as reliable for action guidance, voliting types of belief being tolerated mainly in the private domain, where no public issue is at stake. In other words, the nonvoliting belief acquisitions would be treated very much the way beliefs are treated in our society, as action guides, which as such should be reliable mirrors of the evidence.

Perhaps we can give an evolutionary account of the nonvolitional nature of belief acquisition. To survive, animals need a fairly accurate and spontaneous representation of the world. The cat's action of catching the mouse and the primitive human's running away from the bear would not be aided by intervening volits between the representations of the mouse and the bear and the beliefs that the representations were accurate, nor would it be helpful for us to have to decide to believe our perceptions under normal conditions. Basically, we are credulous creatures. For most believings, most of the time, *contra* Descartes and Kierkegaard, the will has nothing to do with the matter. Beliefs come naturally as that which purports to represent the way the world is so that our actions may have a reliable map by which to steer.

The "*Logic of Belief*" Argument Against Volitionalism

The phenomenological argument gets its force by attacking the second characteristic of an act of voliting: the act must be done in full consciousness. If my analysis is correct, voliting must be a highly abnormal phenomenon, if it exists in any positive form at all. However, I have not ruled out the possibility of some people voliting. In this sense, my analysis has resembled Hume's account in which it is a contingent matter that we do not obtain beliefs by fiat of the will. A second argument will now be advanced that attacks volitionalism primarily on the basis of its third characteristic: that it must be done independently of evidential or truth considerations (I use these terms synonymously to stand for evidence in the broad sense of the term, including the self-evidence of basic beliefs). I call this argument the "logic of belief" argument. It states that the notion of volitional believing involves a conceptual confusion, that it is broadly a logical mistake. It argues there is something incoherent in stating one can obtain or sustain a belief in full consciousness *simply* by a basic act of the will; that is, by purposefully disregarding the evidence connection. This strategy does not altogether rule out the possibility of obtaining beliefs by voliting in less than full consciousness (not truly voliting), but asserts that when full consciousness enters the "belief" will wither from one's noetic structure. One cannot believe in full consciousness "that *p* and I believe that *p* for other than truth considerations." If you understand that to believe *p* is to believe *p* is true and *wishing never makes it so*, then there is simply no epistemic reason for believing *p*. Suppose I say I believe I have $1,000,000 in my checking account, and suppose when you point out to me that there is no reason to believe this, I respond, "I know that there is not the slightest reason to suppose there is $1,000,000 in my checking account, but I believe it anyway, simply because I want to." If you were convinced I was not joking, you would probably conclude I was insane or didn't know what I was talking about.

If I said that I somehow find myself believing I have $1,000,000 but don't know why, we might

suppose a memory trace of having deposited $1,000,000 into my account, or evidence to that effect in the guise of an intuition, caused my belief. But you would be stumped if I denied that and said, "No, I don't have any memory trace regarding placing $1,000,000 into my account. In fact, I'm sure I never placed $1,000,000 into the account. I just find it good to believe it's there, so I have chosen to believe it."

The point is that because beliefs just are about the way the world is and are made true (or false) depending on the way the world is, it is a confusion to believe that any given belief is true simply on the basis of being willed. As soon as the believer, assuming he (or she) understands these basic concepts, discovers the basis of his belief—as being caused by the will alone—he must drop the belief. In this regard, saying, "I believe *p* but only because I want to believe it," has the same incoherence attached to it as G. E. Moore's paradoxical "I believe *p* but it is false that *p*." Structurally, neither are strictly logical contradictions, but both show an incoherence that might be called broadly contradictory.

Robert Audi has objected that my argument only has merit if one supposes the believer is rational, for an irrational believer could continue to believe that *p* in some other sense. However, I think that there is something wrong with describing irrational persons as having a belief here at all. There is a fundamental confusion lurking in their noetic structure that disqualifies them from having that notion ascribed to them in the full sense of the word. That is, it is not necessarily the case that, just because S believes he believes *p*, S *actually* believes *p*, especially if he (or she) also consciously believes not-*p* at the same time. Although we can have contradictory beliefs without knowing that we do, it is hard to understand what a fully conscious contradictory belief would be. In like manner, the fully conscious voliter isn't believing anything when he (or she) believes he has acquired a belief simply by voliting. It is as though he were saying, "To believe anything is to believe it because of some evidence (even self-evidence) E, but to believe what I am now believing is believed nonevidentially." What is being believed?

My formulation builds minimal understanding of the concept of belief and truth or evidence into its premises, but if the reader is sympathetic to

Audi's criticism, we can modify our formula to apply only to rational believing (leaving aside whether irrational believing *in this sense* is possible).

But even if the believer can believe it is his (or her) will causing the belief in cases of doxastic incontinence, the argument would show the believer could not believe that his belief was being caused or sustained in the right way. The rational believer, in full consciousness, would see there must be a truth connection between states of affairs and the belief by virtue of which the belief is true, so the will is essentially unnecessary for the belief—although it may be necessary in order to get into a proper state of mind where he will be able to perceive the evidence perspicuously. Just as there is an instrumental relation between opening one's eyes and seeing whatever one sees, but an intrinsic relation between states of affairs in the world and what one sees, so likewise there is only an instrumental relationship between willing to believe p and believing p, whereas there is an intrinsic relationship between state of affairs S by virtue of which p is true and my belief that p. Once the believer realizes willing never makes it so, he or she must give up the belief the will is decisively or intrinsically sustaining the belief p, although he may believe there is an instrumental relationship. At least, the believer will not be able to believe that the will *alone* is causing him to believe p, but that the evidence is the deciding factor.

There is a clear difference between acting, which is volitional, and acquiring a belief, which is not volitional but an event or a happening. Believing is evidential, in that to believe p is to presuppose that I have evidence for p or that p is self-evident or evident to the senses. I need not have a developed concept of evidence to believe this. Children do not have a full concept of belief, but they tacitly suppose something like this. On reflection, rational adults seem to recognize the connection between a belief and objective states of affairs. In a sense, belief that p seems to imply the thought of a causal chain stretching back from the belief to a primary relationship with the world and so faithfully representing the world. We may have more or less confidence about the preciseness of the way our beliefs represent the world, but some degree seems implicit in every belief state.

Another way to make this same point about the evidentiality of belief is to define propositional belief in terms of a subjective probability index. All believing is believing to a degree of confidence. You may test the approximate degree to which you believe a proposition by imagining how surprised you would be if you found out that the particular belief in question turned out to be false. Suppose we had a way of quantifying the strength of our beliefs by means of a "belief meter." The meter has two rubber balls wired to it, which, when the balls are squeezed, measures the pressure of the squeezes. The subject holds a ball in each hand and is instructed to squeeze the ball in his (or her) right hand when he believes the proposition, and to squeeze the ball in his left hand when he believes the proposition to be false, and to refrain from squeezing when he believes the proposition to be neither true nor false. In addition, the subject is instructed to squeeze the appropriate ball with a pressure appropriate to the *degree* with which he believes the proposition in question. A certain amount of experimentation may be necessary to work the correlations out, but accuracy will be approximated by the help of a truth serum. In this way we might be able to quantify our beliefs into a subjective probability index. For example, it might turn out that Ann discovers she only believes God exists to a probability of 0.6, whereas she believes it will rain today to a probability of 0.8. It might also turn out that Ann discovers she had deceived herself into thinking she had a deep conviction about God's existence, whereas she really only weakly believes in God's existence. (Of course, she could doubt the reliability of the belief meter, but we may suppose it has an excellent track record.)

In principle, I see no reason against the possibility of rough belief quantification just described, but the point is that we already have a satisfactory notion of subjective probability in terms of the relative degrees with which we believe propositions. If believing were the result of our immediate willings, it would not be about the probability of states of affairs obtaining, but simply about our desires. It would be the case that I could come to a judgment that the probability of p on the evidence E was 0.5 and via a volit conclude it was 0.6. Could I in full consciousness make such a leap? It seems as possible as believing "2 + 2 = 4" and then deliberately at the same time believing "2 + 2 = 5."

It may be objected that this argument implies

we must have a concept of probability, but I think we all do have a notion of degrees of belief that entails a rough notion of subjective probability in the manner described. If this argument is sound, the interesting thing is that not only can we not volit a belief, but we cannot even volit a change in the degree with which we believe a proposition. We cannot increase the strength of our belief that p from 0.6 to 0.65 simply by a fiat of the will.

The "logic of belief" argument has not ruled out the logical possibility of voliting but simply rules out as logically odd (in the wider sense of the term) the possibility of acquiring a belief in full consciousness by a fiat of the will without regard to truth considerations. It does not rule out the possibility of obtaining the belief in less than full consciousness or indirectly. The phenomena in these cases seem similar to that of self-deception, where one is not fully aware of what one truly believes. Once someone discovers that he (or she) has self-deceived himself, the logic of the discovery seems to entail the giving up of the false "belief" (the belief the person thought he or she had on a conscious level). Likewise, once someone realizes that the only basis for believing that p is the wanting p to be true, the belief must wither. Hence, if someone could come to have a belief through directly willing to have it, once he (or she) reflected on the acquisition and discovered its illegitimate origin, the person would give it up (unless, of course, he now had evidence for it). He would see on reflection that the purported belief reflects only the content of his will. It has the same status as a product of the imagination.

Consider this similarity between imagining and willing to believe. Take for example, vivid imaginer Imogene, who gets so carried away with her imagination that she sometimes believes her imagination reports. While sitting bored to death in her logic class, she fantasizes that she is swimming in the Bahamas or is being embraced by Warren Beatty. She imagines these things so vividly that for the moment she believes that they are really happening, until the teacher rudely calls on her and breaks the spell of her daydream, thus shattering her transient "beliefs." Perhaps many of our beliefs are formed through the imagination that are more subtle than this and that we never discover, but when we do discover that a belief has its basis in the imagination, we discard it as worthless—and we do so automatically and not by a volit. But voliting and imagining seem to display the very same logic regarding belief acquisition. Both are acquired independently of evidential considerations.

Of course, it is possible that a person may regard his or her wants about reality as counting as *evidence* for propositions. For example, someone might say, "I have found that whenever I want a proposition to be true, amazingly it generally turns out to be so." Here wanting would indirectly cause belief, but not by voliting, but rather by being regarded as reliable evidence, a type of credible testimony. It would still be the case that what causes the believer to believe is evidential and not simply the will's fiat.

If my analysis is correct, there is a deep conceptual confusion in self-consciously believing of any proposition that it has originated through a volit and/or that what sustains one's belief is one's will.[3]

I conclude that voliting seems both psychologically aberrant and conceptually confused. It is psychologically problematic because the feature of demanding full consciousness attaches to acts of will. It is conceptually confused because it neglects the evidential aspect of conscious belief acquisition and sustainment.

Indirect Volitionalism and the Ethics of Belief

Indirectly believing does involve the will. I have argued that we cannot normally believe anything at all simply by willing to do so, for believing aims at truth and is not a basic act or a direct product of the will. If we could believe whatever we chose to believe simply by willing to do so, belief would not be about reality but about our wants. Nevertheless, the will does play an important indirect role in believing. Many of the beliefs that we arrive at are finally the results of our policy decisions. Although believing itself is not an act, our acts determine the sorts of beliefs we end up with. It is primarily because we judge that our beliefs are to some significant degree the indirect results of our actions that we speak of being responsible for them. Although we cannot be said to be directly responsible for them, as though they were actions, we can be said to be indirectly responsible for many of them. If we had chosen differently, if we had been better moral agents, paid attention to the evidence, and so forth, we would have different beliefs than we in fact do have.

To be sure, we are not responsible for all our beliefs, and the degree of responsibility seems to vary in proportion to the amount of evidence available at different times and our ability to attend properly to that evidence. For example, the person who pays attention to a certain matter often comes to have more accurate beliefs than the inattentive person. Attention is generally within our direct control. As long as we agree that the inattentive person could have acted differently, could have been attentive if he (or she) had really wanted to, we can conclude that the inattentive person is responsible for not having the true beliefs he might have had. In the same way we can conclude that the attentive person is responsible for the beliefs he or she has.

Being (indirectly) responsible for our beliefs indicates that praise and blame attach indirectly to our epistemic states, that indirectly beliefs are morally assessable. It may be that I have many beliefs I ought not to have. If I had been a better person, learned to investigate certain matters with the right categories, I might now be endowed with a more accurate system of beliefs and believe many of my present beliefs in different degrees of confidence from my present state of belief.

Many philosophers reject the notion of an ethics of belief. Mill, James, and Meiland believe that there are no special doxastic moral duties. Hume and Price argue that there are only counsels of prudence. Price puts it thus:

> But even if it were in our power to be wholly rational all of the time, it still would not follow that there is anything morally blameworthy about assenting unreasonably (against the evidence or without regard to the evidence) or that we ought to be chastised for doing so. There is nothing wicked about such assents. It is however true, and important, that unreasonable assent is contrary to our *long term interest*. It is to our long term interest to believe true

propositions rather than false ones. And if we assent reasonably (i.e. in accordance with the evidence), it is likely that in the long run the propositions we believe will be more often true than false.[4]

The only "ought" regarding belief acquisition is a prudential ought. A person is free to seek whatever goals he (or she) desires: happiness, salvation, convenience, aesthetic pleasure, and so forth. It is simply in your long-term best interest generally to seek to have true beliefs. However, if you find yourself inclined to sacrifice truth for some other goal, you have every right to do so. We may call this the *libertarian view of doxastic responsibility*. It affirms that believing is a purely private matter. Mill says that each person must be accorded "absolute freedom of opinion on all subjects practical and speculative."[5]

One may readily recognize the virtues of this position. Not many of us want to see totalitarian thought reforms, brainwashing, and government intervention into personal beliefs, in order to help others acquire "true beliefs." The libertarian position is right to emphasize human autonomy with regard to our private selves, and it may even be the case that it is a good thing to have a plurality of opinions in a society. Nevertheless, libertarian-prudentialist doctrine is false: *It sells the truth short.* It does so on two counts: it underestimates the significance of truth for the individual him- or herself, and it ignores the social dimension of truth seeking. Personhood, involving a high degree of autonomy, entails respect for highly justified beliefs. Socially, truth seeking is important, for unless a society has accurate information many of its goals are not likely to be reached. I develop these ideas in the following analysis.

Perhaps the clearest account of a volitional stance on the ethics of belief is Jack Meiland's article "What Ought We to Believe," in which Meiland argues that not only is it sometimes morally *permissible* to believe against the evidence, but that it is sometimes morally *obligatory* to do so. In all cases of belief acquisition "extra-factual considerations are relevant."[6] After presenting Meiland's position against a strict evidentialism and in favor of prescriptive volitional belief acquisition, I show what is wrong with Meiland's position, showing that what is new is not true and what is true is not new. Specifically, I contend there is a more moderate form of evidentialism that escapes Meiland's criticisms and thus provides a middle way between the two extremes of rigid evidentialism and volitionalism. I outline what such a moderate evidentialism with regard to the ethics of belief looks like.

Rigid evidentialism states, following Meiland's interpretation, that one ought to believe propositions if and only if they are backed by sufficient evidence. This position, which, according to Meiland, is found in Descartes, Locke, Clifford, and Chisholm, is largely impervious to subjective factors in belief formation. Chisholm's formulation is cited as a clear expression of this position:

1. Anyone having just the evidence in question is warranted in accepting the conclusion.

2. I am in a position of having that evidence.

3. Therefore, I am justified in accepting the conclusion. (p. 19)

On this account, everyone is epistemically required to come to the same conclusion, given the same evidence. The argument for this position can be spelled out as follows. Suppose Person A is justified on Evidence E in believing that *p*. Suppose, further, that Person B has exactly the same evidence as A has but believes that not-*p*. On the face of it, it seems contradictory to say that although A is justified in believing *p* on E, B is justified in believing not-*p* on E. This suggests that E both justifies belief *p* and not-*p*, but this defies our very notion of justification. Hence, the evidentialist concludes that not both A and B can be justified in believing what they believe on E. If A is justified in believing *p* on E, then B is not, and vice versa. Yet anyone who has the evidence A has is in the same state of being justified as A is, whether he or she knows it or not.

What this argument for evidentialism neglects is a notion of the larger context into which apparently similar evidence comes. Just as a farmer, a real estate dealer, and an artist, all looking at the "same" field, may not see the same field, so evidence always is relative to a person's individuating background beliefs, capacities to interpret data, and expectations. Meiland, rightly, points out that subjective factors play a strong role in our interpretation of evidence and in the formation of beliefs, but over-

steps the evidence when he interprets this subjectivism to include direct volitionalism, the acquisition of beliefs through conscious choices. Classical evidentialism may be too rigid in its notion of justification. It neglects psychological factors, which enter into every belief acquisition. All believing is believing from a perspective, and any type of evidentialism that neglects this perspectival element may be designated "rigid" in that it lacks a proper appreciation for the complexity of evidence gathering and assembling.

A second important feature of Meiland's position on the ethics of belief is his subsuming epistemic duties under the heading of general ethical duties. That is, we have no special epistemic duties that are not already covered by ethical principles *simpliciter*. If we claim that someone has a duty to believe some proposition, we must give moral reasons for that duty, not epistemic ones. Meiland argues on utilitarian grounds that it is often morally required that we act against so-called epistemic requirements of believing according to sufficient evidence. Here Meiland holds a stronger position than James, Chisholm, or Nathanson, who allow for voliting only when the eivdence is insufficient, as a sort of a tie breaker.[7] Meiland maintains that we are sometimes obligated to get ourselves to believe propositions even when we have sufficient evidence to the contrary. However, he does not go as far as Kierkegaard in allowing for believing against even conclusive evidence. When we have conclusive evidence, it is not in our power to believe against the evidence.

The sort of sufficient evidence for a proposition against which we may believe is illustrated in the example of the wife who finds lipstick on her husband's handkerchief, a blonde strand of hair on his suit, and a crumpled piece of paper with a telephone number on it in a woman's handwriting in his pocket. This would constitute sufficient evidence (on the rigid evidentialist account) that the husband is having an affair with another woman and would normally cause the wife to believe that her husband was being unfaithful. However, the wife may have good reason for rejecting the evidence even though she admits it is sufficient to justify belief in her husband's unfaithfulness. She rejects the belief, however, for pragmatic reasons. Suppose the wife closely examines the evidence and decides that if she comes to believe what it points to (or continues to believe that her husband is unfaithful), their marriage will be ruined and great unhappiness will ensue. If, however, she can get herself to believe that her husband is faithful, in spite of the evidence to the contrary, the marriage probably will be saved. She reasons that her husband will very likely get over his infatuation and return to his marital commitment. Suppose she has good evidence for this second belief. Should she not acquire the belief in her husband's faithfulness, in hope of saving her marriage? Perhaps she also justifiably believes that undergoing this volitional process, of somehow acquiring a belief by willing to have it despite the evidence, will do no permanent damage to her noetic structure. After acquiring the belief and letting the belief direct her actions, the marriage will be saved; and after the marriage is saved, she will recall the process she underwent to save the marriage. Now, however, she will be in a position to live with the unwelcome evidence and even speak openly with her husband about it. Given these factors, is not the wife morally obligated to take steps to obtain the belief in her husband's faithfulness?

Unlike the usual volitionalist strategy of advocating voluntary believing only in extreme cases, Meiland makes the rather daring claim that in every case of believing where there is insufficient evidence or sufficient evidence for an unwelcome proposition, extrafactual considerations are relevant considerations (p. 21). Although Meiland believes that believing is within the direct control of our will (except where there is conclusive evidence), he is content to let his case rest on the possibility that we may indirectly cause ourselves to believe against the evidence.

I have four objections to Meiland's position on the ethics of belief: (1) his notion of evidentialism is overly rigid and ignores a broader form of evidentialism that obviates the need for a volitional alternative in most cases of believing; (2) a minor criticism is that Meiland fails to make clear why we may have an obligation to believe against the evidence when it is sufficient but may not have an obligation to believe against the evidence when it is conclusive; (3) his position undervalues the importance of having reliable belief-forming mechanisms and misconstrues the nature of belief acquisitions; and (4) if Meiland's position is interpreted by the principle of charity into making merely the weak claim that sometimes we have a moral duty to override our duty of seeking to have true, justified beliefs, then there is nothing new in his position. Let us look briefly at each of these criticisms.

First, Meiland is correct in criticizing the Clifford-Chisholm line of evidentialism, which focuses on a nonperspectival relationship between evidence and justification. This position seems to neglect or underemphasize the point that evidence is person-relative, so that each person views the data with a different noetic endowment. The Aristotelian and the nominalist who hear the argument from contingency for the existence of God, will each view its soundness differently. But, given their different worldviews, each may well be justified in coming to the belief he does. Although there may be such a thing as *propositional warrant,* which provides objective evidence for a given proposition, justification has mainly to do with what is reasonable for a given person to believe, given his or her noetic structure, background beliefs, ability to pay attention, ability to weigh evidence impartially, ability to interpret the evidence according to certain rules, and the like. A person living in the Middle Ages may well have been warranted in believing that the earth is flat, even though there may have been objective evidence to support the proposition that it is round, evidence that anyone in an ideal situation would have.

Meiland posits an unnecessary dichotomy between objective (sufficient) evidence and subjective factors where the will determines the belief. The only alternatives are not rigid evidentialism and volitionalism. Simply because objective evidence is not the only necessary factor in belief acquisition does not mean that the will can or should decide the matter. One must take into account such subjective factors as unconscious wants and past learning that have been internalized so that we are not aware of the information processing our subconscious self is undertaking. For example, chicken sexers, while failing the strong evidentialist's test of being able to give an account of their evidence, nevertheless probably have evidence for the reliable judgments they consistently make. Given their high success rate in identifying the sex of chicks, it is more reasonable to say that they know but cannot tell us even themselves how they know the chick's sex than to attribute their success to acts of the will (or simply luck).

I am suggesting that a more moderate version of evidentialism includes a recognition of subjective factors in belief acquisition without admitting that the will directly causes belief or that it should cause it indirectly. We don't need to bring in volitions to account for the subjective element in belief formation. An alternative interpretation of one of Meiland's examples will illustrate what I mean. Imagine a defense attorney who agrees with the prosecution and the jury that there is sufficient evidence against his client but, who, nevertheless, continues to believe in his client's innocence despite the evidence. His belief is vindicated years later. This is supposed to show that the attorney has a right to believe his client is innocent in spite of the evidence where there are pragmatic grounds for doing so. I doubt the will is directly involved here at all, and I believe the attorney's belief can be accounted for through my modified version of evidentialism. The attorney, Smith, hears and sees all the evidence E against his client, Brown. He concludes on the basis of E that Brown is probably guilty. But he pauses, introspects, and senses some resistance from within to that conclusion. He finds himself with a tendency to reject the first conclusion in favor of a belief that Brown is innocent. Perhaps for a time he vacillates between two belief tendencies, or he experiences undulating alternate belief states. When he is in court or looking at the evidence in private, he feels a subtle certainty that Brown is guilty, but when he faces Brown, looks him in the eye, and speaks to him, he senses that he must be wrong in believing the evidence that points to Brown's guilt. Perhaps we can say (following Price) Smith half-believes Brown is innocent and half-believes he is guilty, the belief states alternating so frequently that he cannot fully make up his mind. Perhaps the feeling Brown is innocent finally wins out in the battle of Smith's mind. Meiland would explain this alternation and conclusion as making a decision to believe. I doubt whether this description is correct and suggest it is more likely Smith's previous experience with people, especially defendants, both innocent and guilty, has caused him to form reliable beliefs about characteristic features and behaviors of the guilty and innocent, including the "seemingly innocent" and the "seemingly guilty." He is unaware of this large repository of internalized evidence and cannot formulate it. Here, we want to say Smith's reliability at judging character and legal evidence warrants our saying he has internalized skills and sets of inductive generalizations (for example, judging from certain characteristic looks on innocent faces to a conclusion of particular innocence) that cause individual belief occurrences. Smith has data and skills that the jury does not, that a less competent attorney does not, and that the judge may not have.

One can generalize from this case and say with regard to any proposition, *p*, and for any person S, that if S finds himself (or herself) believing *p*, the belief that *p* is *prima facie* evidence for *p* itself relative to S; that is, S is *prima facie* justified in believing *p*. It may not be very strong justification, and S may be forced to weaken his hold on *p* when he cannot defend *p*, but it is some evidence, enough to start with. Furthermore, to the extent that S finds himself a reliable judge in a given area, to exactly that extent is he justified in holding on to a belief tenaciously in the light of evidence to the contrary. Modified evidentialism accepts intuitive judgments as playing an evidential role in believing. If my account of evidentialism is correct, then the motivation for much of Meiland's volitionalism is dissipated. Simply saying that subjective factors enter into our belief acquisitions is not sufficient to justify volitionalism, for in a sense all believing involves subjective factors that are causative in belief formation. (This leads to the second criticism of Meiland's position.)

The *second* criticism of Meiland's position focuses on his distinctions among insufficient evidence, sufficient evidence, and conclusive evidence in relation to the ability to volit. According to Meiland, it is only possible to volit (or indirectly get ourselves into a belief state through volitional means) when the evidence is not conclusive. Hence, it can only be morally required that we volit in those cases. But unless we reduce "conclusive evidence" to the trivially true definiens "that which we cannot will ourselves not to believe," we seem to have a problem; for if I have a moral obligation to believe (through volitional means) against sufficient evidence, why can I not have an obligation to believe (via those same means) against conclusive evidence? The answer cannot be simply that it is easier to do this in the first case. It may be that we must spend more time and effort getting ourselves to believe against conclusive evidence, going to a better hypnotist or whatever, but if our utilitarian cost—benefit analysis specifies that the psychic price is worth paying (for example, we may be able to save our children's sanity or lives by keeping our marriage together by believing that our spouses are faithful even though we catch them in bed committing adultery), then, on Meiland's analysis, we should pay that price. I see no criterion to distinguish between believing against evidence where it is only sufficient and believing against the evidence where it is conclusive. If Meiland responds that there is a likelihood that such manipulations would mess up the subject's mind, we should respond, "What makes you so confident this isn't what happens in every case of purposefully getting ourselves to believe against or in the absence of sufficient evidence?" This leads to the most serious criticism of volitional positions on the ethics of belief.

Third, my main criticism of positions like Meiland's (including William James's) has to do with the importance of having well-justified beliefs and truth seeking in general. We generally believe these two concepts are closely related, so the best way to assure ourselves of having true beliefs is to seek to develop one's belief-forming mechanisms in such ways as to become good judges of various types of evidence, attaining the best possible justification of our beliefs. The value of having the best justified beliefs possible can be defended both on deontological grounds with regard to the individual and on teleological or utilitarian grounds regarding the society as a whole. The deontological argument is connected with our notion of autonomy. To be an autonomous person is to have a high degree of warranted beliefs available on which to base one's actions. There is a tendency to lower freedom of choice as one shrinks the repertoire of well-justified beliefs regarding a plan of action, and because it is a generally accepted moral principle that it is wrong to lessen autonomy or personhood, it is wrong to lessen the degree of justification of one's beliefs on important matters. Hence, there is a general presumption against beliefs by willing to have them. Cognitive voliting is a sort of lying or cheating in that it enjoins believing against what has the best guarantee of being the truth. When a friend or doctor lies to a terminally ill patient about her con-

dition, the patient is deprived of the best evidence available for making decisions about her limited future. She is being treated less than fully autonomously. Although a form of paternalism may sometimes be justified, there is always a presumption against it and in favor of truth telling. We even say that the patient has a right to know what the evidence points to. Cognitive voliting is a sort of lying to oneself, which, as such, decreases one's own freedom and personhood. It is a type of doxastic suicide that may only be justified in extreme circumstances. If there is something intrinsically wrong about lying (making it *prima facie* wrong), there is also something intrinsically wrong with cognitive voliting, either by directly or indirectly. Whether it be Pascal, James, Meiland, Newman, or Kierkegaard, all prescriptive volitionalists (consciously or not) seem to undervalue the principle of truthfulness and its relationship to personal autonomy.

The utilitarian, or teleological, argument against cognitive voliting is fairly straightforward. General truthfulness is a desideratum without which society cannot function. Without it, language itself would not be possible, because it depends on faithful use of words and sentences to stand for appropriately similar objects and states of affairs. Communication depends on a general adherence to accurate reporting. More specifically, it is very important that a society have true beliefs with regard to important issues, so that actions based on beliefs have a firm basis.

The doctor who cheated her way through medical school and who, as a consequence, lacks appropriate beliefs about certain symptoms, may endanger a patient's health. A politician who fails to take into consideration the amount of pollution being given off by large corporations that support his candidacy, may endanger the lives and health of his constituents. Even the passer-by who gives wrong information to a stranger who asks directions may seriously inconvenience the stranger. Here Clifford's point about believing against the evidence is well taken, despite its "all-too-robustious" tone (as James describes it). The shipowner who failed to make necessary repairs on his vessel and "chose" to believe that it was seaworthy, is guilty of the deaths of the passengers. "He had no right to believe on such evidence as was before him."[8] It is because beliefs are action guiding, maps by which we steer, and as such tend to cause actions, that society has a keen interest in our having the best-justified beliefs possible regarding important matters.

Nevertheless, Meiland might reply, while there may be a general duty to seek to have well-justified beliefs, there may be many cases where other considerations override our duty to believe according to the evidence. In fact, these cases may be so numerous that one is tempted to conclude (as Meiland does) that "extrafactual considerations" are relevant to every case of belief acquisition (and, following this logic, relevant to every case of maintaining each of our beliefs). The trouble with this response is that it ignores the sort of intention skill that truth seeking is. It is dispositional, a habit. If it is to be effective at all, it must be deeply engrained within us, so it is not at all easy to dispense with. The wife, if she has been properly brought up as a truth seeker, may simply not be able to believe against the evidence without going through elaborate conditioning processes that might seriously affect her personality and even her personal identity.

Furthermore, our beliefs do not exist in isolation from each other, so that to overthrow one belief may have reverberations throughout our entire noetic structure, affecting many of our other beliefs. Getting oneself to believe against the evidence that supports a belief that *p,* may upset our other justified beliefs *q, r,* and *s,* which in turn may affect still other beliefs. Cognitive voliting, as Bernard Williams has pointed out, "is like a revolutionary movement trying to extirpate the last remains of the *ancien regime.* The man gets rid of this belief that his son is dead, and then there is some belief which strongly implies that his son is dead, and that has to be got rid of. It might be that a project of this kind tends in the end to involve total destruction of the world of reality, to lead to paranoia."[9] After the wife succeeds in believing her husband is innocent, what is the effect of this on her noetic structure? What happens every time she looks at the suit on which the strand of hair was found or sees a handkerchief? What happens every time she sees a strand of blonde hair? every time she sees her husband talking to a blonde? every time she sees a telephone number? Must she repress memories and deny this is important evidence against her spouse's faithfulness? Do we have enough control over our knowledge about our unconscious selves to be able to

predict the final result of volitional believing on our personality and character?

The utilitarian argument against volitional manipulation of our belief mechanisms might be stated this way.

1. Voliting is morally justified only if we have adequate evidence (acquired nonvolitionally) that it will result in better consequences than if we abstain from voliting.

2. But our noetic structure is such that we almost never do have adequate evidence it will produce better consequences.

3. Therefore, voliting is almost never morally justified.

We almost never know how we will be affected by frustrating and manipulating our normal belief-forming mechanisms. Our subconscious realm, where normal beliefs are formed, seems very complex, so that in attempting to influence it over one matter, we may cause unpredictable chain reactions within our noetic structure.

Of course, Meiland might well reply that if, on reflection, the cost is going to be this great, we ought not believe against sufficient evidence in most cases. Perhaps this is a satisfactory reply, and perhaps our main difference is merely one of emphasis: Meiland arguing against rigid evidentialism that makes objective justification an absolute duty and I arguing for a presumption of truth seeking, making it a very high moral duty. These are not incompatible views. However, I think there is more to our difference than this. The difference is rooted in two different views on how evidence is processed and of the possibility of consciously willing to have certain beliefs against what is taken to be good evidence. Meiland simply believes we have more control over our beliefs than I believe we do, and this difference results in a difference about the relevancy of volitional strategies.

Meiland has a pragmatic justification of belief that goes like this:

1. A has sufficient evidence for *p* (there is a strong inclination on A's part to believe *p* or A does believe *p*), but A also has nonevidential reasons for believing not *p*.

2. A decides, after reflection, that it is morally permissible or obligatory to get himself into a position where he believes not-*p*.

3. A takes whatever steps are necessary in order to get into that position, and presumably, A comes to believe not-*p*.

There is something odd about this argument, for it raises the fundamental question (considered in Section I) of whether a rational person can consciously carry out a cognitive volit or sustain a belief while knowing that he or she has obtained the belief solely through a fiat of the will. For example, what happens when the wife, in Meiland's example, reflects on her belief that her husband is innocent? She looks at her belief and looks at the way it was brought about. Can she go on believing her husband is innocent despite the sufficient evidence to the contrary? There seems to be something incoherent about the phenomena of consciously acquiring or sustaining a belief regardless of the perceived evidence against the belief. This brings me to my final criticism of Meiland's position.

Fourth, Meiland may escape all my objections by arguing that while it is always relevant in principle to take pragmatic considerations into account in acquiring (and sustaining) beliefs, it may hardly ever be our actual duty. He may defend his flank by saying he merely wants to show that truth seeking (as the rigid evidentialist conceives of it) is not an absolute moral duty but is overridable in some instances. But if this is all he is saying, his position surely loses much of its brashness and excitement. It may be true, but it is hardly new. Most moral systems since W. D. Ross and including such unlikely bedfellows as Richard Brandt, William Frankena, R. M. Hare, and J. L. Mackie would agree that there are few, if any, moral absolutes, and that truth seeking is not a moral absolute (nonoverridable) but a strong *prima facie* duty. Meiland's position must be stronger than this to be interesting, but if it is stronger than this, it seems implausible.

Criteria for Morally Prescriptive Indirect Volitionalism

Let me conclude this essay by offering a set of criteria by which to decide when it is morally permissible to indirectly volit. I agree with Meiland against Clifford, Gale, and others who contend we ought never under any circumstances to get ourselves to believe anything where the evidence alone doesn't warrant it but simply because we have a need to believe it. Although I think instances of justified voliting (indirectly) are probably exceedingly rare, there may be some. Meiland's example of the wife concerned with saving her marriage may indeed be such a case. Another may be the following. Suppose I gain some information about you that causes me to act in a way you perceive as harmful to your interests and suppose that I have obtained this information in a morally unacceptable way, say, by reading your diary or private correspondence, and that I would not have had this information had I not read this material. Suppose, further, there is a competent psychiatrist who can bring it about, at minimum risk, that I totally forget the information I possess about your private life. Or suppose there is a psychologically harmless pill that will do this same thing. Is it obvious that you would not have a right to demand I take the necessary steps to forget the memory belief I have? Perhaps a certain type of forgiveness involves getting ourselves, through autosuggestion, to forget in part the seriousness of the acts against us. Of course, self-creating beliefs seem the best examples of what may be morally permissible in this area. Suppose you must swim two miles to shore in order to save your life. You have never swum so far and have good evidence you can't do it. However, you reason that if you can get yourself to believe you can swim two miles, the confidence will somehow produce a physiological state giving you a better chance of swimming two miles (although not quite a 50 percent chance). Would you not be justified in getting yourself into that place?

If at times it is morally permissible or even obligatory to volit a belief against sufficient evidence, what conditions must be met? I suggest the following: a prudential condition and two utilitarian conditions (a general and a specific).

1. *A prudential requirement.* The justified volit would have to involve a nonvolitional cost–benefit analysis that might be undermined if the agent were not a dispositional evidentialist. The act must be seen as possible and worth doing on the evidence available. There must be some morally acceptable benefit that outweighs the cost involved in getting the new belief by voliting.

2. *A general utility requirement.* Others must not be significantly harmed by this act, or their harm must not outweigh the benefits that would accrue to the agent, and the benefits must be normally acceptable. Again, the leap is parasitical on evidentialism, for a mistake may be dangerous. For example, if I get myself to believe the world will end shortly (for religious reasons) and then I become secretary of the interior, I may treat the environment so poorly as to hasten the end of the world.

3. *The chain of deception requirement.* This is a special instance of the utility requirement. In getting yourself into a state S where you will believe *p*, which you presently do not believe on the evidence, you will be responsible for a chain of unnecessary false reports. That is, if you were to tell others *p* was the case, you would be lying. Although the self that actually reports *p* will not be lying, that self is spreading a falsehood (or reporting falsely), becoming an unreliable witness and starting a possible chain of false reports. In essence, in willing to deceive your future self, who will sincerely report to others, you are taking on the responsibility for deceiving others. As the beginning of a chain of misinformation, only the most extreme grounds would seem to justify the volit.

If, however, you can make a cost–benefit analysis in the most rigorously evidentialist fashion and can determine that the volit is both psychologically possible and worth the cost of deceiving yourself and possibly others, then perhaps the volit is justified. If you are sure you are not going to bring harm to others or lessen their autonomy significantly and that you will not harm your children by being an unreliable witness, then you might well be justified in acquiring a belief by willing to have it and doing what is necessary to bring it about. But who can be so certain, given the uncertainty of how all these factors will work out in life? James's stranded mountain climber at the edge of the gorge certainly seems to be, for his options are limited. The person who read your diary may also be justified in trying to forget his or her belief. Perhaps the hermit who lives alone on an island is justified, though perhaps he or she has an obligation to place a sign on the dock, warning people who approach that they trespass at their own risk, for the inhabitant has engaged regularly in voliting and may seriously misinform them on certain matters. For the rest of us,

almost all the time, indirect voliting will not be a relevant consideration, but will be an imprudent and immoral act. Because truth matters, and because we can take steps to acquire habits making true beliefs more likely, there is an ethics of belief.

Notes

1 Descartes, *Meditations,* trans. E. Haldane and G. R. T. Ross (Cambridge, England: Cambridge University Press, 1911), Meditation IV and Replies, p. 175.

2 Thomas Aquinas, *Summa Theologica* Part II, Q. 4, Art. 2; Søren Kierkegaard, *Philosophical Fragments,* trans. D. Swenson (Princeton, NJ: Princeton University Press, 1962), p. 104; John Henry Newman, *An Essay in Aid of a Grammar of Assent* (Westminster, MD: Christian Classics, 1973), p. 232; William James, "The Will to Believe" in *Essays in Pragmatism* (New York: Haefner, 1969); Joseph Pieper, *Belief and Faith* (New York: Pantheon Press, 1956), p. 25f; Roderick Chisholm, "Lewis' Ethics of Belief" in Paul Schilpp, ed., *The Philosophy of C. I. Lewis* (Peru, IL: Open Court, 1968); Jack Meiland, "What Ought We to Believe" (*American Philosophical Quarterly, 17,* no. 1 (January 1980), 15–24; and Robert Holyer, "Belief and Will Revisited" (*Dialogue,* 1983).

3 There is one final objection to my thesis that we do not (normally) acquire beliefs by voliting. This objection centers on the phenomenon of self-creative or self-verifying beliefs, the activity described by William James in his classic essay "The Will to Believe," whereby one's deciding to believe is causally operative in creating a state of affairs that makes the belief true. This, the objector claims, seems like a normal case of volitionalism. Suppose you are going to play a game of chess. Your using autosuggestion to get into a state of mind where you believe you will win actually plays a causal role in your winning (it may, of course, have the reverse effect through causing overconfidence). James's own example (with my filling out an interpretation) is of a man trapped at the edge of a crevasse, overlooking a yawning gorge. He calculates that a successful leap is improbable, but it will increase in probability in proportion to his convincing himself that he must get himself to believe what an impartial look at the evidence will not allow. So he volits the belief. Or consider a student who loves philosophy and whose self-identity is centered on the goal of being a good philosopher. She doubts whether she will ever become such, but believes that her chances of becoming good will be increased by believing that she will reach that goal. So she apparently volits and believes without sufficient evidence that she will become a good philosopher. Because of this confidence, she succeeds where she would have otherwise failed. These sort of cases have been used as counterexamples to my arguments against volitionalism.

Two things can be said about such cases. The first is that they are not counterexamples to the thesis that we cannot acquire beliefs by fiat of the will. It seems reasonable to say that a deliberation process went on in each of these cases in which the will *indirectly* caused belief by refocusing the mind on favorable evidence rather than on the unfavorable evidence. No volit is necessary.

For example, caught as I am before the yawning gorge, I ask myself, how in the world am I to attain the presumably necessary belief (which I don't have) that I can jump the gorge. I cannot just acquire it by a fiat, so I hit on the idea of thinking of all the successful long jumps I made in grammar school. I then imagine myself a great Olympic track star. Perhaps a little self-hypnosis helps here. I focus on appropriate successes (real or imaginary), block out negative thoughts (if I can), and finally self-deceive myself to the point where I believe that I believe that I can leap over the crevasse. But all this illustrates is a case of indirect volitional control, not direct control over believing. I have a goal, plan a policy of action, and indirectly come to attain that goal.

The second thing to say is that this example seems to be an instance where a form of self-deception has salutary effects.

[4] H. H. Price, *Belief* (London: Allen & Unwin, 1967), p. 238.

[5] John Stuart Mill, *On Liberty* (London: 1859). Mill continues, "the appropriate region of human liberty . . .

comprises liberty of conscience in the most comprehensive sense: Liberty of thought and feeling, absolute freedom of opinion on all subjects practical and speculative, scientific, moral or theological." The statement is ambiguous, seeming to conflate the right to be protected from doxastic coercion and the right to manipulate our minds as we see fit.

[6] Jack Meiland, "What Ought We to Believe, or the Ethics of Belief Revisited," *American Philosophical Quarterly 17* (January 1980), 15–24. Reprinted in this anthology (the preceding reading).

[7] Chisholm, "Lewis' Ethics of Belief"; Stephen Nathanson, "The Ethics of Belief," in *Philosophy and Phenomenological Research,* 1982.

[8] W. K. Clifford, "The Ethics of Belief," in *Lectures and Essays,* 2d ed. (London: Macmillan, 1866) (Reading X.1 in this anthology).

[9] Bernard Williams, "Deciding to Believe," in *Problems of the Self* (Cambridge, England: Cambridge University Press, 1972).

X.5 *Epistemic Obligations*

Richard Feldman

Richard Feldman is Professor of Philosophy at the University of Rochester. In this essay, he considers the concept of epistemic obligation and distinguishes it from pragmatic and moral obligations. He argues that because epistemic states are not under our direct control, they are not subject to moral or pragmatic assessment but are closer to institutional duties (for example, financial and legal obligations). Next Feldman sets forth an evidentialist account of epistemic duties, arguing against those who deny that there are such duties.

I

Suppose an unfortunate student, Jones, is about to take an oral exam with an unusually difficult teacher. In fact, the failure rate on oral exams with

Reprinted from *Philosophical Perspectives, 2 Epistemology, 1988,* ed. James Tomberlin (Atascadero, CA: Ridgeview Publishing Company, © 1988) by permission of the publisher.

this teacher is grim indeed: only 10% of the students who take the exam pass it. One slightly encouraging fact is that people who are optimistic about their chances for passing the exam tend to do a little better: 20% of them pass it. Apparently, the teacher's evaluations are improved by sincere manifestations of confidence. Let us also suppose that Jones, the student, has no particularly good information about his own abilities on the material to be covered on the tests. Assume next that Jones is a relatively normal person and that he has a strong desire to pass the test. Assume finally that Jones is aware of all of this and is considering the proposition that he will pass the exam.

We may ask what, given this information, Jones ought to believe. Should he believe that he will pass the oral exam?[1] When Jones considers the proposition that he will pass the exam, he must take exactly one of three attitudes toward it: he must either believe it, disbelieve it, or suspend judgment with respect to it. One of these attitudes will be the one that he ought to have.[2]

One may find oneself with conflicting intuitions about what Jones should do. On the one hand, it surely is in Jones's interest to believe that he'll pass; one could hardly blame him for doing whatever he could to improve his chances. Since he wants to pass and knows that the best way to increase his chances is to believe that he'll pass, he should believe that he'll pass. At the very least, this way of thinking about the case makes it seem clear that it is permissible for him to believe that he'll pass. In other words, it is not the case that he ought to believe that he won't pass.

On the other hand, his evidence makes passing look unlikely, and this inclines us to say that believing that he'll pass "flies in the face of the facts." After he finds out that he's failed and we're dealing with his disappointment, we might say that he should have realized that he wouldn't pass. That is, given his information, he should not have believed that he would pass. So, it seems that there is some basis for saying that he shouldn't believe that he'll pass, as well as some basis for saying that he should believe that he'll pass.

The apparent conflict between these inclinations can be resolved easily. The inclination to say that Jones ought to believe that he'll pass concerns a *practical* or *prudential* sense of obligation. Sometimes it makes sense to treat beliefs like other actions and to evaluate their practical or prudential merit. Jones's optimistic belief scores well in this evaluation, and this accounts for our judgment that it is a belief he ought to have. The contrary intuition concerns *epistemic* obligation. The peculiarly epistemic judgment concerns not these practical merits but rather the propriety of a disinterested believer in Jones's situation having that belief. Since Jones's optimistic belief does not come out so well on these grounds, it is epistemically improper. Epistemic obligation, then, concerns obligations to believe to

which the practical benefits of beliefs are not relevant. They are obligations that arise from a purely impartial and disinterested perspective.[3]

Epistemic obligation also differs from *moral* obligation. There may be cases in which having a belief is morally significant. If there are such cases, then it may be that the moral factors lead one to a different belief than the epistemic factors. Thus, for example, one might have a moral duty to trust one's friends and family, thereby making it morally obligatory that one believe their claims. At the same time, one's purely epistemic obligation may well lead the other way. In allowing for this possibility, I may be disagreeing with the well-known claim of William K. Clifford (1886), who said that "It is wrong, always, everywhere, and for every one, to believe anything upon insufficient evidence." (p. 346). If 'wrong' here expresses moral wrongness, as the context suggests it does, then Clifford is claiming that one never is morally permitted to believe what is not supported by one's evidence.[4] And, given what I will argue later, this is equivalent to saying that one is never morally permitted to believe what one is not epistemically permitted to believe. Equivalently, if one epistemically ought to believe something, then, on Clifford's view, one also morally ought to believe it. That, as I said, seems wrong to me, since the moral consequences of an epistemically obligatory belief might be very bad. Thus, I think epistemic and moral obligation are distinct.

This discussion of the ethics of belief, of the moral status of beliefs, suggests an obvious and important issue. It is generally held that something can be obligatory only if it is a free action, only if it is something over which the agent has control. But it is doubtful that beliefs are, for the most part, free, voluntary, or controllable actions. Hence, it seems that there can't be any epistemic obligations to have beliefs. I respond to this claim in the next section. In subsequent sections I will develop an account of what our epistemic obligations are.

II

The objection to there being any epistemic obligations concerns doxastic voluntarism, the view that having a belief is something a person does voluntarily and can control. Alvin Plantinga (1986) has recently defended a version of this objection, arguing that if accepting a "proposition is not up to me, then accepting . . . [that] . . . proposition cannot be a way in which I can fulfill my obligation to the truth, or indeed *any* obligation." (p. 12). Plantinga thinks that it is as absurd to hold that one has epistemic obligations if doxastic voluntarism is false as it is to hold that one has obligations regarding which way to fall—up or down—after one has gone off a cliff.

Plantinga's point can be formulated as a simple argument, which I will call 'The Voluntarism Argument':

1. Doxastic voluntarism is false.

2. If doxastic voluntarism is false, then no one has epistemic obligations.

3. Therefore, no one has epistemic obligations.

The Voluntarism Argument has considerable plausibility. There is a long tradition that makes only voluntary or controllable actions the subject of obligations, so (2) seems true. And it does seem that we can't control our beliefs. In the ordinary course of events, one finds oneself with some beliefs and rather little one can do about them. If revelations about your favorite politician cause you to believe that he is dishonest, then you might wish that you didn't have this belief. Although you may be able to put the matter out of mind, you can't, at will, change your belief about the topic. Similarly, all the perceptual beliefs that you have seem just to come over you. When I go outside on a typical winter day in Rochester, the belief that it is cold and gray outside just comes over me. In general, there is rather little we can do about our beliefs. They seem not to be matters under our control. So, (1) seems to be correct as well.

Despite the apparent truth of (1) and (2), philosophers have denied each premise. Although some philosophers, perhaps Descartes, have thought that beliefs are voluntarily adopted and maintained, few have rejected (1) on this basis. A more plausible reason for rejecting (1) has been advanced by John Heil (1983). His idea is that although we can't "directly" control our beliefs (in some sense of 'direct'), we can indirectly control

them. There are things we can do to alter the ways in which we form beliefs and the kind of information which we receive. I can, for example, study logic and probability theory with the aim of reducing the number of mistaken inferences I draw. I might read the publications of some political or religious groups with the aim of eventually coming to accept the general set of beliefs they support. These and any number of other voluntary actions will affect my beliefs, and I may perform the actions for that very purpose. Hence, I do have some sort of indirect control over my beliefs. And this indirect control over beliefs makes some sort of doxastic voluntarism true, so (1) is false.

Heil is surely right about there being some sense in which we can indirectly control our beliefs. Perhaps, this shows that not every version of doxastic voluntarism is true. However, defenders of The Voluntarism Argument are likely to contend that (1) and (2) are true when 'doxastic voluntarism' is taken to refer to the view that people have the relevant sort of "direct" control over their beliefs. They would argue that indirect control of the sort Heil discusses is not sufficient for there to be epistemic obligations. At most, they would grant that Heil has shown that there can be obligations to perform the sort of belief inducing actions Heil mentions. He has not shown that there can be epistemic obligations to believe or disbelieve anything. I'm inclined to agree with Heil's critics here, although the meanings of 'direct' and 'indirect' are sufficiently obscure to make these issues extremely difficult to sort out.

In any case, we are willing to say of people that they should or should not believe things even in cases in which they do not have the ability to undertake courses of action that might affect their beliefs in the relevant way. So, our intuitive judgments do not limit epistemic obligations to cases in which we have the sort of indirect control Heil describes. Thus, an equally damaging version of The Voluntarism Argument, restricted to cases of this sort, can be constructed.

Examples of the sorts of cases I have in mind are ones in which seemingly unchangeable psychological factors determine one's beliefs. For example, I just can't help believing that I see some tables and chairs now. Moreover, it is unlikely that I could embark upon any course of action, even the study of skepticism, which would lead me to believe otherwise in similar situations. Despite my inability to avoid this belief, this is exactly what I should believe in my current situation. Similarly, as a result of some psychological factors one may be unable to do anything about some of one's beliefs about oneself or one's family. For example, some people never believe that they are successful or talented, no matter what their accomplishments. Such people often should have better opinions of themselves, but there may be nothing they can do to change their negative attitude. Thus, there seem to be epistemic obligations even in cases in which we don't have the limited sort of control Heil describes. But the modified Voluntarism Argument has the conclusion that we don't have epistemic obligations in these cases. Thus defenders of epistemic obligations need a response to that argument that goes beyond Heil's. They need a way to reconcile the apparent truth of doxastic involuntarism with their inclination to ascribe epistemic obligations even in these cases.

Another way to respond to The Voluntarism Argument is to deny (2), the claim that if voluntarism is false, then there are no epistemic obligations. One might reject (2) on the basis of the idea that epistemic obligations pertain not to doxastic states but rather to actions that lead to doxastic states. Thus, my epistemic obligations may be to gather lots of evidence, to listen carefully to critics, and the like. While I grant that there may be obligations to perform actions such as these, I think that this response simply evades the point at issue here. My concern is with obligations to believe and the question is whether there can be any such obligations if doxastic voluntarism is false. The existence of these other obligations, whether they are called 'epistemic obligations' or not, is thus beside the point.

A more promising variant on this objection to (2) has been proposed by Keith Lehrer (1981). Lehrer suggests that the notion of belief should be replaced in some epistemological analyses with that of acceptance. The difference between the two "concerns the element of optionality. Sometimes a person cannot decide what to believe at a moment, but he can decide what to accept. . . . Believing is not an action. Accepting is." (pp. 79–80). Since accepting is an action over which one has control, one can have obligations to accept or not accept

certain propositions. Accounts of these obligations could be constructed that are perfectly analogous to the accounts of obligations to believe that will be considered later. This sort of view preserves the traditional connection between obligation and voluntariness, is consistent with the apparent fact that beliefs are not voluntarily formed or retained, yet makes sense of something like epistemic obligation. I will argue shortly that it is possible to have obligations with respect to involuntary behavior, but those who reject that conclusion may translate all subsequent discussion of obligations regarding beliefs into talk of obligations to accept propositions.[5]

I think that the best response to The Voluntarism Argument is to deny (2) on the grounds that there can be obligations concerning involuntary behavior. It may be true that with respect to *some* sorts of obligation, one has obligations of those sorts only if one has control over the relevant actions, only if one can act (and can avoid acting) in the obligatory way. This seems most clearly true with respect to moral obligation. Perhaps there are also notions of prudential obligation and "all things considered" obligation that obtain only when the person has control over the obligatory behavior. It is never the case that one is obligated, in these senses, to do things one can't avoid doing (or must do).

However, it is equally clear that there are obligations and requirements that obtain in the absence of our ability to fulfill them. Here are some examples. In the beginning of a semester teachers typically tell their students what they are obligated to do as students in the class. We might say that students have an academic obligation to do that work. We also say, more naturally, that they are required to do the work. It often happens that later in the semester students report that they are unable to complete the work. Teachers respond to such claims in any number of ways, but I doubt that any say, "Well, if you can't do it, it follows that you are not required to do it." We are more apt to tell them what we do to students who don't complete their requirements.

To make the case more concrete, and like some Plantinga (1986) considers in his defense of The Voluntarism Argument, suppose a student comes to me and says that he cannot write a term paper because he has a brain lesion that makes him fall asleep whenever he thinks about the paper topic. In this case, it may be best for me to change his requirements or to advise him to switch to another course in which he can fulfill his requirements. His inability plainly does not make it the case that he does not have these academic obligations or course requirements. (His inability makes him not morally required to do the work.) Thus, the student's course requirements include doing work he is unable to do. Similarly, course requirements may include doing something that a student can't refrain from doing. If, somehow, a brain lesion or a malicious demon makes a student unable to avoid doing logic problems identical to those assigned by the logic teacher, it does not follow that he was not required to do those problems. These kinds of obligations or requirements do not imply freedom or control.

Similar considerations apply to some other obligations. When I took out a mortgage on my house I incurred a legal obligation to pay the bank each month a certain sum of money. The amount is roughly equal to my entire monthly salary. If my salary goes down, or I lose my job and I can't pay, I'm sure that officials in the bank's foreclosure department would properly be unimpressed by the argument: "I can't pay you the money you say I owe you; therefore, I have no financial obligation to pay you that money." I still am legally (or financially) obligated to pay, even though I can't do it. On the other hand, if I arrange things so that the money is automatically taken out of my bank account and it is impossible for me to change that, I may be unable to avoid paying the mortgage. I retain my obligation to pay.

I conclude from these examples that there can be non-moral and non-prudential obligations that one can't fulfill and ones that one can't avoid fulfilling. Thus, I think that it is plausible to hold that there can be epistemic obligations that one can't fulfill and ones that one can't avoid fulfilling. Sometimes, one can't believe what one ought to believe and sometimes one can't help believing what one ought to believe. There can be epistemic obligations even if doxastic voluntarism is false.

Some examples, mentioned above, seem to me to give this view support. Normally, while observing the world one forms a lot of perceptual beliefs that are in the relevant sense unavoidable. Yet, many of those beliefs are ones that one should have. For example, when one is looking at a table in clear light one should believe that one sees a table, rather than deny or suspend judgment about the proposition. Fortunately, then, in these cases most of us can't help doing what we epistemically ought to do. But people who are driven to beliefs by hopes, fears, or other emotions may be unable to believe what they epistemically ought to believe.

I can think of two objections to my claim that epistemic obligations don't require doxastic voluntarism. The first grants that some sorts of obligations don't carry implications of freedom and control, but adds that some do and that epistemic obligations are of the latter sort. I've admitted that moral and prudential obligations may obtain only where there is control, but claimed that legal and financial obligations can obtain in the absence of freedom and control. My suggestion is that epistemic obligations are of the latter sort and the response is that they are of the former sort.

I believe that this objection is mistaken. Two remarks are in order. First, I think that the examples support my side. That is, it is natural to say things like "He should (or shouldn't) believe that" even in cases in which there is no freedom or control. The examples already described indicate that. Second, as I hope to show later in this paper, a plausible account of epistemic obligations can be developed which makes it clear that epistemic obligations don't have much to do with freedom and control. Of course, the force of this point turns on the merits of the account to be developed later.

I turn now to the second response to my claim that (2) is false. Recall that my defense relies on the claim that there are some obligations, such as academic and legal ones, that do not require voluntarism. The response is that academic and legal obligations are not, strictly speaking, cases of simple obligation at all. They are, rather, cases of conditional obligation. What's true of the student might be put this way: given that he wants to pass this course, he ought to write the paper. What's true of me is: given that I want to keep my house, I ought to pay my mortgage. Couple these accounts of the obligations present in these cases with the denial of a rule of detachment for obligation statements and one then has the basis for denying that I have presented any cases of obligations that cannot be fulfilled. That is, from these conditional obligations and the facts that the student does want to pass the course and I do want to keep my house, it does not follow that the student ought to do the work or that I ought to pay the mortgage. Hence, we do not yet have cases of unfulfillable unconditional obligations.

If financial and academic obligations are best understood as conditional obligations, and one can have conditional obligations that one cannot fulfill (or cannot avoid fulfilling), then, I think, epistemic obligations can also be understood as conditional obligations that one might be unable to fulfill. If epistemic obligations are best interpreted as conditional obligations, then perhaps they are conditional upon the desire to be epistemically excellent: to say that you epistemically ought to believe *p* is to say that given that you want to achieve epistemic excellence, you ought to believe *p*.

I don't particularly want to defend this analysis. However, I will concede to anyone who insists that the examples I have given of unfulfillable obligations are really only examples of unfulfillable conditional obligations. My claim about epistemic obligations could then be recast as the claim that epistemic obligations are also conditional obligations and they may also be unfulfillable. And if this is the case, then my main claim in this section remains unrefuted: ordinary talk about epistemic obligations, talk about what one ought to believe, carries no implications about doxastic voluntarism. We can, then, look into the nature of epistemic obligations without worrying further about whether doxastic voluntarism is true.

III

I turn next to discussion of the most widely accepted account of what our epistemic obligations are. This view traces back at least to William James (1911). James says,

> There are two ways of looking at our duty in the matter of opinion,—ways entirely different, and yet ways about whose difference the theory of knowledge seems hitherto to have shown little concern. We *must know the truth:* and *we must avoid error,*—these are our first and great commandments as would-be knowers; but they are not two ways of stating an identical commandment, they are two separable laws. . . . By choosing between them we may end by coloring differently our whole intellectual life. . . . For my part, I can believe that worse things than being duped may happen to a man (pp. 17–19).[6]

James states his view in terms of two related "commandments" or imperatives: know the truth and avoid error. In telling us to avoid error, James is telling us that we should not believe falsehoods. And his directive that we know the truth implies that we should believe truths. So, James's idea seems to be that we should believe truths and should not believe falsehoods. His claim that these are two separable and independent commandments can be easily demonstrated. We can succeed in believing lots of truths by believing everything. If one does this (assuming that one can believe both a proposition and its negation), then one will surely have managed to believe all the truths, or at least all the truths among the propositions one considers. But that hardly achieves any sort of epistemic excellence. On the other hand, by believing very little we surely manage to avoid error. But this excessive caution does not achieve epistemic excellence either. It is by attaining a suitable mix of the two goals that we will achieve epistemic excellence. That, according to the Jamesian view, is what we ought to do.

An account of epistemic obligation along Jamesian lines has become a philosophical commonplace. In setting out his own account of epistemic requirements, Roderick Chisholm (1977) cites the passage from James just quoted as his source. Keith Lehrer (1981) uses a notion of reasonableness as the fundamental notion in his account of knowledge, and he says the following about his concept: "When we use the notion of reasonableness in our definition, we mean reasonable for the purpose of pursuing truth. The pursuit of truth involves an interest in obtaining a story free of error, or as much so as we can, and obtaining the whole story, or as much as we can. These combined interests may pull in opposite directions, but they both bear the stamp of legitimacy in the quest of truth." (p. 87). Roderick Firth (1978) discusses, but does not ultimately defend, an analysis of epistemic warrant in terms of "a duty to believe propositions if and only if they are true." (p. 224). The Jamesian flavor in these passages is obvious.

Other writers describe a view very much like James's as 'standard' or 'familiar'. Paul Moser (1985) writes, "A familiar characterization of epistemic obligation states that it is the (prima facie) obligation one has, *qua* truth-seeker, to maximize true belief and to minimize, if not to avoid, false belief." (p. 214). Peter Markie (1986) describes the end (or goal) of believing all and only what is true about the matter under investigation as "the standard epistemic imperative". (p. 37). Richard Foley (1987) says that ". . . a distinctly epistemic goal . . . [is] . . . what epistemologists often have said it to be, now to believe those propositions that are true and now not to believe those propositions that are false." Each of the three writers just mentioned eventually defends an account of epistemic obligation along Jamesian lines and describes such accounts as familiar or standard.

While James's view may seem straightforward enough, there actually is some difficulty in figuring out exactly what his claims amount to. James speaks of "commandments", Chisholm speaks of "requirements", Moser speaks of "obligations", Markie and Foley both speak of "ends" and Markie frames the idea in terms of an imperative. While all of these ideas may be fairly similar, there are differences worthy of our attention, and it is not entirely obvious just how the Jamesian line can be put into plausible account of epistemic obligations.

As a first attempt at a Jamesian view about epistemic obligation, we might try the following:

> (1) S is epistemically obligated to believe *p* if *p* is true and S is epistemically obligated to disbelieve *p* if *p* is false.

(1) is subject to several obvious and decisive objections.

First of all, it is clear that sometimes one epistemically ought to suspend judgement about some propositions. However, (1) implies that everyone should believe every truth and disbelieve every falsehood, thereby leaving no room for suspension of judgment. Suppose a coin I know to be fair has been tossed, I have not seen how it landed, and do not have any other information about how it landed. Surely, I ought to suspend judgment about the proposition that it came up heads. But (1) says that I ought to believe it came up heads if it did come up heads and disbelieve that if it didn't. That's clearly wrong. I ought to suspend judgment in this and many other cases in which I have no good information about the truth value of the proposition in question.

It is equally clear that sometimes people should believe propositions that are in fact false. Suppose that some proposition, *p*, is false but all the evidence anyone has indicates that *p* is true, and some person carefully collects and weighs all the evidence, and then believes *p* on the basis of that evidence. Then surely that person is believing what he epistemically ought to believe. It may be that the evidence is in some sense misleading, but if the person has no way to know that, then the mere falsity of his belief does not demonstrate that he had failed to do what he epistemically should have done. To say, for example, that ancient school children should have believed that the Earth was (roughly) round, since it is roughly round, is to miss the point of epistemic obligation altogether. By believing that the Earth is flat such children were believing exactly what they should have believed, given the situation they were in.

But if (1) is false, and so seriously off the mark, what could James have had in mind in asserting it? And what have others had in mind in endorsing his view? I believe that we can arrive at an answer to these questions by considering an analogy. Investors are often urged to "buy low and sell high". That is, they should buy stocks that are at a low point and will go up and they should sell stocks that are at a high point and will go down. Thus, we might say

> (2) S ought to buy stock x if the price of x will go up and S ought to sell x if the price of x will go down.

While (2) may seem to express some truth, there is at least one straightforward interpretation under which it is plainly false. Suppose that, as a matter of fact, some stock is about to go up, but all available indications are that it is about to go down. Perhaps it has just been discovered that the company's sole product is defective, e.g., house paint that is water-soluble after it dries. There seems to be a clear sense in which, assuming one knows this, one ought not buy the stock. (Ignore the possibility that one might do well by being a "contrarian".) If all the information one has suggests that a stock will go down, then it is a bad idea to buy it. In some sense of 'ought', one ought not buy such stocks. One ought to follow the best indicators of future price that one has. So, (2), at least with "ought' understood this way, is false.

There is, however, some truth in the vicinity of (2). It is:

> (3) One's goals as an investor are to buy stocks that will go up and to sell stocks that will go down.

(3) specifies some *goals* of investing. Although (3) may seem trivial, it is not. You might explain to children who know nothing about the stock market that these are the goals of investing. One could, in fact, disagree about whether (3) is entirely accurate or complete. Some would claim that one's goals are, or should be, different, or at least broader. Profits may not be the only goal. Perhaps investing in companies that meet some political or social values one has is important as well. So (3) is a plausible and non-trivial claim about investment objectives.

More specific investment advice can be seen as advice about how best to satisfy the goal specified in (3). So, when one is told that one ought to buy stocks in companies in expanding rather than declining industries, one is being told about a means to an end. Our obligations, perhaps, are to do what is best (in some sense) to accomplish some end. There is much that remains to be said about all of this. There are, in particular, questions about what exactly counts as the "best" means for achieving these investment ends. But I will ignore these issues for now and return to the epistemic case, which I think is quite similar.

I think that James's remarks are best seen as comments about epistemic ends, not about epistemic obligations. This makes James's view most similar to the one expressed by Foley in the passage quoted above. He has told us what we are to strive for as epistemic agents. He has told us nothing about what means we ought to follow in order to

achieve those ends. Thus, I think that a truth about epistemic ends can be formulated as follows:

> (4) One's goals as a rational believer are to believe things that are true and to avoid believing things that are false.

Again, this may seem trivial, but it isn't. (4) calls our attention to what the proper epistemic ends are. According to this view, it is not to believe things that are edifying or expansive. It is not to believe what makes us feel good. It is not to have opinions that differ from those of our parents. It is to get at the truth. Telling this to children, or to college freshmen, could be useful and enlightening. But (4) leaves open entirely what the proper means to this end are. The passage from James simply has nothing to say about how we ought to go about achieving this end.

Thus, I think that what's true and Jamesian is (4). But (4) isn't a statement about epistemic obligations. One simple statement about obligations somehow connected to (4) is (1). But (1) is false. We have, then, no adequate account of epistemic obligations.

IV

Chisholm (1977) has defended an account of epistemic obligations that is clearly derived from James's account, but which seems to avoid the objections to (1) raised in the previous section. Chisholm writes,

> We may assume that every person is subject to a purely intellectual requirement—that of trying his best to bring it about that, for every proposition *h* that he considers, he accepts *h* if and only if *h* is true. (p. 14).

This statement may be formulated as the following account of epistemic obligation:

> (5) For any proposition *p* and person S, if S considers *p* then S is epistemically obligated to try his best to bring it about that S believes *p* if and only if *p* is true.

This could, of course, be broken up into two principles, one saying that a person is obligated to try to believe *p* if *p* is true and the other saying that the person is obligated to try to avoid believing *p* if *p* is false. Thus Chisholm's view connects with James's in an obvious way. James has said, in principle (4), that the two epistemic ends are to believe truths and to avoid believing falsehoods. Chisholm has said that our epistemic obligation is to try our best to achieve these ends with respect to the propositions we consider.

One obstacle to determining exactly what implications (5) has is the fact that (5) gives no directive about the relative weights given to the obligation to try to believe truths and the obligation to try to avoid believing falsehoods. One might be cautious, and weigh the obligation to try to avoid error more heavily. On the other hand, one might advocate a more adventurous attitude, and emphasize the obligation to try for the truth more strongly. James himself seems to support the latter view, in his remark that he "can believe that worse things than being duped may happen to a man." (1911, p. 19). I think that this is a suggestion to the effect that it is better to be bold, and form beliefs in an effort to get at the truth, than it is to be cautious and avoid belief in an effort to avoid error. I will not pursue this issue, however, because I think that there are more fundamental questions to be raised about (5), and I want to turn to them instead.

I will consider two objections to Chisholm's view. The first objection is that it construes our epistemic obligations far too narrowly, mentioning only obligations to try for the truth and to try to avoid error, omitting many other important epistemic goals. Plantinga (1986) raises this sort of objection in his discussion of Chisholm. He writes, "Obviously, something must be said about *other* epistemic values: the importance of considering *important* propositions, of having beliefs on certain topics, of avoiding unnecessary clutter and trivial dilettantism, etc." (p. 6). Thus, Plantinga thinks Chisholm construes our epistemic obligations too narrowly, considering only our obligation to the truth and ignoring our obligation to be what we might call "good epistemic agents".

I do not wish to deny that there is plausibility in the view that we ought, in some sense, to be good epistemic agents. However, I think that being a good epistemic agent in this sense is irrelevant to the central notion of epistemic obligation, and irrelevant to the sort of obligation with which Chisholm is concerned. Thus I deny that Chisholm has given too narrow an account of our epistemic obligations. I grant, however, that there may be another sort of obligation, distinct from the one with which he is concerned, to which Plantinga is calling attention. Thus, I think that Plantinga's objection to (5) fails.

To see what Chisholm has in mind, it is useful to focus on these questions: given that I am in the situation that I am in, and given that I am considering proposition *p*, what should I do—believe it, disbelieve it, or suspend judgment about it? Which of these three options is epistemically best? In thinking about these questions, one is to consider only these three options and only the end of getting at the truth about *p*. The particularly epistemic aspect of this is supposed to exclude from consideration other factors, such as which attitude would feel good or be comforting or be morally valuable. Also irrelevant to this judgment are the long-term epistemic consequences of adopting the belief. It is the truth about *p* now that matters. Thus, if believing something now would somehow lead me to believe lots of truths later, that long-term epistemic benefit is also irrelevant to this judgment. Foley, in the passage quoted previously, brings out the relevant point by emphasizing the key question related to epistemic obligation is "what should I believe *now*?"

In thinking about this question, being a good epistemic agent in the broader ways that Plantinga mentions is just irrelevant. Whether I have been, am, or will be a good agent—whether I consider important propositions, etc.—has no bearing on what attitude I epistemically ought to take toward *p* now. A person can fulfill the narrower obligations without being a good epistemic agent in the broader sense. He might have the attitude he ought to have toward each proposition he considers even though he spends most of his time considering a sequence of "unimportant" propositions of the form "n + 1 > n" and even if he seeks his intellectual stimulation by going bowling. All that he must do in order to fulfill his narrower epistemic obligations is to have the appropriate attitude toward the propositions he does consider.

Other things that have broader epistemic relevance are also irrelevant to this core notion of epistemic obligation. Consider the suggestion that one ought to seek and consider all relevant evidence. That may be a good idea, but when my question is what I should believe *now,* seeking more evidence just isn't one of my options. Suppose I haven't thought very carefully about some propositions, but the little evidence I have seen suggests that the proposition is true. I ask, "Should I believe that proposition now?" If you tell me that I should seek more evidence, then my original question remains unanswered. Perhaps I should seek more evidence or think about the matter further, but until I have a chance to do that, what should I believe? What should I believe *now?* It is this latter question, I think, that is the central epistemic question, and these issues about epistemic agency are quite clearly irrelevant to it.

It is clear, I think, that there are at least two different questions associated with epistemic obligation. One is the question about what to believe, or what attitude to take toward a particular proposition. This is the question I have been trying to focus on in the preceding paragraphs. There is also a legitimate set of questions about what actions ought to be pursued in an effort to obtain evidence, what issues ought to be the focus of attention and the like. My main point here is that these latter questions are distinct from and independent of the former one. The reason for this, again, is that even if it is true that I should seek more evidence or perform some other action in connection with some proposition, there always remains the question of what attitude I should take toward that proposition now, before (or while) I perform that action.

Sometimes it seems true that a person should seek more evidence concerning some proposition. It is important to realize that this does not imply that the person should suspend judgment about the proposition until that additional evidence is in. Whether I should seek additional evidence typically depends upon how important it is that I get a well-founded belief about the topic in question. An example described by Heil (1986) makes the point well. Suppose that you are in charge of an agency responsible for testing drugs and deciding whether they are to be sold to the public. You might have considerable evidence indicating that a particular drug is safe, sufficient evidence to make it reasonable for you to believe that it is safe. Of your three doxastic options, believing that it is safe is the one you ought to have. At the same time, it may also be true that because of the importance of being right, and the potential risks of allowing an unsafe drug on the market, you ought to seek further evidence about its safety.

This example shows the independence of questions about what actions regarding evidence gathering ought to be performed from questions about what ought to be believed. Since it is this latter sort of obligation with which Chisholm is concerned, the example helps us to see the error in Plantinga's contention that Chisholm has construed epistemic obligations too narrowly.

The example just considered, as well some others to be described below, suggest that the sorts of considerations Plantinga mentions are really relevant to some sort of practical obligations, not to any purely epistemic concerns. Whether the drug tester should seek more evidence seems to be a clear case of a decision problem in which the expected value of the possible actions is to be weighed. If the potential side effects of the drug are severe, more testing may be appropriate. If the drug offers a cure for a serious illness not yet treatable, perhaps foregoing additional testing would be prudent. There seems to be no purely epistemic considerations that decide this matter.

Other cases also suggest that epistemic considerations do not determine what evidence gathering activities are appropriate. To someone who tells me that I should seek additional evidence about some proposition, I might appropriately respond that there are better things for me to do with my time. Maybe it would be better for me to play with my daughter or take my dog for a walk. But these considerations are practical, not epistemological. There are never any purely epistemological considerations that decide these practical questions.

Whether I should be a better epistemic agent is always a practical question. The narrower question about what I should believe now, the question I want to focus on, is the central epistemological question.

Thus, I conclude that this first objection to (5) is mistaken. In thinking that these broader sorts of vaguely epistemological obligations that we may have are relevant to the central notion of epistemic obligation, Plantinga has conflated the epistemic aspects of a broader notion of practical obligation with the central notion of epistemic obligation.

A second objection to Chisholm's view, is, I think, more successful. Chisholm says very little about what counts as "trying one's best", but on at least one plausible interpretation, his view is clearly unsatisfactory. Other, more satisfactory interpretations, are possible, but then the view is in serious need of additional detail.

On Chisholm's view, one's goal is to believe all and only the truths one considers, and one's obligation is to try one's best to achieve that goal. But what counts as trying one's best? Suppose p is a truth I consider. In one straightforward sense of 'try my best to believe truths,' if p is true, then I've tried my best with respect to p if I bring it about that I do believe p. And if p is false, then I've tried my best to avoid error if I've tried in a way that brings it about that I don't believe p. More generally, on one reading of 'try my best to believe truths and avoid falsehood', I've fulfilled my obligation to do this if I've tried in the way that in fact makes me believe all and only truths. What could possibly be a better way to try to achieve a goal than to do what in fact makes one achieve that goal? There's at least one reading of 'try my best' that makes the answer "Nothing". In this sense, one has tried one's best when one has tried in the way that has the best results.

But this reading of 'try my best' saddles (5) with implausible implications that Chisholm surely did not intend. On this reading, when I've done whatever I can to bring it about that I believe truths, then I've done my best. Thus, if there is any way I can try that will make me believe p, and p is true, then I am obligated to try in that way. This is the case even if what I must do is make myself believe what my evidence clearly suggests to be false. Plainly, this is not what Chisholm intended. He surely agrees that there are times when doing one's epistemic best, doing what one epistemically should, will lead to avoidable false beliefs.

I suspect that what Chisholm has in mind is that some general ways or methods to try to believe the truth are better than others and that we epistemically ought to follow the best method. Thus, we might propose the following:

(6) For any proposition p and person S and time t, if S considers p at t, then S is epistemically obligated to believe p at t if and only if, if S were to follow the best available method for trying to believe truths and avoid believing falsehoods at t, then S would believe p at t.

The methods in (6) are limited to methods to be followed at the moment. They are not to include longer term strategies such as looking for lots of evidence. But if this sort of account is to work, some possibly successful ways must be eliminated from the running. For example, one might concoct a way to try for the truth by listing all the truths a person considers and describing the way to try for the truth as trying to believe all the propositions on that list at the appropriate times. Perhaps trying in this way would in fact lead him to believe all the truths. Or, perhaps there is some other way in which the person could try that would have this result. This would saddle (6) with the same absurd consequences as (5). It would have the plainly mistaken result that one is epistemically obligated to believe each of the truths one considers, or at least those one can believe, regardless of the evidence one has and the situation one is in. As we have seen, that is plainly mistaken. The problem, in short, is that there are unnatural and gerrymandered "methods" for trying to believe truths that one could follow. Some of these cooked up methods can be very successful. But their mere success does not make them the ones one ought to follow.

In the next section I will discuss a different account of epistemic obligations. It is possible that the account to be discussed differs from (6) only in that it makes explicit what would have been said in a generous interpretation of (6). It may also be that it is what Chisholm had in mind originally. That is, it may be that the account to be suggested simply specifies what Chisholm was thinking of when he said that one should try one's best to believe truths and avoid believing falsehoods. It has the advantage, however, of avoiding the problems found in formulations (5) and (6).

V

In objecting to (6) I assumed that the best method for trying to believe truths and disbelieve falsehoods is the one that is in fact most effective. There is another way to try to believe truths and perhaps Chisholm would regard this as the best way to do so. In any case, I believe that this other way to try for the truth leads to a more satisfactory account of epistemic obligations.

This other method to try to believe truths and avoid believing falsehoods is to believe what is supported or justified by one's evidence and to avoid believing what is not supported by one's evidence. One who follows this method does not believe things because it feels good to believe them or because of some long-term benefits that result from doing so. One who follows this method just believes at any time exactly what the evidence he then has supports.[7] Thus, I propose:

(7) For any person S and proposition *p* and time *t*, S epistemically ought to believe *p* at *t* if and only if *p* is supported by the evidence S has at *t*.

Since psychological or other factors may force or preclude one from believing what is supported by one's evidence, (7) does not imply that one always can believe, or can avoid believing, what one should believe. It is therefore an account of epistemic obligation that does not require the truth of doxastic voluntarism. Moreover, (7) obviously avoids the successful objections to the other accounts of epistemic obligation previously considered.

In his most recent published discussion of this topic, Chisholm (1986) proposes something along the lines of (7). He writes: "I have previously written, incautiously, that one's primary intellectual duties are to acquire truth and to avoid error. What I should have said is that one's primary intellectual duties are to believe *reasonably* and to avoid believing *unreasonably*" (pp. 90–91). Since what it is reasonable for a person to believe at any time is what is supported by the person's evidence, what

Chisholm says here turns out to be quite similar to (7). To accept (7) as an account of epistemic obligations is not to reject a Jamesian view entirely. (4), the claim that one's epistemic goal is to get at the truth, is consistent with (7) and I believe that it is also true. But one's epistemic duties or obligations concern the way to get to this goal and the epistemically dutiful way to get there is to believe in accordance with one's evidence. That's what one is epistemically obligated to do.[8]

Notes

[1] I will use the phrases 'ought to believe', 'should believe', and 'is obligated to believe' interchangeably. It is possible that there are contexts in which it is useful to distinguish among their meanings, but I don't think the present context is one of those.

[2] It is consistent with the view expressed here that there are also other attitudes one can take toward a proposition. For example, one can hope that it is true or be despondent over its truth. One can also choose to act as if it is true, or take it to be true for the sake of argument or further inquiry. Still, one is always either believing it, disbelieving it, or suspending judgment about it.

[3] It is also possible that there is only one sense of 'ought' at issue here, and that there are conflicting considerations about whether it applies. That is, there are practical considerations supporting the conclusion that Jones ought to believe that he'll pass and epistemic considerations opposing that same conclusion. I believe that the "two senses" resolution is clearly preferable in this case. The reason is just that, upon reflection, it seems clear that the two intended conclusions—that Jones ought to believe that he'll pass and that he ought not to believe that—are compatible.

[4] It is possible that Clifford is making the more modest claim that the fact that a belief is based on insufficient evidence is a factor that counts against its moral permissibility. Other considerations, however, might outweigh this one.

[5] This is not to say that I find Lehrer's notion of acceptance entirely clear. I don't know if accepting is identified with any overt behavior, such as saying that a proposition is true, or any familiar mental activity, such as mentally assenting to it.

[6] This passage, except for the last part, is cited by Chisholm (1977, p. 22).

[7] One who follows this method will also have only epistemically justified beliefs. For an account of epistemic justification that has this implication, see Feldman and Conee (1985).

[8] Earlier versions of this paper were read at Brown University and at the University of Miami. I would like to thank the participants in discussions at those places, as well as Earl Conee, for helpful comments.

References

Chisholm, R.: 1977, *Theory of Knowledge,* 2nd edition, Prentice-Hall, Englewood Cliffs, NJ.

Chisholm, R.: 1986, 'The Place of Epistemic Justification', *Philosophical Topics* 14, pp. 85–92.

Clifford, W. L.: 1866, *Lectures and Essays,* 2nd edition, Macmillan, London.

Feldman, R., and Conee, E.: 1985, 'Evidentialism', *Philosophical Studies* 48, pp. 15–34.

Firth, R.: 1978, 'Are Epistemic Concepts Reducible to Ethical Concepts?' in A. I. Goldman and J. Kim (eds.), *Values and Morals,* D. Reidel, Dordrecht, pp. 215–225.

Foley, R.: 1987, *The Theory of Epistemic Rationality,* Harvard University Press, Cambridge.

Heil, J.: 1983, 'Doxastic Agency', *Philosophical Studies* 43, pp. 355–364.

Heil, J.: 1986, 'Believing Reasonably', presented at The University of Rochester, October, 1986.

James, W.: 1911, *The Will to Believe and Other Essays in Popular Philosophy,* David McKay, New York, 1911.

Lehrer, K.: 1981, 'A Self Profile', in Bogdan, R. (ed.), *Keith Lehrer,* D. Reidel, Dordrecht, pp. 3–104.

Markie, P.: 1986, *Descartes's Gambit,* Cornell University Press, Ithaca.

Moser, P.: 1985, *Empirical Justification,* D. Reidel, Dordrecht.

Plantinga, A.: 1986, 'Chisholmian Internalism', presented at Brown University, November, 1986.

Bibliography

Alston, William. "The Deontological Conception of Epistemic Justification." In William Alston, *Epistemic Justification*. Ithaca, NY: Cornell University Press, 1989.

Chisholm, Roderick. *Perceiving*. Ithaca, NY: Cornell University Press, 1957.

Firth, Roderick. "Are Epistemic Concepts Reducible to Ethical Concepts." In A. I. Goldman and J. Kim, eds., *Values and Morals*. Dordrecht, Netherlands: Reidel, 1978.

Heil, John. "Doxastic Agency." *Philosophical Studies* 43 (1983).

Pojman, Louis. *Religious Belief and the Will*. London: Routledge & Kegan Paul, 1986.

Williams, Bernard. *Problems of the Self*. Cambridge, MA: Cambridge University Press, 1972.